KU-794-468

# MODERN PRODUCTION/ OPERATIONS MANAGEMENT

## WILEY SERIES IN PRODUCTION/OPERATIONS MANAGEMENT

MODERN PRODUCTION/OPERATIONS MANAGEMENT
8TH EDITION
ELWOOD S. BUFFA
RAKESH SARIN

PROJECT MANAGEMENT: A MANAGERIAL APPROACH
JACK R. MEREDITH
SAMUEL MANTEL

THE MANAGEMENT OF OPERATIONS
3RD EDITION
JACK R. MEREDITH

PRODUCTION SYSTEMS: PLANNING, ANALYSIS AND CONTROL
4TH EDITION
JAMES L. RIGGS

DECISION SYSTEMS FOR INVENTORY MANAGEMENT AND PRODUCTION PLANNING
2ND EDITION
EDWARD A. SILVER

THE MANAGEMENT OF QUALITY ASSURANCE
MADHAV SINHA
WALTER O. WILLBORN

# MODERN PRODUCTION/ OPERATIONS MANAGEMENT

## EIGHTH EDITION

**ELWOOD S. BUFFA**

**RAKESH K. SARIN**

**UNIVERSITY OF CALIFORNIA, LOS ANGELES**

**JOHN WILEY & SONS**

**New York Chichester Brisbane Toronto Singapore**

Text design: Karin Gerdes Kincheloe
Cover design: Steve Jenkins

***Library of Congress Cataloging in Publication Data:***

Buffa, Elwood Spencer, 1923–
Modern production/operations management.

(Wiley series in production/operations management)
Includes index.
1. Production management. I. Sarin, Rakesh K.
II. Title. III. Series.

TS155.B723 1987 658.5 86-26802

Printed in Singapore

10 9 8 7 6 5 4

# ABOUT THE AUTHORS

**Elwood S. Buffa** is the Times Mirror Professor at the UCLA Graduate School of Management. His most recent books are, *Meeting the Competitive Challenge: Manufacturing Strategy for U.S. Companies,* Dow Jones–Irwin, Inc., 1984, and, *Corporate Strategic Analysis* (coauthored with Marc Bogue), The Free Press, 1986. He has published many other books and articles in production and manufacturing and management science that deal with both strategic and operations problems. He has engaged in consulting activities in a wide variety of settings during the past twenty-five years, and serves on the board of directors of Planmetrics, Inc. Buffa received his B.S. and MBA degrees from the University of Wisconsin, and his Ph.D. in engineering from the University of California, Los Angeles.

**Rakesh K. Sarin** is professor of production and operations management and decision sciences at the Graduate School of Management of the University of California, Los Angeles. He received his MBA from the Indian Institute of Management, Ahmedabad, and his Ph.D. from the University of California, Los Angeles. Professor Sarin has published many research articles in *Management Science* and *Operations Research* and other journals and is an associate editor of *Management Science.* His current research interests include multicriteria methods for production problems, decision theory and risk analysis.

**To Betty, Chachi, and Anna**

# PREFACE

The decline of the competitive position of U.S. manufactured products in global markets has focused new attention on production and operations management, both in course work in colleges and universities and in business enterprises. The President's Commission on Industrial Competitiveness devoted a great deal of their final report to the issues of productivity, quality, and process technology and their importance in building and maintaining a national competitive position. These are issues that are at the core of production and operations management, and the commission's report provides new and important reasons why every student of management and business administration should have a basic understanding of the field.

The eighth edition marks a major revision of *Modern Production/Operations Management.* In addition, Rakesh Sarin joins as coauthor, providing a fresh approach to the scope and organization of the book as well as to many individual topics. The eighth edition focuses on a simpler but more quantitative step-by-step development. It begins with relatively simple, well-defined subject matter in operations planning and control, such as forecasting and inventory planning and control. Modular information is cumulated toward more complex materials that deal with system design and, finally, the strategic implications of operations.

The opening major section initially deals with the role of operations systems in profitability and competitiveness. How can the operations function make a difference in the ability of an enterprise to compete and survive? Then, types and characteristics of operations systems are discussed in two chapters, one for manufacturing systems and a second for service systems. These chapters are very important in providing initial scope and definition to the course.

The second major section focuses on operations planning and control providing basic knowledge about operations problems that will be valuable in building the students' knowledge base in operations management. In this section, a set of conceptual and analytical tools are presented that are useful in analyzing some well-defined, common, operations management problems. The emphasis is on basic models that capture the key trade-offs involved in the decision. A guide to more advanced materials is provided where appropriate. Chapters dealing with methodology such as linear programming and simulation, are inserted in the sequence needed to deal with chapters on specific operations problems. These methodology chapters may be skipped by instructors whose course has a prerequisite course in management science/operations research.

In keeping with a new emphasis on quality in U.S. manufacturing, two chapters are devoted to this important area, the first dealing broadly with quality assurance and the second devoted to a rather complete coverage of statistical quality control methodology. A full chapter is devoted to Japanese manufacturing systems, reflecting the high interest in these unique methods.

The third major section deals with the design of systems. A special new chapter deals with product–process design, with attention given to the advanced technologies of numerical control, CAD/CAM, robotics, FMS, and the like. The system design section continues with individual chapters on capacity planning, location and distribution, job design, and, finally, facility layout as an expression of the resulting design. Embedded in the sequence is a special chapter on waiting line models, providing an analytical base for the design of service systems, and because most productive system designs must be appraised by more than one criterion, Chapter 21 provides a methodological overview of multicriteria decisions.

Finally, the new emphasis on the role of operations strategy in corporate strategy is reflected in two chapters, the first dealing with a framework for operations strategy formulation and the second dealing with implementation. The final chapter looks to operations systems of the future within the context of the past.

At the end of each chapter there are review questions, and problems and situations (short cases) where appropriate. There are a large number of problems in appropriate chapters arranged with increasing complexity.

## Major Changes in the Eighth Edition

The eighth edition represents several additions and major revisions in almost all the chapters of the previous edition. In terms of new and old materials, most of the materials in the three chapters of Part One are new. The ten chapters of Part Two are largely new, or at least, make innovative use of some existing materials. Only Chapter 11, Project Management, is virtually unchanged from the seventh edition, and even that chapter has some new materials and updating. In Part Three, Chapters 15, 16, 18, 19, and 21 are based largely on new materials, and the two chapters in Part Four on operations strategy are entirely new.

Particularly notable among the new chapters are Chapters 1, 14, 21, 22, and 23, which involve materials not found in most texts on operations management. Chapter 1, which focuses on the role of operations in the overall competitiveness of an enterprise, is a first. This connection has been implied in the past, but it has never been focused on, isolating the competitive priorities that are the province of the operations function. In some ways related to this operations competitiveness, we have presented a full chapter on Japanese manufacturing systems in Chapter 14.

Another first for operations management texts is Chapter 21 on multicriteria decision methods for production problems. Although we have long recognized that most decisions in operations management have multiple criteria, virtually all the formal decision models used involved a single criterion. Here we present methodology for casting decisions in a more realistic, multiple criteria environment.

Finally, with Chapters 22 and 23, we devote two chapters to operations strategy, the first dealing with operations strategy formulation and the second with the implementation of operations strategy. These chapters reflect the growing importance of operations strategy as an integral part of corporate strategy. Every student, whether concentrating in operations management or not, needs to understand operations strategy in order to make decisions that take this important function into account and, even more important, to manage strategically on a day-to-day basis.

Elwood S. Buffa
Rakesh K. Sarin

# ACKNOWLEDGMENTS

Materials in this book have been drawn from a wide variety of sources, including original work by scores of colleagues around the world. The sources of these works are cited where they are discussed in the text, and we hope that we have made no omissions.

Reviewers of the seventh edition and of the revised manuscript provided reactions that were invaluable for the preparation of the eighth edition. They were Solon Morgan of Drexel University; Colonel Allen Grum of the U.S. Military Academy—West Point; James Black of Miami University; Fred Rafaat of Wichita State University; M.H. Safizadeh of Wichita State University; Norman Ware of Eastern Illinois University; and David Carhardt of Bentley College.

We are deeply indebted to these colleagues for taking the time and effort to review such extensive and complex materials and for providing reactions and recommendations for improvement. We recognize that the book is better for their inputs.

The forty or more reviewers of previous editions represent a cross-section of the outstanding professors of production and operations management in the country. They have had an important role in the development and evolution of *Modern Production/Operations Management* over its long life. We sincerely thank them for their many suggestions and comments.

E.S.B.
R.K.S.

# CONTENTS

# PART ONE

# CLASSIFICATION AND IMPORTANCE OF OPERATIONS MANAGEMENT

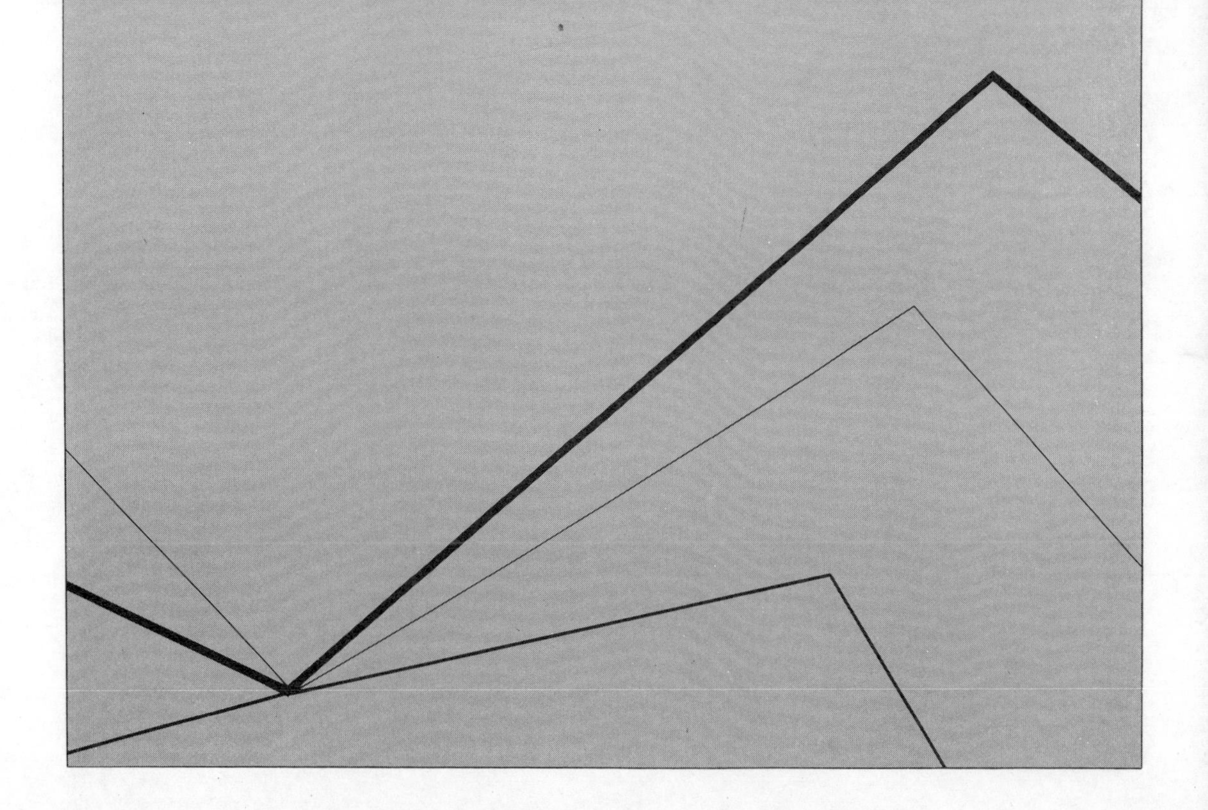

# CHAPTER 1

# OPERATIONS MANAGEMENT IN CORPORATE PROFITABILITY AND COMPETITIVENESS

**What Is a Productive System?**

Examples of Productive Systems
Products versus Services
Services as a Part of the Product
Products as a Part of the Service

**Enterprise Competitiveness and the Operations Function**

Cost
Quality
Dependability as a Supplier
Flexibility/Service

**Operations Strategy—A Key Element in Corporate Strategy**

**The Plan for this Book**

Classification and Importance of Operations Management
Operations Planning and Control
Design of Operational Systems
Operations Strategy and the Firm
Synthesis and Conclusion

**References**

The President's Commission on Industrial Competitiveness states: "Universities need to improve the quality and quantity of their manufacturing-related curriculums. We need more technical courses in process-related subjects and more emphasis on courses in manufacturing management."[1] We heartily agree, and the purpose of this book is to provide effective teaching material to help achieve these objectives. The evidence concerning our global competitiveness indicates that, in order to become competitive, we must manage our productive systems more effectively. This means that top management must place greater emphasis on the operations function, understand it more effectively, and put a higher priority on incorporating it into the enterprise strategy.

Sleeping giants begin to move as corporations throughout the United States realize the importance of the production or operations functions to the success of their businesses; that is, the strategic importance of producing value for the marketplace. This realization has been the result of competition. While competition has always been a potent force in free economies, in recent years its scope has expanded, as over 70 percent of our goods must now operate in a global marketplace.

News stories concerning the loss of market share and jobs to foreign competition have been commonplace in the 1980s, particularly competition from Japanese manufacturers. Not only has the scope of competition become global, but much of the devastating intrusion into both U.S. and foreign markets formerly dominated by U.S. producers has been based on the ability of foreign companies to manufacture at lower costs products of higher quality than American manufacturers could achieve. Cost and quality are characteristics that must be designed into a product in the first place, but achieving them in the final product is the result of carefully managing the

FIGURE 1-1
**AVERAGE ANNUAL PERCENT CHANGE IN PRODUCTIVITY (REAL GROSS DOMESTIC PRODUCT PER EMPLOYED PERSON, 1960–83).**

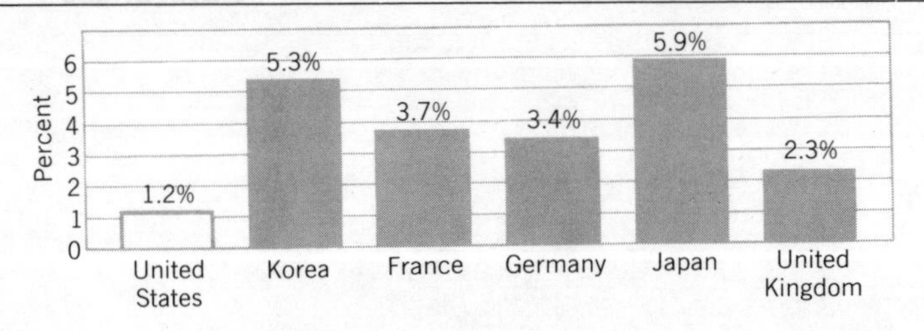


*Source: Global Competition: The New Reality,* Report of the President's Commission on Industrial Competitiveness, Volume I, Superintendent of Documents, U.S. Government Printing Office, Washington, D.C., January 1985.
*Data source:* U.S. Department of Labor, Bureau of Labor Statistics.

[1] *Global Competition: The New Reality,* Report of the President's Commission on Industrial Competitiveness, Superintendent of Documents, U.S. Government Printing Office, Washington, DC, January 1985, p. 24.

FIGURE 1-2
**INTERNATIONAL ADOPTION OF ROBOTS, 1982.**

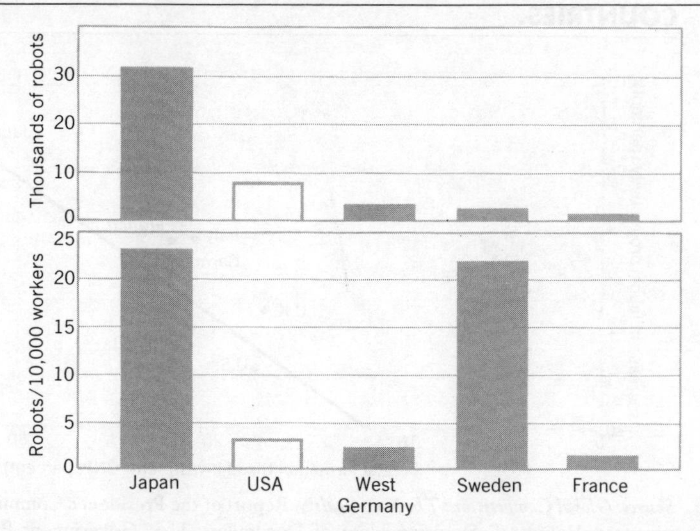


*Source: Global Competition: The New Reality,* Report of the President's Commission on Industrial Competitiveness, Volume I, Superintendent of Documents, U.S. Government Printing Office, Washington, D.C., January 1985.

*Data source:* Society of Manufacturing Engineers, prepared for the International Trade Commission, 1984.

productive resources of a company, and that is what production and operations management is all about.

The Industrial Competitiveness Commission reports that productivity growth since 1960 in the United States has been dismal; we have been outstripped by almost all our trading partners (see Figure 1-1). U.S. productivity growth was actually negative in 1980. From 1960 to 1983, productivity growth in Japan was five times that in the United States, and Japan's actual physical productivity now exceeds that of the United States in steel, transportation equipment, general electrical equipment, and precision machinery.

Related to the productivity record is the Commission's finding that manufacturing technology needs more emphasis.

> Perhaps the most glaring deficiency in America's technological capabilities has been our failure to devote enough attention to manufacturing or "process" technology. It does us little good to design state-of-the-art products, if within a short time our foreign competitors can manufacture them more cheaply. Robots, automation, and statistical quality control were all first developed in the United States, but in recent years they have been more effectively applied elsewhere.[2]

The record with respect to robotics is shown in Figure 1-2, which indicates that the United States is lagging sadly behind Japan and Sweden.

[2] *Global Competition: The New Reality,* p. 20.

FIGURE 1-3
**PRODUCTIVITY GROWTH AND CAPITAL FORMATION FOR SEVERAL COUNTRIES.**

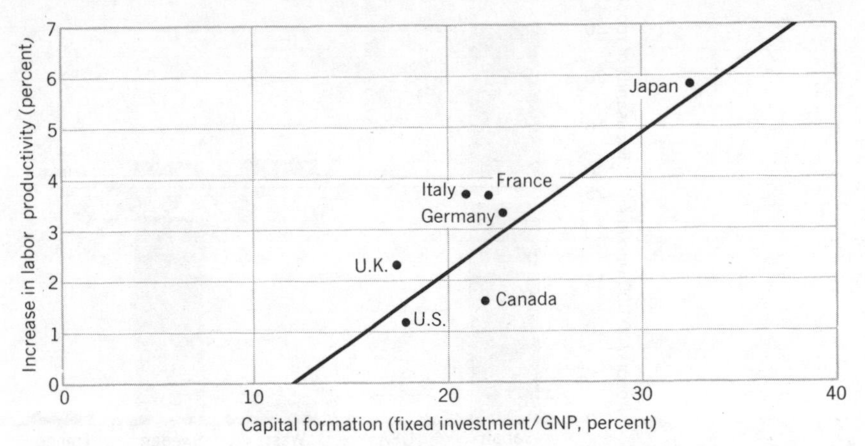


*Source: Global Competition: The New Reality,* Report of the President's Commission on Industrial Competitiveness, Volume I, Superintendent of Documents, U.S. Government Printing Office, Washington, D.C., January 1985.
*Data source:* U.S. Department of Labor, Bureau of Labor Statistics, 1984 and Organization for Economic Cooperation and Development, 1984.

Finally, the Commission Report states, "Countries that invest more tend to be those with the highest rates of growth in productivity."[3] As Figure 1-3 shows so clearly, the United States trails behind its major competitors in capital formation (fixed investment as a percentage of GNP), and the relationship between capital formation and productivity growth is unmistakable. The effect of large and up-to-date capital investment is to provide our work force with the plants and equipment it needs to keep pace with the productivity improvements of our competitors.

## WHAT IS A PRODUCTIVE SYSTEM?

In the most general terms, we define productive systems as *the means by which we transform resource inputs to create useful goods and services as outputs*. This transformation process is diagrammed in Figure 1-4.

The input–conversion–output sequence is a useful way to conceptualize productive systems, beginning with the smallest unit of productive activity, which we commonly refer to as an *operation*. An operation is some step in the overall process of producing a product or service that leads to the final output. For example, in auto assembly, the operation of installing the right-hand door has inputs (the door panel,

[3] *Global Competition: The New Reality,* p. 25.

FIGURE 1-4
**PRODUCTIVE SYSTEMS AS TRANSFORMATION OR CONVERSION PROCESSES.**

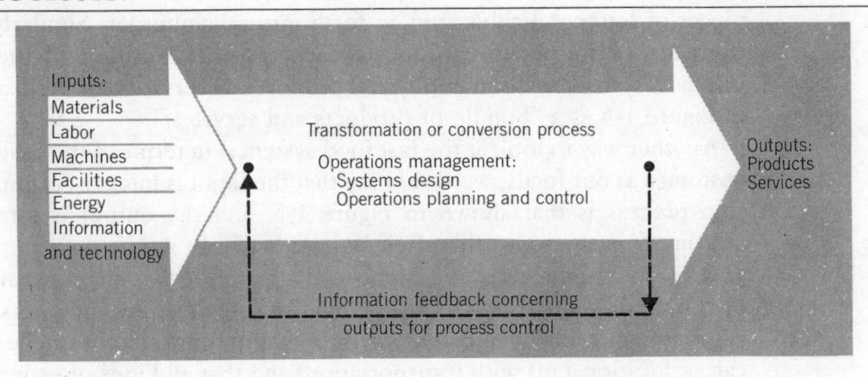


anchor pins and other materials, fixtures to hold the door in place while it is being assembled, etc.), the assembly process itself, and an output (the car body with the door installed), all of which carry assembly forward one more step. Or, taking a service oriented example, obtaining a driver's license commonly involves the step (operation) of paying a fee.

These steps or operations are organized into appropriate sequences to produce larger systems of production. The resource inputs may take a wide variety of forms. In manufacturing operations, the inputs are various raw materials, energy, labor, machines, facilities, information, and technology. In service oriented systems, the inputs are likely to be dominated by labor, but depending on the particular system, inputs common to manufacturing may also be important, as in health care systems, for example. In food service systems, raw materials are an important input. Managing productive systems involves controlling the conversion process and all the variables that affect its performance.

## Examples of Productive Systems

Although many productive systems are very complex, such as electronic assembly, airplane manufacture, steel production, automobile assembly, and many others, we shall use a simple example that is nonetheless a valid productive system. Almost everyone has been to a fast food outlet. We may not think about how carefully the system for producing the food items has been worked out on the one hand or about how much thought has gone into the way you are served on the other. But a fast food outlet is a service oriented system, and the efficiency with which you and your order are handled, including the time required to serve you, and your reaction to the physical surroundings are important factors in how you judge the enterprise and the likelihood that you will return after your first encounter. Of course, the other factors are the quality of the food and its price.

If we look at the system in terms of conversion processes, Figure 1-5 represents some of the most important "operations" or processes. For example, ground meat is "converted" by forming it into patties, frying it, and then assembling it together with pieces of lettuce, pickles, and so forth into a hamburger. Similarly, simple operations are performed to produce french fries. The output of the system in this instance is a combination of physical product and service rendered, and we refer to it in Figure 1-5 as a "bundle of products and services."

Another way to look at the fast food system is in terms of the customer. Using the customer as our focus, we would say that the input is hungry customers, the conversion process is that shown in Figure 1-5, and the output is sated or "satisfied" customers in the sense that their hunger has been gratified.

Table 1-1 summarizes the input–conversion–output characteristics of a number of common productive systems. It indicates the diversity and pervasiveness of such systems in our society and demonstrates that the conversions can be physical, chemical, or locational (as with transportation) and that all kinds of economic activity can be viewed in this productive system format, including manufacturing, services, and public systems.

## Products versus Services

The output in Figure 1-5 was labeled a "bundle of products and services," indicating that the line between product systems and service systems is not necessarily always clear. Nevertheless, there are important differences between them. Products are tangible things that we can carry away with us, whereas services are intangible and perishable and are consumed in the process of their production. Products may be produced to inventory and made available "off-the-shelf," whereas the availability of services requires keeping the productive system that produces them in readiness to produce the services as they are needed. In addition, the person being served often participates in the productive process, as by providing part of the labor in self-serve systems. In product systems, there is very little if any contact between the producers

FIGURE 1-5
**FAST FOOD OUTLET AS A PRODUCTIVE SYSTEM.**

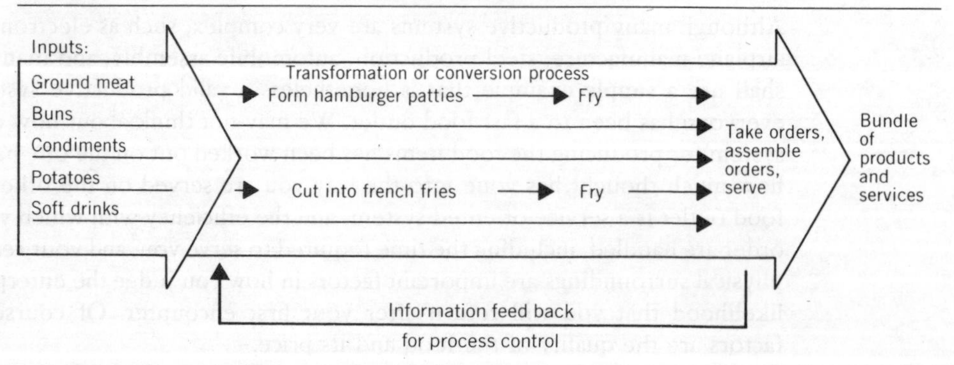

**TABLE 1-1**
**INPUT–CONVERSION–OUTPUT CHARACTERISTICS OF TYPICAL PRODUCTIVE SYSTEMS**

| Productive System | Inputs | Conversion | Outputs |
|---|---|---|---|
| Hospital | Patients | Health | Cured patients |
| Auto factory | Raw materials | Fabrication and assembly of autos | Automobiles |
| Oil refinery | Crude oil | Chemical processes | Gasoline, oil, plastics, etc. |
| Airline | Airplanes, pilots, flight attendants, supplies, customers | Air transportation | Customers transported to destinations |
| Social security | Eligible individuals | Systems for validating eligibility and processing benefits | A measure of economic security for retired persons |

and the users of the product; that is left to distribution and retailing, when customers purchase an item or have it serviced. On the other hand, there is a great deal of contact with the client or customer in service systems. Indeed, much of how individuals rate a service depends on how the service is given. Human contact is almost the essence of many service systems. In product systems, processing to convert raw materials to physical products may involve a multitude of interrelated steps, but the processing required in service systems is usually simple, involving only a few steps.

Other important contrasts between products and services have to do with demand variability, markets, and the location of the productive system. The demand for products certainly varies with time, but that variability tends to be on a weekly, monthly, or seasonal basis. On the other hand, the demand for services is often extremely variable on a short-term basis; that is, weekly, daily, and even hourly variations are common. This extreme short-term variability in the demand for services means that the system must be able to expand and contract its productive capacity rapidly if it is to be cost efficient. Alternatively, service systems can either absorb the costs of overcapacity by designing for peak load conditions, or they can absorb the costs of undercapacity (lost sales and customer dissatisfaction) by designing for something less than peak loads.

Markets served by a productive system for products can be regional, national, or even international. Because of the size of potential markets for products, it is often possible to take advantage of the economies of scale through mechanization and automation. Thus productivity in manufacturing has enjoyed very substantial increases over the years. Conversely, because services cannot be shipped to distant places, a productive system for services must ordinarily serve a local market. Therefore, even though the total market may be national or international (for example, the market for fast foods), the market served by a given productive unit is small, resulting in relatively small units that cannot take great advantage of economies of scale. The location of the productive system is dictated by the location of local markets. If the service system is a nonprofit organization, then the location is dependent on the location of the users, as is the case with post offices, medical clinics, and so on.

The contrasts between product systems and service systems just discussed are summarized in Table 1-2.

## Services as a Part of the Product

If you examine the nature of the delivery system for physical products, the clear line between products and services is much less apparent. Almost all purchases of consumer products involve services as well as the product itself. If you buy an automobile, for example, you buy not only the product but also the guarantee and some servicing of the car.

Services that extend beyond the manufacturer's guarantees and service are usually related to retailing operations. When producers buy products from other producers (raw materials and supplies), they may also be buying services in the form of credit, supply in relation to production schedules, technical advice and service, and so on.

Then, if you look inside the productive system for a product, you may find that services are needed to sustain the production process. For example, there will be machine maintenance, tool cribs to supply the required tools to mechanics, and other internal services.

Finally, services may provide intangible social–psychological benefits that are not easily measured by the senses of touch, smell, sight, sound, and taste. If buying an expensive sports car makes one feel better, can someone else make the judgment that "it isn't worth it" for that person?

TABLE 1-2
**CHARACTERISTICS OF SYSTEMS TO PRODUCE PRODUCTS VERSUS SYSTEMS TO PRODUCE SERVICES**

| Products | Services |
|---|---|
| Tangible | Intangible and perishable; consumed in the process of their production |
| Can be produced to inventory for "off-the-shelf" availability | Availability achieved by keeping the productive system open for services |
| Minimal contact with ultimate consumer | High contact with clients or customers |
| Complex and interrelated processing | Simple processing |
| Demand on system variable on weekly, monthly, and seasonal bases | Demand commonly variable on hourly, daily, and weekly bases |
| Markets served by productive system are regional, national, and international | Markets served by productive system are usually local |
| Large units that can take advantage of economies of scale | Relatively small units to serve local markets |
| Location of system is in relation to regional, national, and international markets | Location dependent on location of local customers, clients, and users |

### Products as a Part of the Service

Similarly, the clear line between products and services in a service oriented system seems to fade. A fast-food operation delivers physical product along with the service. An auto repair service repairs the car and provides the required parts as well. Hospital care involves medication, bandages, X-ray film, and so on.

Thus, although it may be valid to think of systems as primarily producing either products or services, it is better to think in terms of relative emphasis. Some manufacturing systems are predominately the producers of goods and provide very little service. Some service organizations, such as tax consultants, provide almost no physical product as a part of the service. But most productive systems provide a *bundle* of products and services, and an appropriate analysis of the problems of production/operations management should recognize both aspects of the outputs of the system.

## ENTERPRISE COMPETITIVENESS AND THE OPERATIONS FUNCTION

We have alluded to the cost–quality connection in competing for global markets. Indeed, these factors are of great significance, but they are not the only ones. There are four dimensions of competitiveness that measure the effectiveness of the operations function:

- Cost
- Quality
- Dependability as a supplier
- Flexibility/service

### Cost

Although price is the competitive weapon used in the marketplace, profitability is related to the difference between price and cost. Cost is the variable that can allow lower prices that may be profitable. To compete on the basis of price requires an operations function capable of producing at low cost. Therefore, the effects of location, product design, equipment use and replacement, labor productivity, good inventory management, employment of process technology, and so on all contribute to the resulting costs.

It is well known in manufacturing that unit costs are usually reduced as experience is gained through production. It was originally thought that the cost improvement was simply the result of a learning effect among workers, reflecting the development of skill and dexterity that occurs when a task is performed repeatedly. Now, however, this effect is recognized as resulting from a wide variety of additional sources, such as improved production methods and tools, improved product design, standardization, improved material utilization, reduction of system inventories, improved layout and flow, economies of scale, and improved organization. The entire effect might be called *organizational learning.* Actually, the worker learning effect occurs rather quickly and is minor compared to the total organizational learning effect. The cost effects of organizational learning are quantified by the experience curve.

Although all the dimensions of production performance are important in competitiveness, the cost factor is one that is particularly crucial for survival. A survey of 171 of the more than 1000 plant closings during the 1970s by Fortune 500 manufacturers showed that the six most common reasons for plant closings were as shown in Table 1-3. Reasons 1, 3, 4, and 5 all relate to the cost of production and the effectiveness of operations strategy in dealing with costs. The sixth reason reflects in part the effectiveness of the production system in turning out a product of competitive quality.

### Quality

The effectiveness of this factor has been highlighted by Japanese market dominance in consumer electronics, steel, automobiles, and machine tools, where product quality has often been cited as a reason for preferring the products purchased. Customers and clients are often willing to pay more for or wait for delivery of superior products.

### Dependability as a Supplier

A reputation for dependability of supply or even off-the-shelf availability is often a strong competitive weapon. Customers may compromise on cost or even quality in order to obtain on-time delivery when they need an item. The scheduling and coordination of all elements of the productive system determine its ability to produce on time.

TABLE 1-3
**MOST OFTEN CITED REASONS FOR PLANT CLOSINGS**

| Reason | Percent Citing Reason |
|---|---|
| 1. Inefficient or outdated process technology | 46 |
| 2. Lack of sales volume | 27 |
| 3. Price competition from other U.S. companies with better process technology | 25 |
| 4. High labor rates | 21 |
| 5. Price competition from other U.S. companies with lower labor cost, and so on | 17 |
| 6. Superior product performance and features by other U.S. companies | 16 |

*Source:* Roger W. Schmenner, "Every Factory Has a Life Cycle," *Harvard Business Review,* March–April 1983, pp. 121–129.

### Flexibility/Service

How standard is a product or service? Can variations in the product or service be accommodated? The ability to be flexible will depend a great deal on the design of the productive system and the process technology employed. It is probably not worthwhile for a producer of a standardized item in large volume to offer this kind of flexibility. Such a producer would probably respond to a request for variation with the statement, "I am not in that kind of business." Yet there may be a substantial market for that kind of business. Therefore, a competitor could offer such flexibility as a way of competing effectively. What services accompany the sale? Are spare parts readily available? If problems in product performance occur, will the item be serviced quickly and effectively? Flexibility and service, then, are important elements in an enterprise strategy that is provided by the production function.

## OPERATIONS STRATEGY—A KEY ELEMENT IN CORPORATE STRATEGY

Strategy formulation is a process by which a firm determines how it will compete in its industry. It involves goal determination and the development of policies for achieving those goals. The strategy itself must be related to a broad set of external factors, such as industry economic forces and societal values, and to internal factors, such as company strengths and weaknesses and the personal values of key executives. We can think of competitive strategy as a wheel: the firm's goals and the definition of how the firm will compete are in the center, and the spokes of the wheel radiate out through carefully defined key operating policies to the functional areas of the business. Some of these functional areas are as follows:

- Marketing
- Sales
- Target markets
- Product line
- Finance and control
- Engineering and research and development
- Labor
- Purchasing
- Production
- Distribution

Five of the 10 areas listed are extremely important in the performance of the broad operations function. The last three functions (purchasing, production, and distribution) must be carefully related in any modern concept of the operations function. Operations activity thought of as only "production" represents an arbitrary concept. Purchasing provides the material inputs, and the possibility of vertically integrating to include the manufacture of supply items shows how imprecise the line is between "our system" and "their system." The physical distribution system actually involves additional processing steps in the product flow. In other words, the components of the total material flow must be related in the development of key policies that are in line with the competitive strategy.

Engineering, research and development, and labor provide additional key inputs to the operations function. From R&D comes the product design. Will the product be designed for low-cost production? More important, will the product be "designed to cost"; that is, to a target cost? If it is not, a cost leadership strategy begins with a strike against it. Key process technology comes from R&D, and the perception that the R&D function has of itself has an important impact on whether or not it is capable of the process engineering necessary to incorporate the appropriate use of mechanization and automation. This aids in the implementation of a cost leadership strategy. Finally, labor cannot be thought of as being truly separate from production since it also provides crucial input. Job design has a tremendous impact on the cost and quality of products and on whether or not flexibility is feasible in the system.

All the activities in the line of material flow from suppliers through fabrication and assembly and culminating in product distribution must be integrated for a sensible operations strategy formulation. If parts of this flow are left out, there is the risk of an uncoordinated strategy. In addition, the crucial inputs of labor, job design, and technology must be included for an integrated strategy. We conceive of six major components to operations strategy:

- Strategic implications of operating decisions
- Matching the productive system design to market needs
- Capacity and location
- Technological choices
- The work force and job design
- Suppliers and vertical integration

## THE PLAN FOR THIS BOOK

Productive systems share a set of common problems that are the subject of this book. Not all productive systems exhibit all the problems. For example, high personal contact service systems are not likely to have really important inventory or maintenance problems. On the other hand, the operations problems of a system producing so-called "costless" products are likely to be in material supply, packaging, timely performance, and the physical distribution of the product. The plan for the book, nevertheless, covers all the issues, even though every real system may not involve applications for them all.

The material is organized into five major sections:

- Classification and importance of operations management
- Operations planning and control
- Design of operational systems
- Operations strategy and the firm
- Synthesis and conclusion

We shall now discuss the content and rationale of each of these major sections of the book.

## Classification and Importance of Operations Management

The present chapter introduces the notion of what, in fact, a productive system is, and it discusses the four basic criteria for measuring the performance of a productive system. These performance measures are also of great importance to the success of the enterprise as a whole, and they become the bases for linking operations strategy and corporate strategy.

Chapters 2 and 3 deal with the differences between manufacturing systems and service systems, developing the essential characteristics of each system and discussing the variations within each system that we must deal with. For example, the manufacturing system that produces a space vehicle, obviously a low-volume or even a single-unit product, may be quite different from one that produces automobiles. Both are transportation products, but the low product volume and precision requirements of the space vehicle thrust special requirements on the system design. Similarly, the high-volume, low-cost requirements of the auto plant require a quite different design. A similar look at the designs of service systems would examine the customer contact with the system as major variable.

## Operations Planning and Control

Part Two of the book deals with all the issues of the day-to-day, week-to-week, and month-to-month operation of productive systems, which are commonly referred to as "operations planning and control." Each of the nine chapters contribute to the end of providing information, analytical models, and practices that can help managers plan and schedule activities and control these activities once they are planned.

For example, Chapter 4 is about forecasting; it presents methodology that can provide crucial information about expected demand patterns. All the planning activities in operations management require such data and cannot be carried out with intelligence without them. This includes material that deals with inventories, aggregate production planning, and operations scheduling. Chapter 6, on materials requirements planning, deals with special techniques for handling inventory planning and control that are applicable to certain kinds of manufacturing systems, and Chapter 7 deals with the particularly useful mathematical techniques of linear programming, which finds considerable application in production planning. Chapter 9 provides the methodology for simulation, which is useful in operations scheduling, dealt with in Chapter 10, as well as in many other operations management problems that involve system design.

The last four chapters in Part Two deal with special issues. Chapter 11 deals with the special problems and analytical techniques that have developed around large-scale, one-time projects. Such systems are extremely important in the construction and space industries. Chapters 12 and 13 deal with the extremely important topics of quality assurance and statistical quality control methods. Finally, we devote Chapter 14 to a review of the highly effective Japanese manufacturing systems.

## Design of Operational Systems

The eight chapters of Part Three all deal with aspects of the design of systems to produce products and services. The design process begins with product/process technology; it proceeds through capacity planning, location and distribution, and design of processes and jobs; and it culminates in facility layout. Chapters are devoted to each of these major topics. But included at points in this sequence are special chapters that focus on useful analytical methods. For example, a review of waiting line models in Chapter 16 provides an analytical base for the design of service systems. Finally, most productive system designs must be appraised by more than one criterion, so Chapter 21 provides a methodological overview of multicriteria decisions, with production system applications.

## Operations Strategy and the Firm

The operations planning and control and the system design components of production and operations management culminate in the formulation and implementation of an operations strategy. The two chapters of Part Four focus on these broad topics and relate them to the basic strategic thrust of the enterprise. Operations strategy cannot exist by itself in a vacuum.

## Synthesis and Conclusion

The final chapter reviews the past and projects into the future. What will the factory of the future be like? How different will it be from what we know? Will direct labor cease to be a useful resource? If so, how can the resulting social problems be offset?

# REFERENCES

Buffa, E. S., *Meeting the Competitive Challenge: Manufacturing Strategy for U.S. Companies,* Dow Jones-Irwin, Homewood, IL, 1984.

Hayes, R. H., and S. C. Wheelwright, *Restoring Our Competitive Edge: Competing Through Manufacturing,* Wiley, New York, 1984.

Hill, T. J., "Manufacturing Implications in Determining Corporate Policy," *International Journal of Operations & Production Management, 1*(1), 1980, pp. 3–11.

Kantrow, A. M., "The Strategy-Technology Connection," *Harvard Business Review,* July–August 1980, pp. 6–8, 12.

Skinner, W., *Manufacturing: The Formidable Competitive Weapon,* Wiley, New York, 1985.

# CHAPTER 2

# TYPES AND CHARACTERISTICS OF MANUFACTURING SYSTEMS

If we examine the array of products available to the public and to producers, it may seem unreasonable that the productive systems that manufacture them could have common characteristics—the materials vary widely; the sizes, shapes, and weights are diverse; and the applications and uses are equally variegated. But if there were no common characteristics among systems for diverse products—if each system were entirely unique—we could learn nothing transferable by studying production management, and such is not the case. By examining the nature of the product demand in its growth from introduction to maturity and by relating it to the competitive criteria of cost, quality, on-time delivery, and flexibility discussed in Chapter 1, we can develop logical types of manufacturing systems that match marketplace needs. Therefore, the place to start in defining types of manufacturing systems is with product strategies.

## PRODUCT STRATEGIES

Though products occur in great diversity, we seek to classify them in relation to the four competitive criteria. At one extreme, we might have products that are custom in nature; that is, products especially designed to the specifications and needs of customers or clients. Examples are a prototype spacecraft, many producer goods, and construction. A custom product is not available from inventory because it is one of a kind. The emphases in the custom product strategy are on uniqueness, dependability of on-time delivery, quality, and flexibility to change the production process in accordance with changing customer preferences. Cost or price is a lesser consideration. Part of the strategy is to obtain the high profit margins that typically are available for custom designs.

At the other extreme are highly standardized products. Products of this type are available from inventory. They are "off-the-shelf" products because each unit is identical and the nature of demand is such that availability and cost are important elements of competitive strategy. There is very little product differentiation between producers, and there are limited options available in products. The most extreme examples are products that have virtually no variety, such as standard steel and aluminum shapes, and commodities like sugar or gasoline. Important managerial concerns for highly standardized products are dependability of delivery and low cost.

Between the extremes of custom-designed product strategies and highly standardized product strategies, we have mixed strategies that are sensitive to variety, some flexibility, moderate cost, and dependability of supply. In these situations, quality of product is important, but it is not the overwhelming criterion as with custom products. Multiple sizes and types of products are available, possibly from inventory or by order, depending on enterprise strategy. Some of these products are available in fairly low volume, but some, such as automobiles, are available in high volume. The great majority of products available today are in this middle category. Most consumer products are available from inventory. Most producer goods are available by order and may be subject to some special design modifications to meet individual needs, though the basic designs are quite standard.

## The Product Life Cycle

The concept of the product life cycle unifies the previous discussion of product strategies. Figure 2-1 shows products that currently sell in relatively low volume, intermediate volume, and high volume in relation to stages of product introduction, growth, maturity, and decline. If we traced the development of a product now available in high volume in highly standardized form from its original introduction, we would find that it had gone through the first three stages shown in Figure 2-1: introduction at low volume and with custom design; growth in sales, during which variety became more limited; and maturity, during which the product variety became even more limited as the product became basically a commodity. Finally, the product will enter the decline stage as substitutions become available that may be superior in terms of function, quality, cost, or availability.

The product life cycle curve is particularly important in formulating marketing strategies for pricing and market penetration. Of course, one of the objectives in marketing strategy is to find ways to renew the life cycles of products that have matured or are in a state of decline. For example, there has been a market for calculators for a long time. It was satisfied by mechanical calculators for many years. But the mechanical calculator was replaced by the electromechanical calculator, then by the electronic calculator, and most recently by the pocket electronic calculator. Each generation of calculators has had its own product life cycle.

We should note that there are some custom products that are mature but do not go through the phases we have discussed. For example, there is a market for custom-built homes. Architects design such homes and contractors build them to specifications. The industry involved is mature in that it regularly produces custom-designed homes and has refined a system, but if the custom home were produced in volume, it would no longer be a custom home.

FIGURE 2-1
**TYPICAL PRODUCT LIFE CYCLE CURVE FOR THE INTRODUCTION, GROWTH, MATURITY, AND DECLINE IN THE SALES OF PRODUCTS.**

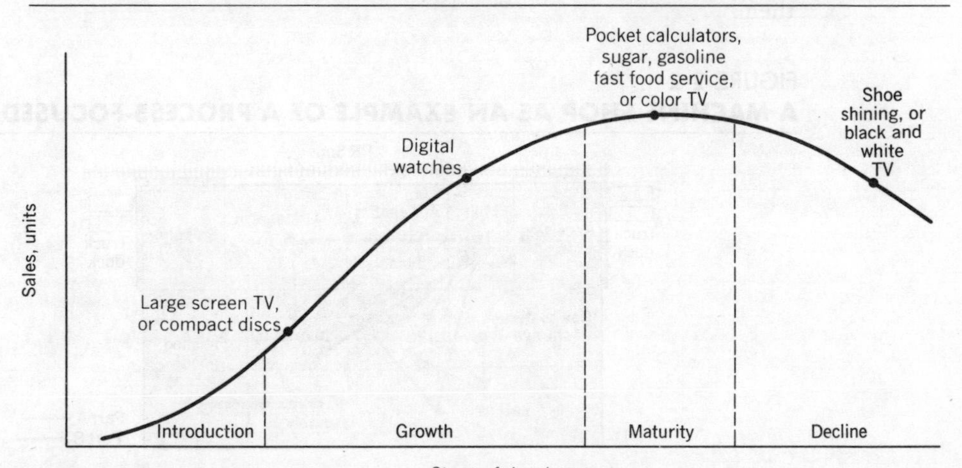

## PRODUCTIVE SYSTEM TYPES

The basic managerial strategies adopted for the productive system must be related to the product strategies. Obviously, it would be inappropriate to use a high-volume process capable of producing millions of gallons to produce an experimental chemical. Again, we should think in terms of alternative strategies for the extremes as well as for the middle ground.

### Process-Focused Systems

A productive system for custom products must be flexible. It must have the ability to produce according to customer or client specifications. For example, an aerospace manufacturer must fabricate special component part designs. The equipment and personnel must be capable of meeting the individual component specifications and of assembling the components in the special configurations of the custom product.

Physical facilities are organized around the nature of the processes, and personnel are specialized by generic process type. For example, in a machine shop we might expect to find milling machine departments, lathe departments, drill departments, and so on. The flow of the item being processed in such productive systems is dictated by individual product requirements, so the routes through the system are variable.

The nature of the demand on the productive system results in intermittent demand for the system's facilities, and each component flows from one process to the next intermittently. Thus, the process-focused system with intermittent demand on process types must be flexible as required by the custom product, and each generic department and its facilities are used intermittently as needed by the custom orders. Figure 2-2 shows an example of a process-focused system in a machine shop. This physical arrangement of the departments by generic type is often called a "job shop" because it is designed to accommodate the needs of individual job orders.

Of course, a productive system of considerable significance in our society that is designed to deal with custom products is the project system. Projects systems have unique methods for planning and control, and we devote Chapter 11 especially to them.

FIGURE 2-2
**A MACHINE SHOP AS AN EXAMPLE OF A PROCESS-FOCUSED SYSTEM.**

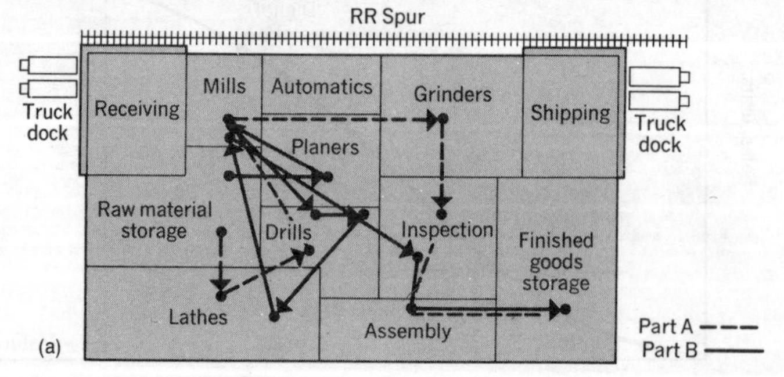

## Product-Focused Systems

By contrast, the nature of the demand on the productive system that produces high-volume, standardized products results in continuous use of the facilities. Also, the material flow may be continuous, as in petroleum refining, or approaching continuous flow, as with automobile fabrication and assembly. Because of the high-volume requirements of such systems, special processing equipment and entire dedicated producing systems can be justified as a productive system strategy. Processing is adapted completely to the product. Individual processes are physically arranged in the sequence required, and the entire system is integrated for a single purpose, like one giant machine. Thus, continuous systems have a product focus. Under these extreme conditions of high demand for standardized products, the production process is integrated and makes use of mechanization and automation to achieve standardization and low cost. Inventories of standardized products may be an important element of production as well as marketing strategy. Figure 2-3 shows an example of a product-focused system involving fabrication and assembly lines.

Between the two extremes of process-focused (intermittent demand) and product-focused (continuous demand) systems, we have systems that must deal with low-volume multiple products and relatively high-volume multiple products. The low-volume multiple-product situation usually involves a process-focused system like that shown in Figure 2-2, but products are produced in *batches*. This allows certain economies of scale in comparison to the job shop system, which is designed to deal with custom products.

The high-volume multiple-product situation is likely to employ a mixed production strategy that combines both the process-focused and product-focused systems illustrated in Figures 2-2 and 2-3. In manufacturing, parts fabrication is often organized on a batch–intermittent basis and final assembly is organized on a line or continuous basis. Because parts fabrication output volume may be substantial but not large enough to justify the continuous use of facilities, parts are produced in economical batches, and the resulting inventories provide an important producing

FIGURE 2-3
**INDUSTRIAL FABRICATION AND ASSEMBLY LINES AS AN EXAMPLE OF A PRODUCT FOCUSED SYSTEM.**

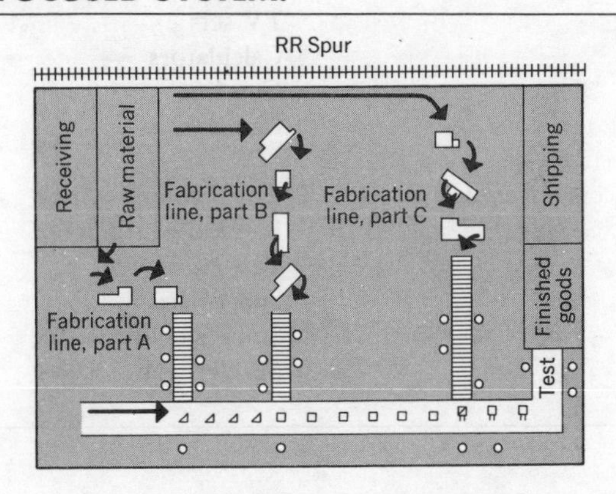

strategy. On the other hand, the nature of assembly makes possible continuous lines dedicated to certain products.

## Production to Stock or to Order

Now, we consider those products that *could* be produced either to stock or to order; that is, a decision is possible. We might decide to produce only to order for important reasons, even though it would be possible to produce to stock. For example, a to-order policy might offer product design flexibility to customers, it might minimize the risk associated with carrying inventories, it might allow a closer control of quality, and so on. On the other hand, we might decide to adopt a to-stock policy for the same type of product for equally valid reasons; for example, to offer better service in terms of availability, to reduce variable costs, and to increase market share by making items available off-the-shelf when customers have the urge to buy.

The choice between a to-order or to-stock inventory policy does not necessarily depend on whether a product-focused or a process-focused physical system has been adopted. For example, one might think that the auto industry, which uses a product-focused system, would certainly be a to-stock producer. But this has not been the case. Each auto is produced for a specific order from a customer or a dealer who has specified the options desired.

Therefore, we have the possibility of two types of systems, product-focused or process-focused, in combination with two possible finished goods inventory policies, to stock or to order, as shown in Table 2-1 with examples.

A reason for emphasizing to-stock and to-order inventory policies is that the management systems for planning and controlling production, scheduling, and in-

TABLE 2-1
**EXAMPLES OF THE TWO DIMENSIONS OF POSITIONING**

| | *Finished Goods Inventory Policy* | |
|---|---|---|
| Type of System | To Stock | To Order |
| Product Focused | *Product Focused/To Stock* | *Product Focused/To Order* |
| | Office copiers | Construction equipment |
| | TV sets | Buses, trucks |
| | Calculators | Experimental chemicals |
| | Gasoline | Textiles |
| | Cameras | Wire and cable |
| | | Electronic components |
| Process Focused | *Process Focused/To Stock* | *Process Focused/To Order* |
| | Medical instruments | Machine tools |
| | Test equipment | Nuclear pressure vessels |
| | Spare parts | Electronic components |
| | Some steel products | Space shuttle |
| | Molded plastic parts | Ships |
| | | Construction projects |

ventory policies are very different, depending on positioning with respect to the market. A to-stock policy results in each item being indistinguishable from the others, so planning and controlling systems can deal with all like items in the same way. A to-order policy means that each order must be controlled separately in a much more complex way; we must be able to respond to individual customers concerning the progress of an order, to quote delivery dates, and to control the progress of each order through the plant.

In practice, there may be a combination of both to-stock and to-order operations because many organizations actually engage in a mixture of product–market situations. Consequently, it is important to realize that even though outputs may appear similar on the surface, very different managerial procedures are usually necessary because of the different policy contexts in which the products are produced.

## PRODUCTIVE SYSTEM POSITIONING STRATEGIES

Now, how should an organization position its productive system in relation to its markets? As the product develops through its life cycle, the productive system goes through a life cycle of its own from a job shop system (process focused, to order) when the product is in its initial stages through intermediate stages to a continuous system (product focused, to stock) when the product is demanded in large volume. (See Figure 2-4.)

FIGURE 2-4
**RELATIONSHIP BETWEEN THE PRODUCT LIFE CYCLE AND PRODUCTIVE SYSTEM TYPES.**

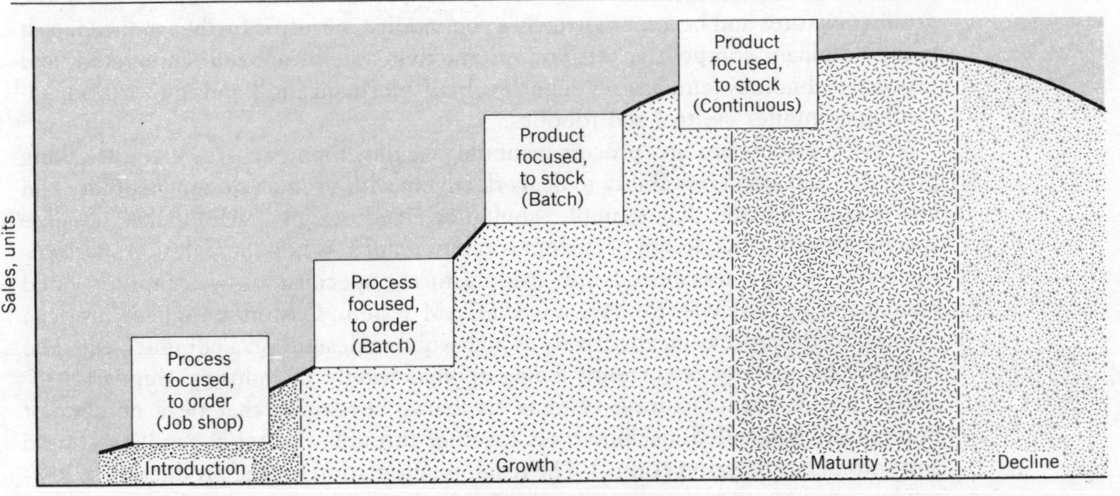

These stages of product and process development are interdependent and feed on each other. There is the obvious dependence of the appropriate type of productive system on the volume of product that is sold. But, in addition, the volume of product sold is dependent in part on costs and in part on the price–quality competitive position, both of which are dependent on the use of the appropriate productive system. The experience curve mentioned in Chapter 1 is a reflection of all of the factors that operate in a productive system to reduce costs and is an important element in a manager's competitive strategy. The results of cost reduction can indeed be used as the basis for aggressive pricing, which may in itself be an important factor in building market share, further building experience, and reinforcing a progression down the curve. For example, in anticipation of a lower cost per unit at larger volumes in future time periods, a firm may price its products even lower than the initial cost of production. In such aggressive pricing, however, risks must be balanced against potential benefits.

## Process Life Cycles and Technology

Another factor correlated with the development of the process life cycle is the employment of rather different levels of process technology at each stage of development. When volumes are low, reflecting a great deal of variety in product designs, the process technology must reflect the need for flexibility. In a machine shop, for example, it might involve employing basic machine tools. Automation has not been available to these low-volume operations in the past, but numerically controlled machines promise to change this situation. As the product volume increases, variety in the line decreases, reinforcing the volume effect, and product-focused facilities become justified. The process technology employed with facilities dedicated to a product becomes specialized, with operations more integrated and more mechanization, automation, and numerically controlled processes used. Finally, when the product matures and becomes virtually a commodity, variety is further reduced, cost is the dominant competitive weapon, productive systems are fully integrated, and process technology emphasizes high levels of mechanization and automation, including computer control and robotics.

Very important product/process technological developments are currently taking place that will affect our ability to deal effectively with product design flexibility and low-volume demand. For example, computer aided design (CAD) makes possible specifications for the design of custom computer chips. When these design specifications are directly transferred into manufacturing specifications—computer aided manufacturing (CAM)—we have a CAD/CAM system. Custom-designed chips can be produced almost as inexpensively as high-volume designs on a per unit basis. The CAD/CAM concept is currently being applied widely in industry. Similarly, so-called flexible manufacturing systems are being developed that tie a number of numerically controlled machine tools together through a material handling system and automatic computer control. The result is automation for the production of low-volume products. These new process technologies will be discussed in greater detail in Chapter 15.

## INTERDEPENDENT PRODUCT LINES

Companies today commonly have complex product lines that may compete in different markets. But even though the products and markets may be different, it may be possible to exploit complementarity and interdependence in the production functions.

Suppose, for example, that a company competes in three basic product markets—color TVs, hand calculators, and digital watches—requiring the following main manufacturing activities:

- Product specific components manufacture
- Integrated circuit manufacture (ICs)
- Housing manufacture
- Accoustical component manufacture
- Assembly

The structure for each of the three product lines is shown in Figure 2-5. The percentage numbers in the boxes indicate the value added by manufacture at each stage for each product, and the vertical length of each box is in proportion to these percentages. The value added by manufacture here is simply the accumulation of the variable costs of manufacture for each product line at each stage. Some of the activities for a given product are independent of the other products, such as the product specific components. However, the other activities are common to at least two of the product lines. For all three products, the largest value added percentage is for integrated circuits (ICs); the next largest is for assembly.

Interdependence provides some advantages in the scale of operations and experience accumulation for ICs and assembly and, to a lesser extent, for plastic housings and acoustical components. Although the volume of ICs required for color TVs might justify process technology of a base level, when the volume of ICs required for all three product lines is taken into account, higher levels of mechanization and automation may be justified. The scale of operations for the combined product lines can contribute to efficiency of operations in ICs, making the company more cost competitive in all three product lines. Furthermore, the larger total volume contributes to organizational learning and the experience curve effecs to which we have alluded. These effects are particularly important for ICs because they represent such a large percentage of the value added for all three products. Cost competitiveness is enhanced for all three products.

Similar concepts apply to assembly operations and, to a lesser extent, to plastic housings and acoustical components. The type of productive system employed for these activities should reflect the process technology available and the total volume; perhaps a product-focused continuous kind of operation would be appropriate.

On the other hand, the manufacturing systems for the product specific components are independent of each other and will reflect the production economics of the lower volumes associated with each product line. The process technology employed will be that appropriate for the smaller volumes, and the rate of experience accumulation will be slower. The type of productive system appropriate may be process focused for production in batches, for example.

FIGURE 2-5
**MANUFACTURING ACTIVITY STRUCTURE FOR A COMPANY PRODUCING COLOR TVs, HAND CALCULATORS, AND DIGITAL WATCHES.**

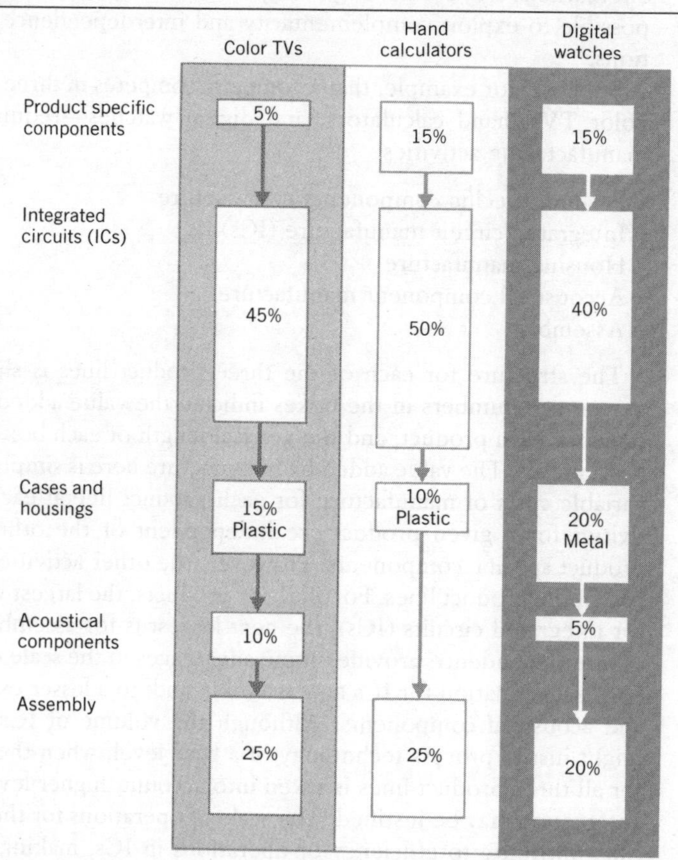


Now suppose that we are considering exiting the color TV business since it has matured and foreign competition is strong. What are the impacts on the production system as a whole and on our competitive position for the other products? What will happen to the scale of IC operations if color TV demand is withdrawn? Will costs of manufacture increase? Will it be necessary to reorganize the IC production system for a different scale of operations? If the change in demand is significant enough, it might dictate a different type of production system for ICs, perhaps a to-order system and/or a process-focused system, where the production economics would result in higher costs. Part of the company's strength and low-cost position in all three product lines stems from the low-cost position in IC components, since they account for the largest value added for all three products. Not only that, but the future position may be affected since less experience in IC manufacture will be accumulated in the future if color TVs are withdrawn.

Now consider the addition of product lines. Unrelated activities will have no positive or negative effects, other than financial ones and those associated with managerial staffing. However, suppose that more products requiring ICs are added. These actions will draw on the low-cost position in ICs and assembly, adding to experience in these areas and perhaps in others. Perhaps the addition of more IC production volume might even justify more advanced process technology and automation. The company would be taking advantage of the structure and the interacting effects.

## ORGANIZATION OF THE OPERATIONS FUNCTION

The nature of the organizational structure that an enterprise chooses for its operations function should be an outgrowth of its strategic choices for the productive system. As noted previously, the choice of productive system type is influenced by the balance of competitive factors that emphasize quality, volume of output and cost, flexibility, and dependability of supply to customers. If the choice based on these competitive factors results in an intermittent system with a process focus, then the organization must be structured to reflect these values, giving primary support to product design flexibility and quality. Conversely, if the choice of productive system type results in a continuous system with a product focus, then the organizational structure must give primary support to dependability of supply to its customers, cost, and price competitiveness. In either situation, we do not mean that the other factors should be ignored but simply that competitive priorities have been established.

### Process-Focused Organizations

Figure 2-6 shows the general structure of a process-focused manufacturing organization. (We show functions because titles vary widely.) The primary supervisory structure follows the physical departmentation. First level supervisors also tend to be experts in the production technology they supervise, and they must coordinate the utilization of people, machines, and material. Higher levels in the production organization involve a broader span of control by managers. The first aggregation of responsibility involves more producing departments, as with the manufacturing manager. But at the plant manager level, the functions that support production are added, such as materials control, quality control, industrial engineering and plant maintenance, and purchasing. On the same level as the plant manager of a single plant operation are the functions of product engineering, finance and accounting, marketing, and personnel and industrial relations. In general, process-focused organizations have highly developed staff functions at higher levels in the organization, and cost and profit responsibility is also at a high level.

In larger organizations, which may operate a number of plants, the plant manager must necessarily have an even larger span of control over additional functions. These usually include at least some aspects of personnel and industrial relations and

FIGURE 2-6
**PROCESS-FOCUSED ORGANIZATIONAL STRUCTURE.**

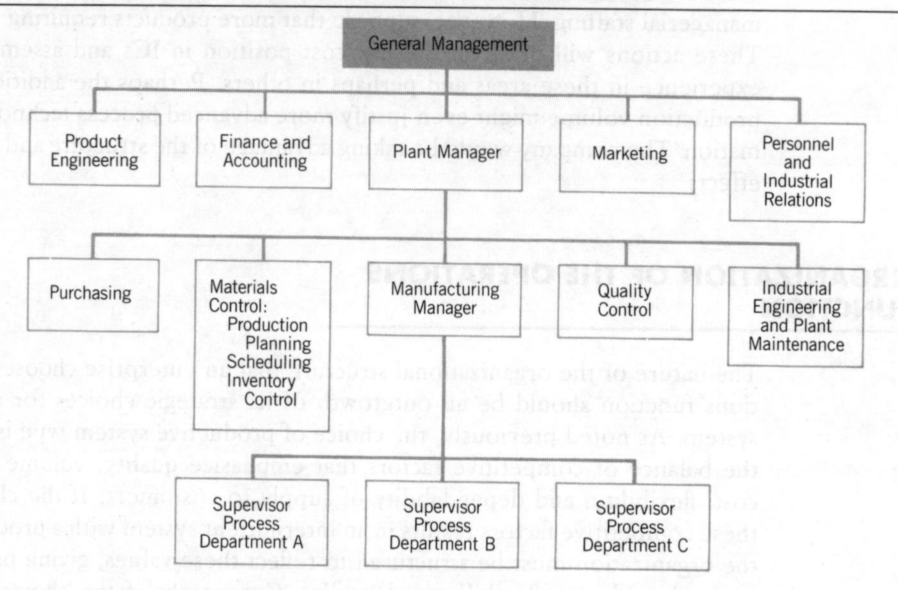


accounting and, depending on the nature of products and plant specialization, may include some aspects of product engineering and marketing. Thus, the production function is apt to be rather hierarchical in nature and usually includes some functions in addition to production at the higher levels. These higher level managers of production systems function as more general managers, and this may account for their generally high salaries.

Why does the process-focused structure give stronger support to the competitive priorities of product flexibility and quality? The product engineering function is separate and independent and is at a high level in the organization. Taking account of individual customer requirements in product design is the responsibility of high level managers, who are not compromised by trade-offs that might be made for the strictly production objectives of standardization and low cost. Quality control is separate and independent from the production organization. The disadvantages of this structure are that management must provide a great deal of coordination between organizational units to make the system work and that cost and supply time are not given high priority in the structure.

## Product-Focused Organizations

Figure 2-7 shows the general structure for a product-focused manufacturing organization. Organization at the primary level is by product or product line. The first level supervisor is primarily responsible for the execution of plans, but he or she is supported by staff experts in production planning and scheduling, inventory control, and quality control who are responsible directly to the manager of the product department. In general, profit and cost responsibility is held by the product groups

FIGURE 2-7
**PRODUCT-FOCUSED ORGANIZATIONAL STRUCTURE.**

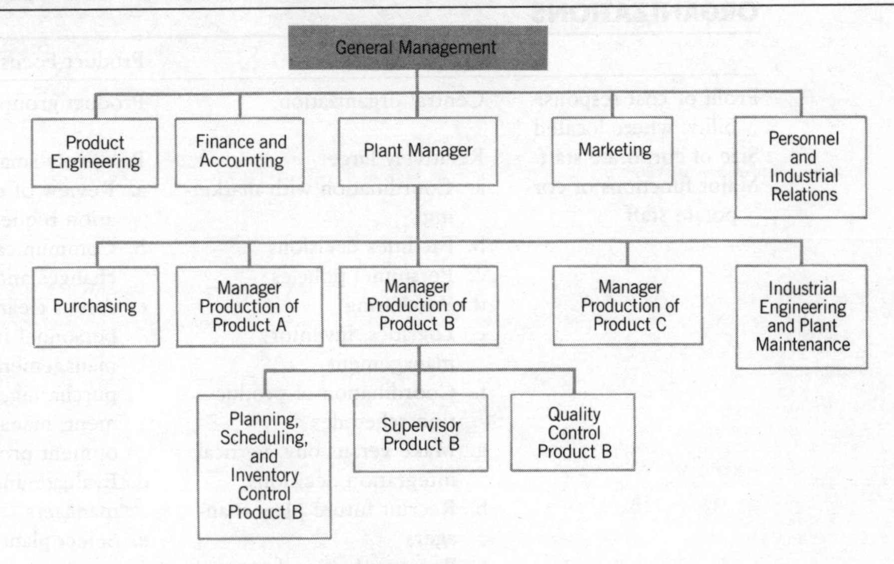


in product-focused organizations; higher level staff provide coordination, but it has much less direct influence over operating decisions.

In the product-focused organization, the close association of the control elements that bear on costs, on-time delivery, and quality makes the entire local organization tuned to perform effectively in achieving these goals. Authority is highly decentralized, which contributes to achieving the specialized objectives of the unit. Each manager of the production of a product line functions more nearly like an independent small organization with relatively little oversight and coordination from corporate levels.

The disadvantages of the product-focused organization are in the lack of flexibility of personnel who may be specialized to a high degree and in the inability of the organization to accommodate customer needs for variations in product design. Table 2-2 compares some of the major differences between process-focused and product-focused organizations.

## IMPLICATIONS FOR THE MANAGER

The two-by-two matrix of basic types of productive systems provides managers with a simple but powerful understanding of the range of systems available and their appropriate application. Whether the market conditions support a process-focused or product-focused system and a to-order or to-stock system can be of the greatest importance in the ultimate competitiveness of a company. Real systems are often a combination of these basic types because of different sizes and styles of the same product or because related product lines can gain economies by aggregating production requirements for common components.

TABLE 2-2
**DIFFERENCES BETWEEN PROCESS AND PRODUCT-FOCUSED ORGANIZATIONS**

| | Process Focus | Product Focus |
|---|---|---|
| Profit or cost responsibility: where located | Central organization | Product groups |
| Size of corporate staff | Relatively large | Relatively small |
| Major functions of corporate staff | a. Coordination with marketing<br>b. Facilities decisions<br>c. Personnel policies<br>d. Purchasing<br>e. Logistics, inventory management<br>f. Coordination of production schedules<br>g. Make versus buy, vertical integration decisions<br>h. Recruit future plant managers<br>i. Review plant performance | a. Review of capital appropriation requests<br>b. Communicate corporate changes and requests<br>c. Act as clearing house for personnel information, management recruiting, purchasing, used equipment, management development programs<br>d. Evaluate and reward plant managers<br>e. Select plant managers and manage career paths—possibly across product group lines |
| Major responsibilities of plant organizations | a. Use materials and facilities efficiently<br>b. Recruit production, clerical, and lower management workers<br>c. Training and development of future department and plant managers<br>d. Respond to special requests from marketing, within limited ranges | a. Coordination with marketing<br>b. Facilities decisions (subject to marketing)<br>c. Purchasing and logistics<br>d. Production scheduling and inventory control<br>e. Make versus buy<br>f. Recruit management |

*Source:* R. H. Hayes and R. W. Schmenner, "How Should You Organize Manufacturing," *Harvard Business Review,* January–February 1978, pp. 105–118.

The positioning of the productive system in relation to markets is of the greatest importance to managers. This positioning should be an integral part of the overall corporate strategy and should include the decision of whether to produce to stock or to order. The concept of the product life cycle provides a rationale for the growth, development, maturation, and decline of products. Managers need to match the appropriate productive system type to their position on the product life cycle. This does not meant that there is a rigid one-to-one relationship between one's position on the product life cycle curve and the exact kind of productive system that is appropriate. Managers may choose to emphasize quality and diversity of multiple products as a way of gaining a competitive advantage. Alternately, a manager in the same basic situation might choose to compete on price and availability with a limited line. The success of enterprises that choose different bases for competing, using their productive system as a weapon, gives evidence that there is no right answer to each situation.

Investment in improved process technology, either by direct purchase or through allocations to research and development, can reduce future costs and improve quality. With dramatic breakthroughs in process technology, a firm could even lower prices, which could provide a very effective competitive weapon. A danger of the effects of highly-integrated, automated systems is the loss of flexibility that results from specialization. But the new technologies of numerically controlled machines, CAD/CAM, and flexible manufacturing systems tend to counterbalance this disadvantage of older automated systems.

Finally, organizational structure should be chosen to give support to the productive system design. In general, organizational structure follows the basic design of the system—if the productive system is designed for process focus, then the organization should be process focused, and vice versa.

# REVIEW QUESTIONS

1. Describe the concept of the product life cycle.
2. Where in their product life cycles would you place the following:
   a. Word processing systems
   b. Electric typewriters
   c. Steel production by the continuous casting process
   d. Sushi bars (Japanese raw fish)
   e. Video disk players
   f. Cassette tape decks
   g. Reel to reel tape decks
3. Define the following terms:
   a. Product-focused system
   b. Process-focused system
   c. Continuous system
   d. Intermittent system
   e. To-order production
   f. To-stock production
4. Why would General Motors, the world's largest auto producer, use a to-order system when they are producing in such large volume?
5. Under what conditions is a process-focused, to-stock system justified?
6. Under what conditions is a product-focused, to-order system justified?

7. We discussed process life cycles. Is there also a process technology life cycle? If so, describe a scenario for such a life cycle illustrated by a product of your choice.
8. How can a company gain a competitive advantage in production cost through its system of related products and product lines? Illustrate with three related product lines of your choice.
9. What are the impacts of a decision to eliminate a product line on the costs of the remaining product lines?
10. What is meant by the productive system/product joint strategy?
11. What are the differences between process-focused and product-focused organizations? Why do these differences occur?

# SITUATION

## The Electronic Relay Company

12. The Electronic Relay Company (ERC) came into being five years ago based on a new product innovation that involved microcircuitry. The new "smart" relays could react much faster and time their action to coordinate with many special needs in complex equipment. Like many new products involving silicon chips, electronic relays had swept the industry and were in great demand because of their versatility and moderate cost.

The relays were used in many types of equipment, and the service requirements were quite variable, depending on the particular application. Although ERC's output included 500 different models each year, they had developed a substantial demand for 10 popular models that seemed to find application in many different end products. ERC was one of several firms in the field that had an excellent engineering staff that could design smart relays to individual customer needs. Sales had increased extremely rapidly, especially in the last two years when they had increased 40 percent each year. Long-term sales forecasts indicated that a 30 percent annual increase was the best estimate for the next five years.

The relays were produced in a flexible process-focused plant only on the basis of special order. The process departments were metal stamping, a small machine shop, electronics assembly, paint, final assembly, and an inspection and test. ERC had a minimum size order of ten, though some recent orders had been as large as 1000. Each order was first routed to engineering for design requirements and then to a cost estimating department for the construction of a bid price and estimated delivery commitment. If the customer accepted the terms, the materials required were ordered and a production order (PO) was issued. The processes required were listed on the PO. The order was routed to the required departments in sequence, was tested, and was finally shipped to the customer. The typical time for production, once the customer had accepted the terms, was six weeks.

Because of the long-term forecasts, the president, Frank Moore, made strategic planning the subject of the next executive committee meeting. The views of the committee members were divergent but were summarized by the VP of manufacturing and VP of marketing. The VP of manufacturing, Tom Hendrick, was strongly for standardizing on relatively few high-demand models and gearing up to produce them in quantity for a mass market.

> There are really only about ten different designs and models when you come right down to it. All the others are just minor variations of these ten. Right now, ten models account for 75 percent of orders. If we could just standardize on these, I could knock 50 percent of the cost out of them. In a couple of years the demand for just those ten would be such that we could automate a line and become the dominant producer in the industry. Let's take the cream of the business and let someone else wrestle with those small special orders.

Dick Lutz, the marketing VP, strongly disagreed:

> We will miss out on a lot of business if we don't give them what they need. They don't all have the same needs in their products. Our people are in touch with the market all the time, and we see some common needs as Tom says, but there are a lot of different situations out there. Sure an order for ten must drive Tom's people nuts, but we charge accordingly. We're making a lot of money from those small orders. Naturally we like the big orders too, and it's true that there is a natural tendency toward standardization because the customer can get a better price on one of our standard models. But let's not shove the market around, let's go with the market.

Vassily Rostopovich, the engineering VP, agreed with Dick Lutz, though not with great vigor. He said:

> We are really good at designing the smart relay to meet individual needs. We have it down to a computer aided design process so we can produce a special design within a couple of days if we have to.

Frank said that he would think over what had been said and draft a position paper on ERC's strategic plan for the next five years for discussion at the next executive committee meeting. What should Frank do? Outline a position paper that you would recommend to Frank.

# REFERENCES

Hayes, R. H., and R. W. Schmenner, "How Should You Organize for Manufacturing," *Harvard Business Review,* January–February 1978, pp. 105–118.

Hayes, R. H., and S. C. Wheelwright, "Link Manufacturing Process and Product Life Cycles," *Harvard Business Review,* January–February 1979.

Hayes, R. H., and S. C. Wheelwright, "The Dynamics of Process–Product Life Cycles," *Harvard Business Review,* March–April 1979a, pp. 127–136.

Shapiro, B. P., "Can Marketing and Manufacturing Coexist?," *Harvard Business Review,* September–October 1977, pp. 104–114.

# CHAPTER 3

# TYPES AND CHARACTERISTICS OF SERVICE SYSTEMS

Many productive systems, such as hospitals, beauty salons, consulting companies, banks, and airlines, do not produce a tangible product that can be stored for later consumption. Instead, the output of such systems is a service—for example, health care, good looks, advice, loans, and transportation—that is consumed in the process of its production. From our day-to-day experience, we know that the cost and quality of services provided even within the same industry can vary a great deal. As consumers, we discriminate among alternative service provisions much the same way as we do for products. Similarly, we have preferences and are willing to pay for different components of service, such as speed, quality, degree of variety, and so forth. Better management of the system that provides the service, consistent with customer preferences and requirements, will lead to greater profitability for the firm. We must therefore understand the nature of the various types of service systems and the associated management tasks that are required to improve a service firm's competitiveness.

## IMPORTANCE OF THE SERVICE SECTOR

During the twentieth century, there has been a gradual but steady shift from the manufacturing sector to the service sector in the U.S. economy. Since about 1945 (the end of World War II), services have steadily increased, from about 33 percent of personal consumption in 1945 to 47 percent in 1980. This trend, shown in Figure 3-1, indicates that expenditures for services have been increasing much faster than those for goods. In 1980, the service sector employed more than two-thirds of the working population and accounted for more than 60 percent of the gross national product. For the first time in history, investment per office worker now exceeds investment per factory worker. With the continuing trend toward a service economy, a greater proportion of future operations managers will be employed by this sector.

In addition to the continuing growth of the service sector, the role of service in the manufacturing sector has been increasing. With increasing automation and the use of computers in the design of a product and its manufacturing process, technical and professional staffs will have a greater role in the actual production of the product than will unskilled workers. Thus, in the factory of the future, the productive process may be guided by design engineers, computer operators, and production planners.

Finally, as discussed in Chapter 1, service is part of the product. When we buy a consumer durable, such as an automobile, a washing machine, or a solar heating system, a guarantee to service the product accompanies the product itself. Often our decision to buy a product is influenced by the services provided with the product. In the future, with greater customization and product variety, the service component of the product will increase. It is anticipated that, by the turn of the century, a customer will be able to walk into an automobile dealership, order a car based on his or her preferences for color, style, optional equipment, and the like, and arrange all necessary financing using a computer terminal. The order will be relayed to the

FIGURE 3-1
**RELATIVE IMPORTANCE OF SERVICES AND GOODS IN PERSONAL CONSUMPTION EXPENDITURES.**

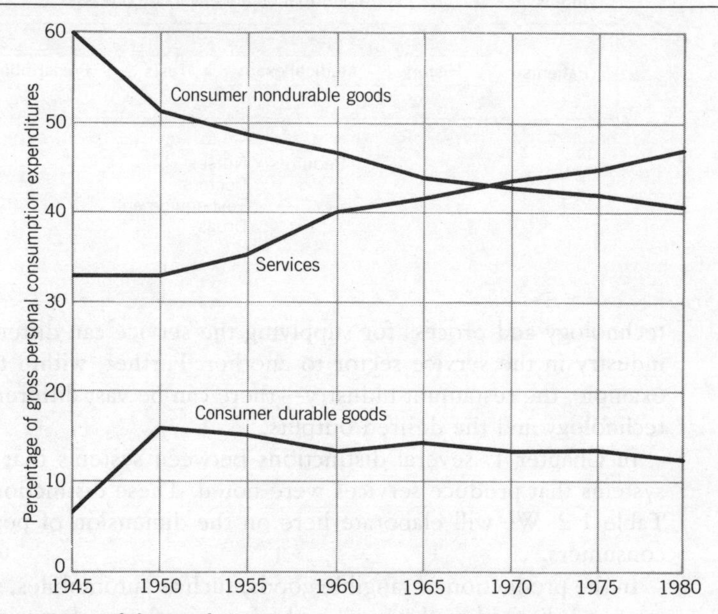


*Source: Economic Report of the President,* 1981.

factory, where a car meeting the customer's specific requirements will be manufactured and readied for delivery in a short time. It is clear that corporate profitability demands that the design and implementation of the service component of a product be strategically evaluated. The integration of product and service is vital for a firm's success, as it influences how a customer perceives the product. Operations managers must therefore direct attention to both the product and the service that accompanies the product.

## DISTINCTIVE FEATURES OF SERVICE SYSTEMS

The inputs to a service productive system are the consumers themselves. The productive process that transforms the inputs into outputs consists of labor, technology, information, and the like. The output of such a system is the altered state of the consumer, for example, a cured patient, a transported traveler, or an informed client. The operations manager can control the design and mix of the productive process to meet customer requirements. In Figure 3-2, a simplified productive process for a doctor's office is shown.

The key distinction between service and manufacturing systems is that services are intangible outputs that are consumed in the process of their production. The

FIGURE 3-2
**DOCTOR'S OFFICE AS A PRODUCTIVE SYSTEM.**

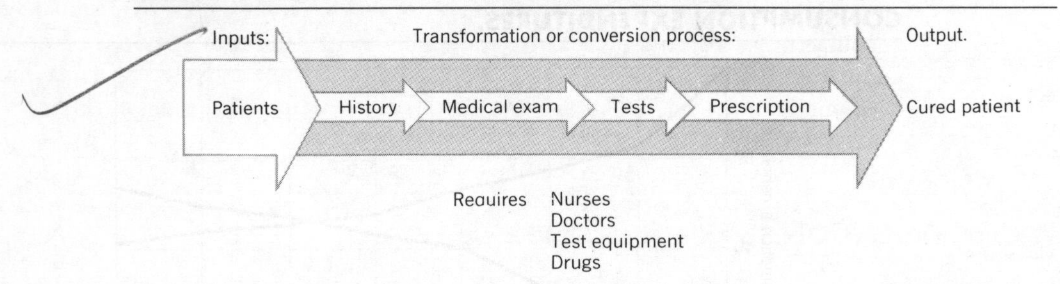


technology and process for supplying the service can differ significantly from one industry in the service sector to another. Further, within the same industry—for example, the restaurant industry—there can be vast differences in both the supply technology and the desired outputs.

In Chapter 1, several distinctions between systems that produce products and systems that produce services were noted. These distinctions were summarized in Table 1-2. We will elaborate here on the dimension of personal contact with the consumers.

In the production of tangible goods, such as automobiles, soap, or beer, customer contact is limited to the retail end, after actual manufacturing has been completed. In the design, planning, and control of the associated manufacturing process, the preferences of consumers are important, but the customer's actual presence is *not*. This anonymity in the productive process allows the attainment of significant manufacturing efficiencies and productivity growth, as has been witnessed in the past 100 years. For example, the number of watches produced per worker has increased a hundred fold since the advent of the watch industry. This has undoubtedly decreased the cost of watches, making them affordable to virtually anyone with moderate means. In the same time span, however, productivity in education may not have even doubled, despite the significant advances in information transmission technology. Therefore, without public subsidy, quality education would be affordable only to those with extensive means. The key distinction is not that the watchmaker now works faster than the teacher but rather that the direct customer (pupil) contact required in education limits sustained growth in productivity without compromising the quality of the service delivered. Gradual increases in the cost of education are not the result of administrative inefficiencies but are intrinsic to the nature of the services provided. An operations manager or policymaker who views progress in terms of cost reduction would likely be frustrated in the field of education. Instead, the emphasis should be on the quality and accessibility of education and on education's contribution to productivity growth in other sectors through well-trained engineers, managers, or physicists.

However, not all services require such a high degree of customer contact. At the other extreme is the telephone industry, which requires little direct customer contact except for operator-assisted telephone calls and directory assistance. In this industry, the cost of the service has steadily decreased while quality improvements have been consistently achieved over time. The productivity growths documented in the telephone industry are large in comparison to those attained by virtually any manufacturing institution. Since considerable insights into the workings of various industries within the service sector of our economy can be provided by using direct customer contact as a variable, we will use it as a primary feature for classifying service systems.

## A CLASSIFICATION OF SERVICE SYSTEMS

The service sector does not consist of a homogeneous group of services. The industries within the service sector are too heterogeneous for a common frame of analysis. We will use here a classification scheme proposed by Baumol (1984) with some modifications. The services can be classified into four categories:

1. Stagnant personal services
2. Substitutable personal services
3. Progressive services
4. Explosive services

### Stagnant Personal Services

These services frequently require direct contact between the customer and the service provider. Some examples are haircutting, live artistic performance, psychiatric counseling, and teaching. Since the quality of such a service is highly correlated with labor time, it is difficult to realize significant productivity gains for these services without an appreciable reduction in quality. It seems evident, for instance, that the amount of time required for a haircut cannot be decreased substantially without some drastic implications. These services offer low innovation potential and are difficult to standardize.

The challenge in managing stagnant personal services is to improve their effectiveness through better management. A substantial gain in productivity in the supporting activities necessary for providing the service can often be realized. For example, copying facilities, overhead projectors, and computers have all contributed to improving the productivity of teachers. Even live artistic performances have benefited from jet travel, which has reduced the total number of artist hours per performance considerably even though actual rehearsal and performance time remains constant over time.

Although productivity gains are minimal in stagnant personal services, the operations manager has several options for strategically placing the service that are consistent with corporate goals. All haircutting shops, for instance, are not alike. One may emphasize low cost with little customization, whereas another may emphasize customization and charge a higher price. Both firms may be successful if managed well, as they cater to different segments of the market. Later in this chapter, strategies available to individual firms will be discussed.

## Substitutable Personal Services

These services also require direct personal contact, and they have characteristics similar to stagnant personal services. However, it is possible to substitute for these services with technological or other alternatives. An example would be the services of a guard that can be replaced by electronic surveillance systems. In the twentieth century, we have seen ovens, washers and dryers, and other household appliances substituted for personal servants (maids, cooks, etc.). Some types of teaching, such as real estate licensing course work, are now conducted using cassettes, tapes, and videos, and the demand for the live instructors has decreased correspondingly.

A great leap in productivity in substitutable personal services is provided by technological innovation. For example, electronic mail may improve the productivity of the mail delivery system manyfold. Television provides access to millions of people of special events that can be viewed in person by only by a few thousand.

It should be noted that while the substitutes for personal services are often less costly, they are often also inferior. A personal cook cannot be compared with an assortment of kitchen devices that make cooking easy. Similarly, watching a concert or a sporting event on TV is not the same as the live performance.

## Progressive Services

These services have two components. One component requires little labor, and considerable cost reductions are possible with it. The second component is highly labor intensive and is much like stagnant personal services. An example is computation services.

In a simplified aggregate view, computation services can be conceptualized as consisting of hardware and software. The cost of hardware per computation has declined steadily; conversely, the cost of software has risen. This is because software is produced by human labor and offers limited productivity growth.

Another example is television broadcasting, where the two components are the transmission and the production of a program. Transmission costs have steadily decreased with advances in the electronics and space industries. However, the production of a television program is highly labor intensive, and consequently, the associated costs continue to increase. Research and development can also be thought of as consisting of two dichotomous components: equipment and human thought.

Progressive services can exhibit phenomenal productivity growth and cost reductions initially. This is due to the relatively important contribution of the first technology intensive component. For example, computer hardware contributes significantly to computation costs; thus, decreases in hardware costs per computation lead to overall cost reductions. Since the costs per unit of output for the second, labor intensive component are increasing, the decline in total cost cannot be sustained for long periods. In this sense, productivity growth is self-extinguishing. This happens because, in due course of time, the relative contribution of the second component exceeds that of the first component. The stagnant nature of the second component dampens productivity growth.

A numerical example illustrates the cost per unit behavior of progressive services. Suppose the share of component 1 is 80 percent in the beginning and that of component 2 is 20 percent. Further, suppose that the cost of the first component is declining at the rate of 30 percent per year and the cost of the second component is rising at the rate of 10 percent per year. For an output of service that costs $100 in year zero (the initial period), the first component costs $80 and the second costs $20. At the end of the first year, the cost of the first component has declined to $80 − (0.3 × $80) = $56, and the cost of the second component has risen to $20 + (0.1 × $20) = $22. Thus, the total cost of the same unit of service has decreased from $100 to $56 + $22 = $78. In a similar manner, we can compute the cost of the two components for year two and so on. The results of these computations are shown in Table 3-1.

From Table 3-1, it is clear that in the first few years there is a decline in the total cost per unit of service. In fact, in just four years the service costs half as much as it did initially. By year seven, however, there is a reversal of this trend and total costs begin to increase. This happens because the relative share of the cost of component 2 is now much larger (85 percent as compared with 20 percent initially) and this stagnant component is increasing in cost. In Figure 3-3, the costs of the two components and the total cost per unit of service are plotted.

An important feature of the progressive service is that the faster the initial decline in total cost per unit of service, the more rapidly cost reduction ceases. This is because the relative share of the first component responsible for cost reductions shrinks rapidly and the service begins to acquire the characteristics of the second

**TABLE 3-1**
**COST BEHAVIOR OF PROGRESSIVE SERVICES**

Initial conditions: $100 worth of service at time 0

| | | Share of component 1 = 80% | | Share of component 2 = 20% | |
|---|---|---|---|---|---|
| | | Rate of decrease in the cost of component 1 = 30%/year | | Rate of increase in the cost of component 2 = 10%/year | |
| Year | Cost of Component 1 | Share of Component 1 in Total Cost | Cost of Component 2 | Share of Component 2 in Total Cost | Total Cost for a Unit of Service |
| 0 | $80.00 | 80.00% | $20.00 | 20.00% | $100.00 |
| 1 | 56.00 | 71.80 | 22.00 | 28.20 | 78.00 |
| 2 | 39.20 | 61.83 | 24.20 | 38.17 | 63.40 |
| 3 | 27.44 | 50.76 | 26.62 | 49.24 | 54.06 |
| 4 | 19.21 | 39.62 | 29.28 | 60.38 | 48.49 |
| 5 | 13.45 | 29.46 | 32.21 | 70.54 | 45.66 |
| 6 | 9.41 | 20.98 | 35.43 | 79.02 | 44.84 |
| 7 | 6.59 | 14.46 | 38.97 | 85.54 | 45.56 |
| 8 | 4.61 | 10.75 | 42.87 | 89.25 | 47.48 |
| 9 | 3.23 | 6.41 | 47.16 | 93.59 | 50.39 |
| 10 | 2.26 | 4.17 | 51.88 | 95.83 | 54.14 |

FIGURE 3-3
**PLOT OF THE COSTS FOR TWO COMPONENTS AND TOTAL COST FOR PROGRESSIVE SERVICES.**

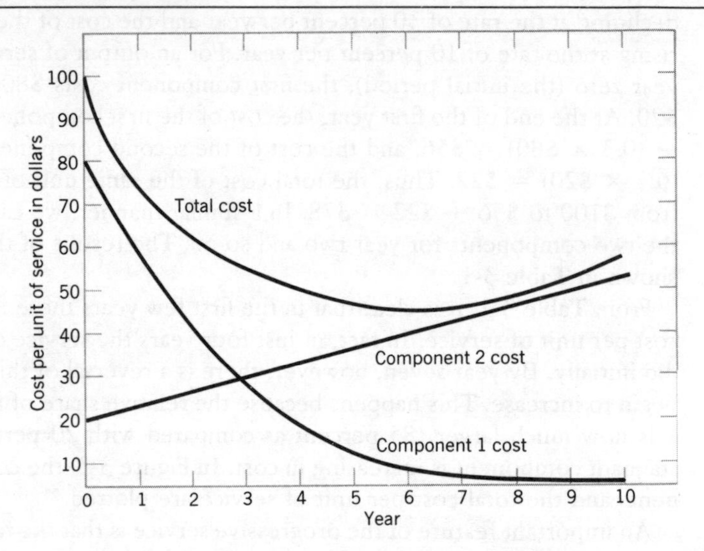


component. If, for example, in Table 3-1, the cost of component 1 decreases at the rate of 50 percent per year rather than 30 percent per year, then the total costs will decline for only the first four years. From the fifth year onwards, the cost per unit will increase.

Progressive services pose a special challenge to operations managers, as the management of the two components of the service will require careful coordination. The rational expectations for these services should not be guided by the initial cost decline and productivity growth but by a longer range view. In the long run, the emphasis should be on improving the performance of the service system as overall costs will not be likely to go down. This has been demonstrated in electronic libraries, where the quality of the service has improved but expected cost savings have not occurred.

## Explosive Services

Explosive services involve virtually no contact between customers and production labor. Telephone communications is one example of such a service. These services offer high innovation potential as technological advances decrease cost substantially. In telephone communications, the technology has progressed from open wires to microwaves, coaxial cables, satellite transmissions, and digital technology. The productivity growth has been enormous, and soon remote parts of the world will be reachable with connections as clear as those for local city calls. In the future, services such as airlines reservations, banking, and shopping may be conveniently conducted using a home computer. These services will experience explosive growth in productivity commensurate with associated technological advances. The benefit to the consumer will be greater variety of services at declining costs.

## PRODUCTIVITY GROWTH POSSIBILITIES

The four categories of services and some examples of them are shown in Table 3-2. It is clear from the examples in Table 3-2 that productivity growth possibilities for each category are significantly different.

The first category offers little or no opportunity for productivity growth. Consequently, the cost of these services will continue to increase.

The second category of services offers an opportunity for cost reduction if substitutes are acceptable. Often, substitutes are of inferior quality. Further, there may be long periods when no substitutes are available, so costs will increase. Even when substitutes become available via technological breakthroughs or price pressures, the substitutes themselves may suffer from "cost disease." This will happen if the initial cost of a substitute is lower but subsequent reductions in the cost are difficult to achieve.

Progressive services provide an enormous opportunity for productivity growth and cost reductions initially. In time, though, the stagnant component of these services will dominate the total cost and, consequently, productivity growth will cease and costs will begin to rise.

Finally, explosive services, which require no direct contact with customers, can take full advantage of any technological breakthroughs. The potential for productivity growth for these services often exceeds that available in the manufacturing sector.

Overall, however, the service sector exhibits a lower productivity growth and offers fewer opportunities for cost reductions than does the manufacturing sector. The management of firms in the service sector therefore poses special challenges. We now shift our discussion from an industry perspective to an individual firm perspective.

**TABLE 3-2**
**A CLASSIFICATION OF SERVICE SYSTEMS**

| Stagnant Personal | Substitutable Personal | Progressive | Explosive |
|---|---|---|---|
| Doctor's office | Personal servants | Broadcasting | Telecommunications |
| Teaching | Full service grocery stores | Computation | Telephone |
| Barber shop | Personal lawyers, accountants | Research and development | |
| Live performance | | | |

## SERVICE STRATEGY OF A FIRM

A service firm must emphasize those dimensions of its service that enable it to achieve a competitive advantage over its competitors. For example, in the health care field, a multispecialty group practice clinic will emphasize its ability to treat acute or complex health problems. Such a clinic consists of an affiliated group of physicians who practice medical specialties and attract patients by referral from a primary care physician or by reputation. In contrast, a primary care clinic consisting of general practitioners, family practitioners, and the like will emphasize the treatment of a full range of health problems and will be responsible for preventive medicine and health education.

The cost of service will be relatively less important for the multispecialty clinic than for the primary care clinic. Because of the different emphasis, the design and control of the process of production and delivery of service will be different for the two types of clinics. For example, a multispecialty clinic may not invest in an automated laboratory where each patient is subjected to a standardized battery of tests that are conducted in an efficient manner. Instead, it may utilize a conventional laboratory for specific tests requested by the physician. The primary care clinic may, however, prefer an automated laboratory, as it provides a low-cost method for obtaining information on the health status of a patient.

The preceding example illustrates that the criteria that a service firm emphasize differ widely. We now discuss some of the criteria that may be relevant in defining the service strategy of a firm.

### Criteria for Competition

A service firm may not be able to perform well on all criteria, such as speed, cost, quality, variety, customization, reliability, and consistency. Full-service brokers, for example, provide personal attention and a greater variety of products, such as forming real estate partnerships, than do discount brokers. However, the commission charged per transaction is higher for the full-service brokers. Similarly, Federal Express delivers packages at great speed but also at a relatively high cost and with limited flexibility. The General Post Office, in contrast, delivers at lower cost and with higher flexibility (in types, sizes, and destinations of packages), but it is significantly slower. A useful way to group various criteria is as follows:

- Cost
- Quality
- Dependability
- Flexibility or customization

The cost criterion is the cost of providing service and may include both capital and operating costs.

The quality of a service can be measured in several different ways, depending on the context. The craftsmanship of the provider, such as a barber or a surgeon, directly influences the quality of the output (the haircut or a successful operation). In some cases, personal attention and speed of service is indicative of quality (e.g., the service of a receptionist). Reliability of output (e.g., financial advice or tax consulting) is also a measure of quality.

The dependability criterion reflects the consistency and the availability of the service when needed. For example, a 24-hour operation will have higher dependability than an 8-hour operation.

Finally, the flexibility or customization criterion measures the ability to provide service according to an individual's requirements. A health club that provides coaching and assistance in designing an exercise program according to each individual member's physical condition and goals will have a higher degree of flexibility than will a health club that only makes the exercise equipment available for use.

It is clear that there are tradeoffs among these criteria and that the simultaneous maximization of each criterion is not possible. For example, if the demand for service fluctuates, as with the arrival rate of customers in a bank, then greater dependability and quality (a shorter wait) can only be achieved by staffing for the peak loads and thus increasing the costs. A reduced level of staffing will reduce costs, but it will undoubtedly increase the waiting time and queue length. Similarly, the Super Cut chain of hair salons charges less, but the degree of customization and the craftsmanship of its workers are relatively low. In contrast, Vidal Sassoon employs highly skilled workers and provides a greater degree of customization in hair designs but charges more per haircut.

These criteria are not necessarily competing, and some technological breakthroughs can improve both the cost per unit and service quality. But, in a relative sense, emphasis on one criterion could lead to a compromise with respect to some other criteria.

## Positioning

Within a given industry, such as the food store industry, a firm may choose to emphasize some criteria over the others, the relative emphasis thus determining the firm's unique positioning in the industry. For example, a mom and pop store depends on personal relationships between the owners and clients, but it has a higher average cost per item. On the other hand, a supermarket uses economies of scale to reduce the average cost per item; however, it tends to be impersonal and does not offer adaptability to individual client's needs.

A service firm must carefully examine and evaluate its position with respect to its competitors in order to determine an effective strategy. In Figure 3-4, a matrix is given that indicates relative positions for different types of firms. A firm can be characterized by the degree of customization it offers in its service and by the characteristics of the service it provides. Of course, this is an incomplete characterization of the position of the firm as several other distinctive features are left out. The matrix, however, provides a starting point for analyzing the position of the firm vis-a-vis its competitors.

FIGURE 3-4
**MATRIX OF RELATIVE POSITIONS OF SERVICE FIRMS.**

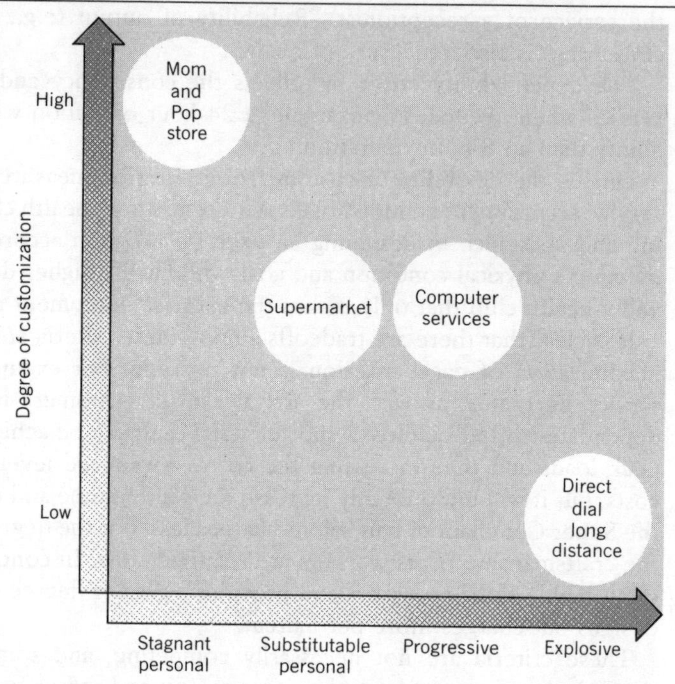


## Operations Decisions

The design and control of the process for producing and delivering service critically depends on the position of the firm. All operations decisions must be consistent with the service criteria that the firm have chosen to emphasize.

A distribution company that emphasizes low cost will operate with few warehouses and low inventory levels in each warehouse. In contrast, a company that emphasizes better service (low delivery time) will have a larger network of warehouses, will incur higher cost of inventory, and will employ faster means of transportation. The cost per unit for the second company will be higher and the delivery time will be lower.

Operations decisions, such as capacity expansion, technological choices, work force and job designs, suppliers, and vertical integration, depend on the service strategy of the firm. A more detailed discussion of these issues is provided in Chapter 21 and 22. Books by Fitzsimmons and Sullivan (1982) and Sasser et al. (1978) are devoted to operations decisions for the firms in the service sector. For the purposes of this introductory chapter, it is sufficient to reiterate that services, in spite of their commonality as intangible products, differ a great deal. Operations managers should recognize these differences and make decisions consistent with the strategy of the firm.

## IMPLICATIONS FOR THE MANAGER

A simple classification of services into four categories—stagnant personal, substitutable personal, progressive, and explosive—provides a manager insights into the productivity improvement possibilities for industries in a particular category. A careful analysis shows that all services to some degree, and some services to an extraordinary degree, have productivity growth and cost reduction possibilities.

Productivity, however, is only one dimension by which the manager should evaluate a service. The manager must also understand the competitive advantage of his or her firm and make decisions that will support and improve the firm's competitive position over time.

The four criteria—cost, quality, dependability, and flexibility—can be used to define the service strategy of the firm. These criteria need to be further specialized for specific situations. A manager should gain a clear understanding of which criteria are relatively more important for his or her firm. All operating decisions should then be consistent with these criteria.

# REVIEW QUESTIONS

1. Services have become more important in our economy, as was indicated by Figure 3-1. It is also generally true that the dominant cost in most services is labor. What are the future prospects for continued rapid increases in productivity in the United States economy if the conversion to services continues?
2. What are the important differences between products and services?
3. Provide an example of each of the four types of services discussed in this chapter.
4. What criteria for defining service strategy will be important for the following firms:
   a. Executive Recruitment Firm
   b. Vending Services
   c. Starving Students Moving Company
   d. Self-Serve Cafeteria
5. The sole objective of an operations manager should be to improve the efficiency and productivity of services. Yes or No? Explain.

# SITUATION

## Medical Costs Soar

6. Medical care is one area that has been the target of critics because of skyrocketing costs. The total U.S. health care bill in 1971 stood at $70 billion per year (about $324 per person per year or about 7 percent of the GNP). These expendi-

FIGURE 3-5
**COMPARATIVE PRICE INDEXES AND INDUSTRIAL OUTPUT PER WORKER-HOUR INDEX (1950 = 100).**

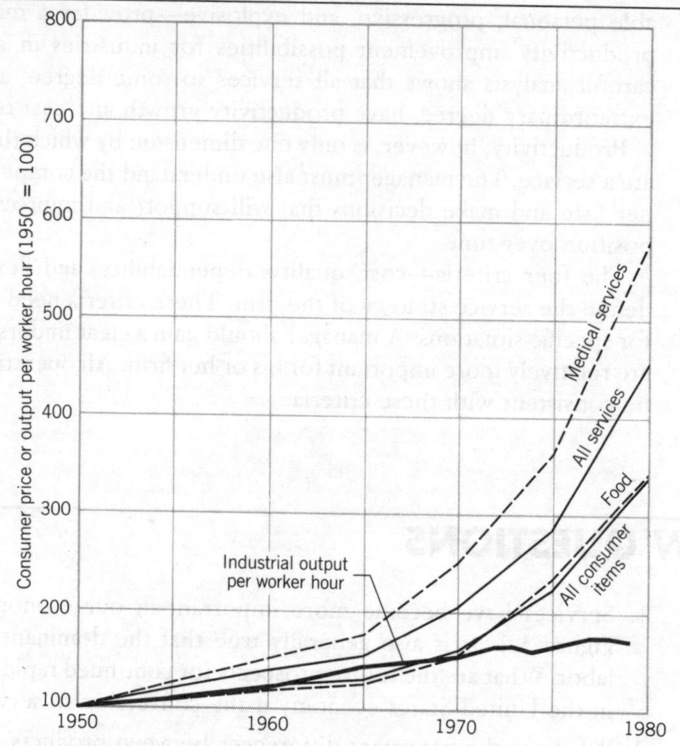


*Source: Economic Report of the President,* 1981.

tures have increased at an average rate of almost 13 percent per year during the last decade.

Figure 3-5 confirms some of the reasons for concern. Since 1950, the price index for medical care has risen from 100 to 582, whereas the general index of consumer prices has risen to only 341. The price index of all services has far outstripped the general index, and medical care has been the price leader. Of course, during the period from 1950 to the present, there have been substantial increases in productivity to help offset the effect of general price increases, as is shown in Figure 3-5. (Output per worker-hour increased from 100 to 173 between 1950 and 1979.) Otherwise, the general price index would undoubtedly have increased more than it did. In general, services have not benefited as much as manufacturing from productivity increases.

From what you know about health care systems, what are the reasons for rising medical costs? What are the most promising areas for cost reductions and productivity increases in this industry?

## REFERENCES

Baumol, W. J., "Productivity Policy and the Service Sector," Discussion Paper #1, Fishman-Davidson Center for the Study of the Service Sector, University of Pennsylvania, Philadelphia, April 1984.

Fitzsimmons, J. A., and R. S. Sullivan, *Service Operations Management,* McGraw-Hill, New York, 1982.

Sasser, W. E., R. P. Olson, and D. D. Wyckoff, *Management of Service Operations: Text, Cases, and Readings,* Allyn & Bacon, Boston, 1978.

# PART TWO

# OPERATIONS PLANNING AND CONTROL

# CHAPTER 4

# FORECASTING FOR OPERATIONS

Planning and control for operations requires an estimate of the demand for the product or the service that an organization expects to provide in the future. Numerous methods for the art and science of forecasting have been developed and reported in the literature. In this chapter, we focus on those methods of forecasting that are specially suited to production/operations situations.

Since forecasting should be an integral part of planning and decision making, the choice of a forecasting horizon (a week or a month, for example), a forecasting method with desired accuracy, and the unit of forecasting (gross dollar sales, individual product demand, etc.) should be based on a clear understanding of how the output of the forecast will be used in the decision process. The field of forecasting is full of instances at both government and individual firm levels where a mass of data was generated that was little used in making the subsequent decisions. The type of information that is needed for inventory planning is significantly different from the type of information that is needed for planning capacity additions. Forecasting should address these different needs and provide data that are appropriate and useful for decision making in these differing contexts.

## REQUIREMENTS OF FORECASTING FOR OPERATIONS

Planning and control for operations takes place at several levels. Therefore, it is unlikely that one kind of forecast can serve all needs. We require forecasts of different time spans to serve as the basis for operating plans developed for different planning horizons. These include (1) plans for current operations and for the immediate future, (2) intermediate-range plans to provide for the capacities of personnel, materials, and equipment required for the next 1 to 12 months, and (3) long-range plans for capacity, locations, changing product and service mix, and the development of new products and services.

The horizon of the forecast must be matched with the decision the forecast will affect. If the decision will deal with activities over the next three months, a one-month forecast would be valueless. On the other hand, it is unwise to select a forecasting model for daily or weekly decisions that has an acceptable error on a monthly or annual basis but poor accuracy for daily or weekly projections. Therefore, a major criterion for model selection is the match between decision time, forecast horizon, and forecasting accuracy.

When developing plans for current operations and for the immediate future (e.g., how many jobs should be released to a shop on a given day or how many tellers should be assigned during the lunch hour on a Friday), the degree of detail required in forecasting is high. The forecast data should be available in a form that can be translated into demands for material, specific labor skills, and time usage of specific equipment. Therefore, forecasts of gross dollar demand, demand by customer or client classification, or demand by broad product or service classifications are of limited value for short-term, daily operational decisions.

For such short-term decisions, we need forecasting methods that are relatively inexpensive to install and maintain and that can be adapted to situations involving a large number of items to be forecast. This means that the data input and storage requirements should be modest and that computerized methods are a likely mechanism for updating forecast data as needed.

For intermediate-range plans, such as plans for monthly production levels or work-force levels, useful forecasts will probably be aggregated by product types. Detailed forecasts for each individual item may not be necessary. Also, since the relative frequency of forecasts is lower and the number of different product types for which forecasts are made is smaller than is the case for the short-term decisions, forecasting methods that require modest cost and effort could be employed.

Long-range plans for capacity, location, and new technologies for plant and equipment require forecasts for the next 1 to 10 years. Because of the longer time involved, these forecasts will necessarily have greater uncertainty and a lower degree of accuracy. Often, the mechanical application of a model is not sufficient to obtain the desired forecast, and subjective inputs from the managers and other knowledgeable people are required. The methods of forecasting should therefore be able to integrate objective data and subjective inputs.

## BASIC CATEGORIES OF FORECASTING METHODS

Forecasting methods can be divided into three main categories:

- Extrapolative or time series methods
- Causal or explanatory methods
- Qualitative or judgmental methods

In some situations, a combination of methods may be more appropriate than a single method.

Extrapolative methods use the past history of demand in making a forecast for the future. The objective of these methods is to identify the pattern in historic data and extrapolate this pattern for the future. This process might seem like driving while looking only through a rear view mirror. However, if the time horizon for which the forecast is made is short, extrapolative methods perform quite well.

Causal methods of forecasting assume that the demand for an item depends on one or more independent factors (e.g., price, advertising, competitor's price, etc.). These methods seek to establish a relationship between the variable to be forecasted and independent variables. Once this relationship is established, future values can be forecasted by simply plugging in the appropriate values for the independent variables.

Judgmental methods rely on experts' (or managers') opinion in making a prediction for the future. These methods are useful for medium to long-range forecasting tasks. The use of judgment in forecasting, at first blush, sounds unscientific and ad hoc. However, when past data are unavailable or not representative of the future, there are few alternatives other than using the informed opinion of knowledgeable people. There are, however, good ways and bad ways to solicit judgments for making a forecast. We will discuss some approaches that structure and formalize the process of soliciting judgments so that individual biases are minimized. Often, in operations situations, judgmental methods are employed in conjunction with extrapolative or causal methods.

## EXTRAPOLATIVE METHODS

Extrapolative methods seek to identify patterns in past data. Most of these patterns depend on four components of demand: horizontal, trend, seasonal, and cyclical. The appropriateness of an extrapolative method will depend on which components of demand are operating in a given situation.

### Components of Demand

The horizontal component of demand exists when the demand fluctuates about an average demand. The average demand remains constant and does not consistently increase or decrease. The sales of a product in the mature stage of the product life cycle may show a horizontal demand pattern.

The trend component of demand refers to a sustained increase or decrease in demand from one period to the next. For example, if the average monthly demand for a product has increased 10 to 15 percent in each of the past few years, then an upward trend in demand exists. The sales of products in the growth stage of the product life cycle tend to show an upward trend, whereas those in decline tend to show a downward trend.

The seasonal component of demand pertains to the influence of seasonal factors that impact demand positively or negatively. For example, the sales of snow blowers will be higher in winter months and lower in summer months every year, indicating a seasonal component in the demand for snow blowers.

The cyclical component of demand is similar to the seasonal component except that seasonality occurs at regular intervals and is of constant length, whereas the cyclic component varies in both time and duration of occurrence. For example, the impact of a recession on the demand for a product will be reflected by the cyclic component. Recessions occur at irregular intervals and the length of time a recession lasts varies. This component is present in most economic data, such as GNP, personal income, and industry sales of such consumer durables as automobiles and major appliances.

### Moving Average Method

The simplest extrapolative method is the moving average method. In this method, two simple steps are needed to make a forecast for the next period from past data.

*Step 1.* Select the number of periods for which moving averages will be computed. This number, $N$, is called an order of moving average.

*Step 2.* Take the average demand for the most recent $N$ periods. This average demand then becomes the forecast for the next period.

To illustrate this method, consider the demand data for a product for which, in the months of February, March, April, May, and June, the demand was 90, 80, 120, 100, and 80 units, respectively. Interest is in making a forecast for the month of July.

*Step 1.* Choose $N = 4$. Other values can also be chosen. Larger $N$ values will have a greater smoothing effect on random fluctuations in demand. Smaller $N$ values will emphasize the more recent demand history. Notice that $N = 1$ will result in the present period's demand being the forecast for the next period.

*Step 2.* Find the average demand for the most recent 4 periods, $N = 4$.

$$\text{Moving average} = \frac{\text{Demand for March, April, May, June}}{4}$$

$$= \frac{80 + 120 + 100 + 80}{4}$$

$$= 95 \text{ units}$$

The forecast for July is therefore 95 units.

Now, suppose the actual demand for July turns out to be 100 units. The forecast for August will be computed by taking the average demand for April, May, June, and July. This forecast will be

$$\frac{120 + 100 + 80 + 100}{4} = 100 \text{ units}$$

Once $N$ is selected, the new moving average for each future period is computed by taking the average demand for the most recent $N$ periods. The disadvantage of this method is that it requires the storage of demand data for $N$ periods for each item. In a production situation where forecasts for a large number of items are to be made, these storage requirements could be significant. Further, this method will not provide good forecasts if the demand data reflect trend or seasonal components. For example, if there is an upward trend in the data, then a forecast made using the moving average method will underestimate the actual demand.

The moving average method gives equal weight to the demand in each of the most recent $N$ periods. We can modify the method, however, by assigning a different weight to each previous period. Exponential smoothing methods, which are discussed next, are convenient for accomplishing the differential weighting of demand in previous periods. Further, these methods can incorporate trend and seasonality components of demand in forecasting.

## Exponential Smoothing Methods

In these methods, the weight assigned to a previous period's demand decreases exponentially as that data gets older. Thus, recent demand data receives a higher weight than does older demand data.

## WHEN TO USE EXPONENTIAL SMOOTHING

Exponential smoothing methods are particularly attractive for production and operations applications that involve forecasting for a large number of items. These methods work best under the following conditions:

- The forecasting horizon is relatively short; for example, a daily, weekly, or monthly demand needs to be forecasted.
- There is little "outside" information available about cause and effect relationships between the demand of an item and independent factors that influence it.
- Small effort in forecasting is desired. Effort is measured by both a method's ease of application and by the computational requirements (time, storage) needed to implement it.
- Updating of the forecast as new data become available is easy and can be accomplished by simply inputting the new data.
- It is desired that the forecast is adjusted for randomness (fluctuations in demand are smoothed) and tracks trends and seasonality.

## BASIC EXPONENTIAL SMOOTHING MODEL

The simplest exponential smoothing model is applicable when there is no trend or seasonality component in the data. Thus, only the horizontal component of demand is present and, because of randomness, the demand fluctuates around an "average demand," which we will call the "base." If the base is constant from period to period, then all fluctuations in demand must be due to randomness. In reality, fluctuations in demand are caused by both changes in the base and random noise. The key objective in exponential smoothing models is to estimate the base and use that estimate for forecasting future demand.

In the basic exponential smoothing model, the base for the current period, $\bar{S}_t$, is estimated by modifying the previous base by adding or subtracting to it a fraction $\alpha$ (alpha) of the difference between the actual current demand $D_t$ and the previous base $\bar{S}_{t-1}$. The estimate of the new base is then

$$\text{New base} = \text{Previous base} + \alpha(\text{New demand} - \text{Previous base}).$$

Or, stated in symbols,

$$\bar{S}_t = \bar{S}_{t-1} + \alpha(D_t - \bar{S}_{t-1}) \tag{1}$$

The smoothing constant, $\alpha$, is between 0 and 1, with commonly used values of 0.01 to 0.30.

Another interpretation of Equation 1 is that the new base is estimated by modifying the previous base, $\bar{S}_{t-1}$, by correcting for the observed error in period $t$. We call $(D_t - \bar{S}_{t-1})$ an observed error for period $t$ because $D_t$ is the actual demand for period $t$ and $\bar{S}_{t-1}$ is our forecast for period $t$.

Equation 1 can be rearranged as follows:

$$\text{New base} = \alpha(\text{New demand}) + (1 - \alpha)(\text{Previous base})$$

or

$$\bar{S}_t = \alpha D_t + (1 - \alpha)\bar{S}_{t-1} \tag{2}$$

Thus, the new base is estimated by simply taking a weighted average of the new demand $D_t$ and the previous base $\bar{S}_{t-1}$.

To illustrate the application of this model, suppose $\alpha = 0.10$, $\bar{S}_{\text{Jan}} = 50$ units, and $D_{\text{Feb}} = 60$ units. The new base for February is computed by using Equation 2:

$$\begin{aligned} \bar{S}_{\text{Feb}} &= 0.1D_{\text{Feb}} + 0.9\bar{S}_{\text{Jan}} \\ &= 0.1(60) + 0.9(50) \\ &= 51 \text{ Units} \end{aligned}$$

So far, we have seen how we can estimate a new base from the information about new demand and the previous base once $\alpha$ has been specified. We now need to make a forecast for the next period (or, more generally, for some specified future period). In the basic exponential smoothing model, since trend and seasonality components are not included in the model, direct extrapolation of $\bar{S}_t$ to infer a forecast is justified. Therefore, the forecast for any future period is taken directly as the computed value of $\bar{S}_t$. Table 4-1 shows the computations and forecasts for the first several months of demand data for a product. It is useful to split the process of forecasting using exponential smoothing models in two steps.

*Step 1.* Estimate the new $\bar{S}_t$ using Equation 2.

*Step 2.* Forecast $T$ periods ahead by extrapolating the base computed in Step 1. The forecast made in period $t$ for $T$ periods ahead, $F_{t,T}$, in the basic exponential smoothing model is simply $\bar{S}_t$.

$$F_{t,T} = \bar{S}_t$$

Usually $T = 1$; that is, the forecast is made for only one period ahead.

## SOME PROPERTIES OF THE EXPONENTIAL SMOOTHING MODEL

First, the method is simple and requires that minimal information be stored for each item. Unlike the moving average method, for which all past $N$ observations must be stored, the exponential smoothing model requires only two pieces of data: the most recent demand and the previous base. The procedure can be easily automated, and the data entry in each period is only the new demand information.

Second, the choice of $\alpha$ allows us to control the weighting of the new demand. For example, if $\alpha = 0.10$, then Equation 2 says that the base in the current period, $\bar{S}_t$, will be determined by adding 10 percent of the new actual demand information, $D_t$, and 90 percent of the previous base. Because the new demand figure, $D_t$, includes possible random variations, we are discounting 90 percent of those variations. Obviously, small values of $\alpha$ will have a stronger smoothing effect than large values. Conversely, large values of $\alpha$ will reflect real changes in actual demand (as well as random variations) more quickly. Thus, if fluctuations in demand are primarily due to randomness, a small $\alpha$ should be chosen. If fluctuations in demand are due to a shifting base, then a higher $\alpha$ should be chosen. To see the extreme cases, set $\alpha = 0$ and $\alpha = 1$ in Equation 2.

$$\text{If } \alpha = 0, \bar{S}_t = \bar{S}_{t-1}$$

TABLE 4-1
**SAMPLE COMPUTATIONS FOR THE BASE $\bar{S}_t$ AND FORECAST USING A BASIC EXPONENTIAL SMOOTHING MODEL WITH $\alpha = 0.2$**

| Month | Actual Demand $D_t$ | Base $\bar{S}_t$ | Forecast |
|---|---|---|---|
| Initial | — | 23.0 | — |
| Jan | 19.36 | 22.27 | 23.0 |
| Feb | 25.45 | 22.90 | 22.27 |
| Mar | 19.73 | 22.27 | 22.90 |
| Apr | 21.48 | 22.11 | 22.27 |
| May | 20.77 | 21.84 | 22.11 |
| Jun | 25.42 | 22.56 | 21.84 |
| Jul | — | — | 22.56 |

In this case, the new base is just the same as the previous base and, therefore, all fluctuations in demand are attributed to randomness.

$$\text{If } \alpha = 1, \bar{S}_t = D_t$$

In this case, the new base is the new demand and the previous base is totally ignored. Thus, it is assumed that the new demand has no randomness and the base has in fact shifted.

Practically speaking, we will not know how much of a fluctuation in demand is due to randomness and how much of it is due to a shift in the base. Forecasts based on a large value of $\alpha$ fluctuate quite a bit, whereas forecasts based on a small value of $\alpha$ are smoother and fluctuate less. Since a small $\alpha$ has a greater smoothing effect on demand, it is usually recommended that an $\alpha$ between 0.01 and 0.30 be chosen. It is also possible to conduct an empirical test in which $\alpha$ is varied and forecast errors are computed for several alternative values of $\alpha$. The value of $\alpha$ that produces minimum forecast error is then chosen. In the next section we will discuss how forecast error can be measured.

Finally, the model given by Equation 2 uses all past demand history. This occurs through the chain of periodic calculations used to produce estimates of the base for each period. In Equation 2, for example, the term $\bar{S}_{t-1}$ was computed from

$$\bar{S}_{t-1} = \alpha D_{t-1} + (1 - \alpha)\bar{S}_{t-2}$$

which includes the previous actual demand $D_{t-1}$. The $\bar{S}_{t-2}$ term was calculated in a similar manner, which included $D_{t-2}$, and so on, back to the beginning of the series. Therefore, the smoothed averages are based on a sequential process that represents all previous actual demands.

It is also important to recognize that at least one year of historical data are required before confidence can be placed in the resulting forecasts. The initial, assumed value of $\bar{S}_t$ has an impact on the early data, but because of the heavier weighting of recent data, the effects of errors in initial values become very small at the end of the initialization process.

## FORECAST ERRORS

Forecast errors are defined as

$$\begin{aligned} e_t &= \text{Forecast error} \\ &= \text{Actual demand for period } t - \text{Forecast for period } t \end{aligned}$$

Forecast errors provide a measure of accuracy and a basis for comparing the performance of alternate models. The error measures commonly used are

1. Average error $(AE) = \dfrac{1}{N}\displaystyle\sum_{t=1}^{N} e_t$

2. Mean absolute deviation $(MAD) = \dfrac{1}{N}\displaystyle\sum_{t=1}^{N} |e_t|$

3. Mean squared error $(MSE) = \dfrac{1}{N}\displaystyle\sum_{t=1}^{N} e_t^2$

4. Mean absolute percentage error $(MAPE) = \dfrac{1}{N}\displaystyle\sum_{t=1}^{N} \left|\dfrac{e_t}{D_t} \times 100\right|$

The average error (*AE*) should be near zero for a larger sample; otherwise, the model exhibits bias. Bias indicates a systematic tendency to forecast high or low values for demand. But *AE* obscures variability because positive and negative errors cancel out.

The mean absolute deviation (*MAD*) provides additional information that is useful in selecting a forecasting model and its parameters. *MAD* is simply the sum of all errors without regard to algebraic sign, divided by the number of observations.

The mean squared error (*MSE*) provides information similar to *MAD*, but it penalizes larger errors. *MSE* is computed by summing the squared individual errors and dividing by the number of observations.

The mean absolute percentage error (*MAPE*) is a relative measure that is computed by dividing the forecast error for period $t$ by the actual demand for period $t$ and thereby computing the percentage error in period $t$.

$$\text{Percentage error in period } t = \frac{\text{Forecast error in period } t}{\text{Demand in period } t} \times 100$$

The percentage error is now summed by ignoring the algebraic sign (that is, by taking its absolute value), and this sum is divided by the number of observations to obtain *MAPE*. *MAPE* gives the decision maker an idea of how much the forecast is off as a percentage of demand. In Table 4-2, the computation of these four measures

TABLE 4-2
**COMPUTATION OF FOUR MEASURES OF FORECAST ERROR**

| Period | Demand | Forecast | Error | $(\text{Error})^2$ | % Error |
|---|---|---|---|---|---|
| 1 | 20 | 18 | + 2 | 4 | +10.00% |
| 2 | 30 | 25 | + 5 | 25 | +16.67 |
| 3 | 10 | 15 | − 5 | 25 | −50.00 |
| 4 | 40 | 30 | +10 | 100 | +25.00 |
| 5 | 30 | 35 | − 5 | 25 | −16.67 |

$$\text{Average error} = \frac{2 + 5 - 5 + 10 - 5}{5} = 1.4$$

$$\text{Mean absolute deviation} = \frac{2 + 5 + 5 + 10 + 5}{5} = 5.4$$

$$\text{Mean squared error} = \frac{4 + 25 + 25 + 100 + 25}{5} = 35.8$$

$$\text{Mean absolute percentage error} = \frac{10 + 16.67 + 50 + 25 + 16.67}{5} = 23.6\%$$

is illustrated. One or more of these measures could be used to compare the performance of alternative forecasting models.

## Classification of Exponential Smoothing Models

The basic exponential smoothing model does not incorporate trend and seasonality components in the demand data for forecasting. Winters (1960) and Pegels (1969) have developed models that are capable of incorporating these effects. The classification of these models is shown in Figure 4-1 with hypothetical demand patterns.

The trend and seasonality components of demand each have three levels; thus, there are nine possible models shown in Figure 4-1. The three levels of the trend component are shown along the rows and those of the seasonality component are shown along the columns.

Demand data can have no trend, a linear trend, or a ratio trend. A linear trend is defined by the units per period by which the expected demand changes (increases or decreases). An example of a linear trend would be an average increase in demand of 10 units per period. A ratio trend is defined by the percentage of demand by which demand is changing, as, for example, when demand increases at an average rate of 15 percent per period. Thus, in a ratio trend, there is a compounding effect on the absolute value of demand.

Similarly, demand data can have no seasonality, additive seasonality, or ratio seasonality. The distinction between additive and ratio seasonality is that the former is defined as the number of units above the average and the latter is defined as a ratio

FIGURE 4-1
**CLASSIFICATION OF EXPONENTIAL SMOOTHING MODELS.**

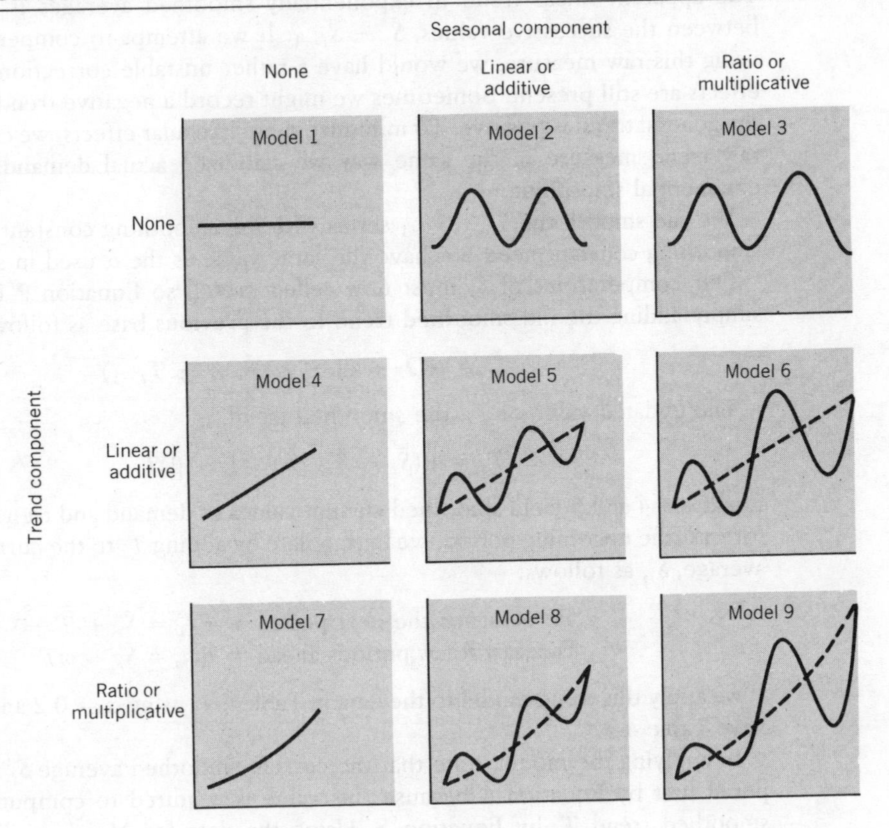


of period sales to average sales. With additive seasonality, therefore, the amplitudes of the demand pattern remain more or less constant; with ratio seasonality, the amplitudes become more pronounced as demand levels increase over time.

The process of forecasting using any one of the nine models shown in Figure 4-1 can be split into two steps. In the first step, the smoothed values of the base, the trend, or the seasonality factor are estimated using the following formula:

$$\bar{S}_t = \alpha A + (1 - \alpha)B \tag{3}$$

where $\alpha$ is a constant between 0 and 1 and $A$ and $B$ vary depending on the chosen model. For example, in the basic exponential smoothing model that we discussed earlier, $A = D_t$ and $B = \bar{S}_{t-1}$. In the second step, these smoothed values are used to make a forecast.

We will discuss, in some detail, how this strategy is used to build a forecasting model for the additive or linear trend case (model 4), the ratio seasonality case (model 3), and the additive trend and ratio seasonality case (model 6).

### LINEAR OR ADDITIVE TREND MODEL

The apparent linear trend in exponentially smoothed averages is the difference between the successive values, $\bar{S}_t - \bar{S}_{t-1}$. If we attempt to compensate for trend using this raw measure, we would have a rather unstable correction since random effects are still present. Sometimes we might record a negative trend when, in fact, the general trend is positive. To minimize these irregular effects, we can stabilize the raw trend measure in the same way we stabilized actual demands, by applying exponential smoothing.

We can smooth the $\bar{S}_t - \bar{S}_{t-1}$ series with the smoothing constant β (beta). This smoothing constant need not have the same value as the α used in smoothing $D_t$.

Our computations of $\bar{S}_t$ must now reflect trend, so Equation 2 is modified by simply adding the old smoothed trend to the previous base as follows:

$$\bar{S}_t = \alpha D_t + (1 - \alpha)(\bar{S}_{t-1} + T_{t-1}) \tag{4}$$

The updated value of $T_t$, the smoothed trend, is

$$T_t = \beta(\bar{S}_t - \bar{S}_{t-1}) + (1 - \beta)T_{t-1} \tag{5}$$

Equations 4 and 5 yield smoothed current values of demand and trend; therefore to forecast the upcoming period, we extrapolate by adding $T_t$ to the current smoothed average, $\bar{S}_t$, as follows:

$$\begin{aligned} \text{Forecast for the next period} &= F_{t,1} = \bar{S}_t + T_t \\ \text{Forecast for } m \text{ periods ahead} &= F_{t,m} = \bar{S}_t + mT \end{aligned} \tag{6}$$

If we apply this trend model to the data in Table 4-1, using $\alpha = 0.2$ and $\beta = 0.1$, we have Table 4-3.

In applying the model, note that the current smoothed average $\bar{S}_t$ must be computed first by Equation 4 because this value is required to compute the current smoothed trend $T_t$ by Equation 5. Using the data for March in Table 4-3, the forecast for April would be computed as follows:

$$\begin{aligned} \bar{S}_{\text{Mar}} &= 0.2 \times 19.73 + 0.8(20.9774 + 0.0990) \\ &= 3.9460 + 16.8610 \\ &= 20.8071 \\ T_{\text{Mar}} &= 0.1(20.8071 - 20.9774) + 0.9 \times 0.0990 \\ &= -0.0170 + 0.0891 \\ &= 0.0721 \\ \text{Forecast (Apr)} &= 20.8071 + 0.0721 \\ &= 20.8792 \end{aligned}$$

The model using a direct estimation of trend is valuable when trend and random variation are present in the data. In addition, the concept is useful in some of the more complex models that combine estimates of average demand, trend, and seasonal components.

The simple, exponentially smoothed forecast and the trend model forecast are plotted in relation to actual demand in Figure 4-2. Because the raw data exhibit a

TABLE 4-3
**SAMPLE COMPUTATIONS FOR TREND MODEL WITH α = 0.2 and β = 0.1**

| Month | Actual Demand $D_t$ | $\bar{S}_t$ Equation 4 | $T_t$ Equation 5 | $F_{t,1}$ Equation 6 |
|---|---|---|---|---|
| Initial | — | 20.0000 | 0 | — |
| Jan | 19.36 | 19.8720 | −0.0128 | — |
| Feb | 25.45 | 20.9774 | 0.0990 | 19.86 |
| Mar | 19.73 | 20.8071 | 0.0721 | 21.08 |
| Apr | 21.48 | 20.9994 | 0.0841 | 20.88 |
| May | 20.77 | 21.0208 | 0.0778 | 21.08 |
| Jun | 25.42 | 21.9629 | 0.1643 | 21.10 |
| Jul | | | | 22.13 |

trend, the simple model lags in its response. The trend model forecast corrects for this lag, so it rises above the simple model forecast after initial conditions lose their effect.

When this model is applied to the three-year record of data in Figure 4-2 with $\alpha = 0.2$ and $\beta = 0.1$, $AE = 0.33$, $MAD = 2.34$, and $MSE = 9.06$. The choice of the two smoothing constants has an important impact on forecast errors. Holding

FIGURE 4-2
**FORECASTS BY SIMPLE EXPONENTIAL SMOOTHING AND BY THE TREND MODEL.**

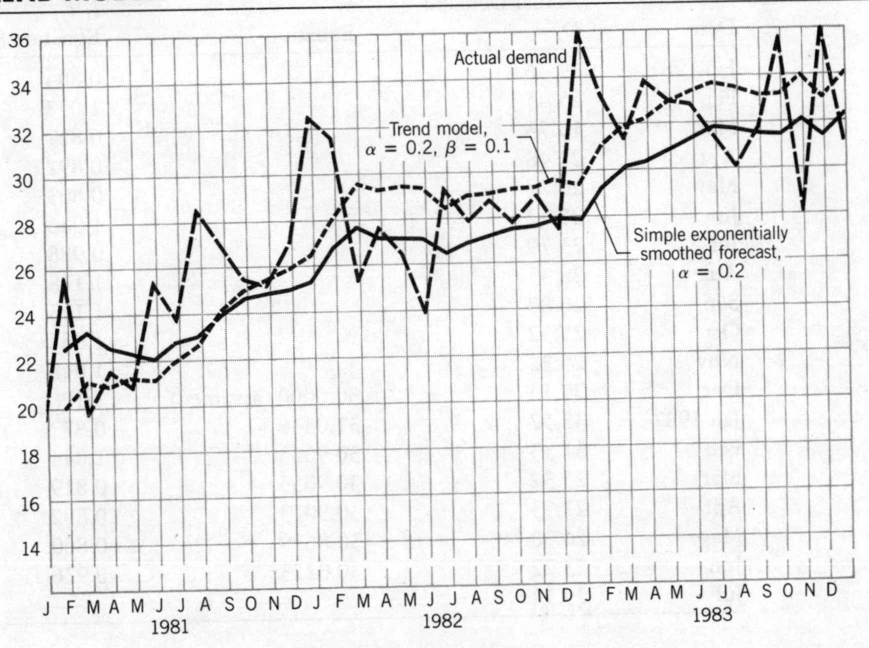

$\alpha$ = 0.2, the same data were run for values of $\beta$ = 0.01, 0.05, 0.1, 0.2, and 0.3. Subsamples yielded $MAD$ = 2.23, 2.16, 2.34, 2.23, and 2.44, respectively. Because the objective in developing a forecasting system is to minimize forecast errors, testing the sensitivity of errors to parameter values is an important step in refining a system.

The initialization process for the trend model requires a longer historical record. Because of the initially assumed values of $\bar{S}_t$ and $T_t$, a two-year history is normally considered to be minimum.

## RATIO SEASONALITY MODEL

The method for taking direct account of seasonal variations is to construct a seasonal index using previous data. For example, if we take the actual demand from Figure 4-2 and divide each monthly demand by the annual average, we get a set of seasonal indices. The average demand during 1981 was 24.07, so the index for January would be 19.36/24.07 = 0.804; for February, it would be 25.45/24.07 = 1.057. These initial indices for 1981, shown in Table 4-4, are used only to initialize the process. A process for updating the indices will be used in succeeding years so that they will reflect changes that may occur.

Given the initial indices, we can normalize actual demand figures by dividing them by the previous year's index for that period, $I_{t-L}$. ($L$ is the number of periods in one

TABLE 4-4
**SAMPLE COMPUTATIONS FOR SEASONAL MODEL WITH $\alpha$ = 0.1, $\gamma$ = 0.3, and $L$ = 12**

| Date | Actual Demand $D_t$ | $\bar{S}_t$ Equation 7 | $I_t$ Equation 8 | $F_{t,1}$ Equation 9 |
|---|---|---|---|---|
| Jan 1981 | 19.36 | | 0.804 | |
| Feb | 25.45 | | 1.057 | |
| Mar | 19.73 | | 0.819 | |
| Apr | 21.48 | | 0.892 | |
| May | 20.77 | | 0.863 | |
| Jun | 25.42 | | 1.056 | |
| Jul | 23.79 | | 0.988 | |
| Aug | 28.35 | | 1.178 | |
| Sep | 26.80 | | 1.113 | |
| Oct | 25.32 | | 1.052 | |
| Nov | 25.22 | | 1.048 | |
| Dec | 27.14 | 30.0000 (assumed) | 1.128 | — |
| Jan 1982 | 32.52 | 31.0448 | 0.877 | — |
| Feb | 31.33 | 30.9043 | 1.044 | 32.81 |
| Mar | 25.32 | 30.9055 | 0.819 | 25.31 |
| Apr | 27.53 | 30.9013 | 0.892 | 27.57 |
| May | 26.38 | 30.8679 | 0.860 | 26.67 |
| Jun | 23.72 | 30.0273 | 0.976 | 32.60 |
| Jul | 29.14 | — | — | 29.67 |

cycle—12 if data are by month, 4 if data are by quarter.) Therefore, if actual demand for February 1982 is $D_t = 31.33$, we divide it by the index for February of the previous year, 1981, $I_{t-12} = 1.057$, to obtain $31.33/1.057 = 29.64$. The effect of this process is to deseasonalize by decreasing adjusted demand during high-demand periods and increasing it during low-demand periods. The deseasonalized smoothed average, $\bar{S}_t$, is then

$$\bar{S}_t = \alpha\left(\frac{D_t}{I_{t-L}}\right) + (1 - \alpha)\bar{S}_{t-1} \tag{7}$$

However, the seasonal indices for 1981 are reflective only of that year's experience. If the seasonal cycle repeated itself consistently each year, using the 1981 indices each year would be appropriate. Because random variations are a component, however, a single year's history as a basis for seasonal indices is normally replaced by some averaging process, such as exponentially weighted averaging. Therefore, we use the following equation to update the seasonal indices, where $\gamma$ (gamma) is the smoothing constant for seasonal indices:

$$I_t = \gamma\left(\frac{D_t}{\bar{S}_t}\right) + (1 - \gamma)I_{t-L} \tag{8}$$

The actual demand $D_t$ is divided by the new smoothed average $\bar{S}_t$, computed by Equation 7, to reflect the amount by which $D_t$ exceeds or falls short of the deseasonalized average. This variation from the deseasonalized average is weighted by the smoothing constant. The old seasonal index is last year's index and is weighted by $1 - \gamma$. The new index $I_t$ is stored, to be used in computations for $\bar{S}_t$ and $I_t$ next year.

The result, after the process has been in operation for several years, is that each seasonal index is based on seasonal variation that occurred $L$, $2L$, $3L$, and so on periods ago. The most recent data are weighted more heavily, depending on the value of the smoothing constant $\gamma$.

To forecast for the upcoming period, $t + 1$, we carry forward the most current smoothed average, $\bar{S}_t$, but we modify it by the seasonal index for the upcoming period, $I_{t-L+1}$. Equation 9 has the effect of reseasonalizing the formerly deseasonalized smoothed average.

$$F_{t,1} = \bar{S}_t I_{t-L+1} \tag{9}$$

And the forecast for $m$ periods ahead $= F_{t,m} = \bar{S}_t I_{t-L+m}$.

Table 4-4 applies the seasonal model to several months of data, using $\alpha = 0.1$ and $\gamma = 0.3$. In applying the model, we compute the current smoothed average $\bar{S}_t$ first by Equation 7 since this value is required to update the seasonal indices by Equation 8 and to compute the forecast by Equation 9.

Using the data for April 1982 in Table 4-4, we compute the forecast for May as follows:

$$\begin{aligned}\bar{S}_{\text{Apr}} &= 0.1\left(\frac{27.53}{0.892}\right) + 0.9 \times 30.9055 \\ &= 3.0863 + 27.8149 \\ &= 30.9012\end{aligned}$$

$$I_{\text{Apr}} = 0.3\left(\frac{27.53}{30.9012}\right) + 0.7 \times 0.892$$
$$= 0.2673 + 0.6244$$
$$= 0.8917$$

$$\text{Forecast (May)} = 30.9012 \times 0.863$$
$$= 26.667$$

For the seasonal model applied to the three-year data record in Figure 4-2, $AE = -0.15$, $MAD = 3.38$, and $MSE = 20.53$ ($\alpha = 0.1, \gamma = 0.3$).

Forecasting accuracy here is not as good with the seasonal model. Why? First, this model does not account for trend, which is a component of the data. Second, an entire year of data is consumed in order to initialize the seasonal indices. The remaining two-year sample may contain some extreme values that carry larger weight in the smaller sample. Third, the seasonal cycles in the data may not be stable from year to year.

As with the trend model, the choice of the smoothing constants affects forecasting errors. Subsamples used to compute $MAD$ for several combinations of values of $\alpha$ and $\gamma$ yield the following:

| | $\gamma$ | | | | |
|---|---|---|---|---|---|
| $\alpha$ | 0.01 | 0.05 | 0.10 | 0.20 | 0.30 |
| 0.1 | 3.67 | 3.60 | 3.54 | 3.44 | 3.38 |
| 0.2 | 3.65 | 3.75 | 3.73 | 3.60 | 3.37 |

## ADDITIVE TREND AND RATIO SEASONALITY MODEL

As might be expected, one can combine the trend model and the seasonal model. The equations to update the smoothed trend and seasonal are the same, but the equation to compute the current value for the smoothed average, $\bar{S}_t$, must reflect both trend and seasonal variations.

$$\bar{S}_t = \alpha\left(\frac{D_t}{I_{t-L}}\right) + (1 - \alpha)(\bar{S}_{t-1} + T_{t-1}) \tag{10}$$

The trend and seasonal index equations are

$$T_t = \beta(\bar{S}_t - \bar{S}_{t-1}) + (1 - \beta)T_{t-1} \tag{11}$$

$$I_t = \gamma\left(\frac{D_t}{\bar{S}_t}\right) + (1 - \gamma)I_{t-L} \tag{12}$$

Finally, to forecast for the upcoming period, $t + 1$, we combine the elements of Equations 6 and 9.

$$F_{t,1} = (\bar{S}_t + T_t)(I_{t-L+1}) \tag{13}$$

To forecast for $m$ periods ahead

$$F_{t,m} = (\bar{S}_t + mT_t)I_{t-L+m}$$

The value of $\bar{S}_t$ must be computed using Equation 10 first because it is used in Equations 11, 12, and 13. As before, computing the updated seasonal index produces an index to be stored for use a year hence. Table 4-5 applies the trend and seasonal model to the first several months of data in Figure 4-2, using smoothing constants of $\alpha = 0.2$, $\beta = 0.3$, and $\gamma = 0.1$. The initial seasonal indices are those used to initialize the seasonal model in Table 4-4.

Using the data in Table 4-5 for May 1982 to forecast for June 1982, computations are as follows

$$\begin{aligned}
\bar{S}_{\text{May}} &= 0.2\left(\frac{26.38}{0.863}\right) + 0.8(34.2099 + 0.7955) \\
&= 6.1136 + 28.0043 \\
&= 34.1179 \\
T_{\text{May}} &= 0.3(34.1179 - 34.2099) + 0.7 \times 0.7955 \\
&= -0.0276 + 0.5569 \\
&= 0.5293 \\
I_{\text{May}} &= 0.1\left(\frac{26.38}{34.1179}\right) + 0.9 \times 0.863 \\
&= 0.0773 + 0.7767 \\
&= 0.8540 \\
\text{Forecast (June)} &= (34.1179 + 0.5293)1.056 \\
&= 36.5874
\end{aligned}$$

With three smoothing constants, the number of possible combinations increases substantially. Berry and Bliemel (1974) show how computer search methods can be used in selecting optimal combinations of the smoothing constants.

The initialization process is somewhat longer with the trend and seasonal model. Historical data are required to initialize the seasonal indices as well as $\bar{S}_t$ and $T_t$. Therefore, a three-year historical record is normally required in order to have confidence in the results.

## INITIALIZATION

When an exponential smoothing model is used for the first time, we need initial values for the base sales, trend, and the seasonal factors. To see this, consider the basic exponential smoothing given by Equation 2.

$$\bar{S}_t = \alpha D_t + (1 - \alpha)\bar{S}_{t-1}$$

To estimate the base sales for the first period, $\bar{S}_1$, we need $\bar{S}_0$. Similarly, initial values for trend and seasonal factors must somehow be obtained to run the model. If no data are available, we must either wait until data are accumulated or we could use our judgment to specify the initial values. After a few periods, the effect of the initial values on the forecast will be minimal.

If past data are available, the demand history is divided into two parts. The first part is used to estimate the initial values, and the second part to estimate the values

TABLE 4-5
**SAMPLE COMPUTATIONS FOR THE TREND AND SEASONAL MODEL WITH $\alpha = 0.2$, $\beta = 0.3$, $\gamma = 0.1$, and $L = 12$**

| Month | Actual Demand $D_t$ | $\bar{S}_t$ Equation 10 | $T_t$ Equation 11 | $I_t$ Equation 12 | $F_{t,1}$ Equation 13 |
|---|---|---|---|---|---|
| Jan 1981 | 19.36 | | | 0.804 | |
| Feb | 25.45 | | | 1.057 | |
| Mar | 19.73 | | | 0.819 | |
| Apr | 21.48 | | | 0.892 | |
| May | 20.77 | | | 0.863 | |
| Jun | 25.42 | | | 1.056 | |
| Jul | 23.79 | | | 0.988 | |
| Aug | 28.35 | | | 1.178 | |
| Sep | 26.80 | | | 1.113 | |
| Oct | 25.32 | | | 1.052 | |
| Nov | 25.22 | | | 1.048 | |
| Dec | 27.14 | 30.0000 (assumed) | 1.0000 (assumed) | 1.128 | — |
| Jan 1982 | 32.52 | 32.8896 | 1.5669 | 0.823 | — |
| Feb | 31.33 | 33.4932 | 1.2779 | 1.045 | 36.42 |
| Mar | 25.32 | 34.0000 | 1.0465 | 0.812 | 28.48 |
| Apr | 27.53 | 34.2099 | 0.7955 | 0.883 | 31.26 |
| May | 26.38 | 34.1179 | 0.5293 | 0.854 | 30.21 |
| Jun | 23.72 | 32.2102 | −0.2017 | 1.024 | 36.59 |
| Jul | 29.14 | — | — | 0.982 | 31.62 |

of the constants $\alpha$, $\beta$, and $\gamma$. To demonstrate this procedure, consider the quarterly sales of a product shown in Table 4-6 for a three-year period.

We will take the data for years 1 and 2 to derive initial values, and we will experiment with alternative values of the coefficients $\alpha$, $\beta$, and $\gamma$ on the data for year 3. The idea is to choose a model that produces the least forecasting error when applied to year 3 data. The forecasts for each quarter in year 3 are made in sequential steps by pretending that the actual sales for the upcoming quarter are unknown.

There is no unique way to obtain initial estimates. If we employ a basic exponential smoothing model, then we only need $\bar{S}_0 = \bar{S}_{\text{year 2, quarter 4}}$. This is obtained by simply taking the average of the average quarterly sales for years 1 and 2.

$$\bar{S}_0 = \frac{\left(\frac{10 + 30 + 50 + 10}{4}\right) + \left(\frac{10 + 40 + 60 + 10}{4}\right)}{2}$$

$$= (25 + 30)/2$$
$$= 27.5$$

In the linear trend model, $T_0$ and $\bar{S}_0$, where the period 0 refers to the quarter 4 of year 2, are obtained by first estimating $T_0$.

TABLE 4-6
**COMPUTATION OF SEASONALITY FACTORS**

| | *Year 1* | | *Year 2* | | | *Year 3* |
|---|---|---|---|---|---|---|
| Quarter | Sales (1) | Seasonality Factors (2) | Sales (3) | Seasonality Factors (4) | *I*-Values (2) + (4)/2 | Sales |
| 1 | 10 | 10/25 | 10 | 10/30 | 0.366 | 20 |
| 2 | 30 | 30/25 | 40 | 40/30 | 1.265 | 60 |
| 3 | 50 | 50/25 | 60 | 60/30 | 2.0 | 90 |
| 4 | 10 | 10/25 | 10 | 10/30 | 0.366 | 20 |
| Average sales | 25 | | 30 | | | 47.5 |

$$
\begin{aligned}
T_0 &= (\text{Average quarterly sales year 2} \\
&\quad - \text{Average quarterly sales year 1})/4 \\
&= (30 - 25)/4 \\
&= 1.25 \text{ units/quarter}
\end{aligned}
$$

$\bar{S}_0$ is now obtained by simply extrapolating the average quarterly sales for year 2, which are centered in the middle of year 2 to quarter 4 of year 2.

$$
\begin{aligned}
\bar{S}_0 &= 30 + (1.25)(1.5) \\
&= 31.875 \text{ units}
\end{aligned}
$$

In the ratio seasonality model, $\bar{S}_0$ is computed the same way as in the basic model: $\bar{S}_0 = 27.5$. To compute the seasonality factors $I_{\text{quarter 1}}$ to $I_{\text{quarter 4}}$, we simply take the average of the seasonality factors for year 1 and year 2 shown in Table 4-6.

In the linear trend ratio seasonality model, $\bar{S}_0$ and $T_0$ can be computed in the same way as in the linear trend model just described; $\bar{S}_0 = 31.875$ units, $T_0 = 1.25$ units/quarter. The seasonality indices are computed as shown in Table 4-6.

Once we know the initial estimates for a chosen model, the constants α, β, and γ are selected and the model is applied to year 3 data. The forecasting error is recorded and the values of α, β, and γ are systemically varied to find the combination that produces the lowest forecast error.

Usually, the choice of a model (e.g., with or without seasonality) can be made by plotting the data and using judgment. It is also possible to experiment with alternative models, and the model with the lowest forecast error can be selected.

## ADAPTIVE METHODS

As we have noted, it is common to use fairly small values for α in exponential smoothing systems in order to filter out random variations in demand. When actual demand rates increase or decrease gradually, such forecasting systems can track the changes rather well. If demand changes suddenly, however, a forecasting system that uses a small value for α will lag substantially behind the actual change. Thus, adaptive response systems have been proposed.

The basic idea of adaptive smoothing systems is to monitor the forecast error and, based on preset rules, to react to large errors by increasing the value of $\alpha$. The value of $\alpha$ in the Trigg and Leach (1967) model is set equal to the absolute value of a tracking signal.

$$\text{Tracking signal} = \frac{\text{Smoothed forecast error}}{\text{Smoothed absolute forecast error}}$$

The smoothing of error is accomplished by using an equation similar to Equation 2. If the error is small, $\alpha$ will be small. If, due to a sudden shift in demand, the error is large, then the tracking signal will be large. Thus, if a step change in demand were to occur because of a radical change in the market, a large error would result. The large error signals that $\alpha$ should increase in order to give greater weight to current demand. The forecast would then reflect the change in actual demand. When actual demand stabilizes at the new level, adaptive systems would reset the value of $\alpha$ to a lower level that filters out random variations effectively. A number of approaches to adaptive response systems have been proposed, see, for example, Chow (1965), Trigg and Leach (1967), and Roberts and Reed (1969).

Adaptive models may be useful for new products for which little historical data are available; the adaptive models should correct and stabilize themselves quickly. If demand shows rapid shifts and little randomness, then adaptive methods may perform well. Such a demand pattern will, however, be uncommon in production inventory situations. Limitations of adaptive methods rest in the greater amounts of historical data, and computer time they require in comparison to the simpler models.

## CAUSAL OR EXPLANATORY METHODS

When we have enough historical data and experience, it may be possible to relate forecasts to factors in the economy that cause the trends, seasonals, and fluctuations. Thus, if we can measure these causal factors and can determine their relationships to the product or service of interest, we can compute forecasts of considerable accuracy.

The factors used in causal models are of several types: disposable income, new marriages, housing starts, inventories, and cost-of-living indices as well as predictions of dynamic factors and/or disturbances, such as strikes, actions of competitors, and sales promotion campaigns. The causal forecasting model expresses mathematical relationships between the causal factors and the demand for the item being forecast. There are two general types of causal models: regression analysis and econometric methods.

### Regression Analysis

Forecasting based on regression methods establishes a forecasting function called a regression equation. The regression equation expresses the series to be forecast in terms of other series that presumably control or cause sales to increase or decrease.

The rationale can be general or specific. For example, in furniture sales we might postulate that sales are related to disposable personal income: if disposable personal income is up, sales will increase, and if people have less money to spend, sales will decrease. Establishing the empirical relationship is accomplished through the regression equation. To consider additional factors, we might postulate that furniture sales are controlled to some extent by the number of new marriages and the number of new housing starts. These are both specific indicators of possible demand for furniture.

Table 4-7 gives data on these three independent variables—housing starts, disposable income, and new marriages—and on the sales of a hypothetical furniture company called the Cherryoak Company. We propose to build a relationship between the observed variables and company sales in which the sales are dependent on, or are caused by, the observed variables. Therefore, sales is termed the "dependent" variable and the observed variables are called the "independent" variables.

Once we know the relationship between the dependent variable (company sales) and the independent variables (housing starts, disposable income, and new marriages), we can use this relationship to forecast company sales.

To summarize, the central idea in regression analysis is to identify variables that influence the variable to be forecasted and establish the relationship between them so that the known values of the independent variables can be used to estimate the unknown or forecasted value of the dependent variable.

If only one independent variable is used to estimate the dependent variable, the relationship between the two is established using *simple regression analysis*. We will illustrate this method with a simple example, and we will return to the more realistic situation in Table 4-7 later to discuss multiple regression, where the effects of more than one causal factor (independent variables) are considered.

## SIMPLE REGRESSION ANALYSIS

Suppose the annual sales of Delicious Fried Chicken stores in a region depend on the annual industry sales for fried chickens in the same region. The sales data for the past 10 years for Delicious and the industry are given in Table 4-8. These data show that in year 9, industry sales were \$8 million and the sales of the Delicious Fried Chicken stores were \$220,000. The objective is to establish the relationship between store sales, $Y$, and industry sales, $X$. We can then use this relationship to forecast the value of the dependent variable $Y$ from the value of the independent variable $X$.

The first step in regression analysis is to plot the data in Table 4-8 as a scatter diagram, as is done in Figure 4-3.

The method of least squares is used to fit a line to the data in Figure 4-3. This method minimizes the sum of the squares of the vertical deviations separating the observed values of the dependent variable $Y$ from the fitted line. A property of the least squares line will be that the positive deviations from the line will be equal to the negative deviations. The least squares line is represented by the equation of a straight line,

$$\hat{Y} = a + bX$$

TABLE 4-7
**DATA FOR 24 YEARS (1947–1970) USED IN PERFORMING REGRESSION ANALYSIS TO FORECAST 1971 SALES OF CHERRYOAK COMPANY**

| Year | Housing Starts (*H*) (thousands) | Disposable Personal Income (*I*) ($ billions) | New Marriages (*M*) (thousands) | Company Sales (*S*) ($ millions) | Time (*T*) |
|---|---|---|---|---|---|
| 1947 | 744 | 158.9 | 2291 | 92.920 | 1 |
| 1948 | 942 | 169.5 | 1991 | 122.440 | 2 |
| 1949 | 1033 | 188.3 | 1811 | 125.570 | 3 |
| 1950 | 1138 | 187.2 | 1580 | 110.460 | 4 |
| 1951 | 1549 | 205.8 | 1667 | 139.400 | 5 |
| 1952 | 1211 | 224.9 | 1595 | 154.020 | 6 |
| 1953 | 1251 | 235.0 | 1539 | 157.590 | 7 |
| 1954 | 1225 | 247.9 | 1546 | 152.230 | 8 |
| 1955 | 1354 | 254.4 | 1490 | 139.130 | 9 |
| 1956 | 1475 | 274.4 | 1531 | 156.330 | 10 |
| 1957 | 1240 | 292.9 | 1585 | 140.470 | 11 |
| 1958 | 1157 | 308.5 | 1518 | 128.240 | 12 |
| 1959 | 1341 | 318.8 | 1451 | 117.450 | 13 |
| 1960 | 1531 | 337.7 | 1494 | 132.640 | 14 |
| 1961 | 1274 | 350.0 | 1527 | 126.160 | 15 |
| 1962 | 1327 | 364.4 | 1547 | 116.990 | 16 |
| 1963 | 1469 | 385.3 | 1580 | 123.900 | 17 |
| 1964 | 1615 | 404.6 | 1654 | 141.320 | 18 |
| 1965 | 1538 | 436.6 | 1719 | 156.710 | 19 |
| 1966 | 1488 | 469.1 | 1789 | 171.930 | 20 |
| 1967 | 1173 | 505.3 | 1844 | 184.790 | 21 |
| 1968 | 1299 | 546.3 | 1913 | 202.700 | 22 |
| 1969 | 1524 | 590.0 | 2059 | 237.340 | 23 |
| 1970 | 1479 | 629.6 | 2132 | 254.930 | 24 |

*Note:* Company sales and disposable per-capita income have been adjusted for the effect of inflation and appear in constant 1959 dollars.

*Source:* G. C. Parker and E. L. Segura, "How to Get a Better Forecast," *Harvard Business Review*, March–April 1971, based on data from *Statistical Abstract of the United States*, Bureau of the Census, Washington, D.C.

where $X$ is the observed value of the independent variable, $\hat{Y}$ is the estimated value of the dependent variable, and $a$ and $b$, respectively, are the intercept and the slope of the line fitted to the sample data. The values of $a$ and $b$ are such that $\Sigma(Y - \hat{Y})^2$ is minimum. These values are given by the following equations:

$$b = \frac{\Sigma XY - n\bar{X}\bar{Y}}{\Sigma X^2 - \bar{X}^2} \tag{14}$$

$$a = \bar{Y} - b\bar{X} \tag{15}$$

TABLE 4-8
**DATA AND INTERMEDIATE COMPUTATIONS FOR REGRESSION ANALYSIS FOR DELICIOUS FRIED CHICKEN**

| Year | Store Sales $Y$ (10 thousand dollars) | Industry Sales $X$ (Million dollars) | $XY$ | $X^2$ | $Y^2$ |
|---|---|---|---|---|---|
| 1 | 9 | 2 | 18 | 4 | 81 |
| 2 | 14 | 4 | 56 | 16 | 196 |
| 3 | 16 | 4 | 64 | 16 | 256 |
| 4 | 18 | 6 | 108 | 36 | 324 |
| 5 | 19 | 6 | 114 | 36 | 361 |
| 6 | 20 | 6 | 120 | 36 | 400 |
| 7 | 18 | 7 | 126 | 49 | 324 |
| 8 | 21 | 7 | 147 | 49 | 441 |
| 9 | 22 | 8 | 176 | 64 | 484 |
| 10 | 23 | 10 | 230 | 100 | 529 |
| Sum | 180 | 60 | 1,159 | 406 | 3,396 |

FIGURE 4-3
**SCATTER DIAGRAM FOR THE DATA IN TABLE 4-8.**

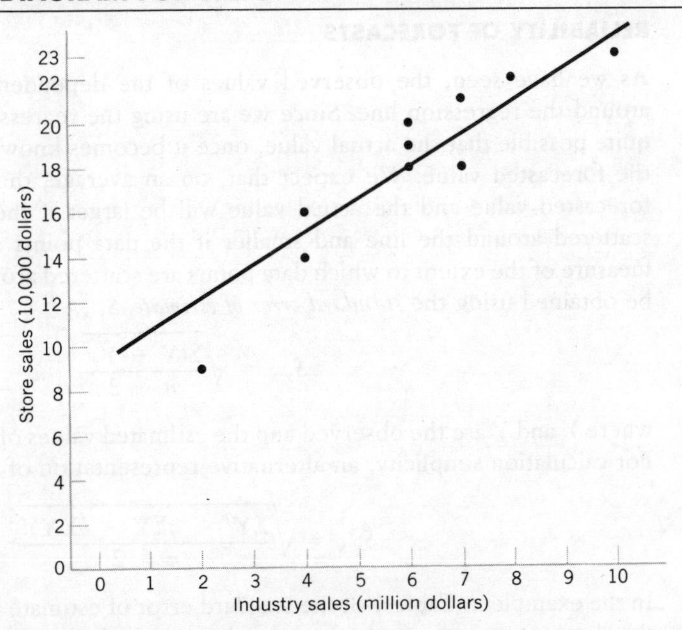

where $n$ is the number of observations in the sample data and $\bar{X}$ and $\bar{Y}$ are the arithmetic means of the variables $X$ and $Y$.

In Table 4-8, the intermediate computations for estimating $a$ and $b$ are shown. From Table 4-8, we compute

$$\bar{X} = \frac{\Sigma X}{n} = \frac{60}{10} = 6$$

$$\bar{Y} = \frac{\Sigma Y}{n} = \frac{180}{10} = 18$$

Now we substitute $n = 10$, $\Sigma XY = 1{,}159$, $\Sigma X^2 = 406$, and $\Sigma Y^2 = 3{,}396$ in Equations 14 and 15 to obtain

$$b = \frac{1{,}159 - (10)(6)(18)}{406 - 10(6)^2} = 1.717$$

$$a = 18 - 1.717(6) = 7.698$$

The regression line is

$$\hat{Y} = 7.698 + 1.717X$$

To use this regression line to forecast the value of the dependent variable, we simply substitute the value of $X$ and compute $\hat{Y}$. For example, if the industry sales in year 11 are estimated to be \$10 million, then the forecast for store sales in year 11 will be

$$\begin{aligned} \hat{Y} &= 7.698 + (1.717)(10) = 24.868 \times \$10{,}000 \\ &= \$248{,}680 \end{aligned}$$

## RELIABILITY OF FORECASTS

As we have seen, the observed values of the dependent variable are scattered around the regression line. Since we are using the regression line to forecast, it is quite possible that the actual value, once it becomes known, will be different from the forecasted value. We expect that, on an average, the deviation between the forecasted value and the actual value will be larger if the data points are widely scattered around the line and smaller if the data points are close to the line. A measure of the extent to which data points are scattered around a regression line can be obtained using the *standard error of estimate*, $S_{y \cdot x}$,

$$S_{y \cdot x} = \sqrt{\frac{\Sigma(Y - \hat{Y})^2}{n - 2}} \tag{16}$$

where $Y$ and $\hat{Y}$ are the observed and the estimated values of the dependent variable. For calculation simplicity, an alternative representation of $S_{y \cdot x}$ is

$$S_{y \cdot x} = \sqrt{\frac{\Sigma Y^2 - a\Sigma Y - b\Sigma XY}{n - 2}} \tag{17}$$

In the example in Table 4-8, the standard error of estimate is 1.595 (× \$10,000). If the data points are scattered randomly around the regression line, then approximately two-thirds of the points should lie within a band drawn one $S_{y \cdot x}$ above and below the regression line. Hence, for $X = 10$ in the year 11, the forecasted store sales, $\hat{Y} = \$248,680$, could be between $\$248,680 \pm 1.595\ (10,000)$ or between $232,730 and $264,630, with two chances out of three of being correct.

The standard error of forecast[1] discussed in statistics books is a refinement of standard error of estimate discussed here. Standard error of forecast accounts for the sampling error in the regression line itself along with the error due to the scatter of data points around the regression line. We do not discuss this concept here; however, we note that the confidence level for the forecasted value will be slightly higher if the standard error of forecast is used.

## COEFFICIENT OF DETERMINATION

In choosing a variable $X$ to forecast the variable of interest $Y$, it is useful to know to what extent $X$ accounts for variation in $Y$. The coefficient of determination, $r^2$, measures the strength of the linear relationship between the two variables.

$$r^2 = 1 - \frac{\Sigma(Y - \hat{Y})^2}{\Sigma(Y - \bar{Y})^2} = 1 - \frac{\text{Unexplained variation}}{\text{Total variation}}$$

For calculation simplicity, an alternative expression for $r^2$ is

$$r^2 = \frac{a\Sigma Y + b\Sigma XY - n\bar{Y}^2}{\Sigma Y^2 - n\bar{Y}^2} \tag{18}$$

For the data in Table 4-8, $r^2 = 0.87$. This means that 87 percent of the variation in the annual store sales is explained by the variation in industry sales and 13 percent has not been explained. If $r^2$ is low, then we should either look for another independent variable or include other variables in the analysis.

## STATISTICAL TESTS

A number of statistical tests can be performed to help determine the appropriateness and accuracy of a regression equation as a forecasting device. Data resulting from these statistical tests are commonly generated automatically in standard regression analysis computer programs. Here, without going into theory or details, we will provide an overview of the statistical tests that a forecast user might be aware of.

Consider a simple example where a regression equation is computed for the relationship between defectives produced by an operator and that operator's work experience.

$$\hat{Y} = 5 - 0.5X$$

$X$ = Work experience of the operator in years
$Y$ = Annual percentage of defectives produced by the operator

[1] The formula for standard error of forecast, $S_f$, is given by

$$S_f = S_{y \cdot x}\sqrt{1 + \frac{1}{n} + \frac{(X_0 - \bar{X})^2}{\Sigma(X - \bar{X})^2}}$$

where $X_0$ is the value of $X$ for which an individual value of $Y$ is to be predicted.

Suppose that this relationship was computed using a sample of 20 operators. For this sample, we can say that for each additional year of work experience, defectives decline by one-half percent ($b = 0.5$). It is quite possible that for a different sample of 20 operators, the values for coefficients $a$ and $b$ differ from 5 and $-0.5$, which were the values for the original sample data. Thus, many different regression lines could be estimated between the same two variables by using different samples. Our estimates are therefore subject to sampling error. The purpose of statistical tests is to estimate the limits within which the values of coefficients computed from sample data are likely to fall. Of course, inferences about relationships in the entire population based on data from a sample can only be made if certain assumptions are satisfied.[2]

The first question of interest to the forecaster is whether it is appropriate to use $X$ values to forecast $Y$ values. If, in our example, $b = -0.5$ is obtained purely by chance, then it makes no sense to use work experience as a causal factor for predicting the percentage of defectives. To ensure that our estimated relationship is valid and that we are justified in using it for prediction, a $t$-test for the slope coefficient is conducted. Packaged computer programs give the $t$-values for all regression coefficients. These computed $t$-values must be larger than the $t$-values read from a table. Except for small samples (less than eight data points), the general rule is that if the absolute value of the computed $t$-value (computer generated) is greater than 2.5, the estimated relationship has a 95 percent confidence level of being valid.

Several other statistical tests are useful for computing confidence intervals for the coefficients, for determining the significance of $r^2$, and for identifying autocorrelations between successive error terms. These tests aid a forecaster in refining regression models until a suitable model is found.

## MULTIPLE REGRESSION

The general concepts of simple regression analysis can be extended to include the effects of several causal factors through multiple regression analysis. The inclusion of additional independent variables might improve the prediction of the dependent variable. For the data in Table 4-7, if we compute the relationship between company sales ($S$) and disposable income ($I$) using simple regression, we obtain the following

$$S = 72.5 + 0.23I \tag{19}$$

The standard error of estimate for this equation is 38.7 and $r^2$ is 0.65. Thus, 35 percent of the variation in sales remains unexplained. In multiple regression analysis, we include additional variables and hope that a greater percentage of the variation in sales can be explained. In this example, the multiple regression equation is

$$S = 49.85 - 0.068M + 0.036H + 1.22I - 19.54T \tag{20}$$

[2] Briefly stated, these assumptions are (1) the population relationship is linear, (2) the standard deviation of the error, $\epsilon = Y - \hat{Y}$, is the same for all values of $X$ (constant variance or homoscedasticity), (3) the $\epsilon$'s are independent of each other, and (4) the $\epsilon$'s are normally distributed so that the distribution of points above and below the regression line roughly follows a normal curve.

where

$S$ = Gross sales per year
49.85 = Base sales or the starting point from which other factors have an influence
$M$ = New marriages during the year
$H$ = New housing starts during the year
$I$ = Disposable personal income during the year
$T$ = Time trend ($T = 1, 2, 3, \ldots, n$)

and the coefficients that precede each of the causal factors represent the extent of the influence of changes in that factor on sales.

The coefficient of determination, $r^2$, for Equation 20 is 0.92, and the standard error of estimate is 11.9, indicating that the value of the equation as a forecasting mechanism is substantially greater than Equation 19.

Equation 20 can be improved as a forecasting mechanism by making additional changes. The factor of new marriages is dropped, and last year's sales ($S_{t-1}$) is substituted to improve overall forecasting accuracy. Also, last year's housing starts ($H_{t-1}$) is substituted for $H_t$ because this allows for the lag we would expect between construction time and the time home furnishing expenditures might be made. The revised equation is

$$\begin{array}{lccccc} S = & -33.51 & + 0.373S_{t-1} & + 0.033H_{t-1} & + 0.672I_t & - 11.03T \\ t\text{-values} & (-2.1) & (2.8) & (2.4) & (5.7) & (-5.1) \end{array} \qquad (21)$$

Forecasting accuracy has improved again, with $r^2 = 0.95$ and the standard error of estimate = 9.7. The computed $t$-values for the coefficients are shown in parentheses under Equation 21. These $t$-values are significant at a 95 percent confidence level; hence, all the variables are relevant for explaining company sales. If the $t$-value for a variable is low, say, 1.0, then we might drop that variable and run the regression with the remaining variables. The forecast for 1970 using Equation 21 is

$$\begin{aligned} S = & -33.51 + 0.373 \times 237.34 + 0.033 \times 1524 \\ & + 0.672 \times 629.6 - 11.03 \times 24 = 263.8 \end{aligned}$$

Note that in order to make a forecast for 1971 in 1970 we will need a projection of personal income for 1971.

When forecasts must be made for longer terms, as when new products and services are contemplated or when new facility locations and capacities are being considered, multiple regression analysis is a logical forecasting method. It requires considerable time and cost because various hypotheses about the effect of various variables may need to be tested. However, standard computer programs for multiple regression are now widely available that ease the burden and reduce the cost of application.

Besides possibly ignoring one or more important variables, one of the great dangers in using regression analysis is assuming that a good fit with historical data will guarantee that a regression equation will be a good forecasting device. This is because there may be a spurious correlation between the independent and the dependent variables. For example, food consumption and movie attendance may show a strong relationship in some countries. Such a relationship could result from an increase in population, which would cause both food consumption and the number of people going to the movies to show an increase. Higher food consumption does not give one an urge to go to the movies, and seeing a movie does not increase appetite. The regression equation itself should be an expression of a good causal theory relating to the factors in the regression model. In addition, we also need an understanding of the potential importance of factors that are not included in the model.

In using regression analysis for forecasting effectively, we should exercise some care when extrapolating beyond the range of observed data in the sample. It is quite possible that within the range of data in the sample, the relationship is linear. Outside this range, the relationship may be nonlinear or may follow a different slope.

When the relationship between the independent variables and the dependent variable is not linear, some transformations of one or more of the variables may provide a better fit to the data. For example, the failure rate of parts ($Y$) may not be linearly related to the number of hours of operation ($X$) because a defective part tends to fail early. However, if the dependent variable is transformed to a new variable, log $Y$, then an equation such as

$$\log \hat{Y} = a + bX$$

may provide a better fit to the data. Several transformations, involving square roots, reciprocals, logarithms, squares, and so forth of one or more of the variables, can be useful in improving the fit to the data.

Finally, the impact of qualitative variables, such as strikes, recessions, new product introduction, and the like on the forecast can be incorporated through the use of *dummy variables*. A dummy variable is an additional variable in the regression equation that takes on a value of 1 if the factor is present and a value of 0 if it is absent. In the forecasting project discussed later, the dummy variable technique for regression analysis is demonstrated.

## Econometric Forecasting Methods

In simplest terms, econometric forecasting methods are an extension of regression analysis and include a system of simultaneous regression equations. If, for example, we attempt to include the effect of price and advertising in Equation 21, then there is the possibility of an interdependence in which our own sales can have an effect on these factors and vice versa.

For example, assume that sales are a function of GNP, price, and advertising. In regression terms, we would assume that all three independent variables are exogenous to the system and are thus not influenced by the level of sales itself or by one another. This is a fair assumption as far as GNP is concerned. But, if we consider price and advertising, the same assumption may not be valid. For example, if the per unit cost is of some quadratic form, a different level of sales will result in a different level of cost. Furthermore, advertising expenditures will influence the price of the product because production and selling costs influence the per unit price. The price, in turn, is influenced by the magnitude of sales, which can also influence the level of advertising. All of this points to the interdependence of all four of the variables. When this interdependence is strong, regression analysis cannot be used. If we want to be accurate, we must express these relationships by developing a system of four simultaneous equations that can deal with the interdependence directly.

Thus, in econometric form, we have

$$\begin{aligned} \text{Sales} &= f(\text{GNP, price, and advertising}) \\ \text{Cost} &= f(\text{production and inventory levels}) \\ \text{Selling expenses} &= f(\text{advertising and other selling expenses}) \\ \text{Price} &= f(\text{cost and selling expenses}) \end{aligned}$$

Instead of one relationship, we now have four. As in regression analysis, we must (1) determine the functional form of each of the equations, (2) estimate in a simultaneous manner the values of their parameters, and (3) test for the statistical significance of the results and the validity of the assumptions.

To date, econometric models have been used largely in connection with relatively mature products where a considerable historical record is available in an industry and for broad economic forecasts. For example, the Corning Glass Works developed econometric models to forecast television tube sales (Chambers et al., 1971). These models were used to forecast sales six months to two years in the future to spot turning points sufficiently in advance to facilitate decisions for production and employment planning.

Industry econometric models have been developed to forecast activity in the forest products industry. Also, the forecasting models for the economy developed at UCLA and the Wharton School are econometric models.

## QUALITATIVE OR JUDGMENTAL METHODS

In this age of management science and computers, why must we resort to qualitative methods to make some of the most important predictions of future demands for products and services, predictions on which great risks involving large investments in facilities and market development hinge? The answer is that where we have no historical records, statistical methods have no validity. Further, past data, even when they exist, may not be representative of future conditions. Estimates of what people think, samplings of how they react to market tests, knowledge of consumer behavior, and analogies to similar situations may be the best we can do. Given this situation, the most scientific approach is to bring as much order as possible to these kinds of judgments. We cannot create data that do not exist. The qualitative methods are of considerable significance, then, because they provide a basis for some important decisions.

### The Delphi Method

*Technological forecasting* is a term used in conjunction with the longest-term predictions, and the Delphi technique is the methodology often used as the vehicle for such forecasting. The objective of the Delphi technique is to probe into the future in hopes of anticipating new products and processes in the rapidly changing environment of today's culture and economy. In the short range, such predictions can also be used to estimate market sizes and timing.

The Delphi technique draws on a panel of experts in a way that eliminates the potential dominance of the most prestigious, the most verbal, and the best salespeople. The object is to obtain expert opinion in the form of a consensus instead of a compromise. The result is pooled judgment, in which both the range of opinion and the reasons for differences of opinion can be seen. The Delphi technique was first developed by the RAND Corporation as a means of achieving these kinds of results. In contrast to conferences and panels where the individuals involved are in direct communication, this technique eliminates the undesirable effects of group interaction.

The panel of experts can be organized in various ways, and it often includes individuals from both inside and outside the organization. Each panel member is an expert on some aspect of the problem, but no one is an expert on the entire problem. In general, the procedure involves the following.

1. Each expert in the group makes independent predictions in the form of brief statements.
2. The coordinator edits and clarifies these statements.
3. The coordinator provides a series of written questions to the experts that include feedback supplied by the other experts.
4. Steps 1 to 3 are repeated several times. In practice, convergence is usually obtained after a small number of rounds.

One of the most extensive probes into the technological future was reported by TRW, Inc. (North and Pyke, 1969).

## Market Surveys

Market surveys and analyses of consumer behavior have become quite sophisticated, and the data that result are extremely valuable inputs for predicting market demand. In general, the methods involve the use of questionnaires, consumer panels, and tests of new products and services. The field is a specialty in itself and beyond our scope.

There is a considerable amount of literature dealing with the estimation of new product performance based on consumer panels (Ahl, 1970) and analytical approaches (Bass, 1969; Claycamp and Liddy, 1969) as well as simulation and other techniques (Bass, King, and Pessemeier, 1968). Proposed products and services can be compared with the products and known plans of competitors, and new market segments can be exploited with variations of product designs and quality levels. In such instances, comparisons can be made using data on existing products. These kinds of data are often the best available to refine the designs of products and facilities for new ventures.

## Historical Analogy and Life Cycle Analysis

Market research studies can sometimes be supplemented by referring to the performance of an ancestor of the product or service under consideration and applying an analysis of the product life cycle curve. For example, the assumption can be made that color television would follow the general sales pattern experienced with black and white television but that it would take twice as long to reach a steady state (Chambers, Mullick, and Smith, 1971). Such comparisons provide guidelines during initial planning phases and may be supplemented by other kinds of analyses and studies as actual demand becomes known. Chase and Aquilano (1977) focus their attention on the life cycle of products in studying the problems of production management.

## Scenario Based Forecasting

Long-range forecasting has been criticized because of its lack of predictive accuracy. Ascher (1978) has documented that the results of long-range forecasts in several areas have been inaccurate because the core assumption upon which the forecasts were predicated proved to be wrong. It is reasonable to assume that the further the forecast horizon, the less accurate the forecast is likely to be. Long-range forecasts, however, are an integral part of long-range planning, so they must be made.

The approach that we discuss now utilizes multiple future scenarios to come up with alternative projections. The decision maker is provided with the conditions under which high or low forecasts would result.

The first step in this approach is to define the variable to be projected, $Y$, and establish its measurement unit. Since a multitude of factors influence the variable $Y$, the next step is to identify these factors. Suppose $X_1, X_2, \ldots, X_n$ are the factors that influence $Y$. An example of $Y$ might be the capacity, measured in megawatts, of solar electric energy sources installed by the year 2000. Examples of $X$ factors might be

$X_1$ = Cost of solar energy in the year 2000
$X_2$ = Demand for energy
$X_3$ = Cost of nuclear, coal, and oil energies
$X_4$ = Oil embargo
$X_5$ = Nuclear slowdown
$X_6$ = Trend of society toward decentralization

The selected factors $X_1, X_2, \ldots, X_n$ must be comprehensive enough to reflect all the relevant concerns about the future and must also be well defined.

Given a combination of some specific levels of these factors, the projection for $Y$ may have to be made by consulting experts or utilizing past data and analogies. Techniques of regression analysis can be used to establish the relationship between $Y$ and $X_1, X_2, \ldots, X_n$. The projection for $Y$ will now vary with the combination of the levels of the factors that is assumed, which is called a *scenario*. Managers may also be interested in knowing which future scenarios are more likely to occur. This would require assessing the probability of occurrence of a certain level of a factor and then combining these for all the factors to come up with a scenario probability. For example, if there are only two factors and each factor has only two levels—that is, each factor either occurs or does not occur—then there are four possible scenarios. If the probability of occurrence for the first factor is 0.8 and that for the second factor is 0.5, then the probability of the scenario consisting of the occurrence of both factors will be $0.8 \times 0.5 = 0.4$. Of course, we implicitly assumed that the probability of the occurrence of the two factors are independent. More sophisticated approaches (e.g., see Linstone and Turoff, 1975; Helmer, 1977; and Sarin, 1979) will be required to quantify scenario probabilities if the factors are interdependent.

## ACCURACY OF FORECASTING METHODS

The accuracy of forecasting methods is one of the most important criteria for comparing alternative methods of forecasting. Cost, ease of application, and specific requirements of a planning situation are other factors that influence the choice of a forecasting method. It is difficult to determine which method will provide the most accurate forecast in a specific situation. However, over the years, considerable empirical evidence has been collected for both hypothetical and real-world data that allow some general conclusions about the relative accuracy of various forecasting methods.

The most significant conclusion, supported by a number of studies, is that more sophisticated methods do not necessarily produce more accurate results than do simpler methods that are easier to apply and less costly to use. There is also solid support in the literature for the view that, in spite of their logical appeal, sophisticated causal models do not outperform time series models (Armstrong, 1978). Further, with exponential smoothing, simpler time series models often give results that compare favorably with more complex time series models; an example is the Box–Jenkins method (Makridakis et al., 1982).

In some important situations, more than one method of forecasting may seem appropriate. The question then is how do we select a method for forecasting. Makridakis and Winkler (1983) empirically estimated the impact of the number and choice of forecasting methods on the accuracy of forecasts when the results of the methods used are simply averaged to provide the final forecast. Their main findings were as follows:

- Forecasting accuracy improves as the forecasts from more methods are combined to provide the final forecast; however, the marginal impact of including an additional method decreases as the number of methods increase.
- The risk of a large error in forecasting that might result from the choice of a wrong method is diminished when the results of two or more methods are combined.
- Variability in forecast accuracy among different combinations of forecasting methods decreases as the number of methods increase.

Thus, a practical alternative when we are unsure about the "best" method of forecasting is simply to take the average of the forecasts of two or more forecasting models.

Based on the empirical evidence reported in the literature, we can reasonably conclude that in production/inventory situations that are characterized by a need for producing forecasts of thousands of items on a routine basis, exponential smoothing is the most cost-effective method of forecasting. With the development of fast and user friendly computer programs, more sophisticated time series forecasting models may become practical for routine production/inventory situations.

## OTHER METHODS OF FORECASTING

Several other methods of forecasting are available, ranging from the relatively simple to the highly sophisticated. We will briefly discuss the conceptual bases of some of these methods.

*Decomposition methods* are extrapolative in nature, but they differ from exponential smoothing methods. The key difference is that, instead of extrapolating a single pattern as is the case with exponential smoothing, each component of demand is extrapolated separately. Thus the extrapolation of the seasonal pattern, the trend pattern, and the cyclical pattern and the smoothing of randomness all take place separately. The forecast is obtained by combining these component patterns.

Box and Jenkins (1970) have proposed a framework for analyzing and modeling time series data. This framework is based on well-developed statistical theory. It provides an approach for identifying patterns in data and a methodology for extrapolating these patterns into the future. The basic framework consists of three stages: identification, estimation, and diagnostic testing.

This method requires considerable expertise on the part of the analyst, and substantial analysis of the data must be performed before a forecasting model is chosen.

The *Fourier series forecasting method* represents time series using a mathematical function consisting of a constant term plus the sum of several sine and cosine terms. The method is useful when data have seasonal patterns.

Finally, the prediction of business cycles is important for decisions that will impact a company's profitability for a long period of time. Measuring leading indicators is one useful technique for identifying business cycles or turning points in time series data. The idea is to identify those indicators, such as housing starts, money supply, and durable new orders, whose present levels influence future business activity.

In Table 4-9, a brief description of the forecasting methods discussed in this chapter is provided along with their potential applications and relative costs.

## IMPLICATIONS FOR THE MANAGER

If there is a single, most important set of data for managers, it is forecast data. Virtually every important decision in operations depends in some measure on a

TABLE 4-9
**METHODS OF FORECASTING**

| Method | General Description | Applications | Relative Cost |
|---|---|---|---|
| | *Time Series Forecasting Models* | | |
| Moving averages | Forecast based on projection from time series data smoothed by a moving average, taking account of trends and seasonal variations. Requires at least two years of historical data. | Short-range forecasts for operations, such as inventory, scheduling, control, pricing, and timing special promotions. | Low |
| Exponential moving averages | Similar to moving averages, but the averages are weighted exponentially to give more recent data heavier weight. Well adapted to computer application and large numbers of items to be forecast. Requires at least two years of historical data. | Same as above. | Low |
| Decomposition | Each component of the time series is extrapolated separately and the results are then combined to produce a forecast. | Medium-range forecasts and forecasts of aggregate data, e.g., air traffic, business activity, etc. | Medium |
| Box–Jenkins | Models a time series by a combination of moving averages and autocorrelation terms. | Short- and medium-range forecasts of sales. | Medium |
| Fourier series least squares fit | Fits a finite Fourier series equation to empirical data, projecting trend and seasonal values. Requires at least two years of historical data. | Same as above. | Low to medium |
| | *Causal Forecasting Methods* | | |
| Regression analysis | Forecasts of demand related to economic and competitive factors that control or *cause* demand, through the least squares regression equation. | Short- and medium-range forecasting of existing products and services; marketing strategies; production and facility planning. | Medium |
| Econometric models | Based on a system of interdependent regression equations. | Same as above. | High |
| | *Predictive Methods* | | |
| Delphi | Expert panel answers a series of questionnaires where the answers to each questionnaire are summarized and made available to the panel to aid in answering the next questionnaire. | Long-range predictions; new products and product development; market strategies; pricing and facility planning. | Medium-high |

**TABLE 4-9**
***(Continued)***

| Method | General Description | Applications | Relative Cost |
|---|---|---|---|
| | *Predictive Methods* | | |
| Market surveys | Testing markets through questionnaires, panels, surveys, tests of trial products, analysis of time series data. | Same as above. | High |
| Historical analogy and life cycle analysis | Prediction based on analysis of and comparison with the growth and development of similar products. Forecasting new product growth based on the S-curve of introduction, growth, and market saturation. | Same as above. | Medium |
| Scenario based forecasting | Uses expert judgment in predicting alternative future scenarios. | Same as above. | High |

forecast of demand. For example, broad aggregate decisions concerning hiring and laying off personnel, the use of facilities, overtime, and the accumulation of seasonal inventories are made in relation to a forecast of expected demand. In service industries, such as hospitals or telephone exchange offices, it is necessary to provide service 24 hours a day, 7 days a week. Scheduling personnel who normally work only 40 hours per week to perform these services must take into account the anticipated demand for service. Inventories of raw materials, work in process, and finished goods are important for the smooth functioning of most service systems. Constructing rational inventory policies depends on forecasts of usage.

Managers are keenly aware of their dependence on forecasts. Indeed, a great deal of executive time is spent worrying about trends in economic and political affairs and how events will affect the demand for products or services. An issue is the relative value of executive opinion versus quantitative forecasting methods. Executives are perhaps most sensitive to events that may have a significant impact on demand. Quantitative techniques are probably least effective in "calling the turn" that may result in sharply higher or lower demand because quantitative methods are based on historical data.

Management science has attempted to automate sensitivity to sharp changes in demand through the use of adaptive systems and causal models. As we noted in our discussion of adaptive forecasting systems, success has been elusive, and it is not clear that the performance of adaptive systems is superior. Causal models suffer the least from sluggishness, since they are designed to reflect the effects on demand caused by indicators in an industry or in the economy.

The manager's choice of forecasting models must take into account the forecasting range required, the accuracy desired, and costs. Exponential smoothing methods are particularly adaptable for short-range forecasting, and they are inexpensive to install. The annual cost of maintaining such systems increases as the forecasting range is shortened, simply because the system must be updated more often.

Exponential smoothing forecasts are particularly adaptable to computer systems because a minimum amount of data needs to be stored for each item to be forecast. Data storage requirements increase as one moves from simple models to the more complex ones that take account of trends and seasonal variations. Whether or not the additional complexity is justified depends on the balance between the forecasting accuracy needed and the costs incurred. The fact that exponential smoothing systems are adaptable to electronic computing makes them particularly attractive for forecasting large numbers of items, as is often required in inventory control.

When the forecasting horizon requirement is somewhat further and an explanation and justification for the forecast is required, causal methods should be favored by management. These conditions are common when managers must make broad-level plans for the allocation of capacity sources that may involve the expansion or contraction of short-term capacity. These aggregate plans are discussed in Chapter 8. They may involve hiring or laying off personnel, the use of overtime, the accumulation of seasonal inventories, the use of back ordering, or the use of subcontracting. These are important managerial decisions, and forecasting accuracy requirements may justify the costs of causal methods.

# REVIEW QUESTIONS

1. What common components of demand do we wish to take into account in a forecasting system for operations?
2. What are the general smoothing effects of a small number of periods (perhaps three to five) in a moving average? What are the effects on the ability of a moving average to track a rapidly changing demand?
3. What are the general smoothing effects of values of $\alpha$ in the 0.01 to 0.20 range in exponential forecasting systems? How do systems with low values of $\alpha$ track rapidly changing demand?
4. Show that exponential forecasting systems actually give weight to all past data.
5. How can one explain the fact that to extrapolate or to forecast using the basic model of Equation 2, we simply use the most current smoothed average $\bar{S}_t$ and phase it forward by one period?
6. If one uses a no-trend model to forecast demand when a trend actually exists, what is the nature of the error that results?
7. What is the raw measure of trend used in the linear trend model? Why do we smooth it?

8. What is the meaning of seasonal indexes? Why do we smooth these indexes for subsequent years rather than simply use the initial values?
9. If we plot a graph between time and deseasonalized demand, what would be its characteristic?
10. What is the general structure of adaptive forecasting systems?
11. What is the rationale behind the Fourier series forecasting method?
12. Distinguish the statistical methodology of causal methods of forecasting from time series methods.
13. As in the Cherryoak Company example used in the text, if we find a regression equation that fits historical data accurately, why can we not assume that it will be a good forecasting device? Why must we have a theory to explain why the equation fits the data?
14. Define the coefficient of determination and the standard error of estimate as measures of forecast reliability in regression analysis.
15. What are the assumptions made in regression analysis?
16. How is econometric forecasting different from regression analysis?
17. When should we use judgmental methods of forecasting?
18. What is the key difference between the Delphi method and the scenario based forecasting method?
19. What is the reasonable approach for combining forecasts if two or more methods of forecasting are used?

## PROBLEMS

20. Consider the following data for an item:

| PERIOD | DEMAND ($D_t$) |
|---|---|
| 1 | 4 |
| 2 | 5 |
| 3 | 4 |
| 4 | 6 |

a. Using a three-period simple moving average method, forecast demand for period 5.

b. Assuming the basic exponential smoothing model with $\alpha = 0.2$ and $\bar{S}_3 = 3$, forecast demand for period 5.

c. Using the linear trend exponential smoothing model, forecast demand for time period 5. Use $\alpha = 0.2$, $\beta = 0.3$, $\bar{S}_3 = 3$, and $T_3 = 1$. What is your forecast for period 6?

21. Unique Video Systems required a quarterly forecast for the upcoming year for its operation planning and budgeting. The following data are available about the past demand history:

| Quarter | 1984 | 1985 | 1986 | 1987 |
|---|---|---|---|---|
| 1 | 10 | 10 | 10 | |
| 2 | 30 | 50 | 50 | |
| 3 | 50 | 50 | 60 | |
| 4 | 10 | 10 | 20 | |

a. Using a linear trend exponential smoothing model, compute the 1987 quarterly forecast. Assume $\alpha = \beta = 0.5$, $\bar{S}_{Q3,1986} = 50$, and $T_{Q3,1986} = 10$.

b. What will be the quarterly forecast for 1987 if the linear trend and ratio seasonality model is employed? Assume $\alpha = \beta = \gamma = 0.5$, $\bar{S}_{Q3,1986} = 50$, $T_{Q3,1986} = 10$, and the seasonality indexes for the four quarters are $I_{Q1} = 0.4$, $I_{Q2} = 1.2$, $I_{Q3} = 2.0$, and $I_{Q4} = 0.4$.

c. Suppose 1987 sales turn out to be Q1 = 30, Q2 = 50, Q3 = 55, and Q4 = 30. What are the forecast errors of the two models in parts a and b above?

22. The enrollment at the Disco-Dance Studio is higher in the first semester than in the second semester. Given the following past data, forecast student enrollment in semester 1 and semester 2 of the upcoming year.

| Semester | 1984 | 1985 | 1986 |
|---|---|---|---|
| 1 | 100 | 90 | |
| 2 | 50 | 30 | |

Use the ratio seasonality model with $\alpha = \gamma = 0.1$, $\bar{S}_{\text{semester 1, 1985}} = 75$, $I_{\text{semester 1, 1985}} = 4/3$, and $I_{\text{semester 2, 1984}} = 2/3$.

23. You have found an old report, parts of which have been eaten by mice, with the following information:

| Month | Demand ($D_t$) | Base Estimate ($\bar{S}_t$) |
|---|---|---|
| 9 | 900 | |
| 10 | 960 | |
| 11 | 942 | |
| 12 | 998 | 934 |

a. Do you need to know the base estimates for previous periods (e.g., $\bar{S}_{11}$) if you wish to make a forecast for period 13 using the basic exponential smoothing model?

b. If the company was using a basic exponential soothing model with $\alpha = 0.2$, what were $\bar{S}_{11}$ and $\bar{S}_{10}$?

24. The total cost of production for a product is related to the number of units produced. The data for the past ten months is as follows:

| Month | Production Cost (in 1000 dollars) | Number of Units Produced (in 1000 units) |
|---|---|---|
| 1 | 30 | 5 |
| 2 | 51 | 10 |
| 3 | 46 | 8 |
| 4 | 22 | 4 |
| 5 | 37 | 6 |
| 6 | 69 | 12 |
| 7 | 21 | 4 |
| 8 | 45 | 7 |
| 9 | 65 | 13 |
| 10 | 55 | 10 |

a. Using regression analysis, determine the relationship between production cost and units produced.

b. Interpret the meaning of the coefficients in the regression line estimated in part a.

c. If the company is planning a production level of 11,000 units for the upcoming month, what is your forecast for the total production cost that the company will incur at this production level?

d. Compute the standard error of estimate for the regression line. What is its interpretation in the context of this problem?

e. What percentage of variation in production cost is explained by the units produced?

25. A newly hired M.B.A. at a toy manufacturer related the month-end retail inventory to the retail sales ($S$) for a month using regression analysis. She found the following relationship

$$I = 3.1 - 0.46S$$

where

$I$ = Inventory in million dollars at month end
$S$ = Sales in million dollars per month

a. What could be the reason for a negative relationship between $I$ and $S$?

b. Are there other ways to estimate or forecast month-end retail inventory?

26. A large supermarket chain with several stores stocks both food and nonfood items. In planning its layout, shelf space utilization, and stocking policies, the management is interested in studying the relationship between total profits and the sales of food and nonfood items. The annual profits for a sample of stores for the previous year were related to the annual sales of food and nonfood items in each store using multiple regression analysis. The following results were obtained:

$$\hat{Y} = -0.62 + 0.21X_1 + 0.34X_2$$

where

$\hat{Y}$ = Estimate of annual profit for a store (million dollars)
$X_1$ = Sales of food items (million dollars)
$X_2$ = Sales of nonfood items (million dollars)

a. If the company expects to sell $2 million of food items per year and $0.5 million of nonfood items per year at a new location, should it open the store?

b. Interpret the coefficients in the regression equation.

c. Suppose $r^2$ for the regression equation is 0.67. What is the meaning of this $r^2$?

d. What can be done to improve the forecasting of profits?

27. The Rapid Growth Company has been experiencing increasing sales for the past few years and expects this growth to continue for the foreseeable future. The sales data for this company for the past 12 years are given below:

| YEAR | SALES (in million dollars) |
|---|---|
| 1 | 0.1 |
| 2 | 0.4 |
| 3 | 0.9 |
| 4 | 0.6 |
| 5 | 1.2 |
| 6 | 2.1 |
| 7 | 2.4 |
| 8 | 1.9 |
| 9 | 3.1 |
| 10 | 3.3 |
| 11 | 3.5 |
| 12 | 4.2 |

a. Use regression analysis to determine the relationship between company sales and time.

b. Bob Bright prefers to use an exponential smoothing model for forecasting company sales. How should he obtain $\bar{S}_{12}$ and $T_{12}$ so that he can make a forecast for period 13?

c. What will be the forecast for company sales for period 13 using regression analysis and using exponential smoothing?

d. What is the relative advantage of using exponential smoothing instead of regression analysis in this situation?

# FORECASTING PROJECT

28. *Note:* This project will require the use of computer program to facilitate computations.

TABLE 4-10
**MONTHLY AVERAGE NUMBER OF INPATIENTS AT A LARGE HOSPITAL**

| Month | 1982 | 1983 | 1984 | 1985 | 1986 | 1987 |
|---|---|---|---|---|---|---|
| Jan | 795 | 780 | 815 | 830 | 820 | 820 |
| Feb | 810 | 820 | 865 | 840 | 880 | 835 |
| Mar | 840 | 825 | 850 | 825 | 875 | 830 |
| Apr | 820 | 815 | 845 | 845 | 890 | 815 |
| May | 800 | 825 | 840 | 830 | 775 | 800 |
| Jun | 765 | 780 | 825 | 810 | 865 | |
| Jul | 745 | 785 | 820 | 770 | 795 | |
| Aug | 740 | 750 | 800 | 795 | 770 | |
| Sep | 750 | 745 | 810 | 805 | 805 | |
| Oct | 820 | 830 | 870 | 815 | 810 | |
| Nov | 840 | 810 | 850 | 850 | 805 | |
| Dec | 755 | 770 | 745 | 790 | 705 | |

**Part 1**

a. Graph the data in Table 4-10. Choose an initial forecasting model for the hospital. For this model estimate the initial values (e.g., $\bar{S}$, $T$, and $I$) using the data for 1982 to 1984.

b. Now, assume some values for the parameters α, β, and γ. Using the initial values in a, make period by period forecasts for 1985, 1986, and the first five months of 1987. Compute the forecast error. Vary the parameters and recompute the forecasts and the forecast errors. Try at least four different combinations of the parameters and select the combination that yields the lowest forecast error.

c. Choose a different forecasting model than you used in part a. Estimate the initial values for this model using the data for 1982 to 1984. As in part b, try several different values of the parameters and make forecasts for the years 1985, 1986, and the first five months of 1987. Compute the forecast errors and pick the combination of parameters that yields the lowest forecast error.

d. Recommend a forecasting model for the hospital. Using your recommended model, make forecasts for the last seven months of 1987

**Part 2**

a. Use regression analysis to forecast the number of patients for the years 1985, 1986, and the first five months of 1987. Compute the forecast error. The instructions for building a regression model using historical time series data follow.

In regression analysis, the dependent variable, $y$, is the monthly average number of patients. The nature of independent variables depends on the type of model assumed. For example, if we wish to capture only the trend component in the data and make no allowance for the seasonality component, then time is taken as an independent variable. If in addition to trend, demand contains a seasonal component, then a dummy variable that takes either a value of 1 or 0 needs to be defined for each period in the seasonal cycle except for one. Thus, 11 dummy variables need to be defined, one for each month. A model with seasonality and trend components can be formulated as follows:

$$y = a + b_1x_1 + b_2x_2 + \ldots + b_{11}x_{11} + b_{12}x_{12}$$

where

$y$ = Monthly average number of patients

$x_1$ = Dummy variable for January, which takes a value of 1 when we forecast for January and a value of 0 when a forecast for any other month is wanted

$x_2$ = Dummy variable for February

.

.

.

$x_{11}$ = Dummy variable for November

$x_{12}$ = Time, for example, $x_{12} = 14$ for February 1983

Note that dummy variable for December is purposely omitted.

This model can be estimated using past data. To obtain the forecast for March 1986, we will use

$$y = a + b_3 + b_{12} \quad (51)$$

Since $x_3 = 1$, $x_{12} = 51$ (time variable) and the remaining dummy variables are set at zero. To obtain the forecast for December 1986, we will use

$$y = a + b_{12} \quad (60)$$

Notice that $x_1$ to $x_{11}$ are all set to zero and the time variable is set at 60. The effect of December's seasonality is captured in the constant term. Thus, December serves as a base month. Of course, we could have chosen any month as a base month. The choice of December as a base month was completely arbitrary. The point is that if we want monthly seasonal factors, then we only need 11 dummy variables. If we want quarterly seasonal factors, then we will need 3 dummy variables.

Table 4-11 shows how dummy variables are assigned for seasonal factors. It is now possible to use a standard regression analysis program to estimate the coefficients. The model then can be used to make forecasts.

b. What other approach can you take to build a regression model for forecasting patient demand? Identify the possible independent variables that you would need for this approach. Do not let your thinking be constrained by the data given in Table 4-10. You could choose variables for which data are not provided here but could be collected in real situations.

TABLE 4-11
**ASSIGNMENT OF DUMMY VARIABLES FOR REGRESSION ANALYSIS**

| | | *Jan* | *Feb* | *Mar* | *Apr* | *May* | *Jun* | *Jul* | *Aug* | *Sep* | *Oct* | *Nov* | *Time* |
|---|---|---|---|---|---|---|---|---|---|---|---|---|---|
| Month | $y$ | $x_1$ | $x_2$ | $x_3$ | $x_4$ | $x_5$ | $x_6$ | $x_7$ | $x_8$ | $x_9$ | $x_{10}$ | $x_{11}$ | $x_{12}$ |
| Jan 1982 | 795 | 1 | 0 | 0 | 0 | 0 | 0 | 0 | 0 | 0 | 0 | 0 | 0 |
| Feb | 810 | 0 | 1 | 0 | 0 | 0 | 0 | 0 | 0 | 0 | 0 | 0 | 2 |
| Mar | 840 | 0 | 0 | 1 | 0 | 0 | 0 | 0 | 0 | 0 | 0 | 0 | 3 |
| Apr | 820 | 0 | 0 | 0 | 1 | 0 | 0 | 0 | 0 | 0 | 0 | 0 | 4 |
| May | 800 | 0 | 0 | 0 | 0 | 1 | 0 | 0 | 0 | 0 | 0 | 0 | 5 |
| Jun | 765 | 0 | 0 | 0 | 0 | 0 | 1 | 0 | 0 | 0 | 0 | 0 | 6 |
| Jul | 745 | 0 | 0 | 0 | 0 | 0 | 0 | 1 | 0 | 0 | 0 | 0 | 7 |
| Aug | 740 | 0 | 0 | 0 | 0 | 0 | 0 | 0 | 1 | 0 | 0 | 0 | 8 |
| Sep | 750 | 0 | 0 | 0 | 0 | 0 | 0 | 0 | 0 | 1 | 0 | 0 | 9 |
| Oct | 820 | 0 | 0 | 0 | 0 | 0 | 0 | 0 | 0 | 0 | 1 | 0 | 10 |
| Nov | 840 | 0 | 0 | 0 | 0 | 0 | 0 | 0 | 0 | 0 | 0 | 1 | 11 |
| Dec | 755 | 0 | 0 | 0 | 0 | 0 | 0 | 0 | 0 | 0 | 0 | 0 | 12 |
| Jan 1983 | 780 | 1 | 0 | 0 | 0 | 0 | 0 | 0 | 0 | 0 | 0 | 0 | 13 |
| Feb | 820 | 0 | 1 | 0 | 0 | 0 | 0 | 0 | 0 | 0 | 0 | 0 | 14 |
| Mar | 825 | 0 | 0 | 1 | 0 | 0 | 0 | 0 | 0 | 0 | 0 | 0 | 15 |
| . | | | | | | | | | | | | | |
| . | | | | | | | | | | | | | |
| . | | | | | | | | | | | | | |
| Jan 1984 | 815 | 1 | 0 | 0 | 0 | 0 | 0 | 0 | 0 | 0 | 0 | 0 | 25 |
| Feb | 865 | 0 | 1 | 0 | 0 | 0 | 0 | 0 | 0 | 0 | 0 | 0 | 26 |
| . | | | | | | | | | | | | | |
| . | | | | | | | | | | | | | |
| . | | | | | | | | | | | | | |
| Dec | 745 | 0 | 0 | 0 | 0 | 0 | 0 | 0 | 0 | 0 | 0 | 0 | 36 |

c. Compare and contrast the appropriateness and usefulness of the exponential smoothing approach and the regression approach for the patient forecasting problem. You should point out advantages and disadvantages of both approaches. What additional information would you need to decide which of the two approaches should be used in a given application?

# SITUATION

## Patient Forecasting for Nurse Scheduling

29. The hospital for which data are given in Table 4-10 is attempting to improve its nurse scheduling system. Initially, it is concentrating on broad planning for the aggregate levels of nursing personnel needed.

In the past, the number of nursing personnel had been determined for the peak demand expected during the year. Under heavy pressure to reduce costs, the hospital administrator is now considering alternatives that take account of shorter-term variations in the patient load. An exponential smoothing model was applied to the 5.5-year historical record, using a smoothing constant of $\alpha = 0.2$. This model resulted in forecasting error measurements of $MAD = 31.9$. The hospital administrator felt that the error was too large, stating that he could do almost as well based on his knowledge of patient fluctuations. For example, he expects a relatively small number of patients in December because those with "elective" medical problems avoid the holiday season; elective cases usually come in the spring.

The administrator is contemplating the use of more sophisticated forecasting models and wonders whether a model that accounts for trends and seasonals would result in greater forecasting accuracy. He also wants advice concerning the possible use of a regression model.

Finally, the hospital administrator is deeply concerned about the 1986 data. The hospital had a record average of 890 patients in April of that year but a record low of only 705 patients in December. He feels that the situation is explainable by the fact that the patient load built up because of the increase in population in the community and that the low in December reflects the opening of enlarged facilities at the nearby county hospital. He wonders, however, what plans he should make for the balance of 1987 and for 1988.

What recommendations would you submit to the hospital administrator?

# REFERENCES


Ahl, D. H., "New Product Forecasting Using Consumer Panels," *Journal of Marketing Research,* 7(2), May 1970, pp. 159–167.

Armstrong, J. S., *Long-Range Forecasting: From Crystal Ball to Computer,* Wiley, New York, 1978.

Ascher, W., *Forecasting: An Appraisal for Policy Makers and Planners,* The Johns Hopkins Press, Baltimore, 1978.

Bass, F. M., "A New Product Growth Model for Consumer Durables," *Management Science, 16*(5), January 1969, pp. 215–227.

Bass, F. M., C. W. King, and E. A. Pessemeier, *Applications of the Sciences in Marketing Management,* Wiley, New York, 1968.

Berry, W. L., and F. W. Bliemel, "Selecting Exponential Smoothing Constants: An Application of Pattern Search," *International Journal of Production Research, 12*(4), July 1974, pp. 483–500.

Berry W. L., V. A. Mabert, and M. Marcus, "Forecasting Teller Window Demand With Exponential Smoothing," *Journal of the Academy of Management, 22*(1), March 1979, pp. 129–137.

Box, G. E. P., and G. M. Jenkins, *Time Series Analysis, Forecasting, and Control,* Holden–Day, San Francisco, 1970.

Chambers, J. C., S. K. Mullick, and D. D. Smith, "How to Choose the Right Forecasting Technique," *Harvard Business Review,* July–August 1971, pp. 45–74.

Chase, R. B. and N. J. Aquilano, *Production and Operations Management* (4th ed.), Irwin, Homewood, Ill., 1985.

Chow, W. M., "Adaptive Control of the Exponential Smoothing Constant," *The Journal of Industrial Engineering, 16*(5), 1965, pp. 314–317.

Claycamp, H. J., and L. E. Liddy, "Prediction of New Product Performance: An Analytical Approach," *Journal of Marketing, 6*(4), November 1969, pp. 414–421.

Helmer, O., *Systematic Use of Experts,* P-3721, Rand Corporation, Santa Monica, California, November 1967.

Linstone, H. A., and M. Turoff, *The Delphi Method: Techniques and Applications,* Addison-Wesley, Reading, Mass., 1975.

Makridakis, S., and R. L. Winkler, "Averages of Forecasts: Some Empirical Results," *Management Science, 29*(9), September 1983, pp. 987–996.

Makridakis, S., S. C. Wheelwright, and V. E. McGee, *Forecasting Methods and Applications,* Wiley, New York, 1983.

North, H. Q., and D. L. Pyke, "Probes of the Technological Future," *Harvard Business Review,* May–June 1969.

Parker, G. G. C., and E. L. Segura, "How to Get a Better Forecast," *Harvard Business Review,* March–April 1971, pp. 99–109.

Pegels, C. C., "Exponential Forecasting: Some New Variations," *Management Science, 12*(5), 1969, pp. 311–315.

Roberts, S. D., and R. Reed, "The Development of a Self-Adaptive Forecasting Technique," *AIEE Transactions, 1*(4), 1969, pp. 314–322.

Sarin, R. K., "An Approach for Long Term Forecasting with an Application to Solar Electric Energy," *Management Science, 25*(6), June 1979, pp. 543–554.

Trigg, D. W., and A. G. Leach, "Exponential Smoothing with an Adaptive Response Rate," *Operational Research Quarterly, 18*(1), March 1967, pp. 53–59.

Winters, P. R., "Forecasting Sales by Exponentially Weighted Moving Averages," *Management Science, 6*(3), April 1960, pp. 324–342.

# CHAPTER 5

# INVENTORY PLANNING AND CONTROL

Control and maintenance of inventory of physical goods is a problem common to all enterprises. For most manufacturing firms, inventory accounts for a large percentage of working capital. There are several reasons for keeping inventory. These include protection against variations in demand, maintaining smooth flow of production by providing a decoupling function between stages of production, and lowering total material cost by taking advantage of quantity discounts. In addition, inventory can actually aid in increasing production rate and lowering manufacturing costs if, through its prudent use, excessive set ups at the bottleneck stage of production are avoided. A company can realize substantial savings by using a rational procedure for inventory management. In this chapter, we discuss procedures for managing independent demand inventory items, where the demand for an item is based on its own usage history and statistical variation. In Chapter 6, we discuss policies for dependent demand items, where demand is determined by production schedules for end products.

## SYMPTOMS OF MISMANAGED INVENTORIES

In many firms, the management of inventory of physical goods is based on the intuitive determinations of the purchasing manager, who decides which items to buy, when to buy them, and what quantities to buy. When a company is small and the number of items to be stocked are few, such informal procedures may work well. However, as a company grows and begins to require a wide variety of inventory items having different usage rates, informal systems tend to create problems that can result in higher costs and interruptions in production and the supply of end items. Unfortunately, detecting mismanaged inventories is not easy, as the symptoms vary a great deal. Some symptoms that should indicate to managers that a scientific management of inventories is required are (1) the total amount of inventory rises faster than the growth of sales; (2) stockouts of items occur, causing interruptions in production or delayed deliveries to customers; (3) clerical costs for procuring, expediting, and maintaining inventories become too high; (4) there is too much quantity in stock for some items and too little for others; and (5) items are missing or misplaced and spoilage and obsolescence rates are too high.

A formal system of inventory management can produce substantial savings for a company. These savings are realized in several different forms, depending on the particular situation of the company. Some common sources of such savings are lower purchase cost, lower interest expenses or an increase in the availability of internal funds, lower operating costs (clerical, expediting, transportation, receiving, etc.), lower production cost per unit, dependable delivery of production, and better customer service in the supply of goods. We will discuss the basic principles and models that are important for designing a formal system of inventory management.

## STOCK POINTS IN A PRODUCTION–DISTRIBUTION SYSTEM

Figure 5-1 identifies the main stock points in a production–distribution system, from the ordering of raw materials and supplies, through the productive process, and culminating in the availability of finished goods for consumption. At the head of the system, stocks of raw materials and supplies are required in order to carry out the productive process at minimum cost and by the required schedule. Inventory policies are developed to determine when to replenish these inventories and how much to order at one time. These issues are compounded by price discounts and by the need to ensure that delays in supply time and temporary increases in requirements will not disrupt operations.

As a part of the conversion process within the productive system, in-process inventories are converted to finished goods inventories. The level of finished goods inventory depends on the policy used for determining production lot sizes and timing and on the usage rates as determined by distributors' orders. High-volume items justify different policies for production and inventory replenishment than those for medium- or low-volume items. Decisions about production lot size and timing are very important regarding the economical use of personnel and equipment. The continuous production of a high-volume item may be justified. On the other hand, low-volume items should probably be produced only periodically and in economic lots. Again, we will need policy guidelines to determine the size of buffer inventories necessary to absorb the effects of production delays and random variations in demand by distributors.

The function of distributors and retailers is to make products available to consumers from finished goods inventories. Distributors and retailers often carry a wide range of items; therefore, replenishment policies that take this kind of complexity into account are required. Commonly, routine orders for a variety of items are periodically placed with each supplier. Price discounts are often an additional factor to consider.

Although the details of problems at each level in the production–distribution system may differ, note that the basic policy issues at each stage pertain to the inventory replenishment process and focus on how much and when to order. There is a general class of problems for which the concepts of economic order quantities

FIGURE 5-1
**MAIN STOCK POINTS IN A PRODUCTION–DISTRIBUTION SYSTEM.**

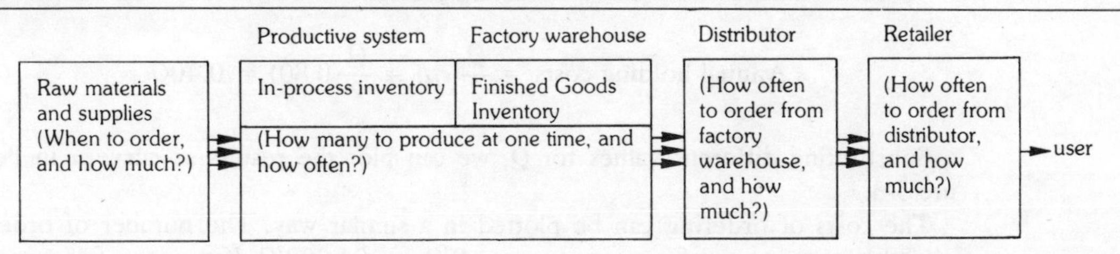

(*EOQ*) provide important insights. We will first develop these concepts within the framework of the size of purchase orders; later, we will see how these concepts may be adapted for inventory problems downstream in the system.

## THE BASIC INVENTORY MODEL

The objective of the basic inventory model is to determine the optimal order quantity that minimizes the total incremental costs of holding inventory and processing orders. The trade-offs that are captured in this model can be illustrated with a simple example.

Suppose that the annual requirement for a particular raw material item is $R = 2000 \times 52 = 104{,}000$ units, or an average of 2000 units per week. If we order in lots of $Q = 10{,}000$ units, then a new lot will be required every five weeks. When a new lot arrives in the warehouse, there will be 10,000 units of this raw material in stock. This inventory will be depleted at the rate of 2000 units per week. At the end of the fifth week, there will be zero inventory and the next lot of 10,000 units will enter the system. Figure 5-2*a* illustrates the changes in inventory levels for this item over time as a result of this order policy. The average inventory level for this situation is one-half the lot size, or $Q/2 = 5000$ units.

If the item is ordered more often in smaller quantities, as shown in Figure 5-2*b*, the associated inventory level will decrease in proportion to the number of units ordered at one time. Since the incremental costs of holding inventory depend on the average inventory level, carrying costs are proportional to the lot size $Q$, the number of items ordered at one time.

From Figure 5-2, we can also see that the total annual cost of placing orders for the order pattern of Figure 5-2*b* will be twice for the order pattern of Figure 5-2*a* because twice as many orders are placed for the same annual requirement. Therefore, we have isolated two types of incremental costs that represent the quantitative criteria for evaluating the inventory system. These are the costs associated with inventory level, or ***holding costs,*** and the costs associated with the number of orders placed, or ***preparation costs.***

In further defining the system, let us construct a graph that shows the general relationship between $Q$ (lot size) and the incremental costs we have isolated. We saw in Figure 5-2 that if $Q$ is doubled, the average inventory level is doubled. Assume a holding cost of $c_H = 80$ cents per year to carry a unit of inventory. (Costs include such items as interest, insurance, and taxes.) Because the average inventory level is $Q/2$, the annual incremental costs associated with inventory are

$$\text{Annual holding costs} = \frac{Q}{2}(c_H) = \frac{Q}{2}(0.80) = 0.40Q \qquad (1)$$

Substituting different values for $Q$, we can plot the results as curve *a* in Figure 5-3.

The costs of ordering can be plotted in a similar way. The number of orders placed per year to satisfy requirements is $R/Q = 104{,}000/Q$. If the costs for prepar-

FIGURE 5-2
**SIMPLIFIED MODEL OF THE EFFECT OF LOT SIZE ON INVENTORY LEVELS.**

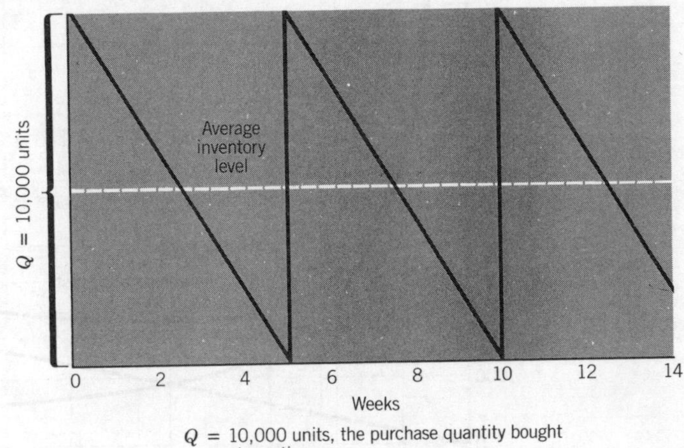


$Q$ = 10,000 units, the purchase quantity bought at one time.
$R$ = 2000 × 52 = 104,000 units, the total annual requirement.
$I$ = $Q$/2 = 5000 units, the average inventory.

*(a)*

$Q$ = 5000 units

0 2 4 6 8 10 12 14

Weeks

$Q$ = 5000 units
$R$ = 104,000 units per year
$I$ = $Q$/2 = 2500 units

*(b)*

ing and following up an order are $c_P$ = \$20, then the total annual incremental costs of ordering are

$$\text{Annual order cost} = \frac{R}{Q}(c_P) = \frac{104{,}000}{Q}(20) = \frac{2{,}080{,}000}{Q} \qquad (2)$$

Therefore, as $Q$ increases, the annual incremental ordering costs decrease. This relationship is plotted as curve $b$ in Figure 5-3, which is obtained by substituting different values of $Q$ into Equation 2.

Curve $c$ in Figure 5-3 shows the total incremental cost curve that results from adding curves $a$ and $b$. This curve represents a model that expresses total annual

FIGURE 5-3
**GRAPHIC MODEL OF A SIMPLE INVENTORY PROBLEM.**

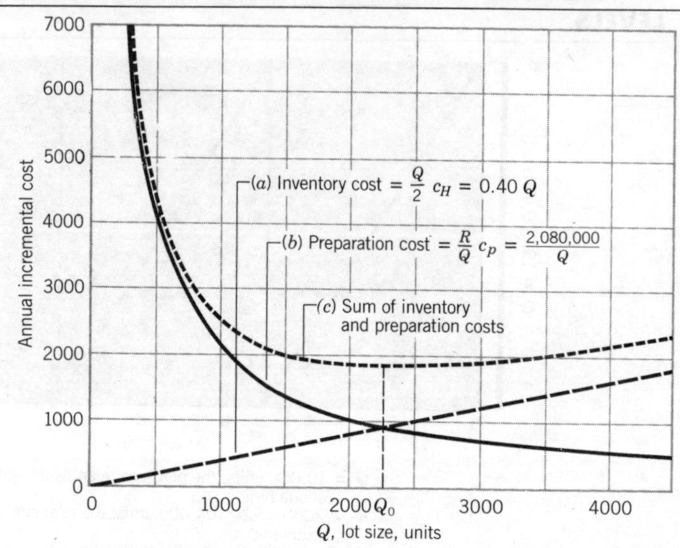


incremental costs as a function of the variables that define the system. The equation for the total cost curve can also be expressed algebraically as the sum of the annual holding and order costs found using Equations 1 and 2.

$$TIC = \frac{Q}{2} \quad c_H \quad + \quad \frac{R}{Q} \quad c_P \qquad (3)$$

$$\begin{pmatrix}\text{Total}\\\text{incremental}\\\text{cost}\end{pmatrix} \quad \begin{pmatrix}\text{Average}\\\text{inventory}\end{pmatrix} \quad \begin{pmatrix}\text{Unit inventory}\\\text{cost per year}\end{pmatrix} \quad \begin{pmatrix}\text{Number}\\\text{of orders}\\\text{per year}\end{pmatrix} \quad \begin{pmatrix}\text{Cost}\\\text{of an}\\\text{order}\end{pmatrix}$$

The variable in Equation 3 that can be manipulated by management is $Q$ (lot size). Uncontrollable variables are the requirements that are related to such factors as consumer demand, taxes, and insurance rates. For this example, the uncontrollable variables are $c_H$ (inventory costs per unit), $R$ (demand or requirements), and $c_P$ (order preparation costs). All the factors that determine $c_H$ and $c_P$ should vary with order size.

## A General Solution

For our simplified model, we can select the optimal policy as that defined by the minimum point on the total incremental cost curve of Figure 5-3, or $EOQ = 2280$. (The symbol $EOQ$ denotes the optimal value of $Q$.) Note that at the optimal point annual holding cost is equal to annual order cost. This is a solution to the specific problem with the given values for $c_H$, $R$, and $c_P$. From Equation 3 for the total incremental cost, we can derive a formula for the minimum point on the curve through the use of differential calculus. We take the derivative of $TIC$ with respect to $Q$ and set $dTIC/dQ$ equal to zero. Solving for $Q$ yields a formula that represents the general solution for the model:

$$EOQ = \sqrt{\frac{2Rc_P}{c_H}} \tag{4}$$

This formula gives the value of $EOQ$ that yields the minimum total incremental cost for the model. Substituting the values in the example

$$EOQ = \sqrt{\frac{2 \times 104{,}000 \times 20}{0.80}} = \sqrt{5{,}200{,}000} = 2280.35 \text{ units}$$

When using Equation 4, it is essential that all constants and variables be expressed in consistent units. For example, if it is desired that the economic order quantity be expressed in dollars, the requirements must also be expressed in dollars. Similarly, if annual requirements are to be expressed in monthly rates, inventory costs must also be expressed as monthly rates. In practice, charts, graphs, and tables based on the formula are often used to minimize computations. More currently, computer programs automatically issue purchase orders for the quantities computed by the formula.

The incremental cost of the optimal solution, $TIC_0$, is obtained by substituting $EOQ$ into Equation 3:

$$TIC_0 = \sqrt{2c_Pc_HR} \tag{5}$$

Substituting the values from our example gives

$$TIC_0 = \sqrt{2 \times 20 \times 0.8 \times 104{,}000} = \sqrt{3{,}328{,}000} = \$1824.28/\text{year}$$

The inventory policy from our example is to order 2280 units each time, which will result in an average number of annual orders of $R/Q = 45.6$. The time between placing and receiving an order, called the *lead time*, determines when an order is placed. For example, if the lead time is one week, then an order should be placed when on hand inventory falls to 2000 units. The inventory level when an order is placed is called the *reorder point*. In the basic model, since the demand is assumed to be known, the reorder point represents the amount of stock required to satisfy demand during the lead time.

## Important Assumptions

The $EOQ$ model is intuitively attractive because it minimizes the obvious incremental costs associated with inventory replenishment. In applying the model, however, there are some important assumptions:

1. Average demand is continuous and constant, represented by a distribution that does not change with time. Therefore, if there is significant trend or seasonality in the average annual requirements, $R$, in Equation 4, the simple model may not be appropriate.
2. Supply lead time is constant. Although this assumption may be reasonable in

many situations, supply lead times are often quite variable. The result of a variable lead time is that the receipt of the order produces excess inventories when lead times are shorter than expected and stockout situations when lead times are longer than expected. The basic model is not appropriate when lead times are variable. Further, the delivery for all $Q$ items is instantaneous rather than over time.

3. Independence between inventory items. The *EOQ* model assumes that the replenishment of one inventory item has no effect on the replenishment of any other inventory item. This assumption is valid in many instances, but exceptions arise when sets of supply items are coupled together by a common production plan.
4. Purchase price, and the cost parameters $c_H$ and $c_P$ are constants.
5. The order quantity, *EOQ*, is equal to the delivery quantities. If delivery lots are smaller, the average inventories in the *EOQ* model are not valid.

There are various ways of dealing with the effects of these assumptions. Indeed, much of the research on inventory models that followed the development of Equation 4 has centered on concepts and techniques for dealing with situations where one or more of the assumptions is not valid.

## Sensitivity Analysis

For a variety of practical considerations (truckload requirements, warehouse space constraints, etc.), it may not be possible to follow *EOQ* policy exactly. Obviously, any deviation from the optimal policy will increase *TIC*; the purpose of sensitivity, or "what if," analysis is to determine the magnitude of corresponding increases in *TIC*.

In our example, the optimal policy is $EOQ = 2280$ units and $TIC_0 = \$1824.28/$year. Now, suppose management wishes to order in lots of 2000. The annual cost of this policy can be obtained from Equation 3

$$TIC(Q = 2000) = \frac{2000}{2} \times 0.80 + \frac{104{,}000}{2000} \times 20$$

$$= \$1840.0/\text{year}$$

Thus, the cost of deviating somewhat from the optimal policy is relatively small: ($1840 − $1824.28) = $15.72. From Figure 5-3, it can be seen that the shape of *TIC* curve $c$ is like a bathtub and therefore the costs increase gradually around *EOQ*.

Similarly, the inputs to the *EOQ* model, $R$, $c_P$, and $c_H$, can only be estimated within some range. Sensitivity analysis can reveal any error in *TIC* due to estimation. Usually, because of the robustness of the model, moderate errors in estimation result only in small increases in *TIC*. Since the model is simple, different types of sensitivity analyses can be conducted by implementing the model on a spread-sheet program (e.g., Lotus 1–2–3) for a personal computer. A general conclusion is that the near optimal performance of the model is not sensitive to the accuracy of cost and demand estimates, the assumption of constant demand, or choices of $Q$ in the neighborhood of $EOQ$. The simple model is therefore quite attractive for practical applications.

## The Effect of Quantity Discounts

The basic economic order quantity formula assumes a fixed purchase price. When quantity discounts enter the picture, the total incremental cost equation is no longer a continuous function of order quantity but becomes a step function with the components of annual inventory cost, ordering cost, and material cost involving the price discount schedule. The total incremental cost equation becomes

$$TIC = c_H Q/2 + c_P R/Q + p_i R \tag{6}$$

where $p_i$ is the price per unit for the $i$th price break and $c_H = p_i F_H$, where $F_H$ is the fraction of inventory value. The procedure is then one of calculation to determine if there is a net advantage in annual ordering plus material costs that counterbalances the increased annual inventory costs.

As an illustration, assume that a manufacturer's requirement for an item is 2000 per year. The purchase price is quoted as \$2 per unit in quantities below 1000, \$1.90 per unit in quantities between 1000 and 1999, and \$1.86 per unit in quantities above 2000. Ordering costs are \$20 per order, and inventory costs are 16 percent of the average inventory value per unit per year, or \$0.32 per unit per year at the \$2 unit price. Equation 4 indicates that the economic order quantity is

$$Q_0 = \sqrt{\frac{2 \times 20 \times 2000}{0.32}} = \sqrt{250{,}000} = 500 \text{ units at the \$2 unit price.}$$

Using the preceding data and Equation 6, we can compute $TIC$ for each of the three price ranges, as is shown in Figure 5-4. (The solid line curves indicate the relationships for valid price ranges.

1. Note that for the \$2 price that applies for a $Q$ of *less than* 1000, $EOQ = 500$ units produces the lowest cost of \$4160 (curve 1).
2. However, for order quantities between 1000 and 1999, the price of \$1.90 per unit applies. When $Q = 1000$, $TIC = \$3992$—a cost saving of \$168 per year as compared to ordering in lots of 500 units (curve 2).
3. Finally, when $Q$ is *greater than or equal to* 2000, the price of \$1.86 per unit applies, and $TIC = \$4038$ at $Q = 2000$ units (curve 3).

The ordering policy with the lowest cost is to take advantage of the first price break, but not the second, and to order in lots of $Q = 1000$ units. Summary calculations are shown in Table 5-1.

With other numerical values, it is possible for curve 2 to have its optimum occur within the middle price range or for curve 3 to have its optimum occur within the upper price range. Therefore, a general procedure such as the following is needed:

1. Calculate the $EOQ$ for each price.
2. Eliminate $EOQ$s that fall outside of valid price ranges.

FIGURE 5-4
**TOTAL INCREMENTAL COST CURVES FOR INVENTORY MODEL WITH THREE PRICE BREAKS: $R$ = 2000 UNITS PER YEAR, $c_P$ = \$20, $F_H$ = 0.16.**

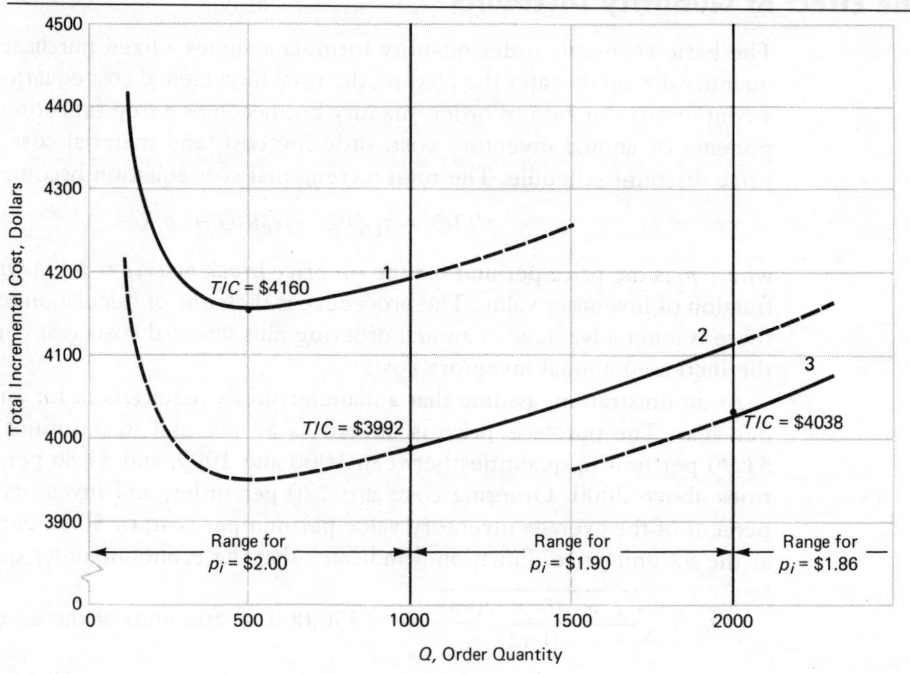


TABLE 5-1
**INCREMENTAL COST ANALYSIS TO DETERMINE NET ADVANTAGE OR DISADVANTAGE WHEN PRICE DISCOUNTS ARE OFFERED**

| | Lots of 500 Units, Price = \$2.00 per Unit | Lots of 1000 Units, Price = \$1.90 per Unit | Lots of 2000 Units, Price = \$1.86 per Unit |
|---|---|---|---|
| Purchase of a year's supply ($p_i \times 2000$) | \$4000 | \$3800 | \$3720 |
| Ordering cost ($20 \times 2000/Q$) | 80 | 40 | 20 |
| Inventory cost (average inventory $\times$ unit price $\times$ 0.16) | 80 | 152 | 298 |
| Total | \$4160 | \$3992 | \$4038 |

3. Calculate *TIC*s for valid *EOQ*s and at price breaks.
4. Select lot size associated with the lowest *TIC*.

## Multiple Products and Resource Constraints

The *EOQ* model treats each inventory item as independent. If there are no resource constraints, the optimal inventory policy for the company is merely to stock *EOQ* of each item. However, in many real systems there are constraints on storage space, amount of investment in inventory, number of orders and deliveries that can be accepted, and so forth. Under such constraints, determining order quantities for individual items may cause resource limitations to be exceeded. For example, the total space available for stocking items may be exceeded if optimal order quantities for each item are determined independently. Therefore, we must look for a cost-effective way to reduce order quantities below *EOQ*'s so that all necessary items can be accommodated in the available space. An example will demonstrate the procedure for adjusting order quantities to meet specified resource limitations.

Consider a department that stocks three items. The warehouse has limited space, and there is therefore an upper limit to the average amount of space that can be allotted to these items. The pertinent data for the items are given in Table 5-2. Management wishes to minimize the total incremental costs of holding and ordering the three items while ensuring that the total average space requirements do not exceed 800 $ft^3$.

The first step in determining inventory policy under resource constraints is to compute *EOQ* for each item and verify whether the resource constraint is indeed violated. In our example, as shown in Table 5-2, the average space needed to stock independent optimal order quantities for each item will be 946 $ft^3$, which exceeds the limit of 800 $ft^3$.

An intuitive, but mathematically optimal, procedure to determine lot sizes $Q_1$, $Q_2$, $Q_3$ for the three items so that the upper limit on the average space allowed is not

TABLE 5-2
**EXAMPLE OF LOT SIZE DETERMINATION WITH RESOURCE CONSTRAINTS**

| | | | | | | $\lambda = .295$ | |
|---|---|---|---|---|---|---|---|
| Item | *R* (Annual Demand) | Cost/Unit | Space in $ft^3$/Unit | *EOQ* | Average Space | *Q* | Average Space |
| A | 15,000 | 8 | 4.7 | 250 | 587 | 199 | 468 |
| B | 21,000 | 3.5 | 0.5 | 447 | 112 | 419 | 105 |
| C | 14,000 | 15 | 2.8 | 176 | 247 | 162 | 227 |
| | | | | | 946 | | 800 |

Cost of ordering = $c_P$ = \$5
Cost of holding = $c_H$ = cost/unit × 0.3

exceeded is to modify the $EOQ$ of Equation 4 by attaching a price to space. Thus,

$$Q_i = \sqrt{\frac{2R_i c_{P_i}}{c_{H_i} + \lambda S_i}} \tag{7}$$

where $R_i$ is annual demand, $c_{P_i}$ is the cost of ordering, $c_{H_i}$ is the cost of holding per unit per year, and $S_i$ the space required per unit for item $i$. The value $\lambda$ indicates the price per unit of space. In Equation 7, the cost of holding in the denominator is inflated by including the price associated with the space required by a unit of item $i$. If $\lambda = 0$, then no price is attached to space and $Q_i = EOQ$. For $\lambda > 0$, the lot size for item $i$ will be smaller than its $EOQ$. For example, if $\lambda = 0.1$ (i.e., the price for space is assumed to be 10 cents per ft$^3$, then by Equation 7, $Q_1 = 229$ ($EOQ_1 = 250$), $Q_2 = 437$ ($EOQ_2 = 447$), and $Q_3 = 171$ ($EOQ_3 = 176$). The average space required will be

$$\frac{229 \times 4.7}{2} + \frac{437 \times 0.5}{2} + \frac{171 \times 2.8}{2} = 887 \text{ ft}^3$$

which is below the 946 ft$^3$ that would be required if $EOQ$ lot sizes were implemented. However, the upper limit for average space is still exceeded. In an iterative manner, the value of $\lambda$ is increased, thereby reducing the lot sizes and space requirements, until the upper limit on space is just met. For our example, $\lambda = 0.295$ and lot sizes of $Q_1 = 199$, $Q_2 = 419$, and $Q_3 = 162$ satisfy the space limit. The total $TIC$ for a policy that meets a resource constraint will be larger than the total $TIC$ of independent $EOQ$ policy. The difference in the two costs indicates the additional cost incurred by a company due to resource limitations. In our example, total $TIC$ for $EOQ$ policy is

$$\sqrt{2 \times 15{,}000 \times 5 \times 2.4} + \sqrt{2 \times 21{,}000 \times 5 \times 1.05} + \sqrt{2 \times 14{,}000 \times 5 \times 4.5} = \$1863.2$$

The total $TIC$ for the policy that satisfies the upper limit on space needed is computed as

$$TIC = \sum_{i=1}^{3} \frac{Q_i c_{H_i}}{2} + \frac{R_i c_{P_i}}{Q_i}$$

$$= \frac{199}{2} \times 2.4 + \frac{15{,}000}{199} \times 5 + \frac{419}{2} \times 1.05$$

$$+ \frac{21{,}000}{419} \times 5 + \frac{162}{2} \times 4.5 + \frac{14{,}000}{162} \times 5$$

$$= \$1882.8$$

A more detailed discussion of resource constraints and their impact on lot sizes is provided in Hadley and Whitin (1963), Chapter 2.

## Japanese Inventory System

In Japanese manufacturing systems, inventories are considered evil and great effort is focused on reducing the levels of inventories. In Chapter 14, we will discuss Japanese manufacturing systems in some detail; here, we will provide a few insights into its relationship to the *EOQ* model.

In Equation 4, if the order cost or set-up cost in a production lot size determination, $c_P$, is reduced, then *EOQ* will also be reduced. Japanese companies invest a great deal of time and effort in modifying equipment and procedures so that set-up times and costs are reduced. Similarly, they deal with suppliers who are in close proximity to the company, and they have long-term commitment so that suppliers deliver small amounts more frequently. In Figure 5-5, the impact of reducing $c_P$ on lot size or order quantity is shown. The reduction in set-up cost is achieved incrementally, a little at a time, over a long duration.

It is also possible to quantify the trade-offs between the costs associated with reducing set-ups and the benefits associated with reducing inventory-related operating costs. In this formulation, both $c_P$ and $Q$ will be variable. In Porteus (1985), a model to determine the optimal levels of $c_P$ and $Q$ simultaneously is proposed. The basic idea is that it often makes sense to invest in reducing set-up costs to achieve a greater overall reduction in operating costs.

Finally, in the Japanese inventory system, a long-term view is taken, which means that the components of holding costs that seem fixed, such as some types of storage

FIGURE 5-5
**IMPACT ON ORDER QUANTITY OF A REDUCTION IN SET-UP OR ORDER COSTS.**

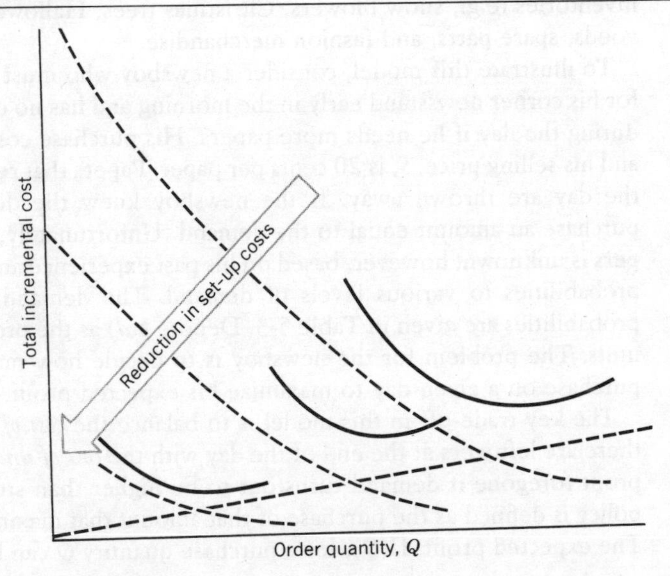

and clerical costs, are actually variable. In Equation 4, this adjustment leads to a larger value of $c_H$ and results in a lower *EOQ*.

The preceding discussion does not imply that the Japanese inventory system can be completely understood or rationalized using the *EOQ* model. The multitudes of benefits that result from reducing inventories exceed the benefits of reducing inventory related operating costs. In Chapter 14, some of these other benefits will be discussed.

## INVENTORY MODELS WITH UNCERTAIN DEMAND

In simple inventory models, we assume that demand and supply lead times are constant. In many real world applications, demand cannot be predicted with certainty and lead times often vary from one order to another. A consequence of this variation is that stockouts may occur if future demand exceeds our estimate or if an order arrives later than expected. It is possible to reduce the risks of stockouts by carrying larger inventories, called *safety stocks* or *buffer stocks;* however, additional costs are incurred by tying up additional funds in inventories and risking the possibility of obsolescence. The objective, then, is to develop a model for determining inventory policy that balances these risks and minimizes expected total incremental costs.

### Single Period Model

We first consider a simple model in which only a single procurement is made over a single, well-defined time period. This model is applicable for stocking seasonal inventories (e.g., snow blowers, Christmas trees, Halloween costumes), perishable goods, spare parts, and fashion merchandise.

To illustrate this model, consider a newsboy who must purchase the newspapers for his corner newsstand early in the morning and has no opportunity to repurchase during the day if he needs more papers. His purchase cost, $C$, is 5 cents per paper and his selling price, $S$, is 20 cents per paper. Papers that remain unsold at the end of the day are thrown away. If the newsboy knew the demand, he would simply purchase an amount equal to the demand. Unfortunately, the demand for newspapers is unknown; however, based on his past experience and sales data, he can assign probabilities to various levels of demand. The demand data and the associated probabilities are given in Table 5-3. Denote $p(d)$ as the probability that demand is $d$ units. The problem for the newsboy is to decide how many papers, $Q$, he should purchase on a given day to maximize his expected profit.

The key trade-off in this model is to balance the *cost of overstocking* the papers if there are leftovers at the end of the day with the *cost of understocking* in terms of the profit foregone if demand turns out to be higher than stock on hand. An optimal policy is defined as the purchase of that amount that maximizes the expected profit. The expected profit, $\Pi(Q)$, for a purchase quantity $Q$ can be calculated as shown in

TABLE 5-3
**NEWSBOY EXAMPLE**

| | | Purchase Quantity $Q$ = 30 | | | |
|---|---|---|---|---|---|
| Demand | Probability | Number Sold | Revenue (dollars) | Cost | Profit |
| 10 | .05 | 10 | 2 | 1.50 | 0.50 |
| 20 | .15 | 20 | 4 | 1.50 | 2.50 |
| 30 | .30 | 30 | 6 | 1.50 | 4.50 |
| 40 | .20 | 30 | 6 | 1.50 | 4.50 |
| 50 | .10 | 30 | 6 | 1.50 | 4.50 |
| 60 | .10 | 30 | 6 | 1.50 | 4.50 |
| 70 | .10 | 30 | 6 | 1.50 | 4.50 |

$$\text{Expected profit} = .05 \times .50 + .15 \times 2.50 + .30 \times 4.50 + .20 \times 4.50 + .10 \times 4.50 + .10 \times 4.50 + .10 \times 4.50 = 4.0$$

Table 5-3 for $Q = 30$. A general expression for expected profit is

$$\Pi(Q) = S\sum_{d=0}^{Q} d\,p(d) + SQ\sum_{d=Q+1}^{\infty} p(d) - CQ \tag{8}$$

$$= \begin{pmatrix}\text{Expected revenue}\\ \text{when demand is less}\\ \text{than or equal to } Q\end{pmatrix} + \begin{pmatrix}\text{Expected revenue}\\ \text{when demand is}\\ \text{more than } Q\end{pmatrix} - \begin{pmatrix}\text{Cost}\\ \text{of}\\ \text{purchase}\end{pmatrix}$$

Using this formula for $Q = 30$ in our example, we obtain:

$$\begin{aligned}\Pi(30) &= .20(10 \times .05 + 20 \times .15 + 30 \times .3) \\ &\quad + .2 \times 30(.2 + .1 + .1 + .1) - .05 \times 30 \\ &= 2.5 + 3 - 1.5 = 4\end{aligned}$$

In order to determine the optimal $Q$, we define the cost of overstocking (the cost of leftover units), $C_o$, and the cost of understocking (forgone profit per unit), $C_u$, and use an incremental analysis approach as in Trueman (1971). In our example, $C_o = C = 5$ cents and $C_u = S - C = 15$ cents. Supposing we have $(Q - 1)$ units, we will stock one more unit if the expected profit from stocking this additional unit is greater than expected loss; otherwise, it will not be advantageous to stock the additional unit. Thus, we *choose the largest* $Q$ so that

| | | | |
|---|---|---|---|
| | Expected profit from stocking an additional unit | > | Expected loss from stocking an additional unit |
| or | $C_u$ × probability demand is greater than or equal to $Q$ | > | $C_o$ × probability demand is less than $Q$ |
| or | $C_u$ Prob. $(D \geq Q)$ | > | $C_o$ Prob. $(D \leq Q)$ |

$$\text{or} \qquad C_u \text{ Prob. } (D \geq Q) \qquad > C_o [1 - \text{Prob. } (D \geq Q)]$$

$$\text{or} \qquad \text{Prob. } (D \geq Q) \qquad > \frac{C_o}{C_o + C_u} \tag{9}$$

Substituting the data from our example in Equation 9, we find that

$$\frac{C_o}{C_u + C_o} = \frac{5}{5 + 15} = .25$$

At $Q = 50$, Prob. $(D \geq 50) = .3$, which is greater than .25; hence, a purchase quantity of 50 units is optimal. The expected profit for $Q = 50$ can be calculated by Equation 8, $\Pi(50) = 4.6$.

The newsboy model can be adapted to a wide variety of situations. For example, if the leftovers can be sold at a price $\ell$, then $C_u = C - \ell$ and optimal $Q$ is computed by Equation 9. The model is also applicable when the probability distribution for demand is continuous, that is, when demand has a normal, uniform, or some other type of distribution.

## Order Quantity—Reorder Point Model

We now consider the situation, commonly faced by materials managers, when an item is continuously demanded, procurement orders for the item can be placed at any time, and the time horizon is sufficiently long that the inventory system can be assumed to operate for all future time. The problem is to determine the size of an order, $Q$, and when that order should be placed, the reorder point, *ROP*. In the basic model, we made the assumption that demand is constant and known. Thus, Equation 4 was used to compute the order quantity, $Q$, and *ROP* was simply set equal to the

FIGURE 5-6
**CHARACTERISTICS OF (Q, ROP) SYSTEM.**

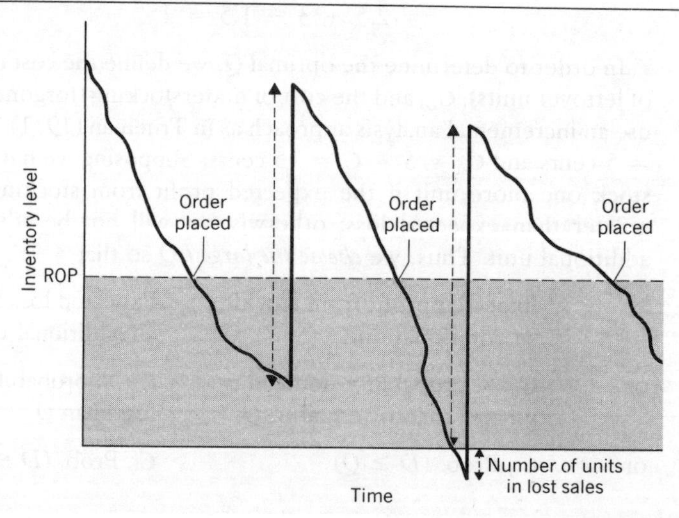

known demand during the lead time. We now discuss the case when demand during the lead time is uncertain.

Figure 5-6 shows the characteristics of the ($Q$, $ROP$) model. When inventory falls to a preset reorder point $ROP$, an order for the quantity $Q$ is placed. Since demand during lead time is uncertain, inventory may sometimes decline to create lost sales or backorders until the order for $Q$ units is received. The objective, therefore, is to select $Q$ and $ROP$ so as to minimize the sum of expected ordering and holding costs and the costs of lost sales or backorders. The model is illustrated with an example.

Suppose that the expected annual demand, $R$, for an item is 90 units. The cost of ordering, $c_P$, is \$5/order; the cost of holding one unit for one year, $c_H$, is \$1/unit/year; the cost of lost sales, $c_S$, is \$5/unit; and the probability distribution for demand during lead time, $DDLT$, is as shown in Table 5-4.

A simple approach to determine $Q$ and $ROP$ that yields results close to optimal is as follows:

*Step 1.* Find $Q$ using the $EOQ$ formula in Equation 4.

$$Q = \sqrt{\frac{2Rc_P}{c_H}} = \sqrt{\frac{2 \times 90 \times 5}{1}} = 30 \text{ units}$$

*Step 2.* Find $ROP$ by choosing the largest value for which

$$\text{Prob. } (DDLT \geq ROP) > \frac{c_H}{c_H + c_S \times \dfrac{R}{Q}} > \frac{1}{1 + 5 \times \dfrac{90}{30}} > .0625 \qquad (10)$$

From Table 5-4, the above inequality is satisfied at $ROP = 3$.

The inventory policy (30, 3) for our example means that when the inventory level falls to 3 units an order for 30 units is placed. The sequential procedure just described has an intuitive interpretation. In Step 1, $Q$ is calculated using the $EOQ$ formula to provide a good approximation when expected lost sales are small. The

**TABLE 5-4**
**DATA AND COMPUTATIONS FOR (Q, ROP) MODEL (ROP = 3 UNITS)**

| Demand During Lead Time | Probability | Physical Inventory Just Before an Order Arrives | Number of Units in Lost Sales |
|---|---|---|---|
| 0 | .30 | 3 | 0 |
| 1 | .25 | 2 | 0 |
| 2 | .30 | 1 | 0 |
| 3 | .10 | 0 | 0 |
| 4 | .05 | 0 | 1 |

Expected demand during lead time $= 0 \times .3 + 1 \times .25 + 2 \times .3 + 3 \times .1 + 4 \times .05 = 1.35$

Expected number of lost sales $= E(S) = 1 \times .05 = 0.05$

Expected physical inventory $= 3 \times .3 + 2 \times .25 + 1 \times .3 = 1.7$

Expected physical inventory $= ROP - E(DDLT) + E(S) = 3 - 1.35 + .05 = 1.7$

determination of *ROP* in Step 2 can be interpreted as a newsboy problem, where demand during lead time is uncertain, *ROP* is the decision variable, $c_H$ is the cost of overstocking, and $c_S(R/Q)$ is the cost of understocking [$c_o = c_H$, $c_u = c_S(R/Q)$]. Notice that $c_S$ is multiplied by the expected number of orders, $R/Q$, per year so that the units of $c_o$ and $c_u$ are consistent. This is because $c_H$ is defined on a yearly basis. Equivalently, we can define $c_o = c_H/(R/Q)$ and $c_u = c_S$ so that both $c_o$ and $c_u$ are measured as costs per order cycle.

Expected total annual incremental costs, $E(TIC)$, for a $(Q, ROP)$ policy is given by:

$$\begin{aligned} E(TIC) &= \text{Expected order cost per year} \\ &\quad + \text{Expected holding cost per year} \\ &\quad + \text{Expected cost of lost sales per year} \\ &= \frac{R}{Q} c_P + \left[\frac{Q}{2} + ROP - E(DDLT) + E(S)\right] c_H + E(S) \frac{R}{Q} c_S \qquad (11) \end{aligned}$$

In Equation 11, annual holding cost consists of two components: $Q/2$ is the average cycle inventory and $[ROP - E(DDLT) + E(S)]$ is the average inventory on hand when an order arrives in the system. A justification of this term is provided in Table 5-4 by a numerical example. The quantity $ROP - E(DDLT)$ is also called the *safety stock* or *buffer stock*.

For the policy (30, 3) total incremental cost is computed using Equation 11. In Table 5-4, $E(DDLT) = 1.35$ and $E(S) = 0.05$ are computed

$$\begin{aligned} E(TIC) &= \frac{90}{30} \times 5 + \left(\frac{30}{2} + 3 - 1.35 + 0.05\right) 1 + 0.05 \times \frac{90}{30} \times 5 \\ &= 15 + 16.70 + 0.75 = 32.45 \end{aligned}$$

As stated previously, the sequential procedure discussed above provides close approximation to the optimal solution. To obtain a better solution, Equation 11 has to be minimized with respect to the decision variables $Q$ and *ROP*. The resulting solution is:

$$Q = \sqrt{\frac{2R[c_P + c_S E(S)]}{c_H}} \qquad (12)$$

and *ROP* is chosen as the largest value such that

$$\text{Prob. } [(DDLT) \geq ROP] > \frac{c_H}{c_H + c_S \dfrac{R}{Q}} \qquad (13)$$

Equations 12 and 13 need to be solved simultaneously in an iterative manner to obtain the optimal values of $Q$ and *ROP*. Iterations are required because Equation 12 requires knowledge of *ROP* so that $E(S)$ can be computed, and Equation 13 uses $Q$ as input.

In the preceding discussion, we have not made a distinction between lost sales and backorder cases. In lost sales cases, on-hand inventory when an order arrives will always be $Q$; in the backorder cases, on-hand inventory is reduced by the number of backorders. The impact of this adjustment on $Q$ and $ROP$ is usually relatively small.

It is also possible to compute the cost of uncertainty in demand. In fact, Japanese inventory systems attempt to eliminate uncertainty in the supply process so that buffer stocks can be eliminated or reduced. The difference between the average annual cost of the ($Q$,$ROP$) model (Equation 11) and that of the $EOQ$ model (Equation 5) represent the annual savings attainable if all uncertainties in demand and supply lead times are eliminated. In our example,

$$TIC(EOQ = 30) = \sqrt{2 \times 90 \times 5 \times 1} = \$30$$

by Equation 5, and

$$TIC(Q = 30, ROP = 3) = \$32.45$$

by Equation 11. Thus, the cost of uncertainty in demand is \$32.45 − \$30 = \$2.45 per year for this item.

The key difference between the $EOQ$ and ($Q$, $ROP$) models is that in the latter demand is uncertain. Therefore, $ROP$ takes into consideration both the expected demand during lead time and safety stock. The level of $ROP$ also governs the average number of lost sales per cycle in the system. To compute $Q$ and $ROP$, an estimate of the cost of lost sales must be available. When such an estimate cannot be made, an alternate service level method may be employed to determine $Q$ and $ROP$.

## Service Level Method to Determine Q and *ROP*

In service level methods, management specifies a policy such as stockouts should not occur more than $x$ percent of the time. Clearly, a smaller $x$ will require a higher level of safety stock and thus a higher $ROP$. In the extreme case, when $x = 0$ percent, management requires the system never to be out of stock, and $ROP$ is therefore set equal to the maximum possible demand during lead time. For other specified levels of $x$ (e.g., 10 percent) $ROP$ is simply determined by the probability distribution for demand during lead time. In the example data in Table 5-4, if $ROP = 1$, then the system will run out of stock 45 percent of the time. If $ROP = 2$, the system will run out of stock 15 percent of the time, which is still more than the management specification. For $ROP = 3$, the system will run out of stock only when demand during lead time is 4, or 5 percent of the time. The level of order quantity is determined by the $EOQ$ formula. Thus, for $x = 10$ percent, $ROP = 3$, and $Q = 30$, as determined using Equation 4.

Alternatively, management may specify that $y$ percent of the units demanded must be provided from stocks on hand. This implies that, on the average, permissible shortages are $(100 - y)$ percent of demand. Thus, the average permissible number of units short per order cycle is $(100 - y/100)Q$. Suppose $y = 99.99$ percent for our example. Then, permissible shortages per cycle will be $(100 - 99.99/100)30 = 0.03$. If we set $ROP = 3$, the expected shortages per cycle as calculated in Table 5-4 will be 0.05, exceeding the constraint specified by management. Therefore, we should increase *ROP*. At $ROP = 4$, expected shortages will be 0. Hence, the policy chosen will be $Q = 30$ and $ROP = 4$.

A specified service level has implications for the range of shortage or lost sales costs. For a given *Q*, higher cost of lost sales or a higher service level both require a larger *ROP* and therefore higher safety stock.

## Practical Methods for Determining Buffer Stocks

Computations for the reorder point (*ROP*) and safety or buffer stocks are simplified considerably if we can justify the assumption that the probability distribution for the demand during lead time follows some particular, well-defined distribution, such as a normal, Poisson, or negative exponential distribution.

First let us recall that buffer stock is defined as the difference between the reorder point and the expected demand during lead time.

$$B = ROP - \bar{D} \tag{14}$$

where *B* is the buffer stock, *ROP* is the reorder point, and $\bar{D}$ is the expected demand during lead time.

We now define $ROP = \bar{D} + n\sigma_D$; that is, the reorder point is the average demand $\bar{D}$ plus some number of standard deviation units, *n*, that is associated with the probability of occurrence of that demand. (In practice, *n* is often called the safety factor.) Substituting this statement of *ROP* in our definition of *B* (Equation 14), we have

$$\begin{aligned} B &= ROP - \bar{D} = (\bar{D} + n\sigma_D) - \bar{D} \\ &= n\sigma_D \end{aligned} \tag{15}$$

This simple statement allows us to determine easily those buffer stocks that meet risk requirements when we know the mathematical form of the demand distribution. The procedure is as follows:

1. Determine whether a normal, Poisson, or negative exponential distribution approximately describes demand during lead time for the case under consideration. This determination is critically important and requires well-known statistical methodology.
2. Set a service level based on (a) managerial policy, (b) an assessment of the balance of incremental inventory and stockout costs, or (c) an assessment of the manager's trade-off between service level and inventory cost when stockout costs are not known.
3. Using the service level, define *ROP* in terms of the appropriate distribution.
4. Compute the required buffer stock from Equation 15, where *n* is the safety factor and $\sigma_D$ is the standard deviation for the demand distribution.

We will illustrate this approach in the context of the normal distribution.

## BUFFER STOCKS FOR THE NORMAL DISTRIBUTION

The normal distribution has been found to describe many demand functions adequately, particularly at the factory level of the supply–production–distribution system (Buchan and Koenigsberg, 1963). Given the assumption of normality and a service level of, perhaps, 95 percent, we can determine $B$ by referring to the normal distribution tables, a small part of which has been reproduced as Table 5-5. The normal distribution is a two-parameter distribution that is described completely by its mean value $\bar{D}$ and the standard deviation $\sigma_D$. Implementing a service level of 95 percent means that we are willing to accept a 5 percent risk of running out of stock. Table 5-5 shows that demand exceeds $\bar{D} + (n\sigma_D)$ with a probability of .05, or 5 percent of the time when $n = 1.645$; therefore, this policy is implemented when $B = 1.645\ \sigma_D$. As an example, if the estimate of $\sigma_D$ is 300 units and $\bar{D} = 1500$ units, assuming a normal distribution, a buffer stock to implement a 95 percent service level would be $B = 1.645 \times 300 = 494$ units. Such a policy would protect against the occurrence of demands up to $ROP = 1500 + 494 = 1994$ units during lead time. Obviously, any other service level policy could be implemented in a similar way.

## DETERMINATION OF DEMAND DURING LEAD TIME

The probability distribution for the demand during lead time can be estimated by observing actual demand over lead time for several instances. These observations can be used to compute the expected value, $\bar{D}$, and the standard deviation, $\sigma_D$, of demand during lead time.

If the lead time is approximately constant but the daily demand rate is normally distributed, then $\bar{D}$ and $\sigma_D$ for the demand during lead time can be derived easily. We assume that daily demands are independent. First, using past observations, we determine the average daily demand and its variance. Suppose the average daily demand is 10 units and its variance is 9 units$^2$. Further, suppose the lead time is 4 days. Now, to calculate $\bar{D}$, we simply multiply the lead time by the average daily demand, or $\bar{D} = 4 \times 10 = 40$ units. The variance of the demand during lead time, $\sigma_D^2$, is computed by multiplying the lead time and the variance of the daily demand. In our example, $\sigma_D^2 = 4 \times 9 = 36$ units. Thus $\sigma_D = 6$ units. The demand during lead time is normally distributed with the mean $\bar{D} = 40$ units and the standard deviation $\sigma_D = 6$ units.

When both the lead time, $L$, and the daily demand rates are variable, then we need to estimate four quantities: the average daily demand, the standard deviation of daily demand, the average lead time, and the standard deviation of lead time. If daily demand as well as lead time are normally distributed, then $\bar{D}$ and $\sigma_D$ can be easily computed. Suppose the average daily demand is 10 units and the average lead time is 4 days. Then,

$$\begin{aligned}\bar{D} &= \text{Average daily demand} \times \text{Average lead time} \\ &= 10 \times 4 \\ &= 40 \text{ units}\end{aligned}$$

TABLE 5-5
**AREA UNDER THE RIGHT TAIL OF THE NORMAL DISTRIBUTION (SHOWING THE PROBABILITY THAT DEMAND EXCEEDS $\bar{D} + n\sigma_D$ FOR SELECTED VALUES OF $n$)**

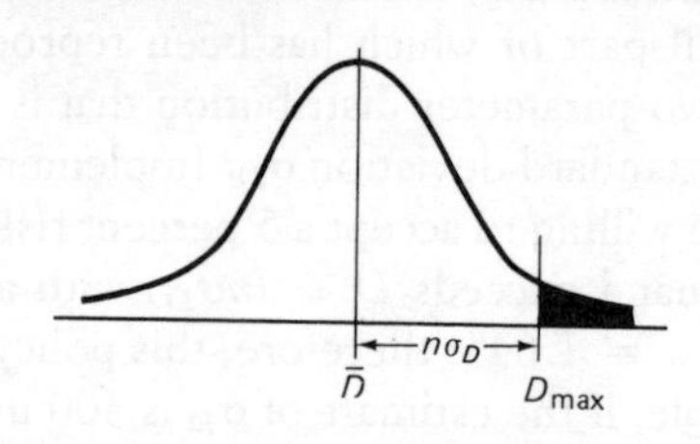


| $D_{max} = \bar{D} + n\sigma_D$ | Probability |
|---|---|
| $\bar{D} + 3.090\sigma_D$ | 0.001 |
| $\bar{D} + 2.576\sigma_D$ | .005 |
| $\bar{D} + 2.326\sigma_D$ | .010 |
| $\bar{D} + 1.960\sigma_D$ | .025 |
| $\bar{D} + 1.645\sigma_D$ | .050 |
| $\bar{D} + 1.282\sigma_D$ | 0.100 |
| $\bar{D} + 1.036\sigma_D$ | .150 |
| $\bar{D} + 0.842\sigma_D$ | .200 |
| $\bar{D} + 0.674\sigma_D$ | .250 |
| $\bar{D} + 0.524\sigma_D$ | .300 |
| $\bar{D} + 0.385\sigma_D$ | 0.350 |
| $\bar{D} + 0.253\sigma_D$ | .400 |
| $\bar{D} + 0.126\sigma_D$ | .450 |
| $\bar{D}$ | .500 |

To compute $\sigma_D^2$, we assume that the variance of daily demand is 9 units and the variance of lead time is 1.08 days. Then,

$$\begin{aligned}\sigma_D^2 &= \text{Average lead time} \times \text{Variance of daily demand} \\ &\quad + (\text{Average daily demand})^2 \times \text{Variance of lead time} \\ &= 4 \times 9 + (10)^2 \times 1.08 \\ &= 36 + 108 \\ &= 144\end{aligned}$$

Thus, $\sigma_D = \sqrt{144} = 12$ units. The demand during lead time is normally distributed, with expected value of $\bar{D} = 40$ units and standard deviation $\sigma_D = 12$ units. We can use this information to determine buffer stock and the reorder point as discussed in the previous section.

## PRODUCTION ORDER QUANTITIES AND PRODUCTION CYCLING

In the process-focused model of productive systems, where demand is independent, as with spare parts, and production is carried out in batches, management must decide how large these batches should be. The concept of *EOQ* represented by Equation 4 can be applied directly, recognizing that preparation costs are the incremental costs of writing production orders, controlling the flow of orders through the system, and setting up machines for the batch; inventory costs are associated with holding in-process inventory.

However, the assumption that an order is received and placed into inventory all at one time is often not true in manufacturing. Equation 4 assumes the general inventory pattern shown in Figure 5-7*a*, where the entire order quantity $Q$ is instantaneously received into inventory. The inventory is then drawn down at the usage rate, and subsequent orders are placed with sufficient lead time so that their receipt coincides with the minimum inventory level.

For many manufacturing situations, the production of the total order quantity takes place over a period of time, and the parts go into inventory in smaller quantities as production continues. This results in an inventory pattern similar to Figure 5-7*b*.

If $Q_P$ is the production order quantity, then Equation 3 for total incremental cost is modified as follows:

$$TIC = \frac{1}{2}\frac{Q_P}{p}(p - r)c_H + \frac{R}{Q_P}c_P \qquad (16)$$

In the above expression, the first component is the holding cost and the second is the production set-up cost. Since $p$ is the production per unit time, it takes $Q_P/p$ time units to produce the production order quantity, $Q_P$. Further $p - r$ units accumulate in inventory per unit time, so in $Q_P/p$ time units, an inventory of $Q_P/p(p - r)$ units will be accumulated. (This is the height of the triangle in Figure 5-7*b*.) We now take the derivative of $TIC$ with respect to $Q_P$ and set $dTIC/dQ_P$ equal to zero. Solving for $Q_P$ yields the following formula:

$$Q_P = \sqrt{\frac{2Rc_P}{c_H\left(1 - \frac{r}{p}\right)}} \qquad (17)$$

where

$r$ = Requirements or usage rate (short term, perhaps daily or weekly)
$p$ = Production rate (on same time basis as for $r$)
$c_P$ = Ordering and set-up cost
$c_H$ = Unit inventory cost
$Q_P$ = Minimum cost production order quantity
$R$ = Annual requirements

The $Q_P$ that results is larger than that which would result from Equation 4. Average inventory is smaller for a given $Q_P$ and the balance between set-up costs and inven-

FIGURE 5-7
**COMPARISON OF INVENTORY BALANCE (*a*) WHEN THE ORDER QUANTITY, Q, IS RECEIVED ALL AT ONE TIME AND (*b*) WHEN Q IS RECEIVED OVER A PERIOD OF TIME.**

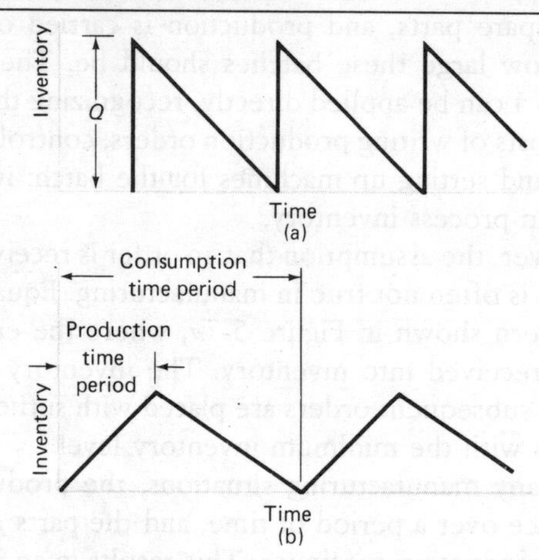


tory costs takes place at a higher value of the order quantity $Q_P$. The number of production cycles per year is $R/Q_P$.

The total incremental cost of the optimal production order quantity is

$$TIC_0 = \sqrt{2c_P c_H R\left(1 - \frac{r}{p}\right)} \tag{18}$$

## INVENTORY CONTROL SYSTEMS

In designing an inventory control system, three questions are relevant:

1. How often should the assessment of stock on hand be made?
2. When should a replenishment order be placed?
3. What should be the size of the replenishment order?

The physical operation and the advantages and disadvantages of three common control systems will be discussed next. In practice, however, several variations of these systems are used.

### Continuous Review Fixed Reorder Quantity System

The structure of the fixed reorder quantity system was illustrated by Figure 5-6. A reorder level is set that allows inventory to be drawn down to the buffer stock level within the lead time if average usage rates are experienced. Replenishment orders are placed in a fixed, predetermined amount that is timed to be received at the end of the supply lead time.

The parameters that define a fixed reorder quantity system are $Q$, the fixed amount ordered at one time, and the reorder point, $ROP$.

Fixed reorder quantity systems are common where a perpetual inventory record is kept or where the inventory level is under sufficiently close surveillance so that notice can be given when the reorder point has been reached. One of the simplest methods for maintaining this close watch on inventory level is the use of the "two-bin" system. In this system, the inventory is physically (or conceptually) separated into two bins, one of which contains an amount equal to the reorder inventory level, $ROP$. The balance of the stock on hand is placed in the other bin, and day-to-day needs are drawn from it until it is empty. At this point, it is obvious that the reorder level has been reached, and a stock requisition is issued. Then stock is drawn from the second bin, which contains an amount equal to the average used during the lead time plus a buffer stock. The stock is replenished when the order is received, the separation into two bins is made again, the cycle is repeated. This system is simple for a stock clerk to understand; however, it requires continuous monitoring of inventory levels.

## Periodic Reorder System

A common alternative system of control fixes the reorder cycle instead of the reorder quantity. In such systems, the inventory status is reviewed on a periodic basis, and an order is placed for an amount that will replenish inventories to a planned maximum level. The reorder quantity therefore varies from one review period to the next.

An economic reorder cycle can be approximated by computing $EOQ$; the economic reorder cycle would then be $EOQ/R$, where $R$ is the annual requirement. For example, if $EOQ = 7500$ units and annual requirements are $R = 100{,}000$ units, then the economic cycle would be $7500/100{,}000 = 0.075$ years, or 3.9 weeks. This would probably be rounded to 4 weeks.

The periodic reorder system has some advantages in production cycling, where high value items require close control, in the control of items that may deteriorate with time, and where a number of items may be ordered from the same supplier. In the latter situation, it may be possible to gain shipping cost advantages by grouping orders normally sent to a common supplier. In addition, the periodic system makes operating efficiencies possible by reviewing the status of all items at the same time. Because of these advantages, the review cycle is commonly set by considerations other than just the individual item economic reorder cycle.

Perhaps the single most important advantage of the periodic reorder system is that the periodic review of inventory and usage levels provides the basis for adjustments to take account of demand changes. This is particularly advantageous with seasonal items. If demand increases, order sizes increase; if demand decreases, order sizes decrease. The main disadvantage of this system is that inventory holding costs are usually higher than those associated with the continuous review system.

### Optional Replenishment System

Control systems that combine regular review cycles and order points are also encountered in practice. In such systems, stock levels are reviewed on a periodic basis, but orders are placed only when inventories have fallen to a predetermined reorder level. At that time, an order is placed to replenish inventories to the level that is sufficient for buffer stocks plus the expected requirements for one cycle, as in the periodic system.

Such systems combine the advantages of periodic review systems and order point systems. These have the lowest total costs; however, the determination of three decision variables is quite difficult.

## ABC CLASSIFICATION OF INVENTORY ITEMS

Equal control effort for all items is not ordinarily justified. First, the different value of inventory items suggests that we should concentrate our attention on higher valued items and be less concerned about lower valued items. For example, Figure 5-8 shows a fairly typical relationship between the percentage of inventory items and the percentage of inventory's total dollar value. Twenty percent of the items account for 60 percent of the inventory's total dollar value in Figure 5-8. The second 20 percent of the items accounts for 20 percent of the value, and finally, the greatest percentage of items (60 percent) accounts for only 20 percent of total inventory value. Because inventory costs are directly associated with inventory value, the potential cost saving from closer control is greatest among the first group of items, which accounts for most of the inventory value.

FIGURE 5-8
**ABC CLASSIFICATION OF INVENTORY ITEMS VERSUS DOLLAR VOLUME.**

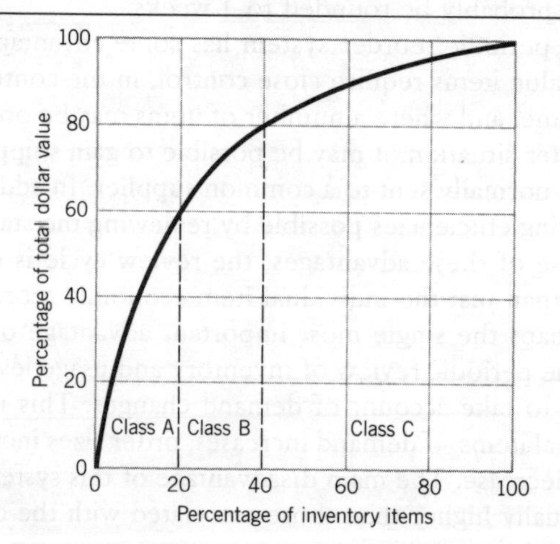


**FIGURE 10-10**
ABC classification of inventory items versus dollar volume.

Second, even though an item may in itself be of low value, it is possible that the cost of a stockout could be considerable. For example, the shortage of a seemingly minor raw material item could cause idle labor costs and loss of production on an entire assembly line. Therefore, for both of the preceding reasons, a classification of inventory items by the degree of control needed allows managers to concentrate their efforts where the returns will be greatest.

### Controls for Class A Items

Close control is required for inventory items that have high stockout costs and those items that account for a large fraction of the total inventory value. The closest control might be reserved for raw materials that are used continuously in extremely high volume. Purchasing agents may arrange contracts with vendors for the continuous supply of these materials at rates that match usage rates. In such instances, the purchase of raw materials is not guided by either economical quantities or cycles. Changes in the rate of flow are made periodically as demand and inventory position changes. Minimum supplies are maintained to guard against demand fluctuations and possible interruptions of supply.

For the balance of Class A items, periodic ordering, perhaps on a weekly basis, provides the necessary close surveillance over inventory levels. Variations in usage rates are absorbed quickly by the size of each weekly order, according to the periodic system or optional system discussed previously. Also, because of the close surveillance, the risk of a prolonged stockout is small. Nevertheless, buffer stocks that provide excellent service levels will be justified for items having large stockout costs.

### Controls for Class B Items

These items should be monitored and controlled by a computer-based system, with periodic reviews by the management. Many of the models discussed in this chapter are relevant for these items. However, model parameters are reviewed less often than with Class A items. Stockout costs for Class B items should be moderate to low, and buffer stocks should provide adequate control for stockouts, even though the ordering occurs less often.

### Controls for Class C Items

Class C items account for the great bulk of inventory items, and carefully designed but routine controls should be adequate. A reorder point system that does not require a physical stock evaluation, such as the "two-bin" system, will ordinarily suffice. For each item, action is triggered when inventories fall to the reorder point. If usage changes, orders will be triggered earlier or later than average, providing the needed compensation. Semiannual or annual reviews of the system parameters should be performed to update usage rates, estimates of supply lead times, and costs that might result in changes in *EOQ*. A periodic review at a long interval can also be used.

## IMPLICATIONS FOR THE MANAGER

It is not uncommon for inventories to represent 20 to 30 percent of the total assets of a manufacturing organization. Even in the nonmanufacturing organizations, inventories of materials and supplies can represent a significant investment. Therefore, inventory replenishment policies are an important aspect of day-to-day managerial control.

The simple concepts of *EOQ* provide the basis for balancing the costs associated with inventory replenishment decisions. Note that the typical total incremental cost curve shown in Figure 5-3 was shallow near the optimum. Thus, managers should be more concerned with operating in the optimum range rather than with slavishly following an *EOQ* based policy. In following an *EOQ* policy, it is important to recognize that the assumption of constant demand is crucial. This assumption is often not true in practice. Seasonal variations and dependent demand in production lot size decisions may favor periodic ordering and other policies coupled with inventory planning.

The concepts underlying the design of buffer stocks and service levels should be of concern to managers. Recognizing the relationship between service level and the cost of stockouts is important if managers are to be able to make good judgments about appropriate service levels.

Most inventory replenishment systems for the low value, Class C items can be automated with computer programs. On the other hand, Class A and some Class B items may require the attention of a responsible executive because decisions about them can be of crucial significance to operating success.

We have developed the concepts of *EOQ*, buffer stocks, and common managerial control systems in the context of raw materials and supplies. Recall from Figure 5-1, however, that there are stock points downstream in the process where similar decisions concerning inventory replenishment are required. The concepts and control systems discussed are, with modification, transferable to the production phase and other stock points.

# REVIEW QUESTIONS

1. What are the relevant costs that management should try to balance in deciding on the size of purchase orders? How do they vary with order size?
2. What is the total incremental cost equation involving
   a. Ordering and inventory costs?
   b. Price discounts?
   c. Shortage costs?
3. What is buffer stock? What is the reason for keeping buffer stock?
4. If p($d$) is the probability of demand during lead time $d$ and *ROP* is the reorder point, write the expressions for expected units short per order cycle and expected units short per year.

5. What happens to the annual expected quantity short if
   a. The buffer stock is increased?
   b. The order size is increased?
   c. Annual requirements double, same order size?
   d. Through a policy change, service level is increased?
   e. Annual requirements double, *EOQ* policy?
   f. Variability of demand increases?
6. What "triggers" a replenishment order in each of the following managerial control systems?
   a. Fixed reorder quantity system
   b. Periodic reorder system
   c. Optional replenishment system
7. Explain the concept of the "two-bin" system.
8. Under what conditions would one use the fixed reorder quantity system in preference to the periodic reorder system and vice versa?
9. As time passes, any inventory control system may become dated as demand, costs, and competitive pressures change. Thus, the periodic review of system parameters is important. What are the parameters that should be reviewed for the fixed reorder quantity and periodic reorder systems?
10. What is the key difference between the newsboy model and the $(Q, ROP)$ model?
11. How would you modify the *EOQ* equation to account for
    a. A constraint on total investment in inventory?
    b. A constraint on total number of orders per year?
12. Develop an expression for expected profit in newsboy model when there is a salvage value of $\ell$ for the leftovers.
13. What are $C_o$ and $C_u$ in newsboy model if there is an explicit cost of holding, $b$, for leftovers?
14. In the $(Q, ROP)$ model, the $Q$ calculated by iterative procedures will always be higher than *EOQ*. Why?
15. What is the cost of uncertainty in demand during lead time?
16. What is the service level method for determining $Q$ and $ROP$? When should it be used?
17. What is ABC classification? What is the criterion used to classify items in the A, B, and C categories?
18. What are the criteria a general manager will use in evaluating the over-all performance of inventory system?
19. In arid and semiarid climates, permanently installed lawn sprinkler systems are used. Automating the control of such systems has been a common procedure for parks and golf courses. More recently, systems have been designed that are

low enough in cost so that homeowners can be relieved of the bother of the watering cycle.

For one such system, the user can set the watering cycle—for example, every 1, 2, or 4 days—and the amount of time the sprinklers are to run—for example, 3, 11, 22, 45, 60, or 90 minutes. In addition, a moisture sensor is implanted in the lawn. If, when the cycle is set to trigger, the moisture sensor indicates that the soil is still moist enough, that cycle will be skipped.

Relate this sprinkler control system to one of the inventory control systems discussed in the text.

# PROBLEMS

20. We have the following data for an item that we purchase regularly: annual requirement, $R$ = 10,000 units; order preparation cost, $c_P$ = \$25 per order; inventory holding cost, $c_H$ = \$10 per unit per year.
    a. Compute the economic order quantity, *EOQ*.
    b. Compute the number of orders that must be placed each year and the annual cost of placing the orders.
    c. Compute the average inventory if *EOQ* units are ordered each time, and compute the annual cost of the inventory.
21. Suppose that the estimate of $c_P$ in problem 20 was in error and should be only \$20 per order. What is the value of *EOQ*? What is the percentage change in *EOQ* for the 20 percent decrease in $c_P$?
22. Suppose that the estimate of $c_H$ in problem 20 was in error and should actually be \$15 per unit per year. What is the value of *EOQ*? What is the percentage change in *EOQ* for the 50 percent increase in $c_H$?
23. A price discount schedule for an item that we purchase is offered as follows: \$1 per unit in quantities below 800, \$0.98 per unit in quantities of 800 to 1599, and \$0.97 per unit in quantities of 1600 or more. Other data are $R$ = 1600 units per year; $c_P$ = \$5 per order; and inventory holding costs are 10 percent of the average inventory value per year, or \$0.10 per unit per year at the \$1 per unit price. The value of *EOQ* using Equation 4, is 400 units. What should the purchase quantity be in order to take advantage of the price discount?
24. Weekly demand for a product, exclusive of seasonal and trend variations, is represented by the empirical distribution shown in Figure 5-9. What safety or buffer stock would be required for the item to ensure that one would not run out of stock more than 15 percent of the time? More than 5 percent of the time? More than 1 percent of the time? (Assume that lead time is one week.)
25. A manufacturer is attempting to set the production lot size for a particular item that is manufactured only periodically. The incremental cost of setting up machines for production is \$40. The inventory holding cost is \$1 per unit per year. The annual requirements for the item are 52,000 and the production rate is 5000 units per week.

FIGURE 5-9

**DISTRIBUTION REPRESENTING RANDOM VARIATION IN WEEKLY SALES, EXCLUSIVE OF SEASONAL AND TREND VARIATIONS.**

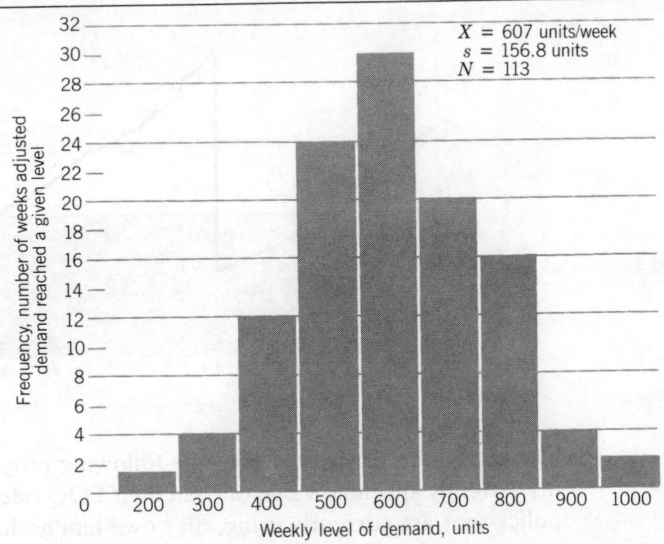


a. What is the most economical manufacturing lot size?

b. How many production runs are needed per year to satisfy the requirements?

c. What considerations should influence the actual lot size selected?

26. Consider the inventory graph in Figure 5-10.

a. What ordering policy is being followed?

b. What is the lead time between when an order is placed and when it is received?

c. If average demand is 150 units/week, how many units of safety stock are being held by the firm?

d. If the lead time calculated in b should double, what order point would be required to maintain the same safety stock level?

27. A firm with a uniform demand for its product currently places an order for 100 units once a month, and there is *no* backlogging. The company has some difficulty in determining $c_H$. However, an analyst may be able to infer an apparent $c_H$ based on the firm's inventory policy. We have the following information:

$$\text{Demand } (R) = 1200 \text{ units per year}$$
$$\text{Set-up cost } (c_P) = \$10 \text{ per set-up}$$
$$\text{Holding cost } (c_H) = ?$$

a. What would holding cost have to be for the current policy to be optimal?

b. Suppose that a management consultant *accurately* specifies that $c_H$ = \$9.60 per unit per year. What optimal lot size does this imply?

FIGURE 5-10
**INVENTORY GRAPH FOR PROBLEM 26.**

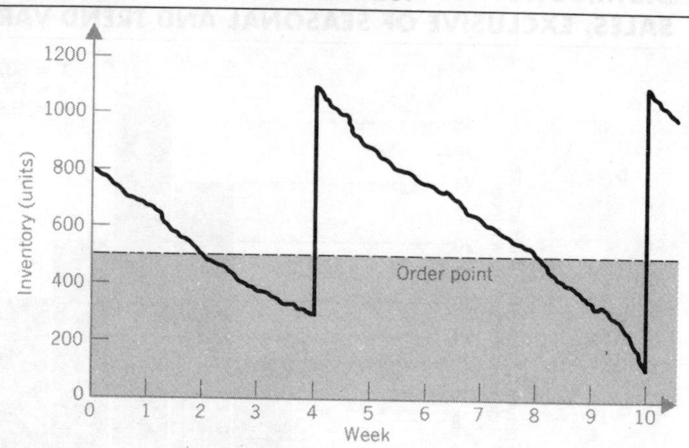


c. The consultant makes the firm the following proposition: If they don't use his correctly specified value of $c_H$ in their EOQ calculations and continue the policy they are currently using, they owe him nothing. However, if they use the $Q$ value based on the correctly specified value of $c_H$, they must pay him \$100 a year.

What should the firm do and why?

28. Consider a product with an average annual demand of approximately 9000 units/year. Order costs are \$250 per order and holding costs are \$2/unit/year. Lead time demand is distributed as follows:

| $D$ | $\phi(D)$ |
|---|---|
| 5 | .10 |
| 10 | .05 |
| 15 | .10 |
| 20 | .20 |
| 25 | .20 |
| 30 | .05 |
| 40 | .05 |
| 50 | .15 |
| 60 | .10 |

a. Assuming shortages are costed at \$1/unit, determine *EOQ* and *ROP* using the sequential method. Determine the expected annual *TIC* of the policy you determine.

b. Assuming that management requires that, on the average, at least 99 percent of the annual demand must be met from inventory, determine the *EOQ* and *ROP* that should be used.

c. Suppose management requires that stockouts should not occur more than 10 percent of the time. What *ROP* level is implied by this management specification?

29. Consider the following data for a product:

Demand = 1000 units/year
Order cost = $4/order
Holding cost = 10% of unit cost/unit-year
Unit cost = $50/unit

| DEMAND DURING LEAD TIME | PROBABILITY |
|---|---|
| 10 | .1 |
| 15 | .3 |
| 20 | .35 |
| 25 | .2 |
| 30 | .05 |

a. What is the annual holding cost of safety stock if management decides to use an *ROP* level of 20 units?
b. Suppose management wants to set the *ROP* so that the risk of a stockout situation during the lead time is only .05. How much safety stock should the company carry?
c. With an *ROP* of 20, how many shortages per year can management expect?

30. A nursery is in the process of deciding how many Christmas trees should be stocked. The trees are sold for $20 and cost $5. The trees can be purchased only once and unsold trees are a complete loss. The probability distribution for demand is as follows:

| DEMAND | PROBABILITY |
|---|---|
| 4000 | .2 |
| 4100 | .3 |
| 4200 | .1 |
| 4300 | .2 |
| 4400 | .1 |
| 4500 | .1 |

a. How many trees should the nursery purchase to maximize its expected profit?
b. What is the expected profit if the nursery purchased the number of trees equal to the expected demand?
c. What is expected number of unsold trees if the nursery purchases the optimal number of trees?
d. If the nursery could find out the demand exactly, how much should it pay for this information?

31. As a manager of the Constrained Warehouse, you are faced with the order quantity decision for two products, A and B. The following table provides the relevant information on these two products:

| Product | Unit Cost | Cost of Ordering/ Order | Annual Demand | Storage Space Required | Holding Cost |
|---|---|---|---|---|---|
| A | \$10 | \$5 | 1000 | 10 $ft^3$/unit | 10% of unit cost/yr |
| B | \$20 | \$10 | 250 | 25 $ft^3$/unit | 10% of unit cost/yr |

Management is concerned that if orders for both products arrive simultaneously, the total storage space available (1500 $ft^3$) may be exceeded. Show how to solve this problem. You may assume that all the other *EOQ* assumptions (e.g., uniform demand) apply.

32. Seers Company orders vacuum cleaners at \$50 each. The annual demand for the past two years has been relatively constant at 500 units/year. The other pertinent information is provided in the following table.

| Year | Order Size | Average Annual Order Cost \$ | Average Annual Holding Cost \$ |
|---|---|---|---|
| 1975 | 50 | 20 | 125 |
| 1976 | 100 | 10 | 250 |

a. What is the cost of placing an order ($c_P$) and the cost of holding each unit per year ($c_H$)?

b. What is the optimal order quantity for the Seers Company?

c. In 1977, the Seers Company estimated that the cost of ordering was somewhere between \$2 and \$10 per order. Annual demand was estimated to be 1000 units. Seers used *EOQ* to determine the optimal order quantity and assumed order cost to be \$4 per order and holding cost to be 10 percent of the unit cost. At the end of the year, the actual order cost was found to be \$9 per order. Had the company known the true cost of placing an order at the beginning of 1977, how much savings could it have realized? (Assume that the other parameters were correctly estimated.)

33. The Delicate Bakery orders ingredient A for bread from an out of town supplier. The lead time as well as the requirements for ingredient A during the lead time are uncertain. The Delicate Bakery has collected the following information using past history:

| Demand during Time Interval between Placing and Receiving an Order | Frequency |
|---|---|
| 5 | 0.20 |
| 10 | 0.30 |
| 15 | 0.10 |
| 20 | 0.20 |
| 25 | 0.20 |

The cost of ordering ingredient A = \$1 per order and the cost of holding = 50 cents per unit per year. Annual requirements are 10,000 units and the bakery requires that 97 percent of the units demanded be met from inventory.

a. Using the sequential method, determine when the bakery should place an order and how much they should order.

b. What is the true service level of your policy in a?

c. What is the average percentage of stockouts in the long run if the policy you recommend in a is followed?

d. If the cost of a shortage, $c_S$, is 2 cents per unit, compute *ROP*. Assume *Q* is as determined in a.

e. What is the implied service level in terms of the percentage of units demanded being satisfied directly from inventory if your policy in d is followed?

34. Cindy Williams operates a consulting business that caters to small business enterprises. One of her clients, a large independent supermarket called Ronnies, has asked Cindy to investigate its order policy for bread, particularly its order policy for Pepperidge Farm Cracked Wheat Bread. Ronnies buys bread from its supplier every week. It pays \$0.35 per loaf and sells it for \$0.65 per loaf. Bread left over at the end of the week is sold back to the supplier for \$0.15 per loaf. Inventory holding costs are negligible, but Ronnies is concerned about the "bad will" consequences of being unable to supply all customer demands. Ronnies estimates the weekly demand for bread to be as follows:

| LOAVES, $d$ | PROB (DEMAND = $d$) |
|---|---|
| 20 | .1 |
| 25 | .05 |
| 30 | .2 |
| 35 | .2 |
| 40 | .1 |
| 45 | .2 |
| 50 | .1 |
| 60 | .05 |

a. Ignoring "bad will" considerations, how many loaves should Ronnies stock each week?

b. What is Ronnies' expected weekly profit (or *EMV*), again ignoring "bad will" losses.

c. *Assuming* that Ronnies stocks 50 loaves of bread, what must Ronnies' estimate of "bad will" loss be per loaf? Please provide a range.

# SITUATIONS

## The Mixing and Bagging Company

35. The Mixing and Bagging Company produces a line of commercial animal feeds in 10 mixes. The production process itself is rather simple, as the company

name implies. A variety of basic grain and filler ingredients is mixed in batches. The mixture is then fed to an intermediate storage hopper, from which it is conveyed to a bagging operation. The bags of feed are then loaded on pallets and moved to the nearby warehouse for storage.

The operations are supervised by a foreman. Direct labor is provided by a full-time worker who operates the mixing and blending equipment, plus four full-time and 10 part-time workers. The foreman is paid $15,000 per year; the mixer-operator, $5 per hour; the other full-time workers, $4 per hour; and the 10 part-time workers, $3 per hour.

The usual routine for a production run is as follows: The foreman receives job tickets from the office indicating the quantities to be run and the formula. The job tickets are placed in the order in which they are to be processed. At the end of a run, the foreman purges the mixing system and ducts of the previous product. This takes 20 minutes.

Meanwhile, the foreman has directed the mixer-operator and the four full-time employees to obtain the required ingredients for the next product from the storeroom. When the mixing equipment has been purged, the mixer-operator loads the first batch of materials according to the formula in the mixer and gets it started. This takes about 10 minutes. The total time spent by the mixer-operator in obtaining materials and loading the mixer is 30 minutes. The four full-time exployees devote the 30 minutes to obtaining materials.

While the previous activities are being performed the foreman turns his attention to the bagger line, which requires a minor change over for bag size and the product identifying label that is sewed to the top of the bag as it is sewed closed.

While the foreman is purging the system, the 10 part-time employees transfer what is left of the last run to the warehouse, which requires about 15 minutes. They are then idle until the bagging operation is ready to start again.

The inventory in the finished goods warehouse is valued according to the sale price of each item, which is about $5 per 100 pounds. The cost of placing the items in the warehouse has been calculated as approximately $0.25 per 100 pounds, based on the time required for one of the part-time workers to truck it to the warehouse and place it in the proper location. The front office has calculated that the storage space in the owned warehouse is worth about $10 per square foot per year, but because the bags are palletized and stacked 12 feet high, this cost has been reduced to only $0.20 per 100 pounds per year. The product mixes are stable, and there is very little risk of obsolescence. There is some loss because uninvited guests (rats, etc.) come in to dine. The total storage and obsolescence costs are estimated as 5 percent of inventory value.

The Mixing and Bagging Company has a factory overhead rate that it applied to materials and direct labor. This overhead rate is currently 100 percent and is applied to the average material cost of $1.87 per 100 pounds plus direct labor costs of $0.13 per 100 pounds. The company earns 8 percent after taxes and can borrow at the local bank at an interest rate of 9 percent.

The factory manager is currently reviewing the bases for deciding the length of production runs for products. He figures that operations are currently at about 85 percent of capacity. He has heard of *EOQ* as a basis for setting the length of production runs. What values should he assign to $c_P$ and $c_H$ for his operations?

## Topanga Gas and Electric

36. Mr. Dale Patterson, Chairman of the Topanga Gas and Electric (TG&E), is reexamining the billing policy of the company. The present policy is to bill all customers once a month. Mr. Patterson feels that a better billing policy would result in faster collection so that more money would be available for alternate uses. He estimates that the released money can easily save 12 percent per annum. Mr. Patterson employed a consultant, Linda Jacobs, to carry out a detailed study of a town in the state. Ms. Jacobs collected the following information:

TOWN (TOPANGA)

| | |
|---|---|
| Number of the household users of electricity | 25,000 |
| Average amount of bill/customer | $6/month |

Ms. Jacobs estimated that the total cost of meter reading, bill preparation, dispatch, collection, and the like is about $3000 for each billing.

The Assistant Engineer of Topanga, Mr. Mike Poor, doubts whether billing time could be reduced to less than once a month. Besides several organizational constraints, he points out that a majority of the customers are in the lower-middle income group and can therefore make payments only after receiving their monthly paychecks. Mr. Poor thinks that more money could be made available by a better collection policy rather than a new billing policy. He notes that about half the customers pay their bills in a few days and about half pay one billing cycle late. Linda has asked Mike what improvements could be made in the present collection policy. The following two main ideas evolved during their discussions.

One is to issue a warning to customers that if the payment is not made within a week of receiving the bill the electric supply will be cut off. Mike pointed out that this policy had worked two years ago when Mr. Young was the Assistant Engineer. Subsequently, however, it was discontinued because the cost of cutting off the connections of slow paying customers was excessive. Mike estimates that, on the average, an additional cost of $1000 per billing period will be incurred if this policy is implemented.

The second idea is to charge slow paying customers a one half percent per month surcharge on the amount due. However, if payment is not received by the next billing period, the electricity is to be cut off. This policy would allow customers more time to make their payments.

For the town of Topanga:

a. Sketch a graph of Topanga's Accounts Receivable (money owed to TG&E) by its customers, assuming a monthly billing cycle. Sketch several cycles. Identify all the relevant parts of the graph.

b. TG&E's goal is to select a combined billing and collection policy. The billing alternatives are (1) billing monthly, (2) billing semimonthly (six times a year), (3) billing quarterly, or (4) billing annually. The collection policy alternatives are (1) to do nothing (continue present policy), (2) to cut-off power after one week, and (3) the ½ percent surcharge. Analyze these alternatives and propose the best plan. *Hint:* For a monthly billing cycle, determine the total incremental costs to TG&E for each of the three collection policies. Repeat for the other billing alternatives.

# REFERENCES

Buchan, J., and E. Koenigsberg, *Scientific Inventory Control,* Prentice-Hall, Englewood Cliffs, N.J., 1963.

Buffa, E. S., and J. G. Miller, *Production–Inventory Systems: Planning and Control,* (3rd ed.), Irwin, Homewood, Ill., 1979.

Hadley, G., and T. M. Whitin, *Analysis of Inventory Systems,* Prentice-Hall, Englewood Cliffs, N.J., 1963.

Peterson, R., and E. A. Silver, *Decision Systems for Inventory Management and Production Planning,* Wiley, New York, 1985.

Porteus, E. L., "Investing in Reduced Setups in the EOQ Model," *Management Science, 31*(8), August 1985, pp. 998–1010.

Trueman, R. E., "Incremental (Marginal) Analysis of Basic Inventory Models," *Decision Sciences, 2,* July 1971, pp. 341–345.

Vollmann, T. E., W. L. Berry, and D. C. Whybark, *Manufacturing Planning and Control Systems,* Irwin, Homewood, Ill., 1984.

# CHAPTER 6

# MATERIAL REQUIREMENTS PLANNING

In manufacturing situations, the demand for raw materials, components, subassemblies, and so forth is dependent on the production plan for the final product. It is therefore possible to determine how many parts or components will be needed in each future time period in the planning horizon once we know the production requirements for the final product. The production requirements for the final product are, in turn, determined by sales forecasts. Material requirements planning methods exploit this information about dependence on demand in managing inventories and controlling the production lot sizes of the numerous parts that go into the making of a final product. In contrast, the methods discussed in Chapter 5 treat the demand for each part (stock keeping unit) as independent and use trigger levels (reorder points) to indicate when orders are to be placed or production is to be started. The managerial objective in using materials requirements planning is to avoid inventory stockouts so that production runs smoothly, according to plans, and to reduce investment in raw materials and work in process inventories.

## REQUIREMENTS PLANNING CONCEPTS

Figure 6-1*a* is an illustration of a simple dinette table that shows the parts or components required. The table consists of a plywood top covered with Formica, four metal legs, and some miscellaneous hardware.

Figure 6-1*b* is a simplified operation process chart showing the sequence of major operations required to fabricate and assemble the table. The glue, screws (two different sizes), plastic feet, and paint are noted as being purchased outside; unlike the other raw materials (e.g., the plywood and metal tubing) they are not processed before use.

Now, if the table is to be a "one-of-a-kind" custom table, the operation process chart of Figure 6-1*b* specifies what must be done and the sequences required. However, if a substantial number of tables are to be made, we have alternatives that make the problem more complex but offer planning and scheduling opportunities for efficient manufacture.

### Bill of Materials

We can abstract a "bill of materials" from Figure 6-1*a*. This document is not simply a materials list but is constructed in a way that reflects the manufacturing process. Of course, the operation process chart of Figure 6-1 does this also, but we want information useful to a material requirements system in a form that can be maintained in a computerized file.

The information that will be particularly significant, in addition to the simple list of parts, will be the dependency structure. For example, if we examine operation 11 in Figure 6-1, there is a subassembly; the plywood top, wood skirts, Formica top, and Formica skirts come together in operation 11 to form a unit. Also, the metal tubing, brackets, paint, and feet form a second subassembly. These two subassem-

FIGURE 6-1
**(*a*) PART COMPONENTS FOR DINETTE TABLE; (*b*) OPERATION PROCESS CHART.**

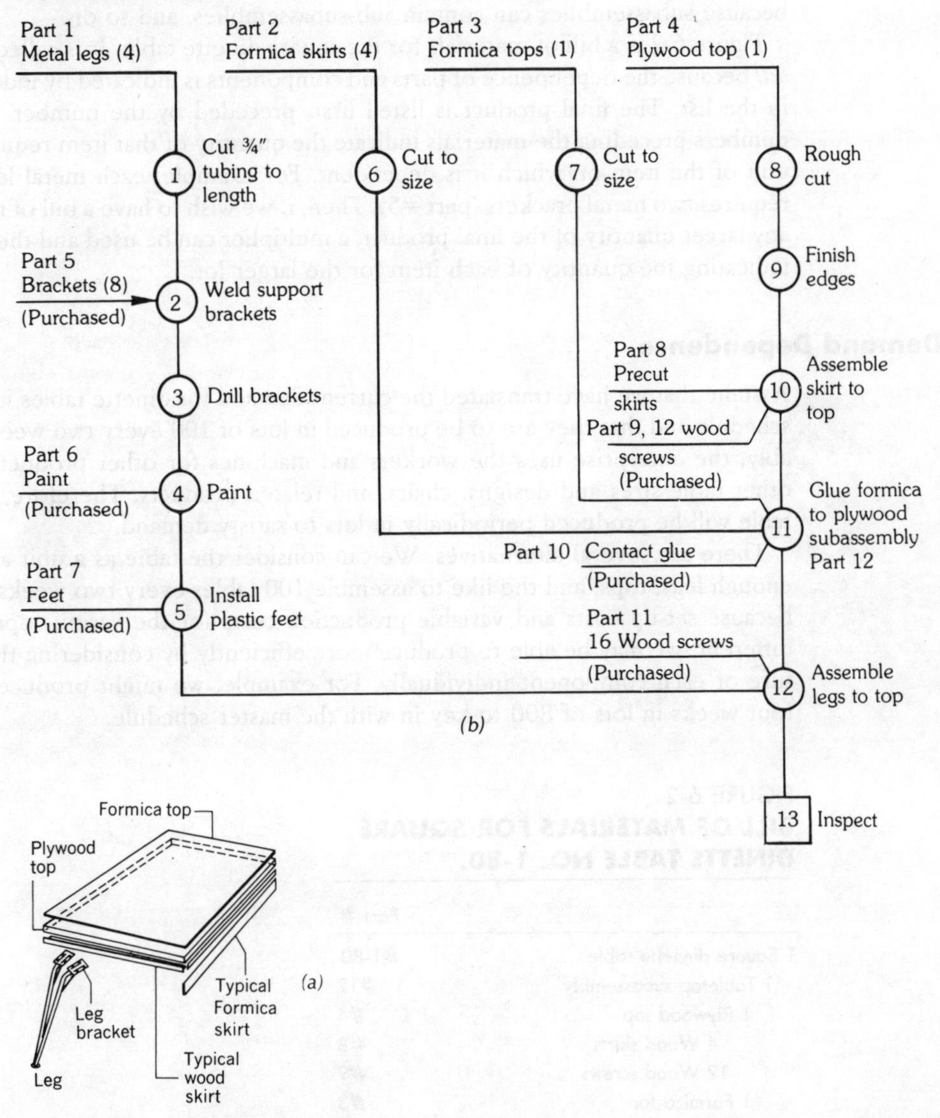


blies can be produced separately in batches and then assembled in operation 12 into finished tables in batches as needed. Indeed, an important reason for dealing with these subassemblies as separate units is that the same leg is used in another product, as we shall see. Therefore, the lot size and timing of the production of legs take on broader significance.

As a result, one important input to a material requirements planning (*MRP*) system is a bill of materials constructed in a way that recognizes the dependence of certain components on subassemblies, which are in turn dependent on the final product. In more complex products, there can be several levels of dependency because subassemblies can contain sub-subassemblies, and so on.

Figure 6-2 is a bill of materials for the square dinette table. It is called an *indented bill* because the dependence of parts and components is indicated by indenting items in the list. The final product is listed first, preceded by the number "1." All the numbers preceding the materials indicate the quantity of that item required for one unit of the item on which it is dependent. For example, each metal leg (part #1) requires two metal brackets (part #5). Then, if we wish to have a bill of materials for any larger quantity of the final product, a multiplier can be used and the list printed indicating the quantity of each item for the larger lot.

## Demand Dependence

Assume that we have translated the current demand for dinette tables into a master schedule and that they are to be produced in lots of 100 every two weeks. Presumably, the enterprise uses the workers and machines for other products, including other table sizes and designs, chairs, and related products. Therefore, the dinette table will be produced periodically in lots to satisfy demand.

There are several alternatives. We can consider the table as a unit and produce enough legs, tops, and the like to assemble 100 tables every two weeks. However, because set-up costs and variable production costs for the various operations are different, we may be able to produce more efficiently by considering the manufacture of each component individually. For example, we might produce legs every four weeks in lots of 800 to key in with the master schedule.

FIGURE 6-2
**BILL OF MATERIALS FOR SQUARE DINETTE TABLE NO. 1-80.**

| | Part # |
|---|---|
| 1 Square dinnette table | #1-80 |
|   1 Tabletop subassembly | #12 |
|     1 Plywood top | #4 |
|       4 Wood skirts | #8 |
|       12 Wood screws | #9 |
|     1 Formica top | #3 |
|     4 Formica skirts | #2 |
|     6 oz Contact cement | #10 |
|   4 Leg subassemblies | #1 |
|     2 3′ Lengths of tubing | #13 |
|     2 Metal brackets | #5 |
|     2 oz Paint | #6 |
|     1 Plastic foot | #7 |
|   16 Wood screws | #11 |

Let us consider the schedule for producing tables every two weeks in lots of 100 and legs every four weeks in lots of 800. Because the demand for the legs is entirely dependent on the *production schedule* for the tables, the time phasing of the leg lots with respect to table lots has a very important impact on the in-process inventory of legs. Tables are produced in lots of 100 in weeks 3, 5, 7, and so on, as shown in Figure 6-3*c*. In Figure 6-3*a*, legs are produced in lots of 800 every four weeks in weeks 1, 5, 9, and so on. Legs go into inventory when the lot is completed and are available for use the following week. They are used in table assembly in weeks 3, 5, 7, and so forth, but they are in inventory one full week before 400 of them are used to produce 100 tables in week 3. The remaining 400 are in inventory during week 4 and are finally used to produce 100 tables in week 5. The average in-process inventory of legs is $\bar{I} = 400$ units.

FIGURE 6-3
**IN-PROCESS INVENTORY OF TABLE LEGS WHEN, (*a*) PRODUCED IN WEEKS 1, 5, 9, ETC. AND (*b*) PRODUCED IN WEEKS 2, 6, 10, ETC. (*c*) TABLES ARE PRODUCED IN WEEKS 3, 5, 7, ETC.**

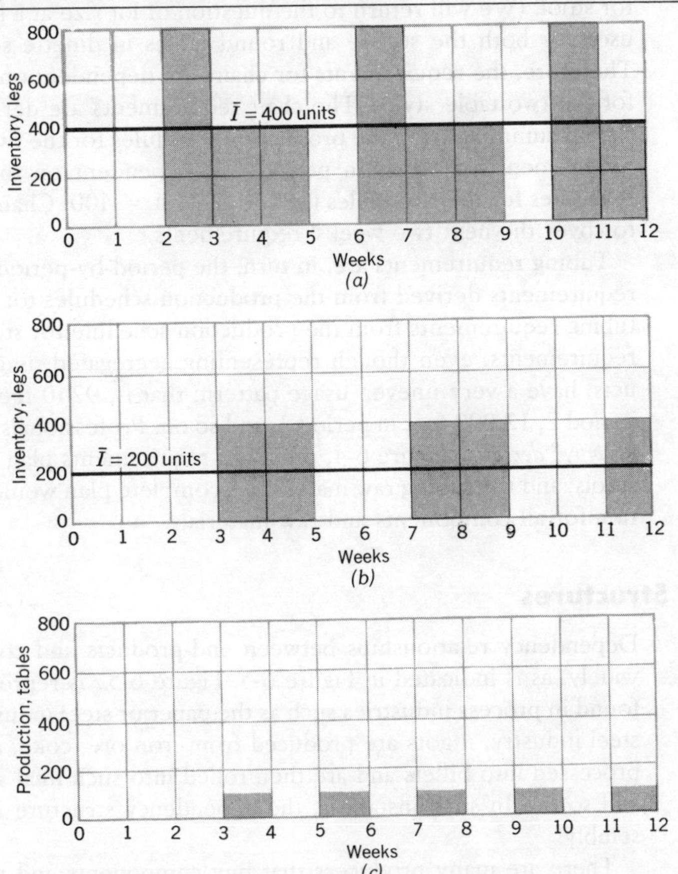

If we produce legs in weeks 2, 6, 10, and so forth, as in Figure 6-3*b*, the in-process inventory is reduced to $\bar{I} = 200$ units. This is true because the revised timing uses 400 legs immediately in week 3 to produce 100 tables. The remaining 400 legs are in inventory during week 4, as with the previous situation, and are used to produce 100 tables in week 5. Therefore, the problem is not simply to produce legs in lots of 800 every 4 weeks, but to time phase the production of legs with respect to the production of the tables, the primary item. The demand for tables is presumably dependent on market factors. However, the production of legs becomes a *requirement* as soon as the table production schedule is set. If the proper time phasing is ignored, the price will be paid in higher in-process inventory of components.

Let us follow through the structure of requirements determination (called the "bill of materials explosion" process) in Figure 6-4. Figure 6-4 culminates in the total requirements for metal tubing needed to produce two different models of dinette tables with accompanying sets of four chairs and a stool. Each product involves the use of metal tubing from which the legs are fabricated. First, the primary demand for the two tables and the stools is indicated by the forecasts for each period. Production schedules to meet the demand for each of the three primary products are set to anticipate demand for two periods ahead for the tables and for four periods ahead for stool. (We will return to the question of lot size at a later point.) The chairs are used for both the square and round tables in dinette sets, four chairs per table. Therefore, the requirements for chairs are dependent on the production schedules for the two table styles. The chair requirements are derived through a period-by-period summing from the production schedules for the two tables. For example, the requirement for chairs in period 1 is dependent on the sum of the production schedules for the two tables $(100 + 0) \times 4 = 400$. Chairs are produced in batches to cover the next two weeks' requirements.

Tubing requirements are, in turn, the period-by-period summation of the tubing requirements derived from the production schedules for tables and chairs plus the tubing requirements from the production schedule for stools. Note that the tubing requirements, even though representing aggregated usage in four different products, have a very uneven usage pattern; that is, 9240 feet in period 1, 960 feet in period 2, 12,000 feet in period 3, and so on. Professionals term such a usage pattern *"lumpy" demand.* Figure 6-4, then, is a requirements plan for the two tables, chairs, stools, and the tubing raw material. A complete plan would provide similar information for all components and raw materials.

## Product Structures

Dependency relationships between end-products and components and parts vary widely, as is indicated in Figure 6-5. Figure 6-5*a* is representative of the structure found in process industries such as the paper or steel industries. For example, in the steel industry, ingots are produced from iron ore, coke, and limestone. Ingots are processed into billets and are then rolled into such final shapes as sheets, I-beams, and so on. In such instances, the dependency structure is linear, involving no assembly.

There are many producers that buy components and parts and assemble them,

FIGURE 6-4
**REQUIREMENTS DETERMINATION FOR SQUARE AND ROUND TABLES, CHAIRS, STOOLS, AND FINALLY TUBING. REQUIREMENTS FOR CHAIRS ARE DEPENDENT ON THE PRODUCTION SCHEDULES FOR TABLES. TUBING REQUIREMENTS ARE DEPENDENT ON THE PRODUCTION SCHEDULES FOR ALL FOUR PRODUCTS.**

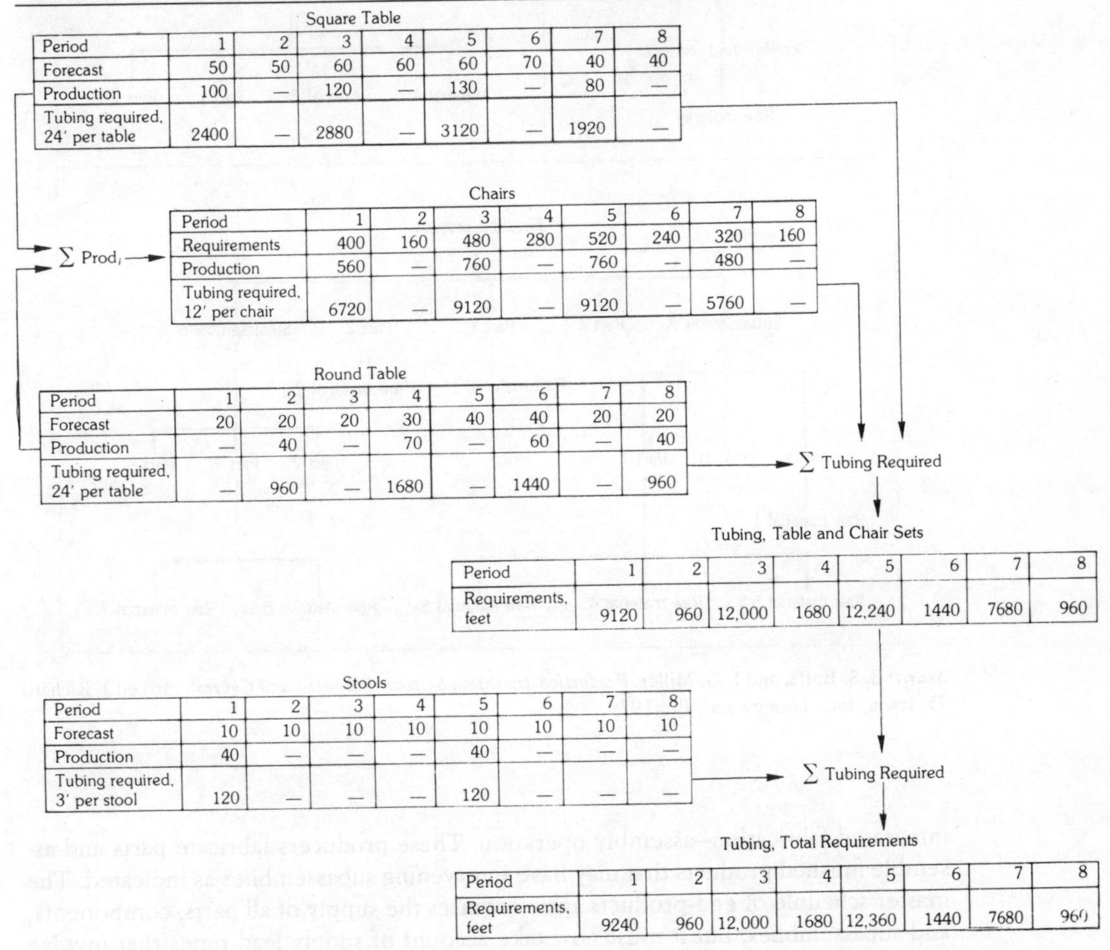


Square Table

| Period | 1 | 2 | 3 | 4 | 5 | 6 | 7 | 8 |
|---|---|---|---|---|---|---|---|---|
| Forecast | 50 | 50 | 60 | 60 | 60 | 70 | 40 | 40 |
| Production | 100 | — | 120 | — | 130 | — | 80 | — |
| Tubing required, 24′ per table | 2400 | — | 2880 | — | 3120 | — | 1920 | — |

Chairs

| Period | 1 | 2 | 3 | 4 | 5 | 6 | 7 | 8 |
|---|---|---|---|---|---|---|---|---|
| Requirements | 400 | 160 | 480 | 280 | 520 | 240 | 320 | 160 |
| Production | 560 | — | 760 | — | 760 | — | 480 | — |
| Tubing required, 12′ per chair | 6720 | — | 9120 | — | 9120 | — | 5760 | — |

Round Table

| Period | 1 | 2 | 3 | 4 | 5 | 6 | 7 | 8 |
|---|---|---|---|---|---|---|---|---|
| Forecast | 20 | 20 | 20 | 30 | 40 | 40 | 20 | 20 |
| Production | — | 40 | — | 70 | — | 60 | — | 40 |
| Tubing required, 24′ per table | — | 960 | — | 1680 | — | 1440 | — | 960 |

Tubing, Table and Chair Sets

| Period | 1 | 2 | 3 | 4 | 5 | 6 | 7 | 8 |
|---|---|---|---|---|---|---|---|---|
| Requirements, feet | 9120 | 960 | 12,000 | 1680 | 12,240 | 1440 | 7680 | 960 |

Stools

| Period | 1 | 2 | 3 | 4 | 5 | 6 | 7 | 8 |
|---|---|---|---|---|---|---|---|---|
| Forecast | 10 | 10 | 10 | 10 | 10 | 10 | 10 | 10 |
| Production | 40 | — | — | — | 40 | — | — | — |
| Tubing required, 3′ per stool | 120 | — | — | — | 120 | — | — | — |

Tubing, Total Requirements

| Period | 1 | 2 | 3 | 4 | 5 | 6 | 7 | 8 |
|---|---|---|---|---|---|---|---|---|
| Requirements, feet | 9240 | 960 | 12,000 | 1680 | 12,360 | 1440 | 7680 | 960 |

with little or no fabrication operations, as is illustrated in Figure 6-5*b*. Examples are many producers of electronic products and some small appliances. In such situations, the product structure is horizontal rather than vertical as with process industries. The master schedule of the finished product requires the supply of all the parts and components at the right time and in the quantities needed. To accomplish these ends, supply lead times from vendors are of great importance in planning and executing the schedule.

Finally, Figure 6-5*c* is illustrative of the very complex structures found in an

FIGURE 6-5
**TYPICAL PRODUCT STRUCTURES FOR DEPENDENT DEMAND FOR (*a*) PROCESS INDUSTRIES, (*b*) ASSEMBLERS WHO PURCHASE COMPONENTS, AND (*c*) INTEGRATED FABRICATION-ASSEMBLY.**

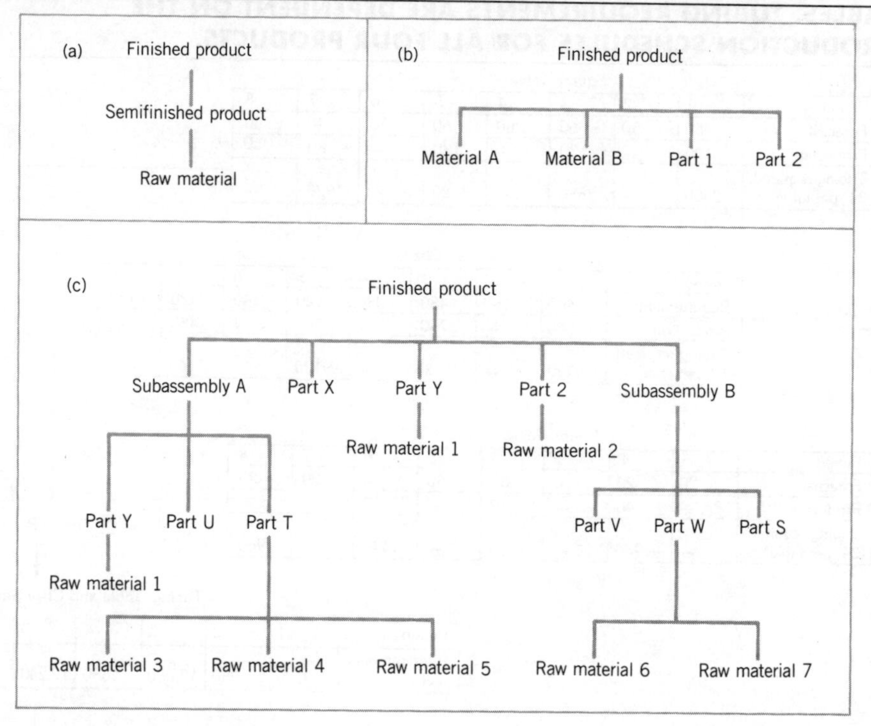


*Source:* E. S. Buffa, and J. G. Miller. *Production-Invention Systems: Planning and Control,* (3rd ed.), Richard D. Irwin, Inc., Homewood, Ill., 1979.

integrated fabrication–assembly operation. These producers fabricate parts and assemble finished products that may have intervening subassemblies as indicated. The master schedule of end-products again requires the supply of all parts, components, and subassemblies, but it must now take account of supply lead times that involve not only vendors but also in-plant fabrication operations. Examples of these hierarchical product structures abound in industry, including automobiles, appliances, machine tools, and so on.

## Forecasting Versus Requirements

The required use of metal tubing for the example dinette table is indicated in Figure 6-4. Suppose that we wish to set up an inventory control system for the tubing so it can be reordered as needed to maintain stock. If the requirements for tubing in Figure 6-4 represent demand, can we apply standard forecasting techniques?

Figure 6-6 shows the application of an exponential forecasting system with $\alpha = 0.1$ to the requirements as demand data. Average actual demand for the eight periods is 5790 feet, and this is taken as the initial value for $\bar{S}_0$. The forecast has the usual smoothing effect.

Now, suppose that tubing is ordered on the basis of the smoothed forecast. If $D_{max}$ were defined as the maximum demand observed in our small sample, then the buffer stock required would be $B = D_{max} - \bar{D} = 12{,}360 - 5790 = 6570$ feet, and the average inventory would be $\bar{I} = Q/2 + B = 5790/2 + 6570 = 9465$ feet.

But, in fact, we do not want to smooth demand because the requirements schedule for tubing is the best forecast that we can obtain. Using exponential smoothing (or any other forecasting technique) here is a misapplication of forecasting because the demand for tubing is dependent. Compare the forecast line with actual demand in Figure 6-6. The forecast errors are very large, $MAD = 5049$. Note that if we provide inventory according to the requirements schedule, the average inventory would be only 5790 feet, or $9465 - 5790 = 3675$ feet less than if we attempted to

FIGURE 6-6
**EFFECT OF USING AN EXPONENTIAL FORECAST ($\alpha = 0.1$) FOR THE DEPENDENT DEMAND OF TUBING.**

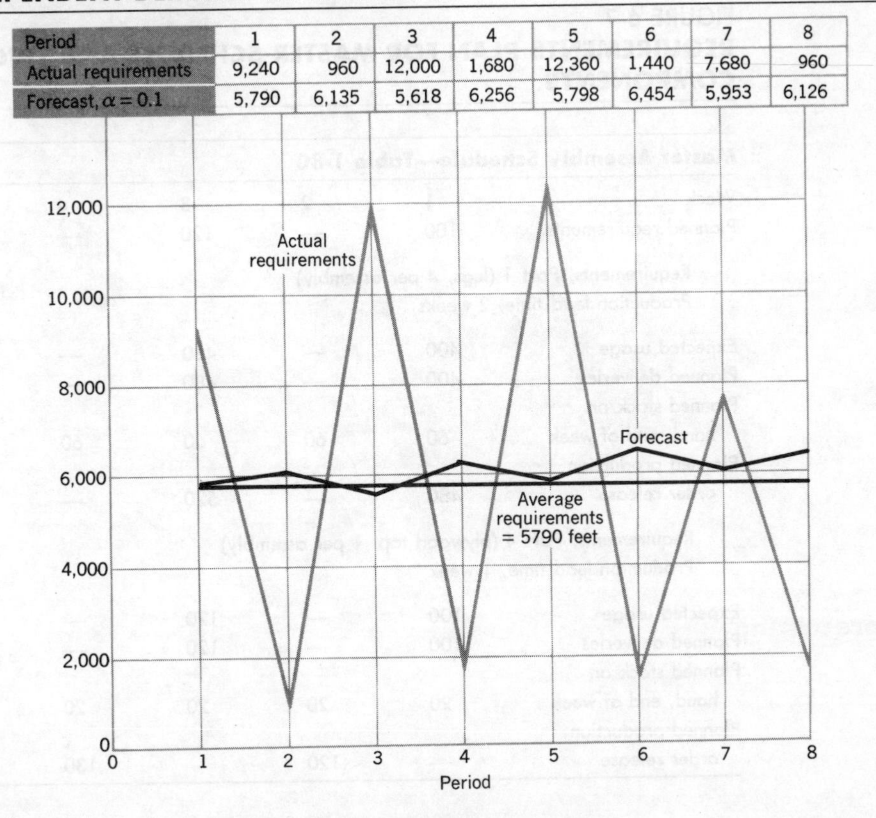

| Period | 1 | 2 | 3 | 4 | 5 | 6 | 7 | 8 |
|---|---|---|---|---|---|---|---|---|
| Actual requirements | 9,240 | 960 | 12,000 | 1,680 | 12,360 | 1,440 | 7,680 | 960 |
| Forecast, $\alpha = 0.1$ | 5,790 | 6,135 | 5,618 | 6,256 | 5,798 | 6,454 | 5,953 | 6,126 |

cover requirements based on the exponential forecasting methodology. Using the forecasting methodology, we must provide a very large buffer stock, and although this buffer stock cannot be completely eliminated in requirements systems, the time phasing of inventory receipts can drastically reduce it. (We will discuss buffer stocks for requirements systems at a later point.)

When then is forecasting applicable in requirements systems? Forecasting is applicable to the primary demand for the tables and stools, not to the dependent components and raw materials. Their requirements are derived directly from the production schedules that have taken into account primary demand and other factors. Therefore, inventory control systems for dependent items will use requirements schedules directly instead of interposing a forecasting system.

The basic ideas of requirements generation developed in connection with the simple example of the tables, chairs, and stools can be carried forward into larger scale for more complex systems. Figure 6-7 shows that the form of the plan normally includes the master schedule for the *independent item* (the finished product) at the head, followed by requirements plans for dependent components that are keyed to the master schedule. In addition, requirements plans normally indicate the production lead time, a planned stock record, and the timing of production order releases phased to take account of production lead times.

FIGURE 6-7
**REQUIREMENTS PLAN FOR MASTER SCHEDULE AND TWO DEPENDENT COMPONENTS.**

| **Master Assembly Schedule—Table 1-80** | | | | | | |
|---|---|---|---|---|---|---|
| Week | 1 | 2 | 3 | 4 | 5 | 6 |
| Planned requirements | 100 | — | 120 | — | 130 | 60 |
| Requirements, Part 1 (legs, 4 per assembly) Production lead time, 2 weeks | | | | | | |
| Expected usage | 400 | — | 480 | — | 520 | 240 |
| Planned deliveries | 400 | — | 480 | — | 520 | — |
| Planned stock on hand, end of week | 60 | 60 | 60 | 60 | 60 | 60 |
| Planned production order release | 480 | — | 520 | — | 320 | — |
| Requirements, Part 4 (plywood top, 1 per assembly) Production lead time, 1 week | | | | | | |
| Expected usage | 100 | — | 120 | — | 130 | — |
| Planned deliveries | 100 | — | 120 | — | 130 | — |
| Planned stock on hand, end of week | 20 | 20 | 20 | 20 | 20 | 20 |
| Planned production order release | — | 120 | — | 130 | — | 80 |

## INVENTORY PLANNING SYSTEMS

Suppose we have an end item A that requires one unit of an important component B per unit of end item. The master schedule indicating the weekly production requirements for the end item A is

| | Week | | | | | | | | | | | |
|---|---|---|---|---|---|---|---|---|---|---|---|---|
| | 1 | 2 | 3 | 4 | 5 | 6 | 7 | 8 | 9 | 10 | 11 | 12 |
| Quantity | 150 | 50 | 70 | 100 | 0 | 150 | 200 | 100 | 0 | 80 | 20 | 160 |

Further, suppose it takes two weeks to produce a batch of component B and the entire batch must be available at the beginning of the week in which this component is to be used. For example, in week 8, 100 units of end item A are to be produced. The production of component B must begin in week 6 so that 100 units of this component are available at the beginning of week 8. The pertinent data for component B is as follows:

COMPONENT B

| | |
|---|---|
| Average Weekly Demand | 100 units |
| Set-up Cost | $90 |
| Inventory Holding Cost | 20 cents/unit/week |

In addition, 170 units of component B are in stock at the beginning of week 1 and 50 units of this component are scheduled to be completed at the beginning of week 2. Our objective is to prepare a materials requirement plan for component B.

In Table 6-1, the net requirements for component B are derived. Row 1 of Table 6-1 shows the gross requirements or the quantity of component B that must be available by the beginning of the week. The numbers in row 1 are derived from the master schedule of end item A. In row 2, on-hand inventory is shown. Since we start out with 170 units of component B, and 150 units are demanded in week 1, at the end of week 1 there will only be 20 units on hand. At the beginning of week 2, 50 units are added to the inventory (shown in row 3) and thus the total inventory is 70 units, out of which 50 units are consumed in week 2, leaving only 20 units on hand. In week 3, 70 units are demanded, but only 20 units are on hand; thus, a net requirement of 50 units is created. The net requirements shown in row 4 reflect the minimum quantity that must be available at the beginning of the week to ensure that stockouts do not occur. The net requirements for week 4 are 100 units as no inventory is on hand and the demand for week 4 is 100 units. Actually, once the on-hand inventory runs out, the net requirement for any future period merely equals the demand (or gross requirements) for that period.

Several options are available to satisfy the net requirements shown in Table 6-1. At one extreme, we can manufacture the quantity sufficient to satisfy the requirements for up to the end of the planning horizon (week 12) in a single batch. The other extreme is to manufacture the quantity sufficient to meet only a single period's

TABLE 6-1
**COMPUTATION OF NET REQUIREMENTS**

| | | *Week* | | | | | | | | | | | |
|---|---|---|---|---|---|---|---|---|---|---|---|---|---|
| | | 1 | 2 | 3 | 4 | 5 | 6 | 7 | 8 | 9 | 10 | 11 | 12 |
| Gross requirements | | 150 | 50 | 70 | 100 | 0 | 150 | 200 | 100 | 0 | 80 | 20 | 160 |
| On-hand inventory[a] | 170 | 20 | 20 | | | | | | | | | | |
| Scheduled receipts[b] | | | 50 | | | | | | | | | | |
| Net requirements | | | | 50 | 100 | 0 | 150 | 200 | 100 | 0 | 80 | 20 | 160 |
| Planned production | | | | | | | | | | | | | |

[a] Measured at the end of each week.
[b] Received at the beginning of each week (50 units are currently being manufactured for delivery at the beginning of week 2).

requirements. The cost of holding inventory and cost of set-up must be considered in determining a decision policy.

## Lot Size Decision Policies

Before considering the alternative lot size policies, let us review some of the key elements of requirements systems that may be helpful in determining appropriate lot size policies. First, we know that demand for components is dependent and must be thought of as requirements generated to key in with the master schedule of the final product. The nature of the demand distributions that result is not uniform and continuous, as may be true for primary items, such as those discussed in Chapter 5, where demand resulted from the aggregation of independent orders from multiple sources. Demand is lumpy because it is dependent and because demand variations are not the result of random fluctuation. Therefore, some of the assumptions that are important in traditional inventory control theory are questionable for dependent items. We must keep these assumptions in mind as we discuss alternative lot size policies. The following comparison of several lot size policies is intended to show how these policies react to lumpy demand and is not intended to be a valid test of these policies in *MRP* systems.

### LOT-FOR-LOT

In this policy, the lot size for a batch is chosen to satisfy the net requirements for a single period. For our example, in Table 6-1, 50 units are required at the beginning of week 3 and, hence, a batch of 50 units is put into production in week 1. Since production lead time is two weeks, this batch will be available at the beginning of week 3. Similarly, since 100 units are required in week 4, production of 100 units is planned to begin in week 2. In Table 6-2, a lot-for-lot policy is employed to determine planned production. The costs of following this policy will be

$$\text{Set-up cost} = 8 \text{ set-ups} \times \$90 \text{ per set-up} = \$720$$

$$\text{Holding cost} = 20 \text{ units in week } 1 \times 0.2 + 20 \text{ units in week } 2 \times 0.2 = \$8$$

$$\text{Total cost for the 12-week period} = \$720 + \$8 = \$728$$

TABLE 6-2
**LOT-FOR-LOT PRODUCTION RULE**

| | | Week | | | | | | | | | | | |
|---|---|---|---|---|---|---|---|---|---|---|---|---|---|
| | | 1 | 2 | 3 | 4 | 5 | 6 | 7 | 8 | 9 | 10 | 11 | 12 |
| Gross requirements | | 150 | 50 | 70 | 100 | 0 | 150 | 200 | 100 | 0 | 80 | 20 | 160 |
| On-hand inventory[a] | 170 | 20 | 20 | 0 | 0 | 0 | 0 | 0 | 0 | 0 | 0 | 0 | 0 |
| Scheduled receipts[b] | | | 50 | 50 | 100 | | 150 | 200 | 100 | | 80 | 20 | 160 |
| Net requirements | | | | 50 | 100 | 0 | 150 | 200 | 100 | 0 | 80 | 20 | 160 |
| Planned production | | 50 | 100 | 0 | 150 | 200 | 100 | 0 | 80 | 20 | 160 | 0 | 0 |

[a]Measured at the end of each week.
[b]Received at the beginning of each week (50 units are currently being manufactured for delivery at the beginning of week 2).

| | | |
|---|---|---|
| Set-up cost | = | \$720 |
| Holding cost | = | \$ 8 |
| Total incremental cost | = | \$728 |

The lot-for-lot policy is cost-effective only when set-up costs are extremely small in relation to holding costs.

## ECONOMIC ORDER QUANTITY (*EOQ*)

In this policy, *EOQ* is calculated based on expected requirements.

$$EOQ = \sqrt{\frac{2Rc_P}{c_H}} = \sqrt{\frac{2 \times 100 \times 90}{0.2}} = 300 \text{ units}$$

The batch size is now simply set to *EOQ*. In our example, a batch must be put into production in week 1 to satisfy requirements in week 3. The lot size for this batch is set equal to *EOQ* the amount of 300 units. In Table 6-3, the performance of *EOQ* policy is shown.

If the net requirements for a period are greater than the *EOQ* amount, then either a multiple of the *EOQ* (e.g., 2 × *EOQ* or 3 × *EOQ*) can be produced or the amount equal to the requirements is produced. Several observations about *EOQ* policy should be made.

First, *EOQ* policy is not optimal in material requirements planning systems because the assumption of constant demand is not met. As compared with a lot-for-lot policy, the set-up costs for an *EOQ* policy will generally be lower and holding costs will be higher. Second, in an *EOQ* policy, extra inventory is unnecessarily carried to the end of the planning horizon. In Table 6-3, for example, the requirements for weeks 10, 11, and 12 are only 260 units, yet 300 units are put into production using the *EOQ* policy. This results in carrying 40 units of excess inventory. Finally, the downstream departments experience a stable demand, but the periodicity of demand fluctuates if an upstream department is using an *EOQ* policy. For example, if three units of part C are required for manufacturing one unit of component B, then, using information from Table 6-3, we can conclude that the gross requirements for part C in weeks 1, 5, and 8 will be 900 units for each period.

TABLE 6-3
**EOQ LOT SIZE POLICY**

| | | *Week* | | | | | | | | | | | |
|---|---|---|---|---|---|---|---|---|---|---|---|---|---|
| | | 1 | 2 | 3 | 4 | 5 | 6 | 7 | 8 | 9 | 10 | 11 | 12 |
| Gross requirements | | 150 | 50 | 70 | 100 | 0 | 150 | 200 | 100 | 0 | 80 | 20 | 160 |
| On-hand inventory[a] | 170 | 20 | 20 | 250 | 150 | 150 | 0 | 100 | 0 | 0 | 220 | 200 | 40 |
| Scheduled receipts[b] | | | 50 | 300 | | | | 300 | | | 300 | | |
| Net requirements | | | | 50 | 100 | 0 | 150 | 200 | 100 | 0 | 80 | 20 | 160 |
| Planned production | | 300 | 0 | 0 | 0 | 300 | 0 | 0 | 300 | 0 | 0 | 0 | 0 |

[a]Measured at the end of each week.
[b]Received at the beginning of each week.

| | | | | |
|---|---|---|---|---|
| Set-up cost | = 3 | × $90 | = | $270 |
| Holding cost | = 1150 | × $0.2 | = | $230 |
| Total incremental cost | = | | | $500 |

## PERIOD ORDER QUANTITY (POQ)

In this policy, the lot size is set equal to the actual requirements in a predetermined fixed number of periods. Thus, the excess inventory that may be carried under an *EOQ* policy is eliminated. To compute the number of periods for which the requirements must be met by a single lot, we use

$$\text{Number of periods} = \frac{EOQ}{\text{Average period demand}}$$

Thus, in our example, 300/100 = 3 periods' requirements must be met by one production batch. Table 6-4 shows the performance of this policy. The advantage of *POQ* policy over *EOQ* policy is in reducing inventory holding costs when requirements are nonuniform because excess inventory is avoided. The requirements for a downstream department will fluctuate with this policy. In our example, the department manufacturing part C will experience demands of 450 units for week 1 and 1350 units for week 4 and so on. (Three units of part C are needed to manufacture one unit of component B.)

## PART-PERIOD TOTAL COST BALANCING

In this policy, holding costs and set-up costs are balanced as closely as possible for each lot size decision. For example, in week 1, we have the following alternatives with the associated costs for holding and set-up.

Manufacture only for one period's demand (week 3)

Holding cost = 0
Set-up cost = $90

TABLE 6-4
**POQ LOT SIZE POLICY**

| | | Week | | | | | | | | | | | |
|---|---|---|---|---|---|---|---|---|---|---|---|---|---|
| | | 1 | 2 | 3 | 4 | 5 | 6 | 7 | 8 | 9 | 10 | 11 | 12 |
| Gross requirements | | 150 | 50 | 70 | 100 | 0 | 150 | 200 | 100 | 0 | 80 | 20 | 160 |
| On-hand inventory[a] | 170 | 20 | 20 | 100 | 0 | 0 | 300 | 100 | 0 | 0 | 180 | 160 | 0 |
| Scheduled receipts[b] | | | 50 | 150 | | | 450 | | | | 260 | | |
| Net requirements | | | | 50 | 100 | 0 | 150 | 200 | 100 | 0 | 80 | 20 | 160 |
| Planned production | | 150 | 0 | 0 | 450 | 0 | 0 | 0 | 260 | 0 | 0 | 0 | 0 |

[a]Measured at the end of each week.
[b]Received at the beginning of each week.

| | | | |
|---|---|---|---|
| Set-up cost | = 3 × $90 | = | $270 |
| Holding cost | = 880 × $0.2 | = | $176 |
| Total incremental cost | = | | $446 |

Manufacture for two periods' demand (weeks 3 and 4)

Holding cost = 100 × 0.2 = $20
Set-up cost = $90

Manufacture for three periods' demand (weeks 3 to 5)

Holding cost = 100 × 0.2 = $20
Set-up cost = $90

Manufacture for four periods' demand (weeks 3 to 6)

Holding cost = 250 × 0.2 + 150 × 0.2 + 150 × 0.2 = $110
Set-up cost = $90

Since a lot size that meets the requirements for four periods (weeks 3 to 6) produces the closest balance between holding costs and set-up costs, it is chosen. Table 6-5 shows the results of this method.

## OTHER METHODS

Many other lot sizing techniques have been considered in the literature (see Orlicky, 1975, Chapter 6). For the single-stage system, the Wagner–Whitin (1958) dynamic programming algorithm produces an optimal solution and the Silver–Meal heuristic provides a good solution. In Wagner–Whitin algorithm, a batch is produced only when on-hand inventory is zero, and lot size is determined so that it exactly matches the net requirements for some number of periods. In multistage systems, however, no simple procedure for obtaining optimal lot sizes exist. The problem can be formulated as a mixed integer programming problem, but for practical problems of even moderate size, the computational time required to solve the model is often prohibitive.

TABLE 6-5
**PART-PERIOD TOTAL COST BALANCING**

| | | Week | | | | | | | | | | | |
|---|---|---|---|---|---|---|---|---|---|---|---|---|---|
| | | 1 | 2 | 3 | 4 | 5 | 6 | 7 | 8 | 9 | 10 | 11 | 12 |
| Gross requirements | | 150 | 50 | 70 | 100 | 0 | 150 | 200 | 100 | 0 | 80 | 20 | 60 |
| On-hand inventory[a] | 170 | 20 | 20 | 250 | 150 | 150 | 0 | 200 | 100 | 100 | 20 | 0 | 0 |
| Scheduled receipts[b] | | | 50 | 300 | | | | 400 | | | | | 60 |
| Net requirements | | | | 50 | 100 | 0 | 150 | 200 | 100 | 0 | 80 | 20 | 60 |
| Planned production | | 300 | 0 | 0 | 0 | 400 | 0 | 0 | 0 | 0 | 60 | 0 | 0 |

[a] Measured at the end of each week.
[b] Received at the beginning of each week.

| | | | | |
|---|---|---|---|---|
| Set-up cost | = 3 | × $90 | = | $270 |
| Holding cost | = 1010 | × $0.2 | = | $202 |
| Total incremental cost = | | | | $472 |

When new demand information becomes available, the timing and lot sizes of production may be altered. Such alterations are unattractive from a practical standpoint. Kropp et al. (1983) have examined this issue of *nervousness* in *MRP* and suggest assigning a penalty cost for changing previously determined schedules.

Biggs, Goodman, and Hardy (1977) developed a multistage production–inventory system model that involves a hierarchical system of part and component manufacture, subassembly, and final assembly. The hierarchical system makes it possible to test alternative lot size policies in an operating system where part and component manufacturing schedules are dependent on final assembly schedules. The final assembly schedule is set in relation to product demand. Thus, the structure permits the testing of lot size policies as they would function in a multistage system. Five lot size policies were tested:

Economic order quantity (*EOQ*)

Periodic reorder system, using the *EOQ* to determine the reorder time cycle

Part-period total cost balancing

Lot-for-lot, in which an order is placed for exactly what is needed in the next period

Wagner–Whitin dynamic programming model

The system performance of the lot size models was evaluated using the following four criteria:

1. Total number of stockouts for final products
2. Total units of stockouts for final products
3. Total number of set-ups, total system
4. Average dollar value of inventory, total system

The results indicate that the part-period total cost balancing and *EOQ* policies were consistently the best performers in the simulation experiments. The dominance of one policy over others depends on the weighting given to the four criteria. The reemergence of the *EOQ* policy as a good performer in a multistage system is explained in part by its excellent performance with respect to final product stockouts. The *EOQ* policy places larger orders fewer times per year and is therefore exposed to the risk of stockout less often. Tests by De Bodt and Van Wassenhove (1983) also confirm that fixed *EOQ* policy does quite well when there is considerable uncertainty in the demand pattern. Based on the simulation experiments, managers may select policies based on their preference for a given weighting of the criteria.

These results must be regarded as preliminary. As with most early simulation experiments, actual shop conditions are only approximated. In this instance, the simulated shop was loaded well under capacity. No lot splitting was permitted, and when "desired" production exceeded capacity, a priority index was used to determine which lots would not be processed. It is difficult to tell how the five lot size policies would have performed if these arbitrary rules had not been imposed and if the load had been varied over a range that included heavy loads. Nevertheless, testing alternative lot size policies within a multistage environment is important and is a step toward resolving the issue of how different lot size policies actually perform.

## Buffer Stocks in Requirements Systems

We have already noted that dependent items are not subject to the kinds of random variations in demand that characterize primary product demand. The demand variability is largely planned and is lumpy in nature. There are sources of variation, however, for which buffer stocks are a logical countermeasure. Buffer stocks in requirements systems are designed to absorb random variations in the *supply* schedule. The time required for processing orders through the system is variable because of such factors as delays, breakdowns, and plan changes. In addition, the actual quantity delivered from production is variable because of scrap. The result is that we need a cushion to absorb variations in supply time and in the quantity actually delivered.

### SAFETY LEAD TIME

If the lead time for manufacturing a component or a part is variable, then stockouts could occur if a batch is not scheduled for production sufficiently in advance of actual requirements. In our example, suppose component B takes normally two weeks to manufacture. However, 10 percent of the time the shop is busy with other orders; therefore, the lead time is really three weeks. Rarely, say one percent of the time, production lead time could be as high as four weeks. Now in this situation, if management desires that stockouts do not occur even one percent of the time, then a batch of component B must be put into production four weeks in advance of the actual net requirements. This would result in much higher inventory holding costs since most of the time production will take less than four weeks and excess inventory will have to be carried. The determination of lead time should therefore balance the cost of holding inventory and cost of stockouts. Attempts should also be made to reduce the variability in lead time by proper scheduling and coordinated production control systems.

## SAFETY STOCK

In some situations, the per period requirements are variable because of sales forecast errors, customer order changes, or production variability in upstream departments. Alternatively, a larger quantity than required may have to be manufactured to adjust for rejects, scraps, and the like. A safety stock is needed to guard against such variability. Safety stock is determined by considering the cost of stockouts and cost of holding excess inventories. Once a safety stock level is determined, the lot size policies discussed earlier are modified to start production when net requirements fall to the level of the safety stock. A requirements plan using an *EOQ* policy for component B in our example is shown in Table 6-6 when the safety stock is assumed to be 200 units. Notice that the inventory level never falls below 200 units in two consecutive periods. This is because as soon as on-hand inventory reaches 200 units, production is triggered for an *EOQ* quantity (300 units) that arrives in the upcoming period.

Caution is warranted in the use of buffer stocks. If sales forecasts are inflated, production lead times are pessimistically estimated to be longer than normal, and orders are triggered when on-hand inventory is still sufficient, the compounding effects could produce very large raw material and work-in-process inventories. This defeats the primary purpose of material requirements planning systems. It is therefore recommended that sufficient efforts be expanded in identifying, isolating, and correcting the causes of variation in lead times or requirements so that safety lead times and safety stocks can be kept at a minimum.

TABLE 6-6
**EOQ POLICY WITH SAFETY STOCK = 150 UNITS**

| | | *Week* | | | | | | | | | | | |
|---|---|---|---|---|---|---|---|---|---|---|---|---|---|
| | | 1 | 2 | 3 | 4 | 5 | 6 | 7 | 8 | 9 | 10 | 11 | 12 |
| Gross requirements | | 150 | 50 | 70 | 100 | 0 | 150 | 200 | 100 | 0 | 80 | 20 | 160 |
| On-hand inventory[a] | 170 | 20 | 20 | 250 | 150[c] | 450 | 300 | 100[c] | 300 | 300 | 220 | 200[c] | 340 |
| Scheduled receipts[b] | | | 50 | 300 | | 300 | | | 300 | | | | 300 |
| Net requirements | | | | 50 | 100 | 0 | 150 | 200 | 100 | 0 | 80 | 20 | 160 |
| Planned production | | 300 | | 300 | | | 300 | | | | 300 | | |

[a]Measured at the end of each week.
[b]Received at the beginning of each week.
[c]Safety stock is reached, triggering production for the upcoming period.

## CAPACITY REQUIREMENTS PLANNING

The requirements plans we have discussed have shown ways of exploiting the knowledge of demand dependence and product structure in order to develop production order schedules. These schedules take account of the necessary timing of production orders, but they assume that the capacity is available when needed. However, capacity constraints are a reality that must be taken into account. Because the *MRP* system contains information in its files about the processing of each production order, we should be able to use that information to determine whether or not capacity problems exist.

As an example, consider just the processing of metal legs beginning with the information contained in Figure 6-4. There are two dinette tables that use the same legs, and Table 6-7 summarizes the leg requirements from Figure 6-4. The bottom line of Table 6-7 gives the production requirements for legs if we accumulate four weeks' future requirements as production orders. Therefore, it is necessary to receive lots of 1320 legs in period 1 and 1240 legs in period 5. Because there is a production lead time of three weeks, these production orders must be released three weeks ahead of the schedule shown in Table 6-7.

From the operation process chart of Figure 6-1*b*, let us consider only the load requirements for the fabrication operations of (1) cut to length, (2) weld support brackets, and (3) drill brackets. The expected time requirements for these three operations are shown in Table 6-8 for each of the two lot sizes we must consider.

If the production orders are released three weeks before the legs are needed for assembly, assume that the cutting operation is planned for the first week, the welding operation for the second week, and the drilling and other minor operations for the third week. Then, the machine hour load for each of the three processes can be projected, as shown in Figure 6-8, so that all operations are completed and the two orders are available in the first and fifth weeks.

Following the same rationale that determined the load effects for the three processes shown in Figure 6-8, a computer program can pick up the loads for all orders for all parts and products in the files of the requirements program and print out a projected load for each work center. For example, the projected weekly load on the drill press work center is shown in Figure 6-9. The accumulated load by weeks is shown as "released load," in hours. The capacity for the 8-week horizon is shown as

TABLE 6-7
**REQUIREMENTS FOR TABLE LEGS FROM PRODUCTION SCHEDULES FOR SQUARE AND ROUND TABLES SHOWN IN FIGURE 6-4 (PRODUCTION LEAD TIME = 3 WEEKS)**

| Period, weeks | 1 | 2 | 3 | 4 | 5 | 6 | 7 | 8 |
|---|---|---|---|---|---|---|---|---|
| Leg requirements, square | 400 | — | 480 | — | 520 | — | 320 | — |
| Leg requirements, round | — | 160 | — | 280 | — | 240 | — | 160 |
| Total leg requirements | 400 | 160 | 480 | 280 | 520 | 240 | 320 | 160 |
| Production requirements | 1320 | — | — | — | 1240 | — | — | — |

TABLE 6-8
**PROCESS TIME REQUIREMENTS FOR LEGS IN LOTS OF 1320 AND 1240**

| Process | Setup Time, Minutes | Run Time, Minutes/unit | *Total Time, Hours, in Lots of* 1320 | 1240 |
|---|---|---|---|---|
| 1. Cut to length | 5 | 0.25 | 5.58 | 5.25 |
| 2. Weld brackets | 10 | 1.00 | 22.16 | 20.83 |
| 3. Drill brackets | 20 | 0.75 | 16.83 | 15.50 |
| 4. Paint | 10 | 0.25 | 5.66 | 5.33 |
| 5. Install feet | 5 | 0.10 | 2.28 | 2.15 |

FIGURE 6-8
**LOAD GENERATION FOR THREE PROCESSES, BASED ON THE PRODUCTION SCHEDULE FOR LEGS. THE TIME REQUIREMENTS ARE FROM TABLE 6-8.**

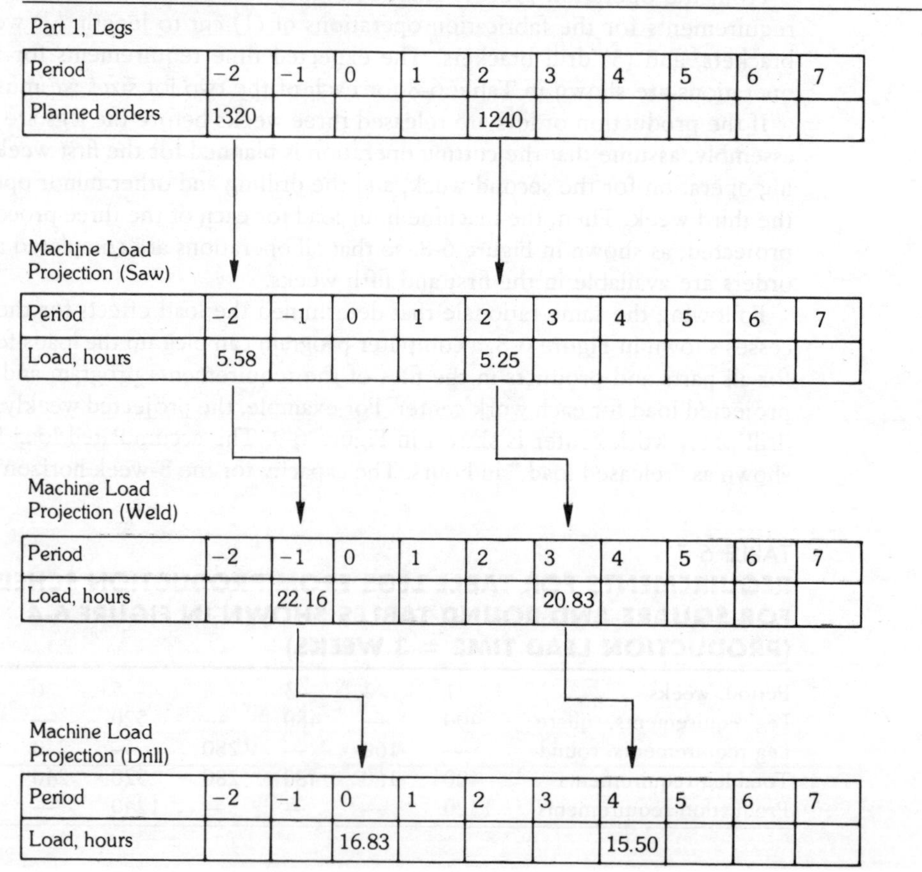

Part 1, Legs

| Period | −2 | −1 | 0 | 1 | 2 | 3 | 4 | 5 | 6 | 7 |
|---|---|---|---|---|---|---|---|---|---|---|
| Planned orders | 1320 | | | | 1240 | | | | | |

Machine Load Projection (Saw)

| Period | −2 | −1 | 0 | 1 | 2 | 3 | 4 | 5 | 6 | 7 |
|---|---|---|---|---|---|---|---|---|---|---|
| Load, hours | 5.58 | | | | 5.25 | | | | | |

Machine Load Projection (Weld)

| Period | −2 | −1 | 0 | 1 | 2 | 3 | 4 | 5 | 6 | 7 |
|---|---|---|---|---|---|---|---|---|---|---|
| Load, hours | | 22.16 | | | | 20.83 | | | | |

Machine Load Projection (Drill)

| Period | −2 | −1 | 0 | 1 | 2 | 3 | 4 | 5 | 6 | 7 |
|---|---|---|---|---|---|---|---|---|---|---|
| Load, hours | | | 16.83 | | | | 15.50 | | | |

FIGURE 6-9
**SAMPLE PROJECTED LOAD REPORT FOR ONE WORK CENTER.**

Projected Weekly Machine Load Report
Work Center 21, Drill Presses
Date: 02/01/80

| Period | 1 | 2 | 3 | 4 | 5 | 6 | 7 | 8 |
|---|---|---|---|---|---|---|---|---|
| Released load, hours | 65 | 71 | 49 | 90 | 81 | 95 | 48 | 62 |
| Capacity, hours | 80 | 80 | 80 | 80 | 80 | 80 | 80 | 80 |
| Available hours | 15 | 9 | 31 | −10 | −1 | −15 | 32 | 18 |

80 hours, the equivalent of two available machines. The available hours in Figure 6-9 then indicate whether or not capacity problems are projected. In periods 4, 5, and 6, there are projected overloads. Given this information, we may wish to anticipate the problem by changing the timing of some orders, meet the overload through the use of overtime, or possibly subcontract some items. In the example shown in Figure 6-9, substantial slack is projected for periods 3 and 7, so it might be possible to smooth the load by releasing some orders earlier.

## COMPUTERIZED *MRP*

The concepts of *MRP* are relatively straightforward, but they clearly require computers for implementation for large numbers of products. When there are many assembled products, perhaps with subassemblies, the number of parts involved can easily be in the thousands. Requirements generation, inventory control, time phasing of orders, and capacity requirements all clearly need to be coordinated. This is a job for computers. *MRP* developed in the computer age for good reasons.

### Benefits

It is estimated that somewhat more than 1000 manufacturers are using computerized *MRP* systems with excellent results. Some of the benefits are obvious. Think of changing schedules as a result of market shifts, changed promises to customers, orders cancellations, or whatever. A computerized *MRP* system can immediately reflect the effects of changed order quantities, cancellations, delayed material deliveries, and so on. A manager can change the master schedule and quickly see the effects on capacity, inventory status, or the ability of the system to meet promises to customers.

One of the important advantages is in capacity requirements adjustments. When planners examine work center load reports, such as that shown in Figure 6-9, they can immediately see possibilities for work load smoothing. It may be possible to pull some demand forward to fill in slack loads. Such actions may reduce idle time and may eliminate or reduce overtime.

### MRP Programs

The structure of *MRP* computer programs is shown in Figure 6-10. The master schedule drives the *MRP* program. The other inputs are product structures, bills of materials, and inventory status. The outputs of the *MRP* program are open and planned orders, net requirements for parts and materials, load reports, and updated and projected inventory status. A variety of other reports can be generated to suit individual needs because the files are maintained so that they can be formulated in a variety of formats.

Figure 6-11 shows a flow diagram for the IBM Requirements Generation System. It includes various lot size policies including the three we discussed, that can be selected.

## MANUFACTURING RESOURCE PLANNING (*MRP* II)

As we discussed, *MRP* is an effective ordering method for dependent demand situations where the placement of an order or the start of a production batch for a part is determined by the timing and usage of the part in a subsequent stage of production. Since *MRP* decisions for a production stage (what to manufacture, how many, and when) are coordinated with decisions for other stages, it is natural to extend *MRP* to include capacity planning, shop floor control, and purchasing. This extended *MRP* is referred to as *closed loop MRP*.

In *MRP* II, financial and marketing functions are tied to the operations function. Since materials and production requirements for each stage of production are determined in *MRP*, these requirements are converted into dollars. We can then have, by each product group category, on-hand inventory in dollars, purchase requirements in dollars, an estimate of labor dollars, and budgets for each department for the planning horizon. In this way, production and finance people work together to ensure that the desired resources are made available to meet the production requirements for the final products.

*MRP* II also facilitates coordination with marketing. To begin with, sales forecasts are inputs to *MRP* as they are used to determine aggregate production plans and the master schedules for each product. The production planner and the marketing product manager then work together on a weekly basis to see whether changes in the master schedules are needed based on individual customer orders. These changes may include changes in the order size, cancellations, and the expediting or postponement of some orders. The marketing manager and the plant manager may meet monthly to update sales forecasts and revise master schedules. Finally, the top managers from production, marketing, and finance together decide the product mix, aggregate production plans by families of products, financial requirements, and pricing strategies.

*MRP* II therefore provides a convenient vehicle for coordinating the efforts of manufacturing, finance, marketing, engineering, and personnel departments toward the common business plan. Since *MRP* II is computerized, the managers can per-

FIGURE 6-10
**STRUCTURE OF MRP COMPUTER PROGRAMS.**

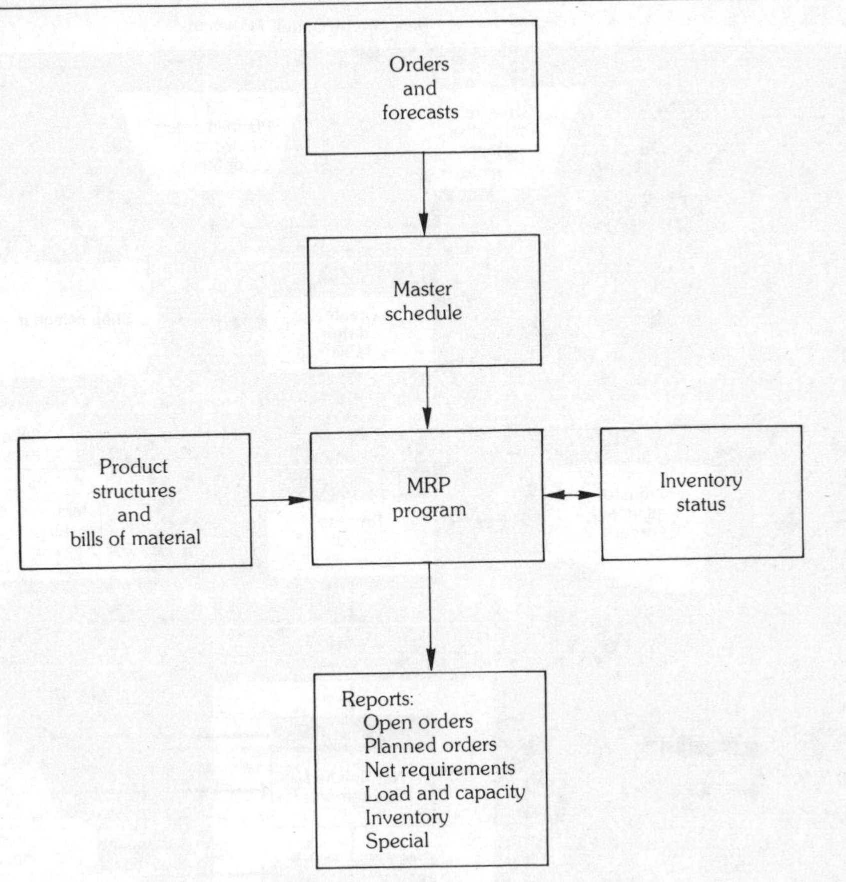


form "what if" analyses to evaluate the implications of their decisions. For example, if the sales forecasts provided by marketing cannot be met with existing capacities, the financial and other implications of alternative decisions, such as subcontracting, scheduling overtime or second shifts, or postponing some customer orders, can be evaluated using the simulation capabilities of *MRP* II.

Another extension of *MRP* concepts is in planning distribution requirements for various central, regional, and branch warehouses. This is called *distribution resource planning* (*DRP*). In simple terms, the idea of *DRP* is to coordinate the decisions at various distribution points in much the same way as *MRP* is used to coordinate decisions at different production stages. Thus, instead of independent control of the same item at different distribution points using *EOQ* methods, the dependent demand at a higher echelon (e.g., a central warehouse) is derived from the requirements of lower èchelon (e.g., regional warehouses). *DRP* is useful for both manufacturing firms (automotive, other consumer durables, etc.) that sell their products

FIGURE 6-11
**COMPUTERIZED REQUIREMENTS GENERATION SYSTEM.**

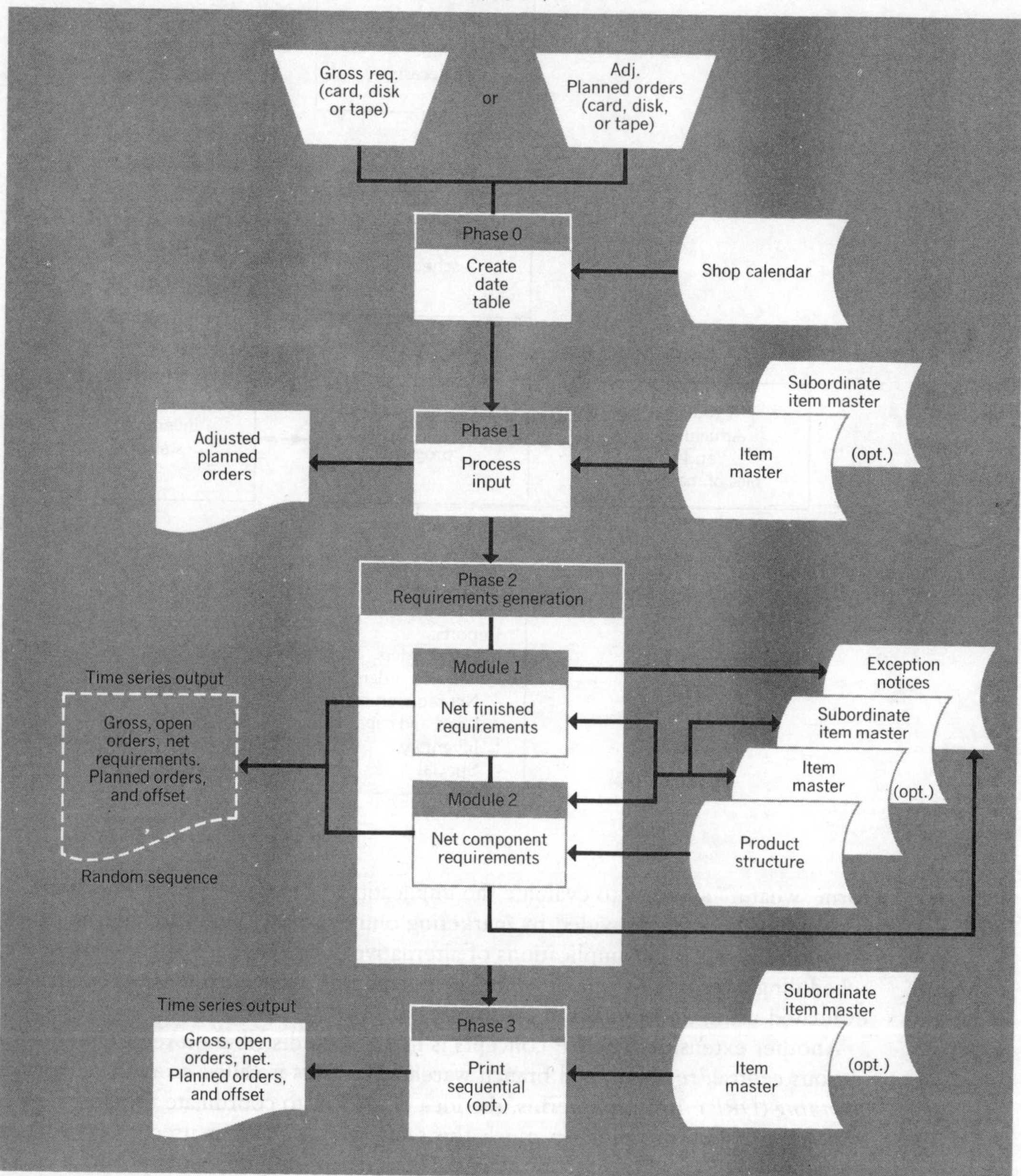


(Courtesy International Business Machines Corporation.)

through several distribution points and purely distributional firms (department stores, supermarkets, etc.).

## OPTIMIZED PRODUCTION TECHNOLOGY (OPT)

*OPT* is a proprietary software package for production planning and scheduling owned by Creative Output, Inc., of Milford, Connecticut. The objective of *OPT* is to schedule production so that production output is maximized. Because of the limited information available about the inner workings of the scheduling procedure used in *OPT*, it is difficult to assess whether *OPT* represents a new methodological approach. Nevertheless, the framework employed by *OPT* contains some useful ideas applicable to a number of production/operations situations. The key distinctive feature of *OPT* is its ability to identify and isolate bottleneck operations and focus on these bottlenecks to determine production plans and schedules for the entire shop. This simple idea could lead to the better utilization of manufacturing resources, resulting in greater productivity and lower costs. We will illustrate the advantage of using a bottleneck operation to drive the planning for the remaining operations by means of a simple example.

Consider two products, 1 and 2, that are manufactured by the process shown in Figure 6-12. The process consists of three operations, A, B, and C. The set-up times and production rates for the three operations are shown in Figure 6-12 and are identical for the two products. We assume that 40 hours per week are available for production and that equal amounts of the two products must be made available at the end of each week.

Clearly, operation B is the bottleneck operation in the production process shown in Figure 6-12. Let us make several observations about the implications of bottleneck operation B for the preceding operation A and the succeeding operation C.

FIGURE 6-12
**PROCESS FLOW FOR AN ILLUSTRATIVE EXAMPLE.**

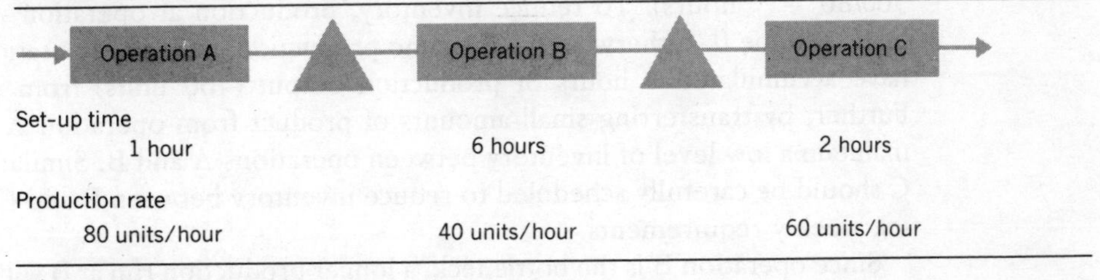


**Other assumptions:**

- **40 hours per week are available for production.**
- **Set-up times and production rates are identical for Products 1 and 2.**
- **Equal amounts of each product must be made available each week.**
- **A new set-up must be made the beginning of the week even if the same product was produced at the end of the previous week.**

First, if operation A, which precedes the bottleneck operation, is not controlled, inventory will accumulate between A and B because A will produce at the rate of 80 units per hour, whereas B will only use the output of A at a rate of 40 units per hour. Second, if the capacity of B is increased by one unit (through overtime or by adding facilities) then the throughput of the entire system will be increased by one unit, resulting in an increase in profit equal to the contribution of the whole product (and *not* merely the relative contribution at stage B). Conversely, a loss in capacity for operation B (through improper scheduling or a maintenance problem) will result in a decrease in profit equal to the contribution of the whole product. Third, an increase in the number of set-ups for operations A and C, to the point these operations themselves become bottlenecks, produces no incremental cost to the company. Thus, fewer set-ups and larger lots for the bottleneck operations and more frequent set-ups and smaller lots for nonbottleneck operations often make economic sense. Finally, note that if the *production lot size* for operation B is 400 units, it is not necessary that we transfer the product to operation C only after all 400 units have been completed at operation B. Doing so will result in a high level of inventory between operations B and C. To reduce this inventory, it may be practical to transfer in lots of 40 (one hour's worth of production) or some other quantity smaller than 400 units. Thus, in general, production lot size and transfer lot size may not be equal. It may be economical to use a larger production lot size and smaller transfer lot size. This distinction is important in *OPT*, and the procedure selects appropriate production and transfer lot sizes for each operation. Since the production and transfer lots may be different, the entire concept of production *EOQ*s is called into question.

We will now illustrate how careful scheduling for operation B will improve the production rate of the system in Figure 6-12. Recall that for product mix considerations we are required to supply equal amounts of products 1 and 2 by the end of a week. A simple rule then is to produce product 1 for the first 20 hours of the week and product 2 for the next 20 hours or vice versa. In this plan, since 6 hours are required for set-ups for bottleneck operation B, we will be able to produce 40 units per hour × 14 hours = 560 units of each product per week. This 560 units of production is limited by the capacity of operation B. Of course, operation A could produce the 560 units in 8 hours (set-up time of one hour + production time of 560/80 = 7 hours). To reduce inventory, production at operation A should not begin at time 0. Otherwise, by the time production begins at operation B, we will have accumulated 5 hours of production output (400 units) from operation A. Further, by transferring small amounts of product from operation A to B we can maintain a low level of inventory between operations A and B. Similarly, operation C should be carefully scheduled to reduce inventory between B and C while meeting weekly requirements.

Since operation B is the bottleneck, a longer production run at B will improve the output. For example, we can produce product 1 for the first entire week and product 2 for the next entire week at operation B. Thus, each product is produced only once in two weeks at operation B. The weekly output for operation B under this plan would be as follows:

| | Week | | | |
|---|---|---|---|---|
| | 1 | 2 | 3 | 4 |
| Product 1 | 1360 | 0 | 1360 | 0 |
| Product 2 | 0 | 1360 | 0 | 1360 |

However, operation C must deliver equal amounts of products 1 and 2 *each* week. To achieve this, 680 units of inventory must be carried between operations B and C. Hence in week 1, operation C will require 680 units of both product 1 and product 2. Since 1360 units of product 1 are produced by operation B, the ending inventory for week 1 for product 1 will be 680 units. However, operation C must draw 680 units of product 2 from beginning inventory to be able to manufacture the requirements for week 1. The inventory position between B and C under this plan will be as follows:

**INVENTORY AT THE END OF EACH WEEK**

| | Week | | | |
|---|---|---|---|---|
| | 1 | 2 | 3 | 4 |
| Product 1 | 680 | 0 | 680 | 0 |
| Product 2 | 0 | 680 | 0 | 680 |

The net result of the second plan (one product per week at operation B) is that the output per week has increased from 560 units to 680 units; however, additional inventory is accumulated between operations B and C. The relative cost of this additional inventory must be weighed against the relative increase in profits due to increased output in the selection of a final plan.

In a realistic example, the variability of production times, fluctuating sales requirements, and conflicts in scheduling multiple products must all be considered simultaneously. Our point in the simple example has been to demonstrate that the bottleneck operation must drive the entire planning and scheduling of a manufacturing shop.

*OPT* produces production plans and detailed schedules using four basic modules.

1. *Buildnet.* This module creates a model of the manufacturing facility using data on work center capabilities (processing and set-up times), routings that describe the flow of product through manufacturing, bills of materials, inventories, and sales forecasts. This model is in the form of a network.
2. *Serve.* The model of the shop is run through an iterative process to determine bottlenecks in the system. Serve resembles *MRP* in its workings, and one of its outputs is a load profile for each of the resources in the model. The most heavily utilized resource could produce a bottleneck in the system and must be examined carefully. Sometimes, rescheduling work from the heavily utilized machine to some other alternate machine may produce satisfactory results.

3. *Split.* The network model of the shop is divided into two parts: critical resources and noncritical resources. The bottleneck operation and all operations that follow it in the order of manufacturing (e.g., subassemblies and assembly) up to customer orders are included in the critical resource portion of the network. The remaining portion of the network includes noncritical resources.
4. *Brain.* The operations in the critical resource portion of the network are scheduled using a module called the Brain of *OPT*. The Brain of *OPT* determines production and transfer lot sizes and the timing of production for each product for the bottleneck operations. Its output is fed to Serve module, which then produces the entire production plan.

There has been considerable discussion of the differences between *MRP* and *OPT*.* We believe that, for dependent demand situations in a multiple fabrication/assembly operation, *MRP* provides a basic planning framework. Several ideas used by *OPT* can be useful for enhancing the workings of *MRP*. Particularly, the active identification of bottlenecks and the adjustment of schedules so that these bottlenecks are used judiciously (by transferring work to an alternate source, reducing set-up times, or scheduling a long run) will improve the effectiveness of *MRP*. Similarly, the goal of reducing inventory in *MRP* can be further enhanced by distinguishing between production lots and transfer lots and by reducing the size of transfer lots. The basic files used in *MRP* are directly usable in *OPT*, so that system conversions can be made.

## IMPLICATIONS FOR THE MANAGER

Managers of process-focused systems face extreme complexities in planning, scheduling, and control. These complexities are at a maximum when the productive system must cope with different levels of dependency of items in assembly, subassembly, and component manufacture. Managers who understand the dependency relationships are better able to create effective systems of planning and control.

The conceptual framework of requirements planning recognizes that the nature of demand for primary products is substantially different from that for the parts and components of the primary products. Demand for parts and components is dependent on the production schedules of the primary items. Often, parts and components are used in more than one primary product, so the requirements schedule for these items are determined by summing the needs indicated on the master schedule for all primary products. The demand dependence of parts and components has profound effects on the policies used to determine the timing of production orders and the size of production lots.

The demand for parts and components is dependent not only on the quantities needed but also on the timing of supply. Because we are dealing with an interlocking

*See Robert E. Fox, "OPT vs. MRP: Thoughtware vs. Software," *Inventories & Production*, Vol. 3, No. 6, November/December 1983. This article traces a specific example through both the *MRP* and *OPT* scheduling processes showing why *OPT* principles produce a superior result.

structure, the components must be ready for use at a precise time. If they are too late, production of primary items will be disrupted and delayed. If they are too early, in-process inventory costs will increase.

Because demand for components is dependent and is usually lumpy, some of the assumptions of traditional inventory models are not valid. For example, demand is not constant, nor is it the result of the aggregation of the independent demands of multiple sources. In short, demand variations for components are not due to random fluctuations. In addition, production and transfer lots are often not equal, nor should they be equal. The result is that the economic order quantity policy sometimes belies its name.

# REVIEW QUESTIONS

1. What are "dependent" and "independent" demand items? What kind of forecasting methods are appropriate for each as a basis for production and inventory control?
2. What is the information contained in
   a. Product structures?
   b. Bills of materials?
   c. Master schedules?
3. If demand is lumpy, why may *EOQ/ROP* methods not be appropriate for scheduling production or controlling inventories?
4. Describe the following methods for lot size decisions in requirements planning.
   a. Lot-for-lot
   b. *EOQ*
   c. *POQ*
   d. Part-period cost balancing
5. What is the rationale for using (a) safety lead time and (b) safety stock in a requirements planning system?
6. Under what situations are *EOQ/ROP* methods suitable for the inventory control of a component or a subassembly for which demand can be derived from the requirement for end items?

# PROBLEMS

7. Figure 6-13 is a cross-classification chart showing the subassemblies, parts, and raw materials that are used in each of nine primary products. For example, reading horizontally, product 1 requires subassembly 11 and part 28; subassembly 11 requires parts 20 and 28; and parts 20 and 28 require purchased parts or raw materials—20 (35) and 28 (31, 33, and 35).

FIGURE 6-13
**CROSS-CLASSIFICATION CHART SHOWING THE COMPLETE EXPLOSION OF A PRODUCT LINE.**

| | | Subassembly | | | | | | | | | | Part | | | | | | | | | | | Purchased part or raw material | | | | | | |
|---|---|---|---|---|---|---|---|---|---|---|---|---|---|---|---|---|---|---|---|---|---|---|---|---|---|---|---|---|---|
| | Item | 10 | 11 | 12 | 13 | 14 | 15 | 16 | 17 | 18 | 19 | 20 | 21 | 22 | 23 | 24 | 25 | 26 | 27 | 28 | 29 | 30 | 31 | 32 | 33 | 34 | 35 | 36 | |
| Finished product | 1 | | 1 | | | | | | | | | | | | | | | | | 1 | | | | | | | | | 1 |
| | 2 | | | 1 | | | | | | | | | | | | | | | | | | 1 | | 1 | | | | | 2 |
| | 3 | | | | 2 | | | | | | 1 | | | | | | | | | | | | | | | | | | 3 |
| | 4 | | | | | 1 | | | | | | 1 | | | | | | | | | | | | | | | | | 4 |
| | 5 | | | | | | 2 | | | | | 2 | | 1 | | | | | | | | | | | | | | | 5 |
| | 6 | 1 | | | | | | 1 | | | | | | | | | | | | | 1 | | | | | | | | 6 |
| | 7 | | | | | | | | 1 | 1 | | | 2 | | | | | | | | | | | | | | | | 7 |
| | 8 | | 1 | | | | | | | | | | | | | | | 1 | | | | | | | | | | | 8 |
| | 9 | | | | | | | | 1 | | | | | 1 | | | | | | | | | | | | | | | 9 |
| Subassembly | 10 | | | | | | | | | | | | | | | 1 | 2 | | | | | | | | | | | | 10 |
| | 11 | | | | | | | | | | | 1 | | | | | | | | 1 | | | | | | | | | 11 |
| | 12 | | | | | | | | | | | | 1 | | | | | | | | 2 | | | | | | | | 12 |
| | 13 | | | | | | | | | | | | | 2 | | 1 | | 2 | | | | | | | | | | | 13 |
| | 14 | | | | | | | | | | | | | | 3 | | 3 | | 4 | | | | | 1 | | | 2 | | 14 |
| | 15 | | | | | | | | | | | | | 3 | | 2 | | | | 2 | | | | | 1 | | | | 15 |
| | 16 | | | | | | | | | | | | | | | | 2 | | | | 1 | | | | | | | 1 | 16 |
| | 17 | | | | | | | | | | | | | | | | | | | | | 1 | | | | | | 1 | 17 |
| | 18 | | | | | | | | | | | | 1 | | | | | 2 | | | | | 1 | | 1 | | | | 18 |
| | 19 | | | | | | | | | | | | | 1 | | | | | | 1 | | | | 1 | | 1 | | | 19 |
| Part | 20 | | | | | | | | | | | | | | | | | | | | | | | | | | 1 | | 20 |
| | 21 | | | | | | | | | | | | | | | | | | | | | | | | | | | 1 | 21 |
| | 22 | | | | | | | | | | | | | | | | | | | | | | 1 | | | 1 | | | 22 |
| | 23 | | | | | | | | | | | | | | | | | | | | | | | 1 | | | | | 23 |
| | 24 | | | | | | | | | | | | | | | | | | | | | | 1 | | | | 1 | | 24 |
| | 25 | | | | | | | | | | | | | | | | | | | | | | | 1 | | | | 1 | 25 |
| | 26 | | | | | | | | | | | | | | | | | | | | | | | | 1 | | | | 26 |
| | 27 | | | | | | | | | | | | | | | | | | | | | | | | | 1 | | | 27 |
| | 28 | | | | | | | | | | | | | | | | | | | | | | 1 | | 2 | | 1 | | 28 |
| | 29 | | | | | | | | | | | | | | | | | | | | | | 1 | | | 2 | | 1 | 29 |
| | 30 | | | | | | | | | | | | | | | | | | | | | | | 1 | | 2 | | 1 | 30 |

a. Prepare an indented bill of materials for one unit of product 1.

b. If one of each of the nine products were produced, how many units of part 20 would be required?

8. Using the dinette table shown in Figure 6-1 as an example for requirements planning, why not produce enough components every two weeks to key in with a schedule of 100 completed tables per two weeks? What are the disadvantages of doing this?

9. Still using the dinette table as an example, suppose that they are produced in lots of 400 in weeks 3, 6, 9, and so on. Legs are produced in lots of 3200 every six weeks. How should the leg production be phased with respect to the table assemblies? Why?

10. The requirements for a motor drive unit to be assembled into a dictating machine follow the assembly schedule for the completed unit. The assembly schedule requires motor drive units with the timing shown in Table 6-9. Other data for the motor drive unit are as follows: Average requirements are $R$ = 115.8 units per week, $c_P$ = \$400 per lot, and $c_H$ = \$4 per unit per week. What is the inventory record and total incremental cost under each of the following lot size policies? Account for differences in the performance of these lot size policies.

    a. Economic lot size

    b. Periodic order quantity model

    c. Part-period total cost balancing

11. The requirements for the motor drive unit described in problem 10 have been stabilized considerably by compensatory promotion of the dictating machine and by designing a line of portable tape recorders that have a general use and a counterseasonal cycle. The tape recorder uses the same motor drive unit. Table 6-10 shows the new requirements schedule. What are the inventory records and total incremental costs for the same three lot size policies? Account for differences in the performance of the three policies.

TABLE 6-9
**REQUIREMENTS SCHEDULE FOR A MOTOR DRIVE UNIT**

| Week number | 1 | 2 | 3 | 4 | 5 | 6 | 7 | 8 | 9 | 10 | 11 | 12 |
|---|---|---|---|---|---|---|---|---|---|---|---|---|
| Requirements, units | 25 | 30 | 75 | 125 | 200 | 325 | 400 | 100 | 0 | 100 | 0 | 10 |

Total requirements for 12 weeks, 1390 units.

TABLE 6-10
**STABILIZED REQUIREMENTS FOR A MOTOR DRIVE UNIT**

| Week number | 1 | 2 | 3 | 4 | 5 | 6 | 7 | 8 | 9 | 10 | 11 | 12 |
|---|---|---|---|---|---|---|---|---|---|---|---|---|
| Requirements, units | 300 | 300 | 300 | 300 | 350 | 350 | 400 | 400 | 350 | 350 | 350 | 325 |

Total requirements for 12 weeks, 4075 units.

12. A toy company manufactures a boxed game for children. There are four departments in the company. The cardboard production department makes cardboard for the game boards. The finished cardboard is shipped to the board fabrication department, which prints the game boards. Dice manufacturing makes the dice for the game. The finished game boards and dice are shipped to the final assembly department, where they are combined into the finished game. Cost, demand, and lead time data for the departments are as follows:

| | Cardboard | Board Fabrication | Dice |
|---|---|---|---|
| Lead time | 2 weeks | 1 week | 2 weeks |
| Average demand/week | 20 | 20 | 40 |
| Ordering cost | \$30/order | \$50/order | \$80/order |
| Carrying cost (per unit per week) | \$2 | \$4 | \$1 |
| Number of finished units per game | 1 unit/game | 1 unit/game | 2 units/game |

a. Diagram the manufacturing process in terms of the four departments.

The final assembly department has determined its requirements for the next eight weeks as follows:

| | Week | | | | | | | |
|---|---|---|---|---|---|---|---|---|
| | 1 | 2 | 3 | 4 | 5 | 6 | 7 | 8 |
| Requirements | 10 | 25 | 0 | 40 | 20 | 35 | 10 | 20 |

b. Given that it takes one game board per finished game and that there are 40 units in beginning inventory, prepare a requirements plan for *board fabrication* using lot-for-lot, *EOQ*, *POQ*, and part-period cost balancing policies.

| | | Week | | | | | | | |
|---|---|---|---|---|---|---|---|---|---|
| | | 1 | 2 | 3 | 4 | 5 | 6 | 7 | 8 |
| Gross requirements | | | | | | | | | |
| On-hand inventory | 40 | | | | | | | | |
| Scheduled receipts | | | | | | | | | |
| Net requirements | | | | | | | | | |
| Planned order release | | | | | | | | | |

c. Compute the total incremental costs of the policies in part b.

13. A company has three components that go into its final assembly process as indicated by the diagram below.

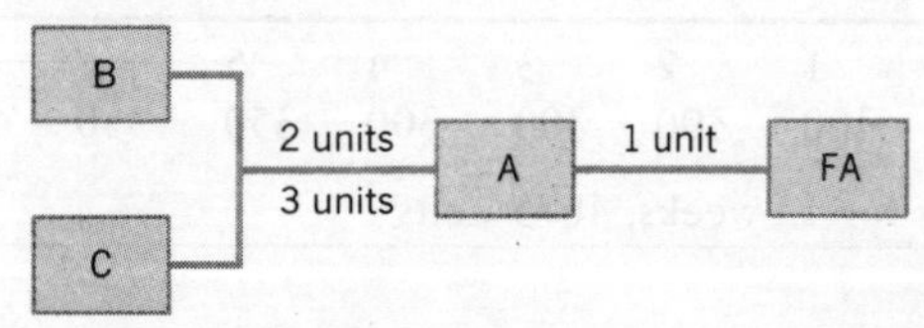

Note that it requires two units of component B and three units of component C to make one unit of component A, and one unit of component A to make one unit in final assembly.

The following table indicates cost, demand, and lead time information for the components.

| | Component A | Component B | Component C |
|---|---|---|---|
| Average demand (units/week) | 30 | 60 | 90 |
| Ordering cost ($/order) | $100 | $540 | $400 |
| Carrying cost ($/unit-week) | $ 2 | $ 2 | $ 1.80 |
| Lead time (weeks) | 2 | 1 | 2 |
| Initial inventory (units) | 72 | 130 | 150 |

The final assembly master schedule is as follows:

| | *Week* | | | | | | | |
|---|---|---|---|---|---|---|---|---|
| | 1 | 2 | 3 | 4 | 5 | 6 | 7 | 8 |
| Demand | 47 | 16 | 34 | 25 | 50 | 40 | 16 | 12 |

a. Prepare a requirements plan for component A using (a) *EOQ* policy and (b) *POQ* policy.

b. Prepare a requirements plan for component C using a lot-for-lot policy. How do the requirement plans for component C differ when *EOQ* or *POQ* policy is used for component A?

c. If the buffer stock for component A is 30 units, prepare a requirements plan for it using a *POQ* policy.

d. If the safety lead time for component A is one week (that is, an allowance of three weeks is made for production lead time), what will be the requirements plan for component A using a *POQ* policy?

e. What is the cost of using the buffer stock of 30 units in part c if true demand turns out to be as anticipated?

f. What is the cost of using the safety lead time of one week in part d if the true lead time is two weeks?

# SITUATIONS

## The Wheel-Pump Dilemma

14. The Wheel Pump Company was originally the Pump Company, but many years ago the owner had an opportunity to bid on a contract to produce steel wheels for one of the smaller automobile companies. The Pump Company was successful in its venture into this new field, and it became a supplier of wheels to the auto industry.

## THE WHEEL BUSINESS

The basic process for wheel production involved stamping hub parts from coil strip steel, rolling rim shapes from steel stock, welding the rolled stock into a circular shape, welding hub parts to the rim, and painting. The fabrication processes were connected by conveyor systems, and once set up for a given type and size of wheel the system ran smoothly. The main production control problems seemed to be in maintaining material supply and quality control and in scheduling types and sizes of wheels to meet customer requirement schedules on two parallel line setups.

## THE PUMP BUSINESS

The original pump business was still flourishing. The company manufactured a line of water pumps used in a variety of applications. There were 10 different models that had some common parts. There was a machine shop that fabricated parts, which were stocked as semifinished items. Production orders were released for these parts based on a reorder with manufacturing lead times of from two to 6 weeks, depending on the item. The intention was to maintain a buffer stock of six weeks' supply. A forecast of demand for each item was updated monthly, using an exponential smoothing system with $\alpha = 0.3$. The relatively large value of $\alpha$ was used to provide fast reaction to demand changes for inclusion in *EOQ* computations. Purchase parts were handled on an *EOQ/ROP* basis, again with a buffer stock of six weeks' supply.

The basic schedule for the assembly of pumps was set monthly in a master schedule. The master schedule was projected for three months, with the first month representing a firm schedule. The most important input to the master scheduling process was a forecast for each model based on an exponential smoothing system merged with knowledge of contracts, orders, and sales estimates from the salespeople. The basic production rule was to produce one month's estimated requirements for the four models with heavy demand and two months' estimated requirements for the six models with smaller demand. These estimates were then adjusted for backorders or excess inventory. The intention was to maintain a buffer inventory of finished goods of two weeks' supply.

Part shortages at assembly were common, and it was the job of expeditors to get rush orders through the shop to keep the assembly of pumps on schedule. Nevertheless, it was often true that pumps could not be assembled completely because of part shortages and had to be set back in the assembly schedule, resulting in stockouts of finished products.

## MATERIAL REQUIREMENTS PLANNING

The two product lines have always been operated as two separate businesses, both in sales and manufacturing, although the manufacturing facilities were located on the same site. The systems common to both product lines were in the accounting and finance functions. On the retirement of the original owner, the firm was sold to a conglomerate, and a professional manager was installed as president. The new president was satisfied that the manufacturing facilities for the two product lines had to be separate, but she felt that the functions of production planning and control could and should be merged. She attended seminars on *MRP* at a local university and was impressed with the integrative nature of the computer-based systems available. She felt that the requirements generation system available as software for the company computer could generate material requirements for both the wheel and pump product lines. She believed that production order releases keyed to sales requirements would be beneficial to both product lines and that the use of the capacity requirements concepts would enable forward planning on the use of overtime and the prevention of finished goods stockouts.

The president called in the vice-president of production and suggested the use of the *MRP* concept. The vice-president of production had served under the previous owner for 10 years and objected. "They are two different businesses, so it won't work," he said.

What do you recommend?

## Planning and Scheduling of Pots and Pans

15. Cookware, Inc. (CI) produces a line of pots and pans in various types and sizes. For example, saucepans are produced in three sizes: 1, 2, and 3 quarts. The saucepans and covers are made of stainless steel with plastic handles. The stainless steel parts are fabricated in plant, and all other parts are purchased according to specifications. Following the fabrication of the stainless steel parts, they are routed to the saucepan (SP) assembly facility for the assembly of handles and covers, packaging, and final movement to the factory warehouse. There are separate assembly facilities for the other products.

### PLANNING AND SCHEDULING

Forecasts for each product are made for four-week planning periods and a 24-week horizon. Master schedules are constructed based on forecasts, capacities, and inventories on hand, and are updated every four weeks. The production runs for each product are set in each four-week period to match the forecast, but the scheduler "eyeballs" the future and tries to average out differences, attempting to stabilize output. Also, inventories of purchased parts are maintained on a monthly basis, with the intention of ordering a one month's supply for items that have a two-week lead time and a two months' supply for items with a four-week lead time. The preparation cost of purchase orders is $c_P = \$20$ and the preparation and set-up costs for fabrication and assembly orders is $c_P = \$75$. The inventory holding cost is 25 percent of the inventory value.

When the master schedule was updated for each four-week planning period, it was forwarded to the assembly department supervisors, the fabrication department supervisor, and the purchasing department, who were responsible for the coordination necessary to have the required parts available according to the master assembly schedule. However, it was the assembly department supervisors who were responsible for the coordination process, and the development of weekly schedules by product for the upcoming eight weeks (two planning periods), because the maintenance of the assembly master schedule was theirs, and it depended on the availability of all required parts. For example, Joe White, the SP assembly department supervisor, coordinated with the fabrication department supervisor for the supply of pans, brackets, and covers, and with the purchasing department for the supply of the required purchased parts.

When asked, Joe White said that the system worked reasonably well except for the part shortages that often occurred. He said that he dealt with problems resulting from the poor match-up between the master schedule and his resources by scheduling short hours or overtime, and by working with the master schedulers to modify the schedule by shifting orders forward or backward in time to smooth the load. He could also lay off or hire new workers and train them within two weeks because the assembly work involved only simple skills. He preferred not to hire workers for temporary load increases, however, because he would have to lay them off soon, and CI's policy was to maintain a stable work force size. The latest forecasts and master schedules for saucepans has just been issued as shown in Table 6-11. Bills of material and other pertinent data are shown in Tables 6-12 to 6-14. Joe is studying the schedule to see if there will be problems with the normal assembly capacity of 4200 pans per week. Joe can increase capacity by scheduling up to 15 percent overtime, which results in 630 additional pans per week.

What actions should he take? What recommendations would you make to Joe White in developing a weekly schedule? Do you have any recommendations for developing better planning, scheduling, and control systems? What should the schedule be for Part 101, given your weekly schedule?

TABLE 6-11
**SIX PERIOD FORECAST AND MASTER SCHEDULE FOR SAUCEPANS (PLANNING PERIOD IS FOUR WEEKS)**

| Model number | July | July–Aug. | Aug.–Sept. | Sept.–Oct. | Oct.–Nov. | Nov.–Dec. |
|---|---|---|---|---|---|---|
| S1, Forecast | 8,000 | 10,000 | 11,000 | 12,000 | 10,000 | 9,000 |
| Schedule | 9,000 | 9,000 | 11,000 | 11,000 | 10,000 | 10,000 |
| S2, Forecast | 3,800 | 3,900 | 4,000 | 4,200 | 4,100 | 4,000 |
| Schedule | 3,800 | 3,800 | 3,800 | 4,200 | 4,200 | 4,200 |
| S3, Forecast | 1,500 | 1,800 | 2,200 | 2,500 | 2,000 | 2,000 |
| Schedule | 1,800 | 1,900 | 2,000 | 2,100 | 2,100 | 2,100 |

TABLE 6-12
**BILL OF MATERIALS AND ASSOCIATED DATA FOR SAUCEPAN S1**

| Part Number | Description | Number Required per Pan | Cost per Pan | Lead Time, Weeks | Current Inventory |
|---|---|---|---|---|---|
| S1 | One-Quart Saucepan | 1 | $2.75 | 4 | 400 |
| 100 | Pan | 1 | 1.50 | 4 | 3,400 |
| 101 | Handle bracket | 1 | 0.15 | 2 | 11,200 |
| 102 | Right handle | 1 | 0.15 | 4 | 3,500 |
| 103 | Left handle | 1 | 0.15 | 4 | 3,800 |
| 104 | Mounting screw | 2 | 0.05 | 2 | 4,000 |
| 105 | Hook ring | 1 | 0.05 | 2 | 2,500 |
| 106 | Pan cover | 1 | 0.45 | 4 | 2,600 |

TABLE 6-13
**BILL OF MATERIALS AND ASSOCIATED DATA FOR SAUCEPAN S2**

| Part Number | Description | Number Required per Pan | Cost per Pan | Lead Time, Weeks | Current Inventory |
|---|---|---|---|---|---|
| S2 | Two-Quart Saucepan | 1 | $3.25 | 4 | 2,300 |
| 200 | Pan | 1 | 1.90 | 4 | 3,400 |
| 101 | Handle bracket | 1 | 0.15 | 2 | 11,200 |
| 102 | Right handle | 1 | 0.15 | 4 | 3,500 |
| 103 | Left handle | 1 | 0.15 | 4 | 3,800 |
| 104 | Mounting screw | 2 | 0.05 | 2 | 4,000 |
| 105 | Hook ring | 1 | 0.05 | 2 | 2,500 |
| 206 | Pan cover | 1 | 0.55 | 4 | 1,000 |

TABLE 6-14
**BILL OF MATERIALS AND ASSOCIATED DATA FOR SAUCEPAN S3**

| Part Number | Description | Number Required per Pan | Cost per Pan | Lead Time, Weeks | Current Inventory |
|---|---|---|---|---|---|
| S3 | Three-Quart Saucepan | 1 | $3.50 | 4 | 900 |
| 300 | Pan | 1 | 2.05 | 4 | 3,400 |
| 101 | Handle bracket | 1 | 0.15 | 2 | 11,200 |
| 102 | Right handle | 1 | 0.15 | 4 | 3,500 |
| 103 | Left handle | 1 | 0.15 | 4 | 3,800 |
| 104 | Mounting screw | 2 | 0.05 | 2 | 4,000 |
| 105 | Hook ring | 1 | 0.05 | 2 | 2,500 |
| 306 | Pan cover | 1 | 0.65 | 4 | 3,600 |

# REFERENCES

Berry, W. L., "Lot Sizing Procedures for Requirements Planning Systems: A Framework for Analysis," *Production and Inventory Management,* 2nd Quarter, 1972, pp. 13–34.

Biggs, J. R., S. H. Goodman, and S. T. Hardy, "Lot Sizing Rules in a Hierarchical Multi-Stage Inventory System," *Production and Inventory Control Management,* 1st Quarter, 1977.

Blumberg, D. F., "Factors Affecting the Design of a Successful MRP System," *Production and Inventory Management, 21,* 4, 4th Quarter, 1980, pp. 50–62.

Buffa, E. S. and J. G. Miller, *Production-Inventory Systems: Planning and Control,* (3rd ed.), Irwin, Homewood, Ill., 1979.

De Bodt, M. and L. Van Wassenhove, "Lot Sizes and Safety Stocks in MRP: A Case Study," *Production and Inventory Management, 24,* 1, 1983, pp. 1–16.

Fox, R. E., "OPT vs. MRP: Thoughtware vs. Software," *Inventories & Production, 3,* 6, November/December 1983.

Holstein, W. K., "Production Planning and Control Integrated," *Harvard Business Review,* May–June 1968.

Kropp, D., R. Carlson, and J. Jucker, "Heuristic Lot-Sizing Approaches for Dealing with MRP System Nervousness," *Decision Sciences, 14,* 2, 1983, pp. 156–186.

New, C., *Requirements Planning,* Halsted, New York, 1973.

Orlicky, J., *Material Requirements Planning,* McGraw-Hill, New York, 1975.

Peterson, R. and E. A. Silver, *Decisions Systems for Inventory Management and Production Planning,* Wiley, New York, 1985.

Rice, J. W. and T. Yoshikawa, "MRP and Motivation: What Can We Learn from Japan?" *Production and Inventory Management,* 2nd Quarter, 1980, pp. 45–52.

Wagner, H. M. and T. M. Whitin, "Dynamic Version of the Economic Lot Size Model," *Management Science, 5,* 1, October 1958.

Wight, O. W., *The Executive's Guide to Successful MRP II,* Oliver Wight, Ltd. Publications, Williston, Vt., 1982.

# CHAPTER 7

# LINEAR PROGRAMMING—A METHODOLOGICAL OVERVIEW

Linear programming is used most often when we are attempting to allocate some limited or scarce resource among competing activities in such a way that a single stated criterion is optimized (either minimized or maximized). Linear programming is one of the most widely used operations research techniques and is applicable to a wide variety of production and operations problems.

## The Meaning of Linearity

In linear models, we *must* use only linear mathematical expressions. In Figure 7-1 we show equations of both linear and nonlinear mathematical expressions, together with their graphs. Figures 7-1*a* and 7-1*b* are graphs of linear expressions, which appear as straight lines. Figures 7-1*c* and 7-1*d* are graphs of nonlinear expressions because the equation in Figure 7-1*c* contains an $x^2$ term and that in Figure 7-1*d* contains the cross product of $x_1x_2$.

Figure 7-1 also illustrates the mathematical form of the constraints. In the shaded portion of Figure 7-1*b*, we see the expression $x_1 - 2x_2 \geq 4$, which states that $x_1 - 2x_2$ must be greater than or equal to ($\geq$) 4. When it is equal to 4, we have the straight line. Otherwise, the constraints of the inequality expression require that all combinations of $x_1$ and $x_2$ be in the shaded portion of the graph. Conversely, all combinations of $x_1$ and $x_2$ that fall above the straight line are not admissible because they do not satisfy the constraint $x_1 - 2x_2 \geq 4$.

Figure 7-1*d* shows a nonlinear constraint expression in the shaded portion of the graph. The constraints of that expression require that all combinations of $x_1$ and $x_2$ be above the curve (in the shaded portion) because the expression states that $x_1 - 2x_1x_2$ must be less than or equal to ($\leq$) 4. Again, when the statement on the left-hand side of the expression is equal to 4, all points fall on the curve.

Mathematical statements of constraints may be less than or equal to ($\leq$), equal to ($=$), and greater than or equal to ($\geq$). *Linear* constraints, illustrated by the expression in the shaded portion of Figure 7-1*b*, will be very important in linear optimization models.

## Elements of the Model Building Process

To develop a linear optimization model, we use the following process:

1. Define the decision variables.
2. Define the objective function, $Z$, a linear equation involving the decision variables that identifies our objective in the problem-solving effort. This equation predicts the effects on the objective function of choosing different values for the decision variables. The objective function is either minimized or maximized. For example, if $Z$ is defined as total production cost, then it is minimized. If $Z$ is defined as total profits, then it is maximized. Other examples of $Z$ include project completion time (minimized), production and distribution costs (minimized), and the production rate of an assembly line (maximized).

FIGURE 7-1
**EXAMPLES OF LINEAR AND NONLINEAR EXPRESSIONS: (a) AND (b) ARE LINEAR; (c) AND (d) ARE NONLINEAR, BECAUSE (c) HAS AN $x^2$ TERM AND (d) CONTAINS THE CROSS PRODUCT TERM $x_1x_2$. THE SHADED PORTIONS OF BOTH (b) AND (d) CONTAIN INEQUALITY EXPRESSIONS DESCRIBING CONSTRAINTS; THAT IS, VALUES OF $x_1$ AND $x_2$ FALLING WITHIN THE SHADED AREAS ARE ADMISSIBLE BUT POINTS BEYOND THE CURVE ARE NOT.**

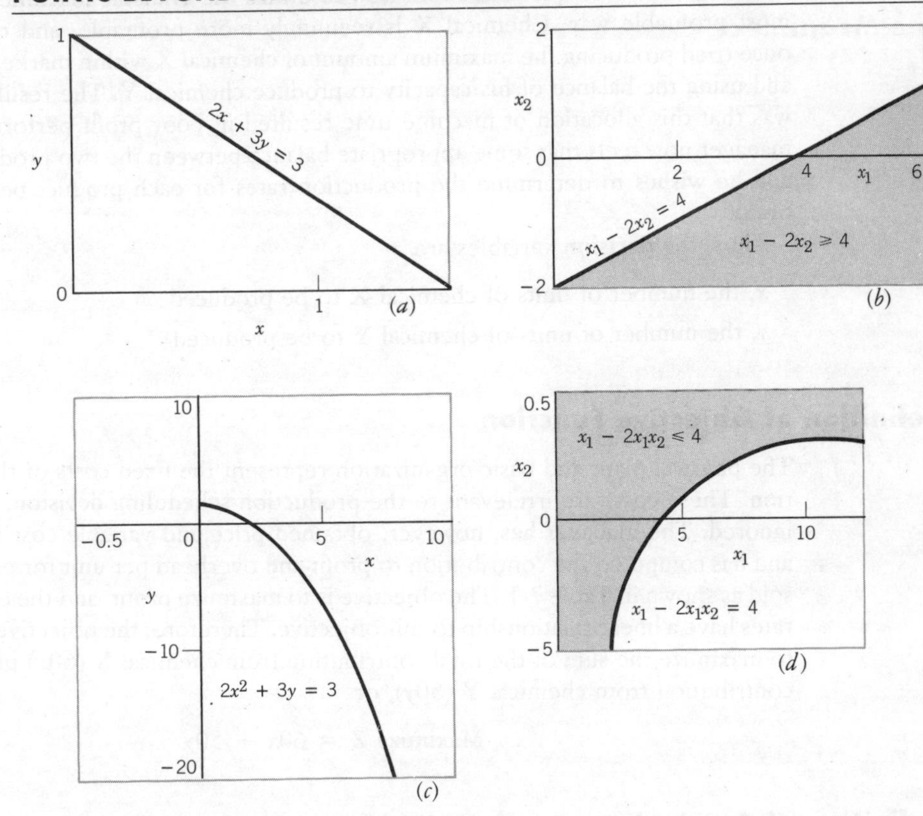


3. Define the constraints, which are linear expressions involving the decision variables that specify the restrictions on the decisions that can be made. *Feasible alternatives* can be generated by selecting values for the decision variables that satisfy these constraints.

## FORMULATION OF A TWO-PRODUCT MODEL

A chemical manufacturer produces two products, which we shall call chemical X and chemical Y. Each product is manufactured by a two-step process that involves blending and mixing in machine A and packaging on machine B. The two products complement each other because the same production facilities can be used for both products, thus achieving better utilization of these facilities.

## Definition of Decision Variables

Since the facilities are shared and the costs and profits from each product are different, there is a question about how to utilize the available machine time in the most profitable way. Chemical X is seemingly more profitable, and the manager once tried producing the maximum amount of chemical X within market limitations and using the balance of his capacity to produce chemical Y. The result, however, was that this allocation of machine time resulted in poor profit performance. The manager now feels that some appropriate balance between the two products is best, and he wishes to determine the production rates for each product per two-week period.

Thus, the decision variables are

$x$, the number of units of chemical X to be produced

$y$, the number of units of chemical Y to be produced

## Definition of Objective Function

The physical plant and basic organization represent the fixed costs of the organization. These costs are irrelevant to the production scheduling decision, so they are ignored. The manager has, however, obtained price and variable cost information and has computed the contribution to profit and overhead per unit for each product sold as shown in Table 7-1. The objective is to maximize profit, and the contribution rates have a linear relationship to this objective. Therefore, the objective function is to maximize the sum of the total contribution from chemical X ($60x$) plus the total contribution from chemical Y ($50y$), or

$$\text{Maximize } Z = 60x + 50y$$

## Definition of Constraints

The processing times for each unit of the two products on the mixing machine, A, and the packaging machine, B, are as follows:

| Product | Machine A (hours/unit) | Machine B (hours/unit) |
|---|---|---|
| Chemical X | 2 | 3 |
| Chemical Y | 4 | 2 |

For the upcoming two-week period, machine A has 80 hours of processing time available and machine B has 60 hours available.

TABLE 7-1
**SALES PRICES, VARIABLE COSTS, AND CONTRIBUTIONS PER UNIT FOR CHEMICALS X AND Y**

| | Sales Price ($p$) | Variable Costs ($c$) | Contribution to Profit and Overhead ($r = p - c$) |
|---|---|---|---|
| Chemical X | $350 | $290 | $60 |
| Chemical Y | 450 | 400 | 50 |

#### MACHINE A CONSTRAINT

Since we are limited by the 80 hours available on the mixing machine A, the total time spent in the manufacture of chemical X and chemical Y cannot exceed the total time available. For machine A, because chemical X requires two hours per unit and chemical Y requires four hours per unit, the total time spent on the two products must be less than or equal to 80 hours; that is,

$$2x + 4y \leq 80$$

#### MACHINE B CONSTRAINT

Similarly, the available time on the packaging machine B is limited to 60 hours. Because chemical X requires three hours per unit and chemical Y requires two hours per unit, the total hours for the two products must be less than or equal to 60 hours; that is,

$$3x + 2y \leq 60$$

#### MARKETING CONSTRAINTS

Market forecasts indicate that we can expect to sell a maximum of 16 units of chemical X and 18 units of chemical Y. Therefore,

$$x \leq 16$$
$$y \leq 18$$

#### MINIMUM PRODUCTION CONSTRAINTS

The minimum production for each product is zero. Therefore,

$$x \geq 0$$
$$y \geq 0$$

## The Linear Optimization Model

We can now summarize a statement of the linear optimization model for the two-product chemical company in the standard linear programming format as follows:

$$\text{Maximize } Z = 60x + 50y$$

subject to

$$\begin{aligned} 2x + 4y &\le 80 && \text{(machine A)} \\ 3x + 2y &\le 60 && \text{(machine B)} \\ x &\le 16 && \text{(demand for chemical X)} \\ y &\le 18 && \text{(demand for chemical Y)} \\ x &\ge 0 && \text{(minimum production for chemical X)} \\ y &\ge 0 && \text{(minimum production for chemical Y)} \end{aligned}$$

## ASSUMPTIONS OF LINEAR PROGRAMMING

A general mathematical model for a linear programming problem such as that of the chemical manufacturer discussed previously is

$$\text{Maximize } Z = c_1x_1 + c_2x_2 + \ldots + c_nx_n$$

Subject to the constraints

$$\begin{aligned} a_{11}x_1 + a_{12}x_2 + \ldots + a_{1n}x_n &\le b_1 \\ a_{21}x_1 + a_{22}x_2 + \ldots + a_{2n}x_n &\le b_2 \\ &\ldots \\ a_{m1}x_1 + a_{m2}x_2 + \ldots + a_{mn}x_n &\le b_m \end{aligned}$$

and,

$$x_1 \ge 0, x_2 \ge 0, \ldots, x_n \ge 0$$

In the preceding formulation $x_j$ is the level of activity J (decision variable), $c_j$ is the increase in $Z$ that would result from each unit increase in $x_j$ (contribution or cost coefficient), $b_i$ is the amount of resource I, and $a_{ij}$ is the amount of resource I consumed by each unit of activity J.

In some situations, the objective function $Z$ may be minimized, or the constraints may involve greater than or equal to ($\ge$) inequality, or they may be represented in equation form with equality ($=$) constraints. Several assumptions are implicitly made in the above formulation. These assumptions are summarized in the following discussion.

### Certainty

All parameters of the model (the $c_j$, $b_i$, and $a_{ij}$ values) are known constants. Since in real world applications we will not know precisely all of these parameter values precisely, sensitivity analysis, discussed later, is a helpful way to ensure the stability of the results obtained.

### Proportionality

Suppose that only one activity, K, is undertaken and that all other activities are set at the zero level. In this case,

$$Z = c_kx_k$$

and the usage of each resource I is equal to $a_{ik}x_k$. Note that both the objective function and the resource usage are proportional to the level of each activity K undertaken by itself. This assumption will exclude a fixed cost for starting up an activity. In our chemical example, we are assuming that the contribution from a product remains proportional to the number of units produced over the entire range. That is, at higher levels of production, the contribution should not go up because of increased production efficiencies. Some types of nonproportionality can be handled by linear programming by appropriately reformulating the problem.

### Additivity

This assumption requires that for any given level of activities ($x_1, x_2, \ldots, x_n$), the total value of the objective function $Z$ and the total usage of each resource equal the sum of the contribution or the resource use of each activity undertaken by itself. Note that proportionality may be satisfied but additivity is violated if there are cross product terms indicating interaction between the activities. For example, the following objectives function has a cross product term involving $x_1$ and $x_2$:

$$Z = c_1x_1 + c_2x_2 + c_3x_1x_2$$

### Divisibility

Each activity in linear programming can take on any fractional value, such as $x_1 = 1.375$. Thus an activity can be divided into fractional levels. If $x_1$ is the number of cars produced, then the divisibility assumption is violated as $x_1$ can take on only integer values. If the numbers involved are large, we can use linear programming as an approximation and round up or down to obtain an integer solution. In general, however, formal models of integer programming will have to be employed if some of the decision variables can take on only integer values.

## SOLUTION OF THE TWO-PRODUCT MODEL

### A Graphical Solution

We can gain some insight into the solution of a linear optimization model by analyzing it graphically. Although this is not a practical approach for solving large linear optimization models of real-world problems, the basic concepts do carry over into those problems.

The constraints of the linear optimization model are shown in Figure 7-2. To see how they were plotted, suppose we consider the machine A constraint

$$2x + 4y \leq 80 \tag{1}$$

The simplest way to show the values of $x$ and $y$ that satisfy an inequality is to plot the straight line corresponding to the equation obtained by replacing the inequality sign

FIGURE 7-2
**GRAPHIC REPRESENTATION OF THE LIMITATIONS IMPOSED BY MACHINE CAPACITY, MARKETING, AND MINIMUM PRODUCTION CONSTRAINTS. THE AREA ENCLOSED BY *abcdef* INCLUDES ALL FEASIBLE SOLUTIONS TO THE MODEL.**

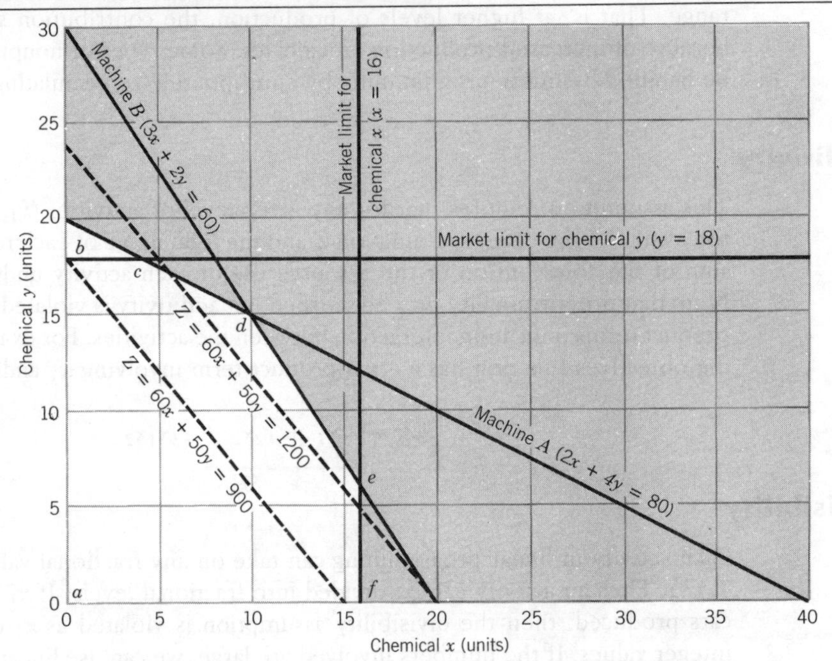


with an equality sign; that is, for this example we plot the line corresponding to the equality

$$2x + 4y = 80 \tag{2}$$

Generally, the easiest way to plot an equality is to find the $x$-intercept, the point on the $x$ axis representing the value of $x$ that satisfies this equality constraint when $y = 0$, and the $y$-intercept, the value of $y$ that satisfies the equality when $x = 0$.

If $y = 0$ in Equation 2, then $2x + 4(0) = 80$ or $2x = 80$. Therefore, $x = 80/2 = 40$ is the $x$-intercept value for Equation 2 as shown in Figure 7-2. If $x = 0$, then $2(0) + 4y = 80$, so $y = 20$ is the $y$-intercept value. Since we know that Equation 2 passes through the two points (40, 0) and (0, 20), the line can be plotted easily.

This straight line represents all the values of $x$ and $y$ that satisfy Equation 2, but what about the $x$ and $y$ pairs that satisfy Inequality 1? All the points that satisfy an inequality lie on one side of the line corresponding to the equation, and all the points that violate the inequality lie on the other side. On which side of the line representing Equation 2 do the points lie that satisfy Inequality 1? The simplest way to decide is often to consider the origin (0, 0) and check to see if the values $x = 0$ and $y = 0$ satisfy the inequality. If they do, then the origin and all other points that lie on the same side of the equality line 2 satisfy Inequality 1. Otherwise, all points on the side of line 2 away from the origin satisfy Inequality 1. In our example, $2(0) + 4(0) = 0$ and $0 \leq 80$, so the origin satisfies Inequality 1.

The solution to a linear optimization model must simultaneously satisfy *all* the constraints of the model. Points that violate one or more of the constraints of the two-product model are in the shaded areas of Figure 7-2. For example, the values $x = 0$ and $y = 20$ satisfy the constraints $2x + 4y \leq 80$ and $3x + 2y \leq 60$, but they violate the constraint $y \leq 18$. Therefore, the point (0, 20) is in the shaded region of Figure 7-2. The solution to our problem lies somewhere within the set of feasible decisions, the solution space *abcdef*. Any production schedule with a combination of amounts $x$ and $y$ that falls outside this solution space is not feasible because it does not simultaneously satisfy all the constraints.

We have also plotted in Figure 7-2 the linear objective function for two values of the total contribution, $Z = \$900$ and $Z = \$1200$. When we set $Z = \$900$, for example,

$$60x + 50y = 900$$

Then, when $x = 0$, the $y$-intercept must be $y = 18$ because $60(0) + 50(18) = 900$; when $y = 0$, we have $60x + 50(0) = 900$ and $x = 900/60 = 15$. The resulting straight line is very simple to plot in Figure 7-2. The portion of the \$900 line that lies within the solution space of points that simultaneously satisfy all of the constraints defines all the feasible solutions that would produce a contribution of $Z = \$900$. Since our objective is to maximize contribution, what happens if we increase $Z$ to \$1200? Since the slope of the objective function has not changed, the line for $Z = \$1200$ is parallel to the \$900 line, and closer to point $d$, as can be seen in Figure 7-2. For this simple problem, it is now rather obvious that if we substituted larger and larger values of $Z$ in the objective function, lines parallel to the \$900 and \$1200 lines would result. A line through point $d$ would define the combination of $x$ and $y$ with the maximum possible contribution within the feasible solution space. Now we will see how this same solution point might be found using a computer program for solving linear optimization models.

## Computer Solution and Interpretation

We will assume that we have a mechanism for solving linear optimization models when they are formulated in the standard format just discussed. Indeed, linear programming computing codes for solving large-scale linear programming problems are commonly available in both interactive mode (available from a time-share terminal) and batch mode. In order to use either of these types of computing programs for the solution of linear optimization models, the problem must be presented to the "black box" in the precise form required. We shall use the software called LINDO to illustrate the solutions to the problems in this chapter (see Schrage, 1984).

Now, let us return to the chemical production problem for which we just formulated the linear optimization model in standard form. Figure 7-3 shows a portion of the computer printout for the problem.

FIGURE 7-3
**THE CHEMICAL PRODUCTION PROBLEM: (*a*) LINDO COMPUTER INPUT AND (*b*) COMPUTER SOLUTION.**

```
MAX     60 CHEMX   + 50 CHEMY
SUBJECT TO
   2)    2 CHEMX   + 4  CHEMY <= 80
   3)    3 CHEMX   + 2  CHEMY <= 60
   4)      CHEMX   <= 16
   5)    CHEMY     <= 18
END
```

(*a*)

```
          LP OPTIMUM FOUND   AT STEP          3

                 OBJECTIVE FUNCTION VALUE

   1)               1350.00000

VARIABLE            VALUE              REDUCED COST
   CHEMX            10.000000             .000000
   CHEMY            15.000000             .000000

ROW                 SLACK               DUAL PRICES
   2)               .000000              3.750000
   3)               .000000             17.500000
   4)               6.000000              .000000
   5)               3.000000              .000000

NO. ITERATIONS=        3
```

(*b*)

## COMPUTER INPUT

In Figure 7-3*a* we see the computer input for the linear optimization model; it is in almost the same from that we have been using. Unless your computer center has made the necessary conversion in the output, as is the case with the computer output we will show, the "<=" will mean "≤" in constraint statements. We need not enter the last two constraints, $x \geq 0$ and $y \geq 0$, because the computer program assumes that none of the decision variables can take on negative values.

## COMPUTER OUTPUT

Figure 7-3*b* shows the solution output. On the line labeled "1)," the optimum value of the objective function is shown, $1350. In other words, it states that $Z = 1350$ in the objective function for an optimal solution.

Next, the values of the variables in the optimum solution are shown under the column heading "VALUE." The column labeled "REDUCED COST" lists the marginal amount by which the objective function coefficient of each variable must change before it would appear in the optimal solution. These are listed as zero in our example because the variables are already in the optimal solution.

Now let us consider variables listed in the solution, *CHEMX* and *CHEMY*. The solution states that their optimal values are 10 and 15 units, respectively. Note that this is point *d* in Figure 7-2, the point where the capacity constraint lines for machines A and B intersect, as we expected, based on our graphical analysis of this problem. This is an important observation that we shall use in understanding how the linear programming algorithm actually works.

Using the solution values of *CHEMX* and *CHEMY*, we insert them in the objective function and compute *Z*:

$$Z = 60 \times 10 + 50 \times 15 = 1350$$

This result checks with the optimum value of *Z* given by the computer solution.

Checking one further bit of logic, if the solution to our problem lies at the intersection of the lines of the two capacity constraint equations, then we should be able to solve the equations for the two lines simultaneously to determine the values of *CHEMX* and *CHEMY* that are common to both equations. First, let us use the equation for machine A and solve for $x$:

$$2x + 4y = 80$$

Therefore,

$$\begin{aligned} x &= 80/2 - 4y/2 \\ &= 40 - 2y \end{aligned}$$

We then substitute this value of $x$ in the constraint equation for machine B:

$$\begin{aligned} 3(40 - 2y) + 2y &= 60 \\ 120 - 6y + 2y &= 60 \\ 4y &= 60 \\ y &= 15 \end{aligned}$$

This value of $y$ checks with our computer solution. Now, we substitute $y = 15$ in the machine A constraint equation to determine the value of $x$,

$$\begin{aligned} 2x + 4(15) &= 80 \\ x &= (80 - 60)/2 \\ &= 10 \end{aligned}$$

Thus, we have verified that the solution to our problem lies at point *d* of Figure 7-2 where the two constraint equations intersect. Another interpretation of this fact is that machines A and B, our two productive resources, are completely utilized in this solution; there is no residual slack machine capacity. This fact is important because any of the other feasible solutions in the polygon *abcdef* of Figure 7-2 would involve some slack capacity in one or both of the two machines. If there had been slack capacity for either of the machines in the optimum solution, that fact would have been indicated in the computer output for the optimum solution. In some more complex problems, there may be slack capacity for a productive resource in the optimum solution.

The computer output also gives us values for "SLACK" and "DUAL PRICES." The nonzero slack values are for constraints 4 and 5, the market constraints. Constraint 4, $CHEMX \leq 16$ was the market limit for that product. The solution simply points out to us that if we produce according to the optimum solution where $CHEMX = 10$, there will be unsatisfied demand (slack) of 6; this fits in with the market constraint because $CHEMX + SLACK4 = 10 + 6 = 16$. Similarly, the value of $SLACK5 = 3$ agrees with the market constraint 5, $CHEMY \leq 18$, because $CHEMY + SLACK4 = 15 + 3 = 18$.

These interpretations of the optimum solution to the chemical production problem are rather simple. The important point is that equivalent interpretations of more complex problems are a straightforward extension of these ideas. The solution will state the combination of variables that optimizes the objective function. Some, but not necessarily all, of the constraints will be controlling constraints, and there will be slack in some of the resources; that is, all the resources will not be fully utilized. In our example, the slack is in the demand for the two products. Note, however, that if the demand for *CHEMY* drops to only 14, that is, $y = 14$, it would become one of the controlling ("tight") constraints, as may be seen in Figure 7-2, and there would be some slack capacity in machine A.

The "DUAL PRICES" column, also called "shadow prices," will be discussed in the next section in connection with sensitivity analysis and additional interpretations of the results.

## SENSITIVITY ANALYSIS AND INTERPRETATION OF RESULTS

If we want only the solution to the problem—the optimal combination of variables, the value of slack variables, and the optimum value of the objective function—we could stop at this point. However, additional valuable information can be obtained from a sensitivity analysis.

Although the optimum solution states what should be done now, given the objective function and the constraints, a sensitivity analysis raises questions about opportunities and perhaps about what could or should be done to improve the solution to the managerial problem.

Figure 7-4 presents the computer output of LINDO in response to the query, "DO RANGE (SENSITIVITY ANALYSIS)?". This output in combination with the DUAL PRICES (shadow prices) output provides additional valuable information.

### Cost Coefficient Ranges (Price Sensitivity)

The contribution rates in the objective function are generally termed *prices*. Recall that the contribution of a unit of *CHEMX* was \$60 and that for a unit of *CHEMY*

FIGURE 7-4
**LINDO SENSITIVITY ANALYSIS FOR THE CHEMICAL PRODUCTION PROBLEM.**

RANGES IN WHICH THE BASIS IS UNCHANGED

| | | COST COEFFICIENT RANGES | |
|---|---|---|---|
| VARIABLE | CURRENT COEF | ALLOWABLE INCREASE | ALLOWABLE DECREASE |
| CHEMX | 60.000000 | 15.000000 | 35.000000 |
| CHEMY | 50.000000 | 70.000000 | 10.000000 |

| | | RIGHTHAND SIDE RANGES | |
|---|---|---|---|
| ROW | CURRENT RHS | ALLOWABLE INCREASE | ALLOWABLE DECREASE |
| 2 | 80.000000 | 8.000000 | 24.000000 |
| 3 | 60.000000 | 12.000000 | 12.000000 |
| 4 | 16.000000 | INFINITY | 6.000000 |
| 5 | 18.000000 | INFINITY | 3.000000 |

was \$50. These contributions are shown as the "CURRENT COEF" values in Figure 7-4, under the general heading "COST COEFFICIENT RANGES." But, what if prices change? Would the changes affect the solution? The upper and lower bounds for prices, shown in Figure 7-4 under the headings "ALLOWABLE INCREASE" and "ALLOWABLE DECREASE," indicate the range of prices (contribution rates) for which the optimum solution ($x = 10, y = 15$) is still optimum. For example, the contribution rate for *CHEMX* could be anywhere in the range of \$60 − \$35 = \$25 to \$60 + \$15 = \$75 and the optimum amount of *CHEMX* and *CHEMY* would still be as indicated in the present solution: 10 units of *CHEMX* and 15 units of *CHEMY*. Of course, the total contribution would change because of the change in the contribution rate, but the *optimal decision* would remain the same.

There is a practical significance to the price sensitivity. For example, the manager might estimate the contribution of *CHEMX* at \$60, but such figures are seldom absolutely precise. Suppose that the contribution is actually somewhere in the \$55 to \$65 range. In this case, the same solution applies. The result is that the use of *rough* estimates of contribution rates is adequate, so we should not spend additional time and money to refine these estimates. Thus, the calculated bounds in relation to managerial judgments help indicate how we should allocate time and money to refine cost information. If the bounds are tight, it may be worthwhile to be precise, but if they are loose, we would gain nothing by attempting to improve the estimates.

## Dual Prices (Shadow Prices)

The dual or shadow prices indicate the value of a marginal unit in the right-hand side of the constraint. For example, recall the meaning of the first constraint for machine A ($2\ CHEMX + 4\ CHEMY \leq 80$). It states that the total available capacity for machine A is 80 hours. What would be the marginal value (in the objective function) of one additional unit of capacity? The answer is given in Figure 7-3*b* as \$3.75. Thus, if the capacity of machine A were 81 hours, the extra hour would add $3.75 to the total contribution *Z*. Conversely, if only 79 hours were available, this amount would be subtracted from the total contribution.

Now observe that the dual price for machine B capacity is $17.50. The marginal value of capacity for machine B is 17.50/3.75 = 4.7 times that for machine A. Thus, the dual prices tell the manager that the opportunity provided by increasing machine B capacity is relatively large, which provides information for the appraisal of expansion proposals for both machines.

The dual prices for constraints 3 and 4 (demands) are zero because these constraints do not limit us in the current solution. If demand for *CHEMY* dropped to 14, then it would become one of the controlling constraints, as we noted previously. The optimum solution would then change. In addition, the shadow price for constraint 4 would become some positive value, indicating a marginal value to increasing demand for *CHEMY* and perhaps providing the manager with information to appraise programs to stimulate demand.

## Right-Hand Side Ranges

We just stated the meaning of the "DUAL PRICES" information in Figure 7-3—the value of marginal units of resources. But, for what ranges are these marginal values valid? Can we increase capacity for machine B to two or three times its present capacity and expect to obtain an additional $17.50 per unit in the objective function? No, there are limits or bounds, and the "RIGHTHAND SIDE RANGES" listed in Figure 7-4 tell us exactly what they are. Taking the capacity of machine B as an example, it is currently 60 hours, as is shown in Figure 7-4 under the "CURRENT RHS" column. We can also see that the dual price is valid in the range of 60 − 12 = 48 hours to 60 + 12 = 72 hours.

Thus, if we could increase the capacity of machine B to 72 hours, we would obtain an additional $17.50 × 12 = $210 in total contribution. We would be able to increase contribution by $210 × 100/1350 = 15.6 percent. On the down side, if we had a breakdown of machine B, for example, and the available hours fell to the lower bound of 48, we would lose $210 in total contribution. The interpretation for the bounds on the capacity of machine A is similar.

Now let us examine the significance of these bounds on the demand for the two products. Take constraint 5, the demand for *CHEMY*, for example. Its lower bound is 15. A dual price of zero still applies if demand falls to 15; that is, the constraint is still ineffective. But, as we have already noted, if demand falls below 15, constraint 5 becomes one of those controlling the solution.

The upper bound for constraint 5 is listed as "INFINITY," indicating that there is no upper bound.

## Summary

Given a linear optimization model stated in the format we have specified, we can use a computer program to provide the optimum combination of decision variables, the optimum value of the objective function, and the values of slack capacity or other resources in the system. In interpreting the solution, however, we can also obtain the value of a marginal unit of each resource (the shadow price) and the range for which this value is valid. In addition, we can obtain the range of prices (contribution rates in our example) in the objective function for which the printed solution is valid.

Understanding the significance of the optimum solution and the sensitivity analysis in the context of the real problem has great value. Decision makers are in a position to appraise various proposals for changing the optimum solution. They should not view the optimum solution as necessarily the final decision, but as a basis for asking "what if" questions. The sensitivity analysis provides information regarding many possible "what if" questions, and it may also suggest variations of the model that may require additional computer runs.

## THE SIMPLEX METHOD

The *simplex method* is a general procedure for solving linear programming problems. This method is remarkably efficient, and it is capable of solving very large problems, involving several hundred or even several thousand variables and constraints, using computers. While a computer code is always used to solve linear programs, it is important to learn how the method works.

We will use a modification of the chemical production problem as a vehicle for discussion. Because we can represent the problem in graphic form and because we already know the optimal solution, we can readily see what is happening at each stage of the algorithm. We will simplify the problem slightly by eliminating the demand constraints. Recall that for the stated problem, these constraints were not effective in dictating the optimal solution anyway. Eliminating them allows a simpler, more direct explanation of the procedure.

### Formulation

The problem is one of allocating time on machines A and B to the two products, chemical X and chemical Y, in such a way that contribution to profit and overhead would be maximized. The time requirements of the two machines for each product were given and the total available time on the two machines was limited. Therefore, the resulting modified linear optimization model is

$$\text{Maximize } Z = 60x + 50y$$

subject to

$$
\begin{aligned}
2x + 4y &\leq 80 && \text{(machine A)}\\
3x + 2y &\leq 60 && \text{(machine B)}\\
x &\geq 0 && \text{(minimum production for chemical X)}\\
y &\geq 0 && \text{(minimum production for chemical Y)}
\end{aligned}
$$

## Graphic Solution

Figure 7-5 shows the constraints plotted on a graph and identifies the feasible solution space, *abcd*, and the previously determined optimal allocation of machine time at point *c*; that is, $x = 10$ units and $y = 15$ units. Recall also that the contribution for the optimal solution was $1350.

In Figure 7-5, we have plotted the linear objective function for two values of total contribution, $Z = \$900$ and $Z = \$1200$. It is now rather obvious for this simple problem that if we substitute larger and larger values of $Z$ in the objective function, lines parallel to the $900 and $1200 lines would result and a line through point *c* would define the combination of $x$ and $y$ with the maximum possible contribution within the feasible solution space. Figure 7-5, then, provides us with a clear picture of the problem and the relationship among the various solutions of the objective function.

## Slack Variables

First, we note the physical meaning of the constraints on the available time for machines A and B. For machine A, because chemical X requires 2 hours per unit and chemical Y requires 4 hours per unit and we are limited to a total of 80 hours, we write the inequality constraint:

$$2x + 4y \leq 80 \tag{1}$$

For machine B, we write the inequality constraint:

$$3x + 2y \leq 60 \tag{2}$$

These inequalities state that the use of machines A and B is *less than* or equal to 80 and 60 hours, respectively; that is, there *could* be idle machine time. To account for any slack available, we could convert Inequalities 1 and 2 into equations by defining *slack variables* to represent the possible idle time. Therefore,

$$2x + 4y + W_A = 80 \tag{3}$$

$$3x + 2y + W_B = 60 \tag{4}$$

where $W_A$ is the idle time for machine A, and $W_B$ is the idle time for machine B. We also require $W_A$ and $W_B$ to be nonnegative ($W_A$, $W_B \geq 0$). The constraints plotted in Figure 7-5 are then lines that indicate the full use of machine A when $W_A = 0$ and of machine B when $W_B = 0$. Solutions that involve some idle time are permissible and would fall below one or both of the constraint lines, which would be within the solution space *abcd*.

The effect of solutions involving slack (idle machine time) is easy to see through examples. Assume that the production schedule is 9 units of chemical X and 14 units of chemical Y. Because 2 hours per unit of chemical X and 4 hours per unit of chemical Y are required of machine A time and because machine A has a total of 80 hours available, we have from Equation 3

$$W_A = 80 - (2)(9) - (4)(14) = 80 - 74 = 6 \text{ hours}$$

Thus, there are 74 productive hours, so the slack idle time for machine A is 6 hours.

FIGURE 7-5
**GRAPHIC SOLUTION OF THE EXAMPLE USED FOR INTERPRETATION OF THE SIMPLEX METHOD.**

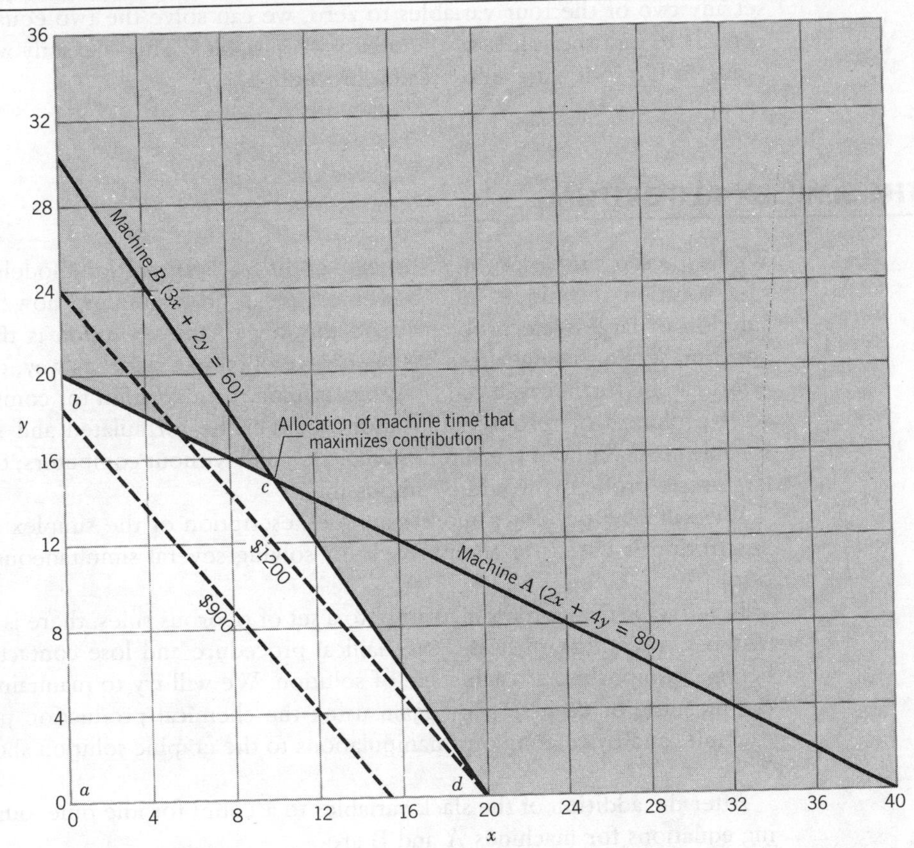


Similarly, the idle time for machine B, from Equation 4, would be

$$W_B = 60 - (3)(9) - (2)(14) = 60 - 55 = 5 \text{ hours}$$

Now examine Figure 7-5 and note that the point $x = 9$, $y = 14$ falls inside the feasible solution space but not on any of the constraint lines. This type of solution is called a *nonbasic solution.*

With the slack variables now included in the formulation, the objective function is actually

$$\text{Maximize } Z = 60x + 50y + (0)W_A + (0)W_B$$

The zero coefficients for the slack variables are appropriate because they make no contribution to profit. The total contribution of the nonbasic solution is

$$Z = (60)(9) + (50)(14) + (0)(6) + (0)(5) = 540 + 700 + 0 + 0 = 1240$$

Let us return to Equations 3 and 4, with four unknown variables plus the objective function. Now, recall from simple algebra that we can solve equations simultaneously if they contain the same number of unknowns as there are equations. If we set any two of the four variables to zero, we can solve the two equations simultaneously to find the values of the other two variables. This is exactly what we will be doing in the following step-by-step procedure.

## THE SIMPLEX ALGORITHM

We have used simple problems to explain linear optimization models and the simplex solution technique. The power of linear programming, however, is in the solution of large-scale problems, and the key to their solution is the simplex algorithm. When the algorithm has been developed in a rigorous way, the computing effort can be further reduced by programming the algorithm for computers. Large-scale problems of resource allocation can then be formulated and solved at reasonable cost. Without the simplex algorithm and without computers, the solution of large-scale problems would be impossible.

We will now present a more rigorous description of the simplex method. This description is based on an approach for solving several simultaneous linear equations.

In reducing the simplex algorithm to a set of rigorous rules, there is a risk that we may begin to think of it as a mechanical procedure and lose contact with what is being accomplished at each stage of solution. We will try to maintain contact with the meaning of each step by again using the chemical production problem as an example, and by relating our manipulations to the graphic solution shown in Figure 7-5.

After the addition of the slack variables to account for idle time, our two restricting equations for machines A and B are

$$2x + 4y + W_A = 80 \tag{5}$$

$$3x + 2y + W_B = 60 \tag{6}$$

An initial solution to this set of equations is found by setting $x = y = 0$, which gives $W_A = 80$ and $W_B = 60$. This solution is easy to see, because $W_A$ has a coefficient of $+1$ in Equation 5 but does not appear in Equation 6, and $W_B$ has a coefficient of $+1$ in Equation 6 but does not appear in Equation 5.

The objective function for this problem can be written as

$$Z = 60x + 50y + (0)W_A + (0)W_B \tag{7}$$

because idle time contributes nothing to profits or overhead. Substituting the initial solution of $W_A = 80$ and $W_B = 60$ into Equation 7 gives

$$Z - 60x - 50y = (0)80 + (0)60 = 0 \tag{8}$$

as the corresponding value of the objective function.

We can combine Equation 8 with Equations 5 and 6 and write

$$
\begin{aligned}
Z - 60x - 50y \qquad\qquad &= 0 \qquad \text{(row 0)}\\
2x + 4y + W_A \qquad &= 80 \qquad \text{(row 1)}\\
3x + 2y \qquad + W_B &= 60 \qquad \text{(row 2)}
\end{aligned}
$$

where all the variables must also be nonnegative. This is the set of *initial equations* that is associated with the initial solution $x = y = 0$, $W_A = 80$, and $W_B = 60$.

## Improving the Initial Solution

To improve the initial solution, we use the test for optimality: "Are there coefficients in the objective function that indicate that $Z$ can be increased?" If there are, we know that we can substitute a variable in the solution that has a higher contribution rate to the objective function than one of the variables now in the solution. Variables with *negative* coefficients in row 0 will improve the objective function if they are brought into the solution.

### IDENTIFYING THE ENTERING VARIABLE AND KEY COLUMN

Any variable with a negative coefficient in row 0 will improve (increase) the objective function if its value is increased from 0. The following rule is useful in selecting the entering variable:

*Rule I.* If there are variables with negative coefficients in row 0, choose the one with the most negative coefficient as the *entering variable.* If there are no variables with negative coefficients in row 0, the current solution is optimal.

In this example, we choose $x$ as the entering variable according to Rule I. This choice determines the "direction of change" in the solution.

The coefficients of the entering variable $x$, $-60$ in row 0, 2 in row 1, and 3 in row 2, will play a key role in the computations of the simplex algorithm. Because these coefficients are arranged vertically as a column of numbers in rows 0, 1, and 2, we designate them as the *key column*.

### IDENTIFYING THE KEY ROW

If $x$ increases by 1 unit, $W_A$ must decrease by 2 units (the coefficient of $x$ in row 1) in order to maintain the equality in row 1, and $W_B$ must decrease by 3 units (the coefficient of $x$ in row 2) to maintain the equality in row 2. If $W_A$ decreases from its initial value of 80 units to 0, $x$ could increase to $80/2 = 40$; if $W_B$ decreases from its initial value of 60, $x$ could increase to $60/3 = 20$. The latter, 20, would be reached first as $x$ increases. Therefore, the relationship between $W_B$ and $x$ in row 2 *limits* the size of $x$, so we designate row 2 as the *key row* in our calculations.

Notice that this result was determined by dividing the right-hand side of each row (ignoring row 0) by the corresponding number in the key column. If the coefficient in the key column for a row were negative or zero, the row would be ignored because increasing the entering variable would not force another variable to zero. This idea can be implemented in the simplex algorithm with a second rule.

*Rule II.* Taking the ratios of the right-hand sides of the rows to the corresponding coefficients of the key column (ignoring zero or negative coefficients), choose the row with the smallest ratio as the *key row.*

Rule II determines the "amount of change" in the solution.

### PIVOTING

We now know the entering variable $x$, the key column of the coefficients of $x$, and the key row, row 2. The coefficient of the entering variable $x$ that is in the key column and in the key row, 3, also plays a special role in the simplex algorithm, so we call it the *key number.* We are now prepared to carry out the *pivoting operation* that determines a revised solution to our linear optimization problem.

The key row was determined by identifying the first nonzero variable to be *decreased to zero* as the entering variable is *increased from zero.* From our Rule II calculations, we know that the variable $x$ will be increased to 20 and the variable $W_B$ will be decreased to 0 in the new solution.

Pivoting requires the following steps:

1. Divide each coefficient in the key row and its right-hand side by the key number.
2. For each row *except* the key row:
   a. Multiply each coefficient of the newly transformed key row (found in step 1 above) by the negative of the coefficient in the key column in the nonlimiting row.
   b. Add the result to the nonlimiting row.

In our example problem, we carry out these steps by dividing row 2 (the key row) by the key number, 3. The result is

$$x + \frac{2y}{3} \qquad + \frac{W_B}{3} = 20 \tag{9}$$

Next, we modify rows 0 and 1 as indicated.

Row 0: multiply Equation 9 by 60 and add to row 0

Row 1: multiply Equation 9 by $-2$ and add to row 1

For row 0, the calculations would be

$$\begin{array}{llll} Z - 60x - 50y & & = 0 & \text{(row 0)} \\ \quad\;\; 60x + 40y & + 20W_B & = 1200 & \text{(Equation 9 multiplied by 60)} \\ \hline Z \qquad\quad - 10y & + 20W_B & = 1200 & \end{array}$$

After carrying out similar calculations for row 1 (check them for yourself), the revised set of equations is

$$Z \quad - 10y \quad + 20W_B = 1200 \qquad \text{(row 0)}$$

$$\frac{8y}{3} + W_A - \frac{2W_B}{3} = 40 \qquad \text{(row 1)}$$

$$x + \frac{2y}{3} \quad + \frac{W_B}{3} = 20 \qquad \text{(row 2)}$$

Notice that in each row there is one variable with a coefficient of 1 that has a coefficient of 0 in the other rows (including row 0). This variable is "in the solution" with a value equal to the number on the right-hand side of the equal sign. In row 0, this variable is $Z$, which equals 1200; in row 1, it is $W_A$, which equals 40; and in row 2, it is $x$, which equals 20. The variables that are "in the solution" are called *basic variables*. The other variables, $y$ and $W_B$ in this case, are required to equal 0 and are called *nonbasic variables*.

When examined closely, pivoting is simply an approach for solving a system of simultaneous equations. Although the arithmetic is a bit tedious, there is nothing about this basic solution strategy that is particularly sophisticated or mathematically "advanced."

In fact, step 2 of the pivoting procedure can be made even more mechanical by using a simple formula. For each row *except* the key row, all the numbers in the revised row can be obtained from the following relationships:

$$\text{New number} = \text{Old number} - \frac{\begin{pmatrix}\text{Corresponding}\\ \text{number of}\\ \text{key row}\end{pmatrix} \times \begin{pmatrix}\text{Corresponding}\\ \text{number of}\\ \text{key column}\end{pmatrix}}{\text{Key number}} \qquad (10)$$

For example,

1. Row 1, constant column

$$\text{New number} = 80 - (60 \times 2)/3 = 40$$

2. Row 1, $x$ column

$$\text{New number} = 2 - (3 \times 2)/3 = 0$$

3. Row 0, $x$ column

$$\text{New number} = -60 - (3 \times -60)/3 = 0$$

The remaining coefficients in row 0 and row 1 can be calculated in the same way (check this yourself).

Accomplishing the pivoting operation completes one *iteration* of the simplex algorithm. One iteration corresponds to a movement from one corner point of the solution space to another adjacent corner point, or from one basic solution to another.

## The Second Iteration

The variable $y$ has the only negative coefficient in row 0, so we know that it should enter the solution by Rule I. The coefficients of $y$, $-10$ in row 0, 8/3 in row 1, and 2/3 in row 2, become the key column. We can determine the key row from the ratios shown in Table 7-2. The minimum ratio of 15 corresponds to row 1, which is designated as the key row according to Rule II. The key number is the coefficient in both the key row and the key column, 8/3.

Performing the pivoting operation, we first divide each coefficient in the key row, row 1, by the key number, 8/3, and obtain

$$y + \frac{3W_A}{8} - \frac{W_B}{4} = 15 \tag{11}$$

We modify rows 0 and 2 as indicated.

Row 0: multiply Equation 11 by 10 and add to row 0.

Row 2: multiply Equation 11 by $-2/3$ and add to row 2.

Alternatively, rows 1 and 2 could be determined by applying Equation 10. The resulting system of equations is

$$Z \quad + \frac{15W_A}{4} + \frac{35W_B}{2} = 1350 \qquad \text{(row 0)}$$

$$y + \frac{3W_A}{8} - \frac{W_B}{4} = 15 \qquad \text{(row 1)}$$

$$x \quad - \frac{W_A}{4} + \frac{W_B}{2} = 10 \qquad \text{(row 2)}$$

By identifying the variable in each row with a coefficient of 1 that has a coefficient of 0 in the other rows, we see that the solution is $Z = 1350$, $x = 10$, and $y = 15$, with $W_A = W_B = 0$. Now both $x$ and $y$ are basic variables, whereas $W_A$ and $W_B$ are nonbasic.

Because there are no variables in row 0 with negative coefficients, this solution is optimal. Note that the coefficients in row 0 yield the shadow prices obtained previously for $W_A$ and $W_B$.

## Summary of the Procedure

The steps of the simplex algorithm may be summarized as follows:

1. Formulate the constraints and the objective function.
2. Develop the set of *initial equations,* using the slack variables in the initial solution.
3. Identify the *entering variable,* the variable with the most negative coefficient in row 0, and the *key column* of coefficients of the entering variable.
4. Identify the *kew row,* the row with the minimum ratio, determined by dividing the right-hand side of each row by the positive coefficient in the key column of

TABLE 7-2
**APPLYING RULE II**

| Row | Current Right-Hand Side | Coefficient of $y$ | Ratio |
|---|---|---|---|
| 1 | 40 | 8/3 | 15 |
| 2 | 20 | 2/3 | 30 |

that row. (If the coefficient is zero or negative, the row is ignored.) This is the limiting row, and all other rows are nonlimiting.

5. Perform the *pivoting operation.*
   a. Divide the key row by the *key number,* the coefficient at the intersection of the key row and the key column.
   b. For each nonlimiting row:
      (1) Multiply the newly transformed key row (found in a) by the negative of the coefficient in the key column of the nonlimiting row.
      (2) Add the result to the nonlimiting row.

   Alternatively, the coefficients for the nonlimiting rows can be calculated from the formula:

$$\text{New number} = \text{Old number} - \frac{\begin{pmatrix}\text{Corresponding}\\ \text{number of}\\ \text{key row}\end{pmatrix} \times \begin{pmatrix}\text{Corresponding}\\ \text{number of}\\ \text{key column}\end{pmatrix}}{\text{Key number}}$$

6. Repeat steps 3 through 5 until all the coefficients in row 0 are nonnegative. An optimal solution then results.
7. The resulting optimal solution is interpreted in the following manner: In each row there is exactly one basic variable with a coefficient of 1 that has a coefficient of 0 in the other rows. This variable is equal to the right-hand side of the row. The value of the objective function is given by the value of $Z$. All other nonbasic variables are zero. The shadow prices, which indicate the value of a marginal unit of each variable not in the solution, are the coefficients of the slack variables in row 0.

The output for the computer solution, including a sensitivity analysis, for the simplified chemical production problem is shown in Figure 7-6.

## THE SIMPLEX TABLEAU

The logic and calculations of the simplex algorithm can be simplified even further by the use of the simplex tableau format for organizing the data. To minimize recopying of $x$, $y$, $W_A$, $W_B$, and $Z$, let us rearrange the two restricting equations, Equations 5 and 6, and the objective function equation, Equation 8, with the variables at the

FIGURE 7-6
**LINDO COMPUTER SOLUTION AND SENSITIVITY ANALYSIS FOR THE SIMPLIFIED CHEMICAL PRODUCTION PROBLEM.**

```
MAX      60X + 50Y
SUBJECT TO
   2)      2X + 4Y <= 80
   3)      3X + 2Y <= 60
END

          LP OPTIMUM FOUND  AT STEP     2

               OBJECTIVE FUNCTION VALUE

   1)          1350.00000

VARIABLE            VALUE              REDUCED COST
       X          10.000000                .000000
       Y          15.000000                .000000

ROW                 SLACK              DUAL PRICES
   2)              .000000                3.750000
   3)              .000000               17.500000

NO. ITERATIONS=        2

         RANGES IN WHICH THE BASIS IS UNCHANGED

                              COST COEFFICIENT RANGES
VARIABLE           CURRENT          ALLOWABLE          ALLOWABLE
                     COEF            INCREASE           DECREASE
       X          60.000000         15.000000          35.000000
       Y          50.000000         70.000000          10.000000
                              RIGHTHAND SIDE RANGES
     ROW           CURRENT          ALLOWABLE          ALLOWABLE
                      RHS            INCREASE           DECREASE
       2          80.000000         40.000000          40.000000
       3          60.000000         60.000000          20.000000
```

heads of columns and the coefficients of these variables in rows to represent the equations. The equal signs have also been dropped.

| $Z$ | $x$ | $y$ | $W_A$ | $W_B$ | | |
|---|---|---|---|---|---|---|
| 1 | −60 | −50 | 0 | 0 | 0 | (row 0) |
| 0 | 2 | 4 | 1 | 0 | 80 | (row 1) |
| 0 | 3 | 2 | 0 | 1 | 60 | (row 2) |

Next, to the right beside constants 80 and 60, we place two columns that identify the variables in the solution and their contribution rates in the objective function, as

TABLE 7-3
**INITIAL SIMPLEX TABLEAU**

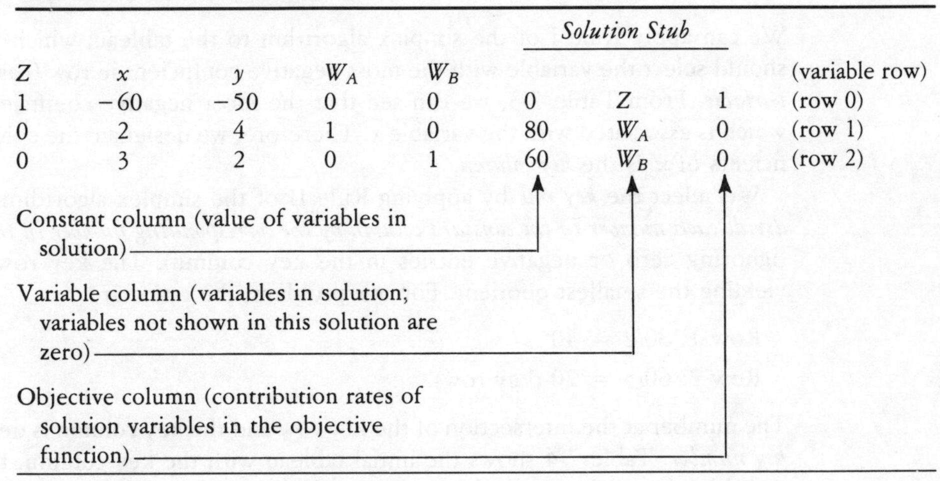

| | | | | | *Solution Stub* | | | |
|---|---|---|---|---|---|---|---|---|
| $Z$ | $x$ | $y$ | $W_A$ | $W_B$ | | | | (variable row) |
| 1 | −60 | −50 | 0 | 0 | 0 | $Z$ | 1 | (row 0) |
| 0 | 2 | 4 | 1 | 0 | 80 | $W_A$ | 0 | (row 1) |
| 0 | 3 | 2 | 0 | 1 | 60 | $W_B$ | 0 | (row 2) |



shown in Table 7-3. This format for a linear optimization model is called the *simplex tableau.* The column of constants plus these two new columns is called the *stub* of the tableau.

Before proceeding, let us name the various parts of the tableau shown in Table 7-3. The variable row simply identifies the variable associated with each of the coefficients in the various columns. Row 0 is the objective function row and contains the negative of the coefficients that show the contribution rates for each of the variables in the objective function. For example, the contribution of $x$ is \$60 per unit, $y$ is \$50 per unit, $W_A$ is zero, and so on.

The solution stub always contains three columns. The constant column shows the value of each of the variables in the solution. The variable column shows the variables that have positive values (basic variables) at a given stage of solution, *and the variables not shown in the variable column have a value of zero.* The objective column shows the contribution rates of the variables in the solution, and these coefficients come from the objective row. For example, in the initial solution, the coefficients below $W_A$ and $W_B$ are zeros.

We must not lose sight of the fact that the numbers in the tableau are the coefficients of the variables in the variable row, and that the numbers in the constant column are the numerical values of the right-hand side of the objective function row 0 and of the constraint equations, rows 1 and 2.

## Improving the Initial Solution

The simplex algorithm can be applied just as before, except that the tableau format allows some additional streamlining of the calculations.

## SELECTING THE KEY COLUMN, KEY ROW, AND KEY NUMBER

We can apply Rule I of the simplex algorithm to the tableau, which says that we should select the variable with the most negative coefficient in row 0 as the *entering variable.* From Table 7-3, we can see that the most negative coefficient is −$60, which is associated with the variable $x$. Therefore, we designate the column of coefficients of $x$ as the *key column.*

We select the *key row* by applying Rule II of the simplex algorithm. That is, *we divide each number in the constant column by the corresponding number in the key column* (ignoring zero or negative entries in the key column). The key row is the row yielding the smallest quotient. For our problem, the ratios are:

Row 1: 80/2 = 40

Row 2: 60/3 = 20 (key row)

The number at the intersection of the key row and the key column is designated the *key number.* Table 7-4 shows the initial tableau with the key column, the key row, and the key number identified.

The pivoting operation can now be accomplished in a mechanical fashion by creating a new tableau. The first step in developing the new tableau is to calculate the coefficients for the *main row.* The main row appears in the same relative position in the new tableau as the key row in the preceding tableau. It is computed by dividing the coefficients of the key row by the key number. Table 7-5 shows this development. The variable and its objective number from the head of the key column, that is, $x$ and 60, are placed in the stub of the main row, replacing $W_B$ and 0 from the previous tableau. The balance of the objective and variable columns in the stub is copied from the previous tableau and the new tableau developed to this point now appears in Table 7-6.

Now all the remaining coefficients in the new tableau can be calculated by applying Equation 10. The completed improved solution is shown in Tableau II in Table 7-7. Note that the solution at this stage is $x = 20$, $W_A = 40$, $y = 0$, and $W_B = 0$ and that the value of the objective function is 1200, as shown in the solution stub.

**TABLE 7-4**
**INITIAL SIMPLEX TABLEAU WITH KEY COLUMN, KEY ROW, AND KEY NUMBER IDENTIFIED**

*Tableau I*

| | $Z$ | $x$ | $y$ | $W_A$ | $W_B$ | | | | |
|---|---|---|---|---|---|---|---|---|---|
| | 1 | −60 | −50 | 0 | 0 | 0 | $Z$ | 1 | (row 0) |
| | 0 | 2 | 4 | 1 | 0 | 80 | $W_A$ | 0 | (row 1) |
| Key row → | 0 | 3 | 2 | 0 | 1 | 60 | $W_B$ | 0 | (row 2) |

Key column (↑ $x$ column); Key number (3)

TABLE 7-5
**SIMPLEX TABLEAU WITH MAIN ROW OF NEW TABLEAU**

*Tableau I*

| $Z$ | $x$ | $y$ | $W_A$ | $W_B$ | | | | |
|---|---|---|---|---|---|---|---|---|
| 1 | −60 | −50 | 0 | 0 | 0 | $Z$ | 1 | (row 0) |
| 0 | 2 | 4 | 1 | 0 | 80 | $W_A$ | 0 | (row 1) |
| 0 | 3 | 2 | 0 | 1 | 60 | $W_B$ | 0 | (row 2) |

*Tableau II*

| | | | | | | | | |
|---|---|---|---|---|---|---|---|---|
| 0 | 1 | 2/3 | 0 | 1/3 | 20 | | | Main row |

TABLE 7-6
**SIMPLEX TABLEAU WITH VARIABLE AND OBJECTIVE COLUMNS COMPLETED**

*Tableau I*

| $Z$ | $x$ | $y$ | $W_A$ | $W_B$ | | | | |
|---|---|---|---|---|---|---|---|---|
| 1 | −60 | −50 | 0 | 0 | 1200 | $Z$ | 1 | (row 0) |
| 0 | 2 | 4 | 1 | 0 | 80 | $W_A$ | 0 | (row 1) |
| 0 | 3 | 2 | 0 | 1 | 60 | $W_B$ | 0 | (row 2) |

*Tableau II*

| | | | | | | | |
|---|---|---|---|---|---|---|---|
| | | | | | | $Z$ | 1 |
| | | | | | | $W_A$ | 0 |
| 0 | 1 | 2/3 | 0 | 1/3 | 20 | $x$ | 60 |

TABLE 7-7
**SIMPLEX TABLEAU WITH FIRST ITERATION COMPLETED**

*Tableau I*

| $Z$ | $x$ | $y$ | $W_A$ | $W_B$ | | | | |
|---|---|---|---|---|---|---|---|---|
| 1 | −60 | −50 | 0 | 0 | 0 | $Z$ | 1 | (row 0) |
| 0 | 2 | 4 | 1 | 0 | 80 | $W_A$ | 0 | (row 1) |
| 0 | 3 | 2 | 0 | 1 | 60 | $W_B$ | 0 | (row 2) |

*Tableau II*

| | | | | | | | | |
|---|---|---|---|---|---|---|---|---|
| 1 | 0 | −10 | 0 | 20 | 1200 | $Z$ | 1 | (row 0) |
| 0 | 0 | 8/3 | 1 | −2/3 | 40 | $W_A$ | 0 | (row 1) |
| 0 | 1 | 2/3 | 0 | 1/3 | 20 | $x$ | 60 | (row 2) |

TABLE 7-8
**SIMPLEX TABLEAU, SECOND AND THIRD ITERATIONS COMPLETED**

*Tableau I*

| $Z$ | $x$ | $y$ | $W_A$ | $W_B$ | | | | |
|---|---|---|---|---|---|---|---|---|
| 1 | −60 | −50 | 0 | 0 | 0 | $Z$ | 1 | (row 0) |
| 0 | 2 | 4 | 1 | 0 | 80 | $W_A$ | 0 | (row 1) |
| 0 | 3 | 2 | 0 | 1 | 60 | $W_B$ | 0 | (row 2) |

*Tableau II*

| | | | | | | | | |
|---|---|---|---|---|---|---|---|---|
| 1 | 0 | −10 | 0 | 20 | 1200 | $Z$ | 1 | (row 0) |
| 0 | 0 | 8/3 | 1 | −2/3 | 40 | $W_A$ | 0 | (row 1) |
| 0 | 1 | 2/3 | 0 | 1/3 | 20 | $x$ | 60 | (row 2) |

*Tableau III*

| | | | | | | | | |
|---|---|---|---|---|---|---|---|---|
| 1 | 0 | 0 | 15/4 | 35/2 | 1350 | $Z$ | 1 | (row 0) |
| 0 | 0 | 1 | 3/8 | −1/4 | 15 | $y$ | 50 | (row 1) |
| 0 | 1 | 0 | −1/4 | 1/2 | 10 | $x$ | 60 | (row 2) |

## Optimal Solution

Next, we examine row 0 of Tableau II in Table 7-7, and we see that the potential for improvement still exists because the coefficient −10 appears under the variable $y$. Thus, $y$ is selected as the key column of Tableau II. Proceeding as before, we obtain the new solution in Tableau III of Table 7-8, which is optimal.

To summarize, the use of the tableau helps to organize the data and calculations of the simplex algorithm, but the results obtained are identical.

The optimum solution is interpreted in the following manner: The solution appears in the stub. The variables shown in the variable column have the values shown in the corresponding rows of the constant column. The value of the objective function is shown in the constant column, row 0. All variables not shown in the stub are zero. The shadow prices that indicate the value of a marginal unit of each variable not in the solution are shown in row 0 of the final solution.

# GOAL PROGRAMMING

In several decision situations, management attempts to satisfy several objectives, involving profits, market share, product diversification, and so forth. Goal programming offers a convenient way of dealing with multiple objectives, and we will illustrate its basic idea using the chemical example discussed earlier.

Suppose the management has two objectives—profits and equity of distribution of the two products X and Y. The second objective might be relevant if each product has its own product manager who desires that equal amounts of each product be delivered to them in each planning period. Further suppose that the goal for the profit objective is 1400. Thus,

$$60x + 50y = 1400 \quad \text{(goal 1)}$$
$$x - y = 0 \quad \text{(goal 2)}$$

We should choose production quantities $x$ and $y$ that come as close as possible to attaining the two goals. This is achieved by choosing $x$ and $y$ such that deviations from the goals are as small as possible. In the simplest case, when the deviations from the respective goals are equally important, we attempt to minimize $Z$ so that

$$Z = |60x + 50y - 1400| + |x - y - 0|$$

where the first term denotes the absolute value of the deviation from goal 1 and the second term denotes the absolute value of the deviation from goal 2. We define $Z_1$ and $Z_2$, which are deviations from the goals that can take either positive or negative values, as follows:

$$Z_1 = 60x + 50y - 1400$$
$$Z_2 = x - y - 0$$

The positive deviation is defined by $Z_i^+$ and the negative deviation by $Z_i^-$. Thus,

$$|Z_1| = Z_1^+ + Z_1^-$$
$$|Z_2| = Z_2^+ + Z_2^-$$

where

$$Z_1 = Z_1^+ - Z_1^-$$
$$Z_2 = Z_2^+ - Z_2^-$$

The goal programming model can now be rewritten as

$$\text{Minimize } Z = |Z_1| + |Z_2| = Z = Z_1^+ + Z_1^- + Z_2^+ + Z_2^-$$

Subject to

$$60x + 50y - 1400 = Z_1^+ - Z_1^- \quad \text{(deviation from goal 1)}$$
$$x - y - 0 = Z_2^+ - Z_2^- \quad \text{(deviation from goal 2)}$$
$$\left.\begin{array}{l} 2x + 4y \le 80 \\ 3x + 2y \le 60 \\ x \le 16 \\ y \le 18 \end{array}\right\} \quad \text{(original problem constraints)}$$
$$x, y, Z_1^+, Z_1^-, Z_2^+, Z_2^- \ge 0 \quad \text{(nonnegativity constraints)}$$

This reformulated model is a simple linear program that can be solved by a computer program.

We can weight the positive and negative deviations for a goal differently. Similarly, we can assign different weights to different goals based on managerial preference. This is easily accomplished by simply modifying the objective function, for example,

$$\text{Minimize } Z = W_1^+ Z_1^+ + W_1^- Z_1^- + W_2^+ Z_2^+ + W_2^- Z_2^-$$

where $W_1^+$, $W_1^-$, $W_2^+$, and $W_2^-$ are weights assigned to the respective deviations. In our example, $W_1^+ = 0$ as a positive deviation for profit should not be penalized. If management considers that falling below the profit goal is five times as important as failing to meet equity of distribution of the two products (goal 2), then $W_1^- = 5$ whereas $W_2^+ = 1$ and $W_2^- = 1$. The equal values for $W_2^+$ and $W_2^-$ imply that the positive and the negative deviation for goal 2 are equally important.

In summary, once we have defined the goals, the strategy in goal programming is to minimize the sum (or the weighted sum) of the deviations from these goals, subject to the constraints that define these deviations and the original problem constraints.

## REVIEW QUESTIONS

1. Which of the following mathematical expressions are linear? Why?
   a. $x + y = 1$
   b. $x^2 + y^2 = 10$
   c. $1/x + 2x = 10$
   d. $x + xy + y = 1$
   e. $x_1 + x_2 + x_3 + x_4 = 1$
2. Outline the model-building process used for developing linear optimization models.
3. Suppose that in the chemical production problems, the availability of time on machine A is drastically reduced to only 40 hours because of a breakdown. How does this change the solution space shown in Figure 7-2? Is it likely to change the optimum number of units of each chemical to produce?
4. Explain the concept of dual or shadow prices. How can a manager use a knowledge of dual prices in decision making?
5. What is the interpretation of the upper and lower bounds on the shadow prices indicated in Figure 7-4? Of what value is this information to a manager?
6. What is the interpretation of the upper and lower bounds on the "prices" given in Figure 7-4? Of what value is this information to the manager?
7. What is the practical value of knowing whether the bounds on one or more prices are "tight"?
8. What is the function of slack variables in the simplex method of solution?
9. What is the physical meaning of slack variables for the following types of constraints?
   a. Constraint on the capacity of a machine
   b. Constraint on the size of the market
   c. Constraint on the total expenditure on advertising in various media

10. What is a feasible solution? A basic solution? Identify both kinds of solutions in Figure 7-1. Can a feasible solution be basic? Must a feasible solution be basic?

# PROBLEMS

11. Once upon a time, Lucretia Borgia invited 50 enemies to dinner. The *piece de resistance* was to be poison. In those crude days only two poisons were on the market, poison X and poison Y. Before preparing the menu, however, the remarkably talented young lady considered some of the restrictions on her scheme:

    a. If she used more than one-half pound of poison, the guests would detect it and refuse to eat.

    b. Lucretia's own private witch, a medieval version of the modern planning staff, once propounded some magic numbers for her in the following doggerel:

       One *Y* and *X* two,
       If less than half,
       Then woe to you.

    c. Poison X will kill 75 and poison Y will kill 200 people per pound.

    d. Poison X costs 100 solid gold pieces per pound, and poison Y costs 400 solid gold pieces per pound.

    After devising a menu to cover up the taste of the poison, Lucretia found she was very short of solid gold pieces. In fact, unless she were very careful she would not be able to schedule another poisoning orgy that month. So she called in her alchemist, a very learned man, and told him about her problem. The alchemist had little experience in solving problems of this type, but he was able to translate the four restrictions into mathematical statements.

    (1) $X + Y \leq 1/2$

    (2) $2X + Y \geq 1/2$

    (3) $75X + 200Y \geq 50$

    (4) $100X + 400Y = \text{cost}$

    Assist the alchemist in solving this problem, using graphic methods. The penalty for failure will be an invitation to Lucretia's dinner.

12. A manufacturer has two products, both of which are made in two steps by machines A and B. The process times for the two products on the two machines are as follows:

| Product | Machine A (hr) | Machine B (hr) |
|---|---|---|
| 1 | 4 | 5 |
| 2 | 5 | 2 |

For the coming period, machine A has 100 hours available and machine B has 80 hours available. The contribution for product 1 is $10 per unit, and for product 2 it is $5 per unit. Using the methods of the simplex algorithm, formulate and solve the problem for maximum contribution.

13. Consider the following linear optimization model:

$$\text{Maximize } Z = 3x_1 + x_2 + 4x_3$$

Subject to

$$6x_1 + 3x_2 + 5x_3 \leq 25$$
$$3x_1 + 4x_2 + 5x_3 \leq 20$$
$$x_1, x_2, x_3 \geq 0$$

After adding slack variables and performing one simplex iteration, we have the following tableau:

| | | | | | | | | |
|---|---|---|---|---|---|---|---|---|
| 1 | −3/5 | 11/5 | 0 | 0 | 4/5 | 16 | $Z$ | 1 |
| 0 | 3 | −1 | 0 | 1 | −1 | 5 | $x_4$ | 0 |
| 0 | 3/5 | 4/5 | 1 | 0 | 1/5 | 4 | $x_3$ | 4 |

If this result is not optimal, perform the next iteration. Indicate the resulting values of the variables and the objective function.

14. Consider the following linear optimization model:

$$\text{Maximize } Z = 3x_1 + 6x_2 + 2x_3$$

Subject to

$$3x_1 + 4x_2 + x_3 \leq 2 \quad \text{(resource A)}$$
$$x_1 + 3x_2 + 2x_3 \leq 1 \quad \text{(resource B)}$$
$$x_1, x_2, x_3 \geq 0$$

Solve this problem for the optimal solution using the simplex method.

15. A company produces three products Brite, Glo, and Chumpy. The labor availability in the three departments involved in manufacturing the three products is limited. The following information provides the relevant data for planning the level of production for each product for the upcoming period:

| | Brite | Glo | Chumpy | Labor Hours Available |
|---|---|---|---|---|
| Contribution/unit | 3 | 5 | 4 | — |
| Dept. A, min./unit | 1.00 | 0.35 | 0.50 | 100 |
| Dept. B, min./unit | 0.30 | 0.20 | 0.40 | 36 |
| Dept. C, min./unit | 0.20 | 0.50 | 0.30 | 50 |

a. Develop a linear programming model for the company and solve it using a computer program to determine the optimal production quantities of the three products. What is the total contribution of your decision?

b. If the labor availability in the three departments can be increased by scheduling, how much will you be willing to pay per hour of overtime in each of the three departments?

16. A precision component, Perfect, can be manufactured using any one of three machines available. The production rate, reject rate, and the operating cost for each machine is different. A machine cannot be operated for more than four hours because it loses the tolerance required to manufacture Perfect. Since there is only one skilled operator, the machines must be operated sequentially. The demand for Perfect is at least 2000 units for the eight-hour shift. The reject rate should not exceed two percent. Taken together, the three machines must operate for eight hours (e.g., one possibility is to operate machine 1 for three hours, machine 2 for one hour, and machine 3 for four hours). The data for the three machines are as follows:

| | Machine 1 | Machine 2 | Machine 3 |
|---|---|---|---|
| Production rate, units/hour | 300 | 200 | 350 |
| Reject rate, percent | 2% | 1% | 4% |
| Operating cost, $/hour | $590 | $520 | $550 |

If the objective is to minimize the total operating costs, how many hours should each machine be operated during the eight-hour shift? What is the total operating cost? What is the daily production rate? Formulate the problem and use a computer program to obtain the solution.

17. A newly founded pharmaceutical company mixes a long life elixir called Eternity from four ingredients. These four ingredients in combination form three compounds that are critical for the effectiveness of Eternity. There must be at least 5 grams of compound A, 100 grams of compound B, and 30 grams of compound C in one gallon of Eternity for it to attain its full potency. The objective is to use the fraction $x_i$ of ingredient I per gallon of Eternity so that the total cost is minimized. The problem formulation is as follows:

$$\text{Min} \quad 800x_1 + 400x_2 + 600x_3 + 500x_4$$

Subject to

$$10x_1 + 3x_2 + 8x_3 + 2x_4 \geq 5 \quad \text{(requirement for A)}$$
$$90x_1 + 150x_2 + 75x_3 + 175x_4 \geq 100 \quad \text{(requirement for B)}$$
$$95x_1 + 25x_2 + 20x_3 + 37x_4 \geq 30 \quad \text{(requirement for C)}$$
$$x_1 + x_2 + x_3 + x_4 = 1 \quad \text{(blend for 1 gallon)}$$
$$x_i \geq 0, \; i = 1 \text{ to } 4$$

The LINDO computer solution and sensitivity analysis for this problem is given in Figure 7-7, which can be used to answer the following questions.

a. Interpret the meaning of the objective function and the decision variable ($x_1$, $x_2$, $x_3$, $x_4$) values.

b. How many grams of compound C are in the optimal mix for Eternity?

FIGURE 7-7
**LINDO COMPUTER SOLUTION AND SENSITIVITY ANALYSIS FOR THE ETERNITY PROBLEM.**

```
MIN      800 X1 + 400 X2 + 600 X3 + 500 X4
SUBJECT TO
    2)   10 X1 + 3 X2 + 8 X3 + 2 X4 >= 5
    3)   90 X1 + 150 X2 + 75 X3 + 175 X4 >= 100
    4)   45 X1 + 25 X2 + 20 X3 + 37 X4 >= 30
    5)     X1 + X2 +J X3 + X4 = 1
END

        LP OPTIMUM FOUND   AT STEP     7

            OBJECTIVE FUNCTION VALUE

    1)          511.111084

VARIABLE            VALUE            REDUCED COST
       X1         .259259               .000000
       X2         .703704               .000000
       X3         .037037               .000000
       X4         .000000             91.111145

ROW                 SLACK             DUAL PRICES
       2)         .000000            -44.444450
       3)       31.666664               .000000
       4)         .000000             -4.444443
       5)         .000000           -155.555542

NO. ITERATIONS=        7

        RANGES IN WHICH THE BASIS IS UNCHANGED

                             COST COEFFICIENT RANGES
VARIABLE          CURRENT           ALLOWABLE           ALLOWABLE
                   COEF              INCREASE            DECREASE
       X1       800.000000          223.636505          119.999954
       X2       400.000000           66.847839          299.999817
       X3       600.000000           85.714249          118.269272
       X4       500.000000            INFINITY           91.111145

                             RIGHTHAND SIDE RANGES
ROW               CURRENT           ALLOWABLE           ALLOWABLE
                    RHS              INCREASE            DECREASE
        2         5.000000            2.375000             .250000
        3       100.000000           31.666664            INFINITY
        4        30.000000             .714286            7.000000
        5         1.000000             .250000             .043478
```

c. If the cost of ingredient 1 decreases from $800 to $700, will the optimal mix change?

d. If the requirements for compound B are changed from 100 grams to 90 grams per gallon, will the optimal solution change? What happens if the requirements for compound A are reduced to 4.99 grams per gallon? What will be the increase or decrease in the optimal cost?

e. If the price for ingredient 3 goes up by $100 per gallon, will the optimal mix change? What if it goes up by $50 per gallon?

f. The minimum cost of $511.11 per gallon needs to be reduced to $500 per gallon. Can this be achieved by relaxing the requirement for compound A? Compound B? Compound C?

18. A flexible manufacturing plant can produce several types of gearboxes and other parts, such as axles, with the same equipment and facilities. Demand considerations require that two types of gearboxes need to be produced for the next two quarters. The demand for the two gearboxes for the upcoming quarters is forecasted to be:

| | GEARBOX A | GEARBOX B |
|---|---|---|
| Quarter 1 | 100 units | 150 units |
| Quarter 2 | 200 units | 150 units |

The initial inventory for gearbox A is 25 units and that for gearbox B is 50 units. The ending inventory desired is 10 units for gearbox A and 25 units for gearbox B. Gearbox A requires 50 machine hours per unit and gearbox B requires 90 machine hours per unit. The total available machine hours for each quarter are 22,000. The cost of carrying inventory is charged to the stock on hand at the end of the quarter and is $90 per unit for gearbox A and $150 per unit for gearbox B. What should be the production quantities for gearboxes A and B in quarters 1 and 2 in order to minimize inventory holding costs? Formulate this problem as a linear program and solve it using a computer program.

19. The Smash Sports Company manufactures a complete line of tennis rackets in three plants. All three types of rackets manufactured (heavy, medium, light) can be produced in any of the three plants, which have total capacities of 550, 650, and 300 units per day, respectively. The contribution of each type of racket to profit varies by plant, due to differing production costs. This information is summarized as follows:

| | *Contribution to Profit* | | |
|---|---|---|---|
| Racket type | Plant 1 | Plant 2 | Plant 3 |
| Heavy | $10 | $8 | $12 |
| Medium | 7 | 9 | 8 |
| Light | 8 | 5 | 4 |

FIGURE 7-8
**LINDO COMPUTER SOLUTION AND SENSITIVITY ANALYSIS FOR THE TENNIS RACKET PROBLEM.**

```
MAX      10 XH1 + 8 XH2 + 12 XH3 + 7 XM1 + 9 XM2 + 8 XM3 + 8 XL1
    + 5 XL2 + 4 XL3
SUBJECT TO
    2)      XH1 + XM1 + XL1  <= 550
    3)      XH2 + XM2 + XL2  <= 650
    4)      XH3 + XM3 + XL3  <= 300
    5)      XH1 + XH2 + XH3  <= 700
    6)      XM1 + XM2 + XM3  <= 850
    7)      XL1 + XL2 + XL3  <= 750
END

      LP OPTIMUM FOUND   AT STEP      1
            OBJECTIVE FUNCTION VALUE

    1)          14650.0000

VARIABLE           VALUE              REDUCED COST
     XH1        400.000000              .000000
     XH2           .000000             3.000000
     XH3        300.000000              .000000
     XM1           .000000             1.000000
     XM2        650.000000              .000000
     XM3           .000000             2.000000
     XL1        150.000000              .000000
     XL2           .000000             4.000000
     XL3           .000000             6.000000

ROW                SLACK              DUAL PRICES
     2)            .000000             8.000000
     3)            .000000             9.000000
     4)            .000000            10.000000
     5)            .000000             2.000000
     6)         200.000000              .000000
     7)         600.000000              .000000

NO. ITERATIONS=     1

     RANGES IN WHICH THE BASIS IS UNCHANGED

                             COST COEFFICIENT RANGES
VARIABLE          CURRENT          ALLOWABLE          ALLOWABLE
                   COEF            INCREASE           DECREASE
     XH1        10.000000          2.000000           2.000000
     XH2         8.000000          3.000000           INFINITY
     XH3        12.000000          INFINITY           2.000000
     XM1         7.000000          1.000000           INFINITY
     XM2         9.000000          INFINITY           3.000000
```

FIGURE 7-8
***(Continued)***

RANGES IN WHICH THE BASIS IS UNCHANGED *(Cont.)*

COST COEFFICIENT RANGES

| VARIABLE | CURRENT COEF | ALLOWABLE INCREASE | ALLOWABLE DECREASE |
|---|---|---|---|
| XM3 | 8.000000 | 2.000000 | INFINITY |
| XL1 | 8.000000 | 2.000000 | 1.000000 |
| XL2 | 5.000000 | 4.000000 | INFINITY |
| XL3 | 4.000000 | 6.000000 | INFINITY |

RIGHTHAND SIDE RANGES

| ROW | CURRENT RHS | ALLOWABLE INCREASE | ALLOWABLE DECREASE |
|---|---|---|---|
| 2 | 550.000000 | 600.000000 | 150.000000 |
| 3 | 650.000000 | 200.000000 | 650.000000 |
| 4 | 300.000000 | 400.000000 | 150,000000 |
| 5 | 700.000000 | 150.000000 | 400.000000 |
| 6 | 850.000000 | INFINITY | 200.000000 |
| 7 | 750.000000 | INFINITY | 600.000000 |

Sales forecasts for the three types of rackets are 700, 850, and 750 units per day. Since production quantities may be limited by capacity constraints, all demand may not be satisfied.

A LINDO computer solution and sensitivity analysis is given in Figure 7-8.

a. What is the optimal solution?
b. Can 200 units of the light rackets be produced per day at plant 1?
c. If the production capacity at plants 1, 2, and 3 can be increased, what is the maximum cost that management should be willing to pay for a unit increase in capacity at plant 1? At plant 2? At plant 3?
d. If the demand for the medium rackets goes up to 900 rackets per day, will the profits of the company increase?
e. If the net contribution of the medium rackets at plant 2 decreases to $5.50 per racket, will the present optimal LINDO solution change? How will you find the new solution?

# REFERENCES

Bierman, H., C. P. Bonini, and W. H. Hausman, *Quantitative Analysis for Business Decisions* (6th ed.), Irwin, Homewood, Ill., 1981.

Buffa, E. S., and J. S. Dyer, *Management Science/Operations Research: Model Formulation and Solution Methods* (2nd ed.), Wiley, New York, 1981.

Daellenbach, H. G., and E. J. Bell, *User's Guide to Linear Programming,* Prentice-Hall, Englewood Cliffs, N.J., 1970.

Eppen, G. D., and F. J. Gould, *Quantitative Concepts for Management: Decision Making Without Algorithms,* Prentice-Hall, Englewood Cliffs, N.J. 1979.

Krajewski, L. J., and H. E. Thompson, *Management Science: Quantitative Methods in Concepts,* Wiley, New York, 1981.

Schrage, L., *Linear, Integer, and Quadratic Programming with LINDO* (and User's Manual), Scientific Press, Palo Alto, Calif., 1984.

CHAPTER 8

# PLANNING AGGREGATE PRODUCTION, WORK FORCE, AND INVENTORY LEVELS

"If demand were only constant, managing productive systems sure would be a lot easier." The sage who made this statement prefers to remain anonymous because he knows that, although it is so true, only a dreamer dares to think about an ideal world. And the sage is not a dreamer but a vice-president of manufacturing who works in the real world of random demand variations and seasonality. He must be concerned with the utilization of facilities and work force and the level of inventories.

> When inventories seem too large, the president complains about the investment tied up and the costs of carrying them. When inventories are low, the marketing vice-president complains about poor service to customers. When I have to lay off workers during a sales slump, the union president complains and sometimes makes threats, and I have even had visitations from the town mayor pleading for whatever employment stabilization measures that are possible.

This manufacturing vice president has the responsibility of producing high quality products at low cost and timed to be available when the market wants them. In addition, he must consider trade-offs between cost and employment stabilization, cost and market timing, and market timing and employment stabilization. When product demand is seasonal, the problems of achieving the needed balance among these factors is much more difficult.

## NATURE OF AGGREGATE PLANNING

Most managers want to plan and control operations at the broadest level through some kind of aggregate planning that bypasses the details of individual products and the detailed scheduling of facilities and personnel. This fact is a good illustration of how managerial behavior actually employs system concepts by starting with the whole. Management would rather deal with the basic relevant decisions of programming the use of resources. This is accomplished by reviewing projected employment levels and by setting activity rates that can be varied within a given employment level by varying the hours worked (working overtime or undertime). Once these basic decisions have been made for the upcoming period, detailed scheduling can proceed at a lower level within the constraints of the broad plan.

What is needed first for aggregate plans is the development of some logical overall unit for measuring output, for example, gallons of paint in the paint industry, cases of beer in the beer industry, perhaps equivalent machine hours in mechanical industries, beds occupied in hospitals, or pieces of mail in a post office.

Management must also be able to forecast for some reasonable planning period, perhaps up to a year, in these aggregate terms. Finally, management must be able to isolate and measure the relevant costs. These costs may be reconstructed in the form of a model that will permit near optimal decisions for the sequence of planning periods in the planning horizon.

Aggregate planning increases the range of alternatives for capacity use that can be considered by management. The concepts raise such broad basic questions as the following: To what extent should inventory be used to absorb the fluctuations in demand that will occur over the next 6 to 12 months? Why not absorb these fluctuations by simply varying the size of the work force? Why not maintain a fairly stable work force size and absorb the fluctuations by changing activity rates by varying work hours? Why not maintain a fairly stable work force and let subcontractors wrestle with the problem of fluctuating order rates? Should the firm purposely not meet all demands? Each of the preceding policies may be termed a *pure strategy* because only one policy is used to smooth production activity.

In most instances, it is probably true that any one of these pure strategies would not be as effective as a balance among them. Each strategy has associated costs. We seek an astute combination of the pure strategies called a *mixed strategy*.

## COSTS

The choices concerning aggregate production, work force, and inventory levels influence several relevant costs. These costs need to be identified and measured so that alternative aggregate plans can be evaluated on a total cost criterion. Some of the cost items that may be relevant are

- Payroll costs
- Costs of overtime, second shifts, and subcontracting
- Costs of hiring and laying off workers
- Costs of excess inventory and backlog
- Costs of production rate changes

The selected cost items that are included in the model should vary with changes in the decision variables. If a cost item, such as the salary of a manufacturing manager, is incurred no matter which aggregate plan is chosen, then this cost is excluded from consideration. The behavior of cost with respect to changes in decision variables is not easy to quantify, however. Often, approximations are made by assuming the costs to be a linear or quadratic function of the appropriate decision variable. These simplifying assumptions permit the use of some simple models, such as linear programming, in the determination of a minimum cost aggregate plan. We will now briefly discuss the behavior of the cost items illustrated in Figure 8-1.

In Figure 8-1*a*, the payroll costs are shown to be close to linear. This assumption may not be appropriate if the supply for labor is limited and incremental additions to the labor pool for higher levels of production can only be made by paying higher rates. In addition, the productivity of labor in relation to the volume of activities, shown in Figure 8-1*b*, makes labor cost per unit a nonlinear function. Viewing labor in the aggregate and not considering substantial changes in basic technology, we would expect the toe of the productivity curve to exhibit start-up difficulties that would be reflected in low output per worker-hour. In the middle range of one-shift operations, the curve may be approximately linear. But, as we approach the limits of one-shift capacity, productivity falls off because of increased congestion, cramped quarters, interference, and delays. There is a logical tendency to try to achieve increased output near the limits of one-shift capacity through the use of overtime for

FIGURE 8-1
**SELECTED COST BEHAVIOR PATTERNS.**

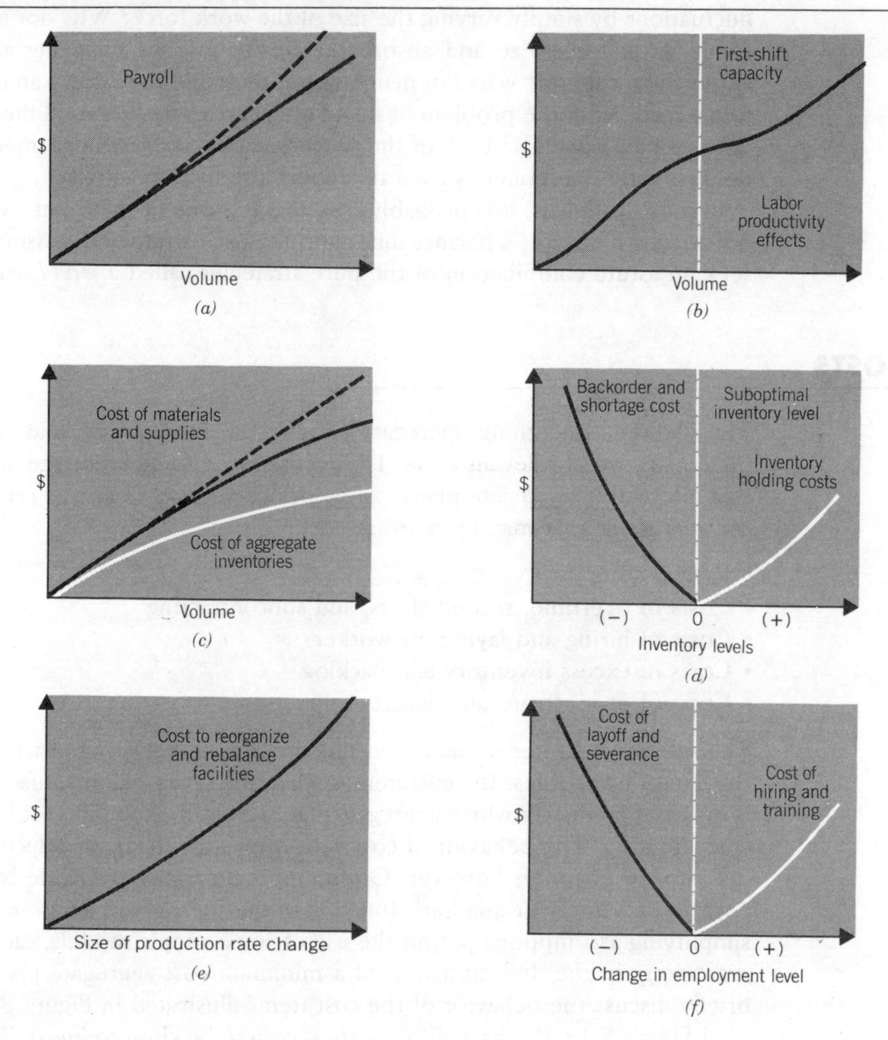


the existing work force, which has a higher cost of marginal productivity. Changes in technology might change the level and contour of the curve, but the general non-linearities would remain.

In Figure 8-1*c*, we see two cost components related to material. We assume that the cost of materials would be linear in relation to volume (the dashed line), but quantity discounts and an aggressive procurement staff should produce economies at higher volumes (the solid line). As volume goes up, the size of the aggregate inventory necessary to maintain the production–distribution process increases also, but not in direct proportion.

In Figure 8-1*d*, we see the relative costs of holding either too much or too little inventory. This presupposes that there exists, for each level of operation, some ideal aggregate inventory for sustaining the productive process. Inventories might vary from this ideal amount for two possible reasons, however. First, they might be different from the ideal levels because of the capriciousness of consumer demand. If demand were less than expected, we would incur extra inventories and the cost of holding them. If demand were greater than expected, we would incur back-order or shortage costs and the possible opportunity costs of lost sales or a lower volume of activity. A second basic reason why aggregate inventories might differ from ideal levels is as a result of conscious managerial design. Management might consciously accumulate extra inventories in a slack demand season to reduce the costs of hiring, layoff, and overtime. These costs of holding too much or too little inventory are probably not linear for larger ranges.

Finally, in Figures 8-1*e* and 8-1*f*, we have included two cost items associated with changes in output and employment levels. When output rates are changed, some costs are incurred in reorganizing and replanning for the new level and in balancing crews and facilities.

When operating near a capacity limit (e.g., single-shift capacity), costs increase and profits decline. This happens due to the behavior of some of the cost components and the decline of labor productivity, the use of overtime, and the relative inefficiency of newly hired labor. When operating near a capacity limit these cost increases are normally greater than the savings in material and inventory costs. When the decision to add a second shift is made, there will be increased semifixed costs in putting on the second shift. As we progress into the second shift volume range, labor productivity will be low initially, reflecting start-up conditions, and a pattern similar to that of the first shift will be repeated.

In some of the analyses of operations management problems, we assume linear approximations of nonlinear cost functions in order to simplify the problems and to conceptualize the models. In many instances, the assumption of linearity is an excellent one, but near a capacity limit it may not be appropriate.

Many costs affected by aggregate and scheduling decisions are difficult to measure and are not segregated in accounting records. Some, such as interest costs on inventory investment, are opportunity costs. Other costs are not measurable, such as those associated with public relations and public image. However, all the costs are real and bear on aggregate planning decisions.

## PROBLEM STRUCTURE

The simplest structure of the aggregate planning problem is represented by the single-stage system shown in Figure 8-2. In Figure 8-2, the planning horizon is only one period ahead; therefore, we call Figure 8-2 a "single-stage" system. The state of the system at the end of the last period is defined by $W_0$, $P_0$, and $I_0$, the aggregate work force size, the production or activity rate, and the inventory level, respectively. The ending state conditions for one period become the initial conditions for the upcoming period. We have a forecast of the requirements for the upcoming

FIGURE 8-2
**SINGLE-STAGE PLANNING DECISION SYSTEM WHERE PLANNING HORIZON IS ONLY ONE PERIOD. $W$ = SIZE OF WORK FORCE, $P$ = PRODUCTION OR ACTIVITY RATE, AND $I$ = INVENTORY LEVEL.**

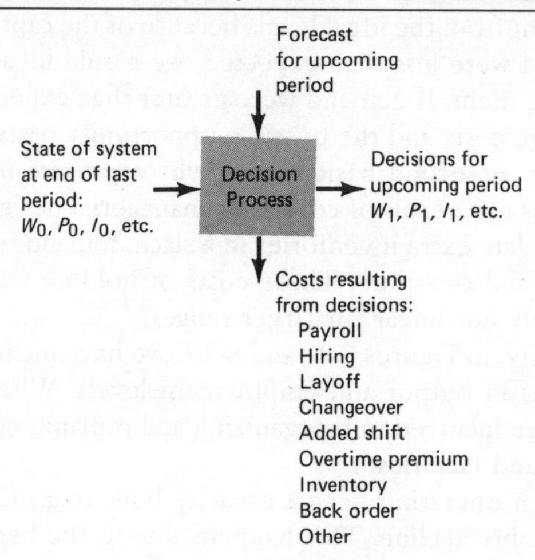


period; through some process, decisions are made that set the size of the work force and production rate for the upcoming period. Projected ending inventory is then, $I_1 = I_0 + P_1 - F_1$, where $F_1$ is forecasted sales.

The decisions made may call for hiring or laying off personnel, thereby expanding or contracting the effective capacity of the productive system. The work force size, together with the decision on activity rate during the period, then determines the required amount of overtime, inventory levels, extent of back-ordering, whether or not a shift must be added or dropped, and other possible changes in operating procedure. The comparative costs that result from alternative decisions on work force size and production rate are of great interest in judging the effectiveness of the decisions made and the decision process used. The comparative cost of a sequence of such alternative decisions are also of interest in judging the applicability of the single-stage model.

Let us suppose that we make a sequence of independent decisions by the structure of the single-stage model of Figure 8-2. If the forecasts for each of the first four periods are progressively decreasing, our decision process responds by decreasing both the work force size and the activity rates in some combination, incurring layoff and changeover costs. Then, for the fifth through tenth periods, if we find the period forecasts are progressively increasing, the decision process for each period calls for hiring personnel and increased activity rates, incurring more hiring and changeover costs. The single-period planning horizon has made each independent decision seem internally logical, but it has resulted in laying off workers only to hire them back again.

If we had been able to look ahead for several periods with an appropriate decision process, we might have decided to stabilize the work force size, at least to some

FIGURE 8-3
**MULTISTAGE AGGREGATE PLANNING DECISION SYSTEM FOR PLANNING HORIZON OF *N* PERIODS.**

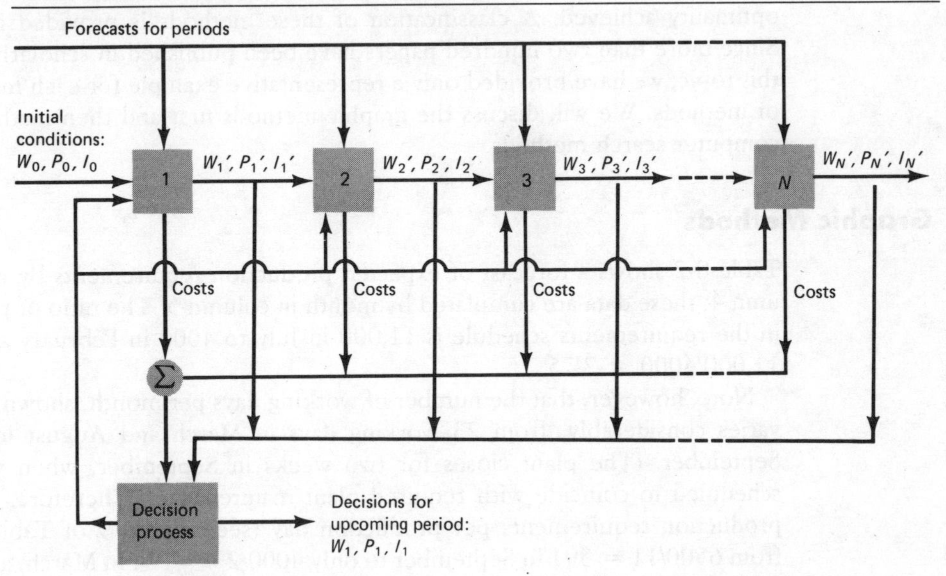


extent, and absorb the fluctuations in demand in some other way. For example, we could have changed the activity rate through the use of overtime and undertime or by carrying extra inventories through the trough in the demand curve. Broadening the planning horizon can improve the effectiveness of the aggregate planning system.

Figure 8-3 shows a multistage aggregate planning system where the horizon has been expanded with forcasts for each period. Our objective is the same as before: to make decisions concerning the work force size and production rate for the upcoming period. In doing so, however, we consider the sequence of projected decisions in relation to the forecasts and their cost effects. The decision for the upcoming period is affected by the future period forecasts, and the decision process must consider the cost effects of the sequence of decisions. The connecting links between the several stages are the *W*, *P*, and *I* values at the end of one period and the beginning of the next. The feedback loop from the decision process may involve some iterative or trial-and-error procedures to obtain a solution.

## DECISION PROCESSES FOR AGGREGATE PLANNING

The aggregate planning problem is the production planning problem of an organization seeking to meet a varying pattern of demand over an intermediate span of time (e.g., a year). Specifically, the managerial decisions in the aggregate planning problem are to set aggregate production rates and work force levels for each period within the planning horizon. There are several approaches available in the literature that differ from one another based on the cost structure assumed and the solution optimality achieved. A classification of these methods is provided in Table 8-1. Since more than two hundred papers have been published in scholarly journals on this topic, we have provided only a representative example for each major category of methods. We will discuss the graphic methods first and then mathematical and computer search methods.

## Graphic Methods

Table 8-2 shows a forecast of expected production requirements by month in column 4; these data are cumulated by month in column 5. The ratio of peak to valley in the requirements schedule is 11,000 in July to 4000 in February and March or 11,000/4000 = 2.75.

Note, however, that the number of working days per month, shown in column 2, varies considerably, from 23 working days in March and August to only 11 in September. (The plant closes for two weeks in September, when vacations are scheduled to coincide with required plant maintenance.) Therefore, the swing in production requirements per production day (see column 9 of Table 8-2) varies from 6500/11 = 591 in September to only 4000/23 = 174 in March, a ratio of 591/174 = 3.40. This substantial variation in daily production requirements is shown on the graph of requirements in Figure 8-4. Developing aggregate schedules that meet these seasonal requirements is part of the problem. Developing aggregate schedules that minimize the incremental costs associated with meeting requirements is the challenge.

Assume that normal plant capacity is 350 units per day. Additional capacity can be obtained through overtime up to a maximum capacity of 410 units per day. The additional cost per unit for units produced during overtime hours is $10.

**Buffer Inventories and Maximum Requirements.** Column 6 of Table 8-2 shows buffer inventories, which are the minimum stocks required. These buffer stocks

**TABLE 8-1**
**CLASSIFICATION OF AGGREGATE PLANNING METHODS**

| | *Cost Structure* | | | |
|---|---|---|---|---|
| Solution Optimality | Linear Cost Model | Quadratic Cost Model | Fixed Cost Model | General Cost Model |
| Optimal solution | Distribution model, linear program | Linear decision rule | Integer program, dynamic programming | Dynamic programming, nonlinear programming |
| Heuristic approximate solution | Decomposition approaches for large problems | Goal programs, Lagrangean relaxation and approximation | Decomposition approach | Search decision rule, simulation analysis |

TABLE 8-2

**FORECAST OF PRODUCTION REQUIREMENTS AND BUFFER INVENTORIES: CUMULATIVE REQUIREMENTS, AVERAGE BUFFER INVENTORIES,[a] AND CUMULATIVE MAXIMUM PRODUCTION REQUIREMENTS**

| (1) Month | (2) Production Days | (3) Cumulative Production Days | (4) Expected Production Requirements | (5) Cumulative Production Requirements. Col. 4 Cumulated | (6) Required Buffer Inventories | (7) Cumulative Maximum Production Requirements. Col. 5 + Col. 6 | (8) Col. 2 × Col. 6 | (9) Production Requirements per Production Day. Col. 4 ÷ Col. 2 |
|---|---|---|---|---|---|---|---|---|
| January | 22 | 22 | 5,000 | 5,000 | 2,800 | 7,800 | 61,600 | 227.3 |
| February | 20 | 42 | 4,000 | 9,000 | 2,500 | 11,500 | 50,000 | 200.0 |
| March | 23 | 65 | 4,000 | 13,000 | 2,500 | 15,500 | 57,500 | 173.9 |
| April | 19 | 84 | 5,000 | 18,000 | 2,800 | 20,800 | 53,200 | 263.2 |
| May | 22 | 106 | 7,000 | 25,000 | 3,200 | 28,200 | 70,400 | 318.2 |
| June | 22 | 128 | 9,000 | 34,000 | 3,500 | 37,500 | 77,000 | 409.1 |
| July | 20 | 148 | 11,000 | 45,000 | 4,100 | 49,100 | 82,000 | 550.0 |
| August | 23 | 171 | 9,000 | 54,000 | 3,500 | 57,500 | 80,500 | 391.3 |
| September | 11 | 182 | 6,500 | 60,500 | 3,000 | 63,500 | 33,000 | 590.9 |
| October | 22 | 204 | 6,000 | 66,500 | 3,000 | 69,500 | 66,000 | 272.7 |
| November | 22 | 226 | 5,000 | 71,500 | 2,800 | 74,300 | 61,600 | 227.3 |
| December | 18 | 244 | 5,000 | 76,500 | 2,800 | 79,300 | 50,400 | 277.8 |
| | | | | | | | 743,200 | |

[a] Average buffer inventory = 743,200/244 = 3045.9 units.

were determined by a judgmental process. Their purpose is to provide for the possibility that market requirements could be greater than expected. When we add the buffer inventories for each month to the cumulative production requirements in column 5, we have the cumulative maximum requirements shown in column 7. Column 8 provides the basis for weighting the buffer inventory by production days and for computing the average buffer inventory of 3045.9 units in the table footnote.

## ALTERNATIVE PLANS

**Plan 1—Level Production.** The simplest production plan is to establish an average output level that meets annual requirements. The total annual requirements are the last figure in the cumulated requirements schedule in column 5 of Table 8-2—76,500 units. Because there are 244 working days, an average daily output of 76,500/244 = 314 units should cover requirements. We may find problems with such a schedule because of timing, but we shall see what to do about these problems later. Our strategy is simple: accumulate seasonal inventory during the slack produc-

FIGURE 8-4
**COMPARISON OF TWO PRODUCTION PLANS THAT MEET REQUIREMENTS.**

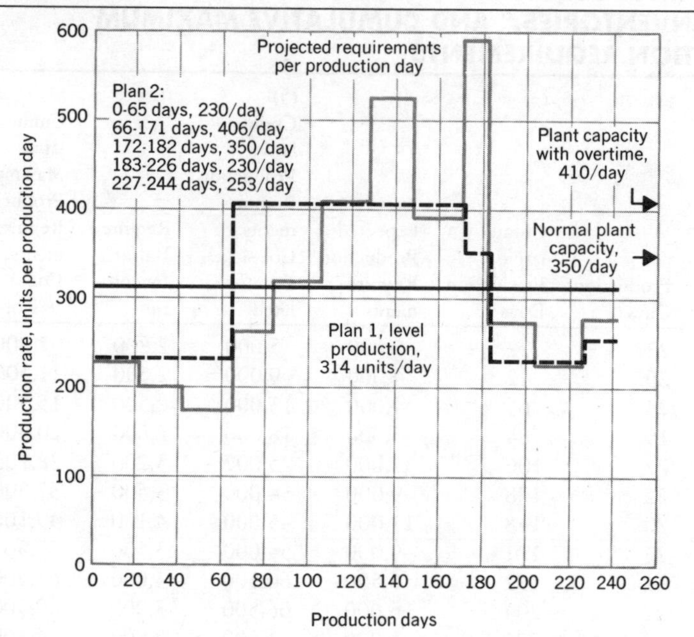


tion requirements months for use during peak requirements months. The level production plan is shown in relation to the production requirements per day in Figure 8-4 as Plan 1.

The inventory requirements for Plan 1 are calculated in Table 8-3. The production in each month is computed in column 3 and is cumulated in column 4 to produce a schedule of units available each month, starting with a beginning inventory of 2800 units, the required buffer inventory in January. Then, by comparing the units available in column 4 with the cumulative maximum requirements schedule in column 5, we can generate the schedule of seasonal inventories in column 6.

The seasonal inventories for Plan 1 in column 6 vary from a maximum of 8376 units in April to a minimum of −3552 in September. The significance of the negative seasonal inventories is that the plan calls for dipping into buffer stocks. In August, we propose to use 1006 units out of the planned buffer of 3500 units, but in September, we actually exceed the planned buffer by 552 units. In other words, the plan would actually require either back-ordering or the expected loss of the sale of 552 units in September. The plan recovers in subsequent months and meets aggregate requirements, but it incurs total shortages for the year of 7738 units.

We decide not to plan to use the buffer inventory since the buffer was designed to absorb unexpected sales increases. (If we *plan* to use them, they lose their buffering function.) How do we adjust the plan to take the negative seasonal inventories into account? All we need to do is increase the beginning inventory by the most negative seasonal inventory balance, −3552 units in September. This new beginning inven-

**TABLE 8-3**
**CALCULATION OF SEASONAL INVENTORY REQUIREMENTS FOR PLAN 1**

| (1) Production Days | (2) Production Rate, Units, per Day | (3) Production in Month, Units, Col. 1 × Col. 2 | (4) Cumulative Units Available. Cumulative Production + Beginning Inv. (2800) | (5) Cumulative Maximum Requirements, from Col. 7 of Table 8-2 | (6) Seasonal Inventory[a] = Col. 4 − Col. 5 | (7) Col. 1 × Col. 6 |
|---|---|---|---|---|---|---|
| 22 | 314 | 6,908 | 9,708 | 7,800 | 1,908 | 41,976 |
| 20 | 314 | 6,280 | 15,988 | 11,500 | 4,488 | 89,760 |
| 23 | 314 | 7,222 | 23,210 | 15,500 | 7,710 | 177,330 |
| 19 | 314 | 5,966 | 29,176 | 20,800 | 8,376 | 159,144 |
| 22 | 314 | 6,908 | 36,084 | 28,200 | 7,884 | 173,448 |
| 22 | 314 | 6,908 | 42,992 | 37,500 | 5,492 | 120,824 |
| 20 | 314 | 6,280 | 49,272 | 49,100 | 172 | 3,440 |
| 23 | 314 | 7,222 | 56,494 | 57,500 | −1,006 | −23,138 |
| 11 | 314 | 3,454 | 59,948 | 63,500 | −3,552 | −39,072 |
| 22 | 314 | 6,908 | 66,856 | 69,500 | −2,644 | −58,168 |
| 22 | 314 | 6,908 | 73,764 | 74,300 | − 536 | −11,792 |
| 18 | 314 | 5,652 | 79,416 | 79,300 | 116 | 2,088 |
| 244 | | | | | | |

[a] Average seasonal inventory (positive values in column 7/days) = 768,010/244 = 3147.6 units.

tory level has the effect of increasing the entire schedule of cumulative units available in column 4 of Table 8-3 by 3552 units. Then, average seasonal inventories will also be increased by 3552 units.

The seasonal inventories for Plan 1 are calculated in Table 8-3 as 3147.6 units, weighted by production days, assuming that we use buffer stocks and record shortages as indicated in column 6. If we revise the plan so that the buffer inventories are not used, the average seasonal inventory would be 3147.6 + 3552 = 6699.6 units.

Assuming that inventory holding costs are $50 per unit per year and that shortage costs are $25 per unit short, we can now compute the relative costs of the variants of Plan 1. If beginning inventories are only 2800 units, the annual inventory costs are 50 × 3147.6 = $157,380, and the shortage costs are 25 × 7738 = $193,450. The total incremental costs are then $350,830.

By comparison, if we decide not to use buffer inventory, the average seasonal inventories are 6699.6 units at a cost of $50 × 6699.6 = $334,980, the total incremental cost for comparison. Given these costs for holding inventories and incurring shortages, it is obviously more economical to plan on larger inventories. In other situations, the reverse might be true. If the cost of shortages is only $20 per unit, it would be slightly more economical to take the risk. Alternatively, if the costs of holding inventories were $62 per unit per year and shortage costs were $25 per unit, then the balance of costs would again favor taking the risk of incurring shortages. Of course, there are other factors that enter into the decision of whether or not to risk incurring shortages, such as the potential of losing market share permanently.

Plan 1 has significant advantages. First, it does not require the hiring or layoff of personnel. It provides stable employment for workers and would be favored by organized labor. Also, scheduling is simple—314 units per day. From an incremental production cost viewpoint, however, it fails to consider whether or not there is an economic advantage in trading off the large seasonal inventory and shortage costs for overtime costs and/or costs incurred in hiring or laying off personnel to meet seasonal variations in requirements.

**Plan 2—Using Hiring, Layoff, and Overtime.** Note from Figure 8-4 that normal plant capacity allows an output of 350 units per day and that an additional 60 units per day can be obtained through overtime work. Units produced on overtime cost an additional $10 per unit in this example.

Up to the normal capacity of 350 units per day, we can increase or decrease output by hiring or laying off labor. A worker hired or laid off affects the net output by 1 unit per day. The cost of changing output levels in this way is $200 per worker hired or laid off, owing to hiring, training, severance, and other associated costs.

Plan 2 offers the additional options of changing basic output rates and using overtime for peak requirements. Plan 2 is shown in Figure 8-4 and involves two basic employment levels: labor to produce at normal output rates of 230 and 350 units per day. Additional variations are achieved through the use of overtime when it is needed. The plan has the following schedule:

0 to 65 days—produce at 230 units per day.

66 to 171 days—produce at 406 units per day (hire 120 workers to increase basic rate without overtime from 230 to 350 units per day; produce 56 units per day at overtime rates).

172 to 182 days—produce at 350 units per day (no overtime).

183 to 226 days—produce at 230 units per day (lay off 120 workers to reduce basic rate from 350 to 230 units per day again).

227 to 244 days—produce at 253 units per day (23 units per day at overtime rates).

The calculations for the seasonal inventory requirements for Plan 2 are similar to those for Plan 1. The seasonal inventory for Plan 2 has been reduced to only 2356 units, 75 percent of Plan 1 with shortages and 35 percent of Plan 1 without shortages.

To counterbalance the inventory reduction, we must hire 120 workers in April and lay off an equal number in October. Also, we have produced a significant number of units at overtime rates from April to September and in December. The costs of Plan 2 are summarized in Table 8-4. The total incremental costs of Plan 2 are $229,320, which is 65 percent of Plan 1 with shortages and 68 percent of Plan 1 without shortages.

Plan 2 is a somewhat more economical plan, but it requires substantial fluctuations in the size of the work force. Whether the social and employee relations conse-

TABLE 8-4
**CALCULATION OF INCREMENTAL COSTS FOR PLAN 2**

| (1) Production Days | (2) Production Rate/Day | (3) Units of Production Rate Change | (4) Units Produced at Overtime Production Rates Greater Than 350 or 230 × Col. 1 |
|---|---|---|---|
| 22 | 230 | –0– | –0– |
| 20 | 230 | –0– | –0– |
| 23 | 230 | –0– | –0– |
| 19 | 406 | 120 | 1,064 |
| 22 | 406 | –0– | 1,232 |
| 22 | 406 | –0– | 1,232 |
| 20 | 406 | –0– | 1,120 |
| 23 | 406 | –0– | 1,288 |
| 11 | 350 | –0– | –0– |
| 22 | 230 | 120 | –0– |
| 22 | 230 | –0– | –0– |
| 18 | 253 | –0– | 414 |
| | | 240 | 6,350 |
| Production rate change costs = 240 × 200 = | | | $ 48,000 |
| (A change in the basic rate of one unit requires the hiring or layoff of one worker at $200 each) | | | |
| Overtime costs at $10 extra per unit = 10 × 6,350 = | | | 63,500 |
| Seasonal inventory cost (2356.4 units at $50 per unit per year) = 50 × 2356.4 = | | | 117,820 |
| Total incremental cost = | | | $229,320 |

quences can be tolerated is a matter for managerial judgment. If the employment fluctuation is greater than management feels can be tolerated, other alternatives involving smaller fluctuations in employment can be computed. Perhaps some of the variations can be absorbed by more overtime work, and in some kinds of industries, subcontracting can be used to meet the most severe peak requirements.

**Plan 3—Adding Subcontracting as a Source.** Suppose that management wishes to consider a third alternative that involves smaller work force fluctuations by using overtime, seasonal inventories, and subcontracting to absorb the balance of requirements fluctuations. Plan 3 has the following schedule:

0 to 84 days—produce at 250 units per day.

85 to 128 days—produce at 350 units per day (hire 100 workers to increase the basic rate from 250 to 350 units per day).

129 to 148 days—produce at 410 units per day (60 units per day produced on overtime, plus 1700 units subcontracted).

149 to 171 days—produce at 370 units per day (20 units per day produced on overtime).

172 to 182 days—produce at 410 units per day (60 units per day produced on overtime, plus 1380 units subcontracted).

183 to 204 days—produce at 273 units per day (23 units per day produced on overtime; lay off 100 workers to reduce employment level from basic rate of 350 to 250 units per day).

205 to 244 days—produce at 250 units per day.

Plan 3 reduces seasonal inventories still further to an average of only 1301 units. Employment fluctuation is more modest, involving the hiring and laying off of only 100 workers. Only 2826 units are produced at overtime rates, but a total of 3080 units are subcontracted at an additional cost of $15 per unit.

Table 8-5 summarizes the costs for all three plans. For the particular example, Plan 3 is the most economical. The buffer inventories are nearly the same for all the plans, so their costs are not included as incremental costs.

Even though Plan 3 involves less employment fluctuation than Plan 2, it may still be felt to be too severe. Other plans involving less fluctuation could be developed and their incremental costs determined in the same way.

## CUMULATIVE GRAPHS

Although Figure 8-4 shows the effects of the production rate changes quite clearly, it is actually somewhat easier to work with cumulative curves, which are shown in Figure 8-5. The procedure is to plot first the cumulative production requirements. The cumulative maximum requirements curve is then simply the former curve with

TABLE 8-5
**COMPARISON OF COSTS OF ALTERNATE PRODUCTION PLANS**

| | Plan 1 | | | |
|---|---|---|---|---|
| Costs | With Shortages | Without Shortages | Plan 2 | Plan 3 |
| Shortages[a] | $193,450 | — | — | — |
| Seasonal inventory[b] | 157,380 | $334,980 | $117,820 | $ 65,070 |
| Labor turnover[c] | — | — | 48,000 | 40,000 |
| Overtime[d] | — | — | 63,500 | 28,260 |
| Subcontracting[e] | — | — | — | 46,200 |
| Totals | $350,830 | $334,980 | $229,320 | $179,530 |

[a] Shortages cost $25 per unit.
[b] Inventory carrying costs are $50 per unit per year.
[c] An increase or decrease in the basic production rate of one unit requires the hiring or layoff of one employee at a hiring and training, or severance, cost of $200 each.
[d] Units produced at overtime rates cost an additional $10 per unit.
[e] Units subcontracted cost an additional $15 per unit.

FIGURE 8-5
**CUMULATIVE GRAPHS OF REQUIREMENTS AND ALTERNATE PRODUCTION PROGRAMS.**

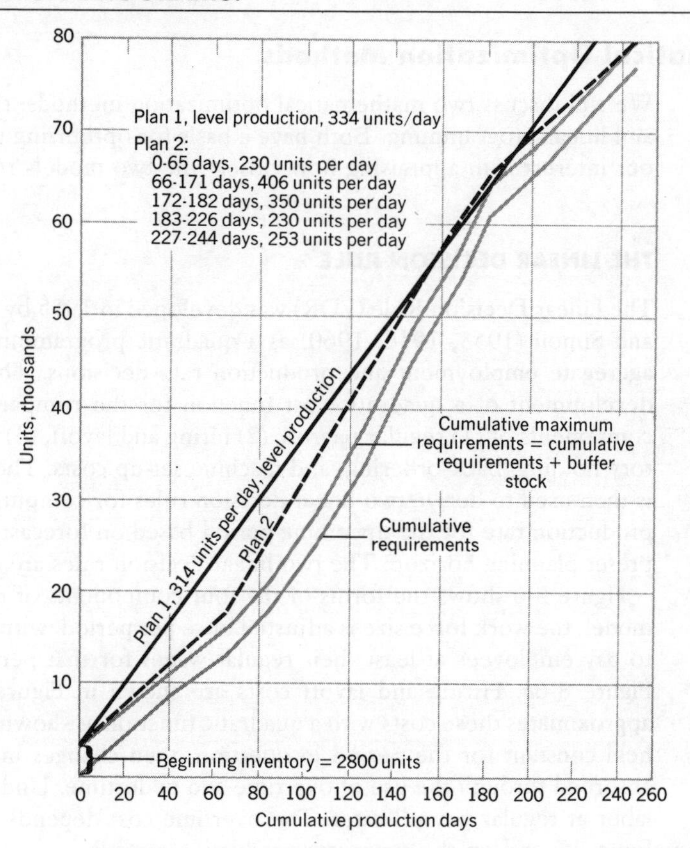


the required buffer inventories added for each period. The cumulative graph of maximum requirements can then be used as a basis for generating alternative program proposals. Any production program that is feasible, in the sense that it meets requirements while providing the desired buffer stock protection, must fall entirely above the cumulative maximum requirements line. The vertical distances between the program proposal curves and the cumulative maximum requirements curve represent the seasonal inventory accumulation for each plan.

Graphic methods are simple and have the advantage of allowing alternative programs to be visualized over a broad planning horizon. The difficulties with graphic methods, however, are the static nature of the graphic model and the fact that the process is in no sense cost or profit optimizing. In addition, the process does not itself generate good programs; it simply compares proposals that have been made.

The alternative plan proposals used in connection with the graphic methods indicate the sensitivity of the plans to the use of various sources of short-term capacity: seasonal inventories, shortages, the use of overtime capacity, and subcontracting.

Mathematical and computer search models attempt to find optimal combinations of these sources of short-term capacity.

## Mathematical Optimization Methods

We will discuss two mathematical optimization methods: the Linear Decision Rule and linear programming. Both have a basis for optimizing the model developed, so our interest is in appraising how closely the two models represent reality.

### THE LINEAR DECISION RULE

The Linear Decision Rule (LDR) was developed in 1955 by Holt, Modigliani, Muth, and Simon (1955, 1956, 1960) as a quadratic programming approach for making aggregate employment and production rate decisions. The LDR is based on the development of a quadratic cost function for the company in question with cost components of (1) regular payroll, (2) hiring and layoff, (3) overtime, and (4) inventory holding, back-ordering, and machine set-up costs. The quadratic cost function is then used to derive two linear decision rules for computing work force level and production rate for the upcoming period based on forecasts of aggregate sales for a preset planning horizon. The two linear decision rules are optimum for the model.

Figure 8-6 shows the forms of the four components of the cost function. In this model, the work force size is adjusted once per period, with an implied commitment to pay employees at least their regular wages for that period. This is indicated in Figure 8-6*a*. Hiring and layoff costs are shown in Figure 8-6*b*; the LDR model approximates these costs with a quadratic function as shown. If the work force size is held constant for the period in question, then changes in production rate can be absorbed through the use of overtime and undertime. Undertime is the cost of idle labor at regular payroll rates. The overtime cost depends on the size of the work force, $W$, and on the aggregate production rate, $P$.

The form of the overtime–undertime cost function in relation to production rate is shown in Figure 8-6*c*; it is also approximated by a quadratic function. Whether overtime or undertime costs will occur for a given decision depends on the balance of costs defined by the horizon time. For example, in responding to the need for increased output, the costs of hiring and training must be balanced against the costs for overtime. Conversely, the response to a decreased production rate would require the balancing of layoff costs against undertime costs.

The general shape of the net inventory cost curve is shown in Figure 8-6*d*. Again, these costs are approximated by a quadratic function in the LDR model.

The total incremental cost function is the sum of the four component cost functions for a particular example. The mathematical problem is to minimize the sum of the monthly combined cost function over the planning horizon time of $N$ periods. The result of this mathematical development is the specification of two linear decision rules that are then used to compute the aggregate size of the work force and the production rate for the upcoming period. These two rules require as inputs the forecast for each period of the planning horizon in aggregate terms, the size of work force, and inventory level in the last period. Once the two rules have been devel-

FIGURE 8-6
**APPROXIMATING THE LINEAR AND QUADRATIC FUNCTIONS USED BY THE LINEAR DECISION RULE (LDR) MODEL.**

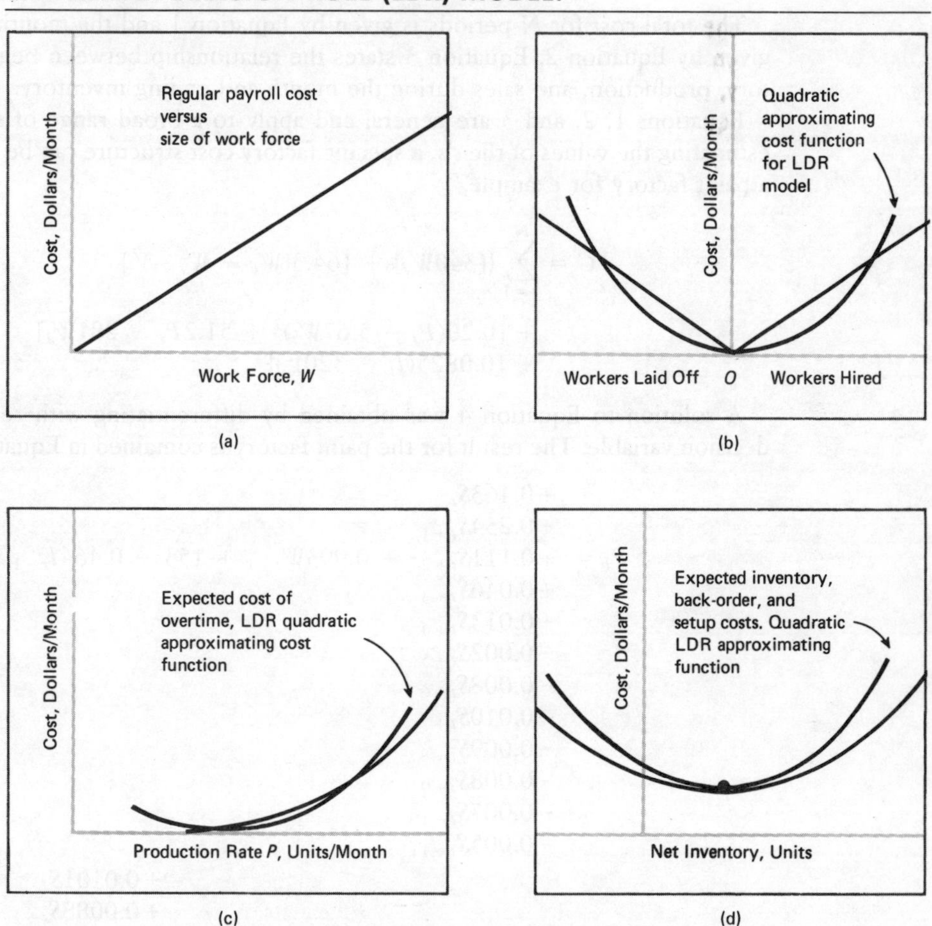


oped for a specific application, the computations needed to produce the decisions recommended by the model require only 10 to 15 minutes by manual methods.

We will now discuss the development of the Linear Decision Rule Model. The problem is to minimize costs over $N$ periods, or

$$\text{Minimize } C = \sum_{t=1}^{N} C_t \tag{1}$$

where

$$\begin{aligned} C_t = [&(c_1 W_t) && \text{(regular payroll costs)} \\ &+ c_2(W_t - W_{t-1})^2 && \text{(hiring and layoff costs)} \\ &+ c_3(P_t - c_4 W_t)^2 + c_5 P_t - c_6 W_t && \text{(overtime costs)} \\ &+ c_7(I_t - c_8 - c_9 S_t)^2] && \text{(inventory connected costs)} \end{aligned} \tag{2}$$

subject to the constraints

$$I_{t-1} + P_t - F_t = I_t \qquad t = 1, 2, \ldots, N \tag{3}$$

The total cost for $N$ periods is given by Equation 1 and the monthly cost, $C_t$, is given by Equation 2. Equation 3 states the relationship between beginning inventory, production, and sales during the month and ending inventory.

Equations 1, 2, and 3 are general and apply to a broad range of situations. By estimating the values of the $c$'s, a specific factory cost structure can be specified. For a paint factory for example,

$$\begin{aligned} C = \sum_{t=1}^{N} \{&[340W_t] + [64.3(W_t - W_{t-1})^2] \\ &+ [0.20(P_t - 5.67W_t)^2 + 51.2P_t - 281W_t] \\ &+ [0.0825(I_t - 320)^2]\} \end{aligned} \tag{4}$$

A solution to Equation 4 was obtained by differentiating with respect to each decision variable. The result for the paint factory is contained in Equations 5 and 6:

$$P_t = \begin{Bmatrix} +0.463S_t \\ +0.234S_{t+1} \\ +0.111S_{t+2} \\ +0.046S_{t+3} \\ +0.013S_{t+4} \\ -0.002S_{t+5} \\ -0.008S_{t+6} \\ -0.010S_{t+7} \\ -0.009S_{t+8} \\ -0.008S_{t+9} \\ -0.007S_{t+10} \\ -0.005S_{t+11} \end{Bmatrix} + 0.993W_{t-1} + 153 - 0.464I_{t-1} \tag{5}$$

$$W_t = 0.743W_{t-1} + 2.09 - 0.010I_{t-1} + \begin{Bmatrix} +0.0101S_t \\ +0.0088S_{t+1} \\ +0.0071S_{t+2} \\ +0.0054S_{t+3} \\ +0.0042S_{t+4} \\ +0.0031S_{t+5} \\ +0.0023S_{t+6} \\ +0.0016S_{t+7} \\ +0.0012S_{t+8} \\ +0.0009S_{t+9} \\ +0.0006S_{t+10} \\ +0.0005S_{t+11} \end{Bmatrix} \tag{6}$$

where

$P_t$ = The number of units of product that should be produced during the forthcoming month $t$.

$W_{t-1}$ = The number of employees in the work force at the beginning of the month (the end of the previous month).

$I_{t-1}$ = The number of units of inventory minus the number of units on back-order at the beginning of the month.

$W_t$ = The number of employees that will be required for the current month $t$. The number of employees that should be hired is therefore $W_t - W_{t-1}$.

$S_t$ = A forecast of number of units of product that will be ordered for shipment during the current month $t$.

Equations 5 and 6 would be used at the beginning of each month. Equation 5 determines the aggregate production rate and Equation 6, the aggregate size of the work force.

**An Example.** An LDR model was developed for a paint company and was applied to a six-year record of known decisions in the company. Two kinds of forecasts were used as inputs: a perfect forecast and a moving average forecast. The actual order pattern was extremely variable, involving both the 1949 recession and the Korean War. The graphic record of actual factory performance for production rates and work force levels compared with the simulated performance of the LDR is shown in Figures 8-7 and 8-8. From company data, costs were reconstructed for actual operation during the six-year period and were projected for the decision rules based on the nonquadratic cost structure originally estimated. The cost difference between the actual company performance and performance with the LDR based on the moving average forecast was $173,000 per year in favor of the LDR.

The LDR has many important advantages. First, the model is optimizing, and once derived, the two decision rules are simple to apply. In addition, the model is dynamic and represents the multistage kind of system that we discussed in connection with Figure 8-3. On the other hand, the quadratic costs structure may have severe limitations, and it probably does not adequately represent the cost structure of many organizations.

## LINEAR PROGRAMMING METHODS

The aggregate planning problem has been developed in the context of distribution models (Bowman, 1956) as well as more general models of linear programming. Methods of linear programming developed for distribution problems have some limitations when they are applied to aggregate planning problems. The distribution model does not account for production change costs, such as those incurred in hiring and laying off personnel. Thus, the resulting programs may call for changes in production levels in one period that require an expanded work force, only to call for the layoff of these workers in a future period. Still, the model has considerable flexibility for including a variety of costs, and it is relatively simple to formulate and use.

The more general linear programming formulation makes it possible to include production level change costs in the model. Hanssmann and Hess (1960) developed a linear optimization model that is entirely parallel with the Linear Decision Rule in

FIGURE 8-7
**COMPARATIVE PERFORMANCE OF THE LINEAR DECISION RULE (LDR) WITH ACTUAL FACTORY PERFORMANCE FOR PRODUCTION RATES.**

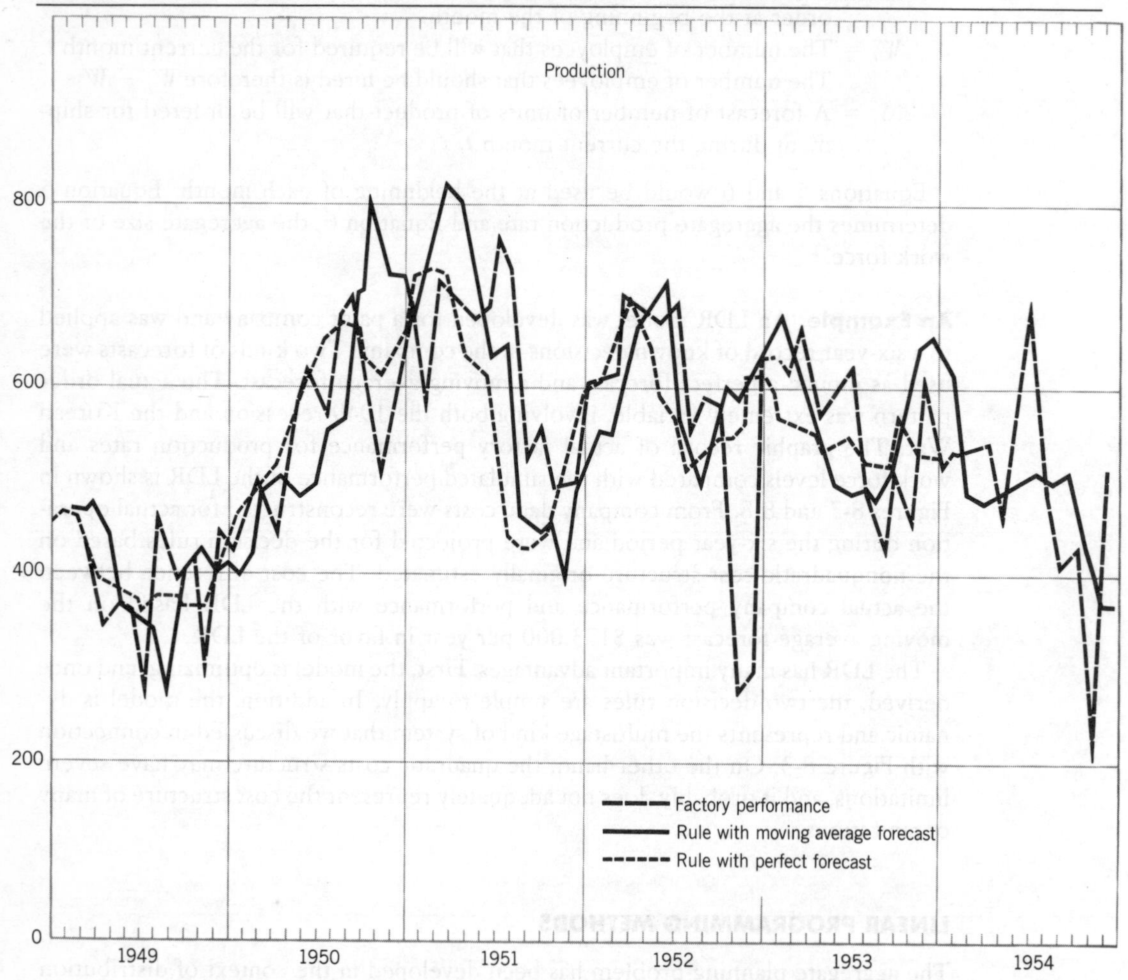


*Source:* C. C. Holt, F. Modigliani, and H. A. Simon, "A Linear Decision Rule for Production and Employment Scheduling," *Management Science, 2*(2), October 1955.

terms of using work force and production rate as independent decision variables and in terms of the cost components it uses. The main differences between the Hanssmann-Hess (H-H) model and LDR model are that in the H-H model all cost functions must be linear and linear programming is the solution technique. One's preference between the two models would depend on the preference for using either the linear or the quadratic cost model in a given application.

There have been many applications of linear programming to the aggregate planning problem. Also, Lee and Moore (1974) have applied the general goal programming format to the aggregate planning problem.

FIGURE 8-8
**COMPARATIVE PERFORMANCE OF THE LINEAR DECISION RULE (LDR) WITH ACTUAL FACTORY PERFORMANCE FOR WORK FORCE SIZE.**

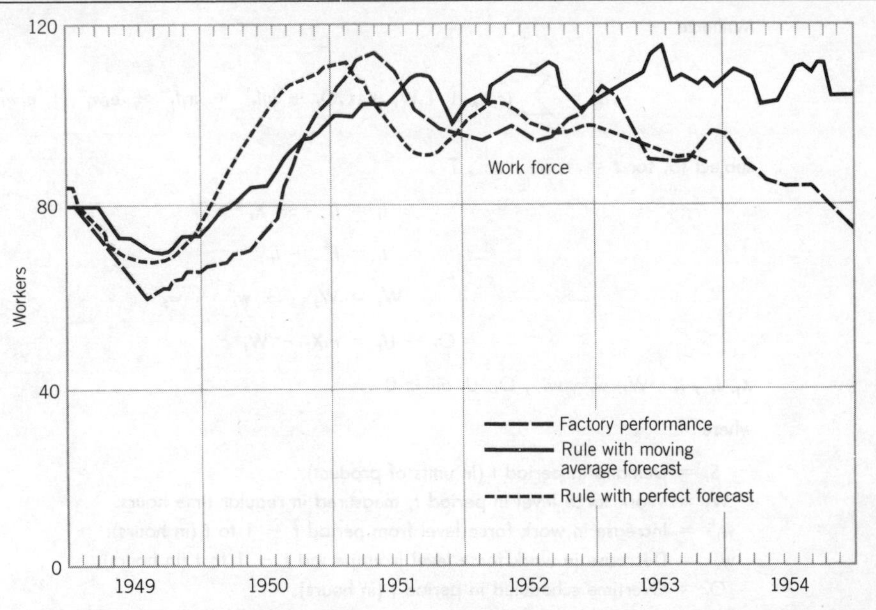


*Source:* C. C. Holt, F. Modigliani, and H. A. Simon, "A Linear Decision Rule for Production and Employment Scheduling," *Management Science, 2*(2), October 1955.

**Generalized Linear Optimization Model for Aggregate Planning.** In the time since Bowman developed the distribution model for aggregate planning, several linear programming formulations have been developed that overcome its disadvantages. Most of these models can be viewed as variations on the general information shown in Figure 8-9 (Equations 7-11).

The objective function (Equation 7) minimizes, over the entire planning horizon of $T$ periods, the sum of regular production costs, regular and overtime labor costs, inventory and backlogging costs, and work force change costs.

Constraint Equation 8 merely states that the ending inventory, $I_t$, equals the beginning inventory plus production during the period minus demand during the period.

Constraint Equation 9 states a further restriction on ending inventory, $I_t$, to take account of the balance between inventory on hand and back-orders.

Constraint Equation 10 states that the work force level in period $t$, $W_t$, measured in regular time hours, is equal to the level of the previous period, $W_{t-1}$, plus any additions or decreases due to hiring or layoff.

Constraint Equation 11 states a required balance between the sum of overtime hours scheduled less undertime or unused capacity in period $t$ and the hours used to produce the number of units scheduled, $X_t$, less the work force size in hours available. This equation ensures that all production occurs on regular time or over-

FIGURE 8-9
**GENERALIZED LINEAR OPTIMIZATION MODEL FOR AGGREGATE PLANNING.**

Minimize

$$Z = \sum_{t=1}^{T} (c_t X_t + \ell_t W_t + \ell'_t O_t + h_t I_t^+ + \pi_t I_t^- + e_t w_t^+ + e'_t w_t^-) \quad (7)$$

subject to, for $t = 1, 2, \ldots, T$

$$I_t = I_{t-1} + X_t - S_t \quad (8)$$

$$I_t = I_t^+ - I_t^- \quad (9)$$

$$W_t = W_{t-1} + w_t^+ - w_t^- \quad (10)$$

$$O_t - U_t = mX_t - W_t \quad (11)$$

$X_t, I_t^+, I_t^-, W_t, w_t^+, w_t^-, O_t, U_t$ all $\geq 0$

where

$S_t$ = Demand in period $t$ (in units of product).
$W_t$ = Work force level in period $t$, measured in regular time hours.
$w_t^+$ = Increase in work force level from period $t - 1$ to $t$ (in hours).
$w_t^-$ = Decrease in work force level from period $t - 1$ to $t$ (in hours).
$O_t$ = Overtime scheduled in period $t$ (in hours).
$U_t$ = Undertime (unused regular time capacity) scheduled in period $t$ (in hours).
$X_t$ = Production scheduled for period $t$ (in units of product).
$I_t^+$ = On-hand inventory at the end of period $t$
$I_t^-$ = Back order position at the end of period $t$.
$m$ = Number of hours required to produce one unit of product.
$\ell_t$ = Cost of an hour's worth of labor on regular time in period $t$.
$\ell'_t$ = Cost of an hour's worth of labor on overtime in period $t$.
$e_t$ = Cost to increase the work force level by one hour in period $t$.
$e'_t$ = Cost to decrease the work force level by one hour in period $t$.
$h_t$ = Inventory carrying cost, per unit held from period $t$ to $t + 1$.
$\pi_t$ = Back order cost, per unit carried from period $t$ to $t + 1$.
$c_t$ = Unit variable production cost in period $t$ (excluding labor).

time. The undertime variable, $U_t$, is a slack variable to take account of the fact that the work force may not always be fully utilized.

Finally, all the variables are restricted to be nonnegative.

## Search Decision Rule (SDR)

A computer search procedure may be used to evaluate systematically a cost or profit criterion function at trial points. When using this procedure, it is hoped that an optimum value may be eventually found, but there is no guarantee. In direct search methods, the cost criterion function is evaluated at a point, the result is compared with previous trial results, and a move is determined on the basis of a set of heuristics ("rules of thumb"). The new point is then evaluated, and the procedure is repeated until it is determined that a better solution that will result in an improved value of the objective function cannot be found or until the predetermined computer time limit is exceeded. Taubert (1968, 1968a) experimented with computer search methods using the paint company data as a vehicle.

The costs to be minimized are expressed as a function of production rates and work force levels in each period of the planning horizon. Therefore, each period included in the planning horizon requires the addition of two dimensions to the criterion function, one for production rate and one for work force size.

Table 8-6 shows a sample of the computer output for the first month of factory operation of the paint company. The computer output gives the first month's deci-

TABLE 8-6
**SDR OUTPUT FOR THE FIRST MONTH OF FACTORY OPERATION (PERFECT FORECAST)**

A. SDR Decisions and Projections

| Month | Sales (gallons) | Production (gallons) | Inventory (gallons) | Work Force (workers) |
|---|---|---|---|---|
| 0 | | | 263.00 | 81.00 |
| 1 | 430 | 471.89 | 304.89 | 77.60 |
| 2 | 447 | 444.85 | 302.74 | 74.10 |
| 3 | 440 | 416.79 | 279.54 | 70.60 |
| 4 | 316 | 380.90 | 344.44 | 67.32 |
| 5 | 397 | 374.64 | 322.08 | 64.51 |
| 6 | 375 | 363.67 | 310.75 | 62.07 |
| 7 | 292 | 348.79 | 367.54 | 60.22 |
| 8 | 458 | 345.63 | 268.17 | 58.68 |
| 9 | 400 | 329.83 | 198.00 | 57.05 |
| 10 | 350 | 270.60 | 118.60 | 55.75 |

B. Cost Analysis of Decisions and Projections (dollars)

| Month | Payroll | Hiring and Layoff | Overtime | Inventory | Total |
|---|---|---|---|---|---|
| 1 | 26,384.04 | 743.25 | 2558.82 | 18.33 | 29,704.94 |
| 2 | 25,195.60 | 785.62 | 2074.76 | 24.57 | 28,080.54 |
| 3 | 24,004.00 | 789.79 | 1555.68 | 135.06 | 26,484.53 |
| 4 | 22,888.86 | 691.69 | 585.21 | 49.27 | 24,215.03 |
| 5 | 21,932.79 | 508.43 | 1070.48 | 0.36 | 23,512.06 |
| 6 | 21,102.86 | 383.13 | 1206.90 | 7.06 | 22,699.93 |
| 7 | 20,473.22 | 220.51 | 948.13 | 186.43 | 21,828.29 |
| 8 | 19,950.99 | 151.70 | 2007.33 | 221.64 | 22,331.66 |
| 9 | 19,395.30 | 171.76 | 865.74 | 1227.99 | 21,660.79 |
| 10 | 18,954.76 | 107.95 | −1395.80 | 3346.46 | 21,012.37 |
| | | | | | 241,530.14 |

*Source:* W. H. Taubert, "Search Decision Rule for the Aggregate Scheduling Problem," *Management Science, 14* (6), February 1968, pp. 343–359.

sion as well as an entire program for the planning horizon of 10 months. In the lower half of the table, the program prints out the component costs of payroll, hiring and layoff, overtime, and inventory and the total of these costs for the entire planning horizon. Thus, a manager is provided not only with immediate decisions for the upcoming month but also with projected decisions based on monthly forecasts for the planning horizon time and the economic consequences of each month's decisions. Of course, the more distant projections lose much of their significance. The projections are updated, with each monthly decision based on the most recent forecast and cost inputs. The total cost of the SDR program exceeds the LDR total by only $806 or 0.11 percent. This difference may be accounted for by the fact that the SDR used a planning horizon of only 10 months as compared to the 12-month horizon used by the LDR.

With the encouraging results of the SDR virtually duplicating the performance of LDR for the paint company, it was decided to test the SDR in more demanding situations. Thus, models were developed for three rather different applications: (1) the Search Company (Buffa and Taubert, 1967), a hypothetical organization involving a much more complex cost model including the possibility of using a second shift when needed; (2) the Search Mill (Redwine, 1971), based on disguised data obtained from a major American integrated steel mill; and (3) the Search Laboratory (Taubert, 1968a), a fictious name for a division of a large aerospace research and development laboratory. All three situations represent significant extensions beyond the paint company applications with highly complex cost models and other factors to challenge the SDR methodology. Results from the Search Laboratory application are discussed in Situation 22.

Flowers and Preston (1977) applied the SDR methodology to work force planning in one department of a tank trailer manufacturer. The department had a work force ranging from 14 to 23 employees, and the company employed a total of 250 to 350 persons. Because the department worked almost exclusively from a backlog of firm orders, the assumption of perfect forecasts was logical and was accepted by management as representing reality. The simplicity of the situation made it possible to restrict decisions to the single variable of work force size. SDR decisions were about three percent less costly than actual decisions. This saving was regarded as significant by management and led to their desire to extend the model to include the entire work force.

Rossin (1985) has used SDR methodology to develop a manager-interactive model. In this model, the manager specifies the objective function and constraints, and a search procedure is then used to obtain solutions for aggregate production, work force, and inventory levels. The procedure is terminated if the manager likes the solution; otherwise, additional constraints or parameters are included in the model and another solution is obtained. This approach is useful in institutions where a manager may not be able to specify the model in complete detail *a priori*. However, when a solution is presented to the manager, he or she can examine it and provide additional information to be included in the model. This approach may make for greater realism in the model formulation and solution process. A flowchart for this procedure is shown in Figure 8-10.

FIGURE 8-10
**MANAGER INTERACTIVE MODEL.**

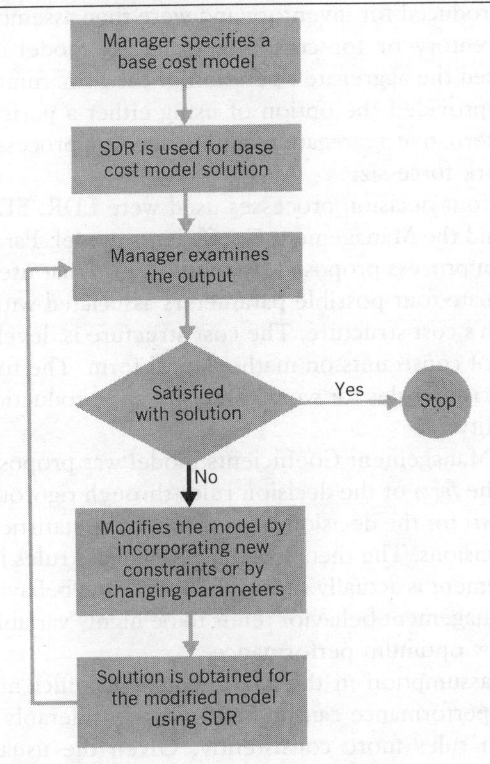


## COMPARATIVE PERFORMANCE OF AGGREGATE PLANNING DECISION PROCESSES

Because the LDR is optimal for a model, it has commonly been used as a standard for comparison by proposers of new decision processes for aggregate planning. The availability of a standard for comparison has been particularly valuable for decision processes that are not mathematically optimal. By substantially duplicating LDR performance on standard problems, such as that of the paint company, the general validity of new methods has been established. Such comparisons, however, fall short of validating the performance of any decision process in real environments. LDR assumes that cost structures are quadratic in form when, in fact, cost functions may take a variety of mathematical forms. Thus, the best evaluation of the comparative performance of alternative decision processes is in the real world, where we are attempting to optimize the costs (or profits) actually found rather than those of a restrictive model.

Lee and Khumawala (1974) report a comparative study carried out in the environment of a firm in the capital goods industry having annual sales of approximately $11 million. The plan was a typical closed job shop manufacturing facility in which parts were produced for inventory and were then assembled into finished products either for inventory or for customer order. A model of the firm was developed that simulated the aggregate operation of the firm. Simulated demand forecasting in the model provided the option of using either a perfect or an imperfect forecast, and four alternative aggregate planning decision processes were used to plan production and work force size.

The four decision processes used were LDR, SDR, Parametric Production Planning, and the Management Coefficients model. Parametric Production Planning is a decision process proposed by Jones (1967) that uses a coarse grid search procedure to evaluate four possible parameters associated with minimum cost performance in the firm's cost structure. The cost structure is developed for the particular firm and is free of constraints on mathematical form. The four parameters are then inserted into decision rules for work force size and production rate. There is no guarantee of optimality.

The Management Coefficients model was proposed by Bowman (1963); it establishes the *form* of the decision rules through rigorous analysis, but it determines the *coefficients* for the decision rules through the statistical analysis of management's own past decisions. The theory behind Bowman's rules is rooted in the assumptions that management is actually sensitive to the same behavior used in analytical models and that management behavior tends to be highly variable rather than consistently above or below optimum performance.

The assumption in the Management Coefficients model, then, is that management's performance can be improved considerably if it simply applies the derived decision rules more consistently. Given the usual dish-shape of cost functions, inconsistency in applying decision rules is more costly than consistently being slightly above or below optimum decisions because such functions are commonly quite flat near the optimum.

## Results

Table 8-7 summarizes comparative profit performance for actual company decisions and the four test decision processes. When the imperfect forecast available to the management of the firm is used, all four decision processes result in increased profits. The minimum mean profit increase over actual company decisions is $187,000 (4 percent), which was obtained by using the Management Coefficients model. The maximum mean increase is $601,000 (14 percent), which was obtained by using SDR. The contrast between the profit figures for the perfect and imperfect forecast gives a measure of the value of more accurate forecast information. Although perfect forecasts increase profits ($119,000 for the SDR for example), forecast accuracy is less significant than the decision process used. Note, for instance, the $601,000 difference between the SDR and company decisions and the $414,000 difference between the SDR and the Management Coefficients model.

TABLE 8-7
**COMPARATIVE PROFIT PERFORMANCE**

| | Imperfect Forecast | Perfect Forecast |
|---|---|---|
| Company decisions | $4,420,000 | — |
| Linear Decision Rule | $4,821,000 | $5,078,000 |
| Management Coefficients model | $4,607,000 | $5,000,000 |
| Parametric Production Planning | $4,900,000 | $4,989,000 |
| Search Decision Rule | $5,021,000 | $5,140,000 |

*Source:* W. B. Lee and B. M. Khumawala, "Simulation Testing of Aggregate Production Planning Models in an Implementation Methodology," *Management Science, 20* (6), February 1974, pp. 903–911.

## MANAGERS' POLICIES FOR DEALING WITH LOAD LEVELING

In addition to aggregate planning, managers use a number of policies to cope with the problems that result from seasonality; among them are the adoption of counter-seasonal products, influencing demand, some interesting organizational adaptations, and legal coordination with other organizations.

### Counterseasonal Products

One of the most common managerial strategies for obtaining good utilization of facilities and work force and stabilizing employment is to acquire counterseasonal products and integrate them into the system. The strategy here is to find product lines that use existing production technology but have a demand pattern that complements that of the existing lines. The classic example is lawn mowers and snow blowers.

Figure 8-11 shows a situation where the original plant load built up to a peak during the summer, resulting in large hiring and layoff costs and high investment in physical capacity for the peak. By adding the proposed product line, the total plant load would be much more level throughout the year. The costs of labor fluctuations are eliminated, the basis for improved labor relations is established, and both labor and facilities utilization are improved. The new peak physical capacity requires only a 50 percent increase over the old, assuming that temporary measures such as overtime can be used for the late summer minipeak. But, physical production should be approximately double. Assuming the same revenue per unit of load, total revenue would double in addition to the other advantages.

Obviously, the decision to adopt a new product line is one that is made at high levels in any organization. The decision involves all the major functional units, but its impact on the production function is very important indeed. Vergin (1966), in his analysis of eight manufacturing organizations, found that the counterseasonal prod-

FIGURE 8-11
**LOAD LEVELING EFFECT OF ADDING A SEASONALLY COMPLEMENTARY PRODUCT LINE TO AN EXISTING PRODUCT LINE.**

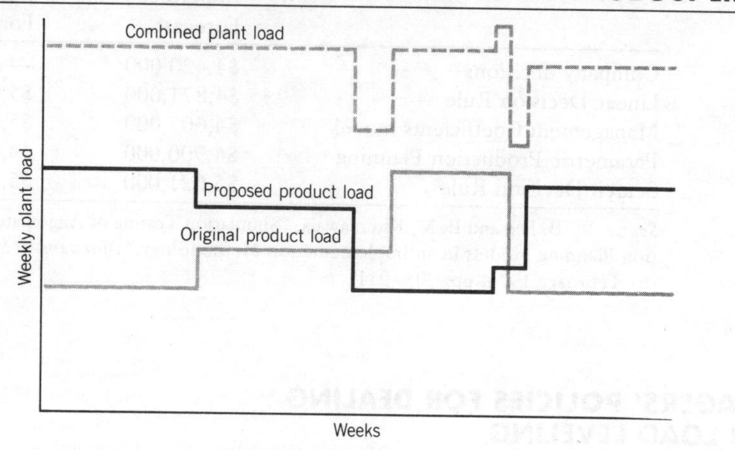


uct was the dominant managerial strategy, almost to the exclusion of other very attractive alternatives, such as aggregate planning.

## Influencing Demand

This well-known managerial practice is illustrated by post-Christmas sales, and the airlines' offerings of special prices during the off-season and for night flights. But these pricing practices have ramifications beyond simply increasing sales. Managers can also influence demand by compensatory allocation of promotion budgets. By stimulating demand during the off-season, managers can help level plant load, which has important effects on costs, capacities, and employment stabilization. As we will see later in this chapter, formal models of aggregate planning have been constructed that make production and marketing decisions jointly in order to approach a system optimum.

## Organizational Adaptations

Managers make fundamental adaptations in their organizations in an attempt to smooth demand in relation to resources that are often fixed. For example, in one of the early applications of aggregate planning, a chocolate factory changed its location to a rural area in order to take advantage of the farm labor available in the fall and winter season. Thus, a hiring and layoff smoothing strategy became compatible with seasonal fluctuations in production. The guaranteed annual wage in the meat packing industry makes it possible to vary the length of the work week without substantial wage variations. Of course, the adoption of counterseasonal products is also an adaptive response.

An interesting organizational adaptation that has implications for seasonal operations is that of Blackburn College.[1] Every student must work for the college 15 hours per week, regardless of his or her financial position. Besides certain educational and operational cost values to such a program, the cost of labor force fluctuations between summer and the academic year is zero. According to the treasurer, "We have a highly intelligent work staff that retires every four years, without pension."

### Coordination with Other Organizations

One of the common managerial strategies has been to subcontract requirements above certain capacity limits when possible. Such a managerial strategy usually involves coordination between two different firms in the marketplace. A larger, integrated firm may make subcontracting arrangements with smaller, more flexible firms operating in the same field. Galbraith (1969) cites examples in the coal and oil-refining industries.

In other situations, managerial strategy may involve coordination between producers and customers in which the producer may be able to increase lot sizes, split lots, or delay or speed up deliveries in order to smooth the work load. In return, the customer receives preferential supply treatment.

Finally, it may be possible for some organizations to form a coalition that can have the effect of smoothing work loads. For example, electric utilities join together in networks of supply that enable them to meet peak demands for the network system as a whole. If each individual utility had to meet its individual peak demands, higher plant investment would be required in the aggregate for each organization. The airlines have found that by sharing equipment when route structures are noncompetitive and counterseasonal, they can achieve somewhat better equipment utilization.

## JOINT DECISIONS AMONG OPERATIONS, MARKETING, AND FINANCE

The entire thrust of aggregate planning and scheduling methods is to employ systems concepts in making key decisions for operations. The results of coordinating decisions about activity levels, work force size, the use of overtime, and inventory levels amply illustrate that these kinds of decisions should be made jointly rather than independently. To make them independently is to suboptimize. But why stop with the operations function? Would even better results be obtained if some key operational decisions were made jointly with key decisions in marketing and finance?

Tuite (1968) proposed merging marketing strategy selection and production scheduling. Holloway (1969) proposed price as an independent variable coupled with allocations of compensatory promotion budgets. Bergstrom and Smith (1970)

[1] "The School That Works," *Time,* May 18, 1981, p. 77.

proposed estimating revenue versus sales curves for each product in each time period, with the amount to be sold considered as a decision variable dependent upon price and possibly other parameters. Finally, Damon and Schramm (1972) proposed joint decisions in production, marketing, and finance. In their model, marketing sector decisions are made with respect to price and promotion expenditures, and finance sector decisions are made with respect to investment in marketable securities and short-term debt incurred or retired. The solution technique used was a computer search methodology similar to the SDR.

## AGGREGATE PLANNING FOR NONMANUFACTURING SYSTEMS

The general nature of aggregate planning and scheduling problems in nonmanufacturing settings is basically similar to that of manufacturing settings in that we are attempting to build a cost or profit model in terms of the key decision variables for short-term capacity. The degrees of freedom in adjusting short-term capacity in nonmanufacturing settings are likely to be fewer, however, because of the absence of inventories and subcontractors as sources of capacity. The result is that the manager is more likely to attempt to control demand through techniques like reservations or to absorb fluctuations in demand rather directly by varying work force size, hours worked, and overtime.

We will not attempt any detailed discussion of aggregate planning in nonmanufacturing systems here because separate chapters deal with operations planning and control in large-scale projects and in service systems. These chapters will include the special problems of both aggregate and detailed schedules in such systems.

## AGGREGATE PLANNING UNDER UNCERTAINTY

In many realistic situations, there is considerable uncertainty in demand estimates. Usually, the uncertainty is greater for time periods that are further into the future. If actual demand does not turn out to be close to what was expected when the aggregate production plan was formulated, excess inventories or stockouts could occur. To see this, consider a simple situation where a company is following a level production plan and accumulating inventory to meet the higher seasonal demand. Three scenarios are possible: demand during high season periods turns out to be the same as expected, higher than expected, or lower than expected. In the first scenario, the company will continue to produce as planned. In the second scenario, the company may have to increase its capacity through overtime, subcontracting, or the like, to meet the higher demand. Since the company is following a level production plan, it should have some inventory already accumulated before the high demand season begins and moderate increases in capacity may be sufficient to meet the additional unexpected demand. In the third scenario, however, the company may get stuck with excess inventories if a considerable stock was accumulated in low season to meet a high season demand that did not materialize. This scenario could be especially costly for companies that introduce new products or models frequently and may face a high obsolescence cost.

Now, consider the case of a company that is following a chase production plan in which production rate is kept low in the off-season and is increased just before the high demand season begins. A chase plan is one that follows demand, and is characterized as "chasing" demand. Again, three scenarios are possible: demand during high season turns out to be as expected, higher than expected, or lower than expected. This company could deal with the first and third scenarios, respectively, by keeping the production rate as planned or by decreasing it. In the second scenario, however, the company may face a stockout situation. This is because in the chase plan the company is probably using close to its maximum capacity during the high season. Thus, there may not be enough flexibility to increase the capacity further to meet the unexpected higher demand. A firm that has several competitors may be vulnerable in this situation as customers may not wait and sales may be lost.

These two situations are summarized in the following table:

| Production Plan | Scenario 1 (Demand as Expected) | Scenario 2 (Demand Lower than Expected) | Scenario 3 (Demand Higher than Expected) |
|---|---|---|---|
| Level | Planned production | Excess inventory | Increase production |
| Chase | Planned production | Reduce production | Lost sales |

To deal with the volatility of demand, a manager will have to consider the trade-offs between the cost of excess inventories and the cost of lost sales. If the cost of excess inventories is high (e.g., due to obsolescence) then caution should be exercised in stockpiling in anticipation of demand. However, if lost sales are to be avoided, then sufficient additional capacity should be kept in reserve to meet unexpectedly high demand.

How should the models discussed in this chapter be modified to deal with uncertainty in demand? One approach is to quantify the uncertainty in demand by a probability distribution and then use an aggregate planning model, such as linear programming, in which the expected demand is replaced by an appropriate fractile of the probability distribution for demand. This fractile could be chosen by service level considerations or by trading-off the cost of lost sales with the cost of excess inventories as in the newsboy model discussed in Chapter 5.

While managers consider uncertainty in demand in formulating an aggregate planning strategy, research in this area is in its infancy. The preceding discussion should be helpful for understanding the nature of the trade-offs involved and how these trade-offs can be reflected in aggregate planning models to determine reasonable, though not optimal, plans.

## IMPLICATIONS FOR THE MANAGER

The aggregate planning problem is one of the most important to managers because it is through these plans that major resources are deployed. Through the mechanisms of aggregate planning, management's interest is focused on the most important aspects of this deployment process; basic employment levels and activity rates are set, and where inventories are available as a part of the strategy, their levels are also set. Given managerial approval of these broad-level plans, the detailed planning and scheduling of operations can proceed within the operating constraints established by the aggregate planning model.

We have discussed the structure of the aggregate planning problem and a number of alternative decision processes. At this point, the graphic methods are probably most frequently used. Mathematical and computer search methods have been developed in an effort to improve on traditional methods by making the process dynamic, optimum seeking, and representative of the multistage nature of the problem. Several models have been of value mainly as stepping stones to more useful models that represent reality more accurately. The most important single stepping stone has been the LDR; however, its original advantage in requiring only simple computations has been largely offset by the computer.

Presently, the computer search methods seem to offer the most promise. Although some of the analytical methods do produce optimum solutions, we must remember that it is the model that is being optimized. The real-world counterpart of the model is also optimized only if the mathematical model duplicates reality. The computer search methods are only optimum seeking by their nature, but they do not suffer from the need to adhere to strict mathematical forms in the model and can therefore more nearly duplicate reality in cost and profit models.

The extension of aggregate planning models to joint decisions among the productions, marketing, and finance functions is most encouraging and demonstrates progress in our ability to employ systems concepts.

Perhaps the greatest single contribution of formal models to aggregate planning is that they provide insight for the manager into the nature of the resource problem faced. Managers need to understand that good solutions ordinarily involve a mixed strategy that uses more than one of the available options of hiring–layoff, overtime, inventories, outside processing, and so forth. The particular balance for a given organization will depend on the balance of costs in that organization. Even if formal models are not used for decision making, they may be useful as managerial learning devices concerning the short-term capacity economics of the enterprise. Judgments about the most advantageous combination of strategies at any particular point in the seasonal cycle can be developed through a gaming process.

The manager must be concerned not only with the direct economic factors that enter the aggregate planning problem but also with the human and social effects of alternative plans. These kinds of variables are not included in formal models; however, by considering a range of alternate plans that meet human and social requirements to varying degrees, managers can make trade-offs between costs and more subjective values. Thus, the formal models can help managers to generate aggregate plans that are acceptable on the basis of broadly based criteria.

Inventories are not available to absorb demand fluctuations in service and nonmanufacturing situations. Although this variable is not available as a managerial strategy, the aggregate planning problem in such organizations is conceptually similar to that in manufacturing organizations. Thus, managers must focus their strategies on hiring and layoff, on the astute use of normal labor turnover, and on the allocation of overtime and undertime. In service-oriented situations, the use of part-time workers is often an effective strategy.

# REVIEW QUESTIONS

1. What is the meaning of the term *aggregate plan*? What are the objectives of aggregate plans? What are the inputs and the nature of the outputs?
2. Place aggregate planning in context with the term *planning horizon*. What is the appropriate planning horizon for aggregate planning?
3. Discuss the relevant cost components involved in aggregate planning decisions.
4. Under what conditions would a single-stage aggregate planning decision system be appropriate?
5. In what ways does a multistage aggregate planning system take account of realities that would in fact affect decisions for production rates and work force size?
6. Appraise graphic methods of aggregate planning.
7. Compare the Linear Decision Rule with the multistage aggregate planning decision system discussed and summarized by Figure 8-3. What compromises with reality, if any, have been made by the LDR model?
8. Compare the Hanssmann-Hess linear programming model of aggregate planning with the multistage decision process discussed and summarized by Figure 8-3. What compromises with reality, if any, have been made in the linear programming model?
9. As a decision system, contrast the SDR with the LDR. What are the advantages and disadvantages of each?
10. Referring to Figure 8-6:
    a. Rationalize why the cost of overtime should increase at an increasing rate as production rates increase.
    b. If the inventory varies from the optimal level (minimum cost level), why would the incremental costs increase at an increasing rate as indicated in Figure 8-6?
11. Criticize the usefulness and validity of the strict aggregate planning concept; that is, making decisions solely in the aggregate terms of work force size and production rate.
12. What is the meaning of the term *capacity* in aggregate planning models? How

does a decision to hire, layoff, or subcontract affect capacity? How does physical or limiting capacity affect these decisions?

13. Cost comparisons between the results of actual managerial decisions and those produced by solving decision rule models are typically made by running both sets of decisions through the cost model and then comparing the results. Does this methodology seem valid? If not, what other approach might be followed?
14. Account for the differences in performance of the several aggregate planning decision systems in the study summarized in Table 8-10.
15. What values are gained by expanding aggregate planning decision systems to produce joint decisions among operations, marketing, and finance? Are there any disadvantages?

# PROBLEMS

16. Table 8-8 gives data that show the projected requirements for the production of a medium-priced camera, together with buffer stock requirements and available production days in each month. Develop a chart of cumulative requirements and cumulative maximum requirements for the year, plotting cumulative production days on the horizontal axis and cumulative requirements in units on the vertical axis.
17. Using the data of Table 8-8, compare the total incremental costs involved in a level production plan, in a plan that follows maximum requirements quite closely, and in some intermediate plan. Normal plant capacity is 400 units per

TABLE 8-8
**PROJECTED PRODUCTION AND INVENTORY REQUIREMENTS**

| Month | Production Requirements | Required Buffer Stocks | Production Days |
|---|---|---|---|
| Jan | 3000 | 600 | 22 |
| Feb | 2500 | 500 | 18 |
| Mar | 4000 | 800 | 22 |
| Apr | 6000 | 1200 | 21 |
| May | 8000 | 1600 | 22 |
| Jun | 12,000 | 2400 | 21 |
| Jul | 15,000 | 3000 | 21 |
| Aug | 12,000 | 2400 | 13 |
| Sep | 10,000 | 2000 | 20 |
| Oct | 8000 | 1600 | 23 |
| Nov | 4000 | 800 | 21 |
| Dec | 3000 | 600 | 20 |
| | 87,500 | 17,500 | 244 |

working day. An additional 20 percent capacity can be obtained through overtime but at an additional cost of $10 per unit. Inventory carrying cost is $30 per unit per year. Changes in production level cost $5000 per 10 units. Extra capacity can be obtained by subcontracting certain parts at an extra cost of $15 per unit. Beginning inventory is 600 units, or must be determined for some plans.

18. Given the data in Table 8-5:
    a. What value of inventory carrying cost would make Plans 1 and 2 equally desirable?
    b. What hiring–layoff cost makes Plans 1 and 2 equally desirable?
    c. What subcontracting cost makes Plans 2 and 3 equal?

19. A manufacturer of containers employed a Linear Decision Rule model to derive two decision rules for setting quarterly production rates and work force levels. These rules are

$$\begin{aligned} P_t &= 0.5S_t + 0.3S_{t+1} + 0.1S_{t+2} - 0.5S_{t+3} \\ &\quad + 1.5W_{t-1} - 0.5I_{t-1} + 150 \\ W_t &= 0.1W_{t-1} + 5 - 0.01I_{t-1} + 0.1S_t \\ &\quad + 0.05S_{t+1} + 0.01S_{t+2} + 0.005S_{t+3}, \end{aligned}$$

where

$P_t$ = The number of containers that should be produced during quarter $t$
$W_t$ = The number of employees in quarter $t$
$S_t$ = A forecast of number of units of containers in quarter $t$

Suppose that at the beginning of quarter 1 the inventory level was 80 and the work force level was 100. Forecasts for quarters 1 to 4 are 600, 500, 300, and 200, respectively.

a. Determine the production rate and work force level for quarter 1.
b. Suppose the actual shipment in quarter 1 was 500 units. What should the production rate and work force levels be for quarter 2 if the forecast for quarter 1 of the next year is 700 units?
c. Suppose in quarter 2, new forecasts are made. These forecasts are

| | |
|---|---|
| Quarter 2 | 400 |
| Quarter 3 | 200 |
| Quarter 4 | 100 |
| Quarter 1 (next year) | 500 |

What should the production rates and work force levels for quarter 2 be this year?

# SITUATIONS

## Aggregate Planning v/s Inventory Management

20. Schwarz and Johnson (1978) have reevaluated the empirical performance of the paint company application of the LDR. The results of the paint company applications of the LDR compared with actual company performance are summarized in Table 8-9. The inventory-related costs (inventory plus back-order costs = 361 + 1566 = 1927) account for 1927 × 100/4085 = 47.2 percent of the company's total performance costs. On the other hand, these costs account for only (451 + 616 = 1067) × 100/3222 = 33.1 percent of the LDR total costs with the moving average forecast and (454 + 400 = 854) × 100/2929 = 29.2 percent of the LDR total costs with the perfect forecast.

    Schwarz and Johnson focus attention on the sources of cost reductions in Table 8-10. They then state the following hypothesis:

    > The LDR (substitute any other aggregate planning model you like) has not been implemented because, despite its conceptual elegance, most of the cost savings of the LDR may be achieved by improved aggregate inventory management alone.

    The authors argue that if company management had begun with an initial gross inventory of 380 units (corresponding to the LDR's ideal *net* inventory of 320 units) as the LDR did, total company costs would have been only $3,228,000. This is approximately the same total cost achieved by the LDR using the moving average forecast. In addition, they state, "More important, *any* initial gross inventory between 380 and 700 would have resulted in total company costs lower than the LDR with moving average forecasts." Schwarz and Johnson state further:

    > Please note that we do not claim that the paint company management was following the "wrong" inventory policy, although, given the firm's "true" back-order and holding costs it would appear that it was. We also do not claim that management could be expected to have made exactly the same sequence of monthly production and work force decisions as they did before, given a higher buffer inventory. We do claim the following: virtually all of the LDR's cost savings could have been obtained without recourse to any aggregate planning model. All that was necessary was a different inventory management policy: in this case, a significantly higher buffer inventory.

    Given the empirical findings by Schwarz and Johnson, do you feel that a company should ignore aggregate planning concepts and simply focus on aggregate inventory management, as is implied in the authors' hypothesis? Would the results have been the same in another organization where the inventory costs were twice that they were in the paint company? Ten times what they were in the paint company? In relation to the preceding two questions, how do you interpret the statement by Schwarz and Johnson: "Please note that we do *not* claim that the paint company management was following the 'wrong' inventory

TABLE 8-9
**COMPARATIVE COSTS IN THOUSANDS FOR THE PAINT COMPANY, 1949–1953**

| | | *Decision Rule* | |
|---|---|---|---|
| Type of Cost | Company Performance | Moving Average Forecast | Perfect Forecast |
| Regular payroll | $1,940 | $1,834 | $1,888 |
| Overtime | 196 | 296 | 167 |
| Inventory | 361 | 451 | 454 |
| Backorders | 1,566 | 616 | 400 |
| Hiring and layoffs | 22 | 25 | 20 |
| Total cost | $4,085 (139%) | $3,222 (110%) | $2,929 (100%) |

*Source:* C. C. Holt, F. Modigliani, and H. A. Simon, "A Linear-Decision Rule for Production and Employment Scheduling," *Management Science, 2*(2), October 1955.

TABLE 8-10
**SOURCE OF MAJOR COST REDUCTIONS FOR THE LDR APPLICATION IN THE PAINT COMPANY**

| | LDR (Moving Average Forecast) versus Company Performance | LDR (Perfect Forecast) versus Company Performance |
|---|---|---|
| Total cost reduction | 4085 − 3222 = 863 | 4085 − 2929 = 1156 |
| Inventory related cost reduction | 1927 − 1067 = 860 | 1927 − 854 = 1073 |
| Percent, inventory to total cost reduction | 99.7% | 92.8% |

policy, although, given the firm's 'true' back-order and holding costs, it would appear that it was"? If we accept Schwarz and Johnson's implied conclusion that only inventory management is needed, what recommendations regarding aggregate planning would you make to organizations that produce no inventoriable product?

## Hospital Admissions Planning

21. The hospital admissions system is used as an overall mechanism for planning and scheduling the use of hospital facilities. The basic unit of capacity is the hospital bed, and bed occupancy level is the variable under management control. Bed occupancy level, in turn, opens up revenue flow from the broadly based health care services of the hospital. The utilization of and resulting revenue from these hospital services depend, in turn, on patient mix selection,

which affects the length of stay of the patients. The demand on other hospital services, such as X-ray and other laboratories, then flows from patient mix.

The problem of operations management is not simply to maximize bed occupancy level because emergency demand must be met and because the cost of services incurred when bed occupancy levels are too high increases rapidly. Thus, an aggregate planning and scheduling model must take account of scheduling the flow of elective arrivals and the patient mix therefrom, as shown in Figure 8-12. This flow can be regulated to a substantial degree because the actual admission date for such cases can be scheduled, and this represents the hospital manager's buffer against the seeming capriciousness of demand. The flow of emergency cases, however, is on a random arrival basis and compounds the problem greatly. The cost-effectiveness of the entire hospital admissions system is dependent on variables that follow probabilistic distributions. Up to 75 percent of total hospital costs are fixed in nature (rooms, beds, laboratory facilities, basic staff). Yet, the demand on hospital services is highly variable in nature.

Do you feel that aggregate planning is a useful concept in hospitals? What form should it take; that is, should it be a cost-minimizing approach, an attempt merely to find feasible solutions, a methodology designed to maximize service to patients, or what? Do you feel that any of the formal models discussed in the chapter can be applied?

FIGURE 8-12
**AN OVERVIEW OF THE HOSPITAL ADMISSIONS PROCESS.**

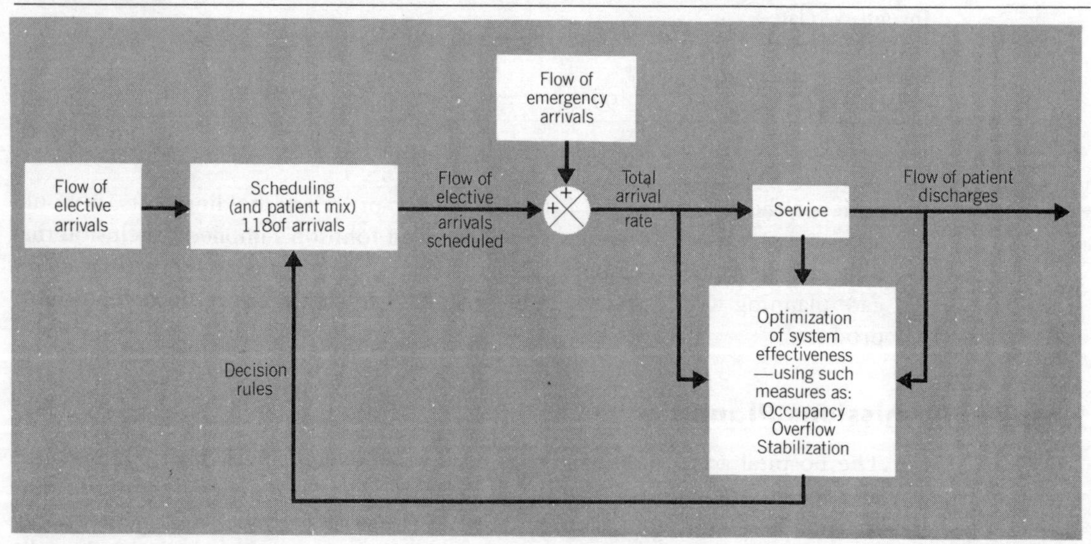


*Source:* J. H. Milsum, E. Turban, and I. Vertinsky. "Hospital Admission Systems: Their Evaluation and Management," *Management Science, 19*(6), February 1973, p. 655.

## Search Laboratory

22. Taubert (1968) developed an aggregate planning cost model for the Search Laboratory, a fictional name for a real company. The laboratory is housed in a 100,000 square foot facility and employs a staff of 400. Approximately 300 members of the staff are classified as direct technical employees, and the balance are indirect administrative support for the operations of the laboratory.

    The laboratory offers a capability through its scientific staff and facilities, and widely fluctuating employment could severely impair this capability. The research programs of the laboratory are funded by both the government and the corporation, and an important part of the operating environment is wide fluctuations in government sales and rapid shifts in technology. Thus, the operations planning problem is defined by the need for employment stability on the one hand and wide fluctuations in government sales on the other.

    Specifically, the operations planning problem is centered in the monthly decision of the director concerning the size of the scientific staff and administrative staff as well as the allocation of the scientific staff to government contracts, corporate research programs, and overhead. Overhead charges arise when there are no contracts or corporate research programs available for scientists. This charge is in addition to the charges normally made to overhead for the usual indirect costs. In effect, then, overhead is used as a buffer to absorb fluctuations in the demand for scientific personnel. The four independent decision variables incorporated in the aggregate planning model are as follows:

    $WG_t$ = Scientific staff allocated to government contracts
    $WR_t$ = Scientific staff allocated to corporate research programs
    $WO_t$ = Scientific staff allocated to overhead
    $WI_t$ = Size of the indirect administrative support staff.

### COST MODEL

Figure 8-13 shows the 12 cost relationships that constitute the components for the cost model of the Search Laboratory. Note that a variety of mathematical relationships are included, such as linear, piecewise linear, constraint, and nonlinear forms. Taubert also built into the model a complete set of equations representing the overhead cost structure used to compute the overhead rate for any given set of decision variables. The resulting overhead rate is then used to compute the monthly government sales volume, which is in turn compared with a cumulative sales target.

The inputs to the decision system are monthly forecasts of contract personnel, research personnel, overhead personnel, and a cumulative sales target that represents the financial plan of the laboratory. The total personnel forecast must be met, and part of the director's operations planning problem is to determine the best combination of decision variables that will accomplish this objective. Failure to meet the personnel requirements increases costs, and the effect is also implemented in the cost model.

FIGURE 8-13
**THE 12 COST RELATIONSHIPS FOR THE SEARCH LABORATORY COST MODEL.**

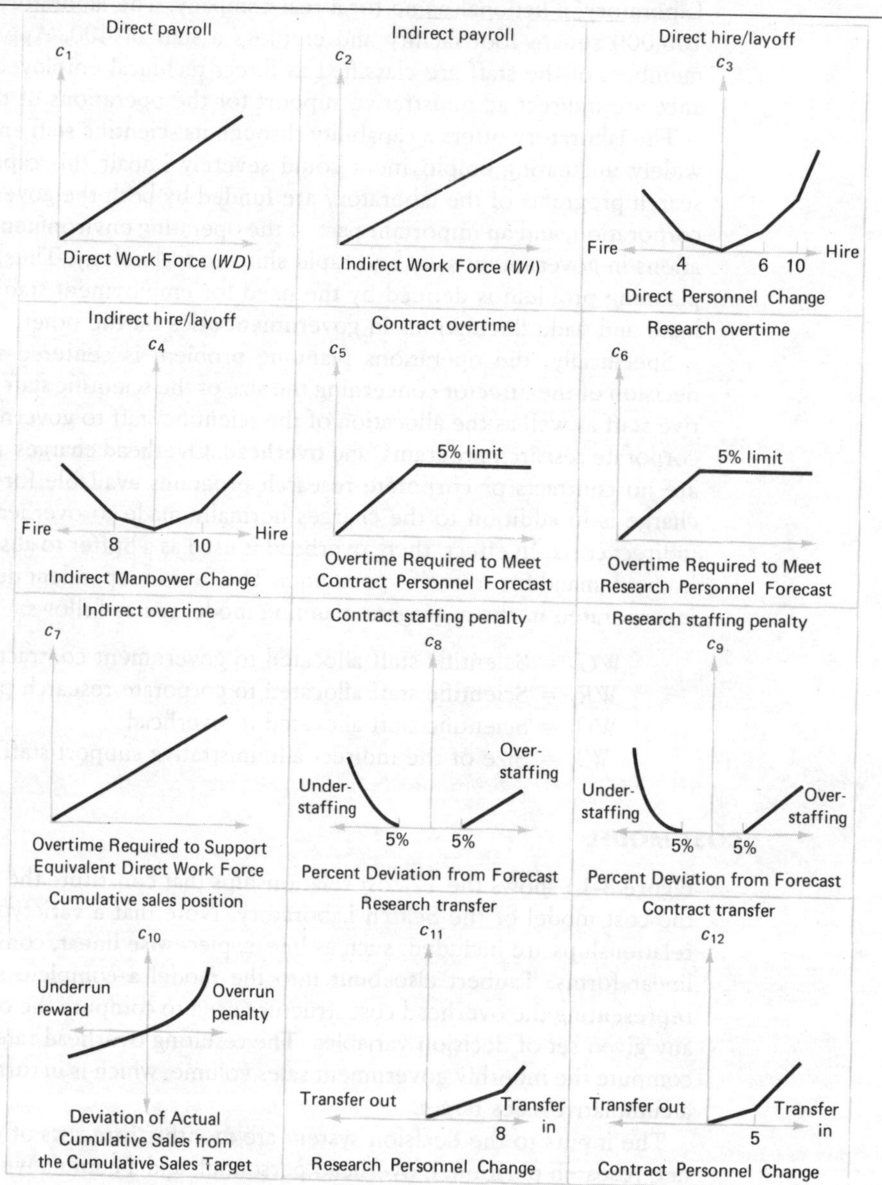


*Source:* W. H. Taubert, "The Search Decision Rule Approach to Operations Planning," unpublished Ph.D. dissertation, UCLA, 1968.

**RESULTS**

Taubert validated the cost model against the financial record of the laboratory over a 5½-year period. Following the validation, the decision system was operated for each month in the 5½-year test period. A 6-month planning horizon was used that required the SDR to optimize a 24-dimension response surface (four decisions per month for the 6-month planning horizon). Figure 8-14 summarizes the comparative results. Figure 8-14*a* shows the contrast between the SDR decisions on contract and research personnel compared with forecasts; Figure 8-14*b* shows a similar comparison of actual management decisions compared with forecasts. Note that the SDR decisions responded much more smoothly to fluctuating personnel forecasts than did actual management decisions.

The costs resulting from the SDR decisions compared with those of actual management decisions indicated that the SDR would have produced cost savings. Over the 5½-year test period, the SDR advantage ranged from a high of 19.7 percent to a low of 5.2 percent and averaged 11.9 percent over the entire test period. The SDR decisions produced lower overhead rates and significant cost reductions in direct payroll, research program staffing, sales target penalties and rewards, and direct hiring costs. It achieved these results largely through the more extensive use of overtime.

If you were the manager of the Search Laboratory, would the aggregate planning system developed be helpful in making decisions? If so, what kinds of decisions? The Search Laboratory is a system without inventories. With inventories not available as a trade-off, are the manager's hands tied? Is there any flexibility left for him or her?

## Aggregate Planning Project

23. An organization has forecasted maximum production requirements for the coming year as follows:

| | | | |
|---|---|---|---|
| January | 400 | July | 580 |
| February | 510 | August | 600 |
| March | 400 | September | 300 |
| April | 405 | October | 280 |
| May | 460 | November | 440 |
| June | 675 | December | 500 |

The present labor force can produce 480 units per month. An employee added to or subtracted from the labor force affects the production rate by 20 units per month. The average salary of employees is \$660 per month and overtime can be used at the usual premium of time and one-half pay up to 10 percent of time for each employee. Therefore, an employee working the maximum overtime could produce the equivalent of an additional two units per month. Hiring and training costs are \$100 per employee, and layoff costs are \$200 per employee.

FIGURE 8-14
**RESULTS OF SDR DECISIONS FOR SEARCH LABORATORY I COMPARED WITH FORECASTS AND ACTUAL MANAGEMENT DECISIONS.**

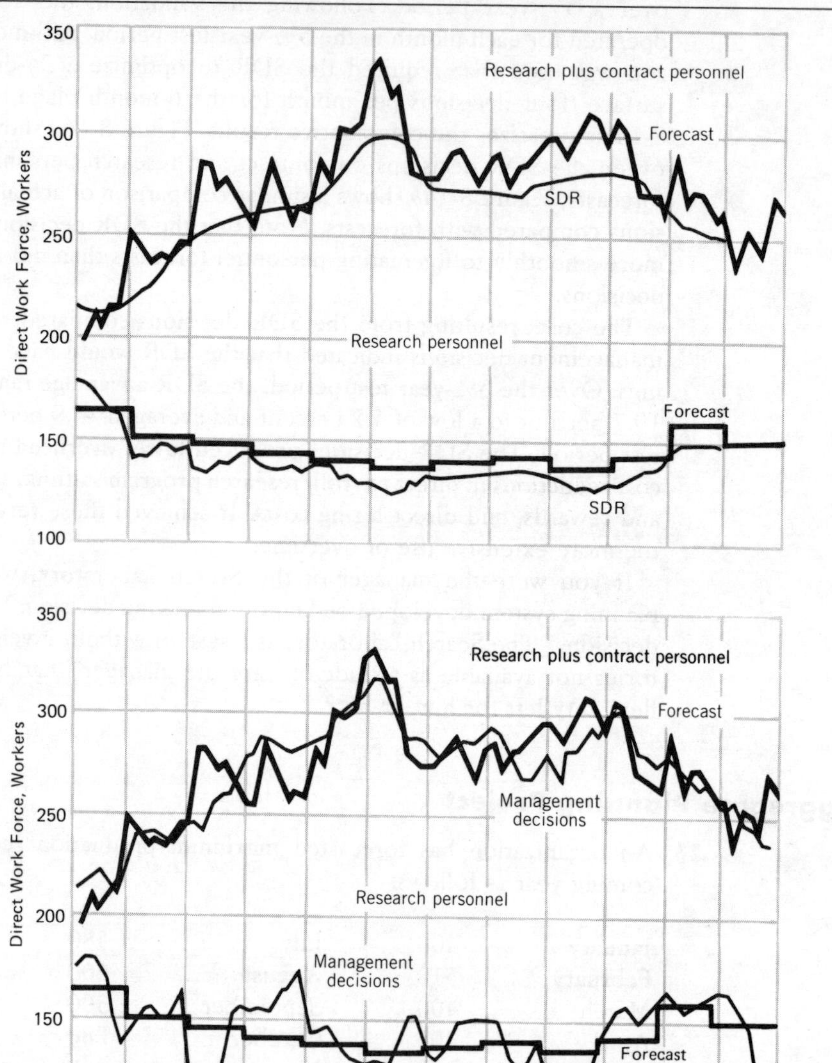


*Source:* W. H. Taubert, "The Search Decision Rule Approach to Operations Planning," unpublished Ph.D. dissertation, UCLA, 1968.

Inventory holding costs are $10 per month per unit, and back-orders cost $50 per unit back-ordered.

a. Assume that the initial inventory is zero and that the present work force level is 24. Formulate a level production plan, a chase production plan, and an intermediate plan using a graphic approach. Evaluate the costs of these three plans. You may employ a worksheet (e.g., Lotus 1-2-3) to set-up this problem.
b. Changeover costs for any increase or decrease in production rates are $3000 per changeover over and above pertinent hiring and layoff costs. These costs include the replanning and rebalancing of production lines and so on. No changeover cost is appropriate when additional production is achieved through the use of overtime. What plan do you recommend? What is the cost of your plan?
c. Formulate the aggregate planning problem as a linear program (ignore changeover costs in part b). Solve the linear program and compare your solution with the one obtained in part a. How would you modify the linear program to incorporate the changeover costs.

# REFERENCES


Bergstrom, G. L. and B. E. Smith, "Multi-Item Production Planning—An Extension of the HMMS Rules," *Management Science, 16* (10), June 1970, pp. 614–629.

Bowman, E. H., "Production Scheduling by the Transportation Method of Linear Programming," *Operations Research, 4* (1), 1956.

Bowman, E. H., "Consistency and Optimality in Managerial Decison Making," *Management Science, 9* (2), January 1963, pp. 310–321.

Buffa, E. S., "Aggregate Planning for Production," *Business Horizons,* Fall 1967.

Buffa, E. S. and W. H. Taubert, "Evaluation of Direct Computer Search Methods for the Aggregate Planning Problem," *Industrial Management Review,* Fall 1967.

Damon, W. W. and R. Schramm, "A Simultaneous Decision Model for Production, Marketing, and Finance," *Management Science, 19* (2), October 1972, pp. 161–172.

Galbraith, J. R., "Solving Production Smoothing Problems," *Management Science, 15* (12), August 1969, pp. 665–674.

Hanssmann, F. and S. W. Hess, "A Linear Programming Approach to Production and Employment Scheduling," *Management Technology, 1,* January 1960, pp. 46–52.

Holloway, C. A., "A Mathematical Programming Approach to Identification and Optimization of Complex Operational Systems with the Aggregate Planning Problem as an Example," unpublished Ph.D. dissertation, 1969.

Holt, C. C., F. Modigliani, and J. F. Muth, "Derivation of a Linear Decision Rule for Production and Employment," *Management Science, 2* (2), January 1956, pp. 159–177.

Holt, C. C., F. Modigliani, J. F. Muth, and H. A. Simon, *Planning, Production, Inventories, and Work Force,* Prentice-Hall, Englewood Cliffs, N.J., 1960.

Holt, C. C., F. Modigliani, and H. A. Simon, "A Linear Decision Rule for Production and Employment Scheduling," *Management Science, 2* (2), October 1955, pp. 1–30.

Jones, C. H., "Parametric Production Planning," *Management Science, 13* (11), July 1967, pp. 843–866.

Krajewski, L. J. and H. E. Thompson, "Efficient Employment Planning in Public Utilities," *Bell Journal of Economics and Management Science,* Spring 1975.

Lee, S. M. and L. J. Moore, "A Practical Approach to Production Scheduling," *Production and Inventory Management,* 1st Quarter 1974, pp. 79–92.

Lee, W. B. and B. M. Khumawala, "Simulation Testing of Aggregate Production Planning Models in an Implementation Methodology," *Management Science, 20* (6), February 1974, pp. 903–911.

Monden, Y., Two-Part Series on Toyota's Production Smoothing: Part One, "Smoothed Production Lets Toyota Adapt to Demand Changes and Reduce Inventory," *Industrial Engineering, 13* (8), August 1981, pp. 42–51; Part Two, "How Toyota Shortened Supply Lot Production Time, Waiting Time and Conveyance Time," *Industrial Engineering, 13* (9), September 1981, pp. 22–30.

Redwine, C. N., "A Mathematical Programming Approach to Production Scheduling in a Steel Mill," Ph.D. dissertation, UCLA, 1971.

Rossin, D. E., "A Manager's Interactive Model for Aggregate Planning," Ph.D. dissertation, University of California, Los Angeles, 1985.

Schwarz, L. B. and R. E. Johnson, "An Appraisal of the Empirical Performance of the Linear Decision Rule," *Management Science, 24* (8), April 1978, pp. 844–849.

Singhal, K., "A Generalized Model for Production Scheduling by Transportation Method of LP," *Industrial Management, 19* (5), September–October 1977, pp. 1–6.

Taubert, W. H., "Search Decision Rule for the Aggregate Scheduling Problem," *Management Science, 14* (6), February 1968, pp. 343–359.

Taubert, W. H., "The Search Decision Rule Approach to Operations Planning," Ph.D. dissertation, UCLA, 1958.

Tuite, M. F., "Merging Market Strategy Selection and Production Scheduling," *Journal of Industrial Engineering, 19* (2), February 1958, pp. 76–84.

Vergin, R. C., "Production Scheduling Under Seasonal Demand," *Journal of Industrial Engineering, 17* (5), May 1966.

# CHAPTER 9

# SIMULATION: A METHODOLOGICAL OVERVIEW

The behavior of a real operational system can be studied by building a model of the system and then experimenting with the model to gather desired information. If the model is simple, then mathematical methods (calculus, mathematical programming, probability theory, etc.) can be used to obtain the information for questions of interest (analytical solutions). Often, however, realistic models of a system are too complex to allow analytical solutions. These models must be studied by means of simulation. In a simulation, the model is evaluated repeatedly to obtain estimates of the characteristics of interest. Experimentation with the model often requires the use of a computer. An example will serve to illustrate the mechanics of simulation.

## A COMPUTED EXAMPLE

Suppose we are dealing with the maintenance of a bank of 30 machines, and, initially, we wish to estimate the level of service that can be maintained by one mechanic. We have the elements of a waiting line situation here, to be covered in Chapter 16, with machine breakdowns representing arrivals, the mechanic acting as a service facility, and repair times representing service times. If the distributions of times between breakdowns and service times followed the negative exponential distribution, the simplest procedure would be to use formulas and calculate the average machine waiting time, the mechanic's idle time, and so forth. However, we can see by inspecting Figures 9-1 and 9-2 that the distributions are not similar to the negative exponential; therefore, simulation is an alternative. The procedure is as follows:

1. *Determine the distributions of times between breakdowns and service times.* If these data were not available directly from records, we would be required to conduct a study to determine them. Figures 9-1 and 9-2 show the distributions of breakdown and repair times for 73 breakdowns.
2. *Convert the frequency distributions to cumulative probability distributions (see Figures 9-3 and 9-4).* This conversion is accomplished by summing the frequencies that are less than or equal to each breakdown or repair time and plotting them. The cumulative frequencies are then converted to probabilities by assigning the number 1.0 to the maximum value.

   As an example, let us take the data in Figure 9-1 and convert them to the cumulative distribution of Figure 9-3. Beginning with the lowest value for breakdown time, 10 hours, there are 4 occurrences, so 4 is plotted on the cumulative chart for the breakdown time of 10 hours. For the breakdown time of 11 hours, there were 10 occurrences, but there were 14 occurrences of 11 hours or less, so the value 14 is plotted for 11 hours. Similarly, for the breakdown time of 12 hours, there were 14 occurrences recorded, but there were 28 occurrences of breakdowns for 12 hours or less.

   Figure 9-3 was constructed from the data in Figure 9-1 by proceeding in this way. When the cumulative frequency distribution was completed, a cumulative

FIGURE 9-1
**FREQUENCY DISTRIBUTION OF THE TIME BETWEEN BREAKDOWNS FOR 30 MACHINES.**

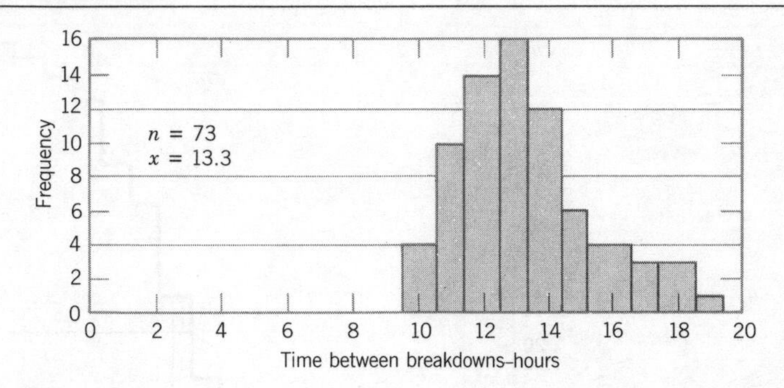


probability scale was constructed at the right of Figure 9-3 by assigning the number 1.0 to the maximum value, 73, and dividing the resulting scale into 10 equal parts. This results in a cumulative empirical probability distribution. From Figure 9-3, we can say that 100 percent of the breakdown time values were 19 hours or less; 99 percent were 18 hours or less, and so on. Figure 9-4 was constructed from the data in Figure 9-2 in a comparable way.

3. *Sample at random from the cumulative distributions to determine specific breakdown times and repair times to use in simulating operation.* We do this by selecting numbers between 001 and 100 at random (representing probabilities in percentages). The random numbers could be selected by any random process, such as drawing numbered chips from a box. The easiest way is to use a table of random numbers, such as that shown in Appendix Table 5. (Pick a starting point in the table at random and then take two-digit numbers in sequence from that column, for example.)

   The random numbers are used to enter the cumulative distributions to obtain time values. An example is shown in Figure 9-3. The random number 30 is

FIGURE 9-2
**FREQUENCY DISTRIBUTION OF THE REPAIR TIME FOR 73 BREAKDOWNS.**

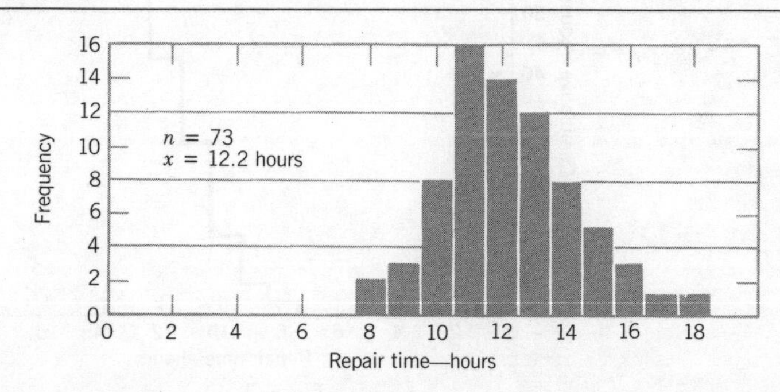

FIGURE 9-3
**CUMULATIVE DISTRIBUTION OF BREAKDOWN TIMES.**

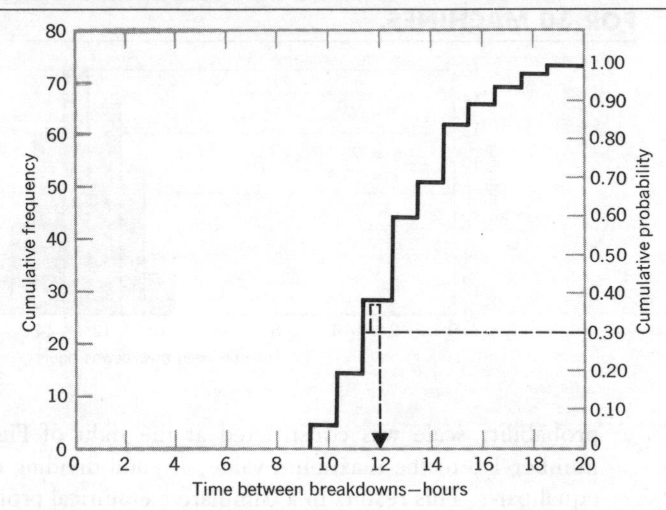


shown to select a breakdown time of 12 hours. We can now see the purpose behind converting the original distribution to a cumulative distribution. Only one breakdown time can be associated with a given random number. In the original distribution, two values would result because of the bell shape of the curve.

By using random numbers to obtain breakdown time values from Figure 9-3 in this fashion, we can obtain breakdown time values in proportion to the probabil-

FIGURE 9-4
**CUMULATIVE DISTRIBUTION OF REPAIR TIMES.**

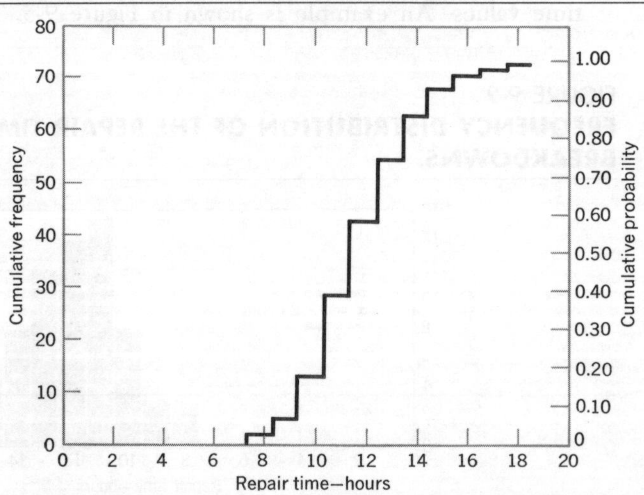

ity of occurrence indicated by the original frequency distribution. We can construct a table of random numbers that select certain breakdown times. For example, reading from Figure 9-3, the random numbers 6 through 19 result in a breakdown time of 11 hours. This is equivalent to saying that 5 percent of the time we would obtain a value of 10 hours, 14 percent of the time we would obtain a breakdown time of 11 hours, and so forth. Table 9-1 shows the random number equivalents for Figures 9-3 and 9-4.

Sampling from either the cumulative distributions of Figures 9-3 and 9-4 or from Table 9-1 will produce breakdown times and repair times in proportion to the original distributions, just as if actual breakdowns and repairs were happening. Table 9-2 gives a sample of 20 breakdown and repair times determined in this way.

4. *Simulate the actual operation of breakdowns and repairs.* The structure of the simulation of the repair operation is shown by the flowchart of Figure 9-5. This operation involves selecting a breakdown time and determining whether or not the mechanic is available. If the mechanic is not available, the machine must wait for service, and the waiting time can be computed. If the mechanic is available, the question is: "Did the mechanic have to wait?" If waiting time was required, we compute the mechanic's idle time. If the mechanic did not have to wait, we select a repair time and proceed according to the flowchart, repeating the overall process as many times as desired and stopping the procedure when the desired number of cycles has been completed.

The simulation of the repair operation is shown in Table 9-3 using the breakdown times and repair times selected by random numbers in Table 9-2. We assume that time begins when the first machine breaks down, and we calculate breakdown times

TABLE 9-1

**RANDOM NUMBERS USED TO DRAW BREAKDOWN TIMES AND REPAIR TIMES IN PROPORTION TO THE OCCURRENCE PROBABILITIES OF THE ORIGINAL DISTRIBUTIONS**

| *Breakdown Times* | | *Repair Times* | |
|---|---|---|---|
| These Random Numbers → | Select These Breakdown Times | These Random Numbers → | Select These Repair Times |
| 1–5 | 10 hours | 1–3 | 8 hours |
| 6–19 | 11 | 4–7 | 9 |
| 20–38 | 12 | 8–18 | 10 |
| 39–60 | 13 | 19–40 | 11 |
| 61–77 | 14 | 41–59 | 12 |
| 78–85 | 15 | 60–75 | 13 |
| 86–90 | 16 | 76–86 | 14 |
| 91–95 | 17 | 87–93 | 15 |
| 96–99 | 18 | 94–97 | 16 |
| 100 | 19 | 98–99 | 17 |
| | | 100 | 18 |

TABLE 9-2
**SIMULATED SAMPLE OF TWENTY BREAKDOWN AND REPAIR TIMES**

| *Breakdown Times* | | *Repair Times* | |
|---|---|---|---|
| Random Number | Breakdown Time from Table 9-1 | Random Number | Repair Time from Table 9-1 |
| 83 | 15 | 91 | 15 |
| 97 | 18 | 4 | 9 |
| 88 | 16 | 72 | 13 |
| 12 | 11 | 12 | 10 |
| 22 | 12 | 30 | 11 |
| 16 | 11 | 32 | 11 |
| 24 | 12 | 91 | 15 |
| 64 | 14 | 29 | 11 |
| 37 | 12 | 33 | 11 |
| 62 | 14 | 8 | 10 |
| 52 | 13 | 25 | 11 |
| 9 | 11 | 74 | 13 |
| 64 | 14 | 97 | 16 |
| 74 | 14 | 70 | 13 |
| 15 | 11 | 15 | 10 |
| 47 | 13 | 43 | 12 |
| 86 | 16 | 42 | 12 |
| 79 | 15 | 25 | 11 |
| 43 | 13 | 71 | 13 |
| 35 | 12 | 14 | 10 |

from that point. The repair time required for the first breakdown was 15 hours, and because this is the first occurrence in our record, neither the machine nor the mechanic had to wait. The second breakdown occurred at 18 hours, but the mechanic was available at the end of 15 hours, waiting 3 hours for the next breakdown to occur.

We proceed in this fashion, adding and subtracting, according to the requirements of the simulation model to obtain the record of Table 9-3. The summary at the bottom of Table 9-3 shows that for the sample of 20 breakdowns, total machine waiting time was 11 hours, and total mechanic's idle time was 26 hours. To obtain a realistic picture, we would have to use a much larger sample. Using the same data on breakdown and repair time distributions, 1000 runs using a computer yielded 15.9 percent machine waiting time and 7.6 percent mechanic's idle time. Of course, the mechanic is presumably paid for an eight-hour day, regardless of the division between idle and service time; however, knowing the idle time available may be a guide to the assignment of "fill-in" work.

FIGURE 9-5
**FLOWCHART SHOWING STRUCTURE OF REPAIR SIMULATION.**

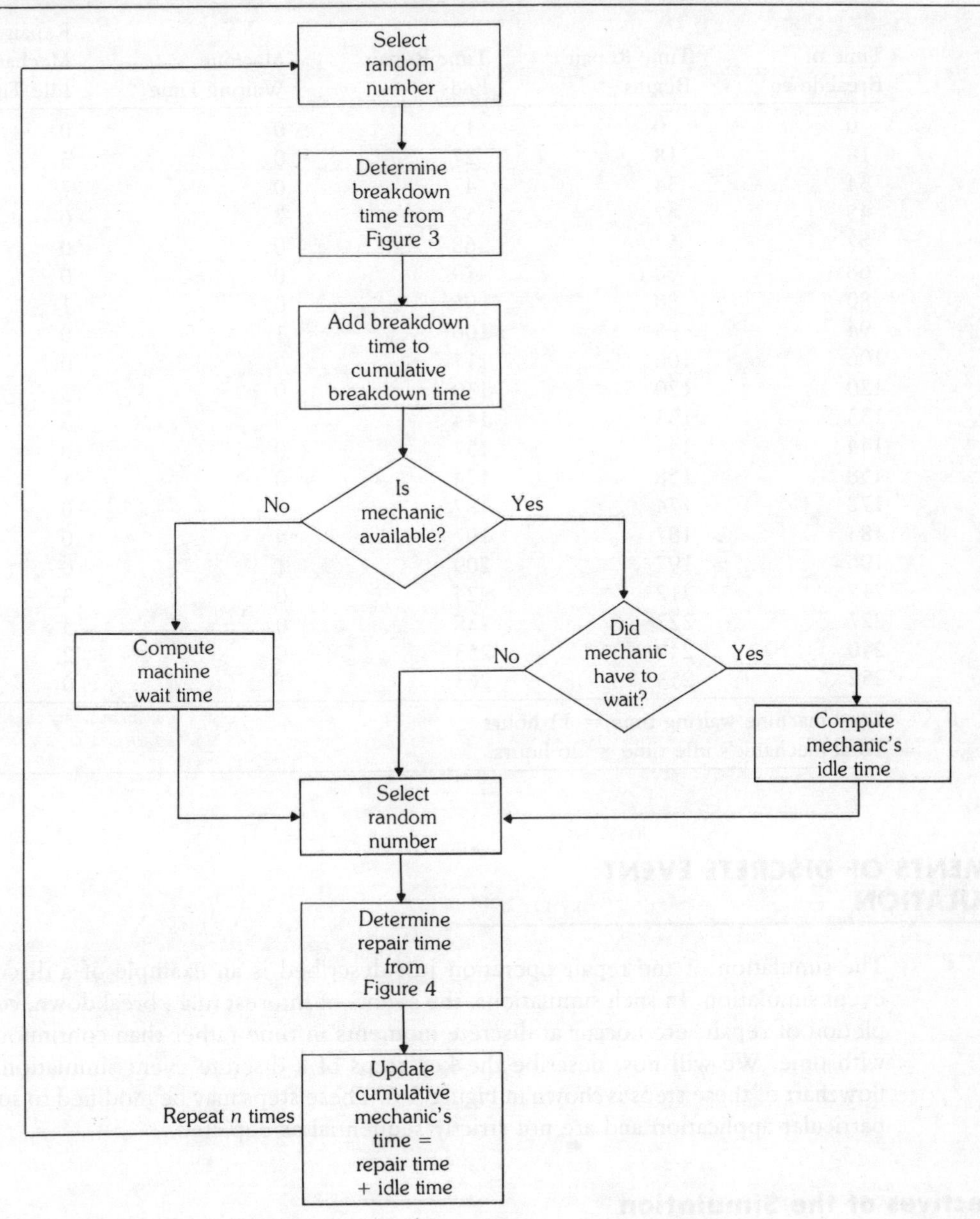

TABLE 9-3
**SIMULATED BREAKDOWN AND REPAIR FOR TWENTY BREAKDOWNS**

| Time of Breakdown | Time Repair Begins | Time Repair Ends | Machine Waiting Time | Repair Mechanic's Idle Time |
|---|---|---|---|---|
| 0 | 0 | 15 | 0 | 0 |
| 18 | 18 | 27 | 0 | 3 |
| 34 | 34 | 47 | 0 | 7 |
| 45 | 47 | 57 | 2 | 0 |
| 57 | 57 | 68 | 0 | 0 |
| 68 | 68 | 79 | 0 | 0 |
| 80 | 80 | 95 | 0 | 1 |
| 94 | 95 | 106 | 1 | 0 |
| 106 | 106 | 117 | 0 | 0 |
| 120 | 120 | 130 | 0 | 3 |
| 133 | 133 | 144 | 0 | 3 |
| 144 | 144 | 157 | 0 | 0 |
| 158 | 158 | 174 | 0 | 1 |
| 172 | 174 | 187 | 2 | 0 |
| 183 | 187 | 197 | 4 | 0 |
| 196 | 197 | 209 | 1 | 0 |
| 212 | 212 | 224 | 0 | 3 |
| 227 | 227 | 238 | 0 | 3 |
| 240 | 240 | 253 | 0 | 2 |
| 252 | 253 | 263 | 1 | 0 |

Total machine waiting time = 11 hours
Total mechanic's idle time = 26 hours

## ELEMENTS OF DISCRETE EVENT SIMULATION

The simulation of the repair operation just described is an example of a discrete event simulation. In such simulations, the events of interest (e.g., breakdown, completion of repair, etc.) occur at discrete moments in time rather than continuously with time. We will now describe the key steps of a discrete event simulation. A flowchart of these steps is shown in Figure 9-6. These steps may be modified to suit a particular application and are not strictly sequential as depicted.

### Objectives of the Simulation

The purpose of conducting a simulation analysis and the decisions for which the simulation results will be used should be clearly specified. The objectives of simulation are many and varied. For example, simulation may be employed to study the behavior of a system to gain insights into its workings. Alternatively, one may use simulation to design a system or to evaluate a few chosen policies. A simulation may

FIGURE 9-6
**ELEMENTS OF DISCRETE EVENT SIMULATION.**

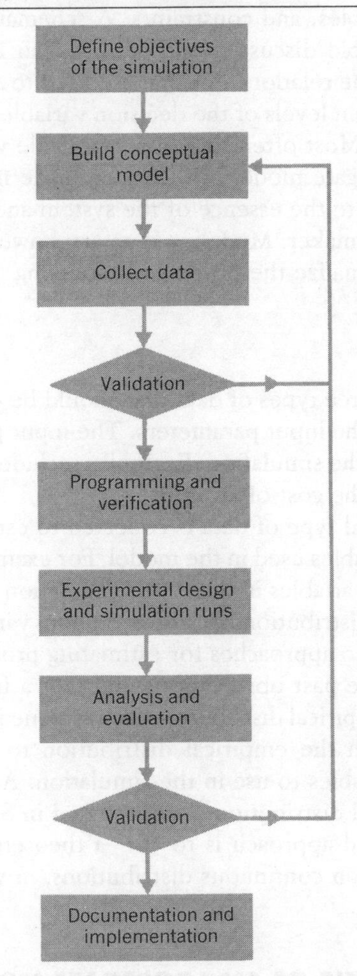


be used to train operators or managers by providing them with feedback on system performance resulting from their decisions. Clarity in specifying the objectives of simulation is most important. The cost and time expended in developing a simulation model will be wasted if the information provided by the model is not useful to the decision maker. The analyst and the managers must interact closely so that the model developed by the analyst is useful and consistent with the intended objectives of the managers.

## Model Building

Once the objectives of the simulation are defined, the next step is to build a conceptual model of the real-world system using mathematical and logical relationships. A useful approach for model building is to start with a simple aggregate model by defining decision variables, uncontrollable variables that influence the outcome, output variables, and constraints. A schematic of such an aggregate model for the repair example discussed earlier is shown in Figure 9-7. The box in Figure 9-7 represents the relationships that are used to *derive* the levels of the output variables from the given levels of the decision variables, the uncontrollable variables, and the constraints. Most often, the uncontrollable variables are random variables.

The aggregate model can then be made more detailed if necessary. The model should capture the essence of the system and should provide useful information to the decision maker. Modeling is an art; however, recently some attempts have been made to formalize the process of modeling (see Geoffrion, 1985).

## Data Collection

There are three types of data that should be collected. The first type of data is used to estimate the input parameters. The input parameters are fixed values that do not vary during the simulation. Examples include the estimate of demand, the yield of a process, or the cost of an item.

The second type of data is collected to estimate probability distributions for the random variables used in the model. For example, repair times and breakdown times are random variables in the repair simulation discussed earlier. We need to estimate probability distributions for these random variables as shown in Figures 9-1 and 9-2. There are two approaches for estimating probability distributions. One approach is simply to use past observations and plot a frequency distribution or histogram to obtain an empirical distribution, as was done in Figures 9-1 and 9-2. We then sample directly from the empirical distribution to determine the specific values of the random variables to use in the simulation. A procedure for drawing a sample from the empirical distribution was discussed in Step 3 of the computed example.

The second approach is to "fit" a theoretical distribution to the collected data. Some common continuous distributions, in which a variable can take on any of an

FIGURE 9-7
**A SCHEMATIC OF AN AGGREGATE MODEL.**

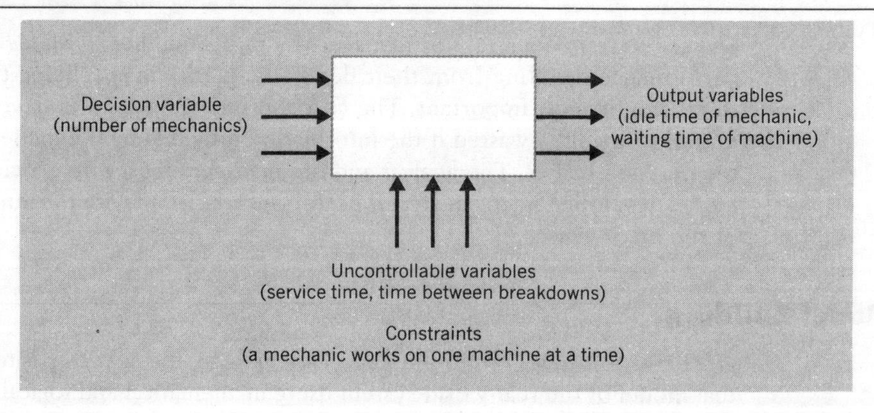

infinite number of possible values, include uniform, exponential, normal, and beta distributions. Discrete distributions, in which a variable can take on one of a finite number of possible values, that are commonly employed in simulation include Bernoulli, binomial, geometric, and Poisson distributions. We need to determine which of the possible theoretical distributions is appropriate for a particular random variable and then estimate its parameter values. In some cases, prior knowledge about the random variable can help us exclude some distributions. For example, repair times should not be generated from a normal distribution because repair times cannot take on negative values. In general, however, we will have to plot the data and use our judgment in selecting an appropriate distribution. Once a particular distribution has been chosen for a random variable, the values of its parameters are estimated from the data. A completely specified probability distribution for the random variable is thereby obtained. Visual inspection and goodness-of-fit tests are used to determine whether the fitted distribution is in agreement with the collected data. Procedures and programs for generating a random representative sample from a specified theoretical distribution are available (see Law and Kelton, 1982, Chapters 5 and 7).

What should we do if we have no data for a random variable of interest? Such a situation may arise in a design simulation for a system that does not actually exist. In these situations, we will have to use either the expert opinion of engineers, managers, vendors, and the like or a historical analogy to subjectively specify distributions.

Finally, the data should be collected on the performance of the real system. For example, real data on the idle time of the mechanic and machine waiting times will be useful in validating the simulation model since the results of the simulation can be compared with actual observations of existing system conditions.

## Validation

Determining whether a simulation model is an accurate representation of a real-world system is called validation. Some degree of validation must take place throughout the simulation study. However, validation during the modeling of the system and when simulation results become available is particularly important. We will discuss validation in some detail later. Here, we wish to emphasize that decision makers must be involved in modeling so that both the actual validity and the perceived validity of the model will be improved. A modeler may not have the insights into the nuances of the mechanics of a system that a manager who is intimately involved with the system will have. Determining whether the parameters, the random variables and their respective probability distributions, and the data collected on system performance are accurate representations of the system is essential for maintaining model validity.

## Programming and Verification

A computer program must be constructed for the simulation model as most real-world simulations require the use of a computer. A modeler can select either a general purpose computing language, such as FORTRAN or PASCAL, or a specially designed simulation language, such as GASP, GPSS, or SIMSCRIPT. These simulation languages often reduce programming time and effort considerably. For example, the capability to generate random variables from a specified distribution is essential for all simulation models. For some specific applications, such as project planning, packaged simulation programs exist that reduce or eliminate the burden of programming. One such package, the Factory Modeling System (FMS) for the logical design of a factory, will be discussed later in the chapter.

Debugging a computer program to ensure that the model performs as intended is called verification. It is useful to debug the program in simple modules or subprograms. A trace, in which the state of the simulated system is printed out after the occurrence of each event, also helps in identifying problems. The simulation model can also be run under simplifying assumptions for which the output can be hand computed.

Once a computer program is debugged, pilot runs of the model are made to ensure that the results do indeed make sense. Appropriate modifications in the model and in the computer program are made based on the results of these tests.

## Experimental Design and Simulation Runs

In some situations, alternative system designs are available for evaluation. For example, we may wish to evaluate the system performance (e.g., the average wait time) for some specified designs. The question of interest in such situations is how to compare alternative designs. If average performances of two systems are compared, we may reach wrong conclusions since average performance is itself a random variable; that is, in one simulation run of a specified length (e.g., 500 customers or 8 hours), the average waiting time for a system may be 2 minutes, but in another simulation run of the same length, it may be 1.8 or 2.3 minutes. Statistical tests that provide confidence intervals for the difference between the performance of two systems will be required to reach a conclusion. A discussion of these various statistical tests is beyond the scope of this book. We emphasize, however, that the pitfall of choosing a system based on an average performance measure for a single simulation run should be avoided.

In many situations, a choice of alternative systems for comparison is available to the modeler. For example, in job shop scheduling, the policy for setting customer due dates, the rules for releasing jobs to the shop, and the priorities for selecting the next job for processing on a machine may be varied to some degree. An informal, trial-and-error approach for evaluating alternative designs may not be efficient. Experimental design methods ensure the systematic exploration of alternatives. As we learn about the performance of the system, the experimental design can be further refined and made to focus precisely on the preferred designs. Factorial design, in which fixed levels are chosen for each relevant factor and possible combinations of the levels of factors are evaluated by simulation, is a useful type of experimental design. For example, if each of three factors in the job shop scheduling example have two levels, then there are eight possible combinations that must be evaluated. If we denote the two due date setting policies as $D_1$ and $D_2$, the two job release rules as $R_1$ and $R_2$, and the two priority rules as $P_1$ and $P_2$, then the system performance, $O_i$, (e.g., number of jobs late) can be studied for all eight possible combinations. This experimental design is shown in Table 9-4. In Table 9-4, the third row shows that when the $D_1$ level for the first factor, the $R_2$ level for the second factor, and the $P_1$ level for the third factor are chosen, then the simulation results produce a performance of $O_3$. Statistical analysis can be used to identify the impact of each factor on system performance and to identify the preferred combination of factors.

The number of possible combinations grows rapidly with the number of factors as well as with the number of factor levels. Fractional factorial designs reduce the number of combinations so that the cost of simulation is not prohibitive.

Once the alternative system designs are selected by appropriate experimental design methods, several other decisions must be made. For each system design to be simulated, starting conditions for the simulation run, the length of the simulation run, and the number of independent simulation runs must also be determined. Starting conditions should be representative of the real system. A job shop that initializes a simulation with no jobs on any machine may produce artificially low values for queues since heavily utilized machines often have jobs in queue from the previous day. The simulation may, of course, be run for a few time periods with starting conditions of no jobs in the system with the data for these warm-up periods then disregarded. The length of the simulation run and the number of independent replications of the simulation are determined by cost considerations and the degree of output precision desired.

Simulation runs are made to provide data on system performance. In making production simulation runs, it is desirable to proceed slowly and to examine the output as it becomes available. Modification of the experimental design may be appropriate in order to improve the efficiency and precision of the results. For example, if the specified levels of a factor do not seem to have much influence on system performance or if the levels of some other factor seem to have particularly significant influence, then it may be desirable to eliminate the first factor from the

**TABLE 9-4**
**FACTORIAL DESIGN FOR JOB SHOP SCHEDULING EXAMPLE**

| Factor Combination | Factor 1 (Due Date Policy) | Factor 2 (Release Rule) | Factor 3 (Priority Rule) | System Performance |
|---|---|---|---|---|
| 1 | $D_1$ | $R_1$ | $P_1$ | $O_1$ |
| 2 | $D_1$ | $R_1$ | $P_2$ | $O_2$ |
| 3 | $D_1$ | $R_2$ | $P_1$ | $O_3$ |
| 4 | $D_1$ | $R_2$ | $P_2$ | $O_4$ |
| 5 | $D_2$ | $R_1$ | $P_1$ | $O_5$ |
| 6 | $D_2$ | $R_1$ | $P_2$ | $O_6$ |
| 7 | $D_2$ | $R_2$ | $P_1$ | $O_7$ |
| 8 | $D_2$ | $R_2$ | $P_2$ | $O_8$ |

experimental design and to explore instead system performance under more detailed levels of the second factor.

## Analysis and Evaluation

The results of production runs should be examined visually as well as analyzed statistically. The purpose of this analysis is to gain insights into the workings of the system and to evaluate alternative policies. Summary measures are useful so that the decision maker is not overwhelmed with information. Sensitivity analysis is conducted to ensure the stability of the results.

## Validation

As we discussed earlier, validation of a simulation model should be carried on throughout the study. Conversations with experts and decision makers, observations of the system, and simple common sense about how the components of a system operate will help in developing a model with high validity. The assumptions of the model should also be tested empirically. For example, if a theoretical probability distribution is a fit for a random variable, such as repair time, then statistical tests can be used to determine the adequacy of the fit. Under some assumptions, the results for system performance can be derived analytically or by manual computation. These results can then be checked against the simulation results. Sensitivity analysis will help in identifying the sensitivity of the output to changes in the values of various inputs. These changes should make qualitative sense; for example, the direction of the change and its magnitude should be within a hypothesized range.

Finally, the output of the simulation can be compared with the observed output of the real system. The prediction of the model should be tested against the actual performance of the system.

## Documentation and Implementation

Good documentation of the assumptions, the model, and the computer program is essential for the continued use of a simulation program. Good documentation permits the use of the simulation by different people in the organization, and it makes it easy to use the simulation model, with appropriate modifications, for other similar applications.

Finally, the intended purpose of the simulation is achieved only if the results are implemented. In some situations, simulation results provide insights for decision making and are not directly implementable. A subjective assessment of the decision makers as to whether they found the simulation results useful should be sought. Fortunately, simulation results have been used in numerous applications, and organizations have indeed found this technique quite useful.

## USES OF SIMULATION

Simulation has been used for a wide variety of applications in production and operations that range from assembly line scheduling to factory design. The various uses of simulation can be grouped into three broad categories:

- Design
- Diagnosis
- Training

A large number of simulation studies fall into the design category, in which alternative system designs (or policies) are evaluated with respect to a specified measure of system performance. Examples include the evaluation of inventory policies, bank teller scheduling, distribution system design, and ambulance location and dispatching.

In some situations, simulation is used to study the behavior of systems under alternative conditions. The intent is not to evaluate alternative policies but merely to diagnose the potential problems that may arise. The diagnostic use of simulation is particularly important for newly installed systems where little experience has been gathered. Simulation can provide managers with insights into the workings of the system that might otherwise require several years to develop. In addition, potential problems that might arise under some specified future conditions can be identified.

Finally, simulation can be used as a tool for training users to perform their tasks effectively. Flight simulators for training pilots have been available for a long time. Recently, "decision simulators" have been developed that provide an interactive visual stimulation of an actual decision-making scenario. The decision maker or user can test the implications of his or her decisions by experimenting with the decision simulator. Immediate feedback accelerates the learning process, and a user can be trained in a short period of time to make decisions that enhance corporate profitability that might otherwise take years of on the job experience. An excellent example of this process is provided in Lembersky and Chi (1984). They developed a decision simulator that allows operators to test different cross-cutting and log-allocating decisions for economic value. This decision simulator was implemented at the Weyerhaeuser Company in 1977, and it continues to yield multimillion-dollar annual profit increases to the company.

## CELLULAR SIMULATION SYSTEMS

Conway (1984) developed a new, interactive, graphical approach to discrete event simulation called cellular simulation. These systems can be implemented on a personal computer. An engineer or a manager can learn to use these systems easily and can develop simulation models using these systems in hours as compared to the weeks usually required to program a model using a standard simulation language. These sysems require no programming and, in fact, are simpler to learn and use than spread-sheet programs such as Lotus 1-2-3. The limitation of the cellular systems is that they are tailored for specific families of applications, such as distribution system modeling, factory modeling, multiproduct production line simulation, and *just-in-time* scheduling. In the future, we believe such systems will be developed for important classes of production problems, which should promote the widespread use of simulation.

We will now describe an application of one of the cellular simulation systems, the Factory Modeling System (FMS), through an example.

### Example

Consider a plant that receives cranberries and processes them for bagging and shipment. A simplified flowchart for the operations involved in cranberry processing is shown in Figure 9-8.

For the purpose of this simulation, we assume that trucks loaded with cranberries arrive continuously so that the cranberries enter the system at a constant rate of 60 tons/hour. These trucks can be unloaded at the rate of 1 minute/ton. The cranberries are stored in bins that have a combined capacity of 200 tons. If the bins are full, the trucks cannot be unloaded, which results in the queuing of the trucks. The cranberries are next destoned and dechaffed. The process capacity for destoning and dechaffing varies between 1 and 2 minutes/ton (30 to 60 tons/hour) and the yield of the process is 95 percent. We assume throughout a uniform probability distribution for process capacity within the specified range. The cranberries are next dried, with the capacity of the drying process ranging from 1.5 to 2 minutes/ton (30 to 40 tons/hour) and a yield of 92 percent. The cranberries are next separated into three classes according to graded quality. The separator has a capacity of 0.9 to 1.5 minutes/ton and yields 98 percent usable cranberries. Finally, the cranberries are bagged at the rate of 1 minute/ton and are shipped for storage. The cranberries rejected from each process (e.g., 5 percent from destone and dechaff) are simply wasted.

FIGURE 9-8
**FLOWCHART FOR CRANBERRY PROCESSING.**

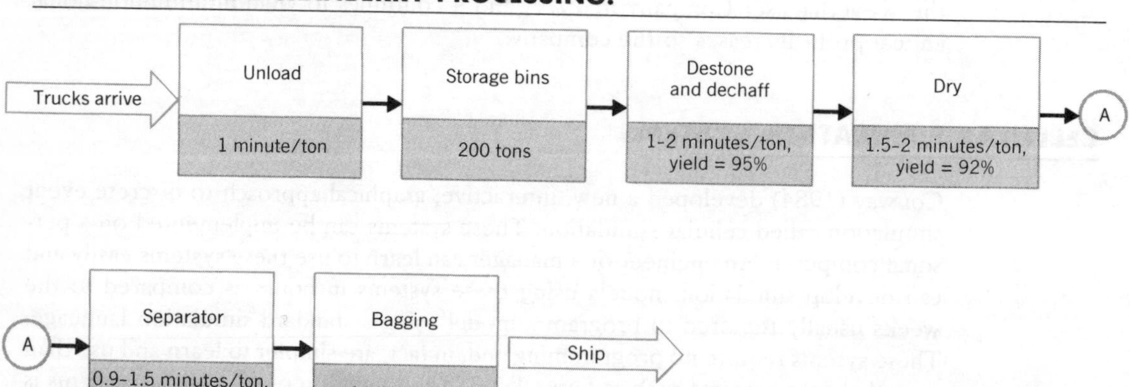

The first objective of the simulation analysis is to

- Determine the capacity of the system in tons/hour.
- Determine the idle capacity for each stage of the process.
- Determine how fast the storage bins fill up, triggering a queuing of the trucks.

The second objective of the simulation analysis is to evaluate the impact on the system if the capacity of a given stage in the system is increased. For our illustration, we will simply increase the capacity of the drying process so that the new drying times are 1.2 to 1.5 minutes/ton. Note that the previous capacity of the drying process was 30 to 40 tons/hour; it is increased to 40 to 50 tons/hour by adding additional dryers.

## The Factory Modeling System (FMS)

The FMS allows the user to construct a working model of the operations of a manufacturing or service firm and then to experiment with the model to observe its performance.

In Figure 9-9, a conceptual model for the cranberry processing operations developed using the FMS is shown. Since the FMS allows the creation of a work center (stage of process), a receiving area, a shipping area, and a storage area, the building of the model literally takes only minutes.

The model was run for 6000 minutes of operations. In Table 9-5, the system capacity and the idle capacities for each stage of the process are given. Figure 9-10 shows that the storage bins were filled in 460 minutes, indicating that the trucks will

FIGURE 9-9
**MODEL OF THE CRANBERRY PROCESSING SYSTEM USING THE FACTORY MODELING SYSTEM (FMS).**

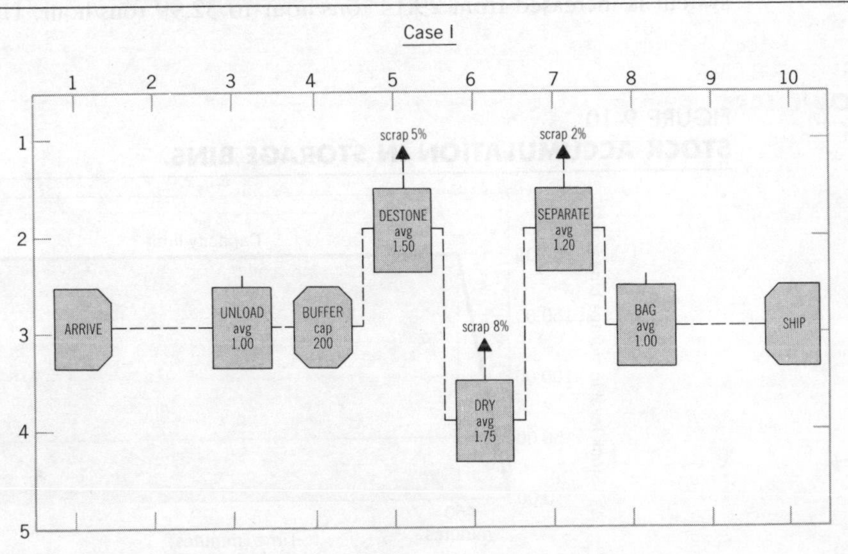

TABLE 9-5
**RESULTS OF 6000 MINUTES OF SIMULATION RUN**

Input: 3598 tons
Output: 2914 tons (29.14 tons/hour)
Yield for the plant: 2914/3598 = 0.8099

| Work Center | Percentage of Time Busy |
|---|---|
| Unload | 59.96% |
| Destone and dechaff | 85.20% |
| Dry | 94.07% |
| Separator | 59.56% |
| Bagging | 48.56% |

begin to queue after that time. With appropriate modifications to the model, we can also plot the number of trucks in queue at various points in time (by assuming a truck capacity). We can also set a termination time for truck arrival beyond which no trucks arrive but processing continues. These details can be easily incorporated in the FMS model.

The average capacity of the processing plant is 29.14 tons/hour. The maximum utilization is for dryers (94.07 percent), indicating a possible bottleneck. Note that the capacities for some stages are variable within a range; therefore, 100 percent utilization may not occur even for a bottleneck stage.

The model for the modified system with additional drying capacity is shown in Figure 9-11. The modified model was also run for 6000 minutes.

Table 9-6 shows the results of adding drying capacity. The average capacity of the system is increased from 29.14 tons/hour to 32.99 tons/hour. Utilization was the

FIGURE 9-10
**STOCK ACCUMULATION IN STORAGE BINS.**

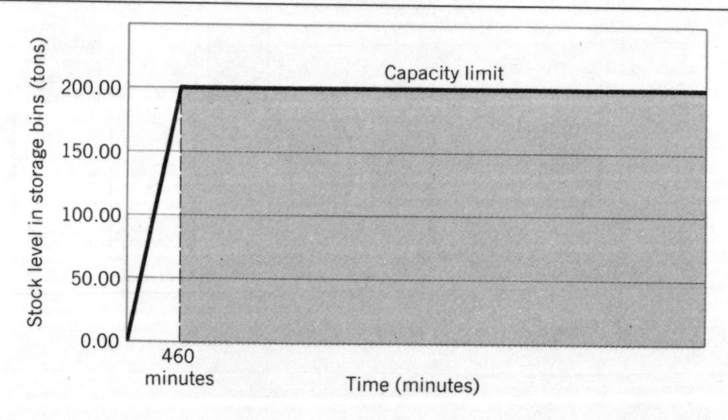

FIGURE 9-11
**MODIFIED MODEL FOR THE CRANBERRY PROCESSING SYSTEM (WITH ADDITIONAL DRYING CAPACITY) USING THE FACTORY MODELING SYSTEM (FMS).**

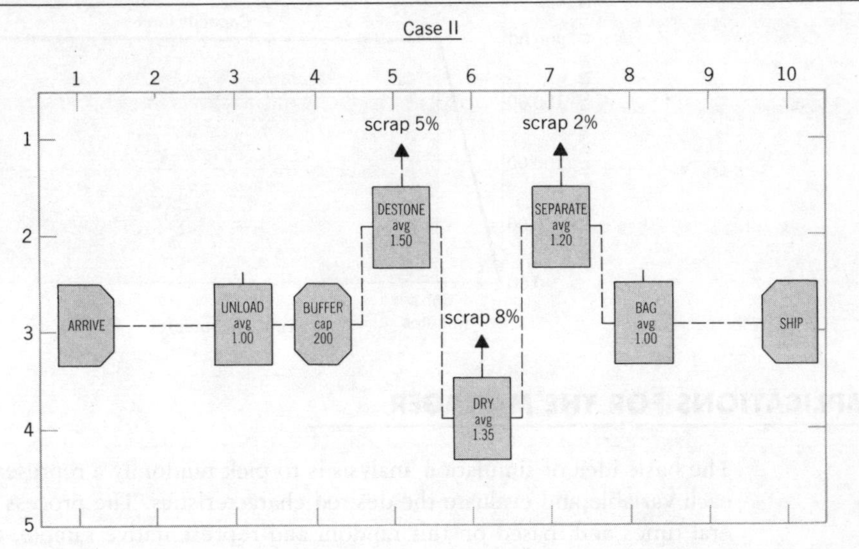


highest for the destone and dechaff process (96.03 percent), indicating a shift of the bottleneck process from drying. Figure 9-12 shows that the storage bins now take 655 minutes to fill up as compared with 460 minutes without the additional drying capacity.

Economic analysis is required to compare the costs of adding additional drying capacity with the benefits of higher output and reduced queuing of trucks.

TABLE 9-6
**RESULTS OF 6000 MINUTES OF SIMULATION RUN WITH ADDITIONAL DRYING CAPACITY**

Input: 4054 tons
Output: 3299 tons (32.99 tons/hour)
Yield for the Plant: 3299/4054 = 0.8137

| Work Center | Percentage of Time Busy |
|---|---|
| Unload | 67.55% |
| Destone and dechaff | 96.03% |
| Dry | 82.47% |
| Separator | 67.36% |
| Bagging | 55.00% |

FIGURE 9-12
**STOCK ACCUMULATION IN STORAGE BINS WITH ADDITIONAL DRYING CAPACITY.**

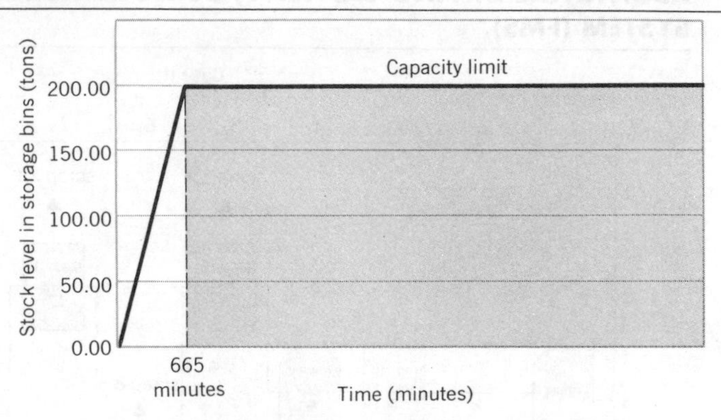


## IMPLICATIONS FOR THE MANAGER

The basic idea of simulation analysis is to pick randomly a representative value for each variable and evaluate the desired characteristics. The process is repeated several times and, based on this random and representative sample, the desired performance measures are estimated. Thus, conceptually we need:

1. A method for randomly selecting a representative sample (which will involve the generation of random variable values by computer).
2. A method for keeping track of the various steps in analysis and for estimating the desired performance measures based on the sample results.

There are several reasons for using simulation analysis, three of which are as follows:

1. *Problem complexity.* If a problem has a large number of variables and complex interactions among the variables, a direct analytical solution may not be possible.
2. *Convenience.* For many problems, there are "packaged routines" on computers for carrying out simulation analysis. Cellular simulation eliminates the burden of programming and makes simulation analysis available to a wide number of users.
3. *Understandability.* The process of obtaining a solution can be easily understood by the user as the steps of the simulation correspond to how a user would go about solving the problem.

Simulation has found wide applicability for various areas of production and operations in both manufacturing and service. We note, however, that simulation, because of its simplicity, should not be substituted where analytical results are possible. If analytical results can be derived for only a part of the model, then simulation should make use of these results as appropriate subroutines in the computer program. Each simulation run produces only an estimate of the model's true performance or output characteristics. Several independent runs are therefore needed to improve confidence in the results.

A manager must clearly understand that simulation results only describe the behavior of the model. If the model is not a valid representation of the actual system, then these results will provide little useful information. Unfortunately, this simple observation is often overlooked because the mass of data and statistics produced by simulation create an impression of authenticity that may not be justified.

We believe that simulation, if properly used, is a powerful tool for a manager in diagnosing, evaluating, and managing the operations system of a firm. We predict a greater use of simulation for decision making as we move toward technologically sophisticated and integrated manufacturing.

# REVIEW QUESTIONS

1. What is the distinction between a model and a system?
2. Why don't we simulate the system directly?
3. What types of data are collected in a simulation?
4. What is the distinction between verification and validation as these terms are defined in the chapter?
5. What is an experimental design?
6. Why are the results of a simulation only estimates and not actual performance characteristics?
7. What is cellular simulation? What are its advantages and its limitations?
8. What are the reasons for using simulation for the analysis and evaluation of policies?

# PROBLEMS

9. A sample of 100 arrivals of customers at a check-out station of a small store yields the following distribution:

| Time between Arrival, Minutes | Frequency |
|---|---|
| 0.5 | 2 |
| 1.0 | 6 |
| 1.5 | 10 |
| 2.0 | 25 |
| 2.5 | 20 |
| 3.0 | 14 |
| 3.5 | 10 |
| 4.0 | 7 |
| 4.5 | 4 |
| 5.0 | 2 |
| | 100 |

A study of the time required to service the customers by adding up the bill, receiving payment, making change, placing packages in bags, and so on, yields the following distribution:

| Service Time, Minutes | Frequency |
|---|---|
| 0.5 | 12 |
| 1.0 | 21 |
| 1.5 | 36 |
| 2.0 | 19 |
| 2.5 | 7 |
| 3.0 | 5 |
| | 100 |

a. Convert the distributions to cumulative probability distributions.

b. Using a simulated sample of 20, estimate the average percentage of customer waiting time and the average percentage of idle time for the server.

10. The manager of a drive-in restaurant is attempting to determine how many carhops he needs during his peak load period. As a policy, he wishes to offer service such that average customer waiting time does not exceed two minutes.

a. How many carhops does he need if the arrival and service distributions are as follows and if any carhop can service any customer?

| Time between Successive Arrivals, Minutes | Frequency | Carhop Service Time, Minutes | Frequency |
|---|---|---|---|
| 0.0 | 10 | 0.0 | 0 |
| 1.0 | 35 | 1.0 | 5 |
| 2.0 | 25 | 2.0 | 20 |
| 3.0 | 15 | 3.0 | 40 |
| 4.0 | 10 | 4.0 | 35 |
| 5.0 | 5 | | |
| | 100 | | 100 |

b. Simulate each alternative for number of carhops with a sample of 20 arrivals.

11. A company maintains a bank of machines that are exposed to severe service, causing bearing failure to be a common maintenance problem. There are three bearings in the machines that cause trouble. The general practice had been to replace the bearings when they failed. However, excessive downtime costs raised the question of whether or not a preventive policy was worthwhile. The company wishes to evaluate three alternative policies:

a. The current practice of replacing bearings that fail.

b. When one bearing fails, replace all three.

c. When one bearing fails, replace that bearing plus any other bearings that have been in use 1700 hours or more.

Time and cost data are as follows:

| | |
|---|---|
| Maintenance mechanic's time: | |
| Replace 1 bearing | 5 hours |
| Replace 2 bearings | 6 hours |
| Replace 3 bearings | 7 hours |
| Maintenance mechanic's wage rate | $3 per hour |
| Bearing costs | $5 each |
| Downtime costs | $2 per hour |

A record of the actual working lives of 200 bearings gives the following distribution:

| Bearing Life, Hours | Frequency |
|---|---|
| 1100 | 3 |
| 1200 | 10 |
| 1300 | 12 |
| 1400 | 20 |
| 1500 | 27 |
| 1600 | 35 |
| 1700 | 30 |
| 1800 | 25 |
| 1900 | 18 |
| 2000 | 15 |
| 2100 | 4 |
| 2200 | 1 |
| | 200 |

Simulate approximately 20,000 hours of service for each of the three alternative policies.

# SITUATIONS

## Circuit Board Company

12. A manufacturer of electrical circuit boards faces the problem of whether to accept a mix of large order sizes. The manufacturer has specialized in small custom orders that require precision work and innovative designs. The present mix of order sizes in a typical month is given in Table 9-7. The concern that the manufacturing manager has about accepting order sizes up to 100 circuit boards per order is that quality problems may arise and delivery time may increase.

A typical order is processed through several operations, which are shown in Table 9-8. The set-up time for each order and the run time per circuit board is also shown in Table 9-8. In addition to actual manufacturing time, the orders require one week for design and ordering materials and an additional week for

TABLE 9-7
**PRESENT MIX OF ORDER SIZES IN A TYPICAL MONTH**

| Order Size (Number of Circuit Boards per Order) | Number of Orders | Total Number of Circuit Boards |
|---|---|---|
| 1 | 10 | 10 |
| 2 | 15 | 30 |
| 4 | 25 | 100 |
| 8 | 5 | 40 |
| 16 | 2 | 32 |
| | 57 | 212 |

scheduling. The reject rate is about five percent and the rework rate is about three percent. With larger orders (order sizes greater than 16), the reject rate is expected to climb to seven percent and the rework rate, to four percent.

The manufacturing manager believes that a simulation study could provide valuable information for the company's decision.

How would you set up a simulation study for the problem? Describe all the steps and the data that you will need to complete the study.

## Should an Automated Teller Be Installed?

13. A bank is considering whether to install an automated teller service for its busy downtown branch. At present, the waiting time for the customers fluctuates greatly. The bank has collected data on the arrival pattern of its customers. The time to process a customer is also variable because of the varying complexity of the transactions. For a typical staffing pattern, the bank has developed a probability distribution for service time. Of course, a change in staffing would influence both the service time and the waiting time for the customers. For example, a person assigned exclusively to handle travelers checks would reduce both the service time and the waiting time.

TABLE 9-8
**OPERATIONS REQUIRED BY A TYPICAL ORDER**

| Operation | Set-up Time/Order (Minutes) | Run Time/Board (Minutes) |
|---|---|---|
| Photograph | 30 | 0 |
| Shear and drill | 40 | 1 |
| Plate and etch | 30 | 4 |
| Configuration | 50 | 1 |
| Drill | 50 | 2 |
| Inspect and pack | 20 | 2 |

The automated teller will be an efficient way to meet the needs of the customers who require some simple transactions. It would also lead to a reduction in the staff level.

The operations manager built a simulation model for branch operations. He ran the simulation for processing 1000 customers, both with the present system and with the automated teller. The model required some assumptions about how many customers will actually use the automated teller. The branch manager considers this and other assumptions he made to be realistic. The waiting time for each customer was computed, and the results obtained can be summarized as follows:

| | | |
|---|---|---|
| Average waiting time with the present system | = | 1.1 minutes |
| Maximum waiting time with the present system | = | 16.3 minutes |
| Average waiting time with the automated teller | | |
| Customers using automated teller | = | 0.25 minutes |
| Customers using branch staff | = | 0.99 minutes |
| Maximum waiting time with the automated teller | | |
| Customers using automated teller | = | 2.9 minutes |
| Customers using branch staff | = | 17.5 minutes |

The maximum waiting time is defined as the largest amount of time that any of the 1000 customers spent in the system. Note that the automated teller option assumes a reduced staffing level; hence, for some customers the average waiting time could indeed increase.

Based on these results, the operations manager recommended that the automated teller option be chosen. He argued that the average wait for customers who use the automated teller is clearly low. Further, the average wait for customers who require the services of the branch staff is also reduced.

How do you interpret the results of the simulation study? Do you see any problem in drawing conclusions based on a single run of 1000 customers? What modifications to the simulation would you make and what type of data would you desire to make a rational decision concerning the problem posed?

## Investment Project

14. An evaluation of the attractiveness of an investment project requires an estimation of the net contribution from the new product line. The net contribution, $\pi$, is determined as follows:

$$\pi = (N \times M) - F$$

where

$N$ = Number of units of the product sold
$M$ = Margin per unit sold
$F$ = Fixed costs of undertaking the project

The number of units sold depends on the size of the market, $S$, and the percentage share of the product, $\alpha$.

$$N = \left(\frac{\alpha}{100}\right)S$$

The company has made the following assessments: $\alpha$ is a uniform distribution between 10 and 30 percent, and $S$ is given by the continuous distribution shown in Figure 9-13. $M$ is given by a discrete distribution:

| $M$ | \$5/unit | \$4/unit | \$3/unit |
|---|---|---|---|
| Probability | .25 | .5 | .25 |

Finally, $F$ is given by a uniform probability distribution between \$5 and \$10 million.

Set up a table to carry out a simulation analysis for the problem to determine the probability distribution for the net contribution from the new product line. By using a random number table, carry out 25 iterations of the simulation, where each iteration consists of randomly selecting the values of $\alpha$, $S$, $M$, and $F$ to derive a value for the net contribution, $\pi$. Based on these 25 iterations or observations, plot a probability distribution for the net contribution.

If you have access to a spreadsheet program, you may wish to carry out 100 or 1000 iterations to obtain a probability distribution for net contribution.

## Medical Clinic

15. Note: This situation requires the use of a cellular simulation program such as the FMS or EXCELL, which are distributed by the Scientific Press.

A medical clinic is in the process of deciding how many modules to include in its automated multitest laboratory. A larger number of modules will increase the capital and operating costs but, hopefully, will result in a higher capacity for the system (measured in number of patients tested per hour).

FIGURE 9-13
**CUMULATIVE DISTRIBUTION FOR THE SIZE OF THE MARKET.**

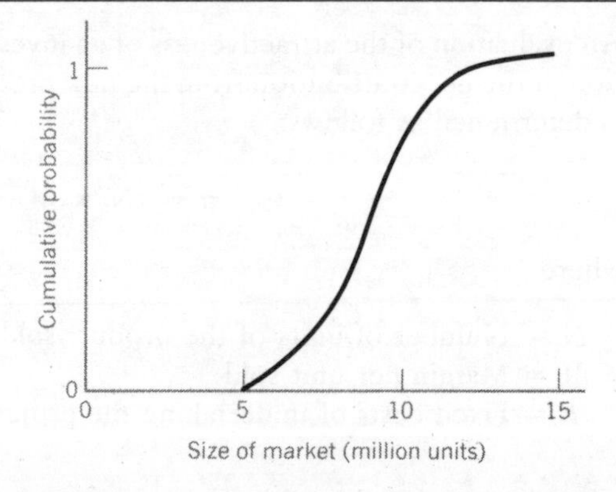

Three configurations that involve four, five, or six modules are under consideration. The incremental costs for the three options are estimated as follows:

| | | |
|---|---|---|
| 4 modules | Base case ($0) | Base case ($0) |
| 5 modules | $30,000 | $4,000/year |
| 6 modules | $50,000 | $10,000/year |

The arrangement of the tests in the modules and the estimated time for a test are shown in Table 9-9. The estimated time that a patient may spend for a test is assumed to follow a uniform distribution within the range indicated in Table 9-9.

Based on the information provided, develop a simulation model for the automated multitest laboratory. Present the output of your simulation program in a format that will be useful to the decision maker.

## Nuclear Camera

16. Note: This situation requires the use of a cellular simulation program such as the FMS or EXCELL, which are distributed by the Scientific Press.

A new plant for the fabrication and assembly of a camera for use in nuclear medicine is to be designed. Two options for assembling the cameras are being considered. One is to use a manual process that has the advantage of flexibility but is slow. The other option is to use a more efficient automated assembly procedure. The automated procedure will be cost-effective only if there is a significant gain in output (30 to 50 percent) and assembly is busy more than 75 percent of the time.

The new plant will consist of three receiving areas. In receiving area R1, raw materials will be received. Receiving area R2 will handle components that will go into the subassemblies. Receiving area R3 will stock subassemblies directly purchased from outside that will be required in the final assembly.

TABLE 9-9
**ARRANGEMENTS AND PROCESSING TIMES FOR TESTS**

| | *Alternative* | | |
|---|---|---|---|
| Module | 4 Modules | 5 Modules | 6 Modules |
| 1 | E and S (6–10) | E (3–6) | E (3–6) |
| 2 | V (4–7) | S (3–4) | S (3–4) |
| 3 | B (4–7) | V (4–7) | V (4–7) |
| 4 | T and A (5–8) | B (4–7) | B (4–7) |
| 5 | — | T and A (5–8) | T (3–4) |
| 6 | — | — | A (2–4) |

( ) = Processing time in minutes
E = Electrocardiography
S = Spirometry
V = Vision
B = Blood Pressure
A = Audiometer

From receiving area R1, raw materials will be drawn and sent to the fabrication shop. The process of fabrication requires 4 to 6 hours per camera.

The output from fabrication and the components from receiving area R2 are sent to a subassembly area. The subassemblies assembled in the shop require 5 to 8 hours per camera.

The subassemblies assembled in house and those purchased from outside are assembled according to customer specifications. This process will require 8 to 16 hours if the manual procedure is used and 4 to 6 hours if the automated procedure is used. The rework rate for the manual procedure is expected to be 10 percent and that for the automated procedure, 20 percent.

Finally, the inspection process requires 5 to 10 hours and the rework rate is expected to be 10 percent. Units that pass inspection are sent to shipping area S1. All rework is done at a separate location in the plant that is equipped with general purpose machines and electrical testing apparatus. The workers employed for rework also have a wide variety of skills. The processing time for rework is highly fluctuating and is expected to be 5 to 20 hours per unit. It is expected that 5 percent of the units sent to the rework station will be complete rejects and must be disregarded. The remaining reworked units are sent to shipping area S2.

Develop a simulation model for the new plant. You may use buffer storage areas anywhere in the process if it improves the workflow, but buffer storage areas take up expensive floor space and should be used judiciously. Based on the runs of your model, provide a recommendation to the plant manager.

# REFERENCES


Conway, R., "A User's Guide to the Factory Modeling System," TR 84–596, Department of Computer Science, Cornell University, Ithaca, New York, March 1984.

Fishman, G. S., *Principle of Discrete Event Simulation,* Wiley, New York, 1978.

Geoffrion, A. M., *Structured Modeling,* Graduate School of Management, UCLA, January 1985.

Law, A. M. and W. D. Kelton, *Simulation Modeling and Analysis,* McGraw-Hill, New York, 1982.

Lembersky, M. R. and Chi, V. H., "Decision Simulators Speed Implementation and Improve Operation," *Interfaces, 14,* July–August, 1984, pp. 1–15.

Maisel, H. and G. Gnugnuoli, *Simulation of Discrete Stochastic Systems,* SRA, Chicago, 1972.

Moore, L. J. and B. W. Taylor, III, "Experimental Investigation of Priority Scheduling in a Bank Check Processing Operation," *Decision Sciences, 8*(4), October 1977.

Reitman, J. *Computer Simulation Applications,* Wiley, New York, 1971.

Schriber, T. J., *Simulation Using GPSS,* Wiley, New York, 1974.

Shannon, R. E., *Systems Simulation: The Art and Science,* Prentice-Hall, Englewood Cliffs, N.J., 1975.

# CHAPTER 10

# OPERATIONS SCHEDULING

In this chapter, we discuss methods of scheduling tasks or operations on available resources so as to achieve some specified objectives. An example of a scheduling problem is to determine the order in which jobs in a manufacturing plant will be completed so that the number of on-time deliveries are maximized. Other examples of scheduling include the running of programs at a computing center, the processing of loan applications by a bank, the landing of aircraft at an airstrip, and performing medical tests on a patient. An arbitrary procedure, such as "first come first served" or scheduling by default, may lead to solutions that are far from optimal with respect to a company's objectives. We hope to demonstrate that, by using scientific procedures for scheduling, a company can achieve significantly better performance on stated objectives.

## JOB SHOP SCHEDULING

In Chapter 2, types and characteristics of alternative production systems were described. While scheduling problems occur to varying degrees in all types of systems, they are particularly salient in job shops. A job shop is a process-focused production system that employs general purpose processors. Production is to order, and a large number of different products are produced, each in relatively small volume. Examples of job shops include machining shops, multispecialty clinics, computer centers, and consulting firms.

A production manager of a job shop will use the results of scheduling in several aspects of decision making. At the broadest level is capacity planning, in which the need for additional capacity and the type of capacity needed are identified. A simulation analysis of forecasted order patterns could reveal bottlenecks and the requirements for additional capacity. In some cases, efficient scheduling can improve the utilization of existing processors (machines) so that expensive additions to capacity can be postponed.

The next level at which the results of scheduling are useful is in decisions concerning order acceptance, due date specifications, and product mix considerations. For example, scheduling may reveal that, given the nature of the processors in a job shop, accepting a mix of smaller volume and larger volume orders and quoting similar due dates for both types of orders create bottlenecks and late deliveries. Management may then wish either to focus on one type of order or to quote differential due dates to avoid bottlenecks and late deliveries.

Further down in the level of detail is shop loading, where the manager must decide on a daily basis how many jobs and which jobs to release to the shop for processing. The criteria of machine utilization and customer service will be important.

Finally, the manager must develop procedures for deciding the order in which the operations of different jobs should be performed on a processor if several operations are competing for the same processor. Simple procedures, such as "first come first served" or random selection, will often produce unacceptable solutions, resulting in delayed deliveries, the unbalanced utilization of processors, and the like. A clear understanding of the nature of scheduling problems at this most detailed level and of the procedures of scheduling will provide inputs to the higher level decisions discussed earlier. We will therefore focus on the job shop scheduling problem at this level of detail. To illustrate the differences among alternative scheduling procedures and the impact of a choice of a scheduling procedure on a desired performance measure, we will examine single processor scheduling in some detail.

## Single Processor Scheduling

Consider a hypothetical automated chemical plant that produces several different products, but only one product can be produced at a time. Suppose that the production manager of the plant has to decide on the scheduling of four products, the production times and due dates for which are shown in Table 10-1. The table shows, for example, that product 4 will require 8 days in manufacturing and that it is due to be delivered in 17 days. The production manager has several alternatives for scheduling the production of these products. For example, he could produce product 1 first and then product 2, followed by product 3 and finally product 4. Alternatively, he could produce product 4 first, product 2 next, then product 1, and finally product 3. In fact, there are $4 \times 3 \times 2 \times 1 = 24$ distinct ways of scheduling the production of these four products. The decision facing the production manager is which one of these possible 24 schedules should be chosen?

This simplified example illustrates the problem of scheduling on a single processor. Single processor or single machine scheduling is of interest for the following reasons:

- There are many situations where an entire plant can be viewed as a single processor, as is the case in chemical manufacturing, paint manufacturing, and the manufacturing of products in automated plants.
- In plants that employ multiple processors, there is often a bottleneck processor that controls the output of the plant because of its limited capacity. The analysis of this bottleneck processor may determine the decisions for the entire plant.
- The analysis of a single processor illustrates many important problems that arise in more complex scheduling situations; therefore, it serves as a building block for understanding the decision problems in these more complex situations.

TABLE 10-1
**SCHEDULING EXAMPLE**

| Product | Production Time, Days | Due Date, Days |
|---|---|---|
| 1 | 4 | 6 |
| 2 | 7 | 9 |
| 3 | 2 | 19 |
| 4 | 8 | 17 |

For the single processor scheduling problem, we will assume that all jobs are available for processing at time zero; that set-up times for the jobs are independent of job sequence and can therefore be included in their processing times; that the processor is continuously available, without breakdown or other interruption, until all the jobs are completed; and that the processing of a job, once begun, is not interrupted until it is completed. These assumptions allow us to limit our attention to *permutation schedules,* which are completely specified by identifying the order in which the jobs will be processed. If $n$ jobs are available for scheduling, then there will be $n!$ possible schedules.

Returning to the example in Table 10-1, the production manager faces precisely the single processor scheduling problem. (Assume that the set-up times are included in the production times and do not vary with the order in which the products are processed.) The choice of a schedule will depend on the *criterion* or objective that the production manager wishes to consider in his or her evaluation. We will now provide notation and definitions and discuss some criteria that are often employed in evaluating the desirability of alternative schedules.

## NOTATION AND DEFINITIONS

Each job in the single processor scheduling model is described by two parameters:

$$p_i = \text{Processing time for job } i$$
$$d_i = \text{Due date for job } i$$

In addition, in some cases, $r_i$, the ready time, release time, or arrival time of job $i$ may be useful. In the models discussed here, all jobs are available for processing at time zero and hence $r_i = 0$ for all jobs.

The definition of $p_i$ includes set-up time for job $i$. If job $i$ is defined as a lot of several identical pieces, then $p_i$ will denote the time required to process the complete lot. The due date, $d_i$, may be set by customer requirements or by internal planning considerations. We will consider the due date to be the time by which a job must be completed; otherwise, the job will be deemed late.

Several variables determine the solution of a scheduling decision. Some of the more important of these are

$$W_i = \text{Waiting time for job } i$$
$$C_i = \text{Completion time of job } i$$
$$F_i = \text{Flow time of job } i$$
$$L_i = \text{Lateness of job } i$$
$$T_i = \text{Tardiness of job } i$$
$$E_i = \text{Earliness of job } i$$

$W_i$ is the amount of time job $i$ has to wait before its processing begins. The first job on the schedule will have zero waiting time, and the second job on the schedule will have to wait by the amount of the processing time of the first job. $C_i$ is simply the time at which the processing of job $i$ is completed. $F_i$ is the amount of time a job spends in the system; thus, $F_i = C_i - r_i$. Since in our case $r_i = 0$, $F_i = C_i$. Lateness, $L_i$, is the amount of time by which the completion time of job $i$ exceeds its due date.

Thus, $L_i = C_i - d_i$. Note that $L_i$ can be either positive or negative. A positive lateness represents a violation of the due date and is called tardiness, $T_i$. Similarly, a negative lateness represents the completion of a job before its due date and is called earliness, $E_i$. Thus, the three measures of schedule, $L_i$, $T_i$, and $E_i$, measure the deviation of the completion time from the due date. Since there is often a penalty associated with not meeting due dates, the tardiness measure is usually used. However, in some cases there may be a penalty for being either too early or too late (e.g., crop harvesting), so both tardiness and earliness measures may be useful.

## CRITERIA AND OBJECTIVE FUNCTIONS FOR SCHEDULING

Several criteria can be employed to evaluate the performance of a schedule. The scheduling criteria chosen in a given situation depend on the objective function of the manager. For example, the underlying objective function or cost function of the company may be such that a penalty is associated with a tardy job, but once a job is delayed, the amount of tardiness does not influence the cost. In this situation, a scheduling criterion that minimizes the number of tardy jobs will be most appropriate for selecting an optimal schedule.

Suppose there are $n$ jobs to be scheduled. Some commonly employed criteria are described in the following material:

$$\text{Mean flow time} = \bar{F} = \frac{1}{n}\sum_{i=1}^{n} F_i$$

This criterion measures the average amount of time that a job spends in the system. Minimization of $\bar{F}$ is appropriate when rapid turnaround is required and when the objective is to keep a low in-process inventory. Rapid turnaround may provide a competitive advantage to the company when customers are sensitive to fast deliveries.

$$\text{Mean tardiness} = \bar{T} = \frac{1}{n}\sum_{i=1}^{n} T_i$$

This criterion is useful when the objective function of the company includes a penalty per unit of time if job completion is delayed beyond a specified due date. For example, a penalty of $X per day may be imposed for each job that is delayed beyond its specified due date.

$$\text{Maximum tardiness} = T_{\max} = \max_i \{T_i\}$$

To compute maximum tardiness, the tardiness for each job is calculated. The job that has the largest tardiness of all the jobs determines $T_{\max}$. For example, if $T_1 = 3$, $T_2 = 5$, $T_3 = 1$, and $T_4 = 4$, then $T_{\max} = 5$ and is determined by job 2. This criterion is useful when the penalty per day for tardiness increases with the amount of tardiness.

$$\text{Number of tardy jobs} = n_T$$

This criterion simply counts the total number of jobs that are not completed by their due dates.

Several other criteria and procedures for selecting a schedule that optimize these criteria have been discussed in Conway, Maxwell, and Miller (1967) and Baker (1974).

## SCHEDULING PROCEDURES

We will now illustrate several scheduling procedures using the example in Table 10-1.

**Shortest Processing Time (SPT) Procedure.** A schedule obtained by sequencing jobs in nondecreasing order of processing times is called a shortest processing time (SPT) schedule. This schedule minimizes mean flow time, $\bar{F}$. In addition, the SPT rule also minimizes mean lateness and mean waiting time. In the example in Table 10-1, the SPT schedule is

$$< 3, 1, 2, 4 >$$

This shows that job 3 is processed first, followed by jobs 1, 2, and 4, in that order. In Table 10-2, the calculations for obtaining the flow time for each job are shown. Job 3 is first in the sequence; hence, its completion time is 2 days. Job 1 is started after job 3 is finished and takes 4 days. Thus, the completion time for job 1 is 6 days. The completion times for the remaining jobs are similarly computed. Since all the jobs are available at time zero, the flow time for each job is identical to its completion time. The mean flow time is computed by simply adding the flow time for each job and dividing by 4.

$$\bar{F} = \frac{(F_1 + F_2 + F_3 + F_4)}{4} = \frac{(6 + 13 + 2 + 21)}{4} = \frac{42}{4} = 10.5$$

It can be checked that no other sequence can produce a better mean flow time than the sequence obtained by the SPT rule. The optimality of the SPT rule can be mathematically proved. By finishing the shorter jobs first, both the turnaround time and the work-in-process inventory are reduced. The SPT procedure is simple to implement and provides good results even in the more complex scheduling situations discussed later.

**Due Date (DD) Procedure.** In the due date procedure, jobs are sequenced in the order of nondecreasing due dates. In our example, job 1 will be sequenced first because it has the earliest due date. The sequence obtained by this rule is

$$< 1, 2, 4, 3 >$$

The due date procedure minimizes the maximum tardiness. In Table 10-3, the computations for individual job tardiness, $T_i$, for the due date sequence are shown. The maximum tardiness is 2 days. No other schedule can produce a tardiness of less than 2 days. For comparison, the maximum tardiness for the SPT schedule is 4 days, as shown in Table 10-2.

TABLE 10-2
**COMPUTATIONS USING THE SPT PROCEDURE FOR THE DATA IN TABLE 10-1**

| Job | Processing Time ($p_i$) | Due Date ($d_i$) | Completion Time for SPT Schedule ($C_i$) | Flow Time ($F_i$) | Tardiness ($T_i$) |
|---|---|---|---|---|---|
| 1 | 4 | 6 | 6 | 6 | 0 |
| 2 | 7 | 9 | 13 | 13 | 4 |
| 3 | 2 | 19 | 2 | 2 | 0 |
| 4 | 8 | 17 | 21 | 21 | 4 |

**Moore Procedure.** The number of jobs tardy for the SPT schedule is 2 (Table 10-2), and for the DD schedule, it is 3 (Table 10-3). The Moore procedure minimizes the total number of tardy jobs. This procedure is described in the following steps.

*Step 1.* Arrange the jobs in nondecreasing order of their due dates (DD schedule). If this sequence yields one or zero tardy jobs, then the DD schedule is optimal and the procedure stops. In our example, 3 jobs are tardy in the DD schedule (Table 10-3), so we proceed to step 2.

*Step 2.* Identify the first tardy job in the DD schedule. In our example, the first tardy job in the DD schedule is job 2, which is marked by an asterisk (*) in the following schedule:

| | | | | |
|---|---|---|---|---|
| DD schedule | <1 | 2* | 4 | 3> |
| Completion time | 4 | 11 | 19 | 21 |
| Due date | 6 | 9 | 17 | 19 |

*Step 3.* Identify the longest job from among the jobs including and to the left of the job marked with the * in the schedule in step 2. That is, we pick the longest job among the jobs that are completed no later than the completion time of the first tardy job in step 2. In our example, jobs 1 and 2 are candidates, and since job 2 has the longer processing time of the two, it is identified.

TABLE 10-3
**COMPUTATIONS USING THE DD PROCEDURE FOR THE DATA IN TABLE 10-1**

| Job | Processing Time ($p_i$) | Due Date ($d_i$) | Completion Time for DD Schedule ($C_i$) | Tardiness ($T_i$) |
|---|---|---|---|---|
| 1 | 4 | 6 | 4 | 0 |
| 2 | 7 | 9 | 11 | 2 |
| 3 | 2 | 19 | 21 | 2 |
| 4 | 8 | 17 | 19 | 2 |

The identified job is removed and the completion times for the remaining jobs are revised.

| | $<1$ | 4 | $3>$ |
|---|---|---|---|
| Completion time | 4 | 12 | 14 |
| Due date | 6 | 17 | 19 |

We now repeat step 2. In our example, all the jobs are now on time, so we terminate the procedure. The Moore schedule is

$$< 1, 4, 3, 2 >$$

which is obtained by simply putting the jobs removed in step 3 at the end of the schedule.

**Weighted Shortest Processing Time (WSPT) Procedure.** If jobs are not of equal importance, then it may be more appropriate to minimize the weighted flow time

$$\sum_{i=1}^{n} w_i F_i$$

where $w_i$ is the weight associated with the flow time of job $i$. The weights reflect the relative importance of individual job flow time. For example, if $w_1 = 1$ and $w_2 = 2$, it is as desirable to reduce the flow time of job 1 by 2 days as it is to reduce the flow time of job 2 by 1 day. Considerations of the relative costs of each job, the importance of the customer requiring a job, and so forth will influence the determination of $w_i$'s.

A simple procedure to minimize the weighted flow time is to compute the weighted processing time, $p_i/w_i$, for each job. Now, the job with the smallest $p_i/w_i$ is scheduled first in the sequence. From the remaining jobs, the job with the lowest $p_i/w_i$ is selected and is placed in the second position in the schedule. The procedure is repeated until all of the jobs are scheduled. Essentially, the schedule is obtained by arranging the jobs in order of nondecreasing $p_i/w_i$ ratios.

**Other Procedures.** Several other procedures for optimizing a specified criterion are available in the literature. However, even for single processor scheduling, optimization for some criteria is quite difficult. For example, no simple procedure exists for minimizing mean tardiness, $\bar{T}$. In such cases, a manager has the choice of using either a simpler procedure that produces good results but cannot guarantee an optimal solution (called a heuristic) or a complex procedure utilizing techniques of combinatorial optimization, which will require the use of a computer and may be expensive to implement but will guarantee optimal results.

Several extensions of the basic single processor scheduling model have been examined in the literature. These include the nonsimultaneous arrival of jobs, the incorporation of dependence among jobs (e.g., a precedence constraint, such as job $i$ must be completed before job $j$), and the allowance for set-up times that depend on the sequence (e.g., the processing of beige paint after black paint may require a higher set-up time than the processing of beige paint after white paint). In addition, probabilistic situations, where the arrival of jobs is uncertain or jobs have random processing times or due dates, have also been examined.

## Flow Shop Scheduling

In many situations, there is more than one processor and a job consists of several operations that are to be performed in a specific order. Moving from a single processor job shop to a multiple processor job shop poses a formidable challenge. We first consider a special job shop case in which the flow of work is unidirectional.

A flow shop is a special type of job shop in which $m$ machines are numbered 1, 2, . . . , $m$ and a job may require a maximum of $m$ operations—one operation on each machine. Further, for every job, if operation $j$ precedes operation $k$, then the machine required for operation $j$ has a lower number than the machine required for operation $k$. An example of a flow shop is shown in Figure 10-1. In Figure 10-1*a*, all the jobs require one operation on each processor; such a shop is called a "pure" flow shop. In Figure 10-1*b*, even though the flow of work is unidirectional, a job may require fewer than $m$ operations and the operations need not be performed on adjacent processors. In Figure 10-1*b*, job 1 is processed on all three processors, job 2 is processed on processors 2 and 3, and job 3 is processed on processors 1 and 3. An example of a flow shop is an assembly line where work progresses from one stage to the next in the same direction. In several manufacturing situations (e.g., the manufacture of printed circuit boards), the same sequence of operations is required for a large number of orders. Further, in many cases, manufacturing can be divided into two stages. One stage is like a flow shop with all jobs having the same sequence, whereas the second stage requires a more complex routing of operations. One

FIGURE 10-1
**SCHEMATIC OF FLOW SHOPS: (*a*) A PURE FLOW SHOP; (*b*) A GENERAL FLOW SHOP.**

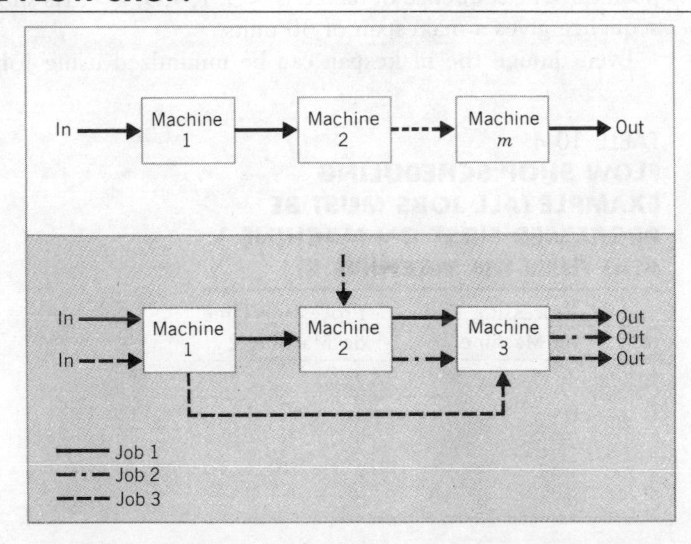

example of such a process is furniture manufacturing, where the front end is a flow shop and customization for upholstery, paint, and the like is accomplished at the back end of the manufacturing process.

To demonstrate scheduling procedures for flow shops, consider the example problem in Table 10-4. In this example, there are two machines and five jobs.

If we schedule the jobs on machines 1 and 2 in the order of the job numbers, we obtain the schedule shown in Figure 10-2*a*. The shaded areas show the amount of time during which a machine is idle. The completion time of last job determines the *makespan* of the schedule, which measures machine utilization. In Figure 10-2*a*, the makespan is 33 units of time.

For the special case of a two-machine flow shop, Johnson's procedure minimizes the makespan. This procedure works as follows:

*Step 1.* Determine the minimum processing time on either machine. In our example, it is 2 for job 3 on machine 1.

*Step 2a.* If the minimum processing time occurs on machine 1, place the associated job in the first available position in the sequence. In our example, job 3 is placed in the first position. Proceed to step 3.

*Step 2b.* If the minimum processing time occurs on machine 2, place the associated job in the last available position in sequence. Proceed to step 3.

*Step 3.* The job sequenced by either step 2*a* or step 2*b* is removed from consideration. The process is repeated, starting with step 1, until all the jobs are sequenced. Ties can be broken arbitrarily.

In our example, once job 3 is removed, the minimum processing time occurs for job 2 on machine 2; hence, by step 2*b*, job 2 is placed last in the sequence. For the remaining jobs, 1, 4, and 5, the minimum processing time occurs for job 5 on machine 2; using step 2*b* again, job 5 is placed in the last available position (the fourth position). Finally, job 4 is placed in the sole available position, the third position. The sequence obtained is < 3, 1, 4, 5, 2 >. As shown in Figure 10-2*b*, this sequence gives a makespan of 30 units.

Even though the makespan can be minimized using Johnson's procedure for a

**TABLE 10-4**
**FLOW SHOP SCHEDULING EXAMPLE (ALL JOBS MUST BE PROCESSED FIRST ON MACHINE 1 AND THEN ON MACHINE 2)**

| Jobs | Processing Time on Machine 1 | Processing Time on Machine 2 |
|---|---|---|
| 1 | 4 | 7 |
| 2 | 6 | 3 |
| 3 | 2 | 3 |
| 4 | 7 | 7 |
| 5 | 8 | 6 |

FIGURE 10-2
**SCHEDULE FOR FLOW SHOP EXAMPLE IN TABLE 10-4. (*a*) SCHEDULE FOR SEQUENCE < 1, 2, 3, 4, 5 > ON EACH MACHINE. (*b*) SCHEDULE USING JOHNSON'S PROCEDURE.**

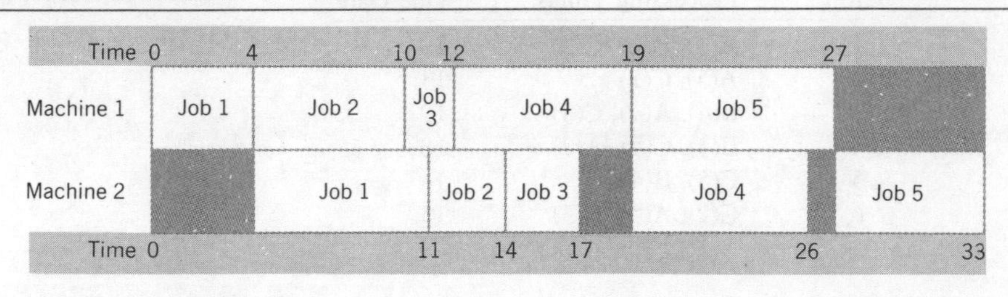


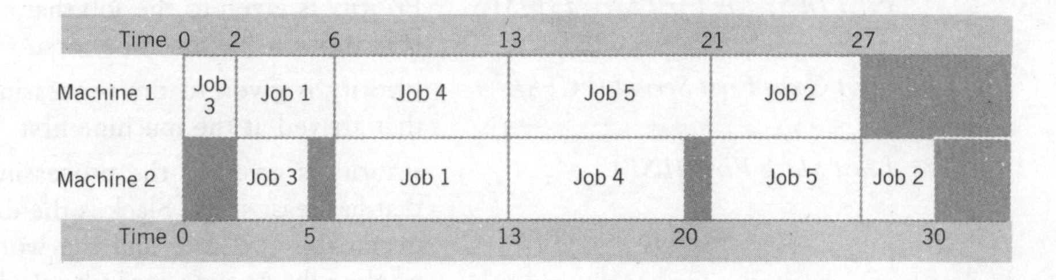


two-machine flow shop, few results are available for other criteria. In fact, for scheduling a flow shop with $m$ machines, one has to rely on combinatorial techniques or heuristic procedures. This shows the difficulty in scheduling and the combinatorial nature of the problem for even a well-structured environment like a flow shop.

## General Job Shop Scheduling

Our conclusion in the preceding discussion of flow shops provides a guide for our introduction to general job shops, in which the flow of work may take any pattern. *There are no optimal rules or procedures for job shops with more than two machines and two jobs.* We will therefore focus on some rules that provide "good" solutions most of the time.

To illustrate the preparation of schedules for general job shops, we will use the example in Table 10-5. Job 3 in this example is due in 12 days, and it must be processed first on machine B for 4 days, then on machine A for 4 days, and finally on machine C for 3 days.

As we begin scheduling with machine A, we face the decision of whether job 1 or job 2 should be scheduled first. Several simple rules can be employed to resolve the choice of a job from a set of available jobs waiting to be processed on the same machine at a given point in time. Some commonly employed rules are

*Earliest Due Date First (EDD).* Priority is given to the job with the earliest due date. (Job 1 will be chosen for scheduling on machine A at time zero.)

TABLE 10-5
**GENERAL JOB SHOP EXAMPLE**

| Job | Sequence and Processing Times | Due Date |
|---|---|---|
| 1 | A(3), B(3), C(2) | 10 |
| 2 | A(5), C(2) | 13 |
| 3 | B(4), A(4), C(3) | 12 |
| 4 | B(3), C(5), A(2) | 18 |
| 5 | C(5), B(4) | 14 |
| 6 | C(2), A(5), B(5) | 15 |

*First In System First Served (FISFS).* Priority is given to the job that arrived in the *shop* (not on the machine) first.

*First Come First Served (FCFS).* Priority is given to the processing of the job that arrived at the machine first.

*Least Slack First (LSF).* Priority is given to the processing of the job that has least slack. Slack is the difference between the due date and the work remaining on the job. At time zero, the slack for job 1 is $10 - (3 + 3 + 2) = 2$ days in our example.

*Shortest Processing Time (SPT).* Priority is given to the job with the shortest processing time on the machine under consideration.

*Least Work Remaining (LWR).* Priority is given to the job with the least amount of total processing remaining to be done.

Several other rules can be devised to select a job from a set of waiting jobs for scheduling on a machine. The managerial objectives are the simplicity of implementation of a rule as well as the attainment of some desired performance, such as reducing the congestion in the shop, improving machine utilization, and meeting job due dates.

Figure 10-3 contains Gantt charts that show the schedules developed using the aforementioned rules. A Gantt chart is prepared by determining the set of jobs waiting for each machine. If more than one job is waiting for a machine, a rule is used to choose a job to be processed next. When the processing of a job on one machine is completed, that job is added to the waiting list for the machine it needs to be processed by next. The procedure is repeated each day (or unit of time) until all the jobs are scheduled.

It is clear from Figure 10-3 that different rules produce different schedules. In Table 10-6, the performance of these rules on the criteria number of jobs tardy, total tardiness, mean flow time, and makespan is evaluated. The relative performance of a rule may change if the problem data are modified. In a static situation where all jobs are available simultaneously, it is possible to compare the perfor-

FIGURE 10-3
**GANTT CHARTS SHOWING THE SCHEDULES DEVELOPED USING ALTERNATIVE RULES FOR THE EXAMPLE IN TABLE 10-5.**

Scheduling Rule: EDD

| Time | 1 | 2 | 3 | 4 | 5 | 6 | 7 | 8 | 9 | 10 | 11 | 12 | 13 | 14 | 15 | 16 | 17 | 18 | 19 | 20 | 21 | 22 |
|---|---|---|---|---|---|---|---|---|---|---|---|---|---|---|---|---|---|---|---|---|---|---|
| Machine A | 1 | 1 | 1 | 2 | 2 | 2 | 2 | 2 | 3 | 3 | 3 | 3 | 6 | 6 | 6 | 6 | 6 | – | – | – | 4 | 4 |
| Machine B | 3 | 3 | 3 | 3 | 1 | 1 | 1 | 5 | 5 | 5 | 5 | 4 | 4 | 4 | – | – | – | 6 | 6 | 6 | 6 | 6 |
| Machine C | 5 | 5 | 5 | 5 | 5 | 6 | 6 | 1 | 1 | 2 | 2 | – | 3 | 3 | 3 | 4 | 4 | 4 | 4 | 4 | – | – |
| Finished jobs | | | | | | | | | 1 | | 2<br>5 | | | | 3 | | | | | | | 4<br>6 |

Scheduling Rule: FISFS

| Time | 1 | 2 | 3 | 4 | 5 | 6 | 7 | 8 | 9 | 10 | 11 | 12 | 13 | 14 | 15 | 16 | 17 | 18 | 19 | 20 | 21 | 22 |
|---|---|---|---|---|---|---|---|---|---|---|---|---|---|---|---|---|---|---|---|---|---|---|
| Machine A | 1 | 1 | 1 | 2 | 2 | 2 | 2 | 2 | 3 | 3 | 3 | 3 | 6 | 6 | 6 | 6 | 6 | 4 | 4 | – | – | – |
| Machine B | 3 | 3 | 3 | 3 | 1 | 1 | 1 | 4 | 4 | 4 | 5 | 5 | 5 | 5 | – | – | – | 6 | 6 | 6 | 6 | 6 |
| Machine C | 5 | 5 | 5 | 5 | 5 | 6 | 6 | 1 | 1 | 2 | 2 | 4 | 4 | 4 | 4 | 4 | 3 | 3 | 3 | – | – | – |
| Finished jobs | | | | | | | | | 1 | | 2 | | | 5 | | | | | 3<br>4 | | | 6 |

Scheduling Rule: FCFS Tie Breaker: FISFS

| Time | 1 | 2 | 3 | 4 | 5 | 6 | 7 | 8 | 9 | 10 | 11 | 12 | 13 | 14 | 15 | 16 | 17 | 18 | 19 | 20 | 21 | 22 |
|---|---|---|---|---|---|---|---|---|---|---|---|---|---|---|---|---|---|---|---|---|---|---|
| Machine A | 1 | 1 | 1 | 2 | 2 | 2 | 2 | 2 | 3 | 3 | 3 | 3 | 6 | 6 | 6 | 6 | 6 | 4 | 4 | – | – | – |
| Machine B | 3 | 3 | 3 | 3 | 4 | 4 | 4 | 1 | 1 | 1 | 5 | 5 | 5 | 5 | – | – | – | 6 | 6 | 6 | 6 | 6 |
| Machine C | 5 | 5 | 5 | 5 | 5 | 6 | 6 | 4 | 4 | 4 | 4 | 4 | 2 | 2 | 1 | 1 | 3 | 3 | 3 | – | – | – |
| Finished jobs | | | | | | | | | | | | | | 2<br>5 | | 1 | | | 3<br>4 | | | 6 |

Scheduling Rule: LS

| Time | 1 | 2 | 3 | 4 | 5 | 6 | 7 | 8 | 9 | 10 | 11 | 12 | 13 | 14 | 15 | 16 | 17 | 18 | 19 | 20 |
|---|---|---|---|---|---|---|---|---|---|---|---|---|---|---|---|---|---|---|---|---|
| Machine A | 1 | 1 | 1 | 6 | 6 | 6 | 6 | 6 | 3 | 3 | 3 | 3 | 2 | 2 | 2 | 2 | 2 | 4 | 4 | – |
| Machine B | 3 | 3 | 3 | 3 | 1 | 1 | 1 | 4 | 4 | 4 | 5 | 5 | 5 | 5 | 6 | 6 | 6 | 6 | 6 | – |
| Machine C | 6 | 6 | 5 | 5 | 5 | 5 | 5 | 1 | 1 | – | 4 | 4 | 4 | 4 | 4 | 3 | 3 | 3 | 2 | 2 |
| Finished jobs | | | | | | | | | 1 | | | | | 5 | | | | 3 | 4<br>6 | 2 |

Scheduling Rule: SPT Tie Breaker: FISFS

| Time | 1 | 2 | 3 | 4 | 5 | 6 | 7 | 8 | 9 | 10 | 11 | 12 | 13 | 14 | 15 | 16 | 17 | 18 | 19 | 20 |
|---|---|---|---|---|---|---|---|---|---|---|---|---|---|---|---|---|---|---|---|---|
| Machine A | 1 | 1 | 1 | 2 | 2 | 2 | 2 | 2 | 6 | 6 | 6 | 6 | 6 | 3 | 3 | 3 | 3 | 4 | 4 | – |
| Machine B | 4 | 4 | 4 | 1 | 1 | 1 | 3 | 3 | 3 | 3 | 5 | 5 | 5 | 5 | 6 | 6 | 6 | 6 | 6 | – |
| Machine C | 6 | 6 | 5 | 5 | 5 | 5 | 5 | 1 | 1 | 2 | 2 | 4 | 4 | 4 | 4 | 4 | – | 3 | 3 | 3 |
| Finished jobs | | | | | | | | | 1 | | 2 | | | 5 | | | | | 4<br>6 | 3 |

FIGURE 10-3
***(Continued)***

Scheduling Rule: LWKR

| Time | 1 | 2 | 3 | 4 | 5 | 6 | 7 | 8 | 9 | 10 | 11 | 12 | 13 | 14 | 15 | 16 | 17 | 18 | 19 | 20 | 21 | 22 | 23 | 24 | 25 | 26 |
|---|---|---|---|---|---|---|---|---|---|---|---|---|---|---|---|---|---|---|---|---|---|---|---|---|---|---|
| Machine A | 2 | 2 | 2 | 2 | 2 | 1 | 1 | 1 | 3 | 3 | 3 | 3 | 4 | 4 | – | – | – | – | – | 6 | 6 | 6 | 6 | 6 | – | – |
| Machine B | 4 | 4 | 4 | 3 | 3 | 3 | 3 | 5 | 5 | 5 | 5 | 1 | 1 | 1 | – | – | – | – | – | – | – | – | – | – | 6 | 6 |
| Machine C | 5 | 5 | 5 | 5 | 5 | 2 | 2 | 4 | 4 | 4 | 4 | 4 | 3 | 3 | 3 | 1 | 1 | 6 | 6 | – | – | – | – | – | – | – |
| Finished jobs | | | | | | | 2 | | | | 5 | | | 4 | 3 | | 1 | | | | | | | | | 6 |

mance of alternative rules. The rule and the associated schedule that meet the managerial objectives may then be selected for implementation.

However, in a dynamic situation where jobs are arriving over time and the universe of jobs in the system is continuously changing, prior knowledge of which rules perform well on the average for some selected measures of performance will be useful.

For dynamic job shops, several studies have been conducted to evaluate the relative performance of various rules (often called dispatching rules). These studies employ computer simulation models, and several of them are reported in Buffa and Miller (1979).

A clear conclusion that can be derived from over a dozen studies is that the SPT rule performs the best if the objective is to minimize shop congestion as measured by the mean flow time or the mean number of jobs in the system. The improved turnaround that can be achieved by using the SPT rule implies lower work-in-process inventories and can provide a competitive sales advantage as well. Note that for the single machine case, the SPT rule was indeed optimal with respect to mean

TABLE 10-6
**A SUMMARY OF THE PERFORMANCE OF THE SCHEDULING RULES ON SEVERAL CRITERIA FOR THE EXAMPLE IN TABLE 10-5**

| | *Criteria* | | | |
|---|---|---|---|---|
| Rule | Number of Tardy Jobs ($n_T$) | Total Tardiness ($\Sigma T_i$) | Mean Flow Time ($\bar{F}$) | Makespan ($F_{max}$) |
| Earliest due date first (EDD) | 3 | 14 | 15 | 22 |
| First in system first served (FISFS) | 3 | 15 | 15.67 | 22 |
| First come first served (FCFS) | 5 | 22 | 17.33 | 22 |
| Least slack (LS) | 4 | 18 | 16.5 | 20 |
| Shortest processing time (SPT) | 3 | 13 | 15.33 | 20 |
| Least work remaining (LWKR) | 3 | 24 | 15.5 | 29 |

flow time. Intuitively, the SPT rule performs well because the progress of jobs with shorter operation times is accelerated by giving them priority. Thus, shop congestion is reduced as jobs are turned around fast and machines are made available for other jobs. However, as can be expected, a few longer jobs may encounter very long delays as they get stuck in the system.

When customer service is a dominant concern, then tardiness-based criteria, such as the proportion of jobs tardy or the mean tardiness, may be relevant. Surprisingly, the SPT rule does very well even for tardiness-based criteria. This result is bewildering because the SPT rule ignores the due dates. However, the selection of best rule critically depends on such factors as the level of the shop load, the procedure for setting due dates, and the tightness of the due dates.

## SCHEDULING FOR BATCH SHOPS

In the preceding discussion of job shop scheduling, the processing time for a job on a given machine was specified. The processing time could be defined as the time required for manufacturing a batch of several identical items, where the entire batch of items is distinct from another batch of items either because of different processing requirements or because each batch is manufactured for a different customer. Job shop analysis is applicable when each job has its own identity (processing requirements, due date, customer type, etc.) and production is customized to the order.

As we discussed in Chapter 2, batch production falls between job shop production and continuous production. It is an extremely common type of production system when the output is inventoriable and is produced in substantial volume, even though the volume may not justify continuous production. In these situations, the manager must determine the lot size for a batch to be produced at one time in addition to scheduling the batch on the facilities. An example of batch production is the bottling of gin, vodka, rum, and the like using the same production facility. The manager must decide how many cases of vodka in a given bottle size (e.g., a quart) should be bottled at one time (the determination of lot size) and when the processing of this batch should begin (the scheduling decision). If 12,000 cases of vodka in a quart size are required in a year, many options, such as to produce 6000 cases twice a year or 3000 cases four times a year, are available. A key trade-off in the determination of the lot size for an item is between set-up costs and inventory holding costs. Another equally important consideration is the requirement to produce a feasible schedule that meets the demand for all items. For example, if set-up costs are low relative to holding costs, indicating small lot sizes, it may not be possible to produce the required quantities of all items within the specified time period if these small lot sizes are employed. This will happen if much of the time is consumed by merely setting up machines, thereby reducing the available production time. In order to meet requirements for different items, larger lot sizes may have to be employed. We will now illustrate this problem of obtaining a feasible schedule, and we will discuss a method for computing lot sizes while maintaining feasibility in scheduling the batches of items under consideration.

## Independent *EOQ* Scheduling

Why not determine lot sizes economically, according to the *EOQ* equations from Chapter 5? *EOQ*s would be computed independently for each item and processed through the system as a lot. Sometimes this decision may be a good one, but quite often the *EOQ* equations are oversimplifications of the true situations, and improved decision policies can be used. Some of the complexities that commonly intrude on the simplicity of *EOQ* equations are as follows:

1. Because of differing requirements, set-up costs, and inventory carrying costs for each job, inventories that result from *EOQ* lots may not last through a complete cycle. Because of stockouts, special orders of smaller size may then be needed, resulting in capacity dilution.
2. When operating near capacity limits, competition for machine and/or worker time may cause scheduling interference. In order to maintain scheduled commitments, lots may be split. Again, a side effect of this is reduced capacity.
3. Sometimes there is a bottleneck machine or process through which all or most of the jobs must be sequenced. Its limited capacity may exert pressure toward smaller lot sizes, diluting capacity in order to meet scheduled commitments on at least a part of job orders.
4. Where parts or products are produced in regular cycles, individual lot sizes are constructed to fit in with the cycles, rather than from the balance of set-up and inventory holding costs for each individual item.
5. The assumption of constant demand is not met, either as a result of seasonal usage or sales or because demand is *dependent* on the production schedules of other parts, subassemblies, or products. This point was dealt with in Chapter 6.
6. The process and transit lot sizes are not equal, so that the inventory structure of the *EOQ* formulation is not valid.

Most of these reasons for deviating from the concepts of the *EOQ* equations lead to smaller lot sizes and to reductions in effective capacity. Under these conditions, relatively larger fractions of the available machine and worker time are devoted to machine set-up. Note that items 1 through 4 in the preceding list all indicate some kind of dependence of the individual lot size on the other orders in the system.

### AN EXAMPLE

Table 10-7 gives data on requirements, costs, and production for 10 products that are processed on the same equipment. The capacity of the equipment is limited to 250 days of usage per year. When the daily production rates for each product listed in column 4 are converted to required production days in column 5, we see that the total annual production requirement of 241 days falls within the 250-day maximum limit (set-up times are included). Our particular interest is in columns 8 through 11 of Table 10-7. The lot sizes are computed using Equation 17[1] from Chapter 5, and

[1] The choice between Equations 4 and 17 depends on whether or not items go into inventory while production progresses. If items do go into inventory during production, inventory builds up at the rate of

TABLE 10-7

**REQUIREMENTS, COSTS, AND PRODUCTION DATA FOR 10 PRODUCTS RUN ON THE SAME EQUIPMENT**

| (1) Product Number | (2) Annual Requirements, $R_i$ | (3) Sales per Production Day (250 days per year), Col. 2/250, $r_i$ | (4) Daily Production Rate, $p_i$ | (5) Production Days Required, Col. 2/Col. 4 | (6) Inventory Holding Cost per Unit per Year, $c_{H_i}$ | (7) Machine Setup Cost per Run, $c_{P_i}$ | (8) *EOQ*, Equation 17 from Chapter 5 | (9) Number of Runs per Year, Col. 2/Col. 8 | (10) Production Days per Lot, Col. 8/Col. 4 | (11) $TIC_0$ Equation 18 from Chapter 5 |
|---|---|---|---|---|---|---|---|---|---|---|
| 1 | 9,000 | 36 | 225 | 40 | $0.10 | $40 | 2928 | 3.1 | 13.0 | $245.93 |
| 2 | 20,000 | 80 | 500 | 40 | 0.20 | 25 | 2440 | 8.2 | 4.9 | 409.88 |
| 3 | 6,000 | 24 | 200 | 30 | 0.15 | 50 | 2132 | 2.8 | 10.7 | 281.42 |
| 4 | 12,000 | 48 | 600 | 20 | 0.10 | 40 | 3230 | 3.7 | 5.4 | 297.19 |
| 5 | 16,000 | 64 | 500 | 32 | 0.02 | 50 | 9578 | 1.7 | 19.2 | 167.04 |
| 6 | 15,000 | 60 | 500 | 30 | 0.50 | 40 | 1651 | 9.1 | 3.3 | 726.64 |
| 7 | 8,000 | 32 | 1000 | 8 | 0.35 | 30 | 1190 | 6.7 | 1.2 | 403.27 |
| 8 | 9,000 | 36 | 900 | 10 | 0.05 | 60 | 4743 | 1.9 | 5.3 | 227.68 |
| 9 | 2,000 | 8 | 125 | 16 | 0.55 | 25 | 441 | 4.5 | 3.5 | 226.89 |
| 10 | 3,000 | 12 | 200 | 15 | 0.20 | 20 | 799 | 3.8 | 4.0 | 150.20 |
| | | | | 241 | | $380 | | | 70.5 | $3136.14 |

the number of runs per year, the production days per lot, and the costs are computed for the independent *EOQ* scheduling of the 10 products.

Because only 1 product can be produced at a time, problems result from an attempt to schedule the 10 products independently (see Table 10-8). Each *EOQ* lot provides inventories to be used at the daily usage rate, $r_i$, of that product. These inventories will be depleted in $EOQ/r_i$ days, as shown in column 4. Therefore, the inventory cycle must be long enough for that product to be recycled. The total number of production days for all 10 products is shown in column 2 as 70.5 days. Scanning column 4, we see that the inventory for products 2, 4, 6, 7, 9, and 10 will be depleted before the cycle can be repeated. The situation, shown graphically for product 2 in Figure 10-4, is called *scheduling interference.*

Clearly, independent scheduling will not provide a feasible solution. This infeasibility is not surprising because the schedule of each product is not independent of the other products since they are all processed on the same equipment, which has limited capacity. We must therefore treat the 10 products as a system. Before considering the alternatives, note that our system is operating near capacity, with 241 production days scheduled, or 241 × 100/250 = 96.4 percent of the days available. Scheduling interference would probably not occur if we were operating at relatively low loads. Under conditions of low load, slack capacity would be available to make the system work.

---

$p - r$, requiring the use of Equation 17, as is assumed in this example. If the situation were such that the entire batch went into inventory at the completion of production, Equation 4 from Chapter 5 would be appropriate.

TABLE 10-8
**CALCULATION OF PRODUCTION DAYS REQUIRED, PEAK INVENTORY, AND NUMBER OF DAYS OF SALES REQUIREMENTS MET BY AN EOQ FOR 10 PRODUCTS**

| (1) Product Number | (2) Production Days Required, $EOQ/p_i$ | (3) Peak Inventory, Production Days × $(p_i - r_i)$ | (4) Days to Deplete $EOQ$, $EOQ/r_i$ |
|---|---|---|---|
| 1 | 13.0 | 2457 | 81.3 |
| 2 | 4.9 | 2058 | 30.6[a] |
| 3 | 10.7 | 1883 | 88.8 |
| 4 | 5.4 | 2980 | 67.3[a] |
| 5 | 19.2 | 8371 | 149.7 |
| 6 | 3.3 | 1452 | 27.5[a] |
| 7 | 1.2 | 1162 | 37.2[a] |
| 8 | 5.3 | 4579 | 131.8 |
| 9 | 3.5 | 410 | 55.1[a] |
| 10 | 4.0 | 752 | 66.6[a] |
| | 70.5 | | |

[a] Items that stock out, inventory lasts less than 70.5 days.

FIGURE 10-4
**INVENTORY LEVELS VERSUS DAYS FOR PRODUCTS 1 AND 2. PRODUCT 2 IS PRODUCED IN THE QUANTITY $Q_p$ = 2440 UNITS, WHICH LASTS ONLY 30.5 DAYS AT THE USAGE RATE OF $r_2$ = 80 UNITS PER DAY.**

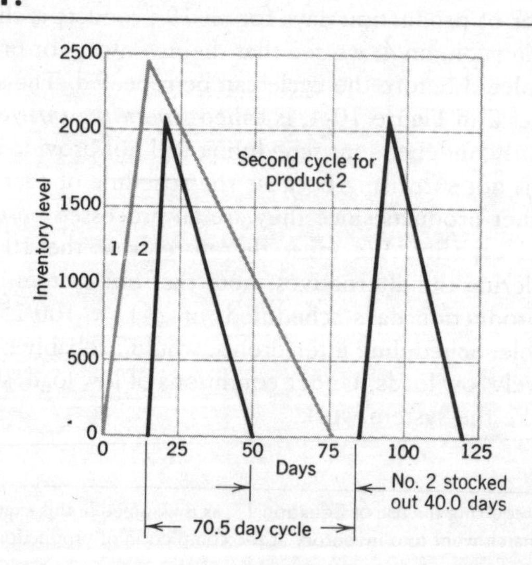

## Common Cycle Scheduling

Perhaps the simplest way to ensure feasible solutions to scheduling interference problems is to adopt some common cycle for all the products and to produce lot quantities for each product that cover usage rates for the cycle. Scanning column 9 of Table 10-7, the number of runs per year ranges from 1.7 to 9.1, with an average of 4.55 runs. A cycle of 4 or 5 runs per year might be reasonable. Table 10-9 gives the key results for a cycle of 4 runs per year. Each product is scheduled for the production of a quantity sufficient to provide 250/4 = 62.5 days' supply.

At the stated usage rates, the inventory of each product will not be depleted before it is recycled. These production lot quantities are computed in column 3 of Table 10-9 as $62.5 \times r_i$. The graphs of inventory build up and depletion follow the same general form as Figure 10-4. The inventory costs are computed in column 7 of Table 10-9, and column 8 gives the costs for four set-ups per year for each product. The total incremental costs for the common cycle scheduling system are shown at the bottom of the table as \$3723.38, \$587.24 greater than the costs for independent scheduling. But, independent scheduling did not provide a feasible solution. The total number of production days required is 60.25 days in column 4 of Table 10-9, leaving a slack capacity of 62.50 − 60.25 = 2.25 days, or 2.25 × 100/62.5 = 3.6 percent.

TABLE 10-9
**CALCULATION OF INVENTORY AND SET-UP COSTS WHEN 10 PRODUCTS ARE PRODUCED FOUR TIMES PER YEAR IN A COMMON CYCLE OF LENGTH, 250/4 = 62.5 DAYS. EACH PRODUCT IS PRODUCED IN A LOT SIZE $Q_i$ SUFFICIENT TO COVER 62.5 DAYS' SUPPLY**

| (1) Product Number | (2) Daily Usage Rate, $r_i$ | (3) Production Lot Quantity, $62.5 \times r_i$ = 62.5 × Col. 2 | (4) Production Days Required, $Q_i/p_i$ = Col. $3/p_i$ | (5) Peak Inventory, Col. 4 × $(p_i - r_i)$ | (6) Inventory Holding Cost per unit per year, $c_{H_i}$ | (7) Annual Inventory Holding Cost (Col. 5 × Col. 6)/2 | (8) Annual Setup Costs, $4 \times c_{P_i}$ |
|---|---|---|---|---|---|---|---|
| 1 | 36 | 2250 | 10.00 | 1890 | \$0.10 | \$94.50 | \$160.00 |
| 2 | 80 | 5000 | 10.00 | 4200 | 0.20 | 420.00 | 100.00 |
| 3 | 24 | 1500 | 7.50 | 1320 | 0.15 | 99.00 | 200.00 |
| 4 | 48 | 3000 | 5.00 | 2760 | 0.10 | 138.00 | 160.00 |
| 5 | 64 | 4000 | 8.00 | 3488 | 0.02 | 34.88 | 200.00 |
| 6 | 60 | 3750 | 7.50 | 3300 | 0.50 | 825.00 | 160.00 |
| 7 | 32 | 2000 | 2.00 | 1936 | 0.35 | 338.80 | 20.00 |
| 8 | 36 | 2250 | 2.50 | 2160 | 0.05 | 54.00 | 240.00 |
| 9 | 8 | 500 | 4.00 | 468 | 0.55 | 128.70 | 100.00 |
| 10 | 12 | 750 | 3.75 | 705 | 0.20 | 70.50 | 80.00 |
| | | | 60.25 | | | \$2203.38 | \$1520.00 |

$TIC$ = inventory + set-up costs = 2203.38 + 1520.00 = \$3723.38

## ECONOMIC COMMON CYCLE SCHEDULING

Because a common cycle can provide a feasible solution as long as the total load is within system capacity, the next question is, "Which cycle should be used, $N = 4, 5, 6$, or what?" Calculations similar to those in Table 10-9 can be made for various cycles. Intuitively, we know that as we increase the number of cycles per year and decrease the lot sizes, annual inventory costs will decrease, but annual set-up costs will increase in proportion to the number of cycles per year. Table 10-10 summarizes costs for common cycles of $N = 4, 5, 8$, and 10 runs per year for the same 10 products. For the alternatives computed, the lowest incremental cost is associated with $N = 5$ runs to cover $250/5 = 50$ days' supply. If one were to select any of the larger number of runs per year as a plan, which would involve more rapid cycling, it would be important to consider the extent to which effective capacity would be reduced. If set-up times were relatively large, the system capacity limit would be reached at these high loads. Remember that set-up times *are not isolated* in our example.

Formal models for common economic cycles for a number of products, $m$, can be derived by methods similar to those used to develop the $EOQ$ formulas.[2] They are slightly more complex, but they are parallel in concept. The total incremental cost equation is developed for the entire set of products, and similar mathematical operations produce the number of production runs that jointly minimize annual inventory costs plus set-up costs for all products.

$$TIC(N) = \sum_{i=1}^{m} c_{P_i} N + \sum_{i=1}^{m} \frac{c_{H_i}}{2} \frac{R_i}{N}\left(1 - \frac{r_i}{p_i}\right)$$

and

$$N_0 = \sqrt{\frac{\sum_{i=1}^{m} c_{H_i} R_i (1 - r_i/p_i)}{2 \sum_{i=1}^{m} c_{P_i}}} \tag{1}$$

Equation 1 requires the multiplication of $c_{H_i}$, $R_i$, and $(1 - r_i/p_i)$ for each individual product in the numerator; these are then summed for all products. The denominator is simply two times the sum of the set-up costs for all products. Since each product is produced after $(1/N_0) \times 12$ months, called the cycle time, the sum of the set-up times plus the sum of the production times for all products must be less than the cycle time. The total incremental cost of an optimal solution is

[2]Equations 1 and 2 assume that production takes place over a period of time and that items go into inventory in smaller quantities as production continues. If this assumption does not apply, and the entire batch goes into inventory all at once, then the $1 - r_i/p_i$ terms in Equation 1 and 2 become 1, and these terms drop out.

TABLE 10-10
**INVENTORY AND SET-UP COSTS FOR COMMON CYCLES OF $N$ = 4, 5, 8, and 10 RUNS PER YEAR FOR 10 PRODUCTS**

| $N$, Cycles per Year | Number of Day's Supply Produced | Average Annual Inventory Cost | Annual Set-up Costs | Total Incremental Costs |
|---|---|---|---|---|
| 4 | 62.50 | $2203.38 | $1520.00 | $3723.39 |
| 5 | 50.00 | 1762.70 | 1900.00 | 3662.70 |
| 8 | 31.25 | 1101.69 | 3040.00 | 4141.69 |
| 10 | 25.00 | 881.35 | 3800.00 | 4681.35 |

$$TIC_0 = \sqrt{2 \sum_{i=1}^{m} c_{P_i} \sum_{i=1}^{m} c_{H_i} R_i \left(1 - \frac{r_i}{p_i}\right)} \qquad (2)$$

Table 10-11 shows the calculations in applying Equations 1 and 2 to the 10-product example. The optimal number of production runs is $N_0$ = 4.82 at a cost of $TIC_0$ = \$3660.13. As a practical matter, one would probably select a number of runs close to the optimal number, based on other considerations because total

TABLE 10-11
**CALCULATION OF THE ECONOMIC NUMBER OF PRODUCTION RUNS PER YEAR, USING EQUATION 1**

| (1) Product Number | (2) $(1 - r_i/p_i)$ from Table 10-7, (1 − Col. 3/Col. 4) | (3) $c_{H_i}R_i(1 - r_i/p_i)$, Col. 6 (Table 10-7) × Col. 2 (Table 10-7) × Col. 2 (this table) | (4) $c_{P_i}$, from Col. 7 of Table 10-7 |
|---|---|---|---|
| 1 | 0.840 | 756.00 | $40 |
| 2 | 0.840 | 3,360.00 | 25 |
| 3 | 0.880 | 792.00 | 50 |
| 4 | 0.920 | 1,104.00 | 40 |
| 5 | 0.872 | 279.04 | 50 |
| 6 | 0.880 | 6,600.00 | 40 |
| 7 | 0.968 | 2,710.40 | 30 |
| 8 | 0.960 | 432.00 | 60 |
| 9 | 0.936 | 1,029.60 | 25 |
| 10 | 0.940 | 564.00 | 20 |
| | | 17,627.00 | $380 |

$$N_0 = \sqrt{\frac{17{,}627}{2 \times 380}} = 4.82 \text{ runs per year}$$

$$TIC_0 = \sqrt{2 \times 380 \times 17{,}627} = \$3660.13$$

incremental cost differences are small near the optimum, as indicated in Table 10-10. In the absence of other overriding considerations, one would probably simply round the number of cycles to $N = 5$ runs per year in our example because the annual cost difference between $N = 5$ and $N_0 = 4.82$ is only $2.57.

The lot size scheduling problem has been the subject of a great deal of research, and improvements over the costs that result from applying Equation 1 have been developed. For example, if a product has a low set-up cost and a high holding cost, then producing it more often will improve costs. Doll and Whybark (1973) provide a procedure that allows different numbers of production runs for different products.

## SCHEDULING FOR HIGH VOLUME CONTINUOUS SYSTEMS

As discussed in Chapter 8, for high volume continuous systems the aggregate plan determines the production levels, work force requirements, and resulting inventory levels in aggregate terms. The scheduling problem for such systems is to develop detailed master schedules for individual end products and for facilities and personnel within the constraints of aggregate plan. Master schedules are stated specifically in terms of the quantities of each individual product to be produced and the time periods for production. For example, the aggregate schedule might call for 1000 units in planning period 1, where the planning period might be a month or perhaps a four-week period. If there were three products, the more detailed master schedule would indicate the quantities of each of the three products to be produced in each week of the planning period, consistent with the aggregate schedule.

As an example, assume that the aggregate schedule calls for a level production rate during the three-period planning horizon. The periods of planning horizons are often months or four-week periods. The latter is particularly convenient because it breaks the year into 52/4 = 13 periods of equal size. The weekly master schedule then conveniently fits most work schedules. In our example we will assume three four-week periods in the planning horizon.

The aggregate plan may have produced the following:

**AGGREGATE PLAN**

| Period.(4 weeks) | Initial | 1 | 2 | 3 |
|---|---|---|---|---|
| Aggregate forecast | — | 1200 | 1100 | 800 |
| Production | — | 1000 | 1000 | 1000 |
| Aggregate inventories | 800 | 600 | 500 | 700 |

Now we must disaggregate the forecasts on a weekly basis for the three products. Suppose that the composition of the forecasts is as follows:

**FORECASTS FOR THREE PRODUCTS**

| Period | 1 | | | | 2 | | | | 3 | | | | |
|---|---|---|---|---|---|---|---|---|---|---|---|---|---|
| Week | 1 | 2 | 3 | 4 | 5 | 6 | 7 | 8 | 9 | 10 | 11 | 12 | Total |
| Product 1 | 100 | 100 | 100 | 100 | 100 | 80 | 75 | 75 | 75 | 75 | 65 | 50 | 995 |
| Product 2 | 150 | 125 | 125 | 100 | 75 | 75 | 75 | 65 | 65 | 65 | 60 | 50 | 1030 |
| Product 3 | 75 | 75 | 75 | 75 | 100 | 120 | 125 | 135 | 135 | 60 | 50 | 50 | 1075 |
| Total | 325 | 300 | 300 | 275 | 275 | 275 | 275 | 275 | 275 | 200 | 175 | 150 | 3100 |
| Period Total | 1200 | | | | 1100 | | | | 800 | | | | 3100 |

The aggregate schedule calls for level production at 1000 units per four-week period. The aggregate forecasts decline, but the forecasts by weeks for the three products follow different patterns. Products 1 and 2 decline, but product 3 increases during the second four-week period, although it declines rapidly in the third four-week period.

The master scheduling problem requires the construction of schedules for each of the products, consistent with the aggregate plan, the forecasts, and planned inventories. Table 10-12 shows a master schedule that fits these requirements. The production plan in Table 10-12*a* indicates the initial cycling among the three products, where productive capacity is allocated to one of the products each week. In the fifth week, the strategy changes to cycle product 3 every other week to take account of the high forecast requirements for that product during the fifth through the ninth weeks. In the tenth week, the plan returns to a three-week cycling of the three products.

The individual product inventory profiles that would result from the master schedule are shown in Table 10-12*b*. Note that the individual inventory balances, $I_t$, are end-of-week figures that result from the simple accounting equation, $I_t = I_{t-1} - F_t + P_t$, where $F_t$ is the forecast and $P_t$ is the production during the week. For example, in Table 10-12*b*, the initial inventory for product 3 is $I_0 = 150$ units, requirements were forecast as $F_1 = 75$ units, and production is scheduled at $P_1 = 250$ units. Therefore, the projected inventory at the end of week 1 is $I_1 = 150 - 75 + 250 = 325$ units, as indicated in Table 10-12*b* for product 3. The total end-of-week inventory is simply the sum of the inventories for the three products. The inventory called for by the aggregate plan was an end-of-period (four-week) figure, so there are deviations from the plan in the first three weeks of each four-week period, but the deviation is zero in the last week of each four-week planning period.

The master scheduling methods indicated by this discussion follow from the simple logic of the disaggregation of aggregate plans. In more complex situations, problems might have occurred because of conflicts in forecast requirements, production capacities, and inventory position, resulting in stockouts. Alternative plans could be tried to see if the problem can be solved. It may be necessary to cycle back to a reevaluation of the aggregate plan, with changes in it possibly being required.

In the master schedule of Table 10-12, no attempt was made to consider the balance between set-up and inventory costs. Optimizing methods for master

TABLE 10-12*a*
**MASTER SCHEDULE FOR THREE PRODUCTS CONSISTENT WITH FORECASTS AND AGGREGATE PRODUCTION PLAN**

| Period | | 1 | | | | 2 | | | | 3 | | | |
|---|---|---|---|---|---|---|---|---|---|---|---|---|---|
| Week | 0 | 1 | 2 | 3 | 4 | 5 | 6 | 7 | 8 | 9 | 10 | 11 | 12 |
| Product 1, production | | — | — | 250 | — | — | 125 | — | 125 | — | 250 | — | — |
| Product 2, production | | — | 250 | — | 250 | — | 125 | — | 125 | — | — | 250 | — |
| Product 3, production | | 250 | — | — | — | 250 | — | 250 | — | 250 | — | — | 250 |
| Total production | | 250 | 250 | 250 | 250 | 250 | 250 | 250 | 250 | 250 | 250 | 250 | 250 |
| Capacity, aggregate plan | | 250 | 250 | 250 | 250 | 250 | 250 | 250 | 250 | 250 | 250 | 250 | 250 |
| Deviation | | 0 | 0 | 0 | 0 | 0 | 0 | 0 | 0 | 0 | 0 | 0 | 0 |

TABLE 10-12*b*
**PRODUCT END-OF-WEEK INVENTORY PROFILES ASSOCIATED WITH MASTER SCHEDULE**

| Period | | 1 | | | | 2 | | | | 3 | | | |
|---|---|---|---|---|---|---|---|---|---|---|---|---|---|
| Week | 0 | 1 | 2 | 3 | 4 | 5 | 6 | 7 | 8 | 9 | 10 | 11 | 12 |
| Product 1, inventory | 400 | 300 | 200 | 350 | 250 | 150 | 195 | 120 | 170 | 95 | 270 | 205 | 155 |
| Product 2, inventory | 250 | 100 | 225 | 100 | 250 | 175 | 225 | 150 | 210 | 145 | 80 | 270 | 220 |
| Product 3, inventory | 150 | 325 | 250 | 175 | 100 | 250 | 130 | 255 | 120 | 235 | 175 | 125 | 325 |
| Total inventory | 800 | 725 | 675 | 625 | 600 | 575 | 550 | 525 | 500 | 475 | 525 | 600 | 700 |
| Inventory, aggregate plan | 800 | 600 | 600 | 600 | 600 | 500 | 500 | 500 | 500 | 700 | 700 | 700 | 700 |
| Deviation | 0 | 125 | 75 | 25 | 0 | 75 | 50 | 25 | 0 | (225) | (175) | (100) | 0 |

scheduling are developed by Hax and Meal (1975) in a hierarchical production planning system.

The master schedule provides the basis for detailed plans concerning material flow, equipment, and personnel schedules. Obviously all materials, components, and subassemblies need to be coordinated with the master schedule; this was the subject of Chapter 6 on "Material Requirements Planning."

## SCHEDULING FOR SERVICE SYSTEMS

Service oriented organizations, such as medical facilities, computer centers, or banks, face unique scheduling problems. For some of these systems, the waiting line models discussed in Chapter 14 or the priority rules discussed earlier in this chapter may provide sufficiently good solutions. These approaches are useful when the arrival of customers or jobs is random. Here we examine methods for scheduling personnel and facilities when the arrivals for service follow a dominant pattern. For example, if the arrivals of patients at a clinic follows a weekly pattern in which a larger number of patients arrive on Mondays and a smaller number arrive on Wednesdays, then we can use an appointment system and the appropriate scheduling of physicians to meet the load. In all of these kinds of systems, demands for service and the time to perform the service may be highly variable. It often appears as though no sensible schedule can be constructed when arrivals for service and service times are random. One solution is to maintain the capability for service at capacity levels that are sufficient to keep the waiting line at certain acceptable average levels; thus, the service facility is idle for some fraction of time so that service can be provided when it is needed. In a sense, the scheduling of the personnel and physical facilities is simple in such situations, being controlled by policies for the hours during which the service is to be offered and for the service level to be available. Schedules are then simple statements of "capacity for service," and personnel and other resources are keyed to these levels. The size of maintenance crews has often been determined on this basis, for example.

Usually, however, we can improve on the system response of simply "keeping hours." Sometimes, overall performance can be improved through the use of a priority system, taking arrivals on other than a first-come-first-served basis. Also, improvements can often result from examining the demand to see if there is a weekly and/or a daily pattern. When a pattern exists, it may be possible to schedule more effectively to improve service facility utilization, shorten average waiting time, or both. Thus, we have three broad groups of situations: the one described by random arrivals at a service center that performs a service requiring variable time, the one where priority systems are the basis for improved scheduling, and the one in which arrivals follow some dominant pattern.

The random arrival, variable service time case is the classic waiting line or queuing problem. When the distribution of arrivals and service times follow a certain known dominant pattern, we can use that information to schedule personnel and facilities.

## Scheduling Personnel and Work Shifts

The objective in scheduling personnel and work shifts is to minimize labor costs, given particular service standards, or to establish some happy compromise between labor costs and service standards. Although our emphasis will be on personnel and shift scheduling itself, it is important to recognize that shift scheduling is part of a larger process. The demand for the service must be forecast and converted to equivalent labor requirements by the hour of the day, the day of the week, and so forth. Scheduling is then done in relation to these requirements. Finally, individual workers must be assigned to work days and shifts.

### NONCYCLIC PERSONNEL SCHEDULES

Suppose that we are faced with hourly requirements that vary from hour to hour, day to day, week to week, and so on. Staffing this operation would require continuous adjustment to the changing requirements. The demand variations might be caused by trend and seasonal factors, holidays, or weather conditions, depending on the nature of the particular operation. These kinds of personnel scheduling situations can be approached through the application of a simple concept, the "first-hour" principle (Browne and Tibrewala, 1975). The first-hour principle can be stated as follows: Assign to start to work in the first period a number of workers equal to the number required for that period. For each subsequent period, assign the exact number of additional workers needed to meet requirements. When workers come to the end of their shifts, do not replace them if they are not needed. This procedure is best explained with the aid of an example. Assume the following sequence of worker requirements for the first 12 hours of a continuous operation (once assigned, workers continue working for an 8-hour shift):

| Period | 1 | 2 | 3 | 4 | 5 | 6 | 7 | 8 | 9 | 10 | 11 | 12 |
|---|---|---|---|---|---|---|---|---|---|---|---|---|
| Requirements, $R_i$ | 5 | 5 | 7 | 8 | 9 | 10 | 15 | 14 | 12 | 10 | 10 | 10 |

In the following schedule, workers are added when they are needed, and we keep a running total of workers on duty during each period. For example, $X_i = 5$ workers are assigned in period 1 to work 8 hours. No additional workers are needed in period 2 because the requirement of 5 workers does not change. However, 2 additional workers must be assigned in period 3 to meet the total requirement of 7. In period 8, a total of $W_i = 15$ workers are on duty. The 5 workers who were assigned in period 1 complete their shifts at the end of period 8, leaving a residual of 10 workers who continue into period 9. But 12 workers are required in period 9, so 2 additional workers must be assigned to start their shifts. In period 10, the requirement for workers drops to 10, so no new workers are assigned. But at the beginning of period 11, the 2 workers who were assigned in period 3 will have completed their shifts, so the total on duty in period 11 drops to 10. At the start of period 12, an additional worker must be assigned to maintain a total of 10 on duty, because the worker assigned in period 4 goes off duty.

| Period | 1 | 2 | 3 | 4 | 5 | 6 | 7 | 8 | 9 | 10 | 11 | 12 |
|---|---|---|---|---|---|---|---|---|---|---|---|---|
| Requirements, $R_i$ | 5 | 5 | 7 | 8 | 9 | 10 | 15 | 14 | 12 | 10 | 10 | 10 |
| Assigned, $X_i$ | 5 | — | 2 | 1 | 1 | 1 | 5 | — | 2 | — | — | 1 |
| On duty, $W_i$ | 5 | 5 | 7 | 8 | 9 | 10 | 15 | 15 | 12 | 12 | 10 | 10 |

The assignment procedure would continue in the same way, in an endless chain, as new requirements became known.

## CYCLIC PERSONNEL SCHEDULES

Now, suppose that we have a stable situation in which the requirements pattern repeats. What is the stable staffing pattern that should be used to meet the cyclic requirements? Propp (1978) has shown that optimal solutions to cyclic staffing problems can be developed by applying the first-hour principle successively to the requirements schedule until the assignment pattern repeats. The repeating schedule is then the optimal cyclic staffing pattern. We use as an example a 24-hour operation with a 12-hour cyclic requirements schedule where employees work only 4-hour shifts, as might be true if the operation were staffed by students who could work only part-time. This situation keeps the computations simpler for illustrative purposes.

| Period | 1 | 2 | 3 | 4 | 5 | 6 | 7 | 8 | 9 | 10 | 11 | 12 |
|---|---|---|---|---|---|---|---|---|---|---|---|---|
| Requirements, $R_i$ | 4 | 6 | 8 | 8 | 9 | 7 | 9 | 7 | 7 | 7 | 6 | 5 |

Following the first hour principle, the assignments would be as follows:

**FIRST CYCLE**

| Period | 1 | 2 | 3 | 4 | 5 | 6 | 7 | 8 | 9 | 10 | 11 | 12 |
|---|---|---|---|---|---|---|---|---|---|---|---|---|
| Requirements, $R_i$ | 4 | 6 | 8 | 8 | 9 | 7 | 9 | 7 | 7 | 7 | 6 | 5 |
| Assigned, $X_i$ | 4 | 2 | 2 | — | 5 | — | 4 | — | 3 | — | 3 | — |
| On duty, $W_i$ | 4 | 6 | 8 | 8 | 9 | 7 | 9 | 9 | 7 | 7 | 6 | 6 |

Continuing with the second cycle, 3 workers who started in period 9 complete their shifts at the end of period 12. Therefore, 3 workers continue, and 1 worker must be assigned to meet the requirement of 4 workers in period 1 of the second cycle. No workers complete their shifts at the end of period 1, so 2 new workers must be assigned in period 2 to meet the requirement of 6 workers, and so on.

**SECOND CYCLE**

| Period | 1 | 2 | 3 | 4 | 5 | 6 | 7 | 8 | 9 | 10 | 11 | 12 |
|---|---|---|---|---|---|---|---|---|---|---|---|---|
| Requirements, $R_i$ | 4 | 6 | 8 | 8 | 9 | 7 | 9 | 7 | 7 | 7 | 6 | 5 |
| Assigned, $X_i$ | 1 | 2 | 5 | — | 2 | — | 7 | — | — | — | 6 | — |
| On duty, $W_i$ | 4 | 6 | 8 | 8 | 9 | 7 | 9 | 9 | 7 | 7 | 6 | 6 |

**THIRD CYCLE**

| Period | 1 | 2 | 3 | 4 | 5 | 6 | 7 | 8 | 9 | 10 | 11 | 12 |
|---|---|---|---|---|---|---|---|---|---|---|---|---|
| Requirements, $R_i$ | 4 | 6 | 8 | 8 | 9 | 7 | 9 | 7 | 7 | 7 | 6 | 5 |
| Assigned, $X_i$ | — | — | 8 | — | 1 | — | 8 | — | — | — | 6 | — |
| On duty, $W_i$ | 6 | 6 | 8 | 8 | 9 | 9 | 9 | 9 | 8 | 8 | 6 | 6 |

**FOURTH CYCLE**

| Period | 1 | 2 | 3 | 4 | 5 | 6 | 7 | 8 | 9 | 10 | 11 | 12 |
|---|---|---|---|---|---|---|---|---|---|---|---|---|
| Requirements, $R_i$ | 4 | 6 | 8 | 8 | 9 | 7 | 9 | 7 | 7 | 7 | 6 | 5 |
| Assigned, $X_i$ | — | — | 8 | — | 1 | — | 8 | — | — | — | 6 | — |
| On duty, $W_i$ | 6 | 6 | 8 | 8 | 9 | 9 | 9 | 9 | 8 | 8 | 6 | 6 |
| Slack, $W_i - R_i$ | 2 | 0 | 0 | 0 | 0 | 2 | 0 | 2 | 1 | 1 | 0 | 1 |

The assignments and the workers on duty for the third and fourth cycles are identical; they would continue to repeat with additional cycles, and they are optimal. The staffing pattern shown in the third and fourth cycles should be applied repetitively as long as the requirements pattern remains stable. The resulting slack of 9 worker-hours in the resources applied is shown in the bottom row of the fourth cycle. The sum of the requirements over the 12-hour period is 83 worker-hours, and 83 + 9 = 92 worker-hours were used.

## WEEKLY SCHEDULES FOR SEVEN-DAY OPERATIONS

Many services and some manufacturing operations must operate on a seven days per week basis, employing labor that normally works approximately 40 hours per week. Legal requirements and company–union work rules result in constraints concerning permissible work periods. One of the simplest constraints is that each worker must be provided with two consecutive days off each week. There are often additional constraints concerning the number of weekend days off, lunch periods, rest breaks, and so on.

Figure 10-5*a* shows a typical situation in which the number of workers required involves a peak requirement of three workers on Wednesday, Thursday, and Friday,

FIGURE 10-5
**(*a*) REQUIREMENTS FOR A SEVEN-DAY PER WEEK OPERATION, (*b*) DAILY SCHEDULE FOR FOUR WORKERS TO MEET REQUIREMENTS, AND (*c*) COMPARISON OF REQUIREMENTS AND WORKERS SCHEDULED WITH SLACK SHOWN.**

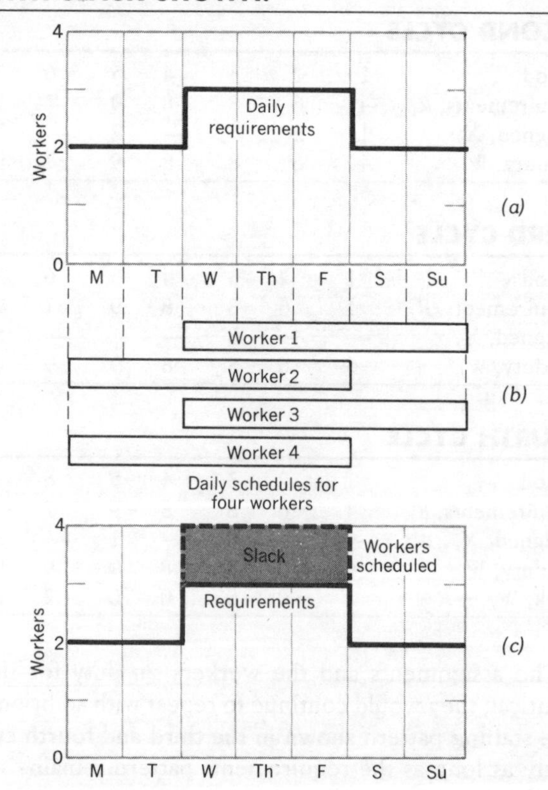

with only two workers being required on the other four days. The weekly labor requirement is the sum of the daily requirements, which is 17 worker-days. If each worker is guaranteed five days of work per week, then the minimum number of workers to staff the operation is four, equaling 20 worker-days and resulting in 3 worker-days of slack capacity.

Figure 10-5*b* shows a configuration of the schedules for four workers that meets the requirements, with each worker having two consecutive days off. Figure 10-5*c* shows the comparison of workers scheduled versus requirements and indicates the location of the slack associated with the peak days of Wednesday, Thursday, and Friday. Obviously, if part-time workers were available and fit in with other possible work rule constraints, a better solution would be to employ three full-time workers plus one part-time worker for two days per week. Such a solution would minimize labor costs, but it provides no slack in the system during the peak load days.

Figure 10-5 provides a framework for the general situation that we wish to analyze. Solutions to this simple situation are fairly obvious, but we need a formal model to analyze such situations efficiently when the problems are larger and more complex.

**Days Off Personnel Schedules.** Suppose that we must staff an operation seven days per week, with the personnel requirements for each day given by the following schedule:

| | M | T | W | Th | F | S | Su |
|---|---|---|---|---|---|---|---|
| Required workers, $R_i$ | 2 | 2 | 2 | 2 | 2 | 2 | 3 |

If each worker is assigned a five-day week with two consecutive days off, we have a seemingly difficult problem. However, if we sum the requirements, they total 15 worker-days. Theoretically, $15/5 = 3$ workers can be assigned to meet requirements, and in this case the objective can be met by the following schedule:

| | M | T | W | Th | F | S | Su |
|---|---|---|---|---|---|---|---|
| Worker 1 | O | O | W | W | W | W | W |
| Worker 2 | W | W | O | O | W | W | W |
| Worker 3 | W | W | W | W | O | O | W |

Days off are indicated by Os, and Ws are days worked. This schedule for three workers meets requirements and is optimal. The schedule is unique, there being no other way of scheduling the three workers to meet the requirements other than simply reversing the days off for workers 1 and 3.

This optimum schedule was generated using simple rules that can be applied to larger problems with somewhat more variable requirements schedules. A computerized algorithm for this problem was developed by Browne (1979, 1980). The algorithm starts with the requirements schedule and assigns days off for worker 1, subtracts the requirements satisfied by worker 1 from the original schedule, and repeats the process until all the workers have been assigned days off. Days worked for each worker are simply the five days that remain after days off are assigned.

We will use another example to explain the process. The requirements schedule at the time we assign days off to worker 1 is:

| | M | T | W | Th | F | S | Su |
|---|---|---|---|---|---|---|---|
| $R_i$ | 3 | 3 | 4 | 3 | 3 | 1 | 2 |

Note that the total requirements for the week are 19 worker-days. The best possible solution will thus require only four workers.

*Step 1.* Identify the maximum staffing requirement for the seven-day week, the next highest staffing requirement, the third highest, and so on, until a unique pair of days off can be identified that has the lowest level of requirements. In the case of ties, choose the pair of days off with the lowest requirements for an adjacent day. If a tie still remains, arbitrarily choose the first of the available tied pairs, assuming that Monday is the beginning of a cycle. The days off assignment should always involve the lowest requirements in the schedule.

The unique pair of days for our example is S–Su. That pair is circled as the assigned days off for worker 1. The unique pair could have been in the middle of the week; for example, if the requirements for the Monday through Sunday schedule were 5–5–2–1–4–4–5, the unique days off would be W–Th.

*Step 2.* The requirements for each work day are reduced by 1, reflecting the days worked by worker 1, to produce a requirements schedule to be used to assign days off for worker 2.

For our example, the original and reduced schedules are as follows. (Note that, because none of the S–Su requirements have been satisfied, they are carried forward to $R_2$.)

| | M | T | W | Th | F | S | Su |
|---|---|---|---|---|---|---|---|
| $R_1$ | 3 | 3 | 4 | 3 | 3 | (1 | 2) |
| $R_2$ | 2 | 2 | 3 | 2 | 2 | 1 | 2 |

Repeat step 1. In $R_2$, the maximum requirement is for three workers, followed by the tied requirements of two workers on Su–M–T and Th–F. The lowest requirement of one worker is on S, which is adjacent to the next lowest requirements of two workers on F and Su. We could choose either F–S or S–Su as the days off assignment for worker 2, so we arbitrarily choose the first of these, F–S. The assignment of F–S as the days off for worker 2 is made by circling these days in $R_2$, and step 2 is repeated. One day is subtracted from worker 2's workdays to produce $R_3$.

| | M | T | W | Th | F | S | Su |
|---|---|---|---|---|---|---|---|
| $R_1$ | 3 | 3 | 4 | 3 | 3 | (1 | 2) |
| $R_2$ | 2 | 2 | 3 | 2 | (2 | 1) | 2 |
| $R_3$ | 1 | 1 | 2 | 1 | 2 | 1 | 1 |

In $R_3$, the maximum requirement is for two workers on W and F followed by ties of one worker required for all other days. We choose the first tied pair, M–T, as the days off assignment for worker 3, and one day is subtracted for each work day in $R_3$ to produce $R_4$.

| | M | T | W | Th | F | S | Su |
|---|---|---|---|---|---|---|---|
| $R_1$ | 3 | 3 | 4 | 3 | 3 | (1 | 2) |
| $R_2$ | 2 | 2 | 3 | 2 | (2 | 1) | 2 |
| $R_3$ | (1 | 1) | 2 | 1 | 2 | 1 | 1 |
| $R_4$ | 1 | 1 | 1 | 0 | 1 | 0 | 0 |

For $R_4$, the unique pair of days off at minimum requirements is S–Su. Reduction of $R_4$ results in 0 requirements for all days, completing the schedule. The work days off can be summarized as follows:

| | M | T | W | Th | F | S | Su |
|---|---|---|---|---|---|---|---|
| Worker 1 | W | W | W | W | W | O | O |
| Worker 2 | W | W | W | W | O | O | W |
| Worker 3 | O | O | W | W | W | W | W |
| Worker 4 | W | W | W | W | W | O | O |
| Workers, $W_i$ | 3 | 3 | 4 | 4 | 3 | 1 | 2 |
| Slack, $S_i = W_i - R_i$ | 0 | 0 | 0 | 1 | 0 | 0 | 0 |

The solution is optimal, because the requirements have been met with four workers. The total slack is one day on Thursday. The slack can be used to generate alternate solutions.

**Weekend Peak Example.** Now suppose that the personnel requirements emphasize a weekend load. The following schedule has a total weekly requirement of 20 worker-days; it can theoretically be satisfied by four workers, each working five days, with two consecutive days off:

| | M | T | W | Th | F | S | Su |
|---|---|---|---|---|---|---|---|
| $R_1$ | 3 | 2 | 2 | 2 | 3 | 4 | 4 |

Applying the choice rules, we obtain the following schedule:

| | M | T | W | Th | F | S | Su |
|---|---|---|---|---|---|---|---|
| $R_1$ | 3 | (2 | 2) | 2 | 3 | 4 | 4 |
| $R_2$ | 2 | 2 | (2 | 1) | 2 | 3 | 3 |
| $R_3$ | (1 | 1) | 2 | 1 | 1 | 2 | 2 |
| $R_4$ | 1 | 1 | 1 | (0 | 0) | 1 | 1 |
| $W_i$ | 3 | 2 | 2 | 2 | 3 | 4 | 4 |
| $S_i$ | 0 | 0 | 0 | 0 | 0 | 0 | 0 |

The solution is optimal with no slack. There are variations in the schedule because of the overlapping days off, but these are actually variations of the same basic schedule, with pairs of workers exchanging days off. The following days-off patterns are also optimal.

| | Days Off Schedule | | | |
|---|---|---|---|---|
| Worker | 1 | 2 | 3 | 4 |
| 1 | T–W | T–W | M–T | W–Th |
| 2 | M–T | M–T | T–W | M–T |
| 3 | W–Th | Th–F | W–Th | T–W |
| 4 | Th–F | W–Th | Th–F | Th–F |

**Rotating Schedules.** The schedules illustrated in our examples are assumed to be fixed. Each employee works a specific cyclic pattern with specified days off. Because of the desire for free weekends, there is the possibility of workers rotating through the several schedules. This creates a different problem because the number of workdays between the individual schedules will vary. For example, the schedule that we used to explain the days-off algorithm resulted in the following:

| | Workdays | Days Off |
|---|---|---|
| Worker 1 | M–F | S–Su |
| Worker 2 | Su–Th | F–S |
| Worker 3 | M–F | S–Su |
| Worker 4 | W–Su | M–T |

If one rotates through these schedules, the number of workdays between days off is variable. Shifting from the first schedule to the second, there are only four workdays between days off; from the second to the third, there are six workdays; and from the third to the fourth, there are zero workdays, there being two consecutive sets of days off. If the sequence of the schedules is changed, the patterns of workdays between days off will also change, but the new pattern will probably also have problems. These variations in the numbers of workdays between rotating schedules are often unacceptable, even though they average out over a period of time.

**Additional Work Rule Constraints.** Baker and Magazine (1977) provide algorithms for days-off constraints in addition to the two consecutive days-off constraint that we have discussed. These more constraining situations include the following:

1. Employees are entitled to every other weekend off and to four days off every two weeks.
2. Employees are entitled to every other weekend off and to two pairs of consecutive days off every two weeks.

When part-time workers can be used, the problem of scheduling personnel is eased somewhat. The scheduling of the part-time workers then becomes an interesting problem.

### USING PART-TIME WORKERS

When demand for service varies significantly but follows a fairly stable weekly pattern, the use of part-time employees can give managers added flexibility. Mabert and Raedels (1976) reported such an application involving eight branch offices of the Purdue National Bank.

## Daily Workshift Scheduling

There are many situations where services for operations are required on a 24-hour basis and where the demand for services is highly fluctuating. For example, Figure 10-6 shows the number of incoming calls at a telephone exchange during a 24-hour period. It is clear from this figure that the telephone company must schedule operators judiciously so that the load is met and the costs are minimized. Hospitals, banks, supermarkets, and police departments all face similar problems in meeting a highly varying demand.

Buffa, Cosgrove, and Luce (1976) have developed an approach for scheduling workers or operators so that requirements are met as closely as possible. The approach begins with a forecast of daily demand (the daily number of calls in the telephone exchange example) that considers seasonal, weekly, and special-day effects as well as trends. This forecast is converted to a distribution of operator requirements by half-hour increments. Based on the distribution of operator requirements, a schedule of tours or shifts is developed and, finally, specific operators are assigned to tours. The key idea in designing shifts to meet load is to utilize flexibility in shift lengths and in the positioning of lunch hours and rest periods. The shifts should meet the constraints imposed by state and federal law, union agreements, company policy, and other practical considerations.

Work shift scheduling problems can be formulated as integer programming problems. However, the solution of large-size, real-world problems by these methods is computationally prohibitive except for some problems with very special structures. Heuristic solutions have been used to obtain very good, though not optimal, solutions for large problems. Integrated systems for scheduling work shifts have been developed in the telephone industry, in the postal service, and for nurse scheduling. These integrated systems make it possible to schedule shifts and personnel for fairly large operations, based on forecasts. Managers of such systems can meet service performance requirements at minimum costs on a routine basis.

# IMPLICATIONS FOR THE MANAGER

The managers of process-focused systems, such as job shops, must balance concerns about work-in-process inventory, machine utilization, meeting customer order due dates, and the like. Scheduling rules define the priority system by which jobs competing for a given machine are selected. A manager must balance performance according to multiple criteria to choose an appropriate rule. The trade-offs among criteria will be dictated by the enterprise strategy, such as cost minimization or on-time delivery.

FIGURE 10-6
**TYPICAL HALF-HOURLY CALL DISTRIBUTION.**

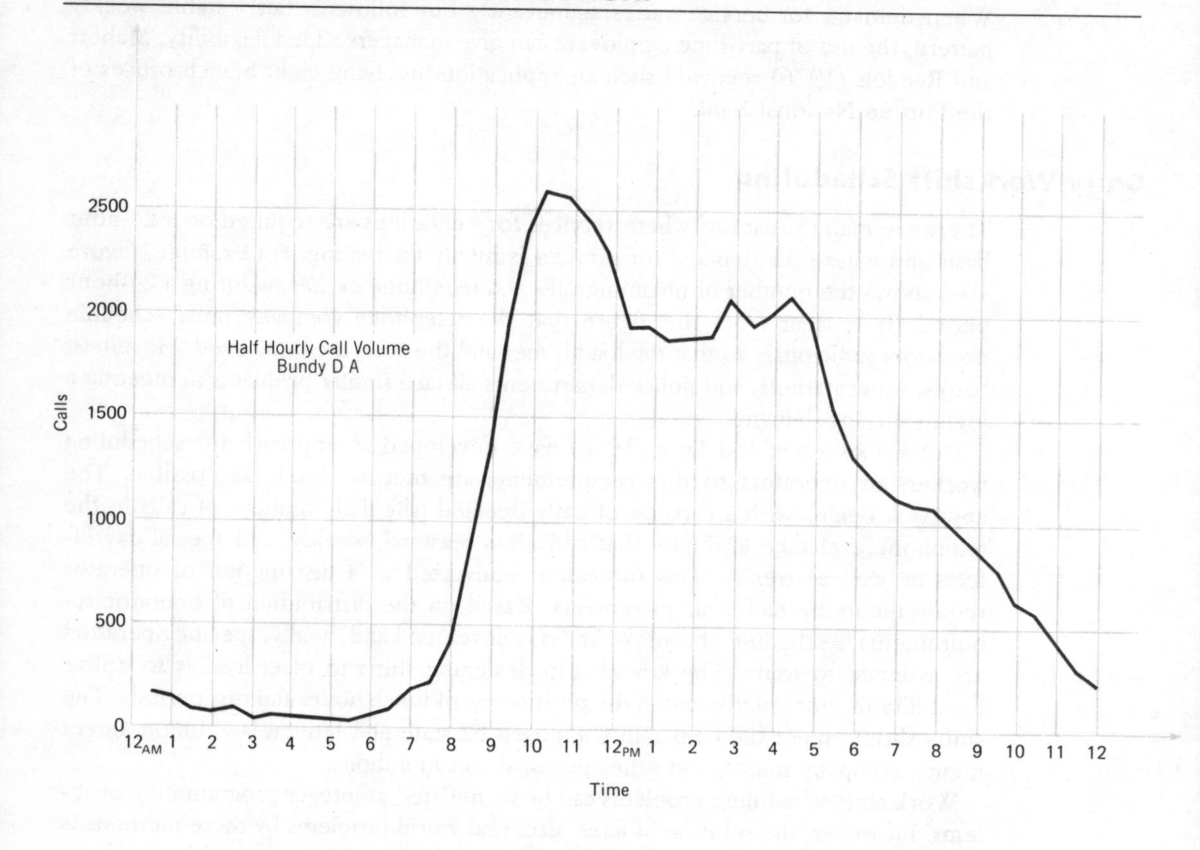


For the managers of batch shops, the relationship between capacity and lot size is important to recognize. Capacity can be diluted by responding to the pressures to meet commitments on rush jobs with lot splitting. Scheduling the use of time-shared equipment often results in pressures to reduce lot sizes in order to meet commitments on a variety of orders. The intensity of these kinds of problems is greatest when an operation is operating near capacity limits. But dilution of capacity in such situations has the effect of intensifying the original problem.

Although *EOQ* concepts can help managers to think in terms of balancing relevant costs, they are seldom applicable in their simple forms. The assumptions of constant demand and lead time are very often not valid, and the assumption of independence among orders fails in most situations unless the system is operating at low load for which the interdependent effects are minimal. Managers who understand these effects seek scheduling systems that treat orders as a part of an interdependent system.

In continuous systems that produce large volumes of a few products, the aggregate plans discussed in Chapter 8 are first derived. The managers of such systems must disaggregate these plans and give careful attention to the product mix. Therefore, the master schedule is of key importance. For these managers, the issues must also consider which products to produce and when, what types of workers must be hired and laid off, what the projected inventory balances for each product are in relation to demand and the production schedule, and which raw materials must be available and when to order them to key in with the production schedule?

Finally, the managers of service systems must schedule work force shifts so that varying demand is met at low cost. The level staffing of many activities, such as nursing care and fire protection, has been the pattern in the past. Certainly, level staffing is the easiest strategy for managers to employ, with the peak requirement determining the staffing level. But level staffing will be expensive in most cases, so managers need to consider alternatives. Scheduling to meet variable requirements is one way that managers can counter the system and remain in control.

Our society seems to demand that more and more services be available throughout the week and often on a 24-hour basis. Supermarkets, health services, food services, and even banks are faced with demand for extended hours. At the same time, we are beginning to consider seriously a variety of alternative work patterns, such as the four-day workweek, the 30-hour workweek, and the 10-hour workday patterns now being discussed. Some of these proposals complicate personnel scheduling, whereas others may provide more flexibility. Formal scheduling models will become even more valuable as the variety of work patterns increases. Fortunately, in most instances, rather simple algorithms can be used to schedule personnel within the constraints of work rules.

## REVIEW QUESTIONS

1. What is the distinction between a scheduling rule and a scheduling criterion?
2. For single processor scheduling, which procedure will minimize the following?
   a. Mean flow time
   b. Maximum tardiness
   c. Number of jobs late
   d. Weighted flow time
3. State the assumptions made in the scheduling models for a single processor.
4. What is a flow shop? For a two machine flow shop, which procedure will minimize maximum flow time?
5. Is there any criterion for which we can use a simple procedure that will provide an optimal solution for the general job shop problem?
6. If a machine is idle and a job is waiting to be processed on it, is it always preferable to schedule that job on the machine in a general job shop? Give a reason for your answer.
7. Why does the SPT rule perform so well for a job shop where jobs are arriving randomly over time? Is there any negative aspect in using the SPT rule?

8. What is the difference in decision variables for scheduling in a job shop and in a batch shop?
9. What is the problem with using independently determined *EOQ*s as batch sizes in a multi-item batch shop?
10. If a common cycle is used for producing all the items in a batch shop, will costs be minimized? Give the reason for your answer.
11. Given the aggregate plan as a constraint to operations scheduling in product-focused systems, what flexibility is left to planners in developing detailed schedules?
12. Why does personnel scheduling in service oriented systems present unique problems?
13. Define the important characteristics of the work shift scheduling problem.

# PROBLEMS

14. The following data are given for a single processor, static job shop:

| Job | 1 | 2 | 3 | 4 | 5 | 6 |
|---|---|---|---|---|---|---|
| Processing time | 3 | 2 | 9 | 4 | 2 | 4 |
| Due date | 17 | 21 | 5 | 12 | 15 | 24 |

   a. Give a schedule that minimizes the average flow time. What is the average flow time for your schedule?

   b. Give a schedule that minimizes maximum tardiness. What is the maximum tardiness for your schedule?

   c. Give a schedule that minimizes the number of tardy jobs. How many jobs are tardy in your schedule?

15. A job shop incurs a cost of $C$ dollars per day for each day a job is in the shop. At the beginning of a month, there are five jobs in the shop. The data for these jobs are given below:

| Job | 1 | 2 | 3 | 4 | 5 |
|---|---|---|---|---|---|
| Processing time (days) | 5 | 3 | 10 | 2 | 4 |
| Due date (days) | 10 | 15 | 20 | 9 | 7 |

   a. If cost per day is $50 for each job, what schedule will minimize total cost?

   b. Suppose job $i$ costs $C_i$ dollars per day for each day it is in the shop.

| Job | 1 | 2 | 3 | 4 | 5 |
|---|---|---|---|---|---|
| Cost $C_i$ | 30 | 10 | 20 | 5 | 50 |

   What schedule will minimize total cost?

16. A bomb squad faces a terrible situation that the members wish had never happened. A terrorist has planted five bombs in an airport building, endangering lives and property. The squad has located all five bombs and must now proceed to dismantle them. Because of limited staffing, the bombs can be

dismantled only sequentially. Unfortunately, there is not much time left, and the squad must choose judiciously the order in which the bombs will be dismantled. The following data represents a reliable estimate by the squad.

| Bomb | 1 | 2 | 3 | 4 | 5 |
|---|---|---|---|---|---|
| Time to dismantle (hours) | 3 | 1 | 2 | 4 | 1 |
| Time remaining before the bomb will explode (hours) | 9.0 | 11.25 | 11.0 | 6.0 | 5.0 |

a. Should the bomb squad dismantle the bombs that take least number of hours to dismantle first?

b. What sequence for dismantling the bombs would you recommend to the squad? What should be the criterion that the squad must optimize?

17. The Reliable word processing center has accepted several jobs that are due in the next few days. A batch of these jobs is assigned to Miss Coco. The pertinent data for these jobs are given below:

| Job | 1 | 2 | 3 | 4 | 5 | 6 |
|---|---|---|---|---|---|---|
| Time to process (days) | 5 | 4 | 3 | 1 | ½ | 2 |
| Due in (days) | 11 | 10 | 16 | 2 | 1 | 3 |

a. Can Miss Coco finish all her jobs on time?

b. Give the schedule that Miss Coco should follow in processing these jobs. Justify your choice of a schedule.

c. If the company pays a penalty of $10 per day for a job that is tardy but receives no reward for jobs finished early, what schedule would you recommend to Miss Coco?

d. If the company receives a reward of $10 per day that a job is early and a penalty of $10 per day that a job is tardy, what schedule would you recommend to Miss Coco?

18. Consider a flow shop that has only two processors. A job is completed first on processor 1 and then on processor 2. The data for 10 jobs are as follow:

| | *Processing Time* | | | | | | | | | |
|---|---|---|---|---|---|---|---|---|---|---|
| Job | 1 | 2 | 3 | 4 | 5 | 6 | 7 | 8 | 9 | 10 |
| Processor 1 | 2 | 7 | 9 | 0 | 3 | 10 | 1 | 5 | 6 | 8 |
| Processor 2 | 6 | 8 | 4 | 10 | 9 | 7 | 5 | 1 | 2 | 3 |
| Due date | 25 | 19 | 30 | 25 | 16 | 55 | 60 | 32 | 45 | 39 |

a. Determine the schedule that minimizes the maximum flow time.

b. What is the maximum flow time for your schedule?

c. How many jobs are tardy in your schedule?

19. For a three machine job shop, the following data are given:

| JOB | JOB ROUTING AND PROCESSING TIMES | DUE DATE |
|---|---|---|
| 1 | B(2), C(5) | 9 |
| 2 | A(6), B(1), C(3) | 15 |
| 3 | B(1), A(4) | 10 |
| 4 | C(3), A(2), B(5) | 12 |
| 5 | A(5), C(4), B(1) | 14 |

   a. Use a Gantt Chart to obtain schedules using the following rules:
      (1) Earliest due date first (EDD)
      (2) Shortest processing time (SPT)
      (3) Least slack time first (LS)
   b. Compute the values of mean flow time, maximum flow time (makespan), total tardiness, and number of jobs tardy for your schedules in part a.
   c. For each day a job is tardy, your shop incurs a penalty of \$50 per day. Further, for each day a job is in the shop a cost of \$5 per day is incurred. What is the total cost of the EDD schedule, the SPT schedule, and the LS schedule?

20. Job orders with the characteristics indicated by the following data are received at a work station:

| Order Number | Due Date | Date and Time Received | Operation Time, Hours | Remaining Operations |
|---|---|---|---|---|
| 1 | May 1 | Apr 18, 9 A.M. | 6 | 3 |
| 2 | Apr 20 | Apr 21, 10 A.M. | 3 | 1 |
| 3 | Jun 1 | Apr 19, 5 P.M. | 7 | 2 |
| 4 | Jun 15 | Apr 21, 3 P.M. | 9 | 4 |
| 5 | May 15 | Apr 20, 5 P.M. | 4 | 5 |
| 6 | May 20 | Apr 21, 5 P.M. | 8 | 7 |

   a. In what sequence should the orders be processed at the work station if the priority dispatch decision rule is
      (1) First come first served
      (2) Shortest processing time first
      (3) Least slack
      (4) Earliest due date first
      (5) Least slack/remaining number of operations first.
   b. Which decision rule do you prefer? Why?

21. Table 10-13 gives data on five products that are produced on the same equipment. Assume that 250 productive days are available per year. The *EOQ*s and associated costs are also shown in the Table.

TABLE 10-13
**DATA FOR FIVE PRODUCTS TO BE PRODUCED ON THE SAME EQUIPMENT**

| (1) Product Number | (2) Annual Requirements, $R_i$ | (3) Daily Requirements, $R_i/250 = r_i$ | (4) Daily Production rate, $p_i$ | (5) Annual Inventory Holding Costs, $c_{H_i}$ | (6) Set-up Costs per Run, $c_{P_i}$ | (7) *EOQ*, Equation 4, Chapter 5 | (8) $TIC_0$, Equation 17, Chapter 5 |
|---|---|---|---|---|---|---|---|
| 1 | 5,000 | 20 | 400 | $1.00 | $40 | 648.89 | $616.44 |
| 2 | 12,500 | 50 | 300 | 0.90 | 25 | 912.87 | 684.65 |
| 3 | 7,000 | 28 | 200 | 0.30 | 30 | 1,275.89 | 329.18 |
| 4 | 16,250 | 65 | 300 | 0.75 | 27 | 1,222.14 | 718.01 |
| 5 | 4,000 | 16 | 160 | 1.05 | 80 | 822.95 | 777.69 |
| | | | | | $202 | | $3,125.97 |

a. If the products are produced in *EOQ* lots, what problems would result?

b. Using the data in Table 10-13, compute the lot sizes that would result from using a common cycle for all products of $N = 6$ and $N = 8$. How many days supply must be produced for each product? Which common cycle do you prefer? Why?

22. Data for a particular job order are set-up time = 10 hours, run time = 1 minute per unit once the set-up is made, $c_P$ = \$150 per set-up, $c_H$ = \$0.12 per unit per year, $R$ = 10,000 units, and $EOQ$ = 5000 units.

    a. What percent dilution in capacity would occur if production were actually in lots of $Q$ = 1000 units instead of *EOQ*?

    b. Suppose that the set-up time = 1 hour and $c_P$ = \$15 per order; then $EOQ$ = 1581 units. What percent dilution in capacity would occur if production is in lots of $Q$ = 300 units instead of *EOQ*?

23. Based on a daily forecast, the number of operators required to meet the hourly load in a telephone exchange on a given day are as follows:

| Period (hour) | 1 | 2 | 3 | 4 | 5 | 6 | 7 | 8 | 9 | 10 | 11 | 12 |
|---|---|---|---|---|---|---|---|---|---|---|---|---|
| Requirements, $R_i$ | 7 | 4 | 2 | 2 | 2 | 2 | 6 | 11 | 20 | 24 | 26 | 27 |
| **Period (hour)** | 13 | 14 | 15 | 16 | 17 | 18 | 19 | 20 | 21 | 22 | 23 | 24 |
| **Requirements, $R_i$** | 23 | 25 | 24 | 23 | 23 | 21 | 21 | 20 | 19 | 17 | 13 | 10 |

a. Using the first-hour principle, what is the staffing pattern for the first 24 hours of operation, assuming a noncyclic situation and an eight-hour shift?

b. What is the staffing pattern assuming a cyclic situation?

24. The following Monday through Sunday schedule of requirements is similar to

that in the days off example used in the text, with the exception that the requirement for Thursday is for four workers:

| | M | T | W | Th | F | S | Su |
|---|---|---|---|---|---|---|---|
| $R_1$ | 3 | 3 | 4 | 4 | 3 | 1 | 2 |

The result is that no slack would be available if four workers could be scheduled with consecutive days off. Is it still possible to use only four workers to meet requirements? If so, are there alternative solutions?

25. A service operation is offered seven days per week. Demand for the service is such that four workers are required throughout the week. Work rules require that each worker be given two consecutive days off each week. How many workers will be required to staff the operation? Develop a schedule of days worked and days off for each worker.
26. Assume that the schedule of requirements in the previous problem is altered only in that the requirement for Sunday is six workers. Is it still possible to schedule the operation with the same number of workers? Does it make any difference whether or not the requirement of six workers occurs on Sunday or on some other day of the week?
27. A service operation requires five workers per day, seven days per week. Total weekly requirements are $5 \times 7 = 35$ worker-days per week. Theoretically, the 35 worker-days can be met with $35/5 = 7$ workers, assuming that each worker must have two consecutive days off. Such a solution would have no slack. Is it possible?

# SITUATIONS

## Minutes to Survival

28. During a heavy fog, eight aircraft were "stacked" over Dragon Airport. Around 6:45 A.M., the weather cleared up. The planes must now be sequenced for landing, so the controller team of two scheduling experts, Freeda and Tom, have to do a rush job.

Not all the aircraft are alike. They differ (because of size and operating characteristics) in *RUT*, the amount of time during which they need exclusive use of the runway; and in *OCT*, their operating cost per unit of time while airborne (mainly due to different fuel consumptions).

| Aircraft | 1 | 2 | 3 | 4 | 5 | 6 | 7 | 8 |
|---|---|---|---|---|---|---|---|---|
| *RUT* (minutes) | 3 | 2 | 4 | 3 | 2 | 4 | 3 | 4 |
| *OCT* ($/minute) | 20 | 10 | 60 | 30 | 20 | 80 | 60 | 40 |

Freeda suggests that, in order to minimize the average operating cost per plane, the plane with the lowest *RUT*/*OCT* should be sequenced first. This way, she argues, the planes that consume more fuel per minute but take less runway time are given priority.

It is now 6:50 A.M. Freeda has signaled the first aircraft, No. 6, to land.

Suddenly, Tom screams, "No!!!" The sequencing has to be altered. Aircraft No. 2, which was to be sequenced last, does not have enough fuel. Many others are also low on fuel. The team knows the remaining flying time for each aircraft, which at 6:50 A.M. is as follows:

| Aircraft | 1 | 2 | 3 | 4 | 5 | 6 | 7 | 8 |
|---|---|---|---|---|---|---|---|---|
| Remaining flying time (minutes) | 20 | 15 | 30 | 26 | 20 | 20 | 31 | 15 |

The planes must start landing by 6:55 A.M. Another factor complicates the decision further. For a normal landing, some clearance time must elapse before one aircraft can land after another. This is because when a 747 lands, for example, the turbulence it causes must dissipate before the next aircraft lands. Clearance time is around two minutes for aircraft No. 6 and No. 8 and is negligible for the others. It is, however, considered safe not to allow any clearance time during an emergency.

a. What landing sequence will minimize the sum of *RUT* and waiting time for all planes?

b. What order of landing will minimize average operating costs?

c. What landing sequence will avoid a crash?

## Fire Department Scheduling

29. Figure 10-7 shows the hourly variation in the demand for fire service for three typical days in New York City. On the average day, the 8 to 9 P.M. peak is 7.7 times the low point that occurs at 6 A.M. The peak for July 4 to July 5 is 3.7 times the peak for the low day in the distribution. Traditional deployment policies in fire departments have been to keep the same number of fire fighters and units on duty around the clock. Also, traditional policies have tried to maintain a "standard response" of personnel and equipment to alarms in most areas at all times.

    What staffing strategy should the fire department adopt in attempting to meet the demand for fire protection service? What risks should the department take with respect to the extreme demand days?

## Mixing and Bagging Company II

30. The Mixing and Bagging Company discussed in a Situation in Chapter 5 has carried through its plan to install *EOQ* scheduling of its products. The idea expressed by the factory manager is to use an order point trigger for each product. He set the order point, $P_i$, for each product to cover average demand for two weeks. When warehouse inventory for an item declines to the order point, an order for the approximate *EOQ* is written and released to the foreman.

    The delay between actual recognition that the inventory level has triggered an order and the order release to the foreman is three days, and the production lead time of two days is felt to be normal. The factory manager thought that it

FIGURE 10-7
**TOTAL FIRE ALARMS RECEIVED IN NEW YORK CITY BY HOUR—1968 DATA.**

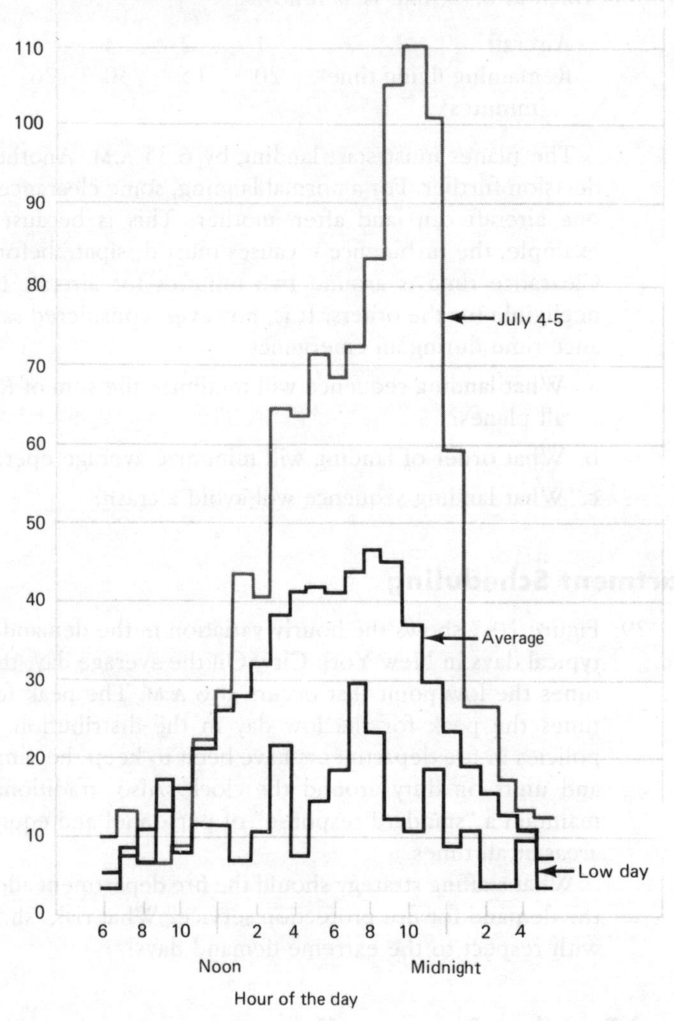


*Source:* E. H. Blum, *Development Research of the New York City Fire Project,* the New York City Rand Institute, R–968, May 1962.

should be possible to get an inventory item in mixed and bagged form replenished in the warehouse within the lead time because of the simple production process. Thus, five working days' (one week's) worth of the two-week inventory supply was planned to be used in replenishment. This left a one-week supply as a buffer against the possibility of especially high demand. The factory manager felt that the extra one-week's supply should cover most situations.

The factory manager has classified the 10 product types into *practical* production lot sizes, based on his *EOQ* calculations. There are three high-demand items that are run in lots of 4000 bags (100 pounds per bag), four intermediate-demand items that are run in lots of 2000 bags, and three low-demand items that are run in lots of 1000 bags. These lot sizes are reasonably close to the *EOQ*s and correspond to units of raw materials and supplies that are easy to deal with. Also, having only three sizes of runs makes the system simple for the supervisor and the production workers.

Using the factory manager's classification, the product demand, lot sizes, and runs per year are summarized in the following table:

| Product | Average Demand (100-pound sacks/year) | Lot Size (100-pound sacks/run) | Average Number of Runs per Year per Product |
|---|---|---|---|
| 3 high demand | 160,000 | 4000 | 40 |
| 4 high demand | 40,000 | 2000 | 20 |
| 3 low demand | 10,000 | 1000 | 10 |

A run of 4000 sacks requires about 590 minutes, including set-up, a run of 2000 sacks requires about 310 minutes, and a run of 1000 sacks requires about 170 minutes. (Each run includes a 30 minute set-up plus 0.14 minutes per bag.) The factory manager figures that the average number of runs with the average mix of order sizes requires only about 34 hours per week of production time on the equipment, including set-up. In other words, the plant is operating at about 85 percent of capacity.

After a short time operating under the new *EOQ* system, the factory manager is puzzled by the results. He is stocking out of some of the high-demand items before the completion of production runs. He has examined demand figures and has found that the demand for these items has been greater than the average because of some seasonality in demand, but he cannot understand why the one-week supply has not taken care of the problem.

The supervisor has said that he has the place "humming," but he has complained that the factory manager is always and forever telling him to produce a given order first because of short supply. "Every order can't be run first," he has said. The number of orders that he has on his production list seems to be growing, and he processes them strictly in the order in which they are received unless told to expedite a particular order. When the foreman was asked what he thought the problem was, he said, "The problem is that the runs are too short for the high-demand items. I spend my time constantly changing over to a new product. I suggest that we make all of the lot sizes larger, but particularly the high-demand items. Perhaps the lot sizes should be 10,000, 5000 and 1000. The small runs of 1000 are okay for the low-demand items, since I can sandwich them in easily."

What is the problem? What are your recommendations to the factory manager?

# REFERENCES

Baker, K. R., *Introduction to Sequencing and Scheduling,* Wiley, New York, 1974.

Baker, K. R., and M. Magazine, "Workforce Scheduling with Cyclic Demands and Days-Off Constraints," *Management Science, 24*(2), October 1977, pp. 161–167.

Berry, W. L., V. A. Mabert, and M. Marcus, "Forecasting Teller Window Demand with Exponential Smoothing," *Academy of Management Journal,* March 1979.

Browne, J. J., "Simplified Scheduling of Routine Work Hours and Days Off," *Industrial Engineering,* December 1979, pp. 27–29.

Browne, J. J., and J. Propp, "Supplement to Scheduling Routine Work Hours," *Industrial Engineering,* July 1980, p. 12.

Browne, J. J., and R. K. Tibrewala, "Manpower Scheduling," *Industrial Engineering,* August 1975, pp. 22–23.

Buffa, E. S., and J. G. Miller, *Production–Inventory Systems: Planning and Control* (3rd ed.), Irwin, Homewood, Ill., 1979.

Buffa, E. S., M. J. Cosgrove, and B. J. Luce, "An Integrated Work Shift Scheduling System," *Decision Sciences,* 7(4), October 1976, pp. 620–630.

Chase, R. B., "Where Does the Customer Fit in a Service Operation," *Harvard Business Review, 56,* 1978, pp. 137–142.

Fitzsimmons, J. A., and R. S. Sullivan, *Service Operations Management,* McGraw-Hill, New York, 1982.

Hax, A. C., and H. C. Meal, "Hierarchical Integration of Production Planning and Scheduling," in *Studies in the Management Sciences, Vol. I, Logistics,* edited by M. A. Geisler, North Holland-American Elsevier, Amsterdam, 1975.

Mabert, V. A., and A. R. Raedels, "The Detail Scheduling of a Part-Time Work Force: A Case Study of Teller Staffing," *Decision Sciences,* 7(4), October 1976.

Mabert, V. A., and M. J. Showalter, "Priority Rules for Check Processing in Branch Banking," *Journal of Operations Management, 1*(1), Summer 1980.

Peterson, R., and E. A. Silver, *Decision Systems for Inventory Management and Production Planning,* Wiley, New York, 1985.

Propp, J. A., *Greedy Solution for Linear Programs With Circular Ones,* IBM Corporation Internal Report, 1978.

Rising, E. J., R. Baron, and B. Averill, "A Systems Analysis of a University-Health-Service Outpatient Clinic," *Operations Research, 21*(5), September–October 1973, pp. 1030–1047.

Sasser, W. E., R. P. Olsen, and D. D. Wyckoff, *Management of Service Operations: Text, Cases, and Readings,* Allyn & Bacon, Boston, 1978.

Tibrewala, R. K., D. Philippe, and J. J. Browne, "Optimal Scheduling of Two Consecutive Idle Periods," *Management Science, 19*(1), September 1972, pp. 71–75.

# CHAPTER 11
# LARGE-SCALE PROJECTS

Our society produces buildings, roads, dams, missiles, ships, and other products of large scale projects. The problems of planning and managing such projects stem from their great complexity and the interdependent nature of the activities that must be performed to complete them. Some projects are one of a kind, such as planning for the first space shuttle mission, whereas others are repeatable, such as building an apartment complex. Even repeatable projects may have many features that are custom designed and therefore lead to significant differences in the required activities from one project to the next. Thus, the focus of the managerial effort in project systems is on the detailed planning, scheduling, and control of each major activity with respect to the project as a whole. In this chapter, we discuss methods of project management that provide managers with the crucial information they need to complete a project successfully.

## ORIGIN OF PROJECT PLANNING

Project planning methods, also called network planning methods, were initially developed independently by two different groups. As an internal project of the DuPont Company, Critical Path Methods (CPM) were developed to plan and control the maintenance of chemical plants. They were subsequently widely used by DuPont for many engineering functions.

Parallel efforts were undertaken by the U.S. Navy at about the same time to develop methods for planning and controlling the Polaris missile project. This project involved 3000 separate contracting organizations and was regarded as the most complex project undertaken to that date. The result was the development of the Performance Evaluation and Review Technique (PERT) methodology.

The immediate success of both the CPM and PERT methodologies may be gauged by the following facts. DuPont's application of the CPM technique to a maintenance project in their Louisville works resulted in a reduction in downtime for maintenance from 125 to 78 hours. The PERT technique was widely credited with helping to shorten by two years the time originally estimated for the completion of the engineering and development program for the Polaris missile.

PERT and CPM are based substantially on the same concepts. As originally developed, PERT was based on probabilistic estimates of activity times that resulted in a probabilistic path through a network of activities and a probabilistic project completion time. CPM, in contrast, assumed constant or deterministic activity times. Actually, both the probabilistic and the deterministic cases are equally applicable to and usable with either technique.

## PERT/CPM PLANNING METHODS

We will use a relatively simple example, the introduction of a new product, to develop the methods used in generating a network representation of a project. The development of a project network may be divided into (1) activity analysis, (2) arrow diagramming, and (3) node numbering.

## Activity Analysis

The smallest unit of productive effort to be planned, scheduled, and controlled is called an *activity*. For large projects, it is possible to overlook the need for some activities because of the great complexity. Therefore, although professional planning personnel are commonly used, the generation of the activity list is often partially done in meetings and round-table discussions that include managerial and operating personnel. Table 11-1 is an activity list for the introduction of a new product.

## Network Diagramming[1]

A network is developed that takes account of the precedence relationships among the activities; it must be based on a complete, verified, and approved activity list. The important information required for these network diagrams is generated by the

TABLE 11-1
**PRECEDENCE CHART SHOWING ACTIVITIES, THEIR REQUIRED SEQUENCE, AND TIME REQUIREMENTS FOR THE NEW PRODUCT INTRODUCTION PROJECT**

| Activity Code | Description | Immediate Predecessor Activity | Time, Weeks |
|---|---|---|---|
| A | Organize sales office | — | 6 |
| B | Hire salespeople | A | 4 |
| C | Train salespeople | B | 7 |
| D | Select advertising agency | A | 2 |
| E | Plan advertising campaign | D | 4 |
| F | Conduct advertising campaign | E | 10 |
| G | Design package | — | 2 |
| H | Set up packaging facilities | G | 10 |
| I | Package initial stocks | H, J | 6 |
| J | Order stock from manufacturer | — | 13 |
| K | Select distributors | A | 9 |
| L | Sell to distributors | C, K | 3 |
| M | Ship stock to distributors | I, L | 5 |

[1] Activities will be diagrammed as occurring on the arcs or arrows. An alternate network diagramming procedure, where activities occur at the nodes, will be discussed later in the chapter. We can refer to the first as an "arcs" network, and the second as a "nodes" network.

following three questions:

1. Which activities must be completed before each activity can be started?
2. Which activities can be carried out in parallel?
3. Which activities immediately succeed other activities?

The common practice is simply to work backwards through the activity list, generating the immediate predecessors for each activity listed, as shown in Table 11-1. The estimated time for each activity is also shown in the table. The network diagram may then be constructed to represent the logical precedence requirements shown in Table 11-1.

### DUMMY ACTIVITIES

Care must be taken in correctly representing the actual precedence requirements in the network diagram. For example, in house construction, consider the immediate predecessor activities for activity *s*, sand and varnish flooring, and activity *u*, finish electrical work. Activity *s* has the immediate predecessors *o* and *t*, finish carpentry and painting, respectively, whereas *u* has a predecessor of only activity *t*, paint. The relationship shown in Figure 11-1*a* does not correctly represent this situation because it specifies that the beginning of *u* is dependent on both *o* and *t*, and this is not true.

To represent the situation correctly, we must resort to the use of a dummy activity that requires zero performance time. Figure 11-1*b* represents the stated requirement. Finish electrical work, *u*, now depends only on the completion of painting, *t*. Through the dummy activity, however, both finish carpentry and painting must be completed before activity *s*, sand and varnish flooring, can be started. The dummy activity provides the logical sequencing relationship. But because the dummy activity is assigned zero performance time, it does not alter computations for project completion time.

Another use of the dummy activity is to provide an unambiguous beginning and ending event or node for each activity. For example, a functionally correct relation-

FIGURE 11-1
**(a) DIAGRAM DOES NOT PROPERLY REFLECT PRECEDENCE REQUIREMENTS BECAUSE U SEEMS TO BE DEPENDENT ON THE COMPLETION OF BOTH O AND T. (b) CREATING TWO NODES WITH A DUMMY ACTIVITY BETWEEN PROVIDES THE PROPER PREDECESSORS FOR BOTH ACTIVITIES S AND U.**

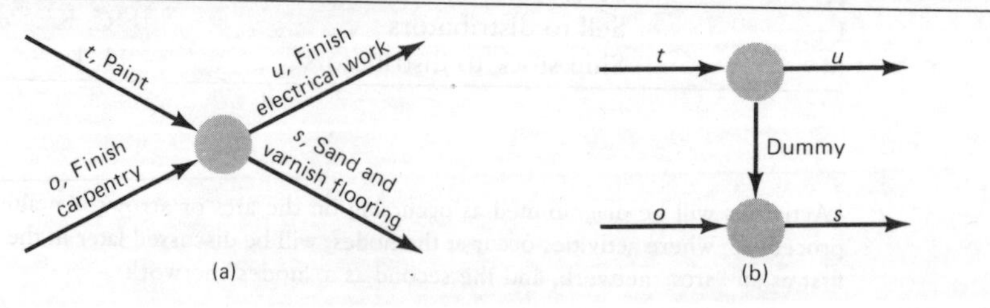

FIGURE 11-2
**(*a*) ACTIVITIES *m* AND *n* MAY BE CARRIED OUT IN PARALLEL, BUT THIS RESULTS IN IDENTICAL BEGINNING AND ENDING EVENTS. (*b*) THE USE OF A DUMMY ACTIVITY MAKES IT POSSIBLE TO SEPARATE ENDING EVENT NUMBERS.**

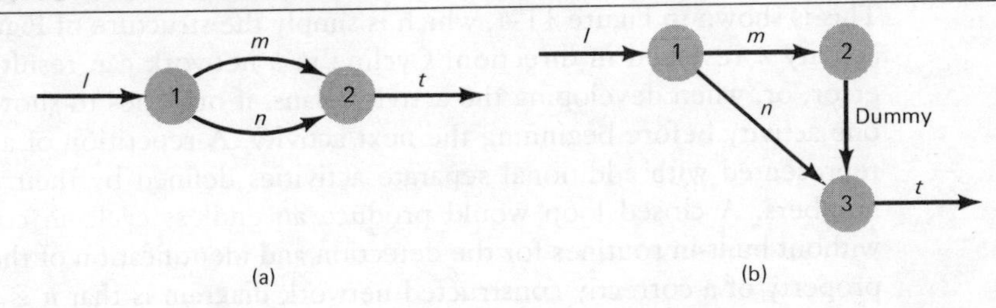


ship might be represented by Figure 11-2*a*, in which two activities have the same beginning and ending nodes. If Figure 11-2*a* were used, however, it would not be possible to identify each activity by its predecessor and successor events because both activities *m* and *n* would begin and end with the same node numbers. This is particularly important in larger networks that employ computer programs for network diagram generation. The computer is programmed to identify each activity by a pair of node numbers. The problem is solved through the insertion of a dummy activity, as shown in Figure 11-2*b*. The functional relationship is identical because the dummy activity requires zero time, but now *m* and *n* are identified by different pairs of node numbers.

Figure 11-3 shows the completed network diagram for the new product introduction project. The activities are identified, their required times in weeks are given, and all the nodes are numbered.

## Node Numbering

The node numbering shown in Figure 11-3 has been done in a particular way. Each arc, or arrow, represents an activity. If we identify each activity by its tail ($i$) and head ($j$) numbers, the nodes are numbered so that for each activity, $i$ is always less

FIGURE 11-3
**ARCS NETWORK DIAGRAM FOR THE NEW PRODUCT INTRODUCTION PROJECT.**

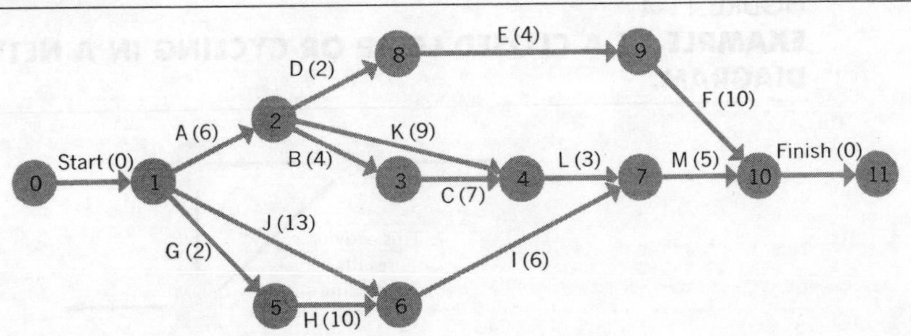

than $j$, $i < j$. The numbers for every arrow are progressive, and no backtracking through the network is allowed. This convention in node numbering is effective in computing programs to develop the logical network relationships and to prevent the occurrence of cycling or closed loops.

A closed loop would occur if an activity were represented as going back in time. This is shown in Figure 11-4, which is simply the structure of Figure 11-2*b* with the activity *n* reversed in direction. Cycling in a network can result through a simple error, or, when developing the activity plans, if one tries to show the repetition of one activity before beginning the next activity. A repetition of an activity must be represented with additional separate activities defined by their own unique node numbers. A closed loop would produce an endless cycle in computer programs without built-in routines for the detection and identification of the cycle. Thus, one property of a correctly constructed network diagram is that it is noncyclical.

## CRITICAL PATH SCHEDULING

With a properly constructed network diagram, it is possible to develop the important schedule data for each activity and for the project as a whole. The data of interest are the minimum time required for completion of the project, the critical activities that can not be delayed or prolonged, and the earliest and latest start and finish times for the activities. An algorithm to compute these data is described below.

### Earliest Start and Finish Times

If we take zero as the starting time for the project, then for each activity there is an earliest starting time, *ES*, relative to the project starting time. This is the earliest possible time that the activity can begin, assuming that all the predecessors also are started at their *ES*. Then, for that activity, its earliest finish time, *EF*, is simply *ES* + activity time.

### Latest Start and Finish Times

Assume that our target time for completing the project is "as soon as possible." This target is called the latest finish time, *LF*, of the project and of the finish activity. For

FIGURE 11-4
**EXAMPLE OF A CLOSED LOOP OR CYCLING IN A NETWORK DIAGRAM.**

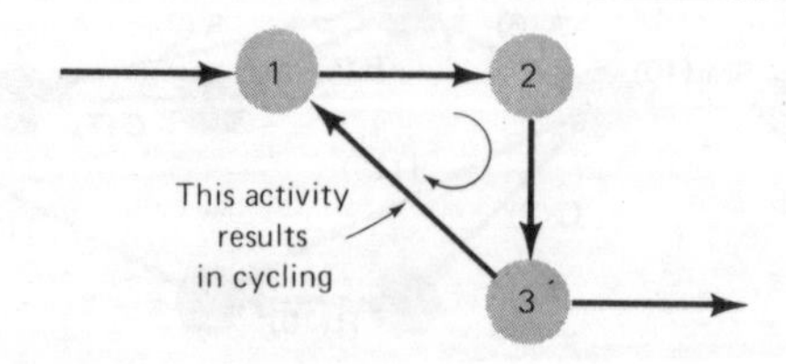

the finish activity, $LF$ will be equal to its earliest finish time, $EF$. The latest start time, $LS$, is the latest time at which an activity can start if the target or schedule is to be maintained. Thus, $LS$ for an activity is $LF$ − activity time.

Existing computer programs may be used to compute these schedule data automatically, requiring as inputs the activities, their performance time requirements, and the precedence relationships established. The computer output might be similar to Figure 11-5, which shows the schedule statistics for all the activities.

## Slack

The total slack for an activity is simply the difference between the computed late start and early start times, $LS - ES$, or between late finish and early finish times, $LF - EF$. The significance of total slack, $TS$, is that it specifies the maximum time that an activity can be delayed without delaying the project completion time. Note that all critical activities have zero total slack in their schedules. All other activities have greater than zero slack.

The free slack, $FS$, shown in Figure 11-5 indicates the time that an activity can be delayed without delaying the $ES$ of any other activity. $FS$ is computed as the

FIGURE 11-5
**SAMPLE COMPUTER OUTPUT OF SCHEDULE STATISTICS AND THE CRITICAL PATH FOR THE NEW PRODUCT INTRODUCTION PROJECT.**

*THE CRITICAL PATH IS*

*START → A → B → C → L → M → FINISH*

*THE LENGTH OF THE CRITICAL PATH IS 25*

| *NODE* | *DURATION* | *EARLY START* | *EARLY FINISH* | *LATE START* | *LATE FINISH* | *TOTAL SLACK* | *FREE SLACK* |
|---|---|---|---|---|---|---|---|
| START | 0.00 | 0.00 | 0.00 | 0.00 | 0.00 | 0.00 | 0.00 |
| A | 6.00 | 0.00 | 6.00 | 0.00 | 6.00 | 0.00 | 0.00 |
| B | 4.00 | 6.00 | 10.00 | 6.00 | 10.00 | 0.00 | 0.00 |
| C | 7.00 | 10.00 | 17.00 | 10.00 | 17.00 | 0.00 | 0.00 |
| D | 2.00 | 6.00 | 8.00 | 9.00 | 11.00 | 3.00 | 0.00 |
| E | 4.00 | 8.00 | 12.00 | 11.00 | 15.00 | 3.00 | 0.00 |
| F | 10.00 | 12.00 | 22.00 | 15.00 | 25.00 | 3.00 | 3.00 |
| G | 2.00 | 0.00 | 2.00 | 2.00 | 4.00 | 2.00 | 0.00 |
| H | 10.00 | 2.00 | 12.00 | 4.00 | 14.00 | 2.00 | 1.00 |
| I | 6.00 | 13.00 | 19.00 | 14.00 | 20.00 | 1.00 | 1.00 |
| J | 13.00 | 0.00 | 13.00 | 1.00 | 14.00 | 1.00 | 0.00 |
| K | 9.00 | 6.00 | 15.00 | 8.00 | 17.00 | 2.00 | 2.00 |
| L | 3.00 | 17.00 | 20.00 | 17.00 | 20.00 | 0.00 | 0.00 |
| M | 5.00 | 20.00 | 25.00 | 20.00 | 25.00 | 0.00 | 0.00 |
| FINISH | 0.00 | 25.00 | 25.00 | 25.00 | 25.00 | 0.00 | 0.00 |

difference between the *EF* for an activity and the earliest of the *ES* times of all immediate successors. For example, activity F has $FS = 3$ weeks. If its earliest finish time is delayed up to three weeks, the *ES* time for no other activity is affected, nor is the project completion time affected. Note also that activity K can be delayed two weeks without affecting activity L, its successor. To compute the *FS* manually, one should examine the network diagram in order to take account of the precedence relationships.

On the other hand, total slack is shared with other activities. For example, activities D, E, and F all have $TS = 3$. If activity D is delayed and thus uses up the slack, then E and F no longer have slack available. These relationships are most easily seen by examining the network diagram, where the precedence relationships are shown graphically.

Actually, there are five different paths from start to finish through the network. The longest, most limiting path requires 25 weeks for the activity sequence START–A–B–C–L–M–FINISH, which is called a critical path. In a small problem such as this one, we could enumerate all the alternative paths to find the longest path, but there is no advantage in doing so because the critical path is easily determined from the schedule statistics, which are themselves useful.

## Manual Computation of Schedule Statistics

Manual computation is appropriate for smaller networks, and it helps to convey the significance of the schedule statistics. To compute *ES* and *EF* manually from the network, we proceed forward through the network as follows, referring to Figure 11-6.

1. Place the value of the project start time in both the *ES* and *EF* positions near the start activity arrow. See the legend for Figure 11-6. We will assume relative values, as we did in the computer output of Figure 11-5, so the number 0 is placed in the *ES* and *EF* positions for the start of the activity. (Note that it is not necessary in PERT to include the start activity with a zero activity duration. It has been included here to make this example parallel in its activity list with the comparable "activities on nodes" example of Figure 11-8. The start and finish activities are often necessary in nodes networks.)
2. Consider any new unmarked activity, all of whose predecessors have been marked in their *ES* and *EF* positions, and mark in the *ES* position of the new activity with the largest number marked in the *EF* position for any of its immediate predecessors. This number is the *ES* time of the new activity. For activity A in Figure 11-6, the *ES* time is 0 because that is the *EF* time of the preceding activity.
3. Add to this *ES* number the activity time, and mark the resulting *EF* time in its proper position. For activity *A*, $EF = ES + 6 = 6$.
4. Continue through the entire network until the "finish" activity has been marked. As we showed in Figure 11-5, the critical path time is 25 weeks, so $ES = EF = 25$ for the finish activity.

FIGURE 11-6
**FLOW OF CALCULATIONS FOR EARLY START, *ES*, AND EARLY FINISH, *EF*, TIMES.**

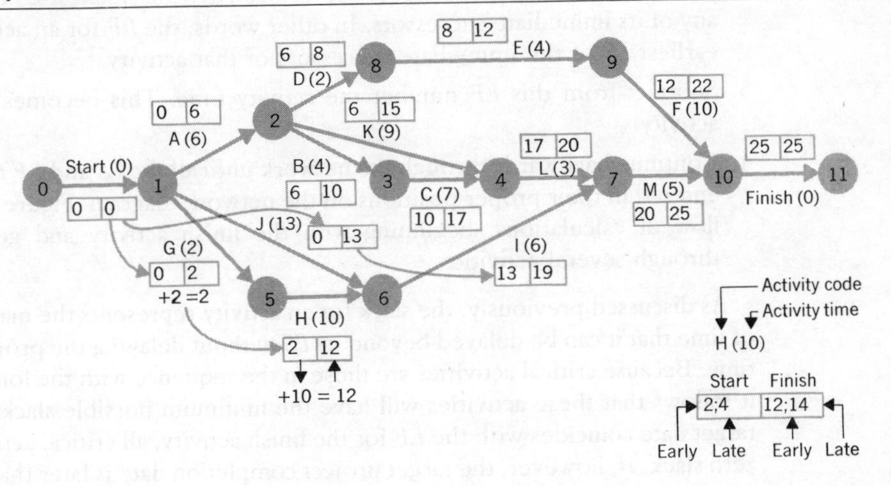


To compute the *LS* and *LF*, we work backwards through the network, beginning with the finish activity. We have already stated that the target time for completing the project is as soon as possible or 25 weeks. Therefore, $LF = 25$ for the finish activity without delaying the total project beyond its target date. Similarly, the *LS* time for the finish activity is *LF* minus the activity time. Since the finish activity requires 0 time units, its $LS = LF$. To compute *LS* and *LF* for each activity, we proceed as follows, referring to Figure 11-7.

FIGURE 11-7
**FLOW OF CALCULATIONS FOR LATE START, *LS*, AND LATE FINISH, *LF*, TIMES.**

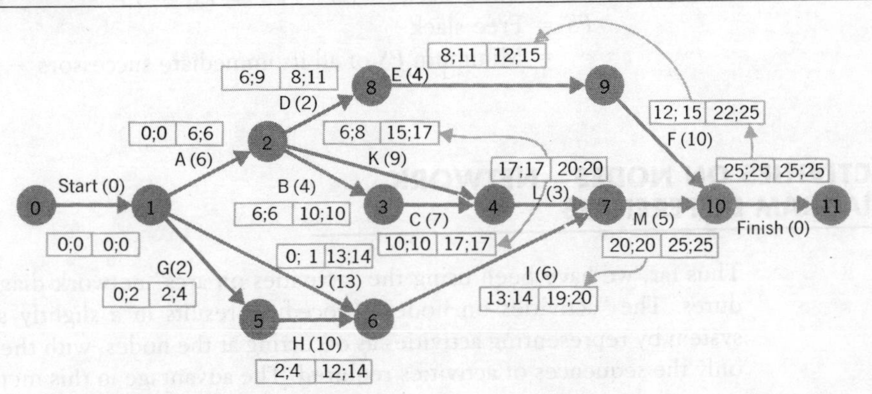

1. Mark the value of *LS* and *LF* in their respective positions near the finish activity.
2. Consider any new unmarked activity, all of whose successors have been marked, and mark in the *LF* position for the new activity the smallest *LS* time marked for any of its immediate successors. In other words, the *LF* for an activity equals the earliest *LS* of the immediate successors of that activity.
3. Subtract from this *LF* number the activity time. This becomes the *LS* for the activity.
4. Continue backwards through the network until all the *LS* and *LF* times have been entered in their proper positions on the network diagram. Figure 11-7 shows the flow of calculations, beginning with the finish activity and going backwards through several activities.

As discussed previously, the slack for an activity represents the maximum amount of time that it can be delayed beyond its *ES* without delaying the project completion time. Because critical activities are those in the sequence with the longest time path, it follows that these activities will have the minimum possible slack. If the project target date coincides with the *LF* for the finish activity, all critical activities will have zero slack. If, however, the target project completion date is later than the *EF* of the finish activity, all critical activities will have slack equal to this time-phasing difference. The manual computation of slack is simply $LS - ES$ or, alternately, $LF - EF$. As noted previously, free slack is the difference between the *EF* for an activity and the earliest *ES* time of all its immediate successors. Thus, free slack is not affected by any time-phasing difference.

In summary, the project and activity schedule data are computed as follows:

$$
\begin{aligned}
ES &= \text{Earliest start of an activity} \\
&= \text{Minimum of } EF \text{ of all its immediate predecessors} \\
EF &= \text{Earliest finish of an activity} \\
&= ES + \text{Activity time} \\
LF &= \text{Latest finish of an activity} \\
&= \text{Minimum } LS \text{ of all its immediate successors} \\
LS &= \text{Latest start of an activity} \\
&= LF - \text{Activity time} \\
TS &= \text{Total slack} = LS - ES = LF - EF \\
FS &= \text{Free slack} \\
&= \text{Minimum } ES \text{ of all its immediate successors} - EF
\end{aligned}
$$

## ACTIVITIES ON NODES—NETWORK DIAGRAM DIFFERENCES

Thus far, we have been using the "activities on arcs" network diagramming procedures. The "activities on nodes" procedure results in a slightly simpler network system by representing activities as occurring at the nodes, with the arrows showing only the sequences of activities required. The advantage in this methodology is that

FIGURE 11-8
**PROJECT GRAPH OF ACTIVITIES ON NODES FOR THE NEW PRODUCT INTRODUCTION PROJECT.**

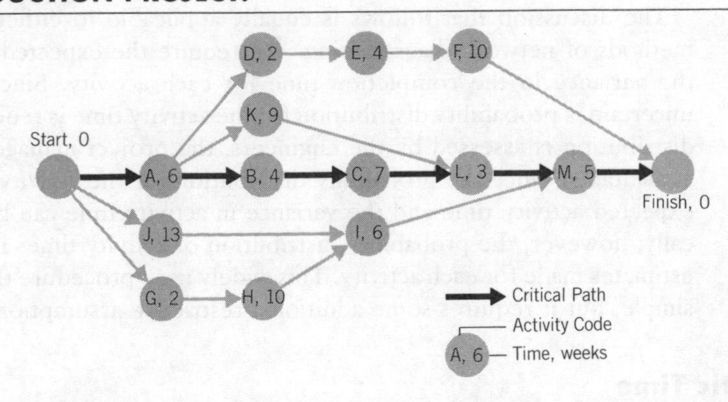


it is not necessary to use dummy activities in order to represent the proper sequencing. Figure 11-8 shows the network for the new product introduction project, which may be compared with the comparable "activities on arcs" network shown in Figure 11-3.

The analysis for developing the early and late start and finish times and slack times is identical with the forward and backward pass procedure previously outlined. The net results of both systems are the schedule statistics that are computed. Because these are the data of interest and because the entire procedure is normally computerized for both methodologies, the choice between the two may depend on other criteria, such as the availability and adaptability of existing computer routines, or the choice may be simply a matter of personal preference.

## PROBABILISTIC NETWORK METHODS

The network methods that we have discussed so far may be termed "deterministic" because estimated activity times are assumed to be fixed constants. No recognition is given to the fact that activity times could be uncertain.

Probabilistic network methods assume the more realistic situation in which uncertain activity times are represented by probability distributions. With such a basic model of the network of activities, it is possible to develop additional data important to managerial decisions. Such data help in assessing planning decisions that might revolve around such questions as the following: What is the probability that the completion of activity A will be later than January 10? What is the probability that the activity will become critical and affect the project completion date? What is the probability of meeting a given target completion date for the project? The nature of the planning decisions based on such questions might involve the allocation or reallocation of personnel or other resources to the various activities in order to derive a more satisfactory plan. Thus, a "crash" schedule involving extra resources might be justified to ensure the on-time completion of certain activities. The extra resources needed are drawn from noncritical activities or from activities for which the probability of criticality is small.

The discussion that follows is equally applicable to either the arc or the node methods of network diagramming. We require the expected completion time and the variance in the completion time for each activity. Since the activity time is uncertain, a probability distribution for the activity time is required. This probability distribution is assessed by the engineers, the project manager, or the appropriate consultants. Once the probability distribution for the activity time is specified, the expected activity time and the variance in activity time can be computed. Historically, however, the probability distribution of activity times is based on three time estimates made for each activity. This widely used procedure that we describe now is simple, but it requires some additional restrictive assumptions.

### Optimistic Time

Optimistic time, $a$, is the shortest possible time to complete the activity if all goes well. It is based on the assumption that there is no more than one chance in a hundred of completing the activity in less than the optimistic time.

### Pessimistic Time

Pessimistic time, $b$, is the longest time for an activity under adverse conditions. It is based on the assumption that there is no more than one chance in a hundred of completing the activity in a time greater than $b$.

### Most Likely Time

Most likely time, $m$, is the single most likely modal value of the activity time distribution. The three time estimates are shown in relation to an activity completion time distribution in Figure 11-9.

### Expected Activity Time

By assuming that activity time follows a beta distribution, the expected time of an activity, $t_e$, is computed as

$$t_e = \frac{a + 4m + b}{6}$$

### Variance of Activity Time

The variance, $\sigma^2$, of an activity time is computed using the formula

$$\sigma^2 = \left(\frac{b - a}{6}\right)^2$$

FIGURE 11-9
**TIME VALUES IN RELATION TO A DISTRIBUTION OF ACTIVITY TIME.**

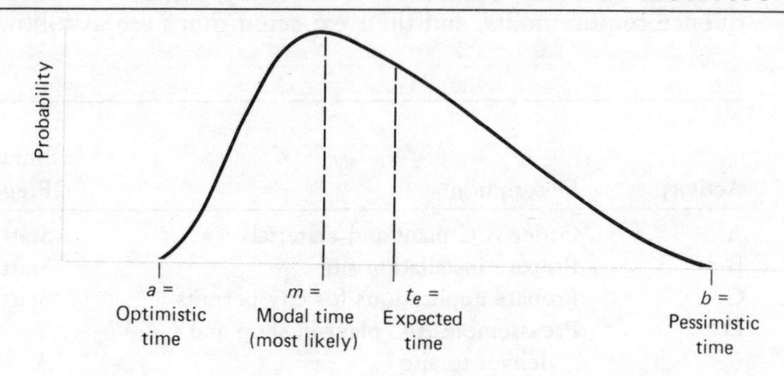


Probability theory provides the basis for applying probabilistic network concepts. First, the sum of a reasonably large number ($n > 30$) of identically distributed random variables is itself a random variable, but it is normally distributed even if the individual random variables are not. Second, the variance of the sum of statistically independent random variables is the sum of the variances of the original random variables.

Translated for network scheduling concepts, we have the following useful statements for large projects with independent activity times:

1. The mean completion time is the mean of a normal distribution, which is the simple sum of the $t_e$ values along a critical path.
2. The variance of the mean project completion time is the simple sum of the variances of the individual activities along a critical path.

We can now use the method described earlier to determine the critical path by substituting $t_e$ for the activity time. The mean and the variance of the project completion time are obtained by summing $t_e$ and $\sigma^2$, respectively, for the activities on the critical path.

We can then use the normal tables to determine the probabilities for the occurrence of a given project completion time estimates. For example, the probability that a project will be completed in less than the mean time is only .50. The probability that a project will be completed in less than the mean time plus one standard deviation is about .84; in less than the mean time plus two standard deviations, .98; and so on.

## Simulation of PERT Networks

The procedure just described could give biased results (overstate the probability of project completion by a given date), particularly if the mean length of the critical path is close to the mean length of other paths that have higher variances. A simulation approach may provide better estimates in such situations.

As an example, assume a simple network involving only the seven activities required to install an air conditioning (A/C) plant. The seven activities, their sequence requirements, and their expected times are as follows:

| Activity | Description | Immediate Predecessors | Expected Time, Weeks |
|---|---|---|---|
| A | Order A/C plant and materials | Start | 4.4 |
| B | Prepare installation site | Start | 5.2 |
| C | Prepare applications for city permits | Start | 4.2 |
| D | Preassemble A/C plant in shop and deliver to site | A | 4.4 |
| E | Obtain city permits | C | 3.0 |
| F | Install ducting and electrical connections | A | 7.6 |
| G | Install A/C system | B, D, E | 4.2 |

The network diagram for the project is shown in Figure 11-10. The critical path can be determined by inspection because it is the longest time path through the network and there are only four paths. The four paths and their times are as follows:

| | |
|---|---|
| A—F | 12.0 weeks |
| B—G | 9.4 weeks |
| A—D—G | 13.0 weeks |
| C—E—G | 11.4 weeks |

The longest time path is A–D–G, requiring 13 weeks. The most important activities to monitor are therefore "Order A/C plant and materials," "Preassemble A/C plant in shop and deliver to site," and "Install A/C system."

We now substitute independent empirical probability distributions for the deterministic activity times, assuming that the beta distribution is not a good approximation to reality. These empirical distributions are superimposed on the network diagram in Figure 11-11. Note that the expected times were calculated directly from these distributions. For example, the expected time for activity B is $.2 \times 4 + .4 \times 5 + .4 \times 6 = 5.2$ weeks.

We can simulate the execution of the network using Monte Carlo sampling (see Chapter 9) of the activity times from each of the distributions. After having drawn a set of simulated activity times at random, we can determine the critical path for that set of activity times, noting the path time and the total project time. By repeating the simulation for a large number of cycles, we can estimate the expected completion time and the probability of a shorter or longer project time.

## SELECTION OF RANDOM NUMBERS

For activity A in Figure 11-11, the assumed probability of a time of 4 weeks is .6, so only random numbers 1 through 6 will result in a time of 4 weeks. The probability that activity A will require 5 weeks is .4, so the random numbers 7 through 0 are

FIGURE 11-10
**NETWORK DIAGRAM FOR THE AIR CONDITIONER PROJECT, WITH DETERMINISTIC ACTIVITY TIMES.**

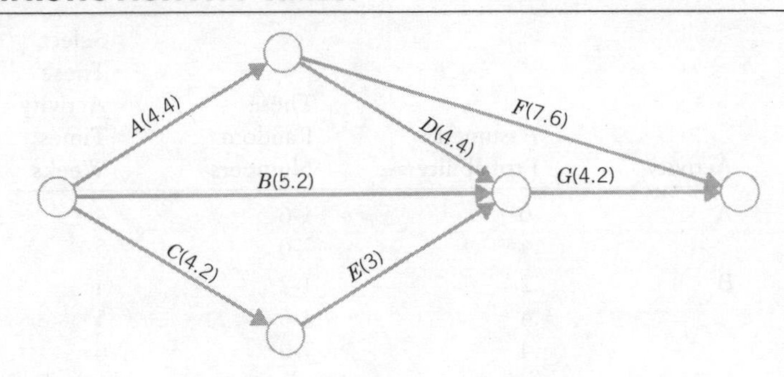


assigned. Table 11-2 shows the random number equivalents for the empirical distributions of all seven activities.

### NETWORK SIMULATION

To simulate the network, we select sets of seven random numbers from Table 5 in the Appendix. For example, a set of random numbers drawn and the equivalent activity times are as follows:

| Activity | A | B | C | D | E | F | G |
|---|---|---|---|---|---|---|---|
| Random number drawn | 7 | 8 | 7 | 1 | 2 | 3 | 8 |
| Activity time | 5 | 6 | 5 | 3 | 2 | 7 | 5 |

FIGURE 11-11
**NETWORK DIAGRAM WITH ACTIVITY TIMES REPRESENTED AS PROBABILITY DISTRIBUTIONS.**

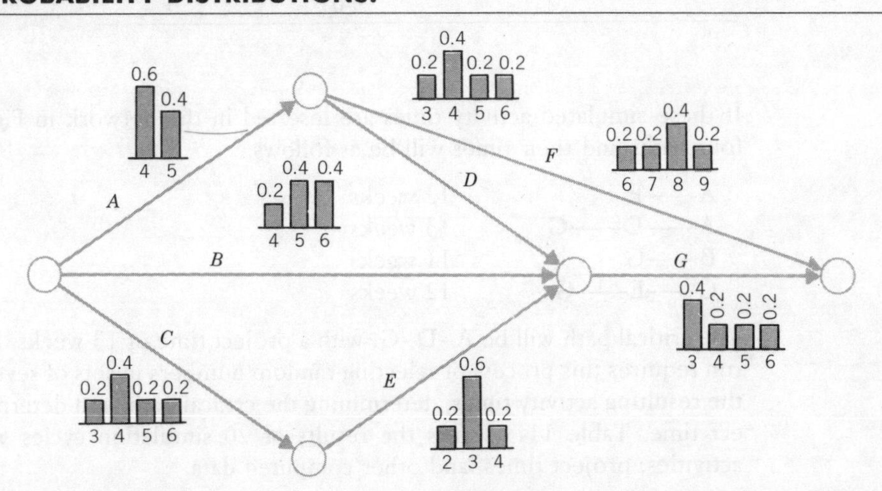

TABLE 11-2
**RANDOM NUMBER EQUIVALENTS FOR SEVEN NETWORK ACTIVITIES**

| Activity | Assumed Probability | These Random Numbers | Select These Activity Times, Weeks |
|---|---|---|---|
| A | .6 | 1-6 | 4 |
| | .4 | 7-0 | 5 |
| B | .2 | 1-2 | 4 |
| | .4 | 3-6 | 5 |
| | .4 | 7-0 | 6 |
| C | .2 | 1-2 | 3 |
| | .4 | 3-6 | 4 |
| | .2 | 7-8 | 5 |
| | .2 | 9-0 | 6 |
| D | .2 | 1-2 | 3 |
| | .4 | 3-6 | 4 |
| | .2 | 7-8 | 5 |
| | .2 | 9-0 | 6 |
| E | .2 | 1-2 | 2 |
| | .6 | 3-8 | 3 |
| | .2 | 9-0 | 4 |
| F | .2 | 1-2 | 6 |
| | .2 | 3-4 | 7 |
| | .4 | 5-8 | 8 |
| | .2 | 9-0 | 9 |
| G | .4 | 1-4 | 3 |
| | .2 | 5-6 | 4 |
| | .2 | 7-8 | 5 |
| | .2 | 9-0 | 6 |

If these simulated activity times are inserted in the network in Figure 11-11, the four paths and their times will be as follows:

| | |
|---|---|
| A——F | 12 weeks |
| A——D——G | 13 weeks |
| B——G | 11 weeks |
| C——E——G | 12 weeks |

The critical path will be A–D–G, with a project time of 13 weeks. Each simulation run requires this process of selecting random numbers in sets of seven, determining the resulting activity times, determining the critical path, and determining the project time. Table 11-3 shows the results of 20 simulation cycles with the critical activities, project times, and other computed data.

TABLE 11-3
**SIMULATION OF 20 TRIALS FOR THE AIR CONDITIONER PLANT INSTALLATION PROJECT COMPLETION TIME**

| Simulation Cycle Number | *Sampled Activity Times (*Indicates "On Critical Path")* A | B | C | D | E | F | G | Project Completion Time |
|---|---|---|---|---|---|---|---|---|
| 1 | 5* | 6 | 4 | 4 | 3 | 8* | 3 | 13 |
| 2 | 5* | 6 | 5 | 3* | 2 | 7 | 5* | 13 |
| 3 | 5* | 5 | 4 | 6* | 2 | 8 | 5* | 16 |
| 4 | 5* | 5 | 5 | 4* | 3 | 6 | 3* | 12 |
| 5 | 5* | 6 | 3 | 3 | 3 | 9* | 4 | 14 |
| 6 | 5 | 4 | 6* | 3 | 3* | 7 | 6* | 15 |
| 7 | 5* | 6 | 5 | 5* | 4 | 8 | 5* | 15 |
| 8 | 4* | 4 | 3 | 6* | 3 | 6 | 5* | 15 |
| 9[a] | 5* | 5 | 6* | 4* | 3* | 6 | 3* | 12 |
| 10 | 5* | 5 | 6 | 5* | 3 | 6 | 3* | 13 |
| 11 | 4 | 6 | 6* | 4 | 3* | 8 | 4* | 13 |
| 12 | 5* | 5 | 4 | 5* | 4 | 8 | 5* | 15 |
| 13 | 4 | 5 | 5* | 3 | 3* | 7 | 6* | 14 |
| 14[a] | 5* | 6 | 4 | 4* | 3 | 7* | 3* | 12 |
| 15 | 5* | 5 | 3 | 4* | 2 | 6 | 6* | 15 |
| 16 | 5* | 5 | 4 | 4* | 4 | 6 | 3* | 12 |
| 17 | 4 | 5 | 6* | 3 | 3* | 8 | 4* | 13 |
| 18 | 4* | 6 | 6 | 6* | 3 | 6 | 6* | 16 |
| 19 | 5* | 5 | 4 | 3 | 3 | 7* | 3 | 11 |
| 20[a] | 4* | 4 | 4 | 6* | 3 | 9* | 3* | 13 |
| Number of Times Critical | 16 | 0 | 5 | 13 | 5 | 5 | 17 | 273 |
| Critical Ratio | 0.80 | 0.0 | 0.25 | 0.65 | 0.25 | 0.25 | 0.85 | |

Average project completion time = 273/20 = 13.65 weeks

[a] Note that on simulation cycles 9, 14, and 20, there were *two* critical paths. For cycle 9, *A–D–G* and *C–E–G* were both critical with the same project completion time of 12 weeks. For cycles 14 and 20, the critical paths *A–D–G* and *A–F* have the same project completion times.

## INTERPRETATION OF RESULTS

The average simulated project time is 13.65 weeks, ranging from 12 to 16 weeks. This information is in itself useful to a manager, but the bottom of Table 11-3 has additional information in the form of the number of times that each activity was critical and the critical ratio.

The critical ratio is the proportion of cycles for which each activity is critical, which is an estimate of the probability that the activity will be critical. Note, for example, that activity F has a critical ratio of only .25, whereas activity G has a critical ratio of .85. Activity B was never on the critical path, so it has a critical ratio of 0.

The critical ratios provide new and valuable information to the manager. Activities A, D, and G should receive the most attention because they are likely to be critical in a high proportion of instances. A larger number of cycles would refine these initial estimates of project completion time and critical ratios. With larger, more complex networks and the need for a large sample, network simulation requires the use of a computer.

## DEPLOYMENT OF RESOURCES

PERT/CPM estimates of the project completion time assume that the resources needed to carry out the activities according to the schedule are available. It is therefore important to understand that PERT/CPM estimates of project completion time are lower bounds that may not be attainable with limited resources. Several useful extensions of basic PERT/CPM methods are possible when the availability and cost of resources influence project scheduling decisions.

### Activity Time/Cost Trade-off Analysis

Consider the simple project for which the pertinent data and the activities on a node diagram are given in Figure 11-12. The table below the network diagram indicates, for example, that activity C normally requires 6 months; however, with additional resources this activity can be completed in less than 6 months. Each month of reduction in the activity time of C will cost $6000, and the minimum possible time for C (the crash time) is 3 months.

The objective in an activity time/cost trade-off analysis is to compute the trade-off between project completion time and the additional cost of resources that are needed to achieve it. In our example, there are two paths A–B–D and A–C–D. If we use the normal activity time, then this project can be completed in 20 months (critical path A–C–D) without any additional cost. To finish the project in 19 months, either activity C or activity D must be reduced by 1 month. (No reduction in A is permissible.) Since it is cheaper to reduce C, the project completion time of 19 months can be achieved by completing C in 5 months. The additional cost of this reduction will be $6000. Now, both paths A–B–D and A–C–D are critical. We have two choices:

Reduce D at a cost of $12,000/month

Reduce B *and* C at a combined cost of $16,000/month

Activity D is reduced by one month with the following results:

| | | |
|---|---|---|
| Project completion time | = | 18 months |
| Additional cost | = | $6,000 + $12,000 = $18,000 |
| New critical paths | = | A——B——D, A——C——D |

FIGURE 11-12
**ACTIVITY TIME/COST TRADE-OFF ANALYSIS EXAMPLE.**

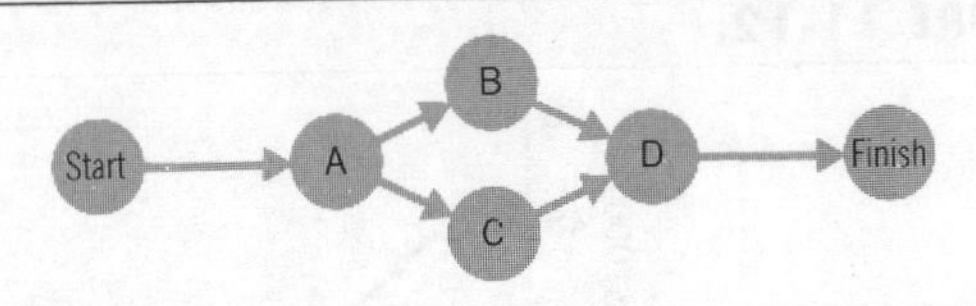


| Activity | Normal Time, Months | Crash Time, Months | Cost of Crashing One Month ($1000) |
|---|---|---|---|
| A | 6 | 6 | — |
| B | 5 | 4 | 10 |
| C | 6 | 3 | 6 |
| D | 8 | 6 | 12 |

Again, activity D is reduced by one month:

Project completion time = 17 months
Additional cost = $18,000 + $12,000 = $30,000
New critical paths = A—B—D, A—C—D

To further reduce the project completion time, both B and C must be reduced since D is at its minimum possible time:

Project completion time = 16 months
Additional cost = $30,000 + $16,000 = $46,000
New critical paths = A—B—D, A—C—D

No further reduction in the project completion time is possible since all the activities in critical path A–B–D are at their minimum possible time. The trade-off curve between the project completion time and the additional costs is plotted in Figure 11-13. This trade-off curve can be used to answer a variety of managerial questions. For example, if each month of reduction in project completion time saves the company $10,000, then it is worthwhile to reduce the project duration to 19 months but not below 19 months as the additional cost of further reduction is $12,000, which is more than the $10,000 savings.

The incremental procedure to adjust activity time for producing the time/cost trade-off curve does not necessarily provide an optimal solution. The following linear program needs to be solved in order to guarantee the lowest additional cost for completing the project by a specified target date.

$n_j$ = Normal time for activity J
$m_j$ = Crash time for activity J
$s_j$ = Cost per unit time of reduction for activity J
$y_j$ = number of units of time (e.g., months in our example) by which activity J is shortened
$x_j$ = Finish time for activity J

FIGURE 11-13
**ACTIVITY TIME/COST TRADE-OFF CURVE FOR THE PROBLEM IN FIGURE 11-12.**

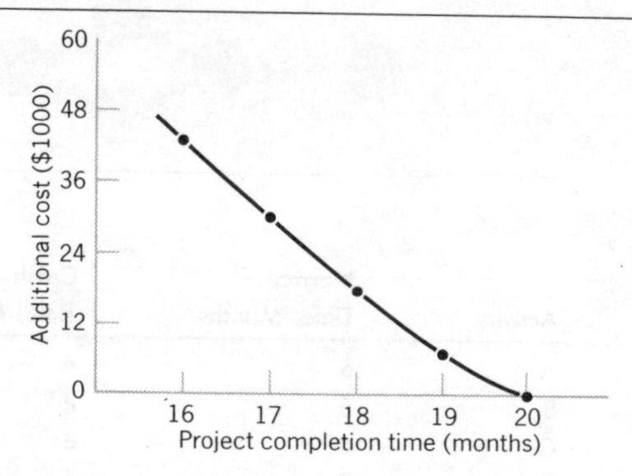


Then, we wish to minimize the cost of crashing subject to the precedence constraints, the target date completion time constraint, and constraints on amount of crashing permitted. For the problem in Figure 11-13, the minimum cost solution for a target completion time of $T$ will be given by the solution of the linear program:

$$\text{Minimize } s_a y_a + s_b y_b + s_c y_c + s_d y_d$$

Subject to

$$\left.\begin{aligned} x_d &\geq x_b + n_d - y_d \\ x_d &\geq x_c + n_d - y_d \\ x_b &\geq x_a + n_b - y_b \\ x_c &\geq x_a + n_c - y_c \\ x_a &\geq n_a - y_a \end{aligned}\right\} \quad \text{(precedence constraints)}$$

$$x_d \leq T \quad \text{(target date constraint)}$$

$$\left.\begin{aligned} y_d &\leq n_d - m_d \\ y_c &\leq n_c - m_c \\ y_b &\leq n_b - m_b \\ y_a &\leq n_a - m_a \end{aligned}\right\} \quad \text{(constraints on amount of crashing permitted)}$$

To construct the time/cost trade-off curve, parameter $T$ is varied. The linear programming approach may be computationally expensive for a large network.

## Resource Smoothing or Load Leveling

In some applications, it may be desirable to minimize the fluctuations in the use of a resource from one period to the next. If we schedule all activities at their earliest start times, it is quite possible that a larger amount of resources will be needed in the early periods and that relatively lower amounts will be needed in the later periods. The specified project completion time could be achieved by shifting some of the activities so that the profile of resource requirements over time is level or has less fluctuation. Such load leveling has the objective of reducing idle labor costs, hiring and separation costs, or the cost of any resource that may be affected by fluctuations in the demand for its use, such as equipment rental.

For simple projects, a scheduler might use activity slack for smoothing peak resource requirements. However, for large and complex projects, a computer-based leveling model may be required.

### Resource Constrained Project Scheduling

In many project situations, resources are available only in fixed amounts. For example, pieces of machinery, the number of design engineers, the budget that can be spent per month, and the like may be limited. The managerial objective in such situations is to minimize the project completion time while not exceeding the given limits on available resources. Since the activities that compete for the same limited resource cannot be scheduled simultaneously, the effect of resource constraints will often be to delay the project completion date relative to the completion date that could be achieved without such restrictions.

An optimal solution for the project completion time with resource constraints requires an integer program that is difficult to solve for practical-sized projects. Several heuristics have been developed and compared (see Davis and Patterson, 1975, for their relative effectiveness). The underlying strategy of these heuristics is to schedule activities on a period-by-period basis so as not to exceed the resource limits. If all eligible activities can not be scheduled due to a resource limit, a *rule* is used to decide which activities should be scheduled and which should be postponed. An example of such a rule is *minimum activity slack*. Using this rule, priority in scheduling is given to those activities with the least slack (slack = latest start time − earliest start time in the critical path analysis). Activity slack is updated in each period to reflect the change in the available slack resulting from the postponement of individual activities. This rule provided the optimal solution in 24 out of 83 test problems in the Davis and Patterson study. Further, it produced the least average percent increase in project duration over the optimal duration (5 to 6 percent above optimum), as compared with several other rules.

## ORGANIZATIONAL STRUCTURES

Given a single project, the manager organizes around the needs of that project, with all functional organizational units focused on achieving the project objectives. The organizational structure is then comparable with the functional organization commonly used in industry. Organizational problems begin when we add a second project. Multiple projects suggest resource sharing with the obvious advantages of better utilization. But how will the resources be shared? By what schedule? Who will decide these issues if there are two project managers? These problems could be solved by simply duplicating the resources and making the two projects independent, but the potential economy advantages of the larger scale of operations would be lost.

FIGURE 11-14
**STRUCTURE OF A MATRIX ORGANIZATION FOR PROJECT MANAGEMENT.**

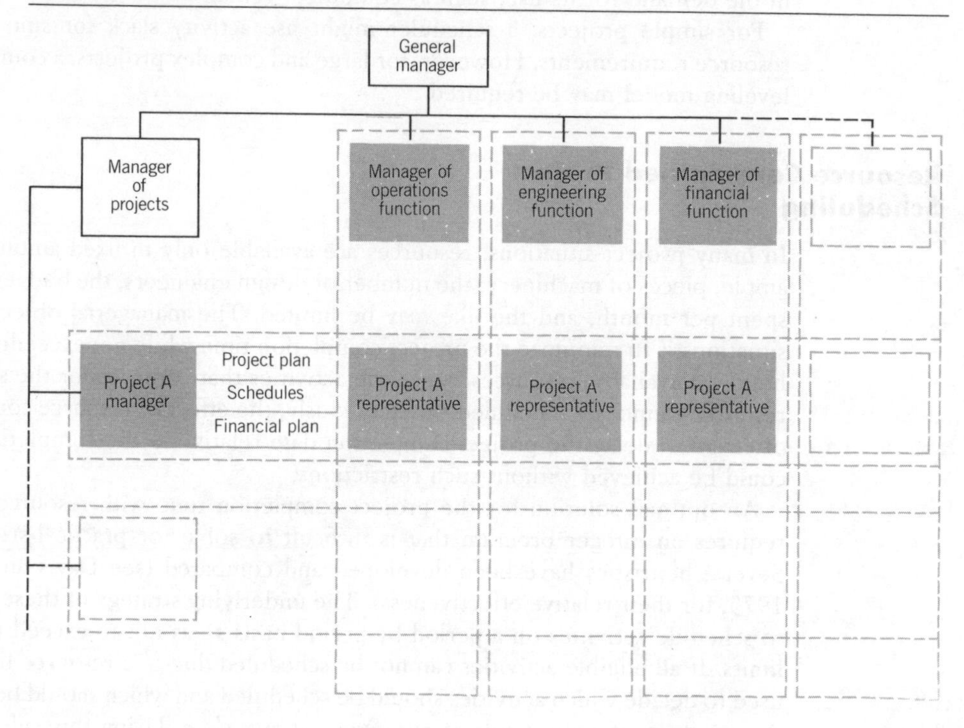


The common organizational form for multiple projects is the matrix organization. Figure 11-14 shows the concept of the matrix organization with the functional managers holding the resources and each project manager coordinating the use of the designated resources for each project. The advantages of the matrix organization are in the efficient use of resources, the coordination across functional departments, and the visibility of project objectives. The disadvantages are in the need for coordination between functional and project managers and the often unbearable situation of the person in the middle (the project representative) who is working for two bosses. Vertically, this person reports to the functional manager, but horizontally the project manager is the boss. If conflicts occur, the person in the middle may be caught there.

## THE PROJECT MANAGER

The nature of the organizational structures for project management and the one-time nature of the projects create a difficult situation for the project manager. The project manager has less than full authority over the project, being in the position of bargaining for resources and their timing with functional managers. At the same time, the uniqueness of each project creates problems that often cannot be foreseen. These problems commonly result in schedule slippage, replanning, and the possible reallocation of resources in order to maintain the project completion schedule.

If the project manager focuses his or her attention on one critical area to the neglect of other important areas, the secondary areas may become critical problems. In short, the project manager must cope with short deadlines, changing situations, rapid-fire decision making, incomplete information, and skimpy authority. The position has all the potential for being one of simply "putting out fires." The issues, then, are to devise means for remaining in control.

Thanhain and Wilemon (1975) report on interviews with 100 project managers concerning the primary sources of conflict during a project. The results indicate the following sources of conflict in three broad phases of a project.

1. *Planning Stage.* Priorities, the required activities, and their sequencing.
2. *Buildup Stage.* Priorities, with the scheduling of activities becoming very important.
3. *Execution.* Scheduling of activities is the primary source of conflict, with the issues concerning the trade-off of the use of resources versus time performance also being very important.

The foregoing typical issues focus on problems of planning, scheduling, and controlling activities. For project managers to remain in control, they need mechanisms that provide a clear logic for planning, a detailed schedule that can be easily updated for all activities, and mechanisms for resource trade-offs. The network planning and scheduling methods discussed in this chapter meet these special needs.

## IMPLICATIONS FOR THE MANAGER

Large-scale projects present managers with unique problems. The managerial issues are rather different from those of the typical manufacturing system. The project manager's problems center on the detailed schedule of activities and a preoccupation with the completion dates of activities, resource budgets, and the project completion date.

The position of project manager requires a particular "breed of cat." A project manager must be someone who can deal with changing deadlines, immediate decisions, and skimpy information, all in a general environment of divided authority. The managerial situation requires special concepts and techniques, and network planning and control systems are the best available today.

Davis (1974a) surveyed the top 400 construction firms and found over 80 percent of the 235 respondents were using network planning methods. Thus, it seems clear that many managers have recognized the practical value of network methods; they are not simply theoretical concepts.

Managers need to be involved in formulating the initial network. Perhaps a majority of the benefits of network methods comes at the planning stage. Given the network and time estimates, managers can have a number of computer runs made to assess alternate plans that involve cost/time trade-offs and resource smoothing. This interaction between the manager and the network model can have enormous benefits.

The control phases of network methods are the most costly. Smaller projects may not justify the cost of obtaining updated information and the periodic rescheduling needed for control. Davis also reported that the primary use of network methods in the construction industry was for project planning rather than for control.

## REVIEW QUESTIONS

1. What are the characteristics of large-scale projects that focus managerial efforts on the detailed scheduling of activities and on project completion dates?
2. In the context of the "activities on arcs" planning methods, define the following terms: activity, event, node, and critical path.
3. For "arcs" planning methods, discuss and interrelate the following three phases:
   a. Activity analysis
   b. Network diagramming
   c. Node numbering
4. What are the functions of dummy activities in an "arcs" network diagram?
5. What is the convention for numbering nodes in an "arcs" network? Why is this convention used?
6. Why must activity networks be noncyclical?
7. Define the following terms: early start (*ES*), early finish (*EF*), latest start (*LS*), latest finish (*LF*), and slack.
8. Outline the procedure for the manual computation of schedule statistics.
9. What are the differences in the construction of the network diagram between the "arcs" and "nodes" methodologies? How can the probabilistic network model provide additional data that are helpful for managerial decisions?
10. Define the following terms as they are used in probabilistic PERT networks: optimistic time, pessimistic time, most likely time, and expected time.
11. Why is the PERT estimate of project completion time biased?
12. Outline the procedure for the manual computation of the activity time/cost trade-off curve.
13. What is meant by load leveling? How may it be accomplished?
14. Provide a rule other than the minimum activity slack rule for scheduling activities when resources are limited.
15. Why is the matrix type of organizational structure used in project management?

TABLE 11-4
**ACTIVITIES, SEQUENCE, AND TIME REQUIREMENTS FOR THE INSTALLATION OF A GAS-FORCED AIR FURNACE**

| Activity Code | Activity Description | Immediate Predecessor Activity | Time, Days |
|---|---|---|---|
| A | Start | — | 0 |
| B | Obtain delivery of furnace unit | A | 10 |
| C | Delivery of piping | A | 5 |
| D | Delivery of dampers and grilles | F | 14 |
| E | Delivery of duct work | F | 10 |
| F | Design duct layout | A | 2 |
| G | Install ducts and dampers | D, E | 12 |
| H | Install grilles | G | 1 |
| I | Install furnace unit | B | 1 |
| J | Install gas piping | C | 5 |
| K | Connect gas pipes to furnace | I, J | 0.5 |
| L | Install electric wiring | B | 2 |
| M | Install controls and connect to electrical system | I, L | 1 |
| N | Test installation | H, K, M | 0.5 |
| O | Clean up | N | 0.5 |

# PROBLEMS

16. Table 11-4 provides data for the project of installing a gas-forced air furnace.
    a. Develop an activity on arc network diagram for the project.
    b. Develop an activity on node network diagram for the project.
    c. Using the manual computation algorithm, compute the following schedule statistics for the furnace installation project:
        (1) *ES*, *EF*, *LS*, *LF* for each activity
        (2) Total slack for each activity
        (3) Free slack for each activity
        (4) Critical path
        (5) Project completion time
17. A simple network consisting of four activities has the following network diagram:

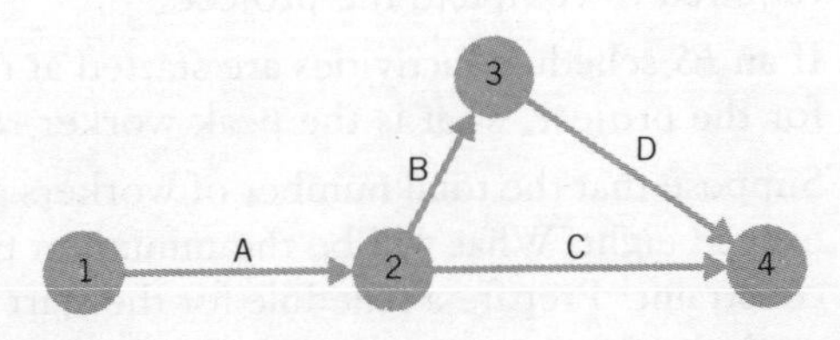

The cost/time relationship for the activities are as follows:

| Activity | Minimum Time, Weeks | Maximum Time, Weeks | Cost/Time Relationship ($1000) |
|---|---|---|---|
| A | 5 | 10 | 100 − (3 × activity time) |
| B | 5 | 10 | 100 − (2 × activity time) |
| C | 10 | 30 | 100 − (2 × activity time) |
| D | 10 | 15 | 100 − (5 × activity time) |

For example, activity A, if completed in 5 weeks would require $85,000, and if completed in 10 weeks, it would require $70,000.

a. What would be the minimum cost of completing this project in 20 weeks?

b. If the desired due date is 33 weeks and the profit mark-up is 20 percent above cost, what should be the bidding price for the project?

c. Suppose a linear program is to be used to obtain the minimum cost schedule for the project completion time of 33 weeks. Formulate the linear program.

18. An arcs diagram for a project is as follows:

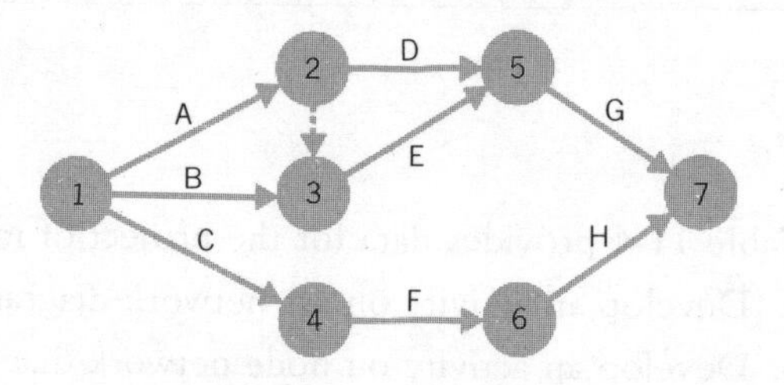


The estimates of completion time for each activity and the number of workers that each activity requires every day are as follows. Activity times cannot be reduced by applying more workers.

| Activity | A | B | C | D | E | F | G | H |
|---|---|---|---|---|---|---|---|---|
| Time (days) | 5 | 3 | 6 | 3 | 4 | 2 | 4 | 2 |
| Number of workers | 4 | 2 | 6 | 5 | 3 | 3 | 4 | 3 |

a. What is the minimum project completion time? How many worker-days are required to complete the project?

b. If an *ES* schedule (activities are started at the earliest start time) is followed for the project, what is the peak worker requirement?

c. Suppose that the total number of workers available on any given day cannot exceed eight. What will be the minimum project completion time with this constraint? Prepare a schedule for the start and finish of each activity for this project.

19. Listed in Table 11-5 is a set of activities, sequence requirements, and estimated activity times for a pipeline renewal project. Figure 11-15 provides the computer output for the project.
    a. Which activities can be delayed beyond the *ES* times without delaying the project completion time of 65 days? Which activities can be delayed without delaying the *ES* of any other activity?
    b. For the data of the pipeline renewal project, suppose that activity H is delayed 12 days. What is the total slack remaining for activity I? What is the remaining free slack for activity I?
    c. Suppose that activity H is not delayed, but I is delayed 14 days. Which activity or activities will be affected? How, and by how many days?
    d. Activity K in the pipeline renewal project is delayed by 2 days. Which activities are affected? How, and by how many days?
    e. In Table 11-6 there is additional information in the form of optimistic, most likely, and pessimistic time estimates for the pipeline renewal project. Compute the expected value and variance of the project completion time.

TABLE 11-5
**ACTIVITIES, SEQUENCE REQUIREMENTS, AND TIMES FOR THE RENEWAL OF A PIPELINE**

| Activity | Activity Code | Code of Immediate Predecessor | Activity Time Requirement (days) | Crew Requirements per Day |
|---|---|---|---|---|
| Assemble crew for job | A | — | 10 | — |
| Use old line to build inventory | B | — | 28 | — |
| Measure and sketch old line | C | A | 2 | — |
| Develop materials list | D | C | 1 | — |
| Erect scaffold | E | D | 2 | 10 |
| Procure pipe | F | D | 30 | — |
| Procure valves | G | D | 45 | — |
| Deactivate old line | H | B, D | 1 | 6 |
| Remove old line | I | E, H | 6 | 3 |
| Prefabricate new pipe | J | F | 5 | 20 |
| Place valves | K | E, G, H | 1 | 6 |
| Place new pipe | L | I, J | 6 | 25 |
| Weld pipe | M | L | 2 | 1 |
| Connect valves | N | K, M | 1 | 6 |
| Insulate | O | K, M | 4 | 5 |
| Pressure test | P | N | 1 | 3 |
| Remove scaffold | Q | N, O | 1 | 6 |
| Clean up and turn over to operating crew | R | P, Q | 1 | 6 |

FIGURE 11-15
**COMPUTER OUTPUT SHOWING THE CRITICAL PATH AND THE SCHEDULE STATISTICS FOR THE PIPELINE RENEWAL PROJECT.**

*THE CRITICAL PATH IS*

*START → A → C → D → G → K → O → Q → R → FINISH*

*THE LENGTH OF THE CRITICAL PATH IS 65*

| *NODE* | *DURATION* | *EARLY START* | *EARLY FINISH* | *LATE START* | *LATE FINISH* | *TOTAL SLACK* | *FREE SLACK* |
|---|---|---|---|---|---|---|---|
| *START* | 0.00 | 0.00 | 0.00 | 0.00 | 0.00 | 0.00 | 0.00 |
| A | 10.00 | 0.00 | 10.00 | 0.00 | 10.00 | 0.00 | 0.00 |
| B | 28.00 | 0.00 | 28.00 | 16.00 | 44.00 | 16.00 | 0.00 |
| C | 2.00 | 10.00 | 12.00 | 10.00 | 12.00 | 0.00 | 0.00 |
| D | 1.00 | 12.00 | 13.00 | 12.00 | 13.00 | 0.00 | 0.00 |
| E | 2.00 | 13.00 | 15.00 | 43.00 | 45.00 | 30.00 | 14.00 |
| F | 30.00 | 13.00 | 43.00 | 16.00 | 46.00 | 3.00 | 0.00 |
| G | 45.00 | 13.00 | 58.00 | 13.00 | 58.00 | 0.00 | 0.00 |
| H | 1.00 | 28.00 | 29.00 | 44.00 | 45.00 | 16.00 | 0.00 |
| I | 6.00 | 29.00 | 35.00 | 45.00 | 51.00 | 16.00 | 13.00 |
| J | 5.00 | 43.00 | 48.00 | 46.00 | 51.00 | 3.00 | 0.00 |
| K | 1.00 | 58.00 | 59.00 | 58.00 | 59.00 | 0.00 | 0.00 |
| L | 6.00 | 48.00 | 54.00 | 51.00 | 57.00 | 3.00 | 0.00 |
| M | 2.00 | 54.00 | 56.00 | 57.00 | 59.00 | 3.00 | 3.00 |
| N | 1.00 | 59.00 | 60.00 | 62.00 | 63.00 | 3.00 | 0.00 |
| O | 4.00 | 59.00 | 63.00 | 59.00 | 63.00 | 0.00 | 0.00 |
| P | 1.00 | 60.00 | 61.00 | 63.00 | 64.00 | 3.00 | 3.00 |
| Q | 1.00 | 63.00 | 64.00 | 63.00 | 64.00 | 0.00 | 0.00 |
| R | 1.00 | 64.00 | 65.00 | 64.00 | 65.00 | 0.00 | 0.00 |
| *FINISH* | 0.00 | 65.00 | 65.00 | 65.00 | 65.00 | 0.00 | 0.00 |

# SITUATIONS

## Pipeline Renewal Company

20. The manager of the Pipeline Renewal Company has always operated on the basis of having detailed knowledge of the required activities. The manager learned the business from the ground up, seemingly having faced virtually all possible crisis types. The network diagram made good sense, but the manager was really intrigued with the schedule statistics that could be derived from the network and the associated activity times.

The manager was bidding on the project for which Table 11-5 represents the basic data. The schedule statistics shown in Figure 11-15 were developed. The estimated times were felt to be realistic and achievable, based on past experience. The bidding was competitive, and time performance was an important

TABLE 11-6
**TIME ESTIMATES FOR THE PIPELINE RENEWAL PROJECT**

| Activity Code | Optimistic Time Estimate ($a$) | Most Likely Time Estimate ($m$) | Pessimistic Time Estimate ($b$) | Expected Time Estimate ($t_e$) |
|---|---|---|---|---|
| A | 8 | 10 | 12 | 10 |
| B | 26 | 26.5 | 36 | 28 |
| C | 1 | 2 | 3 | 2 |
| D | 0.5 | 1 | 1.5 | 1 |
| E | 1.5 | 1.63 | 4 | 2 |
| F | 28 | 28 | 40 | 30 |
| G | 40 | 42.5 | 60 | 45 |
| H | 1 | 1 | 1 | 1 |
| I | 4 | 6 | 8 | 6 |
| J | 4 | 4.5 | 8 | 5 |
| K | 0.5 | 0.9 | 2 | 1 |
| L | 5 | 5.25 | 10 | 6 |
| M | 1 | 2 | 3 | 2 |
| N | 0.5 | 1 | 1.5 | 1 |
| O | 3 | 3.75 | 6 | 4 |
| P | 1 | 1 | 1 | 1 |
| Q | 1 | 1 | 1 | 1 |
| R | 1 | 1 | 1 | 1 |

factor because the pipeline operator would lose some revenue, in spite of the fact that an inventory was developed in activity B, since storage was limited. As a result of these facts, it is common to negotiate penalties for late performance in pipeline renewal contracts.

Because of the uncertainties and risks, the manager estimated the values for $a$, $m$, and $b$ and computed the values for $t_e$ shown in Table 11-6. The manager decided that an attractive completion date would be likely to win the contract. Therefore, the bid promised completion in 70 days, with penalties of $100 per day if the actual completion time was greater than 65 days and $200 per day if it was greater than 70 days. The contract was awarded, Has the manager got a good deal? How likely are the penalties?

After the contract was awarded, the manager became depressed because 5 days were immediately lost because he could not start the job on time due to the interference of other contracts on which he was working. The manager generated the following possible actions to recover schedule time:

a. Shorten the $t_e$ of activity B by 4 days at a cost of $100.

b. Shorten the $t_e$ of activity G by 5 days at a cost of $50.

c. Shorten the $t_e$ of activity A by 2 days at a cost of $150.

d. Shorten the $t_e$ of activity O by 2 days by drawing resources from activity *N*, thereby lengthening its $t_e$ by 2 days.

What should the manager do?

## Pipeline Renewal Company: Labor Deployment Problem

21. The manager of the Pipeline Renewal Company is now concerned with resource utilization. Along with other data, Table 11-5 gives the normal crew requirements per day for each of the activities. By relating this to the *ES* schedule given in Figure 11-15, the manager developed the labor deployment chart shown in Figure 11-16.

    Based on past experience, the manager was aware of the "lumpy" nature of the demand for worker-days on renewal projects. Figure 11-16 verified and dramatized the situation.

    The nature of most of the tasks and skill levels was such that a generalized crew was used that could do all the tasks with few exceptions. For example, activity L has a crew requirement of 25 workers for 6 days, or 150 worker-days. These 150 worker-days may be allocated over many chosen activity times, such as 10 workers for 15 days, or vice versa. The generalized crew provided great flexibility, allowing the reallocation of labor among projects being carried on simultaneously. Also, adjustments for absences or vacations were relatively simple.

    The manager is now thinking of alternatives to Figure 11-16 as ways of allocating labor to projects. There are a number of reasons for being dissatisfied with the current mode of operation. First, the lumpy nature of the typical situation shown in Figure 11-16 often results in idle crew time because of the mismatch between crew sizes and activity times. The company absorbs this idle time. Second, because of mismatches and schedule slippage, it is often necessary to work the crews overtime to meet deadlines. Third, the lumpy nature of demand often results in layoffs or in short-term hiring, with the usual costs of fluctuation in work force size. In addition, the layoffs are a source of discontent among the crews.

    In working with the alternatives, the manager has become aware that some alternatives result in changes in activity times that sometimes affect the critical path. The manager is impressed, however, by the fact that schedule slack can be used to good effect in generating alternatives to Figure 11-16.

    What alternate labor deployment do you recommend? Is the critical path affected by your recommendations?

## Contractor's Dilemma

22. Figure 11-17*a* is a nodes network diagram for a construction contract that shows the time in weeks to complete each activity and the normal schedule estimated costs for each activity. Figure 11-17*b* shows the computer output and indicates an overall project time of 11 weeks, the critical path, and the schedule statistics. The total contractor's cost is \$31,500, but the contract price is \$45,000.

    The contractor's problem is that the costs are based on a normal completion time of 11 weeks, but the customer insists on a completion time of 10 weeks and a penalty for late performance of \$2000 per week. The contract is attractive because it would provide the contractor with a \$13,500 profit. Therefore, the

FIGURE 11-16
**WORKER DEPLOYMENT FOR THE *ES* SCHEDULE USING NORMAL CREW REQUIREMENTS FOR THE PIPELINE RENEWAL PROJECT. ONLY ACTIVITIES REQUIRING THE CREW ARE SHOWN.**

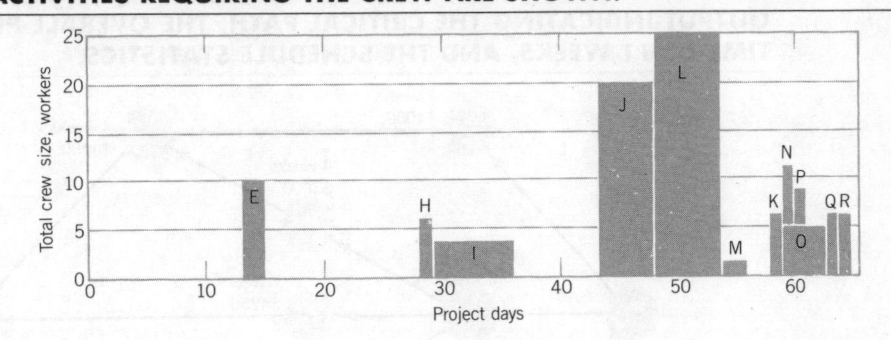


contractor is interested in alternatives that might achieve the 10-week delivery schedule.

The contractor develops cost/time data for several of the activities; the following list indicates the reduction in weeks and the incremental cost:

One week reduction in A, $1500

One week reduction in B, $6000

One week reduction in D, $2000

One week reduction in G, $1500; second week reduction, $2000

The contractor is aware that changes in the activity times are sometimes "tricky" because they may change the critical path. What action should the contractor take?

## Architect's Uncertainty[2]

23. An architect has been awarded a contract to prepare plans and specifications for an urban renewal project. The activities required, their sequencing requirements, and their estimated time requirements are as follows:

| Activity | Description | Immediate Predecessors | Estimated Time, Days |
|---|---|---|---|
| a | Preliminary sketches | — | 2 |
| b | Outline of specifications | — | 1 |
| c | Prepare drawings | a | 3 |
| d | Write specifications | a, b | 2 |
| e | Run off prints | c, d | 1 |
| f | Have specifications printed | c, d | 3 |
| g | Assemble bid packages | e, f | 1 |

[2]This situation requires the application of the concepts of the Monte Carlo simulation.

FIGURE 11-17
**CONSTRUCTION CONTRACT PROJECT: (a) CPM NETWORK DIAGRAM SHOWING TIME IN WEEKS FOR THE COMPLETION OF EACH ACTIVITY AND NORMAL SCHEDULE ACTIVITY COSTS, AND (b) THE COMPUTER OUTPUT INDICATING THE CRITICAL PATH, THE OVERALL PROJECT TIME OF 11 WEEKS, AND THE SCHEDULE STATISTICS.**

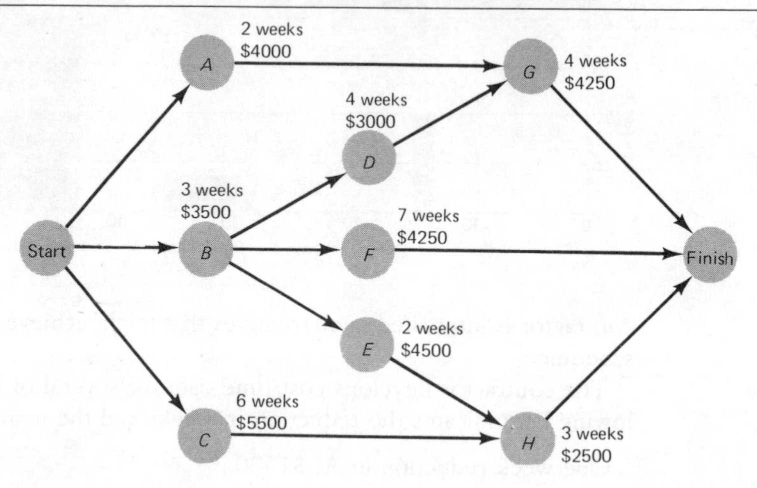


*THE CRITICAL PATH IS*

*START → B → D → G → FINISH*

*THE LENGTH OF THE CRITICAL PATH IS* 11

| *NODE* | *DURATION* | *EARLY START* | *EARLY FINISH* | *LATE START* | *LATE FINISH* | *TOTAL SLACK* | *FREE SLACK* |
|---|---|---|---|---|---|---|---|
| *START* | 0.00 | 0.00 | 0.00 | 0.00 | 0.00 | 0.00 | 0.00 |
| *A* | 2.00 | 0.00 | 2.00 | 5.00 | 7.00 | 5.00 | 5.00 |
| *B* | 3.00 | 0.00 | 3.00 | 0.00 | 3.00 | 0.00 | 0.00 |
| *C* | 6.00 | 0.00 | 6.00 | 2.00 | 8.00 | 2.00 | 0.00 |
| *D* | 4.00 | 3.00 | 7.00 | 3.00 | 7.00 | 0.00 | 0.00 |
| *E* | 2.00 | 3.00 | 5.00 | 6.00 | 8.00 | 3.00 | 1.00 |
| *F* | 7.00 | 3.00 | 10.00 | 4.00 | 11.00 | 1.00 | 1.00 |
| *G* | 4.00 | 7.00 | 11.00 | 7.00 | 11.00 | 0.00 | 0.00 |
| *H* | 3.00 | 6.00 | 9.00 | 8.00 | 11.00 | 2.00 | 2.00 |
| *FINISH* | 0.00 | 11.00 | 11.00 | 11.00 | 11.00 | 0.00 | 0.00 |

(b)

Figure 11-18 is a network diagram for the performance of the project using the deterministic activity times given and showing the critical path as a–c–f–g. The critical path may be identified by inspecting the paths through the network and establishing the critical path as the longest time path or paths.

The architect reexamines the estimated activity times because he is concerned about the effect of unanticipated events, which are common occurrences

FIGURE 11-18
**NETWORK DIAGRAM FOR THE URBAN RENEWAL PROJECT. CRITICAL PATH IS a–c–f–g.**

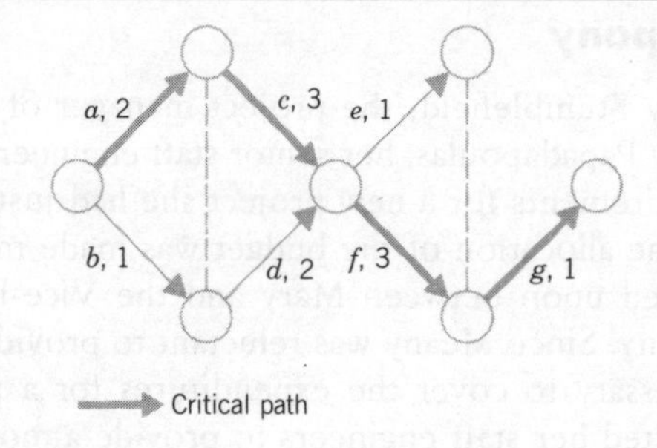


*THE CRITICAL PATH IS*

*START → B → D → G → FINISH*

*THE LENGTH OF THE CRITICAL PATH IS 11*

| *NODE* | *DURATION* | *EARLY START* | *EARLY FINISH* | *LATE START* | *LATE FINISH* | *TOTAL SLACK* | *FREE SLACK* |
|---|---|---|---|---|---|---|---|
| START | 0.00 | 0.00 | 0.00 | 0.00 | 0.00 | 0.00 | 0.00 |
| A | 2.00 | 0.00 | 2.00 | 5.00 | 7.00 | 5.00 | 5.00 |
| B | 3.00 | 0.00 | 3.00 | 0.00 | 3.00 | 0.00 | 0.00 |
| C | 6.00 | 0.00 | 6.00 | 2.00 | 8.00 | 2.00 | 0.00 |
| D | 4.00 | 3.00 | 7.00 | 3.00 | 7.00 | 0.00 | 0.00 |
| E | 2.00 | 3.00 | 5.00 | 6.00 | 8.00 | 3.00 | 1.00 |
| F | 7.00 | 3.00 | 10.00 | 4.00 | 11.00 | 1.00 | 1.00 |
| G | 4.00 | 7.00 | 11.00 | 7.00 | 11.00 | 0.00 | 0.00 |
| H | 3.00 | 6.00 | 9.00 | 8.00 | 11.00 | 2.00 | 2.00 |
| FINISH | 0.00 | 11.00 | 11.00 | 11.00 | 11.00 | 0.00 | 0.00 |

in his office. He comes up with three time estimates for each activity, together with the estimated probabilities of their occurrences as follows:

| | *Optimistic* | | *Estimated* | | *Pessimistic* | |
|---|---|---|---|---|---|---|
| Activity | Time | Probability | Time | Probability | Time | Probability |
| a | 1 | .1 | 2 | .6 | 4 | .3 |
| b | 0.5 | .1 | 1 | .5 | 2 | .4 |
| c | 2 | .2 | 3 | .6 | 5 | .2 |
| d | 1.5 | .1 | 2 | .6 | 3 | .3 |
| e | 0.5 | .1 | 1 | .8 | 1.5 | .1 |
| f | 2 | .3 | 3 | .4 | 4 | .3 |
| g | 0.5 | .1 | 1 | .7 | 1.5 | .2 |

The architect has agreed to finish the project in 10 days, with a $500 per day penalty for each additional day. What advice would you give the architect?

## Constrained Company

24. Mary Stumblefield, the project manager of the Constrained Company, asked Gary Papadapoulas, her senior staff engineer, to prepare a schedule and budget requirements for a new project she had just received.

The allocation of the budget was made monthly according to the time plan agreed upon between Mary and the Vice-President of Finance, Mr. George Meany. Since Meany was reluctant to provide funds for more than the amount necessary to cover the expenditures for a month at a time, Mary always requested her staff engineers to provide a monthly breakdown of costs.

Gary employed the usual procedure for activity analysis to break down the project into activities and obtained the estimates of costs for these activities. These data are shown in Table 11-7.

Gary prepared the following project schedule and monthly budget requirements and submitted them to Mary.

| Beginning of month | 1 | 2 | 3 | 4 | 5 | 6 | 7 | 8 | 9 | 10 |
|---|---|---|---|---|---|---|---|---|---|---|
| Start of activity | a | b, c d, e | — | h | g | f | i | j | — | — |
| Budget ($1000) | 70 | 130 | 130 | 110 | 90 | 160 | 170 | 100 | 100 | 100 |

Mary glanced at the budget and exclaimed, "No way will Meany accept this." Mary told Gary that Meany always tells her to arrange the schedule so as to reduce the expenditures during the initial periods as much as possible. This way, he argues, it is easier for him to obtain funds from the clients as the project

TABLE 11-7
**PROJECT DATA FOR CONSTRAINED COMPANY**

| Activity | Duration Months | Immediate Predecessor | Monthly Cost ($1000) |
|---|---|---|---|
| a | 1 | — | 70 |
| b | 4 | a | 10 |
| c | 3 | a | 40 |
| d | 2 | a | 30 |
| e | 2 | a | 50 |
| f | 2 | b | 80 |
| g | 2 | c | 20 |
| h | 3 | d | 60 |
| i | 1 | g, h | 90 |
| j | 3 | i, e | 100 |

progresses. "Besides," Mary said, "he always gives me a lecture on the present value of money and reminds me of the very high opportunity cost of funds, which he claims is three percent per month." Gary told Mary that he would do his best to revise the budget, but he reminded her that by postponing the start of some activities until later some flexibility would be lost.

After trying several schedules, Gary came up with the suggestion that activities *b* and *e* be postponed by a month, resulting in a postponement of 60,000 dollars in costs. Mary took the revised schedule to Meany for his approval.

Meany told Mary that this project falls in the "B" category and, therefore, no more than $100,000 can be allocated in any one month. "You, of course, also know the company policy that budget requests should be made strictly in accordance with the planned expenditures," he told her. This would mean that in the first month Mary cannot request $100,000 since the only scheduled activity is *a* and it requires $70,000. Mary's reaction was that the stipulated project completion time of one year could not be met under these budget constraints. She also knew of the penalty clause of $1,000 per month delay in the project beyond the due date of one year.

Mary wandered back to her office, wondering whether there might be a good planning aid that would allow her to avoid iterating back and forth with Meany to finalize a budget plan.

a. Does Gary's revised budget lead to a minimum expenditure schedule in the initial periods? If yes, why? If not, provide your own schedule.

b. How long would it take to complete the project with the budget restriction of $100,000 a month?

c. Can you provide Mary with a planning aid to help her in negotiating the budget schedule with Meany?

# REFERENCES


Baker, B. N., and D. L. Wileman, "A Summary of Major Research Findings Regarding the Human Element in Project Management," *IEEE Engineering Management Review,* 9(3), 1981, pp. 56–62.

Buffa, E. S., and J. G. Miller, *Production-Inventory Systems: Planning and Control* (3rd ed.), Irwin, Homewood, Ill., 1979.

Davis, E. W., "CPM Use in Top 400 Construction Firms," *Journal of Construction Division,* ASCE, *100*(01), Proc. Paper 10295, March 1974, pp. 39–49. (a)

Davis, E. W., "Networks: Resource Allocation," *Industrial Engineering,* April 1974, pp. 22–32. (b)

Davis, E. W., "Project Scheduling Under Resource Constraints—Historical Review and Categorization of Procedures," *AIIE Transactions,* 5(4), December 1973, pp. 297–313.

Davis, E. W., and J. H. Patterson, "A Comparison of Heuristic and Optimum Solutions in Resource Constrained Project Scheduling," *Management Science, 21* (8), April 1975, pp. 944–955.

Harrison, F. L., *Advanced Project Management,* Halsted, New York, 1981.
Lee, S. M., L. A. Digman, and G. A. Moeller, *Network Analysis for Management Decisions,* Kluwer–Nijhoff Publishing, Boston, 1981.
Meredith, J. R., and S. J. Mantel, *Project Management,* Wiley, 1985.
Moder, J. J., C. R. Phillips, and E. W. Davis, *Project Management with CPM and PERT* (3rd ed.), Reinhold, New York, 1983.
Smith, L. A., and P. Mahler, "Comparing Commercially Available CPM/PERT Computer Programs," *Industrial Engineering, 10*(4), April 1978, pp. 37–39.
Talbot, B. F., "Resource Constrained Project Scheduling," *Management Science, 28*(10), October, 1982.
Thamhain, H., and D. Wileman, "Conflict Management in Project Life Cycles," *Sloan Management Review, 16*(3), 1975, pp. 31–50.
Wiest, J. D., and F. K. Levy, *A Management Guide to PERT/CPM* (2nd ed.), Prentice-Hall, Englewood Cliffs, N.J., 1977.
Woodwoth, B. M., and C. J. Willie, "A Heuristic Algorithm for Resource Leveling in Multi-Project, Multi-Resource Scheduling," *Decision Sciences, 6*(3), 1975. pp. 525–540.

# CHAPTER 12

# QUALITY ASSURANCE

Product quality has entered the consciousness of managers with a vengeance. It has become crystal clear that high-quality products have a distinct advantage in the marketplace, that market share can be gained or lost over the quality issue. Therefore quality is a competitive priority. We have had formal quality control programs in U.S. companies since the 1940s; important statistical quality control procedures were developed in this country beginning in the early 1930s, and quality control organizations and procedures within companies have been common. Yet something important changed in the global competitive scene in the last ten years or so, and that something was unsurpassed Japanese product quality.

Reports of superior Japanese quality have appeared in the press almost daily during the 1980s. One study is based on the quality performance of nine American and seven Japanese manufacturers of home air conditioners. Table 12-1 summarizes the key results.

The broad findings of the study were as follows:

- The failure rates of air conditioners made by the worst producers, which were all American, were between 500 and 1000 times greater than those made by the best producers, which were all Japanese.
- The average American manufacturer had 70 times as many defects on the assembly line as the average Japanese manufacturer and made 17 times as many service calls during the first year following sale.
- The defect percentages of air conditioners produced by the worst Japanese manufacturers were less than half of those produced by the best American manufacturers.
- Companies with the best quality records also had the highest labor productivity.
- The extra cost of making higher-quality Japanese goods was about half the cost of fixing defective products made by American manufacturers.

The competitive quality and cost advantage of the Japanese home air conditioner products highlight the importance of this chapter on quality assurance and the next chapter on statistical quality control. If the air conditioner study results were an isolated case, there would be no overriding issue, but it is not. Ensuring high quality

TABLE 12-1
**QUALITY CHARACTERISTICS OF NINE AMERICAN AND SEVEN JAPANESE HOME AIR CONDITIONER MANUFACTURERS' PRODUCTS**

| | *Assembly Line Defects* | | *Service Calls* | |
|---|---|---|---|---|
| | Median | Range | Median | Range |
| United States | 63.5 | 7–165 | 10.5 | 5.30–26.5 |
| Japan | 0.95 | 0.15–3.0 | 0.6 | 0.04–2.0 |

*Source:* David A. Garvin, "Quality on the Line," *Harvard Business Review*, September–October, 1983.

is now recognized as being of the greatest significance in maintaining a strong competitive position.

The competitive pressure to produce high quality products has increased greatly in recent years, and Eli Goldratt has characterized the pace of the race by the rapid succession of terms we have adopted and rejected in trying to define what is meant by "quality."

*Yield*—Up to about 1970, the attitude toward quality was reflected in the term "yield." We focused on how many good parts were being produced—"just toss out the bad ones." An acceptable level was thought to be 10%.

*Scrap*—During the 1970s we began to use the term "scrap" to focus on damaged material, and that the level had declined below 10%.

*Quality is Job 1*—By the 1980s, it appeared that even the previous levels were no longer competitive, so slogans like, "quality is job 1," were coined to signal determination to reduce scrap below 1%.

*Parts per Million*—By 1985 the market's perception of quality forced manufacturers toward "zero defects," and the Japanese introduced the intimidating term, "parts per million" to indicate their resolve for quality output.

In this chapter, we will deal with the broader system for assuring that high quality is maintained, the choice of processes, the nature of control procedures for quality of products and services, the maintenance function, and the role of repair and preventive maintenance in ensuring high quality.

We try to control the reliability of productive system outputs as diagrammed in Figure 12-1. The quality and quantity are monitored in some way, and the results are compared with standards. Although we are generally interested in quality measures, changes in output quantity may also be symptomatic of reliability problems. The associated costs of quality and quantity control are derivatives of reliability. When the results are interpreted, we may conclude that the processes are out of adjustment or that something more fundamental is wrong, thus requiring machine repair or possibly retraining in manual operations. If equipment actually breaks down, then the maintenance function is called. Information on output quality and quantity may also be used to form preventive maintenance programs designed to anticipate breakdowns. Thus, although other important interactions have their effects, quality assurance centers on quality control and equipment maintenance.

## THE QUALITY ASSURANCE SYSTEM

Figure 12-1 suggests the nature of control loops for quality and maintenance control. However, it is local in nature and leaves a great deal unsaid. We must ask: Where did the standards come from? What is the nature of the productive system, and is it appropriate for the quality tasks?

Figure 12-2 places the reliability system in context. The organization must set policies regarding the desired quality in relation to markets and needs, investment requirements, return on investment, potential competition, and so forth. For profit-

FIGURE 12-1
**CONTROL LOOPS FOR MAINTAINING SYSTEM RELIABILITY BY MONITORING QUALITY AND QUANTITY OF OUTPUT.**

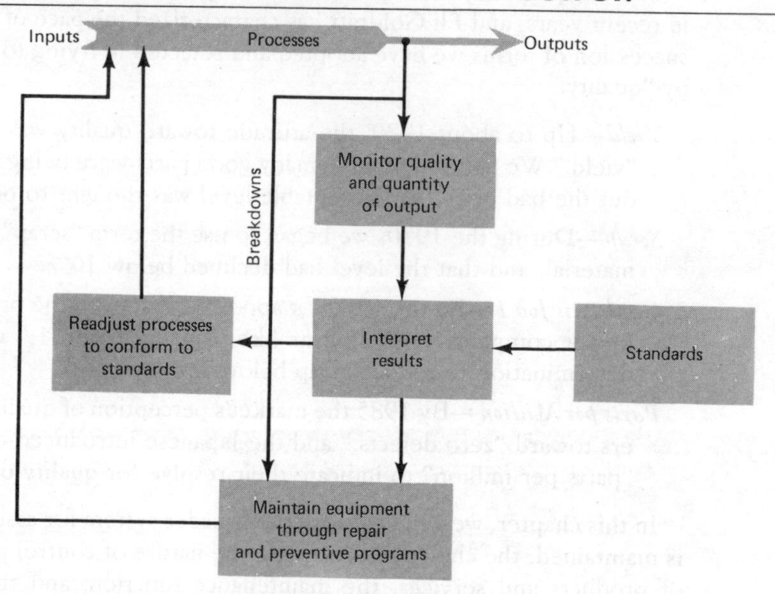


making organizations, this involves the judgment of where in the market the organization has a relative advantage.

For nonprofit organizations, policy setting may involve meeting standards set by legislation and/or by the organization to maximize its position. For example, universities acquire superior academic staffs in order to raise funds, improve the physical plant, obtain outstanding students, and enhance research output. Hospitals may set high standards of care partially to attract the best known physicians, support fund raising programs, and attract interns with the best qualifications. The post office may set standards for delivery delay that accommodate current budgetary levels.

The policies set by management in box 1 of Figure 12-2 provide the guidelines for the design of the organization's products and services. This design process is an interactive one in which the productive system design is both considered in and influenced by the design of products and services, as shown in boxes 2 and 3. For manufacturing systems, the design of products in this interactive fashion is termed *production design*. The interaction affects quality considerations because equipment capability must be good enough to produce at least the intended quality.

Out of the process of the design of products, services and the productive system come specifications of quality standards, as shown in box 4 of Figure 12-2. Here we are dealing with a system of quality standards for materials that are consumed in processes as well as raw materials; standards for the output of processes, such as the specification of dimensions, tolerances, weights, and chemical compositions; and performance standards for components and products. The nature of performance standards for products is well known. For example, manufacturers state the capabili-

FIGURE 12-2
**SCHEMATIC REPRESENTATION OF THE RELATIONSHIPS AMONG POLICIES, DESIGN OF PRODUCTS AND SERVICES, DESIGN OF THE PRODUCTIVE SYSTEM, AND THE MAINTENANCE OF SYSTEM RELIABILITY FOR QUALITY AND QUANTITIES.**

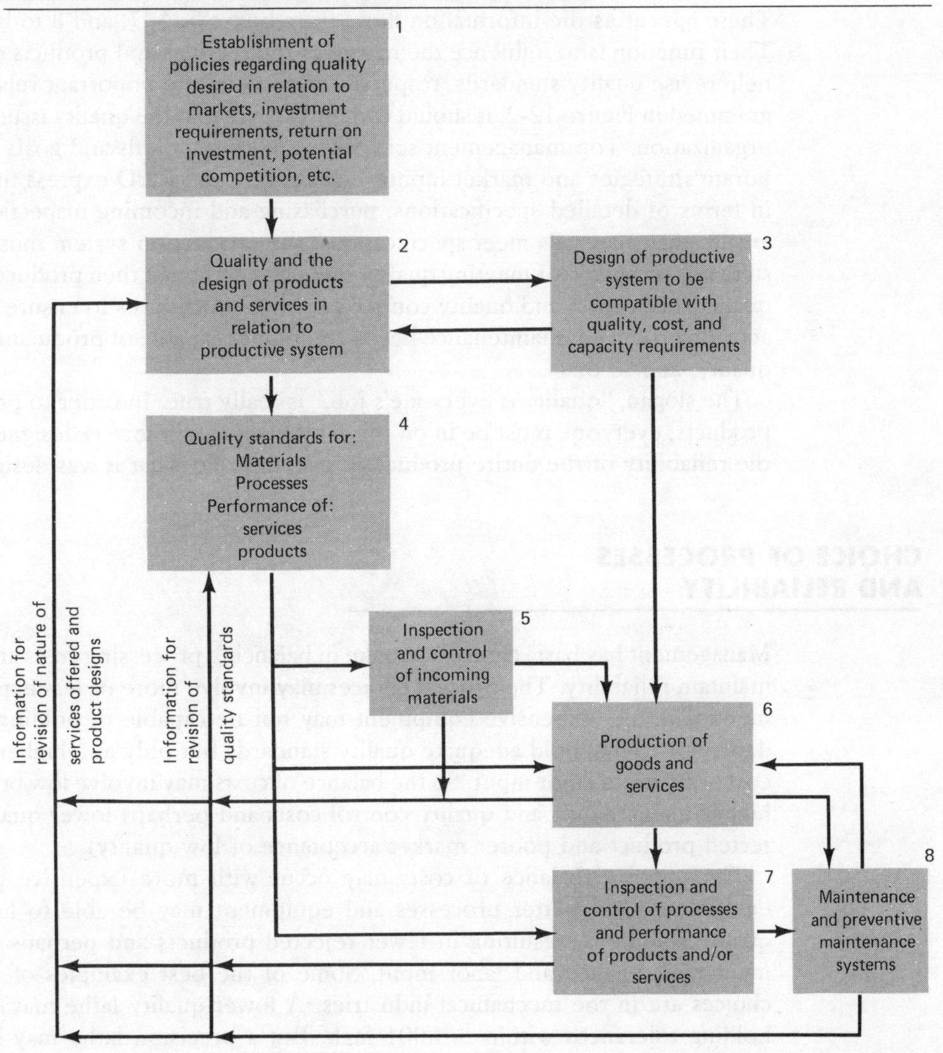


ties of their product: the fidelity range of an amplifier, the acceleration of an automobile, the waterproof finish of a table surface, and the like.

The performance standards of services seem (so far) to be somewhat less formalized. What performance do we expect from postal systems, educational systems, police and fire departments, and medical care systems? This relative lack of formal standards and the difficulty of defining them may be the reasons for the paucity of our knowledge about the control of the quality of services.

Given standards, however, we can set up controls for incoming materials in box 5 and for the processes and performance of products and services in box 7. An interrelated control loop concerns the maintenance of the capabilities of the physical system in box 8 through repair and preventive maintenance programs.

Secondary control loops that seek a system optimum are shown in Figure 12-2. These appear as the information flows from boxes 5, 6, 7, and 8 to boxes 2 and 4. Their function is to influence the nature of the services and products offered and to help revise quality standards, respectively. Beyond the important relationships diagrammed in Figure 12-2, it should convey the fact that the quality issue pervades the organization. Top management sets basic quality standards and goals based on corporate strategies and market inputs; engineering and R&D express these standards in terms of detailed specifications; purchasing and incoming inspection attempt to ensure that materials meet specifications; the production system must be designed so that it is capable of meeting quality standards and must then produce the requisite quality; inspection and quality control establish procedures to ensure that quality is actually produced; maintenance keeps equipment capable of producing the requisite quality; and so on.

The slogan, "quality is everyone's job," is really true. In order to produce quality products, everyone must be in on the act. Quality assurance is designed to maintain the reliability of the entire productive system to do what it was designed to do.

## CHOICE OF PROCESSES AND RELIABILITY

Management has basic choices to make in balancing processing costs and the costs to maintain reliability. The process choices may involve more or less expensive equipment. The less expensive equipment may not be capable of holding quality standards. Or it may hold adequate quality standards but only at a higher maintenance cost or by more labor input. So the balance of costs may involve low process cost but higher maintenance and quality control costs and perhaps lower quality (more rejected product and poorer market acceptance of low quality).

The opposite balance of costs may occur with more expensive processes and equipment. The better processes and equipment may be able to hold improved quality standards, resulting in fewer rejected products and perhaps in less equipment maintenance and labor input. Some of the best examples of these process choices are in the mechanical industries. A lower-quality lathe may be capable of holding tolerances within $\pm 0.001$ inch. But a precision lathe may be capable of holding tolerances within $\pm 0.0001$ inch or better. However, the choice is certainly not always for the precision lathe; it dependes on the product requirements and the balance of costs. These kinds of choices exist generally, although they are not always as clear-cut as the lathe example. Sometimes a more expensive process involves greater labor input with more steps in the productive process.

Figure 12-3 shows the balance between the costs of process choice and the costs of quality assurance. The manager's choice among alternatives should be in the middle range shown, near the minimum cost of the total incremental cost curve.

FIGURE 12-3
**COST BASIS FOR MANAGER'S CHOICE OF PROCESSES AND QUALITY ASSURANCE.**

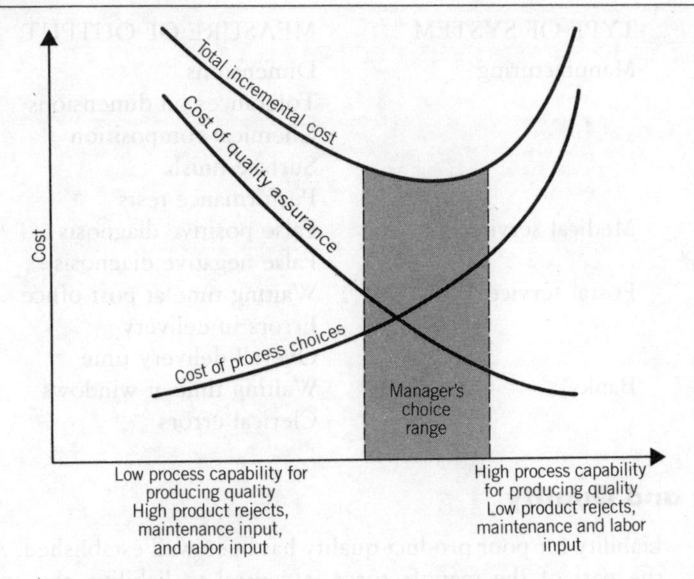


The reason for not stating that the choice should be simply to minimize cost is that the manager's choice should also be influenced by unquantified factors such as market image and acceptance, flexibility of operations, availability of labor with skills to match equipment requirements, and so on.

## CONTROL OF QUALITY

Our general block diagram for control calls for a measurement system to generate information on which to base control actions. In industry, this is the inspection function. Inspectors make measurements that are called for by the quality standards, thereby separating acceptable from nonacceptable units. In addition, the final product must be tested to be sure it performs to standards. However, no control or corrective action is implied. When we link measurement, investigation to determine why an unacceptable product has been produced, and corrective action, we have completed the control loop.

The measures of quality in productive systems are diverse. These measures are perhaps most obvious in manufacturing systems where quality characteristics can be related to objective standards of dimensions, chemical composition, and actual performance tests. Standards for these measures can then be established and regular procedures can be used to measure the critical characteristics to determine if standards are maintained. In service oriented systems, measures of quality are often not as objective. The personal contact required may emphasize the *way* service is given, even though the service is technically adequate. Waiting time is often a criterion for service quality. The following are typical quality measures of the outputs of productive systems:

| TYPE OF SYSTEM | MEASURE OF OUTPUT |
|---|---|
| Manufacturing | Dimensions |
| | Tolerances on dimensions |
| | Chemical composition |
| | Surface finish |
| | Performance tests |
| Medical service | False positive diagnosis |
| | False negative diagnosis |
| Postal service | Waiting time at post office |
| | Errors in delivery |
| | Overall delivery time |
| Banks | Waiting time at windows |
| | Clerical errors |

## Liability and Quality

Liability for poor product quality has been well established. Although negligence on the part of the manufacturer is central to liability, the concept in legal practice extends to include foreseeable use and misuse of the product. Product warranty includes both that expressed by the manufacturer (written and oral) and the implied warranty that the product design will be safe for the user. The uses are not legally restricted to those specified in warranties but include those that may be foreseen. The concept of "foreseeable usage" has often been interpreted to mean that if the product *was* misused, then such use was foreseeable. These legal doctrines place a particularly heavy responsibility on the quality control function, for liability suits can have an important bearing on enterprise survival. See Bennigson and Bennigson (1974) and Eginton (1973) for further discussion of product liability.

Medical malpractice liability has become an important factor in health care costs. Insurance premiums have skyrocketed, and physicians' fees have reflected the increases. Controversy over the control of health care quality has resulted, with emphasis on establishing standards.

## Sampling Information

All processes exhibit variation, and the manager's task is to distinguish between tolerable variation that is representative of the stable system and major changes that result in an unacceptable product. The manager must be aware of the system's inherent capability in order to know when system behavior is abnormal. Thus, because we are dealing with systems that exhibit variation, the manager's control model must be a probabilistic one.

Because of the ongoing nature of processes and their inherent variability, we must usually base quality control decisions on samples. First, we cannot usually examine all the data because the process is continuous and, at best, we have access to a sample at a particular point in time. (In some instances, 100 percent automatic inspection can be incorporated into the process.) Second, even if the entire universe of data were available, it might be uneconomical to analyze it. Third, measurement and inspection sometimes require the destruction of the unit. Fourth, with some products, any additional handling is likely to induce defects and should therefore be avoided. Thus, the sampling of information about the state of incoming raw materials and the control of processes is the common approach on which decisions and control actions are based.

The amount of sampling justified represents another managerial choice. As the amount of sampling increases, approaching 100 percent inspection, the probability of passing defective items decreases, and vice versa. The combined incremental cost curve is again dish shaped. The manager's range of choices is near the minimum cost, but it is a range because unquantified factors must influence the decision.

## Risks and Errors

Because we must normally use samples of data drawn from a system that naturally exhibits variation, we can make mistakes, even in controlled experiments. Figure 12-4 summarizes the nature of the errors and the risks taken; here, we classify the actual state of the system and the decision taken. The process either is in control or it is not; or, similarly, we have a batch of parts or materials that has been generated by a system that either was or was not in control.

As Figure 12-4 shows, we can decide either to accept or to reject the output. If the process is in control—and if, based on our information, we would reject the output—then we have made an error called a *type I error*. We, the producer, risk making such an erroneous decision on the basis of the probabilities that are associated with the inherent variability of the system and the sample size. Logically, this risk is called the *producer's risk* because—if the decision is made—it is the producer who absorbs the loss.

FIGURE 12-4
**ERRORS AND RISKS IN QUALITY CONTROL DECISIONS.**

| True state of system | Decision | |
|---|---|---|
| | Reject output as bad | Accept output as good |
| Process is in control | Type-I error (Producer's risk) | Correct decision |
| Process is out of control | Correct decision | Type-II error (Consumer's risk) |

Similarly, there is a risk that we may accept output as a good product when, in fact, the process is out of control. This decision is called a *type II error* and is termed the *consumer's risk*. In statistical control models, we can preset the probabilities of type I and type II errors.

Philosophically, the concept of the consumer's risk may be in part the cause of American manufacturers' misjudgment of what is really acceptable quality. In fact, from a broader competitive perspective, both risks are the producer's, and we now recognize that the type II risk may be the most serious of the producer's risks since it can result in the loss of customers and market share.

## Kinds of Control

Figure 12-2 shows that, fundamentally, we control quality by controlling (1) incoming materials, (2) processes at the point of production, and (3) the final performance of products and services, with the maintenance system acting in a supporting role. For some products, quality control of product performance includes the distribution, installation, and use phases.

From the point of view of control methods, we can apply statistical control concepts by sampling the output of a process to keep that process in a state of statistical control (process control) or by sampling a *lot* of incoming materials to see whether it is acceptable (acceptance sampling).

In process control, we monitor the actual ongoing process that makes the units. This allows us to make adjustments and corrections as soon as they are needed so that bad units are never produced in any quantity. This procedure is a direct application of the statistical control chart, and, as with acceptance sampling, parallel procedures are available for those situations in which sampling is done by attributes and for those in which measurements are made of variables that measure quality characteristics. Figure 12-5 summarizes the classifications of statistical control models. These control procedures should be used by suppliers to control their processes prior to shipment. The acceptance sampling procedures are designed to ensure the quality of incoming materials.

Acceptance sampling lets us control the level of outgoing quality from an inspection point to ensure that, on the average, no more than some specified percentage of defective items will pass. This procedure assumes that the parts or products have already been produced. We wish to set up procedures and decision rules to ensure that outgoing quality will be as specified or better. In the simplest case of acceptance sampling, we draw a random sample of size $n$ from the total lot $N$ and decide, on the basis of the sample, whether or not to accept the entire lot. If the sample signals a decision to reject the lot, the lot may be subjected to 100 percent inspection during which all bad parts are sorted out, or it may be returned to the original supplier. Parallel acceptance sampling procedures can be used to classify parts as simply good or bad (sampling by attributes) or to make some kind of actual measurement that indicates how good or bad a part is (sampling by variables).

The methods of statistical quality control referred to in Figure 12-5 are of considerable importance in quality assurance, and we devote a special chapter to them (Chapter 13).

FIGURE 12-5
**CLASSIFICATION OF STATISTICAL CONTROL MODELS.**

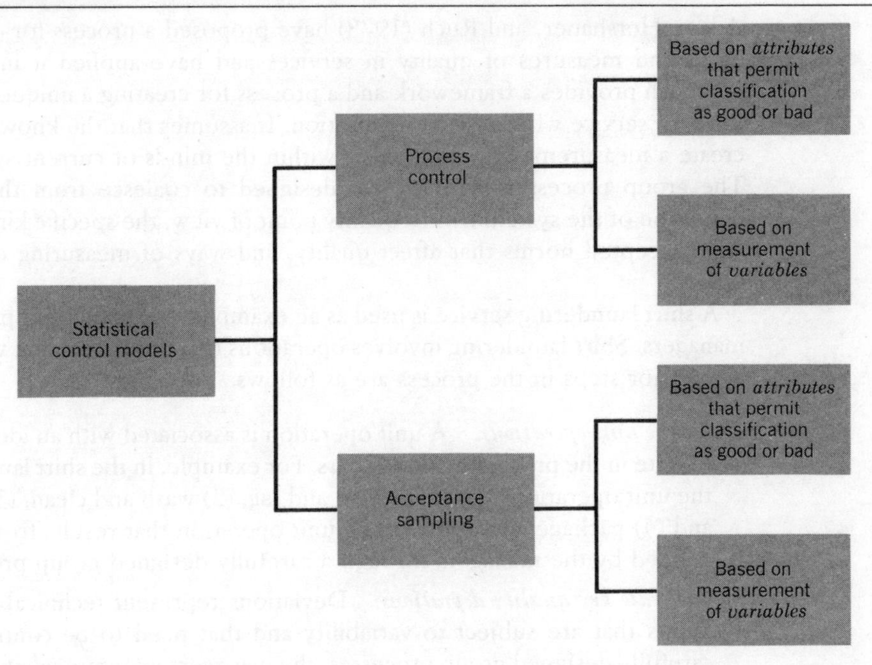


## Controlling the Quality of Services

The previous material dealing with industrial quality control has clear objectives about what to measure and control and sophisticated methodology for accomplishing these ends. In nonprofit organizations, however, the objectives and outputs seem less well defined and the control methodology seems relatively crude.

The profit motive provides a focus for all kinds of managerial controls, including quality. By contrast, nonprofit organizations exist to render service, and their success is judged in those terms. Measuring the quality of the services is difficult in part because the attributes of quality are somewhat more diffuse. Is quality health care measured by the death rate, the length of a hospital stay, or the treatment process used for a specific disease? Is the quality of police protection measured by the crime rate, a feeling of security by citizens, or indexes of complaints of police excesses? (Note the following anomaly: if the size of the police force is increased, crime rates have been observed to increase because more of the crimes committed are acted on and reported.) Is the quality of fire service measured by reaction time, the annual extent of fire damage, or some other factor? In partial answer to these questions, we must note that the quality characteristics of most of these kinds of services are multidimensional and are often controversial, and reducing quality measurement to something comparable to specific dimensions or chemical composition may be impossible.

## A FRAMEWORK FOR CONTROLLING QUALITY OF SERVICES

Adam, Hershauer, and Ruch (1978) have proposed a process for developing standards and measures of quality in services and have applied it in banking. Their approach provides a framework and a process for creating a unique set of measures for each service within each organization. It assumes that the knowledge needed to create a measurement system exists within the minds of current system managers. The group processes involved are designed to coalesce from the managers the definition of the system from a quality point of view, the specific kinds of deviations from accepted norms that affect quality, and ways of measuring each specific deviation.

A shirt laundering service is used as an example to explain their process to system managers. Shirt laundering involves operations that are simple and well understood. The major steps in the process are as follows:

1. *Define unit operations.* A unit operation is associated with an identifiable change in state in the processing that occurs. For example, in the shirt laundering service, the unit operations are (1) receive and tag, (2) wash and clean, (3) dry and press, and (4) package and deliver. The unit operation that results from the process is defined by the managers through a carefully designed group process.
2. *Generate key quality deviations.* Deviations represent technical system requirements that are subject to variability and that need to be controlled. Through carefully designed group processes, the managers generate *what* and *where* in the process deviations may occur. A second step in the process is to distill from the deviations list the key quality deviations. Compared with the industrial quality control systems discussed previously, key quality deviations are equivalent to the dimensions and attributes that need to be controlled because they affect product performance and quality. The key quality deviations are caused by the nature of the items being processed (at entry, in process, or at output) or by the nature of the processes used. In the shirt laundering example, the key quality deviations and the unit operation location where they occur (in parentheses) are as follows:
   a. Number, type, and size of stains in shirts (input, wash and clean)
   b. Number of buttons missing (input, wash and clean, dry and press)
   c. Item identification missing (receive and tag, wash and clean, dry and press)
   d. Wrong availability (package and deliver)
   e. Days until delivery (wash and clean, dry and press, package and deliver)
3. *Generate measures.* Using the key quality deviations as a basis, the managers develop related measures through group processes. For example, for the deviation "number, type, and size of stains," the measures were as follows:
   a. Stain complaints per customer
   b. Worker-hours expended removing stains
   c. Cost of shirt replacement divided by standards for replacements
   d. Number of shirts with a stain divided by total number of shirts received

4. *Evaluation of measures.* As a basis for finalizing the measures developed in step 3, participants are asked to rate each measure in terms of its value in the outcome of the deviation and to rate the strengths of their convictions of that rating. Only measures whose average rating is above a certain threshold are retained in the measurement system.

## APPLICATIONS IN BANKING

The system for developing quality measures was applied to check processing and to the personnel function in three banks.

For check processing, seven unit operations were defined in two banks as the following:

1. Receipt of transfer documents
2. Preparation for processing
3. Processing
4. Reconciling and settlement
5. Preparation for dispatch
6. Dispatch
7. Post processing

In bank C, 93 deviations were defined and were reduced to seven key quality deviations. Sixty measures were then defined related to the key deviations. These measures were evaluated by executives in the organization through the rating process, and a final list of 25 measures was retained. In addition to the more detailed measures, five systemwide measures for check processing were accepted at bank A:

1. Percentage of error-free outgoing cash letters divided by total worker-hours in check processing
2. Dollar amount of "as of" adjustments divided by total dollars processed
3. Percentage of error free outgoing cash letters divided by cost of 1000 letters
4. Total dollar expense of adjusting key deviations divided by total dollar expense in check processing
5. Total worker-hours in adjusting key deviations divided by total worker-hours in check processing

For the personnel function, five unit operations were defined in two banks:

1. Recruit and employ staff
2. Evaluate employee job assignments
3. Compensate employees: review and adjustment for wages, salaries, and benefits
4. Train
5. Administer personnel services to employees and the public

In bank A, 42 deviations were defined and were reduced to 11 key quality deviations. Forty-eight measures were defined related to the key quality deviations. These measures were evaluated by executives through the rating process, and 43 were retained.

Given the measures of *what* to control for service operations, it is necessary to close the control loop. Standards must be set concerning levels of each of the measures that represent acceptable and unacceptable quality, and corrective action must be taken when measurements signal that the system is out of control. Statistical control procedures similar to those used in industrial quality control may then be used.

Although the process for establishing quality measures is complex, it reflects the technical–behavioral emphasis of service systems. It is the first comprehensive effort to establish quality measures in service type operations. The emphasis of the framework on quality measures of service productivity is unique. Most quality control measures in the past have been taken in isolation and have not attempted to relate the measures and the quality control effort to input–output values. The validity of the quality control effort in relation to productivity has been the result of a separate judgment that is usually not explicit.

## THE MAINTENANCE FUNCTION

Quality control procedures are designed to track characteristics of quality and to take action to maintain quality within limits. In some instances, the action called for may be equipment maintenance. The maintenance function then acts in a supporting role to keep equipment operating effectively to maintain quality standards as well as to maintain the quantitative and cost standards of output.

There are alternative policies that may be appropriate, depending on the situation and the relative costs. First, is routine preventive maintenance economical, or will it be less costly to wait for breakdowns to occur and then repair the equipment? Are there guidelines that may indicate when preventive maintenance is likely to be economical? What service level for repair is appropriate when breakdowns do occur? How large should maintenance crews be to balance the costs of downtime versus the crew costs? Should a larger crew be employed in order to give more rapid service at higher cost? In addition, there are longer range decisions regarding the possible overhaul or replacement of a machine.

The decision concerning the appropriate level of preventive maintenance rests on the balance of costs, as indicated in Figure 12-6. Managers will want to select a policy that minimizes the sum of preventive maintenance costs plus repair, downtime, and quality-related costs.

Curve *a* in Figure 12-6 represents the increase in costs that result from higher levels of preventive maintenance. These costs increase because higher levels of preventive maintenance mean that we replace parts before they fail more often, we replace more components when preventive maintenance is performed, and we perform preventive maintenance more frequently. Curve *b* of Figure 12-6 represents the decline in breakdown and repair, downtime, and quality-related costs as the level of preventive maintenance increases. The quality-related costs are too often

FIGURE 12-6
**BALANCE OF COSTS DEFINING AN OPTIMAL PREVENTIVE MAINTENANCE POLICY.**

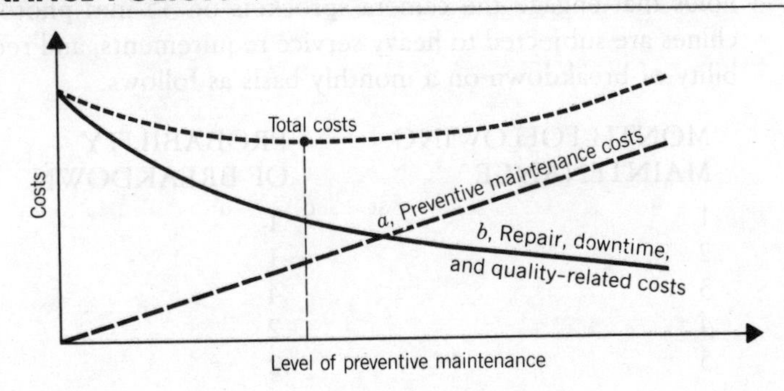


ignored, but they can be of great significance in their impact on product quality directly, management and worker attitudes, and customer reactions. With higher levels of preventive maintenance, we should experience fewer actual breakdowns, and therefore, positive impacts on other costs.

The total incremental cost curve is the sum of curves *a* and *b*. The optimal policy regarding the level of preventive maintenance is defined by the minimum of that curve.

There is a combination of costs that leads to the decision not to use preventive maintenance. Suppose that the costs referred to did not decline as the level of preventive maintenance increased or declined more slowly than preventive maintenance costs increased. Then preventive maintenance would not be justified because the minimum total cost would occur with no preventive maintenance. The optimal policy would then be simply to repair the machine when breakdowns occur.

## Preventive Maintenance (PM)

Assume a preventive maintenance (PM) policy for a single machine that provides for an inspection and perhaps the replacement of parts after the machine has been running for a fixed time. This is the *PM cycle.* It requires an average cost, $C_{PM}$, to accomplish the PM. A certain proportion of breakdowns will occur before the fixed cycle has been completed. For these cases, the maintenance crew will repair the machine, requiring an average cost, $C_R$, for the repair. This is the *repair cycle.* The probability of the occurrence of the two different cycles depends on the specific probability distribution of the time between machine breakdowns and the length of the standard PM cycle. If the distribution of machine breakdown time has a low variability and the standard PM cycle is perhaps only 80 percent of the average run time without breakdowns, actual breakdown would occur rather infrequently, and most cycles would be PM cycles. If the distribution were more variable for the same standard PM period, more actual breakdowns would occur before the end of the standard period. Shortening the standard period would result in fewer actual breakdowns, and lengthening it would have the opposite effect for any distribution.

## A Computed Example

Assume an example where we have $N = 100$ perforating machines that cut the holes that engage the camera sprockets on 35-mm photographic film. These machines are subjected to heavy service requirements, and records indicate the probability of breakdown on a monthly basis as follows:

| MONTH FOLLOWING MAINTENANCE | PROBABILITY OF BREAKDOWN |
|---|---|
| 1 | .1 |
| 2 | .1 |
| 3 | .4 |
| 4 | .2 |
| 5 | .2 |

The breakdown time interval following the last maintenance is called *free run time,* the time that a machine runs free of maintenance, and is a measure of the reliability of the machine. The average free run time can be calculated as follows:

| MONTH FOLLOWING MAINTENANCE ($i$) | PROBABILITY OF BREAKDOWN ($p_i$) | AVERAGE FREE RUN TIME ($i \times p_i$) |
|---|---|---|
| 1 | .1 | 0.1 |
| 2 | .1 | 0.2 |
| 3 | .4 | 1.2 |
| 4 | .2 | 0.8 |
| 5 | .2 | 1.0 |
| | | 3.3 months/breakdown/machine |

The average number of breakdowns for the pool of 100 machines per month is $100/3.3 = 30.3$, giving an indication of the average load on the maintenance crew to service the perforating machines.

Management wishes to determine whether a PM policy would be less costly than simply repairing each machine when it breaks down. The following average cost information is useful:

$$\text{Repair on breakdown, } C_R = \$90$$
$$\text{Preventive maintenance, } C_{PM} = \$30$$

**REPAIR POLICY (RP)**

Evaluating the repair policy cost is simple. It is the average number of repairs per month times the average repair cost, or

$$C_{RP} = 30.3 \times \$90 = \$2727 \text{ per month}$$

## PREVENTIVE MAINTENANCE POLICY (PMP)

When preventive maintenance is used, the assumption is that PM extends the free run time as much as does a repair. We must evaluate the different options of providing such service for various time cycles; that is, monthly, every two months, every three months, and so on. In addition, we must be careful to recognize the effect that preventive maintenance has in extending the free run time of the machines and that, in spite of the preventive maintenance program, some machines will break down and need repair at the higher cost.

The expected number of breakdowns when preventive maintenance is performed on all machines monthly is $B_1$, the total number of machines times the probability of breakdown within a month:

$$B_1 = Np_1 = 100 \times .1 = 10 \text{ machines}$$

The expected number of breakdowns when PMs are performed every two months is the number expected to break down within the first two months, $N(p_1 + p_2)$, plus the number that were repaired in the first month but broke down within the following month, $B_1p_1$:

$$\begin{aligned} B_2 &= N(p_1 + p_2) + B_1p_1 \\ &= 100(.1 + .1) + 10 \times .1 \\ &= 21 \text{ machines} \end{aligned}$$

Similarly, the expected number of breakdowns for a three-month PM cycle is the number that would break down according to the distribution in three months, $N(p_1 + p_2 + p_3)$, plus the number that were repaired in the first month that broke down within the second month, $B_1p_2$, plus the number that were repaired in the second month that broke down again within a month, $B_2p_1$:

$$\begin{aligned} B_3 &= N(p_1 + p_2 + p_3) + B_1p_2 + B_2p_1 \\ &= 100(.1 + .1 + .4) + 10 \times .1 + 21 \times .1 \\ &= 60 + 1 + 2.1 = 63.1 \text{ machines} \end{aligned}$$

The general pattern emerges for standard PM cycles of $n$ months (or other periods of time, such as weeks) is as follows:

$$B_n = N(p_1 + p_2 + p_3 + \ldots + p_n) + B_1p_{n-1} + B_2p_{n-2} + \ldots + B_{n-1}p_1$$

where

$n$ = Number of periods (weeks, months, etc.) in the standard PM cycle
$B_n$ = Number of machines that break down within PM cycle $n$
$N$ = Number of machines
$P_i$ = Probability of breakdown in period $i$

This general equation can be used to evaluate a wide variety of situations since the notation applies to all standard PM cycles, whether weeks, months, or whatever, and to any probability distribution or total number of machines. Applying it to PM cycles of four and five months yields the following:

$$B_4 = 100(.1 + .1 + .4 + .2) + 10 \times .4 + 21 \times .1 + 63.1 \times .1$$
$$= 80 + 4 + 2.1 + 6.31 = 92.41 \text{ machines}$$
$$B_5 = 100 \times 1.0 + 10 \times .2 + 21 \times .4 + 63.1 \times .1 + 92.41 \times .1$$
$$= 125.95 \text{ machines}$$

The calculated $B$ values are then used to compute the preventive maintenance costs as shown in Table 12-2.

The result of Table 12-2 shows that the PM cycle with the minimum cost is two months with a monthly cost of $C_{PMP} = \$2445$. This cost is less than the repair policy cost of \$2727, saving \$282 per month or \$3384 per year.

## Guides to Preventive Maintenance Policy

The decision concerning repair versus preventive maintenance depends on several factors involved in the elements of the calculations we have used. The balance of costs between the two alternatives is sensitive to the following:

- The factor costs, $C_R$ and $C_{PM}$
- The breakdown probability distribution
- Downtime costs
- Quality-related costs

First, in our example, if the factor costs had been different, the economic balance could easily have shifted in favor of the repair policy. If $C_{PM} = \$45$ instead of \$30, as in our calculations, the repair policy wins rather handily over the best PM policy. The cost of PMs increases significantly over those in column *e* of Table 12-2 so that the sum of PM cost and repair cost in column *f* is higher. Not only that, but the best PM period shifts from two months to five months. The recalculated PM policy costs would be as shown in Table 12-3. Note that the higher PM costs per machine make the shorter PM cycles more expensive than they were in Table 12-2, shifting the

TABLE 12-2
**PREVENTIVE MAINTENANCE COSTS FOR THE FIVE PREVENTIVE MAINTENANCE CYCLES ($C_R = \$90$, $C_{PM} = \$30$)**

| (*a*) Preventive Maintenance Cycle (*n*), Months | (*b*) Expected Breakdowns in PM Cycle, $B_i$ | (*c*) Average Number of Breakdowns per Month, (Col. *b*/Col. *a*) | (*d*) Expected Monthly Breakdown Cost, (Col. *c* × \$90) | (*e*) Expected Monthly PM Cost, [(\$30 × 100)/(Col. *a*)] | (*f*) Expected Monthly Cost of Each PM Cycle, (Col. *d* + Col. *e*) |
|---|---|---|---|---|---|
| 1 | 10 | 10 | \$ 900 | \$3000 | \$3900 |
| 2 | 21 | 10.5 | 945 | 1500 | 2445[a] |
| 3 | 63.1 | 21.03 | 1893 | 1000 | 2893 |
| 4 | 92.41 | 23.10 | 2079 | 750 | 2829 |
| 5 | 125.95 | 25.19 | 2267 | 600 | 2867 |

[a] Minimum cost preventive maintenance period = 2 months.

TABLE 12-3
**RECALCULATION OF PREVENTIVE MAINTENANCE COSTS FOR $C_R$ = $90 and $C_{PM}$ = $45**

| (*a*) Preventive Maintenance Cycle (*n*), Months | (*b*) Expected Breakdowns in PM Cycle, $B_i$ | (*c*) Average Number of Breakdowns per Month, (Col. *b*/Col. *a*) | (*d*) Expected Monthly Breakdown Cost, (Col. *c* × $90) | (*e*) Expected Monthly PM Cost, [($45 × 100)/(Col. *a*)] | (*f*) Expected Monthly Cost of Each PM Cycle, (Col. *d* + Col. *e*) |
|---|---|---|---|---|---|
| 1 | 10 | 10 | $ 900 | $4500 | $5400 |
| 2 | 21 | 10.5 | 945 | 2250 | 3195 |
| 3 | 63.1 | 21.03 | 1893 | 1500 | 3393 |
| 4 | 92.41 | 23.10 | 2079 | 1125 | 3204 |
| 5 | 125.95 | 25.19 | 2267 | 900 | 3167[a] |

[a] Minimum cost preventive maintenance period = 5 months.

minimum cost cycle to the fifth month. The result is that much of the advantage of PMs is lost because they are not performed until most of the machines would have broken down and needed repair anyway. At any rate, the results of the economic analysis are quite sensitive to the unit costs $C_R$ and $C_{PM}$.

Second, we have the effect of the breakdown probability distribution. Notice in our previous example that the probability distribution peaked in the third month with a high probability of breakdown of .4. The minimum cost PM cycle in Table 12-2 logically anticipated this peak. Now suppose that the breakdown probability distribution is flat, as follows:

| MONTH FOLLOWING MAINTENANCE | PROBABILITY OF BREAKDOWN |
|---|---|
| 1 | .2 |
| 2 | .2 |
| 3 | .2 |
| 4 | .2 |
| 5 | .2 |

Assuming the original unit costs of $C_R$ = $90 and $C_{PM}$ = $30, let us recalculate the costs for the repair and PM policies. The average machine would break down every 3.0 months, and there would be 100/3 = 33.3 breakdowns per month, resulting in

$$C_{RP} = 33.3 \times \$90 = \$2997$$

The calculations for the PM policies are shown in Table 12-4.

Now the minimum cost PM cycle is four months at a cost of $3166, which is disadvantageous compared to the repair policy cost of $2997. The shape of the probability distribution has made an important difference, shifting the economic advantage from the PM policy to the repair policy. The important characteristic in the original distribution was that its variability was low, so a PM policy could anticipate most of the breakdowns—their timing was more predictable. On the

TABLE 12-4
**RECALCULATION OF PREVENTIVE MAINTENANCE COSTS FOR A FLAT BREAKDOWN PROBABILITY DISTRIBUTION ($C_R$ = $90, $C_{PM}$ = $30)**

| (*a*) Preventive Maintenance Cycle (*n*), Months | (*b*) Expected Breakdowns in PM Cycle, $B_i$ | (*c*) Average Number of Breakdowns per Month, (Col. *b*/Col. *a*) | (*d*) Expected Monthly Breakdown Cost, (Col. *c* × $90) | (*e*) Expected Monthly PM Cost, ($30 × 100)/(Col. *a*) | (*f*) Expected Monthly Cost of Each PM Cycle, (Col. *d* + Col. *e*) |
|---|---|---|---|---|---|
| 1 | 20 | 20 | $1800 | $3000 | $4800 |
| 2 | 44 | 22 | 1980 | 1500 | 3480 |
| 3 | 72.8 | 24.3 | 2184 | 1000 | 3184 |
| 4 | 107.36 | 26.84 | 2416 | 750 | 3166[a] |
| 5 | 148.83 | 29.77 | 2679 | 600 | 3279 |

[a] Minimum cost preventive maintenance period = 4 months.

other hand, the flat distribution has high variability—breakdowns could occur at any time with equal probability. So preventive maintenance programs are generally applicable to breakdown distributions with low variability, allowing us to set a regular PM cycle that forestalls a large fraction of the breakdowns. If we can anticipate breakdowns, we can perform a PM at a lower cost than a repair, and overall maintenance costs will be lower.

Third, downtime costs can modify the conclusions of an economic analysis or should be included in the analysis. When a machine breaks down, it is not uncommon for the business to have to absorb the costs of idle labor. Sometimes this cost is very large, as when an entire production line must be stopped for repair. Under these circumstances, PM is more desirable than a repair policy *if* the PM can take place during second or third shifts, vacations, or lunch hours, when the line is down anyway. An optimal solution under these circumstances would minimize the sum of PM, repair, and downtime costs. The effect of the downtime costs would be to justify shorter PM periods and to justify making repairs more quickly (at higher costs) when they do occur. There are many situations, however, in which extra personnel on a repair job would not speed it up. In such cases, total downtime might be shortened by repair crew overtime on multiple shifts and weekends at higher costs.

Finally, quality-related costs can also modify the conclusions of the economic balance between the repair and PM costs. If equipment is maintained in good repair, quality is maintained in better control, fewer defectives occur, and experience has shown that productivity is improved. Management and worker attitudes and customer confidence and repeat buying patterns may also be improved. High quality has implications for the competitiveness of the firm and may improve market share and profits. Therefore, quality-related costs may dictate a preventive maintenance policy when the strictly maintenance-related costs suggest that a repair policy is logical. Some of these costs may not be measurable, as is true with the factor and downtime costs, but the difference in cost between the repair policy and the PM policy can be used as a yardstick by managers to answer the question, "Are the benefits to quality worth the cost difference?"

The guides to preventive maintenance policy are summarized in Table 12-5.

## Overhaul and Replacement

In maintaining reliability, more drastic maintenance actions are sometimes economical. These decisions concern renewing machines through overhauls or replacing them when they are obsolete. Overhaul and replacement decisions can be related to the capital and operating costs (including maintenance) of the equipment. Figure 12-7 shows that although operating costs are temporarily improved through preventive maintenance, repair, and overhaul, there is a gradual cost increase to the point that replacement is finally justified.

### REPAIR VERSUS OVERHAUL

The decisions concerning the choice between repair and major overhaul normally occur at the time of a breakdown. Many organizations also have regular schedules for overhaul. For example, trucking companies may schedule major engine overhauls after a given number of miles of operation. These major preventive maintenance actions are meant to anticipate breakdowns to avoid the occurrence of downtime at inconvenient times and pehaps to minimize downtime costs.

TABLE 12-5

**SUMMARY GUIDES TO PREVENTIVE MAINTENANCE POLICY**

$C_R$ *versus* $C_{PM}$:

If it costs just as much to perform a PM as it does to repair a machine, then a PM policy will have no advantage, unless large downtime or quality-related costs are involved.

*Breakdown Probability Distributions:*

PM programs are generally applicable to breakdown probability distributions with low variability. The effect of low variability distributions is that we can predict with fair precision when a majority of breakdowns will occur. A standard PM cycle can then be adopted that anticipates breakdowns fairly well.

*Downtime Costs*

The presence of large downtime costs is likely to tip the economic balance in favor of a PM program. If PM can be performed during off hours, when the facilities are down anyway, it is likely to be preferable to a repair policy even if the other economic aspects favor repair.

*Quality Related Costs:*

Negative impact on quality and costs related to quality may justify PM programs and shorter standard PM cycles, even when the balance between PM and repair costs indicates that a repair policy is more economical.

FIGURE 12-7
**OPERATING COST INCREASE WITH TIME WITH TEMPORARY IMPROVEMENTS RESULTING FROM REPAIR, OVERHAUL, AND REPLACEMENT.**

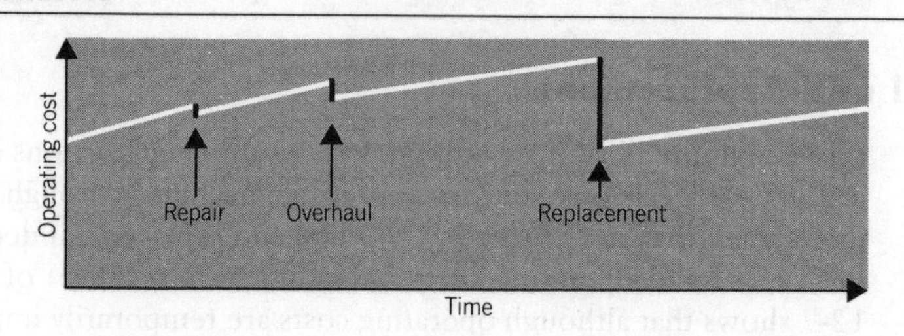


## REPLACEMENT DECISIONS

The choice is not only between overhaul and repair; equipment replacement alternatives lurk in the background and need to be considered as part of a sequential decision strategy. Possible sequences could include repair, overhaul, perhaps a second overhaul, replacement, repair, overhaul, and so on.

Suppose, for example, that a machine is usually overhauled or replaced after two years of service. The present machine was purchased two years ago, and a decision must now be made concerning overhaul or possible replacement. The machine costs $9000 installed, and annual operating costs (including maintenance) were $2000 for the first year and $3000 for the second year. The machine can be overhauled for $5000, but the operating costs for two years will be $2800 and $4000 after the first overhaul and $3500 and $5000 after the second overhaul.

In deciding whether to overhaul or replace at this time, we should consider the available alternative sequences of decisions. For example, we can overhaul or replace at this time. For each of these possible decisions, we have the same options two years hence, and so on. Figure 12-8 shows the simple decision tree structure. In order to compare the alternatives, the future costs are discounted to present value. The four alternative strategies are the following

1. Replace now and in two years (R–R).
2. Replace now and overhaul in two years (R–OH).
3. Overhaul now and replace in two years (OH–R).
4. Overhaul now and again in two years (OH–OH).

Because operating costs increase so rapidly in this example, it might be worthwhile in the present value analysis to see what happens with a longer horizon, perhaps six years. This of course would add more alternative branches to the tree.

This example assumes replacement with an identical machine, but it is often true that alternative machines will have rather different capital and operating costs. New machine designs often have improvements that reduce labor and maintenance costs, and these cost advantages could affect the analysis and the overhaul–replacement decisions.

FIGURE 12-8
**DECISION TREE FOR THE OVERHAUL–REPLACEMENT EXAMPLE.**

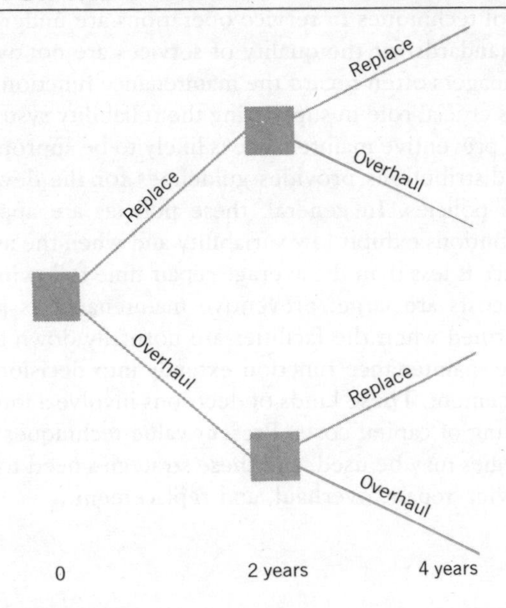


## IMPLICATIONS FOR THE MANAGER

The general concepts of system reliability are important for managers to understand. When productive systems involve a network of activities with many required sequences, it will be difficult to maintain the reliability of the system as a whole. This system unreliability would exist even though each individual operation might be 99 percent reliable. Managers can improve reliability by providing parallel capabilities and slack capacity, although these remedies may be expensive.

The most important techniques available to managers for sustaining reliability are quality control and equipment maintenance systems. The quality control system functions as a primary control loop, and the maintenance system provides reliability in the longer term through a secondary control loop.

Quality control begins in the preproduction planning phases of an enterprise, when policies regarding market strategies are developed. Quality standards are then developed out of the iterative process of product/service design and productive system design. The productive system must be designed so that it is capable of producing the required quality level at reasonable cost.

Monitoring quality levels of output is necessarily a sampling process because the entire output population may not be available for screening and the cost of 100 percent inspection may be too great. The techniques of statistical quality control are often valid and cost-effective mechanisms for managers to employ.

Quality control of services is difficult for a variety of reasons related to the unique character of the services. Attempts are being made to establish a framework for control. Legislation has placed great emphasis on quality control in health care systems, and self-regulation experiments are now developing. Nevertheless, quality control techniques in service operations are underdeveloped, partly because rigorous standards for the quality of services are not available.

Managers often regard the maintenance function as ancillary to operations, ignoring its crucial role in supporting the reliability system. It is important to understand when preventive maintenance is likely to be appropriate. The analysis of breakdown time distributions provides guidelines for the development of preventive maintenance policies. In general, these policies are appropriate when breakdown time distributions exhibit low variability and when the average time for preventive maintenance is less than the average repair time following breakdown. Also, when downtime costs are large, preventive maintenance is preferable to repair if it can be performed when the facilities are normally down anyway.

The maintenance function extends into decisions involving major overhaul and replacement. These kinds of decisions involve a longer time horizon and the proper handling of capital costs. Present value techniques for the evaluation of alternative strategies may be used, and these strategies need to consider sequences of decisions involving repair, overhaul, and replacement.

## REVIEW QUESTIONS

1. What are the primary and secondary feedback control loops in the overall quality assurance system?
2. What measures of quality of output do you think might be important in the following kinds of systems? Be as specific as possible.
   a. A fast-food operation such as McDonalds
   b. A motel
   c. A luxury hotel
   d. Space vehicle manufacture
3. How can you control the aspects of quality that you suggest be measured in your answer to question 2?
4. Define the following terms:
   a. Type I error
   b. Type II error
   c. Producer's risk
   d. Consumer's risk
5. What kinds of control can be exercised in maintaining quality standards?
6. What conditions make acceptance sampling appropriate?
7. What are the criteria of quality in the following?

a. A banking service

b. The postal service

c. An institution of higher learning

d. A hospital

e. The Internal Revenue Service

8. What kinds of costs are associated with machine breakdown?
9. Discuss the general methods by which the reliability of productive systems can be maintained.
10. What is a breakdown time probability distribution?
11. In the model of preventive maintenance discussed in the text, what is the assumption concerning the effect that a PM service has in extending the free run time of machines?
12. In evaluating alternative preventive maintenance periods that might be applicable to a given situation, explain the components of the following function:

$$B_2 = N(p_1 + p_2) + B_1p_1$$

13. Explain the components of the general expression for the number of machines that break down within the standard PM cycle $n$ shown on page 382.
14. Suppose that the unit factor costs, $C_R$ and $C_{PM}$, are equal and downtime and quality-related costs are not important. Would a repair policy or a PM policy be the most economical? Why?
15. Assume the following three breakdown probability distributions:

| Month Following Maintenance | Probability of Breakdown | | |
|---|---|---|---|
| | (1) | (2) | (3) |
| 1 | .5 | .0 | .1 |
| 2 | .1 | .1 | .1 |
| 3 | .1 | .1 | .6 |
| 4 | .1 | .1 | .1 |
| 5 | .1 | .2 | .1 |
| 6 | .1 | .5 | .0 |

Which, if any, of these distributions lend themselves to a preventive maintenance program? Why?

16. It may not be possible to compute quality-related costs. How, then, can they be taken into account in deciding whether or not to adopt a PM program in the face of an economic advantage for a repair policy?
17. What are the general conditions for which preventive maintenance is appropriate?
18. Rationalize why the operating costs for equipment should increase with time, as indicated in Figure 12-7.

# PROBLEMS

19. Maintenance records on 10 machines provide the following data on the probability distribution of breakdowns:

| MONTH FOLLOWING MAINTENANCE ($i$) | PROBABILITY OF BREAKDOWN ($p$) |
|---|---|
| 1 | .5 |
| 2 | .3 |
| 3 | .2 |

a. What is the average time between two successive breakdowns?

b. Compute the average monthly number of breakdowns.

c. If the average cost of a repair is $C_R$ = \$75, what is the annual cost of repair maintenance?

20. Maintenance records on 20 machines provide the following data on the probability distribution of breakdowns:

| MONTH FOLLOWING MAINTENANCE ($i$) | PROBABILITY OF BREAKDOWN ($p$) |
|---|---|
| 1 | .3 |
| 2 | .5 |
| 3 | .2 |

Calculate the expected monthly number of breakdowns if PM policies are installed and PMs are performed:

a. Monthly

b. Every two months

c. Every three months

21. Assume the probability of breakdown distribution in problem 20 for $N = 20$ machines and unit costs of $C_R$ = \$100 and $C_{PM}$ = \$50.

a. Show that a repair policy is most economical.

b. Is the repair policy still most economical if downtime costs are \$25 per breakdown?

c. After examining the analyses of parts *a* and *b* and reports concerning the quality-related problems resulting from machine breakdowns, the vice-president of manufacturing decides to install the PM program anyway. He says, "I can't measure these quality-related costs, but the PM program is worth at least that much to me." What minimum value is the VP placing on the quality-related costs?

22. A company operates a bank of 50 wafer cutters for silicon chip manufacture. The machines operate for two shifts per day and have the following probability of breakdown after maintenance, based on company records:

| MONTH FOLLOWING MAINTENANCE ($i$) | PROBABILITY OF BREAKDOWN ($p$) |
|---|---|
| 1 | .5 |
| 2 | .1 |
| 3 | .1 |
| 4 | .1 |
| 5 | .1 |
| 6 | .1 |

The company has been following a repair policy. It is now considering a PM policy since the discovery that the simple replacement of a single part has the effect of putting a machine back in working order and that this PM service is very inexpensive relative to repair costs incurred once a machine has broken down. The unit factor costs are

$$C_R = \$100$$
$$C_{PM} = \$10$$

Should the company adopt a PM program?

23. A company operates a bank of 100 etching machines for silicon chip manufacture. The machines operate for three shifts per day and have the following probability of breakdown after maintenance, based on company records:

| MONTH FOLLOWING MAINTENANCE ($i$) | PROBABILITY OF BREAKDOWN ($p$) |
|---|---|
| 1 | .0 |
| 2 | .1 |
| 3 | .1 |
| 4 | .1 |
| 5 | .2 |
| 6 | .5 |

The company has been following a PM policy. It is now reconsidering that policy because maintenance costs seem too high. The unit factor costs are

$$C_R = \$100$$
$$C_{PM} = \$75$$

Should the company replace its PM program with a repair policy?

24. A company operates a bank of 50 automatic screw machines. The machines operate for two shifts per day and have the following probability of breakdown after maintenance, based on company records:

| MONTH FOLLOWING MAINTENANCE ($i$) | PROBABILITY OF BREAKDOWN ($p$) |
|---|---|
| 1 | .1 |
| 2 | .1 |
| 3 | .6 |
| 4 | .1 |
| 5 | .1 |

The company has been following a repair policy. It is now considering a PM policy. The unit factor costs are

$$C_R = \$100$$
$$C_{PM} = \$20$$

Should the company adopt a PM program?

# REFERENCES


Adam, E. E., J. C. Hershauer, and W. A. Ruch, *Measuring the Quality Dimension of Service Productivity,* National Science Foundation No. APR 76-07140, University of Missouri—Arizona State University, 1978.

Bennigson, L. A., and A. I. Bennigson, "Product Liability: Manufacturers Beware!" *Harvard Business Review,* May–June 1974.

Boere, N. J., "Air Canada Saves with Aircraft Maintenance Scheduling," *Interfaces,* 7(1), May 1977, pp. 1–13.

"Directory of Software for Quality Assurance and Quality Control," *Quality Progress,* March 1984, pp. 33–53.

Dodge, H. F., and H. G. Romig, *Sampling Inspection Tables* (2nd ed.), Wiley, New York, 1959.

Duncan, A. J., *Quality Control and Industrial Statistics* (4th ed.), Irwin, Homewood, Ill., 1974.

Eginton, W. W., "Minimizing Product Liability Exposure," *Quality Control,* January 1973.

General Electric Company, *User's Guide to Preventive Maintenance Planning and Scheduling,* FAME—Facilities Maintenance Engineering, New York, 1973.

Grant, E. L., and R. S. Leavenworth, *Statistical Quality Control* (5th ed.), McGraw-Hill, New York, 1980.

Higgins, L. R., *Maintenance Engineering Handbook* (3rd ed.), McGraw-Hill, New York, 1977.

Jardine, A. K. S., *Maintenance, Replacement and Reliability,* Wiley, New York, 1973.

Juran, J. M., and F. M. Gryna, *Quality Planning and Analysis: From Product Development Through Usage,* McGraw-Hill, New York, 1970.

Moore, J., *Developing a Preventive Maintenance Program,* Vantage, New York, 1978.

Smith, C. S., *Quality and Reliability: An Integrated Approach,* Pitman, New York, 1969.

# CHAPTER 13

# STATISTICAL QUALITY CONTROL METHODS



(Continued)

The methods of statistical quality control were introduced in 1924 by Walter Shewhart in a Bell Laboratories memorandum. In the following years, Shewhart, Dodge, and others did early work on the concept of acceptance inspection. Much of Shewhart's thinking on these subjects was published in his book, *Economic Control of Quality of Manufactured Product* (1931), in which he introduced the basic concepts of statistical quality control, including the control chart. These concepts have been enlarged and refined and are widely accepted and applied in industry. In fact, they are widely accepted and applied throughout the advanced industrial world, particularly in Japan, where W. Edwards Deming introduced the concepts. Deming, an octogenarian, is the foremost quality control guru and is widely credited for placing Japan in its world leadership position in the quality of its manufactured products.

This chapter assumes that one has read the relevant materials in Chapter 12, on pages 371–375. The classification of the kinds of control shown in Figure 12-5 provides the structure for this chapter. We will discuss the control of both attributes and variables under the basic headings of process control charts and acceptance sampling.

## PROCESS CONTROL CHARTS

In general, variations that occur in a production process fall into two broad categories: *chance* variations and variations with *assignable causes*. Chance variations may have a complex of minor actual causes, none of which can account for a significant part of the total variation. The result is that these variations occur in a random manner, and there is very little that we can do about them, given the process. On the other hand, variations with assignable causes are relatively large and can be traced. In general, assignable causes are the result of

1. Differences among workers
2. Differences among machines
3. Differences among materials
4. Differences due to the interaction between any two or among all three of the preceding causes

A comparable set of assignable causes could be developed for any process. For example, assignable causes for variation in absenteeism might be disease epidemics, changes in interpersonal relations at home or in the employee's work situation, and others.

When a process is in a state of statistical control, variations that occur in the number of defects, the size of a dimension, the chemical composition, the weight, and so on are due only to normal chance variation. With the control chart, we set up standards of expected normal variation due to chance causes. Thus, when variations due to one or more of the assignable causes are superimposed, they "stick out like a sore thumb" and tell us that something basic has changed. Then it is possible to investigate to find the assignable cause and correct it. These statistical control mechanisms are called control charts.

## Conceptual Framework for Control Charts

If we take a set of measurements in sequence, we can arrange the data into a distribution and compute the mean and standard deviation. If we can assume that the data come from a normal population distribution, we can make precise statements about the probability of occurrence associated with the measurements, given in standard deviation units as follows:

68.26 percent of the values normally fall within $\mu \pm \sigma$

95.45 percent of the values normally fall within $\mu \pm 2\sigma$

99.73 percent of the values normally fall within $\mu \pm 3\sigma$

These percentage values represent the area under the normal curve between the given limits; therefore, they state the probability of occurrence for the values that come from the normal distribution that generated the measurements. For example, the chances are 95.45 out of 100 that a measurement taken at random will fall within the $2\sigma$ limits and only 4.55 out of 100 that it will fall outside these limits. These values, as well as decimal values for $\sigma$, come from the table for the normal probability distribution available as Table 6 in the Appendix. The *natural tolerance* of a process, that is, the expected process variation, is commonly taken to be $\mu \pm 3\sigma$. Estimates of the natural tolerance would be based on sample information. We will use the following notation:

$\mu$ = The population mean (parameter)
$\bar{x}$ = The mean of a sample drawn from the population (statistic)
$\sigma$ = The population standard deviation (parameter)
$s$ = The standard deviation of a sample drawn from the population (statistic)

Since we must use sample information to estimate population means and standard deviations, we estimate the natural tolerance of a process by substituting in the sample statistics, $\bar{x} \pm 3s$.

## Kinds of Control Charts

Two basic types of control charts, with variations, are commonly used:

- Control charts for variables
- Control charts for attributes

Control charts for variables are used when the parameter under control is some measurement of a variable, such as the dimension of a part, the time for work performance, and so forth. Variables charts can be based on individual measurements, mean values of small samples, and mean values of measures of variability.

Control charts for attributes are used when the parameter under control is the proportion or fraction of defectives. There are several variations for attributes control charts. Control charts for the number of defects per unit are used when a single defect may not be of great significance but a large number of defects could add up to a defective product, such as the number of blemishes on the surface of a painted surface. We will discuss all of the above types of control charts, providing the bases for their design.

## CONTROL CHARTS FOR VARIABLES

We will first consider a variables chart constructed for samples of $n = 1$ and relate the statistical properties of this simplest of control charts to the more common $\bar{X}$ and $R$ control charts. ($R$-charts are control charts for ranges, which are discussed later in this chapter.)

### Individual Measurements (Samples of One)

If we have established standards for the mean and the standard deviation of a normally distributed variable resulting from normal conditions, we can use these data to construct a control chart. Taking the natural tolerance of the $\pm 3s$ limits as a standard of variation from the mean, we can plot the individual measurements and observe whether the points fall within the $\pm 3s$ control limits or have a tendency to drift beyond one of the control limits. We know that if successive samples are representative of the original population, the probability is small that a sample will fall outside the established control limits. On the other hand, if sample measurements do fall outside the control limits, we have reason to believe that something in the process has changed, the cause for which may be investigated and corrected. Figure 13-1 shows a control chart for samples of $n = 1$ drawn from the distribution of 200 shaft diameters with $\bar{x} = 1.000$ inch and $s = 0.0020$ inch.

The control limits for the control chart in Figure 13-1 are

$$\text{Upper control limit, } UCL = \bar{x} + 3s = 1.000 + 3 \times 0.0020 = 1.0060$$
$$\text{Lower control limit, } LCL = \bar{x} - 3s = 1.000 - 3 \times 0.0020 = 0.9940$$

#### WHAT CONTROL LIMITS?

The process from which the samples were drawn in Figure 13-1 appears to be in control using the $\pm 3s$ control limit criterion. But had $\pm 2s$ control limits been adopted, the next to last point would have been outside limits. There is a 4.55 percent chance that this could have occurred by randomness in the data. The occurrence would have triggered an investigation, and if that investigation indicated that the process had not changed, the cost of conducting the investigation would have been wasted. On the other hand, if the control limits were $\pm 3s$ as shown in Figure 13-1, and the process had in fact changed, the observation would have been ignored

FIGURE 13-1
**DISTRIBUTION FOR SAMPLES OF $n = 1$ AND A CONTROL CHART FOR VARIABLES FOR MEASUREMENTS OF SHAFT DIAMETER.**

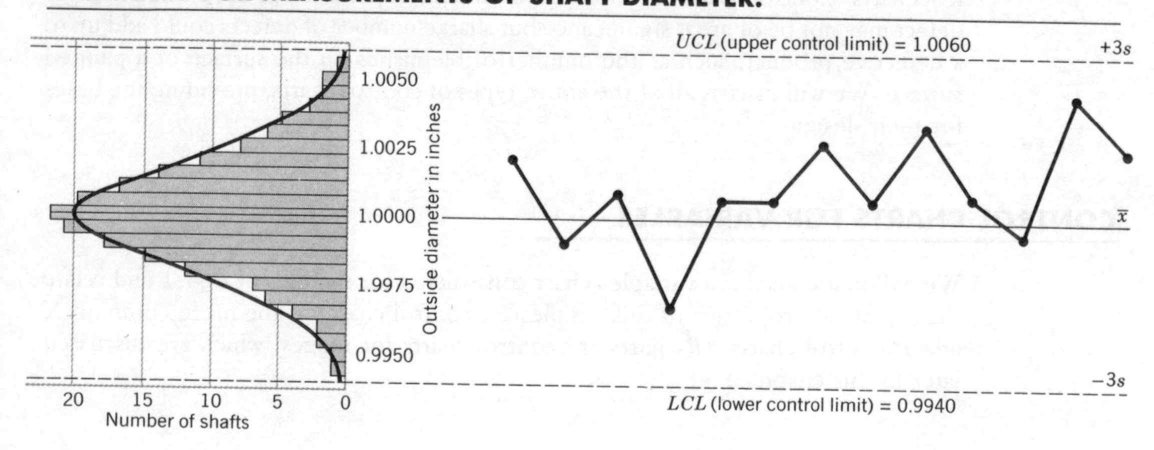


and more scrap product would have been produced in the interim before the change in the process was actually discovered.

Thus, the issue in setting control limits is one of balancing two costs—the cost of investigation and inspection against the cost of losses when no investigation is made. Generally, if the investigation cost is large relative to the possible losses if the process continues out of control, the limits should be fairly broad, perhaps $\pm 3s$. Conversely, if the potential loss is high relative to the cost of investigation, more sensitive control limits are needed.

Usually control charts are constructed for samples larger than one, but the statistical relationships for Figure 13-1 are simple and are of value in understanding the statistical basis of other control charts.

## Sampling Distributions

For Figure 13-1, the control chart based on samples of $n = 1$, the normality of the distribution had already been established. An important reason for taking samples larger than $n = 1$ is that we can side-step the issue of the normality of the population distribution. *Although a population distribution may depart radically from normality, the sampling distribution of means of random samples will be approximately normal if the sample size is large enough.* This statement of the central limit theorem is of great importance, for it gives us some assurance that the probabilities associated with the control limits we design will apply. Actually, deviation from normality in the population distribution can be fairly substantial, yet sampling distributions of the means of samples as small as $n = 4$ or 5 will follow the normal distribution quite closely.

If we take samples of $n = 4$ from the shaft diameter distribution, the means of the samples will form a new distribution with a mean and a standard deviation of its own.

FIGURE 13-2
**RELATIONSHIP BETWEEN THE DISTRIBUTION FOR INDIVIDUAL MEASUREMENTS AND THE SAMPLING DISTRIBUTION OF SAMPLES OF $n = 4$ FOR THE SHAFT DIAMETER DATA.**

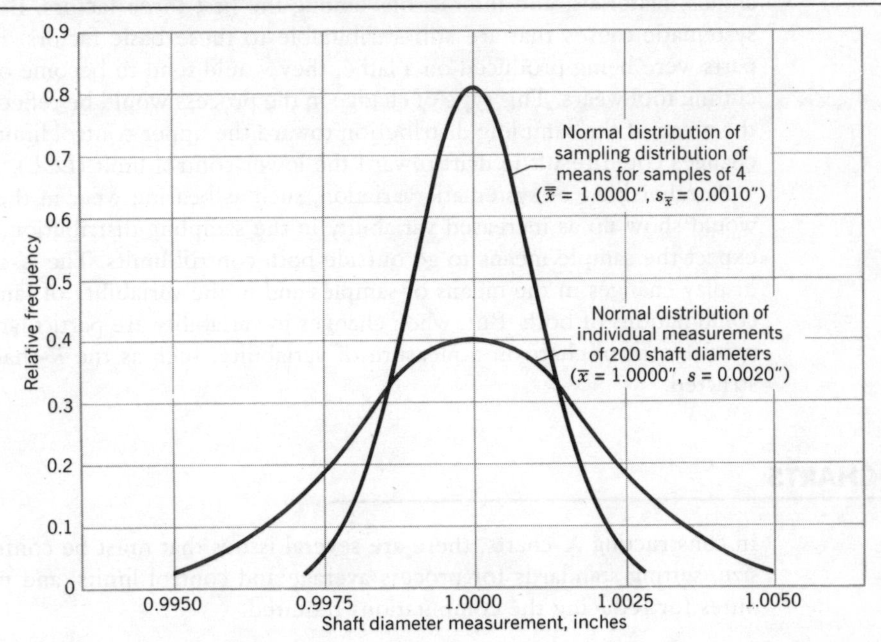


This distribution is called a *sampling distribution of means of* n = 4. To distinguish the statistics from the distribution of individual measurements in Figure 13-2, we use the notation $\bar{\bar{x}}$ for the grand mean of the sampling distribution and $s_{\bar{x}}$ for the standard deviation of the sampling distribution. We expect that $\bar{x}$ and $\bar{\bar{x}}$ will be very nearly equal and that they will be equal in the limit as the number of samples increases.

The standard deviation for the sampling distribution will be much smaller than that for the individual measurements because the variation is reduced by the averaging process within each sample. The resulting relationship between the two distributions for the shaft data is shown in Figure 13-2. The relationship between $s$ and $s_{\bar{x}}$ is given by

$$s_{\bar{x}} = \frac{s}{\sqrt{n}}$$

To construct a control chart for means, we first need to establish standard values for $\bar{\bar{x}}$ *and* $s_{\bar{x}}$ and for the control limits on the sample means. The means of subsequent samples are plotted, and action would be called for if a sample mean should fall outside the control limits. Control mechanisms that employ sample means are called $\bar{X}$ and $R$ control charts.

### Why Sample Means Fall Outside Control Limits

We listed the basic causes earlier as being due to differences among workers, machines, materials, and interactions among the first three factors. But there can be systematic causes that are still attributable to these basic factors. For example, if parts were being produced on a lathe, they would tend to become oversized as the cutting tool wears. This type of change in the process would be reflected in a drift of the mean of the sampling distribution toward the upper control limit (*UCL*). Other changes could result in drift toward the lower control limit (*LCL*).

Another kind of systematic variation, such as bearing wear in the lathe spindle, would show up as increased variability in the sampling distribution, and we would expect the sample means to go outside both control limits. The $\bar{X}$-chart, then, can display changes in the means of samples and in the variability of samples as well as combinations of both. But, when changes in variability are particularly important, a special control chart on a measure of variability, such as the *R*-chart, can be constructed.

## $\bar{X}$-CHARTS

In constructing $\bar{X}$-charts, there are several issues that must be confronted: sample size, setting standards for process average and control limits, and practical procedures for reducing the computations required.

### Sample Size

In industry, sample sizes are usually small for good reasons. First, small samples cost less to gather, inspect, and process. Second, large samples must be taken over a longer time span, and changes could occur within that time, so response might not be timely; out-of-control conditions would not be detected as rapidly, and additional scrap might be produced. Generally, sample sizes of four or five are most common. They anticipate the problems noted, yet they are large enough for the central limit theorem to guarantee normality in the sampling distribution. On the other hand, larger samples have the effect of tightening control limits. Note that sample size is in the denominator of the formula for $s_{\bar{x}}$. Thus, a larger sample size means a smaller $s_{\bar{x}}$. Finer variations in processes can be detected when samples are larger.

### Setting Standards for Process Average and Control Limits

How do we determine that the process average, $\bar{\bar{x}}$, and the control limits are representative of the process when it is in a state of statistical control? If the process were shifting during the period that we were developing information to set these standards, the standards would be meaningless. Nonstandard conditions could result in a shift in the average, the standard deviation, or both.

To guard against this possibility, we compute for a preliminary subgroup a separate $s$ for each of the small samples and then average them. The means of the subgroup samples are plotted on a control chart based on $\bar{\bar{x}} \pm 3s_{\bar{x}}$ to see whether changes in the process average have occurred in the period during which the preliminary data were gathered. To achieve the objectives, the size of the subgroup should be relatively small, perhaps 20 to 25, and the time period over which the preliminary data are gathered should be long enough for any changes in the process that occur between the sampling intervals to be recognized.

## Practical Procedures for Determining $\bar{X}$-Chart Control Limits

The control limits require an estimate of $s_{\bar{x}}$, and although this computation is not onerous, it does require the input of all the data on which the statistic is based. Practitioners in the field have developed short-cut methods for calculating control limits, using the range instead of the standard deviation as a measure of variability. Table 13-1 is a small portion of a table of factors used to convert the average range, $\bar{R}$, to the $3s_{\bar{x}}$ control limits. The procedure is simple. Select the appropriate factor from Table 13-1 for $\bar{X}$-charts, and compute the control limits as follows:

$$\text{Control limits} = \bar{\bar{x}} \pm A_2\bar{R}$$

As an example, if $\bar{\bar{x}} = 2.0000$, $\bar{R} = 0.005$, and $n = 5$, then the factor from Table 13-1 is $A_2 = 0.577$ and the control limits are

$$UCL = 2.0000 + (0.577 \times 0.005) = 2.0000 + 0.0029 = 2.0029$$
$$LCL = 2.0000 - (0.577 \times 0.005) = 2.0000 - 0.0029 = 1.9971$$

The basic calculations for determining the center lines and control limits remain the same, regardless of the variable being measured.

TABLE 13-1
**FACTORS TO CONVERT AVERAGE RANGE, $\bar{R}$, TO VARIABLES CONTROL LIMITS**

| Sample | $\bar{X}$-Chart Control | R-*Chart Control Limits* | |
|---|---|---|---|
| Size, $n$ | Limits, $A_2$ | Lower, $D_3$ | Upper, $D_4$ |
| 3 | 1.023 | 0 | 2.575 |
| 4 | 0.729 | 0 | 2.282 |
| 5 | 0.577 | 0 | 2.115 |
| 6 | 0.483 | 0 | 2.004 |
| 7 | 0.419 | 0.076 | 1.924 |
| 8 | 0.373 | 0.136 | 1.864 |

*Source:* Abstracted from a much larger table of factors useful in the construction of control charts, Table B2 of the A.S.T.M. Manual on Quality Control of Materials, p. 115.

## R-CHARTS—CONTROL CHARTS FOR MEASURES OF VARIABILITY

In calculating the control limits for the $\bar{X}$-chart, the statistics used are the small sample means, and these are the data plotted on the chart. We can just as well use a measure of variability, such as the standard deviation or the range, as the basic statistic. For each sample, we compute a sample standard deviation (or range), and these observations are formed into a distribution that approximates the normal distribution. This new distribution of measures of variability has a mean, a standard deviation, and a range that can be used to construct a control chart. This control chart indicates when the *variability* of the process is greater or less than standard.

In quality control, the statistic chosen is usually the range rather than the standard deviation because of the ease with which the range can be computed in a processing setting. For each sample, the difference between the highest and lowest measurement is plotted on the *R*-chart. The distribution of ranges has an average, $\bar{R}$, and a standard deviation, $s_R$. The $\pm 3s_R$ limits have the same general significance as with the $\bar{X}$-chart.

### Practical Procedures for Determining R-Chart Control Limits

Just as with $\bar{X}$-charts, the computation of the control limits for the *R*-chart has been simplified by using the $\bar{R}$ statistic rather than the standard deviation. Using the data in Table 13-1 for the sample size $n$, select the factors $D_3$ and $D_4$ and calculate the $3s_R$ control limits as follows:

$$UCL_R = D_4\bar{R}$$
$$LCL_R = D_3\bar{R}$$

As an example, if $n = 4$ and $\bar{R} = 3.000$ and from Table 13-1 $D_4 = 2.282$ and $D_3 = 0$, then the control limits for the *R*-chart are

$$UCL_R = 2.282 \times 3.000 = 6.846$$
$$LCL_R = 0 \times 3.000 = 0$$

## EXAMPLES OF $\bar{X}$-CHARTS AND R-CHARTS

Assume a production process for which we wish to set up both an $\bar{X}$-chart and an *R*-chart. In order to initialize the charts, we take 20 samples of $n = 5$ measurements at random as the process continues. These observations are shown in Table 13-2 in columns 2 through 6, each line representing a sample of $n = 5$. Each sample average is given in column 7, and the sample range is given in column 8. The grand mean and the average range are shown at the bottom of these last two columns as $\bar{\bar{x}} = 0.201$, and $\bar{R} = 0.043$, respectively.

TABLE 13-2
**MEASUREMENTS TAKEN IN SEQUENCE ON THE OUTPUT OF A PRODUCTION PROCESS (SAMPLE SIZE IS $N = 20$, $n = 5$)**

| *Sample Number* | *Individual Observations* | | | | | *Sample Average, $\bar{x}$* | *Sample Range, R* |
|---|---|---|---|---|---|---|---|
| (1) | (2) | (3) | (4) | (5) | (6) | (7) | (8) |
| 1 | 0.198 | 0.175 | 0.201 | 0.209 | 0.204 | 0.197 | 0.034 |
| 2 | 0.224 | 0.209 | 0.184 | 0.225 | 0.209 | 0.210 | 0.041 |
| 3 | 0.195 | 0.172 | 0.204 | 0.213 | 0.208 | 0.198 | 0.041 |
| 4 | 0.183 | 0.191 | 0.168 | 0.194 | 0.202 | 0.188 | 0.034 |
| 5 | 0.194 | 0.142 | 0.208 | 0.226 | 0.188 | 0.192 | 0.084 |
| 6 | 0.212 | 0.238 | 0.219 | 0.198 | 0.230 | 0.219 | 0.040 |
| 7 | 0.179 | 0.186 | 0.206 | 0.170 | 0.212 | 0.191 | 0.042 |
| 8 | 0.216 | 0.212 | 0.201 | 0.196 | 0.224 | 0.210 | 0.028 |
| 9 | 0.221 | 0.172 | 0.201 | 0.205 | 0.204 | 0.201 | 0.049 |
| 10 | 0.226 | 0.184 | 0.187 | 0.182 | 0.229 | 0.202 | 0.047 |
| 11 | 0.181 | 0.210 | 0.219 | 0.206 | 0.184 | 0.200 | 0.038 |
| 12 | 0.176 | 0.179 | 0.206 | 0.182 | 0.244 | 0.197 | 0.068 |
| 13 | 0.217 | 0.199 | 0.225 | 0.205 | 0.208 | 0.211 | 0.026 |
| 14 | 0.203 | 0.192 | 0.203 | 0.207 | 0.208 | 0.203 | 0.016 |
| 15 | 0.243 | 0.184 | 0.187 | 0.220 | 0.214 | 0.210 | 0.059 |
| 16 | 0.255 | 0.217 | 0.200 | 0.231 | 0.214 | 0.223 | 0.055 |
| 17 | 0.210 | 0.226 | 0.187 | 0.189 | 0.190 | 0.200 | 0.039 |
| 18 | 0.178 | 0.188 | 0.157 | 0.184 | 0.162 | 0.174 | 0.031 |
| 19 | 0.163 | 0.223 | 0.171 | 0.208 | 0.202 | 0.193 | 0.060 |
| 20 | 0.218 | 0.192 | 0.198 | 0.199 | 0.199 | 0.201 | 0.026 |
| | | | | | | $\bar{\bar{x}} = 0.201$ | $\bar{R} = 0.043$ |

## $\bar{X}$-Charts

First, we compute the preliminary center line and control limits for the $\bar{X}$-chart, as follows:

$$UCL = \bar{\bar{x}} + A_2\bar{R}$$
$$= 0.201 + (0.577 \times 0.043) = 0.226$$
$$LCL = \bar{\bar{x}} - A_2\bar{R}$$
$$= 0.201 - (0.577 \times 0.043) = 0.176$$

The preliminary control limits and the center line for the grand mean are shown in Figure 13-3, with the 20 sample means computed in column 7 of Table 13-2 plotted.

The control chart generally indicates that we have a stable data generating system, with the exception of sample 18, which falls below the *LCL*. It is entirely possible that this sample mean represents one of the chance occurrences of a mean falling outside the $3s_{\bar{x}}$ limits. However, we know that this event occurs with a probability of only .0027, so an investigation is warranted. The investigation reveals that the

FIGURE 13-3
**$\bar{X}$-CHART SHOWING PRELIMINARY AND REVISED PROCESS AVERAGES AND CONTROL LIMITS.**

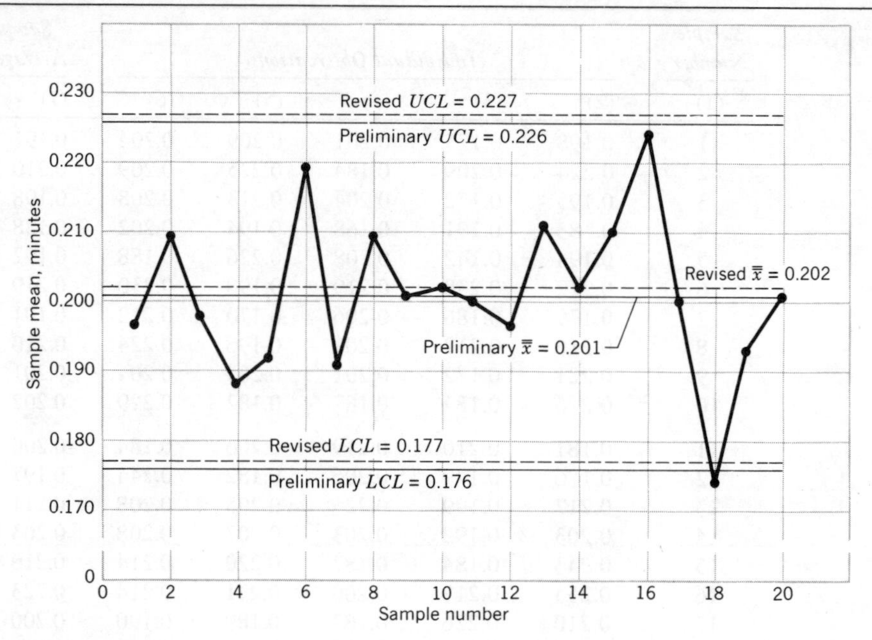


operator had been following a nonstandard method at the time that resulted in the low-valued observation—an assignable cause. Sample 18 is eliminated from the data and a revised grand mean and control limits are computed as $\bar{\bar{x}} = 0.202$ and $\bar{R} = 0.044$. The revised control limits are then

$$UCL = \bar{\bar{x}} + A_2\bar{R} = 0.202 + (0.577 \times 0.044) = 0.227$$
$$LCL = \bar{\bar{x}} - A_2\bar{R} = 0.202 - (0.577 \times 0.044) = 0.177$$

## When to Take Action

Having found sample 18 to be out of limits raises the question, "What patterns of points in a control chart suggest action?" Is action justified only when points go out of limits? The following are good guidelines for when to anticipate troubles by taking investigative action:

- A single point goes out of limits, either above or below
- Two consecutive points are near an upper or lower control limit
- A run of five points above or below the process average
- A five-point trend toward either limit
- A sharp change of level
- Erratic behavior

### R-Charts

The preliminary control limits for an $R$-chart are computed using the $D_3 = 0$ and $D_4 = 2.115$ factors from Table 13-1 as follows:

$$\begin{aligned} UCL &= D_4\bar{R} \\ &= 2.115 \times 0.043 = 0.0909 \\ LCL &= D_3\bar{R} \\ &= 0 \times 0.043 = 0 \end{aligned}$$

Figure 13-4 shows the $R$-chart with the preliminary control limits and the 20 sample ranges plotted. Note that the range for sample 18 does not fall outside the control limits on the $R$-chart. Nevertheless, since it was eliminated from the $\bar{X}$-chart, it must also be eliminated from the $R$-chart; the revised center line and control limits reflect this procedure. The $R$-chart indicates that the variability of the process is normal. The revised center lines and control limits in Figure 13-3 and 13-4 represent reasonable standards for comparison of future samples.

## CONTROL CHARTS FOR ATTRIBUTES

In control charts for attributes, the population is divided into two classifications: defective parts versus good parts, the number of invoices with errors versus error-free invoices in a clerical operation, the number absent versus the number present for absenteeism control, the proportion of idle time versus working time in a work sampling study, and so forth. In every instance where we wish to construct a control chart, we make this "good–not good" distinction.

FIGURE 13-4
**R-CHART SHOWING PRELIMINARY AND REVISED PROCESS AVERAGES AND CONTROL LIMITS.**

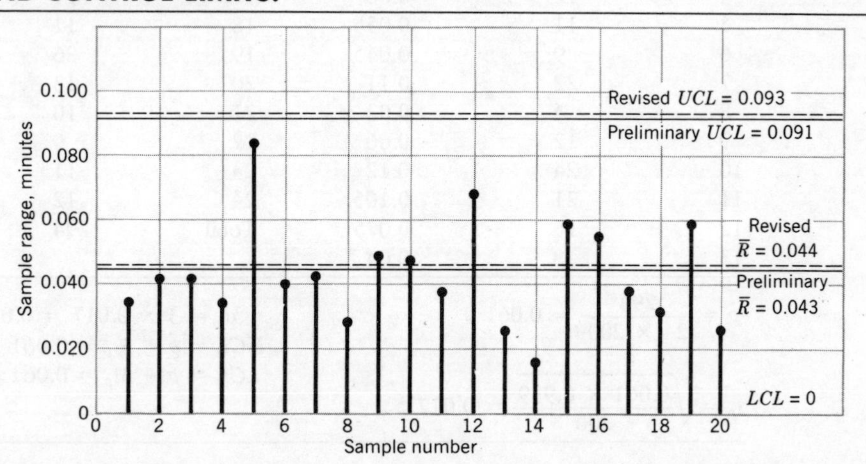

## p-Charts

Control charts for the proportion or fraction of defectives occurring are called *p*-charts; they are based on the binomial distribution. For the binomial distribution, recall that

$$\bar{p} = \frac{x}{N} = \frac{\text{Number of defectives}}{\text{Total number observed}}$$

$$s_p = \sqrt{\frac{\bar{p}(1 - \bar{p})}{n}}$$

where

$n$ = The size of the sample

Following general practice for quality control charts, the control limits are set at the process average of defectives plus and minus three standard deviations, $\bar{p} \pm 3s_p$.

Table 13-3 shows a set of data for the number of defectives found in daily samples of 200 for 24 consecutive production days. First, we want to determine whether the data exhibit statistical control, and then we want to set up a control chart. The daily fraction defective is calculated by dividing each daily figure by the sample size, $n$ = 200. Preliminary figures for $\bar{p}$, $s_p$, and $UCL$ and $LCL$ are also calculated in Table 13-

TABLE 13-3

**RECORD OF NUMBER OF DEFECTIVES AND CALCULATED FRACTION DEFECTIVE IN DAILY SAMPLES OF $n$ = 200**

| Production Day | Number of Defectives | Fraction Defective | Production Day | Number of Defectives | Fraction Defective |
|---|---|---|---|---|---|
| 1 | 10 | 0.05 | 14 | 14 | 0.07 |
| 2 | 5 | 0.025 | 15 | 4 | 0.02 |
| 3 | 10 | 0.05 | 16 | 10 | 0.05 |
| 4 | 12 | 0.06 | 17 | 11 | 0.055 |
| 5 | 11 | 0.055 | 18 | 11 | 0.055 |
| 6 | 9 | 0.045 | 19 | 26 | 0.13 |
| 7 | 22 | 0.11 | 20 | 13 | 0.065 |
| 8 | 4 | 0.02 | 21 | 10 | 0.05 |
| 9 | 12 | 0.06 | 22 | 9 | 0.045 |
| 10 | 24 | 0.12 | 23 | 11 | 0.055 |
| 11 | 21 | 0.105 | 24 | 12 | 0.06 |
| 12 | 15 | 0.075 | Total | 294 | |
| 13 | 8 | 0.04 | | | |

$$\bar{p} = \frac{294}{24 \times 200} = 0.061$$

$$s_p = \sqrt{\frac{0.061 \times 0.939}{200}} = 0.017$$

$$3s_p = 3 \times 0.017 = 0.051$$

$$UCL = \bar{p} + 3s_p = 0.061 + 0.051 = 0.112$$

$$LCL = \bar{p} - 3s_p = 0.061 - 0.051 = 0.010$$

3. These preliminary figures are used to determine whether the process generating the data is in control.

Figure 13-5 shows the resulting plot of the daily proportion defective in relation to the preliminary control limits. Two points are outside of limits, and the point for day 7 is nearly outside the upper limit. Investigation shows nothing unusual for the first point, day 7. For the second point, day 10, it appears that a logical explanation is that three new workers were taken on on that day. The last point, day 19, is explained by the fact that the die had worn and finally fractured that day.

To set up standards for normal variation, we eliminate the data for the days for which we have established assignable causes (days 10 and 19) and recompute $\bar{p}$, *UCL*, and *LCL* as follows:

$$\bar{p} = \frac{244}{200 \times 21} = 0.058$$

$$UCL = 0.058 + 3\sqrt{\frac{0.058 \times 0.942}{200}} = 0.108$$

$$LCL = 0.058 - 3\sqrt{\frac{0.058 \times 0.942}{200}} = 0.008$$

These revised values reflect the variation due to chance causes. We now use them as standards for judging the proportion of defective future samples. If any future samples fall outside these limits, our immediate reaction is that it is highly probable that there is an assignable cause for the unusual observation of proportion defective. We then attempt to determine the cause and correct it before more scrap has been produced.

FIGURE 13-5
**A *p*-CHART FOR EXAMINING PAST DATA AND ESTABLISHING PRELIMINARY AND REVISED CONTROL LIMITS.**

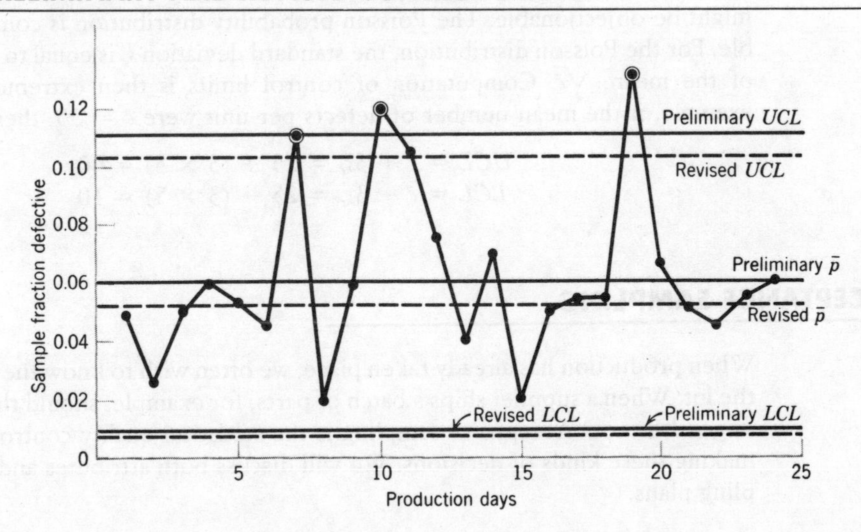

### p-Charts for Variable Sample Size

In the preceding example, the sample size was constant. Often, however, sample sizes vary, as is true when 100 percent inspection is used and output volumes vary from day to day. If sample sizes vary only slightly, control limits may be based on the average sample size. However, when sample sizes vary widely, new control limits can be computed for each sample, which is not an onerous task in today's world of computers.

These control limit computations can be simplified. For example, if $\bar{p} = 0.099$, then $3\sqrt{\bar{p}(1-\bar{p})/n} = 3\sqrt{0.099 \times 0.901}/\sqrt{n} = 0.896/\sqrt{n}$. For each sample then, the square root of the sample size is divided into 0.896 to obtain the $3s_p$ value that must be added to and subtracted from $\bar{p}$ to obtain the individual control limits. Of course, a different $\bar{p}$ requires a new computation of the constant.

Another way to handle this problem of variable sample sizes is to construct a *stabilized* p-*chart* by converting the deviations from the process average into standard deviation units. We compute an $s_p$ for each sample using the short-cut method just discussed (the factor for the example would simply be $0.896/3 = 0.299$) and divide it into the sample variation from $\bar{p}$, $p - \bar{p}$. If the sample proportion defective were $p = 0.084$, $\bar{p} = 0.099$ as before and $n = 95$, then $s_p = 0.299/\sqrt{95} = 0.0306$. Then $(p - \bar{p})/s_p = -0.015/0.0306 = -0.49$ standard deviation units. The control limits are plotted in terms of standard deviation units, and this sample is 0.49 standard deviations below the mean.

### c-Charts—Control Charts for Defects per Unit

Sometimes the parameter to be controlled cannot be expressed as a simple proportion as was true with the $p$-charts. In weaving, for example, the number of defects per 10 square yards of material might be the parameter to be controlled. In such instances, a defect itself might be minor, but a large number of defects per unit area might be objectionable. The Poisson probability distribution is commonly applicable. For the Poisson distribution, the standard deviation $s_c$ is equal to the square root of the mean, $\sqrt{\bar{c}}$. Computation of control limits is then extremely simple. For example, if the mean number of defects per unit were $\bar{c} = 25$, then

$$UCL = \bar{c} + 3s_c = 25 + (3 \times 5) = 40$$
$$LCL = \bar{c} - 3s_c = 25 - (3 \times 5) = 10$$

## ACCEPTANCE SAMPLING

When production has already taken place, we often wish to know the quality level of the lot. When a supplier ships a batch of parts, for example, should they be accepted as good or not? Acceptance sampling is the statistical quality control technique for making these kinds of decisions. We will discuss both attributes and variables sampling plans.

## ACCEPTANCE SAMPLING BY ATTRIBUTES

### Operating Characteristic (OC) Curves

To specify a particular sampling plan, we indicate the sample size, $n$, and the number of defectives in the sample permitted, $c$ (acceptance number), before the entire lot from which the sample was drawn is to be rejected. The *OC* curve for a particular combination of $n$ and $c$ shows how well the plan discriminates between good and bad lots. Figure 13-6 is an *OC* curve for a sampling plan with sample size $n = 100$ and acceptance number $c = 2$. In this plan, if $c = 0$, 1, or 2 defectives are found in the sample of $n = 100$, the lot would be considered acceptable. If more than two defectives are found, the lot would be rejected. If the actual lot quality is 1 percent defectives, the plan in Figure 13-6 would accept the lot about 91.5 percent of the time and reject it about 8.5 percent of the time. Note, however, that if the actual lot quality is somewhat worse than 1 percent defectives—perhaps 5 percent—the probability of accepting the lot falls drastically to about 13 percent. Therefore, if the actual quality is good, the plan provides for a high probability of acceptance, but if the actual quality is poor, the probability of acceptance is low. Thus, the *OC* curve shows how well a given plan discriminates between good and poor quality.

The discriminating power of a sampling plan depends on the size of the sample. Figure 13-7 shows the *OC* curves for sample sizes of 100, 200, and 300, with the acceptance number remaining in proportion to the sample size. Note that the *OC* curve becomes somewhat steeper as the sample size goes up. If we compare the discriminating power of the three plans represented in Figure 13-7, we see that all three would accept lots of about 0.7 percent defectives about 83 percent of the time (approximately the crossover point of the three curves). However, if actual quality falls to 3.0 percent defectives, the plan with $n = 100$ accepts lots about 20 percent

FIGURE 13-6
**OPERATING CHARACTERISTIC (OC) CURVE FOR A SAMPLING PLAN WITH $n = 100$ and $c = 2$.**

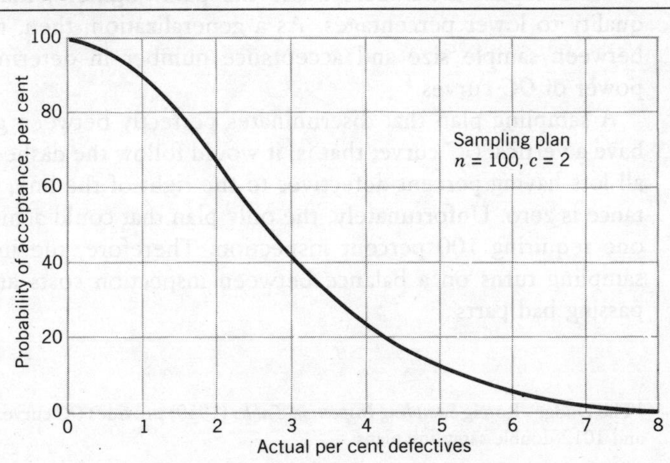

FIGURE 13-7
**OC CURVES FOR DIFFERENT SAMPLE SIZES WITH ACCEPTANCE NUMBERS IN PROPORTION TO SAMPLE SIZES.**

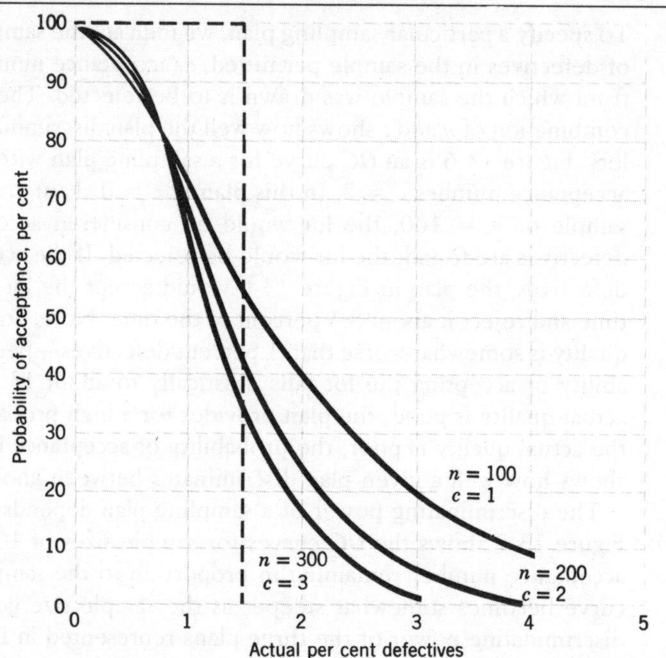


of the time; n = 200 accepts lots about 6 percent of the time; and $n = 300$, less than 1 percent of the time. Plans with larger sample sizes are definitely more effective.

What happens to the *OC* curve if only the acceptance number changes? Figure 13-8 shows *OC* curves for a sample of $n = 50$ and acceptance numbers of $c = 0$, 1, 2, and 3. Note that the effect is mainly to change the level of the *OC* curve, so lower acceptance numbers make the plan "tighter"; that is, they hold outgoing quality to lower percentages. As a generalization, then, there is some interaction between sample size and acceptance number in determining the discriminating power of *OC* curves.[1]

A sampling plan that discriminates perfectly between good and bad lots would have a vertical *OC* curve; that is, it would follow the dashed line in Figure 13-7. For all lots having percent defectives to the right of the line, the probability of acceptance is zero. Unfortunately, the only plan that could achieve this discrimination is one requiring 100 percent inspection. Therefore, the justification of acceptance sampling turns on a balance between inspection costs and the probable costs of passing bad parts.

[1] The Dodge–Romig *Sampling Inspection Tables* (1959) provides *OC* curves for 1148 single sampling plans and 1012 double sampling plans.

FIGURE 13-8
**OC CURVES WITH DIFFERENT ACCEPTANCE NUMBERS FOR A SAMPLE SIZE OF $n = 50$.**

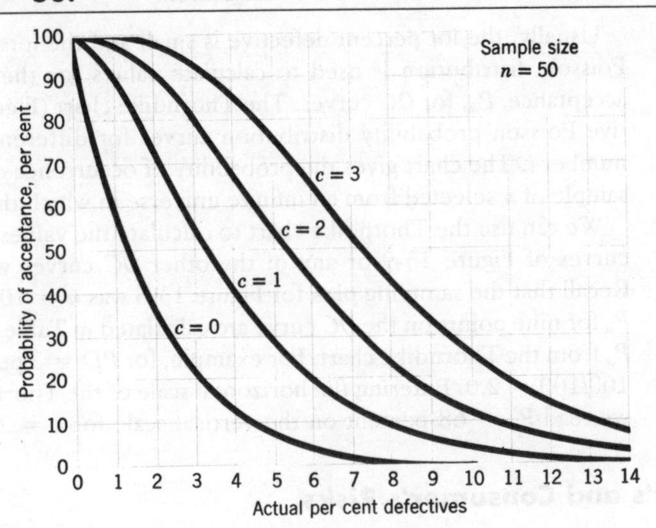


By making sampling plans more discriminating (increasing sample sizes) or tighter (decreasing acceptance numbers), we can approach any desired level of outgoing quality that we please, but at increasing inspection costs. This increased inspection effort would result in lower probable costs of passing defective parts. At some point the combination of these incremental costs is a minimum. This minimum point defines the most economical sampling plan for a given situation. Obviously, if the cost of passing defective products is high, a great deal of inspection is economically justified.

To justify 100 percent inspection of a sample, the probable losses due to the passing of bad products would have to be large in relation to inspection costs, perhaps resulting in the loss of contracts and customers. It is on this basis that the Japanese objective of "zero defects" can be justified. On the other hand, to justify no inspection at all, inspection costs would have to be very large in relation to the probable losses due to passing bad parts. The most usual situation is between these extremes, where there is a risk of not accepting lots that are actually good and a risk of accepting lots that are bad.

## Determining OC Curves

*OC* curves can be constructed from data obtained from normal or Poisson distributions. If lots are large, perhaps greater than 10 times the sample size, probabilities for the *OC* curve can be obtained from the binomial distribution. However, if samples are large, the normal or Poisson approximations are also very good, and they are much more convenient to use. Rules of thumb are as follows:

- If $p'n > 5$, the probabilities can be determined from the normal distribution with a mean $p'$ and standard deviation of $\sqrt{p'(1 - p')/n}$.
- If $p'n \leq 5$, use the Poisson distribution.

Usually, the lot percent defective is small and the lots are relatively large, so the Poisson distribution is used to calculate values for the percentage probability of acceptance, $P_a$, for *OC* curves. The Thorndike chart (Figure 13-9) provides cumulative Poisson probability distribution curves for different values of the acceptance number *c*. The chart gives the probability of occurrence of *c* or fewer defectives in a sample of *n* selected from an infinite universe in which the percent defective is *PD*.

We can use the Thorndike chart to calculate the values for $P_a$ used to plot the *OC* curves of Figure 13-9 or any of the other *OC* curves we have used as examples. Recall that the sampling plan for Figure 13-6 was $n = 100$ and $c = 2$. The values of $P_a$ for nine points on the *OC* curve are calculated in Table 13-4, reading the values of $P_a$ from the Thorndike chart. For example, for $PD = 2$ percent, $PD \times n/100 = 2 \times 100/100 = 2.0$. Entering the horizontal scale of the Thorndike chart with this value, we read $P_a = 68$ percent on the vertical scale for $c = 2$.

## Producer's and Consumer's Risks

The definition of these risks, discussed briefly in Chapter 12, can be made more specific by referring to a typical *OC* curve. Figure 13-10 shows graphically the following four definitions:

*AQL* = Acceptable quality level—lots of this level of quality are regarded as good, and we wish to have a high probability for their acceptance.

$\alpha$ = Producer's risk—the probability that lots of the quality level *AQL* will *not* be accepted. Usually $\alpha = 5$ percent in practice.

*LTPD* = Lot tolerance percent defective—the dividing line selected between good and bad lots. Lots of this level of quality are regarded as poor, and we wish to have a low probability for their acceptance.

$\beta$ = Consumer's risk—the probability that lots of the quality level *LTPD* will be accepted. Usually $\beta = 10$ percent in practice.

When we set the levels for each of these four values, we are determining two critical points on the *OC* curve that we desire, points *a* and *b* shown in Figure 13-10.

## Specification of a Sampling Plan

To specify a plan that meets the requirements for *AQL*, $\alpha$, *LTPD*, and $\beta$, we must find a combination of *n* and *c* with an *OC* curve that passes through points *a* and *b*, as shown in Figure 13-10. The mechanics of actually finding specific plans that fit can be accomplished by using standard tables, charts, or formulas that result in the specification of a combination of *n* and *c* that closely approximates the requirements set for *AQL*, $\alpha$, *LTPD*, and $\beta$.[2]

[2] For example, see H. F. Dodge and H. G. Romig, *Sampling Inspection Tables* (2nd ed.) Wiley, New York, 1959.

FIGURE 13-9

**THE THORNDIKE CHART: CUMULATIVE PROBABILITY DISTRIBUTION CURVES OF THE POISSON DISTRIBUTION.**

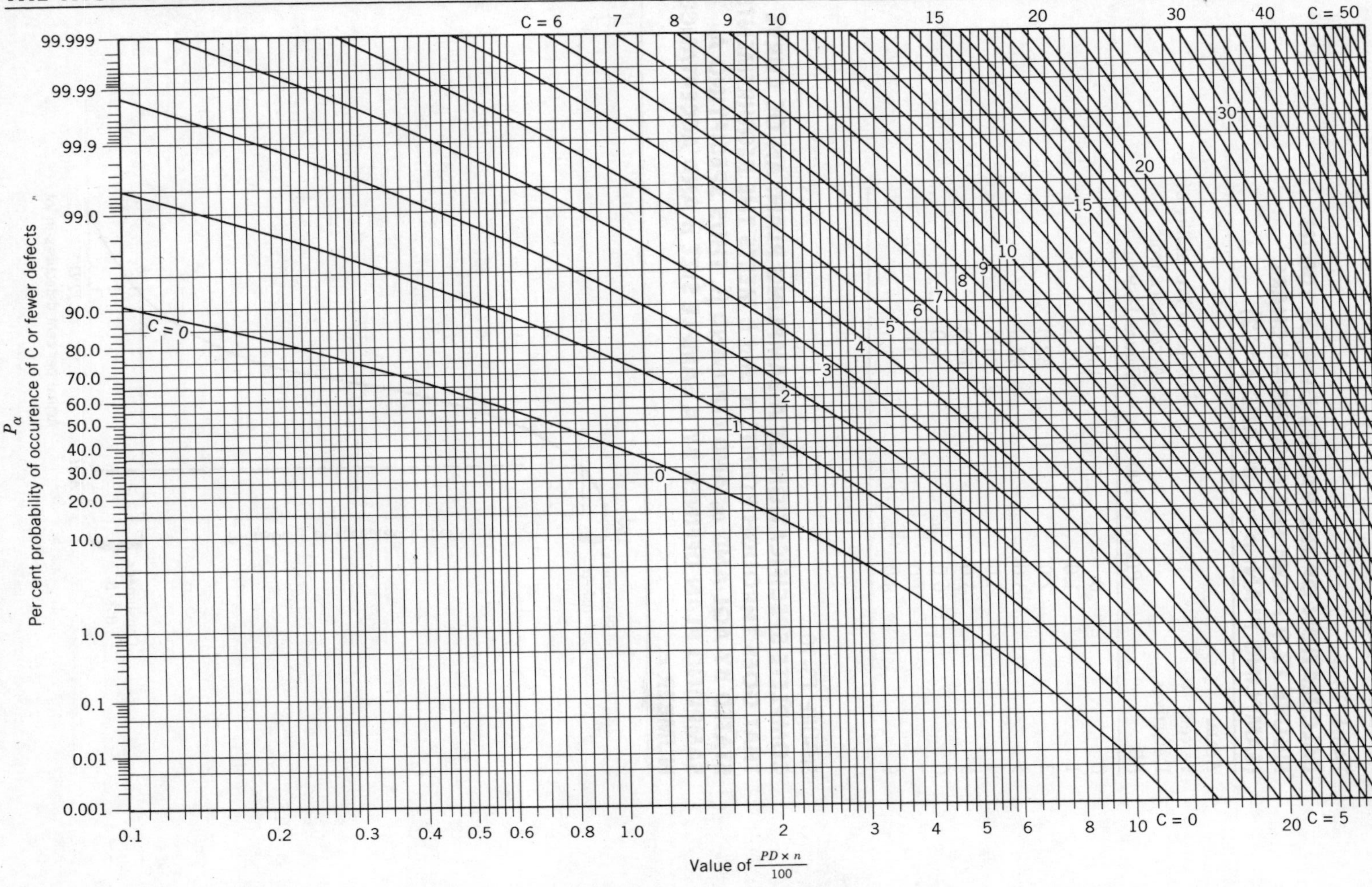


*Source:* Adapted from H. F. Dodge and H. G. Romig, *Sampling Inspection Tables* (2nd ed.), Wiley, New York, 1959.

TABLE 13-4
**CALCULATION OF THE VALUES OF $P_a \times 100$ IN FIGURE 13-9 FROM THE THORNDIKE CHART (SAMPLING PLAN: $n = 100$ AND $c = 2$)**

| Actual Percent Defectives, *PD* | $(PD \times n)/100$ | Percent Probability of Acceptance from Figure 13-9 |
|---|---|---|
| 0 | 0 | 100.0 |
| 1 | 1.0 | 91.5 |
| 2 | 2.0 | 68.0 |
| 3 | 3.0 | 42.0 |
| 4 | 4.0 | 24.0 |
| 5 | 5.0 | 12.0 |
| 6 | 6.0 | 6.0 |
| 7 | 7.0 | 3.0 |
| 8 | 8.0 | 1.5 |

FIGURE 13-10
**COMPLETE SPECIFICATION OF A SAMPLING PLAN. AN OC CURVE THAT GOES THROUGH POINTS *a* and *b* MEETS THE REQUIREMENTS STATED BY *AQL* AND $\alpha$, AND *LTPD* AND $\beta$, THUS SPECIFYING A SAMPLING PLAN DEFINED BY A SAMPLE SIZE *n* AND ACCEPTANCE NUMBER *c*.**

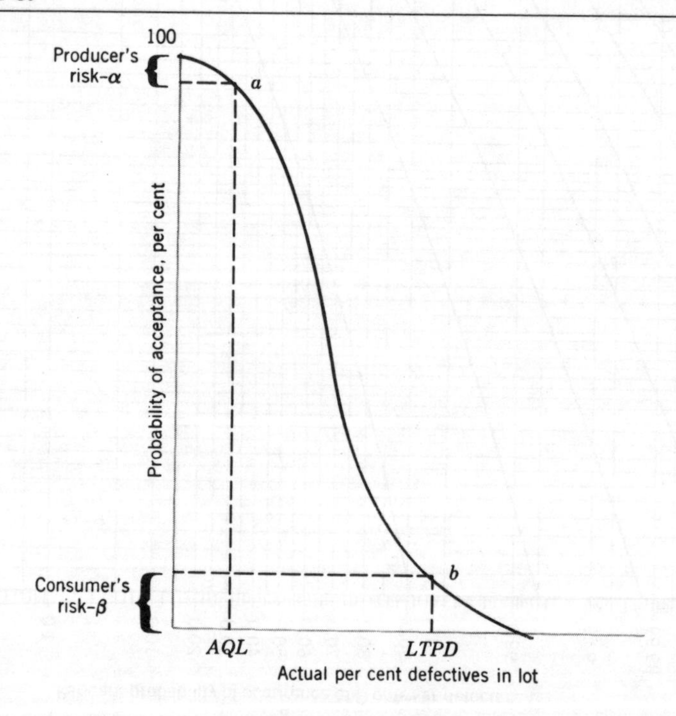

### SPECIFICATION OF $n$ AND $c$ FOR SINGLE SAMPLING PLANS

To specify a plan, we must determine the single sample size $n$ and the acceptance number $c$ that will produce an *OC* curve approximating that specified by the four values *AQL*, $\alpha$, *LTPD*, and $\beta$. This can be done by referring to tables or by using the Thorndike chart.

**An Example.** Assume that we have already specified the characteristics of the *OC* curve desired as

$$AQL = 2 \text{ percent}$$
$$\alpha = 5 \text{ percent}$$
$$LTPD = 8 \text{ percent}$$
$$\beta = 10 \text{ percent}$$

*Step 1.* Tabulate values of $PD \times n/100$ for $P_a = (1 - \alpha) = 95$ percent and $P_a = \beta = 10$ percent for each value of $c$ from the Thorndike chart. For example, for $P_a = 95$ percent and $c = 1$, read $PD \times n/100 = 0.36$, and for $P_a = 10$ percent and $c = 1$, read $PD \times n/100 = 3.9$. Do this for various values of $c$, as in columns 1, 2, and 3 of Table 13-5. Note that in column 2, the *PD* we are referring to is *AQL*, whereas in column 3, it is *LTPD*.

*Step 2.* Compute the ratio of column 3 to column 2 for each of the values of $c$, as in column 4 of Table 13-5. This ratio is *LTPD/PD*. For the plan we seek, we scan column 4 for the ratio $8/2 = 4$, since for our desired plan $LTPD = 8$ and $PD = 2$ percent. The ratio of 4 falls between 4.06 at $c = 4$ and 3.58 at $c = 5$.

*Step 3.* Compute sample sizes as in Table 13-6, deciding whether to hold $\alpha$ fixed and let $\beta$ float, or vice versa. If, for example, we set $c = 4$ and hold $\alpha$ at 5 percent, then $PD \times n/100 = AQL \times n/100 = 1.97$, and we can solve for the sample size $n$:

$$n = \frac{1.97 \times 100}{2} = 99$$

The sampling plan would then be $n = 99$ and $c = 4$.

*Step 4.* Check the resulting value of the risk floated. Using the Thorndike chart, for plan 1, enter with the values of $c = 4$ and $PD \times n/100 = LTPD \times n/100 = 8 \times 99/100 = 7.92$, and read the actual value of $\beta = 10.5$ percent.

Table 13-6 also shows the actual floating values of $\alpha$ and $\beta$ for each of the four plans. Note that for plan 1, the probability of accepting lots of 8 percent quality increases slightly while holding the other specifications. For plan 2, the probability of rejecting lots of good quality increases slightly while holding the specification for $\beta$ and so on. Plans 1 and 2 come closest to meeting the original specifications, and the choice between them depends on the emphasis desired.

TABLE 13-5
**DETERMINATION OF SAMPLING PLANS WITH SPECIFIED *AQL* AND *LTPD* ($\alpha$ = 5 PERCENT, $\beta$ = 10 PERCENT)**

| (1) Acceptance Number | (2) Value of $(PD \times n)/100$ at $P_a$ = 95 percent from Figure 13-9 | (3) Value of $(PD \times n)/100$ at $P_a$ = 10 percent from Figure 13-9 | (4) Ratio of Col. 3 : Col. 2 = *LTPD/AQL* |
|---|---|---|---|
| 1 | 0.36 | 3.9 | 10.83 |
| 2 | 0.80 | 5.3 | 6.63 |
| 3 | 1.35 | 6.7 | 4.96 |
| 4 | 1.97 | 8.0 | 4.06 |
| 5 | 2.60 | 9.3 | 3.58 |
| 6 | 3.30 | 10.5 | 3.18 |
| 7 | 4.00 | 11.8 | 2.95 |
| 8 | 4.70 | 13.0 | 2.77 |

**Other Values of $\alpha$ and $\beta$.** Table 13-5 was constructed for the common values of $\alpha$ and $\beta$, 5 and 10 percent, respectively. But obviously a comparable table could be constructed from the Thorndike chart for any values of $\alpha$ and $\beta$, so the methods described are general.

## Average Outgoing Quality (AOQ) Curves

Figure 13-11 shows the flow of good and rejected parts in a typical sampling plan and provides the structural basis for calculating the average outgoing quality (*AOQ*). The random sample of size $n$ is inspected, and any defectives found in the sample are replaced with good parts. Based on the number of defectives, $c'$, found in the sample, the entire lot is accepted if $c' \leq c$ and is rejected if $c' > c$.

If the lot is rejected, it is subjected to 100 percent inspection, and all defectives found are replaced by good parts. Then, the entire lot of $N$ parts is free of defectives. If, however, the lot is accepted by the sample, we run the risk that some defective parts have passed. The average number of defectives can be calculated.

TABLE 13-6
**SINGLE SAMPLING PLANS FOR c = 4 AND c = 5 WHEN $\alpha$ IS FIXED, ALLOWING $\beta$ TO FLOAT, AND WHEN $\beta$ IS FIXED, ALLOWING $\alpha$ TO FLOAT**

| *c Fixed at 4* | | *c Fixed at 5* | |
|---|---|---|---|
| (1) $\alpha$ = 5 Percent, $\beta$ Floats | (2) $\beta$ = 10 Percent, $\alpha$ Floats | (3) $\alpha$ = 5 Percent, $\beta$ Floats | (4) $\beta$ = 10 Percent, $\alpha$ Floats |
| $n = 1.97 \times 100/2 = 99$ | $n = 8.0 \times 100/8 = 100$ | $n = 2.60 \times 100/2 = 130$ | $n = 9.3 \times 100/8 = 115$ |
| $\beta$ = 10.5 percent | $\alpha$ = 5.5 percent | $\beta$ = 5 percent | $\alpha$ = 3 percent |

FIGURE 13-11
**FLOW OF GOOD AND REJECTED PARTS IN A TYPICAL ACCEPTANCE SAMPLING PLAN SHOWING THE BASIS FOR CALCULATING AVERAGE OUTGOING QUALITY (AOQ).**

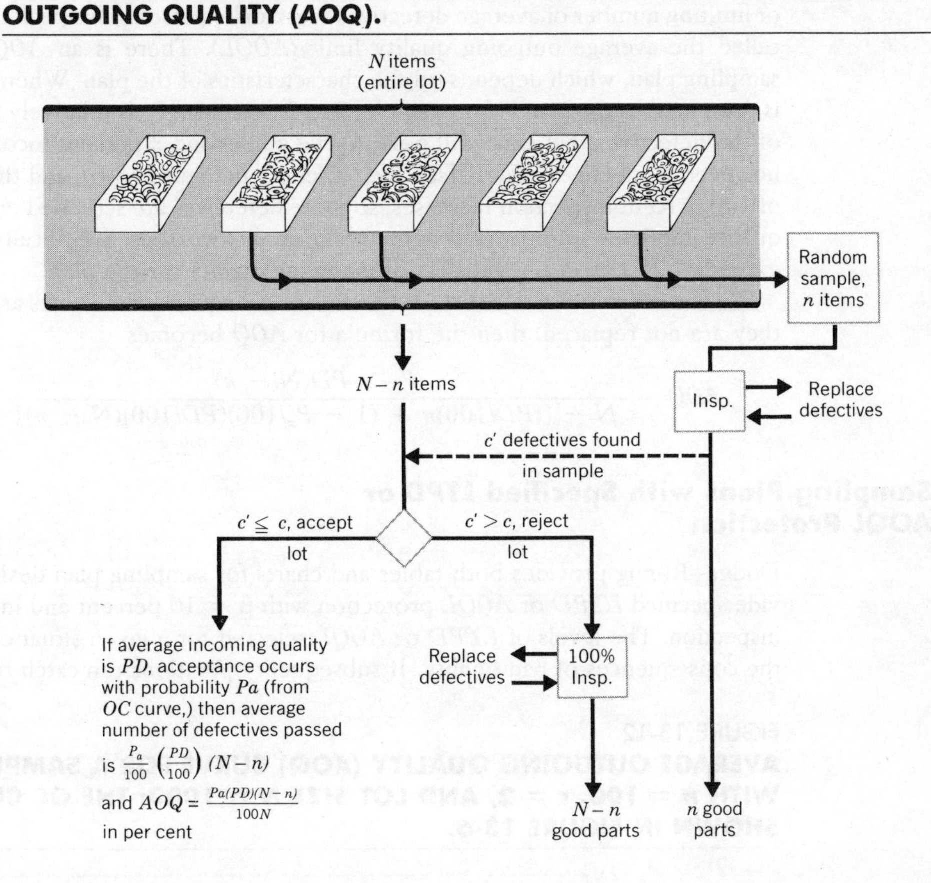


If the average incoming quality is $PD$, acceptance occurs with the probability $P_a$ (taken directly from the $OC$ curve for the $PD$). The average number of defectives is then the product of the fraction defectives received times the number remaining in the lot weighted by the probability that acceptance occurs or $(P_a/100) \times (PD/100) \times (N - n)$. The average outgoing quality $AOQ$ in percent is then:[3]

$$AOQ = \frac{\text{Average number of defectives}}{\text{Number of parts in lot}} \times 100 = \frac{P_a(PD)(N - n)}{100N}$$

From the foregoing relationship, we can develop a curve for any given sampling plan showing the $AOQ$ for any level of incoming quality. Data to plot the curve are generated by assuming different values for incoming quality, determining from the $OC$ curve the $P_a$, and substituting these values in the formula to compute $AOQ$, as

[3]This formula is an approximation, and assumes equal means for each incoming lot.

indicated in Figure 13-12. This *AOQ* curve is based on the *OC* curve of Figure 13-6 for a sampling plan of $n = 100$, $c = 2$, and $N = 1000$.

Note the interesting characteristics of the *AOQ* curve. First, there is a maximum or limiting number of average defectives that can be passed. This peak in the curve is called the average outgoing quality limit (*AOQL*). There is an *AOQL* for every sampling plan, which depends on the characteristics of the plan. When good quality is presented to the plan—for example, 0 to 2 percent—$P_a$ is relatively high, so most of the defectives that exist will pass. As we go beyond 2 percent incoming quality, however, $P_a$ declines rapidly (see the *OC* curve in Figure 13-6), and the probability of 100 percent inspection increases, so more defectives are screened out—outgoing quality improves automatically as incoming quality worsens. Specifically, *AOQ* never exceeds 1.25 percent, regardless of incoming quality for the plan.

We have shown the calculations for the situation where defectives are replaced. If they are not replaced, then the formula for *AOQ* becomes

$$AOQ = \frac{P_a \times PD(N - n)}{N - [(PD/100)n + (1 - P_a/100)(PD/100)(N - n)]} \times 100$$

## Sampling Plans with Specified *LTPD* or *AOQL* Protection

Dodge–Romig provides both tables and charts for sampling plan designs that provide specified *LTPD* or *AOQL* protection with $\beta = 10$ percent and minimum total inspection. The levels of *LTPD* or *AOQL* selected for a given situation depend on the consequences of bad quality. If subsequent operations can catch further defec-

FIGURE 13-12
**AVERAGE OUTGOING QUALITY (AOQ) CURVE FOR A SAMPLING PLAN WITH $n$ = 100, $c$ = 2, AND LOT SIZE $N$ = 1000; THE OC CURVE IS SHOWN IN FIGURE 13-6.**

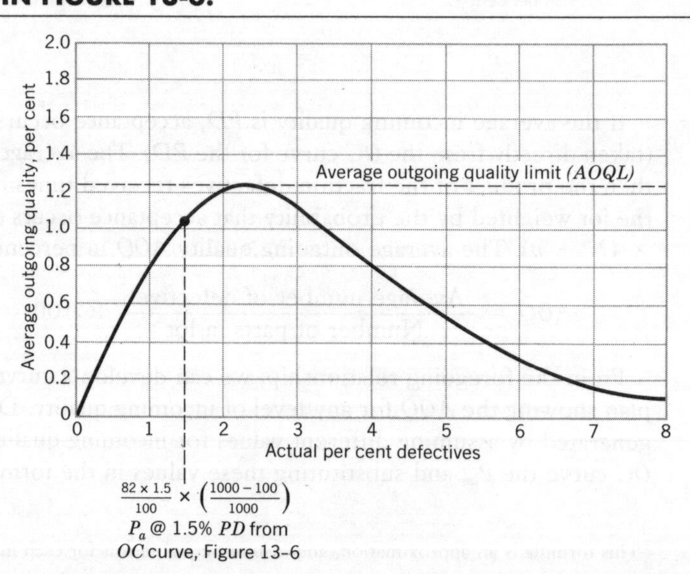

tives without disrupting production, these standards can be fairly loose, but if the lower quality results in high production and quality-related costs, *LTPD* or *AOQL* should be held to low levels.

## Double Sampling Plans

Double sampling has the advantage of lower inspection costs for a given level of protection. It is accomplished by taking a smaller sample initially. Based on the results of this sample, the lot is either accepted, rejected, or no final decision is made. In the last instance, a second sample is drawn and a final decision is made based on the combined samples. The disadvantage of double sampling is that the inspection load varies considerably.

As with single sampling, Dodge–Romig provides both tables and charts to aid in plan design. These aids are constructed both for the situation where one wishes to specify *LTPD* or *AOQL*, with $\beta = 10$ percent, and for minimum total inspection.

## Sequential Sampling Plans

In sequential sampling, samples are drawn at random, as before. But after each sample is inspected, the cumulated results are analyzed and a decision made to (1) accept the lot, (2) reject the lot, or (3) take another sample. Sequential sample sizes can be as small as $n = 1$.

Figure 13-13 shows the graphical structure of a sequential sampling plan. The main advantage of sequential sampling is a reduction in the total amount of inspection required to maintain a given level of protection. In the plan shown in Figure 13-13, a minimum of 15 items must be inspected in order to accept a lot. If the number of rejects on the graph rises such that the point falls on or above the upper line, the

FIGURE 13-13
**SEQUENTIAL SAMPLING PLAN.**

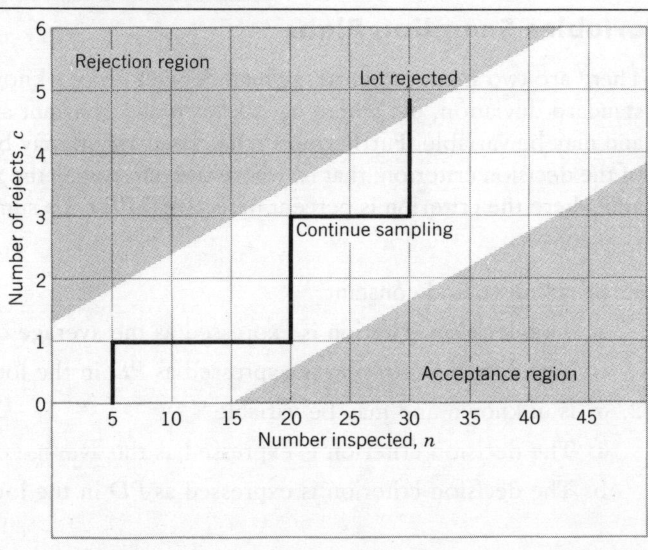

lot is rejected. If the point should fall on or below the lower line, the lot is accepted. Until one of these events occurs, sampling is continued. As before, a sequential sampling plan is specified by the four requirements: *AQL*, α, *LTPD*, and β. In turn, these requirements determine the *OC* curves of the sequential plans that meet the requirements. The disadvantage of sequential sampling is that inspection loads vary considerably. Detailed procedures for the construction of sequential sampling plans are given in Duncan (1974).

### Bases for Selecting Sampling Plans

The relative advantages and disadvantages of alternative sampling plans do not rest on the protection from poor quality that can be achieved. The risks involved depend on the *OC* curve of the plan and can be preset, and specific objectives of *LTPD* or *AOQL* protection can be implemented in all three. Table 13-7 provides the comparison of several factors that influence the choice among the three types of plans.

## ACCEPTANCE SAMPLING BY VARIABLES

In acceptance sampling by variables, we make and record actual measurements instead of simply classifying items as good or bad as in attributes sampling. This difference in procedure changes the details of determining a plan that meets our specifications of *AQL*, α, *LTPD*, and β because the appropriate statistical distribution is now the *normal* distribution instead of distributions for proportions. Conceptually, however, the basic ideas on which the control of outgoing quality is maintained remain the same. The discriminating power of a plan is represented by an *OC* curve, which shows the probability of acceptance for different levels of actual quality presented to the plan. To specify a plan that gives the desired protection requires basically the same procedure as for sampling by attributes.

### Kinds of Variables Sampling Plans

There are two main categories, which depend on our knowledge of the population standard deviation, $\sigma_x$: where $\sigma_x$ is known and constant and where $\sigma_x$ is unknown and may be variable. Furthermore, the classification may be extended to the nature of the decision criterion; that is, where the criterion is the average of measurements and where the criterion is percent defectives (*PD*). To summarize, the classification is as follows:

1. $\sigma_x$ is known and constant
   a. The decision criterion is expressed as the average of measurements, $x_{\bar{a}}$
   b. The decision criterion is expressed as *PD* in the lot
2. $\sigma_x$ is unknown and may be variable
   a. The decision criterion is expressed as the average of measurements, $x_{\bar{a}}$
   b. The decision criterion is expressed as *PD* in the lot

TABLE 13-7
**FACTORS INFLUENCING THE CHOICE AMONG TYPES OF SAMPLING PLANS**

| | *Type of Sampling Plan* | | |
|---|---|---|---|
| Factor | Single | Double | Sequential |
| Protection against rejecting high quality lots and accepting low quality lots | Same | Same | Same |
| Total inspection cost | Highest | Intermediate | Least |
| Amount of record keeping | Least | Intermediate | Most |
| Variability of inspection load | Constant | Variable | Variable |
| Sampling costs when all samples can be taken as needed | Highest | Intermediate | Least |
| Sampling costs when all samples must be drawn at same time | Least | Highest | Intermediate |
| Accurate estimate of lot quality | Best | Intermediate | Worst |
| Sampling costs when dependent on the number of samples drawn | Least | Intermediate | Highest |
| Relationship with suppliers, that is, give more than one chance | Worst | Intermediate | Best |

We will discuss plan design for which $\sigma_x$ is known and constant and the decision criterion is expressed by the average of measurements. Procedures for the situation where $\sigma_x$ is unknown and may be variable may be found in Duncan (1974).

## Variables Sampling Plans Where $\sigma_x$ Is Known and Constant

We will discuss these procedures in the context of an example in which steel bar stock is received in batches from a vendor. It has been determined that a tensile strength of 90,000 pounds per square inch (psi) is required, and we wish to specify that $P_a = 10$ percent for lots of this average tensile strength. Lots with an average tensile strength of 95,000 psi are regarded as good quality, and we wish to specify that $P_a = 95$ percent for lots of this average tensile strength. We have a long history with this supplier, so $\sigma_x$ is known to be 6000 psi, and the measurements are normally distributed. To summarize, our plan specifications are

$$
\begin{aligned}
AQL &= 95{,}000 \text{ psi} \\
\bar{x}_t &= 90{,}000 \text{ psi (equivalent to } LTPD \text{ in attributes sampling)} \\
\alpha &= 5 \text{ percent} \\
\beta &= 10 \text{ percent}
\end{aligned}
$$

We wish to determine a sampling plan that will indicate an acceptance average for sample tests, $\bar{x}_a$, and a sample size $n$ that will accept lots according to our specifications. The acceptance average for sample tests $\bar{x}_a$, is equivalent to acceptance number, $c$, in attributes sampling plans. In other words, when $\bar{x}_a$ is less than the value we determine as critical, the lot from which the sample was drawn will be rejected and returned to the supplier. Lots for which the sample average tensile strength is equal to or greater than $\bar{x}_a$ will be accepted.

The standard deviation of the sampling distribution of means for samples of size $n$ will be $6000/\sqrt{n}$. To be accepted 95 percent of the time, $AQL = 95{,}000$ psi must be $1.645\sigma$ units above the grand mean, $\bar{\bar{x}} = \bar{x}_a$, since 5 percent of the area under a normal curve is beyond $\mu + 1.645\sigma$ (see Table 6 of the Appendix). Therefore, $\bar{x}_a - 95{,}000$ is $1.645\sigma_{\bar{x}}$ units. Then,

$$\bar{x}_a - 95{,}000 = -1.645 \times (6000/\sqrt{n})$$

Also, to ensure that lots of average tensile strength $\bar{x}_t = 90{,}000$ have only a 10 percent chance of acceptance, which ensures that samples with $x_i = 90{,}000$ psi must be $1.282\sigma$ units below the grand mean,

$$\bar{x}_a - 90{,}000 = +1.282 \times (6000/\sqrt{n})$$

We now have two independent equations with two unknowns, $\bar{x}_a$ and $n$. They may be solved simultaneously to yield the following values:

$$\bar{x}_a = 92{,}200 \text{ psi}$$
$$n = 12$$

Figure 13-14 shows the relationships of the various elements of the problem that answer the question, "What is the grand mean, $\bar{\bar{x}}$, and the sample size, $n$, of a normal distribution with $\sigma = 6000$ psi and $\sigma_{\bar{x}} = 6000/\sqrt{n}$?"

The *OC* curve for the plan just described is determined by cumulating the areas under the normal curve for the sampling distribution of sample size $n$. The *OC* curve for this plan is shown in Figure 13-15.

### UPPER AND LOWER TOLERANCE LEVELS

There are often upper *and* lower tolerance levels specified for measurements of part dimensions, chemical content, and so forth. When a measured characteristic may be too small or too large to be useful, these two-sided tolerance levels can be reflected in the specifications of variables sampling plans. A sampling plan would then specify a sample size, with upper and lower average acceptance levels. Two equations must then be written for each limit and solved for $\bar{x}_a$ (upper) and $\bar{x}_a$ (lower) and the integer value of the sample size $n$ that most nearly satisfies the stated risks $\alpha$ and $\beta$.

## Field of Application of Variables Sampling Plans

Obviously, inspection, recording, and computing costs will normally be higher with variables sampling plans than with attributes sampling plans. Then, why use variables plans? The most important reason is that, for a given level of protection, variables plans will require smaller sample sizes and less total inspection. Table 13-8 demonstrates the contrasting sample sizes over a large range. The differences are relatively small for small sample sizes, but if a plan requires a sample size of 750 for attributes sampling, comparable protection could be obtained with a sample of only

FIGURE 13-14
**RELATIONSHIP OF VALUES IN THE TENSILE STRENGTH VARIABLES SAMPLING PLAN TO THE NORMAL CURVE.**

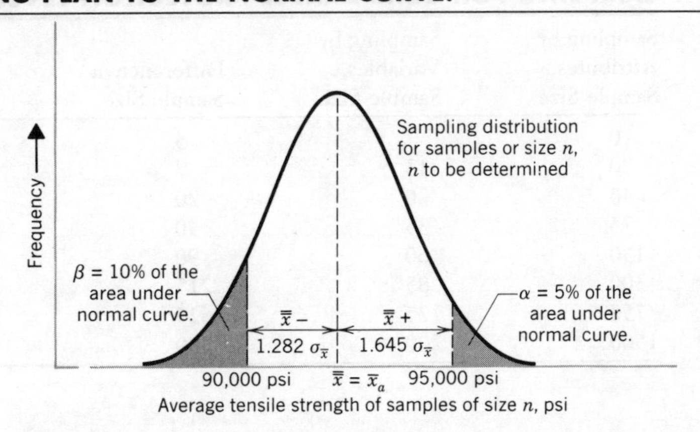


125 for variables sampling. These smaller sample sizes can be very important when the inspection process destroys the part. From an economic point of view, then, variables sampling should be used when the smaller sample size tips the balance of the costs of inspection, scrap, recording, and computing. In addition to the possible cost advantages, the data generated by variables sampling ($\bar{x}$ and $s$) provide additional valuable diagnostic information for controlling production processes.

FIGURE 13-15
**OC CURVE FOR A VARIABLES ACCEPTANCE SAMPLING PLAN FOR THE TENSILE STRENGTH OF STEEL BARS.**

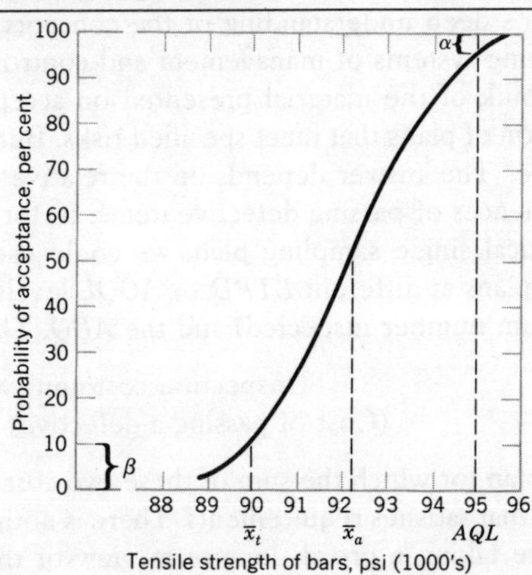

TABLE 13-8
**SAMPLE SIZES FOR VARIABLES VERSUS ATTRIBUTES SAMPLING FOR COMPARABLE PROTECTION LEVELS**

| Sampling by Attributes, Sample Size | Sampling by Variables, Sample Size | Difference in Sample Size | Percentage Difference |
|---|---|---|---|
| 10 | 7 | 3 | 30 |
| 20 | 13 | 7 | 35 |
| 40 | 20 | 20 | 50 |
| 75 | 35 | 40 | 53 |
| 150 | 60 | 90 | 60 |
| 300 | 85 | 215 | 72 |
| 750 | 125 | 625 | 83 |
| 1500 | 200 | 1300 | 87 |

## IMPLICATIONS FOR THE MANAGER

Statistical quality control (*SQC*) is a technical subject, so why should managers have at least the exposure contained in this chapter? First, general managers need to understand just how closely they can control quality; that is, if they are willing to put in the resources to control quality, do the techniques make it possible to achieve high-quality goals? Managers of quality assurance need a deep understanding of all the concepts and techniques. The *SQC* techniques reviewed in this chapter should make it clear that any quality goal can be implemented.

In the past, high quality and high productivity have been treated as a system of trade-offs, the assumption being that you cannot have both of these pluses at the same time. It is now increasingly clear that the two are correlated. Process control puts the emphasis on improving the process so that high quality is produced without high rework and scrap rates—the emphasis is on making it correctly the first time. A manager's deep understanding of the concepts of process control is necessary for developing systems of management and control.

The bulk of the material presented on acceptance sampling has to do with the derivation of plans that meet specified risks. But what should those risks and quality levels be? The answer depends on the relative costs of inspection and the costs or consequences of passing defective items. If, for example, we were searching for an economical single sampling plan, we could use the Dodge–Romig tables to find several plans at different *LTPD* or *AOQL* levels of protection, determining an $I_{min}$ (minimum number inspected) and the *AOQ*. The balance of the costs would be

$$(\text{Inspection cost/unit}) \times (I_{min}/\text{lot}) + (\text{Cost of passing a defective}) \times (AOQ/100 \times N)$$

The plan for which the sum of these two cost components is minimum should be the one that satisfies requirements. There is nothing wrong with this general concept if we are taking a broad, long-term view of the cost of passing a defective. Past practice has taken a narrow, short-term view, however, resulting in quality objectives that characterize $AOQ = 2$ percent defectives as good quality. Meanwhile, our Japanese competitors, using the same statistical quality control techniques taught them by Americans, have adopted much higher quality standards. In fact, "zero defects" has become the objective stated in slogans exhorting Japanese workers on to new heights of quality achievement. The Japanese standards recognize a very high cost of passing a defective, including damage to customer good will and perhaps even loss of market share. If management sets high objectives and standards, acceptance sampling techniques can implement them. *SQC* knows no national boundaries.

Finally, the concepts of *SQC* provide a rigorous base for designing managerial systems on the exception principle. Although the techniques themselves may not be implemented in other settings, the concepts can be employed in many managerial settings.

## REVIEW QUESTIONS

1. What are assignable and chance causes of variation in a process?
2. What are assignable causes of variation in a production process?
3. What is the probability that a measurement drawn from a normal distribution will fall within the $3s$ limits?
4. What is the probability that a measurement drawn from a distribution other than a normal distribution will fall within the $3s$ limits?
5. When the potential loss is high relative to the cost of investigation, should control limits be relatively broad, perhaps $\pm 3s$?
6. Which would be the more sensitive control limits, $\pm 3s$ or $\pm 2s$?
7. Why are variables control charts normally constructed for small samples rather than for individual measurements?
8. What is the relationship between $s_{\bar{x}}$, the standard deviation of the sampling distribution, and $s$, the unbiased estimate of the standard deviation of the population distribution?
9. Outline the procedures required to construct $\bar{X}$ and $R$ control charts.
10. Can $\bar{X}$- and $R$-charts be constructed for measures of variability?
11. What statistical distribution is appropriate for control charts for attributes ($p$-charts)?
12. Could a control chart be constructed that allowed for a continuous change of control limits, as in the situation where a tool might wear as a process progresses?
13. What is the appropriate distribution for control charts for defects per unit ($c$-charts)?
14. What is the area of application of $c$-charts?
15. If sample sizes vary, how can the $p$-chart be modified to take this fact into account?

16. What is a stabilized *p*-chart? What function does it perform?
17. Discuss the concept of statistical control in relation to the general principle of "management control by the exception principle."
18. What is the function of acceptance sampling, and how is it distinguished from other kinds of statistical control?
19. Under what conditions is acceptance sampling appropriate?
20. When is a 100 percent sample justified?
21. What information is provided by an *OC* curve?
22. What is the effect on the *OC* curve of increasing sample size *n*? Of increasing acceptance number *c*?
23. For acceptance sampling by attributes, what is the statistical distribution that is most commonly appropriate? If $p'n$ is greater than 5, what is the distribution that best approximates the binomial distribution?
24. Outline the use of the Thorndike chart in determining *OC* curves for sampling by attributes.
25. Define *AQL*, α, *LTPD*, and β, showing their relationships on a typical *OC* curve.
26. Is it possible to specify exactly the levels of *LTPD*, *AQL*, α, and β in determining an acceptance sampling plan for attributes?
27. What is the function of an *AOQ* curve? Can we specify *AOQL* as one of the design parameters for a plan?
28. Describe the nature of double sampling.
29. What are the advantages and disadvantages of double sampling compared to single sampling?
30. Describe the structure of sequential sampling plans. What are their advantages and disadvantages?
31. Outline the general procedures necessary to construct an acceptance sampling plan for variables.
32. Under what conditions would a variables sampling plan be used?
33. Why is *AOQ* always better than the quality actually produced?
34. How might acceptance sampling procedures be used in the following types of productive systems: a hospital, a drug store, the IRS, the Social Security Administration, an airline, a fast-food restaurant.

# PROBLEMS

35. The mean and the standard deviation for a process for which we have a long record are $\bar{x} = 15.000$ and $s = 4$, respectively. In setting up a variables control chart, we propose to use samples of $n = 4$. What is the standard deviation of the sampling distribution?

36. What are the $\pm 3s$ control limits for a variables control chart on means for the data in problem 35? What are the control limits if the sample size is $n = 1$? What is the implied value of $\bar{R}$?

37. Measurements on the output dimension of a production process are $\bar{\bar{x}} = 4.000$ inch, $\bar{R} = 0.5$ inch, and $n = 6$. What are the center lines and the control limits for an $\bar{X}$-chart and an $R$-chart?

38. Table 13-9 is a record of the number of clerical errors in posting a journal. What is the average error fraction? What is the standard deviation? If a control chart were to be constructed for these data, what kind of chart would it be? What would be the center line and control limits for this chart?

39. For the data in Table 13-9, construct a control chart, plotting the 20 observations given. Is the process in control? If not, what are the revised center line and control limits, assuming that the causes are assignable?

40. Table 13-10 is a record of the number of paint defects per unit for metal desk equipment painted by dipping. What is the average number of defects per unit? What is the standard deviation? If a control chart were to be constructed for these data, what kind of chart would it be? What would be the center line and control limits of the chart?

41. For the data in Table 13-10, construct a control chart, plotting the 20 observations given. Is the process in control? If not, what are the revised center line and control limits, assuming that the causes are assignable?

42. Data are given in Table 13-11 for the number of defective parts in a production process. The sample sizes vary, so it is necessary to construct a $p$-chart with variable control limits. Compute the center line and the variable limits, and plot the data points with their limits on a control chart. Is the process in control?

43. For the data given in Table 13-11, construct a stabilized $p$-chart. Is the process in control?

**TABLE 13-9**
**RECORD OF THE NUMBER OF CLERICAL ERRORS IN POSTING A JOURNAL ($n$ = 200)**

| Sample Number | Number of Errors | Error Fraction | Sample Number | Number of Errors | Error Fraction |
|---|---|---|---|---|---|
| 1 | 11 | 0.055 | 12 | 7 | 0.035 |
| 2 | 7 | 0.035 | 13 | 9 | 0.045 |
| 3 | 4 | 0.020 | 14 | 5 | 0.025 |
| 4 | 1 | 0.005 | 15 | 17 | 0.085 |
| 5 | 5 | 0.025 | 16 | 18 | 0.090 |
| 6 | 13 | 0.065 | 17 | 9 | 0.045 |
| 7 | 6 | 0.030 | 18 | 5 | 0.025 |
| 8 | 5 | 0.025 | 19 | 7 | 0.035 |
| 9 | 3 | 0.015 | 20 | 0 | 0.000 |
| 10 | 0 | 0.000 | Total | 131 | |
| 11 | 5 | 0.025 | | | |

TABLE 13-10
**RECORD OF THE NUMBER OF PAINT DEFECTS PER UNIT FOR METAL DESK EQUIPMENT PAINTED BY DIPPING**

| Item Number | Number of Defects per Unit | Item Number | Number of Defects per Unit |
|---|---|---|---|
| 1 | 19 | 12 | 10 |
| 2 | 16 | 13 | 22 |
| 3 | 23 | 14 | 5 |
| 4 | 11 | 15 | 23 |
| 5 | 15 | 16 | 22 |
| 6 | 12 | 17 | 14 |
| 7 | 17 | 18 | 6 |
| 8 | 11 | 19 | 13 |
| 9 | 20 | 20 | 6 |
| 10 | 15 | | |
| 11 | 13 | | |

TABLE 13-11
**RECORD OF THE NUMBER OF DEFECTIVE PARTS IN A PRODUCTION PROCESS (SAMPLE SIZES VARY)**

| Sample Number | Sample Size | Number of Defective Parts | Proportion Defective |
|---|---|---|---|
| 1 | 95 | 8 | 0.084 |
| 2 | 90 | 6 | 0.067 |
| 3 | 100 | 9 | 0.090 |
| 4 | 105 | 10 | 0.095 |
| 5 | 105 | 8 | 0.076 |
| 6 | 120 | 7 | 0.058 |
| 7 | 115 | 14 | 0.122 |
| 8 | 80 | 7 | 0.088 |
| 9 | 90 | 9 | 0.100 |
| 10 | 80 | 17 | 0.213 |
| 11 | 90 | 12 | 0.133 |
| 12 | 100 | 10 | 0.100 |
| 13 | 100 | 8 | 0.080 |
| 14 | 110 | 10 | 0.091 |
| 15 | 130 | 6 | 0.046 |
| 16 | 100 | 8 | 0.080 |
| 17 | 110 | 9 | 0.082 |
| 18 | 110 | 10 | 0.091 |
| 19 | 90 | 20 | 0.222 |
| 20 | 80 | 10 | 0.125 |
| Totals | 2000 | 198 | |

$\bar{p} = 198/2000 = 0.0990$

44. A single sampling plan is described as $n = 50$ and $c = 1$.
    a. Using the Thorndike chart, determine the values of the percent probability of lot acceptance for actual percent defectives of 0 through 12 in increments of 1.
    b. Plot the results as an *OC* curve.
45. Repeat problem 44, but for a plan where $c = 0$. Plot it on the same diagram, and compare it with the $c = 1$ plan.
46. $AQL = 1.5$ percent, $\alpha = 5$ percent, and $c = 2$. What is the sample size?
47. For the plan in problem 46, if $\beta = 10$ percent, what is *LTPD*?
48. $AQL = 2$ percent, $\alpha = 5$ percent, $LTPD = 6$ percent, and $\beta = 10$ percent. Determine $n$ and $c$ for a single sampling plan that holds rigidly to the specification for $\alpha$. What is the actual value of $\beta$?
49. A producer of computer chips has decided to grant equality to consumers by making $\alpha$ and $\beta$ equal at 5 percent. A further step to ensure high quality is in the standards set: $AQL = 0.5$ percent and $LTPD = 1.5$ percent. With these specifications, the producer is now seeking a single sampling plan to implement the specifications. What plan or plans should she consider?
50. An auditor is sampling a stack of $N = 10{,}000$ invoices to decide if he should accept the work of the clerk involved. He has previous evidence that the error rate has been 0.3 percent, and he is willing to accept this rate 5 percent of the time. However, he is not willing to accept the lot if the error rate is more than 1.5 percent more than 5 percent of the time. What sampling plan should the auditor use?

# SITUATIONS

All the situations in this chapter are based on the 3-inch V-belt pulley shown in Figure 13-16. It should be studied carefully. The pulley is made up of two identical flanges that are formed by presses, a hub that is produced on turret lathes, and a set screw that is purchased. The flanges are spot welded to the hub, and the two flanges are spot welded together, as specified. Finally, the entire pulley is cadmium plated.

## The Hub

51. Trouble has been experienced in holding the tolerance specified for the length of the hub, 1.00 inch ± 0.040 inch. Ten samples of four pulleys each yield the data shown in Table 13-12.
    a. Determine the natural tolerance of the process generating the hub. Is the present turret lathe process capable of meeting the specified tolerance?
    b. Assuming that tool wear is the only predictable variable in the process, at what average hub length should the process be centered whenever a tool change or an adjustment is made? Sketch the distribution relationships and explain.

FIGURE 13-16
**DRAWING OF A V-BELT PULLEY.**

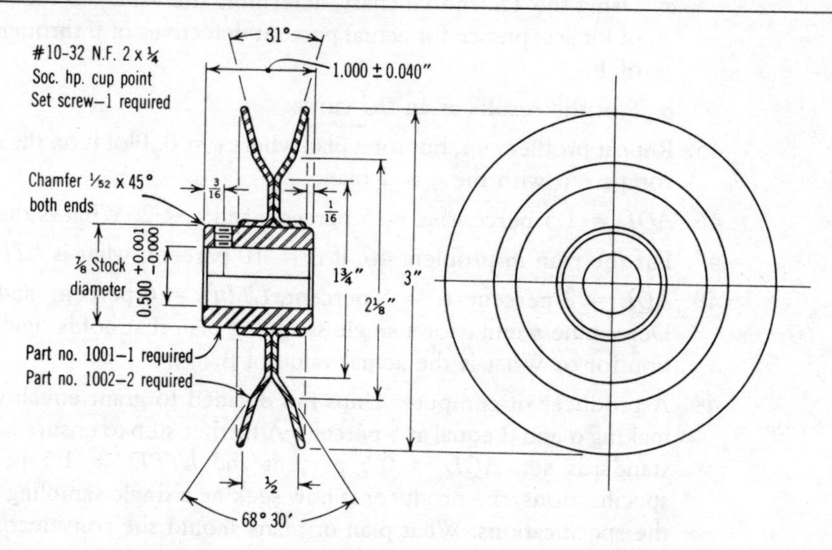


Tolerance of wobble: ±0.010 inch from center. Tolerance on concentricity: ±0.010 inch from center. Fractional tolerances: ±1/64. Angular tolerances: ±1/2 degree. Finish: cadmium plated all over 0.0003 ± 0.0001.

*Notes:* (1) Press fit flanges to hub. (2) Spot weld flanges to hub, two spots each side. (3) Spot weld flanges together, four spots. (4) Flange material: SAE No. 1010 deep-drawn steel. (5) Hub material: SAE No. X1122 cold-finished screw stock.

TABLE 13-12
**TEN SAMPLES OF *n* = 4, PULLEY HUB LENGTH IN INCHES**

| Sample Number | Sample Average, $\bar{x}$ | Sample Range, $R$ |
|---|---|---|
| 1 | 1.007 | 0.013 |
| 2 | 1.008 | 0.022 |
| 3 | 0.991 | 0.018 |
| 4 | 0.993 | 0.014 |
| 5 | 0.998 | 0.019 |
| 6 | 1.008 | 0.026 |
| 7 | 0.996 | 0.024 |
| 8 | 0.995 | 0.011 |
| 9 | 0.999 | 0.021 |
| 10 | 0.995 | 0.024 |
| Totals | 9.990 | 0.192 |

c. Determine preliminary control limits, based on the data given, for $\bar{X}$- and $R$-charts to control the cutoff operation of the turret lathe, assuming samples of $n = 4$.

d. Under normal conditions, the width of the cutoff tool wears at the rate of 0.001 inch per hour of use. Determine the appropriate control limits and the trend of average hub length for the samples of $n = 4$ that reflect the known rate of tool wear. Plot the results. How often should the tool be sharpened and reset if the process is otherwise in control?

e. How will the tool wear affect the control limits and the process average for the $R$-chart?

## Flange Splitting and Wobble

52. When assembling the pulleys by pressing the flanges on the hubs with an arbor press, the flanges tend to split excessively in instances when the hub is relatively large and the flange hole is relatively small and when the flange material is relatively hard, even though all of these factors are within their stated tolerances. In addition, if the press fit between hub and flange is loose, the spot-welding operation tends to pull the flanges off the axis of rotation. As a result, the pulley may be rejected because of excessive "wobble." Inspection of daily production results in rejection of pulleys for these reasons. Table 13-13 is a record of production and rejections for 10 days.

    Construct a $p$-chart with variable control limits and a stabilized $p$-chart, since the amount produced each day varies.

## Plating

53. The plating process for the pulleys can produce defective parts because of either too thick or too thin a plating or because of defective appearance, which shows up in surface defects. Assume that the plating thickness is controlled by a $p$-chart, but the surface defects are controlled by a $c$-chart. Periodic samples of 10 plated pulleys are drawn from the output of the process and inspected, and the number of surface defects are counted. A record of 10 samples is shown in Table 13-14.

    Determine the center line and preliminary control limits, construct the chart, and plot the 10 samples. On the basis of the limited sample of 10, does the process seem to be in control?

## Splitting and Wobble II

54. The bar stock from which the hubs of the V-belt pulley shown in Figure 13-16 are fabricated has the diameter specification of 0.875 inch ± 0.002 inch. This specification is related to the problem of flange splitting and "wobble." When assembling the pulleys by pressing the flanges on the hubs with an arbor press, the flanges tend to split excessively in instances when the hub is relatively large

TABLE 13-13
**TEN-DAY RECORD OF PRODUCTION AND REJECTIONS DUE TO FLANGE SPLITTING**

| Day | Amount Produced | Number of Defectives |
|---|---|---|
| 1 | 5205 | 85 |
| 2 | 6100 | 120 |
| 3 | 5725 | 105 |
| 4 | 5345 | 150 |
| 5 | 4250 | 75 |
| 6 | 3975 | 50 |
| 7 | 4345 | 95 |
| 8 | 5270 | 120 |
| 9 | 6075 | 155 |
| 10 | 7005 | 110 |
| Totals | 53,295 | 1065 |

and the flange hole is relatively small and when the flange material is relatively hard, even though all of these factors are within their stated tolerances. In addition, if the press fit between the hub and flange is loose, the spot-welding operation tends to pull the flanges off the axis of rotation. As a result, the pulleys may be rejected because of excessive "wobble." Bars are ordered in lots of 400. Records indicate that an average of 12 bars in a lot do not meet specifications.

a. It is felt that if 98 percent of the bars meet specifications, this would be good quality. Also, it has been decided that the company should not accept ship-

TABLE 13-14
**PLATING SURFACE DEFECTS IN 10 SAMPLES OF $n = 100$**

| Sample Number | Number of Defects per Sample |
|---|---|
| 1 | 5 |
| 2 | 7 |
| 3 | 2 |
| 4 | 10 |
| 5 | 7 |
| 6 | 11 |
| 7 | 13 |
| 8 | 10 |
| 9 | 4 |
| 10 | 7 |
| Total | 76 |

ments in which as many as 10 percent of the bars do not meet specifications. If $\alpha$ = 5 percent and $\beta$ = 10 percent, what single sampling plan will meet the stated requirements?

b. Determine the *OC* curve for the plan designed in a.

c. What is the *AOQL* of the plan designed in a?

### Rockwell Hardness

55. The flange material for the V-belt pulley of Figure 13-16 must be relatively soft to carry out the press forming operations. Therefore, the material is specified with a Rockwell hardness of 55; a hardness of 60 is regarded as unacceptable. The scrap rate goes up so fast when material with a hardness index above 60 is used that $\beta$ has been set at 5 percent rather than the usual 10 percent; $\alpha$ has also been set at 5 percent. The material is received in 100-feet rolls, 3¼ inches wide, 100 rolls per shipment. We have had considerable experience with the current supplier, so the standard deviation of hardness for individual samples has been well established as $\sigma$ = 2.

a. Determine the Rockwell hardness sample average for acceptance, $x_a$, and the sample size needed for the stated requirements.

b. What variables plan would result if $\beta$ = 10?

c. Determine the *OC* curve for the plan in a.

## REFERENCES

"Directory of Software for Quality Assurance and Quality Control," *Quality Progress,* March 1984, pp. 33–53.

Dodge, H. F., and H. G. Romig, *Sampling Inspection Tables* (2nd ed.), Wiley, New York, 1959.

Duncan, A. J., *Quality Control and Industrial Statistics* (4th ed.), Irwin, Homewood, Ill., 1974.

Grant, E. L., and R. S. Leavenworth, *Statistical Quality Control* (5th ed.), McGraw-Hill, New York, 1980.

Shewhart, W. A., *Economic Control of Quality for Managers and Engineers,* Van Nostrand, Princeton, N.J., 1931.

# CHAPTER 14

# JAPANESE MANUFACTURING SYSTEMS

The competitiveness of Japanese manufactured products has focused attention on their manufacturing systems since the basis of their success has been high-quality, competitively priced products. Indeed, the Japanese market strategy seems to be rooted in their production systems, and the literature is filled with reports of remarkable quality levels, achieved along with lower costs through higher productivity and very low in-process inventories. Some examples of these achievements both in Japan and in Japanese plants in the United States are discussed in the following paragraphs.

Sepehri (1986) reports on a sample of five Japanese companies that employ *just-in-time* (*JIT*) methods—producing the necessary parts in the quantities needed at the time they are needed—as a basis for comparing the results of 13 U.S. companies that have installed *JIT* concepts. The summary results of the five Japanese companies in improving productivity, reducing set-up time, reducing inventory, improving quality, saving space, and reducing lead times are shown in Table 14-1.

The productivity increases are quite remarkable, ranging from a 45 percent increase by Tokai Rika to a 250 percent increase by Canon. The reductions in the set-up times of specific operations by Hitachi and Yanmar suggest that economical batch sizes would be reduced, leading to in-process inventory reductions. Indeed, the inventory reductions reported for all five Japanese companies are indicative of lower cost operations that are responsive to market needs. Quality improvements are significant for all five companies, and all show important space savings and reduced lead times.

In addition, there is the study of room air conditioner quality cited at the beginning of Chapter 12 on quality assurance, in which the Japanese quality levels were extremely high and were coupled with high productivity. The companies with the best quality records also had the highest labor productivity. This union of high quality with high productivity is in contrast with previous conventional wisdom, which commonly held that these two measures represented trade-offs. *How the Japanese achieve high levels in quality and productivity simultaneously will be of central interest in this chapter.*

Japanese firms have also established manufacturing facilities in the United States where they apply their manufacturing techniques. For example, in the early 1970s, Matsushita bought the Motorola TV assembly plant in Franklin, Illinois. The plant had a poor record for both productivity and quality (more than 150 defects per 100 completed sets), but within three years, Matsushita was able to increase productivity by 30 percent and reduce defects to below 4 per 100 sets. However, the quality standards were still not as high as the 0.5 percent achieved in comparable Japanese plants (Wheelwright, 1981).

In 1977, Sanyo bought the Warwick TV plant in Forest City, Arkansas. Sales had declined to such an extent that 80 percent of the plant's capacity had been closed down. Sears owned 25 percent of the stock and had been buying most of Warwick's production output under its own label, but quality had been so poor that Sears had turned to Japanese manufacturers for most of their needs. Within two months after

Sanyo's takeover, quality had been improved from a defect rate of about 30 percent to less than 5 percent while assembly line productivity had improved substantially.[1]

Finally, there is extensive reporting on the Lincoln, Nebraska plant of Kawasaki Motors by Schonberger (1982). Kawasaki opened the plant in 1975 to manufacture motorcycles and added other products later. Originally, the plant was staffed with American managers and workers, but Japanese were installed as top managers in 1981. The *JIT* program was actually started by an American plant manager, based on knowledge he had gained about Kawasaki's Japanese operations, but the Japanese managers completed the conversion of the U.S. plant to Japanese methods.

In order to gain insight into the Japanese methods for guiding operating decisions, we examine the *JIT* concept (see Schonberger, 1982a).

## THE JIT CAUSE–EFFECT CHAIN

When Japanese price–quality competition became so keen, it was originally thought that the reasons were rooted in their culture and in the supports given to life-long employment. The cultural and environmental supports of the work environment are undoubtedly important, but the really important causes are to be found in what happens on the factory floor. Examination of the Japanese operating system produces results that are quite predictable. The system involves a relentless process of improvement, which starts with a drive to reduce production lot sizes.

### Reduction of Lot Sizes

For a given inventory cost, smaller set-up costs result in a smaller *EOQ,* as discussed in Chapter 5. Thus, in practice, smaller set-up costs justify smaller lot sizes and provide greater flexibility for changeovers from one product to another.

This simple logic has formed the basis for many inventory control methods in both the United States and Japan. The difference in practice, however, is that the Japanese do not accept set-up costs as given. Rather, they expend great effort to reduce the set-up costs through tool design, quick clamping devices, and carefully worked out procedures. The objective is to reduce set-up costs to the point that $EOQ = 1$ unit. Of course, if $EOQ = 1$ unit, the immediate benefits are that in-process inventories are reduced and the flexibility to change over production from one product to another is improved. However, reduction in production lot sizes triggers a chain of events involving improved motivation and a focus on *just-in-time* and on scrap and quality control, as shown in Figure 14-1.

[1] Y. Tsurumi. "Productivity: The Japanese Approach," *Pacific Basin Quarterly,* Summer 1981, p. 8. See also, "Sanyo Manufacturing Corporation—Forest City Arkansas," Case #9-682-045, *HBS Case Services,* Harvard Business School.

TABLE 14-1
**SUMMARY RESULTS OF *JUST-IN-TIME* APPLICATIONS IN JAPAN**

| Company | Product Category | Productivity Improvement | Set-up Time Improvement |
|---|---|---|---|
| Canon | Cameras, office equipment, etc. | (Indexed) 100 to 250 Elimination of waste: $15 million in 1976 to $98 million in 1982 | Accessory parts operations: 4 min to 15 sec |
| Hitachi | Home appliances, integrated circuits, computers, industrial transportation, EQ, etc. | (Indexed) 100 to 178 | Sheet metal line: 160 to 5 min<br>Machining Center: 245 to 9 min<br>250 ton die cast: 75 to 3 min |
| Tokai Rika | Automotive parts | (Indexed) 100 to 145; equivalent to 317 people | Die cast: 40 to 2 min, 90 min to 20 sec |
| Toyo Kogo | Automobiles | (Indexed) 100 to 215, 70 to 80% of gain from elimination of waste | Ring gear cutter: 30 min: 30 min in 1976 to 13 min in 1980 |
| Yanmar | Automotive parts | (Indexed) 100 to 191 | Aluminum die cast: 125 to 6 min<br>Cylinder block machining line: 633 to 10 min |

*Source:* Abstracted from Table 1.8, M. Sepehri, *Just in Time, Not Just in Japan: Case Studies of American Pioneers in JIT Implementation,* American Production and Inventory Control Society, Falls Church, Virginia, 1986.

## Motivational Effects and Feedback

If a worker produces a part and passes it directly to the next worker, the second worker can report a defect almost immediately. On being told that the part is defective, the first worker is motivated to find the cause and correct it before large quantities of scrap are produced. The smaller the production lot size, the more immediate the discovery of defects will be. The result is that each pair of operations in the sequence is closely linked and the awareness of the interdependence of the two operations, and particularly the two workers, is enhanced.

If production were in large lots and completed parts were placed in intermediate storage to be withdrawn as needed, this linkage would be destroyed. In many instances, we might not even know which worker produced the defectives to provide the feedback to correct future defects. The system takes advantage of one of

| Inventory Reduction | Quality Improvement | Space Savings | Lead Times |
|---|---|---|---|
| (Indexed) 100 in 1976 to 50 in 1982 | 45% reduction of defects in 3 months (parts machining factory) | Factor of 3 for copier assembly line | Significant |
| (Indexed) 100 in 1977 to 60 in 1981 | Significant | Significant | 20 days to 3 days (S factory) |
| (Indexed) 100 in 1975 to 35 in 1976, 17 days in 1975 to 6 days in 1976 | Significant | Significant Elimination of warehouses, many U-lines | Significant |
| (Indexed) 100 in 1973 to 31 in 1981 | Significant Machine down time reduced to 50 to 60 hours per month | Significant | Significant |
| (Indexed) 100 in 1975 to 35 in 1980, 81 days in 1975 to 29 days in 1980 | Product A defects: 100 to 56 Product B defects: 100 to 18 | Significant | Significant |

the simplest principles of learning, knowledge of results. The fast feedback, *E* in Figure 14-1, leads to a heightened awareness of what probably caused the defect, *F*, producing ideas for controlling defectives in the future.

The three arrows leaving *F* in Figure 14-1 represent three kinds of responses triggered by the worker's heightened awareness of problems and causes. The workers, their supervisors, and staff become involved in generating ideas for controlling defectives, ideas for improving *JIT* delivery performance, and additional ideas for further reducing set-up time and lot sizes.

## Small Group Activities

The close linking of workers and the feeling of responsibility engendered creates committed workers who carry their concerns about all aspects of job performance home with them and into social situations involving coworkers. Schonberger (1982a) contends that quality circles were not really molded from employee partici-

FIGURE 14-1
**EFFECTS OF JIT PRODUCTION.**

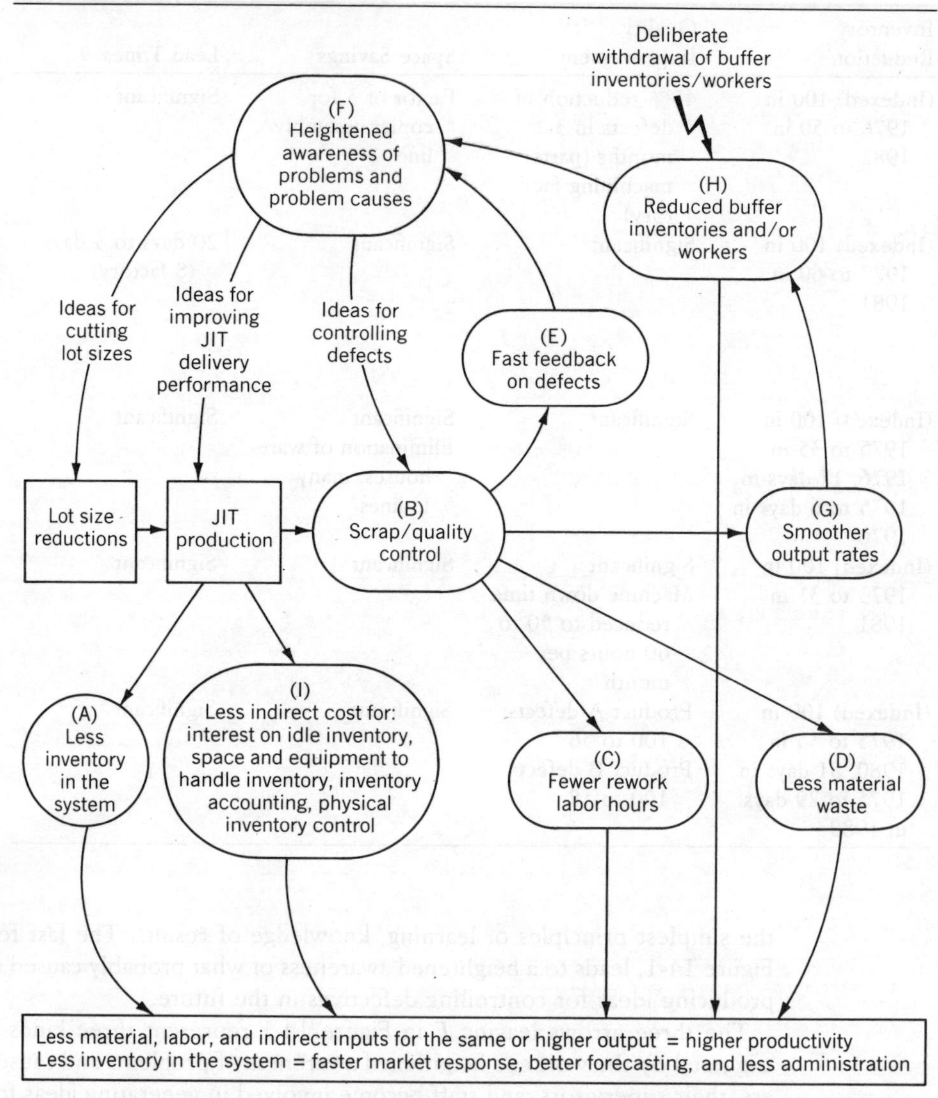


*Source:* Reprinted with permission of the Free Press, a Division of Macmillan, Inc., from Richard J. Schonberger, *Japanese Manufacturing Techniques: Nine Hidden Lessons in Simplicity*, Copyright © 1982 by Richard J. Schonberger.

pation principles but through the worker commitment generated by *JIT* concepts. Quality circles are really self-generated; employee participation is a result of the production situation.

## Withdrawal of Buffer Inventory

Buffer inventories perform the function of asbsorbing variations in flow rates in production systems. One of the direct effects of reducing lot sizes for *JIT* production is lower in-process inventories in the system, as shown by the circle *A* in Figure 14-1. The larger the variations, the larger the buffer inventory required to insulate each operation in the sequence from the effects of lack of material supply. The Japanese recognize the function of buffer inventories, but they deal with it philosophically rather differently.

By systematically removing a portion of the buffer stocks, Japanese managers expose workers to the problems that cause variation in flow. These problems then become goals for problem solution. When the problems that cause variation have been solved, Japanese managers remove more of the insulating buffer stock, revealing the next set of problems that cause variations in flow. The workers are never allowed to become complacent; they are faced with continually perfecting the process. Inventories in the aggregate are reduced, and productivity is improved. This sequence is shown in Figure 14-1 as the loop is closed from *H* to *F* through the heightened awareness of the causes of irregular output, which stimulates ideas for improvement. This result leads to smoother output rates because of fewer interruptions due to quality problems, which reduces the need for buffer stock. The improved scrap and quality control that results from lot size reductions and *JIT* production also results in smoother output rates because there are fewer interruptions in flow that might otherwise occur because of poor quality. We have, in effect, a "hand to mouth" system of supply between operations.

In addition, there are indirect effects that flow from *JIT* production, shown as *I* in Figure 14-1. These include less inventory carrying costs, less space and equipment to handle inventory, less inventory accounting, and a lesser need for physical inventory control.

## Productivity Improvement

The productivity effects of the Japanese operating system are quite pervasive. The close linking among workers that produces the heightened awareness of problems and their causes coupled with management's intervention to reduce buffer inventories produce the production effects shown at the bottom of Figure 14-1:

- Smaller lot size inventories
- Smaller buffer inventories
- Less scrap
- Less direct labor wasted on rework
- Less indirect cost of inventories
- Less space for inventories

- Less equipment to handle inventories
- Less inventory accounting
- Less physical inventory control effort

These productivity improvements result from workers' efforts as a part of a closely linked system. Since most of the system is run by workers and supervisors, the costs of administration are low, and managers are freed to deal with strategic issues.

### Market Effects

While the *JIT* system leads to productivity improvements, the reductions in delays and scrap also improve market response. Production lead times are reduced because of the low cost of changeover, so marketing can promise better delivery dates because the product mix and quantities can be changed quickly as demand and forecasts of demand change. Even forecasting is improved because of the shorter lead times.

## TOTAL QUALITY CONTROL

The concepts of total quality control were originally introduced in Japan by the American consultant W. Edwards Deming in the 1950s. Deming was able to get top managers to install both a philosophy and statistical techniques to foster quality as the prime manufacturing competitive priority. The result was a complete reversal in the quality of Japanese manufactured products, which had formerly had a very bad reputation. (See the chapter-end interview with Deming concerning "The Roots of Quality Control in Japan" presented as Situation 22.)

While quality control is obviously involved in the process described by Figure 14-1, it is only a part of the Japanese concept of total quality control. All plant personnel are inculcated with the view that scrap/quality control, *B* of Figure 14-1, is an end in itself. "Quality at the *source*" is the slogan. It means that error, if any exists, should be caught and corrected at the work place. This is in contrast to the widespread U.S. practice of inspection by sampling after the lot has been produced. In U.S. practice, quality is controlled by inspectors from a quality control department; in Japanese practice, workers and supervisors have the primary responsibility for quality. With quality control at the source, there is fast feedback concerning defects, resulting in fewer rework labor hours and less material waste in addition to the other benefits previously discussed.

### Responsibility for Quality

The key to the Japanese practice is that "the *responsibility* for quality rests with the makers of the part." The workers and the supervisors rather than a staff quality control department bear this responsibility. Schonberger (1982b) states, "If western manufacturers are to close the quality gap with the Japanese, there is no better way to begin than by transferring primary responsibility for quality from the *QC* department to production."

The Japanese consider quality control to be a line function, not a staff function. This fact was highlighted in the Sanyo takeover of the Warwick TV plant cited at the beginning of this chapter. The quality control manager under Warwick's management was made plant manager in the Sanyo reorganization, a clear announcement of a pledge to quality as a line responsibility.[2]

By placing responsibility for quality directly on workers and supervisors, the Japanese implement a commitment to the prevention of defectives. They implement the slogan, "quality at the source," through the following principles:

- Process control, a classic statistical quality control concept, covered in Chapter 13, of checking quality as the process continues and stopping the process if it goes out of control. Whereas U.S. practice is to select a limited number of processes for control, the contrasting Japanese practice is to establish control at each work station.
- Visible, measurable quality is implemented through easy to understand charts and diagrams that keep workers and managers informed about quality.
- Insistence on compliance with quality standards.
- Line-stop authority in the hands of workers in order to implement the insistence on compliance. In capital intensive processes, devices detect poor quality and stop the process automatically.
- Self-correction of errors is the responsibility of each employee, who must rework bad items, usually after regular working hours. By contrast, U.S. plants employ special rework lines as a common practice.
- Expose problems and get them solved; for example, by deliberately removing buffer inventories.
- 100 percent inspection, especially for finished goods.

The duties of the rather small quality control departments in Japanese plants are to monitor production processes to see that standard procedures are followed, to assist in the removal of the causes of defects, and to participate in the audit of supplier plants in order to maintain standards. Receiving inspection of suppliers' materials is usually eliminated; instead, the quality control procedures of the suppliers are relied upon.

## Quality Circles

Whereas the quality control function in the United States developed with a technical staff that functioned by obtaining the cooperation of management and the workers, the Japanese trained the workers themselves in the techniques, as well as management and the technical staff. By training the workers, who are the ones most familiar with day-to-day problems, the Japanese reduced resistance to the introduction of these quantitative models.

[2]"Sanyo Manufacturing Corporation—Forest City Arkansas," Case #9-682-045, *Harvard Case Services*, Harvard Business School.

Workers are organized into teams (3 to 25 members per team) that select, analyze, and present proposed solutions to quality problems. These quality circles involve thousands of people working on problems, raher than only the technical specialist attempting to solve problems and install them through a sales approach. By the beginning of 1979, there were 95,000 registered quality circles with over 900,000 members. It is estimated that only about 15 percent are actually registered; therefore, it appears that over six million workers are involved. In Japan, quality really is everyone's job! (See Blair and Ramsing, 1983, and Konz, 1979.)

In addition to improvements in quality, a large proportion of the solutions to quality problems developed by quality circles also result in improved productivity, as is apparent from the nature of the operating system diagrammed in Figure 14-1.

## KANBAN

The simple *kanban* system of inventory control is an integral part of the *JIT* system of production, and it has received a great deal of attention in the U.S. press. Beginning with the driving mechanism in Figure 14-1 of smaller set-up times, leading to small production lots, the *kanban* system is designed to produce only the number of units needed by a "*pull*" or demand feeding process. It simply adds to all the other effects that result in reduced in-process inventories.

The beauty of the *kanban* system is in its simplicity. A *kanban* is a card of two types: a withdrawal *kanban* and a production-ordering *kanban*. The withdrawal *kanban* shows the quantity of the items that the subsequent process should withdraw from the preceding one. The production-ordering *kanban* shows the quantity that the preceding process should produce. These cards are used within the plant and within suppliers' plants. No complex record keeping is required since each part is produced only in the number required to feed the next operation and just in time for use.

For example, suppose that we are producing products *A, B,* and *C,* and that parts *a* and *b* are produced by the preceding process as shown in Figure 14-2. The worker on the assembly line producing product *A* goes to the fabrication line to withdraw the necessary number of part *a* from the storage location. The worker withdraws the required number of parts, detaches the production-ordering *kanban* and leaves it in place of the parts, and returns to the assembly line with the withdrawal *kanban*. The production-ordering *kanban* is picked up by a worker from the fabrication line as a direction to produce that quantity of part *a*. The *kanban* system provides an additional close link between operations, reinforcing the previous linkages that lead to improved quality and productivity.

In contrast, U.S. systems of inventory control are likely to produce larger lots, reflecting generally larger set-up times, in advance of when they are needed. The large lots go into storage and are used as needed. Thus, there is no real linkage between the operations in the sequence. In contrast to the Japanese system, U.S. systems have been likened to a "*push*" or forced feeding process. In addition, U.S. systems are complex, to the extent of requiring computers to keep track of everything.

FIGURE 14-2
**THE FLOW OF TWO *KANBANS*.**

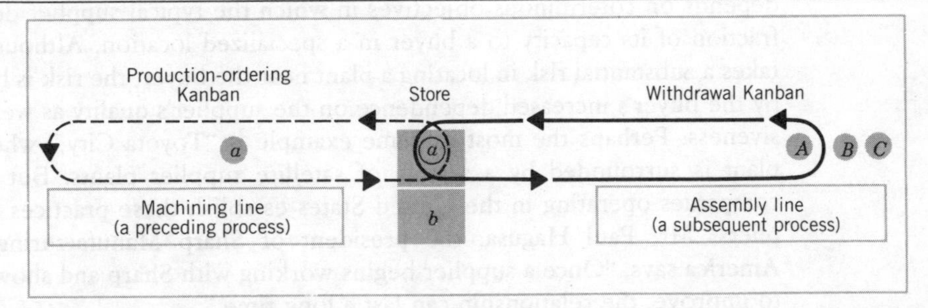


*Source:* Y. Monden, "What Makes the Toyota Production System Really Tick?" *Industrial Engineering, 13*(1), January 1981, pp. 36–46. Reprinted with permission from *Industrial Engineering* magazine, January 1981. Copyright © American Institute of Industrial Engineers, Inc., 25 Technology Park, Atlanta, Norcross, Georgia 30092.

The *kanban* system of inventory control works particularly well in situations where standardized parts and products are cycled in the manufacturing system. It should be noted however, that the Japanese use computer-based systems of inventory control, such as MRP (Materials Requirement Planning), in process-focused systems for low volume manufacturing.

## JIT PURCHASING

The Japanese seem to depend more heavily on suppliers than do U.S. manufacturers, especially in the auto industry. For example, Toyota's purchased materials account for nearly 80 percent of its sales dollar compared to less than 50 percent for General Motors,[3] 60 percent for Ford, and 71 percent for Chrysler.[4]

The characteristics of Japanese *JIT* purchasing are unique, in terms of both general philosophy and in detailed procedures. The term *JIT purchasing* suggests an emphasis on timing, which is true, but it does not suggest the broad philosophical underpinnings of the system. Although the term comes from the emphasis on supplying materials just in time for use on the factory floor, equally important are the close relationships with a few long-term suppliers (approaching sole source in the ideal), geographically close suppliers, loose specifications and contracts, and frequent deliveries of small, exact quantities.

### Long-Term Stable Relationships

The system is designed to provide long-term stable relationships with suppliers that foster mutual confidence so that the supplier will invest in a nearby plant and in

[3] W. J. Abernathy, K. V. Clark, and A. M. Kantrow, "The New Industrial Strategy," *Harvard Business Review,* September–October 1981, pp. 68–81.
[4] "Can Chrysler Keep Its Comeback Rolling," *Business Week,* February 14, 1983.

equipment that will improve productivity and quality. Rather than using the threat of the loss of supply contracts as a means of keeping suppliers in line, the system depends on coterminous objectives in which the typical supplier dedicates a large fraction of its capacity to a buyer in a specialized location. Although the supplier takes a substantial risk in locating a plant near the buyer, the risk is balanced in part by the buyer's increased dependence on the supplier's quality as well as its responsiveness. Perhaps the most extreme example is "Toyota City," where the Toyota plant is surrounded by a system of satellite supplier plants. But even Japanese companies operating in the United States establish these practices with their suppliers. Mr. Paul Hagusa, the president of Sharp Manufacturing Company of America says, "Once a supplier begins working with Sharp and shows a willingness to improve, the relationship can last a long time."[5]

Buyers commonly invest in suppliers' businesses, providing another basis for control. But in addition, control is exercised through constant visits of buyer representatives to the suppliers' plants. Thus, the buyer comes to know the suppliers' strengths and weaknesses and often provides consultation and advice. In addition, suppliers also visit the buyers' plants frequently to gain a better understanding of problems.

## Simple Purchase Agreements

*JIT* purchase agreements tend to be simple, specifying price, specifications, and an overall quantity to be delivered in accordance with long-term production schedules. The specifications are focused on product performance, rather than being highly detailed. These blanket orders provide the umbrella under which actual deliveries are matched to the work center's rate of use, which is often controlled by the use of *kanban* order cards. Every effort is made to stabilize production rates in the buyer's plant so that the flow of materials from the supplier to the buyer can also be established on a steady rate basis.

Whereas the practice in the United States is to specify every conceivable design feature, the Japanese practice is to avoid over specification, leaving the supplier room to innovate. Specifications contain critical dimensions and other performance requirements, but they avoid restrictions that dictate how the product is to be manufactured. The supplier can then employ its expertise to the maximum.

## Small But Frequent Deliveries

The suppliers' proximity contributes to achieving the objective of small but frequent deliveries. In addition, rather than shipping a target quantity plus or minus ten percent or more, the quantity delivered is exact. Instead of counting on receipt, Japanese practice takes advantage of standard packaging so that the count is obvious, and variation from the expected quantity is the exception rather than the rule. The expectation that the quantity delivered will be constant relieves the buyer from the need to hold buffer inventories to guard against the effects of component shortages.

[5] Ibid.

There are many secondary benefits from the *JIT* purchasing system. Inventories are greatly reduced in the buyer's plant since it is working off the suppliers' inventory. Even the suppliers' inventory is smaller because of the nearly continuous supply rate. There is a great deal less paperwork in the system because of the blanket contracts and simpler specifications. As a result of an assured steady flow, suppliers can minimize peak capacity requirements and retain a trained labor force. In addition, proximity makes for easy communication and closer coordination between suppliers' and buyers' engineering and quality control personnel.

## THE TOYOTA PRODUCTION SYSTEM

The roots of the present Japanese manufacturing systems were developed at Toyota, so we will examine that system to see how the various elements fit together in an integrated way. The overall system is shown in Figure 14-3. In order to achieve a continuous flow of production, shown at the top of the inner box leading to Outputs, there are two key concepts on which the system rests: *just-in-time,* and *autonomation.* As we have discussed, *just-in-time* is the objective of producing the necessary units in the quantities needed at the time they are needed. The methods of achieving the objective are of key interest. *Autonomation* is a Toyota coined word that means "autonomous defects control," that is, "worker controlled" quality control.

### Just-in-Time

Accomplishing the *just-in-time* objective rests on systems for determining production methods and the *kanban* system. Both of these concepts contribute to the objective of having the right number of parts or components at the right place at the right time.

#### PRODUCTION METHODS

Processes are designed so that there is less specialization of workers than might be true in the U.S. auto plants. The physical layout is arranged so that a worker can operate two or three different machines, thus providing flexibility in processes that might precede the assembly line. The benefits that result from this organization of multifunctional workers are

- A reduction of inventory between what would otherwise be separate processes
- A decrease in the number of workers required, resulting in a direct increase in productivity
- Increased worker satisfaction because of more broadly defined jobs
- Multifunctional workers can engage in teamwork

There are three elements of job standardization that are included on a standard operation sheet tacked up for all workers to see: cycle time, operations routing, and standard quantity of work in process. Based on the computed cycle time that is

FIGURE 14-3
**THE TOYOTA PRODUCTION SYSTEM.**

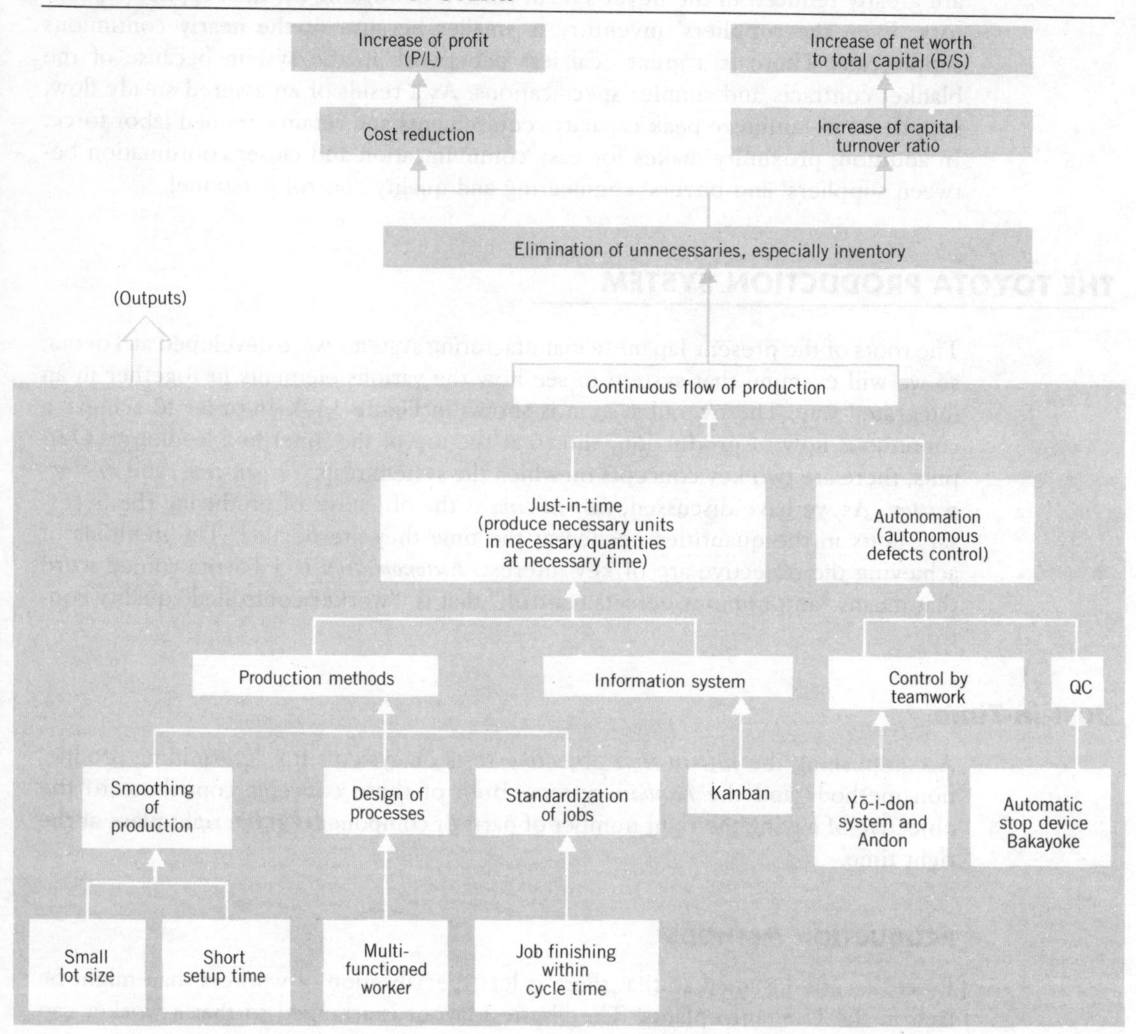


*Source:* Y. Monden. "What Makes the Toyota Production System Really Tick?" *Industrial Engineering, 13*(1), January 1981, pp. 36–46. Reprinted with permission from *Industrial Engineering* magazine, January 1981. Copyright © American Institute of Industrial Engineers, Inc., 25 Technology Park, Atlanta, Norcross, Georgia 30092.

derived from market demand, the aggregate number of workers required to produce one unit of output in the cycle time is determined. Rebalancing may then be necessary to schedule for minimum labor input for a given output objective. The standard routing indicates the exact activities each worker is required to perform correctly in minimum time. The standard quantity of work in process indicates the in-process inventory required for smooth flow.

The smoothing of production is regarded as the most critical element in the just-in-time objective. Workers go to the preceding process to withdraw the required parts of components for their operations using the *kanban* system. If there are fluctuations in the rates at which these materials are withdrawn, then the preceding process must hold buffer in-process inventories to give off-the-shelf service. Variability is amplified as we go upstream in a sequential production process; therefore, the required in-process inventories also increase for upstream processes. This results in the objective of minimizing production fluctuations on the final assembly line by scheduling small lots of individual models and focusing "all out" efforts on minimizing set-up times for all processes.

### Autonomation

Although just-in-time systems control production quantities, the production flow would be interrupted if the items delivered were defective. The *autonomation* system is designed to ensure that, theoretically, 100 percent good units flow to subsequent operations. It is, therefore, an integral part of a well-operating *just-in-time* system. *Autonomation,* meaning "autonomous defects control," depends on both automatic stop devices and worker teamwork.

"In Toyota factories, almost all machines are autonomous," meaning that they are equipped with automatic stopping devices to prevent any large output of defects; *Bakayoke* is one such mechanism.

In manual work, such as occurs on assembly lines, the concept of *autonomation* is implemented by *Andon*; if a worker observes something abnormal, a stop button can be pushed that stops the entire line. The problem is then cleared before defective items are produced in any quantity.

In addition, there is a *Yō-i-don* (which means ready, set, go) system that contributes to *autonomation* as well as to smooth work flow. The *Yō-i-don* system involves teamwork between adjacent operations to make sure that work at the stations is balanced; it involves the *Andon* system when necessary. In the *Yō-i-don* system, when each worker at each station has completed operations, each will press a button. At the end of the cycle time, a red light automatically goes on at each work station where work is not complete. The red lights indicate delays, and the entire line stops until all red lights are off. When this happens, teamwork comes into play, for workers nearby pitch in to help workers who are having difficulty.

## TRANSFER OF JAPANESE METHODS

Given Schonberger's model for how the Japanese manufacturing system works, we need to consider whether or not the concepts can be transferred to the United States or whether the concepts are culturally dependent.

The close linking of workers in the process sequence produces a situation that enables communication and the potential solution of mutual problems. Participation in the solution of problems is a key to the functioning of the system and its success. An authoritarian manager would not fit into the Japanese system.

If it is the situation that closely links workers that is truly unique, then it seems unlikely that it is culturally dependent. Although few people doubt that the Japanese culture supports the values of cooperation and the type of system they have evolved, the same close linking of workers in a U.S. manufacturing system should produce similar results, assuming that worker participation is fostered. Indeed, the system is now being applied in Japanese–U.S. manufacturing operations at Kawasaki, Matsushita, Sanyo, Sharp, and Sony. The management of these plants is Japanese but the workers are American.

But now there are many purely American companies that have installed *JIT* concepts and techniques, companies as American as apple pie, representing "blue chip" concerns as well as smaller ones. There is a growing awareness of these applications as evidenced by the case studies of U.S. companies cited near the beginning of the chapter. Sepehri (1986) summarizes the experience of 13 U.S. companies that have installed *JIT* and gives detailed case studies for nine of them, there being applications in more than one division of some. The 13 companies are Apple Computers; Black & Decker; Derre & Company; Franklin Electric; FMC Corporation; General Electric; Harley Davidson; Hewlett-Packard; IBM; Motorola; Omark Industries; Toyota Motor Manufacturing, U.S.; and 3M.

Perhaps the most interesting observation that emerges is that the sample of six of Sepehri's 13 U.S. companies recorded results, shown in Table 14-2, that are comparable to those recorded by the Japanese firms shown in Table 14-1. This seems to indicate that Sepehri's book title, *Just in Time—Not Just in Japan* is appropriate. The transferability of *JIT* methods to the United States has already happened, and it is spreading rapidly.

## IMPLICATIONS FOR THE MANAGER

The constantly repeating cycle of improvement that is such a clear part of Japanese manufacturing strategy "grinds" away at productivity and quality improvement. Managers should not think of the work force control, quality control, and inventory control as solely operational decisions. They are integral parts of manufacturing strategy, which cannot be implemented without them. Indeed, making operating decisions independently could easily put them at odds with the central strategy. The approach is to integrate the functions related to on-the-job performance with the market strategies.

Wheelwright (1981) cites an example of the broad integrative view of Japanese operating decisions. A directive was received from the executive vice-president of Tokyo Sanyo Electric "to strive for substantial reductions in both raw material and in-process inventories." Such directives in U.S. plants commonly result in ruthless chopping to make the boss happy, but the Sanyo manufacturing managers translated the directive into strategic objectives to

- Standardize parts and components
- Increase the frequency of vendor deliveries
- Develop a mixed-model assembly line for low-volume models

- Reduce set-up and changeover times, resulting in smaller lot sizes and model runs
- Reduce warehouse space needs
- Promote discipline and committment to the policy directive

Thus, they converted what we commonly would have thought to be a short-term fire-fighting action into long-term strategic management. Over a period of years, the program produced impressive results, including reductions in in-process and raw-material inventories from 10 to 1.5 days of supply, in lot sizes from 2 to 3 days' worth to 1 day's worth, and in warehouse space requirements from 80,000 to 20,000 square feet. Overall, the program helped Sanyo achieve a 1975 to 1979 sales increase of 207 percent and a profit increase of 729 percent, demonstrating that operations really are strategic. The emphasis on low set-up times and small production lots sizes produces an environment in which quick changeovers and flexibility are engrained values.

## REVIEW QUESTIONS

1. What is the nature and extent of the improvements effected in Japanese manufacturing plants? What are examples of similar achievements in Japanese plants located in the United States?
2. It is a commonly known Japanese practice to reduce lot sizes. Is this action an uneconomical one; that is, what is the basis for the lot size reductions?
3. What managerial action is the key to the chain reaction resulting in the *JIT* system?
4. What are the worker motivational effects that result from *JIT* production techniques? What is the impact of small lot production on those effects?
5. How does the close linking of workers produce teamwork in production?
6. What is the purpose of Japanese management's withdrawal of buffer inventories? Is this a risky strategy that exposes the system to shutdown if irregularities occur in the system?
7. What are the sources of productivity improvement that result from the Japanese operating system?
8. How is quality control effected within the operating system diagrammed in Figure 14-1?
9. What is the significance of the slogan, "quality at the source" within the concept of the Japanese operating system?
10. In the Japanese system, who is responsible for quality? Who is usually responsible in U.S. plants?
11. What are the principles for implementing the slogan "quality at the source" in the Japanese system?

TABLE 14-2

**SUMMARY RESULTS OF SOME *JUST-IN-TIME* APPLICATIONS IN THE UNITED STATES**

| Company | Product Category | Productivity Improvement | Set-up Time Improvement |
|---|---|---|---|
| Apple Computers (Macintosh) | Microcomputers | Inspection labor from 25 to 9<br>Assembly labor from 22 to 4 | Estimate of 30% (lines mostly dedicated, started *JIT*) |
| Black & Decker (Consumer power tools) | Electrical products | Assembly operators: 24 to 6<br>Support operators: 7 to 5 | Punch press: 1 hour to 1 min<br>Drastic in many areas |
| Deere & Company | Heavy machinery, farm equipment, lawn care equipment | Subassembly: 19 to 35%<br>Welding: 15 to 38%<br>Manufacturing cost: 10 to 20%<br>Material handling: 40% | Presses: 38 to 80%<br>Drills: 24 to 33%<br>Shears: 45%<br>Grinders: 44%<br>Average: 45% |
| General Electric (Housewares) | Electrical appliances | Direct labor: 15%<br>Indirect labor: 25% | Significant, hours to minutes |
| Harley Davidson | Motorcycles | 39% overall productivity increase | Many operations combined, overall set-up reduction: 75% |
| Hewlett Packard | Computers and test systems | 87 to 39 standard hours | 30 to 45% reduction in manual set-up |

*Source:* Abstracted from Tables 1.2 and 1.4, M. Sepehri, ***Just in Time, Not Just in Japan: Case Studies of American Pioneers in JIT Implementation,*** American Production and Inventory Control Society, Falls Church, Virginia, 1986.

12. What is a quality circle? How important is this concept in implementing the concept of total quality control?
13. What is a *kanban?* Why is this system called a "pull" or demand system of inventory control?
14. Explain how a simple *kanban* system works.
15. How do suppliers fit into the *kanban* system in Japan?

| Inventory Reduction | Quality Improvement | Space Savings | Lead Times |
|---|---|---|---|
| Estimate of 90% in WIP and raw material compared to other factories | Scrap and rework: 10%<br>Incoming material: 20% | No need for warehouse<br>Material delivered to point of use | All components less than 2 days<br>Daily schedule |
| Turns: 16 to 30 | Reduced complaints in packaging: 90%<br>100% customer service level | Significant | Products made in weekly lots: 50 to 95% |
| Raw steel: 40%<br>Purchased parts: 7%<br>Crane shafts: 30 to 3 days | Implemented process control charting in 40% of operations | Significant | Significant |
| In-process: 40% | Scrap and rework: 33% | 52,000 sq. ft. | Weeks to days<br>Mixed production<br>Daily vendor delivery |
| Turns up from 5 to 20 | 46% decrease in scrap and rework | 35% reduction in warehouse | All suppliers within 200 miles |
| 60% reduction in WIP and raw material | 35% decrease in warranty | 15% reduction in manufacturing | Weekly or daily delivery |
| PC assembly: 8500 to 5750 square feet | HP corporate helped *JIT*<br>Proud to be among first to implement *JIT/TQC* | PC assembly: 8500 to 5750 square feet | PC assembly: 15 to 1.5 days. |

16. Contrast the differences in typical Japanese and U.S. practices in dealing with suppliers.
17. What is meant by *JIT purchasing?*
18. Define the term *autonomation* as it is used in the Toyota production system. How is it related to the term *automation?*
19. Define the terms *Andon* and *Bakayoke.*
20. Define the term *Yō-i-don.* How is it related to teamwork?

21. Compare the results of *JIT* production in U.S. and Japanese plants as shown by Tables 14-1 and 14-2. Do you feel that Japanese manufacturing methods are culturally and environmentally dependent?

# SITUATION

## The Roots of Quality Control in Japan

22. An Interview with W. Edwards Deming[6]

*Dr. Deming, you said it will take about thirty years for the United States to catch up with Japan. This is a somewhat pessimistic view of the United States. Would you elaborate on this point?*

I don't really know how long it will take. I think it will take thirty years; it should take all of thirty years. I don't think America will catch up with Japan because, so far as I can see, the Japanese system has the advantage over the American system. For example, consider the principle of constancy of purpose, which is absolutely vital and is number one in my Fourteen Points. It refers to planning for the future with constancy of purpose. [See Table 14-3 for Dr. Deming's fourteen points.]

Now in America some companies certainly do have constancy of purpose, but most do not. Most have a president who was brought in to improve the quarterly dividend. That's his job; you can't blame him for doing it. He'll be there a while, then go on to some other place to raise the quarterly dividend there. For instance, someone told me that there were five candidates for president of one of the biggest and most famous of America's companies. When one of them was selected, the other four resigned from the company. Such a thing could not happen in Japan. So you see, the American system is so set up that it cannot use the talents of its people. That's very serious.

People cannot work for the company. They only get out their quota. You can't blame a person for doing the job that is cut out for him since he has to pay his rent and take care of his family. You can't blame him, but you can blame management for a situation in which people cannot work for the company. An employee cannot remain on the job to find out for sure what the job is. The foreman does not have time to help him. As a matter of fact, the foreman may decide a particular person cannot do the job at all and perhaps should be let go. People report equipment out of order and nothing happens. If someone reports equipment out of order more than three or four times, that person is considered

[6] Dr. W. Edwards Deming, recognized as the inspirational force behind the postwar quality control movement in industrial Japan, is the world's foremost authority on the development of quality control standards and procedures for industry. He has been a leading consultant in statistical studies and industrial applications to American and Japanese companies for over 35 years. These edited interviews were given by Dr. Deming to the Pacific Basin Center Foundation on September 8, 1981, and July 28, 1984, and are reproduced here by permission from: *Pacific Basin Quarterly*, Spring/Summer 1985, New York.

TABLE 14-3
**DR. DEMING'S FOURTEEN POINTS**

1. Achieve constancy of purpose
2. Learn a new philosophy
3. Do not depend on mass inspections
4. Reduce the number of vendors
5. Recognize two sources of faults:
   Management and production systems
   Production workers
6. Improve on-the-job training
7. Improve supervision
8. Drive out fear
9. Improve communication
10. Eliminate fear
11. Consider work standards carefully
12. Teach statistical methods
13. Encourage new skills
14. Use statistical knowledge

*Source:* "The Roots of Quality Control in Japan: An Interview with W. Edwards Deming," *Pacific Basin Quarterly,* Spring/Summer 1985.

a troublemaker. If he tries to find out more about the job from the foreman, he is considered a troublemaker. People find out that it is impossible to do what is best for the company or do their best work for the company. They just have to carry on as best they can, given the handicaps.

In addition, people have to use materials that are not suited to the job, and this creates a sense of desperation. There isn't much they can do about it—if they report, or try to do something, they are labeled troublemakers. This situation does not exist in Japan. There, everyone is willing to help everyone else.

*Dr. Deming, as you've mentioned, one of the Fourteen Points emphasizes constancy of purpose. Personally, I learned a great deal from that. Could you elaborate a little more on that point?*

A good way to assess a company's constancy of purpose is to evaluate the source of ultimate authority in that company. To whom does the president of the company answer? Does anybody own the company? Do the owners answer to the stockholders? The stockholders, thousands of them, who want dividends—to whom do they answer? Do they answer to their consciences? Do they answer to a built-in institution? Do they answer to a constitution of the company? Is there a constitution for the company?

Some companies have a constitution. In medical service, for example, you have some constancy of purpose. Not all, but some nursing homes or other medical institutions are under the governance of a religious board, and they're very exact about service. The head of the organization answers to constancy of purpose. There is a constitution with an aim of going beyond the making of dividends.

You have to pay to keep such institutions going, but their job is service. The reason why the public school systems fail in America is because the schools don't answer to anybody. There is no constitution. What is their aim? Is it to teach, or to produce? Is it to help youngsters that have ability to develop that ability, or is it something else? I don't know. The aim is not stated, so the schools are failing.

*We hear that American companies are now changing and adopting such things as quality control. Do you think American companies are heeding your message?*

Many companies are forming QC circles in America without understanding what they're doing. QC circles cannot be effective in the absence of quality control, which means management actively adopting my Fourteen Points. Many companies are forming QC circles because management wants a lazy way to avoid the job of improving quality and productivity. These circles will make a worthwhile contribution if they are given a chance, but QC circles alone are not quality control. Once it becomes obvious that management is working on the Fourteen Points and is trying to do something to make people more effective in their work, then the workers will be creative.

Can you imagine people in a QC circle being effective when half of them will be turned out on the streets when business slacks off? Can you imagine an effective QC circle when half or even fewer of the people involved were rehired after being laid off during a slump? People have to feel secure. That means, according to the word's derivation, "without concern," from the Latin *se* for "without" and *cure* meaning "care" or "concern." Security means being able to speak, ask each other questions, and help one another. There is nothing to hide and no one to please. Most people who work are only trying to please somebody because otherwise they might not have a job.

The lack of constancy of purpose in America is very serious. For example, I received a letter from a man who asked what he could do that would have a lasting benefit for his company. The problem is, the man will probably be where he is for only two more years. At the end of two years, he will either be promoted or he will look for a job with another company. He asked what fire he could start that would continue to burn after he leaves his job, whether he is promoted at the same company or goes elsewhere. It's a very serious question. I don't know if there is an answer.

There is another serious matter in this country: the supposition that quality control consists of a bag of techniques. Quality control is more than just a set of techniques. But you cannot have quality control without physical techniques. One of my Fourteen Points is to remove fear within a company, to make people secure. I don't know of any physical techniques to bring this about. But it is through physical techniques that I discovered the existence of fear. Fear is costing companies a great deal of money and causing a lot of waste in out-of-order machines and rework. Fear causes wasted human effort and wasted materials. It arises because people do not understand their jobs, and have no place to go for help. I don't know of any statistical technique by which to establish constancy of purpose and eliminate fear.

Statistical techniques are certainly necessary for purchasing and selling materials, since without them you cannot measure or understand the quality of what you are buying. American industry and American government, especially the military, are being rooked by the practice of purchasing from the lowest bidder. They are forcing everyone to conform to the lowest price. That is wrong because there is no such thing as price without a measure of quality. Purchasing departments are not prepared to measure quality; they only know arithmetic. They understand that thirteen cents less per thousand pieces translates into so many thousands of dollars per year. But they don't understand that the quality of these pieces may be so bad that it will cause a great deal of trouble.

*You already referred to American management's lack of understanding of quality control for production processes. Could we go back to that?*

Most American managers have no idea how deep the trouble is, and those who do have no idea of what can be done. There is no way for them to learn what to do that I know of.

*In the United States, I have been intrigued by the notion of the trade-off between quality and price and the trade-off between productivity and quality. Here these are seen as different things, and yet your message, which you say the Japanese have accepted, is not to treat quality and price, and productivity and quality, as trade-offs. Why has this been so difficult for Americans to understand?*

Americans simply have no idea of what quality is. Ask almost any plant manager in this country and he'll say it is a trade-off, that you have one or the other. He does not know that you can have both, and that once you have quality, then you can have productivity, lower costs, and a better market position. Here, people don't know this, but they know it in Japan. In 1950 in Japan, I was able to get top management together for conferences to explain what they had to do. No such gathering has ever been held in America and I don't know if anybody has any way of organizing one. In Japan, Mr. Ishikawa of JUSE organized conferences with top management in July 1950, again in August, then six months later, and so on. Top management understood from the beginning what they must do, and that as they improved quality, productivity would increase. They had some examples within six months, and more within a year. News of these examples spread throughout the country, and everyone learned about them because Japanese management was careful to disseminate the information.

The supposition of so many Americans that better quality means more gold plating or polishing, more time spent to do better work, is just not true. Quality improvement means improving the process so it produces quality without rework, quickly and directly. In other words, quality means making it right the first time so you don't have to rework it. By improving the process, you decrease wasted human effort, wasted machine time and materials, and you get a better product. If you decrease rework by six percent, you increase the productivity of a production line by six percent, and increase its capacity by the same amount. Therefore, in many cases, increased capacity could be achieved in this country simply by reducing wasted human effort, machine time, and materials. In this country, better use of existing machinery—not new machinery or automation—is the answer.

*How do you respond to American management's idea that mechanization and automation are cost-saving devices rather than quality-improvement devices? In Japan, mechanization and automation are seen as quality improvement, obviously with cost-saving benefits on the side. But in Japan they're working toward mechanization, automation, and the use of robots as quality-improvement devices.*

New machinery and automation very often bring higher costs, not lower ones. They also bring headaches and troubles which a company is unprepared to handle. The result is that they decrease production, increase costs, lower quality, and create problems the company never had before. The best thing to do is learn to use what you have efficiently. Once you learn that, then there's a possibility you may learn to use more sophisticated equipment. I'm afraid that time is a long way off for this country.

In Japan, now that they're using present equipment successfully and efficiently and cannot extract any more capacity, the only way to increase production is with new automated machinery, because there are no more people to employ. There are no employment agencies in Japan where you can find people to work in plants. In the United States, on the other hand, there are seven million unemployed, maybe half of whom are actually able and willing to work, and are good workers.

*Back in the 1950s, you made a prophetic statement when you told the Japanese that if they pursued this quality-first approach, Japan would dominate the world market and everyone, including the United States, would demand protection from Japanese imports. Did you make that prediction because you were convinced that American industries were not pursuing the proper course of action in this field?*

No, I saw, through the conferences with the top management in Japan, that Japan could do a better job with quality control than America had ever done. Americans had not done well with quality control because they thought of it as a bag of techniques. As a group, management in America never knew anything about quality control. What you had in America, from the intensive statistical courses I started at Stanford University, were brilliant fires and applications all over the country. But when a person changed jobs, the fire burned out and there was nobody in management to keep it going.

We held the first course at Stanford in July 1942, and seventeen people came. Two months later, Stanford University gave another course, and later other universities gave courses. I taught twenty-three of them myself. By that time, they would be attended by fifty or sixty or seventy people. The War Department also gave courses at defense suppliers' factories. Quality control became a big fire. As a matter of fact, courses were given to a total of ten thousand people from eight hundred companies, but nothing happened.

Brilliant applications burned, sputtered, fizzled, and died out. What people did was solve individual problems; they did not create a structure at the management level to carry out their obligations. There was not sufficient appreciation at the management level to spread the methods to other parts of the company.

The man who saw these things first was Dr. Holbrook working at Stanford. He knew the job that management must carry out. He saw it first. We tried, but our efforts were feeble, and the results were zero. We did not know how to do it. In our eight-day courses, we would ask companies to send their top people, but top people did not come. Some came for one afternoon. You don't learn this in one afternoon. So quality control died out in America.

Let me put it this way: more and more, quality control in America became merely statistical methods—the more applications, the better. Instead of finding many problems, we need to find the big problem. Where are the problems? Let's find the big problems first. What methods will help? Maybe no methods will help. Let's be careful—so many things that happen are just carelessness. We don't need control charts for them. We just need some action from management to cut that carelessness. Wrong design? That's management's fault. Recall of automobiles? Management's fault, not the workers' fault.

People started control charts everywhere. The Ford Company had charts all over their assembly plants across the country, one chart on top of another. Quality control "experts" sat and made more and more charts. One man told me his job was to count the number of points out of control every day. But what happened was nothing. Quality control drifted into so-called quality control departments that made charts. They would look at the charts and perhaps tell somebody if something was out of control. The only people who could do anything never saw the charts and never learned anything. That included everybody. Top management never heard or learned anything; people on the production lines did not learn anything. That was totally wrong, because the first step is for management to take on my Fourteen Points, namely, to gain purpose. The Japanese had already accomplished this task. The Japanese were all ready to work on training. JUSE was ready. But in 1950, quality control had practically died out in America. When I went to Japan in 1950, I said to myself, "Why repeat in Japan the mistakes that were made in America? I must get hold of top management and explain to them what their job is, because unless they do their part, these wonderful engineers will accomplish nothing. They will make business applications and then the fire will burn out."

It was at that time I was fortunate enough to meet Mr. Ichiro Ishikawa, who, after three conferences, sent telegrams to forty-five men in top management telling them to come and hear me. Well, I did a very poor job, but I explained what management must do, what quality control is from a management standpoint. For example, I told them to improve incoming materials, which means working with vendors as if they were members of your family, and teaching them. I told them they must learn statistical control of quality. It's a big job.

Incoming materials were wretched, deplorable, and nobody seemed to care. They just thought that industry consisted of taking what you got and doing the best you could. But I explained that that won't do because now you must compete. The consumer you never thought of—to whom you must now export—is in America, Canada, and Europe. Improve agriculture, yes, but the better way—the quicker way, the most effective way—is to export quality. They thought it could not be done. They said they had never done it, that they had a bad reputation. I told them, you can do it—you have to do it, you must. You must learn statistical methods. These methods of quality control must be a part of everybody's job.

At that time, consumer research was unknown in Japan, but the aim of making products was to help somebody. I think they had never thought of the consumer as the most important end of the production line. I told them they must study the needs of the consumer. They must look ahead one year, three years, eight years, to be ahead in new services and new products. As they learned, they must teach everyone else. Well, that was the natural Japanese way. I did not know how much, but I gave them that advice.

*How did you develop your own views, not only of statistical control methods, but also your central message that quality determines productivity?*

By simple arithmetic. If you have material coming in that is difficult to use —and there was plenty of it coming to Japan in 1950—you will produce a lot of wasted human effort, machine time, and materials. There will be a lot of rework, with people occupying time trying to overcome the deficiencies of defective incoming material. So if you have better material coming in, you eliminate waste; production, quality, and productivity go up; costs go down; and your market position is improved.

Well I think that I have put some principles on paper that everybody knew but that, in a sense, nobody knew. They had never been put down on paper. I stated those principles in Japan in the summer of 1950, some for the first time. They're obvious, perhaps, as Newton's laws of motion are obvious. But like Newton's laws, they're not obvious to everyone.

*Is there a company in the United States that has heeded your message? Are there some isolated cases?*

The Nashua Corporation in Nashua, New Hampshire, under the direction of its former president, William E. Conway, was off to a good start. Mr. Conway himself was doing a great deal, not only for his corporation, but for American industry. Almost every day, visiting teams of ten to fifteen people from other companies came to Mr. Conway's offices and plants to hear about what he was doing. He was getting a very good start. The entire company was meant for quality.

*Why is he so different from other American managers?*

I don't know. There are other good companies. Some of them have started lately and they're pushing along. One of the great problems is finding competent statistical consultants. There are very few that can give competent training. One company I work with must train fifty thousand people to discover problems. How long do you think it will take the purchasing department to learn to take quality into consideration along with price? It will take five years or more, and at the end of five years a lot of people will be gone. They will have other jobs. It's going to take a long time. There is no quick road.

## DISCUSSION QUESTIONS

a. Dr. Deming seems to put more emphasis on corporate culture than on quality control methodology. What is necessary to change a corporate culture to be as quality conscious as Deming feels is necessary to compete in global markets?

b. What are the relationships between quality and productivity?

c. If automation continues to be installed in both Japanese and U.S. industry, will the quality problem be solved by technology?

d. What are the future prospects for making the quality of U.S. manufactured products competitive? How can such a goal be achieved, given the current Japanese lead?

## REFERENCES


Bitran, G. R., and L. Chang, "An Optimization Approach to the Kanban System," Working Paper, Sloan School of Management, MIT, March 1985.

Blair, J. D., and K. D. Ramsing, "Quality Circles and Production/Operations Management: Concerns and Caveats" *Journal of Operations Management, 4*(1), November 1983, pp. 1–10.

Crosby, L. B., "The Just-In-Time Manufacturing Process: Control of Quality and Quantity," *Production and Inventory Management, 25*(4), Winter 1984, pp. 110–122.

Deming, W. E., *Quality, Productivity, and Competitive Position,* MIT Press, Cambridge, Mass., 1982.

Garvin, D. A., "Quality on the Line," *Harvard Business Review,* September–October 1983, pp. 65–75.

Goddard, W., "Kanban versus MRP II—Which Is Best for You?," *Modern Materials Handling,* November 5, 1982, pp. 40–48.

Gray, C. S., "Total Quality Control in Japan—Less Inspection, Lower Cost," *Business Week,* July 16, 1981, pp. 23–44.

Hall, R., *Zero Inventories,* Irwin, Homewood, Ill., 1983.

Hayes, R., "Why Japanese Factories Work," *Harvard Business Review,* July–August 1981, pp. 56–66.

Haynsworth, H. C., "A Theoretical Justification for the Use of Just-In-Time Scheduling," *Production and Inventory Management, 25*(1), Spring 1984, pp. 1–3.

Huang, P. Y., L. P. Rees, and B. W. Taylor, "A Simulation Analysis of the Japanese Just-in-Time Technique (with Kanbans) for a Multiline Production System," *Decision Sciences, 14*(3), July 1983, pp. 326–344.

Juran, J. M., "Japanese and Western Quality: A Contrast in Methods and Results," *Management Review,* November 1978, pp. 26–45.

Juran, J. M., "Product Quality—A Prescription for the West: Training and Improvement Programs," *Management Review,* June 1981, pp. 8–14.

Kimura, O., and H. Terada, "Design and Analysis of Pull System, A Method of Multi-Stage Production Control," *International Journal of Production Research, 19*(3), 1981, pp. 241–253.

Konz, S., "Quality Circles: Japanese Success Story," *Industrial Engineering,* October 1979, pp. 24–27.

Lee, S. M., and G. Schwendiman, *Management by Japanese Systems,* Praeger, New York, 1982.

Monden, Y., "Adaptable Kanban System Helps Toyota Maintain Production," *Industrial Engineering, 13*(5), May 1981, pp. 29–46.

Monden, Y., "How Toyota Shortened Supply Lot Production Waiting Time and Conveyance Time," *Industrial Engineering,* September 1981, pp. 22–30.

Monden, Y., *Toyota Production System,* Industrial Engineering and Management Press, Institute of Industrial Engineers, Norcross, Georgia, 1983, pp. 247.

Monden, Y., "Toyota's Production Smoothing Methods: Part II," *Industrial Engineering,* September 1981, pp. 22–30.

Monden, Y., "What Makes the Toyota Production System Really Tick?" *Industrial Engineering, 13*(1), January 1981, pp. 36–46.

Monden, Y., R. Shibakawa, S. Takayanagi, and T. Nagao, *Innovations in Management: The Japanese Corporation,* Industrial Engineering and Management Press, Institute of Industrial Engineers, Norcross, Georgia, 1985.

Nellemann, D. O., and L. F. Smith, "'Just-In-Time' versus 'Just-In-Case' Production/Inventory Systems Borrowed Back From Japan," *Production and Inventory Management, 23*(2), Summer 1982, pp. 12–21.

Rice, J. W., and T. Yoshikawa, "A Comparison of Kanban and MRP Concepts for Control of Repetitive Manufacturing Systems," *Production & Inventory Management, 23*(1), Spring 1982, pp. 1–13.

Rice, J. W., and T. Yoshikawa, "MRP and Motivation: What Can We Learn from Japan," *Production & Inventory Management,* 2nd Quarter 1980, pp. 45–52.

Schonberger, R. J., *Japanese Manufacturing Techniques: Nine Hidden Lessons in Simplicity,* The Free Press, New York, 1982, pp. 260. (a)

Schonberger, R. J., "Production Workers Bear Major Quality Responsibility in Japanese Industry," *Industrial Engineering,* December 1982. (b)

Schroer, B. J., J. T. Black, and S. X. Zhang, "Microcomputer Analyzes 2-Card Kanban System for 'Just-In-Time' Small Batch Production," *Industrial Engineering,* June 1984, pp. 54–65.

Sepehri, M., *Just in Time, Not Just in Japan: Case Studies of American Pioneers in JIT Implementation,* American Production and Inventory Control Society, Falls Church, Virginia, 1986.

Shingo, S., *Study of "Toyota" Production System: From an Industrial Engineering Viewpoint,* Japan Management Association, Tokyo, 1981.

Weiss, A., "Simple Truths of Japanese Manufacturing," *Harvard Business Review,* July–August 1984, pp. 119–125.

Wheelwright, S. C., "Japan—Where Operations Really Are Strategic," *Harvard Business Review,* July–August 1981, pp. 67–74.

# PART THREE

# DESIGN OF OPERATIONAL SYSTEMS

# CHAPTER 15

# PRODUCT/PROCESS DESIGN AND TECHNOLOGICAL CHOICE



(Continued)

With this chapter, we begin Part Three, the "Design of Operational Systems." The preceding major part, dealing with operations planning and control, assumed the existence of a physical system designed with specific competitive objectives in mind. Chapters 2 and 3 discussed the types and characteristics of both manufacturing and service systems, and these materials may be reviewed at this time. Technological choice, capacity planning, location and distribution, process and job design, and facility layout are interrelated issues that contribute to the design of productive systems and are dealt with in separate chapters in Part Three. In addition, waiting line models are particularly important to the design of service systems, and many design decisions have multiple objectives; therefore, two chapters devoted to these methodologies are included in this section.

The competitiveness and profitability of a firm depend in part on the design and quality of the products and services that it produces and on the cost of production. Therefore, the relationship of product innovation to process technology and process innovation is of considerable interest. Predicting the nature and impact of innovation can place one firm in a more competitive position than a firm that does not anticipate these events.

The design of the productive system depends in large part on the design of the products and services to be produced. A product or service designed one way may be costly to produce, but it may be somewhat less costly when designed another way.

## A MODEL FOR PRODUCT AND PROCESS INNOVATION

Recall our discussion in Chapter 2 of the product life cycle and how the productive system goes through a life cycle of its own, evolving from a process-focused system initially, when volumes are low and flexibility is particularly important, to a product-focused system when products have matured. This situation was summarized in Figure 2-4. Now we develop these ideas further with a three-stage model for process and product innovation.

### Stage 1

The first stage begins early in the life of products and processes; initially, innovations are stimulated by needs in the marketplace. Process innovations also are stimulated by the need to increase output rate (see Figure 15-1). In terms of innovation rate, product innovation is high and the initial emphasis is on product performance maximization. There may be the anticipation that new capabilities will, in turn, expand requirements in the marketplace.

Although we may think largely in terms of physical products, service innovations are quite comparable; for example, the initial introduction of such innovative ser-

FIGURE 15-1
**RELATIONSHIPS OF PRODUCT AND PROCESS INNOVATIONS IN A DYNAMIC MODEL.**

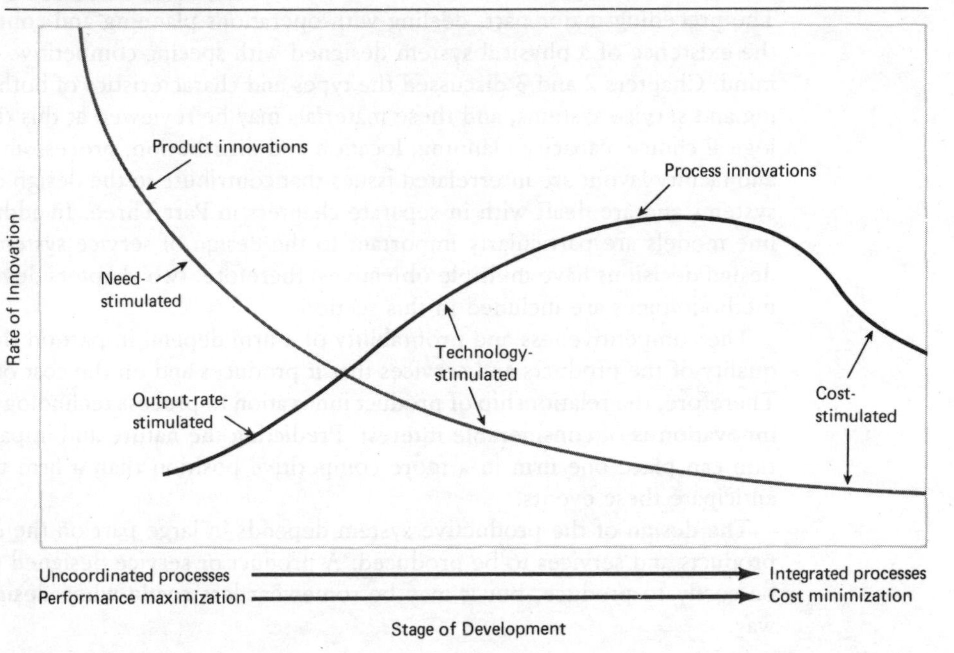


*Source:* J. M. Utterback and W. J. Abernathy, "A Dynamic Model of Process and Product Innovation by Firms," *Omega,* 1975.

vices as social security, no-fault auto insurance, comprehensive health services (e.g., Kaiser Permanente), fast-food services, and so on.

The first phase is called "performance maximization" for products and services and "uncoordinated" for processes. High product innovation rates increase the likelihood that product diversity will be extensive. As a result, the productive process is composed largely of unstandardized and manual operations or operations that rely on general purpose technology. The productive system is likely to be of the process-focused type, but the characterization—uncoordinated—is probably justified in most instances because the relationships between the required operations are still not clear.

## Stage 2

Price competition becomes more intense in the second stage as the industry or product and service group begins to reach maturity. Productive system design emphasizes cost minimization as competition in the marketplace begins to emphasize price. The productive process becomes more capital intensive and more tightly integrated through production planning and control.

At this stage, the production process is often segmented in nature. This is true partly because integration is taking place at a broader level through managerial control systems and partly because the dominant system type is the process focused system. As shown in Figure 15-1, process innovations dominate; however, both process and product innovations are stimulated by technology.

### Stage 3

Finally, as the entire system reaches maturity and saturation, innovations tend to be largely cost stimulated, as indicated in Figure 15-1. Further price competition puts increasing emphasis on cost minimizing strategies, and the production process becomes even more capital intensive and product focused.

The productive process becomes more highly structured and integrated, as illustrated by automotive assembly lines, continuous chemical processes, and such highly automated, large-scale service systems as social security. The productive process becomes so highly integrated that it is difficult to make changes because any change at all creates significant interactions with other operations in the process.

The model of innovation indicates the close relationship between the design and development of products and services and the productive system design. In fact, during the third, or cost-minimizing, stage, the effects of innovation on product cost follow a surprisingly clear pattern. In addition, however, the model demonstrates the close tie-in between the nature of innovation at various times in the product life cycle and the positioning strategy of the enterprise regarding its productive system.

## INTERACTION BETWEEN PRODUCT AND PRODUCTIVE SYSTEM DESIGN

The design of products and services is partially dependent on the productive system design, and vice versa. The concept is so well recognized in the mechanical industries that a term has been coined for the process of designing products from the point of view of producibility—*production design*.

### Production Design

The producibility and minimum possible production cost of a product are established originally by the product designer. The most clever production engineer cannot change this situation; he or she can only work within the limitations of the product design. Therefore, the obvious time to start thinking about basic modes of production for products is while they are still in the design stage. This conscious effort to design for producibility and low manufacturing costs is referred to as "production design," as distinct from functional design. To be sure, the product designer's first responsibility is to create something that meets functional requirements. But once functional requirements are met, there are ordinarily alternative designs, all of which meet functional requirements. Which of these alternatives will minimize production costs and foster product quality?

Given the design, process planning for manufacture must be carried out to specify in careful detail the processes required and their sequence. Production design first sets the minimum possible costs that can be achieved through such factors as the specifications of materials, tolerances, basic configurations, and the methods of joining parts. Final process planning then attempts to achieve that minimum through the specification of processes and their sequence that meet the exacting requirements of the design. Here, process planners may work under the limitations of available equipment. If the volume is great and the design is stable, however, process planners may be able to consider special-purpose process technology, including semiautomatic and automatic processes, and special purpose layouts. In performing their functions, process planners set the basic design of the productive system.

The thesis of a production design philosophy is that design alternatives that still meet functional requirements nearly always exist. Then, for the projected volume of the product, what differences in cost would result? Here we must broaden our thinking because the possible areas of cost that can be affected by design are likely to be more pervasive than we imagine. There are the obvious cost components of direct labor and materials. But perhaps not so obvious are the effects of equipment costs, tooling costs, indirect labor costs, and the nonmanufacturing costs of engineering.

Indirect costs tend to be hidden, but suppose one design requires 30 different parts, whereas another requires only 15 (e.g., the reciprocating automobile engine versus the rotary engine). There are differences in indirect costs as a result of greater paper work and the cost of ordering, storing, and controlling 30 parts instead of 15 for each completed item.

## Design and Redesign

The design process is an iterative one. In a sense, it is never done. New information feeds in from users, and we find ways to improve designs that reduce production costs and improve quality.

As an example of production design and redesign, Bright (1958) describes the development of electric light bulb manufacturing during the period from 1908 to 1955. Initially, a batch process was used that involved manual operations and simple equipment. The conversion from batch to continuous operation was achieved by adopting a systematic layout, standardizing operations, and effecting operation sequence changes. Then, however, the light bulb itself was redesigned a number of times to facilitate process changes and to permit mechanical handling. Finally, an evolution took place in which individual standardized manual operations were replaced by mechanical operations, and these operations were in turn integrated to produce a fully automated process.

## Interchangeable Parts

Designs for component parts need to be specified carefully so that any part from a lot will fit. This is accomplished by establishing tolerances for part dimensions that take into account the manufacturing tolerances of mating parts. The result of design for interchangeable parts is interchangeable assembly. Assembly costs are then much lower than they would be if workers had to select combinations of mating parts that fit.

### Standardization

Custom products are likely to be more costly than standardized products, but managers must attempt a balance that clients and customers will accept. Given the appropriate balance, there are many economic benefits to standardization. The cost items affected are raw materials inventory, in-process inventory, lower set-up costs, longer production runs, improved quality controls with fewer items, opportunities for mechanization and automation, more advantageous purchasing, better labor utilization, lower training costs, and so on.

### Simplification

When two or more parts are finally assembled rigidly together, perhaps the unit can be designed as one piece, thus eliminating an assembly operation. This is often feasible when a single material will meet the service requirements for all the surfaces and cross sections of the part. Another example is the substitution of a plastic snap-on cap in place of a screw-on cap for some applications. The costs of the materials and labor for the snap-on cap are much less. Simplifying the design of services offered has similar implications.

### Modular Designs

If the same component or subassembly can be used in a variety of products, or in a product family, production costs can be reduced. Thus, modular design is one way to offer product variety while holding the number of components and subassemblies to some reasonable level. For the modular components, we can have the advantages that result from volume and the experience curve while offering product variety in the marketplace.

## CLASSIFICATION OF PROCESS TECHNOLOGIES

There are a number of ways to classify process technologies. For example, we could classify them in terms of the nature of the process; that is, processes to change shape or form, chemical processes, information processes, assembly processes, and so on. But we choose to focus on a classification that highlights the historical progression of processes. This classification will also be useful in comparing how each affects the competitive priorities of cost, flexibility, quality, and the ability of the enterprise to perform on time. Thus, we have a three-part classification of process technologies

- Manual
- Mechanized
- Automated

The role of labor and labor costs in these three classifications is high in manual technologies, intermediate in mechanized technologies, and diminishes to near zero in automated technologies. On the other hand, capital costs increase in the reverse order. All three of these types of process technologies are important in operations systems today, depending on product volume, the stability of product design, and competitive requirements.

## General Versus Special Purpose Technologies

Under mechanized and automated technologies we have recognized two subcategories, general and single purpose. But based on product volume and its standardization, a machine could be either dedicated solely to a product or product line, making it a special purpose machine, or it could be general in its application to a wider range of product designs.

General purpose machines have general use capabilities in their fields of application. For example, a typewriter is a general purpose machine—it can be used for various kinds of copy: letters, manuscripts, and some kinds of charts and figures. On the other hand, a typewriter can be made a special purpose machine by adapting it to special uses in accounting. But specialized computer programs can do these accounting tasks much more efficiently, producing the typed accounting reports easily.

In the machine shop, we find the general purpose lathe, drill press, milling machine, and planers, which are capable of performing their functions by generating cylindrical surfaces, holes, and flat surfaces on a wide variety of parts and materials.

General purpose machines find their field of application with low-volume production and changing product designs—situations that demand flexibility. Yet where the situation warrants it, we find special designs of these types of machines meant to produce one part or a group of parts much more efficiently than could their general purpose machine equivalents. Special purpose machines commonly evolve from their general purpose equivalents as the volume of a particular part or product grows and the design stabilizes. With specialized machine designs, higher production rates can be achieved with lower overall costs.

Whether a mechanized technology has lower costs than a manual one depends on the balance of labor and capital costs, though differences in material costs often enter the equation too. But the investment in machines required by mechanization carries with it a risk that there will not be sufficient use of the machine to return its investment plus a profit. The same general concept applies to the economic justification of a special purpose machine compared to its general purpose equivalent. The economic bases for comparing these alternatives are covered later in this chapter and in the supplement to this chapter.

## Progression of Technologies

Since the beginning of the industrial revolution, there has been a continuous substitution of *machine power* for *human power*, and the "mechanized" classification is the result. Progressive mechanization for the production of high-volume standardized parts led to the first automated systems, called "hard automation." But with the advent of computers, and particularly the microprocessor chip, automated processes began to substitute machines for the *control functions* of the human operator as well, opening the field of automation to low-volume products. New and exciting advanced process technologies have been developed, such as

- Robotics
- NC machines (numerically controlled machines where machine tools are computer controlled)
- FMS (flexible manufacturing systems that combine NC machines in flexible systems of production)
- CAD/CAM (computer aided design and manufacturing systems that combine product design and manufacturing instructions)
- CIM (computer integrated manufacturing in which all aspects of manufacturing are integrated through a design and manufacturing data base)
- GT (group technology that organizes planning and facilities for small-lot manufacturing by grouping various parts and products with similar design and production process into efficient systems that can use NC machines, robots, or other advanced technologies)

These advanced technologies find applications in both assembly and parts fabrication. We shall define and deal with each of them, indicating the general way each impacts the competitive dimensions of cost, flexibility, quality, and delivery response and discussing their fields of application.

Figure 15-2 summarizes the development from manual through mechanized and automated processes, branching with mechanized and automated technologies, based on product volume and standardization.

## MANUAL TECHNOLOGY

Manual technology has been the basis for measuring productivity, and throughout the period since the industrial revolution, we have measured much of the economic progress of companies, industries, and even countries based on overall output relative to labor input; that is, on output per worker-hour. Yet in many instances, manual technology may be quite appropriate even in today's high-tech environment. Its advantages are low cost for low-volume, perhaps custom, processes, since little or no capital is generally required, and its inherent flexibility. The combination of labor, material, and capital costs may be difficult to beat in many situations.

Flexibility, both operational and financial, is an important advantage of manual technology. The operational flexibility can be significant for one-of-a-kind or very low-volume products since variations in requirements are easily accommodated. Capacity can usually be expanded or contracted very quickly, unless high skills are required, resulting in cost and schedule flexibility not available in mechanized technologies. Since capital costs are so low, risks are low and financial flexibility is maximized.

Quality control may be more of a problem because of the human error and

FIGURE 15-2
**RELATIONSHIP AND DEVELOPMENT OF MANUAL, MECHANIZED, AND AUTOMATED PROCESSES.**

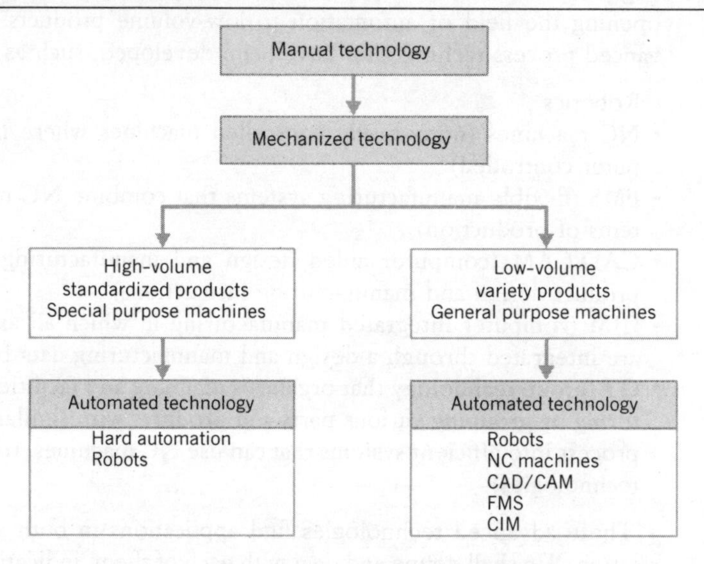


process variation inherent in manual processes. However, for some low volume customized products craftsmen can produce quality superior to mechanized technology. Production cycles may be longer with manual technologies, affecting delivery response time.

## MECHANIZED TECHNOLOGY

Substitutions of machines for human labor began almost as soon as the factory system came into being at the dawn of the industrial revolution, and until a few years ago, mechanized technology was the technology of choice. Substitutions for the power requirements of processes originally supplied by labor were followed by substitutions for all kinds of physical labor inputs. General purpose machines were the first to be developed, and the distinction between general and special purpose machines is important for both mechanized and automated technologies. As the volume of standardized products grew, as occurred in the automobile industry and many others, it became more economical to design machines that were special purpose in nature, dedicated to the production of a single part or product.

Flexibility and cost are the important differences in performance between general and special purpose technologies, and they can have an important bearing on competitive priorities. If the market in which the firm operates or its chosen niche requires flexibility of part or product design, then the firm needs to match this requirement with flexible (general purpose) process technology. If low cost is the primary requirement and product designs are stable, then special purpose technology is the likely choice. But it is difficult to have it both ways. Quality can usually be maintained with either technology, but delivery response may be superior with special purpose technology.

## AUTOMATED TECHNOLOGY

Although automation is new in the sense that its principles have been applied to mechanical and assembly types of processes only relatively recently, the basic ideas are not new. Such automatic processes as the thermostatic control of room temperature have been used for many years, and the common float valve used in toilets automatically fills the tank to a given level and then shuts off. The process industries have used the principles of automation for some time to control chemical processes. But applications of robotics, NC (numerical control of machines), FMS (flexible manufacturing systems), and the coupling of computer aided design (CAD) and computer aided manufacturing (CAM) are quite new and have considerable significance for potential productivity increases in industry.

### Hard Automation

The term "hard automation" means that automation is built in, just as some programs in personal computers are said to be "hard wired." In hard automation, the processing sequence is determined by process and equipment design, as in transfer lines, automatic assembly lines, and some chemical plants such as oil refineries. Usually, hard automation has developed as a natural progression of mechanization as a process becomes highly integrated in the later stages of the product life cycle, and it may incorporate flexible or inflexible robots. These developments occur in the "cost stimulated" portion of our model for product and process innovation diagrammed in Figure 15-1. Typically, changes in process are very expensive to incorporate; that is, hard automation is quite inflexible. By contrast, the programmable types of automation (robots, NC machines, FMS, etc.) are flexible because of the ease and the relatively low cost of changeover.

Some of the most dramatic examples of hard automation are the giant transfer machines used in the auto industry to machine engine blocks, transmission housings, and similar high-volume standardized parts. These machining lines integrate a large number of special purpose machines into a single giant machine that may perform a hundred or more separate machining operations. The system is engineered so that the parts being machined are transferred from operation to operation on a transfer bar at the end of each cycle, each part advancing one station each cycle. Robots are often used as an integral part of the overall process. When the system cycles, each part is positioned and held rigidly in place so that the operations can be carried out. The operations may involve all types of machining processes as well as quality checks and measurements. Completed parts are produced at the end of the line without having been touched by human hands.

These transfer machines have little or no flexibility in the parts they can process, and the costs of modifying them to accommodate part design changes are very high.

The investment required is extremely large, so to be competitive in overall cost with other technologies the volume must be very large and the part design stable.

The automated technologies we will now discuss are all flexible in that they are reprogrammable for changing use requirements. Robots, the first of these technologies discussed, are also used in conjunction with hard automation systems.

## Robotics

After a slow start in the 1960s and 1970s, industrial robots are not only gaining widespread attention, they are being installed rapidly, especially in Japan. Industrial robots are substituted for human manipulation and other functions in highly repetitive production situations. They can move parts, tools, or devices through variable programmed motions and perform a variety of tasks.

What sets industrial robots apart from being simply "cogs in a machine," is that, like human workers, they are reprogrammable. They have most of the advantages and utilized capabilities of typical assembly-line workers and few of the disadvantages: they do not strike; do not mind hot, dirty, dusty conditions; can work long hours without rest breaks; and will not sue if injured.

The Robot Institute of America adopted the following definition of a robot in 1979:

> A robot is a reprogrammable multifunctional manipulator designed to move material, parts, tools, or specialized devices through variable programmed motions for the performance of a variety of tasks.

This definition excludes simpler devices that also serve the automation objective, such as human-controlled manipulators that perform fixed or preset sequences and simple "playbacks" that repeat fixed directions.

### DESIGN CHARACTERISTICS OF ROBOTS

Some of the advanced capabilities being designed into robots in addition to their basic reprogrammability and manipulative skills are virtually all the human senses—vision, tactile sensing, and hand-to-hand coordination. In addition, some robots can be "taught" a sequence of motions in a three-dimensional pattern by moving the end of the arm through the required positions and manipulations. The robot records the pattern in its computer memory and will repeat them on command.

The motions that robots can reproduce seem to duplicate all those that human arms and hands can perform (see Figure 15-3). For example, the jointed arm, spherical motions in both planes, cylinorical rotation, and even complex wrist motions are duplicated in current designs.

### ROBOT APPLICATIONS

There are some unique applications of robots, such as assembling high-explosive shells in government arsenals, picking up hot steel ingots and placing them in presses, handling radioactive rods in nuclear power plants, and other nuclear appli-

FIGURE 15-3
**TYPICAL ROBOT AXES OF MOTION.**

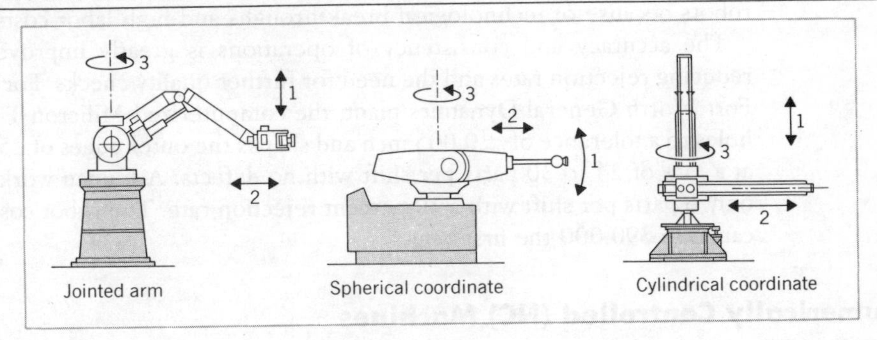


Wrist axes

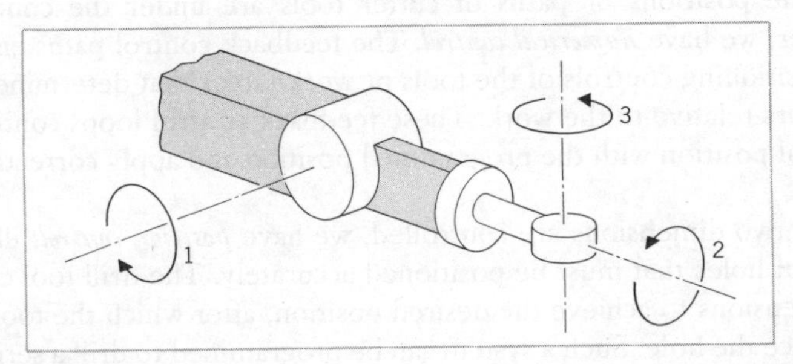


*Source:* L. V. Ottinger, "Robotics for the IE: Terminology, Types of Robots," *Industrial Engineering,* November 1981, p. 30.

cations where human safety requires remote mechanical handling. But by all odds, the dominant applications have been in ordinary manufacturing operations, such as spot welding and material handling. Projections to 1990 foresee large numbers of applications in arc welding and assembly.

The auto industry has been the dominant user, though other industries are rapidly installing robots too, such as electrical machinery, fabricated metals, electronics, and heavy machinery. Currently, for example, General Motors has more than 4000 robots, and it projects 14,000 by 1990. The new Hamtramck plant in Detroit will employ 5000 people in two shifts and 250 robots—160 in the body shop, 70 in the paint shop, and 20 in general assembly.[1]

## ECONOMICS OF ROBOTS

Robots are already economically justified in many situations. Assuming an average original cost of $50,000, they cost in the range of $6 to $8 per hour to operate, including capital and operating costs. Compared to the average steelworker's wage of $26 per hour including benefits or the average autoworker's wage of in excess of

[1] J. B. Tucker, "GM: Shifting To Automatic," *High Technology,* May 1985, pp. 26–29.

$20 per hour, the robot is obviously a bargain. While robots have been available for many years, it is only recently that it has become attractive to replace humans with robots because of technological breakthroughs and high labor costs.

The accuracy and consistency of operations is greatly improved with robots, reducing rejection rates and the need for further quality checks. For example, at the Fort Worth General Dynamics plant, the computerized Milicron T-3 drills a set of holes to a tolerance of ±0.005 inch and shapes the outer edges of 250 types of parts at a rate of 24 to 30 parts per shift with no defects. A human worker can produce only 6 parts per shift with a 10 percent rejection rate. The robot costs $60,000, but can save $90,000 the first year.[2]

## Numerically Controlled (NC) Machines

When the positions or paths of cutter tools are under the control of a digital computer, we have *numerical control.* The feedback control paths emanate from the basic positioning controls of the tools or work tables that determine the position of the cutters relative to the work. These feedback control loops continually compare the actual position with the programmed position and apply correction when necessary.

When two dimensions are controlled, we have *position control,* illustrated by the drilling of holes that must be positioned accurately. The drill tool can be moved in two dimensions to achieve the desired position, after which the tool does the work to produce the hole. Such a system can be programmed to drill a series of accurately positioned holes.

When position control is carried one step further, by controlling three dimensions, we have *contour control,* controlling the actual path of the cutter. Contour control involves a much more complex programming problem because curves and surfaces must often be specified. Contour control systems have great flexibility in terms of the part shapes that can be produced as well as in the change of shapes from job to job. Instead of the part being processed through a sequence of machines or machine centers, it is often possible to perform all the required operations with a single set-up because the cutter can be programmed to make cuts along any path needed to produce the required configuration. Very complex parts can be produced with a single set-up.

One of the great advantages of numerically controlled systems is that the machine tool is not tied up for long periods during set-up because practically all the preparation time is in programming, which does not involve the actual machine tool. In addition, repeat orders require virtually no set-up time. Thus, the field of applicability includes parts that are produced in low volumes. Therefore, through numerically controlled processes, automation is having an important impact on process technology for both high-volume, standardized types of products and low-volume products (even custom designs).

[2]Thomas Dolan, "Automation Moves On," *Barron's,* June 2, 1980.

## Comparative Costs

Figure 15-4 shows an assembly–cost comparison among hard automation, manual methods with labor costing $9 per hour, and programmable automation. The break-even points should be regarded as general, rather than specific, in nature, but they highlight some obvious conclusions. Programmable automation becomes less expensive than manual methods at fairly low annual volumes, and is the lowest-cost method for midrange volumes. Hard automation is less costly than manual methods at fairly high volumes, and it breaks even with programmable automation at an even higher volume. But beyond the break-even point with programmable automation, hard automation is the lowest-cost method and the margin of advantage expands as volume increases.

The reasons for these conclusions lie in the comparative investment costs of the two automation methods—programmable automation is relatively costly to install, but hard automation is much more costly. But when it is economically justified, as in the region beyond three million units per year in Figure 15-4, hard automation has the lowest cost of all methods. Of course, this conclusion assumes that other conditions hold; that is, the volume remains high and changeover requirements do not make the hard automation system obsolete before it has provided its return.

## Computer Aided Design/Computer Aided Manufacturing (CAD/CAM)

Building on the concept of NC manufacturing, one should ask, "How are the computer instructions to the NC machine generated?" If the part design and specifications can be generated on a computer, can the manufacturing instructions for NC

FIGURE 15-4
**COST COMPARISONS FOR THREE ASSEMBLY METHODS.**

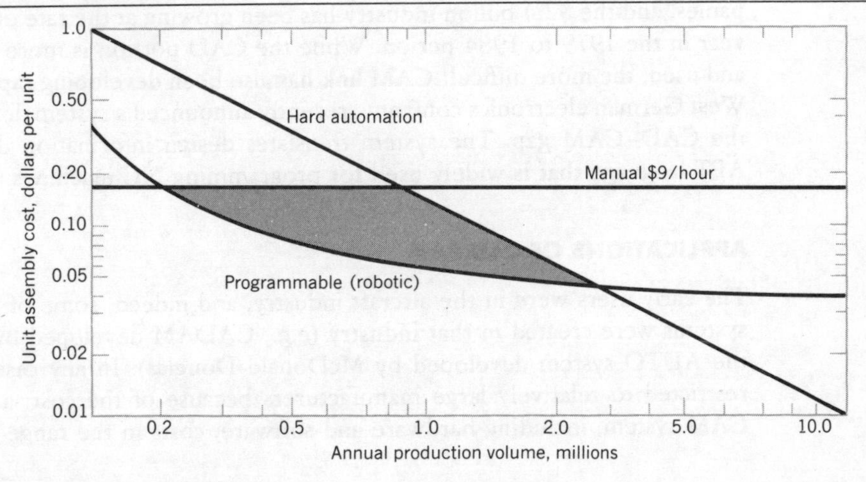


*Source: Iron Age,* July 21, 1980.

machines be generated directly as a translation from the computer-aided part design? Indeed, that is the concept of CAD/CAM, the joining of part design and processing instructions with the aid of a computer.

In the 1960s, engineers at General Motors began working with IBM programmers to develop a system of computer aided design, originally envisioned only as a sophisticated drafting system. The success of the drafting system effort is indicated by the fact that engineering drafting has been virtually eliminated in modern engineering departments. But the more far reaching effects are in the broader concepts of CAD and its connection to CAM. The data specifying the part geometry, for example, is also needed for determining how a cutting tool must move to shape the part. The specification of the cutting path must also take account of the load capacity of the machine, the material from which the part is made, the shape of the cutting tool, the speed and depth of cut, and other variables.

In currently available CAD/CAM systems, the designer sits in front of a computer console screen and can draw on a data bank of existing part designs as the part being designed may be only a variation of a previous design. Programs allow the designer to view the part in any orientation, any scale, or any cross section. Because of the efficiency of the system, the engineering analysis can be done for several alternative design solutions, perhaps analyzing the response of the part to various stresses, without building a prototype. When a design is finalized, the link to CAM is made by producing the manufacturing instructions that will control the machine to produce the part. Manufacturing issues, part of the criteria for a good design, can also be addressed as a part of the analysis.

Because of the efficiency of the CAD/CAM system, the design and manufacture of small lots, and even a custom part, can be low in cost. A CAD/CAM system for designing and manufacturing computer chips has been developed that makes custom designed chips almost as inexpensive to design and manufacture as high-volume, standard designs.

Working CAD/CAM systems are now supplied by a number of software companies, and the $2.4 billion industry has been growing at the rate of 48 percent per year in the 1979 to 1984 period. While the CAD portion is more fully developed and used, the more difficult CAM link has also been developing rapidly. Siemens, a West German electronics company, recently announced a system designed to bridge the CAD–CAM gap. The system translates design information directly into the APT language that is widely used for programming NC machines.[3]

## APPLICATIONS OF CAD/CAM

The early users were in the aircraft industry, and indeed, some of the best known systems were created in that industry (e.g., CADAM developed by Lockheed and the AUTO system developed by McDonald Douglas). In any case, application is restricted to relatively large manufacturers because of the cost; a turnkey CAD/CAM system, including hardware and software, costs in the range of $300,000 to

[3] "Science and Technology," *Business Week*, August 26, 1985, p. 89.

$500,000. However, application is now reasonably diversified in manufacturing, having spread to the largest companies in the following industries:

- Electrical and electronic (Burroughs, Digital Equipment, General Electric, Intel, Texas Instruments, Westinghouse)
- Petroleum and refinery machinery (Exxon, Halliburton, Shell)
- Measurement and analytical instruments (Becton Dickinson, Eastman Kodak, Xerox)
- Transportation (Ford, General Motors, Mercedes Benz, Volkswagen)
- Aerospace (Boeing, Lockheed, McDonnel Douglas, Rockwell, United Technologies)
- Chemicals (Allied Chemical, Dow Chemical, Dupont, Union Carbide)
- Heavy machinery (Caterpillar Tractor, Deere & Company)

### PRODUCTIVITY AND QUALITY IMPROVEMENTS DUE TO CAD/CAM

The effects of an important new technology such as CAD/CAM extend to many functions in an organization, resulting in productivity and quality improvements beyond simply those in manufacturing. The following, some of them items we have already touched on, is a partial list of such effects:

- *Engineering design.* Initial design considers more alternatives, is more efficiently done, and results in better designs. Calculations of area, volume, weight, stress, and the like are best done on a computer. CAD systems can either perform such calculations directly or prepare the data for computation on mainframe computers.
- *Drafting.* Parts with recurring features or parts that are frequently updated can be maintained more efficiently with CAD.
- *Bills of material.* These can easily be produced from data stored in a CAD system.
- *Cost estimating.* CAD systems can correlate, store, and recall graphical and text data for each part for cost estimating purposes.
- *Order entry.* Some manufacturers have integrated order entry with CAD when orders are tied to specific engineering drawings.
- *Manufacturing.* Process planning can be shortened or eliminated through the CAD/CAM coupling. Many commercial systems provide software for producing NC programming tapes and other information used in preparing an order for production.

## Flexible Manufacturing Systems (FMS)

Figure 15-5 shows a schematic layout of an FMS, where NC machines of different types are positioned around a material handling system. The material handling system automatically moves the parts to be processed to computer-directed locations on guided carts or some equivalent material handling mechanism. Robots move the parts to and from the system and, perhaps, to and from the individual machines. The individual NC machines are equipped with tool changers that load

FIGURE 15-5
**SCHEMATIC LAYOUT OF A FLEXIBLE MANUFACTURING SYSTEM.**

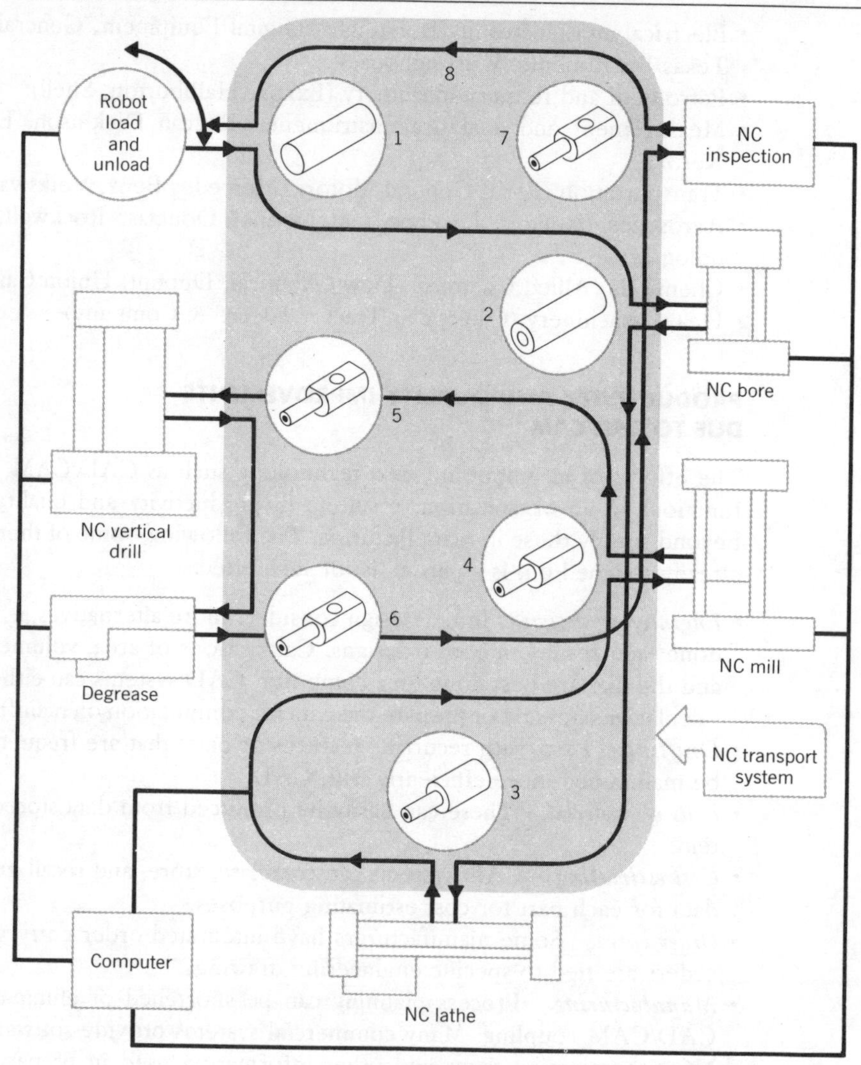


the required tool into the machine, depending on the tool needed for the particular processing job. As with NC machines in general, set-up is solely in the programming of the machines, so they are not tied up during this phase. The entire system, including product changeover, is controlled by its computer, so a wide variety of parts can be produced on the same flexible system.

In Figure 15-5, we show the processing required for a part that goes through an eight-step sequence automatically, including loading and unloading from the FMS. The inserts show the changes in form to produce the final form shown in steps 5, 6, and 7. (Note that the final steps do not involve changes in the form of the part.)

The great potential of FMS technology is that its flexibility, with no machine time for set-up, creates the capacity to manufacture low-cost parts in small volumes. Small lots or even single copies of parts can be produced with the cost of many high-volume production lines. The market for such capability is indicated by the fact that, "75 percent of all machined parts today are produced in batches of 50 or fewer."[4] The flexibility of such systems and their economy for smaller batches suggest smaller plants located closer to markets. Furthermore, producers who can provide flexibility to customers may enjoy a price premium unless or until competitors catch up to the FMS technology.

## APPLICATIONS AND ECONOMICS OF FMS

Flexible manufacturing was pioneered in the United States, but the Japanese are far ahead in the installation of such systems. To date, U.S. manufacturers have bought only a few of these systems, illustrated by GE's electric meter plant in Sommersworth, New Hampshire, which produces 2000 different versions of a meter on the same flexible manufacturing equipment with a total output of more than a million meters per year. Another showcase system in the United States is Deere & Company's $1.5 billion plant in Waterloo, Iowa, which has an FMS for machining 1000 pound castings into finished transmission cases.

The Japanese have been much more aggressive in the installation of FMS systems. Fanuc Ltd., Japan's premier robot producer, has a system near Mount Fuji that makes parts for robots and machine tools that is supervised by a single controller watching operations on closed-circuit TV. The plant cost about $32 million, but Fanuc estimates that the investment required for a conventional plant with similar capacity requiring ten times the labor force would be $320 million. The FMS plant requires 100 employees, one employee to supervise ten machining centers and the others used for maintenance and assembly, making it about five times as labor productive as the conventional plant.[5]

Nearby, Fanuc has an FMS facility for automatically machining and assembling 10,000 electric motors per month. The system involves 60 machining centers and 101 robots. Over 900 types and sizes of motor parts are machined in lots ranging from 20 to 1000 units. Workers perform maintenance during the day, and the robots work at night in eerie darkness.[6]

Near Nagoya in Japan, Yamazaki Machinery Works Ltd. operates a 12-worker $20 million FMS with a three-day turnaround on orders. They estimate that a conventional system would require 215 workers with almost four times the number of machines and a three-month turnaround. Yamazaki estimates that the five-year after tax profit of its FMS will be $12 million compared with only $800,000 for a conventional plant.[7]

The showcase Yamazaki plant is a newer FMS involving 65 computer controlled

[4] G. Bylinski, "The Race to the Automatic Factory," *Fortune,* February 21, 1983, pp. 52–64.
[5] Ibid., G. Bylinski.
[6] Ibid., G. Bylinski.
[7] Ibid., G. Bylinski.

machine tools and 34 robots, all linked with a CAD design center at corporate headquarters. The labor force is 215, compared to an estimated 2500 for an equivalent conventional plant. What is to be produced and the details for processing are controlled from headquarters. Obviously, with a system of such plants, the overhead cost of production planning and control can be reduced compared to the equivalent conventional capacity.[8]

The rush toward advanced production technology has resulted in companies having programmable equipment from many different vendors, often with incompatible ways of packaging and sending information, which cripples the dream of computer integrated manufacturing systems. Individual companies, such as General Motors, have moved to offset this disadvantage by establishing a nonproprietary Manufacturing Automation Protocol (MAP), which specifies a single multichannel coaxial cable for linking incompatible devices in a network and includes a common syntax for exchanging data between their programs.[9]

## GROUP TECHNOLOGY

Group technology is a concept for organizing manufacturing resources to increase productivity in process-focused, small-lot situations involving parts and products that are similar. The idea is to group similar parts, sizes, or types of products, into families based on either their design or processes in order to gain productivity advantages. For a part or product family, similar machines might be grouped together, as in a process-focused system, but the flow of the family of parts or products would be arranged in line fashion. Since the sequence of operations is similar, machines can be arranged in functional groups; these groupings of equipment can be arranged in a sequence that fits the various sizes and types fairly well.

Group technology concepts also include a classification and coding system that is computerized. This coding system exploits the commonalities in the family of parts and products, and in more advanced systems, it can be coupled to CAD/CAM and FMS.

The coding system, then, lends itself to part family programming for numerically controlled production and to group tooling. Part family programming, using a master computer program that accommodates common or similar programming components, reduces programming time and other related costs of production planning for the part family. Similarly, group tooling takes advantage of similar tooling requirements for the family. Design of jigs and fixtures accommodate the entire family, reducing or eliminating the need for individual tooling for each part.

## THE AUTOMATIC FACTORY

Although the "automatic factory" does not exist today, there are portions of factories that are indeed automatic. For example, Seiko has developed a system for the

[8] Ibid., G. Bylinski.

[9] See J. B. Tucker, "GM: Shifting To Automatic," *High Technology,* May 1985, pp. 26–29.

automatic assembly of watches in which no human input to the assembly process is required. A West Coast facility of General Motors manufactures auto wheels automatically, without manual assistance. The raw materials enter at one end as strip steel and coiled bars and are automatically rolled, cut, formed, welded, punched, assembled, painted, and dried. The wheel emerges at the opposite end as a completely finished product.[10]

There are also the FMS systems that we have already discussed: the GE meter plant and the Japanese plants of Fanuc and Yamazaki are nearly automatic, although some components are still processed in manual and mechanized ways. The dream of an automatic factory is close to reality.

## COMPARISON OF MANUFACTURING PROCESS TECHNOLOGIES

Table 15-1 represents a summary of the manual, mechanized, and automated process technologies we have discussed, showing the general fields of application of each and their relative competitive advantages. These comparisons are generalities and are not meant to be detailed appraisals of each dimension and are certainly not meant to be comparisons of each technology for a given job. For example, we indicate that cost is "high" for both manual and general purpose mechanization; this does not mean that they are equally costly for a given job but that neither of these technologies provides a competitive cost advantage.

**TABLE 15-1**
**COMPARISON OF PROCESS TECHNOLOGIES**

| | | *Mechanized* | | *Automated* | | |
|---|---|---|---|---|---|---|
| | Manual | General Purpose | Special Purpose | General Purpose | Special Purpose | Group Technology |
| Field of application | Low volume and custom | Low volume and custom | High volume standardized | Low volume and custom | High volume standardized | Low volume |
| Relative competitive advantage | | | | | | |
| Cost | High | High | Low | Low | Lowest | Low |
| Quality | Variable | High | High | High | High | High |
| Flexibility | High | High | Low | Highest | Lowest | High |
| On-time performance | Lowest | Low | Good | High | High | Good |

[10]D. B. Dallas, "The Advent of the Automatic Factory," *Manufacturing Engineering,* November 1980, pp. 66–76.

# PROCESS TECHNOLOGY IN SERVICE AND NONMANUFACTURING OPERATIONS

Process technology in service and nonmanufacturing operations can be classified in the same manual–mechanized–automated format used for manufacturing process technology. But the greater diversity of the advanced process technology used in service and nonmanufacturing operations does not fit so neatly into the automated scheme that we developed for manufacturing technology. We will discuss process technologies in a few of the myriad of sectors where they have had considerable impact in their fields.

## Distribution and Transport

### CONTAINERIZATION

Containerized shipping is the key to a revolution in distribution and transportation. By standardizing container sizes, it has been possible to develop national and international systems that eliminate most small unit handling and provide highly efficient systems for handling large quantities of goods. Smaller quantities are consolidated into container units for handling. The containers can then be placed on flatbed trucks or railcars for overland transport. The containers are separated from their "wheels" when loaded on cargo vessels for international transport, and the process is reversed when overland transport is required at the destination port. There are many benefits to containerization: better protection from damage and theft resulting in lower insurance rates; better handling times and costs, 1 to 10 times lower; and better utilization of freight vessels because of the faster turnaround time in ports.

Sophisticated computer and telecommunications systems are used to support the needs of container systems. Manifests (cargo lists) are transmitted by telecommunications since the fast turnaround usually results in a ship leaving before they can be completed. Then the containers themselves are an issue: Who owns them? What types are they? Where are they? Where do they go next? What is their condition? How should the supply of containers be allocated to areas for best use? There are also financial questions: Who owes who money, and for what goods and services? The computer and telecommunications technology are an integral part of the operations technology.

Air freight reaps similar benefits from containerization, and the operations problems are parallel, though to date the scale of air freight operations is smaller.

### RESERVATIONS SYSTEMS

It is difficult to remember how airline reservations were once handled, but the present marvels are only about 20 years old. Since the number of passengers carried on airlines has increased by a factor of five in the last 20 years, it may be that the old paper-based system would have fallen by its own weight had electronic systems not been developed. The larger airlines have interconnected national and international systems, and some airlines even have shared systems.

The present system is also an integral part of the check-in procedure, involving seat assignment, arrangement for special meals, baggage check-in, and much more. This operations technology provides better, faster service, with fewer errors and lower costs.

## Warehousing

Computer control has been applied to warehousing—advanced designs will store and retrieve materials on command. Such systems have pallet-loads of material fed on controlled conveyors that carry the pallet to any of several aisles and tranfer it to a storage/retriever stacker. The stacker carries the pallet down the aisle and inserts it into a storage cubicle, all computer directed. Because of the computer direction and control, space-efficient random storage locations can be used instead of dedicated storage spaces. Other designs use carts that are guided to computer directed locations over communications lines buried in the floor. Backing up this system for operating and controlling the physical warehouse is a computer system that deals with storage and retrieval strategy—the allocation of activity among stackers, the distances of alternative locations, and the turnover of older inventory.

Both semiautomatic and automatic order picking systems are in use that involve some of the same types of technology in reverse. Items are picked from storage locations based on an order list in the computer. The stackers, in combination with conveyors or computer-directed carts, assemble the orders and may automatically palletize them for shipment.

## Point of Sale Systems

Mechanization and automation have impacted the operations function in food markets through point of sale systems. The Universal Product Code (the bar code now printed on most product packaging) provides a unique machine readable code for nearly every product. With front-end automation provided by scanners, the checkout clerk simply passes the product over the scanner. The scanner retrieves the price from the central computer and prints the item and the price on a sales slip. Simultaneously, the sale is recorded in an inventory and automatic reordering system. The records produced can also be used for market research, cost control, and the allocation of shelf space.

The technology provides lower costs for check-out, fewer errors, better information for customers on the sales slip, and faster customer service. In addition, the improved data base provides information for market research, cost control, inventory control, and other managerial needs.

## Banking Operations

Advanced technology has changed banking operations in remarkable ways through the check clearing process, computer-based teller equipment, automatic teller equipment (ATMs), and electronic funds transfer, among others.

### CHECK CLEARING

Modern banking operations for check clearing depend on magnetic-ink character recognition (MICR) of codes on all checks. These magnetic characters are machine readable and form the heart of the complex check clearing process. The MICR identifies the individual account (and sometimes the check number), the bank on which the check is drawn, the Federal Reserve District in which the bank is located, and other information involved in routing the check through the system. In addition, the amount of the check must be encoded on the check in magnetic ink as a part of the clearing process.

The clearing process may involve two or more banks, a local clearinghouse, one or more correspondent banks, and one or more Federal Reserve Banks. Yet with the MICR coding, the process is largely an automatic one that operates very smoothly. In addition, the local operations of each bank can operate mostly in electronic mode. To appreciate the enormity of the impact that the MICR encoded check has had on the banking system, its costs, and its reliability, try to imagine how the system once operated manually. But even with MICR encoded checks, the paperwork load is still enormous, so other electronic modes of handling money, such as the debit card, are being pursued. For example, for a large bank such as Chemical Bank in New York, the process of encoding must deal with as much as 3000 pounds of transactions per day. The fact that the load is measured in terms of pounds per day is interesting; noting that there are about 330 transactions per pound, there are as many as 990,000 transactions per day to encode, most of which are checks. Encoding is a manual process, using an encoder machine.

### AUTOMATIC TELLER MACHINES (ATMs)

Linked to computer processing is the development of ATMs. Account holders can get some cash with much less hassle than by going to the bank and can perform some other operations as well. The ATM makes 24-hour service available, and the customer's only cost is to perform some of the labor required, that is, to punch in the required numbers.

Given ATMs, a logical extension is to place an enhanced version in homes and offices, connected by telephone lines to the bank, so that checking account functions of paying bills can substitute for checks. Or, by combining these functions with a debit card and the point of sale front-end automation in super markets, many checks, as well as bad check accounts for markets, could be eliminated. All these developments and more are being discussed as practical ways of automating money transfers.

## FRAMEWORK FOR ANALYZING TECHNOLOGICAL CHOICE

Managers are commonly faced with the problem of choosing which among competing process technologies should be installed. This can be a complex problem because of several factors. First, there may be several alternatives that should be considered. In addition, there may be uncertainties about either the performance of one or more of the alternatives or about future events that could affect the final choice. Second, technological choice usually involves investments over a considerable time horizon, raising the question of how to evaluate the economic effects of the alternatives; that is, what criteria should be used. Finally, the alternatives are commonly not strictly comparable. There may be advantages and disadvantages to each that cannot be reduced to simple economic terms, yet they can be very important in the final choice. Our framework must accommodate these complexities and help to simplify and clarify the process.

## Structuring Alternatives

We must first identify the decision that must be made and the feasible alternative technologies that should be considered. Often, someone is proposing a specific system, and it may become a "favorite" because it has a champion. But good managers should want to compare the economic and other measures of performance of the challengers to the favorite. The development of viable alternatives that really accomplish the processing objectives may be the most important step. The minimum level of comparison should also be considered; that is to do nothing and keep the existing technology.

When the basic alternatives have been developed, the "chance points" should be identified. Here we are attempting to shed light on the uncertainties that may accompany a given alternative. For example, if a given technological alternative still has some development work that must be completed before it could be actually installed, that is a chance point, and we need to assign a probability that it will be successful or that it will be completed by a given time; otherwise, the economic benefits might be affected negatively.

The decision, the alternatives, and the chance points with their probabilities can be represented by a decision tree such as the one shown in Figure 15-6. In this example, we show the decision box, the two alternative new technologies, *A* and *B*, and the "do nothing" alternative. Following alternative *A*, there is a chance point because there is the possibility that there will be a breakthrough in the design of *A* that will make it more economical to operate than it is currently. After consultation with experts in this technology, we assign a probability of $p = .4$ to its success and $p = 1 - .4 = .6$ that it will not be successful. A succession of such chance points might be structured if the situation were more complex.

## Horizon and Choice of Criteria for Decision

The horizon over which we should consider the comparative costs, revenues, and nonquantitative advantages and disadvantages of competing technologies is usually fairly long in technological choice problems. The cost, revenues, and investment amounts are not simply additive; that is, it would not be meaningful to add annual costs and revenues to the fixed investments of alternatives in order to compare

FIGURE 15-6
**STRUCTURE OF DECISION ALTERNATIVES FOR THE EXAMPLE.**

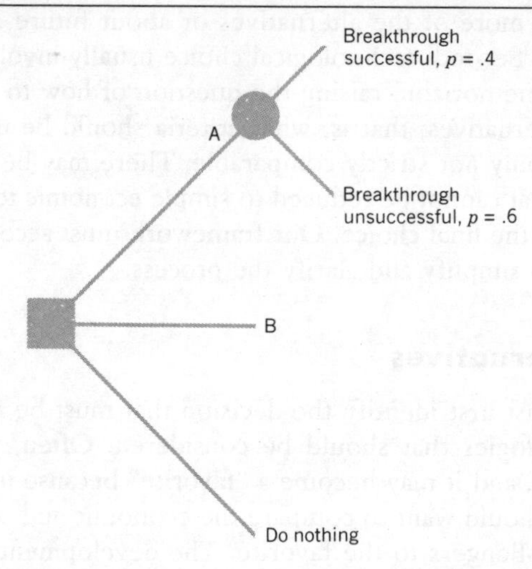


them. Therefore, the relatively long horizon and the presence of investment costs dictates the use of present values as the criteria for measuring the economic costs and benefits of the alternatives. (Present values are discussed in the supplement to this chapter.)

One more complication is imposed by the occurrence of chance points in the decision tree. We must weight the costs and benefits that are affected by the probabilities of occurrence of these chance events. This simply means that, for our example, the present values of the costs associated with successful breakthrough are multiplied by .4, whereas those associated with an unsuccessful effort are multiplied by .6. Since there is risk in these values, they are termed *expected monetary values* (present monetary values in this instance). The total of these weighted present values can then be compared with the present values of *B* and the do nothing alternative. The alternative with the lowest expected monetary value is favored on economic terms, assuming that costs dominate the comparative evaluation. If the financial flows are dominated by revenues, then the alternative with the highest expected monetary value is favored.

## Evaluation of Alternatives and Decision

If all the alternatives are equal in terms of unquantified factors, then the analysis would be complete and the alternative with the lowest expected monetary value would be the appropriate decision, but this is seldom true. Therefore, in order to make a decision, the advantages and disadvantages of the alternatives must be carefully considered. This is commonly a trade-off process. If *B* is lowest in terms of expected monetary value by $10,000, but the manager feels that *A*'s ability to meet higher quality standards is extremely important, *A* might be selected. In coming to this decision, the manager is implicitly placing a value of $10,000 or more on *A*'s qualitative advantage.

In this example, we are using a single criterion under risk, measured by expected monetary values; there are values that we can measure. But as we have indicated, there are also other criteria that enter the manager's decision. The manager takes account of these other values through the informal trade-off process indicated. There are other formal analytical methods for taking multicriteria into account, and we cover them in Chapter 21.

Summarizing then, our framework for analyzing choices among competing technological alternatives is as follows:

- Structure the alternatives
- Set the horizon and choose the criteria for the decision
- Evaluate the alternatives and decide

## An Example

To complete this section on analyzing technological choice, we will provide a computational example that enlarges slightly the structure of the previous example. Figure 15-7 adds a chance point to alternative *B*. The annual costs of operation for alternative *B* will be even more attractive if a new component being developed is successful.

The investment and annual oprating costs for the alternatives are shown in Table 15-2 for each of the conditions. The "do nothing" alternative is largely a manual technology and has no investment requirement. A horizon of five years is adopted as representing the reasonable economic lives of technologies *A* and *B*, interest is at 10

FIGURE 15-7
**DECISION TREE FOR THE COMPUTED EXAMPLE.**

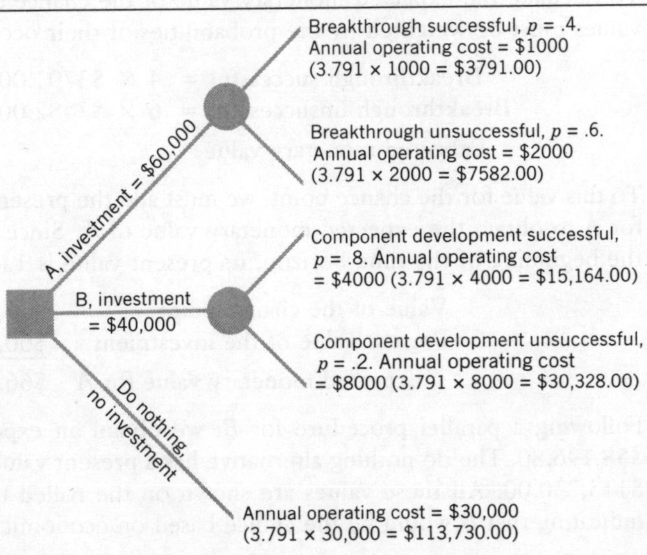

TABLE 15-2
**INVESTMENT AND OPERATING COSTS FOR THE EXAMPLE OF TECHNOLOGICAL CHOICE**

| | *Alternatives* | | |
|---|---|---|---|
| | A | B | Do Nothing |
| Investment required | \$60,000 | \$40,000 | — |
| Annual operating costs: | | | \$30,000 |
| If breakthrough is successful | 1000 | — | — |
| If breakthrough is unsuccessful | 2000 | — | — |
| If component development is successful | — | 4000 | — |
| If component development is unsuccessful | — | 8000 | — |

percent, and the criterion is expected monetary value since there is risk in both alternatives *A* and *B*. From Table 2 in the Appendix, the present value factor for a five-year annuity at 10 percent interest is $PV_a = 3.791$.

In order to evaluate the economic aspects of the three alternatives, we must "roll back" the decision tree by making the computations successively at the ends of branches, then at the chance points, and finally for the alternatives. Beginning with the branches associated with *A*, the present value of the annual operating expenses for a typical branch is a five-year annuity at 10 percent interest:

$$\text{Breakthrough successful} = 3.791 \times \$1000 = \$3791.00$$
$$\text{Breakthrough unsuccessful} = 3.791 \times \$2000 = \$7582.00$$

To calculate the expected monetary value of the chance events, these two present values must be weighted by the probabilities of their occurrence:

| | |
|---|---|
| Breakthrough successful = .4 × \$3791.00 = | \$1516.40 |
| Breakthrough unsuccessful = .6 × \$7582.00 = | 4549.20 |
| Expected monetary value | \$6065.60 |

To this value for the chance point, we must add the present value of the investment for *A* to obtain the expected monetary value of *A*. Since the investment occurs at the beginning of the time horizon, its present value is 1.0:

| | |
|---|---|
| Value of the chance point | \$6,065.60 |
| Present value of the investment | \$60,000.00 |
| Expected monetary value for *A* | \$66,065.60 |

Following a parallel procedure for *B*, we obtain an expected monetary value of \$58,196.80. The do nothing alternative has a present value of 3.791 × \$30,000 = \$113,730.00. All these values are shown on the rolled back tree in Figure 15-8, indicating that *B* would be the choice based on economic grounds only.

FIGURE 15-8
**EXPECTED MONETARY VALUES FOR THE ROLLED BACK DECISION TREE.**

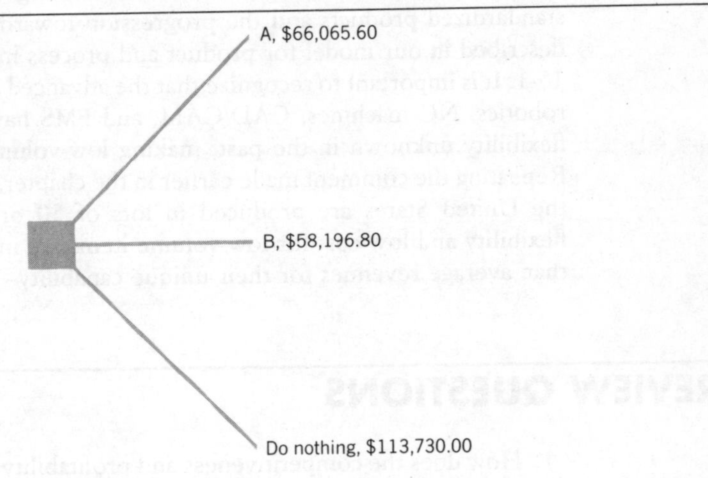


The difference in the expected monetary value between *A* and *B* is $66,065.60 − $58,196.80 = $7868.80. But *A* has the advantage of meeting higher quality standards. The final choice depends on whether the manager thinks that the economic disadvantage of *A* is offset by the quality advantage. The economic analysis allows the manager to quantify this judgment.

## IMPLICATIONS FOR THE MANAGER

This is the first of several chapters that have to do with the *design* of systems to produce products and services. Each of these chapters deal with factors that have a role in setting the system design, but the technology adopted has the greatest influence on the ability of the organization to compete in its arena. The technology sets limits on the productive system's costs, flexibility, quality, and on-time performance. Technological choice provides the junction between product design and process design, making possible joint designs that can achieve competitive objectives. Good managers recognize that process design goes through an evolution or life cycle, just as do products, requiring a dynamic view of process design.

There has been a natural progression from manual, through mechanized, to automated processes since the dawn of the industrial revolution, but managers can still employ all three of these classifications of technology economically today. The issue is always which type of technology is appropriate to the situation. It is true, of course, that all the excitement is around the new advanced technologies, but they are not always the most economical to install. Rather, managers should use a rational framework for making technological choices, and when the most advanced technology is not appropriate for a given application, they should continue to monitor technological alternatives. The situation can and does change as labor continues to become more expensive relative to mechanization and automation.

We have just emerged from a manufacturing era dominated by high-volume, standardized products and the progression toward integrated, inflexible processes described in our model for product and process innovation summarized by Figure 15-1. It is important to recognize that the advanced reprogrammable technologies of robotics, NC machines, CAD/CAM, and FMS have ushered in an era of process flexibility unknown in the past, making low-volume manufacturing also low cost. Repeating the comment made earlier in the chapter, 75 percent of machined parts in the United States are produced in lots of 50 or less. Managers who can offer flexibility and low cost for low-volume items are in a key position to obtain higher than average revenues for their unique capability—a key competitive weapon.

## REVIEW QUESTIONS

1. How does the competitiveness and profitability of a firm depend on the technological choices it makes?
2. Describe the model for product and process innovation. What is the nature of the processes in each of the three stages of the model?
3. How is the model for product and process innovation related to a firm's competitive position?
4. In what ways is process design dependent on the design of the product? How is product design dependent on the design of the processes used to produce it?
5. Define the term *production design.* Give examples.
6. Regarding product design, define the following terms and indicate their significance for production cost:
   a. Interchangeable parts
   b. Standardization
   c. Simplification
   d. Modular design
7. Describe the role of labor in manual, mechanized, and automated technologies. What is the relative capital cost of each?
8. Define the terms *general purpose machines* and *special purpose machines.* What is the general field of application of each? What is their significance in mechanized and automated technologies?
9. Defend the proposition that manual technology is inappropriate in today's high-tech world.
10. Define the term *hard automation.* What is its field of application?
11. What is a transfer machine? What is its general field of application?

12. Define the term *robot.* Is it all-inclusive in terms of automatic devices?
13. What are the design characteristics of robots? Which of the human senses can robots mimic?
14. What does it cost per hour to operate a robot (capital plus operating costs)?
15. What is an NC machine? How long is an NC machine tied up during the set-up process?
16. Describe the general volume levels at which manual, hard automation, and reprogrammable automation break even in overall costs? Account for these break-even levels.
17. What is CAD/CAM?
18. In what industrial sectors has CAD/CAM been applied? What companies within those sectors use CAD/CAM?
19. What are the general areas of CAD/CAM application that have yielded productivity and quality improvements?
20. What is FMS? What is the general field of FMS application? Is the field of FMS application significant in terms of the potential market size for its capability? State statistics.
21. Describe two of the major applications of FMS. Do they appear to be economically justified?
22. What is GT, group technology? What is unique about the concept? What is its field of application?
23. Is the automatic factory a reality? State examples that would appear to justify saying that the automatic factory is a reality.
24. How do the alternative technologies compare in terms of the four competitive priorities of cost, quality, flexibility, and on-time performance?
25. What is the state of process technology in such nonmanufacturing operations as distribution and transport, warehousing, retailing, and banking? Assess the impact of advanced process technologies on costs and quality in each these fields.
26. What framework for analyzing technological choice was discussed in the text?
27. What is the meaning of *expected monetary value?* Why is it a useful criterion for measuring technological alternatives? If there were no chance points in the decision structure, would it be an appropriate criterion?
28. Why are present values used in measuring comparative economic values in technological choice?
29. If a technological alternative has the lowest expected monetary value, why shouldn't it automatically be the clear choice?
30. If one alternative is lower in expected monetary value and another is chosen instead because it can produce a higher quality product, what economic value is implicitly being placed on the quality superiority of the technology chosen?

# PROBLEMS

31. A company is considering two different machines to perform an important operation in their manufacturing process. The first is a standard machine. The second is more expensive, but it has a higher degree of automation incorporated in it, and it is less flexible in the range of jobs it can process than the first. Both meet capacity needs. Comparative data are as follows:

| | MACHINE 1 | MACHINE 2 |
|---|---|---|
| Installed cost | \$20,000 | \$30,000 |
| Estimated economic life | 10 years | 10 years |
| Salvage value | \$5,000 | \$7,000 |
| Labor cost per year | \$12,000 | \$6,000 |
| Maintenance cost per year | \$1,000 | \$3,000 |

The value of money within the organization for investments of this kind is 10 percent.

a. How should the alternatives be structured?

b. What horizon and what decision criteria should be adopted?

c. Which machine is most economical?

d. What decision should be made?

32. After additional efforts to ferret out the cost differences between the two machines in problem 31, it was found that maintenance costs for machine 2 increase rapidly at the rate of \$500 per year. How does this fact change the economics of the situation and the final decision?

33. The manufacturing manager for a company making a line of toys for the high-volume Christmas market is considering options for a particular novelty toy for which market testing has indicated good acceptance. The assumption is that this is a one-season toy.

The plastic and metal parts are fabricated by outside suppliers, and it is possible to have the plastics molder set up to assemble the item completely for a cost of \$1 per unit. Alternately, the toy company can set up work places at a cost of \$1500 and hand assemble the item for an additional variable cost of \$0.75 per unit.

Finally, if the volume warrants it, some aspects of the assembly can benefit from mechanization and line assembly. The line mechanization will cost \$5000 to set up and install, but the variable costs will be only \$0.55 per unit. Market studies indicate a season's sale of 15,000 units and possibly as large as 20,000 units. The value of money within the organization is 10 percent.

a. How should the alternatives be structured?

b. What horizon and what decision criteria should be adopted?

c. Which machine is most economical?

d. What decision should be made?

34. A company has a largely manual technology for performing an operation in their plant, and it is considering two machines to make it somewhat less dependent on the labor supply in the area since labor is in short supply and there has been labor unrest. The annual operating costs for the present situation are $50,000 per year.

Machine *A* costs $100,000 to install and $10,000 per year to operate. Machine *B* is automatic in operation, but it has been developed to date only as a prototype. There is only a probability of .3 that it will be available as a proven production model in time to meet the company's timing requirements. But if it meets timing needs, it would cost $150,000 and would require no direct labor and only $1000 per year for maintenance. Both machines have a projected economic life of five years. The value of money within the organization is 10 percent.

a. How should the alternatives be structured?
b. What horizon and what decision criteria should be adopted?
c. Which machine is most economical?
d. What decision should be made?

# SITUATIONS

## The PANDEX Company—Automation by Crash Schedule

35. The manufacturing manager of the PANDEX Company is considering the technology that should be adopted for a new product that must be available for the market in 18 months. The market forecasts indicate an initial volume of 10,000 units per year and increases of 2000 units per year for the first five years.

The mechanized technology costs $75,000 to install (for two units) and is estimated to have a four-year economic life. The labor and other operating costs are estimated to be $20,000 per year initially, increasing at the rate of $1000 per year. The mechanized technology has the advantage of coming in smaller modular units so that it is expandable in increments. Two units cover projected needs for the five-year projection, but if demand exceeds expectations, another unit could be installed for half the initial costs.

The mechanized technology is a well-known one that is proven in practice; it would be the one of choice were it not for an automated process that is under development. The automated process is projected to cost $125,000 to install, but operating costs are estimated to be only $2000 per year for maintenance. The modular capacity is 50,000 units per year, and the economic life of the system is estimated to be four years.

The problem with the automated technology is with timing. The concepts have been proven with previous development, and a prototype model has been built. But the final development and manufacture of a production model might not meet the PANDEX Company's need to install the equipment within 15 months, which leaves PANDEX only three months to get it into production for product introduction. The equipment manufacturer will give the target date only a 50–50 chance of being attained, but it is willing to give a definite statement on delivery within 6 months.

In order to offset the risks, PANDEX can make a deal with the mechanized equipment manufacturer to promise a "crash" schedule to deliver a system within 6 months following an order to proceed for the premium price of $85,000. This committment would provide PANDEX with enough time to have alternative equipment installed and production tested if the automated equipment manufacturer fails to provide on-time delivery.

The value of money within the organization for investments of this kind is 10 percent.

a. How should the alternatives be structured?
b. What horizon and what decision criteria should be adopted?
c. Which machine is most economical?
d. What decision should be made?

## Nels Jensen's Super Market

36. Nels Jensen started his grocery business 35 years ago in the Lake Tahoe resort community. The combination of good management and well-to-do patrons produced an independent supermarket of unsurpassed quality. One of the hallmarks of Jensen's success model was his emphasis on and definition of the service aspects of his store. Those service aspects were 10 hours of operation every day and minimum customer hassle and waiting time to obtain the desired purchases and get checked out.

A study of some of the major changes that occurred over the years revealed that the nature and quality of service and the system design successively affected each other. When the store was small, employees were stationed in areas to help customers select items, check out, bag, and transfer purchases to the parking lot. Later, with a much larger volume of customers, the system transferred virtually all the selection process to the customer and the system design focused on the check-out stand.

By controlling the number of check-out counters in operation, Jensen set a service standard that he tried to maintain. The standard was set in terms of the time the customer had to wait before being served. Jensen felt that for his clientele, a waiting time of 1.5 minutes was about as long as would be tolerated without complaint. In fact, however, he tried to control waiting time by keeping an eye on the size of the waiting lines. Anytime the lines had two or more people waiting, he would open another check-out counter, even if he had to operate it himself. He then tried to schedule checker shifts to provide capacity for the peak shopping hours. He also trained some of the checkers to do other work, such as pricing and storing stock on display shelves, to provide flexibility in the number of checkers available when peak loads occurred.

Jensen tried several variations of the check-out system. Originally, employees helped to unload the carts to the checkers, but as labor costs increased, this activity was transferred to the customer. Customer complaints resulted. Then, having changed the design of the check-out stand, Jensen tried a system in which the checkers worked directly from the cart. However, the checkers complained of backaches from constantly having to lean over to take items from the carts.

Jensen then modified the system with a new cart and check-out stand design system. This still enabled the checker to work directly from the cart, but did not require leaning over to get items. The new cart–check-out stand system raised the working level. The cart had a hinged end, which the checker opened, placing the bottom of the cart at the check-out stand working level. In this way, all aspects of service could remain the same in terms of waiting time, what the customer had to do to obtain service, and the check-out time.

The next cycle of system design involved what is called *front-end automation*. Measurements made in a survey by Jensen indicated that the average time for a customer in the check-out process was 5.5 minutes, including 1.5 minutes of waiting time. The 4.0 minutes for actual checkout included 2.5 minutes for ringing up the sale and placing the purchases in bags. The balance was payment, which often involved check cashing, as well as some chitchat and other miscellaneous activities. With the advent of item scanning systems, Jensen saw the possibility of improving overall service time by reducing the check-out time itself and possibly reducing labor costs simultaneously.

The scanning systems required that a universal code be placed on products (the bar-pattern codes now commonly used on product packages) that would be read by the scanners. A customer's entire order could then be moved rapidly over the scanner. The system requires the customer to load purchases on a belt that feeds the purchases to the checker, who repositions them to move past the scanning eye. The scanner reads and transmits the information to a computer, which translates the information into prices and a total bill, including sales tax. The checkers' activities are thus confined to scanning, bagging, collecting, and making change.

Although the scanning system has other operating advantages, Jensen is most interested in a possible service improvement, assuming that a productivity increase might justify the scanner's installation on a reasonable basis. The system was partially installed as a test. Measured results indicate that check-out time, exclusive of waiting time prior to check out, has been reduced to an average of 2.4 minutes. In addition, average checker productivity has increased from $252 to $500 in sales per hour, and check-out errors have been reduced by 65 percent. Checkers are paid $4.50 per hour.

Jensen could install the scanning system for the 12 present check-out stands for a lease cost of $7000 per month. Even though only an average of 6 check-out stands are normally in use (current system), if he should decide to install the scanners, he wants the entire system to be automated. His concern is that service be improved in the sense that the customers' time in the system is reduced. On the other hand, the scanner system represents a step backward in that the customers will have to unload their carts and load the conveyor belt. He is not sure how his type of customer will react.

Should Jensen install the scanner system? Why?

## Calculatron—Uncertainties in Process Planning

37. History records that the electronic pocket calculator had a product ancestor known as the mechanical desk calculator, first hand powered and later electrically powered. It was a mechanical marvel, prized by those whose jobs required accurate computations and by organizations that needed both accuracy and relatively high productivity in computations not justified for programming on computers.

Calculatron, Inc., was a major manufacturer of desk calculators and had enjoyed long-term profitability. It had a loyal work force of some semiskilled and some highly skilled employees. Although product improvements had continued over the years, the basic design of Calculatron's product line had been stable for 15 years, and product design changes were carefully implemented to take account of the existing production lines. The market for desk calculators had been an expanding one, and with the advantage of a relatively stable product design, Calculatron had been able to specialize production methods, making continuous improvements in productivity through investments in labor-saving equipment. The productivity increases had helped secure the firm's market position through competitive pricing and had produced profitability and security for both the enterprise and its employees. Employees enjoyed high wages and salaries and excellent pension and other benefits. Employees were organized and affiliated with the AFL–CIO and union–management relationships had been generally very good.

Enter electronic minicircuitry, with microcircuitry and the "chip" on the horizon. The first electronic desk calculator had just been announced by a competitor. Calculatron was not far behind. It had employed a staff of electronic engineers two years previously and had assigned them the task of producing a revolutionary redesign of the product line. The prototypes had already been tested, and the product and production engineers were at work in the production design phase simultaneously, developing preliminary designs of the productive system required to produce the new electronic product line.

Market forecasts indicated a conversion of the former mechanical calculator volume to the electronic, with a "kicker" because a large replacement market was available for the faster, quieter, and more capable electronic machines. The one sour note in the market was the prediction that a pocket-sized calculator would soon be possible if the research and development of microcircuits were to materialize. Reports concerning startling technological innovations in microcircuitry indicated that the probability of a breakthrough was high.

The production engineers are ready to develop final designs of the productive system for the new electronic calculator line. A meeting of the executive committee has been called to examine preliminary plans for production in relation to short and longer term market forecasts and predictions.

a. What kinds of guidelines for the productive system design should the executive committee establish for the production engineers?

b. What plans should Calculatron make for the introduction of the new product line?

c. What kinds of longer term plans should Calculatron make for future product and process innovation in the calculator field?

# REFERENCES


Abernathy, W. J., K. B. Clark, and A. M. Kantrow, "The New Industrial Competition," *Harvard Business Review,* 59(5), September–October 1981, pp. 68–81.

Boyer, C. H., "Lockheed Links Design and Manufacturing," *Industrial Engineering,* 9(1), January 1977, pp. 14–21.

Bright, J. R., *Automation and Management,* Graduate School of Business Administration, Harvard University, Boston, 1958.

Buffa, E. S., *Meeting the Competitive Challenge: Manufacturing Strategy for U. S. Companies,* Irwin, Homewood, Ill., 1984, Chapter 5.

Bylinski, G., "The Race to the Automatic Factory," *Fortune,* February 21, 1983, pp. 52–64.

Gerstenfeld, A., "Technological Forecasting," *Journal of Business, 44*(1), January 1971, pp. 10–18.

Gold, B., "CAM Sets New Rules for Production," *Harvard Business Review,* November–December 1982, pp. 88–94.

Groover, M. P., and E. W. Zimmers, Jr., *CAD/CAM: Computer-Aided Design and Manufacturing,* Prentice-Hall, Englewood Cliffs, N.J., 1984.

Ham, I., K. Hitomi, and T. Yoshida, *Group Technology,* Kluwer-Nijhoff, Boston, 1985.

Utterback, J. M., and W. J. Abernathy, "A Dynamic Model of Process and Product Innovation by Firms," *Omega,* 1975.

Zygmont, J., "Flexible Manufacturing Systems," *High Technology*, October 1986, pp. 22–27.

## SUPPLEMENT TO CHAPTER 15

# CAPITAL COSTS AND INVESTMENT CRITERIA



Capital costs affect decision problems in production/operations management whenever a physical asset or an expenditure that provides a continuing benefit or return is involved. From an accounting point of view, the original capital expenditure must be recovered through the mechanism of depreciation and must be deducted from income as an expense of doing business. The number of years over which the asset is depreciated and the allocation of the total amount to each of these years (i.e., whether depreciation is straight-line or at some accelerated rate) represent alternative strategies that are directed toward tax policy. We must remember that all of these depreciation terms and allocations are arbitrary and have not been designed from the point of view of cost data for decision making.

## OPPORTUNITY COSTS

Suppose that we are discussing an asset that is used for general purpose, such as an over-the-road semitrailer truck. Assume that we own such a truck and that the question is, "How much will it cost us to *own* this truck for one more year?" These costs of owning, or capital costs, cannot be derived from the organization's ordinary accounting records. The cost of owning the truck for one more year depends on its current value. If the truck can be sold on the secondhand market for $5000, this is a measure of its economic value. Because it has value, we have two basic alternatives: we can sell it for $5000 or we can keep it. If we sell, the $5000 can earn interest or a return on an alternate investment. If we keep the truck, we forego the return, which then becomes an *opportunity cost* of holding the truck one more year. Also, if we keep the truck, it will be worth less a year from now, so there is a second opportunity cost, measured by the decrease in salvage value during the year.

The loss of opportunity to earn a return and the loss of salvage value during the year are the costs of continued ownership. They are opportunity costs rather than costs paid out. Nevertheless, they can be quite significant in comparing alternatives that require different amounts of investment. There is one more possible component of capital cost for the next year if the truck is retained, the cost of possible renewals or "capital additions." We are not thinking of ordinary maintenance, here, but of major overhauls, such as a new engine or an engine overhaul, that extend the physical life of the truck for some time. In summary, the capital costs, or the costs of owning the truck, for one more year are as follows:

1. Opportunity costs:
   a. Interest on salvage value at beginning of year
   b. Loss in salvage value during the year
2. Capital additions or renewals required to keep the truck running for at least an additional year

By assuming a schedule of salvage values, we can compute the year-by-year capital costs for an asset. This is done in Table 15-3 for a truck that costs $10,000 initially and for which the salvage schedule is as indicated. The final result is the projected capital cost that is incurred for each year. If we determine the way in which operat-

TABLE 15-3
**YEAR-BY-YEAR CAPITAL COSTS FOR A SEMITRAILER TRUCK, GIVEN A SALVAGE SCHEDULE (INTEREST AT 10%)**

| Year | Year-End Salvage Value | Fall in Salvage Value during Year | Interest on Opening Salvage Value | Capital Cost, Sum of Fall in Value and Interest |
|---|---|---|---|---|
| New | $10,000 | — | — | — |
| 1 | 8,300 | $1700 | $1000 | $2700 |
| 2 | 6,900 | 1400 | 830 | 2230 |
| 3 | 5,700 | 1200 | 690 | 1890 |
| 4 | 4,700 | 1000 | 570 | 1570 |
| 5 | 3,900 | 800 | 470 | 1270 |
| 6 | 3,200 | 700 | 390 | 1090 |
| 7 | 2,700 | 500 | 320 | 820 |
| 8 | 2,300 | 400 | 270 | 670 |
| 9 | 1,950 | 350 | 230 | 580 |
| 10 | 1,650 | 300 | 195 | 495 |

ing and maintenance costs increase as the truck ages, we can plot a set of curves of yearly costs. The combined capital, operating, and maintenance costs curve will have a minimum point. This minimum defines the best cost performance year in the life of the equipment. Beyond that year, the effect of rising maintenance costs more than counterbalances the declining capital costs.

## OBSOLESCENCE AND ECONOMIC LIFE

By definition, when a machine is obsolete, an alternative machine or system exists that is more economical to own and operate. The existence of the new machine does not cause an increase in the cost of operating and maintaining the present machine. Those costs are already determined by the design, installation, and condition of the present machine. However, the existence of the new machine causes the salvage value of the present machine to fall, inducing an increased capital cost. For assets in technologically dynamic classifications, the salvage value schedule falls rapidly in anticipation of typical obsolescence rates. Economic lives are very short. On the other hand, when the rate of innovation is relatively slow, salvage values hold up fairly well.

Table 15-4 compares year-by-year capital costs for two machines that initially cost $10,000 but have different salvage schedules. The value of machine 1 holds better; machine 2 has more severe obsolescence reflected in its salvage schedule. The result is that capital costs in the initial years are greater for machine 2 than for machine 1. The average capital costs for the first five years are

TABLE 15-4
**COMPARISON OF CAPITAL COSTS FOR TWO MACHINES COSTING $10,000 INITIALLY BUT WITH DIFFERENT SALVAGE SCHEDULES (INTEREST AT 10%)**

| *Machine 1* | | | | *Machine 2* | | | |
|---|---|---|---|---|---|---|---|
| Year-End Salvage Value | Fall in Value during Year | Interest at 10% on Opening Value | Capital Cost | Year-End Salvage Value | Fall in Value during Year | Interest at 10% on Opening Value | Capital Cost |
| $10,000 | — | — | — | $10,000 | — | — | — |
| 8,330 | $1,670 | $1,000 | $2,670 | 7,150 | $2,850 | $1,000 | $3,850 |
| 6,940 | 1,390 | 833 | 2,223 | 5,100 | 2,050 | 715 | 2,765 |
| 5,780 | 1,160 | 694 | 1,854 | 3,640 | 1,460 | 510 | 1,970 |
| 4,820 | 960 | 578 | 1,538 | 2,600 | 1,040 | 364 | 1,404 |
| 4,020 | 800 | 482 | 1,282 | 1,860 | 740 | 260 | 1,000 |
| 3,350 | 670 | 402 | 1,072 | 1,330 | 530 | 186 | 716 |
| 2,790 | 560 | 335 | 895 | 950 | 380 | 133 | 513 |
| 2,320 | 470 | 279 | 749 | 680 | 270 | 95 | 365 |
| 1,930 | 390 | 232 | 622 | 485 | 195 | 68 | 263 |
| 1,610 | 320 | 193 | 513 | 345 | 140 | 49 | 189 |

Machine 1 $1913
Machine 2 $2198

Therefore, if the schedules of operating expenses for the two machines were identical, machine 1 would seem more desirable. However, because the timing of the capital costs is different for the two machines, we adjust all figures to their equivalent present values.

## PRESENT VALUES

Because money has a time value, future expenditures will have different present values. Because money can earn interest, $1000 in hand now is equivalent to $1100 a year from now if the present sum can earn interest at 10 percent. Similarly, if we must wait a year to receive $1000 that is due now, we should expect not $1000 a year from now, but $1100. When the time spans involved are extended, the appropriate interest is compounded, and its effect becomes much larger. The timing of payments and receipts can make an important difference in the value of various alternatives.

### Future Single Payments

We know that if a principal amount $P$ is invested at interest rate $i$, it will yield a future total single payment $S$ in $n$ years hence if all the earnings are retained and compounded. Therefore, $P$ in the present is entirely equivalent to $S$ in the future by virtue of the compound amount factor. That is,

$$S = P(1 + i)^n \tag{1}$$

where $(1 + i)^n$ = the compound amount factor for interest rate $i$ and $n$ years.

We can solve for $P$ to determine the present worth of a single payment to be paid $n$ years hence:

$$P = \frac{S}{(1 + i)^n} = S \times PV_{sp} \tag{2}$$

where $PV_{sp} = 1/(1 + i)^n$, the present value of a single payment of $1 to be made $n$ years hence with interest rate $i$. Therefore, if we were to receive a payment of $10,000 in 10 years, we should be willing to accept a smaller but equivalent amount now. If interest at 10 percent were considered fair and adequate, that smaller but equivalent amount would be

$$P = 10{,}000 \times 0.3855 = \$3855$$

because

$$\frac{1}{(1 + 0.10)^{10}} = PV_{sp} = 0.3855$$

Table 1 in the Appendix gives the present values for single future payments or credits; Table 2 gives present values for annuities for various years and interest rates.

## Present Value of Annuities

An *annuity* is a sum that is received or paid periodically and is defined by the following relationship:

$$P = A \times PV_a \tag{3}$$

where

$$PV_a = \frac{1 - (1 + i)^{-n}}{i} \tag{4}$$

where

$A$ = Amount of periodic payment
$PV_a$ = The present value of an annuity
$i$ = Interest rate per period
$n$ = Number of periods

The factors in Table 2 of the Appendix convert the entire series of annual sums to present values for various interest rates and periods.

Consider the present value of receiving $10,000 per year for 10 years with an interest rate of 10 percent.

$$P = \$10{,}000 \times 6.145 = \$61{,}450$$

$$PV_a = \frac{1 - (1 + 0.10)^{-10}}{0.10} = 6.145 \text{ (check in Table 2, Appendix)}$$

As a check of logic, note that the present value of an annuity is simply the sum of the individual single payment present values of the $10,000 amounts received in year 1 plus year 2, and so on. Therefore, the $PV_a$ factor for 10 years at 10 percent (6.145) should be equal to the sum of the individual single payment factors, $PV_{sp}$, for the years 1 to 10 in the 10 percent column in Appendix Table 1. If you add those factors, they total 6.144. The difference is due to rounding in the table.

Now let us return to the example of the two machines. The capital costs for each machine occur by different schedules because of different salvage values. If all future values were adjusted to the present as a common base time, we could compare the totals to see which investment alternative was advantageous. We have done this in Table 15-5, where we have assumed an operating cost schedule in column 2, determined combined operating and capital costs in columns 5 and 6, and listed present values in columns 8 and 9. The present value of the entire stream of expenditures and opportunity costs is $32,405 for machine 1. The net difference in present values for the two machines is shown at the bottom of Table 15-5. Because the operating cost schedule was identical for both machines, the contrast reflects differences in the present worth of the capital costs. Obviously, the method allows for different operating cost schedules as well.

TABLE 15-5
**PRESENT VALUE OF CAPITAL AND OPERATING COSTS FOR THE TWO MACHINES FROM TABLE 15-4 (SCHEDULE OF OPERATING COSTS IS THE SAME FOR BOTH MACHINES; INTEREST AT 10%)**

| | | *Capital Costs (from Table 2)* | | *Combined Operating and Capital Costs* | | Present Worth Factor for Year | *Present Worth of Combined Costs for Year Indicated* | |
|---|---|---|---|---|---|---|---|---|
| Year (1) | Operating Cost (2) | Machine 1 (3) | Machine 2 (4) | Machine 1 (5) | Machine 2 (6) | Indicated[a] (7) | Machine 1 (8) | Machine 2 (9) |
| 1 | $3,000 | $2,670 | $3,850 | $5,670 | $6,850 | 0.909 | $5,154 | $6,227 |
| 2 | 3,200 | 2,223 | 2,765 | 5,423 | 5,965 | 0.826 | 4,490 | 4,939 |
| 3 | 3,400 | 1,854 | 1,970 | 5,254 | 5,370 | 0.751 | 3,946 | 4,033 |
| 4 | 3,600 | 1,538 | 1,404 | 5,138 | 5,004 | 0.683 | 3,509 | 3,418 |
| 5 | 3,800 | 1,282 | 1,000 | 5,082 | 4,800 | 0.621 | 3,156 | 2,981 |
| 6 | 4,000 | 1,072 | 716 | 5,072 | 4,716 | 0.565 | 2,866 | 2,665 |
| 7 | 4,200 | 895 | 513 | 5,095 | 4,713 | 0.513 | 2,614 | 2,418 |
| 8 | 4,400 | 749 | 365 | 5,149 | 4,765 | 0.467 | 2,405 | 2,225 |
| 9 | 4,600 | 622 | 273 | 5,222 | 4,873 | 0.424 | 2,214 | 2,066 |
| 10 | 4,800 | 513 | 189 | 5,313 | 4,989 | 0.386 | 2,051 | 1,926 |
| Totals | | | | | | | $32,405 | $32,898 |

Machine 1, present worth of all future values is total of column (8) less present worth of tenth-year salvage value, i.e., $32,405 − (1610[b] × 0.386) = 32,405 − 621 = $31,784.
Machine 2, $32,898 − (345[b] × 0.386) = 32,898 − 133 = 32,765.
[a] From Table 1 (Appendix).
[b] Tenth-year salvage values from Table 15-4.

There are some difficulties with the methods just described. First, we have assumed that the schedule of salvage values is known, which is not usually true. Second, at some point in the life of the machines, it becomes economical to replace them with identical models. Therefore, a chain of identical machines should be considered for comparative purposes; the machine is replaced in the year in which its operating and capital costs are exactly equal to the interest on the present worth of all future costs. The essence of this statement is that we are seeking a balance between this year's costs (operating and capital costs) and opportunity income from disposal (interest on the present worth of all future costs). When the opportunity income from disposal is the greater of the two, replacement with the identical machine is called for. Most common criteria for comparing alternate capital investments circumvent these problems by (1) assuming an economic life and (2) assuming some standard schedule for the decline in the value of the asset. We will now consider some of these criteria.

## COMMON CRITERIA FOR COMPARING ECONOMIC ALTERNATIVES

Some of the common criteria used to evaluate proposals for capital expenditures and compare alternatives involving capital assets are (1) present values, (2) rate of return, and (3) payoff period. It is recommended that the present value criterion be employed in evaluating alternative capital investments.

## Present Value Criterion

Present value methods for comparing alternatives take the sum of present values of all future out-of-pocket expenditures and credits over the economic life of the asset. This figure is compared for each alternative. If differences in revenue also are involved, their present values must also be accounted for.

### AN EXAMPLE

Suppose we are considering a machine that costs $15,000, installed. We estimate that the economic life of the machine is eight years, at which time its salvage value is expected to be about $3000. For simplicity's sake, we take the average operating and maintenance costs to be $5000 per year. At 10 percent interest, the present value of the expenditures and credits is

| | | | |
|---|---|---|---|
| Initial investment | $= \$15{,}000 \times PV_{sp}$ | $= 15{,}000 \times 1.000 =$ | 15,000 |
| Annual operating and maintenance costs | $= 5000 \times PV_a$ | $= 5000 \times 5.335 =$ | 26,675 |
| | | | 41,675 |
| Less credit of present value of salvage to be received in eight years $=$ | $3000 \times PV_{sp}$ | $= 3000 \times 0.467 =$ | 1,401 |
| | | | $40,274 |

The net total of $40,274 is the present value of the expenditures and credits over the eight-year expected life of the machine. The initial investment is already at present value; that is, $PV_{sp} = 1$. The annual costs of operations and maintenance are an eight-year annuity, so the entire stream of annual costs can be adjusted to present value by the multiplication of $PV_a$ from Appendix Table 2. Finally, the present value of the salvage is deducted. This total could be compared with similar figures for other alternatives over the same eight-year period.

Suppose that another machine is estimated to have a different economic life (perhaps four years). Then, to make the present value totals comparable, we compare two cycles of the four-year machine with one cycle of the eight-year machine. If the operating and maintenance costs increase as the machine ages, the present value of the expenditure in each year would be determined separately by $PV_{sp}$.

## Rate of Return Criterion

One common method of evaluating new projects or comparing alternate courses of action is to calculate a rate of return, which is then judged for adequacy. Usually, no attempts are made to consider interest costs, so the resulting figure is referred to as the "unadjusted" rate of return (i.e., unadjusted for interest values). It is computed as follows:

$$\text{Unadjusted rate of return} = \frac{100(\text{Net monetary operating advantage} - \text{Amortization})}{\text{Average investment}}$$

The net monetary operating advantage reflects the algebraic sum of the incremental costs of operation and maintenance and possible differences in revenue. If the rate computed is a "before-tax" rate, then the amortization—incremental investment/economic life—is subtracted, and the result is divided by the average investment and multiplied by 100 to obtain a percentage return. If an "after-tax" rate is sought, the net increase in income taxes due to the project is subtracted from the net monetary advantage, and the balance of the calculation is as before. Obviously, the adequacy of a given rate of return changes drastically if it is being judged as an after-tax return. The rate of return is that rate, *i*, for which the present value of net monetary operating advantage equals the cost of the initial investment.

## AN EXAMPLE

Assume that new methods have been proposed for the line assembly of a product, each assembly being completed by one individual. The new methods require the purchase and installation of conveyors and fixtures that cost $50,000 installed, including the costs of relayout. The new line assembly methods require five fewer assemblers. After the increased maintenance and power costs are added, the net monetary operating advantage is estimated as $20,000 per year. Economic life is estimated at five years. The unadjusted before-tax return is

$$\frac{20{,}000 - \dfrac{50{,}000}{5}}{\dfrac{50{,}000}{2}} \times 100 = 40 \text{ percent}$$

The after-tax return requires that incremental taxes be deducted. Incremental taxable income will be the operating advantage less increased allowable tax depreciation. Assuming straight-line depreciation and an allowed depreciation term of eight years, incremental taxable income is $20,000 less $50,000/8, or $20,000 − $6,250 = $13,750. Assuming an income tax rate of 50 percent, the incremental tax due to the project is $6875. The after-tax return is therefore

$$\frac{20{,}000 - 6{,}875 - 10{,}000}{25{,}000} \times 100 = \frac{3{,}125 \times 100}{25{,}000} = 12.5 \text{ percent}$$

Whether or not either the before- or after-tax rates calculated in this example are adequate must be judged in relation to the risk involved in the particular venture and the returns possible through alternative uses of the capital.

## Payoff Period Criterion

The payoff period is the time required for an investment to "pay for itself" through the net operating advantage that would result from its installation. It is calculated as follows:

$$\text{Payoff period in years} = \frac{\text{Net investment}}{\text{Net annual operating advantage after taxes}}$$

The payoff period for the conveyor installation that we discussed previously is

$$\frac{\$50{,}000}{\$20{,}000 - 6875} = \frac{\$50{,}000}{\$13{,}125} = 3.8 \text{ years}$$

It is the period of time for the net after-tax advantage to equal exactly the net total amount invested. Presumably, after that period, "it is all gravy"; the $13,125 per year is profit because the invested amount has been recovered. If the economic life of the equipment is five years and 10 percent is regarded as an appropriate rate of after-tax return for the project, what *should* the payoff period be?

Obviously, the period for both capital recovery and return is the five-year economic life. The period that recovers capital only will be somewhat shorter and will depend on the required rate of return. The payoff period is another interpretation that can be given to the present value factors for annuities, $PV_a$, given in Table 2 of the Appendix.

### AN EXAMPLE

As an example, for an economic life of five years and a return rate of 10 percent, $PV_a = 3.791$ from Appendix Table 2. This indicates that capital recovery takes place in 3.791 years. The equivalent of 10 percent compound interest takes place in $5.000 - 3.791 = 1.209$ years. Therefore, any of the $PV_a$ values in Table 2 for a given economic life in years and a given return rate indicate the shorter period in years required to return the investment; they give the payoff period.

The proper procedure would be to estimate economic life and to determine the applicable return rate. Determine from the present value tables the payoff period associated with these conditions. Then compute the actual payoff period of the project in question and compare it with the standard period from the tables. If the computed period is less than or equal to the standard period, the project meets the payoff and risk requirements that are imposed. If the computed value is greater than the table value, the project would earn less than the required rate.

# PROBLEMS

1. A trucking firm owns a five-year-old truck that it is considering replacing. The truck can be sold for $5000, and Blue Book values indicate that its salvage value would be $4000 one year from now. It also appears that the trucker would need to spend $500 on a transmission overhaul if the truck is retained. What are the trucker's projected capital costs for next year? Interest is at 10 percent.

2. What is the present value of the salvage of a machine that can be sold 10 years hence for $2500? Interest is at 10 percent.
3. What is the future value in 25 years of a bond that earns interest at 10 percent and has a present value of $10,000?
4. What interest rate would a $10,000 bond have to earn to be worth $50,000 in 10 years?
5. At 8 percent interest, how many years will it take money to double itself?
6. What is the present value of an income stream of $1500 for 15 years at 10 percent interest?
7. What is the value of an annuity of $2000 per year for 10 years at the end of its life? Interest is at 10 percent.
8. The proud owner of a new automobile states that she intends to keep her car for only two years in order to minimize repair costs, which she feels should be near zero during the initial period. She paid $8000 for the car new, and Blue Book value schedules suggest that it will be worth only $4000 two years hence. She normally drives 10,000 miles per year, and she estimates that her cost of operation is $0.10 per mile. What are her projected capital costs for the first two years, if interest of 6 percent represents a reasonable alternate investment for her?
9. Suppose that we are considering the installation of a small computer to accomplish internal tasks of payroll computation, invoicing, and other routine accounting. The purchase price is quoted as $300,000 and the salvage value five years later is expected to be $100,000. The operating costs are expected to be $100,000 per year, mainly for personnel to program, operate, and maintain the computer. What is the present value of the costs to own and operate the computer over its five-year economic life? The value of money in the organization is 15 percent.
10. An aggressive marketer of a new office copier has made its machine available for sale as well as lease. The idea of buying a copying machine seems revolutionary, but it seems less so when we examine our present costs, which come to $6500 per year for the lease plus per copy charges of 2 cents per page. If we own a machine, the cost of paper and maintenance is projected to be $1500 per year. The new copier costs $10,000, installed, and is assumed to have an economic life of five years and a salvage value of $2000. Assume 50,000 pages per year.
    a. What is the projected unadjusted rate of return if we install the copier?
    b. If incremental taxes for the project are $1000, what is the adjusted rate of return?
11. What is the actual payoff period for the office copier project discussed in problem 10? If interest is 10 percent, what should the minimum payoff period be to make the investment economically sound? Does the office copier project meet the payoff standard?

# REFERENCES

Anthony, R. N., and G. A. Welsch, *Fundamentals of Management Accounting* (3rd ed.), Irwin, Homewood, Ill., 1981.

Copeland, T. E., and J. F. Weston, *Financial Theory and Corporate Policy,* Addison–Wesley, Boston, 1983.

Grant, E. L., and W. G. Ireson, *Principles of Engineering Economy* (5th ed.), Ronald Press, New York, 1970.

Reisman, A., *Managerial and Engineering Economics,* Allyn & Bacon, Boston, 1971.

Thuesen, H. G., W. J. Fabrycky, and G. J. Thuesen, *Engineering Economy* (5th ed.), Prentice-Hall, Englewood Cliffs, N.J., 1977.

Weston, J. F., and T. Copeland, *Managerial Finance* (8th ed.), Dryden Press, Hinsdale, Ill., 1986.

# CHAPTER 16

# WAITING LINE MODELS AND APPLICATIONS TO SERVICE SYSTEM DESIGN

The original work in waiting line theory was done by A. K. Erlang, a Danish telephone engineer. Erlang started his work in 1905 in an attempt to determine the effect of fluctuating demand (arrivals) on the utilization of automatic dial telephone equipment. Since the end of World War II, Erlang's work has been extended and applied to a variety of situations that are now recognized as being described by the general waiting line model.

Many systems in operations management can be formulated as waiting line models (also called *queuing models*). The most common situations are in service systems, such as banks, medical clinics, and supermarkets. But some waiting line situations are embedded in manufacturing systems, as when mechanics go to a tool crib to obtain the tools necessary for the next job or in the typical scheduling of a machine for a variety of jobs. In all these situations, someone or something must wait in line for service. The service is provided by a processing system, followed by a departure process—our typical input–processing–output model for a productive system.

In structuring waiting line models, the inputs are called "arrivals," and the arrival times are controlled by some probabilistic process. The time to process or service the arrivals is also controlled by a probabilistic process. The output rate of such systems depends on the interplay between the random arrivals and the variable service times, and waiting line models are used to predict these values. A common example is found in a bank, where the arrival of customers to do business at a teller window is random, each individual deciding when to go to the bank. The length of the waiting line depends in part on these arrival times. Equally important is the time it takes for a teller to service each individual. These times vary because the time for the human performance of a task is variable and, more important, because each customer requires different services. For instance, the first customer may simply want to make a deposit, whereas the second may want to make a deposit, obtain cash, and pay the gas bill.

The following example of a university outpatient clinic provides a background of the nature of the data needed and the service system design problems involved.

## EXAMPLE OF A SERVICE SYSTEM

The example outpatient clinic at the University of Massachusetts treated an average of 400 to 500 patients per day with a staff that included 12 full-time physicians. Because the physicians had a variety of other duties, only 260 physician-hours per week were available during regular clinic hours, about 22 hours per physician per week. Only about half of the patients were seen by a physician. The others were treated by nurses under a physician's supervision or in specialized subclinics for tests or immunizations.

In aggregate terms, approximately 178 patients per day needed access to an average of 52 available physician-hours. Thus, the average time with a physician was about 17.5 minutes.

## Demand for Service

Part of the difficulty in rendering service can be seen in Figure 16-1. Demand is not uniform through the week, being approximately 20 percent above the average on Mondays, 84 to 88 percent of the average on Thursdays, and increasing slightly on Fridays.

Furthermore, the daily variation is significant. Figure 16-2 shows arrival data for Monday and Thursday (the days with the heaviest and lightest loads, respectively), highlighting the great demand variation during the day, with peaks at 8 A.M., 10 A.M., and 2 P.M. When the arrival data are placed on an interarrival time basis (the time between arrivals), they exhibit a negative exponential distribution, as shown in Figure 16-3.

## Time for Service

The amount of time physicians spent with patients was measured in three separate categories: walk-in, appointment, and second-service times. Figure 16-4 shows histograms of the service times recorded for the three categories. The second-service category represents a return of the patient to the physician following diagnostic tests or other intervening procedures. Although the three distributions are different, they share the common general properties of being skewed to the right and having relatively large standard deviations. Thus the average appointment service time is

FIGURE 16-1
**THE PERCENTAGE OF PATIENTS ARRIVING AT A UNIVERSITY HEALTH SERVICE TO SEE EITHER A PHYSICIAN OR A NURSE.**

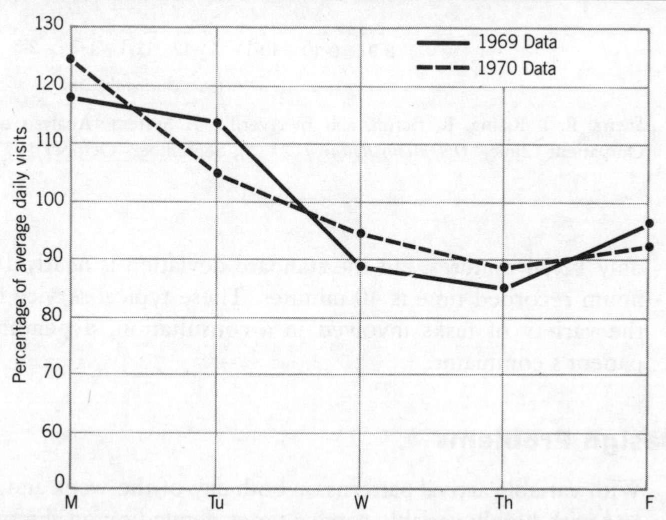


*Source:* E. J. Rising, R. Baron, and B. Averill, "A Systems Analysis of a University-Health-Service Outpatient Clinic," *Operations Research, 21*(5), September–October 1973, p. 1034.

FIGURE 16-2
**THE HOURLY ARRIVALS AT THE UNIVERSITY HEALTH SERVICE (MONDAY AND THURSDAY AVERAGES FOR THE FALL SEMESTERS IN 1969 AND 1970).**

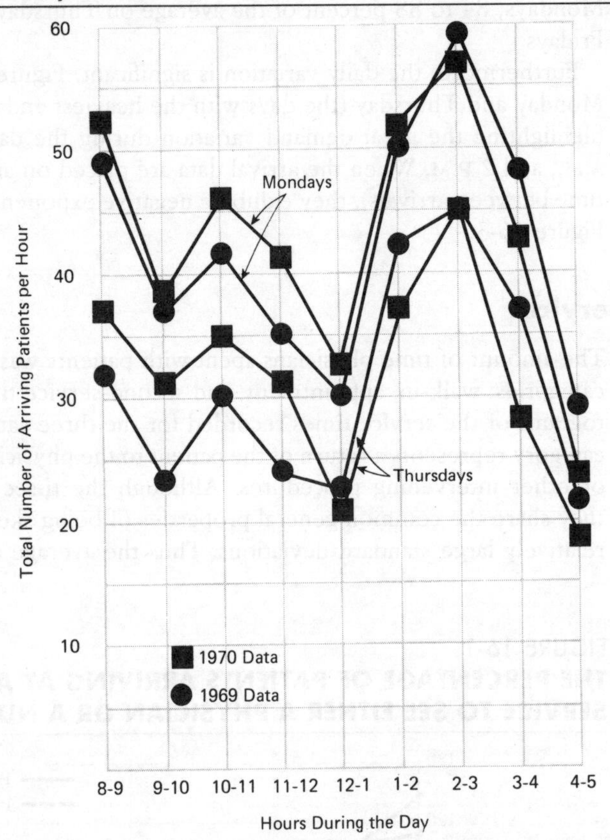


*Source:* E. J. Rising, R. Baron, and B. Averill. "A Systems Analysis of a University-Health-Service Outpatient Clinic," *Operations Research, 21* (5), September–October 1973, pp. 1030–1047.

only 12.74 minutes, but the standard deviation is nearly 10 minutes, and the maximum recorded time is 40 minutes. These typical service time distributions reflect the variety of tasks involved in a consultation, depending on the nature of the patient's complaint.

## System Design Problems

With variable arrival patterns on both day-of-the-week and an hour-of-the-day bases and with highly variable service times depending on the type of patient, important problems result. First, what can be done to schedule appointments so as to smooth the patient load on physicians? How should appointment schedules be arranged

FIGURE 16-3
**THE FREQUENCY DISTRIBUTION OF PATIENT INTERARRIVAL TIMES.**

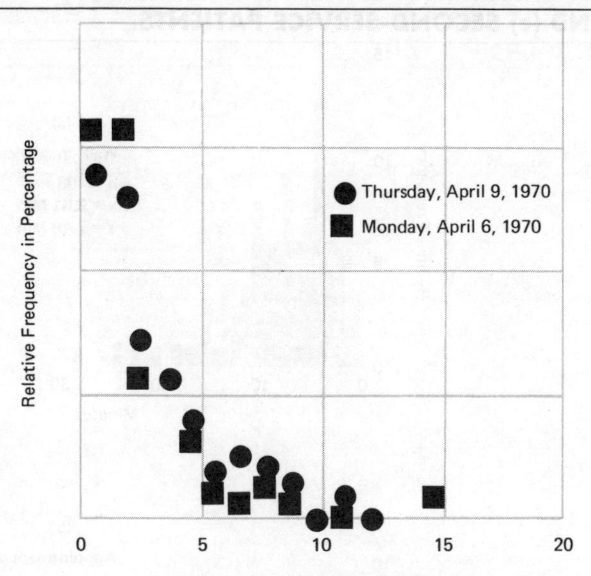


Monday, April 6, 1970: $\bar{x} = 2.167$, $s = 2.402$, $n = 237$. Thursday, April 9, 1970: $\bar{x} = 2.626$, $s = 2.838$, $n = 202$.

*Source:* E. J. Rising, R. Baron, and B. Averill. "A Systems Analysis of a University-Health-Service Outpatient Clinic," *Operations Research, 21*(5), September–October 1973, pp. 1030–1047.

through the week and during the day in light of demand variation? What overall capacity for service is actually needed? How long can patients reasonably be expected to wait for service? Is physician idle time justified? Would a system of priorities help to level loading?

## Schedules for Service Systems

Service oriented organizations face unique scheduling problems. In all of these kinds of systems, demands for service and the time to perform the service may be highly variable. It often appears that no sensible schedule can be constructed if arrivals for service and service times are random. The result would be to maintain the capability for service at levels sufficient to keep the waiting line to certain acceptable average levels; the service facility would be idle for some fraction of the time in order to be able to provide service when it is needed. In a sense, the scheduling of personnel and physical facilities is simple in such situations, being controlled by policies for the hours during which the service is to be available and for the service level to be offered. Schedules are then simple statements of "capacity for service," and personnel and other resources are keyed to these levels. The design for the size of maintenance crews has often been on this basis, for example.

FIGURE 16-4
**HISTOGRAMS OF SERVICE TIME FOR (*a*) WALK-IN, (*b*) APPOINTMENT, AND (*c*) SECOND-SERVICE PATIENTS.**

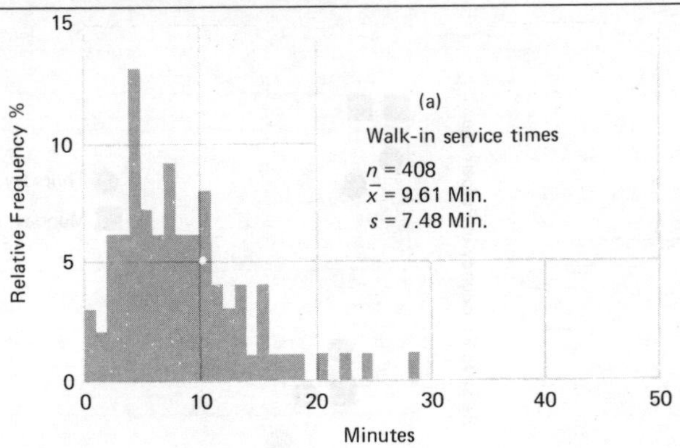


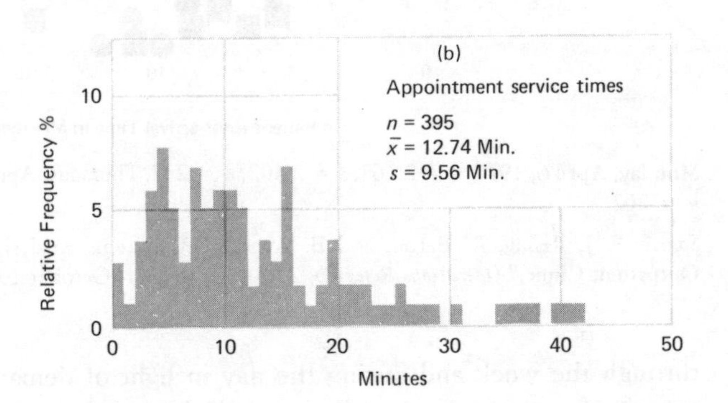


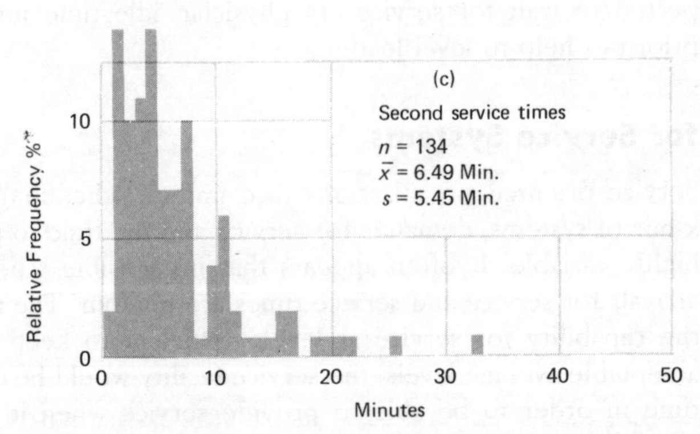


*Source:* E. J. Rising, R. Baron, and B. Averill. "A Systems Analysis of a University-Health-Service Outpatient Clinic," *Operations Research, 21*(5), September–October 1973, pp. 1030–1047.

Usually, however, we can improve on the system response of simply "keeping hours." Sometimes overall performance can be improved by a priority system, taking arrivals on other than a first-come first-served basis. Also, improvements often result from examining the demand to see if there is a weekly and/or daily pattern. When a pattern exists, it may be possible to schedule more effectively to improve service facility utilization, shorten average waiting time, or both. Thus, we have three broad groups of situations: one described by random arrivals at a service center that performs a service requiring variable time, one where priority systems are the basis for improved scheduling, and one in which arrivals follow some dominant pattern.

The random arrival, variable service time case is the classic waiting line or queuing problem. When the distributions of arrivals and service times follow certain known mathematical functions, fairly simple equations describe the flow through the system. These computations can be performed for simple situations such as a single chair barbershop, for a multiple server system such as supermarket check-out stands, or for a serial set of operations such as an assembly line.

One of the variables that may be controllable in waiting line systems is the order of processing of arrivals. For example, in medical facilities, patients will tolerate a priority system that allows emergency cases to be taken first. In machine shops, priority systems are often used to determine the sequence of processing jobs through a service center, as discussed in Chapter 10. Recall that computer simulation of alternate priority rules has shown that certain rules are more effective in getting work through the system on schedule.

When arrivals follow a dominant pattern, we can use that information to schedule personnel and facilities. For example, if arrivals of patients at a clinic followed the weekly pattern shown in Figure 16-1, we could use an appointment system to counterbalance the pattern and smooth the load over the week. Similarly, if the typical daily pattern for physicians' services in a clinic followed that shown in Figure 16-2, it could be counterbalanced both by an appointment system and by having a larger number of physicians on duty during the afternoon hours. If physicians could work different periods or shifts, we might be able to find quite good capacity-service solutions. Thus the entire subject of work shift scheduling becomes an important issue.

## STRUCTURE OF WAITING LINE MODELS

There are four basic waiting line structures that describe the general conditions at a service facility. The simplest structure, shown in Figure 16-5*a*, is our basic module. It is called the *single server case.* There are many examples of this simple module: the cashier at a restaurant, any single-window operation in a post office or bank, or a one-chair barber shop.

If the number of processing stations is increased but still draws on a single waiting line, we have the *multiple servers case* shown in Figure 16-5*b*. A post office with several open windows but drawing on a single waiting line is a common example of a multiple server waiting line structure.

FIGURE 16-5
**FOUR BASIC STRUCTURES OF WAITING LINE SITUATIONS.**

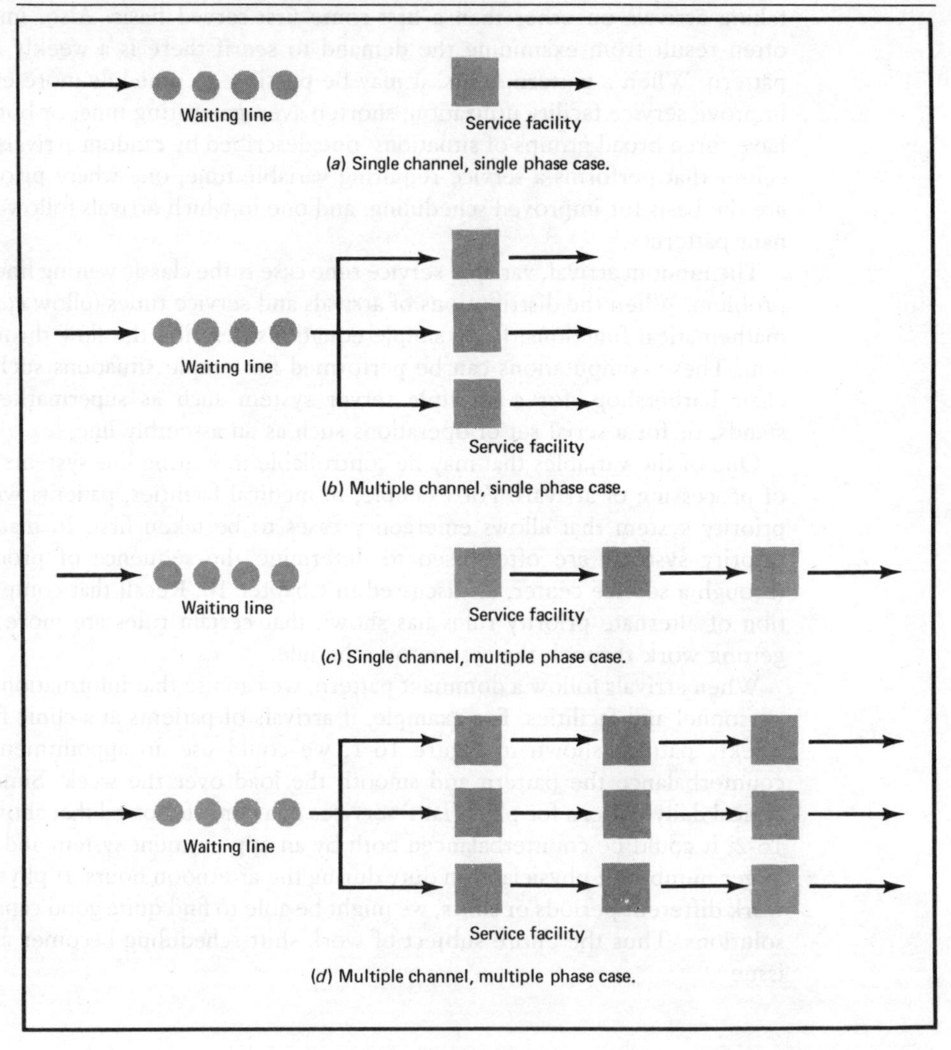


A simple assembly line or a cafeteria line has, in effect, a number of service facilities in series and is an example of the *single servers in series case* shown in Figure 16-5*c*.

Finally, the *multiple servers in series case* can be illustrated by two or more parallel assembly lines as shown in Figure 16-5*d*. Combinations of any or all of the basic four structures can also exist in networks in very complex systems.

The analytical methods for waiting lines are divided into two main categories for any of the basic structures shown in Figure 16-5, depending on the size of the source population of the inputs. When the source population is very large and, in theory at least, the length of the waiting line could grow without fixed limits, the applicable models are termed *infinite waiting line models*. On the other hand, when arrivals come from a small, fixed-size population, the applicable models are termed *finite waiting line models*. For example, if we are dealing with the maintenance of a bank of 20 machines and a machine breakdown represents an arrival, the maximum waiting line is 20 machines waiting for service, and a finite waiting line model is needed. On the other hand, if we operated an auto repair shop, the source population of breakdowns is very large and an infinite waiting line model would provide a good approximation. We will discuss both infinite and finite models.

There are other variations in waiting line structures that are important in certain applications. The "queue discipline" describes the order in which the units in the waiting line are selected for service. In Figure 16-5, we imply that the queue discipline is first come first served. Obviously, there are many other possibilities involving priority systems. For example, in a medical clinic, emergencies and patients with appointments are taken ahead of walk-in patients. In production scheduling systems there has been a great deal of experimentation with alternate priority systems. Because of the mathematical complexity involved, Monte Carlo simulation has been the common mode of analysis for systems involving queue disciplines other than first come first served. Table 16-1 shows the waiting line elements for a number of common situations.

TABLE 16-1
**WAITING LINE MODEL ELEMENTS FOR SOME COMMONLY KNOWN SITUATIONS**

| | Unit Arriving | Service or Processing Facility | Service or Process Being Performed |
|---|---|---|---|
| Ships entering a port | Ships | Docks | Unloading and loading |
| Maintenance and repair of machines | Machine breaks down | Repair crew | Repair machine |
| Assembly line not mechanically paced | Parts to be assembled | Individual assembly operations or entire line | Assembly |
| Doctor's office | Patients | Doctor, staff and facilities | Medical care |
| Purchase of groceries at a supermarket | Customers with loaded grocery carts | Checkout counter | Tabulation of bill, receipt of payment and bagging of groceries |
| Auto traffic at an intersection or bridge | Automobiles | Intersection or bridge with control points such as traffic lights or toll booths | Passage through intersection or bridge |
| Inventory of items in a warehouse | Order for withdrawal | Warehouse | Replenishment of inventory |
| Machine shop | Job order | Work center | Processing |

Finally, the nature of the distributions of arrivals and services is an important structural characteristic of waiting line models. Some mathematical analyses are available for distributions that follow the Poisson or the Erlang process (with some variations) or that have constant arrival rates or constant service times. If distributions are different from these mentioned or are taken from actual records, simulation is likely to be the necessary mode of analysis, as discussed in Chapter 9.

## INFINITE WAITING LINE MODELS

We will not cover all the possible infinite waiting line models but will restrict our discussion to situations involving the first-come first-served queue discipline and the Poisson distribution of arrivals. We will deal initially with the single server case (our basic service facility module); later we will also discuss the multiple server case. Our objective will be to develop predictions for some important measures of performance for waiting lines, such as the mean length of the waiting line and the mean waiting time for an arriving unit.

### Poisson Arrivals

The Poisson distribution function has been shown to represent arrival rates in a large number of real-world situations. It is a discrete function that provides the probability of a given number of arrivals in a unit of time. The Poisson distribution function is given by

$$f(x) = \frac{\lambda^x e^{-\lambda}}{x!} \tag{1}$$

where

$f(x)$ = Poisson distribution function
$\lambda$ = The mean arrival rate
$x$ = The number arriving in one unit of time
$x!$ = $x$ factorial

*Note:* $x!$ is simply $(x)(x-1)\ldots(3)(2)(1)$. For example, $4! = 4 \times 3 \times 2 \times 1 = 24$. $0! = 1$.

For instance, if $\lambda = 4$ per hour, then the probability of $x = 6$ arrivals in 1 hour is

$$f(6) = \frac{4^6 e^{-4}}{6!} = \frac{4096 \times 0.0183}{720} = .104$$

The Poisson distribution for an average arrival rate of $\lambda = 4$ per hour (as well as for other values of $\lambda$) is shown in Figure 16-6. The Poisson distribution is typically skewed to the right. The distribution is simple in that its standard deviation is expressed solely in terms of the mean, $\sigma = \sqrt{\lambda}$.

Evidence that the Poisson distribution does indeed represent arrival patterns in many applications is great. Many empirical studies have validated the Poisson arrival distribution in general industrial operations, traffic flow situations, and various service operations.

FIGURE 16-6
**POISSON DISTRIBUTIONS FOR SEVERAL MEAN ARRIVAL RATES.**

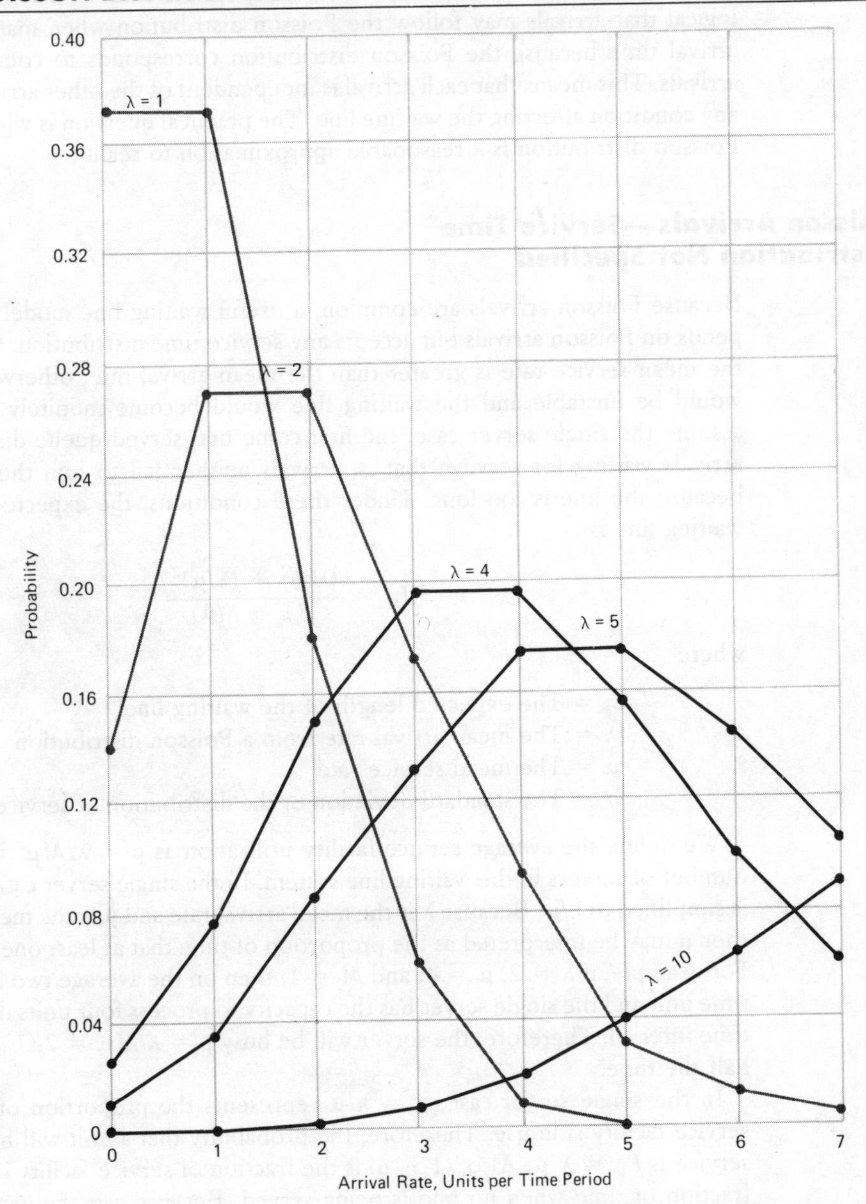


Arrival distributions are sometimes given in terms of the time between arrivals, or interarrival times. The distributions of the time between arrivals often follow the negative exponential distribution. However, if the *number* of arrivals in a given interval are Poisson distributed, then necessarily the times *between* arrivals have a negative exponential distribution, and vice versa.

Although we cannot say that all distributions of arrivals per unit of time are adequately described by the Poisson distribution, we can say that it is usually worth checking to see if it is true, for then a fairly simple analysis may be possible. It is logical that arrivals may follow the Poisson distribution when many factors affect arrival time because the Poisson distribution corresponds to completely random arrivals. This means that each arrival is independent of the other arrivals as well as of any condition affecting the waiting line. The practical question is whether or not the Poisson distribution is a reasonable approximation to reality.

## Poisson Arrivals—Service Time Distribution Not Specified

Because Poisson arrivals are common, a useful waiting line model is one that depends on Poisson arrivals but accepts any service time distribution. We assume that the mean service rate is greater than the mean arrival rate; otherwise, the system would be unstable and the waiting line would become infinitely large. We also assume the single server case, the first-come first-served queue discipline, and all arrivals waiting for service; that is, arrivals neither fail to join the line nor leave because the line is too long. Under these conditions, the expected length of the waiting line is

$$L_q = \frac{(\lambda\sigma)^2 + (\lambda/\mu)^2}{2(1 - \lambda/\mu)} \tag{2}$$

where

$L_q$ = The expected length of the waiting line
$\lambda$ = The mean arrival rate from a Poisson distribution
$\mu$ = The mean service rate
$\sigma$ = The standard deviation of the distribution of service times

We define the average service facility utilization as $\rho = \lambda/M\mu$, where $M$ is the number of servers in the waiting line system. In the single server case, $M = 1$ and $\rho$ is simplified to $\lambda/\mu$. Because $\lambda$ is the mean arrival rate and $\mu$ is the mean service rate, then $\rho$ may be interpreted as the proportion of time that at least one server is busy. For example, if $\lambda = 2$, $\mu = 4$, and $M = 1$, then on the average two units arrive per time unit and the single server has the capacity to process four units during the same time interval. Therefore, the server will be busy $\rho = \lambda/M\mu = 2/(1 \times 4) = 0.5$, or half the time.

In the single server case, $\rho = \lambda/\mu$ represents the proportion of time that the service facility is in use. Therefore, the probability that a unit will have to wait for service is $P_w = \lambda/\mu$. Also, $(1 - \rho)$ is the fraction of service facility idle time or the fraction of time when no one is being served. Because $\rho$ is the expected number being served, the total number in the waiting line plus the expected number being served is the total number in the system, $L$,

$$L = L_q + \lambda/\mu \tag{3}$$

Similar simple logic leads to the formula for expected waiting time in line, $W_q$, and time in the system including service, $W$. The reciprocal of the mean arrival rate is the mean time between arrivals, $1/\lambda$. For example, if $\lambda = 2$ units per hour on the average, then the expected time between arrivals of any two units is $1/2 = 0.5$ hours. The multiplication of the mean time between arrivals and the line length gives the waiting time

$$W_q = L_q/\lambda \tag{4}$$

Therefore, if $\lambda = 2$ units per hour and $L_q = 3$, then one unit arrives in the system every 0.5 hours on the average, but the line is three units long. Thus, units waiting in line must wait three times as long as the time between arrivals, or $3 \times 0.5 = 1.5$ hours, that is, $L_q/\lambda = 3/2 = 1.5$ hours.

Also, the multiplication of the mean time between arrivals and the mean total number in the system, $L$, gives the mean time in the system including service; that is,

$$W = L/\lambda = W_q + 1/\mu \tag{5}$$

The equality in Equation 5 is true because the total time in the system must equal the waiting time plus the time for service. Equations 2, 3, 4, and 5 are useful relationships. The general procedure would be to compute $L_q$ from Equation 2 and then compute the values of $L$, $W_q$, and $W$ as needed, given the value of $L_q$. Note that Equations 2 through 5 deal only with average or long-run equilibrium conditions.

## AN EXAMPLE

Trucks arrive at the truck dock of a wholesale grocer at the rate of 8 per hour and the distribution of the arrivals is a Poisson distribution. The loading and/or unloading time averages 5 minutes, but the estimate of the standard deviation of service time, $\sigma$, is 6 minutes. Truckers are complaining that they spend more time waiting than unloading and the following calculations verify their claim:

$$\lambda = 8/\text{hour};\ \mu = 60/5 = 12/\text{hour};\ s = 6/60 = 1/10 \text{ hours}$$

$$L_q = \frac{(8/10)^2 + (8/12)^2}{2(1 - 8/12)} = 1.63 \text{ trucks in line}$$

$$L = 1.63 + 8/12 = 2.30 \text{ trucks in the system}$$
$$W_q = 1.63/8 = 0.204 \text{ hours, or } 12.24 \text{ minutes in line waiting for service}$$
$$W = 2.30/8 = 0.288 \text{ hours, or } 17.28 \text{ minutes in the system}$$

The calculations yield another verification of logic in that the average truck waits 12.24 minutes in line plus 5 minutes for service, or 17.28 minutes in the system (the small difference is due to rounding). Thus, $W = W_q + 1/\mu$, as indicated in Equation 5.

Let us pause for a moment to reflect on this model. Which are the decision variables and which are the uncontrollable parameters? The service-related variables can be altered by the manager if there is a willingness to invest capital in new capacity or if new procedures can be devised that can reduce the variability of service time. On the other hand, the arrival rate of the trucks is presumably not under managerial control and is therefore a parameter.

The grocer knows, of course, that the problem could probably be solved by expanding the truck dock so that two trucks could be handled simultaneously. This solution, however, would require a large capital expenditure and the disruption of operations during construction. Instead, the grocer notes the very large standard deviation of service time and, on investigation, finds that some orders involve uncommon items that are not stored in a systematic manner. Locating these items takes a great deal of search time.

The grocer revamps the storage system so that all items can be easily located. As a result, the standard deviation is reduced to 3 minutes. Assuming that mean service time is not affected, we have an indication of the sensitivity of the system to changes in the variability of service time. The new values are $L_q = 0.91$, $L = 1.57$, $W_q = 6.8$ minutes, and $W = 11.8$ minutes. Waiting time has almost been cut in half. The truckers are happier, and the grocer has improved the system without a large capital expenditure.

## SERVICE TIME DISTRIBUTIONS

Although there is considerable evidence that arrival processes tend to follow Poisson distributions as has been indicated, service time distributions seem to be much more varied in their nature. This is why the previous model involving Poisson arrivals and an unspecified service time distribution is so valuable. With Equation 2, one can compute the waiting line statistics, knowing only the mean service rate and the standard deviation of service time.

The negative exponential distribution has been one of the prominent models for service time, and there is evidence that in some instances the assumption is valid. However, studies of distributions of arrivals and service times in a Los Angeles machine shop did *not* indicate that the negative exponential model fit the actual service time distributions adequately for all of the machine centers.

### Model for Poisson Input and Negative Exponential Service Times

The negative exponential distribution is completely described by its mean value because its standard deviation is equal to its mean. We can describe this model as a special case of Equation 2. If the service times are adequately described by a negative exponential distribution, then the mean of the distribution is the reciprocal of the mean service rate; that is, $1/\mu$. Therefore, $1/\mu$ is also the standard deviation of the distribution of service times when the distribution is the negative exponential. Equation 6 can easily be derived from Equation 2 when $1/\mu$ is substituted for $\sigma$ (verify this derivation yourself):

$$L_q = \frac{\lambda^2}{\mu(\mu - \lambda)} \tag{6}$$

Also, the probability of $n$ units being in the system at any point in time is

$$P_n = \left(\frac{\lambda}{\mu}\right)^n \left(1 - \frac{\lambda}{\mu}\right) \tag{7}$$

The other relationships between $L_q$, $L$, $W_q$, and $W$ expressed by Equations 3, 4, and 5 hold for the negative exponential service time distributions as well as for the case where no service time distribution is specified. For the sake of simplicity, many individuals prefer to use Equation 2 with the appropriate value of $\sigma$ to reflect the special case.

We can now check to see the effect of exponential service times on waiting line statistics for the truck dock problem. If we assume that the service time in that situation was represented by a negative exponential distribution, then $\sigma = 1/\mu = 1/12$, and the value of $L_q$ from Equation 2 is 1.33. The other waiting line model statistics are $L = 2$, $W_q = 10$ minutes, and $W = 15$ minutes. The values are intermediate between the previous two calculations for the grocer's problem because the value of $\sigma$ is between the two previous values.

## Model for Poisson Input and Constant Service Times

Although constant service times are not usual in actual practice, they may be reasonable assumptions in cases where a machine processes arriving items by a fixed-time cycle. Also, constant service times represent a boundary or lower limit on the value of $\sigma$ in Equation 2. As such, a constant service time is also a special case of Equation 2. The resulting equation for constant service times is

$$L_q = \frac{\lambda^2}{2\mu(\mu - \lambda)} \tag{8}$$

You should derive Equation 8 from Equation 2 by substituting $\sigma = 0$ in Equation 2.

Again, for comparison and to gain insight into what happens in waiting lines, let us see what the result would have been if the grocer could have made service time constant at 5 minutes; that is, if the grocer could have reduced the standard deviation to zero. Substituting in Equation 8, we have $L_q = 0.67$, and $L = 1.33$, $W_q = 5$ minutes, and $W = 10$ minutes. Again, the other relationships between $L_q$, $L$, $W_q$, and $W$ expressed by Equations 3, 4, and 5 hold for the constant service time distribution as well as for the case where no service time distribution is specified.

We can consider Equation 2 as a fairly general model for service time distributions described by the negative exponential or constant service times as special cases. Figure 16-7 shows a graph of $L_q$ for various values of the standard deviation, including the values for the negative exponential distribution and for constant service times. Values of the standard deviation greater than that for the negative exponential distribution occur in distributions termed *hyperexponential*. The extreme values of standard deviation are not representative of values found in practice; however, the tail of the curve in Figure 16-7 is shown to indicate how rapidly $L_q$ increases with variability in the service time distribution.

## Relationship of Queue Length to Utilization

Recall that $\rho = \lambda/M\mu$ represents the service facility utilization. If $\lambda = \mu$, then $\rho = 1$ for the single server case where $M = 1$, and theoretically, the service facility is used

FIGURE 16-7
**RELATIONSHIP BETWEEN WAITING LINE LENGTH, $L_q$, AND THE STANDARD DEVIATION OF SERVICE TIME FOR THE GROCER'S TRUCK DOCK PROBLEM (POISSON INPUT).**

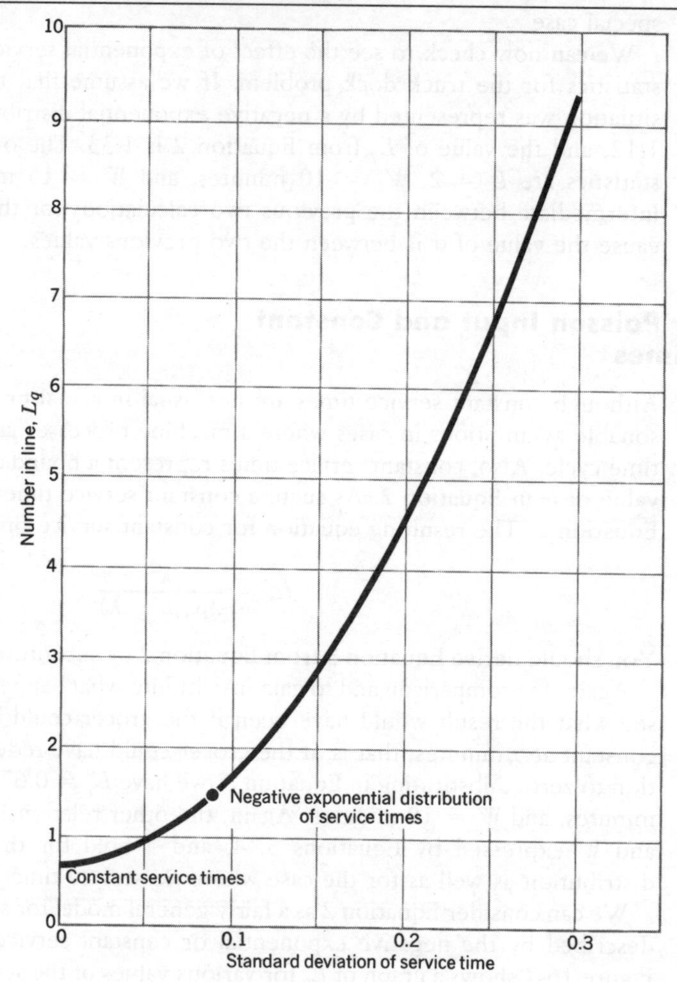


100 percent of the time. But let us see what happens to the length of the queue as ρ varies from 0 to 1. Figure 16-8 summarizes the results for Poisson inputs and exponential service times for a single server. As ρ approaches unity, the number waiting in line increases rapidly and approaches infinity. We can see that this must be true by examining Equations 2, 6, and 8 for $L_q$. In all cases, the denominator goes to zero as ρ approaches unity and the value of $L_q$ becomes infinitely large.

We see now that one of the requirements of any practical system is that $\mu > \lambda$; otherwise, we cannot have a stable system. If units are arriving faster on the average than they can be processed, the waiting line and waiting time will increase continu-

FIGURE 16-8
**RELATIONSHIP OF QUEUE LENGTH TO THE UTILIZATION FACTOR, ρ, FOR A SINGLE SERVER SYSTEM WHERE $M = 1$.**

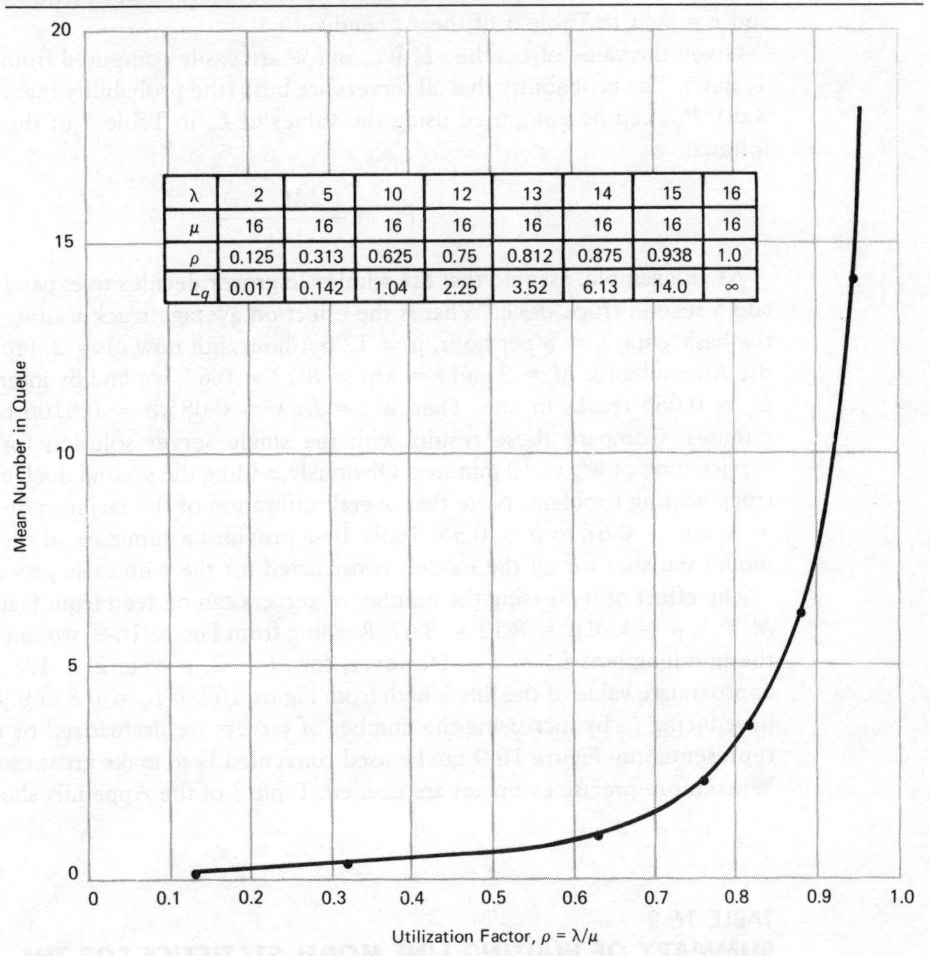


| $\lambda$ | 2 | 5 | 10 | 12 | 13 | 14 | 15 | 16 |
|---|---|---|---|---|---|---|---|---|
| $\mu$ | 16 | 16 | 16 | 16 | 16 | 16 | 16 | 16 |
| $\rho$ | 0.125 | 0.313 | 0.625 | 0.75 | 0.812 | 0.875 | 0.938 | 1.0 |
| $L_q$ | 0.017 | 0.142 | 1.04 | 2.25 | 3.52 | 6.13 | 14.0 | ∞ |

ously and no steady state can be achieved. This simple fact also indicates that there is a value to be placed on idle time in the service facility. *We must trade off the value of rapid service against service facility costs that may include substantial service facility idle time.*

## Multiple Servers

In the multiple servers case, we assume the conditions of Poisson arrivals, exponential service times, first-come first-served queue discipline, and all servers drawing on a single waiting line. The effective service rate, $M\mu$, where $M$ is the number of servers, must be greater than the arrival rate, $\lambda$. The facility utilization factor is $\rho =$

$\lambda/M\mu$, and we define $r = \lambda/\mu$. First, it is necessary to calculate $L_q$, the mean number in the waiting line. The formula for $L_q$ becomes relatively complex in the multiple server case, so we have computed $L_q$ for various values of $M$ (the number of servers) and $r = \lambda/\mu$ in Table 3 of the Appendix.

Given the value of $L_q$, then $L$, $W_q$, and $W$ are easily computed from Equations 3, 4, and 5. The probability that all servers are busy (the probability that there will be a wait), $P_w$, can be computed using the values of $L_q$ in Table 3 of the Appendix as follows:

$$P_w = \frac{L_q(M - r)}{r} \tag{9}$$

As an example, assume that the wholesale grocer decides to expand facilities and add a second truck dock. What is the effect on average truck waiting time? Recall the basic data: $\lambda = 8$ per hour, $\mu = 12$ per hour, but now $M = 2$. From Table 3 of the Appendix for $M = 2$ and $r = \lambda/\mu = 8/12 = 0.67$, we find by interpolating that $L_q = 0.085$ trucks in line. Then $W_q = L_q/\lambda = 0.085/8 = 0.0106$ hours or 0.64 minutes. Compare these results with the single server solution for exponential service time of $W_q = 10$ minutes. Obviously, adding the second dock eliminates the truck waiting problem. Note that overall utilization of the facilities declines from $\rho = \lambda/M\mu = 0.67$ to $\rho = 0.34$. Table 16-2 provides a summary of the waiting line model statistics for all the models constructed for the wholesale grocer example.

The effect of increasing the number of servers can be seen from Figure 16-9. For $M = 1$, $\rho = \lambda/M\mu = 8/12 = 0.67$. Reading from Figure 16-9, we can approximate the line length as $L_q = 1.3$. However, for $M = 2$, $\rho = 8/(2 \times 12) = 0.33$. The approximate value of the line length from Figure 16-9 is $L_q = 0.8$ or 0.9. The effects in reducing $L_q$ by increasing the number of servers are dramatized by the graphical representation. Figure 16-9 can be used conveniently to make gross estimates of $L_q$. When more precise estimates are needed, Table 3 of the Appendix should be used.

**TABLE 16-2**
**SUMMARY OF WAITING LINE MODEL STATISTICS FOR THE WHOLESALE GROCER EXAMPLE ($\lambda$ = 8/hour, $\mu$ = 12/hour)**

| | *Single Dock*, M = 1 | | | | Two Docks, $M = 2$, Negative Exponential Service Time |
|---|---|---|---|---|---|
| | $s = 6$ min | $s = 3$ min | Negative Exponential Service Time, $s = 1/\mu = 5$ min | Constant Service Time, $s = 0$ | |
| $L_q$, trucks in line | 1.63 | 0.91 | 1.33 | 0.67 | 0.085 |
| $L$, trucks in system | 2.30 | 1.57 | 2.00 | 1.33 | 0.752 |
| $W_q$, minutes | 12.24 | 6.80 | 10.00 | 5.00 | 0.64 |
| $W$, minutes | 17.28 | 11.80 | 15.00 | 10.00 | 5.64 |

FIGURE 16-9
**$L_q$ FOR DIFFERENT VALUES OF *M* IN RELATION TO THE UTILIZATION FACTOR ρ (POISSON ARRIVALS AND NEGATIVE EXPONENTIAL SERVICE TIME DISTRIBUTIONS).**

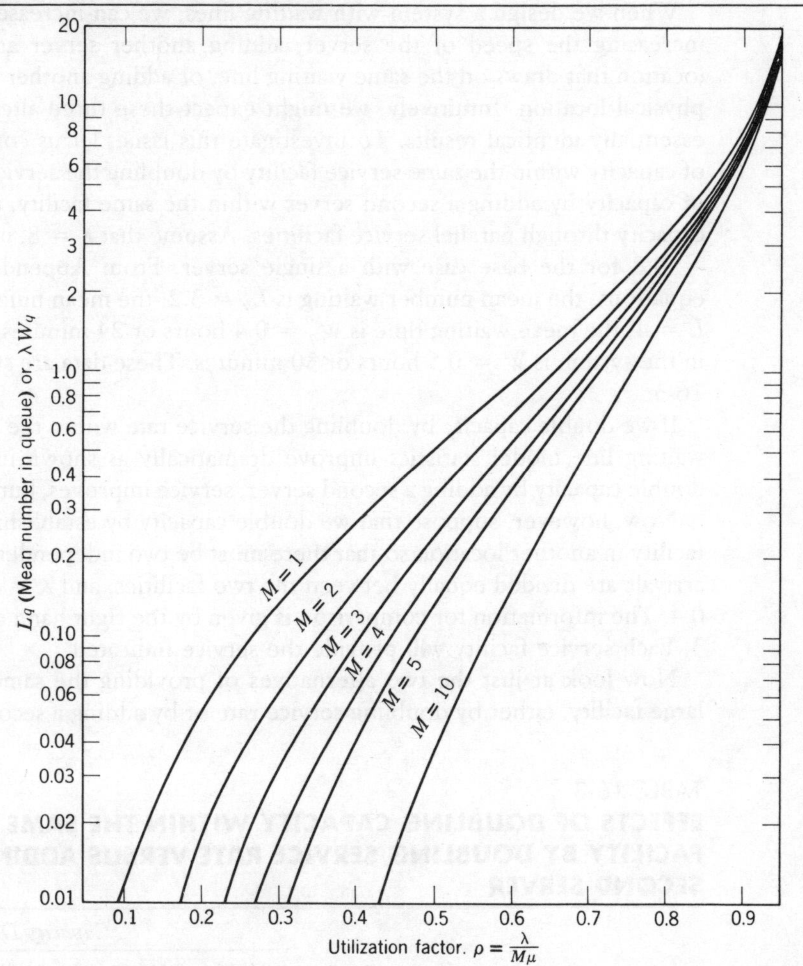


## The Effect of Pooling Facilities

Sometimes managers have the option of organizing the needed capacity into two or more independent facilities or pooling separate facilities into one large facility. If for example, we are faced with a situation where $r = 0.9$ for the single server case, then $L_q$ is approximately 8 from Appendix Table 3. Adding a second server reduces the average line length to $L_q = 0.23$. Adding a third server reduces it to $L_q = 0.03$. The effects on $L_q$ are surprisingly large; that is, we can obtain disproportionate gains in reducing waiting time by increasing the number of servers. We can see intuitively that this might be true from Figure 16-8 because queue length (and waiting time) begins to increase very rapidly at about $\rho = 0.8$ for the single server case represented. A rather small increase in the capacity of the system (a decrease in $\rho$) at these high loads can produce a large decrease in waiting line length and waiting time.

When we design a system with waiting lines, we can increase its service level by increasing the speed of the server, adding another server at the same physical location that draws on the same waiting line, or adding another server at a different physical location. Intuitively, we might expect these three alternatives to produce essentially identical results. To investigate this issue, let us compare the doubling of capacity within the same service facility by doubling the service rate, the doubling of capacity by adding a second server within the same facility, and the doubling of capacity through parallel service facilities. Assume that $\lambda = 8$, $\mu = 10$, and $r = \lambda/\mu = 0.8$ for the base case with a single server. From Appendix Table 3 and the equations, the mean number waiting is $L_q = 3.2$, the mean number in the system is $L = 4$, the mean waiting time is $W_q = 0.4$ hours or 24 minutes, and the mean time in the system is $W = 0.5$ hours or 30 minutes. These data are summarized in Table 16-3.

If we double capacity by doubling the service rate within the same facility, all the waiting line model statistics improve dramatically as shown in Table 16-3. If we double capacity by adding a second server, service improves, but not as dramatically.

Now, however, suppose that we double capacity by establishing a second service facility in another location so that there must be two independent waiting lines. The arrivals are divided equally between the two facilities, and $\lambda = 4$, $\mu = 10$, and $r = 0.4$. The information for comparison is given by the right hand column of Table 16-3. Each service facility will provide the service indicated.

Now look at just the two alternatives of providing the same capacity with one large facility, either by doubling service rate or by adding a second server (the third

TABLE 16-3
**EFFECTS OF DOUBLING CAPACITY WITHIN THE SAME SERVICE FACILITY BY DOUBLING SERVICE RATE VERSUS ADDING A SECOND SERVER**

| | | *Capacity Doubled* | | |
|---|---|---|---|---|
| | Base Case ($M = 1$, $r = 0.8$) | Within Same Facility ($M = 1$, $r = 0.4$) | By Adding Second Server ($M = 2$, $r = 0.8$) | Second Facility Each ($M = 1$, $r = 0.4$) |
| $L_q$[a] | 3.2000 | 0.2666 | 0.1533 | 0.2666 |
| $L = L_q + \lambda/\mu$ | 4.0000 | 0.6666 | 0.9533 | 0.6666 |
| $W_q = L_q/\lambda$ | 0.4000 hr | 0.0333 hr | 0.0192 hr | 0.0667 hr |
| $W = L/\lambda$ | 0.5000 hr or 30.0 min | 0.0833 hr or 5.0 min | 0.1192 hr or 7.15 min | 0.1667 hr or 10.0 min |

[a]Values from Table 3 of the Appendix.

and fourth columns of Table 16-3). Comparing them with two equivalent small facilities in the right-hand column, it is clear that either of the alternatives involving an enlarged single facility gives better service. One large facility definitely provides better service than two equivalent smaller facilities. Looking just at the two alternate ways of doubling capacity within the existing facility, doubling service rate is superior. Although doubling service rate results in a larger waiting line ($L_q = 0.27$ versus 0.15 because sometimes two are being served simultaneously in the $M = 2$ case) and waiting time is proportionately greater, this condition is compensated for by faster service, and the mean number in the system as well as the *total* time in the system are smaller for the system with the higher service rate.

When capacity is doubled by adding a second parallel facility, service is improved but not as dramatically as for either of the other two alternatives. The reason is that service is being provided by two independent systems with two independent waiting lines. Idle capacity in one system cannot be used by the other as would be true if they were both drawing from a single waiting line.

## AN EXAMPLE

A large manufacturing concern with a 100-acre plant had a well-established medical facility, which was located at the plant offices at the eastern edge of the property. Over the years, the plant had grown from east to west and travel time to the medical facility was so great that management was considering dividing the facility. The second unit was to be established near the center of the west end of the plant. A study had been made of weighted travel times for the existing single facility and for the proposed two-facility system. The result indicated that average travel time for the existing large medical facility was 15 minutes. The volume averaged 1000 visits per week or 250 worker-hours for travel time. The two-facility plan would reduce the average travel time to 8 minutes, or 133 worker-hours per week.

The question was, "What would happen to waiting time in the waiting rooms?" For the one large facility, $\lambda = 25$ per hour, and average service time was 20 minutes, or a service rate of $\mu = 3$ per hour, and $r = 25/3 = 8.33$. There were 10 physicians who handled the load. Interpolating in Table 3 of the Appendix, $L_q = 2.45$, and $W_q = 2.45 \times 60/25 = 5.88$ minutes per person or 98 worker-hours per week. Therefore, the travel time plus the waiting time was $250 + 98 = 348$ worker-hours per week.

The plan was to divide the medical staff for the two facilities, and it was assumed that the load would divide equally, so comparable data for the divided facilities were $\lambda = 12.5$ per hour per facility, $\mu = 3$ per hour, $M = 5$, and $r = 4.2$. From Table 3 of the Appendix, $L_q = 3.3269$ and $W_q = 16$ minutes per person or 267 worker-hours per week. The travel plus waiting time for the dual facility plan was therefore $133 + 267 = 400$ worker-hours per week, compared with 348 for the single large facility. Other alternatives could be computed, probably involving an increased medical staff.

The waiting time for the single large facility was 5.88 minutes per person compared with 16.0 minutes per person for the two-facility plan. The large facility gives better service than the two smaller facilities. If we visualize the two decentralized facilities functioning side-by-side, we can see intuitively why waiting time increases. If facility 1 were busy and had patients waiting while at the same time facility 2 happened to be idle, someone from the facility 1 waiting room could be serviced immediately by facility 2, thereby reducing the average waiting time. In this situation the two facilities are drawing from one waiting line. When they are physically decentralized, the facilities must draw on two independent waiting lines and *the idle capacity of one cannot be used by the waiting patients of the other.*

## Costs and Capacity in Waiting Line Models

Although many decisions concerning service systems may turn on the physical factors of line length, waiting time, and service facility utilization, very often system designs will depend on comparative costs for alternatives. The costs involved are commonly the costs of providing the service *versus* the waiting time costs. In some instances the waiting time costs are objective, as when the enterprise employs both the servers and those waiting. The company medical facility just discussed is such a case. The company absorbed all the travel time and waiting time costs as well as the cost of providing the service. In such an instance, a direct cost-minimizing approach can be taken by balancing the waiting costs, or the time-in-system costs, against the costs of providing the service.

When the arriving units are customers, clients, or patients, the cost of making them wait is less obvious. If they are customers, excessive waiting may cause irritation and the loss of goodwill and eventually sales. Placing a value on goodwill, however, is not a straightforward exercise. In public service operations and other monopoly situations, the valuation of waiting cost may be even more tenuous because the individual cannot make alternative choices. In these situations where objective costs cannot be balanced, it may be necessary to set a standard for waiting time; for example, to adjust capacity to keep average waiting time at or below a given number of minutes at supermarket checkout counters.

### AN EXAMPLE

Let us refer to the data for the company internal medical facility. Recall that there were 10 physicians, whom we will assume are paid \$7500 per month, or about \$17,321 per week for the 10 physicians. We also assume that the average hourly wage of the employees coming to the medical facility is \$15. Computations for the single central facility yield a travel time cost of 250 × 15 = \$3750 per week, and a waiting time cost of 98 × 15 = \$1470 per week. The total weekly cost is then \$22,541, including physicians' salaries. First, with the central facility only, how many physicians will minimize affected costs? Using Appendix Table 3, we can determine the average employee waiting time for 9, 10, and 11 physicians and the resulting weekly costs. The results are shown in Table 16-4. Consequently, the present policy of having 10 physicians is a little less costly than having either 9 or 11.

Now, let us consider the dual facility concept, where travel cost is also affected: The travel, waiting, and physicians' cost for the central facility was \$15(250 + 98) +

TABLE 16-4
**UTILIZATION, WAITING TIME, AND COSTS FOR DIFFERENT LEVELS OF MEDICAL SERVICE**

| | Number of Physicians | | |
|---|---|---|---|
| | 9 | 10 | 11 |
| Utilization ($\rho = \lambda/M\mu$) | 0.93 | 0.83 | 0.76 |
| Mean waiting time (min) | 23.4 | 5.88 | 2.26 |
| Weekly waiting time (hr) | 390 | 98 | 38 |
| Cost of waiting time/week | \$ 5,850 | \$ 1,470 | \$ 570 |
| Physicians' cost/week | 15,589 | 17,321 | 19,053 |
| Total affected cost | \$21,439 | \$18,791 | \$19,623 |

\$17,321 = \$22,541 per week. The comparable figures for the dual facilities were \$15(133 + 267) + \$17,321 = \$23,321. Would increased capacity in either or both of the dual facilities improve the affected costs? The answer is no. The weekly travel and waiting costs and service costs for 5 physicians in each facility, 5 in one and 6 in the other, and 6 in each are \$23,321, \$25,056, and \$26,785, respectively.

An important observation concerning the company medical facility is that the unit cost of providing the service is very large and tends to dominate, compared with unit waiting time costs. The physician is paid \$7500 per month whereas the average employee waiting is paid only about \$3000 per month. If the unit costs change relative to each other, the best solution may be different.

## FINITE WAITING LINE MODELS

Many practical waiting line problems that occur have the characteristics of finite waiting line models. This is true whenever the population of machines, people, or items that may arrive for service is limited to a relatively small, finite number. The result is that we must express arrivals in terms of a unit of the population rather than as an average rate. In the infinite waiting line case, the average length of the waiting line is effectively independent of the number in the arriving population, but in the finite case, the number in the waiting line may represent a significant proportion of the arriving population, and therefore the probabilities associated with arrivals are affected. For example, suppose there are 10 machines being serviced by a mechanic and 1 breaks down (arrives for service). Then, there are only 9 that could possibly break down because 1 has been eliminated from the arriving population until it is serviced.

The resulting mathematical formulations are somewhat more difficult computationally than those for the infinite waiting line case. Fortunately, however, finite queuing tables (Peck and Hazelwood, 1958) are available that make the problem solution very simple. Although there is no definite number that we can point to as a dividing line between finite and infinite applications, the finite queuing tables have data for populations from 4 up to 250, and these data may be taken as a general guide. We have reproduced these tables for populations of 5, 10, 20, and 30 in Table 4 of the Appendix to illustrate their use in the solution of finite waiting line problems. The tables are based on a finite model for negative exponential times between arrivals and negative exponential service times and a first-come first-served queue discipline.

## Use of the Finite Queuing Tables

The tables are indexed first by $N$, the size of the population. For each population size, data are classified by $X$, the service factor (comparable to the utilization factor in infinite waiting line models), and by $M$, the number of parallel servers. The service factor $X$ is computed from the following formula:

$$X = \text{Service factor} = \frac{\lambda}{\lambda + \mu}$$

where $\mu$ is the service rate as before, but $\lambda$ is the mean arrival rate *per population unit*. For example, if our time unit is hours and *each population unit* arrives for service every 4 hours on the average, then $\lambda = 1/4 = 0.25$ per hour.

For a given $N$, $X$, and $M$, three factors are listed in the tables: $D$ (the probability of a delay; that is, if a unit calls for service, the probability that it will have to wait), $F$ (an efficiency factor, used to calculate other important data), and $L_q$ (the mean number in the waiting line). To summarize, we define the following factors:

$$W_q = \text{Mean waiting time} = \frac{1}{\mu X}\left(\frac{1 - F}{F}\right)$$

$$\begin{aligned}
L &= \text{Mean number waiting and being served} = L_q + FNX \\
W &= \text{Mean time in system} = W_q + 1/\mu \\
H &= \text{Mean number of units being serviced} = FNX = L - L_q \\
J &= \text{Mean number of units not being served} = FN(1 - X) \\
M - H &= \text{Mean number of servers idle}
\end{aligned}$$

The procedure for a given case is as follows:

1. Determine the mean service rate $\mu$, and the mean arrival rate $\lambda$ per population unit, based on data or measurements of the system being analyzed.
2. Compute the service factor $X = \lambda/(\lambda + \mu)$.
3. Locate the section of the tables listing data for the population size $N$.
4. Locate the service factor calculated in 2 for the given population.
5. Read the values of $D$, $F$, and $L_q$ for the number of servers $M$, interpolating between values of $X$ when necessary.
6. Compute the values for $W_q$, $H$, and $J$ as required by the nature of the problem.

### AN EXAMPLE

A hospital ward has 30 beds in one section, and the problem centers on the appropriate level of nursing care. The hospital management believes that patients should have immediate response to a call at least 80 percent of the time because of possible emergencies. The mean time between calls is 95 minutes *per patient* for the 30 patients. The service time is approximated by a negative exponential distribution and mean service time is 5 minutes.

The hospital manager wishes to staff the ward to give service so that 80 percent of the time there will be no delay. Nurses are paid $15 per hour, and the cost of idle time at this level of service must be considered. Also, the manager wishes to know how much more patients will have to pay for the 80 percent criterion compared with a 50 percent service level for immediate response, which is the current policy.

The *solutions* to the problems posed by the hospital manager are developed through a finite waiting line model. The situation requires a finite model because the maximum possible queue is 30 patients waiting for nursing care, and if 1 patient calls for service, there are only 29 patients who could now possibly call for service. Thus, because of the relatively small population, the potential for more arrivals has been changed by the occurrence of an arrival.

In terms of the finite waiting line model for this situation, the mean service time is 5 minutes ($\mu$ = 0.2/min or 12/hr), the mean time between calls is 95 minutes *per patient* ($\lambda$ = 0.0105/min or 0.632/hr), and, therefore, the service factor is $X = \lambda/(\lambda + \mu) = 0.632/12.632 = 0.05$.

Scanning the finite queuing tables (Table 4 of the Appendix) under population $N = 30$ and $X = 0.05$, we seek data for the probability of a delay of $D = .20$ because we wish to establish service such that there will be no delay 80 percent of the time. The closest we can come to providing this level of service is with $M = 3$ nurses and corresponding data (see Table 4) of $D = .208$, $F = 0.994$, and $L_q = 0.18$. Note that we must select an integer number of servers (nurses).

The cost of this level of service is the cost of employing 3 nurses or 15 × 3 = $45 per hour or $1080 per day, assuming day and night care. The average number of calls waiting to be serviced will be $L_q = 0.18$ and the mean waiting time will be

$$W_q = \frac{1}{\mu X}\left(\frac{1 - F}{F}\right) = \frac{1}{0.2 \times 0.05}\left(\frac{1 - 0.994}{0.994}\right) = 0.6 \text{ minutes}$$

The waiting time is, of course, negligible, which is intended.

The average number of patients being served will be $H = FNX = 0.994 \times 30 \times 0.05 = 1.49$, and the average number of nurses idle will be $3 - 1.49 = 1.51$. The equivalent value of this idleness is 1.51 × 15 × 24 = $543.60 per day.

Finally, the number of nurses needed to provide immediate service 50 percent of the time is $M = 2$ from Table 4 ($D = .571$, $F = 0.963$, and $L_q = 1.11$). The average waiting time under this policy is $W_q = 3.84$ minutes. The average cost to patients of having the one additional nurse to provide the higher level of service is $15 per hour or $360 per day. Divided among 30 patients, the cost is $12 per patient per day.

## REVIEW QUESTIONS

1. Classify the following in terms of the four basic waiting line structures:
   a. Assembly line
   b. Large bank—six tellers (one waiting line for each)
   c. Cashier at a restaurant
   d. One-chair barbershop
   e. Cafeteria line
   f. Jobbing machine shop
   g. General hospital
   h. Post office—four windows drawing from one waiting line
2. Define the following terms:
   a. Arrival process
   b. Queue discipline
   c. Infinite waiting line model
   d. Finite waiting line model
   e. Single server model
   f. Multiple server model
3. Why is queuing felt to be an unacceptable method for dealing with overload conditions in medical systems?
4. What are the assumptions for the waiting line model represented by Equation 2?
5. How is Equation 2 modified if
   a. Service time is constant?
   b. Service time follows the negative exponential distribution?
6. Why are the models associated with finite waiting lines so different from infinite models?

## PROBLEMS

(Table 16-5 provides a summary of waiting line models.)

7. Given a Poisson distribution of arrivals with a mean of $\lambda = 5$ per hour, what is the probability of an arrival of $x = 4$ in 1 hour? What is the probability of the occurrence of 15 minutes between arrivals?
8. The barber of a one-chair shop finds that sometimes customers are waiting but sometimes he has nothing to do and can read sports magazines. He prefers to keep a rather steady pace when he is working, hoping to get blocks of time for reading and keeping up on sports. In the hope of improving his situation, he kept records for several weeks and found that an average of one customer per hour comes in for a haircut (Poisson distribution). It takes him an average of 20

## TABLE 16-5
## SUMMARY OF WAITING LINE MODELS; POISSON ARRIVALS AND FIRST-COME FIRST-SERVED QUEUE DISCIPLINE

| *Infinite Models* | | | | Finite Model, Negative Exponential Service Time, $N = 4 - 250$, Multiple Servers |
|---|---|---|---|---|
| *Single Server Models* | | | Multiple Server Model, Negative Exponential Service Time | |
| Service Time Distribution Not Specified | Negative Exponential Service Time | Constant Service Time | | |
| $L_q = \frac{(\lambda\sigma)^2 + (\lambda/\mu)^2}{2(1 - \lambda/\mu)}$ | $L_q = \frac{\lambda^2}{\mu(\mu - \lambda)}$, or use Appendix Table 3 for $M = 1$ | $L_q = \frac{\lambda^2}{2\mu(\mu - \lambda)}$ | Compute $r = \lambda/\mu$. Use Appendix Table 3 to find $L_q$ for a given value of $M$ | Compute $X = \frac{\lambda}{\lambda + \mu}$. Use Appendix Table 4 to find values of $L_q$, $D$, and $F$ for value of $M$ wanted. |
| $W_q = L_q/\lambda$ | $W_q = L_q/\lambda$ | $W_q = L_q/\lambda$ | $W_q = L_q/\lambda$ | $W_q = \frac{1}{\mu X} \frac{(1 - F)}{(F)}$ |
| $L = L_q + \lambda/\mu$ | $L = L_q + \lambda/\mu$ | $L = L_q + \lambda/\mu$ | $L = L_q + \lambda/\mu$ | $L = L_q + FNX$ |
| $W = W_q + 1/\mu = L/\lambda$ | $W = W_q + 1/\mu = L/\lambda$ | $W = W_q + 1/\mu = L/\lambda$ | $W = W_q + 1/\mu = L/\lambda$ | $W = W_q + 1/\mu$ |
| $\rho = \lambda/M\mu$ | $\rho = \lambda/M\mu$ | $\rho = \lambda/M\mu$ | $\rho = \lambda/M\mu$ | $H = FNX = L - L_q =$ mean number being served |
| | $P_w = \lambda/\mu =$ probability an arrival must wait | | $P_w = L_q(M - r)/r =$ probability an arrival must wait | $J = FN(1 - X) =$ mean number not being served |
| | $P_n = (\lambda/\mu)^n(1 - \lambda/\mu)$ | | | |
| | $P_0 = 1 - \lambda/\mu$ | | $P_0 = \frac{L_q(M - 1)!(M - r)^2}{(r)^{M+1}}$ | $M - H =$ servers idle |

minutes per haircut and the standard deviation of his sample of service times is 5 minutes.

a. What is the average number of customers waiting for service?

b. What is the average customer waiting time?

c. How much of the time does the barber have to read sports magazines?

d. The other barber in town has fallen ill, and our barber's business increases to an average of two customers per hour. What happens to the average number of customers waiting, the average waiting time, and the time available for reading sports magazines?

e. After practicing at home on his children, the barber finds that he can reduce the haircutting time to 10 minutes and the variance to virtually zero by using a bowl and only electric clippers (no scissors). Will this solve the waiting time problem in the interim while the other barber is ill? How would it affect the barber's available reading time?

f. With the other barber ill, our barber finds that his customers are screaming for better service and that his reading time is available only in small increments. He feels under great pressure but is afraid to try the technological improvements he has developed. How can he solve his problem?

9. A taxicab company has four cabs that operate out of a given taxi stand. Customer arrival rates and service rates are described by the Poisson distribution. The average arrival rate is 10 per hour, and the average service time is 20 minutes. The service time follows a negative exponential distribution.
   a. Calculate the utilization factor.
   b. From Table 3 of the Appendix, determine the mean number of customers waiting.
   c. Determine the mean number of customers in the system.
   d. Calculate the mean waiting time.
   e. Calculate the mean time in the system.
   f. What would be the utilization factor if the number of taxicabs were increased from four to five?
   g. What would be the effect of the change in part f on the mean number in the waiting line?
   h. What would be the effect of reducing the number of taxicabs from four to three?
10. A stenographer has five persons for whom he performs stenographic services. Arrival rates are adequately represented by the Poisson distribution, and service times follow the negative exponential distribution. The arrival rate is five jobs per hour. The average service time is 10 minutes. Assume that once an individual assigns a job, she will not bring another job until the first is completed.
    a. Calculate the mean number in the waiting line.
    b. Calculate the mean waiting time.
    c. Calculate the mean number of units being served.
    d. What is the probability that an individual bringing work to the stenographer will have to wait?
11. In the manufacture of photographic film, there is a specialized process of perforating the edges of the 35 mm film used in movie and still cameras. A bank of 20 such machines is required to meet production requirements. The severe service requirements cause breakdowns that must be repaired quickly because of high downtime costs. Because of breakdown rates and downtime costs, management is considering the installation of a preventive maintenance program that they hope will improve the situation.

    The present breakdown rate is three per hour per machine or a time between breakdowns of 20 minutes. The average time for service is only three minutes. The breakdown rate follows a Poisson distribution, and the service times follow a negative exponential distribution. The crew simply repairs the machines in the sequence of breakdown. Machine downtime is estimated to cost $9 per hour, and present repair parts cost an average of $1 per breakdown. Maintenance repairmen are paid $6 per hour. The breakdown rates, service times, and repair parts costs are expected to change with different levels of preventive maintenance, as indicated in Table 16-6.

TABLE 16-6
**EXPECTED CHANGES IN BREAKDOWN RATES, SERVICE TIME, AND COST OF REPAIR PARTS FOR THREE LEVELS OF PREVENTIVE MAINTENANCE**

| Level of Preventive Maintenance | Breakdown Rate (%) | Service Time (%) | Cost of Repair Parts (%) |
|---|---|---|---|
| $L_1$ | −30 | +20 | + 50 |
| $L_2$ | −40 | +35 | + 80 |
| $L_3$ | −50 | +75 | +120 |

What repair crew size and level of preventive maintenance should be adopted to minimize costs?

12. The manager of a large bank has the problem of providing teller service for customer demand, which varies somewhat during the business day from 10 A.M. to 4 P.M. She has a total capacity of six windows and can assign unneeded tellers to other useful work about 60 percent of the time. She also wishes to give excellent service, which she defines in terms of customer waiting time as $W_q \leq 2$ minutes. There is controversy about this service standard, however, with some feeling that the average waiting time should be no longer than 1 minute and others feeling that a 4-minute standard would be adequate.

    In order to give the best service for any situation, the manager has arranged the layout so that customers form a single waiting line from which the customer at the head of the line goes to the first available teller. The arrival pattern is as follows:

    10:00 A.M.–11:30 A.M., $\lambda$ = 1.8 customers per minute
    11:30 A.M.–1:30 P.M., $\lambda$ = 4.8 customers per minute
    1:30 P.M.–3:00 P.M., $\lambda$ = 3.8 customers per minute
    3:00 P.M.–4:00 P.M., $\lambda$ = 4.6 customers per minute

    The arrival distributions follow the Poisson distribution; that is, the mean value of arrivals varies, but the distribution is always Poisson. The average service time is 1 minute and the distribution of service times is approximated by the negative exponential distribution. Tellers are paid $4 per hour.

    The manager wishes to compare the cost of the several standard service policies. Because of the difficulty with reassigning tellers to useful work in all instances, she is also considering the use of part-time tellers.

    What action should be taken by the bank manager?

13. A university must maintain a large and complex physical plant, so plant maintenance is an important support function. The plant maintenance department maintains a crew of six maintenance mechanics who respond to calls for service from department heads and other authorized personnel on the campus. They respond to a wide variety of calls that range from the simple adjustments of room thermostats to the actual repair of plant and equipment. In some in-

stances, extensive work involving specialized personnel may be required, and this is scheduled separately.

During the work day, there are five calls per hour, and the distribution of the call rate is approximated by a Poisson distribution. The average time for service is 60 minutes, including travel time both ways and the actual time to perform the required work, and is approximated by the negative exponential distribution. The wage rate of the mechanics is $8 per hour.

One of the mechanics has just resigned for personal reasons, and the university business manager has refused to replace him because of the budget squeeze. The head of the plant maintenance department is furious and produces a file of complaints from department heads about the slow response to calls for service. The business manager implies that the slow service reflects inefficiency and that it is time for the plant maintenance department to "shape up."

How many maintenance mechanics are economically justified? What action do you feel should be taken?

# SITUATIONS

## The Gasoline Shortage

14. A small town has six gas stations. As gas shortages began to occur during the 1979 oil crisis, the first visible effect was that stations began to close on weekends and to have shorter hours during the week. At any one time, an average of only four stations were open. The average station has two lanes for pumping gas, and only one car can be served at a time in each lane.

    a. Which waiting line model is appropriate to analyze the town gas station problem?

    b. The average station before the shortage had a car arriving for service every 10 minutes on the average. The stations were all "full-service" stations and the average service time was five minutes.

       What are the waiting line model statistics before and after the station closings, assuming that both cases are described adequately by a Poisson process?

    c. As the shortage situation developed, gas station waiting lines continued to grow. It was a field day for the news media, which gave minute by minute bulletins on the progress of the advancing shortage with speculations on when it would end, if it would end, and the likelihood that it would get worse. Station owners reported that their average sale had dropped from 10 to 5 gallons. People were "topping off" their tanks, coming to fill up twice as often. With the smaller sale, the service time was shortened to three minutes; not half as short because the fixed time to give full service had not changed. Tempers were flaring at the stations, and the owners eliminated one lane of service in order to control the situation.

What are the waiting line model statistics for the new situation and how do they compare with the previous statistics?

d. Rules were developed that eliminated full service and required that each customer should not be served unless their gas gages showed ½ tank or less. This policy resulted in an average sale of 10 gallons again. The standard deviation of service time became nearly constant at three minutes.

What are the waiting line model statistics for these new policies, and how do they compare with those in part c? What is your evaluation of the new policies? What do you recommend?

## Smog Emissions Versus Auto Inspection

15. The California Motor Vehicles Department established auto inspection facilities to measure the smog emissions of cars. A typical test center has four parallel service channels. The fee is $15. The four parallel service channels draw on a single waiting line. The arrival rate is $\lambda = 22.8$ cars per hour.

After waiting, service is provided by one of the four service facilities. The data concerning your auto is taken and checked in catalog sources, a physical inspection is made to see if the required smog control equipment is installed in your car, and the data pertinent to your car is typed into a computer terminal. A "hook-up" is made, you start your car, the test is made automatically, and the results are printed out on a computer terminal. If the car passes, you are given the test results and a certificate. If it fails, you are told what modifications or procedures must be followed to pass. With all pertinent activities completed, you drive away, having spent an average of 10 minutes for the services rendered.

a. Assuming that the arrival and service processes are Poisson, what is the mean waiting line length, waiting time, and total time in the system?

b. Additional parallel service channels could be installed, but each new facility requires an additional crew of two workers plus the sophisticated computer-controlled analyzers. These crews and facilities would not serve more cars but would enable the system to give better service. It is estimated that for each additional parallel service facility added, the price would go up by $5 to cover the variable and fixed costs.

Compute the waiting line model statistics for situations involving five and six parallel service facilities and compare them with the results in a.

c. Considering the waiting time, the time in system, and the price that would be charged, which of the three alternative systems would you prefer? Why?

## Journeymen or Apprentices at XACTO?

16. XACTO, Inc., faces a decision of how to allocate its repair crew to various maintenance jobs. It has three journeymen mechanics who are paid $20 per hour and four apprentices who are paid $5 per hour.

XACTO has a bank of ten identical machines that are subjected to severe conditions of temperature and dust, resulting in parts wearing out rapidly. The machines are operated 24 hours per day, seven days per week. Downtime results in idle labor and lost contribution valued at $15 per hour. Maintenance records show that the average breakdown rate per machine is $\lambda = 0.1$ per hour. The average repair time is 1.9 hours for journeymen and 3.7 hours for apprentices. Both arrival and service distributions are representative of a Poisson process.

Should XACTO use journeymen or apprentices for its repair jobs? Why?

## Checkout Service at Food King

17. The manager of a Food King supermarket is reconsidering his service policies. He currently has six checkers working during the busy period, when customers arrive at the rate of $\lambda = 60$ per hour, but he feels that he should be able to get by with only five. The average service time to total the bill, obtain payment (which often requires check cashing), and bag the groceries is $1/\mu = 5$ minutes. Arrival rates and service times follow a Poisson process.

    The corporate objective is to staff the check stands so that the average time for a customer to get through the system is seven minutes or less

    a. How many checkers should be scheduled?
    b. If a bagger is provided in combination with a checker, the service time can be reduced to $1/\mu = 3$ minutes. Checkers are paid $8 per hour and baggers, $3.50 per hour. Is it worthwhile to use baggers?
    c. From the point of view of service, would it be better for the manager to simply add another checker as the union is urging (i.e., over and above the number determined in a), thereby reducing waiting time, or should he use checker–bagger teams, thereby reducing service time?

## Should Truckers Wait at Food King?

18. Food King supermarket maintains a central warehouse from which it supplies all of its stores. In general, each market places orders and obtains daily shipments from the warehouse.

    The general routine is that order pickers assemble orders placed by the stores and load them on one of the five company trucks waiting at the single truck dock. The trucks and their drivers wait in line to obtain their loads on a first-come first-served basis. They then proceed to the store for which the order is destined, unload, and return for another order. Because of the many different routes and distances and traffic problems at different times of the day, the time between arrivals of the trucks at the dock is random, averaging 30 minutes. The loading time follows a negative exponential distribution and averages 15 minutes.

    Truck drivers are paid $15 per hour and the crew of two loaders are each paid $6 per hour. The truckers have complained about the long waiting time, so a sample was taken that showed that truckers did wait an average of 32 minutes. The warehouse manager knows that a second truck dock would probably solve the problem, but this alternative would involve a large capital expenditure plus the disruption of operations during construction.

Tests are made with different crew patterns and it is found that a crew of three can be used to advantage, reducing the loading time to 10 minutes.

a. Is the crew of three loaders more economical than the crew of two?

b. What is the probability that an arriving truck will find at least one truck already in the system?

c. How much of the time is the crew idle? What does the idleness cost?

## Car Wash Crew of 6, 7, or 8?

19. The 10-Minute Car Wash manager has problems in staffing the operation because of the fluctuating demand for car wash service. The crew is used to staff the gas pumps, for vacuum cleaning, to drive cars on the system, and in the wipe and dry operations.

The manager can work with three different crew configurations: eight, seven, and six. With an eight-worker crew, three work the gas pumps, collect fees and vacuum clean; one drives the car on the machine and stays in it, drives it to the wipe and dry area, and runs back to repeat the process; and four wipe and dry. With a crew of seven, the worker who drives and rides through the machine is dropped; a worker from the gas and vacuum area drives a car on the system, and someone from the wipe and dry area drives it off. Finally, with a crew of six, one of the wiper-driers is dropped from the crew.

The mean service times and standard deviations of service times for each of the crew sizes is as follows:

| CREW SIZE | SERVICE TIME, MINUTES | STANDARD DEVIATION, MINUTES |
|---|---|---|
| 8 | 6 | 4 |
| 7 | 7 | 5 |
| 6 | 8 | 9 |

The manager would be happy if he could get most people through the system in 25 minutes overall. The problem is the variability in the number of people who want a wash at any one time. Data were gathered and on a typical Friday-Saturday, the cars arriving for service by a Poisson distribution were as follows:

8:30 A.M.–10:00 A.M., 6 cars per hour
10:00 A.M.–3:00 P.M., 8 cars per hour
3:00 P.M.–5:30 P.M., 5 cars per hour

How should the manager deploy the different crew sizes?

## Tire Manufacturing

20. After tires have been assembled, they go to curing presses where the various layers of rubber and fiber are vulcanized into one homogenous piece and the

final shape, including the tread, is molded. Different tires require somewhat different curing times, which may range up to 90 minutes or more. The press operator can unload and reload a press in $T = 3$ minutes. One operator normally services a bank of curing presses, and each press can be molding tires of a different design, so presses "arrive" for service at nearly random times. The presses automatically open when the preset cure time is complete.

In servicing a bank of 30 presses, the operator ranges over a wide area of approximately 90 feet by 200 feet. Indicator lights flash on, signifying that a press is ready for service. The operator walks to the open press, unloads it, and reloads it. Sometimes, of course, the location of the open press may be quite close to the operator, so his walk is fairly short. In rare instances, the operator is at one extreme of the area and the press requiring service is at the other extreme, requiring a fairly long walk. Thus, the operator's tasks in rendering service are made up of walking plus unloading and reloading the presses. The average time for the operator's activity is $T = 3$ minutes and is approximated by the negative exponential distribution.

When a press is idle, waiting to be serviced, the only costs that continue are the services to the press, mainly the heat supply. The cost of supplying this heat is $8.00 per hour per press. Operators are paid $15.00 per hour, and the contribution per tire is $10.00.

Determine the number of operators that should be used when the average cure time of tires being produced is 80 minutes, for conditions when market demand is less than plant capacity and when it is above plant capacity.

# REFERENCES


Bleuel, W. H. "Management Science's Impact on Service Strategy," *Interfaces,* 6(1), Part 2, November 1975, pp. 4–12.

Cosmetatos, G. P. "The Value of Queueing Theory—A Case Study," *Interfaces,* 9(3), May 1979, pp. 47–51.

Erikson, W. J., "Management Science and the Gas Shortage," *Interfaces,* 4(4), August 1974, pp. 47–51.

Fitzsimmons, J. A., and R. S. Sullivan. *Service Operations Management,* McGraw-Hill, New York, 1982.

Foote, B. L., "A Queuing Case Study of Drive-In Banking," *Interfaces,* 6(4), August 1976, pp. 31–37.

Gilliam, R. R., "An Application of Queueing Theory to Airport Passenger Security Screening," *Interfaces,* 9(4), August 1979, pp. 117–123.

McKeown, P. G., "An Application of Queueing Analysis to the New York State Child Abuse and Maltreatment Register Telephone Reporting System," *Interfaces,* 9(3), May 1979, pp. 20–25.

Paul, R. J., and R. E. Stevens, "Staffing Service Activities with Waiting Line Models," *Decision Sciences, 2,* April 1971, pp. 206–217.

Peck, L. G., and R. N. Hazelwood. *Finite Queuing Tables,* Wiley, New York, 1958.

Vogel, M. A. "Queueing Theory Applied to Machine Manning," *Interfaces,* 9(4), August 1979, pp. 1–8.

# CHAPTER 17
# CAPACITY PLANNING

The long-range operations strategy of an organization is expressed to a considerable extent by capacity plans. It is in connection with capacity planning that the following issues must be considered. What are the market trends, in terms of market size and location and technological innovations? How accurately can these factors be predicted? Is there a technological innovation on the horizon that will have an impact on product or service designs? How will capacity needs be affected by new products? Are there process innovations on the horizon that may affect production methods? Is a more continuous productive system justified in the near future? How are capacity needs affected by process innovations? Will it be profitable to integrate vertically during the planning horizon? In planning new capacity, should existing policies for using overtime and multiple shifts be reviewed? In planning new capacity, should we expand existing facilities or build new plants? What is the optimal plant size? Should a series of smaller units be added as needed, or should larger capacity units be added periodically? Should the policy be to provide a capacity with which some lost sales may be incurred, or is demand to be met?

The foregoing strategic issues must be resolved as a part of capacity planning. In assessing alternatives, the revenues, capital costs, and operating costs may be compared, but managers may need to trade off the possible effects of the strategic issues against economic advantages and disadvantages.

## DEFINITION OF CAPACITY

*Capacity is the limiting capability of a productive unit to produce within a stated time period, normally expressed in terms of output units per unit of time.* But capacity is an elusive concept because it must be related to the intensity with which a facility is used. For example, it may be the policy to work a plant five days per week, one shift per day, to produce a maximum of 1000 units per week. On this basis, one might rate the regular capacity as 1000 output units per week. But this limit can be increased through overtime, resulting in a capacity limit with overtime of 1150 units. By adding a second shift, however, the capacity can be pushed to perhaps 1800 units per week.

Another way of increasing a capacity limit is to engage in subcontracting when it is feasible. Thus, changing policies with respect to the intensiveness with which facilities are used can change capacities without actually adding any new capacity. These alternative sources of capacity can provide managers with important flexibility in making capacity plans.

## MEASURES OF CAPACITY

When output units are relatively homogeneous, capacity units are rather obvious. For example, an auto plant uses numbers of autos, a beer plant uses cases of beer, and a nuclear power plant uses megawatts of electricity.

When output units are more diverse, it is common to use a measure of the availability of the limiting resource as the capacity measure. For example, the airlines use available seat miles (ASMs) as a measure. They do not use "number of seats" because such a measure does not provide an indication of the potential intensiveness of the use of the seats. Similarly, a restaurant would not use seats as a measure because it does not indicate how many "turns" the restaurant can accommodate. Thus, available seat-turns, or the number of people that can be served during meal time, would be an appropriate measure for a restaurant.

Finally, a jobbing machine shop has many different types of equipment for performing a wide variety of machining operations, and the outputs may be unique parts. The value of the labor and material of the outputs could vary widely. Therefore, the capacity of the shop is normally stated as the capacity of the limiting resource, the availability of labor-hours. Labor-hours are used rather than machine hours because there are usually two or three times as many machine hours available as labor-hours; that is, the skilled machinist is the limiting resource.

Table 17-1 shows common capacity measures for a number of different types of organizations.

## PREDICTING FUTURE CAPACITY REQUIREMENTS

Long-range forecasts of demand are difficult to make. There are always contingencies that can have important effects, such as the competitive situation, recessions, wars, oil embargos, or sweeping technological innovations. Therefore, predicting demand also requires an assessment of contingencies. These contingencies are apt to be rather different, depending on the situation. Mature products are likely to have stable and predictable growth, whereas the markets for new products may be quite uncertain.

TABLE 17-1
**MEASURE OF CAPACITY FOR DIFFERENT TYPES OF ORGANIZATIONS**

| Type of Organizations | Capacity Measure |
|---|---|
| Auto plant | Number of autos |
| Steel plant | Tons of steel |
| Beer plant | Cases of beer |
| Nuclear power plant | Megawatts of electricity |
| Airline | Available seat miles (ASMs) |
| Hospital | Available bed-days |
| Movie theater | Available seat-performances |
| Restaurant | Available seat-turns |
| Jobbing machine shop | Available labor-hours |
| School of Business Administration | Available semester or quarter sections |

## Industry Capacity and Competitive Dynamics

Perhaps the most important questions of all to pose are, "Should any capacity be added within the industry?" and the corollary question, "Should this firm be the one to add it?" Answering these questions carefully and with analytical detachment is of the greatest importance. Some of the information needed for the answers may come from long-term projections of demand, but a careful study of the competition's capacity and whatever can be learned about their expansion plans is crucial because strategic capacity moves within an industry can have extremely important price and competitive impacts. We will defer our discussion of the strategic effects of capacity decisions until Chapter 22. The materials in this chapter assume that the decision to add capacity has been made and that planning for the additions is the focus.

## Mature Products with Stable Demand Growth

Many products and services enjoy mature, stable markets. Examples of mature products and commodities are steel, aluminum, fertilizer, cement, and automobiles. Examples of mature services are airline travel and health care. This does not mean that these products and services are not impacted by recessions but that the long-term trend in demand is relatively stable, compared to other situations we describe. In Chapter 4, Table 4-9 summarized prediction and forecasting methods that have value for the longer term. Recall that the predictive methods were the Delphi methods, market surveys, historical and life cycle analyses, and scenario based forecasting. The causal forecasting methods were the regression and econometric models. In addition to these formal predictive methods, executive opinion and extrapolation are common methods for estimating future demand.

Given long-range predictions of demand, we must generate capacity requirements. It is unlikely that these capacity needs will be uniform throughout the productive system. A balance of capacities of subunits exists that reflects the discrete nature of capacity. For example, the existing receiving and shipping operations and factory warehouse area may accommodate a 50 percent increase in output, but the assembly line may already be operating at full capacity and the machine shop, at 90 percent of capacity. The capacity gaps can then be related to future capacity requirements, as shown in Table 17-2.

In Table 17-2, predicted capacity requirements are shown for an enterprise through 1997. The presumption is that these predicted requirements are expected values that take into account contingencies for the situation and a growth rate of approximately 10 percent per year. Optimistic and pessimistic predictions of requirements could also be made.

In Table 17-2, the projected gaps are shown in parentheses. Currently, there is slack capacity in the machine shop and in the receiving, shipping, and warehouse areas. In two years, however, both the machine shop and the assembly line will need additional capacity. These capacity gaps will grow as shown for 1992 and 1997. On the other hand, the receiving, shipping, and factory warehouse capacities will be adequate through 1992.

TABLE 17-2
**PREDICTED REQUIREMENTS, CURRENT CAPACITIES, AND PROJECTED CAPACITY DIFFERENCES**

| | *Capacity, Units per Year* | | | |
|---|---|---|---|---|
| | Current, 1987 | 1989 | 1992 | 1997 |
| Predicted capacity requirements | 10,000 | 12,000 | 15,000 | 20,000 |
| Machine shop capacity | 11,000 | — | — | — |
| Capacity (gap) or slack | 1,000 | (1,000) | (4,000) | (9,000) |
| Assembly capacity | 10,000 | — | — | — |
| Capacity (gap) or slack | — | (2,000) | (5,000) | (10,000) |
| Receiving, shipping, and factory warehouse capacity | 15,000 | — | — | — |
| Capacity (gap) or slack | 5,000 | 3,000 | — | (5,000) |

Identifying the size and timing of projected capacity gaps provides an input for the generation of alternative plans. We may plan to meet demand either by providing the expected required capacity or by partially utilizing alternative sources, or we may absorb some lost sales. We can provide the needed capacity in smaller increments as it is needed or in larger increments that may involve initial slack capacity. We may enlarge existing facilities, establish new producing locations for the additional capacity, or relocate the entire operation.

## New Products and Risky Situations

It is difficult to predict capacity requirements for new products initially or in the rapid development phase of product life cycles. There are also situations involving mature, stable products, such as oil, in which the capacity planning environment is risky owing to unstable political factors. The prediction of capacity requirements in these kinds of situations must place greater emphasis on the distribution of the expected demand. Optimistic and pessimistic predictions can have a profound effect on capacity requirements.

For example, suppose that the product represented in Table 17-2 is in the rapid development stage of its life cycle. There may be considerable uncertainty about the future market because of economic factors and developing competition.

Table 17-3 includes optimistic and pessimistic capacity predictions that affect capacity requirements drastically. The optimistic requirement schedule assumes approximately a 20 percent per year compound growth rate in demand, and the pessimistic schedule assumes only a 5 percent compound growth rate. A 20 percent growth rate might be justified given favorable economic conditions and a slight gain in market share in spite of competition. A 5 percent growth rate might be justified given the success of foreign competition and a smaller market share even though it is assumed that the market as a whole will expand.

Tables 17-4 and 17-5 show the widely differing capacity needs for the optimistic and pessimistic predictions. If we assume the optimistic schedule, we need large

TABLE 17-3
**EXPECTED, OPTIMISTIC, AND PESSIMISTIC PREDICTIONS OF REQUIREMENTS**

| | *Capacity, Units per Year* | | | |
|---|---|---|---|---|
| | Current, 1987 | 1989 | 1992 | 1997 |
| Expected capacity requirements[a] | 10,000 | 12,000 | 15,000 | 20,000 |
| Optimistic requirements | 10,000 | 14,500 | 25,000 | 62,000 |
| Pessimistic requirements | 10,000 | 11,000 | 12,800 | 16,000 |

[a]From Table 17-2.

TABLE 17-4
**PREDICTED REQUIREMENTS, CURRENT CAPACITIES, AND PROJECTED CAPACITY DIFFERENCES FOR THE OPTIMISTIC PREDICTION**

| | *Capacity, Units per Year* | | | |
|---|---|---|---|---|
| | Current, 1987 | 1989 | 1992 | 1997 |
| Predicted optimistic capacity requirements | 10,000 | 14,500 | 25,000 | 62,000 |
| Machine shop capacity | 11,000 | — | — | — |
| Capacity (gap) or slack | 1,000 | (3,500) | (14,000) | (51,000) |
| Assembly capacity | 10,000 | — | — | — |
| Capacity (gap) or slack | — | (4,500) | (15,000) | (52,000) |
| Receiving, shipping, and factory warehouse capacity | 15,000 | — | — | — |
| Capacity (gap) or slack | 5,000 | 500 | (10,000) | (47,000) |

TABLE 17-5
**PREDICTED REQUIREMENTS, CURRENT CAPACITIES, AND PROJECTED CAPACITY DIFFERENCES FOR THE PESSIMISTIC PREDICTION**

| | *Capacity, Units per Year* | | | |
|---|---|---|---|---|
| | Current, 1987 | 1989 | 1992 | 1997 |
| Predicted pessimistic capacity requirements | 10,000 | 11,000 | 12,800 | 16,000 |
| Machine shop capacity | 11,000 | — | — | — |
| Capacity (gap) or slack | 1,000 | — | (1,800) | (5,000) |
| Assembly capacity | 10,000 | — | — | — |
| Capacity (gap) or slack | — | (1,000) | (2,800) | (6,000) |
| Receiving, shipping, and factory warehouse capacity | 15,000 | — | — | — |
| Capacity (gap) or slack | 5,000 | 4,000 | 2,200 | (1,000) |

capacity additions quickly and huge capacity additions within 10 years. If we fail to provide the capacity, we may miss the market, and lost sales could be an important opportunity cost. On the other hand, if we assume the pessimistic schedule, we need only modest amounts of capacity within 5 years that might be provided by multiple shifts and overtime. Even the 10-year capacity gaps seem relatively modest. How do we make capacity plans under such uncertain conditions? We will discuss the use of decision tree analysis to incorporate uncertainties in the evaluation of alternative capacity plans.

## GENERATION OF ALTERNATIVE CAPACITY PLANS

When capacity gaps have been identified, alternative plans can be considered. These alternatives may involve the size and timing of added capacity, the use of overtime and multiple shifts, the use of outside capacity sources, the absorption of lost sales, or the location of new capacity.

### Large or Small Capacity Increments

When an enterprise enjoys stable demand growth, the issues are centered on how and when to provide the capacity rather than *if* capacity should be added. Taking the data for expected capacity requirements from Table 17-2, there is linear growth in capacity requirements of 1000 units per year. One issue is whether capacity should be added more often in smaller increments to keep up with demand (Figure 17-1*a*) or less often in larger increments (Figure 17-1*b*).

Both Figures 17-1*a* and 17-1*b* assume that demand will be met through production, so there will be slack capacity immediately after an addition. The slack capacity declines as requirements increase, and it falls to zero just before the next increment to capacity is installed, if the timing is perfect. Whether smaller or larger increments of capacity will be more economical depends on the balance of incremental capital and the operating costs of a particular organization and on whether or not economies of scale exist. A unit of capacity added now may cost less than a unit added later, yet the slack capacity must be carried as additional overhead until it is actually productive.

### Alternative Sources of Capacity

Another issue in generating capacity plans is whether or not alternative capacity sources can be used near a capacity limit. Figure 17-1 assumes that demand is met through regular productive capacity. Figure 17-2 assumes that the timing of the increments to capacity makes it necessary to use overtime, multiple shifts, and subcontracting where they are feasible. The cost effects of using alternative sources of capacity are the trade-off of some of the costs of carrying slack capacity against the costs of overtime and multiple shifts, productivity losses resulting from pushing capacity beyond normal limits, and the extra costs of subcontracting units of output.

FIGURE 17-1
**CAPACITY INCREMENTS TO MEET REQUIREMENTS (*a*) THROUGH 2000-UNIT INCREMENTS EVERY TWO YEARS AND (*b*) THROUGH 4000-UNIT INCREMENTS EVERY FOUR YEARS.**

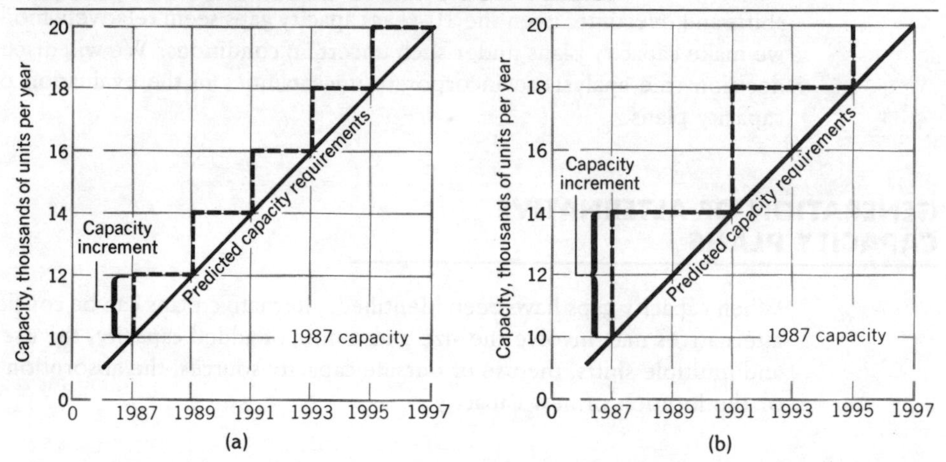


Again, whether or not the use of alternative sources of capacity will be more economical for a particular organization depends on the balance of incremental capital and operating costs.

## Lost Sales

Another alternative to meeting demand through regular productive capacity or alternative capacity sources is to absorb some lost sales. This is a risky strategy

FIGURE 17-2
**CAPACITY INCREMENTS TIMED TO USE ALTERNATIVE SOURCES OF CAPACITY TO MEET REQUIREMENTS**

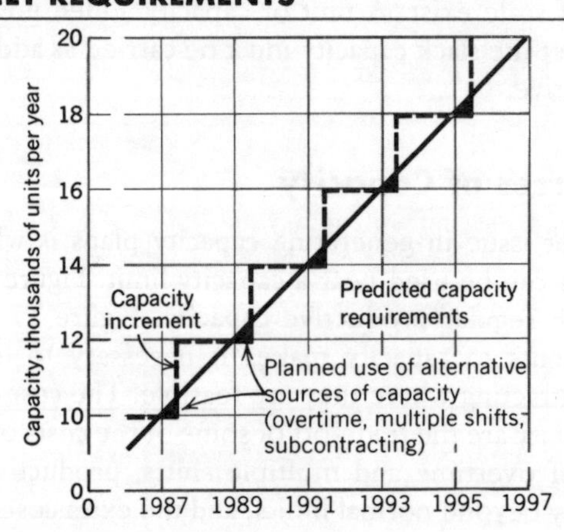

because it is possible that market share could be lost permanently. On the other hand, near capacity limits, contributions decline because of overtime and multiple shift premiums and productivity losses. Thus, absorbing lost sales could be more economical in some situations, yet managers hesitate to take the risk of losing market share. They may be forced into absorbing lost sales at capacity limits, but they would resist the idea of planning to absorb lost sales as a part of a capacity planning strategy.

The question of the location of new capacity is strategically important and involves assessments of market location, system distribution costs, and other factors. We shall defer discussion of location until the next chapter.

## Cost Behavior in Relation to Volume

Figure 17-3 shows a general picture of what happens to costs as volume increases. We are particularly interested in cost behavior at the capacity limits of first and second shifts because this is the condition that prevails when capacity is added.

FIGURE 17-3
**GENERAL STRUCTURE OF COSTS OVER A WIDE RANGE OF VOLUME.**

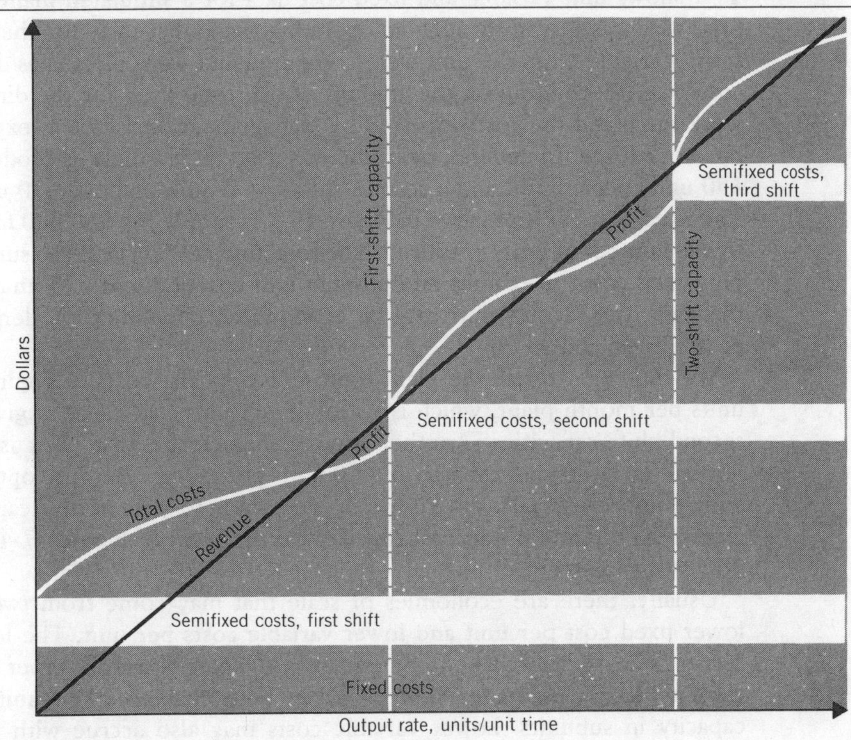


*Source:* E. S. Buffa and W. H. Taubert, "Evaluation of Direct Computer Search Methods for the Aggregate Planning Problem," *Industrial Management Review,* Fall 1967.

Near capacity limits, variable costs increase as a result of the increased use of overtime and subcontracting and because of congestion when facilities are maximally utilized.

On the other hand, when new capacity is first installed, it is not fully utilized unless the expansion is long overdue. Therefore, variable costs for the new capacity are likely to be relatively high, reflecting poor utilization of labor and other resources. But the new capacity relieves the stress on existing facilities, making it possible to eliminate overtime and/or multiple shifts.

The combination of new and existing capacity then reflects a variable cost structure that will improve as the new capacity becomes loaded. The fixed costs of existing capacity are spread over a larger and larger number of units as the volume is driven through the new capacity limits to second and even third shift levels. Thus, the fixed cost per unit declines as existing facilities become more fully utilized. New capacity that is relatively poorly utilized will have high fixed costs per unit.

## Economies of Scale

The nature of the cost structures just discussed suggests that, for a given facility, there should be an optimum output that minimizes fixed plus variable costs. Figure 17-4 shows unit variable and fixed cost data for a simulated manufacturing enterprise that was driven through an operating range that included the use of a second shift. Variable costs per unit were computed and were plotted as data points. Unit costs vary, depending on the amount of overtime used for the direct and indirect work force and the costs incurred by management decisions to expand or contract the work force. In general, overtime was used increasingly as production exceeded 450 units per month, and a second shift was required above 550 units per month. The fixed cost per unit curve in Figure 17-4 is simply the $30,000 fixed cost divided by the number of units produced. The total unit cost curve is the sum of the variable plus fixed costs; it exhibits an optimum unit cost at about 525 units per month. In this case, the second shift may be economical, depending on demand, expansion possibilities, and so on.

We can characterize the plant represented by the costs of Figure 17-4 as a 525 units per month plant, which is its minimum unit cost capacity given the first and second shift capacities. Another way to characterize that plant is in terms of its normal (no overtime) capacity of 450 units per month. Because optimal plant operating points are usually not known, it is common to state normal capacities. In these terms, the minimum unit cost capacity for the plant of Figure 17-4 is $(525/450) \times 100 = 117$ percent of normal.

Usually, there are economies of scale that may come from two basic sources: lower fixed cost per unit and lower variable costs per unit. The lower fixed costs accrue because plant and equipment costs of larger plants are lower in proportion to capacity. Larger plants are likely to have a better balance of subunits with less slack capacity in subunits. Lower variable costs may also accrue with the larger plant because larger volume may justify more mechanization and automation. The result is that minimum unit costs could be substantially less for larger plants, as shown in Figure 17-5.

FIGURE 17-4
**UNIT VARIABLE, FIXED, AND TOTAL COSTS FOR A PLANT IN RELATION TO VOLUME.**

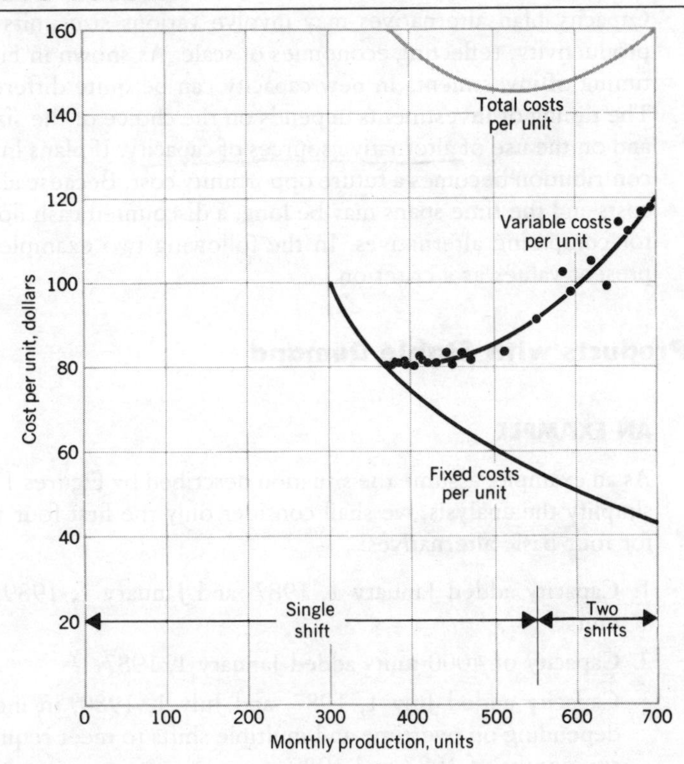


Normal capacity without overtime is 450 units per month, and *minimum unit cost* capacity is 525 units per month.

FIGURE 17-5
**ECONOMIES OF SCALE ILLUSTRATED BY THREE SUCCESSIVELY LARGER PLANTS. *MINIMUM UNIT* COST PLANT SIZES ARE A = 525 UNITS PER MONTH, B = 800 UNITS PER MONTH, AND C = 1000 UNITS PER MONTH.**

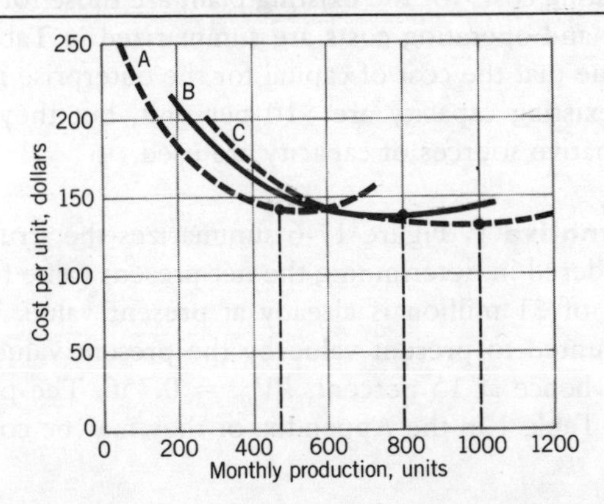

## ECONOMIC EVALUATION OF CAPACITY PLANS

Capacity plan alternatives may involve various size units that may differ in their productivity, reflecting economies of scale. As shown in Figures 17-1 and 17-2, the timing of investments in new capacity can be quite different for alternative plans. The timing of investments depends on the choice of the size of capacity increments and on the use of alternative sources of capacity. If plans involve lost sales, then lost contribution becomes a future opportunity cost. Because all of these costs are future costs and the time spans may be long, a discounted cash flow analysis is appropriate for comparing alternatives. In the following two examples, we shall compute net present values as a criterion.

### Mature Products with Stable Demand Growth

#### AN EXAMPLE

As an example, assume the situation described by Figures 17-1 and 17-2. In order to simplify the analysis, we shall consider only the first four years. We shall compute for four basic alternatives:

1. Capacity added January 1, 1987, and January 1, 1989, in increments of 2000 units.
2. Capacity of 4000 units added January 1, 1987.
3. Capacity added July 1, 1987, and July 1, 1989, in increments of 2000 units, depending on overtime and multiple shifts to meet requirements during the first six months of 1987 and 1989.
4. Capacity of 4000 units added January 1, 1988, depending on overtime and multiple shifts to meet requirements during 1987.

**Costs.** There are economies of scale in the larger plant of 4000 units that are reflected both in the original investment and in the operating costs. Also, units produced using overtime and multiple shifts cost an additional $1.00 per unit. (The operating costs for the existing plant are those for the 2000 unit plant.) The investment and operating costs are summarized in Table 17-6. In the analysis, we shall assume that the cost of capital for the enterprise is 15 percent. Operating costs for the existing capacity are $10 per unit, but they increase to $11 per unit when alternative sources of capacity are used.

**Alternative 1.** Figure 17-6 summarizes the structure of cash flows that must be considered in determining the net present value for Alternative 1. The first investment of $1 million is already at present value. The second investment must be discounted to present value by the present value factor of a single payment two years hence at 15 percent, $PV_{sp} = 0.756$. The present value factors are available from Table 1 in the Appendix, or they may be computed from $PV_{sp} = 1/(1 + i)^n$,

TABLE 17-6
**ORIGINAL INVESTMENT REQUIREMENTS AND OPERATING COSTS**

| Plant Size, Units per Year | Original Investment | Operating Costs per Unit | Operating Costs per Unit When Using Alternative Sources of Capacity |
|---|---|---|---|
| 2000 | $1,000,000 | $10 | $11 |
| 4000 | 1,800,000 | 9 | 10 |

where $i$ = annual interest rate in decimals and $n$ = number of years. For this example, $1/(1 + 0.15)^2 = 0.756$.

The incremental operating costs are related to the actual product produced using the new capacity. When the new capacity comes "on-stream" at the beginning of 1987, it will be entirely slack capacity. Requirements increase linearly as in Figure 17-1*a*, and during the first year, 500 units will be produced by the new capacity. During the second year, 1500 units will be produced, and at the end of the second year the first expansion will be fully utilized.

The fact that only 500 units will be produced from the new capacity during the first year and only 1500 units will be produced during 1988 may be seen from the geometry of Figure 17-7. The production *rate* is increasing linearly to match the requirements, and at the end of the first year, the production rate has increased to 11,000 units. Only one quarter of the 2000-unit capacity of the new facility is used during the first year. The full capacity is represented by the area of the rectangle *abcd*. The number of units produced in 1987, however, is represented by the right

FIGURE 17-6
**PRESENT VALUES FOR ALTERNATIVE 1.**

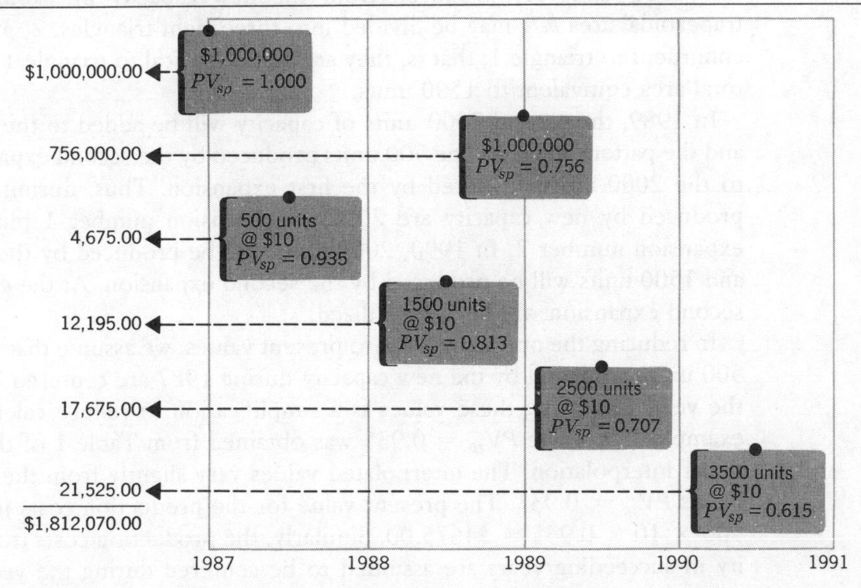

FIGURE 17-7
**GEOMETRIC REPRESENTATION OF UNITS PRODUCED IN 1987 AND 1988 FOR ALTERNATIVE 1.**

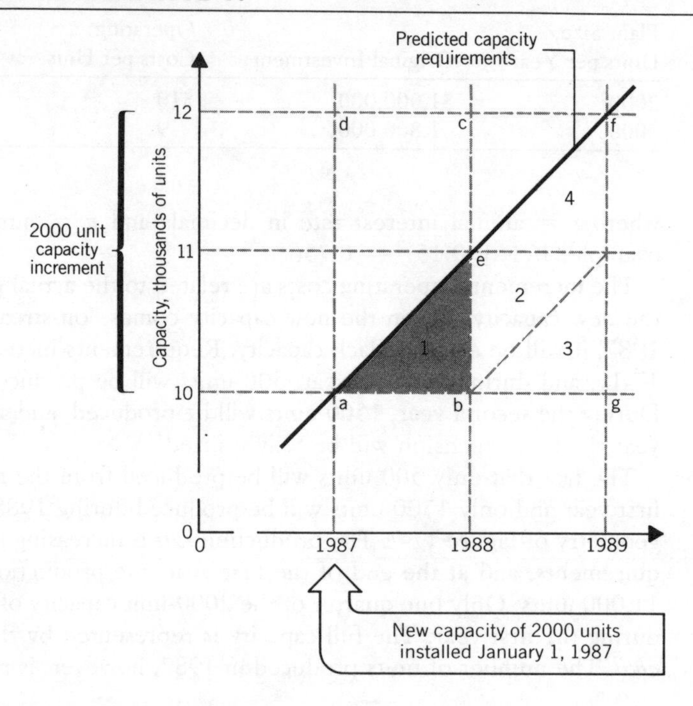


triangle 1, defined by *abe,* which is one quarter of the area of the rectangle. To verify that 1500 units are produced from the new capacity in 1988, note that the trapezoidal area *befg* may be divided into three right triangles, 2, 3, and 4, that are congruent to triangle 1; that is, they are each identical to triangle 1 and represent a total area equivalent to 1500 units.

In 1989, the second 2000 units of capacity will be added to the first expansion, and the pattern repeats. The 500 units produced by the second expansion are added to the 2000 units produced by the first expansion. Thus, during 1989 the units produced by new capacity are 2000 on expansion number 1 plus 500 units on expansion number 2. In 1990, 2000 units will be produced by the first expansion and 1500 units will be produced by the second expansion. At the end of 1990, the second expansion will be fully utilized.

In reducing the operating costs to present values, we assume that the costs for the 500 units produced by the new capacity during 1987 are centered in the middle of the year. Centering these values is a simplification to reduce calculations for this example. The value $PV_{sp} = 0.935$ was obtained from Table 1 of the Appendix by linear interpolation. The interpolated values vary slightly from the formula, which yields $PV_{sp} = 0.933$. The present value for the production costs in 1987, then, is $500 \times 10 \times 0.935 = \$4675.00$. Similarly, the production costs from added capacity in succeeding years are assumed to be centered during the year. The present value factors used are the interpolated values.

Figure 17-6 shows the total present value of the investment and operating costs for two cycles of capacity additions to be $1,812,070. This value will be compared with the values derived by similar methods for the other three alternatives.

**Alternative 2.** Figure 17-8 summarizes the cash flows for Alternative 2. The only investment required is in 1987. The production costs from new capacity are less than those for Alternative 1 because of the economy of scale effect. The economies of scale in capital and operating costs are not sufficient to counterbalance the advantage of Alternative 1, which delays part of the investment in capacity until 1989. Still, Alternative 2 has a strategic advantage of greater slack capacity during the four-year period.

**Alternative 3.** Alternative 3 is similar to Alternative 1 except that each investment in capacity can be delayed for six months by depending on overtime and multiple shifts to meet requirements during that time interval. Recall that using alternative capacity sources results in an incremental cost of $1.00 per unit. See Figure 17-9 for the structure of present values.

The production costs must now reflect the timing and extra cost of the output produced by alternative sources. In 1987, 125 units are produced on the existing capacity during the first six months at $11 per unit (note that the new capacity is not yet available). In this case, the costs are the same as for the new capacity. We have centered these costs at the end of the third month of 1987, and the present value factor of $PV_{sp} = 0.968$ is interpolated from Appendix Table 1. Production costs for the balance of 1987 are centered at the end of the ninth month. Production costs in 1989 are handled in a similar manner. The total present value figure for Alternative 3 shows a net advantage from delaying the investments and obtaining fuller utilization of the new capacity.

FIGURE 17-8
**PRESENT VALUES FOR ALTERNATIVE 2.**

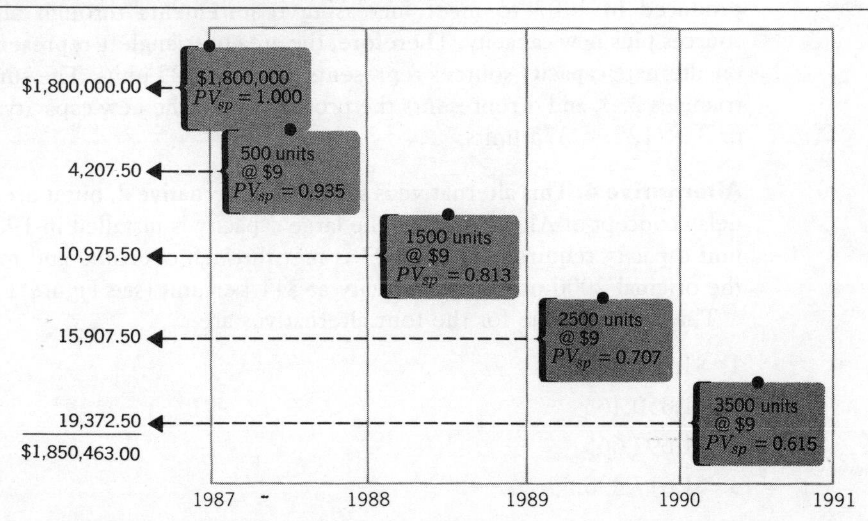

FIGURE 17-9
**PRESENT VALUES FOR ALTERNATIVE 3.**

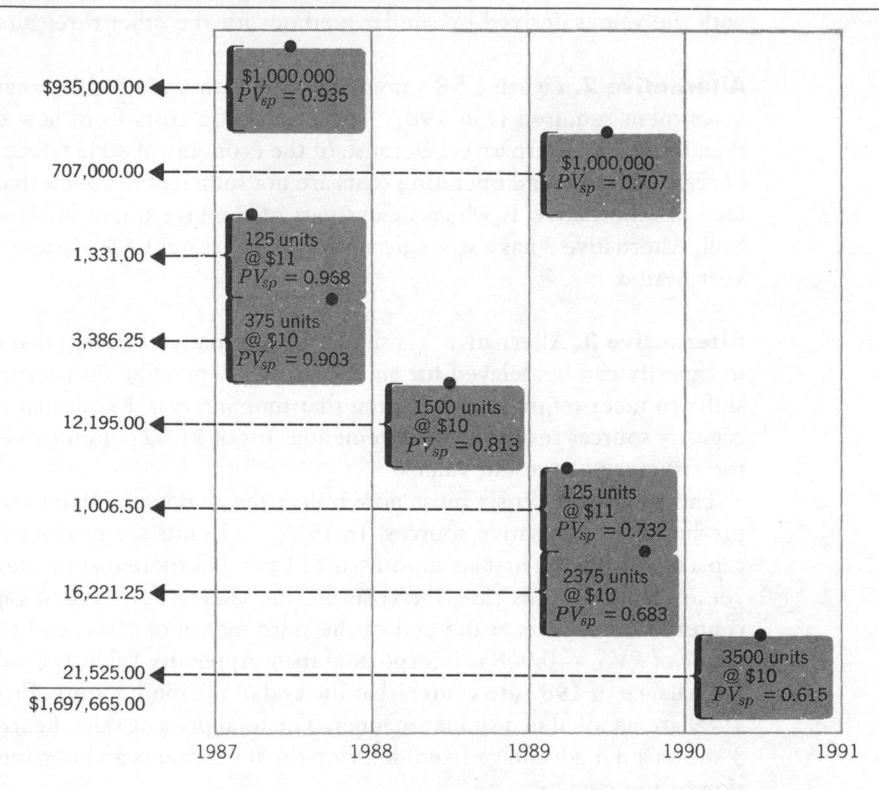


Figure 17-10 shows a geometric representation of the number of units produced on alternate capacity sources, and after the installation of the new capacity of 2000 units on July 1, 1987. Triangle 1 has an area that is one-fourth the area of the large triangle *abc*. The area of the large triangle represents the 500 units that must be produced in 1987 to meet increasing requirements through alternate capacity sources plus new capacity. Therefore, the area of triangle 1 representing production on alternate capacity sources represents 500/4 = 125 units. The sum of the areas of triangles 2, 3, and 4 represents the production on the new capacity installed July 1, or 3 × 125 = 375 units.

**Alternative 4.** This alternative is similar to Alternative 2, but it uses the investment delay concept of Alternative 3. The large capacity is installed in 1988, and the 500-unit capacity requirement in 1987 is met through overtime and multiple shifts on the original 2000 unit plant capacity at $11 per unit (see Figure 17-11).

The present value for the four alternatives are

1. $1,812,070
2. $1,850,463
3. $1,697,665
4. $1,617,398

FIGURE 17-10
**GEOMETRIC REPRESENTATION OF UNITS PRODUCED IN 1987 FOR ALTERNATIVE 3.**

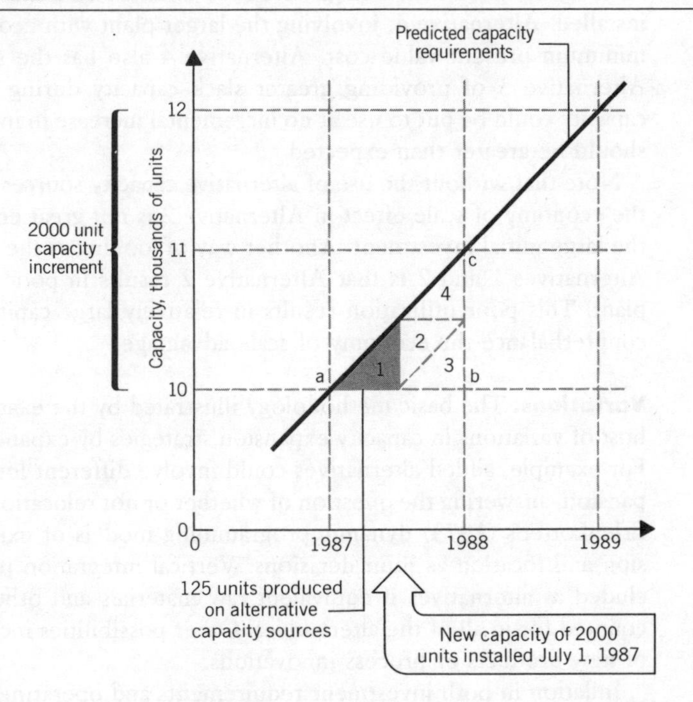


FIGURE 17-11
**PRESENT VALUES FOR ALTERNATIVE 4.**

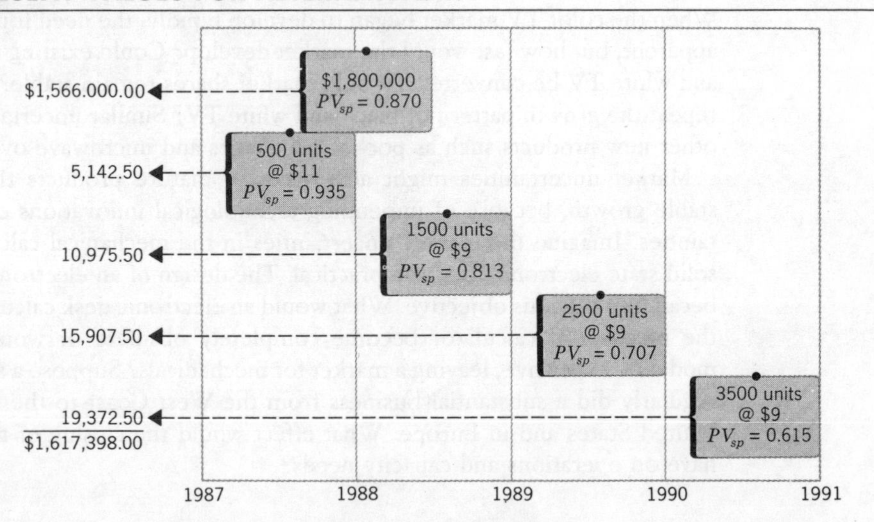

The cost structures in this example favor the use of alternative capacity sources in order to delay capital investments for either the small or large plants. Delaying the investment has the advantage of better utilization of the new capacity when it is installed. Alternative 4, involving the larger plant with economies of scale, has the minimum present value cost. Alternative 4 also has the strategic advantage over Alternative 3 of providing greater slack capacity during the 4 years. This slack capacity could be put to use at no incremental increase in investment cost if demand should be greater than expected.

Note that without the use of alternative capacity sources in Alternatives 1 and 2, the economy of scale effect in Alternative 2 is not great enough to counterbalance the large initial investment. Another way of looking at the cost difference between Alternatives 1 and 2 is that Alternative 2 results in poor utilization of the larger plant. This poor utilization results in relatively large capital costs per unit, which counterbalance the economy of scale advantage.

**Variations.** The basic methodology illustrated by the example can be applied to a host of variations in capacity expansion strategies by expanding the alternatives list. For example, added alternatives could involve different locations coupled with expansion, answering the question of whether or not relocation is justified at this time. Erlenkotter's (1973) dynamic programming models of expansion consider expansion and location as joint decisions. Vertical integration proposals can also be included as alternatives if equivalent raw materials and other affected costs are accounted for in all of the alternatives. Other possibilities include the capacity effects of new products or process innovations.

Inflation in both investment requirements and operating costs can be taken into account by the present value methodology without difficulty. Also, the assumptions regarding the centering of the operating expenses made in the example can be relaxed by constructing a more detailed model.

## New Products and Risky Situations

When the color TV market began to develop rapidly, the need for new capacity was apparent, but how fast would the market develop? Could existing facilities for black and white TV be converted? Would market shares remain stable? Would color TV repeat the growth pattern of black and white TV? Similar uncertainties occurred in other new products such as pocket calculators and microwave ovens.

Market uncertainties might also occur in mature products that have enjoyed stable growth, because of impending technological innovations or political uncertainties. Imagine the market uncertainties in the mechanical calculator field when solid state electronics became practical. The design of an electronic desk calculator became an obvious objective. What would an electronic desk calculator cost? Would the mechanical calculator become completely obsolete or would the electronic model be expensive, leaving a market for mechanicals? Suppose a shipping company regularly did a substantial business from the West Coast to the East Coast of the United States and in Europe. What effect would the closing of the Panama Canal have on operations and capacity needs?

If demands are uncertain, lead times can be important. It may take considerable time for planning, for obtaining government permits that involve environmental impact studies, and for construction. The length of these lead times becomes of even greater importance when planning for products with uncertain demand. Events can occur within the lead times that change the logical alternatives.

Capacity planning in these situations requires an assessment of the risks. The effect of the probability that risky events will occur must be accounted for. If the market is uncertain, a probabilistic prediction of the market provides basic data.

## AN EXAMPLE

Suppose that we are planning future capacity for a product that is in the rapid development phase. Present annual capacity is 20,000 units. New competition is becoming very aggressive, but the enterprise expects to retain its market share. The sales department feels that market share could be increased with aggressive promotion. Estimates of the total market vary, with some feeling that growth might be explosive in the next four to five years. On the other hand, there is the additional uncertainty concerning continuing technological innovation that could stunt the growth of the current line. Thus, expected, optimistic, and pessimistic market predictions are made and assigned probabilities that each might occur. The predictions are converted to capacity requirements per year as follows:

| | 1987, Current | 1988 | 1989 | 1990 | 1991 |
|---|---|---|---|---|---|
| Optimistic ($p$ = .25) | 17,000 | 24,000 | 34,000 | 48,000 | 66,000 |
| Expected ($p$ = .50) | 17,000 | 20,000 | 24,000 | 29,000 | 35,000 |
| Pessimistic ($p$= .25) | 17,000 | 19,000 | 21,000 | 23,000 | 25,000 |

The optimistic requirements are based on the assumption of 40 percent annual growth; the expected, on 20 percent annual growth; and the pessimistic, on only 10 percent annual growth. (Capacities have been rounded.)

**Strategies.** Three alternative strategies are developed, each designed with the three market assumptions in mind. The variable costs of production are the same as for the present capacity because no new process technology is involved. The three alternatives are

1. Install new capacity in 1989, 1990, and 1991 in increments of 15,000 units.
2. Install new capacity in 1989, 1990, and 1991 in increments of 5000 units.
3. Make no capacity additions.

The 15,000-unit capacity additions require an investment of $800,000 each, and the 5000-unit additions require an investment of $300,000 each, reflecting an investment economy for the larger units. *The operating costs per unit are the same for both sizes of capacity additions.* Given each of the three strategies, the outcomes will depend on which requirements schedules actually occur. When requirements exceed capacity, sales are lost, so the cost of lost contribution of \$50 per unit must be taken into account in evaluating the alternatives.

For each of the three strategies, any of the three market assumptions could occur with the stated probabilities. Figure 17-12 is a decision tree representing the strategies and events. In order to evaluate the three alternative strategies, we must compute the present value of each of the nine possible outcomes.

**Present Values of Outcomes.** The present values for each of the three outcomes for each of the three basic strategies are shown in Tables 17-7, 17-8, and 17-9. The calculations for Alternative 1 in Table 17-7 are typical. In Alternative 1*a* of Table 17-7, the optimistic requirements in relation to the proposed capacity with additions provides the basis for computing lost sales. Because there are no operating cost

FIGURE 17-12
**DECISION TREE FOR THE RISKY MARKET EXAMPLE.**

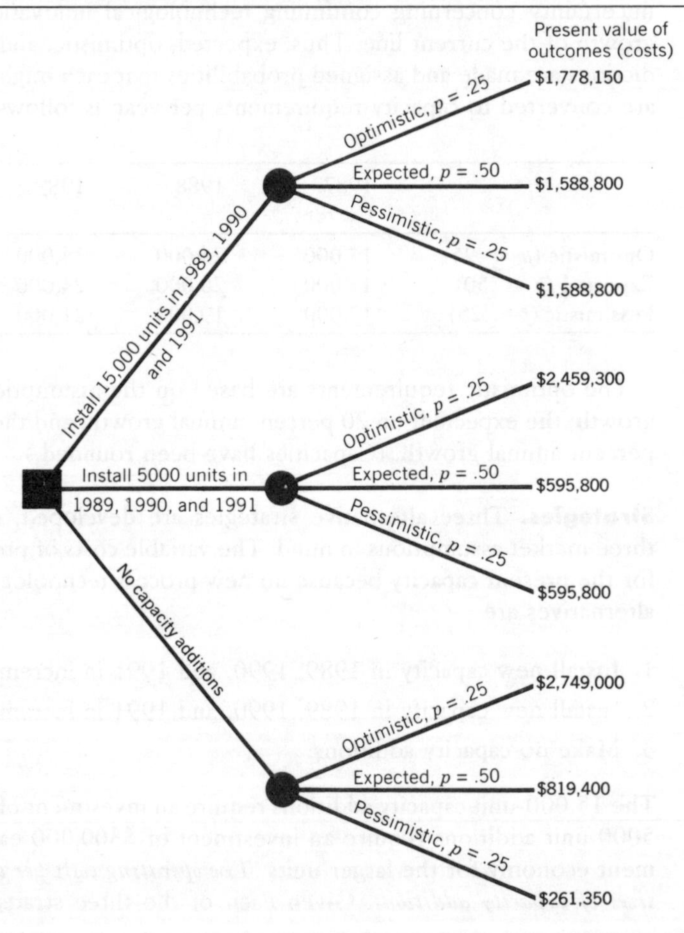

TABLE 17-7
**ALTERNATIVE 1: NEW CAPACITY IN 1989, 1990, AND 1991 IN INCREMENTS OF 15,000 UNITS AT A COST OF $800,000 EACH (INTEREST RATE = 15%)**

| | 1987 | 1988 | 1989 | 1990 | 1991 |
|---|---|---|---|---|---|
| 1*a*: Optimistic requirements | — | 24,000 | 34,000 | 48,000 | 66,000 |
| Proposed additions to capacity | — | — | 15,000 | 15,000 | 15,000 |
| Proposed capacity | 20,000 | 20,000 | 35,000 | 50,000 | 65,000 |
| Lost sales | — | 4,000 | 0 | 0 | 1,000 |
| *Present values:* | | | | | |
| New capacity, 1989, 800,000 × 0.756 = | | | $604,800 | | |
| New capacity, 1990, 800,000 × 0.658 = | | | 526,400 | | |
| New capacity, 1991, 800,000 × 0.572 = | | | 457,600 | | |
| Lost sales, 1988, 4,000 × 50 × 0.813 = | | | 162,600 | | |
| Lost sales, 1991, 1,000 × 50 × 0.535 = | | | 26,750 | | |
| Total | | | $1,778,150 | | |
| 1*b*: Expected requirements | — | 20,000 | 24,000 | 29,000 | 35,000 |
| Proposed additions to capacity | — | — | 15,000 | 15,000 | 15,000 |
| Proposed capacity | 20,000 | 20,000 | 35,000 | 50,000 | 65,000 |
| Lost sales | — | 0 | 0 | 0 | 0 |
| *Present values:* | | | | | |
| New capacity, 1989, 800,000 × 0.756 = | | | $604,800 | | |
| New capacity, 1990, 800,000 × 0.658 = | | | 526,400 | | |
| New capacity, 1991, 800,000 × 0.572 = | | | 457,600 | | |
| Total | | | $1,588,800 | | |
| 1*c*: Pessimistic requirements | — | 19,000 | 21,000 | 23,000 | 25,000 |
| Proposed additions to capacity | — | — | 15,000 | 15,000 | 15,000 |
| Proposed capacity | 20,000 | 20,000 | 35,000 | 50,000 | 65,000 |
| Lost sales | — | 0 | 0 | 0 | 0 |
| *Present values:* | | | | | |
| Same as for 1*b*. | | | $1,588,800 | | |

economies of scale between the large- and small-capacity additions, the operating cost differences among the alternatives are measured by the lost sales.

The present value calculations reduce all future net cash flows in the four-year planning horizon to the planning base period of 1987 at an interest rate of 15 percent. The capacity additions occur two, three, and four years hence, and each is reduced to present value. The lost sales are assumed to be centered within the year that they occur, and the present value factors are interpolated from Table 1 in the Appendix. The present value of the investments and the lost sales costs of $1,778,150 for Alternative 1 is the outcome for that alternative shown in the decision tree of Figure 17-12. All of the cost outcomes shown in Figure 17-12 are computed similarly in Tables 17-7, 17-8, and 17-9.

**Expected Values of the Alternative Strategies.** In order to evaluate the three strategies, we compute their expected values by "rolling back" the decision tree. We

TABLE 17-8
**ALTERNATIVE 2: NEW CAPACITY IN 1989, 1990, AND 1991 IN INCREMENTS OF 5000 UNITS AT A COST OF $300,000 EACH (INTEREST RATE = 15%)**

| | 1987 | 1988 | 1989 | 1990 | 1991 |
|---|---|---|---|---|---|
| 2*a*: Optimistic requirements | — | 24,000 | 34,000 | 48,000 | 66,000 |
| Proposed additions to capacity | — | — | 5,000 | 5,000 | 5,000 |
| Proposed capacity | 20,000 | 20,000 | 25,000 | 30,000 | 35,000 |
| Lost sales | — | 4,000 | 9,000 | 18,000 | 31,000 |
| *Present values:* | | | | | |
| New capacity, 1989, 300,000 × 0.756 = | | | $226,800 | | |
| New capacity, 1990, 300,000 × 0.658 = | | | 197,400 | | |
| New capacity, 1991, 300,000 × 0.572 = | | | 171,600 | | |
| Lost sales, 1988, 4,000 × 50 × 0.813 = | | | 162,600 | | |
| Lost sales, 1989, 9,000 × 50 × 0.707 = | | | 318,150 | | |
| Lost sales, 1990, 18,000 × 50 × 0.615 = | | | 553,500 | | |
| Lost sales, 1991, 31,000 × 50 × 0.535 = | | | 829,250 | | |
| Total | | | $2,459,300 | | |
| 2*b*: Expected requirements | — | 20,000 | 24,000 | 29,000 | 35,000 |
| Proposed additions to capacity | — | — | 5,000 | 5,000 | 5,000 |
| Proposed capacity | 20,000 | 20,000 | 25,000 | 30,000 | 35,000 |
| Lost sales | — | 0 | 0 | 0 | 0 |
| *Present values:* | | | | | |
| New capacity, 1989, 300,000 × 0.756 = | | | $226,800 | | |
| New capacity, 1990, 300,000 × 0.658 = | | | 197,400 | | |
| New capacity, 1991, 300,000 × 0.572 = | | | 171,600 | | |
| Total | | | $595,800 | | |
| 2*c*: Pessimistic requirements | — | 19,000 | 21,000 | 23,000 | 25,000 |
| Proposed additions to capacity | — | — | 5,000 | 5,000 | 5,000 |
| Proposed capacity | 20,000 | 20,000 | 25,000 | 30,000 | 35,000 |
| Lost sales | — | 0 | 0 | 0 | 0 |
| *Present values:* | | | | | |
| Same as for 2*b*. | | | $595,800 | | |

multiply the present value of the cost outcome by the probability of its occurrence and add the three probability weighted values to obtain the expected monetary value for the strategy. This is done for all three strategies in Table 17-10.

Alternative 2, involving the installation of the three 5000-unit capacity additions, produces the lowest expected present value costs. Note that Alternative 2 incurs lost sales only if the optimistic prediction actually materializes, but it requires a much smaller capital investment than Alternative 1. Alternative 3 requires no capital investments, but it incurs large costs of lost sales even for the pessimistic requirements prediction. On balance, then, Alternative 2 is the most economical capacity plan, given the probability of each of the requirements predictions materializing.

Recall, however, that it is not the expected value of costs that will actually materi-

TABLE 17-9
**ALTERNATIVE 3: NO CAPACITY ADDITIONS (INTEREST RATE = 15%)**

| | 1987 | 1988 | 1989 | 1990 | 1991 |
|---|---|---|---|---|---|
| 3*a*: Optimistic requirements | — | 24,000 | 34,000 | 48,000 | 66,000 |
| Proposed capacity | 20,000 | 20,000 | 20,000 | 20,000 | 20,000 |
| Lost sales | — | 4,000 | 14,000 | 28,000 | 46,000 |
| *Present values:* | | | | | |
| Lost sales, 1988, | 4,000 × 50 × 0.813 = | $162,600 | | | |
| Lost sales, 1989, | 14,000 × 50 × 0.707 = | 494,900 | | | |
| Lost sales, 1990, | 28,000 × 50 × 0.615 = | 861,000 | | | |
| Lost sales, 1991, | 46,000 × 50 × 0.535 = | 1,230,500 | | | |
| Total | | $2,749,000 | | | |
| 3*b*: Expected requirements | — | 20,000 | 24,000 | 29,000 | 35,000 |
| Proposed capacity | 20,000 | 20,000 | 20,000 | 20,000 | 20,000 |
| Lost sales | — | 0 | 4,000 | 9,000 | 15,000 |
| *Present values:* | | | | | |
| Lost sales, 1989, | 4,000 × 50 × 0.707 = | $141,400 | | | |
| Lost sales, 1990, | 9,000 × 50 × 0.615 = | 276,750 | | | |
| Lost sales, 1991, | 15,000 × 50 × 0.535 = | 401,250 | | | |
| Total | | $819,400 | | | |
| 3*c*: Pessimistic requirements | — | 19,000 | 21,000 | 23,000 | 25,000 |
| Proposed capacity | 20,000 | 20,000 | 20,000 | 20,000 | 20,000 |
| Lost sales | — | 0 | 1,000 | 3,000 | 5,000 |
| *Present values:* | | | | | |
| Lost sales, 1989, | 1,000 × 50 × 0.707 = | $35,350 | | | |
| Lost sales, 1990, | 3,000 × 50 × 0.615 = | 92,250 | | | |
| Lost sales, 1991, | 5,000 × 50 × 0.535 = | 133,750 | | | |
| Total | | $261,350 | | | |

alize. The actual costs will depend on the actual capacity requirements. If, in fact, the optimistic prediction materializes, the present value of costs under Alternative 2 would be $2,459,300, which is $681,150 greater than if the 15,000 unit additions had been installed. How would managers respond to the situation if by mid-1988 (with the first 5000-unit-capacity addition under construction) it appeared that the optimistic prediction was valid? Of course, they would adjust plans, presumably through a new set of predictions and alternatives. There would be no logic in following through with the original decision of installing the two remaining small-capacity additions.

TABLE 17-10
**EXPECTED VALUES OF THE THREE ALTERNATIVE STRATEGIES**

| | | |
|---|---|---|
| Alternative 1: .25 × 1,778,150 + .50 × 1,588,800 + .25 × 1,588,800 | = | $1,636,137 |
| Alternative 2: .25 × 2,459,300 + .50 × 595,800 + .25 × 595,800 | = | $1,061,675 |
| Alternative 3: .25 × 2,749,000 + .50 × 819,400 + .25 × 261,350 | = | $1,162,288 |

The example is relatively simple in terms of the alternatives selected and in the cost structure represented. With large future costs being involved, managers would probably consider more alternatives and perhaps more than three probabilistic predictions. Also, a more complex cost structure might represent the situation more accurately. But these are straightforward extensions of the same methodology.

## RISKS AND STRATEGIC EFFECTS

Many important effects of alternative capacity plans can be represented in an expanded decision tree. For example, if a technological breakthrough can be assigned a probability of perhaps $p = .30$, then a branch in the tree can be structured for "no breakthrough" ($p = .70$) and "breakthrough" ($p = .30$). Other risks can be handled similarly in the formal decision tree analysis.

Many strategic effects, however, must be evaluated through managerial trade-off. If the most economical plan involves lost sales and possibly a decline in market share, the manager must weigh the lower expected costs against the loss of market share. Specific capacity plans might have an impact on competition, flexibility of operations, market locations, labor policies, market share, and so on.

## FRAMEWORK FOR ANALYZING CAPACITY PLANNING DECISIONS

The capacity planning process fits into the general framework we discussed for analyzing technological choice in Chapter 15. This similarity is not surprising since capacity expansion often involves technological choices and contingencies. We will use the same simple format—structure alternatives, set horizon and criterion, evaluate alternatives and decide—but adapt it to the special nature of capacity planning.

### Structuring Alternatives

Capacity expansion involves extremely important strategic issues that must be addressed before the balance of the planning process can proceed. These issues involve existing industry capacity, where it is located, the nature and strength of the competition, the status of technology in the industry including the potential for technological change within the industry, and so on. These factors have a strong influence on whether or not to pursue an expansion at all as well as on the structuring of alternatives for expansion.

Given a "go" signal for the capacity planning process, alternatives need to be structured around different locations that may have competitive advantages, the process technology that can be used (including the impact of future technological improvements or even radical changes), and the nature of the product and its markets. One of the outcomes will be in terms of the riskiness of the situation, with regard to both the product and its markets (mature or new and risky), and the anticipation of chance occurrences or developments, usually involving technological choices. If the product and its markets are mature and stable and the technology is also stable, then the alternatives are usually straightforword and simple, involving large versus smaller units, economies of scale, the use of alternative sources of capacity, alternative locations, and so on. On the other hand, if the situation is risky for any of the reasons we have discussed, there are probably chance events that need to be taken into account, and a decision tree will prove valuable in analyzing the alternatives. As with the analysis of technological choice, a "do nothing" alternative should be included in the structure of alternatives.

### Horizon and Choice of Criteria for Decision

Capacity expansion invariably involves the creation of assets that have value over long periods. The building and the process equipment normally involve the largest assets of an enterprise, and since the alternatives may involve expenditures and revenues with differing timings, present values should be used to place all of the monetary values on a common basis for comparison. But if we are dealing with risky situations that require decision-tree analysis, then probabilities must be taken into account, and expected monetary values become the criteria as was true with our framework for analyzing technological choice.

### Evaluation of Alternatives and Decision

Although the economic criteria are of great significance in the basic decision to expand capacity, they may yield to qualitative differences in the selection of an alternative. Questions of location and timing may depend on qualitative criteria that cannot be reflected in the economic analysis. Competitive factors among the alternatives may be of extreme importance and may outweigh economic differences among the alternatives in the minds of the decision makers. As with the analysis of technological alternatives, decision makers can make trade-offs between economic and subjective values, thereby "pricing" the subjective advantages. Also, most capacity decision problems involve multiple criteria, in which case the methods discussed in Chapter 21 are of value.

## IMPLICATIONS FOR THE MANAGER

Capacity planning involves top managers in decisions that have important strategic implications. These decisions often have an impact on and are affected by other enterprise functions in addition to operations. They interface with the marketing function in terms of product strategies and market predictions. They interface with engineering and technology in terms of both product and process innovations. Capacity decisions may commit resources that commonly represent the major assets of a firm, requiring financing by debt or equity instruments. Finally, capacity decisions may also set directions for the philosophy governing the productive system design. Will the design emphasize cost and availability, suggesting a product-focused system, or flexibility and quality, suggesting a process-focused system?

Predicting long-range market trends is difficult because events that may cause major demand shifts are unpredictable. Nevertheless, there are many commodities and mature products whose demands seem to be caused by basic trends in population, industrialization, urbanization, and so forth. Causal forecasting models have been shown to be useful for these types of products. Even in these stable product situations, however, economic and political events can have an impact on capacity needs to an extent not foreseen by models based on historical data. Executive opinion, possibly formalized through the Delphi method, may be the basis for these long-range predictions. New product predictions are most often based on these latter methods, often in combination with market surveys and product life cycle analyses.

Given market predictions, the capacity planning options available to managers involve frequent smaller capacity additions versus less frequent larger capacity additions and the use of other sources of capacity, either marginally or as part of an ongoing capacity philosophy. There is no single right choice among these options. Rather, the choice depends on appropriate analyses that provide logical alternatives and evaluation methods. Each situation has its unique growth and cost structure characteristics. In general, deterministic methods are adequate in mature product situations, but probabilistic methods are needed when market predictions are risky.

Although formal economic evaluation is extremely important because of the capital commitments, the result must be regarded as one important input to the decision process. Strategic factors must be weighed and may be the basis for the final choice. With the economic analysis of the alternatives and the identification of the strategic effects of each alternative available, managers can make trade-offs. In effect, the trade-off process allows a pricing of the strategic effects.

## REVIEW QUESTIONS

1. What are the appropriate methods for predicting future requirements for the following?
   a. Electric power
   b. Oil tankers
   c. Hula-hoops
2. Why might there be imbalances in the existing capacities of X-ray, laboratory, intensive care, and other departments in a hospital?
3. A fertilizer company is reviewing its future capacity needs. The company has concluded that its share of the market demand will expand at the rate of 20 percent per year for the next five years. Production is highly capital intensive, and transportation costs for distribution are also important.

   What kinds of alternatives do you think should be considered?

4. How is the capacity planning problem different for mature products that have relatively stable growth patterns than for products that are new or involve risky situations?
5. What are alternative sources of capacity? How do they impact the capacity planning problem?
6. Describe the issues surrounding the choice between large- and small-capacity units.
7. Using the cost–volume relationship shown in Figure 17-3 as a background:
   a. Under what conditions would you expect minimum unit cost plant size (output) to include a second shift?
   b. What are the factors that might result in a larger plant being more cost effective than a smaller one?
8. Define the following terms: *regular capacity, optimal capacity,* and *maximum capacity.*
9. What are the effects of economies of scale on the capacity planning problem?
10. Home computers are now on the market. They are quite powerful, involving keyboard input, video output, and very substantial memory capacities, and they are designed to use rather capable languages such as BASIC. Prices range from $600 to $1500 and are declining.

    If you were tooling up to produce such a product, how would you go about assessing the market for the next five years? What kinds of capacity strategies would you generate? What decision methodology would you use?
11. Referring to question 10, what strategic factors should be weighed and traded off against objective cost–profit results in your strategies?
12. Review the framework for analyzing capacity alternatives. How is it the same as the framework given for analyzing technological choices? How is it different from that framework?
13. Why are present values used in comparing the cash flows in capacity analyses?
14. What are typical factors that might suggest the use of chance events in capacity expansion analyses? What economic criteria would be appropriate under such circumstances?

# PROBLEMS

15. A company is planning an expansion in capacity and two alternatives have been developed for the same site, based strictly on the size of the expansion. The first involves smaller, 2000-unit plants—two units would be installed that would satisfy demand for five years. The units cost $2,500,000 each, installed, and have a ten-year economic life with no salvage value, and each costs $1,000,000 per year to operate.

    The second alternative has scale economies. It is a 4000-unit expansion that costs $8,000,000, installed, has a ten-year economic life with no salvage value, and costs $1,200,000 per year to operate.

The revenue patterns for the two alternatives are identical, there being no lost sales for either. Which alternative would be preferred on economic grounds? Interest is at 10 percent.

16. In problem 15, the equipment supplier for the plant states that it is working on a technological innovation that could make the smaller plant more economical to operate. It estimates the operating costs for the two small units together to be the same as those for the large plant, but the initial costs of the small plant would be $3,500,000 each. The supplier says that the chances are 50-50 that it can prove out the new process in time to install the units by the required schedule. If the project fails to prove out, they can still meet the schedule for the original small plant.

    How does this change the structure of the alternatives? What economic decision criteria should be used? What decision should be made on economic grounds?

17. The Lost Sales Company is considering what to do; it is at two-shift capacity, it is limiting sales, and demand promises to continue to increase at the rate of 20 percent per year. The production manager is against expansion. He says that expansion cannot be justified because labor costs are sky high and, "We have a labor intensive product—there is no point in expansion until we face up to automating to reduce the labor content in our product."

    The sales manager is an expansion advocate. He points to the $100 per unit contribution to profit and overhead available for every unit sold and says "We are losing that amount by not expanding. We could sell 10,000 more units next year if we could produce them."

    The plant and equipment would cost $1,000,000, would have a 15,000 unit capacity per year, and could be on-line in six months, producing 7500 units by year-end. The economic life of the plant and equipment is estimated to be ten years. Interest is at 10 percent.

    a. What is the structure of the alternatives?
    b. What decision criteria should be used?
    c. What economic analysis might resolve the differences between the production and sales managers?

18. The production manager of the Lost Sales Company in problem 17 says he can put on a third shift that would provide a capacity of 600 units per month and risk virtually no capital. The higher labor rate and reduced productivity would cut the contribution to only $80 on the incremental units. He says that he could hire the additional labor and have the third shift operational within three months.

    a. How does this proposal change the structure of alternatives?
    b. What decision should the company make?

19. New alternatives are made available for the example of the economic analysis of a mature product given in the text. The present value calculations for the text example are given in Figures 17-6, 17-8, 17-9, and 17-11.

A radically new process technology that has generated tremendous enthusiasm has been developed by the company engineers. The process has been automated, so capital and material costs dominate; labor costs have been almost eliminated. Therefore, operating costs have been drastically reduced. The result is that two new alternatives have been added to the four given in the text. The two new alternatives involve the possibility of expansion with the automated process and costs as follows:

a. Capacity added January 1, 1987, and January 1, 1989, in increments of 2000 units.

b. Capacity of 4000 units added January 1, 1987.

These plants would be designed for 24-hour operation because of their capital intensive nature. Therefore, other plans involving alternative sources of capacity are not feasible.

There is an economy of scale in the investment cost of the larger plant. The operating costs of the two plant sizes are the same, however, because of the nature of the new process. The investment and operating costs are shown in Table 17-11.

Compute the present values for the two alternatives and compare the results with the four alternatives computed in the text. What decisions should be made? Why?

20. This problem is an extension of the text example for the economic evaluation of a product in its rapid development phase. The decision tree structure is given in Figure 17-12.

A technological breakthrough in an automated production process is now available that can be incorporated with new capital additions. The results would be a dramatic cost decrease of $30 per unit. On the other hand, it is estimated that plant investment costs would increase to $900,000 each for the 15,000-unit plant and $375,000 each for the 5000-unit plant.

The optimistic, expected, and pessimistic requirements schedules as well as the probability estimates remain the same as in the text example. The internal rate of return is 15 percent.

a. What are the present values of each of the nine possible outcomes?

b. What are the expected values of the three alternatives?

c. Which alternative would you choose? Why?

TABLE 17-11
**INVESTMENT AND OPERATING COSTS FOR PROBLEM 19**

| Plant Size, Units per Year | Original Investment | Operating Costs per Unit |
|---|---|---|
| 2000 | $1,300,000 | $1 |
| 4000 | 2,000,000 | 1 |

# SITUATIONS

## SITCOM—Coping with Runaway Capacity Needs

21. SITCOM is a producer of electronic home appliances, including VHS (Video Home System) television recorders, located in northern California. The packaged product weighs about 75 pounds. SITCOM was not the innovator of the system. Rather, its managers sat back and let RCA and others develop the market, and SITCOM is currently producing under license agreements. SITCOM has a conscious strategy of being a follower with new product innovations. It does not have the financial resources to be a leader in research and development.

    SITCOM's strategy is to establish itself in the market as it develops a quality product, waiting for the surge in sales in the product life cycle associated with the rapid development phase. It intends to be ready with the capacity to capitalize on the market surge. SITCOM has proved its competence in marketing and in assembly-type production. The production strategy places great emphasis on parts procurement, quality control of vendors, and materials management in general. This strategy results in the comparatively low capacity costs associated with an assembly operation.

    SITCOM's present opportunity is indicated by the fact that industry sales of VHS recorders have increased 30 percent per year for the past two years, and forecasts for the next year and the two following are even more enticing. SITCOM has established a 10 percent market share position and feels that it can at least maintain this position if it has the needed capacity; it could possibly improve its market share if competitors fail to provide capacity at the time it is needed.

    The forecasts and capacity gaps are indicated in Table 17-12. SITCOM regards the first year forecast as being quite solid, based on its present market share and a compilation of several industry forecasts from different sources. It is less sure about the forecasts for future years, but it is basing these forecasts on patterns for both black and white and color TV sales during their product life cycles.

    SITCOM's VHS model has a factory price of $600. Variable costs are 70 percent of the price. Inventory carrying costs are 20 percent of inventory value, 15 percentage points of which represents the cost of capital. SITCOM's facility planners estimate that a 40,000 unit plant can be built for $5 million and a 100,000 unit plant, for $10 million. Land and labor are available in the area, and either size plant can be built within a year.

    a. What capacity plans do you think SITCOM should make for next year? Why?
    b. What longer term capacity plans should SITCOM make? Why?
    c. What are the implications of these plans for marketing, distribution, and production?

TABLE 17-12
**FORECASTED REQUIREMENTS AND CAPACITY NEEDS FOR SITCOM (PRESENT CAPACITY IS 105 UNITS)**

| | Year | | | | | |
|---|---|---|---|---|---|---|
| | Current Year, 0 | 1 | 2 | 3 | 4 | 5 |
| Forecast, 1000 units | 100 | 140 | 195 | 270 | 350 | 450 |
| Capacity (gap), or slack, 1000 units | 5 | (35) | (90) | (165) | (245) | (345) |

## CHEMCO—Capacity Needs for a New Product

22. CHEMCO is a chemical manufacturing company that has been successful in research and development. It has built its reputation by exploiting its excellent research staff's ability to develop new and useful products. The firm has been able to capitalize on being an innovator, reaping the high profits that result from being first with a product and facing little initial competition. The company has promoted new products strongly, obtaining an identification with them that has carried over into longer-term market dominance in many cases. A recent new product, PRIMEBEEF, seems to have remarkable effects as a cattle feed additive. It results in a higher proportion of high-grade beef.

Having been involved in many new product introductions, CHEMCO has learned to deal with the market uncertainties of new products. Therefore, when the initial market tests for PRIMEBEEF were successful, capacity planning became an issue. CHEMCO developed flexible capacity plans that took account of contingencies. The potential market was large but not certain. It was known that competitors were already attempting imitations. Therefore, part of the strategy was to expand output as soon as possible to establish CHEMCO's market position. The capacity planning issues were centered in plant size and the expandability of a small plant, should that be the decision. After making market estimates, CHEMCO decided on a 10-year planning horizon.

### MARKET SCENARIOS

Marketing predictions could be framed in several scenarios that were structured as follows with probability estimates:

a. Demand would be high initially, product identification would be successful, and demand would remain high. Probability = .60.
b. Demand would be high in the initial two years, but competition would be so keen that demand would be low thereafter (third through tenth years). Probability = .10.
c. Demand would be initially low and would remain low. The product would never be very successful. Probability = .30.

From the above three scenarios, CHEMCO noted that the probability of an initial (first two years) high demand was $p = .70$, which formed the basis for a capacity strategy that would start with a small plant that could be expanded after two years if demand was in fact high during the initial period.

### ALTERNATIVES

Two basic capacity strategies were based on the market predictions. Alternative 1—build a large plant costing \$3 million. Alternative 2—build a small but expandable plant initially costing \$1 million. If initial demand is high, decide within two years whether or not to expand the plant at a cost of \$2,200,000. This decision involved risks also because even if initial demand is high ($p = .70$), the probability is only $p = .60$ that it will be high thereafter. Therefore, the conditional probability that demand will be high following a decision to expand is $p = .60/.70 = .86$.

### REVENUE PATTERNS

Estimates of annual income were made under the assumptions of each demand pattern as follows:

a. A large plant with high volume would yield \$1 million annually in cash flow.
b. A large plant with low volume would yield only \$100,000 annually because of high fixed costs and inefficiencies.
c. A small plant with low demand would be economical and would yield annual cash income of \$300,000.
d. A small plant, during an initial period of high demand, would yield \$450,000 per year, but this yield would drop to \$400,000 yearly in the long run because of competition. (The market would be larger than under c, but would be divided up among competitors.)
e. If the small plant were expanded to meet sustained high demand, it would yield \$700,000 cash flow annually and would be less efficient than a large plant built initially.
f. If the small plant were expanded but high demand was not sustained, estimated annual cash flow would be \$50,000.

### ANALYSIS AND DECISION

CHEMCO decided that the capacity planning program was definitely risky and that a careful analysis should be made before attempting a decision. The president of the company stated that he wished to preserve CHEMCO's historical record of maintaining an 18 percent before tax return on investments. He also raised the questions of whether or not the company had all the information it needed and whether there were other strategies that should be considered.

What analysis should be made? What should CHEMCO do?

# REFERENCES

Armstrong, J. S., and M. C. Grohman, "A Comparative Study of Methods for Long-Range Market Forecasting," *Management Science, 19*(2), October 1972, pp. 211–221.

Basu, S., and R. G. Schroeder, "Incorporating Judgments in Sales Forecasts: Application of the Delphi Method at American Hoist & Derrick," *Interfaces,* 7(3), May 1977, pp. 18–27.

Buffa, E. S., and J. S. Dyer. *Management Science/Operations Research: Model Formulation and Solution Methods* (2nd ed.), Chapter 14, Wiley, New York, 1981.

Bulow, J. J., "Holding Idle Capacity to Deter Entry," *The Economic Journal, 95,* March 1985, pp. 178–182.

Erlenkotter, D. "Sequencing Expansion Projects," *Operations Research, 21,* 1973, pp. 542–553.

Esposito, F. F., and L. Esposito, "Excess Capacity and Market Structure," *Review of Economics and Statistics, 56,* May 1974, pp. 189–194.

Huettner, D. *Plant Size, Technological Change, and Investment Requirements,* Praeger, New York, 1974.

Manne, A. S. (Ed.), *Investments for Capacity Expansion: Size, Location, and Time Phasing.* MIT Press, Cambridge, Mass., 1967.

# CHAPTER 18

# LOCATION AND DISTRIBUTION

The strategic significance of facility location is connected with capacity decisions. Indeed, the issue of capacity expansion immediately raises the companion issue of where to expand in order to tie in effectively with the distribution network. We have separated the materials into two chapters because the approaches to the subproblems are quite different and to divide the materials into manageable units.

The location of facilities involves a commitment of resources to a long-range plan. Thus, predictions of the size and location of markets are of great significance. Given these predictions, we establish facilities for production and distribution that require large financial outlays. In manufacturing organizations, these capital assets have enormous value, and even in service organizations, the commitment of resources may be very large. Location and distribution take on even greater significance because these plans represent the basic strategy for accessing markets and may have significant impacts on revenue, costs, and service levels to customers and clients.

It is not immediately obvious that location is a dominant factor in the success or failure of an enterprise. Indeed, it is not uniformly important for all kinds of enterprises. Decentralization within industries must mean that many good locations exist or that the location methods used could not discriminate among alternative locations.

General technological constraints will commonly eliminate most of the possible locations. Or, to take the opposite point of view, a technological requirement may dominate, so that activity is then oriented toward the technical requirement. For example, mining is raw material oriented, beer is water oriented, aluminum reduction is energy oriented, and service activities, including sales, are consumer or client oriented in their locations. If some technological requirements, such as the location of raw materials, water, or energy, does not dominate, then manufacturing industries are often transportation oriented.

The criterion for the choice of location should be profit maximization for economic activities. If the prices of products are uniform in all locations, then the criterion becomes one of minimizing relevant costs.

If the costs of all inputs are independent of location, but product prices vary, then the criterion for locational choice becomes maximum revenue. In such instances, locations will gravitate to the location of consumers, and the general effect will be to disperse or decentralize facilities.

If all prices and costs are independent of location, then choice will be guided by proximity to potential customers or clients, to similar and competing organizations, and to centers of economic activity in general.

## INDUSTRIAL PLANT LOCATIONS

In most plant location models, the objective is to minimize the sum of all costs affected by location. Some items of cost, such as freight, may be higher for city *A* and lower for city *B*, but power costs, for example, may have the reverse pattern. We are seeking the location that minimizes costs on balance. In attempting to

The effect of Equation 2 is that the site with the minimum cost will have $OFM_i = 1$, and the site with the maximum cost will have $OFM_i = 0$. The sites with intermediate levels of cost are assigned $OFM_i$ values by the linear interpolation. For example, site 3 in Table 18-1 will have

$$OFM_3 = \frac{5.5 - 4.1}{5.5 - 3} = \frac{1.4}{2.5} = 0.56$$

The subjective factor measure, $SFM_i$, for each site is influenced by the relative weight of each subjective factor and the evaluation of site $i$ relative to all other sites for each of the subjective factors. This results in the following statement:

$$SFM_i = \sum_k (SFW_k \times SW_{ik}) \tag{3}$$

where

$SFW_k$ = The weight of subjective factor $k$ relative to all subjective factors
$SW_{ik}$ = The evaluation of site $i$ relative to all potential sites for subjective factor $k$

Note that $\Sigma SFW_k = 1$, $0 \leq SFW_k \leq 1$, $0 \leq SW_{ik} \leq 1$, and $SW_{ik}$ for the site with the best score or performance on the subjective factor $k$ is 1 and for the site with the worst score or performance on the subjective factor $k$ is 0. A method to obtain $SW_{ik}$ is simply to use a rating system by which the sites are rated on a 0 to 1 scale with respect to their relative desirability on the subjective factor $k$. In Chapter 21, formal methods for using preference theory to evaluate multidimensional alternatives such as sites will be discussed.

Finally, the objective factor decision weight, $X$, must be determined. This factor establishes the relative importance of the objective and subjective factors in the overall location problem. The decision is commonly based on managerial judgment that requires a careful analysis of the trade-off between cost and the combined effect of the subjective factors.

With all the data inputs, Equation 1 can be used to compute the location measure, $LM_i$, for each site, and the site that receives the largest $LM_i$ is selected.

For our example in Table 18-1, the objective, subjective, and overall location measures for the six sites are summarized in Table 18-2*a*. The computation for subjective factor measure for the six sites is given in Table 18-2*b*. In the Table 18-2*b*, the weight for each subjective factor is given in parentheses below the factor. The evaluation of each site on a subjective factor is obtained using a rating scale with a range of 0 to 1. For $X = 0.8$, site 6 produces the largest overall location measure and, hence, is the most preferred. For $X > 0.85$, site 1 is the most preferred. Actually, this example problem boils down to a choice between site 1 and site 6, the choice depending on the level of $X$ selected by the management.

TABLE 18-2*a*
**LOCATION MEASURE FOR SIX SITES (X = 0.8)**

| Site | Objective Factor Measure | Subjective Factor Measure (from Table 18-2*b*) | Location Measure |
|---|---|---|---|
| 1 | 1.00 | 0.40 | 0.88 |
| 2 | 0.00 | 0.55 | 0.11 |
| 3 | 0.56 | 0.65 | 0.578 |
| 4 | 0.80 | 0.375 | 0.715 |
| 5 | 0.64 | 0.475 | 0.607 |
| 6 | 0.92 | 0.875 | 0.911 |

TABLE 18-2*b*
**CALCULATION OF SUBJECTIVE FACTOR MEASURE**

| Site | Availability of Transportation (0.2) | Availability of Labor (0.3) | Managerial Control (0.3) | Support of Community (0.2) | Subjective Factor Measure |
|---|---|---|---|---|---|
| 1 | 0.50 | 0.50 | 0.00 | 0.75 | 0.40 |
| 2 | 1.00 | 0.00 | 0.50 | 1.00 | 0.55 |
| 3 | 0.50 | 0.50 | 1.00 | 0.50 | 0.65 |
| 4 | 0.00 | 0.75 | 0.50 | 0.00 | 0.375 |
| 5 | 0.50 | 0.00 | 0.75 | 0.75 | 0.475 |
| 6 | 0.75 | 1.00 | 0.75 | 1.00 | 0.875 |

## COMPETITION AS A CRITICAL LOCATION FACTOR

The location of competition and the anticipated competitive reaction to a locational choice can be of extreme importance. The example of the multiattribute model could include competition as a suggested subjective factor, and perhaps it belongs there in many situations. But, listed there among several other factors, it appears to take on a benign status, its effects to be traded off routinely among the other factors.

In many situations, however, competition and competitive reaction may be a critical or dominant factor in locational choice. It can operate within the multiattribute framework as a critical factor and eliminate locations from further consideration, or it can become a component criterion that dictates a locational choice. This can happen when one location seems to be clearly the best from the point of view of the competition, even though there may be advantages in objective and subjective criteria for other locations. Perhaps this is why managers may trust a location model only for more routine problems but override the model for important location decisions.

## OPERATIONS RESEARCH BASED LOCATION MODELS

In many situations the criterion of interest for choosing among alternative locations can be adequately represented by a single quantifiable objective function, such as dollar cost, time, or distance. However, in spite of a single criterion, the location problem is difficult because the number of alternatives may be too many (sometimes infinite) to allow simple enumeration. Techniques developed in operations research are useful in identifying the optimal location(s) with moderate computing requirements. We will discuss here some of the simplest models that should serve to illustrate the usefulness of the operations research techniques for location and distribution. More details for the models discussed here and several of their extensions can be found in Francis and White (1974) and Hansen et al. (1983).

### Single-Facility Location

Suppose there are $m$ users whose locations are determined by points in a plane as shown in Figure 18-1. The objective is to determine the location of the facility for which total travel costs are minimized. The total cost is the sum of the costs incurred for servicing each user. We define the location of the facility by the coordinates $(x,y)$. The distance to user $i$ from the facility, $d_i$, is given by the length of the line segment connecting the user $i$ to the facility:

$$d_i = \sqrt{(x_i - x)^2 + (y_i - y)^2}$$

where $(x_i,y_i)$ are the coordinates of the user $i$. If $w_i$ is the cost per mile to serve $i$th user, then the total cost of locating facility at $(x,y)$ is given by

$$C(x,y) = \sum_{i=1}^{m} w_i d_i = \sum_{i=1}^{m} w_i \sqrt{(x_i - x)^2 + (y_i - y)^2} \tag{4}$$

FIGURE 18-1
**SINGLE FACILITY LOCATION.**

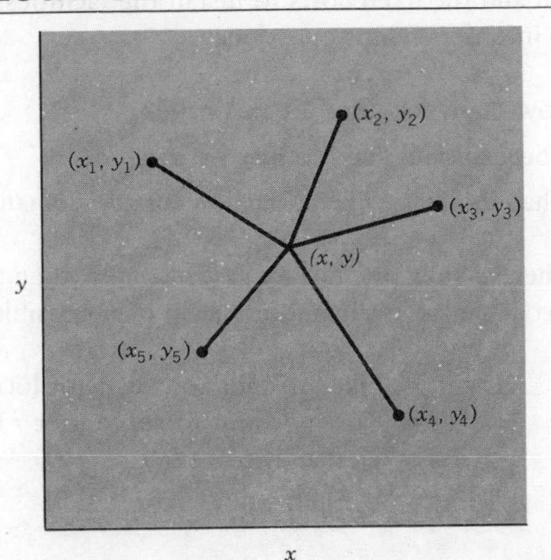

This problem is called the Weber problem in the literature, and a satisfactory procedure for solving it is given in Kuhn and Kuenne (1962). For the special case where all $w_i$s are equal, the minimization of Equation 4 is achieved by locating the facility such that

$$x = \frac{\Sigma x_i}{m}$$

and

$$y = \frac{\Sigma y_i}{m}$$

Some examples of one-facility location problems are the location of a hospital, a fire station, a police station, a power plant, and a warehouse.

Two types of extensions for the single-facility location problem have been examined. One deals with the nature of the objective function. For example, instead of minimizing the sum of the travel costs as in Equation 4, one may minimize the maximum cost borne by any user. A different objective function is minimized if the distance between the facility and the user is measured as the sum of the absolute values of the differences between their abscissae and their ordinates ($|x_i - x| + |y_i - y|$). The second type of extension involves the incorporation of locational constraints that reduce the range of permitted locations. The model can also be extended to incorporate multiple facilities that serve $m$ users. In the next section, we discuss the multifacility location problem when a facility can only be located at one of a number of finite identified points or sites rather than on a continuum of points on a plane.

## Multifacility Location

Suppose there are $m$ users or markets whose locations and demands are known. These demands must be met from a set of facilities that can be located at any of the $n$ identified sites. The objective is to minimize the total cost of production and distribution and the fixed costs to install the facilities. This problem requires answers to three interdependent questions:

1. How many facilities are required?
2. Where should each facility be located?
3. What should be the allocation for the demand of a user to various facilities?

If there is only one facility to be located, then this problem is relatively simple, as total cost can be evaluated for each of $n$ possible locations. Let us define

$F_j$ = Fixed installation costs for locating a facility at site $j$
$c_{ij}$ = Cost per unit to serve user $i$ from the facility at $j$
$D_i$ = Demand for user $i$

The facility is located at the site $j$, which minimizes

$$\text{Total cost} = F_j + \sum_{i=1}^{n} c_{ij} D_i \tag{5}$$

The first component in Equation 5 represents the fixed costs (land, building, taxes, etc.) for installing the facility, and the second component represents the total cost of production and distribution to meet the demand. If the production cost per unit is identical at all locations, then $c_{ij}$ will reflect only the transportation cost per unit for shipments from site $j$ to user $i$.

## DISTRIBUTION METHODS

Another simplification of the general location–allocation problem that is of considerable interest is the simple distribution or transportation problem. In this problem, we assume that the location for facilities are known along with their capacities. The question of interest is to determine how much of each user's demand should be met from each facility so that the total cost of production and distribution is minimized. Although this problem can be formulated as a linear program, specialized procedures called distribution methods can solve it efficiently. We will discuss the distribution methods in some detail and then we will return to the general location and allocation problem.

When the locations of facilities and users are specified, the problem of minimizing total production and distribution costs while meeting the demands for each user is formulated as

$$\text{Min} \sum_{j=1}^{n} \sum_{i=1}^{m} c_{ij} x_{ij} \tag{6}$$

subject to:

$$\sum_{j=1}^{n} x_{ij} = D_i \,, \; i = 1 \text{ to } m \tag{7}$$

$$\sum_{i=1}^{m} x_{ij} \leq U_j \,, \; j = 1 \text{ to } n \tag{8}$$

$$x_{ij} \geq 0 \;, \; i = 1 \text{ to } m, \; j = 1 \text{ to } n \tag{9}$$

Equations 6–9 represent the distribution model where

$c_{ij}$ = Unit cost of production and distribution to serve user $i$ from facility $j$
$x_{ij}$ = Number of units supplied from facility $j$ to user $i$
$D_i$ = Total demand for user $i$
$U_j$ = Total capacity for facility $j$

Equation 6 represents the total cost of production and distribution. Equation 7 ensures that all demand for user $i$ is met. Equation 8 ensures that all shipments from facility $j$ do not exceed its capacity. Finally, all allocations are restricted to be nonnegative by Equation 9. We demonstrate a solution procedure for this problem by means of an example. Efficient computer programs exist for solving these distribution problems. The manual procedure described here provides insights into how allocations can be changed to improve the objective function and a connection with the history of the development of these methods.

## Example Problem

Assume the distribution situation of the Pet Food Company. There are three factories, located in Chicago, Houston, and New York, that produce some identical products. There are five major distribution points that serve various market areas in Atlanta, Buffalo, Cleveland, Denver, and Los Angeles. The three factories have capacities that determine the availability of product, and the market demand in the five major areas determines the requirements to be met. The problem is to allocate available products at the three factory locations to the five distribution points so that demand is met and distribution costs are minimized for the system.

Data for our illustrative problem are shown in Table 18-3. There are 46,000 cases per week available at the Chicago plant, 20,000 at the Houston plant, and 34,000 at the New York plant for a total of 100,000 cases per week of pet food. Demands in the five market areas are indicated in the bottom row of the table and also total 100,000 cases per week. Equality of availability and demand is not a necessary requirement for solution, and this issue is discussed later in this section.

The figures for the units available and the units required are commonly termed the *rim conditions*. Table 18-3 also shows the distribution costs per 1000 cases for all combinations of factories and distribution points. These figures are shown in the small boxes; for example, the distribution cost between the Chicago plant and the Atlanta distribution point is \$18 per 1000 cases. For convenience in notation, the plants are labeled A, B and C, and the distribution points are labeled, V, W, X, Y, and Z. Table 18-3 is called a *transportation table* or a *distribution table.*

### AN INITIAL SOLUTION

We will establish an initial solution in an arbitrary way, ignoring the distribution costs. Beginning in the upper left-hand corner of the transportation table (called the northwest corner), note that A has 46 (times 1000) cases available and V needs 27 (times 1000). We assign the 27 from A to V. (See Table 18-4 where circled numbers represent assigned product; e.g., the 27 in box AV means that 27,000 cases are to go from A to V.) We have not used up A's supply, so we move to the right under column W and assign the maximum possible to the route AW, which is 16. We still have not used up A's supply, so we move to the right under column X and assign the balance of A's supply, 3, to X.

Examining the requirements for X, we note that it has a total requirement of 28, so we drop down to row B and assign the balance of X's requirements, 15, from B's

## TABLE 18-3

## TRANSPORTATION TABLE FOR THE PET FOOD COMPANY (QUANTITIES OF PRODUCT AVAILABLE AT FACTORIES AND REQUIRED AT DISTRIBUTION POINTS AND DISTRIBUTION COSTS PER THOUSAND CASES

| From Factories / To Distr. Points | Atlanta (V) | Buffalo (W) | Cleveland (X) | Denver (Y) | Los Angeles (Z) | Available from Factories (1000) |
|---|---|---|---|---|---|---|
| Chicago (A) | 18 | 16 | 12 | 28 | 54 | 46 |
| Houston (B) | 24 | 40 | 36 | 30 | 42 | 20 |
| New York (C) | 22 | 12 | 16 | 48 | 44 | 34 |
| Required at Distribution Points (1000) | 27 | 16 | 18 | 10 | 29 | 100 |

## TABLE 18-4

## NORTHWEST CORNER INITIAL SOLUTION

| From Factories / To Distr. Points | Atlanta (V) | Buffalo (W) | Cleveland (X) | Denver (Y) | Los Angeles (Z) | Available from Factories (1000) |
|---|---|---|---|---|---|---|
| Chicago (A) | 18 (27) | 16 (16) | 12 (3) | 28 | 54 | 46 |
| Houston (B) | 24 | 40 | 36 (15) | 30 (5) | 42 | 20 |
| New York (C) | 22 | 12 | 16 | 48 (5) | 44 (29) | 34 |
| Required at Distribution Points (1000) | 27 | 16 | 18 | 10 | 29 | 100 |

Total distribution cost

| | |
|---|---|
| AV, 27 × 18 = | $ 486 |
| AW, 16 × 16 = | 256 |
| AX, 3 × 12 = | 36 |
| BX, 15 × 36 = | 540 |
| BY, 5 × 30 = | 150 |
| CY, 5 × 48 = | 240 |
| CZ, 29 × 44 = | 1276 |
| | $2984 |

supply of 20. We then move to the right again and assign the balance of B's supply, 5, to Y. We continue in this way, stair-stepping down the table until all the arbitrary assignments have been made as in Table 18-4. Note that we have seven squares with assignments ($n$ rows + $m$ columns − 1) and eight open squares without assignments. This requirement for ($m + n - 1$) assignments avoids degeneracy, which will be discussed later. Table 18-4 is the northwest corner initial solution.

Methods for obtaining better starting solutions are available. Computer solutions, however, reduce the need to be overly concerned about starting solutions for small to moderate size problems.

### TEST FOR OPTIMALITY

Because the northwest corner solution in Table 18-4 was established arbitrarily, it is not likely to be the best possible solution. Therefore, we need to develop a method for examining each of the open squares in the transportation table to determine if improvements can be made in total distribution costs by shifting some of the units to be shipped to other routes. In making the shifts, we must be sure that any new solution satisfies the supply and demand restrictions shown in the rim conditions of the transportation table.

In evaluating each open square, the following steps are used:

*Step 1.* Determine a closed path, starting at the open square being evaluated and "stepping" from squares with assignments back to the original open square. Right angle turns in this path are permitted only at squares with assignments and at the original open square. Because only the squares at the turning points are considered to be on the closed path, both open and assigned squares may be skipped over.

*Step 2.* Beginning at the square being evaluated, assign a plus sign and then alternate minus and plus signs at the assigned squares on the corners of the path.

*Step 3.* Add the unit cost in the squares with plus signs, and subtract the unit costs in the squares with minus signs. If we are minimizing costs, the result is the net change in cost per unit from the changes made in the assignments. If we are maximizing profits, the result is the net change in profit.

*Step 4.* Repeat steps 1, 2, and 3 for each open square in the transportation table.

Steps 1 and 2 involve assigning a single unit to the open square and then adjusting the shipments in the squares with assignments until all the rim conditions are satisfied.

Step 3 simply calculates the cost (or contribution to profit) that would result from such a modification in the assignments. If we are minimizing costs and if the net changes are all greater than or equal to zero for all the open squares, we have found an optimal solution. If we are maximizing profits and the net changes are less than or equal to zero or all the open squares, we have found an optimal solution.

The application of these steps to open square BV is shown in Table 18-5. In this case, the closed path forms a simple rectangle. The net change in total distribution costs resulting from shifting one unit to route BV is

$$24 - 18 + 12 - 36 = -18$$

**TABLE 18-5**
**EVALUATION OF SQUARE BV FOR POSSIBLE IMPROVEMENT (THE CHANGE IN TOTAL DISTRIBUTION COST RESULTING FROM SHIFTING ONE UNIT TO ROUTE BV IS 24 − 18 + 12 − 36 = −18)**

| From Factories \ To Distr. Points | Atlanta (V) | Buffalo (W) | Cleveland (X) | Denver (Y) | Los Angeles (Z) | Available from Factories (1000) |
|---|---|---|---|---|---|---|
| Chicago (A) | 18; (−) 27 | 16; 16 | 12; (+) 3 | 28; +22 | 54; +52 | 46 |
| Houston (B) | 24; (+) −18 | 40; 0 | 36; 15 (−) | 30; 5 | 42; +16 | 20 |
| New York (C) | 22; −38 | 12; −46 | 16; −38 | 48; 5 | 44; 29 | 34 |
| Required at Distribution Points (1000) | 27 | 16 | 18 | 10 | 29 | 100 |

This value is entered in the bottom left-hand corner of the square BV in Table 18-5. The evaluation of open squares does not always follow a simple rectangular path. For example, the closed path for evaluating square CV is shown in Table 18-6, and the net change in total distribution cost resulting from shifting one unit to route CV is

$$22 - 18 + 12 - 36 + 30 - 48 = -38$$

**TABLE 18-6**
**EVALUATION OF SQUARE CV FOR POSSIBLE IMPROVEMENT (THE CHANGE IN TOTAL DISTRIBUTION COST RESULTING FROM SHIFTING ONE UNIT TO ROUTE CV IS 22 − 18 + 12 − 36 + 30 − 48 = −38)**

| From Factories \ To Distr. Points | Atlanta (V) | Buffalo (W) | Cleveland (X) | Denver (Y) | Los Angeles (Z) | Available from Factories (1000) |
|---|---|---|---|---|---|---|
| Chicago (A) | 18; (−) 27 | 16; 16 | 12; (+) 3 | 28 | 54 | 46 |
| Houston (B) | 24 | 40 | 36; (−) 15 | 30; 5 (+) | 42 | 20 |
| New York (C) | 22; (+) −38 | 12 | 16 | 48; 5 (−) | 44; 29 | 34 |
| Required at Distribution Points (1000) | 27 | 16 | 18 | 10 | 29 | 100 |

The net changes in total distribution cost for all the open squares are shown in Table 18-5 in the lower left-hand corner of each open square.

## IMPROVING THE SOLUTION

Because each negative net change indicates the amount by which the total distribution cost will decrease if one unit is shifted to the route of that cell, we will be guided by these evaluations as indexes of potential improvement. Notice in Table 18-5 that four of the open squares indicate potential improvement, three indicate that costs would increase if units were shifted to those routes, and one indicates that costs would not change if units were shifted to its route. Which change should be made first in determining a new, improved solution? One reasonable rule for small problems and hand solutions is to select the square with the most negative index number when we are minimizing costs. Therefore, we choose square CW.

To improve the solution, we carry out the following steps for square CW:

*Step 1.* Identify again the closed path for the chosen open square, and assign the plus and minus signs around the path as before. Determine the minimum number of units assigned to a square on this path that is marked with a minus sign.

*Step 2.* Add this number to the open square and to all other squares on the path marked with a plus sign. Subtract this number from the squares on the path marked with a minus sign. This step is a simple accounting procedure for observing the restrictions of the rim conditions.

The closed path for open square CW is + CW − AW + AX − BX + BY − CY. The minimum number of units in a square with a minus sign is 5 in CY. Thus, we add 5 units to squares CW, AX, and BY, and we subtract 5 units from squares AW, BX, and CY. This reassignment of units generates a new solution, as shown in Table 18-7.

Taking Table 18-7 as the current solution, we repeat the process, reevaluating all open squares, as shown in Table 18-7. Note that there are now only two open squares with negative index numbers, indicating potential improvement. Following our previous procedure, open square BZ indicates that the largest improvement could be made by shifting assignments to that route.

## AN OPTIMAL SOLUTION

The process is continued until all open squares show no further improvement. At this point, an optimal solution has been obtained and is shown in Table 18-8, in which all the index numbers for open squares are either positive or zero. Alternative optimal solutions also exist. The total distribution cost required by the optimal solution is $2446, which is $538 less than the original northwest corner solution. Although this 18 percent improvement is impressive, we should note that we started with a rather poor initial solution. Better starting solutions can be obtained for simple problems by making initial assignments to the most promising routes while observing the restrictions of the rim conditions and being sure that there are exactly $n + m - 1$ assignments. Solutions with $n + m - 1$ assignments are called

TABLE 18-7
**NEW SOLUTION RESULTING AFTER SHIFTING 5 UNITS TO SQUARE CW (THE NUMBER OF UNITS THAT COULD BE SHIFTED TO CW WAS LIMITED TO 5 BY SQUARE CY IN THE PREVIOUS SOLUTION)**

| From Factories \ To Distr. Points | Atlanta (V) | Buffalo (W) | Cleveland (X) | Denver (Y) | Los Angeles (Z) | Available from Factories (1000) |
|---|---|---|---|---|---|---|
| Chicago (A) | 18 (27) | 16 (11) | 12 (8) | 28 +22 | 54 +6 | 46 |
| Houston (B) | 24 −18 | 40 0 | 36 (10) | 30 (10) | 42 −30 | 20 |
| New York (C) | 22 +8 | 12 (5) | 16 +8 | 48 +46 | 44 (29) | 34 |
| Required at Distribution Points (1000) | 27 | 16 | 18 | 10 | 29 | 100 |

basic solutions, solutions with fewer assignments are called degenerate, and solutions with more than $n + m - 1$ assignments are called nonbasic solutions.

## Unequal Supply and Demand

Now suppose that supply exceeds demand as shown in Table 18-9. The total available supply is still 100,000 cases; however, the aggregate demand at the five distri-

TABLE 18-8
**AN OPTIMAL SOLUTION (EVALUATION OF ALL OPEN SQUARES IN THIS TABLE RESULTS IN NO FURTHER IMPROVEMENT, TOTAL DISTRIBUTION COST = $2446)**

| From Factories \ To Distr. Points | Atlanta (V) | Buffalo (W) | Cleveland (X) | Denver (Y) | Los Angeles (Z) | Available from Factories (1000) |
|---|---|---|---|---|---|---|
| Chicago (A) | 18 (27) | 16 +6 | 12 (18) | 28 (1) | 54 +14 | 46 |
| Houston (B) | 24 +2 | 40 +30 | 36 +22 | 30 (9) | 42 (11) | 20 |
| New York (C) | 22 0 | 12 (16) | 16 0 | 48 +16 | 44 (18) | 34 |
| Required at Distribution Points (1000) | 27 | 16 | 18 | 10 | 29 | 100 |

TABLE 18-9
**DISTRIBUTION TABLE WITH SUPPLY EXCEEDING DEMAND: OPTIMUM SOLUTION**

| From Factories \ To Distr. Points | Atlanta (V) | Buffalo (W) | Cleveland (X) | Denver (Y) | Los Angeles (Z) | Dummy | Available from Factories (1000) |
|---|---|---|---|---|---|---|---|
| Chicago (A) | [18] (25) | [16] 8 | [12] (11) | [28] (10) | [54] 14 | [0] 4 | 46 |
| Houston (B) | [24] 4 | [40] 30 | [36] 22 | [30] 0 | [42] (20) | [0] 2 | 20 |
| New York (C) | [22] 0 | [12] (15) | [16] (7) | [48] 16 | [44] (7) | [0] (5) | 34 |
| Required at Distribution Points (1000) | 25 | 15 | 18 | 10 | 27 | 5 | 100 |

bution points totals only 95,000 cases. This situation can be handled in the problem by creating a dummy distribution point to receive the extra 5000 cases. The nonexistent distribution point is assigned zero distribution costs as shown because the product will never be shipped. The optimal solution then assigns 95,000 of the 100,000 available units in the most economical way to the five real distribution points and assigns the balance to the dummy distribution point. Table 18-9 shows an optimal distribution plan for this situation.

When demand exceeds supply, we can resort to a modification of the same technique. We create a dummy factory to take up the slack. Again zero distribution costs are assigned to the dummy factory because the product will never be shipped. The solution then assigns the available product to the distribution points in the most economical way, indicating which distribution points should receive "short" shipments, so that the total distribution costs are minimized.

## Degeneracy in Distribution Problems

Another aspect of the mechanics of developing a solution is the condition known as degeneracy. Degeneracy occurs in distribution problems when, in shifting assignments to take advantage of a potential improvement, more than one of the existing assignments goes to zero. Degeneracy also occurs if an initial solution does not meet the $m + n - 1$ requirement for the number of allocations.

We can resolve the degeneracy, however, by regarding one of the two squares in which allocations have disappeared as an allocated square with an extremely small allocation, which we will call an $\epsilon$ (epsilon) allocation.

Conceptually, we will regard the $\epsilon$ allocation as infinitesimally small, so that it does not affect the totals indicated in the rim. The $\epsilon$ allocation, however, does make it possible to meet the $m + n - 1$ restriction on the number of allocations so that evaluation paths may be established for all open squares. The $\epsilon$ allocation is simply manipulated as though it were no different from the other allocations.

## LOCATION–ALLOCATION DECISION: AN EXAMPLE

The Pet Food Company has experienced increasing demand for its dog food and cat food products, particularly in the South and Southwest. As a result of this market expansion, the company is now considering the construction of a new plant with a capacity of 20,000 cases per week.

Surveys have narrowed the choice to three general locations: Denver, Los Angeles, and Salt Lake City. Because of differences in local wage rates and other costs, the estimated production costs per thousand cases are different, as indicated in Table 18-10. The distribution costs from each of the proposed plants to the five distribution points and the new estimated market demands in each area are also shown in Table 18-10. The production costs at the existing plants in Chicago, Houston, and New York are $270, $265, and $275 per thousand cases, respectively.

These data are summarized in the three distribution tables shown in Table 18-11, one for each of the three possible configurations that include the new plant at Denver, Los Angeles, or Salt Lake City. Because production costs vary in the alternative locations, we must minimize the sum of production costs plus distribu-

TABLE 18-10
**PRODUCTION AND DISTRIBUTION COSTS, PLANT CAPACITIES, AND MARKET DEMANDS FOR THE PET FOOD COMPANY, EXISTING AND PROPOSED PLANTS**

| | *Distribution Costs per 1000 Cases to These Markets Centers* | | | | | Normal Plant Capacity, 1000 Cases per Week | Production Cost per 1000 Cases |
|---|---|---|---|---|---|---|---|
| | Atlanta (V) | Buffalo (W) | Cleveland (X) | Denver (Y) | Los Angeles (Z) | | |
| Existing plants | | | | | | | |
| Chicago (A) | 18 | 16 | 12 | 28 | 54 | 46 | 270 |
| Houston (B) | 24 | 40 | 36 | 30 | 42 | 20 | 265 |
| New York (C) | 22 | 12 | 16 | 48 | 44 | 34 | 275 |
| Proposed plants | | | | | | | |
| Denver (D) | 40 | 40 | 35 | 2 | 31 | 20 | 262 |
| Los Angeles (E) | 57 | 70 | 64 | 31 | 3 | 20 | 270 |
| Salt Lake (F) | 50 | 50 | 46 | 14 | 19 | 20 | 260 |
| Market demand 1000 cases per week | 30 | 18 | 20 | 15 | 37 | | |

TABLE 18-11

**OPTIMUM PRODUCTION—DISTRIBUTION SOLUTIONS FOR THREE PROPOSED LOCATIONS FOR THE ADDITIONAL PET FOOD COMPANY PLANT**

### *(a)* NEW PLANT AT DENVER

| From Factories \ To Distr. Points | Atlanta (V) | Buffalo (W) | Cleveland (X) | Denver (Y) | Los Angeles (Z) | Available from Factories (1000) |
|---|---|---|---|---|---|---|
| Chicago (A) | 288 (30) | 286 | 282 (16) | 298 | 324 | 46 |
| Houston (B) | 289 | 305 | 301 | 295 | 307 (20) | 20 |
| New York (C) | 297 | 287 (18) | 291 (4) | 323 | 319 (12) | 34 |
| New Plant at Denver | 302 | 302 | 297 | 264 (15) | 293 (5) | 20 |
| Required at Distribution Points (1000) | 30 | 18 | 20 | 15 | 37 | 120 |

Production cost = $32,310
Distribution cost = 2,565
Total $34,875

### *(b)* NEW PLANT AT LOS ANGELES

| From Factories \ To Distr. Points | Atlanta (V) | Buffalo (W) | Cleveland (X) | Denver (Y) | Los Angeles (Z) | Available from Factories (1000) |
|---|---|---|---|---|---|---|
| Chicago (A) | 288 (26) | 286 | 282 (20) | 298 | 324 | 46 |
| Houston (B) | 289 | 305 | 301 | 295 (15) | 307 (5) | 20 |
| New York (C) | 297 (4) | 287 (18) | 291 | 323 | 319 (11) | 34 |
| New Plant at Los Angeles | 327 | 340 | 334 | 301 | 273 (20) | 20 |
| Required at Distribution Points (1000) | 30 | 18 | 20 | 15 | 37 | 120 |

Production cost = $32,470
Distribution cost = 1,941
Total $34,411

TABLE 18-11
***(Continued)***

**(c) NEW PLANT AT SALT LAKE CITY**

| From Factories \ To Distr. Points | Atlanta (V) | Buffalo (W) | Cleveland (X) | Denver (Y) | Los Angeles (Z) | Available from Factories (1000) |
|---|---|---|---|---|---|---|
| Chicago (A) | 288 (30) | 286 | 282 (16) | 298 | 324 | 46 |
| Houston (B) | 289 | 305 | 301 | 295 (15) | 307 (5) | 20 |
| New York (C) | 297 | 287 (18) | 291 (4) | 323 | 319 (12) | 34 |
| New Plant at Salt Lake City | 310 | 310 | 306 | 274 | 279 (20) | 20 |
| Required at Distribution Points (1000) | 30 | 18 | 20 | 15 | 37 | 120 |

Production cost = $32,270
Distribution cost = 2,580
Total $34,850

tion costs. For example, the typical item of cost represented by the Chicago–Atlanta square in Table 18-11 is made up of the production cost at Chicago of $270 plus the distribution cost from Chicago to Atlanta of $18 from Table 18-10 or $270 + 18 = $288 per week. Similarly, for the proposed plant at Salt Lake City, the cost shown in the Salt Lake City–Buffalo square in Table 18-11 is the production cost at Salt Lake City of $260 plus the Salt Lake City to Buffalo distribution cost of $50, or $260 + $50 = $310 per week.

The important question now is: Which location will yield the lowest production plus distribution costs for the system of plants and distribution centers?

To answer this question, we solve the three linear programming distribution problems, one for each combination. Table 18-11 shows the optimum solution for each configuration. In this instance, the objective cost factors favor the Los Angeles location. The Los Angeles location results in the lowest production plus distribution cost of $34,411 per week. The Los Angeles location is $439 per week (almost $23,000 per year) less costly than the Salt Lake City location and $464 per week (more than $24,000 per year) less costly than the Denver location. The Los Angeles location is less costly because the lower distribution costs more than compensate for the higher production costs, as compared with the other two alternatives.

The combined production–distribution analysis, then, provides input concerning the objective factor costs (*OFC*) in the multiattribute location model discussed previously. The subjective factors would be evaluated as before, and a final decision would be based on both objective and subjective factors and the relative weights placed on them.

## GENERAL LOCATION–ALLOCATION MODEL

In the pet food example, we assumed that only one plant will be constructed at one of the three locations. For this problem we solved three linear programming distribution problems—one for each location—and recommended the location that produced the minimum total cost. In general, however, the number of facilities to be installed are also variable. There may be $n$ potential sites and one, two and so on up to $n$ facilities can be located to serve $m$ users. We can indeed solve distribution problems corresponding to each possible combination of number and location of facilities. This will, however, lead to impractically large numbers of distribution problems $(2^n - 1)$ for even a moderate $n$. The general model is given by

$$\text{Minimize} \sum_{j=1}^{n} \sum_{i=1}^{m} c_{ij} x_{ij} + \sum_{j=1}^{n} F_j Y_j \tag{10}$$

subject to

$$\sum_{j=1}^{n} x_{ij} = D_i, \; i = 1 \text{ to } m \tag{11}$$

$$\sum_{i=1}^{m} x_{ij} = U_j Y_j, \; j = 1 \text{ to } n \tag{12}$$

$$Y_j = 0 \text{ or } 1, \; j = 1 \text{ to } n, \text{ and } x_{ij} \geq 0 \text{ for all } i \text{ and } j \tag{13}$$

The objective function in Equation 10 consists of the production and distribution costs and the fixed costs of locating a plant. Equation 11 ensures that all demand for each user is satisfied. Equation 12 ensures that the all supply from a facility does not exceed its capacity. Equation 13 defines $Y_j$ to be 1 if a facility is located at site $j$ and 0 otherwise. All allocations $x_{ij}$ are constrained to be nonnegative.

An efficient procedure for solving the general location–allocation problem is Bender's decomposition (see Erlenkotter, 1978). We observe that if we fix the number and location of facilities, then we have a standard distribution or transportaton problem. The efficient procedures exploit this characteristic in obtaining the solution for the original problem.

## OFFSHORE LOCATIONS

The lure usually held out to manufacturers to locate offshore in foreign countries has been the relatively cheap labor available in some areas. Although rapidly increasing wages in many foreign countries have changed this situation in recent years, this argument still can be made for many foreign areas.

For a particular manufacturer, the important question is: *Is a net advantage available in a foreign location?* There are several important reasons why there may not be.

Wage levels themselves are not the important parameter; rather, labor costs will determine the advantage or disadvantage. Wages can be high and labor costs can be simultaneously low. The equating factor is productivity. Although the American worker is paid a relatively large wage rate, the relatively large capital investment per worker multiplies his or her efforts through special tools, mechanization, and automation.

Of course, the temptation is to assume that we can couple the advantage of lower wages with high productivity by using the same levels of mechanization and managerial practice abroad. The difference in basic production economics in these two contrasting situations must be noted. Because labor is inexpensive relative to capital in some foreign locations, we may find it wise to use relatively more labor and less expensive machinery in these situations. The resulting productivity and final labor costs thus would be more in line with those usually achieved in the foreign environment. The most economic manufacturing methods and techniques are not necessarily those with the greatest possible mechanization but are those that, for a given situation, strike a balance between the costs of labor and capital costs.

There are many costs in addition to labor to consider. If there is a net labor cost advantage, will it be counterbalanced by higher costs of materials, fuel and power, equipment, credit, transportation, and so on?

Studies of production costs in the United States and abroad, involving companies with both domestic and foreign operations, have indicated considerable variability in the relative advantage or disadvantage of foreign locations. Apparently, there are some products, industries, or companies that are favored by the structure of foreign costs; however, these same conditions are unfavorable to others. Products in industries that have a relatively high labor content seemed to have lower costs abroad. On the other hand, industries whose cost structures are dominated by materials, energy, and capital have higher costs abroad.

## WAREHOUSE LOCATION

Whereas industrial plant location is often oriented toward dominant factors, such as raw material sources or even the personal preferences of owners, warehouse location is definitely distribution oriented. Although the particular site choice will be affected by subjective factors, such as those included in the multiattribute model, the focus of interest in the warehouse location problem is on minimizing distribution costs. One reason why warehouse location is interesting is that the problem occurs more frequently than plant location and can be evaluated by objective criteria.

Earlier efforts in logistics and distribution management attempted to define the most appropriate customer zones for existing warehouses. These graphical approaches centered on the determination of lines of constant delivery costs. Since the 1950s, however, there have been a variety of attempts to deal with warehouse location as a variable to be determined using mathematical programming, heuristic and simulation approaches, and branch and bound methods.

The general nature of the problem is to determine warehouse location within the constraints of demand in customer zones in such a way that distribution cost is minimized for a given customer service level. Warehouse capacity is determined as a part of the solution. Customer service is defined in terms of delivery days, thus limiting the number of warehouses that can service a given zone. Distribution costs are the sum of transportation costs, customer service costs, and warehouse operating costs. The warehouse operating costs break down into costs that vary with volume, fixed costs of leasing or depreciation, and fixed payroll and fixed indirect costs.

First, let us dispose of the possibility of calculating the distribution costs of all warehouse–customer zone combinations and simply selecting the combination that has the minimum cost property. The impracticality of the enumeration approach is discussed by Khumawala and Whybark (1971).

Consider the following characteristics of a medium-sized manufacturing firm that distributes only in the United States:

1. 5000 customers or demand centers
2. 100 potential warehouse locations
3. 5 producing plants
4. 16 products
5. 4 shipping classes
6. 100 transportation rate variables involving direction of shipment, product, geographical area, minimum costs, rate breaks, and so forth.

One single evaluation can be made by making an assignment of customers to warehouses for each of the product lines and then using a computer to search for the minimum freight rates for that assignment. This would determine the total cost of that particular warehouse location alternative. Each other assignment would be evaluated in the same way until all were complete and the least cost alternative found. Although this seems feasible, the company described above has over 12 million alternate distribution systems. Even if the evaluation of each alternative could be performed in just three seconds, the evaluation of all alternatives would take over one year of computer time at 24 hours per day.

Since the "brute force" approach is impractical, we must consider techniques that make some trade-off with reality through simplifying assumptions. We will discuss three practical approaches that have been used in large-scale applications.

## Esso—The Branch and Bound Technique

Effroymson and Ray (1966) developed a model that involves a procedure using branch and bound methods and linear programming to produce optimal solutions with reasonable computing time. The location system was applied in the Esso Company to several location problems involving 4 plants, 50 warehouses, and 200 customer zones. The procedure involves the application of rules for including or excluding warehouse locations, depending on whether or not their competitive savings cover their fixed costs of operation. Linear programming is used at points in the procedure to compute lower bound costs. By following out the branches, computing upper and lower bound costs, warehouse locations can be either definitely included in the optimum solution or excluded, leading to the final optimum solution. An example of the procedure together with a case history is given in Atkins and Shriver (1968).

## Hunt–Wesson Foods, Inc.—An Application of Mathematical Programming

Hunt–Wesson Foods, Inc., produces several hundred distinguishable commodities at 14 locations and distributes nationally through 12 distribution centers. The company decided to undertake a study of its distribution system, particularly the location of distribution warehouses. Five changes in location were indicated involving the movement of existing distribution centers as well as the opening of new ones. The cost reductions resulting from the study were estimated to be in the low seven figures.

Geoffrion and Graves (1974) formulated the Hunt–Wesson distribution problem in such a way that the multicommodity linear programming subproblem decomposes into as many independent classical transportation problems as there are commodities. The resulting problem structure included 17 commodity classes, 14 plants, 45 possible distribution center sites, and 121 customer zones. Thus, three levels of distribution were accounted for—plants, distribution centers or warehouses, and customer zones.

Demand for each commodity in each customer zone was known. Demand was satisfied by shipping via regional distribution centers (warehouses), with each customer zone being assigned exclusively to a warehouse. Upper and lower limits were set on the annual capacity of each warehouse. Warehouse location sites were selected to minimize total distribution costs, which were composed of fixed plus variable cost components.

The Hunt–Wesson warehouse location study indicates that the cost reductions possible are of great significance. Geoffrion and Graves state that similar results were obtained in an application for a major manufacturer of hospital supplies with 5 commodity classes, 3 plants, 67 possible warehouse locations, and 127 customer zones.

## Ralston Purina—An Application of Simulation

Markland (1973) applied a computer simulation methodology in evaluating field warehouse location configurations and inventory levels for the Ralston Purina Company.

The basic structure of product flow is a multilevel, multiproduct distribution system involving plant warehouses, field warehouses, wholesalers, and, finally, retail grocers. Shipments from the five warehouses may go to other plant warehouses, to field warehouses, or to wholesalers. Inventories are maintained at the plant warehouse, field warehouse, and wholesaler levels. Also, shipments may go from any of the five field warehouses to any of the 29 demand analyses areas representing the wholesale level or to any of the other field warehouses.

### MODEL STRUCTURE

The distribution system was modeled in the basic format of system dynamics as a dynamic feedback control sysem where product flow is the main control variable. Product flow and inventory level equations were written to represent all flow combinations and inventory levels at plant and field warehouses. Constraints on maximum inventory levels at plant and field warehouses as well as constraints on maximum plant production capacity were established.

### SAMPLE RESULTS

The system was simulated for six different field warehouse configurations and for different inventory service levels. The number of field warehouses was varied from zero to the existing five. Thirty-two field warehouse location patterns were tested, involving combinations of warehouses, using a procedure of dropping warehouses from the existing pattern. In the example given, Ralston Purina saved $132,000 per year by consolidating field warehouses from five to three. The proposed elimination of intermediate warehouses as a policy would have increased costs by $240,000 per year compared with the optimal policy of using only three field warehouses. In addition to the preceding result, it was found that an 85 percent inventory service level minimized distribution cost.

The three warehouse location methodologies discussed are apparently all quite powerful and capable of dealing with problems of practical size. The real advantage of the simulation methodology is that nonlinear costs can be represented easily and that the other features, such as inventory policy, can be included. The advantages of the Hunt–Wesson application are in its capability for handling extremely large-scale systems and in its representing the "storage in transit" costs that are important for firms such as Hunt–Wesson and Ralston Purina. Finally, the branch and bound procedure is efficient in terms of computing time.

## LOCATION OF SERVICE FACILITIES

For location analysis, services can be distinguished into two categories: *fixed services* and *delivered services*. The fixed services are consumed at the facilities where they are supplied. Some examples of fixed services are those supplied by health service, banks, theaters, and food outlets. In contrast, the delivered services, such as sanitation and emergency services (police, fire, and ambulance), are consumed where they are demanded.

There are often multiple objectives that must be considered simultaneously in determining the location of a service facility. In operations research based approaches, the total access cost often represents the objective function for the fixed services and the total delivery cost for the delivered services. The costs can be expressed in money, time, distance, or some other appropriate units.

In delivered services, both the location and the designation of response areas for each facility need to be determined. Emergency services, such as ambulances, fire protection, and police protection, require rapid response. The random nature of the timing and frequency of calls for service, in combination with varying times for response and service, place the problem within the general framework of a waiting line situation. But the managers of such systems would have to provide an extremely large and expensive capacity in order to meet the response standards imposed if facilities were provided for peak demand. These facilities would necessarily be idle most of the time. Since queuing of calls to any great extent is not acceptable, deployment strategies have been used to provide service at reasonable cost. Thus, locations become mobile for ambulances and police protection through two-way communication systems. Instead of always returning to a home base, ambulances and patrol cars may be redeployed in transit. In fire protection systems, units may be relocated (redeployed) when a major fire occurs in order to minimize expected response time if another major fire were to break out.

## IMPLICATIONS FOR THE MANAGER

The emphasis in industrial plant location is to minimize costs; however, we are speaking of longer run costs, and many intangible factors may influence future costs. Thus, a manager is faced with making trade-offs between tangible costs in the present and a myriad of subjective factors that may influence future costs. The multiattribute model provides a framework for the integration of objective and subjective factors using preference theory to assign weights to factors in a consistent manner.

Multiplant location is influenced by existing locations because each location considered must be placed in economic perspective with the existing plants and market areas. Each alternative location considered results in a different allocation of capacity to markets, and the manager's objective is to minimize costs for the system as a whole.

Although it is often true that plant location (particularly the location of individual versus multiple plants) is dominated by the owner's or manager's personal preference for location, warehouse location is dominated by the cost criterion. Here, the managerial objective of minimizing distribution costs can be enhanced considerably through the use of well-developed computer-assisted distribution planning systems.

The very nature of service operations requires a manager to seek locations based on an analysis of the location of users. Thus, whereas warehouses and many industrial plant locations are distribution oriented, the location of service operations is user oriented. Service facilities must be decentralized and relatively local in nature in order to bring the service rendered to the users. The bases on which locations in relation to users are chosen depend largely on the nature of the system.

## REVIEW QUESTIONS

1. In the concepts of locational choice, what is meant by a location oriented toward a technical requirement? Give examples.
2. In locational choice, under what conditions must the criterion be maximum profit? Maximum revenue? Minimum relevant costs?
3. In the multiattribute location model, how is a critical factor weighted? An objective factor?
4. In the multiattribute location model, what is the rationale for weighting subjective factors?
5. In the multiattribute location model, how are the relative weights between objective and subjective factors determined in the overall location problem? Are location choices sensitive to this relative weighting?
6. How can differences in capital expenditure requirements between locations be traded off against differences in variable costs?
7. How is the problem of locating a single plant different from that of locating an additional plant in an existing system of production facilities?
8. Define the warehouse location problem.

## PROBLEMS

9. A company has factories at A, B, and C, which supply warehouses at D, E, F, and G. Monthly factory capacities are 70, 90, and 115, respectively. Monthly warehouse requirements are 50, 60, 70, and 95, respectively. Unit shipping costs are as follows:

| | *To* | | | |
|---|---|---|---|---|
| From | D | E | F | G |
| A | $17 | $20 | $13 | $12 |
| B | $15 | $21 | $26 | $25 |
| C | $15 | $14 | $15 | $17 |

Determine the optimum distribution for this company to minimize shipping costs.

10. A company has factories at A, B, and C, which supply warehouses, D, E, F, and G. Monthly factory capacities are 300, 400, and 500, respectively. Monthly warehouse requirements are 200, 240, 280, and 340, respectively. Unit shipping costs are as follows:

| From | To D | E | F | G |
|---|---|---|---|---|
| A | $ 7 | $ 9 | $ 9 | $ 6 |
| B | $ 6 | $10 | $12 | $ 8 |
| C | $ 9 | $ 8 | $10 | $14 |

Determine the optimum distribution for this company to minimize shipping costs.

11. A company has factories at A, B, and C, which supply warehouses at D, E, F, and G. Monthly factory capacities are 250, 300, and 200, respectively, for regular production. If overtime production is utilized, the capacities can be increased to 320, 380 and 210, respectively. Incremental unit overtime costs are $5, $6, and $8 per unit, respectively. The current warehouse requirements are 170, 190, 130, and 180, respectively. Unit shipping costs between the factories and warehouses are

| From | To D | E | F | G |
|---|---|---|---|---|
| A | $ 8 | $ 9 | $10 | $11 |
| B | $ 6 | $12 | $ 9 | $ 7 |
| C | $ 4 | $13 | $ 3 | $12 |

Determine the optimum production–distribution for this company to minimize cost.

12. A Company with factories at A, B, C, and D supplies warehouses at E, F, G, and H. Monthly factory capacities are 100, 80, 120, and 90, respectively, for regular production. If overtime production is utilized, the capacities can be increased to 120, 110, 160, and 140, respectively. Incremental unit overtime costs are $5, $2, $3, and $4, respectively. Present incremental profits per unit, excluding shipping costs, are $14, $9, $16, and $27, respectively, for regular production. The current monthly warehouse requirements are 110, 70, 160, and 130, respectively. Unit shipping costs are as follows:

| From | To E | F | G | H |
|---|---|---|---|---|
| A | $ 3 | $ 4 | $ 5 | $ 7 |
| B | $ 2 | $ 9 | $ 6 | $ 8 |
| C | $ 4 | $ 3 | $ 8 | $ 5 |
| D | $ 6 | $ 5 | $ 4 | $ 6 |

Determine the optimum production–distribution for this company. (Hint: This problem requires that you maximize profits.) What simple change in the procedures makes it possible to maximize rather than minimize?

# SITUATIONS

## A New Warehouse

13. A company supplies its products from three factories and five distribution warehouses. The company has been expanding its sales efforts westward and in the South and Southwest. It has been supplying these markets from existing distribution centers, but current volume in the new locations has raised the question of the advisability of a new warehouse location.

    Three possible locations are suggested because of market concentrations: Denver, Houston, and New Orleans. Data concerning capacities, demands, and costs are given in Table 18-12. Based on these data, which warehouse location should be chosen? What additional criteria might be invoked to help make a choice? How should management decide whether or not to build the new warehouse or to continue to supply from the existing warehouses? Hint: Three linear programming distribution tables must be formulated, solved, and compared.

## Should a Plant Be Closed?

14. A company has three plants located in Detroit; Hammond, Indiana; and Mobile, Alabama that distribute to five distribution centers located at Milwaukee; Cleveland; Cincinnati; Erie, Pennsylvania; and Mobile, Alabama. Table 18-13 shows distribution costs per unit, together with data on production costs at regular and overtime, fixed costs when the plants are operating and when they are shut down, plant capacities at regular time and the additional output available at overtime, and market demands.

    The problem facing the company is that the demand for their products has

TABLE 18-12
**PRODUCTION COSTS, DISTRIBUTION COSTS, PLANT CAPACITIES, AND MARKET DEMANDS FOR SITUATION 13**

| To Distribution Center | *Distribution Costs per Pair, Handling, Warehousing, and Freight* | | | | | | | | | |
|---|---|---|---|---|---|---|---|---|---|---|
| | *Existing Warehouses* | | | | | *Proposed New Warehouses* | | | Normal Weekly Capacity Pairs | Unit Production Cost |
| From Plants | Atlanta | Buffalo | Cincinnati | Cleveland | Milwaukee | Denver | Houston | New Orleans | | |
| Atlanta | $0.27 | $0.46 | $0.43 | $0.45 | $0.48 | $0.65 | $0.58 | $0.55 | 25,000 | $2.62 |
| Chicago | 0.49 | 0.48 | 0.42 | 0.44 | 0.32 | 0.50 | 0.54 | 0.60 | 20,000 | 2.68 |
| Detroit | 0.50 | 0.38 | 0.41 | 0.36 | 0.42 | 0.55 | 0.60 | 0.65 | 27,000 | 2.70 |
| Forecast: weekly market demand, pairs | 8000 | 15,000 | 11,000 | 13,000 | 9000 | 16,000 | 16,000 | 16,000 | | |

TABLE 18-13
**DISTRIBUTION COSTS, PRODUCTION COSTS, FIXED COSTS, PLANT CAPACITIES, AND MARKET DEMANDS FOR SITUATION 14**

| | *Distribution Costs per Unit* | | | | | | | *Fixed Costs* | |
|---|---|---|---|---|---|---|---|---|---|
| From Plants | Milwaukee | Cleveland | Cincinnati | Erie | Mobile | Normal Weekly Capacity, Units | Unit Production Cost | When Operating | When Shut Down |
| Detroit—reg. | $0.50 | $0.44 | $0.49 | $0.46 | $0.56 | 27,000 | $2.80 | $14,000 | $6000 |
| Detroit—OT | | | | | | 7,000 | 3.52 | | |
| Hammond—reg. | 0.40 | 0.52 | 0.50 | 0.56 | 0.57 | 20,000 | 2.78 | 12,000 | 5000 |
| Hammond—OT | | | | | | 5,000 | 3.48 | | |
| Mobile—reg. | 0.56 | 0.53 | 0.51 | 0.54 | 0.35 | 25,000 | 2.72 | 15,000 | 7500 |
| Mobile—OT | | | | | | 6,000 | 3.42 | | |
| Forecast: weekly market demand, units | 9000 | 13,000 | 11,000 | 15,000 | 8000 | | | | |

fallen somewhat owing to an economic recession. The forecasts indicate that the company cannot expect rapid recovery from the demand levels shown in Table 18-13. The company is considering the possibility of closing a plant, but it is also quite sensitive to the impact of such an action on employee, union, and community relationships. The nature of its products requires semiskilled personnel for a substantial fraction of the labor force in each plant.

a. What configuration of production plants operating and product distribution system would be most economical?
b. How do you, as the manager of this operation, trade off the economic advantages of minimum cost operation for the recession period against the subjective factors? What decision should you make as manager?

Hint: Four linear programming distribution tables must be formulated, solved, and compared, one with all plants operating, and one each with one of the plants shut down and capacity being met by the other two through overtime, if necessary.

## Woods of Grand Rapids in North Carolina

15. The Woods Furniture Company of Grand Rapids is an old-line producer of quality wood furniture. The company is still located at the original plant site in a complex of buildings and additions to buildings. The plant is bursting at the seams again and is in need of further expansion. There is no room left for expansion at the old site, so a variety of alternatives has been considered in and around Grand Rapids. The final alternatives include the removal of all rough mill operations to a second site in town and the building of an entirely new plant on available property about five miles outside of town.

At that point, the treasurer comes to the president with a deal she has uncovered through a contract with a North Carolina wood supplier. The town of Lancaster, North Carolina, is anxious to bring in new industry and is willing to make locating there very attractive. After considerable discussion, it is agreed that Woods should at least listen to a proposal. It turns out that the inducements are substantial. They include a free site large enough for Woods' operations, plus options to buy adjacent land for expansion at an attractive price within five years, no city taxes for five years, the building of an access road to the property, and the provision of all utilities to the site at no cost.

After hearing the proposal, Woods' officers retire to an executive committee meeting. In a burst of enthusiasm, the treasurer moves that the proposal be accepted.

a. What additional information should Woods obtain in order to evaluate the proposal?

b. How should the Woods Company make the location decision?

c. Should Woods accept the proposal from the Town of Lancaster, North Carolina?

## The Brown–Gibson Model at Pumpo Pump

16. The Pumpo Pump Company is current located in the industrial district of a large city, and several problems have led to the decision to relocate. First and most important, the present site is old and inefficient, and there is no room left for easy expansion. A contributing factor is high labor rates, which translate almost directly into high labor costs in the products.

The company has been able to operate with an independent union, and the president feels that relationships have been excellent. Recently, there has been a great deal of pressure for the union to affiliate with the Teamsters. Although this is not the major reason for moving, the president hopes that a carefully planned move may avoid future labor problems, which he feels would have an adverse effect on the company. As the search for a new site continues, the president seems to place more and more emphasis on this labor relations factor.

The search has finally narrowed to four cities, and comparative data are shown in Table 18-14. Objective factor costs that can be measured and that seem to be affected by alternative locations are shown in Table 18-14*a*. The president is surprised by the range in these costs, city D having costs 1.9 times those of city A.

Seven subjective factors have been isolated as having importance, and the search staff has made a preliminary rating of each factor (see Table 18-14*b*). The first six factors were rated on a scale of "excellent, plentiful, very good, good, adequate, or fair." The seventh factor, union activity, was rated "active, significant, moderate, or negligible."

When the summary data were presented to the president, he was impressed, but he expressed concern about how to equate the various objective and subjec-

TABLE 18-14
**(*a*) OBJECTIVE FACTOR COSTS, MILLIONS OF DOLLARS PER YEAR AND (*b*) SUBJECTIVE FACTORS FOR FOUR SITES FOR THE PUMPO PUMP COMPANY**

| | *Objective Factors* | | | | | | | |
|---|---|---|---|---|---|---|---|---|
| | Labor | Transportation | Real Estate Taxes | Fuel | State Taxes | Electric Power | Water | Total Objective Factor Costs |
| City A | 1.50 | 0.60 | 0.03 | 0.04 | 0.02 | 0.04 | 0.02 | 2.25 |
| City B | 1.60 | 0.70 | 0.05 | 0.06 | 0.04 | 0.07 | 0.03 | 2.55 |
| City C | 1.85 | 0.60 | 0.06 | 0.06 | 0.05 | 0.05 | 0.03 | 2.70 |
| City D | 3.45 | 0.50 | 0.10 | 0.06 | 0.08 | 0.06 | 0.05 | 4.30 |

(*a*)

| | *Subjective Factors* | | | | | | |
|---|---|---|---|---|---|---|---|
| | Labor Supply | Type of Labor | Attitude | Appearance | Transportation | Recreation | Union Activity |
| City A | Adequate | Good | Good | Fair | Good | Good | Significant |
| City B | Plentiful | Excellent | Very good | Good | Very good | Very good | Negligible |
| City C | Plentiful | Excellent | Very good | Good | Good | Very good | Negligible |
| City D | Plentiful | Excellent | Good | Good | Very good | Very good | Active |

(*b*)

tive factors and requested further study. The search staff has decided to use the multiattribute location model.

a. Compute the objective factor measure (*OFM*) using Equation 2.
b. Compute the subjective factor decision weights ($SFW_k$), the relative weights to be assigned to each subjective factor. In order to do this, allocate 100 chips among the subjective factors. The number of chips assigned to a factor reflects its relative importance. The subjective factor decision weight is simply number of chips allocated to the factor divided by 100.
c. Determine site evaluations (*SW*) for each factor. The determination of site evaluations for each factor requires a rating procedure. Ratings of each site for each subjective factor must be made, one factor at a time. The data rating each factor for each site given in Table 18-14*b* serve as a guide for the weighting process. The result of this step is a table that gives the site evaluations for each subjective factor; that is, a 7 by 4 table of 28 site evaluations.
d. Compute the subjective factor measure (*SFM*) for each of the four sites using Equation 3. For each site, *SFM* is the sum of the successive multiplication of the factor weights determined previously by the site evaluations for each factor. For each site, there are seven such multiplications that produce the *SFM* for that site.

e. Compute the final location measure (*LM*) for each site. In order to do this, you must decide on the proportion of the decision weight that you wish to place on objective factors. This is a judgmental process, but you should be able to justify why you have chosen a given objective factor decision weight, $X$. Given the selection of a value of $X$, the final location measures are calculated using Equation 1.

f. How sensitive is the final decision as indicated by the *LM*s to variation in the objective factor decision weight, $X$? If the value you have selected for $X$ were to change slightly, would the location selected by the model change?

g. Given the results of the multiattribute model for the Pumpo Pump Company, what decision do you think should be made? Are you satisfied that the model has allowed you to make the necessary trade-offs among objective and subjective factors and that your values (the decision maker's) have been properly and effectively represented in the trade-off process?

# REFERENCES


Atkins, R. J., and R. H. Shriver, "New Approach to Facilities Location," *Harvard Business Review.* May–June 1968, pp. 70–79.

Brown, P. A., and D. F. Gibson, "A Quantified Model for Facility Site Selection—Application to a Multipoint Location Problem," *AIEE Transactions,* 4, March 1972, pp. 1–10.

Effroymson, M. A., and T. A. Ray, "A Branch-Bound Algorithm for Plant Location," *Operations Research, 14,* May–June 1966, pp. 361–368.

Eppen, G. D., and F. J. Gould, *Introductory Management Science,* Prentice-Hall, Englewood Cliffs, N.J., 1984.

Erlenkotter, D. E., "A Dual-Based Procedure for Incapacitated Facility Location," *Operations Research, 26,* 1978, pp. 992–1009.

Francis, R. L., and J. A. White, *Facility Layout and Location: An Analytical Approach,* Prentice-Hall, Englewood Cliffs, N.J., 1974.

Geoffrion, A. M., and G. W. Graves, "Multicommodity Distribution System Design by Benders Decomposition," *Management Science, 20*(5), January 1974, pp. 822–844.

Hansen, P., D. Peeters, and J. F. Thisse, "Public Facility Location Models: A Selective Survey," in *Locational Analysis of Public Facilities.* J. F. Thisse and H. G. Zoller (eds.), North-Holland Publishing Company, Amsterdam, 1983.

Khumawala, B. M., and D. C. Whybark, "A Comparison of Some Recent Warehouse Location Techniques," *The Logistics Review, 7,* 1971.

Krajewski, L. J., and H. E. Thompson, *Management Science: Quantitative Methods in Concepts,* Wiley, New York, 1981.

Kuhn, H. W., and R. E. Kuenne, "An Efficient Algorithm for the Numerical Solution of the Generalized Weber Problem in Spatial Economics," *Journal of Regional Science, 4,* 1962, pp. 21–33.

Markland, R. E., "Analyzing Geographically Discrete Warehouse Networks by Computer Simulation," *Decision Sciences, 4,* April 1973.

# CHAPTER 19

# DESIGN OF PROCESSES, JOBS, AND WORK MEASUREMENT



*(Continued)*

The core of most productive systems today is still a complex of technology and people. Even though automation is making strong inroads, processes usually involve some combination of humans and machines. We will concentrate our attention in this chapter on the blending of technology and people as components of a productive system. Because productive systems are such a blend, they are often called *sociotechnical systems*. We will also consider some of the special design problems encountered in integrating jobs and processes into systems. Finally, we will discuss work measurement and the methodologies used to measure the labor content of products and services for planning purposes and often as a basis for wage payment.

## CRITERIA AND VALUES

From the time of the Industrial Revolution to the present, the main pressures influencing the designs of processes and jobs have been labor productivity improvement and economic optimization. Present-day technology and enormous markets for many products and services have fostered specialization, and that principle has been applied throughout industry and is currently being applied in service and nonmanufacturing systems.

The specific technology involved limits the extent to which division of labor *can* be pursued, and market size limits how far it *will* be pursued. But within these limits, managers usually have a wide range of choices of job and process designs involving different degrees of labor specialization. It was assumed that finely divided jobs were better because they would increase productivity and that other factors were correlated with productivity, and incentive pay schemes were used to maintain workers' motivation.

Beginning in the early 1930s, however, another criterion was proposed as a counterbalance—job satisfaction. Studies indicated that workers responded to other factors in the work situation besides pay. In the late 1940s, the value of the job satisfaction criterion developed from a morale-building program at IBM. The term *job enlargement* was coined to describe the process of reversing the trend toward specialization. Practical applications of job enlargement were written up in the literature, describing improvements in productivity and quality levels resulting from jobs of broader scope.

We will discuss two views of the job design process: the technological view that has been the dominant one and the sociotechnical view that has gained prominence following World War II.

## TECHNOLOGICAL VIEW OF PROCESS PLANNING AND JOB DESIGN

Although the general methods we will describe were developed in manufacturing systems, they have been adapted to and widely used in many other settings, such as offices, banks, and hospitals.

## Product Analysis

The product or service to be produced is first analyzed, primarily from a technological point of view, to determine the processes required. Schematic and graphic models are commonly developed to help visualize the flow of materials and the relationships among parts.

### ASSEMBLY CHARTS

The assembly chart can be useful for making preliminary plans regarding subassemblies, where purchased parts are used in the assembly sequence, and for appropriate general methods of manufacture. The assembly chart is often called a "Gozinto" chart, for the words, "goes into." Figure 19-1 is an assembly chart for a simple capacitor. Notice how clearly the chart shows the relationship of the parts, the sequence of assembly, and which groups of parts make up subassemblies. The chart is a schematic model of the entire manufacturing process at one level of detail.

### OPERATION PROCESS CHARTS

Assuming that the product is already designed, we have complete drawings and specifications of the parts, their dimensions and tolerances, and the materials to be used. The engineering drawings specify locations, sizes, and tolerances for holes to be drilled and surfaces to be finished for each part. With this information, the most economical equipment, processes, and sequences of processes can be specified by a process planner. Figure 19-2 is an example of an operation process chart for the same capacitor for which the assembly chart of Figure 19-1 was prepared.

An operation process chart is a summary of all required operations and inspections. It is a general plan for production. Although the focus of such charts is on the technological processing required, it is obvious that the jobs to be performed by humans have also been specified. Some discretion in the makeup of jobs still exists, especially in the assembly phase; however, it is clear that "technology is in the saddle."

## Analysis of Human–Machine Relationships

Given the product analysis and the required technological processing, individual job designs become the focus. The concepts and methods used have been developed over a long period, beginning with the scientific management era of the early 1900s. The professional designers of processes and jobs in industry have been industrial engineers. In the post–World War II period, psychologists and physiologists have contributed concepts and methods concerning the role of humans in productive systems, thus broadening the technological view.

FIGURE 19-1
**ASSEMBLY OR "GOZINTO" CHART FOR A SIMPLE CAPACITOR.**

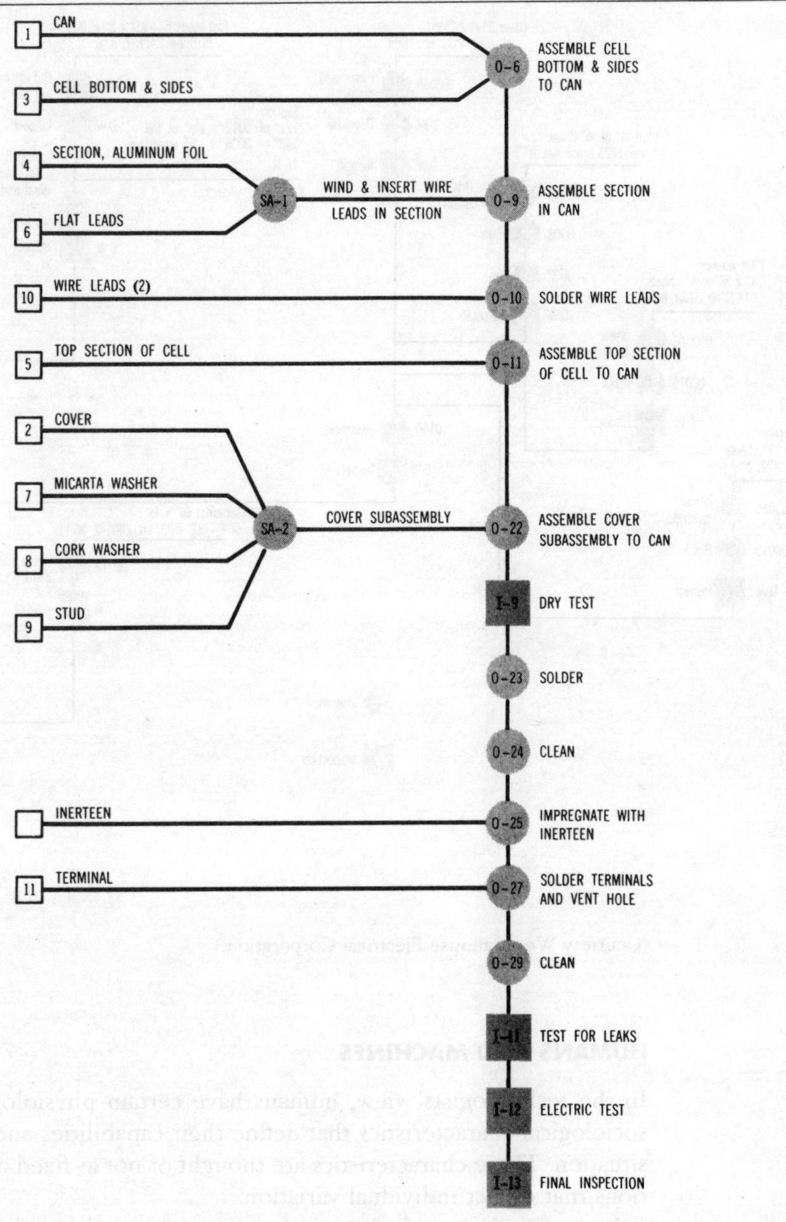

FIGURE 19-2
**OPERATION PROCESS CHART FOR A SIMPLE CAPACITOR.**

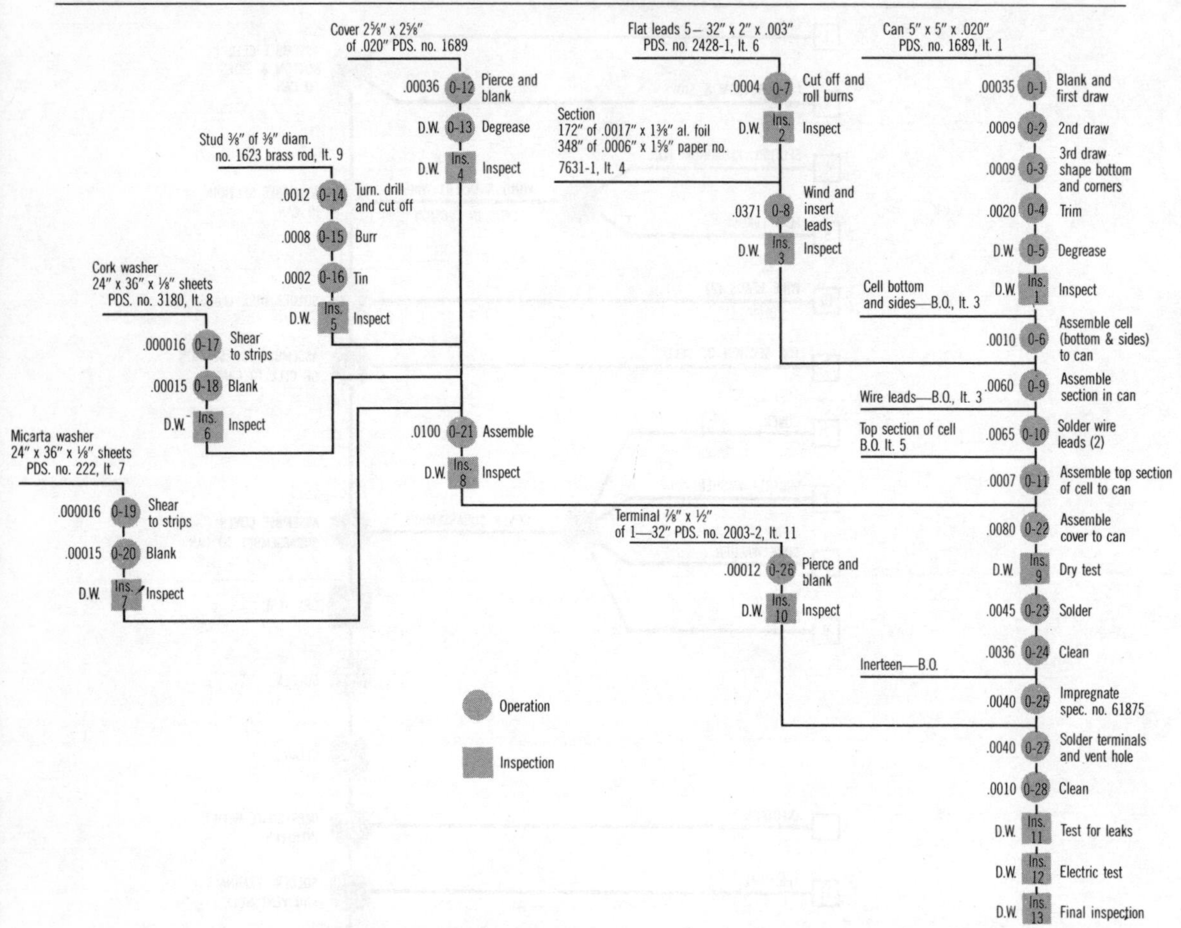


(Courtesy Westinghouse Electrical Corporation.)

## HUMANS AND MACHINES

In the technologists' view, humans have certain physiological, psychological, and sociological characteristics that define their capabilities and limitations in the work situation. These characteristics are thought of not as fixed quantities but as distributions that reflect individual variation.

In performing work, human functions are envisioned in three general classifications:

1. Receiving information through the various sense organs.
2. Making decisions based on information received and information stored in the memory of an individual.

3. Taking action based on decisions. In some instances, the decision phase may be virtually automatic because of learned responses, as with a highly repetitive task. In others, the decisions may involve extensive reasoning and the result may be complex.

Note that the general structure is that of a closed-loop automated system. Wherein lies the difference? Are automated machines like humans? Yes, in this model of humans in the system, machines and humans are alike in certain important respects. Both have sensors, stored information, comparators, decision makers, effectors, and feedback loops. The difference is in the humans' tremendous range of capabilities and in the limitations imposed by physiological and sociological characteristics. Thus, machines are much more specialized in the kinds and ranges of tasks they can perform. Machines perform tasks as faithful servants reacting mainly to physical factors. Humans, however, react to their psychological and sociological environments as well as to the physical environment.

## Conceptual Framework for Human–Machine Systems

We have noted that humans and machines can be thought of as performing similar functions in work tasks, although they each have comparative advantages. The functions they perform are represented in Figure 19-3.

Information is received by the *sensing function.* Sensing by humans is accomplished through the sense organs. Machine sensing can parallel human sensing through electronic or mechanical devices. Machine sensing is usually much more specific or single purpose in nature than is the broadly capable human sensing.

*Information storage* for humans is provided by memory or by access to records. Machine information storage can be obtained by magnetic tape or disk, punched cards, and cams and templates.

FIGURE 19-3
**FUNCTIONS PERFORMED BY WORKER OR MACHINE COMPONENTS OF WORKER–MACHINE SYSTEMS.**

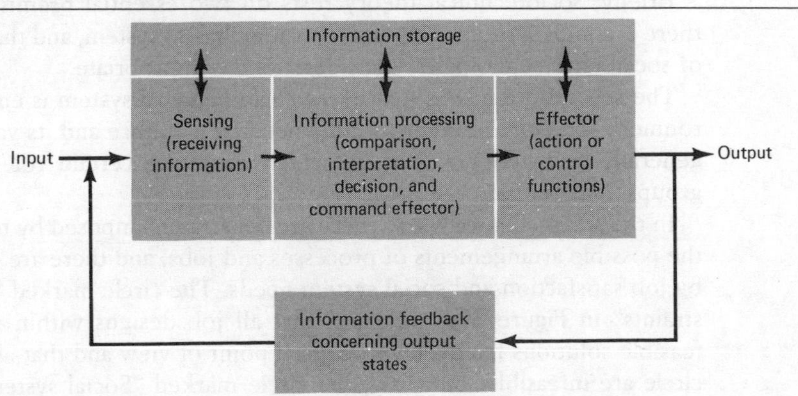

The function of *information processing and decision making* is to take sensed and stored information and produce a decision. The processing could be as simple as making a choice between two alternatives, depending on input data, or very complex, involving deduction, analysis, or computing to produce a decision for which a command is issued to the effector.

The effector or *action function* occurs as a result of decisions and commands and may involve the triggering of control mechanisms by humans or machines or a communication of decisions. Control mechanisms would, in turn, cause something physical to happen, such as moving the hands or arms, starting a motor, or increasing or decreasing the depth of a cut on a machine tool.

*Input and output* are related to the raw materials or the thing being processed. The output represents some transformation of the input. The processes themselves may be of any type: chemical, processes to change shape or form, assembly, transport, or clerical.

*Information feedback* concerning the output states is an essential ingredient because it provides the basis for control. Feedback operates to control the simplest hand motion through the senses and the nervous system. For machines, feedback concerning the output states provides the basis for machine adjustment. Automatic machines couple the feedback information directly so that adjustments are automatic (closed-loop automation). When machine adjustments are only periodic, based on information feedback, the loop is still closed but not on a continuous and automatic basis. Obviously, automation is the ultimate in the technological view of job design.

## THE SOCIOTECHNICAL VIEW OF PROCESS PLANNING AND JOB DESIGN

In the sociotechnical view, the concepts and methods of the technological view are mechanistic, with humans thought of as machines or, worse, as just links in machines. This view states that, without question, the central focus of the technological approach is technology itself and that technology is taken as a given without exploring the full range of the possible alternatives.

Briefly, sociotechnical theory rests on two essential premises. The first is that there is a joint system operating, a sociotechnical system, and that joint optimization of social and technological considerations is appropriate.

The second premise is that every sociotechnical system is embedded in an environment. The environment is influenced by a culture and its values and by a set of generally accepted practices, in which there are certain roles for organizations, groups, and people.

In the sociotechnical view, there are constraints imposed by technology that limit the possible arrangements of processes and jobs, and there are constraints imposed by job satisfaction and social system needs. The circle marked "Technological constraints" in Figure 19-4 indicates that all job designs within the circle represent feasible solutions from a technological point of view and that all points outside the circle are infeasible. Similarly, the circle marked "Social system constraints" indi-

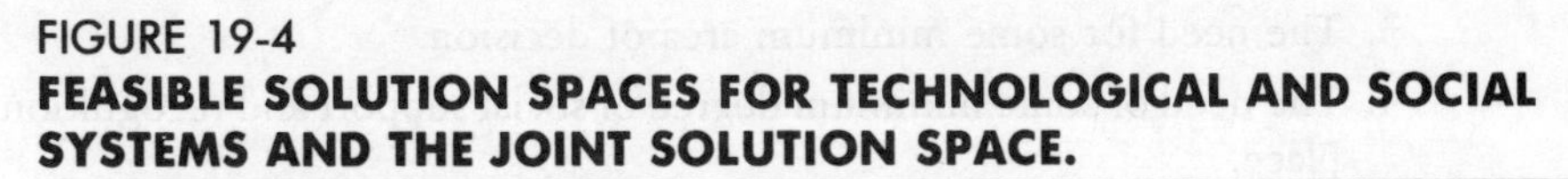

FIGURE 19-4
**FEASIBLE SOLUTION SPACES FOR TECHNOLOGICAL AND SOCIAL SYSTEMS AND THE JOINT SOLUTION SPACE.**

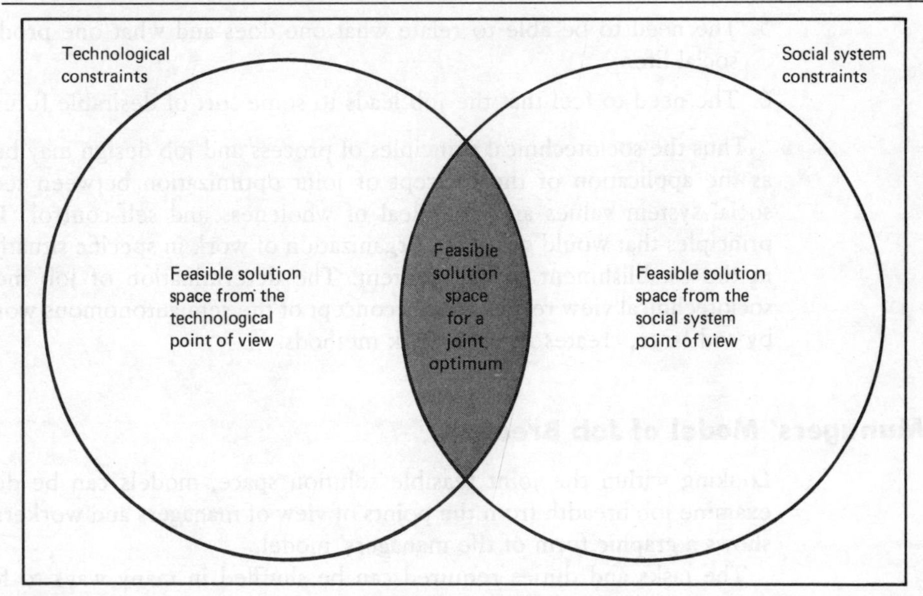


cates that all job designs within the circle represent feasible solutions from the sociological–job satisfaction point of view. Within the shaded area of overlap between the two circles, we have a solution space that meets the constraints of both technology and the social system. The shaded area defines the only solutions that can be considered as feasible in joint terms. Our objective, then, is to consider jointly the economic and social system variables and find the best solution. Because optimization is not a clearly defined process in job design, we seek solutions that are acceptable.

## Psychological Job Requirements

Englestad (1972) developed a set of psychological job requirements. These requirements are an interpretation of empirical evidence that suggests that workers prefer tasks of a substantial degree of wholeness, in which the individual has control over the materials and the processes involved:

1. The need for the content of a job to be reasonably demanding in terms other than sheer endurance yet provide at least a minimum of variety (not necessarily novelty).
2. The need for being able to learn on the job (which implies standards and knowledge of results) and to go on learning. Again, there is a question of neither too much nor too little.

3. The need for some minimum area of decision.
4. The need of some minimum degree of social support and recognition in the work place.
5. The need to be able to relate what one does and what one produces to one's social life.
6. The need to feel that the job leads to some sort of desirable future.

Thus the sociotechnical principles of process and job design may be summarized as the application of the concept of joint optimization between technology and social system values and the ideal of wholeness and self-control. These are the principles that would guide the organization of work in specific situations, resulting in the establishment of job content. The determination of job methods in the sociotechnical view results from a concept of the semiautonomous work group that, by and large, creates its own work methods.

## Managers' Model of Job Breadth

Looking within the joint feasible solution space, models can be developed that examine job breadth from the points of view of managers and workers. Figure 19-5 shows a graphic form of the managers' model.

The tasks and duties required can be shuffled in many ways to form the continuum of narrow versus broad job designs. For example, in auto assembly, jobs can be finely divided, as with conventional auto assembly lines, or at the opposite extreme, one worker or a team can assemble the entire vehicle. This kind of job enlargement can be termed *horizontal. Vertical* enlargement could be envisioned where jobs incorporate varying degrees of quality control, maintenance, repair, supply, and even supervisory functions.

The curves in Figure 19-5 are rationalized as follows (Scoville argues for the shape of the curves rather than for any specific numerical solution):

1. The wage costs curve reflects low productivity for both very narrow and very broad jobs, with a minimum wage cost (maximum productivity) somewhere in the middle range. Training costs go up as the scope of jobs increase, whereas turnover costs are most important for narrow jobs. Thus, the wage costs curve declines to a minimum and increases thereafter as job breadth increases.
2. Material, scrap, and quality control costs are high with narrowly defined jobs owing to lack of motivation. Penalties are also high for broadly defined jobs because the advantages of division of labor are lost.
3. Supervisory costs decline with broader jobs because that function is progressively incorporated with lower level jobs through job enlargement.
4. Capital costs per worker rise on the assumption that capital–labor cost ratios and inventory cost of goods in process both increase. The capital–labor ratio for narrow jobs is low, reflecting the use of simple tools. The capital per worker for skilled, broader jobs, however, reflects the worker's capability to use several machines as needed; for example, an X-ray technician may use different machines for different types of X rays.

FIGURE 19-5
**MANAGERS' MODEL OF JOB BREADTH.**

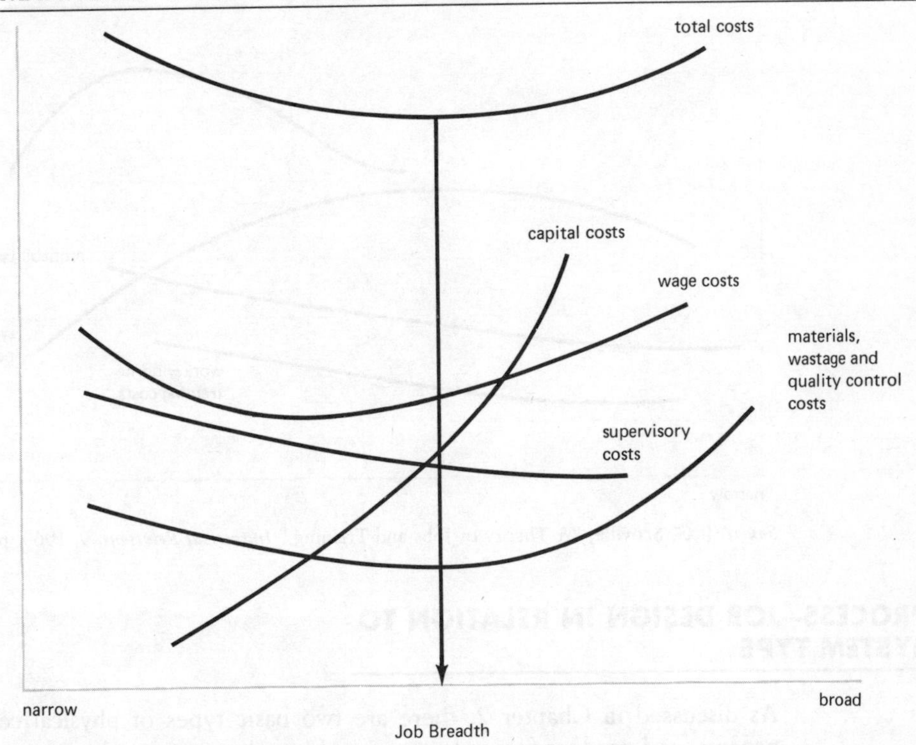


*Source:* J. G. Scoville, "A Theory of Jobs and Training," *Industrial Relations*, 9, 1969, pp. 36–53.

The total cost curve in Figure 19-5 is the sum of the individual cost component curves and reflects an optimum where managers would choose to operate. As with all cost allocation problems, where each extreme strategy involves a cost, the joint optimum must be somewhere between the extremes. The pure strategies cannot represent the optimum because the low cost solution necessarily results from a balance of costs.

## Workers' Model of Job Breadth

A model of job breadth from the workers' viewpoint is shown graphically in Figure 19-6. The wage–productivity and employment probability curves are multiplied to produce the discounted expected earnings curve. If one then subtracts the worker-borne training costs, a net economic benefits curve may be obtained, which has a maximum near the broad end of the spectrum.

These models indicate that there are optimum job designs from an economic point of view. However, because the factors that enter the two points of view are different, it is unlikely that managers and workers could agree on how work should be organized, accounting in part for the conflict between management and labor concerning job design.

FIGURE 19-6
**WORKERS' MODEL OF JOB BREADTH.**

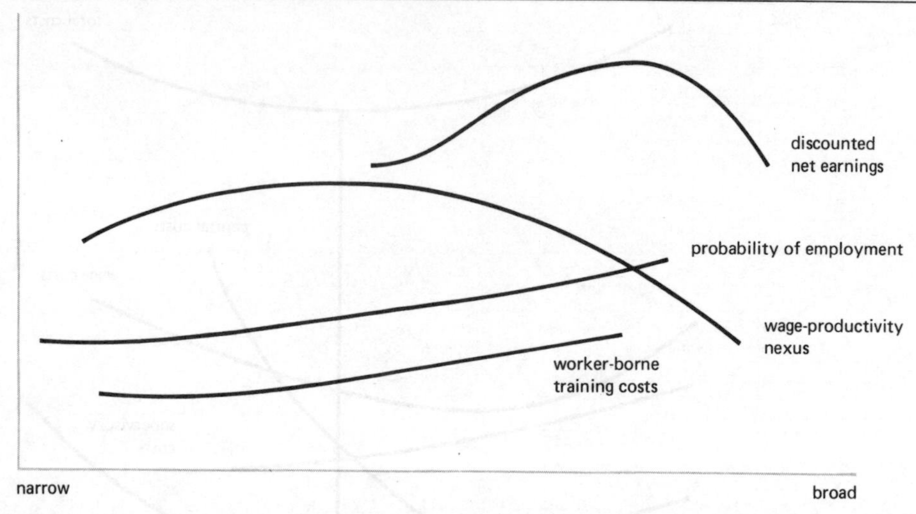


*Source:* J. G. Scoville, "A Theory of Jobs and Training," *Industrial Relations,* 9, 1969, pp. 36–53.

## PROCESS–JOB DESIGN IN RELATION TO SYSTEM TYPE

As discussed in Chapter 2, there are two basic types of physical configurations, process- and product-focused systems. Although many actual systems are combinations of these two extremes, the two types illustrate the nature of the jobs that result.

Recall the discussion of productive system strategies in relation to product strategies introduced in Chapter 2. At one extreme, where product volumes are low and variety, flexibility, and quality are the prime strategies, the economical production system will be a process-focused system. Such a solution results in relatively good utilization of equipment by time sharing it for various jobs requiring a certain production technology.

At the other extreme, for products that are standardized and produced in high volume, there is little if any difference in process requirements from unit to unit. Specialization in the form of product-focused systems is economically justified. Between the extremes, we find mixed types of systems.

The appropriateness of a given system type for supporting the competitive strategy depends on the economics of alternative solutions. For example, if plant, equipment, and other resources were costless, we would set up separate product-focused facilities for each product. Each product would have its own production line. Because these factors of production are not free, we must have sufficient utilization of facilities to justify "single-product" lines. For an oil refinery or a steel mill, a very high utilization is important because of the immense capital requirements. For a fast-food operation, perhaps 50 percent utilization is sufficient.

### Job Breadth Versus System Type

Process-focused systems are associated with a functional process configuration. Departments are generic in type, with all of the operations of a given type being done within that department. For example, in a machine shop, the grinding department performs all kinds of metal work involving grinding. The department has a range of grinding equipment, so it has relatively broad capability within the skill category. There are many examples of other systems where functional process configurations are employed, for example, hospitals, municipal offices, and so on.

The job designs that are associated with functionally laid out systems tend to be relatively broad, though specialized. For example, mechanics in the grinding department can usually perform a wide variety of such work. Normally, they are trained to operate several machines because this breadth offers flexibility. Similarly, an X-ray department in a hospital does a broad range of X-ray work. The variety of work in both situations stems both from the more general nature of the operations in the departments and from the fact that each job order received may be slightly different. Such functional systems require employees who can perform within a skill category. They are specialized, but their skills are more closely related to craft specialties. There is repetition in the work in the sense that an experienced X-ray technician has probably taken all the common types of X rays previously, but there is a continuing mix of job orders that lends variety to the work.

Product-focused systems are associated with line-type operations, where the flow is organized entirely around the product being produced. Each operation being performed must fit into the flow in a highly integrated manner. The operations are highly repetitive. Each employee performs just a few elements of the work that, in themselves, may seem unrelated because of the "balance" among operations required to obtain smooth flow. The balance among operations is critical to making the system function as an efficient, high-output system. The higher the output requirements and the more work stations along the line, the greater the likelihood the system will be balanced with a short, repetitive cycle that restricts the content of each individual job.

## RESTRICTIVE WORK RULES—IMPACT ON PRODUCTIVITY

An important reality in job design practice results from contractual agreements between management and labor concerning work rules. These rules are of every conceivable type, including featherbedding (the practice of padding labor requirements), restrictions concerning the scope of jobs (particularly craft jobs), hours of work, seniority in filling vacancies, "bumping" during layoffs, bases for wages, restrictions on incentive pay standards, and so on. One of the manifestations of restrictive work rules is a large number of job classifications, with workers in each classification restricted to doing the work described. Thus, for example, a mechanic could not do any electrical work. If an electrical problem arises, the mechanic must stop work at that point and wait for someone with the correct job classification to do the electrical work. All these restrictive practices are widespread, though their extensiveness is difficult to document.

## Effects of Work-Rule Changes

The effects of restrictive work rules are to limit flexibility and reduce productivity. Loss of jobs to foreign competition and the 1981–1983 recession put heavy pressure on labor unions to agree to work-rule changes. These changes were mainly in job assignments—cutting crew sizes, enlarging jobs by adding duties, and eliminating unneeded jobs—but they also included hours of work, seniority rules, wages, incentive pay that reflects changed job conditions, allowing team members to rotate, and allowing management to change crew structures as technology changes. The industries affected were in virtually all segments, including airlines, autos, construction, meat packing, petroleum, railroads, rubber, steel, and trucking.[1]

The effects of these work-rule changes were very substantial in improving productivity. In the rubber industry, the changes increased productivity by 10 percent, and hourly output per worker in oil refining increased 10 to 15 percent. At Jones & Laughlin Steel, labor-hours per ton of steel were reduced from 6 to 3.5.[2]

Most of the work-rule changes simply make operations more efficient by combining duties, eliminating featherbedded jobs, allowing more flexibility in work assignments, and so on. But some of the work-rule changes actually change the system in more fundamental ways, such as the reduction of job classifications from 200 to fewer than 100 at TRW's Cleveland plant, resulting in fundamentally more flexibility in task assignments. The most dramatic shifts foretell revolutionary changes in the organization of work in U.S. industry, experimenting with team organization and completely relaxed work rules within units. GM's Saturn Project labor contract has features that hold great promise for future work structures.

## The GM–UAW Saturn Labor Contract[3]

The GM Saturn Project appears to be a bold experiment in self-management and consensus decision making. Representatives of the UAW will sit on all planning and operating committees, and work teams will not be supervised by supervisors. "Work Units," or teams, composed of 6 to 15 workers led by an elected UAW councelor will form the basic productive group, and they will be self-organizing, deciding who will do which tasks, maintaining their own equipment, ordering supplies, and setting relief and vacation schedules for group members. These teams will be responsible for controlling variable costs and quality.

[1] See "Work-Rule Changes Quietly Spread as Firms Try to Raise Productivity," *The Wall Street Journal,* January 25, 1983.

[2] See "A Work Revolution in U.S. Industry: More Flexible Rules on the Job Are Boosting Productivity," *Business Week,* May 16, 1983.

[3] See "How Power Will Be Balanced on Saturn's Shop Floor: GM and Its Auto Workers Launch a Bold Experiment in Self-Management," *Business Week,* August 5, 1985.

Each group of three to six work units will form a "work unit module," led by a company advisor, providing the first managerial input. The advisors provide liaison with experts in engineering, marketing, personnel, and other units, and they provide information to and from the "Business Unit," which will manage the entire plant. The Business Unit has the broad responsibility to coordinate all plant operations and is made up of company representatives, an elected union official, and specialists. To complete the innovative organizational structure, two additional committees are envisioned, both of which have union representation: the "Manufacturing Advisory Committee," which provides oversight for the Saturn complex, and the "Strategic Advisory Committee," which does long-term planning.

The new structure at Saturn will replace the typical organizational structure of assembly plants, which had six layers of management. This hierarchy was headed by a plant manager, but before encountering a production worker, there were the following layers: production manager, general superintendent, production superintendent (5 per shift), general supervisor (15 per shift), and supervisor/foreman (90 per shift).

Of course, the Saturn experiment will be watched, but it involves many elements that should produce positive results. First, it completely relaxes work rules, providing the kind of flexibility available to Japanese managers. But, in addition, Saturn uses team and self-organizing work unit concepts that have been experimented with previously with positive results.

## PERFORMANCE STANDARDS

Performance standards provide data that are basic to many decision-making problems in production/operations management. The performance standard is of critical importance because labor cost is a very important factor, influencing many decisions. For example, decisions to make or buy parts, to replace equipment, or to select certain manufacturing processes require estimates of labor costs.

Performance standards also provide basic data used in day-to-day operation. For example, scheduling or loading machines demands a knowledge of the projected time requirements. For custom manufacture, we must be able to give potential customers a bid price and a delivery date. The bid price is ordinarily based on expected costs for labor, materials, and overhead plus profit. Labor cost is often the largest single component in such situations. To estimate labor cost requires an estimate of how long it will take to perform the various operations. These estimates are also required for computing the capacity of the production process, and provide input to the estimation of delivery times for customers.

Finally, performance standards provide the basis for labor cost control. By measuring worker performance in comparison with standard performance, indexes can be computed for individual workers, whole departments, divisions, or even plants. These indexes make it possible to compare performance on completely different kinds of jobs. Standard labor costing systems and many incentive wage payment systems are based on performance standards.

## INFORMAL STANDARDS

Every organization has performance standards of sorts. Even when they do not exist formally, supervisors have standards in mind for the various jobs based on their knowledge of the work and past performance. These types of standards are informal. Standards based on supervisors' estimates and past performance data have weaknesses, however. First, in almost all such situations, methods of work performance have not been standardized. Therefore, it is difficult to state what output rate, based on past records, is appropriate because past performance data may have been based on various methods. A second major defect in standards based on estimates and past performance records is that they are likely to be too strongly influenced by the working speeds of the individuals who held the jobs. Were those workers high or low performers? The formal methodology of work measurement is designed to offset the disadvantages of informal performance standards.

## WORK–TIME DISTRIBUTIONS

We wish to set up standards that are applicable to the working population, not just to a few selected people within that population. The standards problem is comparable in some ways to that of designing a lever with the proper mechanical advantage to match the capabilities of workers. But not just any worker; the force required to pull the lever should accommodate perhaps 95 to 99 percent of the population so that anyone who comes to the job will have the necessary strength.

Figure 19-7 shows the results of a study of 500 people doing an identical task. The distribution shows that average performance time varies from 0.28 minute to 0.63 minute per piece. If past records reflected data from one or more individuals taken at random from the population of 500, a standard based on their performance might not fit the whole population very well. On the other hand, if we have good data concerning the entire distribution, as in Figure 19-7, we can set up standards that probably would be appropriate for everyone. The common pratice is to set the standard so that it accommodates about 95 percent of the population. For Figure 19-7, a standard performance time of about 0.48 minute is one that about 95 percent of the individuals exceeded. If we pegged the standard at this level, we would expect that practically all employees on the job should be able to meet or exceed the standard.

Some managers feel that it is not wise to quote minimum performance standards such as these for fear that they will encourage relatively poor performance. In this framework, standard performance is about the average of the distribution (0.395 minute for Figure 19-7), and we expect that most workers will produce at about the standard, that some will fall below, and that some will exceed the standard. Both systems of quoting standards are used, although the practice of quoting *minimum acceptable values* is more common than that of quoting average values.

Using the minimum acceptable level as a standard of performance, we find that the normal time for the data of Figure 19-7 is 0.48 minute, the level exceeded by 95 percent of the sample. The total standard time is then given by

FIGURE 19-7
**PERCENTAGE DISTRIBUTION OF THE PERFORMANCE OF 500 PEOPLE PERFORMING A WOOD BLOCK POSITIONING TASK.**

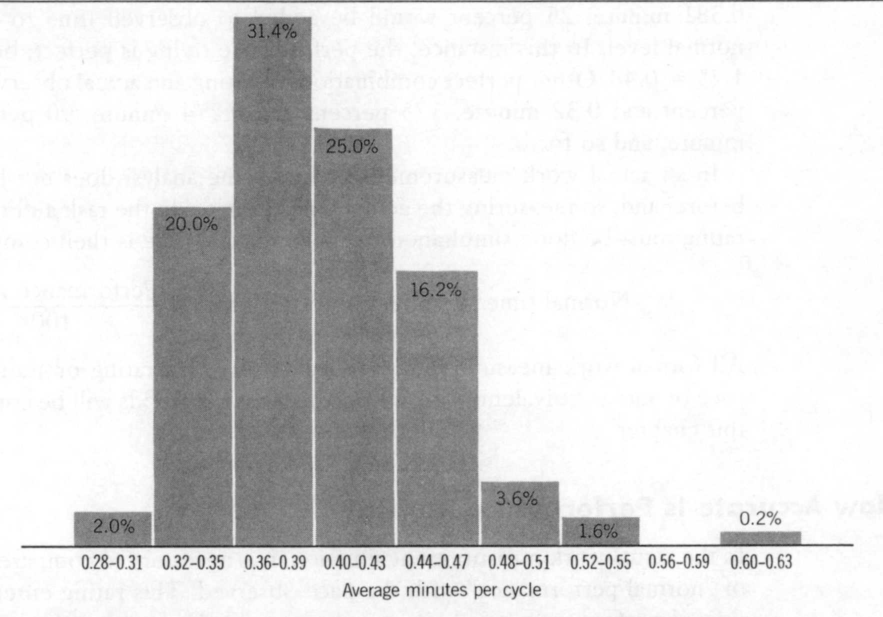


*Source:* Adapted from R. M. Barnes, *Motion and Time Study: Design and Measurement of Work* (7th ed.), Wiley, New York, 1980.

Total standard time = Normal time
+ Standard allowance for personal time
+ Allowance for measured delays normal to the job
+ Fatigue allowance

We will discuss the several allowances later, but the central question now is: How do we determine normal time in the usual situation when only one or a few workers are on the job? The approach to this problem used in industry is called *performance rating.*

## PERFORMANCE RATING

Performance rating is a critically important part of any formal means of work measurement. To be able to rate accurately requires considerable experience. A pace or performance level is selected as standard. An analyst observes this pace and compares it with various other paces, learning to judge pace level as a percentage of the standard pace. For Figure 19-7, the cycle time of 0.48 minute was termed "normal," and the pace or rate of output associated with this time is the normal pace. A pace of work that is 25 percent faster would require proportionately less time per cycle, or

0.48/1.25 = 0.381 minute. If a skilled analyst observed a worker performing the task on which Figure 19-7 is based and rated the performance at 125 percent of normal while simultaneously measuring the actual average performance time as 0.381 minute, 25 percent would be added to observed time to adjust it to the normal level. In this instance, the performance rating is perfect, because 0.381 × 1.25 = 0.48. Other perfect combinations of rating and actual observed time are 150 percent and 0.32 minute, 175 percent and 0.274 minute, 90 percent and 0.533 minute, and so forth.

In an actual work measurement situation, the analyst does not have the answer beforehand, so measuring the actual time taken to do the task and the performance rating must be done simultaneously. The normal time is then computed as

$$\text{Normal time} = \text{Actual observed time} \times \frac{\text{Performance rating}}{100}$$

All formal work measurement systems involve this rating or judging of working pace or some equivalent procedure. Alternative methods will be considered later in this chapter.

### How Accurate Is Performance Rating?

In the actual work measurement situation, it is necessary to compare a mental image of "normal performance" with the pace observed. This rating enters the computation of performance standards as a factor, and the final standard can be no more accurate than the rating. How accurately can experienced people rate? Controlled studies in which films have been rated indicate a standard deviation of 7 to 10 percent. In other words, experienced people probably hold to these limits about 68 percent of the time. Therefore, the effect of the element of judgment in current work measurement practice is considerable.

## WORK MEASUREMENT SYSTEMS

All practical work measurement systems involve (1) the measurement of actual observed time and (2) the adjustment of observed time to obtain "normal time" by means of performance ratings. The alternative systems that we will discuss combine these factors in somewhat different ways. The work measurement systems are

- Stopwatch time studies
- Work sampling
- Standard data work measurement systems

### Stopwatch Methods

The most prevalent approach to work measurement currently used involves a stopwatch time study and the simultaneous performance rating of the operation to determine normal time. Electronic timing devices are now often used instead of the conventional stopwatch. The general procedure is as follows:

1. Standardize methods for the operation; that is, determine the standard method, specifying work place layout, tools, sequence of elements, and so on. Record the resulting standard practice.
2. Select for study an operator who is experienced and trained in the standard methods.
3. Determine the elemental structure of the operation for timing purposes. This may involve a breakdown of the operation into elements and the separation of the elements that occur during each cycle for those that occur only periodically or randomly. For example, tool sharpening might be required each 100 cycles to maintain quality limits. Machine adjustments might occur at random intervals.
4. Observe and record the actual time required for the elements, making simultaneous performance ratings.
5. Determine the number of observations required to yield the desired precision of results based on the sample data obtained in step 4. Obtain more data as required.
6. Compute normal time.

$$\text{Normal time} = \text{Average observed actual time} \times \frac{\text{Average rating factor}}{100}$$

7. Determine allowances for personal time, delays, and fatigue.
8. Determine standard time:

$$\text{Standard time} = \text{Normal times for elements} + \text{Time for allowances}$$

## BREAKDOWN OF ELEMENTS

The common practice is to divide the total operation into elements rather than to observe the cycle as a whole. There are several reasons why this practice is followed:

1. The element breakdown helps to describe the operation in some detail, indicating the step-by-step procedure followed during the study.
2. More information is obtained that may be valuable for comparing times for like elements on different jobs and for building up a handbook of standard data times for common elements in job families. With standard data for elements, cycle times for new sizes can be forecast without additional study.
3. A worker's performance level may vary in different parts of the cycle. With an element breakdown, different performance ratings can be assigned to different elements where the overall cycle is long enough to permit separate evaluation of performances.

In breaking down an operation into elements, it is common practice to make elements a logical component of the overall cycle, as illustrated in Figure 19-8. For

## FIGURE 19-8
## STOPWATCH TIME STUDY OF A DRILLING OPERATION MADE BY THE CONTINUOUS METHOD.

### OBSERVATION SHEET

| | |
|---|---|
| SHEET 1 OF 1 SHEETS | DATE |
| OPERATION Drill ¼″ Hole | OP. NO. D-20 |
| PART NAME Motor Shaft | PART NO. MS-267 |
| MACHINE NAME Avey | MACH. NO. 2174 |
| OPERATOR'S NAME & NO. S.K. Adams 1347 | MALE ☑ FEMALE ☐ |
| EXPERIENCE ON JOB 18 Mo. on Sens. Drill | MATERIAL S.A.E. 2315 |
| FOREMAN H. Miller | DEPT. NO. DL 21 |

| BEGIN 10:15 | FINISH 10:38 | ELAPSED 23 | UNITS FINISHED 20 | ACTUAL TIME PER 100 115 | NO. MACHINES OPERATED 1 |
|---|---|---|---|---|---|

| ELEMENTS | SPEED | FEED | | 1 | 2 | 3 | 4 | 5 | 6 | 7 | 8 | 9 | 10 | SELECTED TIME |
|---|---|---|---|---|---|---|---|---|---|---|---|---|---|---|
| 1. Pick Up Piece and Place in Jig | | | T | .12 | .11 | .12 | .13 | .12 | .10 | .12 | .12 | .14 | .12 | |
| | | | R | .12 | .29 | .39 | .54 | .66 | .77 | .92 | 8.01 | 14 | .32 | |
| 2. Tighten Set Screw | | | T | .13 | .12 | .12 | .14 | .11 | .12 | .12 | .13 | .12 | .11 | |
| | | | R | .25 | .41 | .51 | .68 | .77 | .89 | 7.04 | .14 | .26 | .43 | |
| 3. Advance Drill to Work | | | T | .05 | .04 | .04 | .04 | .05 | .04 | .04 | .04 | .03 | .04 | |
| | | | R | .30 | .45 | .55 | .72 | .82 | .93 | .08 | .18 | .29 | .47 | |
| 4. DRILL ¼″ HOLE | 980 | H | T | .57 | .54 | .56 | .51 | .54 | .58 | .52 | .53 | .59 | .56 | |
| | | | R | .87 | .99 | 3.11 | 4.23 | 5.36 | 6.51 | .60 | .71 | .88 | 11.03 | |
| 5. Raise Drill from Hole | | | T | .04 | .03 | .03 | .03 | .03 | .03 | .03 | .03 | .04 | .03 | |
| | | | R | .91 | 2.02 | .14 | .26 | .39 | .54 | .63 | .74 | .92 | .06 | |
| 6. Loosen Set Screw | | | T | .06 | .06 | .07 | .06 | .06 | .06 | .06 | .06 | .07 | .08 | |
| | | | R | .97 | .08 | .21 | .32 | .45 | .60 | .69 | .80 | .99 | .14 | |
| 7. Remove Piece from Jig | | | T | .08 | .09 | .08 | .08 | .09 | .08 | .07 | .08 | .09 | .07 | |
| | | | R | 1.05 | .17 | .29 | .40 | .54 | .68 | .76 | .88 | 10 08 | .21 | |
| 8. Blow Out Chips | | | T | .13 | .10 | .12 | .14 | .13 | .12 | .13 | .12 | .12 | .11 | |
| | | | R | .18 | .27 | .41 | .54 | .67 | .80 | .89 | 9.00 | .20 | .32 | |
| 9. | | | T | | | | | | | | | | | |
| | | | R | | | | | | | | | | | |
| 10. (1) | | | T | .12 | .11 | .13 | .14 | .12 | .12 | .11 | .13 | .12 | .12 | .12 |
| | | | R | 11.44 | .56 | .69 | .82 | .87 | 17.01 | 18.09 | .21 | .31 | .42 | |
| 11. (2) | | | T | .12 | .14 | .12 | .11 | .12 | .10 | .13 | .15 | .12 | .11 | .12 |
| | | | R | .56 | .70 | .81 | .93 | .99 | .11 | .22 | .36 | .43 | .53 | |
| 12. (3) | | | T | .04 | .04 | .04 | .03 | .04 | .04 | .04 | .04 | .04 | .04 | .04 |
| | | | R | .60 | .74 | .85 | .96 | 16.03 | .15 | .26 | .40 | .47 | .57 | |
| 13. (4) | | | T | .54 | .53 | .55 | .52 | .57 | .54 | .50 | .53 | .55 | .54 | .54 |
| | | | R | 12.14 | 13.27 | 14.40 | 15.48 | .60 | .69 | .76 | .93 | 21 02 | 22.11 | |
| 14. (5) | | | T | .03 | .03 | .03 | .03 | .03 | .03 | .03 | .03 | .03 | .03 | .03 |
| | | | R | .17 | .30 | .43 | .51 | .63 | .72 | .79 | .96 | .05 | .14 | |
| 15. (6) | | | T | .06 | .06 | .06 | .07 | .06 | .05 | .06 | .06 | .05 | .06 | .06 |
| | | | R | .23 | .36 | .49 | .58 | .69 | .77 | .85 | 20.02 | .10 | .20 | |
| 16. (7) | | | T | .08 | .08 | .09 | .08 | .08 | .07 | .08 | .06 | .08 | .08 | .08 |
| | | | R | .31 | .44 | .58 | .66 | .77 | .84 | .93 | .08 | .18 | .28 | |
| 17. (8) | | | T | .14 | .12 | .10 | .09 | .12 | .14 | .15 | .11 | .12 | 12 | .12 |
| | | | R | .45 | .56 | .68 | .75 | .89 | .98 | 19.08 | .19 | .30 | 22.40 | |
| 18. | | | T | | | | | | | | | | | 1.11 |
| | | | R | | | | | | | | | | | |

| SELECTED TIME 1.11 | RATING 100% | NORMAL TIME 1.11 | TOTAL ALLOWANCES 5% | STANDARD TIME 1.17 |
|---|---|---|---|---|

Overall Length 12″ Drill ¼″ Hole
1″ 1″ ¾″

TOOLS, JIGS, GAUGES: Jig No. D-12-33
Use H.S. Drill ¼″ Diam.
Hand Feed
Use Oil - S4

TIMED BY J.B.M.

*Source:* R. M. Barnes, *Motion and Time Study: Design and Measurement of Work* (7th ed.), Wiley, New York, 1980.

example, element 1, "pick up piece and place in jig," is a fairly homogeneous task. Note that element 4, "drill ¼-inch hole," is the machining element, following the general practice to separate machining time from handling time. Finally, constant elements are usually separated from elements that might vary with size, weight, or some other parameter.

## ADEQUACY OF SAMPLE SIZE

We are attempting to estimate, from the sample times and performance ratings observed, a normal time of performance. The precision desired will determine how many observations will be required. For example, if we wanted to be 95 percent sure that the resulting answer, based on the sample, was within ±5 percent, we would calculate the sample size $n$ required from a knowledge of the mean and standard deviation of our sample data. If we wanted greater confidence or closer precision, the sample size would have to be larger.

Figure 19-9 is a convenient chart for estimating required sample sizes to maintain a ±5 percent precision in the answer for 95 and 99 percent confidence levels. To use the chart, calculate the mean value, $\bar{x}$, and the standard deviation, $s$, based on the sample data. The "coefficient of variation" is the percentage variation, $100(s_x/\bar{x})$. The chart is entered with the coefficient of variation, and the sample size is read off for the confidence level desired. The most common confidence level in work measurement is 95 percent.

Using the sample study of Figure 19-8, was $n = 20$ adequate for estimating the overall cycle within a precision of ±5 percent and a confidence level of 95 percent? Table 19-1 shows the calculation of the coefficient of variation for the cycle times as about 5 percent. From Figure 19-9, a sample of $n = 4$ would be adequate to maintain a precision within ±5 percent of the correct mean cycle time 95 percent of the time. For a confidence level of 99 percent, $n = 10$. Our actual sample of 20 was more than adequate.

The reason that the small sample size was adequate is because the variability of the readings is small in relation to the mean cycle time, so a good estimate of cycle time is obtained with only a few observations. This is commonly true of operations dominated by a machine cycle. In this case, the actual drill time is almost half of the total cycle, and the machining time itself does not vary much.

If all we wanted was an estimate of the cycle time, we could stop at this point. Suppose, however, that we want estimates of each of the average element times adequate for future use as elemental standard data. Was the sample size of $n = 20$ adequate for each of these elements? Using element 1 as an example, the mean element time is $\bar{x} = 0.121$ minute, the standard deviation is $s = 0.0097$ minute, and the coefficient of variation is 8 percent. From Figure 19-9, we see that we should have taken a sample of $n = 10$ for a 95 percent confidence level and $n = 20$ for a 99 percent confidence level. The reason a larger sample is needed for element 1 than for the entire cycle is that element 1 is somewhat more variable than is the total cycle (a coefficient of variation of 8 percent compared with only 5 percent for the cycle). Therefore, if data on each of the elements are needed, the element for which the largest sample size is indicated from Figure 19-9 dictates the minimum sample

FIGURE 19-9
**CHART FOR ESTIMATING THE SAMPLE SIZE REQUIRED TO OBTAIN MAXIMUM CONFIDENCE INTERVALS OF ±5 PERCENT FOR GIVEN COEFFICIENT VARIATION VALUES.**

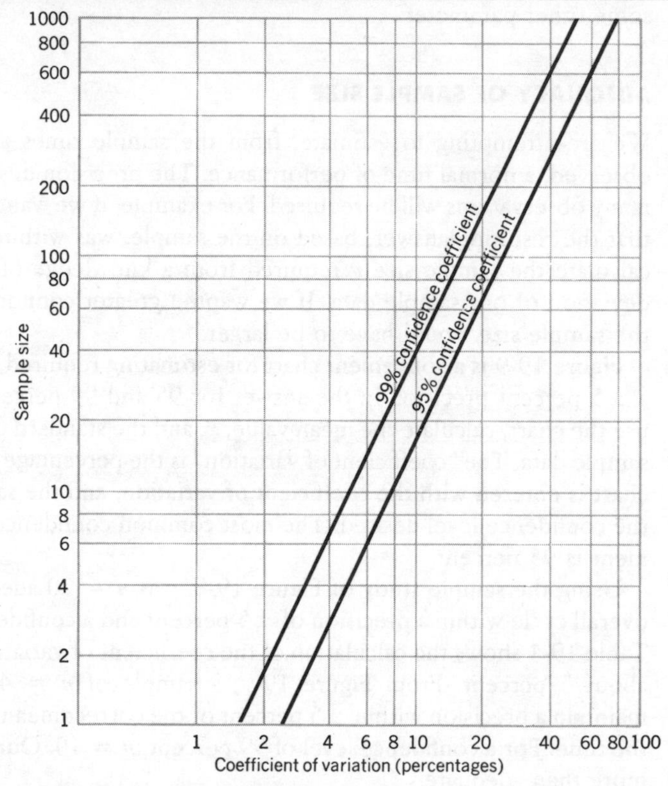


*Source:* A. Abruzzi, *Work Measurement,* Columbia University Press, New York, 1952.

size for the study. This procedure ensures the precision and confidence requirements for the limiting element and yields better results than this on all other elements.

## PROCEDURES FOR ENSURING CONSISTENCY OF SAMPLE DATA

A single study always leaves open the question, "Were the data representative of usual operating conditions?" If a similar study were made on some other days of the week or during some other hour of the day, would the results be different? This question suggests the possibility of dividing the total sample into smaller subsamples taken at random times. Then, by setting up control limits based on an initial sample, we can determine if the subsequent data taken are consistent. That is, did all the data come from a common universe?[4]

[4] For detailed procedures with appropriate charts for estimating sample sizes, precision limits, and control limits, see Barnes (1980).

TABLE 19-1

**CYCLE TIMES FROM FIGURE 19-8, AND CALCULATED MEAN VALUE, STANDARD DEVIATION, COEFFICIENT OF VARIATION, AND REQUIRED SAMPLE SIZES FROM FIGURE 19-9**

| Cycle Number | Cycle Time (minutes) | Cycle Time (squared) | Cycle Number | Cycle Time (minutes) | Cycle Time (squared) |
|---|---|---|---|---|---|
| 1 | 1.18 | 1.395 | 11 | 1.13 | 1.280 |
| 2 | 1.09 | 1.190 | 12 | 1.11 | 1.235 |
| 3 | 1.14 | 1.300 | 13 | 1.12 | 1.255 |
| 4 | 1.13 | 1.280 | 14 | 1.07 | 1.145 |
| 5 | 1.13 | 1.280 | 15 | 1.14 | 1.300 |
| 6 | 1.13 | 1.280 | 16 | 1.09 | 1.190 |
| 7 | 1.09 | 1.190 | 17 | 1.10 | 1.215 |
| 8 | 1.11 | 1.235 | 18 | 1.11 | 1.235 |
| 9 | 1.20 | 1.440 | 19 | 1.11 | 1.235 |
| 10 | 1.12 | 1.255 | 20 | 1.10 | 1.215 |
| | | | Sum | 22.40 | 25.150 |

$$\bar{x} = \frac{22.40}{20} = 1.12$$

$$s = \sqrt{\frac{\Sigma x_i^2 - \frac{(\Sigma x_i)^2}{n}}{n-1}} = \sqrt{\frac{25.150 - \frac{(22.40)^2}{20}}{19}} = 0.057$$

$$\text{Coefficient of variation} = \frac{0.057 \times 100}{1.12} = 5.09\%$$

From Figure 19-9:

$$n \approx 4 \text{ @ } 95\% \text{ confidence level}$$
$$n \approx 10 \text{ @ } 99\% \text{ confidence level}$$

## Work Sampling

The unique thing about work sampling is that it accomplishes the results of the stopwatch study without the need for an accurate timing device. Work sampling was first introduced to industry by L. H. C. Tippett in 1934 and has been in common use since about 1950.

If we wish to estimate the proportion of time that a worker or a group of workers spends working and the proportion of time spent not working, we can perform long-term time studies in which we measure the work time, the idle time, or both. This would probably take a day or longer, and after measuring, we would not be sure that the term of the study covered representative periods of work and idleness.

Instead, suppose that we make a large number of *random* observations in which we simply determine whether the operator is working or idle and tally the results (see Figure 19-10). The percentages of the tallies recorded in the "working" and "idle"

FIGURE 19-10
**WORK SAMPLING TALLY OF WORKING AND IDLE TIME.**

| | Tally | Number | Per cent |
|---|---|---|---|
| Working | 卌 卌 卌 卌 卌 卌 卌 卌 卌<br>卌 卌 卌 卌 卌 卌 卌 卌 卌 卌 / | 96 | 88.9 |
| Idle | 卌 卌 // | 12 | 11.1 |
| Total | | 108 | 100.0 |

classifications are estimates of the actual percentage of time that the worker was working and idle. Herein lies the fundamental principle behind work sampling: *the number of observations is proportional to the amount of time spent in the working or idle state.* The accuracy of the estimate depends on the number of observations, and we can preset precision limits and confidence levels.

## NUMBER OF OBSERVATIONS REQUIRED

The statistical methods of work sampling depend on the distributions for proportions. Recall that

$$\bar{p} = \frac{x}{n} = \frac{\text{Number observed in classification}}{\text{Total number of observations}}$$

and

$$s_p = \sqrt{\frac{(\bar{p}(1-\bar{p})}{n}}$$

From these formulas for a mean proportion and the standard deviation of a proportion, charts and tables have been developed that give directly the number of observations required for a given value of $\bar{p}$, precision limits, and the 95 percent confidence level.[5]

The number of observations required is fairly large. For example, to maintain a precision in the estimate of $\bar{p}$ of $\pm 1.0$ percentage point at the 95 percent confidence level, 10,000 observations are required if $\bar{p}$ is in the neighborhood of 50 percent. About 3600 observations are required to hold an estimated $\bar{p} = 10$ percent between 9 and 11 percent. Smaller samples are required for looser limits. Although these numbers of observations seem very large, the nature of the observation required is merely a recognition of whether or not the employee is working or possibly a classification of worker activity into various reasons for idleness.

## MEASURING DELAYS AND ALLOWANCES

One common use of work sampling is to determine the percentage of time that workers are actually spending for personal time and for delays that are a part of the

[5] More complete information on sample sizes is available in Barnes (1957).

job. The resulting information could then be used as the basis for the percentage allowances that enter into the calculation of standard time.

### DETERMINING PERFORMANCE STANDARDS

If we knew (1) how many pieces were produced during the total time of a study and (2) the performance rating for each observation of work time, we could compute normal time as follows:

$$\text{Normal time} = \frac{\begin{pmatrix}\text{Total}\\ \text{time of}\\ \text{study in}\\ \text{minutes}\end{pmatrix} \times \begin{pmatrix}\text{Work time}\\ \text{in decimals}\\ \text{from work}\\ \text{sampling study}\end{pmatrix} \times \begin{pmatrix}\text{Average}\\ \text{performance}\\ \text{rating in}\\ \text{decimals}\end{pmatrix}}{\text{Total number of pieces produced}}$$

Standard time is then computed as before:

$$\text{Standard time} = \text{Normal time} + \text{Allowances for delays, fatigue, and personal time}$$

### STANDARDS FOR NONCYCLIC ACTIVITIES

Although work sampling can be used in most situations, its most outstanding field of application is in the measurement of noncyclical types of work where many different tasks are performed but there is no set cycle pattern or regularity. In many jobs, the frequency of tasks within the job is based on a random demand function. For example, a storeroom clerk may fill requisitions, unpack and put away stock, deliver material to production departments, clean up the storeroom, and so on. The frequency and time requirements of some of these tasks depend on factors outside the control of the clerk. To determine such production standards by stopwatch methods would be difficult or impossible. Work sampling fits this situation ideally because, through its random sampling approach, reliable estimates of time and performance for these randomly occurring tasks can be obtained.

## Standard Data Work Measurement Systems

Two kinds of standard data are used: universal data based on minute elements of motion (often called *universal data* or *microdata*) and standard data for families of jobs (often called *macrostandard data* or *element standard data*).

### UNIVERSAL STANDARD DATA

Universal standard data give time values for fundamental types of motions, so complete cycle times can be synthesized by analyzing the motions required to perform the task. Fundamental time values of this nature can be used as building blocks for forecasting the standard time, provided that the time values are properly gathered and that the various minute motion elements required by the tasks are analyzed perfectly.

The result provided by these synthetic standards is an estimate of the normal time for the task. Standard time is then determined as before by adding allowances for delay, fatigue, and personal time.

Does performance rating enter into standards developed from universal data? Not for each standard developed because the analyst simply uses the time value from the table for a given motion. However, performance rating was used to develop the time values that are in the tables, so the rating factor enters the system, but not for each occasion that the data are used.

Many people feel that universal standard data lead to greater consistency of standards because analysts are not called on to judge working pace in order to develop a standard. This does not mean that judgment is eliminated from the use of universal standard data systems, however. A great deal of judgment is required in selecting the appropriate classifications of motion to use in analyzing an operation. An inexperienced person ordinarily will not be able to perform these selections accurately enough for the purpose of determining production standards.

Using universal standard data as the sole basis for determining production standards is not common. In most cases where data of this kind are used, they are employed in conjunction with some other technique, such as a stopwatch study or work sampling. The reason for this methodology seems to be that most organizations feel more comfortable when some actual direct measurement of the work involved has been made.

## STANDARD DATA FOR JOB FAMILIES

Standard data for job families give normal time values for major elements of jobs (macrostandard data). Also, time values for machine set-up and for different manual elements are given, so a normal time for an entirely new job can be constructed through an analysis of blueprints to see what materials are specified, what cuts must be made, how the work piece can be held in the machine, and so forth. Unlike the universal standard data discussed previously, however, the time values for these elements have been based on actual previous stopwatch studies or other measurements of work within the job family.

In these previous studies, the operations were consistently broken down into common elements until, finally, a system of data emerged that showed how the "normal element time" varied with size, depth of cut, material used, the way the work piece was held in the machine, and the like. At that point, the data themselves could be used to estimate production standards without a separate study actually being performed on every different part. Again, although an individual performance rating does not enter each application of the standard data, it was used in constructing the data originally. As before, final production standards are determined by adding allowances for delays, fatigue, and personal time to the normal cycle time derived from the standard data. Macrostandard data are in common use, especially in machine shops where distinct families have a long-standing tradition. The occurrence of this kind of standard data is likely to exist wherever job families exist or when parts or products occur in many sizes and types. Macrostandard data have a large field of application where short runs of custom parts and products occur. In these instances, if we attempt to determine production standards by actual measurement, the order may be completed by the time the production standard has been determined. The result will be of no value unless the identical part is reordered.

## ALLOWANCES IN PERFORMANCE STANDARDS

Allowances are commonly added to the computed normal time for delay, fatigue, and personal time. Allowances for delay and fatigue depend on the nature of the operation. They may not exist for some activities. The usual approach is to express allowances in percentage of the total available time. Thus, a 10 percent allowance over an 8-hour (480-minute) day is the equivalent of 48 minutes.

### Delay Allowances

Delay allowance must be based on actual measurement of the magnitude of the delays. Although a stopwatch study can be used, work sampling provides a much more efficient means of obtaining accurate data because delays often occur randomly. Work sampling expresses its measurement of delays directly in terms of a percentage of the total available time.

### Fatigue and Personal Allowances

For some very heavy industrial jobs, an employee might work 20 minutes and rest 20 minutes. This type of very heavy work is not common today, but it occurs often enough for a continuing interest to be maintained in the subject of physical fatigue and rest allowances.

Unfortunately, we still lack an accepted framework for the establishment of rest allowances based on any rational or scientific measurements. In most instances, schedules of *fatigue allowances* for various types of work based on general acceptability are used, and they are often the subject of agreements between labor and management.

Allowances for *personal time* provide at least a minimum amount of time that the worker can be away from the job. This personal time allows a break from both the physical and the psychological stresses that a job may contain and is, in a sense, a minimum fatigue allowance. The minimum allowance is normally 5 percent of the total available time.

### Application of Allowances in Performance Standards

The usual interpretation of the meaning of percentage allowances is that they allow a percentage of the total available time. A personal time allowance of 5 percent translates into $0.05 \times 480 = 24$ minutes of personal time in a normal 8-hour day. If the normal time has been measured as 1.20 minutes per piece, then the personal time must be prorated properly to the normal time in computing the standard time per piece:

$$\text{Standard time} = \text{Normal time} \times \frac{100}{100 - \text{Percentage allowance}}$$

$$= 1.20 \times \frac{100}{95} = 1.263 \text{ minutes per piece}$$

If all of the allowances for delay, fatigue, and personal time are expressed as percentages of the total available time, they can be added together to obtain a single total percentage allowance figure. Then, standard time can be computed from normal time by a single calculation using the preceding formula.

## WAGE INCENTIVES

In spite of the emphasis on job satisfaction and other nonmonetary incentives for workers, monetary incentives remain an extremely strong motivation, and wage incentives are one of the most important uses of work measurement data. A survey by Rice (1977) showed that in a sample of 1500 firms, including government and nonmanufacturing firms, 89 percent used time standards and 44 percent used wage incentives (see Table 19-2). The survey shows that the time study is the dominant method for setting production standards and that the simplest wage incentive plans, piece rates and standard hour plans, are the most used. Wage incentives are also being applied in service operations. For example, a 1986 survey[6] of 1900 banks showed that 28 percent of those responding have wage incentives in place compared to 17 percent in a similar survey in 1982. But wage incentives are much more prevalent in large banks: 68 percent of banks with over a billion dollars in assets use incentive compensation.

*Piece rate* plans are the simplest wage incentives. If the piece rate is $0.50 per unit and a worker produces 75 units per day, earnings are $37.50 for the day. Piece rates could be based on work measurement and a standard hourly pay rate, but ordinarily they are not, negotiation or management fiat being the basis for setting rate.

*Standard hour plans* are the most widely used of the wage incentive plans, and they are based on time standards and hourly pay rate standards called base rates. Suppose that work measurement produces a time standard of 1 minute per unit, and the base rate is $10 per hour. If a worker averages 1 minute per unit, then he or she earns standard hours at the normal rate, and the hourly pay rate will be $10 per hour. In an 8-hour day, that worker would earn 8 standard hours or $80. But if the worker averages only 0.80 minutes per unit, producing $1/0.8 = 1.25$ times the standard hours allowed, then the earned standard hours would be $1.25 \times 8 = 12.5$ or $125

[6] "Incentive Compensation Spreading in Banking Industry," *The Productivity Letter,* American Productivity Center, Houston, Texas, 5(10), March 1986.

TABLE 19-2
**APPLICATION OF WORK MEASUREMENT AND WAGE INCENTIVES**

| | | | |
|---|---|---|---|
| Percent using time standards | 89 | Percent using wage incentives | 44 |
| Time study | 90 | Piece work | 40 |
| Elemental data for job families | 61 | Standard hour | 61 |
| Universal standard data | 32 | Sharing plan | 19 |
| Work sampling | 21 | Plantwide bonuses | 5 |
| Historical estimates | 44 | Profit sharing | 8 |
| Others | 3 | Others | 9 |

*Note:* Some companies use more than one method.

*Source:* R. S. Rice, "Survey of Work Measurement and Wage Incentives," *Industrial Engineering,* July 1977, pp. 18–31.

for the day. Normally, there is a guarantee of the base pay rate in standard hour plans, and the worker receives all the direct labor benefits from his or her own productivity gains. The company gains from fuller utilization of facilities and in the long term from the smaller capital investment per worker.

Though not as widely used as the standard hour plans, direct labor productivity benefits, called gain-sharing plans, can be shared in various proportions between the worker and the company. The plantwide bonus and profit sharing plans referred to in Table 19-2 are not normally tied to work measurement plans.

## IMPLICATIONS FOR THE MANAGER

Managers need to recognize that the basic design of the productive system is an important element of strategic planning, and that job design can help implement the broader enterprise strategy. Many of the problems of the operations manager stem from employees' dissatisfaction with the nature of their jobs. Labor disputes erupt over issues referred to as working conditions and require endless hours of negotiations and grievance hearings for settlement. Even when the issues are not stated in terms of job design, job satisfaction, or dehumanization at the work place, it is often felt that these are the real issues. If the structure of processes, jobs, and choice of system type took account of the workers' model of job breadth, psychological job requirements, and job enrichment principles, perhaps the operations manager would face fewer labor disputes resulting from these causes.

Although alterations in the process and job design structures can be made in existing organizations, managers have the greatest opportunity for innovation when new facilities are being planned. It is during these opportune times that fundamental alternatives to the organization of work can be considered most easily, as with the GM Saturn Project.

Managers need to know about the results of studies of alternative job design structures, the fundamental conflict between the managers' and the workers' models of job breadth, psychological job requirements, and the success of semiautonomous work groups in designing their own work methods. If the process and job design structure and the system type have conflict built into them, the resulting operating problems may be severe.

Aside from the job design aspects, product or line flow is appropriate only under certain conditions. The volume of activity necessary to justify specialized line operations is relatively large and requires a standardized product or service—variations are difficult to incorporate into line systems. The conflict between job specialization and job satisfaction is a difficult one for managers. Specialization has many benefits to society and to an individual enterprise. There seems to be little question that specialized line-type operations are easier to plan for, easier to schedule, easier to control, require less space per unit of capacity, and so on. Yet specialized jobs create a work environment that raises social responsibility issues for managers.

It seems unlikely that large-scale productive systems can or should be converted from line operations to process-focused systems. On the other hand, managers need to raise questions about feasible alternatives that may exist within the joint socio-technical solution space. Experience has shown that there are often solutions to process and job design problems that satisfy both sets of criteria if there is a genuine effort to find them.

In choosing the appropriate system type, managers should carefully relate the problem to the job design question. Process-focused systems allow somewhat broader jobs, though there is specialization within general areas. Product-focused systems are likely to produce narrowly designed jobs. But the choice of productive system type also has a great impact on the enterprise strategy in relation to its chosen markets.

## REVIEW QUESTIONS

1. What are the factors that limit the extent of division of labor in practice?
2. What is job enlargement? How was it originated?
3. What is the technological view of process planning and job design?
4. What are the tools of product analysis? How are job designs affected by their use?
5. In the technologist's view, what are humans' functions in performing work?
6. What is the sociotechnologist's view of process planning and job design?
7. What are Englestad's psychological job requirements? Are they compatible with the technological view of job design?
8. What is the nature of the managers' model of job breadth? Of the workers' model of job breadth? Do they result in the same kinds of job designs?
9. Which view of job design do you think is most practical? Most humane? Most likely to succeed in the long term?
10. How does a process-focused system design affect job designs? How does a product-focused system design affect job designs?

11. What is the nature of the organization of work in the GM Saturn Project? Do you think it will work? Why?
12. What are performance standards? How are they used in industry?
13. What are informal standards? What are their advantages and defects?
14. Define the following terms:
    a. Normal time
    b. Standard time
    c. Allowance
15. What is performance rating? Why is it a necessary part of work measurement? How accurate is performance rating?
16. Describe the procedure for stopwatch work measurement.
17. In stopwatch work measurement, why is the job broken down into elements, rather than being timed as a whole?
18. What are the methods for ensuring an adequate sample size in stopwatch work measurement? For ensuring consistency of sample data?
19. What is work sampling? How does it work?
20. How can work sampling be used to measure delays and allowances? To determine performance standards?
21. What are universal standard data? How can they be used to determine performance standards?
22. What are standard data for job families? How are they used to determine performance standards?
23. What is a piece rate?
24. Describe the functioning of a standard hour incentive plan.

# SITUATIONS

## Toys and Job Design at the Hovey and Beard Company

25. The following is a situation that occurred in the Hovey and Beard Company, as reported by J. V. Clark.[7]

    This company manufactured a line of wooden toys. One part of the process involved spray painting partially assembled toys, after which the toys were hung on moving hooks that carried them through a drying oven. The operation, staffed entirely by women, was plagued with absenteeism, high turnover, and low morale. Each woman at her paint booth would take a toy from the tray beside her, position it in a fixture, and spray on the color according to the required pattern. She then would release the toy and hang it on the conveyor

[7] From J. V. Clark, "A Healthy Organization," *California Management Review, 4,* 1962.

hook. The rate at which the hooks moved had been calculated so that each woman, once fully trained, would be able to hang a painted toy on each hook before it passed beyond her reach.

The women who worked in the paint room were on a group incentive plan that tied their earnings to the production of the entire group. Since the operation was new, they received a learning allowance that decreased by regular amounts each month. The learning allowance was scheduled to fall to zero in six months because it was expected that the women could meet standard output or more by that time. By the second month of the training period, trouble had developed. The women had progressed more slowly than had been anticipated, and it appeared that their production level would stabilize somewhat below the planned level. Some of the women complained about the speed that was expected of them, and a few of them quit. There was evidence of resistance to the new situation.

Through the counsel of a consultant, the supervisor finally decided to bring the women together for general discussions of working conditions. After two meetings in which relations between the work group and the supervisor were somewhat improved, a third meeting produced the suggestion that control of the conveyor speed be turned over to the work group. The women explained that they felt that they could keep up with the speed of the conveyor but that they could not work at that pace all day long. They wished to be able to adjust the speed of the belt, depending on how they felt.

After consultation, the supervisor had a control marked, "low, medium, and fast" installed at the booth of the group leader, who could adjust the speed of the conveyor anywhere between the lower and upper limits that had been set. The women were delighted and spent many lunch hours deciding how the speed should be varied from hour to hour throughout the day. Within a week, a pattern had emerged: the first half-hour of the shift was run on what the women called "medium speed" (a dial setting slightly above the point marked "medium"). The next two and one-half hours were run at high speed, and the half-hour before lunch and the half-hour after lunch were run at low speed. The rest of the afternoon was run at high speed, with the exception of the last 45 minutes of the shift, which were run at medium speed.

In view of the women's report of satisfaction and ease in their work, it is interesting to note that the original speed was slightly below medium on the dial of the new control. The average speed at which the women were running the belt was on the high side of the dial. Few, if any, empty hooks entered the drying oven, and inspection showed no increase of rejects from the paint room. Production increased, and within three weeks the women were operating at 30 to 50 percent above the level that had been expected according to the original design.

Evaluate the experience of the Hovey and Beard Company as it reflects on job design, human relationships, and the supervisor's role. How would you react as the supervisor to the situation where workers determine how the work will be performed? If you were designing the spray painting set-up, would you design it differently?

## Automation in the Warehouse

26. The following situation is drawn from an article by G. Woolsey.[8]

A Canadian manufacturer of heavy equipment had installed an automated warehouse as a base for the worldwide supply of spare parts for their equipment. The automated system involved filling orders for spare parts that would ultimately be packed and shipped. Orders were coded by a clerk, indicating the item and its location, using a keyboard and a cathode ray tube (CRT) information display. In the warehouse, forklift operators also had a small CRT on the truck that listed the necessary items and locations to complete an order.

The trucks were routed to the correct position in the warehouse by a computer, the trucks being guided by wires in the floor. On arrival at the correct location, the truck raised the operator automatically to the proper level so that the item could be picked out of the bin. The truck operator then pressed a button to indicate that the particular item had been obtained. The computer then routed the truck and operator to the next station to pick another item. When all the items for an order had been filled, the computer routed the truck back to the packing and shipping location. The process was then repeated for the next order.

The only control that operators had over their trucks was a "kill" button that could stop them in case of an impending collision. This never happened because the computer program knew the position of all the trucks and programmed them around each other. If the operator stepped off the truck, a "dead man" control stopped the truck.

The automated system had replaced a conventional order picking system in which forklift truck operators performed essentially the same process manually.

On installation, the automated system ran smoothly with virtually zero errors in picking items. Then, however, errors increased to new record levels, absenteeism became a problem, and there were some examples of what appeared to be sabotage. The warehouse supervisor was particularly outraged because the company had agreed to a massive across-the-board pay increase for operators in order to get the union to accept the new computer system. The union had argued that the operators now worked with a computer and that the job was more complex.

What is the problem? Should the multimillion dollar automated system be scrapped? Should the jobs be redesigned? What do you propose?

## Job Design in a Sweatshop

27. Read the following except from an article with these questions in mind:

a. Is there a rational explanation for the situation described in the article? Should the system be redesigned to broaden jobs? Why? If you were a

[8] From G. Woolsey, "Two Digressions on Systems Analysis: Optimum Warehousing and Disappearing Orange Juice," *Interfaces*, 7(2), February 1977, pp. 17–20.

consultant to the owner–manager of the enterprise described, what would you recommend?

b. If you were a worker in this kind of factory, what kinds of satisfaction would you be able to obtain from your work? Do you think that these kinds of satisfactions are adequate for the average industrial worker? How pervasive do you think the situation described is in American industry?

## WORKING IN A SOUTHERN SWEATSHOP: A REPORT

*by Mimi Conway*[9]

Until the time when I made the voluntary transition from professional-class suburbanite to piece-work employee in a Southern garment factory, a second was almost a meaningless unit of time. It was soon to become a very meaningful measure of my economic health and welfare.

I had been an investigative reporter for 10 years before I became dissatisfied with the limitations of journalistic probings into the human condition. I wanted to write fiction, which is, to me, emotional truth. The novel I had in mind necessitated my capturing the rhythms of life on an American assembly line, the sort of life that Labor Day weekend commemorates. For this purpose, and to earn a living while I wrote, I applied for factory work.

A small apparel factory hired me. When I walked into the windowless corrugated metal building in the industrial park on the outskirts of town—the workplace equivalent to the trailer camps that many of the apparel workers lived in—I began learning about working in America in a way new to me.

I began working as a "legger," simultaneously operating three hissing presses that put the permanent-press crease into military pants. "Making production" meant making perfect creases in 650 pant legs a day, 81 legs each hour, one leg every 42 seconds. In exchange for this I received the minimum wage.

I had not expected that the more experienced leggers would be generous and sharing with what they had learned about working optimally: The cooperative spirit among these workers surprised me. After all, I was an outsider and a Northerner.

On the other hand, I had not expected to find physical work so demanding. Clipboard and stop watch in hand, the absentee factory owner's relative would often pause by my presses suggesting how to save a few seconds in the way I smoothed the cloth before releasing the press hoods. Satisfied that I was working at my physical limit, he moved on to the next worker, and the next.

My goal was to work as fast as I could without either making mistakes or getting hurt. The hot metal hoods had no safety catches, and they sometimes crashed without warning. Like other leggers, I had mild burns on my fingers and arms. The knowledge that burned or bandaged hands made reaching my

[9]Reprinted with permission from: *Los Angeles Times* Opinion Section, Sunday, September 2, 1979.

production quota impossible and the fear of being seriously hurt kept me alert. I did not want to be maimed as had leggers before me.

To get through the day, I learned to accept the pressure—a kind of numbed attentiveness—of working with dangerous equipment. And I became inured to the particular kind of sharp leg pains that come from standing on cement for eight and nine hours a day. I even joined the other workers in bolting down lunch in order to steal 10 minutes of our half-hour break back at the machines in order to fill our daily quota.

I had much more trouble accepting the fact that production levels were set by the fastest worker, although that is illegal. It was standard practice for the efficiency expert to revise the quotas upward when too many workers were able to make it.

Nor did I get used to the fact that our employer guaranteed neither a steady paycheck nor fixed hours. When, for example, equipment broke down further up the line or sufficient material had not been prepared for the end-production workers to process, we were sent home in the middle of the day, without pay. More frequently, we were required to work overtime. What rankled was not being told about extra work until just before clock-out time, when the parking lot was already filled with waiting cars of cranky children and husbands needing to get to other factories for second-shift work. Most Friday afternoons we were told we had to work at least a half day on Saturday.

On the last line of production, where the temperature was constantly over 100 degrees, my fellow production workers, sweating women in sleeveless shirts, the "oven girl," the "bundle girls," the "leggers" and the "toppers"—were the youngest, strongest women in the plant. At the other end of the long room, where it was not suffocatingly hot, mostly older women bent over sewing machines, making pockets, button holes, zippers, belt loops, every component of military pants.

The factory was filled with long rows of toiling grandmothers, and daughters, sisters-in-law and cousins, all women except for the boss, the efficiency expert, the mechanics and some of the inspectors. In this small Southern factory, operating under a U.S. government contract, everyone was white except for two Asians and a single black woman.

The women I worked with had an attitude of strength and unity. Several times the best legger walked off her presses when one of the hoods thudded down unexpectedly; it gave others the courage to do the same. Another legger quit after getting a severe shock from the steam gun we used to remove imperfect creases. After that, we repeatedly complained to the plant manager about the condition of the equipment until it was repaired properly.

Much of what I learned in the apparel factory was from the women with whom I worked. But I never learned why all of us worked so hard. We knew that when our machines were broken, the allowances for "lost time" were insufficient. We knew we were making only the minimum wage. Yet we worked harder and harder, the only visible reward being the job well done, the satisfaction of making production, and, of course, the bottom line: keeping our jobs in a region and at a time when work was scarce. As best I could figure it, the women I worked with were courageous in trying to fight what they could and were silent in the face of what they were powerless to change alone.

At the time, I did not know that textiles are the bedrock of the Southern economy. The industry's $16 billion to $18 billion in sales annually is 30 percent to 50 percent higher than the volume of Southern agricultural sales. Textiles account for one-quarter of the jobs in five Southern states.

Nor did I know that textile manufacturers pay the lowest industrial wages in the nation. Mill workers earn $75 a week less than the average American factory workers. And textiles is the only major U.S. industry that is not unionized.

# REFERENCES

Barnes, R. M., *Motion and Time Study: Design and Measurement of Work* (7th ed.), Wiley, New York, 1980.

Barnes, R. M., *Work Sampling* (2nd ed.), Wiley, New York, 1957.

Carlisle, B., "Job Design Implications for Operations Managers," *International Journal of Operations and Production Management, 3*(3), 1983, pp. 40–48.

Davis, L. E., and J. C. Taylor (eds.), *Design of Jobs,* Penguin Books, Middlesex, England, 1972.

Englestad, P. H., "Socio-Technical Approach to Problems of Process Control," in *Design of Jobs,* L. E. Davis and J. C. Taylor (eds.), Penguin Books, Middlesex, England, 1972.

McCormick, E. J., *Human Factors Engineering* (3rd ed.), McGraw-Hill, New York, 1970.

Mundel, M. E., *Motion and Time Study* (5th ed.), Prentice-Hall, Englewood Cliffs, N.J., 1978.

Niebel, B. W., *Motion and Time Study* (7th ed.), Irwin, Homewood, Ill., 1982.

Rice, R. S., "Survey of Work Measurement and Wage Incentives," *Industrial Engineering,* 9(7), July 1977, pp. 18–31.

Scoville, J. G., "A Theory of Jobs and Training," *Industrial Relations, 9,* 1969, pp. 36–53. Also in L. E. Davis and J. C. Taylor (eds.), *Design of Jobs,* Penguin Books, Middlesex, England, 1972.

# CHAPTER 20

# FACILITY LAYOUT AND ASSEMBLY LINE BALANCING

The facility layout is the integrating phase of the design of productive systems. It is the physical expression of the technological choices, the capacity requirements, the process and job designs, the material handling, and the communication systems that interconnect the processes.

## BASIC LAYOUT TYPES AND COMPETITIVE PRIORITIES

The competitive priorities that determine the choice between process- and product-focused systems also dominate in determining the basic layout type for a given system. If the competitive priorities are for flexibility and quality, suggesting a process-focused system, then the technological choices and the organization of jobs make a *functional layout* of facilities logical, such as the machine shop layout shown in Figure 20-1*a*. If cost and product availability dominate the competitive priorities, indicating a product-focused system, then the technological choices and job designs indicate a *line layout,* such as the layout for the production of a high-volume, standardized product shown in Figure 20-1*b*. But, in making choices of system type, there are some important issues of a system design nature that can impact the decision, and we discuss them under the headings for each layout type.

## FUNCTIONAL LAYOUT FOR PROCESS-FOCUSED SYSTEMS

Many examples of functional layouts can be found in practice, for instance, in manufacturing, hospitals and medical clinics, large offices, municipal services, and libraries. In every situation, the work is organized according to the function performed. The machine shop is one of the most common examples, and the name and much of our knowledge of functional layout results from the study of such manufacturing systems. Table 20-1 summarizes the typical departments or service centers that occur in several generic types of functionally laid out systems.

In all the generic types of functional systems, the item being processed (part, product, information, or person) normally goes through a processing sequence, but the work done and the sequence of processing vary. At each service center, the specification of what is to be accomplished determines the details of processing and the time required. For each service center, we have the general conditions of a waiting line (queuing) system with random arrivals of work and random processing rates. When we view a functional layout as a whole, we can visualize it as a network of queues with variable paths or routes through the system, depending on the details of the processing requirements.

FIGURE 20-1
**(*a*) FUNCTIONAL LAYOUT PATTERN FOR PROCESS FOCUS AND (*b*) LINE LAYOUT PATTERN FOR PRODUCT FOCUS.**

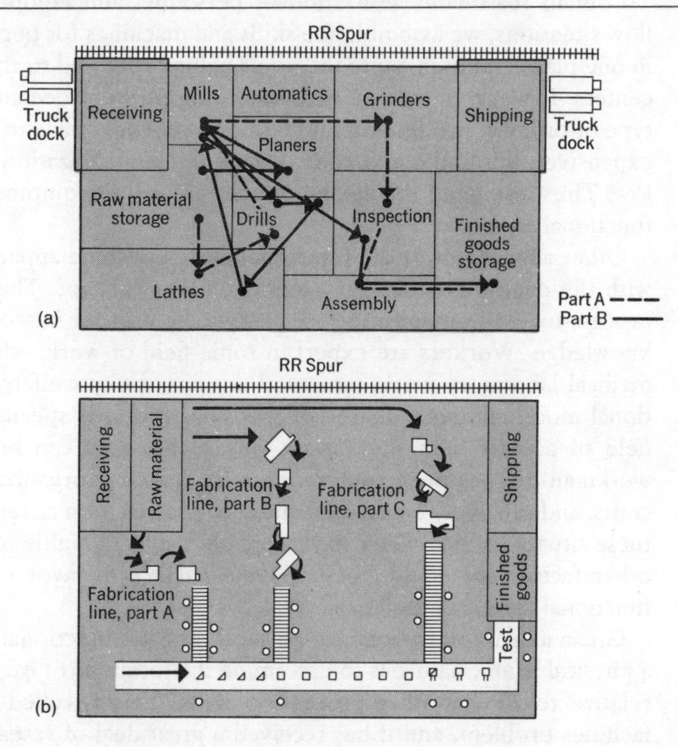


TABLE 20-1
**TYPICAL DEPARTMENTS OR SERVICE CENTERS FOR VARIOUS GENERIC TYPES OF PROCESS-FOCUSED SYSTEMS**

| Generic System | Typical Departments or Service Centers |
|---|---|
| Machine shop | Receive, stores, drill, lathe, mill, grind, heat-treat, inspection, assembly, ship |
| Hospital | Receiving, emergency, wards, intensive-care, maternity, surgery, laboratory, x-ray, administration, cashier, etc. |
| Medical clinic | Initial processing; external examination; eye, ear, nose and throat; x-ray and fluoroscope; blood tests; electrocardiograph and electro-encephalograph; laboratory; dental; final processing |
| Engineering office | Filing, blueprint, product support, structural design, electrical design, hydraulic design, production liaison, detailing and checking, secretarial pool |
| Municipal offices | Police dept., jail, court, judge's chambers, license bureau, treasurer's office, welfare office, health dept., public works and sanitation, engineer's office, recreation dept., mayor's office, town council chambers |

## Decision to Organize Facilities by Process

To obtain reasonable utilization of personnel and equipment in process-focused flow situations, we assemble the skills and machines for performing a given function in one place and then route the items being processed to the appropriate functional centers. If we tried to specialize according to the processing requirements of each type of order in production line fashion, we would have to duplicate many kinds of expensive skills and equipment. The equipment utilization would probably be very low. Thus, the need for flexibility *and* reasonable equipment utilization suggests a functional layout.

Other advantages of the functional design become apparent when it is compared with the continuous flow or production line concept. The jobs that result from a process-focused organization are likely to be broader in scope and require more job knowledge. Workers are expert in some field of work, whether it is heat-treating, medical laboratory work, structural design, or city welfare. Even though the functional mode implies a degree of specialization, it is specialization within a generic field of activity, and the variety within that field can be considerable. Pride in workmanship has been traditional in this form of organization of work by trades, crafts, and relatively broad specialties. Job satisfaction criteria seem easier to meet in these situations than when specialization results in highly repetitive activities and, if other factors are equal, could tip the balance in favor of a process focus and a functional layout of facilities.

Given a decision to organize physical facilities functionally, the major problem of a physical layout nature is to determine the locations of each of the processing areas relative to all the other processing areas. This is called the relative location of facilities problem, and it has received a great deal of research attention.

## Relative Location of Facilities Problem

In a machine shop, should the lathe department be located adjacent to the mill department? In a hospital, should the emergency room be located adjacent to intensive care? In an engineering office, should product support be located adjacent to electrical design? In municipal offices, should the welfare and health department offices be adjacent to each other? The locations will depend on the need for one pair of facilities to be adjacent (or close) to each other relative to the need for other pairs of facilities to be adjacent or close to each other. We must allocate locations based on the relative gains and losses for the alternatives and seek to minimize some measure of the cost of having facilities nonadjacent.

### CRITERIA

We are attempting to measure the interdepartmental interactions required by the nature of the system. How much business is carried on between departments, and how do we measure it? In manufacturing systems, material must be handled from department to department, in offices, people walk between locations to do business

TABLE 20-2
**CRITERIA FOR DETERMINING THE RELATIVE LOCATION OF FACILITIES IN PROCESS-FOCUSED SYSTEMS**

| Generic System | Criterion |
|---|---|
| Manufacturing | Interdepartment material handling cost |
| Hospital | Cost of personnel walking between departments |
| Medical clinic | Walking time of patients between departments |
| Offices | Cost of personnel walking between areas and equipment or face-to-face contacts between individuals |

and communicate; and in hospitals, patients must be moved and nurses and other personnel must walk from one location to another. Table 20-2 summarizes the criteria for four systems.

By their very nature, functional layouts have no fixed path of work flow. We must aggregate for all paths and seek a combination of relative locations that optimizes the criterion. Although this location combination may be poor for some paths through the system, in the aggregate it will be the best arrangement of locations.

### COMPLEXITY OF THE RELATIVE LOCATION PROBLEM

Figure 20-2 shows, in schematic form, 6 process areas arranged on a grid. If any of the 6 departments can be located in any of the 6 alternative locations, there are $6! = 720$ possible arrangements, of which 90 are different in terms of their effects on the cost of interdepartmental transactions. For this trivial problem, we could consider enumerating all the different location combinations, comparing aggregate costs, and selecting the combination with the minimum cost. However, the number of combinations to evaluate increases rapidly as we increase the number of departments. For just 9 departments on a $3 \times 3$ grid, we have more than 45,000 combinations. For 20 departments arranged on a $4 \times 5$ grid we have $608 \times 10^{15}$ combinations. Therefore, we must rule out enumeration as a practical approach.

## Operation Sequence Analysis

An early graphical approach to the problem, called operation sequence analysis, led to a powerful computerized model, which we will also examine.[1] Operation sequence analysis maintains close contact with the nature of the problem and is useful for relatively small problems.

We will use a private industrial clinic that performs services under contract for a number of business and industrial firms as an example. These services include medical examinations for new employees as well as annual physical examinations for all employees. The clinic performs eight types of examination sequences, depending on the details of the individual contracts. Many people who have been examined

[1] See E. S. Buffa, "Sequence Analysis for Functional Layouts," *Journal of Industrial Engineering*, 6(2), March–April 1955.

FIGURE 20-2
**THERE ARE 6! = 720 POSSIBLE ARRANGEMENTS OF THE SIX PROCESS AREAS IN THE SIX LOCATIONS OF THE GRID.**

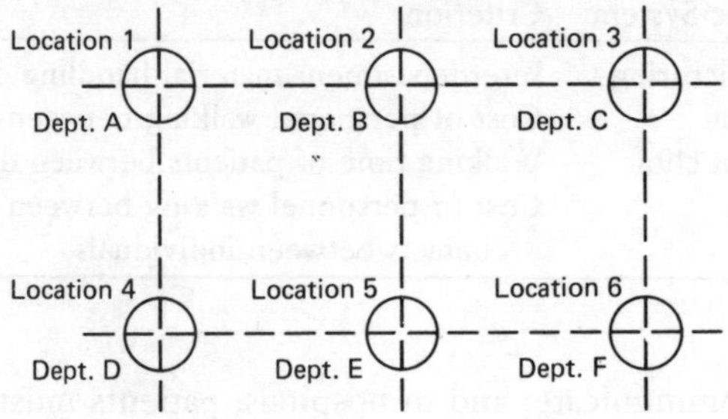

Location 1 Location 2 Location 3
Dept. A Dept. B Dept. C
Location 4 Location 5 Location 6
Dept. D Dept. E Dept. F

have complained about excessive walking because of the clinic layout. The director of the clinic wants to know what a good solution would look like.

### STEP 1—THE LOAD SUMMARY

Table 20-3 represents a one-month sample of the flow among the 11 departments, aggregating over all types of examinations, called a load summary. It summarizes the flow among all combinations of departments. If we were dealing with a new product for which there were no historical data, the part and product routings and system volumes could be used to estimate the flow densities.

### STEP 2—SCHEMATIC REPRESENTATION

The information contained in the load summary is placed in an equivalent schematic diagram in which circles represent the functional service centers. Connecting lines are labeled to indicate the intensity of travel or transactions between centers in either direction. Figure 20-3 is a first solution, which is obtained merely by placing the work centers on a grid following the logic of the pattern indicated by the load summary.

### STEP 3—SOLUTION IMPROVEMENT

The initial solution may be improved by inspecting the effect of changes in location. When an advantageous change is found, the diagram is altered. For example, in Figure 20-3 work center 4 has a total of 300 trips to or from work centers that are not adjacent; that is, to or from work centers 2 and 6. If work center 4 is moved to the location between 2 and 6, all loads to and from 4 become adjacent.

Further inspection shows that 200 nonadjacent trips occur between work centers 6 and 8. Is an advantageous shift possible? Yes. By moving 9 down and placing 8 in the position vacated by 9, the number of nonadjacent trips is reduced from 200 to 100. Figure 20-4 shows the diagram with these changes incorporated.

Further inspection reveals no further obvious advantageous shifts in location.

TABLE 20-3
**LOAD SUMMARY: SAMPLE OF NUMBER OF TRIPS PER MONTH BETWEEN ALL COMBINATIONS OF DEPARTMENTS FOR AN INDUSTRIAL MEDICAL CLINIC**

| *From* | | *To* | | | | | | | | | | |
|---|---|---|---|---|---|---|---|---|---|---|---|---|
| *Departments* | | 1 Initial Processing | 2 Eye Examination | 3 Ear, Nose and Throat | 4 X-ray and Fluoroscope | 5 Blood Tests | 6 Blood Pressure Check | 7 Respiratory Check | 8 Electrographic | 9 Laboratory | 10 Dental Examination | 11 Final Processing |
| Initial Processing | 1 | | 600 | | | | | | | | | |
| Eye Examination | 2 | | | 400 | 100 | | | 100 | | | | |
| Ear, Nose, and Throat | 3 | | | | 350 | 50 | | | | | | |
| X-ray and Fluoroscope | 4 | | | | | | 100 | 450 | | | | |
| Blood Tests | 5 | | | | | | | 50 | | | | |
| Blood Pressure Check | 6 | | | | 100 | | | | | 150 | 100 | |
| Respiratory Check | 7 | | | | | | 50 | | 450 | 100 | | |
| Electrographic | 8 | | | | | | 200 | | | 250 | | |
| Laboratory | 9 | | | | | | | | | | 500 | |
| Dental Examination | 10 | | | | | | | | | | | 600 |
| Final Processing | 11 | | | | | | | | | | | |

Figure 20-4 has a trip-distance rating of $2 \times 100 = 200$, that is, 100 trips $\times$ 2 units of grid distance. For larger problems, grid distance becomes an important part of the measure of effectiveness because frequently used work centers might be separated by many grid units. Figure 20-4 represents a good solution because most of the work centers are adjacent to the other work centers involving interdepartmental flow.

### STEP 4—THE BLOCK DIAGRAM

The block diagram is developed by substituting estimated areas for the small circles in the schematic diagram. Initially, this can be done with block templates to find an arrangement that is compatible with both the flow pattern of the schematic diagram and the various size requirements for the departments. Figure 20-5 shows such an initial block diagram. Although the essential character of the schematic diagram is retained, Figure 20-5 obviously does not yet represent a practical solution. Varying the shapes of departments will enable us to fit the system into a rectangular configuration and meet possible shape and dimension restrictions that may be imposed by the site, the existing building, or the desired configuration of a new building. Figure 20-6 shows such a block diagram.

FIGURE 20-3
**INITIAL GRAPHIC SOLUTION DEVELOPED FROM THE LOAD SUMMARY OF TABLE 20-3.**

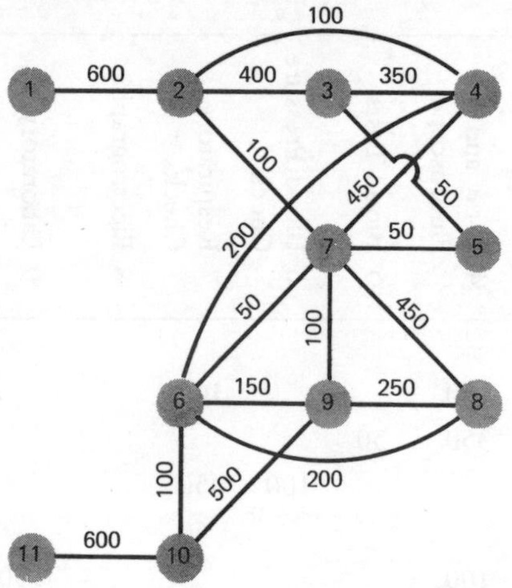

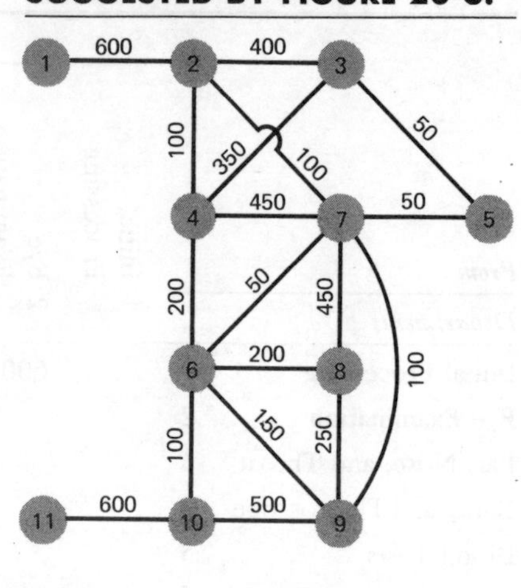


FIGURE 20-4
**SCHEMATIC DIAGRAM INCORPORATING CHANGES SUGGESTED BY FIGURE 20-3.**

The final block diagram represented by Figure 20-6 becomes an input for a detailed layout. The detailed layout phase would undoubtedly require minor shifts in space allocation and shape, but the basic relationships would be retained.

## CRAFT (Computerized Relative Allocation of Facilities)

The graphical approach to the determination of the relative location of departments has obvious limitations. Its effectiveness depends on the individual analyst's insight, and as the number of activity centers increase, the effectiveness of the technique breaks down. Practical problems in facility location often involve 20 or more activity centers, and this number is already at the limit for the feasible use of the operation sequence analysis technique. To overcome this limitation, a computerized relative allocation of facilities technique (CRAFT) was developed, which easily handles up to 40 activity centers and has other important advantages. Versions of CRAFT are now available for microcomputers.

### THE CRAFT PROGRAM[2]

The CRAFT program takes as input data matrices of interdepartmental flow and interdepartmental unit transaction costs together with a representation of a block

[2] See G. C. Armour and E. S. Buffa, "A Heuristic Algorithm and Simulation Approach to Relative Location of Facilities," *Management Science*, 9(1), 1963, pp. 294–309; E. S. Buffa, G. C. Armour, and T. E. Vollmann, "Allocating Facilities with CRAFT," *Harvard Business Review*, *42*(2), March–April 1964, pp. 136–159; and T. E. Vollmann and E. S. Buffa, "The Facilities Layout Problem in Perspective," *Management Science*, *12*(10), June 1966, pp. 450–468.

FIGURE 20-5
**INITIAL BLOCK DIAGRAM. ESTIMATED AREAS ARE SUBSTITUTED FOR CIRCLES IN THE SCHEMATIC DIAGRAM OF FIGURE 20-4.**

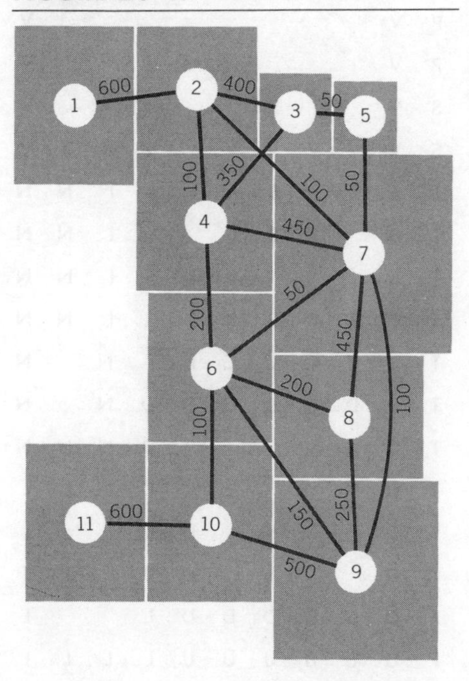


FIGURE 20-6
**BLOCK DIAGRAM THAT TAKES ACCOUNT OF RECTANGULAR BUILDING SHAPE.**

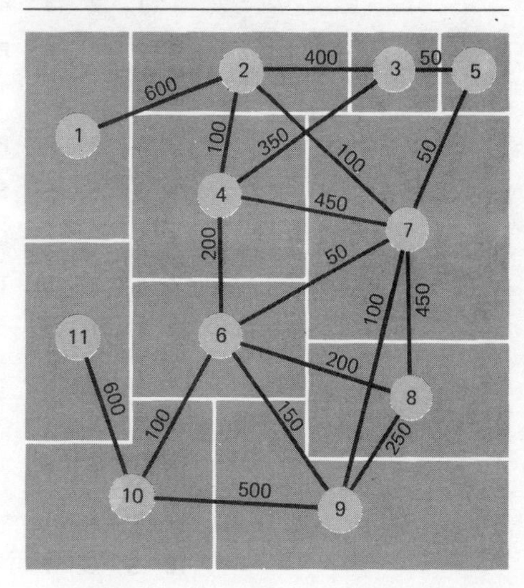


layout. The block layout that is fed in may be the existing layout or any arbitrary starting solution if a new facility is being developed. The program calculates geographic department centers and an estimate of total interaction costs for the input layout. The governing heuristic algorithm then asks: What change in interaction costs would result if locations of departments were exchanged? Within the computer, the locations of the activity centers are exchanged, and the interaction costs are recomputed. Whether the result is an increase or a decrease, the difference is recorded in the computer's memory. The program then asks the same question for other combinations of departments and again records cost differences. It proceeds in this way through all combinations of exchanges. The present algorithm involves either two- or three-way exchanges.

When the cost differences for all such combinations have been computed, the program selects the exchange that would result in the largest reduction, makes the exchange in locations on the block diagram, and then prints out the new block layout, the new total interaction cost, the cost reduction effected, and the departments involved in the exchange. Figure 20-7 is an example of the block diagram portion of the output for an application for a precision manufacturer in the aerospace industry.

FIGURE 20-7
**SAMPLE CRAFT BLOCK DIAGRAM OUTPUT FOR AN APPLICATION FOR A PRECISION MANUFACTURER IN THE AEROSPACE INDUSTRY.**

| | 1 | 2 | 3 | 4 | 5 | 6 | 7 | 8 | 9 | 10 | 11 | 12 | 13 | 14 | 15 |
|---|---|---|---|---|---|---|---|---|---|---|---|---|---|---|---|
| 1 | P | P | P | P | P | V | V | V | V | V | V | V | V | V | V |
| 2 | P | | | | P | V | | | | | | | | | V |
| 3 | S | P | P | P | P | V | | | | | | | | | V |
| 4 | S | S | S | S | S | V | | | | | | | | | V |
| 5 | S | | | S | S | V | V | V | V | V | V | V | V | V | V |
| 6 | S | S | S | T | T | B | B | B | B | M | I | I | I | N | N |
| 7 | T | T | T | | T | B | | | B | I | | | I | N | N |
| 8 | T | T | | | T | B | | | | B | I | | I | N | N |
| 9 | R | R | T | | T | B | B | B | B | B | I | | I | N | N |
| 10 | R | R | T | | T | C | C | C | C | C | I | I | N | | N |
| 11 | R | R | T | | T | D | D | D | D | D | D | D | N | | N |
| 12 | G | G | T | | T | D | | | | | | D | N | N | N |
| 13 | G | G | T | | T | D | | | | | | D | L | L | L |
| 14 | G | G | T | T | T | D | | | | | D | L | | | L |
| 15 | G | Q | Q | Q | Q | D | | | | | D | L | | | L |
| 16 | G | Q | Q | F | F | D | D | D | D | D | D | L | | | L |
| 17 | F | F | F | | F | U | U | U | U | U | U | L | L | L | L |
| 18 | F | | | | F | U | | | | | U | H | H | H | L |
| 19 | F | F | F | | F | U | | | | | U | H | E | E | E |
| 20 | J | J | J | F | F | U | U | U | U | U | U | E | | | E |
| 21 | J | J | J | A | A | K | K | K | K | K | K | E | | | E |
| 22 | A | A | A | | A | K | | | | | K | E | | | E |
| 23 | A | A | A | A | A | K | K | K | K | K | E | E | E | E | E |
| 24 | O | O | O | O | O | O | O | O | O | O | O | O | O | O | O |
| 25 | O | | | | | | | | | | | | | | O |
| 26 | O | | | | | | | | | | | | | | |
| 27 | O | O | | | | | | | | | | | | | O |
| 28 | O | | O | O | O | O | O | O | O | O | O | O | O | O | O |

TOTAL COST 900.93 EST COST REDUCTION 3.38 MOVEA Q MOVEB G MOVEC

*Source:* E. S. Buffa, G. C. Armour, and T. E. Vollmann, "Allocating Facilities with CRAFT," *Harvard Business Review, 42*(2), March–April 1964, pp. 136–159.

The basic procedure is then repeated, generating a second and a third improved block layout, and so on. Finally, when the procedure indicates that no further cost-reducing location exchanges can be made, the final block layout is printed out. This becomes the basis for a detailed template layout of the facility.

The program has the capacity for handling 40 activity centers. Any departmental location can be held fixed simply by specifying in the instructions that the department (or departments) is not a candidate for exchange. This feature has great practical importance because existing layouts cannot be completely rearranged. Fixed locations may develop when costly heavy equipment has been installed, or the location of receiving or shipping facilities may be determined by the location of roads or railroad spurs. Finally, it is often desirable to treat the locations of some work groups as fixed points in the layout. A subsequent development also enables the CRAFT program to include relocation costs as well as interaction costs in the computer program for relayout (Hicks and Cowan, 1976).

### APPLICATIONS OF CRAFT

The CRAFT program has been widely used in both manufacturing and nonmanufacturing situations. To the authors' knowledge, it has been used in four aircraft plants, two of the largest automobile companies, two computer manufacturers, a pharmaceutical manufacturer, a meat packer, a precision machine shop, a movie studio, and a hospital. Since the program has been freely available and has been circulated widely, many other applications have undoubtedly been made.

A powerful three-dimensional version of CRAFT has been developed by Roger V. Johnson (1982), which makes it possible to deal with the large-scale problems associated with space allocation and layout of space in multistory buildings.

## Project Systems and Fixed-Position Assembly

Large-scale projects are common in today's economy. In terms of facility utilization, they are intermittent systems, and their physical layout deserves a special comment. Examples of familiar large-scale projects are huge aerospace projects, such as the Polaris missile project, aircraft assembly, ship building, or large construction projects. Some of these kinds of projects involve basically conventional manufacturing systems to produce components that go into the project itself. The systems that manufacture these components will be typical of either functional or line manufacturing systems.

The heart of the project concept, however, lies in the assembly process, which is usually done on a fixed-position basis, either by necessity (as with buildings, dams, and bridges) or for reasons of economy (as with missiles, aircraft, ships, and other very large projects). In these fixed-position assembly situations, the equivalent of functional centers are commonly arranged around the unit being constructed in "staging areas." Some of the staging areas will be storage locations where material or components are inventoried until needed in the process. Other areas may involve some degree of fabrication or prefabrication before final assembly on the major unit.

The proximity of a staging area to the major unit may depend on frequency of use and travel time between the staging area and the unit. For example, in constructing a skyscraper, the heating and air conditioning unit need only be installed once; however, forming lumber and reinforcing steel will be used continuously throughout the rough construction stages. The general concepts of the computer location algorithms apply to project systems as well as to the kinds of situations already discussed. Because the project is commonly a one-time system, however, formal location procedures have not been used in practice, although the potential for use is valid.

## LINE LAYOUT FOR PRODUCT-FOCUSED SYSTEMS

In line layout, typified by Figure 20-1*b*, equipment is dedicated to parts and products, and if the same process is needed elsewhere in the system, it is duplicated, almost regardless of utilization.

Production line concepts have found their greatest field of application in assembly rather than in fabrication. This is true because machine tools commonly have fixed machine cycles, making it difficult to achieve balance between successive operations. The result can be poor equipment utilization and relatively high costs when production line concepts are applied to fabrication operations. In assembly operations, where the work is more likely to be manual, balance is much easier to obtain because the total job can be divided into smaller elements. If station 10 is too short whereas 16 is too long, part of the work of station 16 probably can be transferred to station 10 (perhaps the tightening of a single bolt). Because very little equipment is involved in assembly, its utilization may not be of great importance.

### Decision to Organize Facilities by Product

The managerial decision to organize facilities with a product focus and a line layout involves important requirements, and there are some consequences affecting the work force that should be weighed carefully.

The following conditions should be met if facilities are to be organized as a product-focused system,

1. Adequate volume for reasonable equipment utilization
2. Reasonably stable product demand
3. Product standardization
4. Part interchangeability
5. Continuous supply of materials

When the conditions for product-focused systems are met, significant economic advantages can result. The production cycle is speeded up because materials approach continuous movement. Since very little manual handling is required, the cost of material handling is low. In-process inventories are lower compared with those of batch processing because of the relatively fast manufacturing cycle. Because aisles are not used for material movement and in-process storage space is minimized, less total floor space is commonly required than for an equivalent functional system, even though more individual pieces of equipment may be required. Finally, the control of the flow of work (production control) is greatly simplified for product-focused systems because routes are direct and mechanical. No detailed scheduling of work to individual work places and machines is required because each operation is an integral part of the line. Scheduling the line as a whole automatically schedules the component operations.

Given the decision for designing a line layout, a major problem is subdividing the work so that smooth flow can result. The subdivision process is called *line balancing*.

## Line Balancing Concepts

Figure 20-8 shows a wooden toy car, the parts of which are named and numbered. We will use the assembly of the car to illustrate the concepts of precedence requirements, cycle time, and capacity specification and the meaning of optimum solutions.

### PRECEDENCE REQUIREMENTS

By examining the toy car, we can see the sequence restrictions that must be observed in its assembly. For example, the hubcaps must be installed on the wheels prior to subsequent assembly steps to ensure that the wood axle is not broken as a result of impact. Finally, the wheels cannot be assembled until the axle has been inserted in the car body.

These sequences must be observed because the toy car cannot be assembled correctly in any other way. On the other hand, it makes no difference whether the headlights are assembled before or after the wheels are assembled. Similarly, whether the front or rear wheels are assembled first is irrelevant.

The task sequence restrictions for assembling the toy car are summarized in Table 20-4. In general, the assembly tasks listed in the table are broken down into the smallest whole activity. For each task, we note in the right-hand column the task or tasks that must immediately precede it. Tasks *a* and *e* can take any sequence because no tasks need precede them. However, task *b* (install right headlight) must be preceded by task *a* (position body to conveyor). Only the immediate predecessor tasks are listed to avoid redundancy. The precedence restrictions in Table 20-4 are summarized in the diagram in Figure 20-9.

### CYCLE TIME AND CAPACITY

Now we can proceed with the grouping of tasks to obtain balance. But balance at what rate of output? What is to be the capacity of the line? This is an important point and one that makes the line balancing problem difficult. If there were no capacity restrictions, the problem would be simple; one could take the lowest common multiple approach. For example, if we had three operations that required 3.2, 2.0,

FIGURE 20-8
**TOY CAR WITH PARTS AND ASSEMBLY DETAILS.**

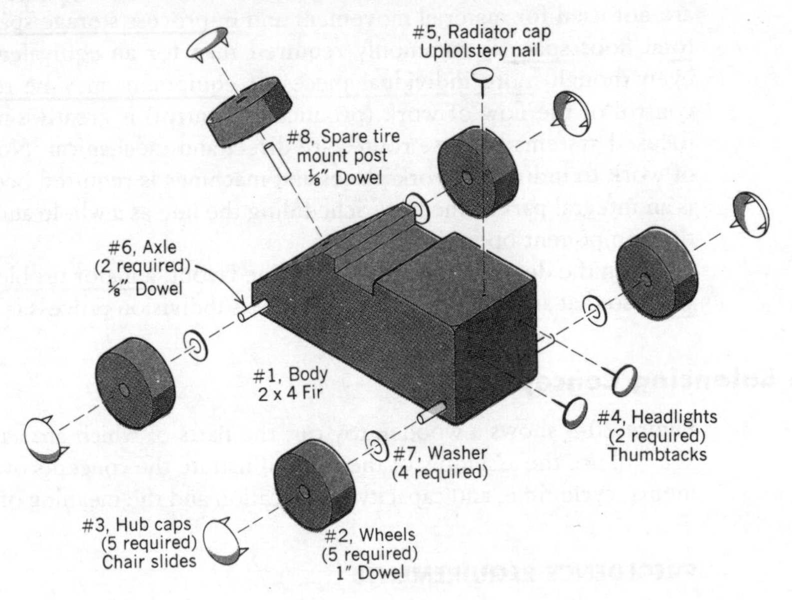


and 4.0 minutes, respectively, we could provide eight work places for the first, five for the second, and ten for the third. The capacity of the line would be 150 units per hour at each of the operations, and the cycle time would be 0.4 minutes. But capacity would then be specified by balance rather than by market considerations. For this illustration, we assume market studies justify a capacity of about 2600 toy cars per day or an average cycle time of 11 seconds.

## OPTIMUM SOLUTIONS

To meet this capacity requirement, no station could be assigned more than 11 seconds of work on the tasks shown in Figure 20-9. The total of all task times is 53 seconds. Therefore, with an 11-second cycle, (53/11 = 4.8) five stations are the minumum possible. Any solution that requires more than five stations would increase direct labor costs. Figure 20-10 shows a solution that assumes five stations. Furthermore, line capacity is determined by the "bottleneck" operation, the slowest operation in the sequence.

Although this example is simple, it illustrates the concepts of assembly line balancing. As the product becomes more complex, the relationships among tasks that end up within jobs may be more disjointed. As the enterprise is rewarded for its success by public acceptance of its product, volume increases and lines are rebalanced for smaller cycle times to achieve higher output rates, further restricting the content of jobs.

TABLE 20-4

**LIST OF ASSEMBLY TASKS SHOWING PERFORMANCE TIMES AND SEQUENCE RESTRICTIONS FOR THE TOY CAR ASSEMBLY**

| Task | Task Description | Performance Time, Seconds | Task Must Follow Task Listed Below |
|---|---|---|---|
| *a* | Position body to conveyor | 2 | — |
| *b* | Install right headlight | 3 | *a* |
| *c* | Install left headlight | 3 | *a* |
| *d* | Install radiator cap | 3 | *a* |
| *e*-1 | Install hubcap on spare tire | 4 | — |
| *e*-2 | Install hubcap on wheel | 4 | — |
| *e*-3 | Install hubcap on wheel | 4 | — |
| *e*-4 | Install hubcap on wheel | 4 | — |
| *e*-5 | Install hubcap on wheel | 4 | — |
| *f* | Assemble spare tire post on spare tire | 2 | *e*-1 |
| *g* | Assemble spare tire subassembly to body | 2 | *a,f* |
| *h*-1 | Press axle on wheel | 2 | *e*-2 |
| *h*-2 | Press axle on wheel | 2 | *e*-3 |
| *i*-1 | Assemble washer to wheel-axle subassembly | 1 | *h*-1 |
| *i*-2 | Assemble washer to wheel-axle subassembly | 1 | *h*-2 |
| *j*-1 | Assemble front wheel-axle-washer subassembly to body | 2 | *a, i*-1 |
| *j*-2 | Assemble back wheel-axle-washer subassembly to body | 2 | *a, i*-2 |
| *k*-1 | Assemble washer to front axle | 1 | *j*-1 |
| *k*-2 | Assemble washer to back axle | 1 | *j*-2 |
| *l*-1 | Press second wheel on front axle | 2 | *e*-4, *k*-1 |
| *l*-2 | Press second wheel on back axle | 2 | *e*-5, *k*-2 |
| *m* | "Drive" car off conveyor | 2 | *b,c,d,g,l* |

## Alternatives to Meet Job Satisfaction Requirements

The production line concept epitomizes division of labor and specialization and is the target of considerable criticism. The general line balancing techniques do not seem to leave a door open for the discussion of job design alternatives. The process starts with the determination of a cycle time that meets output rate needs and progresses toward the generation of stations (jobs) made up of tasks that meet the needs of the cycle and do not violate the technological constraints. Job satisfaction as a criterion seems to have no role in this process. But are there alternatives that will allow us to address the question of the degree of fractionation of jobs while retaining the production line concept?

### MULTIPLE STATIONS AND PARALLEL LINES

Given a capacity or production rate requirement, we can meet that requirement with a single line with a cycle time *c*, or with two parallel lines with a cycle time 2*c*, or

FIGURE 20-9
**PRECEDENCE DIAGRAM REPRESENTING THE SEQUENCE REQUIREMENTS SHOWN IN TABLE 20-4 FOR THE TOY CAR ASSEMBLY EXAMPLE. NUMBERS INDICATE THE TASK PERFORMANCE TIMES.**

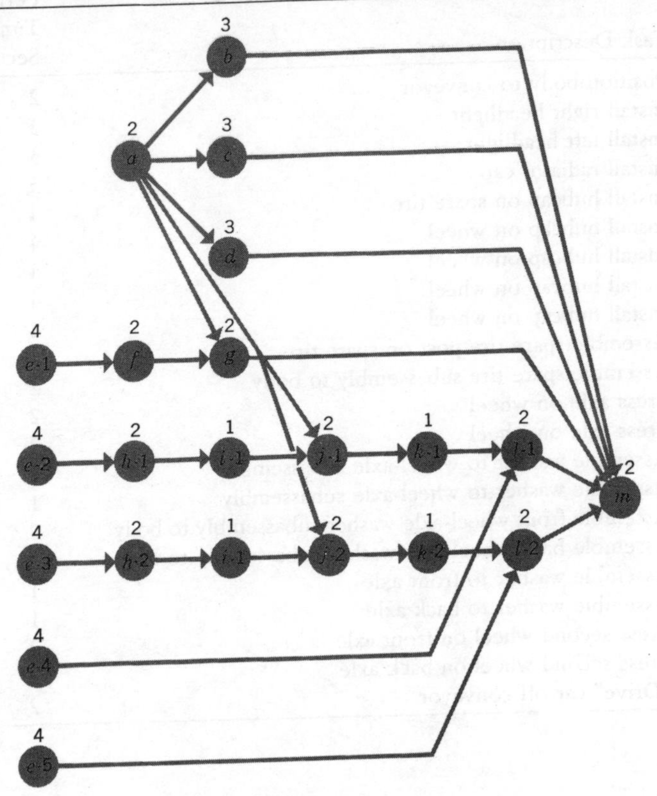


with three parallel lines with a cycle time $3c$, and so forth. Line balancing programs have been developed that enable us to use multiple parallel lines. As the number of parallel lines increases, so does the scope of jobs; and finally, we have complete horizontal job enlargement. The point is that alternatives do exist, even with the line organization of work.

In addition to increasing job scope, there are a number of advantages that result from the parallel line–multiple station concept. First, from the line balancing point of view, balance may be easier to achieve because the larger cycle time offers a greater likelihood of attaining a good fit with low residual idle time. This is particularly true when some of the task times are nearly equal to the single-line cycle time. Furthermore, a multiple-line design increases the flexibility of operations enormously. Output gradations are available; that is, one can have one, two, three, or more lines operating or not operating, and one can work overtime or undertime with all of the line combinations. There are fewer dependent operations; for example, if there is a difficulty with an operation in line 1, it may not affect line 2. A machine breakdown in line 1 need not stop the operation of line 2.

FIGURE 20-10
**A SOLUTION TO THE TOY CAR ASSEMBLY LINE BALANCING EXAMPLE. CYCLE TIME = 11 SECONDS; IDLE TIME = 2 SECONDS AT STATION 5.**

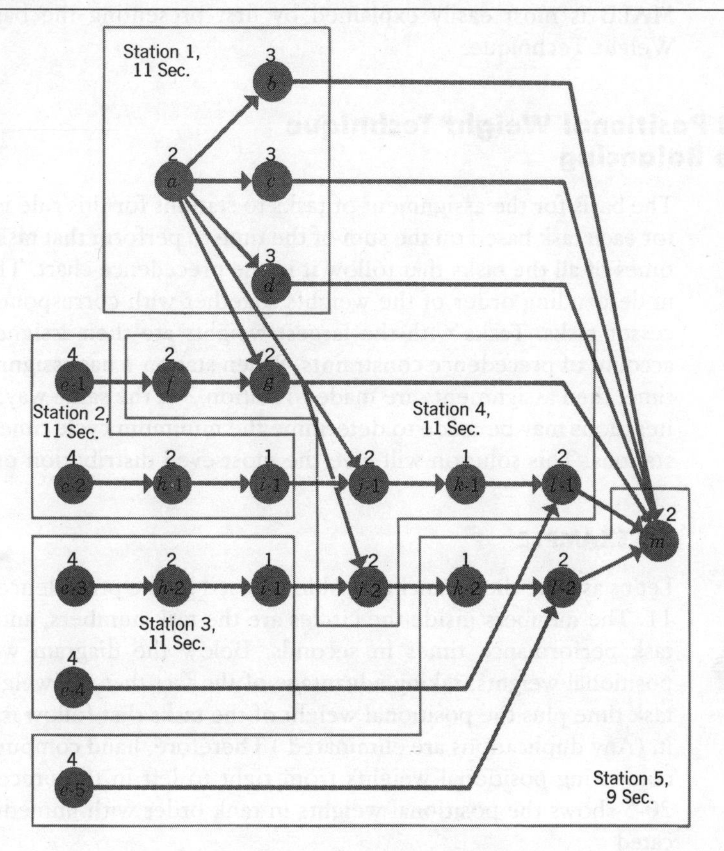


From a human organization viewpoint, the parallel line–multiple station concept has all the advantages of horizontal job enlargement. Work groups can be smaller and more cohesive. A team spirit may be engendered by competition among line teams on the bases of output, quality, safety, and other dimensions. On the other hand, capital investment is likely to increase with parallel line designs because of the duplication of equipment.

## COMPUTERIZED LINE BALANCING TECHNIQUES

Practical line balancing problems are relatively large-scale, involving up to 1000 tasks and 200 stations. Therefore, the algorithms need to be computerized so that optimal solutions can be generated in a relatively short time. As an example, we will present the basic Ranked Positional Weight Technique, followed by an improvement called MALB, a heuristic technique that has been computerized. The improvement by Mansoor (1964) went relatively unnoticed until it was computerized for large-scale problems by Dar-El (1973). (Dar-El and Mansoor are the same person.) MALB is most easily explained by first presenting the basic Ranked Positional Weight Technique.

## Ranked Positional Weight Technique for Line Balancing

The basis for the assignment of tasks to stations for this rule is to determine weights for each task based on the sum of the time to perform that task plus the performance times of all the tasks that follow it in the precedence chart. The tasks are then listed in descending order of the weights together with corresponding immediate predecessor tasks. Tasks with the largest weights are then assigned to station 1, taking account of precedence constraints. When station 1 has assignments that fill the cycle time, then assignments are made to station 2 in the same way, and so on. Successive iterations may be made to determine the minimum cycle time for a given number of stations. This solution will give the most even distribution of work across stations.

### AN EXAMPLE

Let us assume the balancing problem posed by the precedence diagram of Figure 20-11. The numbers inside the circles are the task numbers, and those outside are the task performance times in seconds. Below the diagram we have calculated the positional weights, taking advantage of the fact that the weight for a task is its own task time plus the positional weight of the tasks that follow it and are dependent on it. (Any duplications are eliminated.) Therefore, hand computing time is reduced by computing positional weights from right to left in the precedence diagram. Table 20-5 shows the positional weights in rank order with immediate predecessors indicated.

Next, consider the range of possible solutions. Note that the largest task time is $t = 45$ seconds for task 3, and the sum of all task times is 185 seconds. Therefore, the maximum number of stations that we wish to consider is $185/45 = 4.1$ or 4. We could have, then, 4, 3, 2, or 1 station. Figure 20-12 shows the balance delay graphs for 4, 3, and 2 stations. Balance delay, $d$, is defined as

$$d = \frac{100(nc - \Sigma t_i)}{nc} \tag{1}$$

where

$n$ = Number of stations on the line
$c$ = Cycle time
$t_i$ = Task times

and $n$, $c$, and $t_i$ are integer numbers.

The minimum possible balance delays in Figure 20-12 are 1.6, 0.5, and 0.5

FIGURE 20-11
**PRECEDENCE DIAGRAM SHOWING TASKS REQUIRED (CIRCLES WITH NUMBERS) AND TECHNOLOGICAL SEQUENCE REQUIREMENTS.**

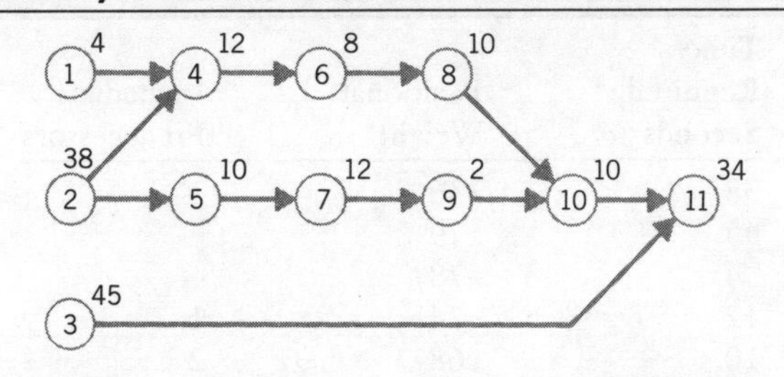


| Task Number | Task Time | Plus Positional Weight of Task Number | Positional Weight |
|---|---|---|---|
| 11 | 34 | — | 34 |
| 10 | 10 | 11 | 44 |
| 9 | 2 | 10 | 46 |
| 7 | 12 | 9 | 58 |
| 5 | 10 | 7 | 68 |
| 8 | 10 | 10 | 54 |
| 6 | 8 | 8 | 62 |
| 4 | 12 | 6 | 74 |
| 1 | 4 | 4 | 78 |
| 2 | 38 | 4, 5 (less times for Tasks 10 and 11) | 136 |
| 3 | 45 | 11 | 79 |
| | 185 seconds | | |

The numbers outside the circles are task times in seconds. Positional weights are calculated below the diagram as the sum of the task times plus the positional weights of the tasks that immediately follow (less any adjustments for duplications). For example, the times for tasks 10 and 11 are duplicated in the positional weights of tasks 4 and 5; therefore, in computing the positional weight for task 2 we have 38 + 74 + 68 − (10 + 34) = 136.

percent for 4, 3, and 2 stations, respectively. Assume that output requirements are for approximately 40 units per hour; therefore, a cycle time in the range of 60 to 70 seconds would provide the needed capacity. From Figure 20-12, we see that a cycle time of 62 seconds will in fact produce a minimum balance delay with 3 stations. We will therefore determine the balance for 3 stations with a minimum cycle time.

The basic ranked positional weight technique procedure is then as follows:

1. Select the task with the highest positional weight and assign it to the first work station.
2. Calculate the unassigned time for the work station by calculating the cumulative time for all the tasks assigned to the station and subtracting this sum from the cycle time.
3. Select the task with the next highest positional weight and attempt to assign it to the work station after making the following checks:

TABLE 20-5
**TASKS IN RANK ORDER OF POSITIONAL WEIGHT WITH IMMEDIATE PREDECESSORS INDICATED**

| Task Number | Time Required, Seconds | Positional Weight | Immediate Predecessors |
|---|---|---|---|
| 2 | 38 | 136 | — |
| 3 | 45 | 79 | — |
| 1 | 4 | 78 | — |
| 4 | 12 | 74 | 1, 2 |
| 5 | 10 | 68 | 2 |
| 6 | 8 | 62 | 4 |
| 7 | 12 | 58 | 5 |
| 8 | 10 | 54 | 6 |
| 9 | 2 | 46 | 7 |
| 10 | 10 | 44 | 8, 9 |
| 11 | 34 | 34 | 3, 10 |

a. Check the list of already assigned tasks. If the "immediate predecessor" tasks have been assigned, precedence will not be violated; proceed to step 3b. If the immediate predecessor tasks have not been assigned, proceed to step 4.

b. Compare the task time with the unassigned time. If the task time is less than the station unassigned time, assign the task and recalculate the unassigned time. If the task time is greater than the unassigned time, proceed to step 4.

FIGURE 20-12
**BALANCE DELAY GRAPHS FOR THE BALANCE PROBLEM OF FIGURE 20-11.**

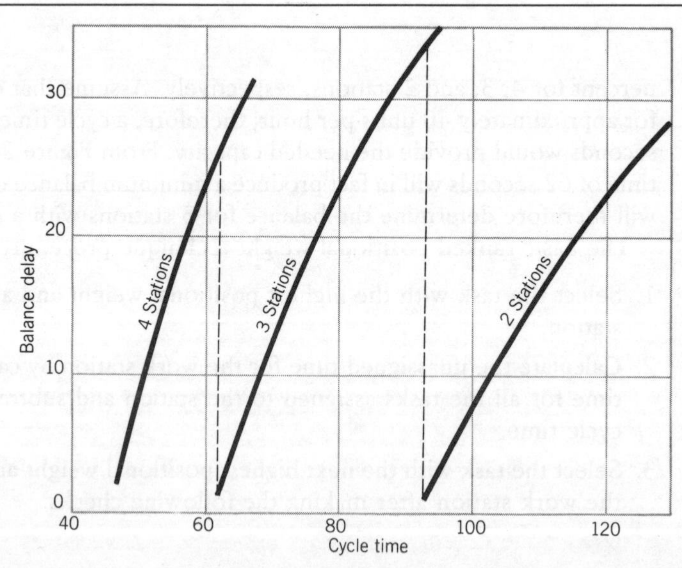

4. Continue to select, check, and assign tasks, if possible, until one of the following two conditions has been met:
   a. All tasks have been assigned.
   b. No unassigned work unit remains that can satisfy both the precedence requirements and the "less than the unassigned time" requirement.
5. Assign the unassigned task with the highest positional weight to the second work station, and continue through the preceding steps in the same manner.
6. Continue assigning tasks to stations until all tasks have been assigned.

Using these assignment rules, we generate Table 20-6 as a solution to the problem. This is the best solution possible with these assignment rules. If one attempts a solution at $c = 63$ seconds by the assignment rules, it is impossible to assign all tasks to only 3 stations. Referring to Figure 20-12, this solution for $c = 64$ seconds has a balance delay of 3.5 percent and slack units not assigned of $S = 7$ seconds.

## MALB—A Heuristic Technique for Large-Scale Problems

Dar El (Mansoor) improves on the solution presented in Table 20-6 by allowing backtracking after the initial assignments have been made to test other combinations of task times to see if they yield improvement.

TABLE 20-6
**ASSIGNMENTS OF TASKS TO STATIONS BY RANK POSITIONAL WEIGHT TECHNIQUE FOR THREE STATIONS AND A CYCLE TIME OF c = 64 SECONDS (SLACK TIME IS S = 7 Seconds)**

| Task Number | Weight | Predecessors | Time | Cumulative Station Time | Unassigned Time | Remarks |
|---|---|---|---|---|---|---|
| | | | *Assignments to Station 1* | | | |
| 2 | 136 | None | 38 | 38 | 26 | Assigned |
| ~~3~~ | ~~79~~ | ~~None~~ | ~~45~~ | ~~83~~ | | $> c$ |
| 1 | 78 | None | 4 | 42 | 22 | Assigned |
| 4 | 74 | 1, 2 | 12 | 54 | 10 | Assigned |
| 5 | 68 | 2 | 10 | 64 | 0 | Assigned |
| | | | *Assignments to Station 2* | | | |
| 3 | 79 | None | 45 | 45 | 19 | Assigned |
| 6 | 62 | 4 | 8 | 53 | 11 | Assigned |
| ~~7~~ | ~~58~~ | ~~5~~ | ~~12~~ | ~~69~~ | | $> c$ |
| 8 | 54 | 6 | 10 | 63 | 1 | Assigned |
| | | | *Assignments to Station 3* | | | |
| 7 | 58 | 5 | 12 | 12 | 52 | Assigned |
| 9 | 46 | 7 | 2 | 14 | 50 | Assigned |
| 10 | 44 | 8, 9 | 10 | 24 | 40 | Assigned |
| 11 | 34 | 3, 10 | 34 | 58 | 6 | Assigned |

### MALB ASSIGNMENT RULES

Dar-El's modified rules are as follows:

1. Begin by selecting the lowest cycle time corresponding to each of the number of work stations possible by, for example, referring to the balance delay graphs. Record the slack units available.
2. Select the task with the highest positional weight and assign it to the first work station.
3. Calculate the unassigned time for the station by calculating the cumulative time for all the tasks assigned to the station and subtracting this sum from the cycle time.
4. Select the task with the next highest positional weight and attempt to assign it to the station after making the following checks:
   a. Check the list of already assigned tasks. If the immediate predecessor tasks have been assigned, precedence will not be violated; proceed to step 4b. If the immediate predecessor tasks have not been assigned, proceed to step 5.
   b. Compare the task time with the unassigned time. If the task time is less than the station unassigned time, assign the task and recalculate the unassigned time. If the task time is greater than the unassigned time, proceed to step 5.
5. Continue to select, check, and assign tasks, if possible, until one of the following two conditions is met:
   a. A combination is obtained where the remaining unassigned time is less than or equals the slack units available; proceed to step 8.
   b. No unassigned task remains that can satisfy both the precedence and the unassigned time requirements; proceed to step 6.
6. Cancel each assigned task in turn, starting with the one having the lowest positional weight (the last one assigned) and, working back, go through steps 4 and 5 until either:
   a. A combination is obtained where the remaining unassigned time is less than or equals the slack units available; proceed to step 8.
   b. All combinations possible have unassigned times in excess of the slack units available so that no solution is possible; proceed to step 7.
7. Select a cycle time having one more unit and start again with step 2.
8. Assign the unassigned task with the highest positional weight to the second station and proceed through the preceding steps in the same manner.
9. Continue assigning tasks to stations until all the tasks have been assigned.

Note that rules 2, 3, 4, 5, 8, and 9 are the same as the rules for the basic procedure with a minor modification to rule 4. The important modifications are to rules 1, 6, and 7. Applying these rules to the same problem, Dar-El produces the solution shown in Table 20-7 with a cycle time of $c = 62$ seconds, one slack unit unassigned, and a balance delay of only 0.5 percent. Dar-El shows similar results for 4 stations and 2 stations. The comparative results are shown in Table 20-8.

TABLE 20-7
**ASSIGNMENT OF TASKS TO STATIONS RESULTING FROM APPLICATION OF DAR-EL'S RULES ($c$ = 62 SECONDS, $S$ = 1 SECOND IN STATION 2)**

| *Station 1* | | *Station 2* | | *Station 3* | |
|---|---|---|---|---|---|
| Task Number | Time, Seconds | Task Number | Time, Seconds | Task Number | Time, Seconds |
| 2 | 38 | 3 | 45 | 6 | 8 |
| 5 | 10 | 1 | 4 | 8 | 10 |
| 7 | 12 | 4 | 12 | 10 | 10 |
| 9 | 2 | | | 11 | 34 |
| Totals | 62 | | 61 | | 62 |

## COMBINATION LAYOUTS

There are variants of the functional and line types of layouts that commonly occur. First, many layouts are a combination of functional and line layouts, usually with fabrication operations being organized functionally and assembly being laid out in line fashion. The reasons the combinations occur are that the line layout requirements discussed are not always met for fabrication operations, particularly with regard to poor equipment utilization. Since fabrication machinery involves large investments, lower costs for this portion of the system can be obtained by time-sharing equipment for a variety of parts and products. Therefore, even though the other requirements stated for a product focus may apply to the fabrication portion of the system, a combination process–product system is more appropriate.

## GROUP TECHNOLOGY LAYOUT

Recall from our discussion of Group Technology (GT) in Chapter 15 that the concept exploits advantages that accrue from the computerized classification and

TABLE 20-8
**COMPARATIVE RESULTS BETWEEN BASIC MALB ASSIGNMENT RULES FOR THE SAMPLE PROBLEM IN FIGURE 20-11**

| | *Basic Positional Weight Rules* | | | *MALB Assignment Rules* | | |
|---|---|---|---|---|---|---|
| | *Number of Stations* | | | *Number of Stations* | | |
| | 2 | 3 | 4 | 2 | 3 | 4 |
| Minimum cycle time, seconds | 97 | 64 | 52 | 94 | 62 | 48 |
| Balance delay, percent | 4.5 | 3.5 | 11 | 1.5 | 0.5 | 3.5 |
| Unassigned slack time, seconds | 9 | 7 | 23 | 3 | 1 | 7 |

coding of part families to increase productivity for small lot manufacture. One of the advantages is in the layout of the physical facilities. GT layout takes a position between functional and line layouts, providing some of the advantages offered by each basic type.

## Applicability of GT Layout

In general terms, if the production lot size, $Q$, is large with respect to the number of different products or parts, $P$, we have the classic situation applicable to line layout. In the high $Q/P$ ratio situation, the large volume and low variety leads to dedicated equipment to exploit the advantages of line layout. At the other end of the $Q/P$ spectrum, we have the classic conditions for functional layout—small lot sizes and a large variety of parts and products. GT layout is applicable to the case where the $Q/P$ ratio is moderate and wewish to find layout patterns that share the advantages of both pure layout types. Figure 20-13 maps the appropriate layout types in relation to the $Q/P$ ratio.

There are three common GT layout patterns that offer advantages in material handling efforts, work organization, and job design: the GT flow line, the GT cell, and the GT center.

## The GT Flow Line

When product families are closely related and the $Q/P$ ratio is near the higher portion of the range applicable to GT layout, it is possible to "have your cake and eat it too," as shown in Figure 20-14*a*. Because of the close relationships among the products, the processing of each product or product family follows very nearly the same processing route. Therefore, horizontally in Figure 20-14*a* we have line flow within a family, but vertically we have processing centers not unlike those found in a functional layout. Thus, we have the advantages of line flow, with low in-process inventories and cycle times, but we also have much of the flexibility of a functional layout in that similar process types are located together, making it possible to obtain excellent equipment utilization and broader job designs.

An excellent example of a GT flow line is actually quite old. The Simmonds Saw Company had product families of saws that required approximately the same kinds of processes. Therefore, they reaped the benefits of line and functional layouts simultaneously as shown in Figure 20-15. Note that the basic physical layout is functional, with departments such as forging and welding, grinding, and so on, but the products flow through the process departments in about the same sequence as in a line layout.

## The GT Cell

When the processing flow for families of parts is different, the GT flow line is not appropriate. For this situation, all the operations for one or more of the families of parts are accomplished by a GT cell that contains the necessary equipment. The cell concept is then replicated to accommodate different families of parts, as illustrated

FIGURE 20-13
**APPLICATION OF LAYOUT TYPES IN RELATION TO THE Q/P RATIO.**

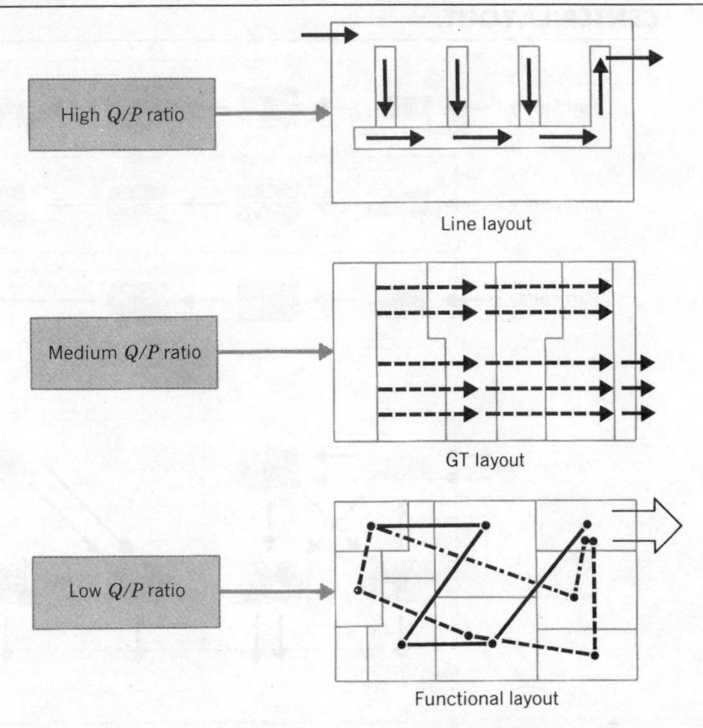


in Figure 20-14*b*. The cell concept represents a compromise between the GT flow line and the GT center, discussed in the following section.

### The GT Center

Figure 20-14*c* shows the GT center concept, which groups similar processing equipment together as does the functional layout but locates the equipment so that a part family can be processed by the same equipment as far as possible.

So, we have three variations of GT layout, the GT flow line being close in concept to the line layout, the GT center being close in concept to the functional layout, and the GT cell occupying a middle ground between them. All take advantage of the similarities of part families to the extent possible.

## SERVICE FACILITY LAYOUT

The layout of service systems can be very important for achieving the client–customer goal of fast service. Fast service is supported by point of sale systems, sometimes with scanners. Self-service is emphasized to provide fast service and to reduce costs, and convenience may be provided with equipment such as automatic tellers for banking operations.

FIGURE 20-14
**(*a*) GT FLOW LINE LAYOUT, (*b*) GET CELL LAYOUT, AND (*c*) GT CENTER LAYOUT.**

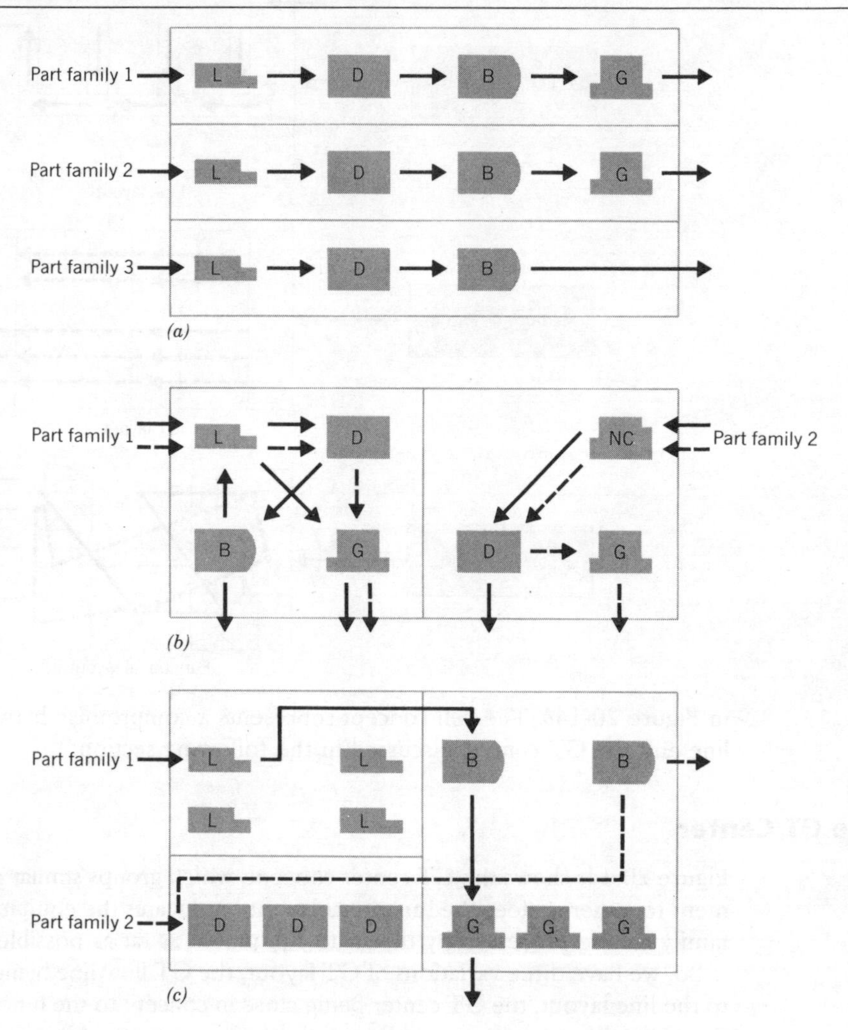


With the common emphasis in service systems on direct contact with the customer, attention should be focused on the waiting line structures presented in Figure 16-5. The single-channel, single-phase case may be thought of as a basic service facility module. Flow to the service facility, as well as the exit flow, needs careful planning to provide enough space for the waiting lines in ways that do not conflict. Well-designed systems provide for exiting without interfering with the waiting lines.

Basic service layouts follow the formats in manufacturing, being functional or line or a combination of the two. The production line approach to fast-food service is common, but the line layout also occurs in many other services, such as some

FIGURE 20-15
**SIMMONDS SAW COMPANY GT FLOW LINE.**

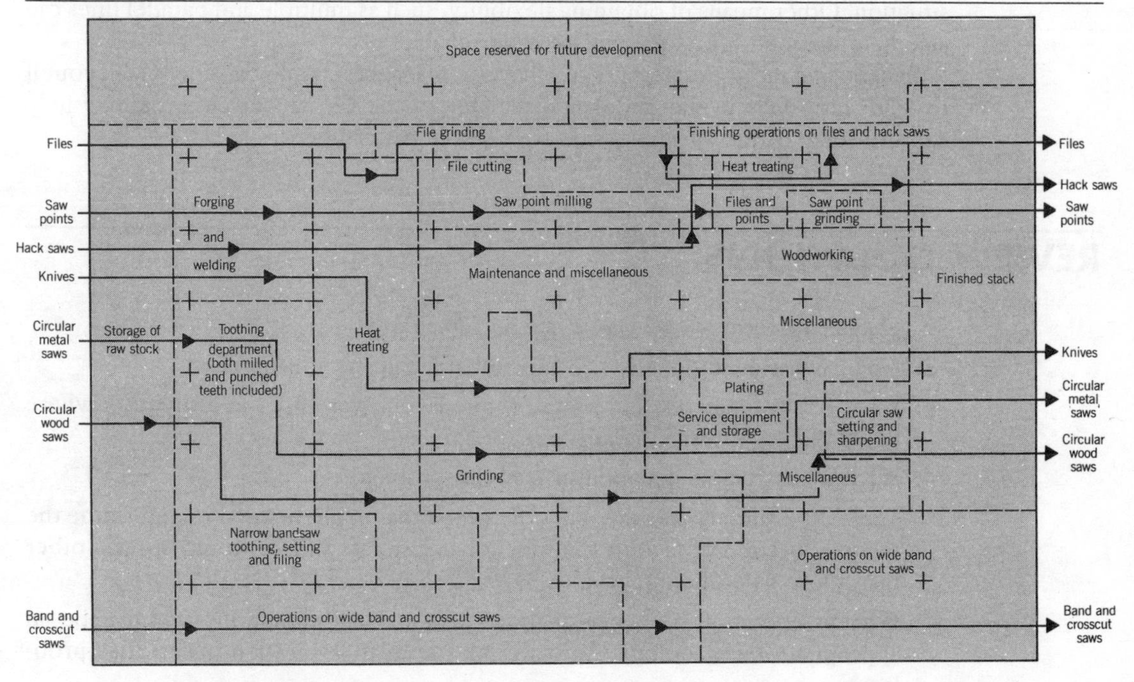


*Source:* F. E. Folts, *Introduction to Industrial Management,* McGraw-Hill, New York, 1963.

medical clinics and some high-volume office operations. In fact, as with manufacturing, when there are high-volume, standardized products, we find line layouts. Functional layout is common with many service operations, too, such as general offices, banks, general hospitals, and municipal offices.

## IMPLICATIONS FOR THE MANAGER

A clear understanding of the appropriateness of different layout flow patterns is needed. Aside from the job design aspects, product or line flow layout is appropriate only under certain conditions. The volume of activity necessary to justify specialized line operations is relatively large and requires a standardized product or service; variations are difficult to incorporate into line systems as compared to functional layouts. The conflict between job specialization and job satisfaction is a difficult one for managers. Specialization has many benefits to society and to an individual enterprise. There seems to be little question that specialized line-type operations are easier to plan for, are easier to schedule and control, require less space per unit of capacity, and so on. Yet specialized jobs create a work environment that raises social responsibility issues for managers.

The power of computerized line balancing systems to produce excellent solutions in short turnaround time is important in many situations. Computerized programs help managers to react to needed changes in output rate by rebalancing lines for different cycle times, providing flexibility in what may seem to be an inflexible situation. Other means of obtaining flexibility, such as multiple and parallel lines can also help broaden job scope and provide reliability.

In choosing the appropriate type of layout, managers should consider GT layout if the *Q/P* ratio falls in the middle range. One of the GT layout patterns may help capture some of the advantages of both classic patterns.

## REVIEW QUESTIONS

1. Define the terms *functional layout* and *line layout.*
2. Under what conditions would functional layout be appropriate?
3. What disadvantages would accrue if line layout were used in a situation where functional layout was the appropriate choice?
4. What is the relative location of facilities problem?
5. Table 20-2 summarizes the types of criteria that might be used to determine the relative location of facilities in functional systems. Where would criteria other than those listed be important?
6. What is operation sequence analysis? Under what conditions would it be an appropriate methodology for analyzing the relative location of facilities problem?
7. What is the CRAFT program? How does it function?
8. What type of layout is appropriate for project systems?
9. What is fixed position layout?
10. In the decision to organize for a product focus, why is each of the following factors a condition that should be met?
    a. Adequate volume for reasonable equipment utilization
    b. Reasonably stable product demand
    c. Product standardization
    d. Part interchangeability
    e. Continuous supply of material
11. Define the nature of the line balance problem.
12. How is the cycle time determined that is used in line balancing problems?
13. Define the term *balance delay.*
14. What is the nature of an optimal solution in a line balancing problem?
15. How is it possible to introduce the question of appropriate job breadth into the process for designing and balancing production lines?
16. Describe the Ranked Positional Weight Technique for line balancing. Outline the basic procedure.

17. How does the MALB procedure improve on solutions generated by the Ranked Positional Weight Technique?
18. Outline the MALB assignment rules.
19. What is the significance of the *Q/P* ratio in choosing layout patterns?
20. Under what conditions is GT layout appropriate?
21. Differentiate among the GT flow line, the GT cell, and the GT center.

# PROBLEMS

22. Consider the schematic diagram shown in Figure 20-4. Can you improve it?
23. A manufacturing concern has four departments, and the flow between departments is as follows:

| | *To* | | | |
|---|---|---|---|---|
| From | A | B | C | D |
| A | | 2 | | 2 |
| B | 2 | | 4 | |
| C | | 3 | | 1 |
| D | 2 | | 1 | |

a. Using the operations sequence analysis technique, how should the departments be arranged?

b. Now suppose that the area requirements are as follows:

Department A—3600 square feet
Department B—2400 square feet
Department C—2400 square feet
Department D—1600 square feet

Sketch the block diagram based on your answer in a.

c. Now assume that the four departments are located in two separate buildings that are 100 feet apart. The two buildings have floor areas of $60 \times 100 = 6000$ square feet housing Departments A and C and $40 \times 100 = 4000$ square feet housing Departments B and D, respectively. What should be the space allocation to the four departments if the material handling costs are as follows:

| | *To* | | | |
|---|---|---|---|---|
| From | A | B | C | D |
| A | | 1 | 1 | 2 |
| B | 1 | | 1 | 2 |
| C | 1 | 1 | | 2 |
| D | 2 | 2 | 2 | |

24. An organization does job machining and assembly and wishes to relayout its production facilities so that the relative location of departments reflects the average flow of parts through the plant somewhat better. In Table 20-9 we show an operation sequence summary for a sample of seven parts with approximate area requirements for each of the 13 machine or work centers. The number in the columns headed by each of the parts indicate the number of the work center to which the part goes next. Just below the sequence summary is shown a summary of production per month and the number of pieces handled at one time through the shop for each part.
    a. Develop a load summary showing the number of loads per month going between all combinations of work centers.
    b. Develop an idealized schematic layout that minimizes nonadjacent loads.
    c. Develop a block diagram that reflects the approximate area requirements and that results in an overall rectangular shape.
25. A layout study was made in the engineering office of a large aerospace manufacturer. Initially, the study focused on the flow of work through the system, but it was difficult to generate meaningful cost data on this basis.

    The search for realistic measures of effectiveness finally narrowed down to the relative location of people in the organization as required by their face-to-face contacts with others in the organization. It was decided to collect data on fact-to-face contacts initiated by each person for a one-month period and to

TABLE 20-9
**OPERATIONS SEQUENCE SUMMARY FOR PROBLEM 24**

| Machine or Work Center | Area, Square Feet | Work Center Number | *Part* A | B | C | D | E | F | G |
|---|---|---|---|---|---|---|---|---|---|
| Saw | 50 | 1 | | 2 | 2 | | | | 2 |
| Centering | 100 | 2 | | 4 | 3 | | | | 3 |
| Milling machines | 500 | 3 | 5 | 9 | 5 | 5 | | 4 | 4 |
| Lathes | 600 | 4 | | 5,7 | 7 | | 5 | 10 | 5 |
| Drills | 300 | 5 | 8 | 3 | 4 | 11 | 7 | | 6 |
| Arbor press | 100 | 6 | | | | | 11 | | 7 |
| Grinders | 200 | 7 | | 12 | 12 | | 6 | | 8 |
| Shapers | 200 | 8 | 9 | | | 3 | | | 9 |
| Heat treat | 150 | 9 | 11 | 4 | | | | | 10 |
| Paint | 100 | 10 | | | | | | 11 | 11 |
| Assembly bench | 100 | 11 | 12 | 13 | 13 | 13 | 13 | 13 | 12 |
| Inspection | 50 | 12 | 13 | 11 | 11 | | | | 13 |
| Pack | 100 | 13 | | | | | | | |
| *Production Summary* | | | | | | | | | |
| Pieces per month | | | 500 | 500 | 1600 | 1200 | 400 | 800 | 400 |
| Pieces per load | | | 2 | 100 | 40 | 40 | 100 | 100 | 2 |
| Loads per month | | | 250 | 5 | 40 | 30 | 4 | 8 | 200 |

TABLE 20-10
**NUMBER OF FACE-TO-FACE CONTACTS PER MONTH IN AN ENGINEERING OFFICE FOR PROBLEM 25**

| | *To* | | | | | | | | | |
|---|---|---|---|---|---|---|---|---|---|---|
| *From* | A Filing | B Supervision | C Blueprint | D Product Support | E Structural Design | F Electrical Design | G Hydraulic Design | H Production Liaison | I Detailing and Checking | J Secretarial Pool |
| A Filing | | 15 | | | | 5 | | 10 | | 15 |
| B Supervision | 20 | | 25 | 40 | 100 | 90 | 80 | 160 | 85 | 60 |
| C Blueprint | | | | | | | | | | |
| D Product Support | 10 | 15 | | | | | 20 | 280 | | 10 |
| E Structural Design | 50 | 20 | 600 | | | 40 | | | 340 | 50 |
| F Electrical Design | | | 475 | | | | | 160 | 270 | 60 |
| G Hydraulic Design | 10 | | 460 | 20 | | | | 140 | 320 | 45 |
| H Production Liaison | 20 | | | 200 | 160 | 190 | 240 | | | 680 |
| I Detailing and Checking | | 210 | 690 | 40 | 190 | 240 | 80 | | | 20 |
| J Secretarial Pool | | 25 | | | | | | 15 | | |

accumulate this data in the form of the matrix of Table 20-10. The entire department was divided into 10 groups or areas as indicated in Table 20-10. Each cell value indicates the number of face-to-face contacts initiated by that group; for example, 15 from A to B. Table 20-11 summarizes the area requirements for each group as well as the average hourly wage paid in each group. Figure 20-16 shows the present block layout.

TABLE 20-11
**AREA REQUIREMENTS AND AVERAGE WAGE RATES FOR 10 GROUPS IN A LARGE ENGINEERING OFFICE**

| | Group | Area | Average Hourly Wage |
|---|---|---|---|
| A | Filing | 20 × 15 = 300 sq. ft. | $2.25 |
| B | Supervision | 30 × 15 = 450 sq. ft. | 5.00 |
| C | Blueprinting | 40 × 15 = 600 sq. ft. | 2.10 |
| D | Product support | 25 × 20 = 500 sq. ft. | 2.70 |
| E | Structural design | 65 × 25 = 1625 sq. ft. | 4.50 |
| F | Electrical design | 25 × 35 = 875 sq. ft. | 4.50 |
| G | Hydraulic design | 45 × 30 = 1350 sq. ft. | 4.50 |
| H | Production liaison | 20 × 70 = 1400 sq. ft. | 2.70 |
| I | Detailing and checking | 70 × 25 = 1750 sq. ft. | 3.60 |
| J | Secretarial pool | 70 × 15 = 1050 sq. ft. | 2.40 |
| | | 90 × 110 = 9900 sq. ft. | |

FIGURE 20-16
**EXISTING BLOCK LAYOUT FOR 10 GROUPS WITHIN A LARGE ENGINEERING OFFICE.**

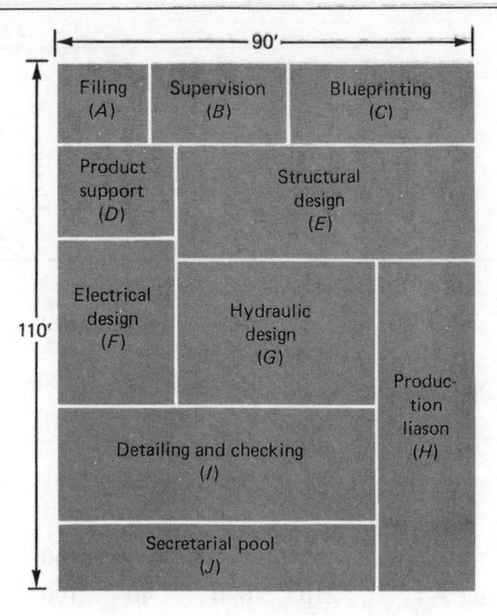


TABLE 20-12
**TASKS, PERFORMANCE TIMES, AND PRECEDENCE REQUIREMENTS FOR PROBLEM 26**

| Task | Performance Time, Minutes | Task Must Follow Task Listed Below |
|---|---|---|
| *a* | 4 | — |
| *b* | 3 | *a* |
| *c* | 5 | *b* |
| *d* | 2 | — |
| *e* | 4 | *c* |
| *f* | 6 | *e* |
| *g* | 2 | — |
| *h* | 3 | *dg* |
| *j* | 5 | *h* |
| *k* | 2 | — |
| *l* | 3 | *k* |
| *m* | 4 | *l* |

Prepare a new block layout within the constraints of the overall size of the layout shown in Figure 20-16.

26. Table 20-12 shows a list of assembly tasks with sequence restrictions and performance times. Construct a precedence diagram for the assembly. Balance the line for an output rate of 10 units per hour.
27. Using the Ranked Positional Weight Technique and the data from Table 20-12,
    a. Balance the line for a 10-minute cycle time. How many stations are required, and what balance delay results?
    b. Balance the line for a 9-minute cycle time. How many stations are required, and what balance delay results?
    c. Balance the line for a 9-minute cycle time. How many stations are required, and what balance delay results?
28. Using the solution for a 10-minute cycle time using the Ranked Positional Weight Technique in the preceding problem, can improvements be made using the MALB assignment rules?

# REFERENCES

Armour, G. C., and E. S. Buffa, "A Heuristic Algorithm and Simulation Approach to Relative Location of Facilities," *Management Science, 9*(1), 1963, pp. 294–309.

Buffa, E. S., G. C. Armour, and T. E. Vollmann, "Allocating Facilities with CRAFT," *Harvard Business Review, 42*(2), March–April 1964, pp. 136–159.

Buxey, G. M., "Assembly Line Balancing with Multiple Stations," *Management Science, 20*(6), February 1974, pp. 1010–1021.

Dar-El, E. M. (Mansoor), "MALB—A Heuristic Technique for Balancing Large Scale Single-Model Assembly Lines," *AIIE Transactions, 5*(4), December 1973.

Francis, R. L., and J. A. White, *Facility Layout and Location: An Analytical Approach*, Prentice-Hall, Englewood Cliffs, N.J., 1974.

Gunther, R. E., G. D. Johnson, and R. S. Peterson, "Currently Practiced Formulations of the Assembly Line Balance Problem," *Journal of Operations Management, 3*(4), August 1983, pp. 209–221.

Ham, I., K. Hitomi, and T. Yoshida, *Group Technology: Applications to Production Management*, Kluwer-Nijhoff Publishing, Boston, 1985. See Chapter 9 on "Layout Planning for Group Technology."

Hicks, P. E., and T. E. Cowan, "CRAFT-M for Layout Rearrangement," *Industrial Engineering, 8*, May 1976, pp. 30–35.

Johnson, R. V., "SPACECRAFT for Multi-Floor Layout Planning," *Management Science, 28*(4), April 1982.

Lew, P., and P. M. Brown, "Evaluation and Modification of CRAFT for an Architectural Methodology," in *Emerging Methods in Environmental Design and Planning*, G. T. Moore (ed.), MIT Press, Cambridge, Mass., 1970.

Mansoor, E. M. (Dar-El), "Assembly Line Balancing—An Improvement on the Ranked Positional Weight Technique," *Journal of Industrial Engineering, 15*(5), March–April 1964.

Nugent, C. E., T. E. Vollmann, and J. Ruml, "An Experimental Comparison of Techniques for the Assignment of Facilities to Locations," *Operations Research, 16*(1), January–February 1968, pp. 150–173.

Ritzman, L. P., "The Efficiency of Computer Algorithms for Plant Layout," *Management Science, 18*(5), January 1972, pp. 240–248.

Vollmann, T. E., and E. S. Buffa, "The Facilities Layout Problem in Perspective," *Management Science, 12*(10), June 1966, pp. 450–468.

CHAPTER 21

# MULTIPLE CRITERIA DECISION METHODS FOR PRODUCTION PROBLEMS

Production managers seek to attain low production costs, high quality of products, quick response to demand, and the flexibility to produce a variety of goods that match customers' tastes and specifications. These multiple concerns, useful in enhancing a firm's competitive position and profitability, must be considered in the design of a production system and in determining numerous planning and control decisions. Unfortunately, a factory or an operating system is seldom able to produce optimal results for all criteria simultaneously. Trade-offs must be made. Although the necessity of making trade-offs among multiple conflicting objectives or criteria has been recognized in the literature, few formal methods have been proposed to aid a manager in making such trade-offs. Almost all of the literature in production management deals with optimization on a single criterion, whereas nearly all real-world decisions involve balancing multiple concerns and criteria. In this chapter, we provide a framework for analyzing production problems that incorporates multiple criteria, and we discuss several methods that are useful in obtaining solutions for these problems.

## EXAMPLES OF PRODUCTION PROBLEMS WITH MULTIPLE CRITERIA

Consider a scheduling problem in which a manager must determine the sequence for the manufacture of some customized products with a common set of labor and facilities. In selecting a sequence, the manager may wish to balance machine utilization, work-in-process inventory, and on-time deliveries. Often, a sequence that is optimal (produces the best results) for one criterion may produce an unacceptable level for some other criterion. In fact, a manager may finally select a sequence that is not optimal with respect to any single criterion but provides a good solution for all the criteria of interest.

In materials management, at an aggregate level, a manager may be interested in balancing investment in inventory, the cost of running the department, and the service level provided. For example, a simple annual ordering of parts and components to satisfy the anticipated demand and adequate buffer stock may result in low cost of running the purchasing department and excellent service level but may require unacceptably high investment in inventory.

In selecting the location for a new plant, a manager may wish to balance land and building costs, delivery time to customers, labor availability, ability to attract professional and technical personnel, among other factors. The economic considerations alone may not be sufficient, as managers have other qualitative but strategically important concerns for location, capacity expansion, and technology choice decisions.

Finally, in formulating a manufacturing strategy, trade-offs among cost, quality, dependability, and flexibility must be explicitly considered. These trade-offs determine the unique positioning of a firm within the industry. A company may place a high weight on the cost criterion and gear its manufacturing organization and plant to low cost production. Another company may emphasize customization and therefore will choose a flexible process and emphasize flexibility in its production planning methods. The relative weights placed on different criteria will determine many other intermediate manufacturing positions.

No single method of analysis will be sufficient to deal with all of the different types of decision problems that occur in production and operations. Based on the nature of the decision problem and the type of information available, different methods may be suitable for different problems.

## PROBLEM STATEMENT AND DEFINING CRITERIA

Consider a simple situation in which there are $N$ decision alternatives denoted $a_1, a_2, \ldots, a_N$. The desirability of each alternative is measured on $m$ criteria. The performance of the alternative $a_j$ on the $i^{\text{th}}$ criterion is denoted $f_i^j$. Table 21-1 depicts this notation. To illustrate the notation, consider a site location problem. Each site is denoted by $a_j$; for example, $a_1$ = Cleveland, $a_2$ = Detroit, and so on. The criteria that are relevant in selecting a site may be capital costs (land, plant, equipment, and construction), labor availability, operating costs (determined by wages, electricity, water, taxes, etc.), and availability of transportation. Further, suppose that the capital costs are measured in millions of dollars, labor availability is measured as the percentage of factory labor requirements that can be met from the local labor pool, operating costs are measured by per unit cost of production, and the availability of transportation is measured on a subjective scale as *excellent, very good, good, fair,* and *poor.* Note that multicriteria decision methods do not preclude the use of subjectively measured criteria. However, the subjective scale must be precisely defined. For example, "excellent" transportation is meant to convey that air, rail, and truck transportation is easily available. "Poor" transportation may be defined as meaning that the company must employ its own fleet of trucks to transport goods as no local transportation is available in the area.

### TABLE 21-1
### NOTATION FOR MULTICRITERIA DECISION PROBLEM

| | *Criteria* | | | |
|---|---|---|---|---|
| Alternatives | 1 | 2 | . . . | $m$ |
| $a_1$ | $f_1^1$ | $f_2^1$ | . . . | $f_m^1$ |
| $a_2$ | $f_1^2$ | $f_2^2$ | . . . | $f_m^2$ |
| . | | | | |
| . | | | | |
| . | | | | |
| $a_N$ | $f_1^N$ | $f_2^N$ | . . . | $f_m^N$ |

In this example:

Criterion 1 = Capital cost (million dollars)
Criterion 2 = Labor availability (percentage of factory labor that can be hired locally)
Criterion 3 = Operating cost ($/unit)
Criterion 4 = Availability of transportation (excellent, very good, good, fair, poor)

If the capital cost for the Cleveland location is 50 million dollars, then in our notation $f_1^1 = 50$. Similarly, if transportation in the Detroit area is rated as excellent, then $f_4^2$ = excellent.

Two questions now arise. How should one identify criteria for a given decision problem? What should be the desirable properties in defining a set of criteria?

A casual approach for identifying criteria is to observe how a manager is presently making decisions. How does he or she rationalize or explain his or her decisions? For example, if a manager considers the waiting time, the length of the queue, and the salary paid to tellers in staffing decisions for a branch of a bank, then these are the criteria that must be considered in analysis. A literature survey or an analysis of the inputs and outputs of the system under consideration will often suggest criteria. For important strategic decisions, a hierarchical approach for structuring the objectives and criteria may be useful. To illustrate this approach, consider a manufacturing firm's decision to add capacity. The decision may include where the capacity is to be added (location), the size of the addition, and the technology to be employed (manual versus automatic).

In Figure 21-1, a hierarchy of objectives is shown. The lowest level in the figure represents the criteria that will be used in evaluating alternative decisions. Obviously, the relative importance of each criterion will depend on managerial preference, which in turn is influenced by the competitive position of the firm. How far should this hierarchy be carried downward? Unnecessary detail or a large number of criteria are seldom useful; experience and managerial judgment should guide this critical choice. The key issue is that each criterion must be clearly stated and must be measurable to the extent that, by knowing a level for a criterion, the decision maker obtains an understanding of the degree to which the associated objective can be achieved and is able to meet his or her preferences for different possible levels of that criterion.

The set of criteria should be complete so that no concern of the decision maker is excluded. Using the capacity addition decision as an example, if the employment of domestic labor is a relevant concern, then it must be included as a criterion. Further, the set of criteria must not be redundant so that the double counting of outcomes is avoided. Finally, the number of criteria should be kept as small as possible while maintaining understandability and measurability. Too broad an objective (e.g., a consumer's view of quality) must be broken down further; however, a large number of criteria for measuring a consumer's view of quality may not be appropriate as the subsequent analysis might become too cumbersome if the size of the criteria set is not kept at a manageable level.

FIGURE 21-1
**A HIERARCHY OF OBJECTIVES FOR CAPACITY ADDITION DECISIONS.**

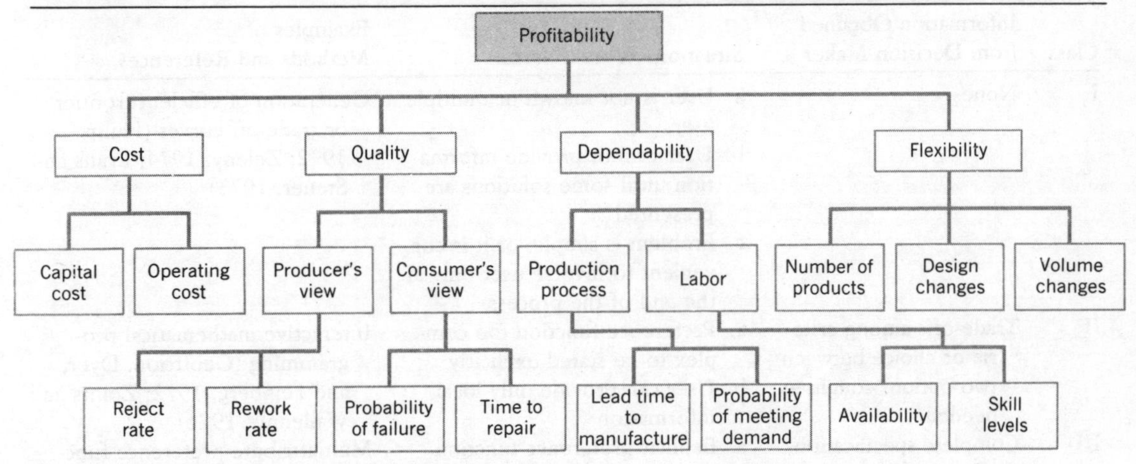


A clear understanding of corporate goals and managerial preferences, as well as some creative thinking, are necessary in specifying a set of criteria. This exercise alone goes a long way toward clarifying the relevant issues and selecting decision alternatives. Formal evaluation schemes, discussed later, are useful, but the damage done by the incomplete or inappropriate specification of criteria cannot be repaired through the sophistication of the evaluation method.

## A CLASSIFICATION OF MULTIPLE CRITERIA DECISION METHODS

The key objective of all multicriteria methods is to formalize and capture the trade-offs among criteria of interest. We will provide a basic understanding of three broad classes of multicriteria methods. Table 21-2 summarizes the features of these three classes of methods.

Multiple criteria decision methods can be distinguished along several dimensions. From a decision maker's perspective, a classification scheme based on the information required from him or her to implement the method is useful. In such a classification, the first class of methods is one in which the decision maker supplies no information during the analysis phase. Since the essential information about the decision maker's trade-offs among criteria is not conveyed, these methods provide only a trade-off curve (also called efficient frontier, nondominated solutions, or pareto optimal solutions) among criteria. The decision maker can then choose a preferred point, reflecting his or her inherent preferences, from the trade-off curve. Alternatively, formal methods can be employed to elicit the decision maker's preference function, which can in turn be used to evaluate the points on the trade-off curve; the optimal decision is identified as the point that maximizes the utility or value specified by the decision maker.

**TABLE 21-2**
**A CLASSIFICATION OF MULTICRITERIA METHODS**

| Class | Information Obtained from Decision Maker | Situations Where Useful | Examples of Methods and References |
|---|---|---|---|
| I | None | a. User is not known or multiple users<br>b. User cannot provide information until some solutions are presented<br>c. Problem is simple, or it is convenient to involve user only at the end of the process | Generation of efficient frontier or trade-off curves (Philip, 1972; Zeleny, 1974; Evans and Steuer, 1973) |
| II | Trade-offs among criteria or choice between two options sought as needed | a. Preference function too complex to be stated explicitly<br>b. User can provide only local information | Interactive mathematical programming (Geoffrion, Dyer, and Feinberg, 1972; Zoints and Wallenius, 1976) |
| III | Complete specification of trade-offs and preference function | a. Explicit preference function can be obtained<br>b. Problem is of strategic nature and, therefore, thinking is focused on values (preferences) desirable before the decisions are evaluated | Multiattribute preference function theory (Keeney and Raiffa, 1976; Dyer and Sarin, 1979) |

In the second class of methods, the decision maker is an integral part of the analytical process. Information is solicited from the decision maker about his or her preferences for various levels of attainment on the criteria of interest. Based on this information, the method progresses to achieve better solutions, with more information sought from the decision maker as it is needed. This sequential approach terminates when an acceptable or the most preferred decision is identified. These methods are interactive in nature, as information from the decision maker is essential for continuing the progress of the method toward the preferred decision.

Finally, in the third class of methods, the decision maker is asked to supply complete information about his or her preferences and trade-offs among criteria. A preference function (utility or value function) is then constructed based on the elicited information. Once the preference function is completely known, the selection procedure substitutes the preference function for an objective function.

Hybrid procedures, which combine the strategies employed in the three classes of methods just described, have also been developed. Other classification schemes can also be developed based on whether the outcomes of the decisions are known or unknown, whether the time horizon over which the outcomes occur is modeled as single or multiple time periods, whether the decision alternatives are finite or infinite, whether there is a single decision maker or a group of decision makers, whether the competitive reaction is implicitly considered or explicitly modeled, and similar questions. Keeney and Raiffa (1976) provide an extensive discussion of some of these topics.

## EFFICIENT FRONTIER OR TRADE-OFF METHOD

Suppose $f_1(x)$ and $f_2(x)$ denote the performance or achievement levels (also referred to as the outcomes or consequences) on two criteria when a decision $x$ is chosen. A decision $x$ *dominates* a decision $y$ whenever both of the following occur:

1. $f_i(x)$ is at least as good as $f_i(y)$ for all $i$
2. $f_i(x)$ is better than $f_i(y)$ for at least one $i$

Since decision $x$ is at least as good as decision $y$ for all criteria and is better for at least one criterion, it is reasonable to exclude decision $y$ from consideration.

Now suppose that we plot all the possible values of $f_1$ and $f_2$ for decision $x$ as shown in Figure 21-2. We assume that higher levels of $f_1$ and $f_2$ are more desirable. In Figure 21-2*a*, decision $x$ is a continuous variable and there are therefore an infinite number of possible outcomes. In Figure 21-2*b*, decision $x$ has a finite number of alternatives (e.g., 15 possible sites) and there are therefore only a finite number of possible consequences. The set of darkened points in Figure 21-2 is called the efficient frontier (the pareto optimal set or the trade-off curve). The key

FIGURE 21-2
**THE TRADE-OFF CURVES FOR TWO ATTRIBUTE CASES. (*a*) INFINITE CONSEQUENCES. (*b*) FINITE CONSEQUENCES.**

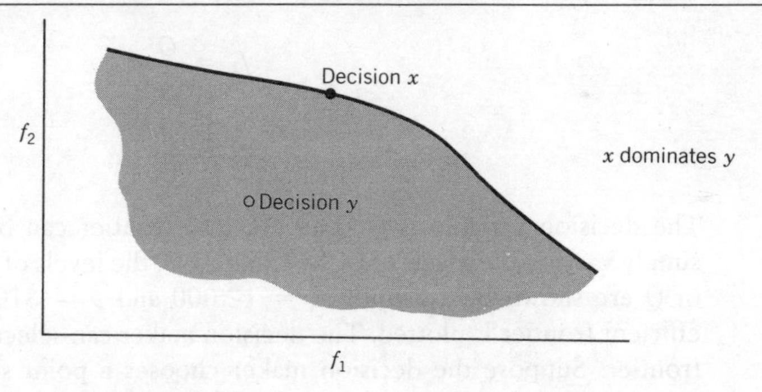


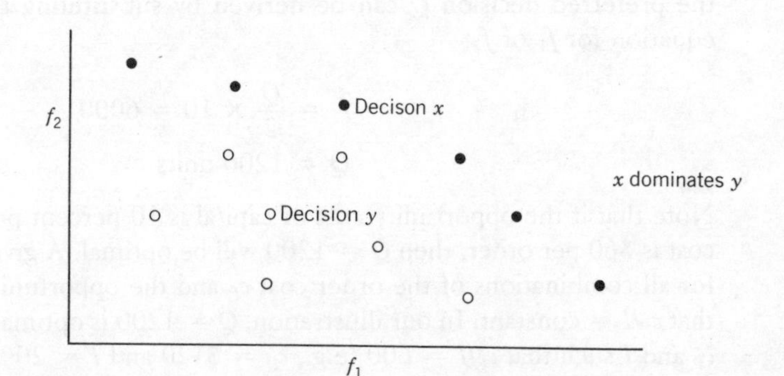

characteristic of the efficient frontier is that every point on it is nondominated. In other words, any point that is not on the efficient frontier or trade-off curve is dominated by some point on the efficient frontier. Managerially speaking, no matter what the underlying preference function (objective function or cost function), the most preferred decision (the optimal decision) must correspond to one of the points on the efficient frontier.

When there are only two criteria of interest, the choice of a final decision may become obvious if an efficient frontier is made available to the decision maker. But how does one obtain the efficient frontier? Three general approaches for constructing the efficient frontier are possible, and we will discuss each using an example.

## Direct Construction of the Efficient Frontier

Suppose that in an inventory planning decision there are two criteria of interest:

$f_1$ = The average investment in inventory
$f_2$ = The work load on the system measured by the number of orders placed per year

Using the notation introduced in Chapter 5, let $R$ be the annual demand, $p$ be the purchase cost per unit, and $Q$ be the order quantity. The demand is known and is constant per unit of time period. Thus,

$$f_1 = \frac{Q}{2} p$$

$$f_2 = \frac{R}{Q}$$

The decision variable is $Q$. The efficient frontier can be constructed directly by simply varying the levels of $Q$. In Table 21-3, the levels of $f_1$ and $f_2$ for several values of $Q$ are shown by assuming $R = 12{,}000$ and $p = \$10$/unit. In Figure 21-3 the efficient frontier is plotted. The decision maker can select a point from the efficient frontier. Suppose the decision maker chooses a point shown in Figure 21-3 that corresponds to 10 orders per year and an average investment of \$6000. The value of the preferred decision $Q$ can be derived by substituting the chosen point in the equation for $f_1$ or $f_2$.

$$f_1 = \frac{Q}{2} \times 10 = 6000$$
$$Q = 1200 \text{ units}$$

Note that if the opportunity cost of capital is 10 percent per annum and the order cost is \$60 per order, then $Q = 1200$ will be optimal. A given point will be optimal for all combinations of the order cost $c_P$ and the opportunity cost of capital $I$ such that $c_P/I$ = constant. In our illustration, $Q = 1200$ is optimal for all combinations of $c_P$ and $I$ such that $c_P/I = 600$ (e.g., $c_P = \$120$ and $I = 20\%$, or $c_P = \$30$ and $I =$

TABLE 21-3
**COMPUTATION OF $f_1$ AND $f_2$ FOR THE INVENTORY PROBLEM ($R$ = 12,000, $p$ = $10/UNIT)**

| Order Quantity, $Q$ | Average Investment in Inventory, $f_1 = (Q/2)p$ | Work Load or Annual Number of Orders, $f_2 = R/Q$ |
|---|---|---|
| 500 | 2,500 | 24 |
| 1,000 | 5,000 | 12 |
| 2,000 | 10,000 | 6 |
| 4,000 | 20,000 | 3 |
| 6,000 | 30,000 | 2 |
| 12,000 | 60,000 | 1 |

5%). Of course, if the explicit cost function is available, then the selection of the preferred point from the efficient frontier will not require managerial input. Actually, in this case the managerial input has been obtained and quantified in the form of a cost function. The efficient frontier approach is useful when the cost function is complicated to the point that it cannot be specified completely. For the more complicated case of uncertain demand, Gardner and Dannenbring (1981) provide an approach for constructing an efficient frontier for a three criteria inventory problem.

FIGURE 21-3
**EFFICIENT FRONTIER FOR THE INVENTORY PROBLEM.**

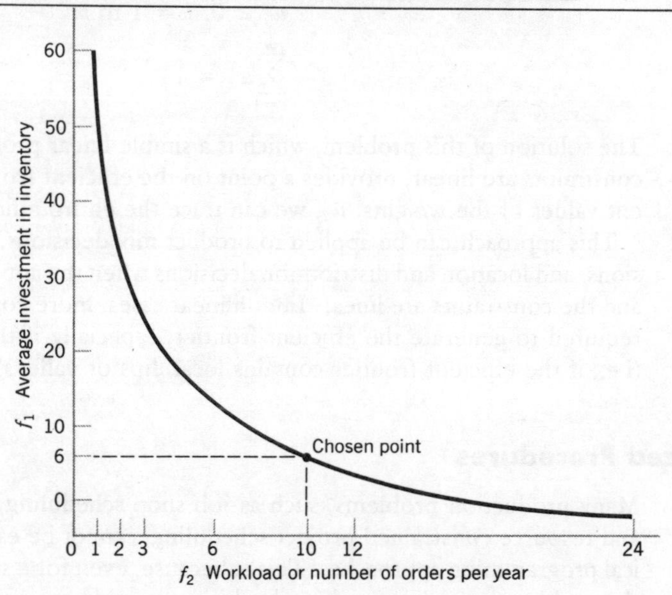

## Mathematical Programming Approach

Consider a project planning example where the two criteria of interest are

$$f_1 = \text{Project completion time}$$
$$f_2 = \text{Cost of crashing activities}$$

In Chapter 11, we formulated this problem as a linear programming problem. To construct the efficient frontier or trade-off curve between $f_1$ and $f_2$, we simply solve the problem:

$$\text{Minimize } f_2$$

$$\text{Subject to: precedence constraints, and } f_1 \leq T$$

Now, we systematically vary $T$, the completion time, to obtain the efficient frontier shown in Figure 21-4. The efficient frontier is piecewise linear because $f_1$ and $f_2$ as well as all the constraints are linear in this problem. The key idea in this approach is that one criterion is contained in the constraint set and is parametrically varied to minimize the other criterion. The approach is also applicable when there are more than two criteria. In this more general case, all but one criterion must be brought into the constraint set and the remaining criterion is successfully optimized by varying the right-hand sides of the criteria in the constraint set.

Another approach for obtaining the efficient frontier is to use a linear weighted average method. In this approach, we optimize

$$w_1 f_1 + w_2 f_2 + w_3 f_3 + \ldots + w_m f_m$$

subject to specified constraints, where

$$w_i \geq 0, \ i = 1 \text{ to } m$$

$$\sum_{i=1}^{m} w_i = 1$$

The solution of this problem, which is a simple linear program if all the $f_i$s and the constraints are linear, provides a point on the efficient frontier. By choosing different values of the weights, $w_i$, we can trace the entire efficient frontier.

This approach can be applied to product mix decisions, aggregate planning decisions, and location and distribution decisions when the appropriate criteria functions and the constraints are linear. In nonlinear cases, more complex procedures will be required to generate the efficient frontier, especially if the problem is nonconvex (i.e., if the efficient frontier contains local dips or valleys).

## Specialized Procedures

Many production problems, such as job shop scheduling, assembly line balancing, and resource constrained project scheduling, cannot be easily solved by mathematical programming approaches. This is because, even for a single criterion, the size of the problem is too large to be solved in reasonable computational time. Specialized

FIGURE 21-4
**EFFICIENT FRONTIER FOR PROJECT PLANNING EXAMPLE.**

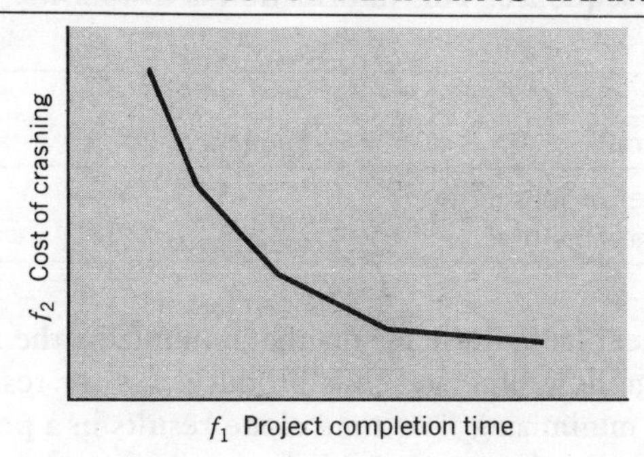


procedures that exploit problem characteristics are needed to solve such problems. Unfortunately, the transferability of these specialized procedures to other problems is negligible at this point in time. In the future, when specialized procedures are developed for a large class of important problems, some pattern of similarity may emerge.

We will demonstrate the construction of the efficient frontier for a single machine job shop scheduling problem when $n$ jobs are available for processing at time zero. The processing time $p_i$ and the due date $d_i$ for each job $i$ is known. The two criteria of interest are

$$f_1 = \text{Number of jobs tardy}$$
$$f_2 = \text{Average flow time}$$

The procedure for constructing the trade-off curve between $f_1$ and $f_2$ has been developed in Nelson, Sarin, and Daniels (1986). We will illustrate this procedure using a simple example.

In Table 21-4 the data for our example are presented. The optimal solution for the number of jobs tardy criterion is given by the Moore sequence, and the optimal

TABLE 21-4
**DATA FOR SINGLE MACHINE SCHEDULING PROBLEM**

| Job | Processing Time ($P_i$) | Due Date ($d_i$) |
|---|---|---|
| 1 | 5 | 245 |
| 2 | 10 | 15 |
| 3 | 30 | 40 |
| 4 | 50 | 55 |
| 5 | 60 | 100 |
| 6 | 90 | 190 |

solution for the average flow time criterion is given by the shortest processing time (SPT) sequence. This information is as follows:

| Criterion | Sequence | Number of Jobs Tardy | Average Flow Time |
|---|---|---|---|
| Number of jobs tardy | 2–3–5–6–1–4 | 1 | 130.00 |
| Average flow time | 1–2–3–4–5–6 | 4 | 93.30 |

It is clear from these results that minimizing the number of jobs tardy alone ignores average flow time and thus produces a poor result on this criterion. On the other hand, minimizing flow time alone results in a poor performance on the number of jobs tardy criterion. It is likely that a manager may prefer a good solution on both criteria rather than an optimal solution on one criterion that has an associated poor solution on the second criterion.

To construct the efficient frontier between $f_1$ and $f_2$ for this problem, several characteristics of the problem are exploited. First, note that there will be only 4 efficient points, one each corresponding to the number of tardy jobs equal to 1, 2, 3, and 4. This is because we cannot reduce the number of tardy jobs below 1 as the Moore sequence provides the fewest number of tardy jobs. Further, even if we permit more than 4 tardy jobs, the average flow time cannot be reduced below 93.3 (the flow time associated with the SPT sequence). Since the average flow time of 93.3 is achieved with 4 tardy jobs, a solution that cannot provide a better flow time but contains more than 4 jobs tardy cannot be on the efficient frontier (it is dominated by the SPT solution).

Another characteristic of this problem is that a job that is early in SPT sequence remains early in a solution that is on the efficient frontier. Thus, jobs 1 and 2, early in the SPT sequence in our example, can be forced to remain early in other sequences that are evaluated in a search for an efficient point.

Thus, as shown in Figure 21-5, a tree procedure can be used to construct the efficient frontier. The first node in the tree corresponds to the SPT sequence and has two jobs, 1 and 2, early. We now need a solution for three jobs early. So we evaluate the node in which jobs 1, 2, and 3 are early, and so on. Level 2 of the tree in Figure 21-5 shows these nodes. Some nodes are eliminated by a dominance rule that we will not discuss here. The key intuition is that if the problem data satisfy some properties, then the dominated node can be eliminated from consideration.

A given node (e.g., the first node on level 2 of the tree, which requires the jobs 1, 2, and 3 to be early) is evaluated by forcing the tardiness of the early jobs to be zero and then minimizing average flow time. The values of average flow time and the number of jobs tardy are shown adjacent to each node in Figure 21-5. The asterisk (*) depicts the node that corresponds to the efficient solution.

The efficient frontier for this problem is shown in Figure 21-6. It should be noted that no matter what the underlying objective function of the manager, as long as it is comprised of only the average flow time and the number of jobs tardy criteria, the only sequences of interest out of the possible 6! = 720 sequences are the four sequences shown in Figure 21-6. We are ignoring the alternative sequences that

FIGURE 21-5
**THE TREE PROCEDURE FOR CONSTRUCTING EFFICIENT SOLUTIONS FOR THE SCHEDULING PROBLEM.**

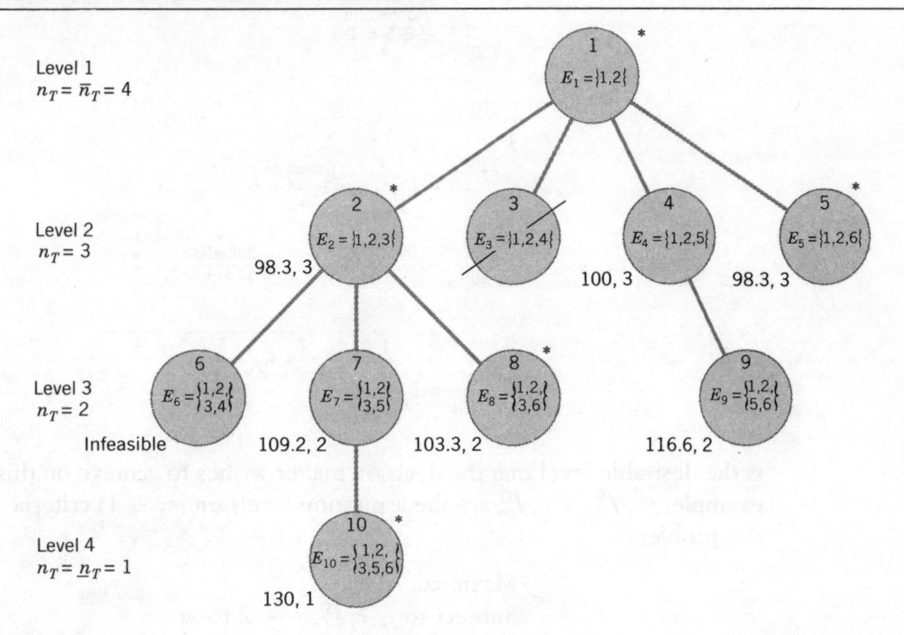


provide solutions identical to those in Figure 21-6 in making this assertion. The manager can now pick an appropriate schedule from the efficient solutions. For example, he might prefer a schedule that provides 2 jobs tardy and 90.3 average flow time. In a conventional approach of optimizing on a single criterion, such a schedule is not available for selection.

## INTERACTIVE PROCEDURES FOR EXPLORING THE EFFICIENT FRONTIER

The construction of the efficient frontier is useful only when there are no more than three criteria of interest *or* when the number of efficient solutions is relatively small. Interactive procedures require that some information be elicited from the decision maker about his or her preferences concerning the relevant criteria. This information is utilized either in exploring the efficient frontier or in reaching a new improved solution. Before we consider a formal interactive procedure, let us discuss an informal interactive approach in order to gain some insight into what we mean by interaction and how the information elicited from the decision maker can be utilized to progress from one solution to the next.

To illustrate this informal procedure, consider $m$ criteria, the decision maker setting aspiration levels for all but one criterion. The aspiration level for a criterion

FIGURE 21-6
**EFFICIENT SOLUTIONS FOR THE SCHEDULING PROBLEM.**

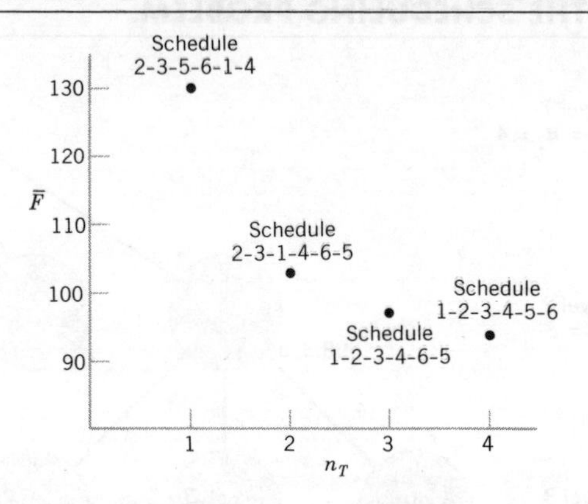


is the desirable level that the decision maker wishes to achieve on this criterion. For example, $f_2^0, f_3^0, \ldots, f_m^0$ are the aspiration levels on $(m - 1)$ criteria. We now solve the problem:

Maximize $f_1(x)$
Subject to $f_i \geq f_i^0$, $i = 2$ to $m$,
and other problem specific constraints.

The solution obtained is examined and new aspiration levels are set based on the information contained in the present solution. For example, if the value of $f_1$ was too small with respect to what the decision maker expects to achieve on criterion 1, then the aspiration levels on the other criteria may be lowered. By this trial and error procedure, the decision maker learns what solutions are achievable and, hopefully, something about his or her preference as well. After a few iterations, the decision maker may wish to stop if he or she thinks a satisfactory solution has been acheived. We refer to this as an informal procedure because convergence to the most preferred solution is not guaranteed. Further, full utilization of information, such as shadow prices or marginal rates of substitution between criteria, has not been exploited. It is a satisficing approach, not an optimizing one.

Geoffrion, Dyer, and Feinberg (1972) presented a formal and rigorous procedure for interactive optimization. This procedure is illustrated with an example they used to implement their procedure.

The example is an aggregate planning problem for a school of management. The faculty of the school may be viewed as engaging in three primary activities: formal teaching, school service (e.g., administration and curriculum development), and such activities as research and student counseling. The formal teaching occurs at three levels: graduate, lower-division undergraduate, and upper-division undergraduate. The basic planning unit of output is the equivalent course section, and all activities are related to that equivalence. Thus, "course releases" are given for such items as administrative activities, curriculum development and research so that the overall allocation of faculty effort can be planned in terms of equivalent course section capacity.

Figure 21-7 summarizes an aggregate planning and scheduling model for such a school. The major features of the model are the identification of the variables under school control, those not controllable by the school (such as policies, procedures, and restrictions), and the multiple criteria and output by which the resulting aggregate schedules are judged. The capacity to carry on the various activities is complicated by the differing roles of the various kinds of faculty. For example, lecturers provide only teaching service; they are assigned eight quarter courses per academic year but no administrative, committee, or other assignments. Regular faculty teach five quarter courses per year, but they carry on many other activities, such as counseling, committee service, and research. Teaching assistants assist in courses and sometimes teach sections of courses in the ratio of one full-time assistant for six equivalent course sections. University rules permit only faculty with certain qualifications to teach graduate level courses, upper-division undergraduate courses, and so on.

Thus, the administrators are forced to think in terms of various decision alterna-

FIGURE 21-7
**AGGREGATE PLANNING MODEL FOR A SCHOOL OF MANAGEMENT.**

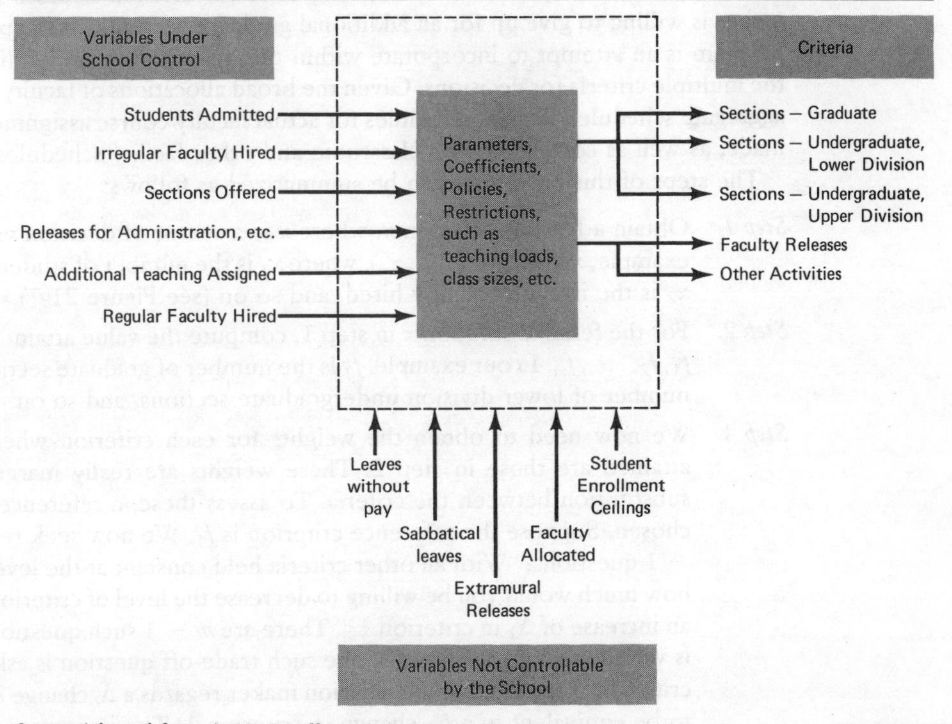


*Source:* Adapted from A. M. Geoffrion, J. S. Dyer, and A. Feinberg, "An Interactive Approach for Multicriterion Optimization, with an Application to the Operation of an Academic Department," *Management Science, 19*(4), December 1972, pp. 357–368.

tives in filling vacancies in the faculty, as well as in deciding on the other variables under their control. The number of students admitted can be controlled, the aggregate number of course sections can be varied, and the amount of equivalent non-teaching activities can be manipulated.

The central university administration determines certain upper limits on capacity through its budget allocations for faculty and student enrollments, and leaves of absence and extramural releases reduce the capacity available in the planning period.

The criteria and output listed on the right of Figure 21-7 are in fact the unique conception of the school model. As outputs, they represent the aggregate schedule for courses of different levels to be offered plus faculty time spent in other ways. However, they are also the dimensions of a multiple criteria problem on which the decision maker's preference for a given mix of activities is defined.

The decision model is actually interactive between the decision maker and a computational model in which the decision maker estimates weights for his or her preference for each of the outputs. Given these weights, a mathematical programming algorithm allocates available faculty time to courses at the several levels, releases, research, and additional activities. The computer output of the results is then examined, and the weights are altered if necessary. The weights, in fact, are expressive of the decision maker's preference for the relative emphasis among criteria. They are estimates of marginal substitution rates between each pair of criteria; for example, how many sections of lower-division courses the decision maker is willing to give up for an additional graduate section. This approach to the problem is an attempt to incorporate within the quantitative model dimensions of the multiple criteria for decisions. Given the broad allocations of faculty effort in the aggregate schedule, detailed schedules for actual faculty course assignments must be made, as well as correlated with classroom and other facility schedules.

The steps of this procedure can be summarized as follows:

*Step 1.* Obtain a feasible solution $x$, where $x$ is a vector of decision variables. For example, $x = (x_1, x_2, \ldots, x_n)$, where $x_1$ is the number of students admitted, $x_2$ is the irregular faculty hired, and so on (see Figure 21-7).

*Step 2.* For the feasible solution $x$ in step 1, compute the value attained on criteria $f_1, f_2, \ldots, f_m$. In our example, $f_1$ is the number of graduate sections, $f_2$ is the number of lower division undergraduate sections, and so on.

*Step 3.* We now need to obtain the weights for each criterion when the levels attained are those in step 2. These weights are really marginal rates of substitution between the criteria. To assess these, a reference criterion is chosen. Suppose the reference criterion is $f_1$. We now seek response to $m - 1$ questions, "With all other criteria held constant at the levels in step 2, how much would you be willing to decrease the level of criterion $i$ to obtain an increase of $\Delta_1$ in criterion 1?" There are $m - 1$ such questions because $i$ is varied from 2 to $m$; that is, one such trade-off question is asked for each criterion. Suppose that the decision maker regards a $\Delta_i$ change in criterion $i$ to be equivalent to a $\Delta_1$ change in criterion 1. The importance weight for criterion $i$, $w_i$, is

$$w_i = -\frac{\Delta_1}{\Delta_i}$$

At this step we have $w_1, w_2, \ldots, w_m$. (Note that $w_1 = 1$)

*Step 4.* Now we solve the mathematical programming problem

$$\text{Maximize} \sum_{i=1}^{m} w_i f_i(x)$$

subject to the problem constraints. The new solution $x'$ is now obtained. The new solution provides updated values for the decision variables $(x'_1, x'_2, \ldots, x'_n)$ and updated associated levels on $m$ criteria. In Figure 21-8, some representative old values and new values are plotted for three criteria.

*Step 5.* Now we have to determine a step size, $t$, which, loosely speaking, represents how far from the previous levels the decision maker wishes the new levels to move. If he or she prefers the new level, then $t = 1$. Alternatively, he or she may prefer intermediate levels shown by the dotted line in Figure 21-8. Specifically, we plot $f_i[x + t(x' - x)]$ where $x = (x_1, x_2, \ldots, x_n)$ represents the previous decision variables, $x' = (x'_1, x'_2, \ldots, x'_n)$ represents the new decision variables, and $0 \leq t \leq 1$.

*Step 6.* We have now obtained new levels for $m$ criteria in step 5. We again seek marginal rates of substitution or importance weights for the criteria. If the importance weights do not change, the most preferred solution is the current one and the procedure terminates. If the importance weights do indeed change, then the procedure is repeated starting with step 4.

FIGURE 21-8
**SELECTION OF STEP SIZE.**

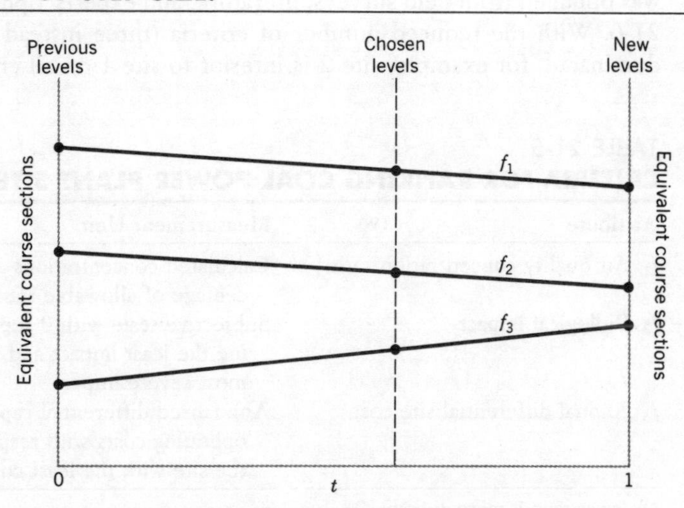

The key characteristic of the procedure just described is that the information elicited from the decision maker helps in the progress of the mathematical programming algorithm. In practical situations, the termination should occur rapidly. When the underlying preference function is a linear function of the criteria, the procedure will terminate in exactly one iteration. Some extensions of this method and descriptions of other applications are provided by Wehrung (1975) and Oppenheimer (1977).

Zionts and Wallenius (1976) propose a method within the framework of the simplex algorithm for linear programming that sequentially solicits certain trade-off information from the decision maker. This approach utilizes the concept of the efficient solution as a key element of the interactive strategy. This approach requires relatively simple information, consisting of the answers to some yes–no questions (ordinal information) rather than more difficult indifference judgments in the Geoffrion, Dyer, and Feinberg approach.

## COMPLETE SPECIFICATION OF THE PREFERENCE FUNCTION

In some production and operations situations, it may be desirable to interrogate the decision maker to quantify his or her preference function for the criteria of interest. The preference function can then be used to evaluate decision alternatives. Using a site location example, we will demonstrate how a preference function can be calibrated. The details for this example are in Sarin (1980).

Thirteen candidate sites for a 1500-megawatt coal-fired power plant were identified in the states of Washington, Oregon, Idaho, Wyoming, and Montana. In the original study, these sites were evaluated on six criteria; however, for the purposes of our illustration, we will consider only three criteria, which are listed in Table 21-5. The expected outcome or level for each of the 13 sites on the three criteria was obtained from field surveys, literature, and experts' opinion are shown in Table 21-6. With the reduced number of criteria (three instead of six), some sites are dominated, for example, site 2 is inferior to site 1 on all criteria.

TABLE 21-5
**CRITERIA FOR RANKING COAL POWER PLANT SITES**

| Attribute | Measurement Unit | Range |
|---|---|---|
| $f_1$ Air quality concentration ratio[a] | Calculated concentrations as a percentage of allowable standard | 25–100% |
| $f_2$ Biological impact | Subjective scale with 0 representing the least impact and 10 the most severe impact | 0–10 |
| $f_3$ Annual differential site cost | Annualized differential capital and operating costs with respect to the site with the least cost | \$0–60 million |

[a] A lower ratio is more desirable.

TABLE 21-6
**LEVELS OF CRITERIA ON SITES**

| Site | Air Quality (percentage of standard) | Biological Impact (10-point scale) | Differential Annual Cost (million dollars) |
|---|---|---|---|
| $S_1$ | 60 | 6 | $ 0 |
| $S_2$ | 90 | 5 | 5 |
| $S_3$ | 75 | 1 | 4 |
| $S_4$ | 30 | 2 | 9 |
| $S_5$ | 35 | 2 | 1 |
| $S_6$ | 30 | 2 | 10 |
| $S_7$ | 95 | 2 | 4 |
| $S_8$ | 65 | 1 | 4 |
| $S_9$ | 100 | 0 | 6 |
| $S_{10}$ | 55 | 10 | 28 |
| $S_{11}$ | 100 | 2 | 36 |
| $S_{12}$ | 70 | 2 | 43 |
| $S_{13}$ | 40 | 3 | 32 |

Our objective is to rank the 13 sites. A procedure for ranking these sites is to assess the preference function of the decision maker for the three criteria. The levels of the criteria for the sites are substituted in the preference function to obtain relative rank ordering of the sites. A site with a higher preference value is preferred to a site with a lower preference value. The procedure for constructing the preference function is described in the following steps.

## Step 1—Determining the Form for the Preference Function

The preference function $P$ can be decomposed into some simple forms if the decision maker's preferences for various combinations of the levels of criteria satisfy certain conditions. The simplest and the most widely used form is the weighted additive form:

$$P(f_1, f_2, f_3) = w_1v_1(f_1) + w_2v_2(f_2) + w_3v_3(f_3) \quad (1)$$

where $w_i$ is the importance weight and $v_i$ is the value function for each criterion. The weights and the value functions are scaled so that

$$\Sigma w_i = 1, \quad 0 \leq w_i \leq 1$$

and

$$v_i \text{ (best level)} = 1$$
$$v_i \text{ (worst level)} = 0, \text{ for } i = 1 \text{ to } m$$

How do we know whether it is appropriate to represent the preference function in the weighted additive form? In order to verify the legitimacy of this form, we need to check a condition called *difference independence* for each criterion. Essentially, this condition means that the magnitude of the difference in the strength of preference between two levels of criterion $i$ does not change when the fixed levels of the other criteria are changed.

To verify difference independence, for example, for the biological impact criterion, the decision maker (or expert) will be given two values $f_2 = 2$ and $f_2 = 8$, such that $f_2 = 2$ is preferred to $f_2 = 8$. Now, the expert is asked whether his or her strength of preference is going from $f_2 = 8$ to $f_2 = 2$ is influenced by the fixed levels of the remaining criteria. If the levels of other criteria do not influence the difference in the strength of preference between $f_2 = 2$ and $f_2 = 8$, then criterion 2 is considered difference independent of the remaining criterion.

If difference independence fails to hold, then we have two options. One is to use a more complicated model that allows for interaction among criteria. The second is to redefine the criteria so that difference independence does indeed hold. Fortunately, the additive form is quite robust and, in most situations, will produce low errors even when there are moderate interactions among criteria.

## Step 2—Constructing Single Dimensional Value Functions

In Equation 1, we need to assess $v_i(f_i)$, the value function for criterion $i$. A simple method for assessing these value functions is to use a 100 point rating scale on which 0 indicates the worst level and 100 indicates the best level. In Figure 21-9, such a rating scale is shown. The different levels of an attribute are rated on this scale to represent the strength of preference of the decision maker. The value of a level of a criterion is simply the rating/100. Thus the best level a criterion can take on always has a value of 1 and the worst level has a value of 0.

The ratings and the values for the 13 sites on the three criteria are shown in Table 21-7. These ratings and values reflect the desirability of various levels for a criterion. Next we determine the importance weights for each criterion.

## Step 3—Determining Importance Weights for the Criteria

We first identify the most important criterion. Suppose it is annual differential cost, $f_3$, in our example. We now ask the following question: "Suppose there is a hypothetical site A that has $f_1 = 100$ percent (the worst level) and $f_3 = 0$ million dollars (the best level). There is another hypothetical site B that has $f_1 = 30$ percent (the best level). What should the level of $f_3$ for the site B be so that you are indifferent about choosing between site A or B?"

Suppose that in our example the answer to this question is $f_3 = 4$ million dollars.

FIGURE 21-9
**RATING SCALE.**

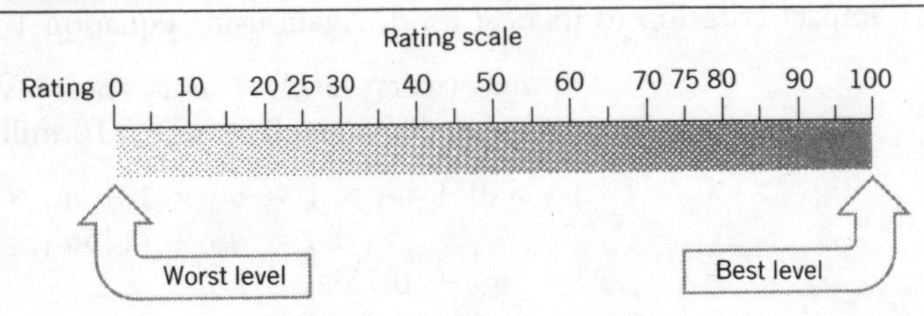


This means that the decison maker is willing to pay \$4 million for improving the worst value on criterion 1 to the best value. Using Equation 1 we have,

$$
\begin{aligned}
w_1 v_1 \text{ (worst level)} &+ w_3 v_3 \text{ (best level)} \\
= w_1 v_1 \text{ (best level)} &+ w_3 v_3 \text{ (4 million)} \\
w_1 \times 0 + w_3 \times 1 &= w_1 \times 1 + w_3 \times 0.90 \\
w_3 &= w_1 \times 1 + 0.9 w_3 \\
w_3 - 0.9 w_3 &= w_1 \\
0.1 w_3 &= w_1
\end{aligned} \tag{2}
$$

Notice that $v_3$ (4 million) is obtained from the rating scale discussed in step 2.

We now ask a similar question: "Suppose there is a hypothetical site A that has $f_2 = 10$ (the worst level) and $f_3 = 0$ million dollars (the best level). There is another hypothetical site B that has $f_2 = 0$ (the best level). What should the level of $f_3$ for site B be so that you are indifferent about choosing between site A or B?" Suppose

TABLE 21-7
**RATINGS AND VALUES OF SITES ON THREE CRITERIA**

| | Criterion | | | | | |
|---|---|---|---|---|---|---|
| | *Air Quality* | | *Biological Impact* | | *Differential Cost* | |
| Site | Rating | Value ($v_1$) | Rating | Value ($v_2$) | Rating | Value ($v_3$) |
| $S_1$ | 75 | 0.75 | 70 | 0.70 | 100 | 1.00 |
| $S_2$ | 20 | 0.20 | 75 | 0.75 | 88 | 0.88 |
| $S_3$ | 50 | 0.50 | 95 | 0.95 | 90 | 0.90 |
| $S_4$ | 100 | 1.00 | 90 | 0.90 | 80 | 0.80 |
| $S_5$ | 98 | 0.98 | 90 | 0.90 | 98 | 0.98 |
| $S_6$ | 100 | 1.00 | 90 | 0.90 | 75 | 0.75 |
| $S_7$ | 10 | 0.10 | 90 | 0.90 | 90 | 0.90 |
| $S_8$ | 70 | 0.70 | 95 | 0.95 | 90 | 0.90 |
| $S_9$ | 0 | 0.00 | 100 | 1.00 | 85 | 0.85 |
| $S_{10}$ | 85 | 0.85 | 0 | 0.00 | 35 | 0.35 |
| $S_{11}$ | 0 | 0.00 | 90 | 0.90 | 16 | 0.16 |
| $S_{12}$ | 60 | 0.60 | 90 | 0.90 | 0 | 0.00 |
| $S_{13}$ | 95 | 0.95 | 80 | 0.80 | 25 | 0.25 |

the answer to this question is $f_3$ = 10 million dollars, reflecting that the decision maker is willing to pay $10 million to improve the worst level for the biological impact criterion to its best level. Again using equation 1 we have,

$$\begin{aligned} w_2 v_2 \text{ (worst level)} + w_3 v_3 \text{ (best level)} \\ = w_2 v_2 \text{ (best level)} + w_3 v_3 \text{ (10 million)} \\ w_2 \times 0 + w_3 \times 1 = w_2 \times 1 + w_3 \times 0.75 \\ w_3 = w_2 + 0.75 w_3 \\ w_3 - 0.75 w_3 = w_2 \\ 0.25 w_3 = w_2 \end{aligned} \tag{3}$$

Again, $v_3$ (10 million) is obtained from the rating scale discussed in step 2. We also know that

$$w_1 + w_2 + w_3 = 1 \tag{4}$$

We have three equations, 2, 3, and 4, and three unknowns, $w_1$, $w_2$, and $w_3$. Substituting Equations 2 and 3 in Equation 4, we get

$$\begin{aligned} 0.1 w_3 + 0.25 w_3 + w_3 = 1 \\ 1.35 w_3 = 1 \\ w_3 = \frac{1}{1.35} \approx 0.75 \end{aligned}$$

From equation 2, $w_1 = 0.1 \times 0.75 = 0.075$. Using Equation 4, $w_2 = 1 - w_1 - w_3 = 1 - 0.75 - 0.075 = 0.175$. Thus, the importance weights for the three criteria are $w_1 = 0.075$, $w_2 = 0.175$, and $w_3 = 0.75$.

## Step 4—Computing the Overall Values

In Table 21-8, the computations of the overall values for each of the sites $S_1$ to $S_{13}$ are shown. Equation 1 is used to compute the weighted value. For example, for the site $S_3$, the values of the three criteria from Table 21-7 are 0.50, 0.95, and 0.90, respectively. The overall value is computed using Equation 1:

$$\begin{aligned} w_1 v_1 + w_2 v_2 + w_3 v_3 = 0.075 \times 0.50 + 0.175 \times 0.95 + 0.75 \times 0.90 \\ = 0.87875 \end{aligned}$$

These overall preference values, shown in the last column of Table 21-8, provide the relative ranking of each site. For example, site $S_5$ is the highest ranked as it has the highest overall value. Site $S_1$ is ranked second as it has a higher overall value than all the sites except site $S_5$.

## Step 5—Sensitivity Analysis

Since both the ratings for the different levels of the criteria and the importance weights are subjectively derived, it is useful to analyze the impact of changing some of these values on the relative ranking of the sites. Alternatively, if several decision makers are involved in the process, it is quite possible that they differ in their

TABLE 21-8
**COMPUTATION OF OVERALL PREFERENCE VALUES (INDIVIDUAL CRITERION VALUES FROM TABLE 21-7)**

| | *Criterion* | | | |
|---|---|---|---|---|
| Site | Air Quality $w_1 = 0.075$ | Biological Impact $w_2 = 0.175$ | Differential Cost $w_3 = 0.75$ | Overall Value (Equation 1) |
| $S_1$ | 0.75 | 0.70 | 1.00 | 0.92875 |
| $S_2$ | 0.20 | 0.75 | 0.88 | 0.80625 |
| $S_3$ | 0.50 | 0.95 | 0.90 | 0.87875 |
| $S_4$ | 1.00 | 0.90 | 0.80 | 0.83250 |
| $S_5$ | 0.98 | 0.90 | 0.98 | 0.96600 |
| $S_6$ | 1.00 | 0.90 | 0.75 | 0.79500 |
| $S_7$ | 0.10 | 0.90 | 0.90 | 0.84000 |
| $S_8$ | 0.70 | 0.95 | 0.90 | 0.89375 |
| $S_9$ | 0.00 | 1.00 | 0.85 | 0.81250 |
| $S_{10}$ | 0.85 | 0.00 | 0.35 | 0.32635 |
| $S_{11}$ | 0.00 | 0.90 | 0.16 | 0.27750 |
| $S_{12}$ | 0.60 | 0.90 | 0.00 | 0.20250 |
| $S_{13}$ | 0.95 | 0.80 | 0.25 | 0.39875 |

assignments of ratings or importance weights. Sensitivity analysis clarifies whether such differences are relevant in selecting the most preferred site. In many situations, we have found that disagreements on ratings or on importance weights do not change the ranking. If, however, the differences in opinion about the ratings or the importance weight do indeed have an influence on the final ranking, then an open discussion or additional information must be used to reconcile the differing viewpoints.

## IMPLICATIONS FOR THE MANAGER

In defining a company's manufacturing strategy, managers must identify the relative emphasis of alternative criteria, such as cost, quality, dependability, and flexibility. Simultaneous maximization—attempting to achieve the best on all criteria—is not often possible. This is because the plant, equipment, labor, technology, and process that can achieve a higher performance on one criterion may not be appropriate for achieving high performance on some other criterion. Once the relative priorities among the manufacturing criteria are established, all decisions must support and be consistent with them.

The trade-offs between competing concerns and criteria are central in most managerial decisions. In this chapter, we have provided an overview of some methods that may be useful to a manager in systematically thinking about such trade-offs. Further, we have shown that some standard operations models that optimize a single criterion can be extended to include the multiple criteria often present in real-world situations.

An essential feature of the multicriteria methods is that inputs from managers are required to obtain a final solution. With advances in the use of computers and graphic displays, it is quite possible that in the near future systems will be developed that will involve the managers in the model formulation and solution for effective multiple criteria problem solving. Intuitive consideration of multiple criteria is a reality in every manager's decision making. We hope that formal methods will aid in clarifying issues and will provide helpful information to the managers.

## REVIEW QUESTIONS

1. Give one example each of a decision problem in production management from the manufacturing sector and the service sector that involves multiple criteria.
2. What are the three classes of multiple criteria decision methods discussed in the chapter?
3. How can you identify the criteria in a given decision problem?
4. What are the desirable properties in defining a set of criteria?
5. Choose a decision problem in a production area and define the criteria that you consider to be relevant for your decision problem. Clearly specify the units of measurement for each criterion.
6. What is an efficient frontier?
7. What are the methods for constructing an efficient frontier?
8. Can any arbitrary solution from the efficient frontier be chosen for implementation?
9. Briefly discuss the essential steps in the interactive mathematical programming approach for multicriteria decisions.
10. Suppose, the total cost of a schedule is determined by

$$\bar{F} + Kn_T, \; K > 0$$

where $\bar{F}$ is the average flow time and $n_T$ is the number of jobs tardy, and $K$ is the constant that reflects the trade-off between $\bar{F}$ and $n_T$. Can we interpret the cost function as a preference function? How?

11. When can we use Equation 1 to rank order multicriteria decision alternatives such as sites?
12. What is the procedure for obtaining importance weights for the criteria of interest?

## PROBLEMS

13. A manufacturer purchases transformers at a cost of \$100 per unit. The annual requirements are 2450 units. Plot a trade-off curve between average investment

in inventory and work load measured in terms of number of orders placed per year. Assume that the order size $Q$ varies from 15 days' requirements to 3 months' requirements.

a. The present policy is to order once a month. Plot this point on the trade-off curve. Now suppose that a change in the order policy is contemplated. Using the trade-off curve, can you summarize the impact of a change in ordering policy if it is changed to (1) an order every two weeks and (2) an order every two months.

b. Suppose the order cost is $90 per order (including freight, handling, etc.) and the cost of capital is 10 percent. Can you use this information and trade-off curve to identify the optimal policy? Compare it with the optimal policy that is derived by using *EOQ* equation.

14. The precedence diagram and the task times for an assembly line shop are as follows:

| Task | Immediate Predecessor | Task Time (Minutes) |
|---|---|---|
| a | — | 3 |
| b | a | 6 |
| c | a | 7 |
| d | a | 5 |
| e | a | 2 |
| f | b,c | 4 |
| g | c,d | 5 |
| h | f,g | 5 |

Assume an 8-hour day for the daily production rate.

a. Plot a trade-off curve between the daily production rate and the number of work stations.

b. If the desired production rate is 40 units per day (cycle time = 10 minutes), what is the optimal number of work stations? Use the trade-off curve in part *a* to answer this question.

c. Balance delay, $d$, is defined as

$$d = \frac{100(nc - \Sigma t_i)}{nc}, \; d \geq 0$$

where

$n$ = Number of work stations on the line
$c$ = Cycle time
$t_i$ = Task times

and $n$, $c$, and $t_i$ are integers.

Plot the curves between the balance delay and the cycle time for $n$ = 1, 2,

3, and 4. Is it possible to find a feasible assignment of tasks corresponding to every point on these curves?

15. In planning production in aggregate terms, the production manager of a company considers two criteria:

$C$ = Total annual costs of payroll and inventory
$N$ = Total number of hirings and firings during the year

The quarterly requirements for the product are

| | |
|---|---|
| Quarter 1 | 100 units |
| Quarter 2 | 400 units |
| Quarter 3 | 500 units |
| Quarter 4 | 200 units |

Each worker is paid $4000 per quarter and is capable of producing 10 units per quarter. The size of the present workforce is 15. Inventory carrying costs are $40 per unit per quarter. No overtime or shortages are permitted. It is assumed that the beginning inventory and the ending inventory are zero.

a. Construct a trade-off curve between the two criteria using the linear programming approach. The formulation for the linear program for this problem is

$$\text{Min } C = 4000 \sum W_t + 40 \sum I_t$$

subject to

$$I_{t-1} + P_t - D_t = I_t, \quad t = 1 \text{ to } 4$$
$$P_t \leq 10\, w_t, \quad t = 1 \text{ to } 4$$
$$W_t - W_{t-1} = H_t - F_t, \; t = 1 \text{ to } 4$$
$$\sum H_t + \sum F_t \leq N$$
$$I_0 = I_4 = 0, \; w_0 = 15, \text{ all variables} \geq 0$$

where

$W_t$ = Number of workers on payroll in period $t$
$I_t$ = Inventory at the end of period $t$
$P_t$ = Production in period $t$
$D_t$ = Demand in period $t$
$H_t$ = Number of workers hired in period $t$
$F_t$ = Number of workers fired in period $t$

b. How can the manager use the trade-off curve in determining a preferred production plan?

16. A manager has to choose one of the available sets of equipment. The equipment sets differ in purchase cost, operating cost, reject rate for the parts produced by the equipment, and length of operating life. The levels for these four criteria and the ratings assigned to these levels are summarized in the following table. The importance weights for the four criteria are also shown.

| | Purchase Cost ($) (0.3)[a] | | Operating Cost ($/unit) (0.1)[a] | | Reject Rate (%) (0.3)[a] | | Life (years) (0.3)[a] | |
|---|---|---|---|---|---|---|---|---|
| | Level | Rating | Level | Rating | Level | Rating | Level | Rating |
| Equipment 1 | 50,000 | 100 | 10 | 0 | 8 | 0 | 8 | 30 |
| Equipment 2 | 80,000 | 0 | 8 | 100 | 5 | 100 | 10 | 100 |
| Equipment 3 | 60,000 | 60 | 9 | 90 | 7 | 60 | 10 | 100 |
| Equipment 4 | 70,000 | 30 | 8 | 100 | 6 | 30 | 7 | 0 |

[a] Importance weight

a. Which equipment should be purchased?

b. If the importance weights for all criteria are identical (0.25 each), which equipment should be purchased?

17. A manufacturer of color TVs was considering several options for capacity expansion and location in the mid 1970s. These options were evaluated on the following criteria:

$f_1$ = Differential capital cost
$f_2$ = Direct production cost/set
$f_3$ = Ease of control (five-point subjective scale)
$f_4$ = Flexibility to design changes (five point subjective scale)

Although other criteria, such as reject rate, dependability of production, labor availability, and the like were of interest, they did not have significant impacts on the relative desirability of the three final contenders. The levels for the three final contenders and their ratings on the four criteria are given in the following table. These ratings were determined by a management team.

| | Criteria | | | | | | | |
|---|---|---|---|---|---|---|---|---|
| | $f_1$ | | $f_2$ | | $f_3$ | | $f_4$ | |
| Alternative | Level | Rating | Level | Rating | Level | Rating | Level | Rating |
| 1. U.S. production (automated process) | $5 million | 0 | $150 | 75 | 5 | 100 | 3 | 50 |
| 2. U.S. production (manual process) | 0 | 100 | 160 | 0 | 4 | 90 | 5 | 100 |
| 3. Offshore production | 0 | 100 | 125 | 100 | 1 | 0 | 2 | 0 |

a. If all the criteria were equally weighted, which option was the most preferred?

b. The marketing group felt that flexibility was the most important criterion, as new design changes were being introduced almost every year. Further, they felt that the company must offer state-of-the-art product features to compete effectively. The group provided the following trade-offs:

(1) $f_1 = 5$ million, $f_4 = 5$ points is indifferent to $f_1 = 0$ million, $f_4 = 4$ points

(2) $f_2 = \$160$, $f_4 = 5$ points is indifferent to $f_2 = \$125$, $f_4 = 3$ points

(3) $f_3 = 1$ point, $f_4 = 5$ points is indifferent to $f_3 = 5$ points, $f_4 = 3$ points

Based on these trade-offs, determine the importance weights for the four criteria. The rating for $f_4 = 4$ is 75. Which option was most preferred using the evaluations provided by the marketing group?

c. The production and finance groups felt that the unit cost was the most important criterion because in a maturing market the pressures on them would be to reduce unit costs. Further, they believed that the marketing group would be forced to cut prices if foreign producers flooded the market with low-cost televisions. The trade-offs provided by these groups were as follows:

(1) $f_1 = 5$ million, $f_2 = \$125$ is indifferent to $f_1 = 0$ million, $f_2 = \$150$

(2) $f_2 = \$125$, $f_3 = 1$ point is indifferent to $f_2 = \$140$, $f_3 = 5$ points

(3) $f_2 = \$125$, $f_4 = 1$ point is indifferent to $f_2 = \$145$, $f_4 = 5$ points

Based on these trade-offs, derive the importance weights for the four criteria. The rating for $f_2 = \$140$ is 50 and for $f_2 = \$145$ is 60. Which option was the most preferred?

d. How will you attempt to reconcile the differences in the evaluations of the groups?

# SITUATIONS

## Manufacturing Strategy Design

18. Fine and Hax (1985) propose a methodology for designing manufacturing strategy. To illustrate their process, they describe an application for Packard Electric, a component division of General Motors. They further focus on Packard's wire and cable strategic business unit (SBU), which has four plants: three near division headquarters in Warren, Ohio, and one in Clinton, Mississippi. Packard's sales are mostly to General Motors. Packard has been under pressure to reduce costs, improve quality, and improve product development. Fine and Hax describe an important step in designing manufacturing strategy, which is to establish the competitive standing of each major product line with respect to the four manufacturing criteria: cost, quality, delivery, and flexibility.

    In the following table, an assessment of the relative importance of the four criteria for each product line is made. This is done by distributing 100 points among the four criteria. Further, an assessment is made of the competitive performance of each product on the four criteria. These assessments are made on a five-point scale:

− − = Very high weakness
− = Mild weakness
E = Even
+ = Mild strength
+ + = Very high strength

| | Criteria | | | | | | | |
|---|---|---|---|---|---|---|---|---|
| | *Cost* | | *Quality* | | *Delivery* | | *Flexibility* | |
| Product Line | Importance Weight | Performance | Importance Weight | Performance | Importance Weight | Performance | Importance Weight | Performance |
| 1. Cable | 30 | + + | 40 | − | 20 | E | 10 | − |
| 2. Printed circuits | 20 | − − | 50 | E | 20 | + | 10 | + |
| 3. Copper rod | 20 | + | 40 | + | 30 | + + | 10 | − |

a. Interpret the information provided in the table.
b. How will you use the information in the table in operational decisions?
c. Using the concepts presented in this chapter, can you provide a better way to assess importance weights and performance levels?

## Scheduling with Multiple Criteria

19. Nelson, Sarin, and Daniels (1986) present a procedure for constructing an efficient frontier for a scheduling problem in which the three criteria of interest are

$$\bar{F} = \text{Average flow time}$$
$$n_T = \text{Number of jobs tardy}$$
$$T_{\max} = \text{Maximum tardiness}$$

The efficient points for the scheduling problem described in this chapter (Table 21-4) are as follows:

| Sequence | $\bar{F}$ | $n_T$ | $T_{\max}$ |
|---|---|---|---|
| 2–3–5–6–1–4 | 780 | 1 | 190 |
| 2–3–5–6–4–1 | 825 | 1 | 185 |
| 2–3–1–4–6–5 | 620 | 2 | 145 |
| 2–3–5–1–4–6 | 655 | 2 | 100 |
| 2–3–5–4–1–6 | 700 | 2 | 95 |
| 2–3–1–4–5–6 | 590 | 3 | 55 |
| 2–3–4–5–6–1 | 775 | 3 | 50 |
| 1–2–3–4–5–6 | 560 | 4 | 55 |

a. How will you choose a schedule from the efficient solutions?
b. If the cost function is $\bar{F} + 150n_T + 3T_{\max}$, which schedule will be optimal?
c. What other factors may be relevant in a manager's choice of a schedule?

# REFERENCES


Dyer, J. S., and R. K. Sarin, "Measurable Multiattribute Value Functions," *Operations Research,* 27, 1979, pp. 810–822.

Evans, J. P. and R. E. Steuer, "A Revised Simplex Method for Linear Multiple Objective Programs," *Mathematical Programming, 5,* 1973, pp. 54–72.

Fine, C. F. and A. C. Hax, "Manufacturing Strategy: A Methodology and an Illustration," *Interfaces, 15,* November–December 1985, pp. 28–46.

Gardner, E. S. and D. G. Dannenbring, "Using Optimal Policy Surfaces to Analyze Aggregate Inventory Tradeoffs," *Management Science, 25*(8), August 1979, pp. 709–720.

Geoffrion, A., J. S. Dyer, and A. Feinberg, "An Interactive Approach for Multi-Criterion Optimization, with an Application to the Operation of an Academic Department," *Management Science, 19,* 1972, pp. 367–368.

Keeney, R. L. and H. Raiffa, *Decisions With Multiple Objectives: Preferences and Value Tradeoffs,* Wiley, New York, 1976.

Nelson, R. T., R. K. Sarin, and R. L. Daniels, "Scheduling with Multiple Performance Measures: The One-Machine Case," *Management Science, 32*(4), April 1986, pp. 464–479.

Oppenheimer, K. R., *A Proxy Approach to Multi-Attribute Decision Making,* Ph.D. Dissertation, Department of Engineering–Economic Systems, Stanford University, March 1977.

Philip, J., "Algorithms for the Vector Maximization Problem," *Mathematical Programming, 2,* 1972, pp. 207–229.

Sarin, R. K., "Ranking of Multiattribute Alternatives and an Application to Coal Power Plant Siting," in *Multiple Criteria Decision Making: Theory and Applications,* G. Fandel and T. Gal (eds.), Springer Verlag, Berlin, 1980.

Wehrung, D. A., *Mathematical Programming Procedures for the Interactive Identification and Optimization of Preferences in a Multi-Attributed Decision Problem,* Ph.D. Dissertation, Graduate School of Business, Stanford University, May 1975.

Zeleny, M., *Linear Multiobjective Programming,* Springer Verlag, New York, 1974.

Zoints, S. and J. Wallenius, "An Interactive Programming Method for Solving the Multiple Criteria Problem," *Management Science, 22,* 1976, pp. 652–663.

# PART FOUR

# OPERATIONS STRATEGY AND THE FIRM

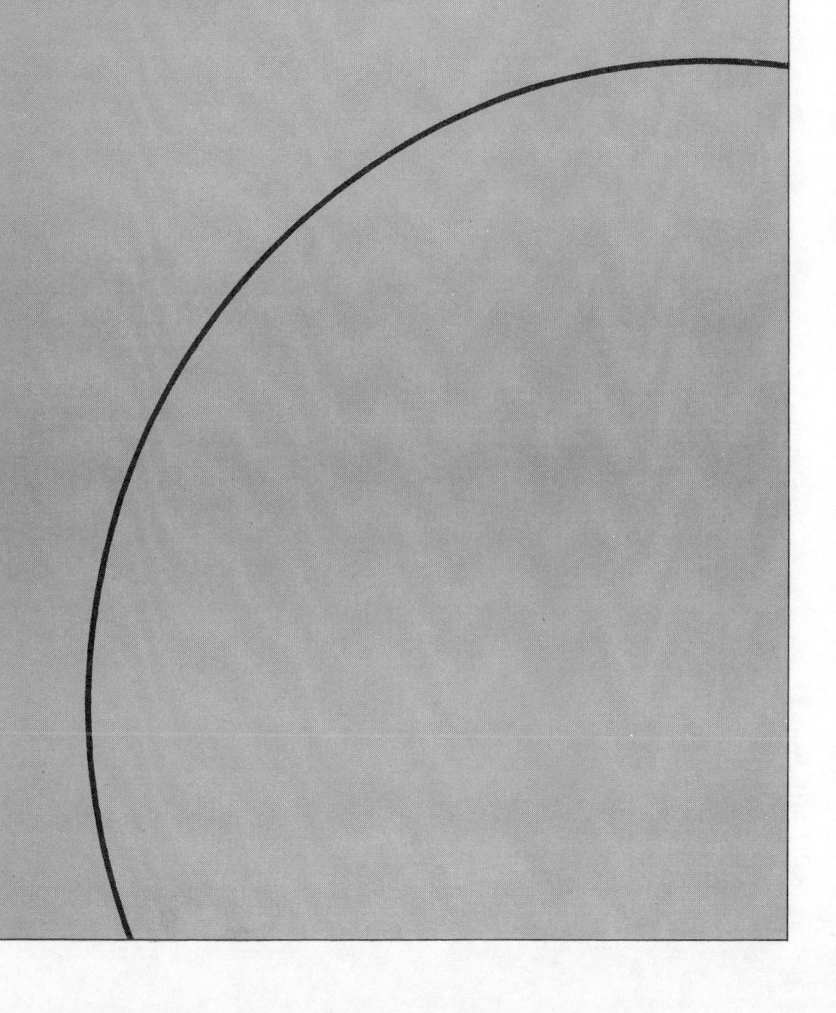

CHAPTER 22

# FRAMEWORK FOR OPERATIONS STRATEGY FORMULATION



*(Continued)*

Most of the topics covered in the book to this point have had strategic implications, at least in some facet. This should not be surprising since all bear on the competitive priorities of cost, quality, flexibility, and on-time performance or dependability in some important way. But in discussing each of the topics in operations planning and control and the design of operational systems, we dealt with that topic from a local perspective, concentrating on the concepts and techniques for implementing good policies in that area of operations management.

For example, when we discussed capacity planning in Chapter 17, we assumed that the decision to expand capacity had already been made and that our task was to plan effectively for the new capacity. Now, however, we will take a broader view of analyzing and formulating operations strategy, in which we will be interested in the strategic use of capacity in achieving the ends of the enterprise. We will attempt to shed light on the broader question of whether or not capacity should be expanded given the competitive situation and the structure and status of the industry and its competitors. Our objective will be to provide a basis for analyzing and formulating operations strategy that can be integrated into a cohesive enterprise strategy.

## GENERIC ENTERPRISE STRATEGIES AND THE OPERATIONS FUNCTION

Porter (1980) classifies three generic enterprise strategies: overall cost leadership, differentiation, and focus. We will substitute the term *segmentation* for focus, since focus is used to mean something different in operations management. Our interest will be particularly on the role of the operations function in each of these generic strategies. The three strategies are

- Overall cost leadership (*low cost* and *high product availability,* usually off-the-shelf)
- Differentiation (*high quality, innovative* in product dęsign, and *flexible*)
- Market segmentation (in terms of meeting the special needs of a particular market, providing lower costs for that market segment, or both)

Overall cost leadership and differentiation are industry wide strategies, but market segmentation, by definition, applies to only a portion of the market. Only one of these strategies is usually employed by a particular business unit; however, different strategies can and should be employed by different business units within the same company.

### Overall Cost Leadership

This strategy requires the concentration of the operations system on all the elements of system design that make low cost possible: in-line operations; fabrication and assembly lines; equipment dedicated to a restricted mix of products; capital intensity in the form of specialized equipment, mechanization, automation, and robotics, all especially designed for the specific operations problem; and, commonly, specialized and narrowly defined job designs.

Usually, the cost leadership strategy also involves production to stock since part of the strategy is to make the product available on demand or off-the-shelf. Where economies of scale are possible, they are used in this strategy, as are the benefits that come from cumulative organizational learning and the experience curve (to be discussed later in this chapter). Products and services are designed for producibility. The organizational structure places emphasis on cost control and on getting product out the door so as to minimize lost sales from not having the product available. Specialization also makes cost minimization possible in other functional areas, such as R&D, service, sales, advertising, personnel, and so on.

Low cost and product availability drives the entire strategy and, indeed, the entire organization. Quality, service, and flexibility are not ignored; however, they are not the emphasis. Nevertheless, it is difficult to have it both ways—by specializing facilities, labor, and the entire organization, a trade-off is made. A single purpose facility is not very flexible; it cannot be easily retooled to make a different product. Quality controls are built into the line operations, but it is not feasible to give the same attention to quality in manufacturing a Honda as is given in building a Rolls Royce. The entire momentum of the design of the system and the organization is given to minimizing costs and maintaining the flow of products.

The low cost producer in an industry will earn higher than average returns, giving it a defense against competitors. The low cost position provides excellent entry barriers in terms of economies of scale and cost advantages. Even product substitutes have a more difficult task in competing because of low cost and availability. The strategy also provides bargaining power in relation to the potential vertical integration of both suppliers and buyers for the efficient producer in comparison to less efficient producers. Many prominent manufacturers have built their competitive strategies around low cost and high availability: Anheuser Busch with beer; Eastman Kodak with photographic film and paper; Texas Instruments with silicon chips, hand calculators, and digital watches; and many others.

There are risks in following the cost leadership strategy. The production system becomes inflexible. If consumer preferences take a sharp turn or if technological changes make product designs, plant, and equipment obsolete, the enterprise may have to reinvest huge sums in order to recover. One of the most dramatic examples of the risks of inflexibility in the low cost strategy was Henry Ford's standardized Model T.[1] Beginning in 1908, Henry Ford embarked on a conscious policy of price and cost reduction that reduced the price from more than $5000 to nearly $3000 in 1910 (in 1958 constant dollars). From that point, the price declined 15 percent for each doubling of cumulative output during the Model T era, culminating in a 1926 price of about $750. Market share increased from 10.7 percent in 1910 to a peak of 55.4 percent in 1921. However, beginning in the middle 1920s, General Motors successfully focused the competitive arena on product innovation. The Ford Com-

[1] W. J. Abernathy and K. Wayne, "The Limits of the Learning Curve," *Harvard Business Review,* September–October 1974, pp. 109–119.

pany was so completely organized to produce a low-cost, standardized product that the effects of the change in consumer preferences nearly sunk the enterprise. Although the company's strategy had been a roaring success during the long period of stable consumer behavior, it had become a business "dinosaur" and could not adapt easily to the realities of the changed environment.

## Differentiation

The firm attempts to differentiate itself from the pack by offering something that is perceived by the industry (and its customers) as being unique. It could be the high quality (Rolls Royce or Mercedes Benz), innovation (Hewlett Packard), or the willingness to be flexible in product design (Ferrari or Maserati). All these examples of quality, innovation, and flexibility have extremely important implications for the production system and the way it is designed and managed. The requirement is to be flexible in order to cope with the demands on the system. Brand image is important to this strategy. There may be other ways that an organization differentiates itself; for example, a strong dealer network (Zenith), an extremely well-designed distribution system (Gillette or Hunt Wesson), or excellent service.

This strategy does not ignore costs, just as the cost leadership strategy does not ignore quality, but the central thrust of the productive system and, indeed, of the entire organization is on the unique character of the company's products and services. Cost and availability are less important in the company's priorities since customers may be willing to pay a little more and even wait in order to have a more unique product.

In relation to industry competitors, a company with a differentiation strategy has less competition from both its direct competitors and from potential substitutes because of the uniqueness of its position. Its customers have greater brand loyalty and, therefore, less price sensitivity. Differentiation draws higher margins, so the higher costs are less important. Barriers to entry are provided, and higher margins make potential competition from suppliers' forward integration less important.

Still there are risks. Customers will tolerate only some maximum premium for uniqueness. If cost control becomes lax or if the cost of providing the uniqueness is beyond the customers' willingness to pay, then advantage can turn to disadvantage. Since many of the ways of providing high quality, innovation, and flexibility are labor intensive, inflation in labor costs relative to the inflation in the costs of other factors can price the product out of the market.

## Market Segmentation

Market segmentation is developed in terms of meeting the special needs of a particular market, providing lower costs for that market segment, or both. Whereas the first two strategies are industry-wide, market segmentation focuses on a particular customer group, a segment of the broad product line, a geographic portion of the market, or some other profitable niche of the market. It selects a market segment on some basis and tries to do an outstanding job of serving that market. The industry-wide leaders cannot serve all segments of the market equally well, so there are important niches for specialists. Perhaps, everyone but the industry leaders should be looking for a comfortable but viable niche.

The segmentation strategy can take an approach that combines one of the first two strategies with it. For example, a supplier of Sears for a particular appliance must undoubtedly have a low-cost substrategy in order to meet the requirements of the nation's number one retailer.

Another example is the firm that limits itself to small special orders within an industry dominated by giants who cannot serve this market niche very well. Yet, there may be a substantial market for small special orders. In order to serve this segment of the market, manufacturing facilities must be flexible enough to handle all types and sizes in small volume. There must be frequent changeover of machines for the many different types of orders that flow through the shop. The equipment must be flexible enough to handle the variety.

Therefore, although segmentation can emulate either of the first two strategies in a more limited way, it is unlikely that a firm using it could ever achieve the market share of the industry leaders who are attempting industry-wide strategies. The segmented firm is likely to be smaller, perhaps lacking the financial resources to attempt an industry-wide strategy.

The segmented firm need not compete directly with the giants of the industry. It may, however, have more of a problem dealing successfully with suppliers because it does not have the leverage of a large producer, and it may be more of a target of forward integration from suppliers and backward integration from customers.

Finally, not all industries seem to have opportunities for all three strategies. For example, in most commodities, cost and availability are the only factors of importance. In industries where entry barriers are low and exit barriers high, the competition may be so intense that the only feasible strategies are either differentiation or segmentation.

### Competing and the Operations Function

It should be clear from our discussion of the three generic enterprise strategies that the operations function plays a central role. A low-cost producer that makes its products available off-the-shelf must depend on its operations function, and its operations strategy must be coordinated to achieve its goal. A differentiated firm is one that has, among other characteristics, a flexible producing system. If its image is one of providing the highest quality, it must be that the operations system has that unique capability. A firm that attempts to succeed through market segmentation had better have a coordinated operations strategy that meshes carefully with the corporate strategy.

## THE EXPERIENCE CURVE PHENOMENON

It is a well established fact in manufacturing that, as experience is gained through production, unit costs are reduced. Originally, this cost improvement was attributed to a learning effect among workers such as the division of labor effect noted by

Adam Smith (i.e., the development of a skill or dexterity when a single task was performed repetitively). Now, however, the effect is recognized as resulting from a wide variety of additional sources, such as changes in production methods and tools, improved product design from the point of view of producibility, standardization, changes in layout and improved flow, economies of scale, better inventory control, improved scheduling and plant utilization, and improvements in organization. Actually, the worker learning effect is one that usually occurs rather quickly.

The concepts of the experience curve (also called the learning curve) were first formalized in the aircraft industry during World War II, though there is currently a general recognition of its applicability and usefulness. Studies of production costs of military aircraft showed that with each doubling of the *cumulative* total output of a model of an aircraft, the unit costs were reduced by 20 percent. Thus, the second unit costs only 80 percent of the first, the fourth unit costs 80 percent of the second, the hundredth unit costs 80 percent of the fiftieth, and so on. This is formalized mathematically as

$$c_n = c_1 n^{-b} \tag{1}$$

where

$c_n$ = The cost of the $n$th item
$c_1$ = The cost of the first item
$n$ = The cumulative output in units
$b$ = A parameter depending on the rate of unit cost decrease

The graph of Equation 1 for a specific example where $c_1 = \$10$ and $b = 0.322$ is the nonlinear cost reduction curve shown in Figure 22-1. In practice, however, the more usual representation of the experience curve has been on log–log graph paper so that Equation 1 plots as a straight line. Taking the log of both sides of Equation 1, we have

$$\log c_n = \log c_1 - b(\log n)$$

and

$$b = \frac{\log c_1 - \log c_n}{\log n} \tag{2}$$

Noting that log 1 = 0 and log 2 = 0.3010, we can represent the first doubling of cumulative output and derive a simple formula for computing the value of $b$ for any experience curve:

$$b = \frac{\log 1 - \log (P/100)}{\log 2} = \frac{-\log (P/100)}{0.3010} \tag{3}$$

where $P$ is the unit cost percentage associated with the learning curve.

Taking a specific example in which the first unit costs \$1, the second unit would cost \$0.80 for an 80 percent experience curve. Substituting these figures in Equation 3 gives us

$$b = \frac{-\log 80/100}{0.3010} = \frac{-\log 0.8}{0.3010} = \frac{0.0969}{0.3010} = 0.3220$$

FIGURE 22-1
**FORM OF 80 PERCENT EXPERIENCE CURVE ($c_n = 10n^{-0.322}$) PLOTTED WITH LINEAR SCALES.**

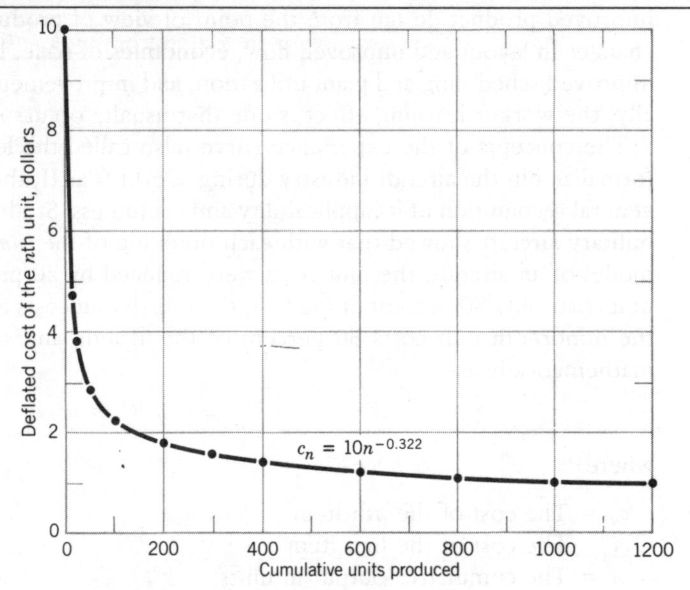


Thus, the 80 percent experience curve has the specific equation of

$$c_n = c_1 n^{-0.322} \tag{4}$$

To compute the cost of the $n$th unit, one simply inserts the desired value of $n$ and the cost of the first unit, $c_1$, in either Equation 1 or 2 for a given value of $b$. The graph of the example where $c_1 = \$10$ for an 80 percent experience curve is shown in Figure 22-1 as plotted with linear scales and in Figure 22-2 as plotted on log–log paper. The parameter $b$ for experience curves with other percents of unit cost reduction for doubling cumulative output can be computed in a similar way.

Table 22-1 provides values of the parameter $b$ for common experience curve percentages. The table also provides calculated values of the term $n^{-b}$ in Equation 1 for various values of $n$, the cumulative number of units produced. The cost of the $n$th unit can then be calculated as the product of the cost of the first unit, $c_1$, and the corresponding table value. For example, for a 95 percent experience curve, the table value for $n^{-b}$ when $n = 100{,}000$ is 0.4266. Therefore, if the first unit costs \$150, the 100,000th unit would cost $150 \times 0.4266 = \$63.99$.

The assumption that the unit cost is reduced by a constant percentage for each doubling of cumulative output makes it easy to plot the curve as a straight line on log–log paper without using the equations directly. For the example graphed in Figure 22-2, plot the cost for the first unit, $n = 1$, $c_1 = \$10$; then plot $n = 2$, $c_2 = 0.8 \times 10 = \$8$. These two points are sufficient to draw the straight line. Additional check points can be calculated, such as $n = 4$, $c_4 = 0.8 \times 8 = \$6.40$, and so on.

FIGURE 22-2
**THE EXPERIENCE CURVE $c_n = 10n^{-0.322}$ PLOTTED ON LOG–LOG GRAPH PAPER.**

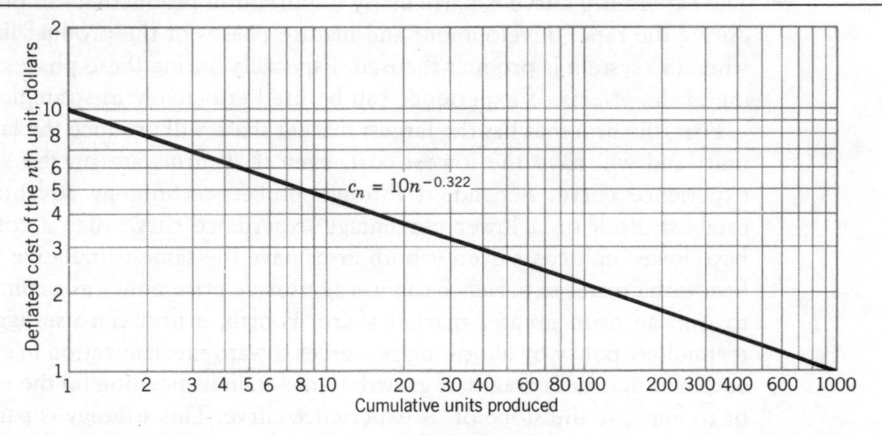


TABLE 22-1
**VALUES OF $b$ AND $n^{-b}$ FOR COMMON EXPERIENCE CURVE PERCENTAGES**

| | Experience Curve Percentages | | | | | | |
|---|---|---|---|---|---|---|---|
| | 99 | 95 | 90 | 85 | 80 | 75 | 70 |
| $b$ | 0.0145 | 0.0740 | 0.1520 | 0.2345 | 0.3220 | 0.4151 | 0.5146 |
| $n$, Cumulative Output, Units | $n^{-b}$ | | | | | | |
| 5 | 0.9769 | 0.8877 | 0.7830 | 0.6856 | 0.5956 | 0.5127 | 0.4368 |
| 10 | 0.9672 | 0.8433 | 0.7047 | 0.5828 | 0.4764 | 0.3845 | 0.3058 |
| 50 | 0.9449 | 0.7486 | 0.5518 | 0.3996 | 0.2837 | 0.1971 | 0.1336 |
| 100 | 0.9354 | 0.7112 | 0.4966 | 0.3396 | 0.2270 | 0.1478 | 0.0935 |
| 500 | 0.9138 | 0.6314 | 0.3888 | 0.2329 | 0.1352 | 0.0758 | 0.0408 |
| 1,000 | 0.9047 | 0.5998 | 0.3499 | 0.1979 | 0.1081 | 0.0568 | 0.0286 |
| 5,000 | 0.8838 | 0.5324 | 0.2740 | 0.1357 | 0.0644 | 0.0291 | 0.0125 |
| 10,000 | 0.8750 | 0.5058 | 0.2466 | 0.1153 | 0.0515 | 0.0219 | 0.0087 |
| 100,000 | 0.8563 | 0.4266 | 0.1738 | 0.0672 | 0.0245 | 0.0084 | 0.0027 |
| 1,000,000 | 0.8185 | 0.3597 | 0.1225 | 0.0392 | 0.0117 | 0.0032 | 0.0008 |

*Note:* Table values for $n^{-b}$ can be used in Equation 1 to calculate unit costs for the $n$th item, $c_n$, given $c_1$. For example, for an 85 percent experience curve and $c_1 = \$150$, the cost of the 5,000th unit is $c_{5,000} = 150 \times$ (Table value for 85 percent and $n = 5000$) $= 150 \times 0.1357 = \$20.36$.

## Strategic Implications of the Experience Curve

The experience curve is particularly important in productivity improvement results during the rapid development and mature phases of the product life cycle, usually when the system is product-focused. Especially during these phases, an understanding of the effects of experience can be used effectively in strategic planning.

First, the firm that has the largest market share will produce the largest number of units and will have the lowest cost, even if all firms are on the same percentage experience curve. Second, if through process-technology advantages a firm can establish itself on a lower percentage experience curve than a competitor, it will have lower unit costs even if both firms have the same cumulative output. Third, a firm with greater experience can use aggressive price policy as a competitive weapon to gain an even greater market share. Fourth, a firm can use aggressive process technology policy by allocating resources toward mechanization in earlier stages and automation in later stages of growth to maintain its position on the experience curve or to improve the slope of its experience curve. This strategy is particularly important in the mature phase of the product life cycle where competition is focused on cost.

## Limitations of the Experience Curve

Perhaps the greatest limitation of the experience curve is that the benefits finally run out simply because of product obsolescence, as is indicated by the product life cycle curve. But even before maturity is reached, the cost reductions due to experience will provide smaller and smaller returns. This is apparent from the shape of the curve in Figure 22-1; early experience provides large returns, but as the product matures, it becomes much more difficult to obtain further cost reductions.

As the product goes through the stages of life cycle development, the productive system also matures, going through the stages of custom volume (job shop), to low volume (batch), high volume, and very high volume (systems with a product focus). Another way to view what is happening as the productive system evolves is to note that it is becoming much less flexible and more and more capital intensive. This evolution is a large part of what makes the experience curve work, but at the same time, it makes the firm vulnerable to radical changes in consumer tastes and product obsolescence.

## Experience Curve for Process-Focused Systems

In process-focused systems, we do not have the opportunity to learn what comes from constant repetition of an activity. Also, the lower volume makes it less likely that improvements will result from mechanization and automation or from flow improvements in layout.

Nevertheless, there is cost improvement in these kinds of systems. Process-focused systems learn how to serve their customers and clients better through improved order processing, better labor assignment and scheduling, better tool design, improved layout, and so on. The results of experience are more difficult to document because we do not have a specific product produced over a period of time for which we can accumulate cost data. Nevertheless, the cost improvement phenomenon exists in process-focused systems, though the net effect is less dramatic than it is in product-focused systems.

## THE ROLE OF PRODUCTIVITY IMPROVEMENT

Comparative productivity statistics for six countries[2] show that from 1960 to 1980 U.S. productivity increases averaged only 2.7 percent and that there was an actual decline of −0.3 percent in 1980. Japan averaged a productivity increase of 9.4 percent during the same period; France averaged 5.6 percent; and West Germany, 5.4 percent. These productivity improvement differences among countries have obvious implications for global competitive advantages and disadvantages, especially when coupled with hourly wage rate differences for some industries such as the automobile and steel industries.

But does increased productivity in an industry lead to market growth, or vice versa, and ultimately to profitability? There is evidence that it does. For example, Figure 22-3*a* shows the relationship between productivity growth and output growth for a large cross-section of the U.S. industrial portfolio during 1972–1976, the period chosen being one during which the United States was falling behind. In general terms, the industries with higher output growth had higher productivity growth; that is, those in the upper left-hand quadrant, such as industrial chemicals, other chemicals, and beverages. Those with lower productivity changes had lower output growth, as was the case with footwear, nonferrous metals, and iron and steel.

The experience curve suggests that growth is related to productivity; therefore, it is not surprising that high or low growth relates to high- or low-productivity sectors. Whether productivity or growth is the primary generator is not the issue. A probable theory is that they feed on each other in a reinforcing cycle. In any case, we observe that there is a general relationship.

To carry the analysis one step further, it can also be shown that there is a general relationship between output growth and returns to stockholder's equity. The prescription seems straightforward—growth and productivity in a reinforcing cycle lead to increased profitability. Earlier in our history, when our domestic markets were more secure and dominated the strategies of U.S. firms, the prescription seemed to work fairly well. International competition was not a vital issue. After all, the United States was the largest world market for most products. We tended to manufacture and sell for our own large markets, and by being productive, we could compete in both domestic and international markets.

[2] See P. Capdevielle and D. Alvarez, "International Comparisons of Trends in Productivity and Labor Costs," *Monthly Labor Review, 104*(12), December 1981, pp. 14–20.

FIGURE 22-3
**PRODUCTIVITY VERSUS OUTPUT GROWTH FOR (*a*) THE U.S. INDUSTRIAL PORTFOLIO, 1972–1976, AND (*b*) THE JAPANESE INDUSTRIAL PORTFOLIO, 1970–1976.**

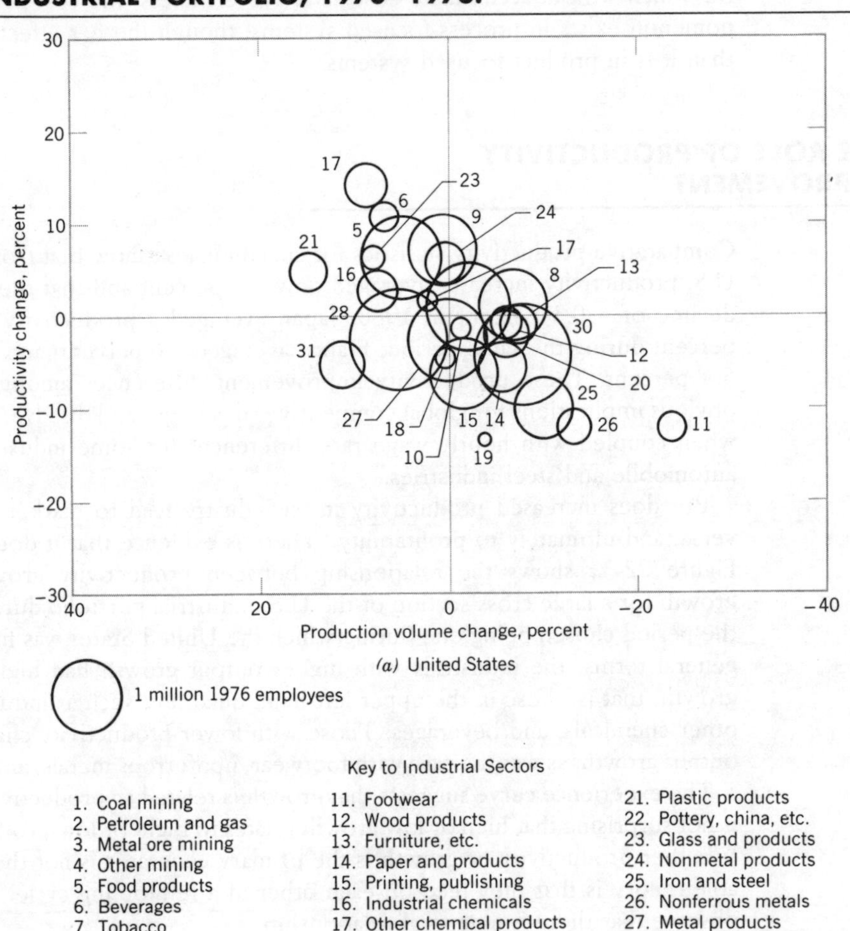


Key to Industrial Sectors

1. Coal mining
2. Petroleum and gas
3. Metal ore mining
4. Other mining
5. Food products
6. Beverages
7. Tobacco
8. Textiles
9. Cloths
10. Leather and products
11. Footwear
12. Wood products
13. Furniture, etc.
14. Paper and products
15. Printing, publishing
16. Industrial chemicals
17. Other chemical products
18. Petroleum refineries
19. Petroleum, coal products
20. Rubber products
21. Plastic products
22. Pottery, china, etc.
23. Glass and products
24. Nonmetal products
25. Iron and steel
26. Nonferrous metals
27. Metal products
28. General machinery
29. Electrical machinery
30. Transport equipment

But that prescription is not sufficient for firms not sheltered from foreign competition to compete in international markets. As some experts have remarked, "If one considers potential exposure to import penetration, over 70 percent of our goods must now operate in an international marketplace."[3] Some markets have become

[3] Ira C. Magaziner and Robert B. Reich, *Minding America's Business: The Decline and Rise of the American Economy*, Vintage Books, New York, 1983, p. 32. See pp. 69–72 for a discussion of sheltered and traded businesses.

FIGURE 22-3
***(Continued)***

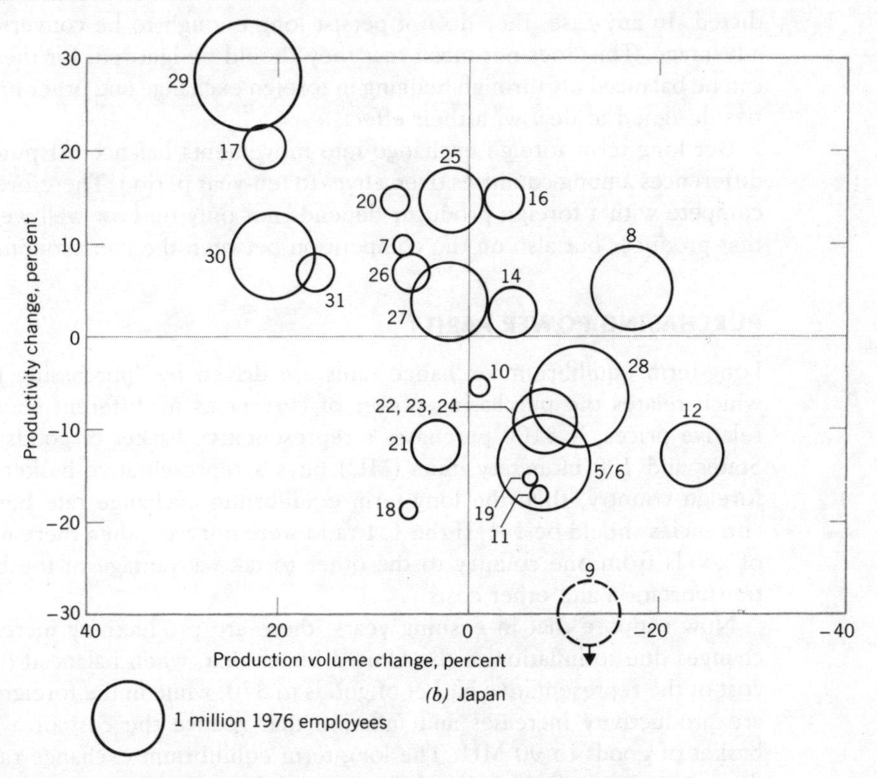


*(b)* Japan

Source: United Nations Yearbook of Industrial Statistics, OECD, 1972–1976.

globalized with further product standardization and even greater emphasis on the benefits that stem from the experience curve and productivity increases.

A competitor in a given country could have significant advantages in factor costs, such as labor, materials, and energy, and it could have a significant productivity advantage. Of course, the factor costs and productivity advantages can result in substantially lower manufacturing costs, all adding to the net effect of being productive within an industry. In addition, however, productivity enters into the international competitive equation through international exchange rates.

A company could be moderately successful in productivity improvement and could even have some factor cost advantages, could obtain relatively low costs and large growth, and could be in a position to compete effectively with domestic rivals, but exchange rates could wipe out the advantage in international markets. To understand productivity effects in international competition, we must establish a broader framework. We must first understand long-term foreign exchange rate movements.

## Some Exchange Rate Effects[4]

Short-term exchange rates are subject to variations that probably cannot be predicted. In any case, they do not persist long enough to be converted to strategic advantage. This does not mean that they should be ignored, for the risks involved can be balanced off through hedging in foreign exchange and other important activities designed to deal with their effects.

But long-term foreign exchange rate movements balance off purchasing power differences among countries over a five- to ten-year period. Therefore, our ability to compete with a foreign producer depends not only on how well we do relative to that producer but also on the competition between the two economies.

### PURCHASING POWER PARITY[5]

Long-term equilibrium exchange rates are driven by "purchasing power parity," which relates the purchasing power of currencies in different countries through relative prices. If $100 purchases a representative basket of goods in the United States and 100 monetary units (MU) buys a representative basket of goods in a foreign country, then the long-term equilibrium exchange rate between the two currencies should be 1 : 1. If the 1 : 1 ratio were not true, then there would be a flow of goods from one country to the other to take advantage of the bargain, within transportation and other costs.

Now suppose that in ensuing years, there are productivity increases and price changes due to inflation in the United States that, when balanced out, reduce the cost of the representative basket of goods to $70, while in the foreign country there are productivity increases and inflation that reduce the cost of a representative basket of goods to 90 MU. The long-term equilibrium exchange rate would then float from the previous 1 : 1 to 7 : 9, or $1 would exchange for 9/7 = 1.29 MU of the foreign currency.

The movement of exchange rates is controlled by the relative productivity improvement and inflation of the two economies, represented by aggregate price levels. For example, if the 1960–1980 average annual productivity improvements in the United States and Japan of 3.0 and 9.4 percent, respectively, were compounded over that 20-year period, aggregate U.S. productivity would be 1.80 times its initial level, compared to 6.72 times the initial level in Japan; that is, if the initial indexes of productivity were both 100, the 1980 indexes would be 180 for the United States and 672 for Japan.

The relative influence on prices in the two countries would be in relation to these productivity improvements. If inflation were the same in both countries, then the

[4] See E. S. Buffa and M. C. Bogue, "Productivity and the Exchange Rate," *National Productivity Review*, Fall 1985, pp. 32–46; and M. C. Bogue and E. S. Buffa, *Corporate Strategic Analysis*, Free Press, New York, 1986.

[5] For a discussion of exchange rate determination, see Alan C. Shapiro, *Multinational Financial Management*, Allyn & Bacon, Boston, 1982, Chapter 4; and Henry J. Gailliot, "Purchasing Power Parity as an Explanation of Long-Term Changes in Exchange Rates," *Journal of Money, Credit and Banking*, August 1970, pp. 348–357.

*relative* price changes would reflect only the influence of productivity improvement. But if inflation averaged 4 percent in the United States and 3 percent in Japan for the 20-year period, then the relative prices would reflect a net inflation in the United States averaging 1 percent (4 percent inflation minus 3 percent productivity increase), whereas the Japanese would enjoy the net effect of a 6.4 percent average productivity–inflation change in price levels. Over the 20-year period, the relative price changes would be reflected in exchange rate adjustments because the purchasing power of the two currencies would have changed. Of course, there may be short-term policies that move exchange rates from their purchasing power parity values, but in the long run, the fundamental forces return the exchange rate to stable equilibrium values.

Now, where do the costs and prices of individual products enter the equation? In a large diversified economy, such as that of the United States, the effect on exchange rates of a single product is minuscule. Through the aggregation of prices in the representative basket of goods, it has an effect, of course. On the other hand, through the exchange rate, the productivity improvement of our economy has an enormous effect on the prices of export products in foreign countries and on the prices of foreign goods in U.S. markets. Thus, the productivity achievements of an individual company for a product are dwarfed by the productivity progress of the economy as a whole. This leads to the following statement: *To compete effectively in a particular international market, we must be at least as productive in that field relative to our own economy as our international competitor is relative to its economy.* The managerial significance of this statement is that productivity improvement takes on an even more important role in corporate strategy.

If we achieve a 20 percent improvement in productivity over a 10-year period, for example, while our economy as a whole achieves the same percentage productivity improvement, we could take pride in our achievement, but we would have just kept up with our economy. If our *domestic* competitors had achieved only a 5 percent productivity improvement during the same period, we would have gained a 15 percentage point cost advantage in real terms. Much of the cost–competitive process in the domestic situation is under our control, in terms of how we manage internally, how innovative we are with technology, and so on.

However, if a foreign competitor achieved only a 5 percent productivity improvement in an economy that was stagnant with zero net improvement, it would be better off than we by 5 percentage points because it had performed better than its economy. This may seem paradoxical, but it reflects the workings of long-term international monetary exchange. Examples will help clarify this important concept of strategic analysis.

### EXAMPLE 1

Assume an example in the context of the preceding discussion, where we start with a product, perhaps a piece of machinery, a machine tool, or an automobile, whose initial costs here and in a foreign country are 5000 monetary units (MU), reflecting parity initially; that is, a 1 : 1 exchange rate. Over a period, perhaps ten years, the U.S. producer achieves a 20 percent productivity improvement (a $1000 cost reduction to 80 percent of the earlier price) in an economy that improved by 20 percent. During the same period, a foreign producer achieved a 5 percent productivity increase (a 250 MU cost reduction to 95 percent of the earlier price) in an economy that did not improve at all in the aggregate. The second row of Table 22-2 shows the domestic cost improvement of each producer.

The long-term equilibrium exchange rate would reflect the productivity changes during the period: 80 (U.S.) to 100 (foreign), or 8:10; $1 United States = 10/8 = 1.25 MU (foreign), assuming equal inflation within the two countries. The bottom two rows of Table 22-2 indicate the cost of each product in the other country in its monetary units, not including transportation and import duties.

The $1000 cost improvement in productivity achieved by the U.S. producer relative to the 250 MU cost improvement achieved by the foreign producer has reversed and become a 5000 MU − 4750 MU = 250 MU *disadvantage* for the U.S. producer competing in the foreign country, before transportation and duty. On the other hand, the foreign producer has a $4000 − $3800 = $200 *advantage* in competing against the U.S. producer's product in the United States, before transportation and duty.

Of course, in this example, the disadvantage for the U.S. producer competing in the foreign country and the foreign producer's competitive advantage in the U.S. would be even greater if the U.S. producer's productivity improvement were less than the 20 percent national aggregate and/or the foreign producer's improvement were more than 5 percent greater than its country's zero improvement.

**EXAMPLE 2**

These effects are clarified and confirmed by the case where each producer improves productivity only to the same extent as its own economy, even though in absolute terms the U.S. producer has a far better record of productivity than the foreign competitor. For example, if the U.S. producer achieves only a 20 percent productivity improvement during a period when the economy achieves 20 percent and the

**TABLE 22-2**
**FOREIGN PRODUCER'S ADVANTAGE**

| | U.S. Producer | Foreign Producer |
|---|---|---|
| Initial cost (exchange rate, 1:1) | $5000 | 5000 MU |
| Cost within each producer's country after productivity improvement | 0.8 × 5000 = $4000 | 0.95 × 5000 = 4750 MU |
| Cost of U.S. product in the foreign country after monetary exchange | 10/8 × 4000 = 5000 MU | |
| Cost of foreign product in the U.S. after monetary exchange | | 8/10 × 4750 = $3800 |

foreign producer achieves a zero percent improvement in a stagnant economy—that is, if both producers do just as well as their economies—the calculations shown in Table 22-3 confirm that cost–price competition will be a standoff. The U.S. producer's 20 percent productivity improvement receives no reward in the international marketplace.

On the other hand, if the U.S. producer increased productivity 30 percent while the economy improved by 20, and the foreign producer improved only 5 percent in a stagnant economy, for example, then the advantage would be with the U.S. producer.

Of course, these examples assume that each producer had equal initial costs, and this is not likely to be true. Nevertheless, the examples show the effects of competitor productivity differences in relation to national productivity differences over a period of time.

## Implications of Exchange-Rate Effects

With this perspective on global operations management competition, it is interesting to look at two industries that have had difficulty competing internationally in recent times, steel and automobiles.

### THE STEEL INDUSTRY

During the 1977–1982 period, the Japanese steel industry was about 50 percent larger than that of its nearest national competitor, the United States, whose steel industry was shrinking by about 10 percent per year. In Figure 22-3, the iron and steel industry (25) is one of the industrial sectors in Japan that was substantially more productive than the Japanese economy as a whole during the 1970–1976 period, a time of intense competitive pressure on U.S. producers. On the other hand, in the U.S. industrial portfolio for the 1972–1976 period, the iron and steel industry was somewhat less productive than the U.S. economy as a whole.

**TABLE 22-3**
**A STANDOFF**

| | U.S. Producer | Foreign Producer |
|---|---|---|
| Initial cost (exchange rate, 1 : 1) | \$5000 | 5000 MU |
| Cost within each producer's country after productivity improvement | 0.8 × 5000 = \$4000 | 1.00 × 5000 = 5000 MU |
| Cost of U.S. product in the foreign country after monetary exchange | 10/8 × 4000 = 5000 MU | |
| Cost of foreign product in the U.S. after monetary exchange | | 8/10 × 5000 = \$4000 |

The reasons for the poor competitive position of our steel industry are commonly assigned to low productivity because of old process technology and high factor costs, including transportation and energy costs and wages and labor costs. Advantages and disadvantages in productivity and in the factor costs of raw materials, energy, and labor enter into the results of the cost–experience curve, helping to account for comparative performance.

**Steel Industry Productivity Comparisons.** Taking the 1960–1970 period of steel productivity improvement in the United States, Japan, West Germany, and Canada, U.S. productivity was the highest, 66.7 tons per 1000 worker-hours, followed by Canada, West Germany, and Japan (see Table 22-4). During the following 10-year period, U.S. steel industry productivity increased by 24.9 percent, and it still had the highest productivity of the four countries in 1970. But Japanese productivity had increased by an astounding 203.3 percent, with West Germany's and Canada's increases being 70.2 and 49.9 percent, respectively. In terms of our analysis, the U.S. steel industry lagged behind our economy as a whole, whereas the productivity increases of the steel industries of the other countries, particularly Japan, had outpaced their own economies.

The 1970–1980 period demonstrates the same kind of general relationships; with an aggregate 10-year increase of only 15.4 percent, the U.S. steel industry productivity lagged behind its own economy. Meanwhile, Japan, West Germany, and Canada recorded 10-year increases of 83.5, 54.1, and 65.9 percent, respectively. By 1980, Japan had the highest productivity of 136.9 tons per 1000 worker-hours, followed by Canada and West Germany, and the United States had the lowest.

## THE AUTOMOBILE INDUSTRY

The automobile and steel industries have much in common in terms of the types of problems they face in international competition, and Japan is the nemesis for both. In addition, they have another touch point—the auto industry is the largest single

TABLE 22-4
**COMPARATIVE STEEL PRODUCTIVITY: THE UNITED STATES, JAPAN, WEST GERMANY, AND CANADA**

| | *Productivity, Tons per 1000 Worker-Hours* | | |
|---|---|---|---|
| | 1960 | 1970 | 1980 |
| United States | 66.7 | 83.3 | 96.1 |
| Japan | 24.6 | 74.6 | 136.9 |
| West Germany | 38.9 | 66.2 | 102.0 |
| Canada | 47.3 | 70.9 | 117.6 |

*Source:* Presentation by Paul Marshall at the UCLA–AISI Conference on "Strategies for the U.S. Steel Industry in the 1980s" and the American Iron and Steel Institute.

customer of the steel industry. The reverse side of the coin is that steel is a major factor cost for automobiles. In addition, there is the wage differential problem of the U.S. auto industry wage rates with respect to general wage levels in the U.S. compared with Japanese auto wages relative to general wages in Japan.

How did the U.S. auto industry perform relative to the U.S. economy, and how did the Japanese auto industry perform relative to its economy? Examining Figure 22-3*a* shows that industry number 30, transport equipment, which includes the auto industry, had negative growth and productivity change during the 1972–1976 period in the United States. However, this industry was one of the star performers during the 1970–1976 period in Japan. Therefore, we should not be surprised to hear in the news that the Japanese have costs that appear to be about $2000 to $2500 less per car than those of U.S. automakers. How much of the difference in costs are real, reflecting better operations management, and how much represents an amplification of cost differences through the exchange rate due to the differential productivity improvement record is a key question.

## Productivity Improvement and Operations Strategy

Given the imperatives resulting from the cost leadership strategy and some types of segmentation strategies that emphasize cost and the concepts of the experience curve, all coupled with the amplifying effects of productivity increase differences, an operations strategy that emphasizes all kinds of productivity improvements seems essential. Depending on the particular industry, this may mean large investments in plant and equipment, with particular emphasis on advanced process technology.

Productivity improvement is an imperative in operations strategy for all firms. In order to remain competitive, a firm must continually seek ways of reducing costs; profits are the difference between prices and costs, and prices are not normally under direct managerial control. It is with firms following the low-cost strategies in one form or another that the concepts of the experience curve and productivity improvement become crucial. This applies even to those firms operating in a sheltered domestic environment. For those firms operating in global markets, productivity improvement needs to become a managerial religion, in part because strong foreign competitors are giving so much attention to it but also because of the amplification of productivity differences through the exchange rate, as we have discussed.

It is largely through operations strategy that productivity improvement becomes implemented. If the basic positioning of the type of productive system mismatches the market, then productivity improvement is hampered by an inappropriate system. The wrong technology can be a result, or jobs and processes may be poorly designed to achieve market objectives. The systems for planning, scheduling, and control may be mismatched, together with all kinds of operating decisions. Productivity improvement cannot be left to the experience curve phenomenon, as something that will simply happen as volume cumulates. It must be managed as a conscious part of operations strategy.

## THE SIX BASIC COMPONENTS OF OPERATIONS STRATEGY

All of the activities in the line of material flow from suppliers through fabrication and assembly and culminating in product distribution must be integrated for sensible operations strategy formulation. Leaving any part out can lead to uncoordinated strategies. In addition to materials, the other crucial inputs of labor, job design, and technology must be parts of the integrated strategy.

The six components of operations strategy are:

- Positioning the productive system
- Capacity/location decisions
- Product and process technology
- Work force and job design
- Strategic implications of operating decisions
- Suppliers and vertical integration

These components are basic to operations strategy because there is a wide managerial choice available within each, and each affects the long-term competitive position of the firm by impacting cost, quality, product availability, and flexibility/service.

### Positioning the Productive System

If production is not made a part of corporate strategy, then the likelihood of a mismatch between system and markets is high, with resulting conflicts, usually between the marketing and production functions. A firm without a unified strategy that includes the operations function is likely to anticipate obtaining low cost, high quality, product availability, and flexibility/service from its production system all at the same time, not realizing that one cannot optimize all these dimensions simultaneously, that there are trade-offs between them. A firm that attempts to be "all things" in its production system is likely to compromise all four dimensions of production competence and end up "stuck in the middle" with low margins.

#### FIRST EXAMINE PRODUCT–PROCESS STRATEGIES

Looking at the product and productive system types jointly, it is useful to think of product volume as the independent variable and the productive system type as the dependent variable, as represented by Figure 22-4. As the product develops through its life cycle, the productive system goes through a life cycle of its own, from a job shop system (process focused, to order) when the product is in its initial stages through intermediate stages to a continuous system (product focused, to stock) when the product is demanded in large volume.

These stages of product and process development are interdependent and feed on each other. There is the obvious dependence of the appropriate type of productive system on the volume of product that is sold. In addition, the volume of product sold is dependent in part on costs and the price–quality competitive positions,

FIGURE 22-4
**RELATIONSHIP BETWEEN PRODUCT VOLUME AND THE TYPE OF PRODUCTIVE SYSTEM OVER A RANGE OF VOLUMES OCCURRING DURING THE PRODUCT LIFE CYCLE.**

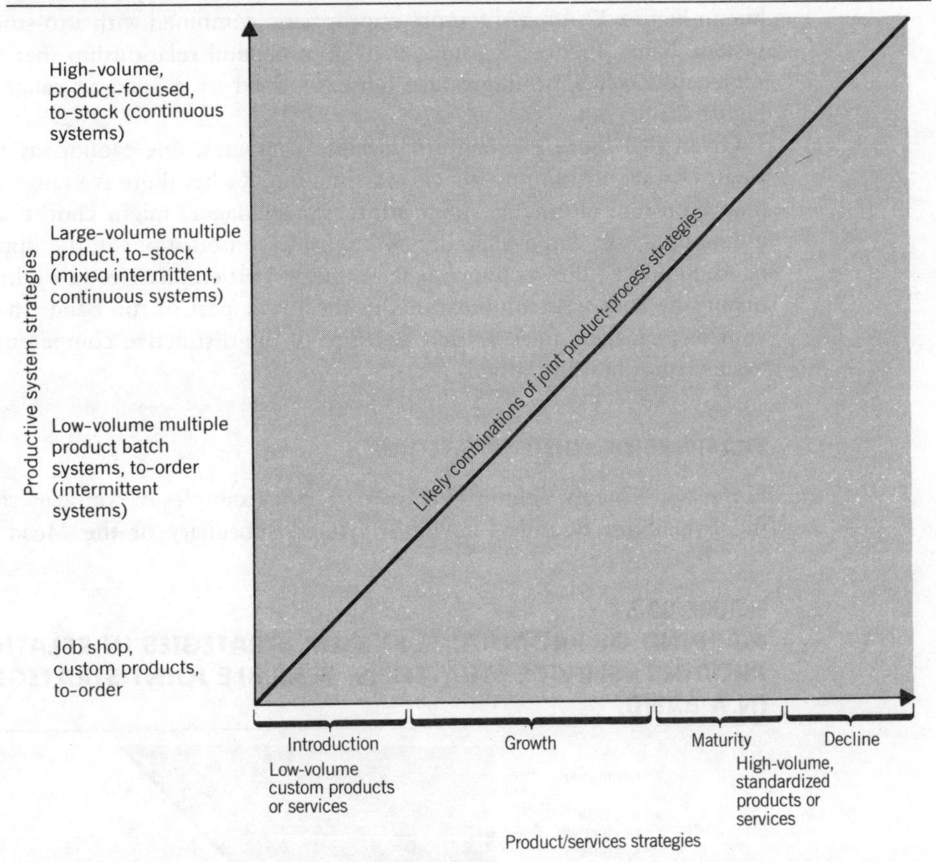


which is dependent on the use of the appropriate productive system. The experience curve is a reflection of all of the factors that operate in a productive system to reduce costs and is an important element in a manager's competitive strategy. The results of the experience curve can be used as the basis for aggressive pricing that may, in itself, be an important factor in building market share, further building experience and resulting in a further progression down the curve. For example, in anticipation of a lower cost per unit at larger volumes in future time periods, a calculator firm may price its products lower than the initial cost of production. In such aggressive pricing, however, risks must be balanced with potential benefits.

But would a firm always follow the strategy implied by the diagonal line of Figure 22-4? As we have noted, process-focused systems provide flexibility and are somewhat more adaptable to product variety and to high-quality production. Thus, where the manager's strategy is focused on providing service, high quality, and meeting customer's individual needs, combinations between product volume and productive system types that are below the line in Figure 22-4 may be more appropriate, probably combined with production to order. On the other hand, if the manager's strategy is focused on price and off-the-shelf availability, combinations above the line in Figure 22-4 may be more appropriate, combined with a to-stock production system. Thus, Figure 22-4 may provide a general relationship that should be observed, but actual strategies are better defined by a band or range, as shown in Figure 22-5.

Given that there is a band of feasible strategies, one cannot say that there is a single correct positioning for a given situation. Rather there is a range of choices that may represent alternative joint strategies. Managers might choose a strategy that emphasizes cost and availability by choosing combinations in the upper part of the band. Similarly, they could choose a strategy that emphasizes flexibility, choice, and quality by choosing combinations in the lower part of the band. In making these choices, managers need to take account of the distinctive competencies that their organization has developed.

## EXAMPLES OF JOINT STRATEGIES

Hayes and Wheelwright (1979a) give specific examples of company strategies using the Lynchburg Foundry, a wholly owned subsidiary of the Mead Corporation.

FIGURE 22-5
**MAPPING OF PRODUCTIVE SYSTEM STRATEGIES IN RELATION TO PRODUCT–SERVICE STRATEGIES. FEASIBLE JOINT STRATEGIES OCCUR IN A BAND.**

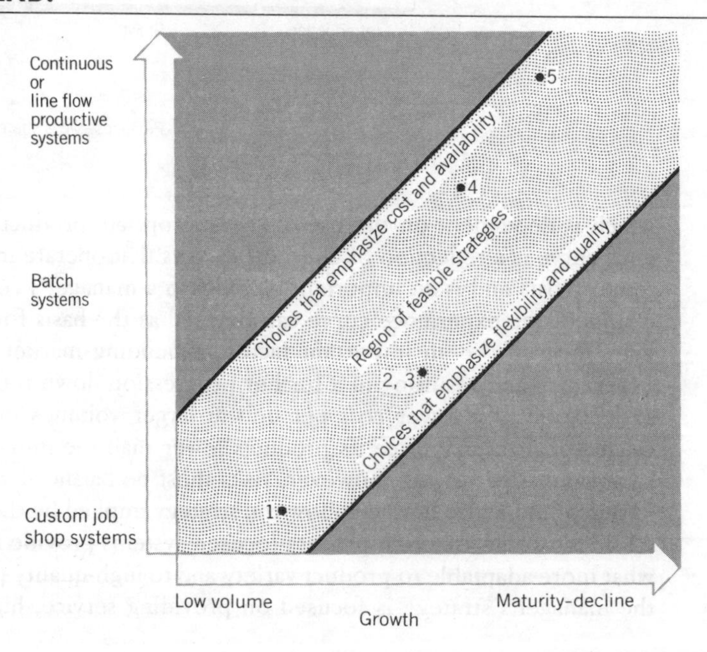

Lynchburg has five plants in Virginia and surrounding states. The five plants represent different points in Figure 22-5. One plant is a job order shop that makes one-of-a-kind products; its joint strategy is represented by point 1 in the lower left region of Figure 22-5. Two plants are organized to produce a variety of products in batches. These plants involve a strategy in the lower middle range in which emphasis has been placed on the flexibility required by multiple products (points 2 and 3). A fourth plant is designed as a line-flow set-up to produce only a few auto part castings; its joint strategy is represented by point 4 in the upper middle range, where cost and availability are emphasized. Finally, the fifth plant is an automated pipe facility producing a highly standardized item in huge quantity on a continuous basis. The joint strategy for the fifth plant is represented by point 5 to the left side of the upper right region of Figure 22-5.

The Lynchburg examples indicate that an enterprise may need to employ different joint strategies for different product–process situations. The resulting planning and control policies and procedures need to be reflective of these quite different strategies; a uniform set of operations planning and control policies would be quite inappropriate.

It is unlikely that a strategy can remain static over long periods. As products or services mature in their life cycles, consumer preferences become known, designs become refined, and volumes build, and the appropriate joint strategy must reflect these changes. Normally, the progression involves a more capital intensive productive process that is more integrated, and there is necessarily a loss of flexibility.

## FOCUS

An observation concerning the producing strategy of the Lynchburg Foundry to note is that each of the five plants has been specialized in some way. By specializing each plant, managers have a more restricted scope that allows them to deal with more limited objectives, presumably making it possible for them to do their jobs more effectively. The advantages of specialization apply to managerial tasks as well as to other forms of work.

Skinner (1985) has referred to this concept of specialization by a producing facility as "the focused factory." These concepts are closely linked with the overall enterprise strategy and, indeed, are an integral part of that strategy.

> A factory that focuses on a narrow product mix for a particular market niche will outperform the conventional plant, which attempts a broader mission. Because its equipment, supporting systems, and procedures can concentrate on a limited task for one set of customers, its costs and especially its overheads are likely to be lower than those of the conventional plant. But, more important, such a plant can become a competitive weapon because its entire apparatus is focused to accompany the particular manufacturing task demanded by the company's overall strategy and marketing objective. (p. 72)

Thinking in terms of the five plants of the Lynchburg Foundry, each had been given a focus. The first was focused on one-of-a-kind products. Two plants were positioned to produce multiple products in batches. The fourth was focused on the production of a few auto part castings in high volume, and the fifth was a highly automated pipe factory that was focused entirely on that product. The managers of each facility were presented with a narrower range of customer types to supply that had unique requirements for quality, costs, and delivery. Although the Lynchburg Foundry is a large organization, the same general concepts can apply to individual product lines in a smaller organization.

The opposite producing strategy would have been to attempt to gain "economies of scale" by assembling all of these diverse objectives in one huge manufacturing facility managed centrally through common control systems. Presumably, the overhead per unit of output should be lower, but there is a trade-off in terms of meeting the diverse objectives of the several businesses that are involved.

## POSITIONING STRATEGY FOR SERVICE SYSTEMS

Managers of service systems also have choices about how to match the nature of the productive system to the market situation. In the case of service systems, however, the productive system is often intimately bound up with the marketing and service concept. The impression that the service system makes on clients and customers is affected by the way the service is given by personnel and by the way the system is designed.

Fast-food operations emphasize low cost and availability with a limited menu. Looking at an individual outlet, the volume is usually high, the product standardized, and the process is product focused. The joint strategy is represented by a point on or above the diagonal line, perhaps in the middle volume range. But when the system as a whole is examined, with multiple standardized modules, central purchasing, distribution, and some central processing of food, we would characterize the joint strategy as being of high volume and above the diagonal line.

There are, however, restaurant chains that replicate a module of more traditional menus with large selection and individual service. This service system is more nearly like the low- to high-volume, multiple-product system, using a process-focused productive system. Such restaurant chains are emphasizing quality and service, but customers must wait for meals to be prepared, and cost is much less a criterion. These chains are below the diagonal line in Figure 22-4, and they move to the right as overall volume develops, paced largely by the opening of new units. Again, the experience curve provides cost reductions from a variety of sources, but the dominant effect results from economies of scale.

There are many other contrasting examples where managers of service systems make choices concerning the position of their productive system in relation to the nature of the market. In health care, there is the general hospital versus the clinic or specialized medical facilities. In package delivery, there is the Post Office versus the specialized services of UPS, Federal Express, and so on.

## POSITIONING IS THE KEY

Although all the elements of operations strategy are important and all need to be woven together to form a coordinated strategy, if the positioning of the system is wrong, the operations strategy will be ineffective. It should be an integral part of the overall corporate strategy and should include both the system type and the to-stock versus to-order decision.

One of the most common mistakes in positioning strategy is to attempt the production of products with fundamentally different market requirements within the same basic production system. The result is that the match between market requirements and the production system is out of sync for some of the products. As a result, costs may be out of line, quality may not receive the necessary emphasis, or delivery times may not meet requirements. Another common mistake is the failure to recognize the dynamics of the process life cycle, which necessitates the basic redesign of the production system as the product goes through its life cycle.

## Making Capacity/Location Decisions Strategic

G. Heileman Brewing Company, the nation's fourth largest brewer, is making a strong move to penetrate the South, where its sales are only two percent of the regional total. By acquiring a modern plant in Georgia as a part of its battle for control of the Pabst Brewing Company, Heileman was establishing a beachhead. "When you buy a battleship, you start a war," explained Russell Cleary, Heileman's chairman and CEO.[6] It could have built new capacity, but it is paying only about $17.50 per barrel for the existing brewing capacity, compared to the $50 per barrel that new capacity would cost. Furthermore, by brewing the beer in Georgia instead of brewing it at other plants in Maryland and Indiana and shipping it at high cost to the South, Heileman will be able to cut prices, if necessary, to increase market share.

Videotape prices in the United States and elsewhere began to decline rapidly in 1982 when Fuji Photo Film, Hitachi Maxell, and TDK collectively increased capacity by over 90 percent. This massive capacity increase was installed just as industry-wide annual growth rates in sales declined to a relatively modest 40 percent. While consumers reaped the benefit of very low tape prices, the supply–demand imbalance created havoc in the industry, and it was expected that the overcapacity would not be absorbed for at least two years.

Dow Chemical Company, headed for overcapacity in basic chemicals, is shifting its product strategy toward higher margin, specialty chemical products. While overcapacity in its basic chemical operations is not the only reason for the shift, its existence in polyethylene capacity, for example, promised low margins for the future. Dow's announcement that it would end polyethylene capacity expansion projects in progress in South Korea, Saudi Arabia, and Yugoslavia, and that it would add specialty chemical capacity, had great significance for the industry.[7]

In March 1983, Domtar Incorporated, Canada's largest maker of fine papers, announced that it would double the capacity of its paper mill in Windsor, Quebec.[8]

[6] *The Wall Street Journal,* February 13, 1983.
[7] *Business Week,* January 31, 1983.
[8] *Wall Street Journal,* March 29, 1983.

The announcement was quite factual, but it indicated that the mill to be enlarged was operating at a loss. In addition, the announcement stated that the mill "benefits, however, from a good wood supply and is near the U.S. border, for increased access to that market. It provides the best location for significant increases in productive capacity." To whom was the announcement really directed? How did the announcement to increase capacity fit in with the company's strategy?

The preceding news items dealing with capacity and location all suggest the importance of capacity/location decisions. In fact, these kinds of decisions are the most significant ones made in terms of the amount of capital involved and the amount of care with which they should be made from a strategic point of view. The risks are great because future demand is uncertain at best. But in making such decisions, forecasting competitors' behavior is even more important than predicting demand. For example, if too many competitors add capacity, as in the videotape case, all firms in the industry are likely to suffer. Once installed, new capacity remains, and overcapacity can be a problem for the company and the industry far into the future.

The issue of capacity expansion immediately raises the companion issues of *where* to expand in order to improve the firm's competitive position, how to counter competitors' moves, and how to tie new capacity into the distribution network effectively.

## THE PLAGUE OF OVERCAPACITY

Excess capacity is a curse, except in situations where explosively increasing demand is nearly certain. Otherwise, overcapacity carries with it both higher overhead costs per unit and lower industry prices. The result is a cost–price squeeze.

There are a number of technological factors that make it difficult to avoid overcapacity, at least in the short run. If capacity is to be added, it must be in a unit of economic scale, perhaps large enough to produce excess capacity for some time before increasing demand can absorb it. Steel production, oil refining, and beer plants are all cases in which the capacity added must be in relatively large units. The long lead times involved in adding capacity increase the risk and make it necessary to watch closely the actions of competitors. A firm that is slow to act may be left out as result of risk aversion, whereas a firm that acts quickly will achieve a cost advantage through experience and may increase its market share; thus, all firms are pressured to act, and the result may be a capacity glut.

An innovation in production technology, such as the oxygen process and continuous casting in steel making, has the effect of attracting investment in the new technology to take advantage of the lower costs and improved quality associated with it, even though adequate industry capacity exists. However, if the exit barriers are high, the existing technology is likely to remain in production and prolong the agony of overcapacity. The result is an industry overcapacity with pressure on the costs of the old capacity as its volumes decline and approach break-even levels. Industry overcapacity produces downward pressure on prices, resulting in a cost–price squeeze that is felt particularly by operators of older, high-cost facilities.

## MANAGING THE CAPACITY EXPANSION PROCESS

A large part of the problem is in managing the potential or real overcapacity in the company and in the industry. The appropriate capacity moves can be rather obvious when new products are in their rapid growth phases. Since the potential costs of lost sales are so great in these instances, capacity expansion is usually clearly justified.

Otherwise, management problems are centered on capacity gaming, incorporated with a rational process for determining options, assessing future demands and technological impacts, and evaluating financial flows. The financial evaluation is terribly important but rather mechanical and does not accurately represent the nature of the managerial problem. The issue is, *which* numbers to insert in the analysis. Given those numbers, comparative evaluation of alternatives is straightforward.

## CAPACITY GAMING

Taking the measure of competitors is critical, in part to avoid when possible the potentially disastrous effects of industry overcapacity. In addition, signaling competitors that an expansion is imminent and that it will be in a certain location may be an effective warning for competitors not to go "head-to-head" with an expansion of their own.

The news announcements earlier regarding capacity/location decisions may have been of this capacity gaming type. Heileman Brewery, with its announced plans for expansion into the southern market, may have been signaling its intentions. But it was also indicating to competitors that its muscles were strong and that it had the advantages of low cost but modern capacity and an already proven marketing strategy to ensure success. Dow Chemical's announcement seems to offer *quid pro quo*: a withdrawal of expansion plans in basic chemicals for a strong intrusion into the specialty chemicals market. Domtar's announcement—intended to test the reaction of other companies—that it would double the capacity at its Windsor, Quebec, papermill may be particularly important in an industry that has suffered the effects of overcapacity in the past. Both the capacity expansion and its location are important in this instance; the wood supply near Windsor couples advantageous costs with the target U.S. market just across the border.

## MULTINATIONAL ACTIVITY BASES

The strategic location of activities in multinational settings is an important element in operations strategy. Where manufacturing facilities are involved, three alternate forms can have significant impacts on a variety of costs and other advantages and disadvantages. Different forms for organizing production facilities have been proposed, and we will discuss three: central location, the multidomestic form, and rationalized exchange.

The central structure establishes one basic location for production and ships the product from it to all markets. For example, a Boeing 747 is made in Seattle and flown to the customer. Similarly, if a foreign customer wants Dupont Nomex or

Kevlar, new high-tenacity fibers, they are made in the United States and shipped overseas. Centralized facilities provide scale advantages and the accumulation of experience at the system rates for all activities. But centralization does not deal with local content rules that exist in many countries, nor with the problems of monetary exchange and short-term exchange rate movements.

In the multidomestic form, a microcosm of operations is established in each of the countries in which the company competes. The advantages are in terms of marketing in having a presence in a country, in easily meeting local content rules, and in providing service. The disadvantages are in fluctuating exchange rates, the cost position of small-scale plants, and the fact that experience curve effects are restricted by the multiple plant organization. Although the total volume may be large, experience is accumulated at the lower activity levels of each plant. Massey–Ferguson in the farm equipment field is an example of the multidomestic form.

Rationalized exchange, the third form, is particularly applicable to complex assembled products and involves allocating component manufacture to the countries in which business is done. For an automobile, for example, transmissions may be made in one country, engines in a second, bodies in a third, assembly in a fourth, and so on. By carefully designing the system of inputs and outputs, local content rules are satisfied and the monetary flows are also kept in balance as the completed autos are shipped back to each country for sale. The operating advantages are of considerable importance: each specialized plant is of a large enough scale for efficient operations, experience is accumulated at the activity level for the total volume for each component, and each plant is focused on a limited set of activities for manufacturing as well as management. In addition to the advantages in operations, there is a balanced foreign exchange exposure. Much of the problem of dealing with exchange rate fluctuations is eliminated through the balancing of monetary inputs and outputs. Rationalized exchange, then, seems to combine all the advantages when the nature of the business makes it an appropriate alternative. Both the Ford Motor Company and IBM in Europe are organized on the basis of rationalized exchange.

### CAPACITY/LOCATION DECISIONS AS OPERATIONS STRATEGY

Poor capacity expansion decisions can virtually negate good operations strategy in other dimensions. The overcapacity that results from any of the structural causes discussed or from ineffective capacity gaming can place a manufacturer in a cost–price vise even if operations strategy is otherwise excellent in relation to competitors. Advanced technology now available will in the future make production capacity more flexible and therefore less subject to the effects of product and schedule changes. Those firms that develop the facilities with the greatest flexibility will have a competitive edge in reacting to major shifts in product design and demand.

## Product and Process Technology

A company can have its production system positioned just right in relation to market requirements and still be technologically obsolete. The appropriate technology must be used to support the chosen strategy.

### SLOW ADOPTION OF ADVANCED PROCESS TECHNOLOGY

The charge has been made that "during the past decades, American managers have increasingly relied on principles which prize analytical detachment and methodological elegance over insights into the subtleties and complexities of strategic decisions, based on experience."[9] The analytical detachment and methodological elegance referred to here are the discounted cash flow and short-term financial measurements, such as return on investment (ROI), and their rigid use that produce a short-term mind set. These techniques place an emphasis on whether or not a new technology will become profitable this year or next year. They have been used as a substitute for managerial insight and judgment concerning the long-term viability of an innovation.

Not only has management's attention been focused on mergers and acquisitions, but its related focus on short-term performance has mitigated against important investments in expensive new and existing technologies, let alone longer-term investments in R&D. Meanwhile, Japanese industries have invested heavily in advanced process technology, accounting in part for their low-cost, high-quality products.

## Work Force and Job Design

With the rise of organized labor in the 1930s, the personnel and industrial relations functions developed as counterpoise to organized labor and, as with other staff functions, absorbed a great deal of the powers of the line organization. It seems odd that the crucial issues of wage determination (which translates into labor costs), design of work rules, and job design have become virtually staff functions, since these are critical components of operations strategy that should be integrated with system positioning, process technology, and other elements of a coordinated operations strategy.

The staff specialists, doing the best they could, looked at their problem as a system of trade-offs. Their attitude was "Give a little here and there in order to get something," which amounted to an industrial equivalent to political appeasement "Peace at almost any price—peace in our time."

But what are the "hard" constraints that cannot be transgressed? When does one cripple the organization's ability to stay the course? Somehow the guiding hand that should have been in touch with the total, long-term implications was missing. The process has been good for neither labor nor management, which has become evident as firm after firm and industry after industry have lost their markets to foreign competition, with jobs perhaps permanently lost to foreign competitors.

Collective bargaining should command the attention of top management. Also, a new balance in the management collective bargaining team needs to be established.

[9] See Robert H. Hayes and William J. Abernathy, "Managing Our Way to Economic Decline," *Harvard Business Review,* July–August 1980, 58(4), pp. 67–77.

This may require a broader balance in the educational and experience backgrounds of both operations and industrial relations executives. The end result should be the recognition that most of the results of collective bargaining agreements become a part of operations strategy and should be a conscious part of that strategy rather than a "happening." This does not mean that staff specialists should not exist, but it does mean that their activities need to be coordinated with operations strategy and that the long-term competitive implications of proposed labor agreements must be assessed more carefully.

Finally, the advances in process technology have set the stage for revolutionary changes in the labor–management relationships. Employment in manufacturing in the coming 10 to 20 years will decline, not only as a proportion of the work force but also in absolute numbers. A large fraction of the remaining jobs will be of a new character and scope. The dividing line between jobs in management and production will be less clear, and part of operations strategy in the future will involve rethinking the labor–management relationship in the light of this change.

There is a strong tie between the work force and job design and operations strategy. Labor is a key input to all the dimensions of the production system within which manufacturers compete: cost, quality, dependability as a supplier, and flexibility/service. The worker's role in the system is crucial to the success of an organization. Therefore, work rules, job design, team organization, wage rates, and the entire labor–management relationship become extremely important elements in operations strategy. This is true in spite of the fact that advanced process technology is reducing the numbers of workers needed in direct manufacturing operations. Labor is still and will continue to be an important input for the forseeable future, though the nature of jobs will change.

## Making Operating Decisions Strategic

Operating decisions are not usually thought to be strategic—each decision seems to be of relatively small importance in the broad sweep. But can these decisions be made in a way that has strategic impact? The Japanese have been particularly successful in creating effective operating systems that have strategic significance in reducing costs and controlling quality.

The "driver" of the operating system is the reduction of operation set-up costs. The effect of lowering set-up costs is to alter the balance between set-up and inventory costs, lowering the economic order quantity (*EOQ*). The Japanese expend every possible effort toward reducing the set-up costs through tool design, quick clamping devices, carefully worked out procedures, and so on. The ultimate objective is to reduce set-up costs to $EOQ = 1$ unit.

Of course, if $EOQ = 1$ unit, or even very small quantities, the immediate and obvious benefits are that in-process inventories are reduced and the flexibility to change production from one product to another is maximized. Furthermore, reduction in production lot sizes triggers a perhaps more important chain of events involving improved motivation and a focus on scrap and quality control and on *just-in-time* (*JIT*).

The reason for the quality improvement derives from the human behavior pattern that results from *JIT* production. If a worker produces a part and passes it directly to the next worker, the second worker will report a defect almost immediately. On hearing that the part is defective, the first worker is motivated to discover the cause and correct it before large quantities of scrap are produced. The smaller the production lot size, the more immediate the discovery of defects will be. *Each pair of operations in the sequence is closely linked,* and therefore, the awareness of the interdependence of the two workers is enhanced. Furthermore, the immediate feedback creates a problem-solving behavior pattern between pairs of workers, who are motivated to be creative in developing ideas for job-related improvements of all kinds. The constantly repeating cycle of improvement gradually enhances productivity and quality.

We should not make a distinction between long-term strategic issues and short-term operating ones. There is usually little argument against the proposition that questions of capacity, process technology, and labor costs have strategic significance. But inventory, quality, and other factory-floor issues tend to be dismissed, as if "operations" had no long-term importance. Yet, quality, cost, and on-time delivery of products can be extremely important in the basic strategy of the firm.

## Strategies Regarding Suppliers and Vertical Integration

The operations system includes all the component and raw material inputs as well as the in-plant processes. As we look upstream to these inputs, we are concerned—just as in the case of in-plant processes—about cost, quality, on-time availability, and flexibility/service. The relative importance of these criteria in judging supplier effectiveness is controlled by the overriding strategy of the firm, as is the case with the operations function as a whole.

In dealing with suppliers, there are many operational issues that need attention, and these are not to be minimized. However, the focus of our attention is on the strategic issues of choosing among alternative suppliers, judging the strength of our own position in dealing with suppliers, and using our strengths effectively. In choosing among suppliers, it is worthwhile to examine each from the viewpoint of how that supplier regards your organization. How does that supplier view you as a customer? Is your business significant to the supplier? Are you a costly customer for the supplier to service? Is the supplier's basic strategy one of low cost, or is the supplier differentiated or in a specific segment? There needs to be a fit or compatibility of the supplier's objectives with your own to achieve overall strategic goals.

Supplier relations in the United States tend to be based on arms-length negotiations that are often unstable from the supplier's viewpoint. We use the threat of taking our business elsewhere or, indeed, of integrating backwards and producing the component in house. On the other hand, the Japanese just-in-time (*JIT*) purchasing, one of the unique elements in Japanese operations management strategy, involves the development of long-term, stable relationships with suppliers.

Finally, since supplier processes are really an extension of manufacturing processes, the question of whether or not to integrate backwards and develop internal capacity to produce a component must be considered. What are the conditions under which vertical integration is an appropriate strategy? What are the appropriate analyses that reveal short- and long-term economic benefits?

### SUPPLIER RELATIONSHIPS AND VERTICAL INTEGRATION AS STRATEGY

Purchasing and relationships with suppliers must be consciously formulated to be part of the operations strategy. The result should depend on the operations strategy's relative emphasis on cost, quality, product availability, and flexibility/service. Suppliers' performance is often as important as in-plant processes in achieving objectives.

In examining supplier relationships and purchasing strategy, the issue of whether or not vertical integration is a logical step is always a question. But more fundamental is the nature of the vertical integration issue, which is basically different from the concerns dominating the mergers and acquisitions craze that has held sway in recent years. In vertical integration decisions, the emphasis is on the logic of a change within the strategy of the firm to produce something of economic value. It is not an investment portfolio concept.

## FORMULATING AND IMPLEMENTING OPERATIONS STRATEGY

The six basic components we have discussed do not in themselves constitute a strategy—they must be integrated into a managerial framework that relates the components and provides a basis for implementing the strategy. We might think of the components as a wheel surrounding operations strategy formulation, with careful interweaving of the relationships among the components, as illustrated in Figure 22-6. For example, the strategy concerning job and process designs needs to be coordinated carefully with the strategic plans for product/process technology, which in turn needs to be coordinated with capacity/location strategies. These strategies must also be related to the positioning strategy, and so on. Rather than showing all these interconnections in Figure 22-6, we depend on the interconnections through the operations strategy formulation process in the center of the diagram. Finally, all the elements of operations strategy must be related to the enterprise strategy, shown surrounding the entire process.

An operations strategy audit can expose the status of the current strategy, whether it is a unconscious one or one that has been carefully developed. Beyond the audit, the *process* of operations strategy formulation and implementation is not far different from that developed for enterprise strategy, for which a large amount of literature exists.

## IMPLICATIONS FOR THE MANAGER

Operations strategy is relatively new, both in terms of how it is seen by top managers and in terms of it being a separate, definable subject of inquiry. The attention of top managers was captured when it became clear in the late 1970s and early 1980s that the reason for the poor competitive position of many U.S. companies and,

FIGURE 22-6
**THE WHEEL OF OPERATIONS STRATEGY.**

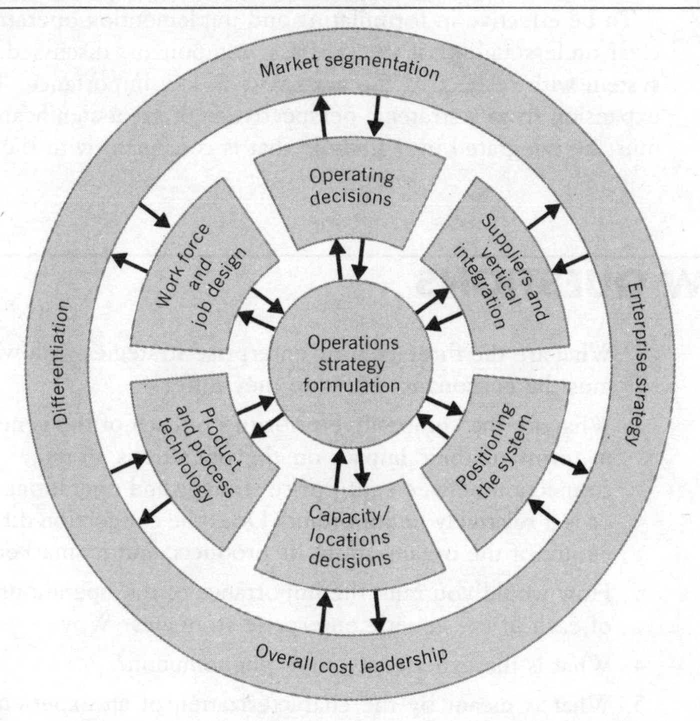


indeed, whole industries was high cost and low quality, both central to the operations function. Prior to that time, the operations function had been largely ignored by top managers.

Operations strategy must, of course, fit in with the basic strategy of an enterprise, whether that strategy is cost leadership, differentiation, or market segmentation. Regardless of the basic strategy, it is clear that the operations strategy must be carefully coordinated with it since that function is so centrally involved in any of the basic strategies.

The concept of the experience curve is of great importance to cost leadership and some segmented strategies. But costs do not necessarily decline automatically without managerial effort. Productivity improvement has long been regarded as important for maintaining a healthy market position, but the blistering pace set by Japanese producers in many industries has made it clear that company survival can depend on close attention to this important objective. Since such a large fraction of manufacturing *and* service operations are now exposed to global competition, an understanding of the exchange-rate effects of differences in productivity improvement among international competitors is extremely important. It is not good enough to be only as productive as a foreign competitor; we must be at least as productive relative to our own economy as the foreign competitor is relative to its economy. This fact places extremely heavy responsibility on operations executives to keep pace with technological change and to implement productivity-enhancing process technology as rapidly as feasible.

To be effective in formulating and implementing operations strategy, we need a clear understanding of the six basic components discussed. The positioning of the system with respect to the market is of key importance. Thinking about capacity expansion from a strategic perspective is of great significance, and all six elements must be integrated into a whole that is consonant with the enterprise strategy.

## REVIEW QUESTIONS

1. What are the three generic enterprise strategies with which operations strategy must be consonant? How do they differ?
2. What are the competitive priorities of each of the generic enterprise strategies in terms of their impact on the operations strategy? Do you think that the connection between enterprise strategy and operations strategy is a strong one, or is it relatively unimportant? Does the connection differ significantly with the nature of the organization, its products, and its markets?
3. How would you rank the importance of the operations function to the success of each of the generic enterprise strategies? Why?
4. What is the experience curve phenomenon?
5. What is meant by the characterization of an experience curve as being a 90 percent curve?
6. Why is the experience curve usually plotted on log–log graph paper?
7. If the cumulative volume doubles from its previous level, what happens to unit cost if there is an 80 percent experience curve?
8. How could a firm use the experience curve as a part of its competitive strategy?
9. Are there limitations to the benefits of the experience curve? Are there any dangers in its use?
10. Experience curves seem most applicable to high-volume, standardized products where product-focused systems would be appropriate. Are they also applicable to process-focused systems?
11. Explain the concept of purchasing power parity. To what range of price movements does it apply?
12. Describe the connection between productivity improvement differences between two international competitors and the productivity improvement differences between the two economies in which the two companies operate.
13. The following statement is quoted from the chapter: "To compete effectively in a particular international market, we must be at least as productive in that field relative to our own economy as our international competitor is relative to its economy." How does the effect of this concept affect a producer of steel? Automobiles? Fast-foods? Electric power generation?

14. Given the concepts of the experience curve and the exchange rate effects on productivity improvements, what role do you feel productivity improvement should play in operations strategy? How would you implement that role in an organization?
15. What are the six basic components of operations strategy? Are they independent of each other?
16. What is meant by the positioning decision in operations strategy?
17. What is a productive system/product joint strategy?
18. How would you describe the productive system/product joint strategies of each of the following:
    a. Post Office
    b. United Parcel Service (UPS)
    c. Federal Express Company (FEC)
19. Does the concept of "positioning" apply to service operations? Give examples.
20. What is meant by the term *focus* in productive systems?
21. What are the risks of emphasizing focus in a managerial strategy?
22. Why are capacity/location decisions of strategic importance?
23. Why is overcapacity a problem of strategic importance in operations strategy?
24. What is meant by the term *capacity gaming*?
25. Which should have primacy in formulating operations strategy, the positioning decision or the selection of process technology?
26. What roles do job design and the work force play in operations strategy? To what other basic components in operations strategy are they most closely related?
27. Since by their nature, operating decisions have effect over the short term, how can they be regarded as having strategic significance?
28. Purchasing is often regarded as a separate function from operations. Why should it be regarded as being a part of operations strategy?
29. Contrast the Japanese concept of just-in-time purchasing with the more common U.S. practice.
30. Why should vertical integration be regarded as a part of operations strategy? Why isn't it simply a top management function to decide whether or not to integrate forward or backward?
31. Examine Figure 22-6. Why is it not sufficient to specify each of the six basic components independently in formulating operations strategy?

# PROBLEMS

32. If the first unit of an item costs \$10, and the system follows a 90 percent experience curve, what is the equation for the cost of the $n$th unit, $c_n$? What is the cost of the 100th unit produced?

33. Assume a 92 percent experience curve, and the following data:

$$c_1 = \$10$$
$$n = 1000 \text{ cumulative units}$$

What is the value of the parameter $b$?

34. What is the cost of the 1000th unit in the previous problem? Use either Equation 1 or Equation 2.

35. A manufacturer of robots produced its first unit at a cost of $c_1 = \$50{,}000$, and it feels that an 80 percent learning curve is appropriate. The marketing manager estimates that the company can sell 5000 units in the first five years. What will the 5000th unit cost? Use Table 22-1.

36. Another way of looking at the experience curve is in terms of the effects on productivity. If unit cost is decreasing, then productivity is increasing. The productivity of the $n$th unit, $p_n$, could be expressed as

$$p_n = p_1 n^d$$

where

$p_n$ = The productivity of the $n$th unit
$p_1$ = The productivity of the first unit
$d$ = A parameter depending on the rate of productivity increase

Notice that the parameter $d$ is positive because we have an increasing productivity function instead of the decreasing cost function for the experience curve. If the productivity of the first unit were taken as 1.0 as an index of productivity, what would the productivity be for the 100th unit if productivity increases 10 percent for each doubling of cumulative output?

37. In 1965, the exchange rate between the United States and another country was 150 MU per dollar. By 1985, productivity in the United States had increased 40 percent while inflation had increased 60 percent. In the foreign country, productivity had increased 80 percent, but inflation was 100 percent during the 20-year period. What would be the long-term equilibrium exchange rate in 1985?

38. Assume a product costs \$5000 to produce in the United States and 5000 MU to produce in a foreign country. The exchange rate at that time was 1:1. Over a period of 10 years, the U.S. producer increased productivity 30 percent while the productivity of the U.S. economy improved by 20 percent. Meanwhile, the foreign producer improved productivity by only 5 percent in an economy that was stagnant; that is, there was no net improvement.

    a. What is the long-term equilibrium exchange rate at the end of the 10-year period?

    b. Calculate the cost reductions for each producer during the 10-year period.

    c. Calculate the cost of the U.S. product in the foreign country after monetary exchange.

    d. Calculate the cost of the foreign product in the U.S. after monetary exchange.

    e. Which producer has an exchange-rate advantage?

# SITUATIONS

## When Experience Curves Really Count

39. Two firms are competing in the same market with products that are considered to be substitutes for each other. Firm A is an old established firm with a great deal of experience; cumulative production to date has been 100,000 units. Some years ago, it produced its first unit at a cost of $c_1 = \$100$, and it has been enjoying a 95 percent experience curve ever since. Firm A is the price leader, with current prices set at $85 per unit, which other producers followed until Firm B entered the market with a $40 price. The president of Firm A is astounded that Firm B is so foolish as to try to compete with it since its experience in the field is so great.

    Firm B has just entered the market after spending a great deal on the research and development of new process technology. After setting up the initial highly automated plant, the cost of the first unit was $150. The news got around the industry, and on hearing it, the president of Firm A laughed and said, "another bust for automation." Since establishing the plant, Firm B has allocated funds generously to the research and development of process technology and has made significant improvements in the original plant.

    Firm B initially priced its product at the industry rate of $85 per unit, but it soon dropped its price to its present $40. This price policy has turned the industry upside down and business has been brisk indeed—Firm B has already produced 5000 units. Having kept careful records on costs, the president of Firm B notes gleefully that it is on an 85 percent experience curve. He is particularly delighted because, having originally been a plant manager for Firm A, he is aware of its costs and experience curve data.

    The president of Firm A is puzzled. "How can Firm B undercut us? It must be losing money on every unit; it is actually pricing below our cost!"

    How do you analyze this situation? Can Firm A possibly make out with its present price policy?

## The Woes of the U.S. Steel Industry—A Case for Operations Strategy

40. This situation uses the data in Table 22-4 regarding productivity in four steel producing countries. In 1970, the U.S. industry still had the highest productivity of the four countries; that is, 83.3 tons per worker-hour. But between 1960 and 1970 the U.S. industry increased productivity by only 24.9 percent, while the Japanese industry increased productivity by 203.3 percent.

    The ratio of constant yen to constant dollars was about 445 in 1960 and had shifted to 350 by 1970. Obviously, U.S. producers still had a cost advantage in 1970, but they had increased productivity less than the U.S. economy, while Japanese steel producers had outpaced their economy.

    During the 1970–1980 period, U.S. steel producers fell further behind, increasing productivity only 15.4 percent during the 10-year period, while

Japanese producers increased productivity by 83.5 percent. The ratio of constant yen to constant dollars fell to about 200 by 1980.

Prepare a one-page statement entitled, "The Woes of the U.S. Steel Industry—A Case for Operations Strategy," using the above information and other additional information you may have, that accounts for the wave of steel plant closings in the 1982–1983 recession period.

# REFERENCES


Abernathy, W. J., and K. Wayne, "The Limits of the Learning Curve," *Harvard Business Review,* September–October 1974, pp. 109–119.

Banks, R. L., and S. C. Wheelwright, "Operations vs. Strategy: Trading Tomorrow for Today," *Harvard Business Review,* May–June 1979, pp. 112–120.

Baumol, W. J., and K. McLennan, *Productivity Growth and U.S. Competitiveness,* Oxford University Press, New York, 1985.

Bogue, M. C., and E. S. Buffa, *Corporate Strategic Analysis,* Free Press, New York, 1986.

Buffa, E. S., *Meeting the Competitive Challenge: Manufacturing Strategy for U. S. Companies,* Irwin, Homewood, Ill., 1984.

Buffa, E. S., "Meeting the Competitive Challenge with Manufacturing Strategy," *National Productivity Review,* Spring 1985, pp. 155–169.

Buffa, E. S., and M. C. Bogue, "Productivity and the Exchange Rate," *National Productivity Review,* 5(1), Winter 1985–86, pp. 32–46.

Capdevielle, P., and D. Alvarez, "International Comparisons of Trends in Productivity and Labor Costs," *Monthly Labor Review, 104*(12), December 1981, pp. 14–20.

Fine, C. H., and A. C. Hax, "Manufacturing Strategy: A Methodology and an Illustration," *Interfaces, 15*(6), November–December 1985, pp. 27–47.

Hayes, R. H., and W. J. Abernathy, "Managing Our Way to Economic Decline," *Harvard Business Review, 58*(4), July–August 1980, pp. 67–77.

Hayes, R. H., and K. B. Clark, "Why Some Factories Are More Productive Than Others," *Harvard Business Review,* September–October 1986, pp. 66–73.

Hayes, R. H., and S. C. Wheelwright, "The Dynamics of Process–Product Life Cycles," *Harvard Business Review,* March–April 1979, pp. 127–136. (a)

Hayes, R. H., and S. C. Wheelwright, "Link Manufacturing Process and Product Life Cycles," *Harvard Business Review,* January–February 1979. (b)

Hayes, R. H., and S. C. Wheelwright, *Restoring Our Competitive Edge: Competing Through Manufacturing,* Wiley, New York, 1984.

Leontief, W., and F. Duchin, *The Future Impact of Automation on Workers,* Oxford University Press, New York, 1986.

Porter, M. E., *Competitive Strategy: Techniques for Analyzing Industries and Competitors,* Free Press, New York, 1980.

Schoeffler, S., R. D. Buzzell, and D. F. Heany, "The Impact of Strategic Planning on Profit Performance," *Harvard Business Review,* March–April 1974.

Skinner, W., *Manufacturing: The Formidable Competitive Weapon,* Wiley, New York, 1985.

Skinner, W., "Manufacturing—Missing Link in Corporate Strategy," *Harvard Business Review,* May–June 1969, p. 136.

Skinner, W., "The Focused Factory," *Harvard Business Review,* May–June 1974, p. 113.

Skinner, W., "Operations Technology: Blind Spot in Strategic Management," *Interfaces, 14*(1), January 1984.

Wheelwright, S. C., "Japan—Where Operations Really Are Strategic," *Harvard Business Review, 59*(4), July–August 1981, pp. 67–74.

Wheelwright, S. C., "Reflecting Corporate Strategy in Manufacturing Decisions," *Business Horizons,* February 1978, pp. 57–65.

# CHAPTER 23

# IMPLEMENTING OPERATIONS STRATEGY

In the previous chapter, we dealt with many of the important elements of operations strategy formulation: the relationships of operations strategy to the three generic enterprise strategies; the experience curve and its implications for strategy formulation; the important role of productivity, with special emphasis on the exchange-rate effects; and, finally, the six basic components of operations strategy formulation. However, the best conceptions of strategy are useless unless they are implemented effectively.

In this chapter, we will provide contrasting examples of how operations strategy has actually been put into practice in both manufacturing and service oriented companies, and we will review some of the important elements in the strategy formulation and implementation process.

The objective of presenting comparative company strategies is to examine the important role of operations in each and to observe how the different enterprise strategies, or missions, have focused on the operations competitive priorities. For each company, we will then identify the elements of operations strategy emphasized.

## IMPLEMENTING OPERATIONS STRATEGIES IN MANUFACTURING SYSTEMS

Manufacturing strategy must be linked to the larger scope of corporate strategy, which is commonly characterized as a mission. The mission can usually be described in a few words that describe the nature of the target markets. Although we have stated that corporate success often depends on manufacturing strategy, it should be clear that "the tail cannot wag the dog"—manufacturing strategy must be congruent with corporate strategy.

The elements of manufacturing strategy may be extremely important in a competitive struggle, as with the battle between Bowmar and Texas Instruments (TI) in pocket calculators. Bowmar was first in the field and had initially established a strong position. A major difference in the manufacturing strategies of the two had to do with the components in the value-added stream in which each participated. An important element in the value-added stream for pocket calculators was the integrated circuit "chip"—the heart of the product. Bowmar had no manufacturing position in chips; they were an outside supply item. TI, on the other hand, was a major producer of chips. Furthermore, it was far down the experience curve in the production of chips, and it used them in other consumer products besides pocket calculators. TI sold chips to other producers of consumer electronic products, including Bowmar, and could put on price pressure in calculator markets in part because of its low cost position in chips. Bowmar finally went bankrupt because it was unable to match TI's low prices and still be profitable.

## Generic Strategies and Manufacturing Missions

The three generic strategies discussed in the previous chapter are broad generalizations. For example, two firms could be following market segmentation strategies, but on closer examination, their strategies may not be the same. Their target markets could be quite different and their manufacturing missions could be very different.

One of the classic comparisons is the one made between Hewlett Packard (HP) and Texas Instruments (TI) in the calculator, instrument, and microcomputer markets (Buffa, 1984). Both hi-tech firms emphasize new product introductions as the center piece of their corporate strategies. But HP concentrates on market segments in which new product introductions are focused on product performance and technology. These new products provide larger margins initially. When these markets begin to draw tough price competition and lower margins, HP goes on to other innovations, leaving its competitors to fight for the larger-volume, lower-margin business. HP focuses on the leading edge of technology, and to be congruent, its manufacturing strategy must provide facilities, organization, and systems that are flexible in accommodating product design changes and the need for high quality.

Texas Instruments also produces many new hi-tech products but with the objective of exploiting the potentially large-volume markets that may follow new product introductions. Thus, from the inception of a new product, TI is interested in "production design" as well as product performance. It intends to follow the product through the several stages of its life cycle, exploiting the high-volume, lower-margin markets. For such a product, TI will have accumulated a great deal of experience and can be price competitive and profitable. To be congruent with TI's corporate mission, manufacturing must design a broader range of strategies that deal with the requirements of new product introductions on the one hand and with product standardization, rapid productivity improvements, consistent quality, and product availability (to stock) on the other hand.

Thus the term, "overall cost leader" does not adequately describe TI in terms that are useful for implementing manufacturing strategy. Neither do the terms, "market segmentation" or "differentiation" adequately describe HP's corporate strategy in terms that are meaningful for manufacturing strategy.

Richardson, Taylor, and Gordon (1985) have developed six categories of corporate missions to which manufacturing strategy implementation can be related. We will use their six corporate mission characteristics as a framework for describing how a number of firms have implemented their manufacturing strategies. These six corporate missions are

- Technology frontiersman
- Technology exploiters
- Technological serviceman
- Customizers
- Cost-minimizing customizers
- Cost minimizers

## Technology Frontiersman

In the foregoing comparison of Hewlett Packard and Texas Instruments, HP was the technology frontiersman. Its mission is to remain on the leading edge of technology with new product innovations. What this means for manufacturing strategy is that flexibility and quality are the dominant manufacturing competitive priorities. Price and off-the-shelf availability are of lesser significance. The production system and supporting organization and controls must retain the flexibility necessary to deal with the continuing flow of new products and must not sacrifice high quality as a trade-off for lower production costs.

The elements of manufacturing strategy that are emphasized to implement the HP mission are, first, in the positioning of the entire system to emphasize flexibility and quality. Second, the nature of the production job to be implemented emphasizes people, and the design of jobs and work systems is of crucial importance in achieving high quality and maintaining flexibility. Also, in order to achieve these ends, the strategic nature of operating decisions must be emphasized. Finally, such complex, hi-tech products require a dependence on suppliers of high-quality components on a timely schedule. These dimensions of implementing the technology frontiersman mission in HP's manufacturing strategy are summarized in Table 23-1.

## Technology Exploiters

The outstanding example of the technology exploiter is Texas Instruments. Like HP, TI brings out a steady stream of new products, but unlike HP, it follows the product life cycle through to maturity. This aspect of the corporate mission means that the manufacturing strategy must not only retain the flexibility to deal with new products, but it must be able to capitalize on product success with low production costs in order to compete in price-competitive markets. Therefore, product development has a closer link with design for low cost manufacture or "production design." The processing system must evolve through its life cycle as the product life cycle develops through the volume requirements of introduction, growth, and maturity.

The manufacturing competitive priorities (see Table 23-1) must jointly emphasize flexibility and cost and, in addition, must be able to convert quickly to a "make to stock system" to make products readily available in the marketplace. New elements appear in the list of elements of manufacturing strategy to be emphasized. Because of the emphasis on cost, productivity becomes an overriding concern through process technology. Also, capacity and its location are central to the manufacturing strategy in order to provide sufficient capacity so that sales are not lost and to take advantage of market–plant location advantages or advantageous factor costs, such as low labor cost areas.

## Technological Serviceman

Firms in this category of missions also rely on technological leadership, but they concentrate on custom service to low-volume markets, though the dollar volume is

TABLE 23-1
**CORPORATE MISSIONS AND LINKS TO MANUFACTURING STRATEGIES**

| Characterization | Description of Mission | Corporate Examples | Manufacturing Competitive Priorities Impacting Design of Physical Facilities, Organization Design, Planning and Control Systems | Elements of Manufacturing Strategy Emphasized |
|---|---|---|---|---|
| Technology frontiersman | R&D driven; constant new product introductions; price competitive markets abandoned | Hewlett Packard | Flexibility, quality, suppliers | Positioning, job design, operating decisions |
| Technology exploiters | New products, but follows life cycle through to maturity; product development linked with production design and emphasis on low costs | Texas Instruments | Flexibility and cost, availability | Positioning, process technology, capacity location, operating decisions, suppliers |
| Technological serviceman | Custom service on complex system for low-volume customers and markets; excellence in product design | Boeing, Rockwell Missile Division | Flexibility, quality | Positioning, process technology, operating decisions, suppliers |
| Customizers | Job shop manufacturing; build to custom designs; low volume | Hughes Satellite Division, Rockwell Space Vehicle Division | Flexibility, quality | Positioning, process technology, operating decisions, suppliers |
| Cost minimizing customizers | Low volume mature products manufactured to individual customer designs | Shipyards, some large construction firms | Cost, on-time delivery, flexibility | Positioning, process technology, suppliers |
| Cost minimizers | High-volume producers of standardized commodity-type products; long runs or continuous production | P&G Household Products, Eastman Kodak (amateur film), Norton Abrasives | Cost, availability, quality | Positioning, process technology, capacity/location, job design, operating decisions, vertical integration |

not necessarily low. Boeing is an excellent example. It customizes its commercial aircraft to the specifications of airline customers. In order to do so, Boeing must maintain a very flexible manufacturing system. Also, the nature of the product requires high quality; compromises on quality would have very negative effects in the marketplace. Rockwell Missile Division faces similar manufacturing competitive priorities, where potential losses to the customer from quality compromises dominates the strategic choices.

Positioning the manufacturing system to achieve the manufacturing priorities of flexibility and quality is central, but process technology choices are also significant in the manufacturing strategy. Operating decisions must be made strategically, and these complex products require dependence on a system of reliable suppliers.

### Customizers

Customizers have the job shop manufacturing mission. They build to the custom designs of the customer in low volumes. The Satellite Division of Hughes Aircraft, for instance, must emphasize flexibility and quality. Quality defects could mean huge losses to customers that have been indemnified by insurance policies. Similarly, the Rockwell Space Vehicle Division deals with an even lower volume in terms of units, requiring a greater emphasis on flexibility and quality. Compromises on quality cannot be tolerated because of the potential economic and human losses. As indicated in Table 23-1, the elements of manufacturing strategy emphasized are those of the technological serviceman: positioning, process technology, operating decisions, and dependable suppliers. Because of the low volumes, advantages can be found in the use of numerically controlled machine tools, FMS, and other forms of low-volume process technology.

### Cost-Minimizing Customizers

The difference between customizers, just discussed, and cost-minimizing customizers is that the latter deal with mature, low-volume products for which the cost of manufacture is important. Otherwise, the products are built to individual customer designs, requiring the skills of both the cost minimizer and the customizer. The manufacturing competitive priorities are focused on low cost, on-time delivery and flexibility.

Shipyards and some large construction firms may be in this mission classification. The most important elements of manufacturing strategy that are emphasized by cost-minimizing customizers are in positioning the system type to the low volume and flexibility needs of the market. In addition, however, because of the cost-minimizing requirements for low-volume manufacture, there are opportunities to apply the automation technologies of numerically controlled processes and FMS.

### Cost Minimizers

The manufacturers of high-volume, standardized products are the cost minimizers in our scheme of missions. They produce products that have developed sufficient volume to justify long production runs or even continuous manufacture and that may have progressed to the maturity or decline phase of the product life cycle. There are many examples of firms in this mission category, such as Procter & Gamble Household Products, Eastman Kodak (amateur film), Norton Abrasives, and so on. These firms must be cost competitive and must usually produce to stock so that the product is available in the marketplace; controlled, consistent quality is also important.

All the six elements of the manufacturing strategy have some significance in implementing the manufacturing mission. Processes tend to be integrated, with heavy emphasis on productivity-enhancing automation. Capacity and its location is important in providing low distribution costs and good delivery service. *Just-in-time* purchasing and inventory concepts may be used to minimize inventory costs, and vertical integration of steps in the raw material supply, manufacturing, and distribution process may contribute to low-cost operations.

## IMPLEMENTING OPERATIONS STRATEGY IN SERVICE SYSTEMS

We select the food business, since nearly everyone has had direct experience with McDonald's and Burger King, and though more expensive, many have been to a Benihana restaurant. Everyone would classify the first two as fast-food restaurants, but Benihana has at least some fast-food characteristics, with its limited menu and its aim to process customers in one hour through a highly standardized system. Certainly, though, Benihana is different from the other two, and we will identify some of these differences.

### The Enterprise Strategies

The generic strategy of each enterprise forms a frame of reference for its operations strategy and is closely related to it. McDonald's and Burger King are in the growing fast-food industry. In 1985, McDonald's was the largest with 6500 outlets in the United States and more than 8000 worldwide; recently it has been adding a new restaurant every 17 hours. Over six percent of the American population eat at a McDonald's restaurant every day. Its strongest competitors are Kentucky Fried Chicken, with 4500 U.S. outlets; Pizza Hut, with 4300; Burger King, with 3500; and Wendy's, with 3300. The fast-food industry is comprised of more than 340 chains with 60,000 outlets in the United States.[1]

#### MCDONALD'S

McDonald's generic strategy is to be the overall cost leader in the hamburger segment of the fast-food industry, and in recent years it has had about a 35 percent market share.[2] McDonald's aims for low cost; fast service; good, consistent quality in the food served; and very high standards of cleanliness and service.

The menu is very limited and is completely standardized, with virtually no options offered. (Their slogan is, "We Do It All for You.") The service is extremely fast, with a combined waiting plus service time of just over two minutes. The prices for the quality of food are very low, and as advertising consistently tells fast-food

[1] See Philip Langdon, "Burgers! Shakes!," *The Atlantic Monthly,* December 1985, pp. 75–89.
[2] For details concerning each of the three companies, see the relevant cases in the reference list at the end of the chapter. For the sake of consistency, policies, systems, and data are assumed to be those described at the time of the cases.

consumers, the volume is tremendous, with billions of hamburgers having been produced and sold.

McDonald's revenues were growing at a brisk 29 percent annual rate during the 1970s, through 5951 restaurants worldwide (4998 in the United States) in 1980. The number of units was growing at an average annual rate of 15 percent.

## BURGER KING

Second place Burger King, with its 11 percent market share of the hamburger fast-food business, has the familiar slogan, "Have It Your Way." The complete jingle commonly used in their advertisements is

Hold the pickles,
Hold the lettuce,
Special orders
Don't upset us.
All we ask is that you
Let us serve it your way.

In spite of the slogan, Burger King's menu is also very limited and standardized. It does not really push the idea of making everything to order; rather its personnel will tailor-make items if the customer wants them to, but they clearly prefer standardized output, similar to McDonald's. In addition, its service is fast, but not as fast as McDonald's (just over four minutes of waiting plus service time). Burger King also takes pride in quality and low cost to customers, but its prices run about 10 percent higher than McDonald's.

Though smaller than McDonald's, Burger King was also growing rapidly in the 1970s (26 percent per year), and by 1980 it had 2766 units worldwide (2640 in the United States), less than half the total number of McDonald's units. Other comparisons show McDonald's systemwide revenues were about three times those of Burger King's, and its revenues per unit were about 36 percent greater than Burger King's.

Burger King's enterprise strategy in 1980 seems to be slightly different from McDonald's, but it is not truly a "differentiated" strategy. It offers some customizing by allowing limited choices in how to "dress" the hamburgers, but it hopes that customers will take standard burgers without special orders. The enterprise strategy seems to be "low cost, fast service, and controlled quality," as was McDonald's, but with some customization.

## BENIHANA

Benihana is in a different segment of the restaurant business from that occupied by Burger King and McDonald's, but many would argue that it is fast food with a flair and a much higher average per person check ($6 for lunch and $10 for dinner in the early 1970s, compared to average 1980 checks of $2.24 for McDonald's and $2.50 for Burger King).

Units are located in major cities and some medium sized ones. High-quality ingredients are cooked and served at a teppanyaki table,[3] at which 8 guests are seated, by a native Japanese chef who combines cooking with a display of "knifesmanship" that can be quite dazzling.

Benihana's has a differentiated enterprise strategy in the broad restaurant business. It does not approach the volume of McDonald's or even Burger King, but the exotic environment, the "show," the fast service, and the low costs provide high margins for Benihana, making its differentiation strategy a profitable one. It is not clear that customers view Benihana as a fast-food outlet—the exotic decor, personalized service, and certainly the meal cost are not characteristics associated with the usual fast-food restaurant. On the other hand, the limited menu, the standard processing through the system, and the clock-work speed of the service are hallmarks of the fast-food business. Since Benihana is differentiated from fast-food as well as standard restaurants, it is in competition for the "dining out" dollar, but it does not compete directly with others as McDonald's and Burger King do with each other.

## The Operations Strategies of McDonald's and Burger King

As is commonly true in service systems, the concept of the strategy and the operations or delivery system are unified. In a very real sense, the operations strategy *is* the strategy. To be sure, the basic strategy must reflect coordination with advertising and marketing, financial plans and budgets, and so on. But if the operations strategy fails, the concept does too—it is the key to the success or failure of the entire enterprise.

The implementation of the operations strategy must reflect the subtle differences that each enterprise's strategy implies. Therefore, we need to ask how the differences between the strategies of McDonald's and Burger King, for example, are implemented in their operations strategies. How do the processing systems take account of these differences? How has the technology employed been adapted to the strategy? How do the control systems reflect the differences? Later, we will also consider how Benihana's operations strategy is designed to achieve the seemingly anomalous objectives of fast standardized food, large average check, exotic surroundings, and a show.

### POSITIONING

The two hamburger fast-food giants seemingly have similar strategies—high volume; low prices; limited menu; fast, courteous service; and controlled quality. But Burger King has appealed to differing consumer preferences with its "Have It Your Way" slogan. The customization of Burger King's product is centered on pickles and lettuce—the dressing of the burger—not on a fundamentally wider menu choice.

[3] A gas fired, steel griddle with a 9.5 inch wood border around which eight guests are seated.

Otherwise, Burger King emulates McDonald's with a production-line approach to food service.

The relative positioning of the two systems in terms of the product–process grid is shown in Figure 23-1. McDonald's is at the high end of the product volume scale, and it certainly has a line-flow process. Having chosen to standardize rather completely, it is positioned slightly above the center line. Its choice emphasizes cost and availability. Burger King has lower volume and a modified line flow process, but it has chosen to offer some choice, emphasizing flexibility to a degree. Thus, differences imposed on the operations strategy by the enterprise strategy are likely to deal with the issue of customization.

## PROCESS FLOW AND TECHNOLOGY

Figures 23-2 and 23-3 provide aggregate level flows of the activities of the customers and servers and manufacture of hamburgers for McDonald's and Burger King. Of course, there are other processing activities for other sandwiches, fries, and so forth, but we have concentrated on the hamburger, since most orders involve them.

As far as the customer is concerned, there are two important differences. At McDonald's, paying occurs at the time the food is ordered and delivered, whereas at Burger King, the order must be prepared before it can be delivered to the customer, with payment occurring in between. (Orders must be transmitted, instead of simply being filled, in order to accommodate the special orders.) The second difference is in the total of waiting plus service time—2 minutes, 3 seconds for McDonald's versus 4 minutes, 5 seconds for Burger King—a net effect of the impact of the small customization offered by Burger King on customer service.

The server tasks are combined in one person for McDonald's; they include taking orders, presenting the food to the customers, and accepting payment and making change. The need to accommodate customization at Burger King is solved by the loudspeaker system to communicate the orders and a counter person to assemble the orders on a tray and give the completed orders to the customers. Having two people in the service role does not mean that the direct labor costs have doubled because there is a different balancing of the required tasks at Burger King, but it does indicate that the small customization offered by Burger King has impacted the system design.

The processing system and technology employed reveal two major differences. First, Burger King uses a continuous-chain broiler to cook hamburgers, with a microwave oven at the end, whereas McDonald's employs a grill. Second, Burger King has an extra in-process inventory between the chain broiler and the assembly operation.

We will take the in-process inventory issue first. Even though the customization offered by Burger King is small, it requires variable assembly time, which in turn requires the in-process stock point as a buffer. Both produce to finished goods inventory, but Burger King's finished goods are standardized items, not the special orders.

The in-process stock point performs the classic inventory function of decoupling activities in a sequence so that each may be carried on relatively independently; that

FIGURE 23-1
**RELATIVE POSITIONING OF MCDONALD'S, BURGER KING, AND BENIHANA.**

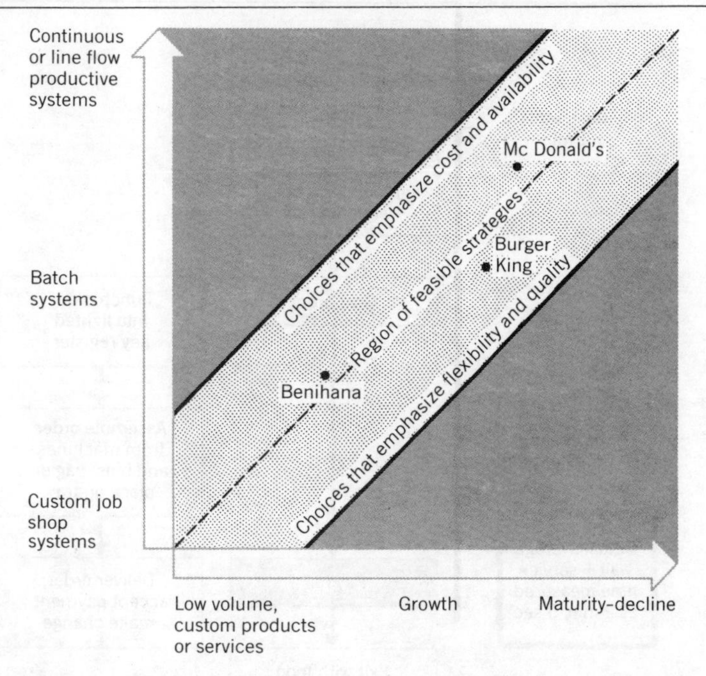


is, patty production can run efficiently at a constant rate for a period of time whereas the rate of hamburger assembly can be adapted to the demand variations of the more customized burgers. Also, Burger King uses the microwave oven to reheat, providing some flexibility in combination with the broiler.

By contrast, the completely standardized McDonald's product can be produced on a balanced production line to finished goods stock. Both process flow systems are rebalanced with different team sizes for varying production rates to match requirements at different times of the day.

One of the results of the two process-flow configurations is in the four- versus two-minute waiting plus service times offered to customers. Customization, no matter how small, exacts a price. McDonald's can offer a lower price and faster service by standardizing.

It is interesting to note that Burger King, which offers a degree of customization, chose a continuous-chain broiler technology that cooks every burger for exactly 80 seconds, and McDonald's, the epitome of standardization, chose the more flexible grill technology.[4] The continuous broiler needs only loading and unloading, whereas

[4]The broiling process involves a grate with radiant heat sources. A grill has a flat surface that is heated from below.

FIGURE 23-2
**CUSTOMERS, SERVERS, AND HAMBURGER PROCESS FLOW FOR MCDONALD'S.**

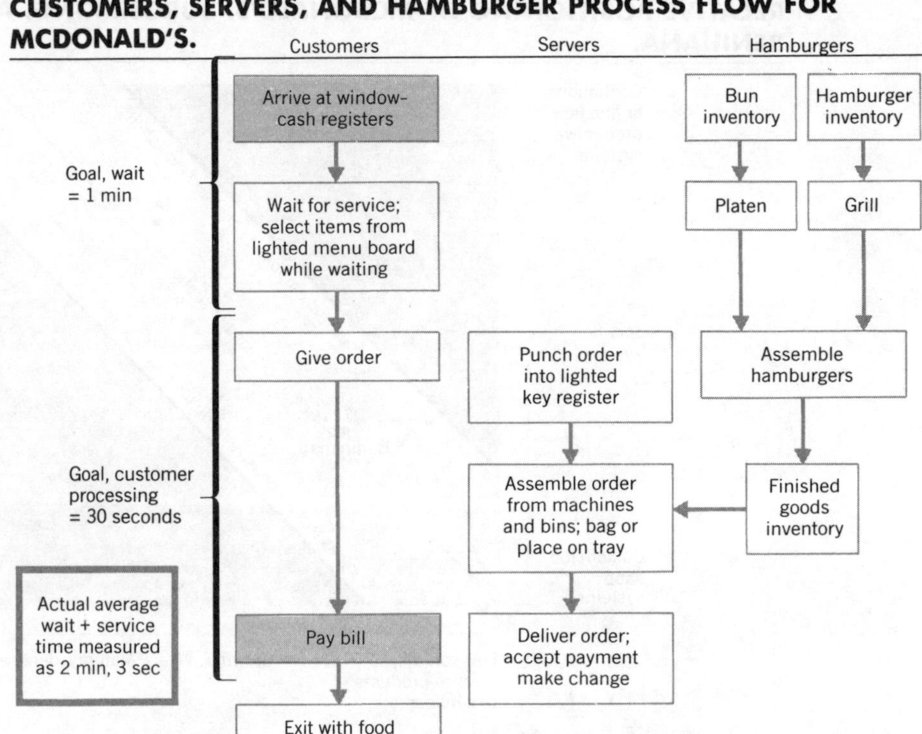


the grill must have constant operator attention to cooking times and turning the patty, which requires timers with signal lights and buzzers.

Both technologies have their positive attributes. The continuous broiler requires somewhat less attention and, at low loads, less labor. The cooking-time flexibility of the grill allows a "rare–medium–well done" choice (which is not offered) and the ability to cook different thicknesses of patties or other items, such as eggs.

## OPERATING DECISIONS

Another impact of Burger King's make-to-order policy is in the system required for controlling orders. Special requirements must be communicated to those workers who must customize the product. Thus, their earlier microphone and later TV screen systems for conveying the details of orders to all concerned were necessary to implement the customizing positioning strategy. These strategies for dealing with special orders are very important, for if the special orders are mixed up, customer dissatisfaction results and there might be increased scrap. For McDonald's, with no customization, no added communications system is necessary. Customers can even change their minds at the last minute since all that it requires is for the server to switch a Big Mac for a Hamburg in the bins and charge the correct price.

FIGURE 23-3
**CUSTOMERS, SERVERS, AND HAMBURGER PROCESS FLOW FOR BURGER KING.**

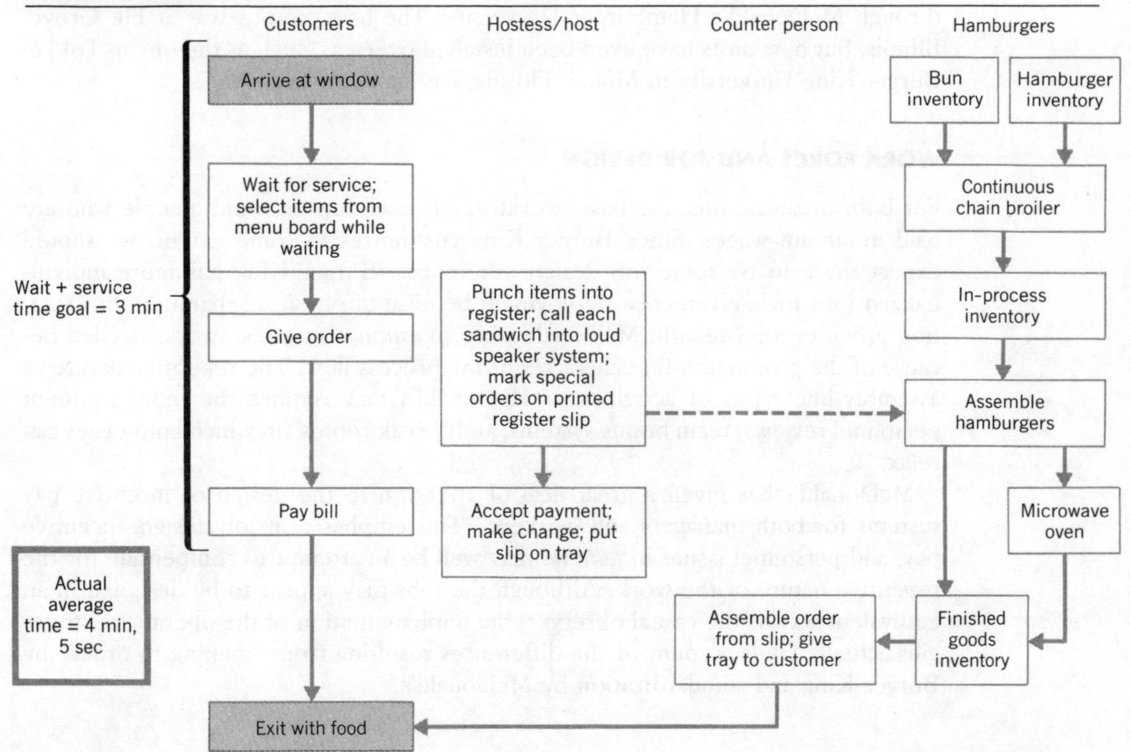


An important operating decision is in setting the short-term capacity levels for the system. Since the physical configuration is set by its design and cannot be changed in the short term, short-term capacity is determined by crew scheduling. Although both firms seem to have equivalent information on which to base these decisions, the bottleneck operation at assembly for Burger King seems to pose additional problems in providing the required capacity at peak loads—a direct result of the "Have It Your Way" positioning of the system.

Quality control is of extreme importance to both organizations, as demonstrated by the lengths to which each goes to ensure the implementation of this element of operations strategy. In a food service organization, quality extends beyond the characteristics of the physical product itself to include the way the product is served and the appearance and cleanliness of the place in which it is served. To control all these aspects of quality, both McDonald's and Burger King use regular, unannounced visits by staff members from headquarters to prepare detailed reports concerning the service, quality characteristics of the food, and cleanliness of the restaurant inside and outside. McDonald's area supervisors, for example, typically make four unannounced visits per month to each unit, sampling all meal times, both during the week and on the weekend. Every aspect of the quality of operations is scored and appropriate comments are recorded.

There is an emphasis on training managers to achieve these and other goals through McDonald's Hamburger University. The first campus was at Elk Grove, Illinois, but new units have even been installed overseas, such as the one in Tokyo. Burger King University in Miami, Florida, has similar objectives.

### WORK FORCE AND JOB DESIGN

For both organizations, the basic workforce is made up of young people who are paid minimum wages. Since Burger King customizes to some extent, we should expect there to be some job design differences. Burger King has more individualized jobs for a given crew deployment because of physical separation, but rotation provides job breadth. McDonald's has an emphasis on teamwork, needed because of the production-line character of the process flow. The repetitive nature of assembly-line types of activities at McDonald's may require the more frequent personnel reviews, team bonus systems, and "break rooms" in which employees can relax.

McDonald's has given a great deal of attention to the design of incentive pay systems for both managers and workers.[5] This emphasis on job design, incentive pay, and personnel issues in general may well be an attempt to compensate for the repetitive nature of the work. Although the jobs may appear to be designed in an equivalent way to the casual observer, the implementation of the operations strategies actually takes account of the differences resulting from "making to order" by Burger King and standardization by McDonald's.

### CAPACITY/LOCATION DECISIONS

The cases listed under References at the end of the chapter are centered on delivery systems and do not give much attention to capacity/location issues. But it is clear from the growth rates quoted for both McDonald's and Burger King that these are issues of great importance for their operating strategies. Both organizations seem to make capacity/location decisions from a competitive–strategic perspective, locating new units to maintain a capacity presence. If a Burger King exists in a general location, it seems likely that a McDonald's does also, and vice versa.

### SUPPLIERS AND VERTICAL INTEGRATION

The design and organization of individual units fosters low cost, particularly for McDonald's. In addition, the existence of a large multiunit system provides opportunities for larger scale manufacturing of patties, buns, and other materials used coupled with efficient distribution to units in a given area. The structure could operate through a system of local suppliers, or it could be vertically integrated, but

[5] See "McDonald's" Case #9-673-062, *HBS Case Services,* Harvard Business School.

in either case, close working relationships between suppliers and users are essential. Also, the perishability of the items provides a natural emphasis on *just-in-time* delivery performance.

## Benihana's Operations Strategy

As with McDonald's and Burger King, Benihana's operations are central to its enterprise strategy. It is the operations strategy that makes it possible for the following contrasts in costs between Benihana and a typical restaurant:[6]

| | Benihana | Typical Restaurant |
|---|---|---|
| Labor costs, percent of sales | 10–12 | 30–35 |
| Food costs, percent of food sales | 30–35 | 38–48 |
| Beverage costs, percent of beverage sales | 20 | 25–30 |
| Rent, percent of sales | 5–7 | 5–9 |

These costs are the major ones involved in operating a restaurant, and if revenues are comparable to the typical restaurant, it is obvious that a Benihana restaurant would be more profitable. The other side of the enterprise strategy coin provides the market differentiation that maintains the steady flow of customers to a limited menu, with customers willing to pay reasonably high prices. This involves the advertising and promotion of the knife show, the exotic Japanese environment, native Japanese chefs, and the like. The focus of our interest, though, is the operations strategy and, particularly, the methods by which low costs are achieved.

### POSITIONING

Benihana has positioned itself a little above the diagonal line shown in Figure 23-1 compared with the typical restaurant. (If compared with McDonald's and Burger King, it would be below the diagonal, offering somewhat more flexibility and quality than Burger King.) The objective, from an operations strategy perspective, is to emphasize low costs and speed of service. The service time is about one hour—nothing like the service times of McDonald's and Burger King—which is short compared with the typical restaurant and is controlled and quite consistent. If the service time were too fast, customers might be dissatisfied, but here low service time is closely related to the low-cost objectives of good facility utilization.

The low-cost operations strategy is implemented by a coordinated system design that has the following dimensions:

- Functions of waiter and chef are combined in a relatively low-skilled job since the menu is simple and limited.

[6]"Benihana of Tokyo" Case #9-673-057, *HBS Case Services,* Harvard Business School.

- Wages are lower because of imported native Japanese chefs and other workers and because all direct laborers are tipped employees.
- Productivity is high because of communal dining and the pacing of the chef to achieve high table turnover.
- Food costs are lower because the limited menu reduces waste and provides opportunities for purchasing discounts.
- Beverage costs are lower because the alcohol ingredients of the exotic drinks promoted on the menu (rum, gin, and vodka) are relatively inexpensive and the drink prices are relatively high.
- Rent costs are relatively lower because the system design utilizes practically the entire restaurant as revenue producing space since no separate kitchen is required.

The implementation of Benihana's positioning as a low-cost, high-quality restaurant has been very cleverly accomplished. Unlike McDonald's and Burger King, Benihana cannot make the trade-off between cost and the quality of service—the customers are paying relatively high prices. The personalized service, food quality, and the exotic environment seem to provide an acceptable balance for the methods used to cut costs and speed service to achieve high table turnover.

## PROCESS FLOW AND TECHNOLOGY

The process flow begins with the bar as a staging area to assemble groups of eight guests to be seated. The flow times are balanced so that time is allowed to serve two drinks. The limited menu makes ordering simple and fast, there being few decisions to be made.

The teppanyaki cooking technology is flexible and can be used to cook all the items. The chef/waiter need not be a highly trained chef because of the limited menu and the simple grilling process used to cook everything.

The combination of communal dining with strangers, attention riveted on the display of knifesmanship—no deep, time-consuming conversations are possible—low cooking time, and fast pacing by the chef all contribute to a one-hour service time and a high table turnover. The result is that the design of the process flow and technology employed help implement the low-cost operations strategy.

## OPERATING DECISIONS

The layout of a typical Benihana restaurant provides small central kitchen and storage space. The small storage space, coupled with the perishability of the raw materials, implements a just-in-time inventory philosophy and minimizes inventories. The limited menu reduces waste, compared to the typical restaurant.

The most important purchased item is the prime-grade beef, tightly specified to maintain high food-quality standards. The quality of the meat is further maintained by pretrimming fat. Finally, quality is maintained by the heavy emphasis on training and by experienced traveling chefs' periodic inspections of each unit.

Low inventories help implement the low-cost operations strategy, and quality controls help implement the strategic image of a first-class restaurant.

### WORK FORCE AND JOB DESIGN

By recruiting and training in Japan, Benihana is provided with a devoted, flexible, and somewhat beholden work force, willing to accept low base wages, which means a low payroll cost to Benihana. Worker earnings, however, can be substantial when gratuities are included, and the fast growing organization provides promotional opportunities.

The Benihana system configuration results in the broader job design of the chef/waiter, which has its own beneficial results in terms of job satisfaction. The chef, usually a position that is not rewarded by gratuities, shares in the largesse in some proportion to his or her effort and skill.

### CAPACITY/LOCATION DECISIONS

High traffic in a business district forms the primary basis for site selection. The multiunit system draws on the accumulated experience of corporate staff to implement this important dimension of operations strategy.

### SUPPLIERS AND VERTICAL INTEGRATION

There are as many as three or four Benihana restaurants in some large metropolitan areas; however, this is a small number, probably not justifying vertically-integrated manufacturing operations. But close working relations with suppliers are important to support the low-cost, high-quality aspects of this operations strategy.

The enterprise and operations strategies of Benihana are closely linked. By differentiating itself from the typical restaurant, Benihana is able to combine a low-cost strategy with the image of a high-quality, full-service restaurant and to earn high returns.

## THE STRATEGY FORMULATION AND IMPLEMENTATION PROCESS

Operations strategy must fit in with overall enterprise strategy. Indeed, past practice in many organizations has assumed that this interlocking would take place without consciously making operations strategy a part of the enterprise strategy formulation, with disappointing results. Whether or not a strategy formulation exercise has taken place as a conscious effort, a strategy exists even if by default.

Usually, some internal or external event triggers a reevaluation of the enterprise strategy: a loss of market share, degenerating cost or quality position, changes in the operating environment, new product or process technologies, deregulation, substantial price changes of raw materials or energy, and so on. Note that some of the triggering events are operations oriented, such as cost and quality position, technological changes, and price changes of ingredients.

A thorough strategic analysis involves an examination of the major competitors in the industry and its markets, revealing the structural strengths and weaknesses of the participants. Following such an analysis, there are usually only a few viable strategies available. Analysts and consultants can be very useful in this process, but they cannot formulate the strategies for a company, nor can they implement them. The value trade-offs and the assumption of risks are managerial functions.

## Making Operations Strategy Internally Consistent

A useful approach for formulating a consistent strategy is to involve different managerial groups in prioritizing the four operations criteria: cost, quality, dependability, and flexibility. For the specific situation of a particular firm, these criteria should be defined precisely. For example, for one firm quality may be indicated by the failure rate of the product whereas for another it may be indicated by fine workmanship.

Based on the competitive analysis and the strengths of the firm, each managerial group is asked to provide relative weights for the four criteria. A sample of these weights for a hypothetical firm, assigned by the production and marketing groups, is given in Table 23-2. Note that the sum of the weights is 100.

It is clear from Table 23-2 that the production group puts more emphasis on cost and quality, whereas the marketing group considers that the firm should emphasize flexibility. If these differences persist, then the two groups will not be coordinating their efforts and decisions toward a common mission for the firm. An acrimonious relationship between the two groups may develop. Further, the company may lose its competitive advantage as the production group may fail to satisfy marketing's requirements of customization, an element that they feel is important in accessing the market niche the firm occupies.

An open and full discussion between the two groups must take place. The consensus weights are shown in the last row of Table 23-2. What is important is not agreement on numbers but agreement on the common mission of the enterprise. The process of assigning numbers merely forces a harder examination of the trade-offs and the priorities for different criteria. In our example, the consensus emerges toward emphasizing flexibility and quality. Assigning a higher importance weight to the flexibility criterion means that the company would prefer to have a wider variety of product features and designs *even though* the cost per unit may be higher than that of competitors.

TABLE 23-2
**PRIORITY WEIGHTS FOR OPERATIONS CRITERIA**

| | *Criteria* | | | |
|---|---|---|---|---|
| | Cost | Quality | Dependability | Flexibility |
| Operations group | 50 | 20 | 20 | 10 |
| Marketing group | 20 | 30 | 10 | 40 |
| Consensus | 25 | 30 | 10 | 35 |

A significant advantage of assigning importance weights to the appropriate operations criteria is that the managers are given an opportunity to reveal their assumptions about the product's market environment and the company's relative strength within this environment. Further, they are forced to provide a rationale for their viewpoints. What emerges is a deeper understanding of the other views and an appreciation of the trade-offs and compromises that must be made.

In our example, the marketing group will have to realize that in order to provide flexibility in product designs and features, the operations function will have to compromise on unit production cost and may incur higher labor and capital costs. Similarly, the production group will have to realize that their emphasis on reducing costs at the expense of reducing flexibility is not in the interest of the firm. This convergence of viewpoints and the internalization of the common values should help in designing a coherent strategy.

## Organizational and Managerial Commitment

A successful strategic planning exercise requires the involvement and commitment of top managers, and an indication of this commitment is the allocation of resources to strategic planning. Equally important is the involvement and commitment of the key people—those in marketing, personnel, finance, R&D, and, of course, operations. These people must make the strategy work, and their involvement in and commitment to strategy formulation are essential to effective implementation.

## Top Down or Bottom Up

In smaller organizations or single-product companies, the corporate and strategic business unit (SBU) plans are likely to be virtually the same. In larger organizations, there may be a variety of product markets, and the corporate strategic plans must embrace the plans of the SBUs. In the latter instance, the corporate plans are not simply an assembly of the individual SBU plans; corporate strategy decisions may assign different roles for different SBUs in the corporate portfolio.

Portfolio analysis is beyond our present scope, but it can be of great importance in SBU strategy development and, in particular, significant to the operations and marketing functions in the characters developed for them and the resource allocations made to them. In multi–SBU situations, the relationships among the process technologies of the SBUs and between the raw materials and end-products can be of great significance in the operations strategy development at the corporate as well as the individual SBU levels.

Elements of strategic plans can be dictated from the top to the relevant SBUs, or the strategy can be molded around the individual SBU strategies. Achieving the appropriate balance between corporate and SBU plans is not a simple matter. Bottom-up plans never seem to aggregate to a balanced corporate portfolio, but top-down planning constrains SBUs in terms of missions to be accomplished, resources available, and so on. On the other hand, the top-down approach overlooks the advantages of SBU staff involvement in the process, perhaps forcing an SBU into an undesirable strategy or starving it of the resources it needs to maintain a technological advantage.

## Developing SBU Plans for Operations

There are four important steps in the process of developing SBU plans for the operations function:

- Analyze the situation—*the operations audit*
- *Develop strategic alternatives*
- *Select a strategy* in harmony with the enterprise strategy
- Formulate detailed plans and budgets to *implement the strategy*

These steps are not independent of each other; rather they involve cycling back to previous steps as new information is developed in subsequent ones.

### THE OPERATIONS AUDIT

The purpose of an audit is to take stock, to obtain a realistic estimate of the status of the operations function and how effective it is in giving life to the enterprise strategy.

The categories for inquiry are the six basics of operations strategy discussed in the previous chapter, but in each category, we need to assess objectively how well the strategic element is being implemented, which means comparisons with standards. But what standards? Strategic standards are found in the performance of competitors. What technology is employed by competitors? What quality standards are being maintained by competitors? What are their costs? What kinds of delivery times can customers obtain from competitors? What are the locations of competitor capacities, and how are they related to markets? Are there structural differences in product lines, scale of operations, and markets that give certain competitors operations advantages? The list can become very long, but these are crucial questions for which comparative data among all competitors, including the subject firm, are needed if strategic planning for operations is to be effective.

The operations audit requires objectivity. It may be difficult for internal staff to see its own operations in a true light; thus, outside analysts and consultants may have an important role to perform in this regard.

A product of the operations audit should be an assessment of the status of the operations strategy. One approach to summarize the results of the audit is to ask the managers to specify how well each of the six elements of operations strategy are currently performed. Such an assessment is provided for our hypothetical company in Table 23-3. The numbers in this status assessment are based on a 100-point scale and indicate the level of attainment for a specified criterion.

There are two ways to think about these ratings. One is to assign ratings with respect to competitors. For example, a rating of 100 may denote the highest attainment on a criterion, that is, the company is the industry leader. A rating of zero denotes the worst performance in the industry. A rating of 50 may denote a median performance, a rating of 75 may denote performance within the top twenty-five

TABLE 23-3
**PRESENT STATUS OF THE OPERATIONS FUNCTION'S PERFORMANCE RELATIVE TO THE OPERATIONS STRATEGY**

| | *Criteria* | | | |
|---|---|---|---|---|
| (Priority Weights) | (25) | (30) | (10) | (35) |
| Elements of Operations Strategy | Cost | Quality | Dependability | Flexibility |
| 1. Positioning | 50 | 90 | 50 | 75 |
| 2. Process flow and technology | 90 | 75 | 75 | 25 |
| 3. Capacity/location decisions | 75 | 80 | 75 | 30 |
| 4. Work force and job design | 100 | 75 | 30 | 30 |
| 5. Operating decisions | 80 | 90 | 75 | 25 |
| 6. Suppliers and vertical integration | 90 | 90 | 50 | 25 |

percent, and so on. A score of 90 for the impact of element No. 2, process flow and technology, on the cost criterion signifies that the company's process and technology is capable of producing at low cost; that is, 90 percent of the competitors have a higher cost of production than the company.

For some cases, the ratings may be based on a relative comparison with what can be achieved by the organization. For example, for the operating decisions element, a rating of 25 on the flexibility criterion signifies that the company places low emphasis on this criterion when planning for inventory, production, and capacity decisions. However, a rating of 90 on the quality criterion indicates that the company places extremely high emphasis on the quality implications of its operating decisions. In these cases, 100 points indicate the highest level that the organization can attain on a criterion, zero the lowest, 50 points the moderate level, and so on.

From Table 23-3, it is clear that our hypothetical company is set up for low cost production but emphasizes high quality (or consistent quality). The production system will have difficulty, however, in responding to new design features and customization as flexibility is given low priority in the five basic elements of operations strategy. Curiously, however, in the positioning element, flexibility is given a higher rating than cost. This may be because positioning is largely determined by the marketing group. As indicated in Table 23-2, the marketing group prefers to compete by segmenting the market and by providing the design features appropriate for each segment. This mismatch must undoubtedly produce strains on manufacturing. The marketing group must also face some problems in slow response to customers' needs and longer lead times for delivery.

## DEVELOP STRATEGIC ALTERNATIVES

The audit provides insights into existing problem areas, and it also highlights some possible directions. In developing alternatives, however, it is important to keep the enterprise's strategic goals in sight. What are we trying to achieve? Where are the important problems with current strategies and their implementation? Is there sufficient capacity? Is the current technology the appropriate one? If we are not cost competitive, what strategies can change that situation? Are there emerging technologies in products, processes, or both that need to be implemented or at least watched carefully? Are there operations control technologies whose installation could solve or improve current operations performance deficiencies?

The above questions are typical of those that should be considered in developing possible strategic alternatives. Although the six basics of operations strategy form a broad outline, the alternative strategies should be specific to the company and its industry.

In Table 23-4, the planned status of the operations function relative to the four criteria is provided. For each of the elements, specific alternatives must be developed to realize the planned levels of achievement. For example, our hypothetical company probably employs low skilled workers who are paid low wages (see Table 23-3). However, since the quality level produced by these workers is high, inspection processes must be thorough to achieve a consistent high level of quality. This can be accomplished, as shown by the case of McDonald's discussed earlier. Now, with a much greater emphasis on flexibility and quality (Table 23-4), skilled workers need to be substituted or the labor force may require extensive retraining.

Similarly, it is likely that more design engineers and perhaps fewer industrial engineers are required and that a larger scope of work instead of narrowly defined jobs, greater discretion on the shop floor rather than in central control, and the like may be needed to turn around the work force and job design element. The key point is that the achievement levels in Table 23-4 should not be merely a "wish list." The managers must provide specific alternatives to establish clearly how the transition from the present levels in Table 23-3 to the planned levels in Table 23-4 can be made. Vague platitudes and abstract plans will not suffice.

Of course, there is no unique right way to move from the present levels to the planned levels. Several alternatives must be considered. Further, when specific alternatives are evaluated, the planned levels may be adjusted somewhat. For example, strong emphasis on both the flexibility and quality criteria may require decisions that increase capital costs and may result in substantial increases in unit production costs. The company may revise the planned levels in view of these findings.

**TABLE 23-4**
**PLANNED STATUS OF THE OPERATIONS FUNCTION RELATIVE TO THE OPERATIONS STRATEGY**

| | Criteria | | | |
|---|---|---|---|---|
| (Priority Weights) | (25) | (30) | (10) | (35) |
| Elements of Operations Strategy | Cost | Quality | Dependability | Flexibility |
| 1. Positioning | 25 | 90 | 50 | 90 |
| 2. Process flow and technology | 50 | 75 | 50 | 75 |
| 3. Capacity/location decisions | 25 | 100 | 50 | 75 |
| 4. Work force and job design | 25 | 100 | 75 | 100 |
| 5. Operating decisions | 50 | 90 | 50 | 80 |
| 6. Suppliers and vertical integration | 25 | 90 | 75 | 100 |

### SELECT A STRATEGY

The assumption is that enterprise goals and strategies guided the development of the alternatives, but those goals and strategies need to be highlighted again in selecting an operations strategy. The selected strategy must have "strategic fit." It must help achieve the enterprise mission.

In addition, it must have organizational fit. The operations strategy must be implemented to be effective, and a brilliant strategy can fall flat if it does not fit the organization. The difficulties with organizational fit commonly occur with new and emerging technologies—product, process, or operations control—where existing personnel or organizational structure is not well adapted to the strategy. Lack of organizational fit does not mean that the strategy is poor, but it may mean that it cannot be implemented now—that some organizational development is necessary before one can hope for implementation.

One of the most common difficulties faced by operations managers occurs during the growth phase as the process technology evolves. If staff members have grown up with a system requiring customization, they often have difficulty adapting to the needs of a higher volume, more standardized system.

### IMPLEMENT THE STRATEGY

The strategy developed must be communicated to everyone who has a role in its implementation. Policies and procedures must be established, role assignments made, and resources allocated in the form of budgets to achieve the results.

Since the technology and production environments constantly change in even the most stable industries, implementation is an ongoing process rather than a one-shot allocation of resources. During the course of implementation and in the subsequent time periods, several decisions will have to be made. These decisions must be evaluated on criteria consistent with the operations strategy.

Of course, the criteria that define operations strategy may seem too broad to evaluate specific alternatives for a given decision. For example, the choice of equipment for which bids have been obtained from several vendors is most appropriately evaluated on specific criteria, such as capital cost, operating cost, versatility, set-up time, ease of installation, reject rate, vendor's reputation and after-sales service, and the like. However, a clear assessment must be made of how the equipment choice may influence operations priorities, even in a small way. This is because such incremental decisions, taken together, may result in an unconscious change in operations priorities, resulting in a gradually widening gap between what operations can deliver and what the customers and the marketing group require.

The internalization of the manufacturing priorities and the corporate mission by the managers at all levels, including the work force, is the *only* way to ensure that the implementation indeed achieves the desired goals.

## Corporate Level Operations Strategy

Just as corporate strategy should not be simply an assemblage of SBU strategies, neither should operations strategy be simplistically related at the SBU and corporate levels. The questions to be raised at the corporate level have to do with the possible interrelationships among the individual SBU operations strategies. These interrelationships are likely to be in terms of the products of one SBU that can be raw materials for another, the scale of operations, the location of capacities for interrelated items, and technology. An operations activity analysis that shows the value added at each stage and the interrelationships of materials, parts, and components for the corporation as a whole is useful.

### Strategic Operations Management

Once the strategy has been set, operations decisions must be made in a strategic way. Perhaps the most important reason for involving operations managers in the strategic planning process is to facilitate their strategic thinking so that the decisions can reflect the strategy more effectively, particularly operating decisions for which the temptation to think "short term" is greatest. This linking of short-term decisions with long-term objectives is an area where Japanese operations managers seem to get particularly high marks.[7]

## IMPLICATIONS FOR THE MANAGER

It is often true that the generic enterprise strategies are closely related to the operations functions and that in many instances they are actually operations strategies for dominating markets or segments of markets. Particularly in the cases of McDonald's and Burger King, the enterprise and operations strategies were virtually coterminous. We showed, through the examples of the companies, how operations strategies were implemented to achieve goals. What may seem like subtle differences in strategy can have an important impact in the way the strategy is implemented.

Operations strategy at the corporate level should not be simply the accumulation of the plans made for individual SBUs in a multiunit corporation. Corporatewide policies and strategies need to be reviewed, and individual SBU strategies related to them.

Operations strategy formulation and implementation must be a part of enterprise strategy and must be carefully coordinated with it. In order for the process to be successful, there must be organizational and managerial commitment and, preferably, the involvement of those who are charged with implementation. The position of the operations audit in the process is particularly important, for it is here that comparisons are made with competitors, the logical standards by which to measure. Given the audit and the self-evaluation that is involved, the steps of developing alternatives and selecting a strategy are more likely to fall into place more easily. But the implementation stage is crucial, and its success will depend in part on the resources allocated to its achievement and on the strategic and organizational fit of the operations strategy.

[7] See S. C. Wheelwright, "Japan—Where Operations Really Are Strategic," *Harvard Business Review*, August 1981, pp. 67–74.

# REVIEW QUESTIONS

1. How are the enterprise strategies or missions of Hewlett Packard (HP) and Texas Instruments (TI) for accessing markets similar? How are they different?
2. Referring to question 1, how are the competitive priorities of cost, quality, on-time delivery, and flexibility affected by the differences in HP's and TI's missions?
3. Discuss the nature of the following six corporate missions as frameworks for manufacturing strategy implementation:
   a. Technology frontiersman
   b. Technology exploiters
   c. Technological serviceman
   d. Customizers
   e. Cost-minimizing customizers
   f. Cost minimizers
4. In which portions of the product life cycle does the technology exploiter participate? The technology frontiersman? Which would have the more difficult managerial problems, the frontiersman or the exploiter? Does the answer to the last question agree with what you know about HP and TI?
5. In implementing the missions of HP and TI, which of the elements of operations strategy are most significant? Are they the same? If not, why not?
6. For which of the six missions listed in question 3 is "system positioning" an important element of operations strategy? Why?
7. What is the difference between the technological serviceman and the technological frontiersman, since both rely on technological leadership and both emphasize low-volume markets? Why is Boeing a good example of a technological serviceman?
8. In the list of corporate missions, the customizer is described as a job shop manufacturer, building to custom design in low volume, with flexibility and quality being the prime competitive priorities. Why would the example companies, Hughes Satellite Division and Rockwell Space Vehicle Division, be regarded as cost-minimizing customizers rather than customizers?
9. How are the elements of manufacturing strategy modified between customizers and cost-minimizing customizers?
10. Cost minimizers are the producers of the high-volume, standardized, commodity-type products. Why is it that availability and quality appear in the list of manufacturing priorities for the example companies, P&G, Kodak, and Norton Abrasives? Why is cost not the only priority?
11. Why does capacity/location appear on the list of elements of manufacturing strategy emphasized for cost minimizers but not for the previous five missions?
12. Describe the corporate strategies or missions of McDonald's, Burger King, and Benihana. How are they similar? How are they different?

13. Which offers the greater degree of customization, Burger King or Benihana?
14. McDonald's, Burger King, and Benihana can be compared to manufacturing operations in that they produce a product along with their services. Using the six missions that we used to classify manufacturers, how would you classify the three food outlets?
15. Thinking just in terms of the impact on the customer, what effect does the customization offered by Burger King have on the customer as compared with McDonald's?
16. Thinking just in terms of the impact on those who serve the customer directly, what effect does the customization offered by Burger King have on the activities of servers as compared with McDonald's?
17. Thinking just in terms of the impact on the process flow and technology, what is the effect of the customization offered by Burger King as compared with McDonald's?
18. Using your answer to question 14 as a background, discuss the premise that Benihana is a fast-food operation.
19. How do you account for the low costs achieved by Benihana as compared with the typical restaurant?
20. How does the process flow and technology employed by Benihana contribute to its low-cost operation?
21. How do the operating decisions, work force, and job design at Benihana restaurants contribute to its low-cost operation?
22. How important is the supply system and vertical integration to the success of a service firm such as McDonald's? Benihana?
23. What kinds of events that trigger the reevaluation of enterprise strategy are operations oriented?
24. How can a firm go about deciding on the relative importance of cost, quality, dependability as a supplier, and flexibility as competitive priorities? How can differences be reconciled?
25. Discuss "top down" versus "bottom up" approaches to strategy planning.
26. Outline the process for developing SBU strategic plans for the operations function.
27. What is an operations audit, and what is its function in developing an operations strategy?
28. Outline a step by step process for conducting an operations audit.
29. How can the goals generated for a future operations strategy be related to the results of an operations audit?
30. What is meant by the term *strategic fit* in characterizing a strategy?
31. What is the role of operations strategy in a corporation in which there are a number of individual business units (SBUs)?
32. What is the meaning of the term *strategic operations management*?

# PROJECT

## Strategy Planning at Turbo Corporation

33. The TURBO Corporation, a consumer electronics company, is engaged in strategic planning for the 1990s for the major functions of the company, including manufacturing, marketing, engineering and R&D, accounting and control, personnel and industrial relations, and finance. TURBO has had considerable success in the past, but many of the products on which it built that success have matured, and with more intense price competition, margins have narrowed.

    TURBO has maintained a central manufacturing facility, gaining scale economies, and has central technologies in electronics assembly. Many of its products use common activities, such as circuit board manufacture, plastics molding for cabinets, and component manufacture as well as the assembly process itself. In order to compete effectively, TURBO has emphasized long runs of items and a stable product mix to spread the set-up costs over large numbers of units. The vice-president of manufacturing takes great pride in the fact that TURBO is far down the experience curve in many of the basic activities. She feels that cost and controlled quality are the really important priorities at TURBO and that these priorities must be nurtured in the future strategic plans that are developed.

    The marketing group at TURBO has been very effective in promoting and selling the company's products, but in recent times, they have found the market to be changing. First, there has been heavy price competition for the existing products. Even more disturbing to them is the fact that competitors have been rolling out new products that offer attractive features, providing competition for TURBO's product line on other bases than price and quality. Customers seem willing to pay higher prices for the new products. On approaching the manufacturing vice-president to tool up to produce product variations, the marketing vice president has received resistance because of the short runs that would be involved and the increase in the number of items to be produced.

    The vice-president of engineering and R&D, and the marketing vice-president seem to sing on key, however, both wishing to differentiate the product line with new products. The vice-president of engineering and R&D has aggressively recruited well-trained electronics engineers on the basis that TURBO would provide them with an exciting environment employing the latest technology, and now he wants to put them to work designing new products.

    The chief accountant seems neutral on the entire issue. She says that she has a flexible cost accounting system that can accommodate any number of products, as long as she is provided with the budget.

    The director of personnel and industrial relations has provided the labor necessary to staff the existing production jobs, which are largely repetitive ones. The company is organized by the AFL–CIO Electrical Workers Union. Contract negotiations are currently under way, with wages and work rules being prime issues.

The finance vice-president runs a tight, "ROI–oriented" financial system, demanding that all products or production expansion meet internal hurdle rates derived from a target of 15 percent return on equity for the company. She is more interested in maintaining the target equity return than in the strategies by which it may be achieved.

### STRATEGY FOR THE FUTURE

The strategic planning committee, made up of the CEO, the executive vice-president, and the vice-presidents and directors of each of the seven areas already discussed have been presented with studies of the market structure, the industry structure, forecasts of future demand, price trends, and positioning in the value-added structure of the major competitors by consultants and other experts. Finally, the CEO has summarized what he sees as the wave of the future of the company in the following list of statements, which he characterizes as guidelines to strategy:

(1) We must meet well-defined customer needs in market segments. This is the most important thing we can do to be successful in the next decade.

(2) We must be very responsive to changes in market requirements and to competitive thrusts.

(3) We must staff and organize to be able to roll out new products at a rate unheard of in this organization.

(4) Our product quality must be perceived as being the best in the industry in terms of performance, "fit and finish," and appearance.

(5) Manufacturing must develop a high degree of flexibility in order to be able to respond to the need to bring out new products, initially in low volume, but at competitive costs.

(6) We must become leaders in the development and use of advanced process technology for automated assembly as well as other appropriate applications of automation.

### GROUP TASKS

Organize into teams that mirror the members of the strategic planning committee, with representatives from each of the major functions plus the CEO and executive vice-president. Each person should be assigned one of the roles, which should be represented logically but vigorously to discuss positions in order to generate consensus weights for the four competitive priorities for the manufacturing function, similar to those illustrated in Table 23-2.

## REFERENCES

"Benihana of Tokyo," Case #9-673-057, *HBS Case Services,* Harvard Business School.

Bogue, M. C., and E. S. Buffa, *Corporate Strategic Analysis,* Free Press, New York, 1986.

Buffa, E. S., *Meeting the Competitive Challenge: Manufacturing Strategy for U. S. Companies,* Irwin, Homewood, Ill., 1984.

"Burger King Corporation," Case #9-681-045, Rev. 6/81, *HBS Case Services,* Harvard Business School.

Fine, C. H., and A. C. Hax, "Manufacturing Strategy: A Methodology and an Illustration," *Interfaces, 15*(6) November–December, 1985, pp. 27–47.

Hayes, R. H., and Kim B. Clark, "Explaining Observed Productivity Differential Between Plants: Implications for Operations Research, *Interfaces, 15*(6), November–December, 1985, pp. 3–14.

Hayes, R. H., and K. B. Clark, "Why Some Factories Are More Productive Than Others," *Harvard Business Review,* September–October 1986, pp. 66–73.

Hayes, R. H., and S. C. Wheelwright, *Restoring Our Competitive Edge: Competing Through Manufacturing,* Wiley, New York, 1984.

"Hewlett-Packard: Where Slower Growth Is Smarter Management," *Business Week,* June 9, 1975, pp. 50–58.

"McDonald's," Case #9-673-062, *HBS Case Services,* Harvard Business School.

"McDonald's Corporation" (Condensed), Case #9-681-044, Rev. 2/82, *HBS Case Services,* Harvard Business School.

Porter, M. E., *Competitive Advantage: Creating and Sustaining Superior Performance,* Free Press, New York, 1985.

Porter, M. E., *Competitive Strategy: Techniques for Analyzing Industries and Competitors,* Free Press, New York, 1980.

Richardson, P. R., A. J. Taylor, and J. R. M. Gordon, "A Strategic Approach to Evaluating Manufacturing Performance, *Interfaces, 15*(6), November–December, 1985, pp. 15–27.

Rosenfeld, D. B., R. D. Shapiro, and R. E. Bohn, "Implications for Cost-Service Trade-offs on Industry Logistics Structures," *Interfaces, 15*(6), November–December, 1985, pp. 47–65.

Skinner, W., *Manufacturing: The Formidable Competitive Weapon,* Wiley, New York, 1985.

# PART FIVE

# SYNTHESIS AND CONCLUSION

# CHAPTER 24

# PERSPECTIVES ON OPERATIONS SYSTEMS OF THE FUTURE

M*odern* production and operations management embraces both manufacturing and nonmanufacturing systems and includes the full range of the contents of this book. A firm's approach for relating operations management issues to the other functional areas of the business, to the business itself, and to the relevant product–market environment can make the crucial difference in profitability, mere survival, or bankruptcy.

To manage operations effectively in today's environment requires an understanding of product–process technology as well as modern decision-making technology. Some of the concepts involved in a modern view of operations management are quantitative, often requiring computers for solution, as with linear programming solutions to problems of aggregate planning, location, and distribution. In recent years, the importance of the operations function in corporate strategy has been recognized and integrative concepts have been developed to formulate operations strategy and its link with the corporate strategy. We have covered both the quantitative and qualitative concepts in the preceding 23 chapters.

Production and operations management have not always been quantitative, scientific, and a part of advanced computer technology. To gain perspective, we must look back more than 250 years to see the flow of ideas that developed the field to its present state so that we can also look forward to envision the operations systems of the future.

## HISTORICAL PERSPECTIVE

There are four dominant themes that, when related to one another, describe our progress in developing the effective systems for producing goods and services that we know today: the changing nature of products and markets; the development of product and process technology; the evolution of organizational form and structure related to information, decision making, and control technology; and productivity as a broad measure of the economic viability of the productive systems that we have developed.

## BEGINNINGS—THE INDUSTRIAL REVOLUTION

We do not know who conceived the first productive systems, but we do know that the great monuments of the ancient world required both technical know-how and managerial systems. These systems made it possible to organize resources and make the grand plans that were executed with such admirable results. Examples are the Egyptian pyramids and sphinxes at Giza, built in about 2500 B.C.; the Greek Parthenon, built in about 440 B.C., the Great Wall of China, built in about 214 B.C.; and the construction marvels of the Roman world—aqueducts, public buildings, roads, and temples—which span a period from at least 400 B.C. to 100 B.C.

During and following the period of the building of the ancient monuments, a wide variety of products were produced through the handicraft system. Something akin to a production and operations management system began to develop with the Industrial Revolution, since it was during that period that the factory system began to evolve from the handicraft system where production took place in homes. A series of changes in industrial techniques and economic conditions made possible the development of larger productive units, though markets were still largely local and products were largely customized and handcrafted. Though we do not have records of productivity statistics for these early periods, we are sure that it was very low compared to modern times or even the later 1800s, when the era of keeping productivity statistics began.

### Substitution of Machine Power for Manpower

In 1764, James Watt made improvements on the steam engine that made it a practical power source. This event was the beginning of a long period of replacing human muscle power with machines that extends to the modern era. Other major technological developments that increased the power available to do work were the internal combustion engine, which offered greater mobility; electricity and power generation and distribution; transportation; and many others.

The substitution of external power for human power has been the source of most of the productivity increases that have occurred in the past 200 years in all kinds of activities in factories, construction, and agriculture. Indeed, the common measure of productivity in terms of output per worker-hour regards labor as the resource of significance, focusing on the labor substitution process that has been ongoing during the same period.

## ADAM SMITH

As technology marched on, outstanding intellectual personalities took notice of the developing Industrial Revolution. The first person to provide a rationale for the production function in business enterprise was Adam Smith. In 1776, Smith wrote his landmark book, *An Inquiry Into the Nature and Causes of the Wealth of Nations,* in which he observed three basic economic advantages that result from the division of labor. These advantages were (1) the development of a skill or dexterity when a single task is performed repetitively, (2) the saving of time normally lost in changing from one activity to the next, and (3) the invention of machines or tools that seemed normally to follow when people specialized their efforts on tasks of restricted scope. These specialization principles have been applied with ever increasing frequency from Smith's time until the present. Specialization in human activity touches everyone today.

## CHARLES BABBAGE

Over fifty years after Smith wrote his book, the mathematician Charles Babbage augmented the principles of the division of labor and raised a number of provocative questions about production organization and economics. The first mathematician to bring a scientific mind and method to bear on production problems, Babbage questioned many existing practices of the time in his book, *On the Economy of Machinery and Manufactures* (1832). Babbage agreed with Smith on the three principles of the division of labor, but he noted that the great economist had overlooked a fourth, that the wage that must be paid was dictated by the highest or rarest skill required of an activity. Therefore, by specializing jobs with homogeneous skills "just the amount of skill needed could be purchased," giving insight into the principle of limiting skills as a basis of pay, which is widely practiced today.

Babbage made another significant contribution, but this one was in the product–process technology field. He invented the first digital computer. It was a mechanical computer that had no immediate impact on operations practice, but its successors were to have a profound effect.

The factory system continued to develop, producing products of higher quality and lower cost than were available from the handicraft system and fostering larger markets. Increasing volumes in turn led to lower costs in a reinforcing cycle. Thus by 1850, national markets had developed for high-volume, standardized products. Until the turn of the century, this continuing development of markets drew on the ability of the productive system to produce good quality at low cost, but the basic structure of these systems did not change.

The owner–managers of businesses remained aloof from how the production process was carried out. The workers themselves did whatever production planning seemed minimally necessary and determined how to produce based on their skills and experience, all guided by traditional methods. "Boondoggling" and featherbedding were common practices and were easy to implement in the impassive atmosphere since owner–managers seldom ventured onto the shop floor. But this stagnant climate within industry was ripe for a hero with the courage to attack the complacency that had developed.

## FREDERICK W. TAYLOR AND SCIENTIFIC MANAGEMENT

Taylor entered industry originally as a worker and therefore had a clear understanding of the existing system, its strong traditions, and its general apathetic atmosphere. In this static environment, Taylor initiated a tidal wave of change in managerial philosophy that shook many organizations from top to bottom.

The essence of Taylor's scientific management philosophy was that the scientific method could and should be applied to all managerial problems. The methods by which work was accomplished should be determined by management through scientific investigation. In his book, *Principles of Scientific Management* (1919), Taylor stated four new duties of management, which may be summarized as follows:

1. The development of a science for each element of human work to replace the old rule-of-thumb methods.
2. The scientific selection, training, and development of workers instead of the old practice of allowing workers to choose their own tasks and train themselves as best they could.
3. The development of a spirit of hearty cooperation between workers and management to ensure that work would be carried out in accordance with scientific procedures.
4. The division of work between workers and management in almost equal shares, each group taking over the work for which it was best fitted, instead of the former condition in which most of the work and responsibility fell on the workers.

These four ideas led to a great deal of new thinking about industrial organization, and they are an integral part of present day managerial thinking. Entire fields of managerial specialization have developed from Taylor's principles. For example, under the general heading of point 1, the fields of methods engineering and work measurement have developed, with research areas of experimental psychology, physiology, and ergonomics. From points 2 and 3, the field of personnel management developed, with its techniques of personnel selection and placement together with the organizational function of industrial relations. From point 4 developed the basic managerial function of planning and control and the functional organization, which was also a Taylor idea.

Taylor was also known for some pioneering experiments in wage payment and in the scientific procedures for such tasks in the steel industry as metal machining, pig iron handling, and shoveling. In his metal cutting experiments, he used tons of metal over a period of 10 years, which resulted in specifications for the feeds and speeds that could be used for different metals and tool materials. In connection with these experiments, he discovered high speed steel in collaboration with Maunsel White, which made him wealthy and allowed him to spend the bulk of his later life furthering his philosophy of scientific management.

## Taylor's Followers

Many individuals worked within Taylor's general philosophy and made contributions of their own. Henry L. Gantt developed the Gantt chart, which was used extensively for the scheduling and control of operations before faster, more flexible computer methods replaced them. Carl Barth and Harrington Emerson worked in the field of wage incentives. Frank and Lillian Gilbreth developed motion study and fostered the concept of "the one best way."

Taylor believed that his important contributions were in his general philosophy rather than in any of his specific discoveries, the latter being merely applications of "scientific management" to specific situations. But the science of management was slow to develop, partly because the really important tools were not yet available and partly because of the natural resistance to new, unsettling ideas. The mathematical techniques to cope with probability and variation were not known in Taylor's time, nor were techniques available to cope with large-scale programming problems. The complexity of managerial problems required computers, but they were not to be available in practical form for more than fifty years.

## 1900–1950—AN ERA OF REMARKABLE PROGRESS

During the 1900–1950 period, productivity in terms of output per worker-hour increased by more than four times (see Figure 24-1), reflecting progressive mechanization in the earlier years and automation near the end of the period. Within the 50-year period, there were landmark events, some of which simply marked growth and some of which must have been the generators of progress. Henry Ford made the moving assembly line a practical fact in 1919, and it is associated with the reality of national markets for high-volume, standardized products that became the hallmark of U.S. manufacturing excellence. In the true spirit of Taylor's scientific management philosophy, there were early formulations of models of operations problems. F. W. Harris formulated the classic *EOQ* inventory model in 1914. This contribution was the forerunner to the extensive use of mathematical models in operations management today and, indeed, their use in other fields of management. Another similar development occurred in 1931 when Walter Shewhart introduced statistical quality control concepts and methods to industry. This event not only impacted the

FIGURE 24-1
**ONE HUNDRED YEARS OF PRODUCTIVITY GROWTH. OUTPUT PER WORKER-HOUR IN UNITED STATES MANUFACTURING, 1870–1980.**

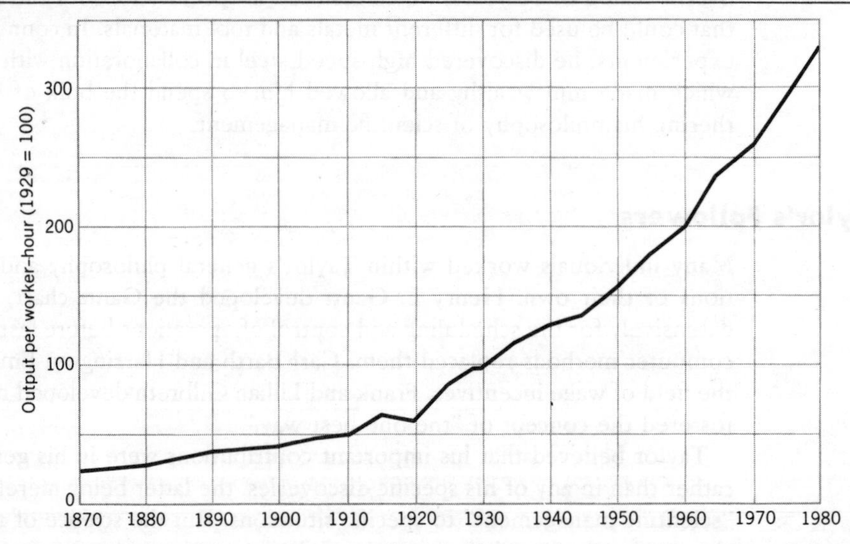


*Sources:* J. W. Kendrick, ***Productivity Trends in the United States,*** Princeton University Press, Princeton, N.J., and the Bureau of Labor Statistics.

field of quality control, but it paved the way for the acceptance of probability and statistical concepts in forecasting, inventory control, and so on.

Near the end of this fifty-year period, a new impact on the field of operations management was made apparent by trends in consumer expenditures and employment patterns. Service systems had become so important in our economy that their effectiveness as operations systems was important and became a subject for study along with manufacturing systems. Percentage expenditures for services surpassed those for consumer nondurable goods. Currently, employment in service operations exceeds that in manufacturing.

The stage was being set for the current era of dynamic changes in markets, technology, organization, and information and decision-making technology. These and the following events are shown in historical perspective in Table 24-1.

## THE CURRENT ERA

The beginning of the current era is selected as 1950 to correspond roughly with the beginning of the use of computers in operations management. The extraordinary impact of electronic computers on operations management has been pervasive, extending into product–process technology, information systems, and decision-making and control technology.

During World War II, research into war operations produced new mathematical and computing techniques that were applied to war operations problems. These problems had many attributes that were similar to operations problems in industry, and applications began of what would be called management science. It was scientific management, but with more powerful tools. All the mathematical methods that have been discussed in this text are a part of that development: In the order in which they appear in the text, these include forecasting models, inventory models, MRP, linear programming, aggregate production planning models, simulation, PERT/CPM, SQC, waiting line models, and location and distribution models.

Not all the developments in this era were quantitative in character. In the early 1950s, there were important experiments that questioned the fractionation of jobs that had continued unabated since the dawn of the Industrial Revolution. Experiments with job enlargement at IBM suggested that division of labor had lost the workers' interest. Experiments with teams and semiautonomous work groups in Great Britain indicated higher productivity and job satisfaction.

### Computers and Management Science

The practical use of some of the foregoing quantitative models was dependent on the development of computers. For example, linear programming without computers would have had a small field of application. MRP is essentially a computer-based information system. Simulation usually requires large samples and is therefore computer dependent. Projects large enough to require PERT/CPM also call for computer solutions. Significant location and distribution problems require computers for solution, as do significant line balance problems.

TABLE 24-1
**TWO HUNDRED FIFTY YEARS IN THE DEVELOPMENT OF PRODUCTION AND OPERATIONS MANAGEMENT**

| Date Line | U.S. Productivity, 1929 = 100 | Nature of Products and Markets | Product–Process Technology | Organization, Information Systems, and Decision Making and Control Technology |
|---|---|---|---|---|
| 1750 | | Local markets, handcrafted products | Industrial revolution<br>Substitution of machine power for human power<br>James Watt—steam engine | Home manufacturing replaced by factory system for many products. |
| | | | | Adam Smith—principles of division of labor recognized and practiced |
| 1800 | | | Eli Whitney—interchangeable parts | |
| | | | Charles Babbage invents first digital computer | Charles Babbage—limiting skills as a basis of pay |
| 1850 | | National markets for high-volume, standardized products develop | | |
| | 25 | | | |
| 1900 | 40 | | | Frederick W. Taylor, father of scientific management |
| | | National markets for high-volume, standardized products the hallmark of U.S. manufacturing | Henry Ford—moving assembly line | F. W. Harris—first inventory model<br>Walter Shewhart—SQC |
| | | Service systems an important fraction of total markets | | |
| 1950 | 160 | | Electronic computers<br>Numerical control of machines | Management science models applied in POM<br>Job enlargement and team concepts |
| | 200 | Global markets for high-volume, standardized products, but 75% of parts produced in lots of 50 or less | Robotics<br>CAD/CAM | |
| | 260 | | | Computers in planning and control (e.g., MRP) |
| | 340(est.) | | Flexible manufacturing systems | JIT concepts at Toyota<br>Operations strategy becomes important |
| 2000 | ? | | | |
| | | Global markets, demand for customization and flexibility ← | ← Automatic factory ← | Computer integrated decision making and control |

### Computers and Product–Process Technology

The substitution of machines for human power did not end with the advent of computers; it continues to this day. But computers have added an entirely new dimension of substitution. Even with power substitution, humans retained the unique capabilities of sensing and control. But with the automation technologies of numerical control of machines and robotics combined into flexible manufacturing systems, these human functions are substituted for by machines. The result is that machines seem to have few restraints limiting their application other than economic justification. These automation technologies coupled with soon to be realized extensive CAD/CAM capabilities mean that the technological barrier to the automatic factory has virtually been removed.

### Global Competition Impacts Operations

In the period following World War II, when U.S. products dominated world markets, top managers seemed to have almost forgotten about operations. They seemed to feel that the production problem was solved by our technological lead. But global competition in high-volume, standardized products proved to be extremely strong, particularly from Japanese producers. In addition, we note that although high-volume, standardized products seem to dominate our thinking about global markets, 75 percent of the parts produced by U.S. industry are produced in lots of 50 or less. This observation provides food for thought concerning the future competitive arena for operations.

While attention was riveted on technology, computers, and advanced decision-making and control methodologies, the Japanese were quietly perfecting the simple systems dependent on the *JIT* concepts discussed in Chapter 14. Though the Japanese certainly had not ignored the use of advance product–process technology, their operating systems contributed strongly to high quality and productivity. With competition based on quality and cost being so intense, operations strategy is currently a hot topic.

## PROGRESS MEASURED BY PRODUCTIVITY

The effectiveness of a sector of the economy is commonly measured by its productivity—outputs relative to some measure of inputs—and the most common basis is labor productivity. The record of labor productivity measured in terms of output per worker-hour in the U.S. from 1870 to 1983 is shown in Figure 24-1, and key labor productivity figures are listed next to the date line in the historical perspective in Table 24-1.

## Rationale for Productivity Improvements

The effects of the progress of the development of production and operations management through the decades can be read in the productivity curve. For example, the productivity progress during the fifty-year period from 1870 to 1920 reflects growing markets and the substitution of machine power for human power; external power sources multiplied human inputs and resulted in increased labor productivity.

The slope of the curve increases at an increasing rate from 1920 until about 1970. Several factors combined to produce the excellent performance during this period. First, there was the continued substitution of machine power for muscle power, but after about 1950, the character of machines changed and began to include computation and control as well as power. These technological effects were combined with better information systems and better decision-making and control technology. Scientific management based on Frederick Taylor's principles probably had its effects, but these were later augmented by management science applications. Better management of all kinds must be credited with part of the excellent productivity record during the fifty-year period.

## The Productivity Crisis

Beginning somewhere around 1970, increases in U.S. productivity began to lag behind the increases in other countries, causing great concern for global competitiveness. For example, in the 1973–1980 period, the average percentage change in manufacturing productivity for six countries shows the United States with the lowest increase:

| United States | Canada | Japan | France | West Germany | United Kingdom |
|---|---|---|---|---|---|
| 1.7 | 2.2 | 6.8 | 4.9 | 4.8 | 1.9 |

*Source:* P. Capdevielle and D. Alverez, "International Trends in Productivity and Labor Costs, *Monthly Labor Review,* December 1981, pp,. 14–20.

In fact, U.S. productivity changes were actually −2.4 percent in 1974, and −0.3 percent in 1980. This leveling off of productivity improvement came at a time when the product–process technologies of *NC,* robotics, *CAD/CAM,* and *FMS* were all available. The failure of U.S. industry to install these and other advanced technologies aggressively (as compared to Japanese manufacturers, for example) may have contributed to the poor performance. The advanced technologies of all types—product–process, information, and decision making and control—are at the core of the vision and hope for operations systems of the future.

Another issue to be considered is the basis for measuring productivity, which is focused on the profitable substitution of capital for labor, however, labor costs have been reduced to only about 15 percent, on the average. But what is the productivity

FIGURE 24-2
**PRODUCTIVITY TRENDS IN U.S. PRIVATE BUSINESSES 1973–1984 (1977 = 100).**

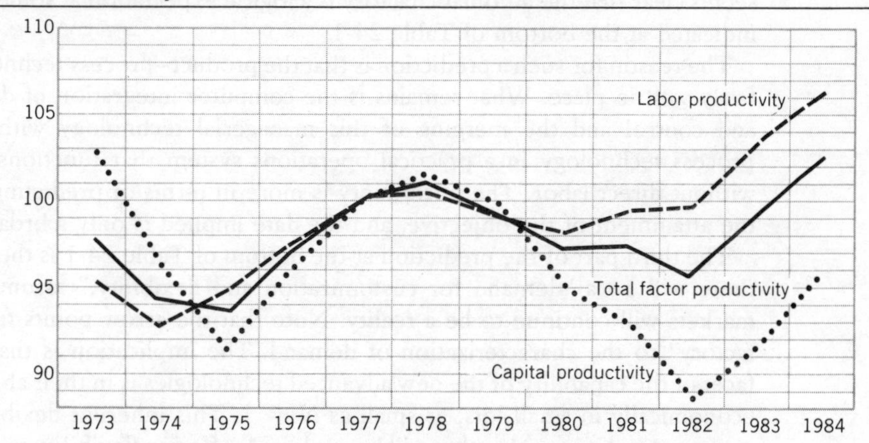


*Source:* Bureau of Labor Statistics and *Productivity Perspectives,* 1986 Edition, American Productivity Center, Houston, TX, 1986.

of capital as well as of the other major resource inputs of material, energy, and so forth? Thus, a broader measure of productivity[1] seems to be called for since labor has become a much smaller proportion of costs and may be eliminated in many future systems.

For example, Figure 24-2 provides a 12-year graph of labor, capital, and total factor productivity for U.S. private businesses, emphasizing the low productivity values during the recession periods of 1973–1976 and 1981–1982, and the substantial recovery through 1984. Total factor productivity is somewhat lower than labor productivity because capital productivity has been so low since 1980. Although all three measures have increased substantially since their lows in 1982, capital productivity remains a problem.

## OPERATIONS SYSTEMS OF THE FUTURE

Predicting the future is always risky, but it is nonetheless a fascinating endeavor. We need to think in terms of both manufacturing and nonmanufacturing systems. The directions for manufacturing systems may be somewhat clearer than for nonmanufacturing systems, in part because nonmanufacturing systems are so diverse.

[1] For example, measures of inputs, including labor, material, capital, and energy, were used to measure total factor productivity in companies in R. H. Hayes and K. B. Clark, "Explaining Observed Productivity Differentials Between Plants: Implications for Operations Research," *Interfaces, 15*(6), November–December 1985, pp. 3–14.

## Future Manufacturing Systems

If one takes the approach of forecasting on the basis of trends that are apparent, it seems clear that the automatic factory is a logical expectation at some future date, as indicated at the bottom of Table 24-1.

The reason for such a prediction is that the product–process technology is already fairly well in place. What remains is the computer integration of decision making and control and the merging of this managerial technology with the product–process technology in a practical operations system that functions automatically, without direct labor. The uncertainty is more in terms of predicting the date than the attainment of the objective, and the date implied is only a broad estimate.

The third part of the prediction at the bottom of Table 24-1 is the statement that there will be a "demand for customization and flexibility," assuming that global markets will continue to be a reality. Note that the arrow points from "automatic factory" to the characterization of demand. The implication is that an important facet of the capability of the new advanced technologies is in their ability to produce economically in small lots, as small as $N = 1$. This inherent flexibility provides a revenue producing value that will be exploited, offering flexibility to customers for a price. But competition will then force flexibility and customization as a competitive priority on all producers, incorporating it as an expectation of the market. Thus, the capability of the automatic factory will introduce this new value into the market, and we will enjoy the fruits of custom product designs to a degree not available since the handicraft system was outmoded by the factory system.

### THE COMPUTER INTEGRATED FACTORY OF THE FUTURE

The system would be linked by computing systems as shown in Figure 24-3 and would be able to manufacture essentially perfect, customized products with no direct labor required. Each of the six major components communicates with the other components and with corporate headquarters (not shown) through computers.

Orders would be fed by telecommunications networks through the marketing function, providing a crucial link with the customer. The orders could include the customer's desired customization, in a fashion described by General Motors in connection with its futuristic SATURN project.

New products would be conceived on the *CAD* system, where libraries of data, previous designs, engineering standards, and so on would be available and used for efficient and accurate designs. But the design process would not be independent of the manufacturing processes that would be used. The close linking of *CAD* and *CAM* provide the unified basis for product design based on both functional and manufacturing considerations. The same data bases would be passed back and forth between product design and production design to ensure the design of the most efficient processes for production.

The *CAM* data are passed directly to the fabrication section where the computer-aided system fabricates the necessary parts, which are then physically transferred to computer aided assembly through robotic materials movement. Quality checks are automatic, as are product tests for performance. Materials are then moved by robots

FIGURE 24-3
**COMPUTER INTEGRATED FACTORY OF THE FUTURE**

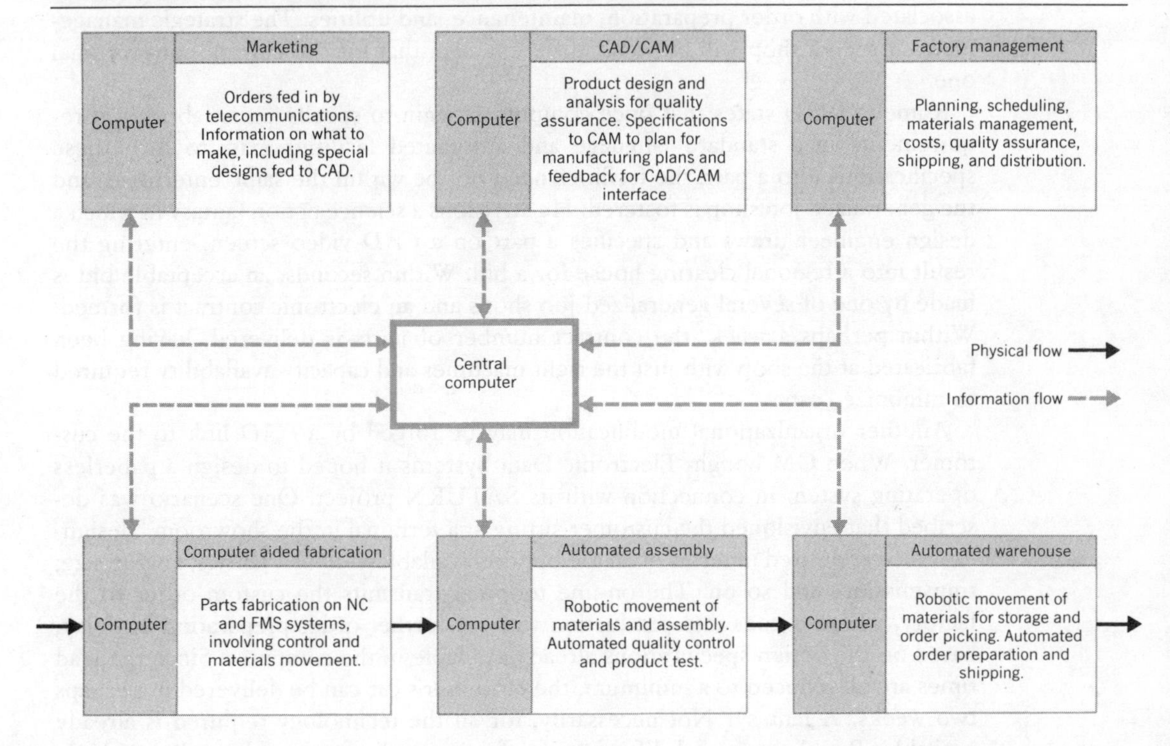


to an automated warehouse where they are packed and shipped or stored automatically if necessary. Storage, however, would not follow the usual pattern. The automated warehouse also functions to supply off-the-shelf items, which can be order picked automatically, and to store purchased parts for the assembly process, which again would be automatically picked according to the requirements schedule.

Factory management in the futuristic scheme is focused on planning, scheduling, materials management, costs, quality assurance, maintenance, and shipping and distribution.

## ALTERED INDUSTRIAL STRUCTURES

The technological changes will impose new and different ways of doing business. The producer who views automation technology as merely another cost reduction tool will have missed the real opportunity. One of the new types of enterprises likely to emerge is the general purpose machine shop, with numerically controlled machine tools, robots for handling materials, and a *CAD*-parts design capability. This new "job shop" will respond quickly and reliably to a wide variety of requirements, with a rapid flow of totally different jobs on different machines. Since virtually all the costs of operation are fixed and largely sunk, the central objective will be to maximize flow through the system. As long as capacity is available, the incremental cost associated with adding one more order is the material cost plus the costs associated with order preparation, maintenance, and utilities. The strategic management of such a shop will be vastly different than that for the current conventional one.

Rumelt (1981) states that once computers begin to specify parts fabrication requirements in a standard language and automated facilities exist to turn these specifications into a part, the facilities need not be within the same enterprise, and the generalized job shop is fostered. He envisions a science fiction fantasy in which a design engineer draws and specifies a part on a *CAD* video screen, entering the result into a regional clearing house for a bid. Within seconds, an acceptable bid is made by one of several generalized job shops and an electronic contract is formed. Within perhaps a week, the contract number of parts is delivered, having been fabricated at the shop with just the right machines and capacity availability required to minimize costs.

Another organizational modification may be forged by a *CAD* link to the customer. When GM bought Electronic Data Systems it hoped to design a paperless operating system in connection with its SATURN project. One scenario was described that envisioned the customer sitting at a terminal in the showroom "designing" the car desired in terms of all the options available—colors, fabrics, engine size, transmission, and so on. The on-line terminal transmits the custom order to the factory, where it goes into production without further order preparation or delay, based on the design specifications already available in the computer. Since the lead times are all reduced to a minimum, the customer's car can be delivered in perhaps two weeks. A fantasy? Not necessarily, for all the technology required is already available. But the new and different interface with the customer coupled with assembly-line automation provides a new market force that fosters product variety and customization because of a *CAD/CAM* linkage.

Finally, there may be a dramatic shift in manufacturing location; we may even manufacture some products in space. There are some products, pharmaceuticals for example, for which zero gravity makes possible a purity not attainable on earth. Again technology makes possible an advance in manufacturing undreamed of in the past.

## Future Nonmanufacturing Systems

The great diversity of nonmanufacturing operations makes generalizations difficult, so we will focus on a few areas as we did in discussing process technologies in nonmanufacturing operations in Chapter 15.

### HIGH CUSTOMER CONTACT SYSTEMS

Many of the service oriented systems of interest will be affected by computer networks that can be used by both individuals and companies and by conversion to a virtually cashless society based on electronic funds transfer. Of course, electronic funds transfers are already common within the banking system, but we are concerned with a more pervasive system available to all who might have funds to transfer, including individuals. Presumably to use the system, some sort of computer terminal will be available to the user.

The availability of such basic systems makes possible a massive change in the way many forms of business are conducted. Instead of going to many places of business, as is done currently, communication takes place via computer link to shop and pay for many items. The current public acceptance of catalog ordering is a step in this direction, but instead of mail ordering and paying by credit card or check, one would simply select the vendor from the terminal, browse through the vendor's video catalog, select items, and pay by electronic funds transfer. At the vendor's end, after automatic verification of funds, the order would be picked by an automated system and shipped, the shipping label being printed as a part of the system.

Many formerly high customer contact systems will be converted to low customer contact by the above scenario, altering the operations system by the way business is done. Paying all kinds of bills will be accomplished with such systems. Airline reservations can be incorporated—the customer browses through schedules, queries the system concerning the availability of the desired flights, and pays by funds transfer, and the ticket is automatically mailed out. Grocery shopping can be done by such a system—purchases are ordered through the system and are either delivered or picked up at a given time. The groceries would, of course, be picked from shelves or bins by an automatic system. The point of sale systems now thought to represent advanced technology would be obsolete.

## LOW CUSTOMER CONTACT SYSTEMS

Many low customer contact systems that produce a product, such as fast-food outlets, are very much like factories in terms of the processing in which they engage. We are not suggesting, however, that McDonald's would develop a completely automated system to produce hamburgers. It is not that the technology is not available to allow such as system. Indeed, an automated system could introduce greater choice into hamburger production than is true currently, probably at no greater cost than to produce a completely standard hamburger by an automated system. The issue is the volume. Each McDonald's outlet, although high-volume in fast-food terms, may not have sufficient volume to justify the high capital costs necessary to install an automated system, unless labor costs were to increase exorbitantly.

One of the low customer contact systems discussed in Chapter 15 was the bank check clearing process. That process was described as being highly automated and efficient in today's terms, at least in comparison to check clearing prior to *MICR* encoding (Magnetic Ink Character Recognition). Of course, that system would be virtually obsolete if electronic funds transfer were widely adopted, and funds flow between banks would be largely bypassed by the electronic system. The small amounts of cash needed by individuals could be furnished by *ATMs*, or supermarkets and others could furnish cash since their accounts would be immediately credited from the customer's accounts; bad checks would be an anachronism.

Warehousing, distribution, and transport will be impacted by the simple *JIT* concepts now being applied with accelerating speed. Although the warehousing systems will continue to apply automated storage–retrieval systems, the quantities needed to be stored will be reduced by the tightened lead times resulting from more frequent *JIT* deliveries. Transportation will continue to emphasize containerization, but transportation modes will shift toward more air freight, reflecting lower air freight costs, the need for *JIT* delivery, and the lower pipeline inventories resulting from shorter delivery times.

## CONCLUDING COMMENTS

It is through productive systems that goods and services are produced in our society. Their effective design, control, and management has been the focus of this entire text. Economies that supply their citizens with a high standard of living are the ones that have effective productive systems—we can only divide what we have produced.

The managers who run the shops, services, or projects have important and exciting positions. From a social point of view they contribute *directly* to the creation of goods and services. The operating management positions themselves involve the development of strategies as well as the day-to-day management of resources and people. The decisions made are crucial to the success of an organization. They determine whether or not the products and services are of the appropriate quality and cost and whether they are delivered to the consumers in a timely fashion. Image makers can build on product attributes that exist, but only the operating managers can build the case on which the image can be erected.

# REFERENCES

"Automation U.S.A.: How GM, IBM, Westinghouse, GE, and Apple are Leading the Way," Special Issue, *High Technology,* 5(5) May 1985, pp. 23–47. (The Special Issue has eight articles including five dealing with the status of automation in each of the above five companies.)

Baumol, W. J., and K. McLennen, *Productivity Growth and U.S. Competitiveness,* Oxford University Press, New York, 1985.

Bylinsky, G., "A New Industrial Revolution Is On the Way," *Fortune,* October 5, 1981, pp. 106–114.

Bylinsky, G., "The Race to the Automatic Factory," *Fortune,* February 21, 1983, pp. 52–64.

Cook, N. H., "Computer-Managed Parts Manufacturing," *Scientific American,* February 1975, pp. 22–29.

Gerwin, D., "Do's and Don'ts of Computerized Manufacturing," *Harvard Business Review,* March–April 1982, pp. 107–116.

Ginzberg, E., "The Mechanization of Work," *Scientific American,* September 1982, pp. 67–75.

Giuliano, V. E., "The Mechanization of Office Work," *Scientific American,* September 1982, pp. 124–135.

Gun, T. G., "The Mechanization of Design and Manufacturing," *Scientific American,* September 1982, pp. 86–109.

Kops, L., Editor, *Towards the Factory of the Future,* The American Society of Mechanical Engineers, New York, 1980, pp. 115.

Leonief, W., and F. Duchin, *The Future Impact of Automation on Workers,* Oxford University Press, New York, 1986.

*Productivity Perspectives,* 1986 Edition, American Productivity Center, Houston, TX, 1986.

Rumelt, R. P. "The Electronic Reorganization of Industry," Paper presented at the "Global Management in the 1980s" Conference of the Strategic Management Society, London, October 1981.

Taylor, F. W., *Principles of Scientific Management,* Harper and Brothers, New York, 1919. Reprinted in *Scientific Management,* Harper and Brothers, New York, 1947.

# APPENDIX

## TABLES

Table 1. $PV_{sp}$, Present-Value Factors for Future Single Payments

Table 2. $PV_a$, Present-Value Factors for Annuities

Table 3. Values of $L_q$ for $M = 1$ to 15, and Various Values of $r = \lambda/\mu$. Poisson Arrivals, Negative Exponential Service Times

Table 4. Finite Queuing Tables

Table 5. Table of Random Digits

Table 6. Areas Under the Normal Curve

## TABLE 1
## $PV_{sp}$, PRESENT-VALUE FACTORS FOR FUTURE SINGLE PAYMENTS

| Years Hence | 1% | 2% | 4% | 6% | 8% | 10% | 12% | 14% | 15% | 16% | 18% | 20% |
|---|---|---|---|---|---|---|---|---|---|---|---|---|
| 1 | 0.990 | 0.980 | 0.962 | 0.943 | 0.926 | 0.909 | 0.893 | 0.877 | 0.870 | 0.862 | 0.847 | 0.833 |
| 2 | 0.980 | 0.961 | 0.925 | 0.890 | 0.857 | 0.826 | 0.797 | 0.769 | 0.756 | 0.743 | 0.718 | 0.694 |
| 3 | 0.971 | 0.942 | 0.889 | 0.840 | 0.794 | 0.751 | 0.712 | 0.675 | 0.658 | 0.641 | 0.609 | 0.579 |
| 4 | 0.961 | 0.924 | 0.855 | 0.792 | 0.735 | 0.683 | 0.636 | 0.592 | 0.572 | 0.552 | 0.516 | 0.482 |
| 5 | 0.951 | 0.906 | 0.822 | 0.747 | 0.681 | 0.621 | 0.567 | 0.519 | 0.497 | 0.476 | 0.437 | 0.402 |
| 6 | 0.942 | 0.888 | 0.790 | 0.705 | 0.630 | 0.564 | 0.507 | 0.456 | 0.432 | 0.410 | 0.370 | 0.335 |
| 7 | 0.933 | 0.871 | 0.760 | 0.665 | 0.583 | 0.513 | 0.452 | 0.400 | 0.376 | 0.354 | 0.314 | 0.279 |
| 8 | 0.923 | 0.853 | 0.731 | 0.627 | 0.540 | 0.467 | 0.404 | 0.351 | 0.327 | 0.305 | 0.266 | 0.233 |
| 9 | 0.914 | 0.837 | 0.703 | 0.592 | 0.500 | 0.424 | 0.361 | 0.308 | 0.284 | 0.263 | 0.225 | 0.194 |
| 10 | 0.905 | 0.820 | 0.676 | 0.558 | 0.463 | 0.386 | 0.322 | 0.270 | 0.247 | 0.227 | 0.191 | 0.162 |
| 11 | 0.896 | 0.804 | 0.650 | 0.527 | 0.429 | 0.350 | 0.287 | 0.237 | 0.215 | 0.195 | 0.162 | 0.135 |
| 12 | 0.887 | 0.788 | 0.625 | 0.497 | 0.397 | 0.319 | 0.257 | 0.208 | 0.187 | 0.168 | 0.137 | 0.112 |
| 13 | 0.879 | 0.773 | 0.601 | 0.469 | 0.368 | 0.290 | 0.229 | 0.182 | 0.163 | 0.145 | 0.116 | 0.093 |
| 14 | 0.870 | 0.758 | 0.577 | 0.442 | 0.340 | 0.263 | 0.205 | 0.160 | 0.141 | 0.125 | 0.099 | 0.078 |
| 15 | 0.861 | 0.743 | 0.555 | 0.417 | 0.315 | 0.239 | 0.183 | 0.140 | 0.123 | 0.108 | 0.084 | 0.065 |
| 16 | 0.853 | 0.728 | 0.534 | 0.394 | 0.292 | 0.218 | 0.163 | 0.123 | 0.107 | 0.093 | 0.071 | 0.054 |
| 17 | 0.844 | 0.714 | 0.513 | 0.371 | 0.270 | 0.198 | 0.146 | 0.108 | 0.093 | 0.080 | 0.060 | 0.045 |
| 18 | 0.836 | 0.700 | 0.494 | 0.350 | 0.250 | 0.180 | 0.130 | 0.095 | 0.081 | 0.069 | 0.051 | 0.038 |
| 19 | 0.828 | 0.686 | 0.475 | 0.331 | 0.232 | 0.164 | 0.116 | 0.083 | 0.070 | 0.060 | 0.043 | 0.031 |
| 20 | 0.820 | 0.673 | 0.456 | 0.312 | 0.215 | 0.149 | 0.104 | 0.073 | 0.061 | 0.051 | 0.037 | 0.026 |

## TABLE 2
## $PV_a$, PRESENT-VALUE FACTORS FOR ANNUITIES

| Years (n) | 1% | 2% | 4% | 6% | 8% | 10% | 12% | 14% | 15% | 16% | 18% | 20% |
|---|---|---|---|---|---|---|---|---|---|---|---|---|
| 1 | 0.990 | 0.980 | 0.962 | 0.943 | 0.926 | 0.909 | 0.893 | 0.877 | 0.870 | 0.862 | 0.847 | 0.833 |
| 2 | 1.970 | 1.942 | 1.886 | 1.883 | 1.783 | 1.736 | 1.690 | 1.647 | 1.626 | 1.605 | 1.566 | 1.528 |
| 3 | 2.941 | 2.884 | 2.775 | 2.673 | 2.577 | 2.487 | 2.402 | 2.322 | 2.283 | 2.246 | 2.174 | 2.106 |
| 4 | 3.902 | 3.808 | 3.630 | 3.465 | 3.312 | 3.170 | 3.037 | 2.914 | 2.855 | 2.798 | 2.690 | 2.589 |
| 5 | 4.853 | 4.713 | 4.452 | 4.212 | 3.993 | 3.791 | 3.605 | 3.433 | 3.352 | 3.274 | 3.127 | 2.991 |
| 6 | 5.795 | 5.601 | 5.242 | 4.917 | 4.623 | 4.355 | 4.111 | 3.889 | 3.784 | 3.685 | 3.498 | 3.326 |
| 7 | 6.728 | 6.472 | 6.002 | 5.582 | 5.206 | 4.868 | 4.564 | 4.288 | 4.160 | 4.039 | 3.812 | 3.605 |
| 8 | 7.652 | 7.325 | 6.733 | 6.210 | 5.747 | 5.335 | 4.968 | 4.639 | 4.487 | 4.344 | 4.078 | 3.837 |
| 9 | 8.566 | 8.162 | 7.435 | 6.802 | 6.247 | 5.759 | 5.328 | 4.946 | 4.772 | 4.607 | 4.303 | 4.031 |
| 10 | 9.471 | 8.983 | 8.111 | 7.360 | 6.710 | 6.145 | 5.650 | 5.126 | 5.019 | 4.833 | 4.494 | 4.192 |
| 11 | 10.368 | 9.787 | 8.760 | 7.887 | 7.139 | 6.495 | 5.988 | 5.453 | 5.234 | 5.029 | 4.656 | 4.327 |
| 12 | 11.255 | 10.575 | 9.385 | 8.384 | 7.536 | 6.814 | 6.194 | 5.660 | 5.421 | 5.197 | 4.793 | 4.439 |
| 13 | 12.134 | 11.343 | 9.986 | 8.853 | 7.904 | 7.103 | 6.424 | 5.842 | 5.583 | 5.342 | 4.910 | 4.533 |
| 14 | 13.004 | 12.106 | 10.563 | 9.295 | 8.244 | 7.367 | 6.628 | 6.002 | 5.724 | 5.468 | 5.008 | 4.611 |
| 15 | 13.865 | 12.849 | 11.118 | 9.712 | 8.559 | 7.606 | 6.811 | 6.142 | 5.847 | 5.575 | 5.092 | 4.675 |
| 16 | 14.718 | 13.578 | 11.652 | 10.106 | 8.851 | 7.824 | 6.974 | 6.265 | 5.954 | 5.669 | 5.162 | 4.730 |
| 17 | 15.562 | 14.292 | 12.166 | 10.477 | 9.122 | 8.022 | 7.120 | 6.373 | 6.047 | 5.749 | 5.222 | 4.775 |
| 18 | 16.398 | 14.992 | 12.659 | 10.828 | 9.372 | 8.201 | 7.250 | 6.467 | 6.128 | 5.818 | 5.273 | 4.812 |
| 19 | 17.226 | 15.678 | 13.134 | 11.158 | 9.604 | 8.365 | 7.366 | 6.550 | 6.198 | 5.877 | 5.316 | 4.844 |
| 20 | 18.046 | 16.351 | 13.590 | 11.470 | 9.818 | 8.514 | 7.469 | 6.623 | 6.259 | 5.929 | 5.353 | 4.870 |

TABLE 3

**VALUES of $L_q$ FOR $M = 1$ TO 15, AND VARIOUS VALUES OF $r = \lambda/\mu$. POISSON ARRIVALS, NEGATIVE EXPONENTIAL SERVICE TIMES**

| | Number of Service Channels M | | | | | | | | | | | | | | |
|---|---|---|---|---|---|---|---|---|---|---|---|---|---|---|---|
| r | 1 | 2 | 3 | 4 | 5 | 6 | 7 | 8 | 9 | 10 | 11 | 12 | 13 | 14 | 15 |
| 4.0 | | | | | 2.2164 | 0.5694 | 0.1801 | 0.0590 | 0.0189 | | | | | | |
| 4.2 | | | | | 3.3269 | 0.7837 | 0.2475 | 0.0827 | 0.0273 | 0.0087 | | | | | |
| 4.4 | | | | | 5.2675 | 1.0777 | 0.3364 | 0.1142 | 0.0389 | 0.0128 | | | | | |
| 4.6 | | | | | 9.2885 | 1.4867 | 0.4532 | 0.1555 | 0.0541 | 0.0184 | | | | | |
| 4.8 | | | | | 21.6384 | 2.0708 | 0.6071 | 0.2092 | 0.0742 | 0.0260 | | | | | |
| 5.0 | | | | | | 2.9375 | 0.8102 | 0.2786 | 0.1006 | 0.0361 | 0.0125 | | | | |
| 5.2 | | | | | | 4.3004 | 1.0804 | 0.3680 | 0.1345 | 0.0492 | 0.0175 | | | | |
| 5.4 | | | | | | 6.6609 | 1.4441 | 0.5871 | 0.1779 | 0.0663 | 0.0243 | 0.0085 | | | |
| 5.6 | | | | | | 11.5178 | 1.9436 | 0.6313 | 0.2330 | 0.0883 | 0.0330 | 0.0119 | | | |
| 5.8 | | | | | | 26.3726 | 2.6481 | 0.8225 | 0.3032 | 0.1164 | 0.0443 | 0.0164 | | | |
| 6.0 | | | | | | | 3.6828 | 1.0707 | 0.3918 | 0.1518 | 0.0590 | 0.0224 | | | |
| 6.2 | | | | | | | 5.2979 | 1.3967 | 0.5037 | 0.1964 | 0.0775 | 0.0300 | 0.0113 | | |
| 6.4 | | | | | | | 8.0768 | 1.8040 | 0.6454 | 0.2524 | 0.1008 | 0.0398 | 0.0153 | | |
| 6.6 | | | | | | | 13.7692 | 2.4198 | 0.8247 | 0.3222 | 0.1302 | 0.0523 | 0.0205 | | |
| 6.8 | | | | | | | 31.1270 | 3.2441 | 1.0533 | 0.4090 | 0.1666 | 0.0679 | 0.0271 | 0.0105 | |
| 7.0 | | | | | | | | 4.4471 | 1.3471 | 0.5172 | 0.2119 | 0.0876 | 0.0357 | 0.0141 | |
| 7.2 | | | | | | | | 6.3135 | 1.7288 | 0.6521 | 0.2677 | 0.1119 | 0.0463 | 0.0187 | |
| 7.4 | | | | | | | | 9.5102 | 2.2324 | 0.8202 | 0.3364 | 0.1420 | 0.0595 | 0.0245 | 0.0097 |
| 7.6 | | | | | | | | 16.0379 | 2.9113 | 1.0310 | 0.4211 | 0.1789 | 0.0761 | 0.0318 | 0.0129 |
| 7.8 | | | | | | | | 35.8956 | 3.8558 | 1.2972 | 0.5250 | 0.2243 | 0.0966 | 0.0410 | 0.0168 |
| 8.0 | | | | | | | | | 5.2264 | 1.6364 | 0.6530 | 0.2796 | 0.1214 | 0.0522 | 0.0220 |
| 8.2 | | | | | | | | | 7.3441 | 2.0736 | 0.8109 | 0.3469 | 0.1520 | 0.0663 | 0.0283 |
| 8.4 | | | | | | | | | 10.9592 | 2.6470 | 1.0060 | 0.4288 | 0.1891 | 0.0834 | 0.0361 |
| 8.6 | | | | | | | | | 18.3223 | 3.4160 | 1.2484 | 0.5286 | 0.2341 | 0.1043 | 0.0459 |
| 8.8 | | | | | | | | | 40.6824 | 4.4806 | 1.5524 | 0.6501 | 0.2885 | 0.1298 | 0.0577 |
| 9.0 | | | | | | | | | | 6.0183 | 1.9368 | 0.7980 | 0.3543 | 0.1603 | 0.0723 |
| 9.2 | | | | | | | | | | 8.3869 | 2.4298 | 0.9788 | 0.4333 | 0.1974 | 0.0899 |
| 9.4 | | | | | | | | | | 12.4189 | 3.0732 | 1.2010 | 0.5287 | 0.2419 | 0.1111 |
| 9.6 | | | | | | | | | | 20.6160 | 3.9318 | 1.4752 | 0.6437 | 0.2952 | 0.1367 |
| 9.8 | | | | | | | | | | 45.4769 | 5.1156 | 1.8165 | 0.7827 | 0.3588 | 0.1673 |
| 10.0 | | | | | | | | | | | 6.8210 | 2.2465 | 0.9506 | 0.4352 | 0.2040 |

**TABLE 3**
***(Continued)***

| r | 1 | 2 | 3 | 4 | 5 | 6 | 7 | 8 | 9 | 10 | 11 | 12 | 13 | 14 | 15 |
|---|---|---|---|---|---|---|---|---|---|---|---|---|---|---|---|
| | Number of Service Channels M | | | | | | | | | | | | | | |
| 0.10 | 0.0111 | | | | | | | | | | | | | | |
| 0.15 | 0.0264 | 0.0008 | | | | | | | | | | | | | |
| 0.20 | 0.0500 | 0.0020 | | | | | | | | | | | | | |
| 0.25 | 0.0833 | 0.0039 | | | | | | | | | | | | | |
| 0.30 | 0.1285 | 0.0069 | | | | | | | | | | | | | |
| 0.35 | 0.1884 | 0.0110 | | | | | | | | | | | | | |
| 0.40 | 0.2666 | 0.0166 | | | | | | | | | | | | | |
| 0.45 | 0.3681 | 0.0239 | 0.0019 | | | | | | | | | | | | |
| 0.50 | 0.5000 | 0.0333 | 0.0030 | | | | | | | | | | | | |
| 0.55 | 0.6722 | 0.0449 | 0.0043 | | | | | | | | | | | | |
| 0.60 | 0.9000 | 0.0593 | 0.0061 | | | | | | | | | | | | |
| 0.65 | 1.2071 | 0.0767 | 0.0084 | | | | | | | | | | | | |
| 0.70 | 1.6333 | 0.0976 | 0.0112 | | | | | | | | | | | | |
| 0.75 | 2.2500 | 0.1227 | 0.0147 | | | | | | | | | | | | |
| 0.80 | 3.2000 | 0.1523 | 0.0189 | | | | | | | | | | | | |
| 0.85 | 4.8166 | 0.1873 | 0.0239 | 0.0031 | | | | | | | | | | | |
| 0.90 | 8.1000 | 0.2285 | 0.0300 | 0.0041 | | | | | | | | | | | |
| 0.95 | 18.0500 | 0.2767 | 0.0371 | 0.0053 | | | | | | | | | | | |
| 1.0 | | 0.3333 | 0.0454 | 0.0067 | | | | | | | | | | | |
| 1.2 | | 0.6748 | 0.0904 | 0.0158 | | | | | | | | | | | |
| 1.4 | | 1.3449 | 0.1778 | 0.0324 | 0.0059 | | | | | | | | | | |
| 1.6 | | 2.8444 | 0.3128 | 0.0604 | 0.0121 | | | | | | | | | | |
| 1.8 | | 7.6734 | 0.5320 | 0.1051 | 0.0227 | 0.0047 | | | | | | | | | |
| 2.0 | | | 0.8888 | 0.1739 | 0.0398 | 0.0090 | | | | | | | | | |
| 2.2 | | | 1.4907 | 0.2770 | 0.0659 | 0.0158 | | | | | | | | | |
| 2.4 | | | 2.1261 | 0.4305 | 0.1047 | 0.0266 | 0.0065 | | | | | | | | |
| 2.6 | | | 4.9322 | 0.6581 | 0.1609 | 0.0426 | 0.0110 | | | | | | | | |
| 2.8 | | | 12.2724 | 1.0000 | 0.2411 | 0.0659 | 0.0180 | | | | | | | | |
| 3.0 | | | | 1.5282 | 0.3541 | 0.0991 | 0.0282 | 0.0077 | | | | | | | |
| 3.2 | | | | 2.3856 | 0.5128 | 0.1452 | 0.0427 | 0.0122 | | | | | | | |
| 3.4 | | | | 3.9060 | 0.7365 | 0.2085 | 0.0631 | 0.0189 | | | | | | | |
| 3.6 | | | | 7.0893 | 1.0550 | 0.2947 | 0.0912 | 0.0283 | 0.0084 | | | | | | |
| 3.8 | | | | 16.9366 | 1.5184 | 0.4114 | 0.1292 | 0.0412 | 0.0127 | | | | | | |

TABLE 4
## FINITE QUEUING TABLES

POPULATION 5

| $X$ | $M$ | $D$ | $F$ | $L_q$ |
|---|---|---|---|---|
| 0.012 | 1 | 0.048 | 0.999 | 0.005 |
| 0.019 | 1 | 0.076 | 0.998 | 0.010 |
| 0.025 | 1 | 0.100 | 0.997 | 0.015 |
| 0.030 | 1 | 0.120 | 0.996 | 0.020 |
| 0.034 | 1 | 0.135 | 0.995 | 0.025 |
| 0.036 | 1 | 0.143 | 0.994 | 0.030 |
| 0.040 | 1 | 0.159 | 0.993 | 0.035 |
| 0.042 | 1 | 0.167 | 0.992 | 0.045 |
| 0.044 | 1 | 0.175 | 0.991 | 0.045 |
| 0.046 | 1 | 0.183 | 0.990 | 0.050 |
| 0.050 | 1 | 0.198 | 0.989 | 0.055 |
| 0.052 | 1 | 0.206 | 0.988 | 0.060 |
| 0.054 | 1 | 0.214 | 0.987 | 0.065 |
| 0.056 | 2 | 0.018 | 0.999 | 0.005 |
| | 1 | 0.222 | 0.985 | 0.075 |
| 0.058 | 2 | 0.019 | 0.999 | 0.005 |
| | 1 | 0.229 | 0.984 | 0.080 |
| 0.060 | 2 | 0.020 | 0.999 | 0.005 |
| | 1 | 0.237 | 0.983 | 0.085 |
| 0.062 | 2 | 0.022 | 0.999 | 0.005 |
| | 1 | 0.245 | 0.982 | 0.090 |
| 0.064 | 2 | 0.023 | 0.999 | 0.005 |
| | 1 | 0.253 | 0.981 | 0.095 |
| 0.066 | 2 | 0.024 | 0.999 | 0.005 |
| | 1 | 0.260 | 0.979 | 0.105 |
| 0.068 | 2 | 0.026 | 0.999 | 0.005 |
| | 1 | 0.268 | 0.978 | 0.110 |
| 0.070 | 2 | 0.027 | 0.999 | 0.005 |
| | 1 | 0.275 | 0.977 | 0.115 |
| 0.075 | 2 | 0.031 | 0.999 | 0.005 |
| | 1 | 0.294 | 0.973 | 0.135 |
| 0.080 | 2 | 0.035 | 0.998 | 0.010 |
| | 1 | 0.313 | 0.969 | 0.155 |
| 0.085 | 2 | 0.040 | 0.998 | 0.010 |
| | 1 | 0.332 | 0.965 | 0.175 |
| 0.090 | 2 | 0.044 | 0.998 | 0.010 |
| | 1 | 0.350 | 0.960 | 0.200 |
| 0.095 | 2 | 0.049 | 0.997 | 0.015 |
| | 1 | 0.368 | 0.955 | 0.255 |
| 0.100 | 2 | 0.054 | 0.997 | 0.015 |
| | 1 | 0.386 | 0.950 | 0.250 |
| 0.105 | 2 | 0.059 | 0.997 | 0.015 |
| | 1 | 0.404 | 0.945 | 0.275 |
| 0.110 | 2 | 0.065 | 0.996 | 0.020 |
| | 1 | 0.421 | 0.939 | 0.305 |
| 0.115 | 2 | 0.071 | 0.995 | 0.025 |
| | 1 | 0.439 | 0.933 | 0.335 |
| 0.120 | 2 | 0.076 | 0.995 | 0.025 |
| | 1 | 0.456 | 0.927 | 0.365 |
| 0.125 | 2 | 0.082 | 0.994 | 0.030 |
| | 1 | 0.473 | 0.920 | 0.400 |
| 0.130 | 2 | 0.089 | 0.993 | 0.035 |
| | 1 | 0.489 | 0.914 | 0.430 |
| 0.135 | 2 | 0.095 | 0.993 | 0.035 |
| | 1 | 0.505 | 0.907 | 0.465 |
| 0.140 | 2 | 0.102 | 0.992 | 0.040 |
| | 1 | 0.521 | 0.900 | 0.500 |
| 0.145 | 3 | 0.011 | 0.999 | 0.005 |
| | 2 | 0.109 | 0.991 | 0.045 |
| | 1 | 0.537 | 0.892 | 0.540 |
| 0.150 | 3 | 0.012 | 0.999 | 0.005 |
| | 2 | 0.115 | 0.990 | 0.050 |
| | 1 | 0.553 | 0.885 | 0.575 |
| 0.155 | 3 | 0.013 | 0.999 | 0.005 |
| | 2 | 0.123 | 0.989 | 0.055 |
| | 1 | 0.568 | 0.877 | 0.615 |
| 0.160 | 3 | 0.015 | 0.999 | 0.005 |
| | 2 | 0.130 | 0.988 | 0.060 |
| | 1 | 0.582 | 0.869 | 0.655 |
| 0.165 | 3 | 0.016 | 0.999 | 0.005 |
| | 2 | 0.137 | 0.987 | 0.065 |
| | 1 | 0.597 | 0.861 | 0.695 |
| 0.170 | 3 | 0.017 | 0.999 | 0.005 |
| | 2 | 0.145 | 0.985 | 0.075 |
| | 1 | 0.611 | 0.853 | 0.735 |
| 0.180 | 3 | 0.021 | 0.999 | 0.005 |
| | 2 | 0.161 | 0.983 | 0.085 |
| | 1 | 0.638 | 0.836 | 0.820 |
| 0.190 | 3 | 0.024 | 0.998 | 0.010 |
| | 2 | 0.177 | 0.980 | 0.100 |
| | 1 | 0.665 | 0.819 | 0.905 |
| 0.200 | 3 | 0.028 | 0.998 | 0.010 |
| | 2 | 0.194 | 0.976 | 0.120 |
| | 1 | 0.689 | 0.801 | 0.995 |
| 0.210 | 3 | 0.032 | 0.998 | 0.010 |
| | 2 | 0.211 | 0.973 | 0.135 |
| | 1 | 0.713 | 0.783 | 1.085 |
| 0.220 | 3 | 0.036 | 0.997 | 0.015 |
| | 2 | 0.229 | 0.969 | 0.155 |
| | 1 | 0.735 | 0.765 | 1.175 |
| 0.230 | 3 | 0.041 | 0.997 | 0.015 |
| | 2 | 0.247 | 0.965 | 0.175 |
| | 1 | 0.756 | 0.747 | 1.265 |
| 0.240 | 3 | 0.046 | 0.996 | 0.020 |
| | 2 | 0.265 | 0.960 | 0.200 |
| | 1 | 0.775 | 0.730 | 1.350 |
| 0.250 | 3 | 0.052 | 0.995 | 0.025 |
| | 2 | 0.284 | 0.955 | 0.225 |
| | 1 | 0.794 | 0.712 | 1.440 |
| 0.260 | 3 | 0.058 | 0.994 | 0.030 |
| | 2 | 0.303 | 0.950 | 0.250 |
| | 1 | 0.811 | 0.695 | 1.525 |
| 0.270 | 3 | 0.064 | 0.994 | 0.030 |
| | 2 | 0.323 | 0.944 | 0.280 |
| | 1 | 0.827 | 0.677 | 1.615 |
| 0.280 | 3 | 0.071 | 0.993 | 0.035 |
| | 2 | 0.342 | 0.938 | 0.310 |
| | 1 | 0.842 | 0.661 | 1.695 |
| 0.290 | 4 | 0.007 | 0.999 | 0.005 |
| | 3 | 0.079 | 0.992 | 0.040 |
| | 2 | 0.362 | 0.932 | 0.340 |
| | 1 | 0.856 | 0.644 | 1.780 |
| 0.300 | 4 | 0.008 | 0.999 | 0.005 |
| | 3 | 0.086 | 0.990 | 0.050 |
| | 2 | 0.382 | 0.926 | 0.370 |
| | 1 | 0.869 | 0.628 | 1.860 |
| 0.310 | 4 | 0.009 | 0.999 | 0.005 |
| | 3 | 0.094 | 0.989 | 0.055 |
| | 2 | 0.402 | 0.919 | 0.405 |
| | 1 | 0.881 | 0.613 | 1.935 |
| 0.320 | 4 | 0.010 | 0.999 | 0.005 |
| | 3 | 0.103 | 0.988 | 0.060 |
| | 2 | 0.422 | 0.912 | 0.440 |
| | 1 | 0.892 | 0.597 | 2.015 |
| 0.330 | 4 | 0.012 | 0.999 | 0.005 |
| | 3 | 0.112 | 0.986 | 0.070 |
| | 2 | 0.442 | 0.904 | 0.480 |
| | 1 | 0.902 | 0.583 | 2.085 |
| 0.340 | 4 | 0.013 | 0.999 | 0.005 |
| | 3 | 0.121 | 0.985 | 0.075 |
| | 2 | 0.462 | 0.896 | 0.520 |
| | 1 | 0.911 | 0.569 | 2.155 |
| 0.360 | 4 | 0.017 | 0.998 | 0.010 |
| | 3 | 0.141 | 0.981 | 0.060 |
| | 2 | 0.501 | 0.880 | 0.600 |
| | 1 | 0.927 | 0.542 | 2.290 |
| 0.380 | 4 | 0.021 | 0.998 | 0.010 |
| | 3 | 0.163 | 0.976 | 0.120 |
| | 2 | 0.540 | 0.863 | 0.685 |
| | 1 | 0.941 | 0.516 | 2.420 |
| 0.400 | 4 | 0.026 | 0.997 | 0.015 |
| | 3 | 0.186 | 0.972 | 0.140 |
| | 2 | 0.579 | 0.845 | 0.775 |
| | 1 | 0.952 | 0.493 | 2.535 |
| 0.420 | 4 | 0.031 | 0.997 | 0.015 |
| | 3 | 0.211 | 0.966 | 0.170 |
| | 2 | 0.616 | 0.826 | 0.870 |
| | 1 | 0.961 | 0.471 | 2.645 |
| 0.440 | 4 | 0.037 | 0.996 | 0.020 |
| | 3 | 0.238 | 0.960 | 0.200 |
| | 2 | 0.652 | 0.807 | 0.965 |
| | 1 | 0.969 | 0.451 | 2.745 |
| 0.460 | 4 | 0.045 | 0.995 | 0.025 |
| | 3 | 0.266 | 0.953 | 0.235 |
| | 2 | 0.686 | 0.787 | 1.065 |
| | 1 | 0.975 | 0.432 | 2.840 |
| 0.480 | 4 | 0.053 | 0.994 | 0.030 |
| | 3 | 0.296 | 0.945 | 0.275 |
| | 2 | 0.719 | 0.767 | 1.165 |
| | 1 | 0.980 | 0.415 | 2.925 |
| 0.500 | 4 | 0.063 | 0.992 | 0.040 |
| | 3 | 0.327 | 0.936 | 0.320 |
| | 2 | 0.750 | 0.748 | 1.260 |
| | 1 | 0.985 | 0.399 | 3.005 |
| 0.520 | 4 | 0.073 | 0.991 | 0.045 |
| | 3 | 0.359 | 0.927 | 0.365 |
| | 2 | 0.779 | 0.728 | 1.360 |
| | 1 | 0.988 | 0.384 | 3.080 |

TABLE 4
***(Continued)***

| $X$ | $M$ | $D$ | $F$ | $L_q$ |
|---|---|---|---|---|
| POPULATION 5, Cont. | | | | |
| 0.540 | 4 | 0.085 | 0.989 | 0.055 |
| | 3 | 0.392 | 0.917 | 0.415 |
| | 2 | 0.806 | 0.708 | 1.460 |
| | 1 | 0.991 | 0.370 | 3.150 |
| 0.560 | 4 | 0.098 | 0.986 | 0.070 |
| | 3 | 0.426 | 0.906 | 0.470 |
| | 2 | 0.831 | 0.689 | 1.555 |
| | 1 | 0.993 | 0.357 | 3.215 |
| 0.580 | 4 | 0.113 | 0.984 | 0.080 |
| | 3 | 0.461 | 0.895 | 0.525 |
| | 2 | 0.854 | 0.670 | 1.650 |
| | 1 | 0.994 | 0.345 | 3.275 |
| 0.600 | 4 | 0.130 | 0.981 | 0.095 |
| | 3 | 0.497 | 0.883 | 0.585 |
| | 2 | 0.875 | 0.652 | 1.740 |
| | 1 | 0.996 | 0.333 | 3.335 |
| 0.650 | 4 | 0.179 | 0.972 | 0.140 |
| | 3 | 0.588 | 0.850 | 0.750 |
| | 2 | 0.918 | 0.608 | 1.960 |
| | 1 | 0.998 | 0.308 | 3.460 |
| 0.700 | 4 | 0.240 | 0.960 | 0.200 |
| | 3 | 0.678 | 0.815 | 0.925 |
| | 2 | 0.950 | 0.568 | 2.160 |
| | 1 | 0.999 | 0.286 | 3.570 |
| 0.750 | 4 | 0.316 | 0.944 | 0.280 |
| | 3 | 0.763 | 0.777 | 1.115 |
| | 2 | 0.972 | 0.532 | 2.340 |
| 0.800 | 4 | 0.410 | 0.924 | 0.380 |
| | 3 | 0.841 | 0.739 | 1.305 |
| | 2 | 0.987 | 0.500 | 2.500 |
| 0.850 | 4 | 0.522 | 0.900 | 0.500 |
| | 3 | 0.907 | 0.702 | 1.490 |
| | 2 | 0.995 | 0.470 | 2.650 |
| 0.900 | 4 | 0.656 | 0.871 | 0.645 |
| | 3 | 0.957 | 0.666 | 1.670 |
| | 2 | 0.998 | 0.444 | 2.780 |
| 0.950 | 4 | 0.815 | 0.838 | 0.810 |
| | 3 | 0.989 | 0.631 | 1.845 |
| POPULATION 10 | | | | |
| 0.016 | 1 | 0.144 | 0.997 | 0.03 |
| 0.019 | 1 | 0.170 | 0.996 | 0.04 |
| 0.021 | 1 | 0.188 | 0.995 | 0.05 |
| 0.023 | 1 | 0.206 | 0.994 | 0.06 |
| 0.025 | 1 | 0.224 | 0.993 | 0.07 |
| 0.026 | 1 | 0.232 | 0.992 | 0.08 |
| 0.028 | 1 | 0.250 | 0.991 | 0.09 |
| 0.030 | 1 | 0.268 | 0.990 | 0.10 |
| 0.032 | 2 | 0.033 | 0.999 | 0.01 |
| | 1 | 0.285 | 0.988 | 0.12 |
| 0.034 | 2 | 0.037 | 0.999 | 0.01 |
| | 1 | 0.302 | 0.986 | 0.14 |
| 0.036 | 2 | 0.041 | 0.999 | 0.01 |
| | 1 | 0.320 | 0.984 | 0.16 |
| 0.038 | 2 | 0.046 | 0.999 | 0.01 |
| | 1 | 0.337 | 0.982 | 0.18 |
| 0.040 | 2 | 0.050 | 0.999 | 0.01 |
| | 1 | 0.354 | 0.980 | 0.20 |
| 0.042 | 2 | 0.055 | 0.999 | 0.01 |
| | 1 | 0.371 | 0.978 | 0.22 |
| 0.044 | 2 | 0.060 | 0.998 | 0.02 |
| | 1 | 0.388 | 0.975 | 0.25 |
| 0.046 | 2 | 0.065 | 0.998 | 0.02 |
| | 1 | 0.404 | 0.973 | 0.27 |
| 0.048 | 2 | 0.071 | 0.998 | 0.02 |
| | 1 | 0.421 | 0.970 | 0.30 |
| 0.050 | 2 | 0.076 | 0.998 | 0.02 |
| | 1 | 0.437 | 0.967 | 0.33 |
| 0.052 | 2 | 0.082 | 0.997 | 0.03 |
| | 1 | 0.454 | 0.963 | 0.37 |
| 0.054 | 2 | 0.088 | 0.997 | 0.03 |
| | 1 | 0.470 | 0.960 | 0.40 |
| 0.056 | 2 | 0.094 | 0.997 | 0.03 |
| | 1 | 0.486 | 0.956 | 0.44 |
| 0.058 | 2 | 0.100 | 0.996 | 0.04 |
| | 1 | 0.501 | 0.953 | 0.47 |
| 0.060 | 2 | 0.106 | 0.996 | 0.04 |
| | 1 | 0.517 | 0.949 | 0.51 |
| 0.062 | 2 | 0.113 | 0.996 | 0.04 |
| | 1 | 0.532 | 0.945 | 0.55 |
| 0.064 | 2 | 0.119 | 0.995 | 0.05 |
| | 1 | 0.547 | 0.940 | 0.60 |
| 0.066 | 2 | 0.126 | 0.995 | 0.05 |
| | 1 | 0.562 | 0.936 | 0.64 |
| 0.068 | 3 | 0.020 | 0.999 | 0.01 |
| | 2 | 0.133 | 0.994 | 0.06 |
| | 1 | 0.577 | 0.931 | 0.69 |
| 0.070 | 3 | 0.022 | 0.999 | 0.01 |
| | 2 | 0.140 | 0.994 | 0.06 |
| | 1 | 0.591 | 0.926 | 0.74 |
| 0.075 | 3 | 0.026 | 0.999 | 0.01 |
| | 2 | 0.158 | 0.992 | 0.08 |
| | 1 | 0.627 | 0.913 | 0.87 |
| 0.080 | 3 | 0.031 | 0.999 | 0.01 |
| | 2 | 0.177 | 0.990 | 0.10 |
| | 1 | 0.660 | 0.899 | 1.01 |
| 0.085 | 3 | 0.037 | 0.999 | 0.01 |
| | 2 | 0.196 | 0.988 | 0.12 |
| | 1 | 0.692 | 0.883 | 1.17 |
| 0.090 | 3 | 0.043 | 0.998 | 0.02 |
| | 2 | 0.216 | 0.986 | 0.14 |
| | 1 | 0.722 | 0.867 | 1.33 |
| 0.095 | 3 | 0.049 | 0.998 | 0.02 |
| | 2 | 0.237 | 0.984 | 0.16 |
| | 1 | 0.750 | 0.850 | 1.50 |
| 0.100 | 3 | 0.056 | 0.998 | 0.02 |
| | 2 | 0.258 | 0.981 | 0.19 |
| | 1 | 0.776 | 0.832 | 1.68 |
| 0.105 | 3 | 0.064 | 0.997 | 0.03 |
| | 2 | 0.279 | 0.978 | 0.22 |
| | 1 | 0.800 | 0.814 | 1.86 |
| 0.110 | 3 | 0.072 | 0.997 | 0.03 |
| | 2 | 0.301 | 0.974 | 0.26 |
| | 1 | 0.822 | 0.795 | 2.05 |
| 0.115 | 3 | 0.081 | 0.996 | 0.04 |
| | 2 | 0.324 | 0.971 | 0.29 |
| | 1 | 0.843 | 0.776 | 2.24 |
| 0.120 | 4 | 0.016 | 0.999 | 0.01 |
| | 3 | 0.090 | 0.995 | 0.05 |
| | 2 | 0.346 | 0.967 | 0.33 |
| | 1 | 0.861 | 0.756 | 2.44 |
| 0.125 | 4 | 0.019 | 0.999 | 0.01 |
| | 3 | 0.100 | 0.994 | 0.06 |
| | 2 | 0.369 | 0.962 | 0.38 |
| | 1 | 0.878 | 0.737 | 2.63 |
| 0.130 | 4 | 0.022 | 0.999 | 0.01 |
| | 3 | 0.110 | 0.994 | 0.06 |
| | 2 | 0.392 | 0.958 | 0.42 |
| | 1 | 0.893 | 0.718 | 2.82 |
| 0.135 | 4 | 0.025 | 0.999 | 0.01 |
| | 3 | 0.121 | 0.993 | 0.07 |
| | 2 | 0.415 | 0.952 | 0.48 |
| | 1 | 0.907 | 0.699 | 3.01 |
| 0.140 | 4 | 0.028 | 0.999 | 0.01 |
| | 3 | 0.132 | 0.991 | 0.09 |
| | 2 | 0.437 | 0.947 | 0.53 |
| | 1 | 0.919 | 0.680 | 3.20 |
| 0.145 | 4 | 0.032 | 0.999 | 0.01 |
| | 3 | 0.144 | 0.990 | 0.10 |
| | 2 | 0.460 | 0.941 | 0.59 |
| | 1 | 0.929 | 0.662 | 3.38 |
| 0.150 | 4 | 0.036 | 0.998 | 0.02 |
| | 3 | 0.156 | 0.989 | 0.11 |
| | 2 | 0.483 | 0.935 | 0.65 |
| | 1 | 0.939 | 0.644 | 3.56 |
| 0.155 | 4 | 0.040 | 0.998 | 0.02 |
| | 3 | 0.169 | 0.987 | 0.13 |
| | 2 | 0.505 | 0.928 | 0.72 |
| | 1 | 0.947 | 0.627 | 3.73 |
| 0.160 | 4 | 0.044 | 0.998 | 0.02 |
| | 3 | 0.182 | 0.986 | 0.14 |
| | 2 | 0.528 | 0.921 | 0.79 |
| | 1 | 0.954 | 0.610 | 3.90 |
| 0.165 | 4 | 0.049 | 0.997 | 0.03 |
| | 3 | 0.195 | 0.984 | 0.16 |
| | 2 | 0.550 | 0.914 | 0.86 |
| | 1 | 0.961 | 0.594 | 4.06 |
| 0.170 | 4 | 0.054 | 0.997 | 0.03 |
| | 3 | 0.209 | 0.982 | 0.18 |
| | 2 | 0.571 | 0.906 | 0.94 |
| | 1 | 0.966 | 0.579 | 4.21 |
| 0.180 | 5 | 0.013 | 0.999 | 0.01 |
| | 4 | 0.066 | 0.996 | 0.04 |
| | 3 | 0.238 | 0.978 | 0.22 |
| | 2 | 0.614 | 0.890 | 1.10 |
| | 1 | 0.975 | 0.549 | 4.51 |
| 0.190 | 5 | 0.016 | 0.999 | 0.01 |
| | 4 | 0.078 | 0.995 | 0.05 |
| | 3 | 0.269 | 0.973 | 0.27 |

**TABLE 4**
***(Continued)***

| X | M | D | F | $L_q$ |
|---|---|---|---|---|
| POPULATION 10, Cont. | | | | |
| | 2 | 0.654 | 0.873 | 1.27 |
| | 1 | 0.982 | 0.522 | 4.78 |
| 0.200 | 5 | 0.020 | 0.999 | 0.01 |
| | 4 | 0.092 | 0.994 | 0.06 |
| | 3 | 0.300 | 0.968 | 0.32 |
| | 2 | 0.692 | 0.854 | 1.46 |
| | 1 | 0.987 | 0.497 | 5.03 |
| 0.210 | 5 | 0.025 | 0.999 | 0.01 |
| | 4 | 0.108 | 0.992 | 0.08 |
| | 3 | 0.333 | 0.961 | 0.39 |
| | 2 | 0.728 | 0.835 | 1.65 |
| | 1 | 0.990 | 0.474 | 5.26 |
| 0.220 | 5 | 0.030 | 0.998 | 0.02 |
| | 4 | 0.124 | 0.990 | 0.10 |
| | 3 | 0.366 | 0.954 | 0.46 |
| | 2 | 0.761 | 0.815 | 1.85 |
| | 1 | 0.993 | 0.453 | 5.47 |
| 0.230 | 5 | 0.037 | 0.998 | 0.02 |
| | 4 | 0.142 | 0.988 | 0.12 |
| | 3 | 0.400 | 0.947 | 0.53 |
| | 2 | 0.791 | 0.794 | 2.06 |
| | 1 | 0.995 | 0.434 | 5.66 |
| 0.240 | 5 | 0.044 | 0.997 | 0.03 |
| | 4 | 0.162 | 0.986 | 0.14 |
| | 3 | 0.434 | 0.938 | 0.62 |
| | 2 | 0.819 | 0.774 | 2.26 |
| | 1 | 0.996 | 0.416 | 5.84 |
| 0.250 | 6 | 0.010 | 0.999 | 0.01 |
| | 5 | 0.052 | 0.997 | 0.03 |
| | 4 | 0.183 | 0.983 | 0.17 |
| | 3 | 0.469 | 0.929 | 0.71 |
| | 2 | 0.844 | 0.753 | 2.47 |
| | 1 | 0.997 | 0.400 | 6.00 |
| 0.260 | 6 | 0.013 | 0.999 | 0.01 |
| | 5 | 0.060 | 0.996 | 0.04 |
| | 4 | 0.205 | 0.980 | 0.20 |
| | 3 | 0.503 | 0.919 | 0.81 |
| | 2 | 0.866 | 0.732 | 2.68 |
| | 1 | 0.998 | 0.384 | 6.16 |
| 0.270 | 6 | 0.015 | 0.999 | 0.01 |
| | 5 | 0.070 | 0.995 | 0.05 |
| | 4 | 0.228 | 0.976 | 0.24 |
| | 3 | 0.537 | 0.908 | 0.92 |
| | 2 | 0.886 | 0.712 | 2.88 |
| | 1 | 0.999 | 0.370 | 6.30 |
| 0.280 | 6 | 0.018 | 0.999 | 0.01 |
| | 5 | 0.081 | 0.994 | 0.06 |
| | 4 | 0.252 | 0.972 | 0.28 |
| | 3 | 0.571 | 0.896 | 1.04 |
| | 2 | 0.903 | 0.692 | 3.08 |
| | 1 | 0.999 | 0.357 | 6.43 |
| 0.290 | 6 | 0.022 | 0.999 | 0.01 |
| | 5 | 0.093 | 0.993 | 0.07 |
| | 4 | 0.278 | 0.968 | 0.32 |
| | 3 | 0.603 | 0.884 | 1.16 |
| | 2 | 0.918 | 0.672 | 3.28 |
| | 1 | 0.999 | 0.345 | 6.55 |
| 0.300 | 6 | 0.026 | 0.998 | 0.02 |
| | 5 | 0.106 | 0.991 | 0.09 |
| | 4 | 0.304 | 0.963 | 0.37 |
| | 3 | 0.635 | 0.872 | 1.28 |
| | 2 | 0.932 | 0.653 | 3.47 |
| | 1 | 0.999 | 0.333 | 6.67 |
| 0.310 | 6 | 0.031 | 0.998 | 0.02 |
| | 5 | 0.120 | 0.990 | 0.10 |
| | 4 | 0.331 | 0.957 | 0.43 |
| | 3 | 0.666 | 0.858 | 1.42 |
| | 2 | 0.943 | 0.635 | 3.65 |
| 0.320 | 6 | 0.036 | 0.998 | 0.02 |
| | 5 | 0.135 | 0.988 | 0.12 |
| | 4 | 0.359 | 0.952 | 0.48 |
| | 3 | 0.695 | 0.845 | 1.55 |
| | 2 | 0.952 | 0.617 | 3.83 |
| 0.330 | 6 | 0.042 | 0.997 | 0.03 |
| | 5 | 0.151 | 0.986 | 0.14 |
| | 4 | 0.387 | 0.945 | 0.55 |
| | 3 | 0.723 | 0.831 | 1.69 |
| | 2 | 0.961 | 0.600 | 4.00 |
| 0.340 | 7 | 0.010 | 0.999 | 0.01 |
| | 6 | 0.049 | 0.997 | 0.03 |
| | 5 | 0.168 | 0.983 | 0.17 |
| | 4 | 0.416 | 0.938 | 0.62 |
| | 3 | 0.750 | 0.816 | 1.84 |
| | 2 | 0.968 | 0.584 | 4.16 |
| 0.360 | 7 | 0.014 | 0.999 | 0.01 |
| | 6 | 0.064 | 0.995 | 0.05 |
| | 5 | 0.205 | 0.978 | 0.22 |
| | 4 | 0.474 | 0.923 | 0.77 |
| | 3 | 0.798 | 0.787 | 2.13 |
| | 2 | 0.978 | 0.553 | 4.47 |
| 0.380 | 7 | 0.019 | 0.999 | 0.01 |
| | 6 | 0.083 | 0.993 | 0.07 |
| | 5 | 0.247 | 0.971 | 0.29 |
| | 4 | 0.533 | 0.906 | 0.94 |
| | 3 | 0.840 | 0.758 | 2.42 |
| | 2 | 0.986 | 0.525 | 4.75 |
| 0.400 | 7 | 0.026 | 0.998 | 0.02 |
| | 6 | 0.105 | 0.991 | 0.09 |
| | 5 | 0.292 | 0.963 | 0.37 |
| | 4 | 0.591 | 0.887 | 1.13 |
| | 3 | 0.875 | 0.728 | 2.72 |
| | 2 | 0.991 | 0.499 | 5.01 |
| 0.420 | 7 | 0.034 | 0.993 | 0.07 |
| | 6 | 0.130 | 0.987 | 0.13 |
| | 5 | 0.341 | 0.954 | 0.46 |
| | 4 | 0.646 | 0.866 | 1.34 |
| | 3 | 0.905 | 0.700 | 3.00 |
| | 2 | 0.994 | 0.476 | 5.24 |
| 0.440 | 7 | 0.045 | 0.997 | 0.03 |
| | 6 | 0.160 | 0.984 | 0.16 |
| | 5 | 0.392 | 0.943 | 0.57 |
| | 4 | 0.698 | 0.845 | 1.55 |
| | 3 | 0.928 | 0.672 | 3.28 |
| | 2 | 0.996 | 0.454 | 5.46 |
| 0.460 | 8 | 0.011 | 0.999 | 0.01 |
| | 7 | 0.058 | 0.995 | 0.05 |
| | 6 | 0.193 | 0.979 | 0.21 |
| | 5 | 0.445 | 0.930 | 0.70 |
| | 4 | 0.747 | 0.822 | 1.78 |
| | 3 | 0.947 | 0.646 | 3.54 |
| | 2 | 0.998 | 0.435 | 5.65 |
| 0.480 | 8 | 0.015 | 0.999 | 0.01 |
| | 7 | 0.074 | 0.994 | 0.06 |
| | 6 | 0.230 | 0.973 | 0.27 |
| | 5 | 0.499 | 0.916 | 0.84 |
| | 4 | 0.791 | 0.799 | 2.01 |
| | 3 | 0.961 | 0.621 | 3.79 |
| | 2 | 0.998 | 0.417 | 5.83 |
| 0.500 | 8 | 0.020 | 0.999 | 0.01 |
| | 7 | 0.093 | 0.992 | 0.08 |
| | 6 | 0.271 | 0.966 | 0.34 |
| | 5 | 0.553 | 0.901 | 0.99 |
| | 4 | 0.830 | 0.775 | 2.25 |
| | 3 | 0.972 | 0.598 | 4.02 |
| | 2 | 0.999 | 0.400 | 6.00 |
| 0.520 | 8 | 0.026 | 0.998 | 0.02 |
| | 7 | 0.115 | 0.989 | 0.11 |
| | 6 | 0.316 | 0.958 | 0.42 |
| | 5 | 0.606 | 0.884 | 1.16 |
| | 4 | 0.864 | 0.752 | 2.48 |
| | 3 | 0.980 | 0.575 | 4.25 |
| | 2 | 0.999 | 0.385 | 6.15 |
| 0.540 | 8 | 0.034 | 0.997 | 0.03 |
| | 7 | 0.141 | 0.986 | 0.14 |
| | 6 | 0.363 | 0.949 | 0.51 |
| | 5 | 0.658 | 0.867 | 1.33 |
| | 4 | 0.893 | 0.729 | 2.71 |
| | 3 | 0.986 | 0.555 | 4.45 |
| 0.560 | 8 | 0.044 | 0.996 | 0.04 |
| | 7 | 0.171 | 0.982 | 0.18 |
| | 6 | 0.413 | 0.939 | 0.61 |
| | 5 | 0.707 | 0.848 | 1.52 |
| | 4 | 0.917 | 0.706 | 2.94 |
| | 3 | 0.991 | 0.535 | 4.65 |
| 0.580 | 8 | 0.057 | 0.995 | 0.05 |
| | 7 | 0.204 | 0.977 | 0.23 |
| | 6 | 0.465 | 0.927 | 0.73 |
| | 5 | 0.753 | 0.829 | 1.71 |
| | 4 | 0.937 | 0.684 | 3.16 |
| | 3 | 0.994 | 0.517 | 4.83 |
| 0.600 | 9 | 0.010 | 0.999 | 0.01 |
| | 8 | 0.072 | 0.994 | 0.06 |
| | 7 | 0.242 | 0.972 | 0.28 |
| | 6 | 0.518 | 0.915 | 0.85 |
| | 5 | 0.795 | 0.809 | 1.91 |
| | 4 | 0.953 | 0.663 | 3.37 |
| | 3 | 0.996 | 0.500 | 5.00 |
| 0.650 | 9 | 0.021 | 0.999 | 0.01 |
| | 8 | 0.123 | 0.988 | 0.12 |
| | 7 | 0.353 | 0.954 | 0.46 |
| | 6 | 0.651 | 0.878 | 1.22 |

TABLE 4
***(Continued)***

| X | M | D | F | $L_q$ |
|---|---|---|---|---|
| POPULATION 10, Cont. | | | | |
| | 5 | 0.882 | 0.759 | 2.41 |
| | 4 | 0.980 | 0.614 | 3.86 |
| | 3 | 0.999 | 0.461 | 5.39 |
| 0.700 | 9 | 0.040 | 0.997 | 0.03 |
| | 8 | 0.200 | 0.979 | 0.21 |
| | 7 | 0.484 | 0.929 | 0.71 |
| | 6 | 0.772 | 0.836 | 1.64 |
| | 5 | 0.940 | 0.711 | 2.89 |
| | 4 | 0.992 | 0.571 | 4.29 |
| 0.750 | 9 | 0.075 | 0.994 | 0.06 |
| | 8 | 0.307 | 0.965 | 0.35 |
| | 7 | 0.626 | 0.897 | 1.03 |
| | 6 | 0.870 | 0.792 | 2.08 |
| | 5 | 0.975 | 0.666 | 3.34 |
| | 4 | 0.998 | 0.533 | 4.67 |
| 0.800 | 9 | 0.134 | 0.988 | 0.12 |
| | 8 | 0.446 | 0.944 | 0.56 |
| | 7 | 0.763 | 0.859 | 1.41 |
| | 6 | 0.939 | 0.747 | 2.53 |
| | 5 | 0.991 | 0.625 | 3.75 |
| | 4 | 0.999 | 0.500 | 5.00 |
| 0.850 | 9 | 0.232 | 0.979 | 0.21 |
| | 8 | 0.611 | 0.916 | 0.84 |
| | 7 | 0.879 | 0.818 | 1.82 |
| | 6 | 0.978 | 0.705 | 2.95 |
| | 5 | 0.998 | 0.588 | 4.12 |
| 0.900 | 9 | 0.387 | 0.963 | 0.37 |
| | 8 | 0.785 | 0.881 | 1.19 |
| | 7 | 0.957 | 0.777 | 2.23 |
| | 6 | 0.995 | 0.667 | 3.33 |
| 0.950 | 9 | 0.630 | 0.938 | 0.62 |
| | 8 | 0.934 | 0.841 | 1.59 |
| | 7 | 0.994 | 0.737 | 2.63 |
| POPULATION 20 | | | | |
| 0.005 | 1 | 0.095 | 0.999 | 0.02 |
| 0.009 | 1 | 0.171 | 0.998 | 0.04 |
| 0.011 | 1 | 0.208 | 0.997 | 0.06 |
| 0.013 | 1 | 0.246 | 0.996 | 0.08 |
| 0.014 | 1 | 0.265 | 0.995 | 0.10 |
| 0.015 | 1 | 0.283 | 0.994 | 0.12 |
| 0.016 | 1 | 0.302 | 0.993 | 0.14 |
| 0.017 | 1 | 0.321 | 0.992 | 0.16 |
| 0.018 | 2 | 0.048 | 0.999 | 0.02 |
| | 1 | 0.339 | 0.991 | 0.18 |
| 0.019 | 2 | 0.053 | 0.999 | 0.02 |
| | 1 | 0.358 | 0.990 | 0.20 |
| 0.020 | 2 | 0.058 | 0.999 | 0.02 |
| | 1 | 0.376 | 0.989 | 0.22 |
| 0.021 | 2 | 0.064 | 0.999 | 0.02 |
| | 1 | 0.394 | 0.987 | 0.26 |
| 0.022 | 2 | 0.070 | 0.999 | 0.02 |
| | 1 | 0.412 | 0.986 | 0.28 |
| 0.023 | 2 | 0.075 | 0.999 | 0.02 |
| | 1 | 0.431 | 0.984 | 0.32 |
| 0.024 | 2 | 0.082 | 0.999 | 0.02 |
| | 1 | 0.449 | 0.982 | 0.36 |
| 0.025 | 2 | 0.088 | 0.999 | 0.02 |
| | 1 | 0.466 | 0.980 | 0.40 |
| 0.026 | 2 | 0.094 | 0.998 | 0.04 |
| | 1 | 0.484 | 0.978 | 0.44 |
| 0.028 | 2 | 0.108 | 0.998 | 0.04 |
| | 1 | 0.519 | 0.973 | 0.54 |
| 0.030 | 2 | 0.122 | 0.998 | 0.04 |
| | 1 | 0.553 | 0.968 | 0.64 |
| 0.032 | 2 | 0.137 | 0.997 | 0.06 |
| | 1 | 0.587 | 0.962 | 0.76 |
| 0.034 | 2 | 0.152 | 0.996 | 0.08 |
| | 1 | 0.620 | 0.955 | 0.90 |
| 0.036 | 2 | 0.168 | 0.996 | 0.08 |
| | 1 | 0.651 | 0.947 | 1.06 |
| 0.038 | 3 | 0.036 | 0.999 | 0.02 |
| | 2 | 0.185 | 0.995 | 0.10 |
| | 1 | 0.682 | 0.938 | 1.24 |
| 0.040 | 3 | 0.041 | 0.999 | 0.02 |
| | 2 | 0.202 | 0.994 | 0.12 |
| | 1 | 0.712 | 0.929 | 1.42 |
| 0.042 | 3 | 0.047 | 0.999 | 0.02 |
| | 2 | 0.219 | 0.993 | 0.14 |
| | 1 | 0.740 | 0.918 | 1.64 |
| 0.044 | 3 | 0.053 | 0.999 | 0.02 |
| | 2 | 0.237 | 0.992 | 0.16 |
| | 1 | 0.767 | 0.906 | 1.88 |
| 0.046 | 3 | 0.059 | 0.999 | 0.02 |
| | 2 | 0.255 | 0.991 | 0.18 |
| | 1 | 0.792 | 0.894 | 2.12 |
| 0.048 | 3 | 0.066 | 0.999 | 0.02 |
| | 2 | 0.274 | 0.989 | 0.22 |
| | 1 | 0.815 | 0.881 | 2.38 |
| 0.050 | 3 | 0.073 | 0.998 | 0.04 |
| | 2 | 0.293 | 0.988 | 0.24 |
| | 1 | 0.837 | 0.866 | 2.68 |
| 0.052 | 3 | 0.080 | 0.998 | 0.04 |
| | 2 | 0.312 | 0.986 | 0.28 |
| | 1 | 0.858 | 0.851 | 2.98 |
| 0.054 | 3 | 0.088 | 0.998 | 0.04 |
| | 2 | 0.332 | 0.984 | 0.32 |
| | 1 | 0.876 | 0.835 | 3.30 |
| 0.056 | 3 | 0.097 | 0.997 | 0.06 |
| | 2 | 0.352 | 0.982 | 0.36 |
| | 1 | 0.893 | 0.819 | 3.62 |
| 0.058 | 3 | 0.105 | 0.997 | 0.06 |
| | 2 | 0.372 | 0.980 | 0.40 |
| | 1 | 0.908 | 0.802 | 3.96 |
| 0.060 | 4 | 0.026 | 0.999 | 0.02 |
| | 3 | 0.115 | 0.997 | 0.06 |
| | 2 | 0.392 | 0.978 | 0.44 |
| | 1 | 0.922 | 0.785 | 4.30 |
| 0.062 | 4 | 0.029 | 0.999 | 0.02 |
| | 3 | 0.124 | 0.996 | 0.08 |
| | 2 | 0.413 | 0.975 | 0.50 |
| | 1 | 0.934 | 0.768 | 4.64 |
| 0.064 | 4 | 0.032 | 0.999 | 0.02 |
| | 3 | 0.134 | 0.996 | 0.08 |
| | 2 | 0.433 | 0.972 | 0.56 |
| | 1 | 0.944 | 0.751 | 4.98 |
| 0.066 | 4 | 0.036 | 0.999 | 0.02 |
| | 3 | 0.144 | 0.995 | 0.10 |
| | 2 | 0.454 | 0.969 | 0.62 |
| | 1 | 0.953 | 0.733 | 5.34 |
| 0.068 | 4 | 0.039 | 0.999 | 0.02 |
| | 3 | 0.155 | 0.995 | 0.10 |
| | 2 | 0.474 | 0.966 | 0.68 |
| | 1 | 0.961 | 0.716 | 5.68 |
| 0.070 | 4 | 0.043 | 0.999 | 0.02 |
| | 3 | 0.165 | 0.994 | 0.12 |
| | 2 | 0.495 | 0.962 | 0.76 |
| | 1 | 0.967 | 0.699 | 6.02 |
| 0.075 | 4 | 0.054 | 0.999 | 0.02 |
| | 3 | 0.194 | 0.992 | 0.16 |
| | 2 | 0.545 | 0.953 | 0.94 |
| | 1 | 0.980 | 0.659 | 6.82 |
| 0.080 | 4 | 0.066 | 0.998 | 0.04 |
| | 3 | 0.225 | 0.990 | 0.20 |
| | 2 | 0.595 | 0.941 | 1.18 |
| | 1 | 0.988 | 0.621 | 7.58 |
| 0.085 | 4 | 0.080 | 0.997 | 0.06 |
| | 3 | 0.257 | 0.987 | 0.26 |
| | 2 | 0.643 | 0.928 | 1.44 |
| | 1 | 0.993 | 0.586 | 8.28 |
| 0.090 | 5 | 0.025 | 0.999 | 0.02 |
| | 4 | 0.095 | 0.997 | 0.06 |
| | 3 | 0.291 | 0.984 | 0.32 |
| | 2 | 0.689 | 0.913 | 1.74 |
| | 1 | 0.996 | 0.554 | 8.92 |
| 0.095 | 5 | 0.031 | 0.999 | 0.02 |
| | 4 | 0.112 | 0.996 | 0.08 |
| | 3 | 0.326 | 0.980 | 0.40 |
| | 2 | 0.733 | 0.896 | 2.08 |
| | 1 | 0.998 | 0.526 | 9.48 |
| 0.100 | 5 | 0.038 | 0.999 | 0.02 |
| | 4 | 0.131 | 0.995 | 0.10 |
| | 3 | 0.363 | 0.975 | 0.50 |
| | 2 | 0.773 | 0.878 | 2.44 |
| | 1 | 0.999 | 0.500 | 10.00 |
| 0.105 | 5 | 0.046 | 0.999 | 0.02 |
| | 4 | 0.151 | 0.993 | 0.14 |
| | 3 | 0.400 | 0.970 | 0.60 |
| | 2 | 0.809 | 0.858 | 2.84 |
| | 1 | 0.999 | 0.476 | 10.48 |
| 0.110 | 5 | 0.055 | 0.998 | 0.04 |
| | 4 | 0.172 | 0.992 | 0.16 |
| | 3 | 0.438 | 0.964 | 0.72 |
| | 2 | 0.842 | 0.837 | 3.26 |
| 0.115 | 5 | 0.065 | 0.998 | 0.04 |
| | 4 | 0.195 | 0.990 | 0.20 |
| | 3 | 0.476 | 0.958 | 0.84 |
| | 2 | 0.870 | 0.816 | 3.68 |
| 0.120 | 6 | 0.022 | 0.999 | 0.02 |

## TABLE 4
***(Continued)***

| $X$ | $M$ | $D$ | $F$ | $L_q$ |
|---|---|---|---|---|
| POPULATION 20, Cont. | | | | |
| | 5 | 0.076 | 0.997 | 0.06 |
| | 4 | 0.219 | 0.988 | 0.24 |
| | 3 | 0.514 | 0.950 | 1.00 |
| | 2 | 0.895 | 0.793 | 4.14 |
| 0.125 | 6 | 0.026 | 0.999 | 0.02 |
| | 5 | 0.088 | 0.997 | 0.06 |
| | 4 | 0.245 | 0.986 | 0.28 |
| | 3 | 0.552 | 0.942 | 1.16 |
| | 2 | 0.916 | 0.770 | 4.60 |
| 0.130 | 6 | 0.031 | 0.999 | 0.02 |
| | 5 | 0.101 | 0.996 | 0.08 |
| | 4 | 0.271 | 0.983 | 0.34 |
| | 3 | 0.589 | 0.933 | 1.34 |
| | 2 | 0.934 | 0.748 | 5.04 |
| 0.135 | 6 | 0.037 | 0.999 | 0.02 |
| | 5 | 0.116 | 0.995 | 0.10 |
| | 4 | 0.299 | 0.980 | 0.40 |
| | 3 | 0.626 | 0.923 | 1.54 |
| | 2 | 0.948 | 0.725 | 5.50 |
| 0.140 | 6 | 0.043 | 0.998 | 0.04 |
| | 5 | 0.131 | 0.994 | 0.12 |
| | 4 | 0.328 | 0.976 | 0.48 |
| | 3 | 0.661 | 0.912 | 1.76 |
| | 2 | 0.960 | 0.703 | 5.94 |
| 0.145 | 6 | 0.051 | 0.998 | 0.04 |
| | 5 | 0.148 | 0.993 | 0.14 |
| | 4 | 0.358 | 0.972 | 0.56 |
| | 3 | 0.695 | 0.900 | 2.00 |
| | 2 | 0.969 | 0.682 | 6.36 |
| 0.150 | 7 | 0.017 | 0.999 | 0.02 |
| | 6 | 0.059 | 0.998 | 0.04 |
| | 5 | 0.166 | 0.991 | 0.18 |
| | 4 | 0.388 | 0.968 | 0.64 |
| | 3 | 0.728 | 0.887 | 2.26 |
| | 2 | 0.976 | 0.661 | 6.78 |
| 0.155 | 7 | 0.021 | 0.999 | 0.02 |
| | 6 | 0.068 | 0.997 | 0.06 |
| | 5 | 0.185 | 0.990 | 0.20 |
| | 4 | 0.419 | 0.963 | 0.74 |
| | 3 | 0.758 | 0.874 | 2.52 |
| | 2 | 0.982 | 0.641 | 7.18 |
| 0.160 | 7 | 0.024 | 0.999 | 0.02 |
| | 6 | 0.077 | 0.997 | 0.06 |
| | 5 | 0.205 | 0.988 | 0.24 |
| | 4 | 0.450 | 0.957 | 0.86 |
| | 3 | 0.787 | 0.860 | 2.80 |
| | 2 | 0.987 | 0.622 | 7.56 |
| 0.165 | 7 | 0.029 | 0.999 | 0.02 |
| | 6 | 0.088 | 0.996 | 0.08 |
| | 5 | 0.226 | 0.986 | 0.28 |
| | 4 | 0.482 | 0.951 | 0.98 |
| | 3 | 0.813 | 0.845 | 3.10 |
| | 2 | 0.990 | 0.604 | 7.92 |
| 0.170 | 7 | 0.033 | 0.999 | 0.02 |
| | 6 | 0.099 | 0.995 | 0.10 |
| | 5 | 0.248 | 0.983 | 0.34 |
| | 4 | 0.513 | 0.945 | 1.10 |
| | 3 | 0.838 | 0.830 | 3.40 |
| | 2 | 0.993 | 0.587 | 8.26 |
| 0.180 | 7 | 0.044 | 0.998 | 0.04 |
| | 6 | 0.125 | 0.994 | 0.12 |
| | 5 | 0.295 | 0.978 | 0.44 |
| | 4 | 0.575 | 0.930 | 1.40 |
| | 3 | 0.879 | 0.799 | 4.02 |
| | 2 | 0.996 | 0.555 | 8.90 |
| 0.190 | 8 | 0.018 | 0.999 | 0.02 |
| | 7 | 0.058 | 0.998 | 0.04 |
| | 6 | 0.154 | 0.991 | 0.18 |
| | 5 | 0.345 | 0.971 | 0.58 |
| | 4 | 0.636 | 0.914 | 1.72 |
| | 3 | 0.913 | 0.768 | 4.64 |
| | 2 | 0.998 | 0.526 | 9.48 |
| 0.200 | 8 | 0.025 | 0.999 | 0.02 |
| | 7 | 0.074 | 0.997 | 0.06 |
| | 6 | 0.187 | 0.988 | 0.24 |
| | 5 | 0.397 | 0.963 | 0.74 |
| | 4 | 0.693 | 0.895 | 2.10 |
| | 3 | 0.938 | 0.736 | 5.28 |
| | 2 | 0.999 | 0.500 | 10.00 |
| 0.210 | 8 | 0.033 | 0.999 | 0.02 |
| | 7 | 0.093 | 0.995 | 0.10 |
| | 6 | 0.223 | 0.985 | 0.30 |
| | 5 | 0.451 | 0.954 | 0.92 |
| | 4 | 0.745 | 0.874 | 2.52 |
| | 3 | 0.958 | 0.706 | 5.88 |
| | 2 | 0.999 | 0.476 | 10.48 |
| 0.220 | 8 | 0.043 | 0.998 | 0.04 |
| | 7 | 0.115 | 0.994 | 0.12 |
| | 6 | 0.263 | 0.980 | 0.40 |
| | 5 | 0.505 | 0.943 | 1.14 |
| | 4 | 0.793 | 0.852 | 2.96 |
| | 3 | 0.971 | 0.677 | 6.46 |
| 0.230 | 9 | 0.018 | 0.999 | 0.02 |
| | 8 | 0.054 | 0.998 | 0.04 |
| | 7 | 0.140 | 0.992 | 0.16 |
| | 6 | 0.306 | 0.975 | 0.50 |
| | 5 | 0.560 | 0.931 | 1.38 |
| | 4 | 0.834 | 0.828 | 3.44 |
| | 3 | 0.981 | 0.649 | 7.02 |
| 0.240 | 9 | 0.024 | 0.999 | 0.02 |
| | 8 | 0.068 | 0.997 | 0.06 |
| | 7 | 0.168 | 0.989 | 0.22 |
| | 6 | 0.351 | 0.969 | 0.62 |
| | 5 | 0.613 | 0.917 | 1.66 |
| | 4 | 0.870 | 0.804 | 3.92 |
| | 3 | 0.988 | 0.623 | 7.54 |
| 0.250 | 9 | 0.031 | 0.999 | 0.02 |
| | 8 | 0.085 | 0.996 | 0.08 |
| | 7 | 0.199 | 0.986 | 0.28 |
| | 6 | 0.398 | 0.961 | 0.78 |
| | 5 | 0.664 | 0.901 | 1.98 |
| | 4 | 0.900 | 0.780 | 4.40 |
| | 3 | 0.992 | 0.599 | 8.02 |
| 0.260 | 9 | 0.039 | 0.998 | 0.04 |
| | 8 | 0.104 | 0.994 | 0.12 |
| | 7 | 0.233 | 0.983 | 0.34 |
| | 6 | 0.446 | 0.953 | 0.94 |
| | 5 | 0.712 | 0.884 | 2.32 |
| | 4 | 0.924 | 0.755 | 4.90 |
| | 3 | 0.995 | 0.576 | 8.48 |
| 0.270 | 10 | 0.016 | 0.999 | 0.02 |
| | 9 | 0.049 | 0.998 | 0.04 |
| | 8 | 0.125 | 0.992 | 0.16 |
| | 7 | 0.270 | 0.978 | 0.44 |
| | 6 | 0.495 | 0.943 | 1.14 |
| | 5 | 0.757 | 0.867 | 2.66 |
| | 4 | 0.943 | 0.731 | 5.38 |
| | 3 | 0.997 | 0.555 | 8.90 |
| 0.280 | 10 | 0.021 | 0.999 | 0.02 |
| | 9 | 0.061 | 0.997 | 0.06 |
| | 8 | 0.149 | 0.990 | 0.20 |
| | 7 | 0.309 | 0.973 | 0.54 |
| | 6 | 0.544 | 0.932 | 1.36 |
| | 5 | 0.797 | 0.848 | 3.04 |
| | 4 | 0.958 | 0.708 | 5.84 |
| | 3 | 0.998 | 0.536 | 9.28 |
| 0.290 | 10 | 0.027 | 0.999 | 0.02 |
| | 9 | 0.075 | 0.996 | 0.08 |
| | 8 | 0.176 | 0.988 | 0.24 |
| | 7 | 0.351 | 0.967 | 0.66 |
| | 6 | 0.592 | 0.920 | 1.60 |
| | 5 | 0.833 | 0.828 | 3.44 |
| | 4 | 0.970 | 0.685 | 6.30 |
| | 3 | 0.999 | 0.517 | 9.66 |
| 0.300 | 10 | 0.034 | 0.998 | 0.04 |
| | 9 | 0.091 | 0.995 | 0.10 |
| | 8 | 0.205 | 0.985 | 0.30 |
| | 7 | 0.394 | 0.961 | 0.78 |
| | 6 | 0.639 | 0.907 | 1.86 |
| | 5 | 0.865 | 0.808 | 3.84 |
| | 4 | 0.978 | 0.664 | 6.72 |
| | 3 | 0.999 | 0.500 | 10.00 |
| 0.310 | 11 | 0.014 | 0.999 | 0.02 |
| | 10 | 0.043 | 0.998 | 0.04 |
| | 9 | 0.110 | 0.993 | 0.14 |
| | 8 | 0.237 | 0.981 | 0.38 |
| | 7 | 0.438 | 0.953 | 0.94 |
| | 6 | 0.684 | 0.893 | 2.14 |
| | 5 | 0.892 | 0.788 | 4.24 |
| | 4 | 0.985 | 0.643 | 7.14 |
| 0.320 | 11 | 0.018 | 0.999 | 0.02 |
| | 10 | 0.053 | 0.997 | 0.06 |
| | 9 | 0.130 | 0.992 | 0.16 |
| | 8 | 0.272 | 0.977 | 0.46 |
| | 7 | 0.483 | 0.944 | 1.12 |
| | 6 | 0.727 | 0.878 | 2.44 |
| | 5 | 0.915 | 0.768 | 4.64 |
| | 4 | 0.989 | 0.624 | 7.52 |
| 0.330 | 11 | 0.023 | 0.999 | 0.02 |
| | 10 | 0.065 | 0.997 | 0.06 |
| | 9 | 0.154 | 0.990 | 0.20 |

**TABLE 4**
***(Continued)***

| X | M | D | F | $L_q$ |
|---|---|---|---|---|
| POPULATION 20, Cont. | | | | |
| | 8 | 0.309 | 0.973 | 0.54 |
| | 7 | 0.529 | 0.935 | 1.30 |
| | 6 | 0.766 | 0.862 | 2.76 |
| | 5 | 0.933 | 0.748 | 5.04 |
| | 4 | 0.993 | 0.605 | 7.90 |
| 0.340 | 11 | 0.029 | 0.999 | 0.02 |
| | 10 | 0.079 | 0.996 | 0.08 |
| | 9 | 0.179 | 0.987 | 0.26 |
| | 8 | 0.347 | 0.967 | 0.66 |
| | 7 | 0.573 | 0.924 | 1.52 |
| | 6 | 0.802 | 0.846 | 3.08 |
| | 5 | 0.949 | 0.729 | 5.42 |
| | 4 | 0.995 | 0.588 | 8.24 |
| 0.360 | 12 | 0.015 | 0.999 | 0.02 |
| | 11 | 0.045 | 0.998 | 0.04 |
| | 10 | 0.112 | 0.993 | 0.14 |
| | 9 | 0.237 | 0.981 | 0.38 |
| | 8 | 0.429 | 0.954 | 0.92 |
| | 7 | 0.660 | 0.901 | 1.98 |
| | 6 | 0.863 | 0.812 | 3.76 |
| | 5 | 0.971 | 0.691 | 6.18 |
| | 4 | 0.998 | 0.555 | 8.90 |
| 0.380 | 12 | 0.024 | 0.999 | 0.02 |
| | 11 | 0.067 | 0.996 | 0.08 |
| | 10 | 0.154 | 0.989 | 0.22 |
| | 9 | 0.305 | 0.973 | 0.54 |
| | 8 | 0.513 | 0.938 | 1.24 |
| | 7 | 0.739 | 0.874 | 2.52 |
| | 6 | 0.909 | 0.777 | 4.46 |
| | 5 | 0.984 | 0.656 | 6.88 |
| | 4 | 0.999 | 0.526 | 9.48 |
| 0.400 | 13 | 0.012 | 0.999 | 0.02 |
| | 12 | 0.037 | 0.998 | 0.04 |
| | 11 | 0.095 | 0.994 | 0.12 |
| | 10 | 0.205 | 0.984 | 0.32 |
| | 9 | 0.379 | 0.962 | 0.76 |
| | 8 | 0.598 | 0.918 | 1.64 |
| | 7 | 0.807 | 0.845 | 3.10 |
| | 6 | 0.942 | 0.744 | 5.12 |
| | 5 | 0.992 | 0.624 | 7.52 |
| 0.420 | 13 | 0.019 | 0.999 | 0.02 |
| | 12 | 0.055 | 0.997 | 0.06 |
| | 11 | 0.131 | 0.991 | 0.18 |
| | 10 | 0.265 | 0.977 | 0.46 |
| | 9 | 0.458 | 0.949 | 1.02 |
| | 8 | 0.678 | 0.896 | 2.08 |
| | 7 | 0.863 | 0.815 | 3.70 |
| | 6 | 0.965 | 0.711 | 5.78 |
| | 5 | 0.996 | 0.595 | 8.10 |
| 0.440 | 13 | 0.029 | 0.999 | 0.02 |
| | 12 | 0.078 | 0.995 | 0.10 |
| | 11 | 0.175 | 0.987 | 0.26 |
| | 10 | 0.333 | 0.969 | 0.62 |
| | 9 | 0.540 | 0.933 | 1.34 |
| | 8 | 0.751 | 0.872 | 2.56 |
| | 7 | 0.907 | 0.785 | 4.30 |
| | 6 | 0.980 | 0.680 | 6.40 |
| | 5 | 0.998 | 0.568 | 8.64 |
| 0.460 | 14 | 0.014 | 0.999 | 0.02 |
| | 13 | 0.043 | 0.998 | 0.04 |
| | 12 | 0.109 | 0.993 | 0.14 |
| | 11 | 0.228 | 0.982 | 0.36 |
| | 10 | 0.407 | 0.958 | 0.84 |
| | 9 | 0.620 | 0.914 | 1.72 |
| | 8 | 0.815 | 0.846 | 3.08 |
| | 7 | 0.939 | 0.755 | 4.90 |
| | 6 | 0.989 | 0.651 | 6.98 |
| | 5 | 0.999 | 0.543 | 9.14 |
| 0.480 | 14 | 0.022 | 0.999 | 0.02 |
| | 13 | 0.063 | 0.996 | 0.08 |
| | 12 | 0.147 | 0.990 | 0.20 |
| | 11 | 0.289 | 0.974 | 0.52 |
| | 10 | 0.484 | 0.944 | 1.12 |
| | 9 | 0.695 | 0.893 | 2.14 |
| | 8 | 0.867 | 0.819 | 3.62 |
| | 7 | 0.962 | 0.726 | 5.48 |
| | 6 | 0.994 | 0.625 | 7.50 |
| 0.500 | 14 | 0.033 | 0.998 | 0.04 |
| | 13 | 0.088 | 0.995 | 0.10 |
| | 12 | 0.194 | 0.985 | 0.30 |
| | 11 | 0.358 | 0.965 | 0.70 |
| | 10 | 0.563 | 0.929 | 1.42 |
| | 9 | 0.764 | 0.870 | 2.60 |
| | 8 | 0.908 | 0.791 | 4.18 |
| | 7 | 0.977 | 0.698 | 6.04 |
| | 6 | 0.997 | 0.600 | 8.00 |
| 0.520 | 15 | 0.015 | 0.999 | 0.02 |
| | 14 | 0.048 | 0.997 | 0.06 |
| | 13 | 0.120 | 0.992 | 0.16 |
| | 12 | 0.248 | 0.979 | 0.42 |
| | 11 | 0.432 | 0.954 | 0.92 |
| | 10 | 0.641 | 0.911 | 1.78 |
| | 9 | 0.824 | 0.846 | 3.08 |
| | 8 | 0.939 | 0.764 | 4.72 |
| | 7 | 0.987 | 0.672 | 6.56 |
| | 6 | 0.998 | 0.577 | 8.46 |
| 0.540 | 15 | 0.023 | 0.999 | 0.02 |
| | 14 | 0.069 | 0.996 | 0.08 |
| | 13 | 0.120 | 0.992 | 0.16 |
| | 12 | 0.311 | 0.972 | 0.56 |
| | 11 | 0.509 | 0.941 | 1.18 |
| | 10 | 0.713 | 0.891 | 2.18 |
| | 9 | 0.873 | 0.821 | 3.58 |
| | 8 | 0.961 | 0.738 | 5.24 |
| | 7 | 0.993 | 0.648 | 7.04 |
| | 6 | 0.999 | 0.556 | 8.88 |
| 0.560 | 15 | 0.035 | 0.998 | 0.04 |
| | 14 | 0.095 | 0.994 | 0.12 |
| | 13 | 0.209 | 0.984 | 0.32 |
| | 12 | 0.381 | 0.963 | 0.74 |
| | 11 | 0.586 | 0.926 | 1.48 |
| | 10 | 0.778 | 0.869 | 2.62 |
| | 9 | 0.912 | 0.796 | 4.08 |
| | 8 | 0.976 | 0.713 | 5.74 |
| | 7 | 0.996 | 0.625 | 7.50 |
| 0.580 | 16 | 0.015 | 0.999 | 0.02 |
| | 15 | 0.051 | 0.997 | 0.06 |
| | 14 | 0.129 | 0.991 | 0.18 |
| | 13 | 0.266 | 0.978 | 0.44 |
| | 12 | 0.455 | 0.952 | 0.96 |
| | 11 | 0.662 | 0.908 | 1.84 |
| | 10 | 0.835 | 0.847 | 3.06 |
| | 9 | 0.941 | 0.772 | 4.56 |
| | 8 | 0.986 | 0.689 | 6.22 |
| | 7 | 0.998 | 0.603 | 7.94 |
| 0.600 | 16 | 0.023 | 0.999 | 0.02 |
| | 15 | 0.072 | 0.996 | 0.08 |
| | 14 | 0.171 | 0.988 | 0.24 |
| | 13 | 0.331 | 0.970 | 0.60 |
| | 12 | 0.532 | 0.938 | 1.24 |
| | 11 | 0.732 | 0.889 | 2.22 |
| | 10 | 0.882 | 0.824 | 3.52 |
| | 9 | 0.962 | 0.748 | 5.04 |
| | 8 | 0.992 | 0.666 | 6.68 |
| | 7 | 0.999 | 0.583 | 8.34 |
| 0.650 | 17 | 0.017 | 0.999 | 0.02 |
| | 16 | 0.061 | 0.997 | 0.06 |
| | 15 | 0.156 | 0.989 | 0.22 |
| | 14 | 0.314 | 0.973 | 0.54 |
| | 13 | 0.518 | 0.943 | 1.14 |
| | 12 | 0.720 | 0.898 | 2.04 |
| | 11 | 0.872 | 0.837 | 3.26 |
| | 10 | 0.957 | 0.767 | 4.66 |
| | 9 | 0.990 | 0.692 | 6.16 |
| | 8 | 0.998 | 0.615 | 7.70 |
| 0.700 | 17 | 0.047 | 0.998 | 0.04 |
| | 16 | 0.137 | 0.991 | 0.18 |
| | 15 | 0.295 | 0.976 | 0.48 |
| | 14 | 0.503 | 0.948 | 1.04 |
| | 13 | 0.710 | 0.905 | 1.90 |
| | 12 | 0.866 | 0.849 | 3.02 |
| | 11 | 0.953 | 0.783 | 4.34 |
| | 10 | 0.988 | 0.714 | 5.72 |
| | 9 | 0.998 | 0.643 | 7.14 |
| 0.750 | 18 | 0.031 | 0.999 | 0.02 |
| | 17 | 0.113 | 0.993 | 0.14 |
| | 16 | 0.272 | 0.980 | 0.40 |
| | 15 | 0.487 | 0.954 | 0.92 |
| | 14 | 0.703 | 0.913 | 1.74 |
| | 13 | 0.864 | 0.859 | 2.82 |
| | 12 | 0.952 | 0.798 | 4.04 |
| | 11 | 0.988 | 0.733 | 5.34 |
| | 10 | 0.998 | 0.667 | 6.66 |
| 0.800 | 19 | 0.014 | 0.999 | 0.02 |
| | 18 | 0.084 | 0.996 | 0.08 |
| | 17 | 0.242 | 0.984 | 0.32 |
| | 16 | 0.470 | 0.959 | 0.82 |
| | 15 | 0.700 | 0.920 | 1.60 |
| | 14 | 0.867 | 0.869 | 2.62 |
| | 13 | 0.955 | 0.811 | 3.78 |
| | 12 | 0.989 | 0.750 | 5.00 |

TABLE 4
***(Continued)***

| X | M | D | F | $L_q$ |
|---|---|---|---|---|
| **POPULATION 20, Cont.** | | | | |
| | 11 | 0.998 | 0.687 | 6.26 |
| 0.850 | 19 | 0.046 | 0.998 | 0.04 |
| | 18 | 0.201 | 0.988 | 0.24 |
| | 17 | 0.451 | 0.965 | 0.70 |
| | 16 | 0.703 | 0.927 | 1.46 |
| | 15 | 0.877 | 0.878 | 2.44 |
| | 14 | 0.962 | 0.823 | 3.54 |
| | 13 | 0.991 | 0.765 | 4.70 |
| | 12 | 0.998 | 0.706 | 5.88 |
| 0.900 | 19 | 0.135 | 0.994 | 0.12 |
| | 18 | 0.425 | 0.972 | 0.56 |
| | 17 | 0.717 | 0.935 | 1.30 |
| | 16 | 0.898 | 0.886 | 2.28 |
| | 15 | 0.973 | 0.833 | 3.34 |
| | 14 | 0.995 | 0.778 | 4.44 |
| | 13 | 0.999 | 0.722 | 5.56 |
| 0.950 | 19 | 0.377 | 0.981 | 0.38 |
| | 18 | 0.760 | 0.943 | 1.14 |
| | 17 | 0.939 | 0.894 | 2.12 |
| | 16 | 0.989 | 0.842 | 3.16 |
| | 15 | 0.999 | 0.789 | 4.22 |
| **POPULATION 30** | | | | |
| 0.004 | 1 | 0.116 | 0.999 | 0.03 |
| 0.007 | 1 | 0.203 | 0.998 | 0.06 |
| 0.009 | 1 | 0.260 | 0.997 | 0.09 |
| 0.010 | 1 | 0.289 | 0.996 | 0.12 |
| 0.011 | 1 | 0.317 | 0.995 | 0.15 |
| 0.012 | 1 | 0.346 | 0.994 | 0.18 |
| 0.013 | 1 | 0.374 | 0.993 | 0.21 |
| 0.014 | 2 | 0.067 | 0.999 | 0.03 |
| | 1 | 0.403 | 0.991 | 0.27 |
| 0.015 | 2 | 0.076 | 0.999 | 0.03 |
| | 1 | 0.431 | 0.989 | 0.33 |
| 0.016 | 2 | 0.085 | 0.999 | 0.03 |
| | 1 | 0.458 | 0.987 | 0.39 |
| 0.017 | 2 | 0.095 | 0.999 | 0.03 |
| | 1 | 0.486 | 0.985 | 0.45 |
| 0.018 | 2 | 0.105 | 0.999 | 0.03 |
| | 1 | 0.513 | 0.983 | 0.51 |
| 0.019 | 2 | 0.116 | 0.999 | 0.03 |
| | 1 | 0.541 | 0.980 | 0.60 |
| 0.020 | 2 | 0.127 | 0.998 | 0.06 |
| | 1 | 0.567 | 0.976 | 0.72 |
| 0.021 | 2 | 0.139 | 0.998 | 0.06 |
| | 1 | 0.594 | 0.973 | 0.81 |
| 0.022 | 2 | 0.151 | 0.998 | 0.06 |
| | 1 | 0.620 | 0.969 | 0.93 |
| 0.023 | 2 | 0.163 | 0.997 | 0.09 |
| | 1 | 0.645 | 0.965 | 1.05 |
| 0.024 | 2 | 0.175 | 0.997 | 0.09 |
| | 1 | 0.670 | 0.960 | 1.20 |
| 0.025 | 2 | 0.188 | 0.996 | 0.12 |
| | 1 | 0.694 | 0.954 | 1.38 |
| 0.026 | 2 | 0.201 | 0.996 | 0.12 |
| | 1 | 0.718 | 0.948 | 1.56 |
| 0.028 | 3 | 0.051 | 0.999 | 0.03 |
| | 2 | 0.229 | 0.995 | 0.15 |
| | 1 | 0.763 | 0.935 | 1.95 |
| 0.030 | 3 | 0.060 | 0.999 | 0.03 |
| | 2 | 0.257 | 0.994 | 0.18 |
| | 1 | 0.805 | 0.918 | 2.46 |
| 0.032 | 3 | 0.071 | 0.999 | 0.03 |
| | 2 | 0.286 | 0.992 | 0.24 |
| | 1 | 0.843 | 0.899 | 3.03 |
| 0.034 | 3 | 0.083 | 0.999 | 0.03 |
| | 2 | 0.316 | 0.990 | 0.30 |
| | 1 | 0.876 | 0.877 | 3.69 |
| 0.036 | 3 | 0.095 | 0.998 | 0.06 |
| | 2 | 0.347 | 0.988 | 0.36 |
| | 1 | 0.905 | 0.853 | 4.41 |
| 0.038 | 3 | 0.109 | 0.998 | 0.06 |
| | 2 | 0.378 | 0.986 | 0.42 |
| | 1 | 0.929 | 0.827 | 5.19 |
| 0.040 | 3 | 0.123 | 0.997 | 0.09 |
| | 2 | 0.410 | 0.983 | 0.51 |
| | 1 | 0.948 | 0.800 | 6.00 |
| 0.042 | 3 | 0.138 | 0.997 | 0.09 |
| | 2 | 0.442 | 0.980 | 0.60 |
| | 1 | 0.963 | 0.772 | 6.84 |
| 0.044 | 4 | 0.040 | 0.999 | 0.03 |
| | 3 | 0.154 | 0.996 | 0.12 |
| | 2 | 0.474 | 0.977 | 0.69 |
| | 1 | 0.974 | 0.744 | 7.68 |
| 0.046 | 4 | 0.046 | 0.999 | 0.03 |
| | 3 | 0.171 | 0.996 | 0.12 |
| | 2 | 0.506 | 0.972 | 0.84 |
| | 1 | 0.982 | 0.716 | 8.52 |
| 0.048 | 4 | 0.053 | 0.999 | 0.03 |
| | 3 | 0.189 | 0.995 | 0.15 |
| | 2 | 0.539 | 0.968 | 0.96 |
| | 1 | 0.988 | 0.689 | 9.33 |
| 0.050 | 4 | 0.060 | 0.999 | 0.03 |
| | 3 | 0.208 | 0.994 | 0.18 |
| | 2 | 0.571 | 0.963 | 1.11 |
| | 1 | 0.992 | 0.663 | 10.11 |
| 0.052 | 4 | 0.068 | 0.999 | 0.03 |
| | 3 | 0.227 | 0.993 | 0.21 |
| | 2 | 0.603 | 0.957 | 1.29 |
| | 1 | 0.995 | 0.639 | 10.83 |
| 0.054 | 4 | 0.077 | 0.998 | 0.06 |
| | 3 | 0.247 | 0.992 | 0.24 |
| | 2 | 0.634 | 0.951 | 1.47 |
| | 1 | 0.997 | 0.616 | 11.52 |
| 0.056 | 4 | 0.086 | 0.998 | 0.06 |
| | 3 | 0.267 | 0.991 | 0.27 |
| | 2 | 0.665 | 0.944 | 1.68 |
| | 1 | 0.998 | 0.595 | 12.15 |
| 0.058 | 4 | 0.096 | 0.998 | 0.06 |
| | 3 | 0.288 | 0.989 | 0.33 |
| | 2 | 0.695 | 0.936 | 1.92 |
| | 1 | 0.999 | 0.574 | 12.78 |
| 0.060 | 5 | 0.030 | 0.999 | 0.03 |
| | 4 | 0.106 | 0.997 | 0.09 |
| | 3 | 0.310 | 0.987 | 0.39 |
| | 2 | 0.723 | 0.927 | 2.19 |
| | 1 | 0.999 | 0.555 | 13.35 |
| 0.062 | 5 | 0.034 | 0.999 | 0.03 |
| | 4 | 0.117 | 0.997 | 0.09 |
| | 3 | 0.332 | 0.986 | 0.42 |
| | 2 | 0.751 | 0.918 | 2.46 |
| 0.064 | 5 | 0.038 | 0.999 | 0.03 |
| | 4 | 0.128 | 0.997 | 0.09 |
| | 3 | 0.355 | 0.984 | 0.48 |
| | 2 | 0.777 | 0.908 | 2.76 |
| 0.066 | 5 | 0.043 | 0.999 | 0.03 |
| | 4 | 0.140 | 0.996 | 0.12 |
| | 3 | 0.378 | 0.982 | 0.54 |
| | 2 | 0.802 | 0.897 | 3.09 |
| 0.068 | 5 | 0.048 | 0.999 | 0.03 |
| | 4 | 0.153 | 0.995 | 0.15 |
| | 3 | 0.402 | 0.979 | 0.63 |
| | 2 | 0.825 | 0.885 | 3.45 |
| 0.070 | 5 | 0.054 | 0.999 | 0.03 |
| | 4 | 0.166 | 0.995 | 0.15 |
| | 3 | 0.426 | 0.976 | 0.72 |
| | 2 | 0.847 | 0.873 | 3.81 |
| 0.075 | 5 | 0.069 | 0.998 | 0.06 |
| | 4 | 0.201 | 0.993 | 0.21 |
| | 3 | 0.486 | 0.969 | 0.93 |
| | 2 | 0.893 | 0.840 | 4.80 |
| 0.080 | 6 | 0.027 | 0.999 | 0.03 |
| | 5 | 0.088 | 0.998 | 0.06 |
| | 4 | 0.240 | 0.990 | 0.30 |
| | 3 | 0.547 | 0.959 | 1.23 |
| | 2 | 0.929 | 0.805 | 5.85 |
| 0.085 | 6 | 0.036 | 0.999 | 0.03 |
| | 5 | 0.108 | 0.997 | 0.09 |
| | 4 | 0.282 | 0.987 | 0.39 |
| | 3 | 0.607 | 0.948 | 1.56 |
| | 2 | 0.955 | 0.768 | 6.96 |
| 0.090 | 6 | 0.046 | 0.999 | 0.03 |
| | 5 | 0.132 | 0.996 | 0.12 |
| | 4 | 0.326 | 0.984 | 0.48 |
| | 3 | 0.665 | 0.934 | 1.98 |
| | 2 | 0.972 | 0.732 | 8.04 |
| 0.095 | 6 | 0.057 | 0.999 | 0.03 |
| | 5 | 0.158 | 0.994 | 0.18 |
| | 4 | 0.372 | 0.979 | 0.63 |
| | 3 | 0.720 | 0.918 | 2.46 |
| | 2 | 0.984 | 0.697 | 9.09 |
| 0.100 | 6 | 0.071 | 0.998 | 0.06 |
| | 5 | 0.187 | 0.993 | 0.21 |
| | 4 | 0.421 | 0.973 | 0.81 |
| | 3 | 0.771 | 0.899 | 3.03 |
| | 2 | 0.991 | 0.664 | 10.08 |
| 0.105 | 7 | 0.030 | 0.999 | 0.03 |
| | 6 | 0.087 | 0.997 | 0.09 |
| | 5 | 0.219 | 0.991 | 0.27 |

TABLE 4
***(Continued)***

| X | M | D | F | $L_q$ |
|---|---|---|---|---|
| POPULATION 30, Cont. | | | | |
| | 4 | 0.470 | 0.967 | 0.99 |
| | 3 | 0.816 | 0.879 | 3.63 |
| | 2 | 0.995 | 0.634 | 10.98 |
| 0.110 | 7 | 0.038 | 0.999 | 0.03 |
| | 6 | 0.105 | 0.997 | 0.09 |
| | 5 | 0.253 | 0.988 | 0.36 |
| | 4 | 0.520 | 0.959 | 1.23 |
| | 3 | 0.856 | 0.857 | 4.29 |
| | 2 | 0.997 | 0.605 | 11.85 |
| 0.115 | 7 | 0.047 | 0.999 | 0.03 |
| | 6 | 0.125 | 0.996 | 0.12 |
| | 5 | 0.289 | 0.985 | 0.45 |
| | 4 | 0.570 | 0.950 | 1.50 |
| | 3 | 0.890 | 0.833 | 5.01 |
| | 2 | 0.998 | 0.579 | 12.63 |
| 0.120 | 7 | 0.057 | 0.998 | 0.06 |
| | 6 | 0.147 | 0.994 | 0.18 |
| | 5 | 0.327 | 0.981 | 0.57 |
| | 4 | 0.619 | 0.939 | 1.83 |
| | 3 | 0.918 | 0.808 | 5.76 |
| | 2 | 0.999 | 0.555 | 13.35 |
| 0.125 | 8 | 0.024 | 0.999 | 0.03 |
| | 7 | 0.069 | 0.998 | 0.06 |
| | 6 | 0.171 | 0.993 | 0.21 |
| | 5 | 0.367 | 0.977 | 0.69 |
| | 4 | 0.666 | 0.927 | 2.19 |
| | 3 | 0.940 | 0.783 | 6.51 |
| 0.130 | 8 | 0.030 | 0.999 | 0.03 |
| | 7 | 0.083 | 0.997 | 0.09 |
| | 6 | 0.197 | 0.991 | 0.27 |
| | 5 | 0.409 | 0.972 | 0.84 |
| | 4 | 0.712 | 0.914 | 2.58 |
| | 3 | 0.957 | 0.758 | 7.26 |
| 0.135 | 8 | 0.037 | 0.999 | 0.03 |
| | 7 | 0.098 | 0.997 | 0.09 |
| | 6 | 0.226 | 0.989 | 0.33 |
| | 5 | 0.451 | 0.966 | 1.02 |
| | 4 | 0.754 | 0.899 | 3.03 |
| | 3 | 0.970 | 0.734 | 7.98 |
| 0.140 | 8 | 0.045 | 0.999 | 0.03 |
| | 7 | 0.115 | 0.996 | 0.12 |
| | 6 | 0.256 | 0.987 | 0.39 |
| | 5 | 0.494 | 0.960 | 1.20 |
| | 4 | 0.793 | 0.884 | 2.48 |
| | 3 | 0.979 | 0.710 | 8.70 |
| 0.145 | 8 | 0.055 | 0.998 | 0.06 |
| | 7 | 0.134 | 0.995 | 0.15 |
| | 6 | 0.288 | 0.984 | 0.48 |
| | 5 | 0.537 | 0.952 | 1.44 |
| | 4 | 0.828 | 0.867 | 3.99 |
| | 3 | 0.986 | 0.687 | 9.39 |
| 0.150 | 9 | 0.024 | 0.999 | 0.03 |
| | 8 | 0.065 | 0.998 | 0.06 |
| | 7 | 0.155 | 0.993 | 0.21 |
| | 6 | 0.322 | 0.980 | 0.60 |
| | 5 | 0.580 | 0.944 | 1.68 |
| | 4 | 0.860 | 0.849 | 4.53 |
| | 3 | 0.991 | 0.665 | 10.05 |
| 0.155 | 9 | 0.029 | 0.999 | 0.03 |
| | 8 | 0.077 | 0.997 | 0.09 |
| | 7 | 0.177 | 0.992 | 0.24 |
| | 6 | 0.357 | 0.976 | 0.72 |
| | 5 | 0.622 | 0.935 | 1.95 |
| | 4 | 0.887 | 0.830 | 5.10 |
| | 3 | 0.994 | 0.644 | 10.68 |
| 0.160 | 9 | 0.036 | 0.999 | 0.03 |
| | 8 | 0.090 | 0.997 | 0.09 |
| | 7 | 0.201 | 0.990 | 0.30 |
| | 6 | 0.394 | 0.972 | 0.84 |
| | 5 | 0.663 | 0.924 | 2.28 |
| | 4 | 0.910 | 0.811 | 5.67 |
| | 3 | 0.996 | 0.624 | 11.28 |
| 0.165 | 9 | 0.043 | 0.999 | 0.03 |
| | 8 | 0.105 | 0.996 | 0.12 |
| | 7 | 0.227 | 0.988 | 0.36 |
| | 6 | 0.431 | 0.967 | 0.99 |
| | 5 | 0.702 | 0.913 | 2.61 |
| | 4 | 0.930 | 0.792 | 6.24 |
| | 3 | 0.997 | 0.606 | 11.82 |
| 0.170 | 10 | 0.019 | 0.999 | 0.03 |
| | 9 | 0.051 | 0.998 | 0.06 |
| | 8 | 0.121 | 0.995 | 0.15 |
| | 7 | 0.254 | 0.986 | 0.42 |
| | 6 | 0.469 | 0.961 | 1.17 |
| | 5 | 0.739 | 0.901 | 2.97 |
| | 4 | 0.946 | 0.773 | 6.81 |
| | 3 | 0.998 | 0.588 | 12.36 |
| 0.180 | 10 | 0.028 | 0.999 | 0.03 |
| | 9 | 0.070 | 0.997 | 0.09 |
| | 8 | 0.158 | 0.993 | 0.21 |
| | 7 | 0.313 | 0.980 | 0.60 |
| | 6 | 0.546 | 0.948 | 1.56 |
| | 5 | 0.806 | 0.874 | 3.78 |
| | 4 | 0.969 | 0.735 | 7.95 |
| | 3 | 0.999 | 0.555 | 13.35 |
| 0.190 | 10 | 0.039 | 0.999 | 0.03 |
| | 9 | 0.094 | 0.996 | 0.12 |
| | 8 | 0.200 | 0.990 | 0.30 |
| | 7 | 0.378 | 0.973 | 0.81 |
| | 6 | 0.621 | 0.932 | 2.04 |
| | 5 | 0.862 | 0.845 | 4.65 |
| | 4 | 0.983 | 0.699 | 9.03 |
| 0.200 | 11 | 0.021 | 0.999 | 0.03 |
| | 10 | 0.054 | 0.998 | 0.06 |
| | 9 | 0.123 | 0.995 | 0.15 |
| | 8 | 0.249 | 0.985 | 0.45 |
| | 7 | 0.446 | 0.963 | 1.11 |
| | 6 | 0.693 | 0.913 | 2.61 |
| | 5 | 0.905 | 0.814 | 5.58 |
| | 4 | 0.991 | 0.665 | 10.05 |
| 0.210 | 11 | 0.030 | 0.999 | 0.03 |
| | 10 | 0.073 | 0.997 | 0.09 |
| | 9 | 0.157 | 0.992 | 0.24 |
| | 8 | 0.303 | 0.980 | 0.60 |
| | 7 | 0.515 | 0.952 | 1.44 |
| | 6 | 0.758 | 0.892 | 3.24 |
| | 5 | 0.938 | 0.782 | 6.54 |
| | 4 | 0.995 | 0.634 | 10.98 |
| 0.220 | 11 | 0.041 | 0.999 | 0.03 |
| | 10 | 0.095 | 0.996 | 0.12 |
| | 9 | 0.197 | 0.989 | 0.33 |
| | 8 | 0.361 | 0.974 | 0.78 |
| | 7 | 0.585 | 0.938 | 1.86 |
| | 6 | 0.816 | 0.868 | 3.96 |
| | 5 | 0.961 | 0.751 | 7.47 |
| | 4 | 0.998 | 0.606 | 11.82 |
| 0.230 | 12 | 0.023 | 0.999 | 0.03 |
| | 11 | 0.056 | 0.998 | 0.06 |
| | 10 | 0.123 | 0.994 | 0.18 |
| | 9 | 0.242 | 0.985 | 0.45 |
| | 8 | 0.423 | 0.965 | 1.05 |
| | 7 | 0.652 | 0.923 | 2.31 |
| | 6 | 0.864 | 0.842 | 4.74 |
| | 5 | 0.976 | 0.721 | 8.37 |
| | 4 | 0.999 | 0.580 | 12.60 |
| 0.240 | 12 | 0.031 | 0.999 | 0.03 |
| | 11 | 0.074 | 0.997 | 0.09 |
| | 10 | 0.155 | 0.992 | 0.24 |
| | 9 | 0.291 | 0.981 | 0.57 |
| | 8 | 0.487 | 0.955 | 1.35 |
| | 7 | 0.715 | 0.905 | 2.85 |
| | 6 | 0.902 | 0.816 | 5.52 |
| | 5 | 0.986 | 0.693 | 9.21 |
| | 4 | 0.999 | 0.556 | 13.32 |
| 0.250 | 13 | 0.017 | 0.999 | 0.03 |
| | 12 | 0.042 | 0.998 | 0.06 |
| | 11 | 0.095 | 0.996 | 0.12 |
| | 10 | 0.192 | 0.989 | 0.33 |
| | 9 | 0.345 | 0.975 | 0.75 |
| | 8 | 0.552 | 0.944 | 1.68 |
| | 7 | 0.773 | 0.885 | 3.45 |
| | 6 | 0.932 | 0.789 | 6.33 |
| | 5 | 0.992 | 0.666 | 10.02 |
| 0.260 | 13 | 0.023 | 0.999 | 0.03 |
| | 12 | 0.056 | 0.998 | 0.06 |
| | 11 | 0.121 | 0.994 | 0.18 |
| | 10 | 0.233 | 0.986 | 0.42 |
| | 9 | 0.402 | 0.967 | 0.99 |
| | 8 | 0.616 | 0.930 | 2.10 |
| | 7 | 0.823 | 0.864 | 4.08 |
| | 6 | 0.954 | 0.763 | 7.11 |
| | 5 | 0.995 | 0.641 | 10.77 |
| 0.270 | 13 | 0.032 | 0.999 | 0.03 |
| | 12 | 0.073 | 0.997 | 0.09 |
| | 11 | 0.151 | 0.992 | 0.24 |
| | 10 | 0.279 | 0.981 | 0.57 |
| | 9 | 0.462 | 0.959 | 1.23 |
| | 8 | 0.676 | 0.915 | 2.55 |
| | 7 | 0.866 | 0.841 | 4.77 |
| | 6 | 0.970 | 0.737 | 7.89 |
| | 5 | 0.997 | 0.617 | 11.49 |

TABLE 4
***(Continued)***

| $X$ | $M$ | $D$ | $F$ | $L_q$ |
|---|---|---|---|---|
| POPULATION 30, Cont. | | | | |
| 0.280 | 14 | 0.017 | 0.999 | 0.03 |
| | 13 | 0.042 | 0.998 | 0.06 |
| | 12 | 0.093 | 0.996 | 0.12 |
| | 11 | 0.185 | 0.989 | 0.33 |
| | 10 | 0.329 | 0.976 | 0.72 |
| | 9 | 0.522 | 0.949 | 1.53 |
| | 8 | 0.733 | 0.898 | 3.06 |
| | 7 | 0.901 | 0.818 | 5.46 |
| | 6 | 0.981 | 0.712 | 8.64 |
| | 5 | 0.999 | 0.595 | 12.15 |
| 0.290 | 14 | 0.023 | 0.999 | 0.03 |
| | 13 | 0.055 | 0.998 | 0.06 |
| | 12 | 0.117 | 0.994 | 0.18 |
| | 11 | 0.223 | 0.986 | 0.42 |
| | 10 | 0.382 | 0.969 | 0.93 |
| | 9 | 0.582 | 0.937 | 1.89 |
| | 8 | 0.785 | 0.880 | 3.60 |
| | 7 | 0.929 | 0.795 | 6.15 |
| | 6 | 0.988 | 0.688 | 9.36 |
| | 5 | 0.999 | 0.575 | 12.75 |
| 0.300 | 14 | 0.031 | 0.999 | 0.03 |
| | 13 | 0.071 | 0.997 | 0.09 |
| | 12 | 0.145 | 0.992 | 0.24 |
| | 11 | 0.266 | 0.982 | 0.54 |
| | 10 | 0.437 | 0.962 | 1.14 |
| | 9 | 0.641 | 0.924 | 2.28 |
| | 8 | 0.830 | 0.861 | 4.17 |
| | 7 | 0.950 | 0.771 | 6.87 |
| | 6 | 0.993 | 0.666 | 10.02 |
| 0.310 | 15 | 0.017 | 0.999 | 0.03 |
| | 14 | 0.041 | 0.998 | 0.06 |
| | 13 | 0.090 | 0.996 | 0.12 |
| | 12 | 0.177 | 0.990 | 0.30 |
| | 11 | 0.312 | 0.977 | 0.69 |
| | 10 | 0.494 | 0.953 | 1.41 |
| | 9 | 0.697 | 0.909 | 2.73 |
| | 8 | 0.869 | 0.840 | 4.80 |
| | 7 | 0.966 | 0.749 | 7.53 |
| | 6 | 0.996 | 0.645 | 10.65 |
| 0.320 | 15 | 0.023 | 0.999 | 0.03 |
| | 14 | 0.054 | 0.998 | 0.06 |
| | 13 | 0.113 | 0.994 | 0.18 |
| | 12 | 0.213 | 0.987 | 0.39 |
| | 11 | 0.362 | 0.971 | 0.87 |
| | 10 | 0.552 | 0.943 | 1.71 |
| | 9 | 0.748 | 0.893 | 3.21 |
| | 8 | 0.901 | 0.820 | 5.40 |
| | 7 | 0.977 | 0.727 | 8.19 |
| | 6 | 0.997 | 0.625 | 11.25 |
| 0.330 | 15 | 0.030 | 0.999 | 0.03 |
| | 14 | 0.068 | 0.997 | 0.09 |
| | 13 | 0.139 | 0.993 | 0.21 |
| | 12 | 0.253 | 0.983 | 0.51 |
| | 11 | 0.414 | 0.965 | 1.05 |
| | 10 | 0.608 | 0.931 | 2.07 |
| | 9 | 0.795 | 0.876 | 3.72 |
| | 8 | 0.927 | 0.799 | 6.03 |
| | 7 | 0.985 | 0.706 | 8.82 |
| | 6 | 0.999 | 0.606 | 11.82 |
| 0.340 | 16 | 0.016 | 0.999 | 0.03 |
| | 15 | 0.040 | 0.998 | 0.06 |
| | 14 | 0.086 | 0.996 | 0.12 |
| | 13 | 0.169 | 0.990 | 0.30 |
| | 12 | 0.296 | 0.979 | 0.63 |
| | 11 | 0.468 | 0.957 | 1.29 |
| | 10 | 0.663 | 0.918 | 2.46 |
| | 9 | 0.836 | 0.858 | 4.26 |
| | 8 | 0.947 | 0.778 | 6.66 |
| | 7 | 0.990 | 0.685 | 9.45 |
| | 6 | 0.999 | 0.588 | 12.36 |
| 0.360 | 16 | 0.029 | 0.999 | 0.03 |
| | 15 | 0.065 | 0.997 | 0.09 |
| | 14 | 0.132 | 0.993 | 0.21 |
| | 13 | 0.240 | 0.984 | 0.48 |
| | 12 | 0.392 | 0.967 | 0.99 |
| | 11 | 0.578 | 0.937 | 1.89 |
| | 10 | 0.762 | 0.889 | 3.33 |
| | 9 | 0.902 | 0.821 | 5.37 |
| | 8 | 0.974 | 0.738 | 7.86 |
| | 7 | 0.996 | 0.648 | 10.56 |
| 0.380 | 17 | 0.020 | 0.999 | 0.03 |
| | 16 | 0.048 | 0.998 | 0.06 |
| | 15 | 0.101 | 0.995 | 0.15 |
| | 14 | 0.191 | 0.988 | 0.36 |
| | 13 | 0.324 | 0.975 | 0.75 |
| | 12 | 0.496 | 0.952 | 1.44 |
| | 11 | 0.682 | 0.914 | 2.58 |
| | 10 | 0.843 | 0.857 | 4.29 |
| | 9 | 0.945 | 0.784 | 6.48 |
| | 8 | 0.988 | 0.701 | 8.97 |
| | 7 | 0.999 | 0.614 | 11.58 |
| 0.400 | 17 | 0.035 | 0.999 | 0.03 |
| | 16 | 0.076 | 0.996 | 0.12 |
| | 15 | 0.150 | 0.992 | 0.24 |
| | 14 | 0.264 | 0.982 | 0.54 |
| | 13 | 0.420 | 0.964 | 1.08 |
| | 12 | 0.601 | 0.933 | 2.01 |
| | 11 | 0.775 | 0.886 | 3.42 |
| | 10 | 0.903 | 0.823 | 5.31 |
| | 9 | 0.972 | 0.748 | 7.56 |
| | 8 | 0.995 | 0.666 | 10.02 |
| 0.420 | 18 | 0.024 | 0.999 | 0.03 |
| | 17 | 0.056 | 0.997 | 0.09 |
| | 16 | 0.116 | 0.994 | 0.18 |
| | 15 | 0.212 | 0.986 | 0.42 |
| | 14 | 0.350 | 0.972 | 0.84 |
| | 13 | 0.521 | 0.948 | 1.56 |
| | 12 | 0.700 | 0.910 | 2.70 |
| | 11 | 0.850 | 0.856 | 4.32 |
| | 10 | 0.945 | 0.789 | 6.33 |
| | 9 | 0.986 | 0.713 | 8.61 |
| | 8 | 0.998 | 0.635 | 10.95 |
| 0.440 | 19 | 0.017 | 0.999 | 0.03 |
| | 18 | 0.041 | 0.998 | 0.06 |
| | 17 | 0.087 | 0.996 | 0.12 |
| | 16 | 0.167 | 0.990 | 0.30 |
| | 15 | 0.288 | 0.979 | 0.63 |
| | 14 | 0.446 | 0.960 | 1.20 |
| | 13 | 0.623 | 0.929 | 2.13 |
| | 12 | 0.787 | 0.883 | 3.51 |
| | 11 | 0.906 | 0.824 | 5.28 |
| | 10 | 0.970 | 0.755 | 7.35 |
| | 9 | 0.994 | 0.681 | 9.57 |
| | 8 | 0.999 | 0.606 | 11.82 |
| 0.460 | 19 | 0.028 | 0.999 | 0.03 |
| | 18 | 0.064 | 0.997 | 0.09 |
| | 17 | 0.129 | 0.993 | 0.21 |
| | 16 | 0.232 | 0.985 | 0.45 |
| | 15 | 0.375 | 0.970 | 0.90 |
| | 14 | 0.545 | 0.944 | 1.68 |
| | 13 | 0.717 | 0.906 | 2.82 |
| | 12 | 0.857 | 0.855 | 4.35 |
| | 11 | 0.945 | 0.793 | 6.21 |
| | 10 | 0.985 | 0.724 | 8.28 |
| | 9 | 0.997 | 0.652 | 10.44 |
| 0.480 | 20 | 0.019 | 0.999 | 0.03 |
| | 19 | 0.046 | 0.998 | 0.06 |
| | 18 | 0.098 | 0.995 | 0.15 |
| | 17 | 0.184 | 0.989 | 0.33 |
| | 16 | 0.310 | 0.977 | 0.69 |
| | 15 | 0.470 | 0.957 | 1.29 |
| | 14 | 0.643 | 0.926 | 2.22 |
| | 13 | 0.799 | 0.881 | 3.57 |
| | 12 | 0.910 | 0.826 | 5.22 |
| | 11 | 0.970 | 0.762 | 7.14 |
| | 10 | 0.993 | 0.694 | 9.18 |
| | 9 | 0.999 | 0.625 | 11.25 |
| 0.500 | 20 | 0.032 | 0.999 | 0.03 |
| | 19 | 0.072 | 0.997 | 0.09 |
| | 18 | 0.143 | 0.992 | 0.24 |
| | 17 | 0.252 | 0.983 | 0.51 |
| | 16 | 0.398 | 0.967 | 0.99 |
| | 15 | 0.568 | 0.941 | 1.77 |
| | 14 | 0.733 | 0.904 | 2.88 |
| | 13 | 0.865 | 0.854 | 4.38 |
| | 12 | 0.947 | 0.796 | 6.12 |
| | 11 | 0.985 | 0.732 | 8.04 |
| | 10 | 0.997 | 0.667 | 9.99 |
| 0.520 | 21 | 0.021 | 0.999 | 0.03 |
| | 20 | 0.051 | 0.998 | 0.06 |
| | 19 | 0.108 | 0.994 | 0.18 |
| | 18 | 0.200 | 0.988 | 0.36 |
| | 17 | 0.331 | 0.975 | 0.75 |
| | 16 | 0.493 | 0.954 | 1.38 |
| | 15 | 0.633 | 0.923 | 2.31 |
| | 14 | 0.811 | 0.880 | 3.60 |
| | 13 | 0.915 | 0.827 | 5.19 |
| | 12 | 0.971 | 0.767 | 6.99 |
| | 11 | 0.993 | 0.705 | 8.85 |
| | 10 | 0.999 | 0.641 | 10.77 |

TABLE 4
***(Continued)***

POPULATION 30, Cont.

| X | M | D | F | $L_q$ |
|---|---|---|---|---|
| 0.540 | 21 | 0.035 | 0.999 | 0.03 |
| | 20 | 0.079 | 0.996 | 0.12 |
| | 19 | 0.155 | 0.991 | 0.27 |
| | 18 | 0.270 | 0.981 | 0.57 |
| | 17 | 0.421 | 0.965 | 1.05 |
| | 16 | 0.590 | 0.938 | 1.86 |
| | 15 | 0.750 | 0.901 | 2.97 |
| | 14 | 0.874 | 0.854 | 4.38 |
| | 13 | 0.949 | 0.799 | 6.03 |
| | 12 | 0.985 | 0.740 | 7.80 |
| | 11 | 0.997 | 0.679 | 9.63 |
| | 10 | 0.999 | 0.617 | 11.49 |
| 0.560 | 22 | 0.023 | 0.999 | 0.03 |
| | 21 | 0.056 | 0.997 | 0.09 |
| | 20 | 0.117 | 0.994 | 0.18 |
| | 19 | 0.215 | 0.986 | 0.42 |
| | 18 | 0.352 | 0.973 | 0.81 |
| | 17 | 0.516 | 0.952 | 1.44 |
| | 16 | 0.683 | 0.920 | 2.40 |
| | 15 | 0.824 | 0.878 | 3.66 |
| | 14 | 0.920 | 0.828 | 5.16 |
| | 13 | 0.972 | 0.772 | 6.84 |
| | 12 | 0.993 | 0.714 | 8.58 |
| | 11 | 0.999 | 0.655 | 10.35 |
| 0.580 | 23 | 0.014 | 0.999 | 0.03 |
| | 22 | 0.038 | 0.998 | 0.06 |
| | 21 | 0.085 | 0.996 | 0.12 |
| | 20 | 0.167 | 0.990 | 0.30 |
| | 19 | 0.288 | 0.980 | 0.60 |
| | 18 | 0.443 | 0.963 | 1.11 |
| | 17 | 0.612 | 0.936 | 1.92 |
| | 16 | 0.766 | 0.899 | 3.03 |
| | 15 | 0.883 | 0.854 | 4.38 |
| | 14 | 0.953 | 0.802 | 5.94 |
| | 13 | 0.985 | 0.746 | 7.62 |
| | 12 | 0.997 | 0.690 | 9.30 |
| | 11 | 0.999 | 0.632 | 11.04 |
| 0.600 | 23 | 0.024 | 0.999 | 0.03 |
| | 22 | 0.059 | 0.997 | 0.09 |
| | 21 | 0.125 | 0.993 | 0.21 |
| | 20 | 0.230 | 0.986 | 0.42 |
| | 19 | 0.372 | 0.972 | 0.84 |
| | 18 | 0.538 | 0.949 | 1.53 |
| | 17 | 0.702 | 0.918 | 2.46 |
| | 16 | 0.837 | 0.877 | 3.69 |
| | 15 | 0.927 | 0.829 | 5.13 |
| | 14 | 0.974 | 0.776 | 6.72 |
| | 13 | 0.993 | 0.722 | 8.34 |
| | 12 | 0.999 | 0.667 | 9.99 |
| 0.650 | 24 | 0.031 | 0.999 | 0.03 |
| | 23 | 0.076 | 0.996 | 0.12 |
| | 22 | 0.158 | 0.991 | 0.27 |
| | 21 | 0.281 | 0.982 | 0.54 |
| | 20 | 0.439 | 0.965 | 1.05 |
| | 19 | 0.610 | 0.940 | 1.80 |
| | 18 | 0.764 | 0.906 | 2.82 |
| | 17 | 0.879 | 0.865 | 4.05 |
| | 16 | 0.949 | 0.818 | 5.46 |
| | 15 | 0.983 | 0.769 | 6.93 |
| | 14 | 0.996 | 0.718 | 8.46 |
| | 13 | 0.999 | 0.667 | 9.99 |
| 0.700 | 25 | 0.039 | 0.998 | 0.06 |
| | 24 | 0.096 | 0.995 | 0.15 |
| | 23 | 0.196 | 0.989 | 0.33 |
| | 22 | 0.339 | 0.977 | 0.69 |
| | 21 | 0.511 | 0.958 | 1.26 |
| | 20 | 0.681 | 0.930 | 2.10 |
| | 19 | 0.821 | 0.894 | 3.18 |
| | 18 | 0.916 | 0.853 | 4.41 |
| | 17 | 0.967 | 0.808 | 5.76 |
| | 16 | 0.990 | 0.762 | 7.14 |
| | 15 | 0.997 | 0.714 | 8.58 |
| 0.750 | 26 | 0.046 | 0.998 | 0.06 |
| | 25 | 0.118 | 0.994 | 0.18 |
| | 24 | 0.240 | 0.986 | 0.42 |
| | 23 | 0.405 | 0.972 | 0.84 |
| | 22 | 0.587 | 0.950 | 1.50 |
| | 21 | 0.752 | 0.920 | 2.40 |
| | 20 | 0.873 | 0.883 | 3.51 |
| | 19 | 0.946 | 0.842 | 4.74 |
| | 18 | 0.981 | 0.799 | 6.03 |
| | 17 | 0.995 | 0.755 | 7.35 |
| | 16 | 0.999 | 0.711 | 8.67 |
| 0.800 | 27 | 0.053 | 0.998 | 0.06 |
| | 26 | 0.143 | 0.993 | 0.21 |
| | 25 | 0.292 | 0.984 | 0.48 |
| | 24 | 0.481 | 0.966 | 1.02 |
| | 23 | 0.670 | 0.941 | 1.77 |
| | 22 | 0.822 | 0.909 | 2.73 |
| | 21 | 0.919 | 0.872 | 3.84 |
| | 20 | 0.970 | 0.832 | 5.04 |
| | 19 | 0.991 | 0.791 | 6.27 |
| | 18 | 0.998 | 0.750 | 7.50 |
| 0.850 | 28 | 0.055 | 0.998 | 0.06 |
| | 27 | 0.171 | 0.993 | 0.21 |
| | 26 | 0.356 | 0.981 | 0.57 |
| | 25 | 0.571 | 0.960 | 1.20 |
| | 24 | 0.760 | 0.932 | 2.04 |
| | 23 | 0.888 | 0.889 | 3.03 |
| | 22 | 0.957 | 0.862 | 4.14 |
| | 21 | 0.987 | 0.823 | 5.31 |
| | 20 | 0.997 | 0.784 | 6.48 |
| | 19 | 0.999 | 0.745 | 7.65 |
| 0.900 | 29 | 0.047 | 0.999 | 0.03 |
| | 28 | 0.200 | 0.992 | 0.24 |
| | 27 | 0.441 | 0.977 | 0.69 |
| | 26 | 0.683 | 0.953 | 1.41 |
| | 25 | 0.856 | 0.923 | 2.31 |
| | 24 | 0.947 | 0.888 | 3.36 |
| | 23 | 0.985 | 0.852 | 4.44 |
| | 22 | 0.996 | 0.815 | 5.55 |
| | 21 | 0.999 | 0.778 | 6.66 |
| 0.950 | 29 | 0.226 | 0.993 | 0.21 |
| | 28 | 0.574 | 0.973 | 0.81 |
| | 27 | 0.831 | 0.945 | 1.65 |
| | 26 | 0.951 | 0.912 | 2.64 |
| | 25 | 0.989 | 0.877 | 3.69 |
| | 24 | 0.998 | 0.842 | 4.74 |

TABLE 5
## TABLE OF RANDOM DIGITS

| | | | | | | | | | |
|---|---|---|---|---|---|---|---|---|---|
| 03689 | 33090 | 43465 | 96789 | 56688 | 32389 | 77206 | 06534 | 10558 | 14478 |
| 43367 | 46409 | 44751 | 73410 | 35138 | 24910 | 70748 | 57336 | 56043 | 68550 |
| 45357 | 52080 | 62670 | 73877 | 20604 | 40408 | 98060 | 96733 | 65094 | 80335 |
| 62683 | 03171 | 77109 | 92515 | 78041 | 27590 | 42651 | 00254 | 73179 | 10159 |
| 04841 | 40918 | 69047 | 68986 | 08150 | 87984 | 08887 | 76083 | 37702 | 28523 |
| 85963 | 06992 | 65321 | 43521 | 46393 | 40491 | 06028 | 43865 | 58190 | 28142 |
| 03720 | 78942 | 61990 | 90812 | 98452 | 74098 | 69738 | 83272 | 39212 | 42817 |
| 10159 | 85560 | 35619 | 58248 | 65498 | 77977 | 02896 | 45198 | 10655 | 13973 |
| 80162 | 35686 | 57877 | 19552 | 63931 | 44171 | 40879 | 94532 | 17828 | 31848 |
| 74388 | 92906 | 65829 | 24572 | 79417 | 38460 | 96294 | 79201 | 47755 | 90980 |
| 12660 | 09571 | 29743 | 45447 | 64063 | 46295 | 44191 | 53957 | 62393 | 42229 |
| 81852 | 60620 | 87757 | 72165 | 23875 | 87844 | 84038 | 04994 | 93466 | 27418 |
| 03068 | 61317 | 65305 | 64944 | 27319 | 55263 | 84514 | 38374 | 11657 | 67723 |
| 29623 | 58530 | 17274 | 16908 | 39253 | 37595 | 57497 | 74780 | 88624 | 93333 |
| 30520 | 50588 | 51231 | 83816 | 01075 | 33098 | 81308 | 59036 | 49152 | 86262 |
| 93694 | 02984 | 91350 | 33929 | 41724 | 32403 | 42566 | 14232 | 55085 | 65628 |
| 86736 | 40641 | 37958 | 25415 | 19922 | 65966 | 98044 | 39583 | 26828 | 50919 |
| 28141 | 15630 | 37675 | 52545 | 24813 | 22075 | 05142 | 15374 | 84533 | 12933 |
| 79804 | 05165 | 21620 | 98400 | 55290 | 71877 | 60052 | 46320 | 79055 | 45913 |
| 63763 | 49985 | 88853 | 70681 | 52762 | 17670 | 62337 | 12199 | 44123 | 37993 |
| 49618 | 47068 | 63331 | 62675 | 51788 | 58283 | 04295 | 72904 | 05378 | 98085 |
| 26502 | 68980 | 26545 | 14204 | 34304 | 50284 | 47730 | 57299 | 73966 | 02566 |
| 13549 | 86048 | 27912 | 56733 | 14987 | 09850 | 72817 | 85168 | 09538 | 92347 |
| 89221 | 78076 | 40306 | 34045 | 52557 | 52383 | 67796 | 41382 | 50490 | 30117 |
| 97809 | 34056 | 76778 | 60417 | 05153 | 83827 | 67369 | 08602 | 56163 | 28793 |
| 65668 | 44694 | 34151 | 51741 | 11484 | 13226 | 49516 | 17391 | 39956 | 34839 |
| 53653 | 59804 | 59051 | 95074 | 38307 | 99546 | 32962 | 26962 | 86252 | 50704 |
| 34922 | 95041 | 17398 | 32789 | 26860 | 55536 | 82415 | 82911 | 42208 | 62725 |
| 74880 | 65198 | 61357 | 90209 | 71543 | 71114 | 94868 | 05645 | 44154 | 72254 |
| 66036 | 48794 | 30021 | 92601 | 21615 | 16952 | 18433 | 44903 | 51322 | 90379 |
| 39044 | 99503 | 11442 | 81344 | 57068 | 74662 | 90382 | 59433 | 48440 | 38146 |
| 87756 | 71151 | 68543 | 08358 | 10183 | 06432 | 97482 | 90301 | 76114 | 83778 |
| 47117 | 45575 | 29524 | 02522 | 08041 | 70698 | 80260 | 73588 | 86415 | 72523 |
| 71572 | 02109 | 96722 | 21684 | 64331 | 71644 | 18933 | 32801 | 11644 | 12364 |
| 35609 | 58072 | 63209 | 48429 | 53108 | 59173 | 55337 | 22445 | 85940 | 43707 |
| 73703 | 70069 | 74981 | 12197 | 48426 | 77365 | 26769 | 65078 | 27849 | 41311 |
| 42979 | 88161 | 56531 | 46443 | 47148 | 42773 | 18601 | 38532 | 22594 | 12395 |
| 12279 | 42308 | 00380 | 17181 | 38757 | 09071 | 89804 | 15232 | 99007 | 39495 |

## TABLE 6
## AREAS UNDER THE NORMAL CURVE

Areas under the normal curve to the left of $x$ for decimal units of $\sigma'$ from the mean, $\bar{x}'$

| $x$ | Area | $x$ | Area | $x$ | Area | $x$ | Area |
|---|---|---|---|---|---|---|---|
| $\bar{x}' - 3.0\sigma'$ | .0013 | $\bar{x}' - 1.5\sigma'$ | .0668 | $\bar{x}' + .1\sigma'$ | .5398 | $\bar{x}' + 1.6\sigma'$ | .9452 |
| $\bar{x}' - 2.9\sigma'$ | .0019 | $\bar{x}' - 1.4\sigma'$ | .0808 | $\bar{x}' + .2\sigma'$ | .5793 | $\bar{x}' + 1.7\sigma'$ | .9554 |
| $\bar{x}' - 2.8\sigma'$ | .0026 | $\bar{x}' - 1.3\sigma'$ | .0968 | $\bar{x}' + .3\sigma'$ | .6179 | $\bar{x}' + 1.8\sigma'$ | .9641 |
| $\bar{x}' - 2.7\sigma'$ | .0035 | $\bar{x}' - 1.2\sigma'$ | .1151 | $\bar{x}' + .4\sigma'$ | .6554 | $\bar{x}' + 1.9\sigma'$ | .9713 |
| $\bar{x}' - 2.6\sigma'$ | .0047 | $\bar{x}' - 1.1\sigma'$ | .1357 | $\bar{x}' + .5\sigma'$ | .6915 | $\bar{x}' + 2.0\sigma'$ | .9772 |
| $\bar{x}' - 2.5\sigma'$ | .0062 | $\bar{x}' - 1.0\sigma'$ | .1587 | $\bar{x}' + .6\sigma'$ | .7257 | $\bar{x}' + 2.1\sigma'$ | .9821 |
| $\bar{x}' - 2.4\sigma'$ | .0082 | $\bar{x}' - .9\sigma'$ | .1841 | $\bar{x}' + .7\sigma'$ | .7580 | $\bar{x}' + 2.2\sigma'$ | .9861 |
| $\bar{x}' - 2.3\sigma'$ | .0107 | $\bar{x}' - .8\sigma'$ | .2119 | $\bar{x}' + .8\sigma'$ | .7881 | $\bar{x}' + 2.3\sigma'$ | .9893 |
| $\bar{x}' - 2.2\sigma'$ | .0139 | $\bar{x}' - .7\sigma'$ | .2420 | $\bar{x}' + .9\sigma'$ | .8159 | $\bar{x}' + 2.4\sigma'$ | .9918 |
| $\bar{x}' - 2.1\sigma'$ | .0179 | $\bar{x}' - .6\sigma'$ | .2741 | $\bar{x}' + 1.0\sigma'$ | .8413 | $\bar{x}' + 2.5\sigma'$ | .9938 |
| $\bar{x}' - 2.0\sigma'$ | .0228 | $\bar{x}' - .5\sigma'$ | .3085 | $\bar{x}' + 1.1\sigma'$ | .8643 | $\bar{x}' + 2.6\sigma'$ | .9953 |
| $\bar{x}' - 1.9\sigma'$ | .0287 | $\bar{x}' - .4\sigma'$ | .3446 | $\bar{x}' + 1.2\sigma'$ | .8849 | $\bar{x}' + 2.7\sigma'$ | .9965 |
| $\bar{x}' - 1.8\sigma'$ | .0359 | $\bar{x}' - .3\sigma'$ | .3821 | $\bar{x}' + 1.3\sigma'$ | .9032 | $\bar{x}' + 2.8\sigma'$ | .9974 |
| $\bar{x}' - 1.7\sigma'$ | .0446 | $\bar{x}' - .2\sigma'$ | .4207 | $\bar{x}' + 1.4\sigma'$ | .9192 | $\bar{x}' + 2.9\sigma'$ | .9981 |
| $\bar{x}' - 1.6\sigma'$ | .0548 | $\bar{x}' - .1\sigma'$ | .4602 | $\bar{x}' + 1.5\sigma'$ | .9332 | $\bar{x}' + 3.0\sigma'$ | .9987 |
| | | $\bar{x}'$ | .5000 | | | | |

$\sigma'$ units from the mean, $\bar{x}'$, associated with given values of the area under the normal curve to the left of $x$

| $x$ | Area | $x$ | Area |
|---|---|---|---|
| $\bar{x}' - 3.090\sigma'$ | .001 | $\bar{x}' + 3.090\sigma'$ | .999 |
| $\bar{x}' - 2.576\sigma'$ | .005 | $\bar{x}' + 2.576\sigma'$ | .995 |
| $\bar{x}' - 2.326\sigma'$ | .010 | $\bar{x}' + 2.326\sigma'$ | .990 |
| $\bar{x}' - 1.960\sigma'$ | .025 | $\bar{x}' + 1.960\sigma'$ | .975 |
| $\bar{x}' - 1.645\sigma'$ | .050 | $\bar{x}' + 1.645\sigma'$ | .950 |
| $\bar{x}' - 1.282\sigma'$ | .100 | $\bar{x}' + 1.282\sigma'$ | .900 |
| $\bar{x}' - 1.036\sigma'$ | .150 | $\bar{x}' + 1.036\sigma'$ | .850 |
| $\bar{x}' - .842\sigma'$ | .200 | $\bar{x}' + .842\sigma'$ | .800 |
| $\bar{x}' - .674\sigma'$ | .250 | $\bar{x}' + .674\sigma'$ | .750 |
| $\bar{x}' - .524\sigma'$ | .300 | $\bar{x}' + .524\sigma'$ | .700 |
| $\bar{x}' - .385\sigma'$ | .350 | $\bar{x}' + .385\sigma'$ | .650 |
| $\bar{x}' - .253\sigma'$ | .400 | $\bar{x}' + .253\sigma'$ | .600 |
| $\bar{x}' - .126\sigma'$ | .450 | $\bar{x}' + .126\sigma'$ | .550 |
| $\bar{x}'$ | .500 | | |

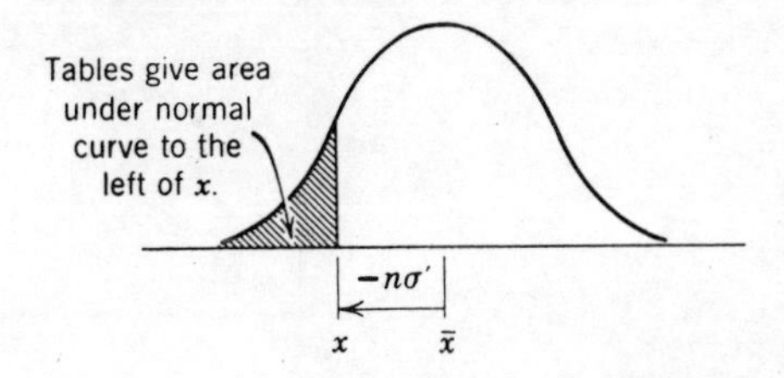
Tables give area
under normal
curve to the
left of x.
−nσ′
x
x̄

# INDEX

Printed and Bound by KIN KEONG PRINTING CO. PTE. LTD. – Republic of Singapore.